HANDBOOK OF INDUSTRIAL ORGANIZATION
VOLUME 3

HANDBOOKS IN ECONOMICS

10

Series Editors

KENNETH J. ARROW
MICHAEL D. INTRILIGATOR

ELSEVIER

AMSTERDAM • BOSTON • HEIDELBERG • LONDON
NEW YORK • OXFORD • PARIS • SAN DIEGO
SAN FRANCISCO • SINGAPORE • SYDNEY • TOKYO
North-Holland is an imprint of Elsevier

N·H

HANDBOOK OF INDUSTRIAL ORGANIZATION

VOLUME 3

Edited by

MARK ARMSTRONG
Department of Economics, University College London

and

ROBERT PORTER
Department of Economics, Northwestern University

ELSEVIER

AMSTERDAM • BOSTON • HEIDELBERG • LONDON
NEW YORK • OXFORD • PARIS • SAN DIEGO
SAN FRANCISCO • SINGAPORE • SYDNEY • TOKYO
North-Holland is an imprint of Elsevier

N·H

North-Holland is an imprint of Elsevier
Radarweg 29, PO Box 211, 1000 AE Amsterdam, The Netherlands
Linacre House, Jordan Hill, Oxford OX2 8DP, UK

First edition 2007

Library of Congress Cataloging-in-Publication Data
A catalog record for this book is available from the Library of Congress

British Library Cataloguing in Publication Data
A catalogue record for this book is available from the British Library

ISBN-13: 978-0-444-82435-6

ISSN: 0169-7218 (Handbooks in Economics series)
ISSN: 1573-448X (Handbook of Industrial Organization series)

For information on all North-Holland publications
visit our website at books.elsevier.com

Printed and bound in The Netherlands

07 08 09 10 11   10 9 8 7 6 5 4 3 2 1

INTRODUCTION TO THE SERIES

The aim of the *Handbooks in Economics* series is to produce Handbooks for various branches of economics, each of which is a definitive source, reference, and teaching supplement for use by professional researchers and advanced graduate students. Each Handbook provides self-contained surveys of the current state of a branch of economics in the form of chapters prepared by leading specialists on various aspects of this branch of economics. These surveys summarize not only received results but also newer developments, from recent journal articles and discussion papers. Some original material is also included, but the main goal is to provide comprehensive and accessible surveys. The Handbooks are intended to provide not only useful reference volumes for professional collections but also possible supplementary readings for advanced courses for graduate students in economics.

KENNETH J. ARROW and MICHAEL D. INTRILIGATOR

CONTENTS OF THE HANDBOOK

VOLUME I

PART 1: DETERMINANTS OF FIRM AND MARKET ORGANIZATION

PART 2: ANALYSIS OF MARKET BEHAVIOR

PREFACE TO THE HANDBOOK OF INDUSTRIAL ORGANIZATION, VOLUME 3

This volume is the third in the *Handbook of Industrial Organization* series (hereafter, the HIO). The first two volumes were published simultaneously in 1989, under the editorship of Richard Schmalensee and Robert Willig. The first two volumes were quite successful, by several measures. Many of the chapters were widely cited, many chapters appeared on graduate reading lists, some have continued to appear even recently, and we understand that the two volumes are among the best sellers in the Handbook of Economics Series. However, the field of industrial organization has evolved since then. Moreover, as Schmalensee and Willig acknowledge in their Preface, the original HIO volumes had some gaps. The purpose of this volume is to fill in some of those gaps, and to report on recent developments. The aim is to serve as a source, reference and teaching supplement for industrial organization, or industrial economics, the microeconomics field that focuses on business behavior and its implications for both market structures and processes, and for related public policies.

The first two volumes of the HIO appeared at roughly the same time as Jean Tirole's (1988) book. Together, they helped revolutionize the teaching of industrial organization, and they provided an excellent summary of the state of the art. Tirole's book explicitly is concerned with the relevant theory, and several commentators noted that the first two HIO volumes contained much more discussion of the theoretical literature than of the empirical literature. In most respects, this imbalance was an accurate reflection of the state of the field. Since then, the empirical literature has flourished, while the theoretical literature has continued to grow, although probably not at the pace of the preceding 15 years.

This volume consists of ten chapters, presented in the alphabetic order of their authors. We briefly summarize them, and indicate how they correspond to chapters in the first two volumes of the HIO.

Mark Armstrong and David Sappington describe developments in regulation. Their chapter can be viewed as a successor to the chapter by David Baron in the original HIO, and to a lesser extent those by Ronald Braeutigam and by Roger Noll. Relative to the Baron chapter, this chapter focuses more on practical regulatory policies and on multi-firm regulation.

Kyle Bagwell discusses advertising, which received a brief treatment only in passing in the first two HIO volumes. More generally, this chapter fills a larger gap, as we know of no thorough modern survey of this literature.

Steven Berry and Peter Reiss describe empirical models of entry and exit that infer aspects of firms' competitive environment from the number of competitors in a market.

The focus is on within industry comparisons, say for example on differences across separate geographical markets for the same product.

As dynamic theoretical models increase in complexity, in order to reflect a wide variety of possible economic environments, it has become increasingly difficult to obtain analytic characterizations of equilibrium outcomes. Ulrich Doraszelski and Ariel Pakes survey methods for deriving numerical solutions in such games. With increases in computer processing speed and memory, it has become possible to analyze a richer set of environments, and to revisit issues such as mergers, where long run effects on entry and investment may be paramount. Applications of these numerical solution methods have just begun to be introduced in the empirical analysis of dynamic oligopoly games, and we believe that some important advances will occur in the near future.

Joseph Farrell and Paul Klemperer discuss lock-in and compatibility. These issues are prominent in markets where there are either direct or indirect benefits to purchasing the same product as many other customers, or where there are other costs associated with switching products. Again, this topic was not covered substantively in the first two HIO volumes.

Ken Hendricks and Robert Porter describe the empirical literature on auction markets. Auctions are an important trading process, and they have been widely adopted in sales of public assets. Economics has informed the design of auction mechanisms, as well as the analysis of bidding, such as the detection of collusion.

Patrick Rey and Jean Tirole discuss the literature on foreclosure, whereby output in one market is restricted by the exercise of market power in another market. Related chapters in the earlier HIO, by Martin Perry, by Janusz Ordover and Garth Saloner and by Michael Katz, touch on these issues. There have been a number of subsequent developments, spurred on in part by several antitrust cases.

Lars Stole discusses price discrimination. His chapter expands on Hal Varian's earlier chapter in the HIO. Varian's discussion largely focuses on monopoly price discrimination, while Stole's chapter is primarily devoted to the more recent literature on price discrimination in oligopoly markets.

John Sutton describes the determinants of market structure, including the size distribution of firms and industry turnover. In contrast to the related chapter by Berry and Reiss, the focus is largely on differences across industries. This chapter is a successor to the chapters by John Panzar, by Richard Schmalensee, and by Wesley Cohen and Richard Levin in the original HIO volumes.

Finally, Michael Whinston discusses horizontal integration. His companion book [Whinston (2006)] also discusses vertical integration and vertical restraints and related antitrust policies. This chapter succeeds that by Alexis Jacquemin and Margaret Slade in the original HIO volumes. It provides an up-to-date account of the latest theory in the area, as well as coverage of empirical techniques which are now used in antitrust policy.

The ten chapters cover a wide range of material, but there remain some important subjects that are not covered in this volume or the prior two HIO volumes. We had hoped that there would be a chapter on the intersection between industrial organization and corporate finance. There is also no discussion of the large empirical literature on estimating demand for differentiated products. Ackerberg et al. (2007), Nevo (2000) and Reiss and Wolak (2007) provide useful discussions, all emphasizing econometric issues. Another unfilled gap is the empirical literature on research and development, expanding on the earlier HIO surveys by Jennifer Reinganum on the theory and by Cohen and Levin on empirical work. Finally, a remaining gap is "behavioral IO", i.e., the study of markets in which consumers and/or firms exhibit myopia, hyperbolic discounting, or some other form of bounded rationality. This area is still in its infancy, but Ellison (2006) provides an initial survey of the terrain.

Acknowledgements

This volume has had a checkered history. It was originally to have been edited by Tim Bresnahan and John Vickers. Tim and John commissioned about a dozen chapters. However, before many had advanced beyond a rough outline, both Tim and John stepped down in order to take government positions in Washington and London, respectively. We agreed to succeed them, but the transition process resulted in some delays. We retained several of the original chapters, and commissioned some new chapters. Tim and John deserve credit for much of the important groundwork. We owe a large debt to the authors of the following chapters, who have taken their assignments seriously, and who were responsive to the various comments and suggestions they received. We would also like to thank Kenneth Arrow and Michael Intriligator for their support in providing guidance throughout the process. Valerie Teng of North-Holland capably provided administrative assistance at various stages of this project.

MARK ARMSTRONG
University College London

ROBERT PORTER
Northwestern University

References

Ackerberg, D., Benkard, L., Berry, S., Pakes, A. (2007). "Econometric tools for analyzing market outcomes". In: Heckman, J., Leamer, E. (Eds.), Handbook of Econometrics, vol. 6. Elsevier. In press.

Ellison, G. (2006). "Bounded rationality in industrial economics". In: Blundell, R., Newey, W., Persson, T. (Eds.), Advances in Economics and Econometrics: Theory and Applications, Ninth World Congress, vol. 2. Cambridge Univ. Press.

Nevo, A. (2000). "A practitioner's guide to estimation of random-coefficients Logit models of demand". Journal of Economics and Management Strategy 9, 513–548.

Reiss, P., Wolak, F. (2007). "Structural econometric modeling: Rationales and examples from industrial organization". In: Heckman, J., Leamer, E. (Eds.), Handbook of Econometrics, vol. 6. Elsevier. In press.

Tirole, J. (1988). The Theory of Industrial Organization. MIT Press, Cambridge, MA.

Whinston, M. (2006). Lectures on Antitrust Economics. MIT Press, Cambridge, MA.

CONTENTS OF VOLUME 3

Chapter 27

RECENT DEVELOPMENTS IN THE THEORY OF REGULATION

MARK ARMSTRONG

Department of Economics, University College London

DAVID E.M. SAPPINGTON

Department of Economics, University of Florida

Contents

Handbook of Industrial Organization, Volume 3
Edited by M. Armstrong and R. Porter

DOI: 10.1016/S1573-448X(06)03027-5

Abstract

This chapter reviews recent theoretical work on the design of regulatory policy, focusing on the complications that arise when regulated suppliers have better information about the regulated industry than do regulators. The discussion begins by characterizing the optimal regulation of a monopoly supplier that is better informed than the regulator about its production cost and/or consumer demand for its product. Both adverse selection ("hidden information") and moral hazard ("hidden action") complications are considered, as are the additional concerns that arise when the regulator's intertemporal commitment powers are limited. The chapter then analyzes the design of practical policies, such as price cap regulation, that are often observed in practice. The design of regulatory policy in the presence of limited competitive forces also is reviewed. Yardstick regulation, procedures for awarding monopoly franchises, and optimal industry structuring are analyzed. The chapter also analyzes the optimal pricing of access to bottleneck production facilities in vertically-related industries, stressing the complications that arise when the owner of the bottleneck facility also operates as a retail producer.

Keywords

Regulation, Monopoly, Asymmetric information, Liberalization

JEL classification: D42, D60, D82, L12, L13, L43, L51

1. Introduction

Several chapters in this volume analyze unfettered competition between firms. Such analyses are instrumental in understanding the operation of many important industries. However, activities in some industries are determined in large part by direct government regulation of producers. This is often the case, for example, in portions of the electricity, gas, sanitation, telecommunications, transport, and water industries. This chapter reviews recent analyses of the design of regulatory policy in industries where unfettered competition is deemed inappropriate, often because technological considerations render supply by one or few firms optimal.

The discussion in this chapter focuses on the complications that arise because regulators have limited knowledge of the industry that they regulate. In practice, a regulator seldom has perfect information about consumer demand in the industry or about the technological capabilities of regulated producers. In particular, the regulator typically has less information about such key industry data than does the regulated firm(s). Thus, a critical issue is how, if at all, the regulator can best induce the regulated firm to employ its privileged information to further the broad interests of society, rather than to pursue its own interests.

As its title suggests, this chapter will focus on recent theoretical contributions to the regulation literature.[1] Space constraints preclude detailed discussions of the institutional features of individual regulated industries. Instead, the focus is on basic principles that apply in most or all regulated industries.[2] The chapter proceeds as follows. Section 2 considers the optimal regulation of a monopoly producer that has privileged information about key aspects of its environment. The optimal regulatory policy is shown to vary with the nature of the firm's private information and with the intertemporal commitment powers of the regulator, among other factors. The normative analysis in Section 2 presumes that, even though the regulator's information is not perfect, he is well informed about the structure of the regulatory environment and about the precise manner in which his knowledge of the environment is limited.[3]

Section 3 provides a complementary positive analysis of regulatory policies in a monopoly setting where the regulator's information, as well as his range of instruments, may be much more limited. The focus of Section 3 is on regulatory policies that perform "well" under certain relevant circumstances, as opposed to policies that are optimal in the specified setting. Section 3 also considers key elements of regulatory policies that have gained popularity in recent years, including price cap regulation.

[1] The reader is referred to Baron (1989) and Braeutigam (1989), for example, for excellent reviews of earlier theoretical contributions to the regulation literature. Although every effort has been made to review the major analyses of the topics covered in this chapter, every important contribution to the literature may not be cited. We offer our apologies in advance to the authors of any uncited contribution, appealing to limited information as our only excuse.

[2] We also do not attempt a review of studies that employ experiments to evaluate regulatory policies. For a recent overview of some of these studies, see Eckel and Lutz (2003).

[3] Throughout this chapter, we will refer to the regulator as "he" for expositional simplicity.

Section 4 analyzes the design of regulatory policy in settings with multiple firms. This section considers the optimal design of franchise bidding and yardstick competition. It also analyzes the relative merits of choosing a single firm to supply multiple products versus assigning the production of different products to different firms. Section 4 also explains how the presence of unregulated rivals can complement, or complicate, regulatory policy.

Section 5 considers the related question of when a regulated supplier of a monopoly input should be permitted to compete in downstream markets. Section 5 also explores the optimal structuring of the prices that a network operator charges for access to its network. The design of access prices presently is an issue of great importance in many industries where regulated suppliers of essential inputs are facing increasing competition in the delivery of retail services. In contrast to most of the other analyses in this chapter, the analysis of access prices in Section 5 focuses on a setting where the regulator has complete information about the regulatory environment. This focus is motivated by the fact that the optimal design of access prices involves substantial subtleties even in the absence of asymmetric information.

The discussion concludes in Section 6, which reviews some of the central themes of this chapter, and suggests directions for future research.

2. Optimal monopoly regulation

2.1. Aims and instruments

The optimal regulation of a monopoly supplier is influenced by many factors, including:

1. the regulator's objective (when he is benevolent);
2. the cost of raising revenue from taxpayers;
3. the range of policy instruments available to the regulator, including his ability to tax the regulated firm or employ public funds to compensate the firm directly;
4. the regulator's bargaining power in his interaction with the firm;
5. the information available to the regulator and the firm;
6. whether the regulator is benevolent or self-interested; and
7. the regulator's ability to commit to long-term policies.

The objective of a benevolent regulator is modeled by assuming the regulator seeks to maximize a weighted average of consumer (or taxpayer) surplus, S, and the rent (or net profit), R, secured by the regulated firm. Formally, the regulator is assumed to maximize $S + \alpha R$, where $\alpha \in [0, 1]$ is the value the regulator assigns to each dollar of rent. The regulator's preference for consumer surplus over rent (indicated by $\alpha < 1$) reflects a greater concern with the welfare of consumers than the welfare of shareholders. This might be due to differences in their average income, or because the regulator cares about the welfare of local constituents and many shareholders reside in other jurisdictions.[4]

The second factor – the cost of raising funds from taxpayers – is captured most simply by introducing the parameter $\Lambda \geqslant 0$. In this formulation, taxpayer welfare is presumed to decline by $1 + \Lambda$ dollars for each dollar of tax revenue the government collects. The parameter Λ, often called the *social cost of public funds*, is strictly positive when taxes distort productive activity (reducing efficient effort or inducing wasteful effort to avoid taxes, for example), and thereby create deadweight losses. The parameter Λ is typically viewed as exogenous in the regulated industry.[5]

The literature generally adopts one of two approaches. The first approach, which follows Baron and Myerson (1982), abstracts from any social cost of public funds (so $\Lambda = 0$) but presumes the regulator strictly prefers consumer surplus to rent (so $\alpha < 1$). The second approach, which follows Laffont and Tirole (1986), assumes strictly positive social costs of public funds (so $\Lambda > 0$) but abstracts from any distributional preferences (so $\alpha = 1$). The two approaches provide similar qualitative conclusions, as does a combination of the two approaches (in which $\Lambda > 0$ and $\alpha < 1$). Therefore, because the combination introduces additional notation that can make the analysis less transparent, the combination is not pursued here.[6]

The central difference between the two basic approaches concerns the regulated prices that are optimal when the regulator and firm are both perfectly informed about the industry demand and cost conditions. In this benchmark setting, the regulator who faces no social cost of funds will compensate the regulated firm directly for its fixed costs of production and set marginal-cost prices. In contrast, the regulator who finds it costly to compensate the firm directly (since $\Lambda > 0$) will establish Ramsey prices, which exceed marginal cost and thereby secure revenue to contribute to public funds. Because the marginal cost benchmark generally facilitates a more transparent analysis, the ensuing analysis will focus on the approach in which the regulator has a strict preference for consumer surplus over rent but faces no social cost of public funds.

The third factor – which includes the regulator's ability to compensate the firm directly – is a key determinant of optimal regulatory policy. The discussion in Section 2 will follow the strand of the literature that presumes the regulator can make direct payments to the regulated firm. In contrast, the discussion of practical policies in Section 3 generally will follow the literature that assumes such direct payments are not feasible (because the regulator has no access to public funds, for example).

The fourth factor – the regulator's bargaining power – is typically treated in a simple manner: the regulator is assumed to possess all of the bargaining power in his interaction

[4] Baron (1988) presents a positive model of regulation in which the regulator's welfare function is determined endogenously by a voting process.

[5] In general, the value of Λ is affected by a country's institutions and macroeconomic characteristics, and so can reasonably be viewed as exogenous to any particular regulatory sector. Laffont (2005, pp. 1–2) suggests that Λ may be approximately 0.3 in developed countries, and well above 1 in less developed countries.

[6] As explained further below, the case where $\alpha = 1$ and $\Lambda = 0$ is straightforward to analyze.

with the regulated firm. This assumption is modeled formally by endowing the regulator with the ability to offer a regulatory policy that the firm can either accept or reject. If the firm rejects the proposed policy, the interaction between the regulator and the firm ends. This formulation generally is adopted for technical convenience rather than for realism.[7]

The fifth factor – the information available to the regulator – is the focus of Section 2. Regulated firms typically have better information about their operating environment than do regulators. Because of its superior resources, its ongoing management of production, and its frequent direct contact with customers, a regulated firm will often be better informed than the regulator about both its technology and consumer demand. Consequently, it is important to analyze the optimal design of regulatory policy in settings that admit such adverse selection (or "hidden information") problems.

Two distinct adverse selection problems are considered in Section 2.3. In the first setting, the firm is better informed than the regulator about its operating cost. In the second setting, the firm has privileged information about consumer demand in the industry. A comparison of these settings reveals that the properties of optimal regulatory policies can vary substantially with the nature of the information asymmetry between regulator and firm. Section 2.3 concludes by presenting a unified framework for analyzing these various settings.

Section 2.4 provides some extensions of this basic model. Specifically, the analysis is extended to allow the regulator to acquire better information about the regulated industry, to allow the firm's private information to be multi-dimensional, and to allow for the possibility that the regulator is susceptible to capture by the industry (the sixth factor listed above). Section 2.5 reviews how optimal regulatory policy changes when the interaction between the regulator and firm is repeated over time. Optimal regulatory policy is shown to vary systematically according to the regulator's ability to make credible commitments to future policy (the seventh factor cited above).

Regulated firms also typically know more about their actions (e.g., how diligently managers labor to reduce operating costs) than do regulators. Consequently, it is important to analyze the optimal design of regulatory policy in settings that admit such moral hazard (or "hidden action") problems. Section 2.6 analyzes a regulatory moral hazard problem in which the firm's cost structure is endogenous.

2.2. Regulation with complete information

Before analyzing optimal regulatory policy when the firm has privileged knowledge of its environment, consider the full-information benchmark in which the regulator is omniscient. Suppose a regulated monopolist supplies n products. Let p_i denote the price of

[7] Bargaining between parties with private information is complicated by the fact that the parties may attempt to signal their private information through the contracts they offer. Inderst (2002) proposes the following alternative to the standard approach in the literature. The regulator first makes an offer to the (better informed) monopolist. If the firm rejects this offer, the firm can, with some exogenous probability, respond with a final take-it-or-leave-it offer to the regulator.

product i, and let $\mathbf{p} = (p_1, \ldots, p_n)$ denote the corresponding vector of prices. Further, let $v(\mathbf{p})$ denote aggregate consumer surplus and $\pi(\mathbf{p})$ denote the monopolist's profit with price vector $\mathbf{p}$. The important difference between the analysis here and in the remainder of Section 2 is that the regulator knows the functions $v(\cdot)$ and $\pi(\cdot)$ perfectly here.

2.2.1. *Setting where transfers are feasible*

Consider first the setting where the regulator is able to make transfer payments to the regulated firm and receive transfers from the firm. Suppose the social cost of public funds is Λ. To limit the deadweight loss from taxation in this setting, the regulator will extract all the firm's rent and pass it onto taxpayers in the form of a reduced tax burden. (The regulator's relative preference for profit and consumer surplus, i.e., the parameter α, plays no role in this calculation.) Since a \$1 reduction in the tax burden makes taxpayers better off by \$$(1 + \Lambda)$, total welfare with the price vector $\mathbf{p}$ is

$$v(\mathbf{p}) + (1 + \Lambda)\pi(\mathbf{p}). \tag{1}$$

A regulator should choose prices to maximize expression (1) in the present setting. In the special case where $\Lambda = 0$ (as presumed in the remainder of Section 2), prices will be chosen to maximize total surplus $v + \pi$. Optimal prices in this setting are marginal-cost prices. This ideal outcome for the regulator will be called the *full-information outcome* in the ensuing analysis. When $\Lambda > 0$, prices optimally exceed marginal costs (at least on average). For instance, in the single-product case, the price p that maximizes expression (1) satisfies the Lerner formula

$$\frac{p - c}{p} = \left[\frac{\Lambda}{1 + \Lambda}\right]\frac{1}{\eta(p)}, \tag{2}$$

where c is the firm's marginal cost and $\eta = -pq'(p)/q(p)$ is the elasticity of demand for the firm's product (and where a prime denotes a derivative).

2.2.2. *Setting where transfers are infeasible*

Now consider the setting in which the regulator cannot use public funds to finance transfer payments to the firm and cannot directly tax the firm's profit. Because the regulator cannot compensate the firm directly in this setting, the firm must secure revenues from the sale of its products that are at least as great as the production costs it incurs. When the firm operates with increasing returns to scale, marginal-cost prices will generate revenue below cost. Consequently, the requirement that the firm earn non-negative profit will impose a binding constraint on the regulator, and the regulator will choose prices to maximize total surplus $(v(\mathbf{p}) + \pi(\mathbf{p}))$ while ensuring zero profit for the firm ($\pi(\mathbf{p}) = 0$). This is the Ramsey–Boiteux problem.[8] (Again, the regulator's relative preference for profit and consumer surplus plays no meaningful role here.) In the single-product case, the optimal policy is to set a price equal to the firm's average cost of production. If we let λ denote the Lagrange multiplier associated with the break-even constraint ($\pi(\mathbf{p}) = 0$), then under mild regularity conditions, Ramsey–Boiteux prices maximize $v(\mathbf{p}) + (1 + \lambda)\pi(\mathbf{p})$, which has the same form as expression (1). Thus, optimal prices in the two problems – when transfers are possible and there is a social cost of public funds, and when transfers are not possible – take the same form. The only difference is that the "multiplier" Λ is exogenous to the former problem, whereas λ is endogenous in the latter problem and chosen so that the firm earns exactly zero profit.[9]

2.3. Regulation under adverse selection

In this section we analyze simple versions of the central models of optimal regulation with private, but exogenous, information.[10] The models are first discussed under the headings of private information about cost and private information about demand. The ensuing discussion summarizes the basic insights in a unified framework.

2.3.1. Asymmetric cost information

We begin the discussion of optimal regulatory policy under asymmetric information by considering an especially simple setting. In this setting, the regulated monopoly sells one product and customer demand for the product is known precisely to all parties. In particular, the demand curve for the regulated product, $Q(p)$, is common knowledge, where $p \geqslant 0$ is the unit price for the regulated product. The only information asymmetry concerns the firm's production costs, which take the form of a constant marginal cost c together with a fixed cost F. Three variants of this model are discussed in turn. In the first variant, the firm has private information about its marginal cost alone, and this cost is exogenous and is not observed by the regulator. In the second variant, the firm is privately informed about both its fixed and its marginal costs of production. The regulator knows the relationship between the firm's exogenous marginal and fixed costs, but cannot observe either realization. In the third variant, the firm can control its marginal cost and the regulator can observe realized marginal cost, but the regulator is

[8] Ramsey (1927) examines how to maximize consumer surplus while employing proportional taxes to raise a specified amount of tax revenue. Boiteux (1956) analyzes how to maximize consumer surplus while marking prices up above marginal cost to cover a firm's fixed cost.

[9] In the special case where consumer demands are independent (so there are no cross price effects), Ramsey prices follow the "inverse elasticity" rule, where each product's Lerner index $(p_i - c_i)/p_i$ is inversely proportional to that product's elasticity of demand. More generally, Ramsey prices have the property that an amplification of the implicit tax rates $(p_i - c_i)$ leads to an equi-proportionate reduction in the demand for all products [see Mirrlees (1976), Section 2].

[10] For more extensive and general accounts of the theory of incentives, see Laffont and Martimort (2002) and Bolton and Dewatripont (2005), for example.

not fully informed about the fixed cost the firm must incur to realize any specified level of marginal cost.

In all three variants of this model, the regulator sets the unit price p for the regulated product. The regulator also specifies a transfer payment, T, from consumers to the regulated firm. The firm is obligated to serve all customer demand at the established price. The firm's rent, R, is its profit, $\pi = Q(p)(p - c) - F$, plus the transfer T it receives.

Unknown marginal cost[11] For simplicity, suppose the firm produces with constant marginal cost that can take one of two values, $c \in \{c_L, c_H\}$. Let $\Delta^c = c_H - c_L > 0$ denote the cost differential between the high and low marginal cost. The firm knows from the outset of its interaction with the regulator whether its marginal cost is low, c_L, or high, c_H. The regulator does not share this information, and never observes cost directly. He views marginal cost as a random variable that takes on the low value with probability $\phi \in (0, 1)$ and the high value with probability $1 - \phi$. In this initial model, it is common knowledge that the firm must incur fixed cost $F \geqslant 0$ in order to operate.

In this setting, the full-information outcome is not feasible. To see why, suppose the regulator announces that he will implement unit price p_i and transfer payment T_i when the firm claims to have marginal cost c_i, for $i = L, H$.[12] When the firm with cost c_i chooses the (p_i, T_i) option, its rent will be

$$R_i = Q(p_i)(p_i - c_i) - F + T_i. \tag{3}$$

In contrast, if this firm chooses the alternative (p_j, T_j) option, its rent is

$$Q(p_j)(p_j - c_i) - F + T_j = R_j + Q(p_j)(c_j - c_i).$$

It follows that if the low-cost firm is to be induced to choose the (p_L, T_L) option, it must be the case that

$$R_L \geqslant R_H + \Delta^c Q(p_H). \tag{4}$$

Therefore, the full-information outcome is not feasible, since inequality (4) cannot hold when both $R_H = 0$ and $R_L = 0$.[13]

To induce the firm to employ its privileged cost information to implement outcomes that approximate (but do not replicate) the full-information outcome, the regulator pursues the policy described in Proposition 1.[14]

[11] This discussion is based on Baron and Myerson (1982). The qualitative conclusions derived in our simplified setting hold more generally. For instance, Baron and Myerson derive corresponding conclusions in a setting with non-linear costs where the firm's private information is the realization of a continuous random variable.

[12] The revelation principle ensures that the regulator can do no better than to pursue such a policy. See, for example, Myerson (1979) or Harris and Townsend (1981).

[13] This conclusion assumes it is optimal to produce in the high-cost state. This assumption will be maintained throughout the ensuing discussion, unless otherwise noted.

[14] A sketch of the proofs of Propositions 1 through 4 is provided in Section 2.3.3.

PROPOSITION 1. *When the firm is privately informed about its marginal cost of production, the optimal regulatory policy has the following features*:

$$p_L = c_L; \qquad p_H = c_H + \frac{\phi}{1-\phi}(1-\alpha)\Delta^c; \tag{5}$$

$$R_L = \Delta^c Q(p_H); \qquad R_H = 0. \tag{6}$$

As expression (6) reveals, the regulator optimally provides the low-cost firm with the minimum possible rent required to ensure it does not exaggerate its cost. This is the rent the low-cost firm could secure by selecting the (p_H, T_H) option. To reduce this rent, p_H is raised above c_H. The increase in p_H reduces the output of the high-cost firm, and thus the number of units of output on which the low-cost firm can exercise its cost advantage by selecting the (p_H, T_H) option. (This effect is evident in inequality (4) above.) Although the increase in p_H above c_H reduces the rent of the low-cost firm – which serves to increase welfare when c_L is realized – it reduces the total surplus available when the firm's cost is c_H. Therefore, the regulator optimally balances the expected benefits and costs of raising p_H above c_H. As expression (5) indicates, the regulator will set p_H further above c_H the more likely is the firm to have low cost (i.e., the greater is $\phi/(1-\phi)$) and the more pronounced is the regulator's preference for limiting the rent of the low-cost firm (i.e., the smaller is α).

Expression (5) states that the regulator implements marginal-cost pricing for the low-cost firm. Any deviation of price from marginal cost would reduce total surplus without any offsetting benefit. Such a deviation would not reduce the firm's expected rent, since the high-cost firm has no incentive to choose the (p_L, T_L) option. As expression (6) indicates, the firm is effectively paid only c_L per unit for producing the extra output $Q(p_L) - Q(p_H)$, and this rate of compensation is unprofitable for the high-cost firm.

Notice that if the regulator valued consumer surplus and rent equally (so $\alpha = 1$), he would not want to sacrifice any surplus when cost is c_H in order to reduce the low-cost firm's rent. As expression (5) shows, the regulator would implement marginal-cost pricing for both cost realizations. Doing so would require that the low-cost firm receive a rent of at least $\Delta^c Q(c_H)$. But the regulator is not averse to this relatively large rent when he values rent as highly as consumer surplus.

This last conclusion holds more generally as long as the regulator knows how consumers value the firm's output.[15] To see why, write $v(p)$ for consumer surplus when the price is p, and write $\pi(p)$ for the firm's profit function (a function that may be known only by the firm). Suppose the regulator promises the firm a transfer of $T = v(p)$ when it sets the price p. Under this reward structure, the firm chooses its price to maximize $v(p) + \pi(p)$, which is just social welfare when $\alpha = 1$. The result is marginal-cost pricing. In effect, this policy makes the firm the residual claimant for social surplus, and

[15] See Loeb and Magat (1979). Guesnerie and Laffont (1984) also examine the case where the regulator is not averse to the transfers he delivers to the firm.

thereby induces the better-informed party to employ its superior information in the social interest. Such a policy awards the entire social surplus to the firm. However, this asymmetric distribution is acceptable in the special case where the regulator cares only about total surplus.[16] (Section 3.2.2 explains how, in a dynamic context, surplus can sometimes be returned to consumers over time.)

Countervailing incentives[17] In the foregoing setting, the firm's incentive is to exaggerate its cost in order to convince the regulator that more generous compensation is required to induce the firm to serve customers. This incentive to exaggerate private information may, in some circumstances, be tempered by a countervailing incentive to understate private information. To illustrate this effect, consider the following model.

Suppose everything is as specified above in the setting where realized costs are unobservable, with one exception. Suppose the level of fixed cost, F, is known only to the firm. It is common knowledge, though, that the firm's fixed cost is inversely related to its marginal cost, c.[18] In particular, it is common knowledge that when marginal cost is c_L, fixed cost is F_L, and that when marginal cost is c_H, fixed cost is $F_H < F_L$. Let $\Delta^F = F_L - F_H > 0$ denote the amount by which the firm's fixed cost increases as its marginal cost declines from c_H to c_L. As before, let $\Delta^c = c_H - c_L > 0$.

One might suspect that the regulator would suffer further when the firm is privately informed about both its fixed cost and its marginal cost of production rather than being privately informed only about the latter. This is not necessarily the case, though, as Proposition 2 reveals.

PROPOSITION 2. *When the firm is privately informed about both its fixed and its marginal cost*:

(i) *If* $\Delta^F \in [\Delta^c Q(c_H), \Delta^c Q(c_L)]$ *then the full-information outcome is feasible (and optimal)*;
(ii) *If* $\Delta^F < \Delta^c Q(c_H)$ *then* $p_H > c_H$ *and* $p_L = c_L$;
(iii) *If* $\Delta^F > \Delta^c Q(c_L)$ *then* $p_L < c_L$ *and* $p_H = c_H$.

Part (i) of Proposition 2 considers a setting where the variation in fixed cost is of intermediate magnitude relative to the variation in variable cost when marginal-cost pricing is implemented. The usual incentive of the firm to exaggerate its marginal cost does

[16] This conclusion – derived here in an adverse selection setting – parallels the standard result that the full-information outcome can be achieved in a moral hazard setting when a risk-neutral agent is made the residual claimant for the social surplus. Risk neutrality in the moral hazard setting plays a role similar to the assumption here that distributional concerns are not present ($\alpha = 1$). The moral hazard problem is analyzed in Section 2.6 below.

[17] The following discussion is based on Lewis and Sappington (1989a). See Maggi and Rodriguez-Clare (1995) and Jullien (2000) for further analyses.

[18] If fixed costs increased as marginal costs increased, the firm would have additional incentive to exaggerate its marginal cost when it is privately informed about both fixed and marginal costs. Baron and Myerson (1982) show that the qualitative conclusions reported in Proposition 1 persist in this setting.

not arise at the full-information outcome in this setting. An exaggeration of marginal cost here amounts to an overstatement of variable cost by $\Delta^c Q(c_H)$. But it also constitutes an implicit understatement of fixed cost by Δ^F. Since Δ^F exceeds $\Delta^c Q(c_H)$, the firm would understate its true total operating cost if it exaggerated its marginal cost of production, and so will refrain from doing so. The firm also will have no incentive to understate its marginal cost at the full-information solution. Such an understatement amounts to a claim that variable costs are $\Delta^c Q(c_L)$ lower than they truly are. This understatement outweighs the associated exaggeration of fixed cost (Δ^F), and so will not be advantageous for the firm.

When the potential variation in fixed cost is either more pronounced or less pronounced than in part (i) of Proposition 2, the full-information outcome is no longer feasible. If the variation is less pronounced, then part (ii) of the proposition demonstrates that the qualitative distortions identified in Proposition 1 arise.[19] The prospect of understating fixed cost is no longer sufficient to eliminate the firm's incentive to exaggerate its marginal cost. Therefore, the regulator sets price above marginal cost when the firm claims to have high marginal cost in order to reduce the number of units of output ($Q(p_H)$) on which the firm can exercise its cost advantage.

In contrast, when the variation in fixed cost Δ^F exceeds $\Delta^c Q(c_L)$, the binding incentive problem for the regulator is to prevent the firm from exaggerating its fixed cost via understating its marginal cost. To mitigate the firm's incentive to understate c, part (iii) of Proposition 2 shows that the regulator sets p_L below c_L. Doing so increases beyond its full-information level the output the firm must produce in return for incremental compensation that is less than cost when the firm's marginal cost is high. Since the firm is not tempted to exaggerate its marginal cost (and thereby understate its fixed cost) in this setting, no pricing distortions arise when the high marginal cost is reported.

One implication of Proposition 2 is that the regulator may gain by *creating* countervailing incentives for the regulated firm. For instance, the regulator may mandate the adoption of technologies in which fixed costs vary inversely with variable costs. Alternatively, he may authorize expanded participation in unregulated markets the more lucrative the firm reports such participation to be (and thus the lower the firm admits its operating cost in the regulated market to be).[20]

Unknown scope for cost reduction[21] Now consider a setting where the regulator can observe the firm's marginal cost, but the firm's realized cost is affected by its (unobserved) cost-reducing effort, and the regulator is uncertain about the amount of effort required to achieve any given level of marginal cost.

[19] If $\Delta^F < \Delta^c Q(\hat{p}_H)$, where $\hat{p}_H = c_H + \frac{\phi}{1-\phi}(1-\alpha)\Delta^c$ is the optimal price for the high-cost firm identified in expression (5), then the price for the high-cost firm will be $p_H = \hat{p}_H$. Thus, for sufficiently small variation in fixed costs, the optimal pricing distortion is precisely the one identified by Baron and Myerson. The optimal distortion declines as Δ^F increases in the range $(\Delta^c Q(\hat{p}_H), \Delta^c Q(c_H))$.

[20] See Lewis and Sappington (1989a, 1989b, 1989c) for formal analyses of these possibilities.

[21] This is a simplified version of the model proposed in Laffont and Tirole (1986) and Laffont and Tirole (1993b, chs. 1 and 2). Also see Sappington (1982).

Suppose there are two types of firm. One (type L) can achieve low marginal cost via expending relatively low fixed cost. The other (type H) must incur greater fixed cost to achieve a given level of marginal cost. Formally, let $F_i(c)$ denote the fixed cost the type $i = L, H$ firm must incur to achieve marginal cost c. Each function $F_i(\cdot)$ is decreasing and convex, where $F_H(c) > F_L(c)$ and where $[F_H(c) - F_L(c)]$ is a decreasing function of c. The regulator cannot observe the firm's type, and views it as a random variable that takes on the value L with probability $\phi \in (0, 1)$ and H with probability $1 - \phi$. As noted, the regulator can observe the firm's realized marginal cost c in the present setting, but cannot observe the associated realization of the fixed cost $F_i(c)$.

Because realized marginal cost is observable, the regulator has three policy instruments at his disposal. He can specify a unit price (p) for the firm's product, a transfer payment (T) from consumers to the firm, and a realized level of marginal cost (c). Therefore, for each $i = L, H$ the regulator announces that he will authorize price p_i and transfer payment T_i when the firm claims to be of type i, provided marginal cost c_i is observed. The equilibrium rent of the type i firm, R_i, is then

$$R_i = Q(p_i)(p_i - c_i) - F_i(c_i) + T_i. \tag{7}$$

As in inequality (4) above, the constraint that the low-cost firm does not claim to have high cost is

$$R_L \geqslant R_H + F_H(c_H) - F_L(c_H). \tag{8}$$

Net consumer surplus in state i is $v(p_i) - T_i$. Using equality (7), this net consumer surplus can be written as

$$v(p_i) + Q(p_i)(p_i - c_i) - F_i(c_i) - R_i. \tag{9}$$

Notice that the regulator's choice of prices $\{p_L, p_H\}$ does not affect the incentive constraint (8), given the choice of rents $\{R_L, R_H\}$. Therefore, price will be set equal to realized marginal cost (i.e., $p_i = c_i$) in order to maximize total surplus in (9). This conclusion reflects Laffont and Tirole's "incentive-pricing dichotomy": prices (often) should be employed solely to attain allocative efficiency, while rents should be employed to motivate the firm to produce at low cost.[22] This dichotomy represents a key difference between Baron and Myerson's (1982) model in which costs are exogenous and unobservable and Laffont and Tirole's (1986) model in which costs are endogenous and observable. In the former model, price levels are distorted in order to reduce the firm's rent. In the latter model, price levels are not distorted given the induced costs, but cost distortions are implemented to limit the firm's rent.

If the regulator knew the firm's type, he would also require the efficient marginal cost, which is the cost that maximizes total surplus $\{v(c) - F_i(c)\}$. However, the full-information outcome is not feasible when the regulator does not share the firm's

[22] For further analysis of the incentive-pricing dichotomy, including a discussion of conditions under which the dichotomy does not hold, see Laffont and Tirole (1993b, Sections 2.3 and 3.6).

knowledge of its technology. To limit the type-L firm's rent, the regulator inflates the type-H firm's marginal cost above the full-information level, as reported in Proposition 3.

PROPOSITION 3. *When the firm's marginal cost is observable but endogenous, the optimal regulatory policy has the following features*:

$$p_L = c_L; \qquad p_H = c_H; \tag{10}$$

$$Q(c_L) + F_L'(c_L) = 0; \tag{11}$$

$$Q(c_H) + F_H'(c_H) = -\frac{\phi}{1-\phi}(1-\alpha)\big(F_H'(c_H) - F_L'(c_H)\big) > 0, \tag{12}$$

$$R_L = F_H(c_H) - F_L(c_H) > 0; \qquad R_H = 0. \tag{13}$$

Expression (11) indicates that the type-L firm will be induced to operate with the cost-minimizing technology. In contrast, expression (12) reveals that the type-H firm will produce with inefficiently high marginal cost. This high marginal cost limits the rent that accrues to the type-L firm, which, from inequality (8), decreases as c_H increases. As expression (12) reveals, the optimal distortion in c_H is more pronounced the more likely is the firm to have low cost (i.e., the larger is $\phi/(1-\phi)$) and the more the regulator cares about minimizing rents (i.e., the smaller is α). The marginal cost implemented by the low-cost firm is not distorted because the high-cost firm is not tempted to misrepresent its type.[23,24]

2.3.2. Asymmetric demand information

The analysis to this point has assumed that the demand function facing the firm is common knowledge. In practice, regulated firms often have privileged information about consumer demand. To assess the impact of asymmetric knowledge of this kind, consider the following simple model.[25]

The firm's cost function, $C(\cdot)$, is common knowledge, but consumer demand can take one of two forms: the demand function is $Q_L(\cdot)$ with probability ϕ and $Q_H(\cdot)$

[23] The regulator may implement other distortions when he has additional policy instruments at his disposal. For example, the regulator may require the firm to employ more than the cost-minimizing level of capital when additional capital reduces the sensitivity of realized costs to the firm's unobserved innate cost. By reducing this sensitivity, the regulator is able to limit the rents that the firm commands from its privileged knowledge of its innate costs. See Sappington (1983) and Besanko (1985), for example.

[24] Extending the analysis of Guesnerie and Laffont (1984), Laffont and Rochet (1998) examine how risk aversion on the part of the regulated firm affects the optimal regulatory policy in a setting where the firm's realized marginal cost is observable and endogenous. The authors show that risk aversion introduces more pronounced cost distortions, reduces the rent of the firm, and may render realized marginal cost insensitive to the firm's innate capabilities over some ranges of capability.

[25] The following discussion is based on Lewis and Sappington (1988a).

with probability $1 - \phi$, where $Q_H(p) > Q_L(p)$ for all prices p. The firm knows the demand function it faces from the outset of its relationship with the regulator. The regulator never observes the prevailing demand function. Furthermore, the regulator never observes realized cost or realized demand.[26] The firm is required to serve all customer demand and will operate as long as it receives non-negative profit from doing so.

As in the setting with countervailing incentives, the regulator's limited information need not be constraining here. To see why in the simplest case, suppose the firm's cost function is affine, i.e., $C(q) = cq + F$, where q is the number of units of output produced by the firm. In this case, the regulator can instruct the firm to sell its product at price equal to marginal cost in return for a transfer payment equal to F. Doing so ensures marginal-cost pricing and zero rent for the firm for both demand realizations, which is the full-information outcome. When marginal cost is constant, the full-information pricing policy (i.e., $p = c$) is common knowledge because it depends only on the firm's (known) marginal cost of production.[27]

More surprisingly, Proposition 4 states that the regulator can also ensure the full-information outcome if marginal cost increases with output.

PROPOSITION 4. *In the setting where the firm is privately informed about demand*:

(i) *If* $C''(q) \geqslant 0$, *the full-information outcome is feasible* (*and optimal*);

(ii) *If* $C''(q) < 0$, *the regulator often*[28] *sets a single price and transfer payment for all demand realizations.*

When marginal cost increases with output, the full-information price for the firm's product p increases with demand, and the transfer payment to the firm T declines with demand. The higher price reflects the higher marginal cost of production that accompanies increased output. The reduction in T just offsets the higher variable profit the firm secures from the higher p. Since the reduction in T exactly offsets the increase in variable profit when demand is high, it more than offsets any increase in variable profit from a higher p when demand is low. Therefore, the firm has no incentive to exaggerate demand. When demand is truly low, the reduction in T that results when demand is exaggerated more than offsets the extra profit from the higher p that is authorized. Similarly, the firm has no incentive to understate demand when the regulator offers the firm two choices that constitute the full-information outcome. The understatement of demand calls forth a price reduction that reduces the firm's profit by more than the

[26] If he could observe realized costs or demand, the regulator would be able to infer the firm's private information since he knows the functional forms of $C(\cdot)$ and $Q_i(\cdot)$.

[27] This discussion assumes that production is known to be desirable for all states of demand.

[28] The precise meaning of "often" is made clear in Section 2.3.3. To illustrate, pooling is optimal when the two demand functions differ by an additive constant and $C(\cdot)$ satisfies standard regularity conditions.

corresponding increase in the transfer payment it receives.[29] In sum, part (i) of Proposition 4 states that the full-information outcome is feasible in this setting.[30]

Part (ii) of Proposition 4 shows that the same is not true when marginal cost declines with output. In this case, the optimal price p declines as demand increases in the full-information outcome.[31] In contrast, in many reasonable cases, the induced price p cannot decline as demand increases when the firm alone knows the realization of demand. A substantial increase in the transfer payment T would be required to compensate the firm for the decline in variable profit that results from a lower p when demand is high. This increase in T more than compensates the firm for the corresponding reduction in variable profit when demand is low. Consequently, the firm cannot be induced to set a price that declines as demand increases. When feasible prices increase with demand while full-information prices decline with demand, the regulator is unable to induce the firm to employ its private knowledge of demand to benefit consumers. Instead, he chooses a single unit price and transfer payment to maximize expected welfare. Thus, when the firm's cost function is concave, it is too costly from a social point of view to make use of the firm's private information about demand.[32]

Notice that in the present setting where there is no deadweight loss involved in raising tax revenue, the relevant full-information benchmark is marginal-cost pricing. As noted in Section 2.1, when a transfer payment to the firm imposes a deadweight loss on society, Ramsey prices become the relevant full-information benchmark. Since the implementation of Ramsey prices requires knowledge of consumer demand, the regulator will generally be unable to implement the full-information outcome when he is ignorant about consumer demand, even when the firm's cost function is known to be convex. Consequently, the qualitative conclusion drawn in Proposition 4 does not extend to the

[29] Lewis and Sappington (1988a) show that the firm has no strict incentive to understate demand in this setting even if it can ration customers with impunity. The authors also show that the arguments presented here are valid regardless of the number of possible states of demand. Riordan (1984) provides a corresponding analysis for the case where the firm's marginal cost is constant up to an endogenous capacity level. Lewis and Sappington (1992) show that part (i) of Proposition 4 continues to hold when the regulated firm chooses the level of observable and contractible quality it supplies.

[30] Biglaiser and Ma (1995) analyze a setting in which a regulated firm produces with constant marginal cost and is privately informed about both the demand for its product and the demand for the (differentiated) product of its unregulated rival. The authors show that when the regulator's restricted set of instruments must serve both to limit the rents of the regulated firm and to limit the welfare losses that result from the rival's market power, the optimal regulatory policy under asymmetric information differs from the corresponding policy under complete information. Therefore, part (i) of Proposition 4 does not always hold when the regulated firm faces an unregulated rival with market power.

[31] This will be the case when the marginal cost curve is less steeply sloped than the inverse demand curve, and so the regulator's problem is concave and there exists a unique welfare-maximizing price that equals marginal cost in each state.

[32] A similar finding emerges in Section 2.5, where the regulator's intertemporal commitment powers are limited. In that setting, it can be too costly to induce the low-cost firm to reveal its superior capabilities, because the firm fears the regulator will expropriate all future rent. Consequently, the regulator may optimally implement some pooling in order to remain ignorant about the firm's true capabilities.

setting where transfer payments to the firm are socially costly. In contrast, the qualitative conclusions drawn in Propositions 1, 2 and 3 persist in the alternative setting when transfer payments are socially costly, provided the full-information prices are Ramsey prices rather than marginal-cost prices.

2.3.3. *A unified analysis*

The foregoing analyses reveal that the qualitative properties of optimal regulatory policies can vary substantially according to the nature of the firm's private information and its technology. Optimal regulated prices can be set above, below, or at the level of marginal cost, and the full-information outcome may or may not be feasible, depending on whether the firm is privately informed about the demand function it faces, its variable production costs, or both its variable and its fixed costs of production. The purpose of this subsection is to explain how these seemingly disparate findings all emerge from a single, unified framework.[33] This section also provides a sketch of the proofs of the propositions presented above. Consequently, this section is somewhat more technical than most. The less technically-oriented reader can skip this section without compromising understanding of subsequent discussions.

This unifying framework has the following features. The firm's private information takes on one of two possible values, which will be referred to as state L or state H. The probability of state L is $\phi \in (0, 1)$ and the probability of state H is $1 - \phi$. The firm's operating profit in state i when it charges unit price p for its product is $\pi_i(p)$. The firm's equilibrium rent in state i is $R_i = \pi_i(p_i) + T_i$, where p_i is the price for the firm's product and T_i is the transfer payment from the regulator to the firm in state i.

The difference in the firm's operating profit at price p in state H versus state L will be denoted $\Delta^\pi(p)$. For most of the following analysis, this difference is assumed to increase with p. Formally,

$$\Delta^\pi(p) \equiv \pi_H(p) - \pi_L(p) \quad \text{and} \quad \frac{\mathrm{d}}{\mathrm{d}p}\Delta^\pi(p) > 0. \tag{14}$$

The "increasing difference" property in expression (14) reflects the standard single crossing property.[34] Its role, as will be shown below, is to guarantee that the equilibrium price in state H is higher than in state L.

The regulator seeks to maximize the expected value of a weighted average of consumer surplus and rent. The social cost of public funds is assumed to be zero. Consumer surplus in state i given price p is the surplus (denoted $v_i(p)$) from consuming

[33] This material is taken from Armstrong and Sappington (2004). Guesnerie and Laffont (1984) and Caillaud et al. (1988) provide earlier unifying analyses of adverse selection models in the case where private information is a continuously distributed variable. Although the qualitative features of the solutions to continuous and discrete adverse selection problems are often similar, the analytic techniques employed to solve the two kinds of problems differ significantly.

[34] The single crossing property holds when the firm's marginal rate of substitution of price for transfer payment varies monotonically with the underlying state. See Cooper (1984) for details.

the product at price p, minus the transfer, T_i, to the firm. Written in terms of rent $R_i = \pi_i(p_i) + T_i$, this weighted average of consumer surplus and rent in state i is

$$S_i + \alpha R_i = v_i(p_i) - T_i + \alpha\big(\pi_i(p_i) + T_i\big) = w_i(p_i) - (1-\alpha)R_i. \tag{15}$$

Here, $w_i(p) \equiv v_i(p) + \pi_i(p)$ denotes total unweighted surplus in state i when price p is charged, and $\alpha \in [0, 1]$ is the relative weight placed on rent in social welfare. Therefore, expected welfare is

$$W = \phi\big\{w_L(p_L) - (1-\alpha)R_L\big\} + (1-\phi)\big\{w_H(p_H) - (1-\alpha)R_H\big\}. \tag{16}$$

The type i firm will agree to produce according to the specified contract only if it receives a non-negative rent. Consequently, the regulator faces the two participation constraints

$$R_i \geqslant 0 \quad \text{for } i = L, H. \tag{17}$$

If the regulator knew that state i was the prevailing state, he would implement the price p_i^* that maximizes $w_i(\cdot)$ while ensuring $R_i = 0$. This is the full-information benchmark, and involves marginal-cost pricing. If the regulator does not know the prevailing state, he must ensure that contracts are such that each type of firm finds it in its interest to choose the correct contract. Therefore, as in expressions (4) and (8) above, the regulator must ensure that the following incentive compatibility constraints are satisfied:

$$R_L \geqslant R_H - \Delta^\pi(p_H), \tag{18}$$

$$R_H \geqslant R_L + \Delta^\pi(p_L). \tag{19}$$

Adding inequalities (18) and (19) implies

$$\Delta^\pi(p_H) \geqslant \Delta^\pi(p_L). \tag{20}$$

The increasing difference assumption in expression (14) and inequality (20) together imply the equilibrium price must be weakly higher in state H than in state L in any incentive-compatible regulatory policy, i.e.,

$$p_H \geqslant p_L. \tag{21}$$

The following conclusion aids in understanding the solution to the regulator's problem.

LEMMA 1. *If the incentive compatibility constraint for the type i firm does not bind at the optimum, then the price for the other type of firm is not distorted, i.e.,* $p_j = p_j^*$.[35]

[35] The surplus functions $w_i(p_i)$ are assumed to be single-peaked.

To understand this result, suppose the incentive compatibility constraint for the type-H firm, inequality (19), does not bind at the optimum. Then, holding R_L constant – which implies that neither the participation constraint nor the incentive compatibility constraint for the type-L firm is affected – the price p_L can be changed (in either direction) without violating (19). If a small change in p_L does not increase welfare $w_L(p_L)$ in (16), then p_L must (locally) maximize $w_L(\cdot)$, which proves Lemma 1.

Now consider some special cases of this general framework.

When is the full-information outcome feasible? Recall that in the full-information outcome, the type-i firm sets price p_i^* and receives zero rent.[36] The incentive constraints (18) and (19) imply that this full-information outcome is attainable when the regulator does not observe the state if and only if

$$\Delta^\pi(p_H^*) \geqslant 0 \geqslant \Delta^\pi(p_L^*). \tag{22}$$

The pair of inequalities in (22) imply that the full-information outcome will not be feasible if the firm's operating profit $\pi(p)$ is systematically higher in one state than the other (as when the firm is privately informed only about its marginal cost of production, for example). If the full-information outcome is to be attainable, the profit functions $\pi_H(\cdot)$ and $\pi_L(\cdot)$ must cross: operating profit must be higher in state H than in state L at the full-information price p_H^*, and operating profit must be lower in state H than in state L at the full-information price p_L^*.

Recall from part (i) of Proposition 4 that the full-information outcome is feasible in the setting where the firm's convex cost function $C(\cdot)$ is common knowledge but the firm is privately informed about the demand function it faces. In this context, demand is either high, $Q_H(\cdot)$, or low, $Q_L(\cdot)$, and the profit function in state i is $\pi_i(p) = pQ_i(p) - C(Q_i(p))$. To see why the full-information outcome is feasible in this case, let $q_i^* \equiv Q_i(p_i^*)$ denote the firm's output in state i in the full-information outcome. Since $C(\cdot)$ is convex:

$$C(Q_i(p_j^*)) \geqslant C(q_j^*) + C'(q_j^*)(Q_i(p_j^*) - q_j^*). \tag{23}$$

To show that inequality (22) is satisfied when prices are equal to marginal costs, notice that

$$\begin{aligned}
\pi_i(p_j^*) &= p_j^* Q_i(p_j^*) - C(Q_i(p_j^*)) \\
&\leqslant p_j^* Q_i(p_j^*) - \{C(q_j^*) + C'(q_j^*)(Q_i(p_j^*) - q_j^*)\} \\
&= p_j^* q_j^* - C(q_j^*) \\
&= \pi_j(p_j^*).
\end{aligned} \tag{24}$$

[36] The single-crossing condition $\frac{\mathrm{d}}{\mathrm{d}p}\Delta^\pi > 0$ is not needed for the analysis in this section.

The inequality in expression (24) follows from inequality (23). The second equality in expression (24) holds because $p_j^* = C'(q_j^*)$. Consequently, condition (22) is satisfied, and the regulator can implement the full-information outcome.

Part (i) of Proposition 2 indicates that the full-information outcome is also feasible in the setting where the demand function facing the firm is common knowledge, the firm is privately informed about its constant marginal c_i and fixed costs F_i of production, and the variation in fixed cost is intermediate in magnitude. To prove this conclusion, we need to determine when the inequalities in (22) are satisfied. Since $\pi_i(p) = (p - c_i)Q(p) - F_i$ in this setting, it follows that

$$\Delta^\pi(p) = \Delta^F - \Delta^c Q(p). \tag{25}$$

Therefore, since full-information prices are $p_i^* \equiv c_i$, expression (25) implies that the inequalities (22) will be satisfied if and only if $\Delta^c Q(c_L) \geqslant \Delta^F \geqslant \Delta^c Q(c_H)$, as indicated in Proposition 2.

Price distortions with separation Suppose that profit is higher in state L than in state H for all prices, so that $\Delta^\pi(p) < 0$. In this case, only the type-H firm's participation constraint in (17) will be relevant, and this firm will optimally be afforded no rent.[37] In this case, the incentive compatibility constraints (18)–(19) become

$$-\Delta^\pi(p_L) \geqslant R_L \geqslant -\Delta^\pi(p_H).$$

Again, since rent is costly, it is only the lower bound on R_L that is relevant, i.e., only the incentive compatibility constraint (18) is relevant.

Therefore, expression (16) reduces to

$$W = \phi\{w_L(p_L) + (1-\alpha)\Delta^\pi(p_H)\} + (1-\phi)w_H(p_H). \tag{26}$$

Notice that this expression for W incorporates both the type-H firm's participation constraint and the type-L firm's incentive compatibility constraint.

Maximizing expression (26) with respect to p_L and p_H implies:

$$p_L = p_L^* \quad \text{and } p_H \text{ maximizes} \quad w_H(p) + \frac{\phi}{1-\phi}(1-\alpha)\Delta^\pi(p). \tag{27}$$

Since $\Delta^\pi(p)$ increases with p, expression (27) implies that $p_H \geqslant p_H^*$. When full-information prices are ordered as in inequality (21), it follows that $p_H \geqslant p_H^* \geqslant p_L^* = p_L$, and therefore the monotonicity condition (21) is satisfied. Therefore, (27) provides the solution to the regulator's problem. In particular, the regulator will induce the firm to set different prices in different states, and the type H firm's price will be distorted above the full-information level, p_H^*. This distortion is greater the more costly are rents (the lower is α) and the more likely is state L (the higher is ϕ).

[37] Since rents are costly in expression (16) and the incentive compatibility constraints (18)–(19) depend only on the difference between the rents, at least one participation constraint must bind at the optimum.

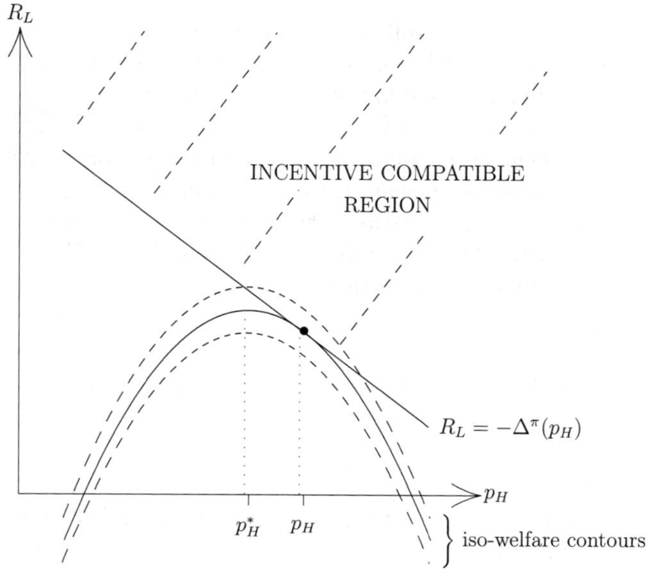

Figure 27.1. Price distortions with separation.

This analysis is presented in Figure 27.1, which depicts outcomes in terms of p_H and R_L. (The remaining choice variables are R_H, which is set equal to zero at the optimum, and p_L, which is set equal to p_L^* at the optimum.) Here, the incentive compatible region is the set of points $R_L \geqslant -\Delta^\pi(p_H)$, and the regulator must limit himself to a contract that lies within this set. Expression (16) shows that welfare contours in (p_H, R_L) space take the form $R_L = (\frac{1}{1-\alpha})(\frac{1-\phi}{\phi})w_H(p_H) + k_o$, where k_o is a constant. Each of these contours is maximized at $p_H = p_H^*$, as shown in Figure 27.1. (Lower contours indicate higher welfare.) Therefore, the optimum is where a welfare contour just meets the incentive compatible region, which necessarily involves a price p_H greater than p_H^*. Increasing α, so that distributional concerns are less pronounced, or reducing ϕ, so that the high-cost state is more likely, steepens the welfare contours, and so brings the optimal choice of price p_H closer to the full-information price p_H^*.

These qualitative features characterize the optimal regulatory policy in many settings, including the Baron–Myerson setting of Proposition 1 where the firm is privately informed about its marginal cost of production. In this setting, $\pi_i(p) = Q(p)(p-c_i)-F$, and so $\Delta^\pi(p) = -\Delta^c Q(p)$. Therefore, expression (27) implies that the optimal price for the high-cost firm is as given in expression (5) of Proposition 1. Notice that in the context of the Baron–Myerson model, welfare in expression (26) can be written as

$$W = \phi\{v(p_L) + Q(p_L)(p_L - c_L)\} + (1-\phi)\{v(p_H) + Q(p_H)(p_H - \hat{c}_H)\}, \tag{28}$$

where

$$\hat{c}_H = c_H + \frac{\phi}{1-\phi}(1-\alpha)\Delta^c. \tag{29}$$

Here, $\hat{c}_H$ is simply p_H in expression (5).[38] Expression (28) reveals that expected welfare is the same in the following two situations: (a) the firm has private information about its marginal cost, where this cost is either c_L or c_H; and (b) the regulator can observe the firm's marginal cost, where this cost is either c_L or $\hat{c}_H$. (Of course, the firm is better off under situation (a).) Thus, the effect of private information on welfare in this setting is exactly the effect of inflating the cost of the high-cost firm according to formula (29) in a setting with no information asymmetry. Under this interpretation, the prices in expression (5) are simply marginal-cost prices, where the "costs" are increased above actual costs to account for socially undesirable rents caused by asymmetric information.

Similar conclusions emerge in the Laffont–Tirole model with observed but endogenous marginal cost, as in Proposition 3. Here, once it is noted that price is optimally set equal to the realized and observed marginal cost ($p_i \equiv c_i$), the problem fits the current framework precisely. Specifically, $\pi_i(p_i) = -F_i(p_i)$, and so $\Delta^\pi(p) = F_L(p) - F_H(p) < 0$, which is assumed to increase with p. Also, $w_i(p) = v(p) - F_i(p)$. Therefore, expression (27) yields expression (12) in Proposition 3.

Pooling It remains to illustrate why the regulator might sometimes implement the same contract in both states of the world. As suggested in the discussion after Proposition 4, pooling (i.e., $p_H = p_L$) may be optimal if $p_L^* > p_H^*$, so that prices in the full-information outcome do not satisfy the necessary condition for incentive compatibility, inequality (21).

To illustrate this observation, consider the setting where the firm's strictly concave cost function is common knowledge and the firm is privately informed about its demand function. Because marginal cost declines with output in this setting, the full-information prices satisfy $p_L^* > p_H^*$. Whether the single-crossing condition (14) is satisfied depends on joint effects of the cost function and the variation in demand. One can show, for instance, that if $Q_H(\cdot) \equiv Q_L(\cdot) + k_1$ where k_1 is a constant, then the single-crossing condition will be satisfied if the cost function satisfies certain standard regularity conditions.

To see that pooling is optimal in this setting, suppose to the contrary that separation ($p_L \neq p_H$) is implemented at the optimum. Then it is readily verified that exactly one of the incentive compatibility constraints (18) or (19) binds, and so, from Lemma 1, the full-information price p_i^* is implemented in one state.[39] Suppose state L is the relevant

[38] The adjusted cost $\hat{c}_H$ is often referred to as the "virtual cost".

[39] If the single-crossing condition holds, both incentive constraints can only bind when $p_L = p_H$. If neither constraint binds, then $p_L = p_L^*$ and $p_H = p_H^*$, which cannot be incentive compatible when $p_L^* > p_H^*$.

state, so that $p_L = p_L^*$ and (18) binds:

$$R_L = R_H - \Delta^\pi(p_H). \tag{30}$$

An analysis analogous to that which underlies expressions (23) and (24) reveals that $\pi_H(p_L^*) \geqslant \pi_L(p_L^*)$ when $C(\cdot)$ is concave, i.e., $\Delta^\pi(p_L^*) \geqslant 0$. Since inequality (21) requires $p_H > p_L^*$ and since $\Delta^\pi(\cdot)$ is an increasing function of p, it follows that $\Delta^\pi(p_H) > 0$. Since at least one participation constraint (17) binds, expression (30) implies

$$R_L = 0; \qquad R_H = \Delta^\pi(p_H). \tag{31}$$

Therefore, expected welfare in expression (16) simplifies to

$$W = \phi w_L\big(p_L^*\big) + (1-\phi)\big\{w_H(p_H) - (1-\alpha)\Delta^\pi(p_H)\big\}. \tag{32}$$

Since $p_H > p_H^*$, it follows that the $\{\cdot\}$ term in expression (32) is decreasing in p_H if $w_H(\cdot)$ is single-peaked in price. Since a small reduction in p_H does not violate any participation or incentive compatibility constraint and increases the value of the regulator's objective function, the candidate prices $\{p_L^*, p_H\}$ cannot be optimal. A similar argument holds if inequality (19) is the binding incentive constraint. Therefore, by contradiction, $p_L = p_H$ in the solution to the regulator's problem.[40]

Notice that, in contrast to the pricing distortions discussed above (e.g., in expression (27)), pooling is not implemented here to reduce the firm's rent. Even if the regulator valued rent and consumer surplus equally (so $\alpha = 1$), pooling would still be optimal in this setting. Pooling arises here because of the severe constraints imposed by incentive compatibility.

2.4. Extensions to the basic model

The analysis to this point has been restrictive because: (i) the regulator had no opportunity to obtain better information about the prevailing state; and (ii) the regulator was uninformed about only a single "piece" of relevant information. In this section, two alternative information structures are considered. First, the regulator is allowed to obtain some imperfect information about the realized state, perhaps through an audit. Two distinct settings are examined in this regard: one where the regulator always acts in the interests of society, and one where the firm may bribe the regulator to conceal potentially damaging information. The latter setting permits an analysis of how the danger of regulatory capture affects the optimal design of regulation. Second, the firm is endowed with superior information about more than one aspect of its environment. We illustrate each of these extensions by means of natural variants of the Baron–Myerson model discussed in Section 2.3.1.

[40] Laffont and Martimort (2002, Section 2.10.2) provide further discussion of when pooling will arise in models of this sort.

2.4.1. Partially informed regulator: the use of audits

First consider the setting where the firm is privately informed about its exogenous constant marginal cost of production ($c \in \{c_L, c_H\}$). Suppose that an imperfect public signal $s \in \{s_L, s_H\}$ of the firm's cost is available, which is realized after contracts have been signed. This signal is "hard" information in the sense that (legally enforceable) contracts can be written based on this information. This signal might be interpreted as the output of an audit of the firm's cost, for example. Specifically, let ϕ_i denote the probability that low signal s_L is observed when the firm's marginal cost is c_i for $i = L, H$. To capture the fact that the low signal is likely to be associated with low cost, assume $\phi_L > \phi_H$.[41]

Absent bounds on the rewards or penalties that can be imposed on the risk-neutral firm, the regulator can ensure marginal-cost pricing without ceding any rent to the firm in this setting. He can do so by conditioning the transfer payment to the firm on the firm's report of its cost and on the subsequent realization of the public signal. Specifically, let T_{ij} be the regulator's transfer payment to the firm when the firm claims its cost is c_i and when the realized signal turns out to be s_j. If the firm claims to have a high cost, it is permitted to charge the (high) unit price, $p_H = c_H$. In addition, it receives a generous transfer payment when the signal (s_H) suggests that its cost is truly high, but is penalized when the signal (s_L) suggests otherwise. These transfer payments can be structured to provide an expected transfer which just covers the firm's fixed cost F when its marginal cost is indeed c_H, i.e.,

$$\phi_H T_{HL} + (1 - \phi_H) T_{HH} = F. \tag{33}$$

At the same time, the payments can be structured to provide an expected return to the low-cost firm that is sufficiently far below F that they eliminate any rent the low-cost firm might otherwise anticipate from being able to set the high price ($p_H = c_H$), i.e.,

$$\phi_L T_{HL} + (1 - \phi_L) T_{HH} \ll F. \tag{34}$$

The transfers T_{HL} and T_{HH} can always be set to satisfy equality (33) and inequality (34) except in the case where the signal is entirely uninformative ($\phi_L = \phi_H$). The low-cost firm can simply be offered its (deterministic) full-information contract, with price p_L equal to marginal cost c_L and transfer $T_{LH} = T_{LL}$ equal to the fixed cost F. This pair of contracts secures the full-information outcome. Thus, even an imprecise monitor of the firm's private cost information can constitute a powerful regulatory instrument when feasible payments to the firm are not restricted and when the firm is risk neutral.[42]

[41] Another way to model this audit would be to suppose the regulator observes the true cost with some exogenous probability (and otherwise observes "nothing"). This alternative specification yields the same insights. A form of this alternative specification is explored in Section 2.4.2, which discusses regulatory capture.

[42] This insight will play an important role in the discussion of yardstick competition in Section 4.1.2, where, instead of an audit, the signal about one firm's cost is obtained from the report of a second firm with correlated costs. Crémer and McLean (1985), Riordan and Sappington (1988) and Caillaud, Guesnerie and Rey (1992) provide corresponding conclusions in more general settings.

When the maximum penalty that can be imposed on the firm ex post is sufficiently small in this setting, the low-cost firm will continue to earn rent.[43] To limit these rents, the regulator will implement the qualitative pricing distortions identified in Proposition 1.[44] Similar rents and pricing distortions will also arise if risk aversion on the part of the firm makes the use of large, stochastic variations in transfer payments to the firm prohibitively costly.[45]

If the regulator has to incur a cost to receive the signal from an audit, the regulator will have to decide when to purchase the signal.[46] If there were no constraints on the size of feasible punishments, the full-information outcome could be approximated arbitrarily closely. The regulator could undertake a costly audit with very small probability and punish the firm very severely if the signal contradicts the firm's report. In contrast, when the magnitude of feasible punishments is limited, the full-information outcome can no longer be approximated. Instead, the regulator will base his decision about when to purchase the signal on the firm's report. If the firm announces it has low cost, then no audit is commissioned, and price is set at the full-information level. In contrast, if the firm claims to have high cost, the regulator commissions an audit with a specified probability.[47] The frequency of this audit is determined by balancing the costs of auditing with the benefits of improved information.

2.4.2. *Partially informed regulator: regulatory capture*

The discussion in this section relaxes the assumption that the regulator automatically acts in the interests of society.[48] For simplicity, consider the other extreme in which the regulator aims simply to maximize his personal income. This income may arise from two sources. First, the firm may attempt to "bribe" the regulator to conceal information that is damaging to the firm. Second, and in response to this threat of corruption, the regulator himself may operate under an incentive scheme, which rewards him when he

[43] See Baron and Besanko (1984a), Demougin and Garvie (1991), and Gary-Bobo and Spiegel (2006), for example.

[44] See Baron and Besanko (1984b).

[45] See Baron and Besanko (1987b).

[46] See Baron and Besanko (1984b) and Laffont and Martimort (2002, Section 3.6).

[47] The importance of the regulator's presumed ability to commit to an auditing policy is apparent. See Khalil (1997) for an analysis of the setting where the regulator cannot commit to an auditing strategy.

[48] This discussion is based on Laffont and Tirole (1991b) and Laffont and Tirole (1993b, ch. 11). To our knowledge, Tirole (1986a) provides the first analysis of these three-tier models with collusion. Demski and Sappington (1987) also study a three-tier model, but their focus is inducing the regulator to monitor the firm. (The regulator incurs a private cost if he undertakes an audit, but the firm does not attempt to influence the regulator's behavior.) Spiller (1990) provides a moral hazard model in which, by expending unobservable effort, the regulator can affect the probability of the firm's price being high or low. In this model, the firm and the political principal try to influence the regulator's choice of effort by offering incentives based on the realized price.

reveals this damaging information. This incentive scheme is designed by a "political principal", who might be viewed as the (benevolent) government, for example.[49]

To be specific, suppose the firm's marginal cost is either c_L or c_H. The probability of the low-cost (c_L) realization is ϕ. Also, suppose that conditional on the firm's cost realization being low, the regulator has an exogenous probability ζ of being informed that the cost is indeed low. Conditional on a high-cost realization, the regulator has no chance of being informed.[50] The probability that the regulator is informed (which implies that the firm has low cost) is $\psi = \phi\zeta$. The probability that the regulator is uninformed is $1 - \psi$. The probability of the cost being low, conditional on the regulator being uninformed, therefore, is

$$\phi^U = \frac{\phi(1-\zeta)}{1-\phi\zeta} < \phi.$$

The information obtained by the regulator is "hard" in the sense that revelation of the regulator's private signal that cost is low proves beyond doubt that the firm has low cost. Therefore, when the regulator admits to being informed, the (low-cost) firm is regulated with symmetric information and so the firm receives no rent. However, if the regulator claims to be uninformed, the principal is unable to confirm this is in fact the case. The principal is unable to determine whether the firm and regulator have successfully colluded and the regulator is concealing the damaging information he has actually obtained.

Suppose the regulator must be paid at least zero by the principal in every state.[51] Also suppose the principal pays the regulator an extra amount s when the regulator admits to being informed. Assume for now that the principal induces the regulator to reveal his information whenever he is informed, i.e., that the principal implements a "collusion-proof" mechanism. In this case, when the regulator announces he is uninformed, the probability that the firm has low cost is ϕ^U. This probability becomes the relevant probability of having a low-cost realization when calculating the optimal regulatory policy in this case.

[49] An alternative formulation would have the regulator commission an auditor to gather information about the firm. The firm might then try to bribe the auditor to conceal detrimental information from the regulator.

[50] Laffont and Tirole (1993b, ch. 11) model the information structure more symmetrically by assuming the regulator is informed about the true cost with probability ζ whether the cost is high or low. However, when the regulator learns the cost is high, the firm has no interest in persuading him to conceal this information. Since the possibility that the regulator might learn that cost is high plays no significant role in this analysis of capture (but complicates the notation) we assume the regulator can obtain information only about a low cost realization.

[51] The ex post nature of this participation constraint for the regulator is important. If the regulator were risk neutral and cared only about expected income, he could be induced to reveal his information to the political principal at no cost. (This could be done by offering the regulator a high reward when he revealed information and a high penalty when he claimed to be uninformed, with these two payments set to ensure the regulator zero expected rent, in a manner similar to that described in Section 2.4.1 above.) In addition, by normalizing the regulator's required income to zero, we introduce the implicit assumption that the regulator is indispensable for regulation, and the political principal cannot do without his services and cannot avoid paying him his reservation wage.

Suppose it costs the firm \$$(1+\theta)$ to increase the income of the regulator by \$1. The deadweight loss θ involved in increasing the regulator's income may reflect legal restrictions designed to limit the ability of regulated firms to influence regulators unduly, for example. These restrictions include prohibitions on direct bribery of government officials. Despite such prohibitions, a firm may find (costly) ways to convince the regulator of the merits of making decisions that benefit the firm. For instance, the firm may provide lucrative employment opportunities for selected regulators or agree to charge a low price for a politically-sensitive service in return for higher prices on other services. For simplicity, we model these indirect ways of influencing the regulator's decision as an extra marginal cost θ the firm incurs in delivering income to the regulator. For expositional ease, we will speak of the firm as "bribing" the regulator, even though explicit bribery may not actually be undertaken.[52]

It is clear from Proposition 1 that the low-cost firm will optimally be induced to set a price equal to its cost. Suppose that when the regulator is uninformed, the contract offered to the high-cost firm involves the price p_H. Assuming the rent of the high-cost firm, R_H, is zero, expression (4) implies the rent of the low-cost firm (again, conditional on the regulator being uninformed) is $\Delta^c Q(p_H)$.

The low-cost firm will find it too costly to bribe the informed regulator to conceal his information if

$$(1+\theta)s \geqslant \Delta^c Q(p_H), \tag{35}$$

where, recall, s is the payment from the principal to the regulator when the latter reports he has learned the firm has low cost. Expression (35) ensures the corruptible regulator is truthful when he announces he is ignorant about the firm's cost.

Suppose the regulator's income receives weight $\alpha_R \leqslant 1$ in the political principal's welfare function, while the rent of the firm has weight α. Then, much like expression (16), total expected welfare under this "collusion-proof" regulatory policy is

$$W = \psi\big[w_L(c_L) - (1-\alpha_R)s\big] + (1-\psi)\big[\phi^U\big\{w_L(c_L) - (1-\alpha)R_L\big\} + \big(1-\phi^U\big)w_H(p_H)\big].$$

Since payments from the political principal to the regulator are socially costly, inequality (35) will bind at the optimum. Consequently, total expected welfare is

$$W = \psi\left[w_L(c_L) - \frac{1-\alpha_R}{1+\theta}\Delta^c Q(p_H)\right] + (1-\psi)\big[\phi^U\big\{w_L(c_L) - (1-\alpha)\Delta^c Q(p_H)\big\} + \big(1-\phi^U\big)w_H(p_H)\big]. \tag{36}$$

Before deriving the price p_H that maximizes expected welfare, consider when the political principal will design the reward structure to ensure the regulator is not captured, i.e., when it is optimal to satisfy inequality (35). If the principal does not choose

[52] If explicit bribery were undertaken, θ might reflect the penalties associated with conviction for bribing an official, discounted by the probability of conviction.

s to satisfy (35), then the firm will always bribe the regulator to conceal damaging information, and so the regulator will never admit to being informed. In this case, the best the principal can do is follow the Baron–Myerson regulatory policy described in Proposition 1, where the policy designer has no additional private information. From expression (26), expected welfare in this case is

$$W = \phi\{w_L(c_L) - (1-\alpha)\Delta^c Q(p_H)\} + (1-\phi)w_H(p_H). \tag{37}$$

Using the identity $\psi + (1-\psi)\phi^U = \phi$, a comparison of welfare in (36) and (37) reveals that the political principal is better off using the corruptible (but sometimes well informed) regulator – and ensuring he is sufficiently well rewarded so as not to accept the firm's bribe – whenever $(1+\theta)(1-\alpha) > 1-\alpha_R$. In particular, if the regulator's rent receives at least as much weight in social welfare as the firm's rent, it is optimal to employ the regulator's information. Assume for the remainder of this section that this inequality holds.

Maximizing expression (36) with respect to p_H yields

$$p_H = \underbrace{c_H + \frac{\phi^U}{1-\phi^U}(1-\alpha)\Delta^c}_{\text{Baron–Myerson price}} + \underbrace{\frac{\psi}{(1-\psi)(1+\theta)(1-\phi^U)}(1-\alpha_R)\Delta^c}_{\text{extra distortion to reduce firm's stake in collusion}}. \tag{38}$$

From expression (5) in Proposition 1, when the regulator is uninformed and there is no scope for collusion, the optimal price for the high-cost firm is the first term in expression (38). The second term in (38) is an extra distortion in the high-cost firm's price that limits regulatory capture. The expression reveals that the danger of capture has no effect on optimal prices only when: (i) payments to the regulator have no social cost (i.e., when $\alpha_R = 1$), or (ii) it is prohibitively costly for the firm to bribe the regulator (so $\theta = \infty$).

The price for the high-cost firm is distorted further above cost when capture is possible because, from expression (35), a higher price for the high-cost firm reduces the rent that the low-cost firm would make if the informed regulator concealed his information. This reduced rent, in turn, reduces the bribe the firm will pay the regulator to conceal damaging information, which reduces the (socially costly) payment to the regulator that is needed to induce him to reveal his information. Most importantly, when there is a danger of regulatory capture, prices are distorted from their optimal levels when capture is not possible in a direction that reduces the firm's "stake in collusion", i.e., that reduces the rent the firm obtains when it captures the regulator. Interestingly, the possibility of capture – something that would clearly make the firm better off if the regulator were not adequately controlled – makes the firm worse off once the political principal has optimally responded to the threat of capture.

This discussion has considered what one might term the optimal response to the danger of capture and collusion.[53] We return to the general topic in Section 3.4.2, which focuses more on pragmatic responses to capture.

[53] In the same tradition, Laffont and Martimort (1999), building on Kofman and Lawarrée (1993), show how multiple regulators can act as a safeguard against capture when the "constitution" is designed optimally. In

2.4.3. Multi-dimensional private information

In practice, the regulated firm typically will have several pieces of private information, rather than the single piece of private information considered in the previous sections. For instance, a multiproduct firm may have private information about cost conditions for each of its products. Alternatively, a single-product firm may have privileged information about both its technology and consumer demand.

To analyze this situation formally, consider the following simple multiproduct extension of the Baron and Myerson (1982) model described in Section 2.3.1.[54] Suppose the firm supplies two products. The demand curve for each product is $Q(p)$ and demands for the two products are independent. The constant marginal cost of producing either product is either c_L or c_H.[55] The firm also incurs a known fixed cost, F. Thus, the firm can be one of four possible types, denoted $\{LL, LH, HL, HH\}$, where the type-ij firm incurs cost c_i in producing product 1 and cost c_j in producing product 2. Suppose the unconditional probability the firm has a low-cost realization for product 1 is ϕ. Let ϕ_i be the probability the firm has a low-cost realization for product 2, given that its cost is c_i for product 1. The cost realizations are positively correlated across products if $\phi_L > \phi_H$, negatively correlated if $\phi_L < \phi_H$, and statistically independent if $\phi_L = \phi_H$. To keep the analysis simple, suppose the unconditional probability of a low-cost realization for product 2 is also ϕ. In this case, states *LH* and *HL* are equally likely, so

$$\phi(1-\phi_L) = (1-\phi)\phi_H. \tag{39}$$

The regulator offers the firm a menu of options, so that if the firm announces its type to be ij, it must set the price p^1_{ij} for product 1, p^2_{ij} for product 2, and in return receive the transfer T_{ij}. The equilibrium rent of the type-ij firm under this policy is

$$R_{ij} = Q\big(p^1_{ij}\big)\big(p^1_{ij} - c_i\big) + Q\big(p^2_{ij}\big)\big(p^2_{ij} - c_j\big) - F + T_{ij}.$$

The participation constraints in the regulator's problem take the form $R_{ij} \geqslant 0$, of which only $R_{HH} \geqslant 0$ is relevant. (If the firm is one of the other three types, it can claim to have high cost for both products, and thereby make at least as much rent as R_{HH}.) There are twelve incentive compatibility constraints, since each of the four types of firm must have no incentive to claim to be any of the remaining three types. However, in this symmetric situation, one can restrict attention to only the constraints that ensure low-cost types do

the later paper, the presence of several regulators, each of whom observes a separate aspect of the firm's performance, relaxes relevant "collusion–proofness" constraints. The earlier paper focuses on the possibility that an honest regulator can observe when another regulator is corrupted, and so can act as a "whistle-blower".

[54] The following is based on Dana (1993) and Armstrong and Rochet (1999).

[55] Multi-dimensional private information is one area where the qualitative properties of the optimal regulatory policy can vary according to whether the firm's private information is discrete or continuous. One reason for the difference is that in a continuous framework it is generally optimal to terminate the operation of some firms in order to extract further rent from other firms. This feature can complicate the analysis (Armstrong, 1999, Section 2). Rochet and Stole (2003) survey the literature on multi-dimensional screening.

not claim to have high costs.[56] The symmetry of this problem ensures that only three rents are relevant: R_{HH}, R_{LL} and R_A. R_A is the firm's rent when its cost is high for one product and low for the other. ('*A*' stands for 'asymmetric'. We will refer to either the type-*LH* or the type-*HL* firm as the 'type-*A*' firm.) Similarly, there are only four prices that are relevant: p_{LL} is the price for both products when the firm has low cost for both products; p_{HH} is the price for both products when the firm has a high cost for both products; p_L^A is the price for the low-cost product when the firm has asymmetric costs, while p_H^A is the price for the high-cost product when the firm has asymmetric costs.

Much as in expression (16) for the single-product case, expected welfare in this setting is

$$\begin{aligned} W = {} & 2\phi(1-\phi_L)\{w_L(p_L^A) + w_H(p_H^A) - (1-\alpha)R_A\} \\ & + \phi\phi_L\{2w_L(p_{LL}) - (1-\alpha)R_{LL}\} \\ & + (1-\phi)(1-\phi_H)\{2w_H(p_{HH}) - (1-\alpha)R_{HH}\}. \end{aligned} \tag{40}$$

(Here, $w_i(p) = v(p) + Q(p)(p - c_i)$, where $v(\cdot)$ again denotes consumer surplus.) The incentive compatibility constraint that ensures the type-*A* firm does not claim to be the type-*HH* firm is

$$\begin{aligned} R_A & \geqslant Q(p_{HH})(p_{HH} - c_H) + Q(p_{HH})(p_{HH} - c_L) - F + T_{HH} \\ & = R_{HH} + \Delta^c Q(p_{HH}), \end{aligned} \tag{41}$$

where $\Delta^c = c_H - c_L$. Similarly, the incentive compatibility constraint that ensures the type-*LL* firm does not claim to be a type-*A* firm is

$$R_{LL} \geqslant R_A + \Delta^c Q(p_H^A). \tag{42}$$

Finally, the incentive compatibility constraint that ensures the type-*LL* firm does not claim to be a type-*HH* firm is

$$R_{LL} \geqslant R_{HH} + 2\Delta^c Q(p_{HH}). \tag{43}$$

The participation constraint for the type-*HH* firm will bind, so $R_{HH} = 0$. The type-*A* firm's incentive compatibility constraint (41) will also bind, so $R_A = \Delta^c Q(p_{HH})$. Substituting these rents into (42) and (43) implies the rent of the type-*LL* firm is

$$R_{LL} = \Delta^c Q(p_{HH}) + \max\{\Delta^c Q(p_H^A), \Delta^c Q(p_{HH})\}.$$

Substituting these rents into expected welfare (40) implies welfare is

$$W = 2\phi(1-\phi_L)\{w_L(p_L^A) + w_H(p_H^A) - (1-\alpha)\Delta^c Q(p_{HH})\}$$

[56] It is straightforward to verify that the other incentive compatibility constraints are satisfied at the solution to the regulator's problem in this symmetric setting. Armstrong and Rochet (1999) show that in the presence of negative correlation and substantial asymmetry across markets, some of the other incentive compatibility constraints may bind at the solution to the regulator's problem, and so cannot be ignored in solving the problem.

$$+ \phi\phi_L\{2w_L(p_{LL}) - (1-\alpha)2\Delta^c Q(p_{HH})\}$$
$$+ (1-\phi)(1-\phi_H)2w_H(p_{HH}) \tag{44}$$

if $p_H^A \geqslant p_{HH}$, and

$$W = 2\phi(1-\phi_L)\{w_L(p_L^A) + w_H(p_H^A) - (1-\alpha)\Delta^c Q(p_{HH})\}$$
$$+ \phi\phi_L\{2w_L(p_{LL}) - (1-\alpha)\Delta^c[Q(p_{HH})$$
$$+ Q(p_H^A)]\} + (1-\phi)(1-\phi_H)2w_H(p_{HH}) \tag{45}$$

if $p_H^A \leqslant p_{HH}$.

The policy that maximizes welfare consists of the prices $\{p_{LL}, p_{HH}, p_L^A, p_H^A\}$ that maximize the expression in (44)–(45). Some features of the optimal policy are immediate. First, since the prices for low-cost products (p_{LL} and p_L^A) do not affect any rents, they are not distorted, and are set equal to marginal cost c_L. This generalizes Proposition 1.[57] Second, the strict inequality $p_H^A > p_{HH}$ cannot be optimal. To see why, notice that when this inequality holds, expression (44) is the relevant expression for welfare. In expression (44), price p_H^A does not affect rent. Consequently, $p_H^A = c_H$ is optimal. But the value of p_{HH} that maximizes expression (44) exceeds cost c_H. Therefore, the inequality $p_H^A \geqslant p_{HH}$ must bind if (44) is maximized subject to the constraint $p_H^A \geqslant p_{HH}$. In sum, attention can be restricted to the case where $p_H^A \leqslant p_{HH}$, and so (45) is the appropriate expression for welfare.

The remaining question is whether $p_H^A = p_{HH}$ or $p_H^A < p_{HH}$ is optimal. If the constraint that $p_H^A \leqslant p_{HH}$ is ignored, the prices that maximize (45) are:

$$p_H^A \quad \text{maximizes} \quad 2w_H(\cdot) - \frac{\phi_L}{1-\phi_L}(1-\alpha)\Delta^c Q(\cdot), \quad \text{and} \tag{46}$$

$$p_{HH} \quad \text{maximizes} \quad 2w_H(\cdot) - \frac{1-(1-\phi)(1-\phi_H)}{(1-\phi)(1-\phi_H)}(1-\alpha)\Delta^c Q(\cdot). \tag{47}$$

Clearly, the price p_{HH} in (47) exceeds the price p_H^A in (46) whenever

$$\phi_L \leqslant 1-(1-\phi)(1-\phi_H), \tag{48}$$

which is equivalent to the condition $\phi_L \leqslant 2\phi_H$.[58] This inequality states that the correlation between the cost realizations is not too pronounced. When this condition is satisfied, expressions (46) and (47) provide the two high-cost prices.

[57] Armstrong and Rochet (1999) show that when there is negative correlation and conditions are very asymmetric across the two markets, it is optimal to introduce distortions even for efficient firms. The distortions take the form of below-cost prices.

[58] This non-trivial manipulation involves using expression (39) to write $\phi = \phi_H/(1+\phi_H-\phi_L)$, and substituting this into inequality (48).

When there is strong positive correlation, so $\phi_L \geqslant 2\phi_H$, the constraint $p_H^A \leqslant p_{HH}$ binds. Letting $p_H = p_H^A = p_{HH}$ denote this common price, (45) simplifies to

$$W = 2\{\phi[w_L(c_L) - (1-\alpha)\Delta^c Q(p_H)] + (1-\phi)w_H(p_H)\},$$

which is just (twice) the standard single-product Baron–Myerson formula. (See expression (26) for instance.) Therefore, with strong positive correlation, the solution is simply the Baron–Myerson formula (5) for each product. This discussion constitutes the proof of Proposition 5.[59]

PROPOSITION 5. *The optimal policy in the symmetric multi-dimensional setting has the following features*:

(i) *There are no pricing distortions for low-cost products, i.e.,* $p_{LL} = p_L^A = c_L$.

(ii) *When there is strong positive correlation between costs (so* $\phi_L \geqslant 2\phi_H$*), the regulatory policy for each product is independent of the firm's report for the other product. The policy for each product is identical to the policy described in Proposition* 1.

(iii) *When cost correlation is weak (so* $\phi_L \leqslant 2\phi_H$*), interdependencies are introduced across products. In particular,*

$$p_H^A = c_H + \frac{\phi_L}{2(1-\phi_L)}(1-\alpha)\Delta^c, \quad \textit{and}$$

$$p_{HH} = c_H + \frac{1-(1-\phi)(1-\phi_H)}{2(1-\phi)(1-\phi_H)}(1-\alpha)\Delta^c \geqslant p_H^A.$$

Part (i) of Proposition 5 provides the standard conclusion that price is set equal to cost whenever the low cost is realized. Since the binding constraint is to prevent the firm from exaggerating, not understating, its costs, no purpose would be served by distorting prices when low costs are reported. Part (ii) provides another finding that parallels standard conclusions. It states that in the presence of strong positive cost correlation, the optimal policy is the same for each product and depends only on the realized cost of producing that product. Furthermore, this optimal policy replicates the policy that is implemented in the case of uni-dimensional cost uncertainty, as described in Proposition 1. Thus, in the presence of strong correlation, the two-dimensional problem essentially is transformed into two separate uni-dimensional problems. The reason for this result is the following. When there is strong positive correlation, the most likely realizations are type *LL* and type *HH*. Consequently, the most important incentive compatibility constraint is that the type-*LL* firm should not claim to be type *HH*. This problem is analogous to the single-product Baron–Myerson problem, and so the optimal policy in this two-dimensional setting parallels the optimal policy in the uni-dimensional Baron–Myerson setting.

[59] In the knife-edge case where $\phi_L = 2\phi_H$, the policies in parts (ii) and (iii) of this proposition generate the same optimal welfare for the regulator.

Part (iii) reveals a major difference between the two-dimensional and uni-dimensional settings. It states that in the presence of weak cost correlation, when the firm has a high cost for one product, its price is set closer to cost for that product when its cost is low for the other product than when its cost is high for the other product. The less pronounced distortion when the asymmetric pair of costs $\{c_L, c_H\}$ is realized is optimal because this realization is relatively likely with weak cost correlation.[60] In contrast, the simultaneous realization of high cost for both products is relatively unlikely. So the expected loss in welfare from setting p_{HH} well above cost c_H is small. Furthermore, this distortion reduces the attraction to the firm of claiming to have high cost for both products in the relatively likely event that the firm has high cost for one product and low cost for the other.

A second regulatory setting in which the firm's superior information is likely to be multi-dimensional occurs when the firm is privately informed about both its cost structure and the consumer demand for its product. Private cost and demand information enter the analysis in fundamentally asymmetric ways. Consequently, this analysis is more complex than the analysis reviewed above. It can be shown that it is sometimes optimal to require the regulated firm to set a price below its realized cost when the firm is privately informed about both its demand and cost functions. Setting a price below marginal cost can help discourage the firm from exaggerating the scale of consumer demand.[61]

2.5. Dynamic interactions

Now consider how optimal regulatory policy changes when the interaction between the regulator and the regulated firm is repeated. To do so most simply, suppose their interaction is repeated just once in the setting where the firm is privately informed about its unobservable, exogenous marginal cost of production. We will employ notation similar to that used in Section 2.3.1. For simplicity, suppose the firm's cost $c \in \{c_L, c_H\}$ is perfectly correlated across the two periods.[62] Let $\phi \in (0, 1)$ be the probability the firm has low marginal cost, c_L, in the two periods. The regulator and the firm have the same discount factor $\delta > 0$. The demand function in the two periods, $Q(p)$, is common knowledge. The regulator wishes to maximize the expected discounted weighted sum of consumer surplus and rent. The firm will only produce in the second period if it receives non-negative rent from doing so, just as it will only produce in the first period if it anticipates non-negative expected discounted rent from doing so.

[60] Notice from part (iii) that in the extreme case where the type-*LL* realization never occurs, i.e., when $\phi_L = 0$, the prices of the type-*A* firm will not be distorted.

[61] See Lewis and Sappington (1988b) and Armstrong (1999) for analyses of this problem.

[62] See Bolton and Dewatripont (2005, Section 9.1.4) for a similar account of regulatory dynamics in the context of the Laffont and Tirole (1993b) model. See Baron and Besanko (1984a) and Laffont and Martimort (2002, Section 8.1.3) for an analysis of the case where the firm's costs are imperfectly correlated over time and where the regulator's commitment powers are unimpeded.

The ensuing discussion analyzes three variants of dynamic regulation that differ according to the commitment abilities of the regulator. The discussion is arranged in order of decreasing commitment power for the regulator.

2.5.1. *Perfect intertemporal commitment*

This first case is the most favorable one for the regulator because he can commit to any dynamic regulatory policy. In this case, the regulator will offer the firm a long-term (two-period) contract. The regulatory policy consists of a pair of price and transfer payment options $\{(p_L, T_L), (p_H, T_H)\}$ from which the firm can choose. In principle, these options could differ in the two time periods. However, it is readily verified that such variation is not optimal when costs do not vary over time. Consequently, the analysis in this two-period setting with perfect intertemporal regulatory commitment parallels the static analysis of Proposition 1, and the optimal dynamic policy simply duplicates the single-period policy in each period.

PROPOSITION 6. *In the two-period setting with regulatory commitment, the optimal regulatory policy has the following features*:

(i) *Prices in each of the two periods are*[63]

$$p_L = c_L, \qquad p_H = c_H + \frac{\phi}{1-\phi}(1-\alpha)\Delta^c.$$

(ii) *Total discounted rents are*

$$R_L = (1+\delta)\Delta^c Q(P_H), \qquad R_H = 0.$$

Once the regulator has observed the choice made by the firm in the first period, he would like to change the second-period policy to rectify the two undesirable features of the optimal regulatory policy under asymmetric information. Recall from Proposition 1 that the high-cost firm charges a price that is distorted above its marginal cost and the low-cost firm obtains a socially costly rent. By the second period, the regulator is fully informed about the firm's cost. Therefore, if the firm has revealed it has high cost, the regulator would like to reduce the firm's price to the level of its cost. Here, the temptation is not to eliminate rent (i.e., to "expropriate" the firm), but rather to achieve more efficient pricing. In this case, therefore, there is scope for mutually beneficial modifications to the pre-specified policy. Alternatively, if the firm has revealed it has low cost, the regulator would like to keep the price the same but eliminate the firm's rent. In this instance, the danger is that the regulator may expropriate the firm. Such a change in regulatory policy would not be mutually improving. These two temptations are the subject of the two commitment problems discussed next.

[63] This is a special case of part (ii) of Proposition 5.

The regulator with full commitment power does not succumb to these temptations. Instead, the regulator optimally commits not to use against the firm in the second period any cost information he infers from the firm's first-period actions. The regulator does this in order to best limit the rent that accrues to the firm with low cost.

2.5.2. Long-term contracts: the danger of renegotiation

Now consider the case where the regulator has "moderate" commitment powers.[64] Specifically, the regulator and the firm can write binding long-term contracts, but they cannot commit not to renegotiate the original contract if both parties agree to do so (i.e., if there is scope for Pareto gains ex post). Thus, the regulator cannot credibly promise to leave in place a policy that he believes to be Pareto inefficient in the light of information revealed to him. However, the regulator can credibly promise not to use information he has obtained to eliminate the firm's rent. In particular, because a policy change requires the consent of both parties, the regulator cannot reduce the rent of the low-cost firm below the level of rent it would secure if it continued to operate under the policy initially announced by the regulator.

In essence, this renegotiation setting presumes that the regulator can commit to provide specified future rent to the firm, but not to how that rent will be delivered (i.e., to the particular prices and transfers that generate the rent). The firm is indifferent as to how its rent is generated. However, the composition of rent affects the firm's incentives to reveal its cost truthfully.

The optimal policy with full commitment (Proposition 6) is no longer possible with renegotiation. The fact that the firm chose p_H initially implies that it has high cost in the second period, and, therefore, that mutual gains could be secured by reducing price to c_H in the second period. In the renegotiation setting, then, whenever definitive cost information is revealed in the first period, the regulator will always charge marginal-cost prices in the second period. It is apparent that this policy is not ideal for the regulator, since the regulator with full commitment powers could implement this policy, but chooses not to do so.

Formally, activity in the renegotiation setting proceeds as follows. First, the regulator announces the policy that will be implemented in the first period and the policy that, unless altered by mutual consent, will be implemented in the second period. Second, the firm chooses its preferred first-period option from the options presented by the regulator. After observing the firm's first-period activities and updating his beliefs about the firm's capabilities accordingly, the regulator can propose a change to the policy he announced initially.[65] If he proposes a change, the firm then decides whether to accept the change.

[64] This discussion is based on Laffont and Tirole (1990a) and Laffont and Tirole (1993b, ch. 10). For an alternative model of moderate commitment power, see Baron and Besanko (1987a).

[65] All parties can anticipate fully any modification of the original policy that the regulator will ultimately propose. Consequently, there is no loss of generality in restricting attention to renegotiation-proof policies, which are policies to which the regulator will propose no changes once they are implemented. See Laffont and Tirole (1993b, pp. 443–447) for further discussion of this issue.

If the firm agrees to the change, it is implemented. If the firm does not accept the change, the terms of the original policy remain in effect.

It is useful as a preliminary step to derive the optimal *separating* contracts in the renegotiation setting, that is to say, the optimal contracts that fully reveal the firm's private information in the first period. Suppose the regulator offers the type-i firm a long-term contact such that, in period 1 the firm charges the price p_i and receives the transfer T_i, and in the second period the firm is promised a rent equal to R_i^2. In this case, given discount factor δ, the total discounted rent of the type-i firm is

$$R_i = Q(p_i)(p_i - c_i) - F + T_i + \delta R_i^2.$$

By assumption, the firm's cost level is fully revealed by its choice of first-period contract. Because the regulator will always provide the promised second-period rent in the most efficient manner, he will set the type i firm's second-period price equal to c_i and implement the transfer payment that delivers rent R_i^2. Therefore, the incentive compatibility constraint for the low-cost firm, when it foresees that the second-period price will be c_H if it claims to have high cost, is

$$\begin{aligned} R_L &\geqslant Q(p_H)(p_H - c_L) - F + T_H + \delta\{Q(c_H)(c_H - c_L) + R_H^2\} \\ &= R_H + [Q(p_H) + \delta Q(c_H)]\Delta^c. \end{aligned} \tag{49}$$

If the incentive compatibility constraint (49) binds and the participation constraint of the high-cost firm binds (so $R_H = 0$), then total discounted welfare is

$$\begin{aligned} W = {} & \phi\{w_L(p_L) + \delta w_L(c_L) - (1-\alpha)\Delta^c[Q(p_H) + \delta Q(c_H)]\} \\ & + (1-\phi)\{w_H(p_H) + \delta w_H(c_H)\}. \end{aligned} \tag{50}$$

Maximizing expression (50) with respect to the remaining choice variables, p_L and p_H, reveals that the first-period prices are precisely those identified in Proposition 1 (and hence also those in part (i) of Proposition 6). Notice in particular that when separation is induced, first-period prices are not affected by the regulator's limited commitment powers. Limited commitment simply forces the regulator to give the low-cost firm more rent.

It is useful to decompose the expression for welfare in (50) into the welfare achieved in the first period and the welfare achieved in the second period. Doing so reveals

$$\begin{aligned} W = {} & \underbrace{\phi\{w_L(c_L) - (1-\alpha)\Delta^c Q(p_H)\} + (1-\phi)w_H(p_H)}_{\text{welfare from Baron–Myerson regime}} \\ & + \delta \underbrace{[\phi\{w_L(c_L) - (1-\alpha)\Delta^c Q(c_H)\} + (1-\phi)w_H(c_H)]}_{\text{welfare from Loeb–Magat regime}}. \end{aligned} \tag{51}$$

Since price p_H in expression (51) is the optimal static price in Proposition 1, welfare in the first period is precisely that achieved by the Baron–Myerson solution to the static problem. Because both prices are set equal to cost in the second period when separation is induced, second-period welfare is the welfare achieved when both firms offer marginal-cost prices, and the low-cost firm is offered the high rent ($\Delta^c Q(c_H)$) to ensure incentive compatibility.[66] This second-period policy is not optimal, except in the extreme setting where $\alpha = 1$, in which case intertemporal commitment power brings no benefit for regulation. The reduced welfare represents the cost that arises (when separation is optimal) from the regulator's inability to commit not to renegotiate.

However, the optimal regulatory policy will not always involve complete separation in the first period.[67] To see why most simply, consider the discounted welfare resulting from a policy of complete pooling in the first period. Under the optimal pooling contract, the firm charges the same price $\tilde{p}$, say, in the first period, regardless of its cost. The high-cost firm obtains zero rent and the low-cost firm obtains rent $\Delta^c Q(\tilde{p})$ in the first period. Clearly, such a policy yields lower welfare than the level derived in the Baron–Myerson regime in the first period. However, it has the benefit that at the start of the second period the regulator has learned nothing about the firm's realized cost, and so there is no scope for renegotiation. In particular, in the second period, the optimal policy will be precisely the Baron–Myerson policy of Proposition 1.

Thus, compared to the optimal separating equilibrium in (51), the pooling regime results in lower welfare in the first period and higher welfare in the second. Much as in expression (51), total discounted welfare under this policy is

$$W = \underbrace{\phi\{w_L(\tilde{p}) - (1-\alpha)\Delta^c Q(\tilde{p})\} + (1-\phi)w_H(\tilde{p})}_{\text{welfare from pooling regime}}$$
$$+\,\delta \underbrace{\left[\phi\{w_L(c_L) - (1-\alpha)\Delta^c Q(p_H)\} + (1-\phi)w_H(p_H)\right]}_{\text{welfare from Baron–Myerson regime}}.$$

Whenever the discount factor δ is sufficiently large (i.e., substantially greater than unity), the second-period welfare gains resulting from first-period pooling will outweigh the corresponding first-period losses, and a separating regulatory policy is not optimal. A pooling policy in the first period can be viewed as a (costly) means by which the regulator can increase his commitment power.

Thus, some pooling will optimally be implemented whenever the regulator and the firm value the future sufficiently highly.[68] When separation is not optimal, the precise details of the optimum are intricate. In rough terms, when the discount factor δ is small

[66] Recall the discussion in Section 2.3.1 of the policy suggested by Loeb and Magat (1979).

[67] In fact, when private information is distributed continuously (not discretely, as presumed in this chapter), a fully-separating first-period set of contracts is never optimal (although it is feasible) – see Laffont and Tirole (1993b, Section 10.6).

[68] Complete pooling is never optimal for the regulator. Reducing the probability that the two types of firm are pooled to slightly below 1 provides a first-order gain in first-period welfare by expanding the output of the low-cost firm toward its efficient level. Any corresponding reduction in second-period welfare is of second-order magnitude because, with complete pooling, the optimal second-period regulatory policy is precisely the policy that is optimal in the single-period setting when ϕ is the probability that the firm has low costs.

enough, the separation contracts derived above are optimal. As δ increases, a degree of pooling is optimal and the amount of pooling increases with δ.[69]

This particular commitment problem is potentially hard to overcome because it arises simply from the possibility that the regulator and firm mutually agree to alter the terms of a prevailing contract. In practice, an additional problem is that political pressure from consumer advocates, for example, might make it difficult for the regulator knowingly to continue to deliver rent to the regulated firm. This problem is discussed next.

2.5.3. *Short-term contracts: the danger of expropriation*

Now consider the two-period setting of Section 2.5.2 with one exception: the regulator cannot credibly commit to deliver specified second-period rents.[70] In other words, the regulator cannot specify the policy he will implement in the second period until the start of that period. In this case, the low-cost firm will be reluctant to reveal its superior capabilities, since such revelation will eliminate its second-period rent. In contrast to the renegotiation model, there are no long-term contracts in this setting that can protect the firm against such expropriation.

The optimal separating regulatory policy in the no-commitment setting can be derived much as it was derived in the renegotiation setting of Section 2.5.2. Suppose the regulator offers the two distinct options (p_L, T_L) and (p_H, T_H) in the first period, and the type-i firm chooses the (p_i, T_i) option with probability one. Because the firm's first-period choice fully reveals its second-period cost, second-period prices will be set equal to marginal costs, and the transfer will be set equal to the firm's fixed cost of production. Because the firm never receives any rent in the second period in this separating equilibrium, the rent of the type-i firm over the two periods is $R_i = Q(p_i)(p_i - c_i) - F + T_i$. Therefore, to prevent the low-cost firm from exaggerating its cost in the first period, it must be the case that

$$
\begin{aligned}
R_L &\geqslant Q(p_H)(p_H - c_L) - F + T_H + \delta\Delta^c Q(c_H) \\
&= R_H + \left[Q(p_H) + \delta Q(c_H)\right]\Delta^c. \qquad (52)
\end{aligned}
$$

Thus, the low-cost firm must be promised a relatively large first-period rent, R_L, to induce it to reveal its superior capabilities. Notice that expression (52) is precisely the

[69] See Laffont and Tirole (1993b, ch. 10) for details of the solution. Notice that the revelation principle is no longer valid in dynamic settings without commitment. That is to say, the regulator may do better if he considers contracts other than those where the firm always reveals its type. See Bester and Strausz (2001) for a precise characterization of optimal contracts without commitment. (Laffont and Tirole did not consider all possible contracts (see p. 390 of their book), but Bester and Strausz show that the contracts Laffont and Tirole consider include the optimal contracts.) For additional analysis of the design of contracts in the presence of adverse selection and renegotiation, see Rey and Salanié (1996), for example.

[70] This discussion is based on Laffont and Tirole (1988a) and Laffont and Tirole (1993b, ch. 9). Freixas, Guesnerie and Tirole (1985) explore a related model that considers linear contracts.

incentive compatibility constraint (49) for the low-cost firm in the setting with renegotiation. Assuming incentive constraint (52) binds and the participation constraint for the high-cost firm binds, welfare is given by expressions (50) and (51). Natural candidates for optimal first-period prices are derived by maximizing this expression with respect to p_L and p_H, which provides the prices identified in Proposition 1.

However, in contrast to the static analysis (and the renegotiation analysis), it is not always appropriate to ignore the high-cost firm's incentive compatibility constraint when the regulator has no intertemporal commitment powers. This constraint may be violated if the firm can refuse to produce in the second period without penalty. In this case, the high-cost firm may find it profitable to understate its first-period cost, collect the large transfer payment intended for the low-cost firm, and then terminate second-period operations rather than sell output in the second period at a price (c_L) below its cost c_H.[71]

To determine when the incentive compatibility constraint for the high-cost firm binds, notice that when the constraint is ignored and $R_H = 0$, the regulator optimally sets $p_L = c_L$ and $T_L = [Q(p_H) + \delta Q(c_H)]\Delta^c + F$. Consequently, the high-cost firm will not find it profitable to understate its cost under this regulatory policy if

$$0 \geqslant Q(c_L)(c_L - c_H) - F + T_L = \big[Q(p_H) + \delta Q(c_H) - Q(c_L)\big]\Delta^c. \tag{53}$$

When p_H is as specified in Equation (5) in Proposition 1, expression (53) will hold as a strict inequality when the discount factor δ is sufficiently small. Therefore, for small δ, the identified regulatory policy is the optimal one when the regulator cannot credibly commit to future policy.[72] Just as in the renegotiation setting, first-period prices are not affected by the regulator's limited commitment powers. Limited commitment simply forces the regulator to compensate the low-cost firm in advance for the second-period rent it foregoes by revealing its superior capabilities in the first period.

When the regulator and firm do not discount the future highly, inequality (53) will not hold, and so the incentive compatibility constraint for the high-cost firm may bind. To relax this constraint, the regulator optimally increases the incremental first-period output ($Q(p_L) - Q(p_H)$) the firm must deliver when it claims to have low cost. This increase is accomplished by reducing p_L below c_L and raising p_H above the level identified in expression (5) of Proposition 1. The increased output when low cost is reported reduces the profit of the high-cost firm when it understates its cost. The profit reduction arises

[71] Laffont and Tirole call this the "take the money and run" strategy. This possibility is one of the chief differences between the setting with renegotiation and the setting with no commitment. Under renegotiation, transfers and rents can be structured over time so that this strategy is never profitable for the high-cost firm. In particular, the renegotiation model gives rise to a more standard structure (i.e., the "usual" incentive compatibility constraints bind) than the no-commitment model.

[72] When private information is distributed continuously (rather than discretely as presumed in this chapter), it is never feasible (let alone optimal) to have a fully-revealing first-period set of contracts. Because the firm obtains zero rent in the second period under any contract that induces full separation in the first period, a firm would always find it profitable to mimic a slightly less efficient firm. This deviation will introduce only a second-order reduction in rent in the first period, but a first-order increase in rent in the second period. See Laffont and Tirole (1993b, Section 9.3).

because the corresponding increase in the transfer payment is only c_L per unit of output, which is compensatory for the low-cost firm, but not for the high-cost firm.

Although these distortions limit the firm's incentive to understate its cost, they also reduce total surplus. Beyond some point, the surplus reduction resulting from the distortions required to prevent cost misrepresentation outweigh the potential gains from matching the second-period price to the realized marginal cost. Consequently, the regulator will no longer ensure the low-cost and high-cost firm always set distinct prices. Instead, the regulator will induce the distinct types of the firm to implement the same price in the first period with positive probability (i.e., partial pooling is implemented).

These conclusions are summarized in Proposition 7.

PROPOSITION 7. *In the two-period setting with no regulatory commitment, the optimal regulatory policy has the following features*:

(i) *When δ is sufficiently small that inequality* (53) *holds, the prices identified in Proposition* 1 *are implemented in the first period, and the full-information outcome is implemented in the second period.*

(ii) *For larger values of δ, if separation is induced in the first period, p_L is set below c_L and p_H is set above the level identified in Proposition* 1. *The full-information outcome is implemented in the second period.*

(iii) *When δ is sufficiently large, partial pooling is induced in the first period.*

The pooling identified in property (iii) of Proposition 7 illustrates an important principle.[73] When regulators cannot make binding commitments regarding their use of pertinent information, welfare may be higher when regulators are denied access to the information. To illustrate, when a regulator cannot refrain from matching prices to realized production costs, welfare can increase as the regulator's ability to monitor realized production costs declines. When the regulator is unable to detect realized cost reductions immediately, the firm's incentives to deliver the effort required in order to reduce cost are enhanced. As a result, profit and consumer surplus can both increase.[74]

Another important feature of the outcome with no commitment (and also with renegotiation) is that, at least when δ is sufficiently small that first-period separation is optimal, the firm benefits from the regulator's limited commitment powers. One might expect that a regulator's inability to prevent himself from expropriating the firm's rents would make the firm worse off. However, notice that the high-cost firm makes no rent whether

[73] Notice that a lack of intertemporal commitment presents no problems for regulation when the static problem involves complete pooling (as is the case, for instance, when demand is unknown and the firm has a concave cost function). At the other extreme, when the full-information optimum is feasible in the static problem (e.g., when demand is unknown and the cost function is convex) there is no further scope for expropriation in the second period. Consequently, the regulator again does not need any commitment ability to achieve the ideal outcome in this dynamic context.

[74] See Sappington (1986). This conclusion is closely related to the principles that inform the optimal length of time between regulatory reviews of the firm's performance. See Section 3.2.3.

the regulator's commitment powers are limited or unlimited, and so is indifferent between the two regimes. Without commitment, expression (52) reveals that the low-cost firm makes discounted rent $[Q(p_H) + \delta Q(c_H)]\Delta^c$. With commitment, Proposition 6 reveals that the corresponding rent is only $[Q(p_H) + \delta Q(p_H)]\Delta^c$. Because $p_H > c_H$ and so $Q(c_H) > Q(p_H)$, the firm gains when the regulator cannot credibly promise to refrain from expropriating the firm.

Of course, in practice a regulator can exploit the firm's sunk physical investments as well as information about the firm's capabilities. We return to the general topic of policy credibility and regulatory expropriation in Section 3.4.1.

2.6. *Regulation under moral hazard*

To this point, the analysis has focused on the case where the firm is perfectly informed from the outset about its exogenous production cost. In practice, a regulated firm often will be uncertain about the operating cost it can achieve, but knows that it can reduce expected operating cost by undertaking cost-reducing effort. The analysis in this section considers how the regulator can best motivate the firm to deliver such unobservable cost-reducing effort.[75]

The simple moral hazard setting considered here parallels the framework of Section 2.3.3 where there are two states, denoted L and H (which could denote different technologies or different demands, for example). State L is the socially desirable state. As before, let $\phi \in (0, 1)$ be the probability that state L is realized. However, the parameter ϕ is chosen by the firm in the present setting. The increasing, strictly convex function $D(\phi) \geqslant 0$ denotes the disutility incurred by the firm in securing the probability ϕ. The regulator cannot observe the firm's choice of ϕ, which can be thought of as the firm's effort in securing the favorable L state. The regulator can accurately observe the realized state, and offers the firm a pair of utilities, $\{U_L, U_H\}$, where the firm enjoys the utility U_i when state i is realized.[76] Because of the uncertainty of the outcome, the firm's attitude towards risk is important, and so we distinguish between 'utility' and 'rent'. (In the special case where the firm is risk neutral, the two concepts coincide.)

The firm's expected utility when it delivers the effort required to ensure success probability ϕ (i.e., to ensure that state L occurs with probability ϕ) is

$$U = \phi U_L + (1 - \phi)U_H - D(\phi) \geqslant U^0, \tag{54}$$

where the inequality in expression (54) indicates that the firm must achieve expected utility of at least U^0 if it is to be willing to participate. The firm's optimal choice of

[75] We are unaware of a treatment of the regulatory moral hazard problem that parallels exactly the problem analyzed in this section. For recent related discussions of the moral hazard problem, see Laffont and Martimort (2002, chs. 4 and 5) and Bolton and Dewatripont (2005, ch. 4). See Cowan (2004) for an analysis of optimal risk-sharing between consumers and the regulated firm in a full information framework.

[76] If the regulator could not observe the realized state in this setting, an adverse selection problem would accompany the moral hazard problem. See Laffont and Martimort (2002, Section 7.2) for an analysis of such models.

ϕ can be expressed as a function of the incremental utility it anticipates in state L, $\Delta^U = U_L - U_H$. The magnitude of Δ^U represents the *power* of the incentive scheme used to motivate the firm. Formally, from expression (54) the firm's equilibrium level of effort, denoted $\hat{\phi}(\Delta^U)$, satisfies:

$$D'(\hat{\phi}(\Delta^U)) \equiv \Delta^U. \tag{55}$$

Equilibrium effort $\hat{\phi}$ is an increasing function of the power of the incentive scheme, Δ^U.

For simplicity, suppose the regulator seeks to maximize expected consumer surplus.[77] Suppose that in state i, if the firm is given utility U_i, the maximum level of consumer surplus available is $V_i(U_i)$. (We will illustrate this relationship between consumer surplus and the firm's utility shortly.) Therefore, the regulator wishes to maximize

$$V = \phi V_L(U_L) + (1 - \phi) V_H(U_H),$$

subject to the participation constraint (54) and the equilibrium effort condition $\phi = \hat{\phi}(\Delta^U)$ as defined by expression (55). Given the presumed separability in the firm's utility function, the participation constraint (54) will bind at the optimum. Therefore, we can re-state the regulator's problem as maximizing social surplus

$$W = \phi W_L(U_L) + (1 - \phi) W_H(U_H) - D(\phi), \tag{56}$$

where $W_i(U_i) \equiv V_i(U_i) + U_i$, subject to $\phi = \hat{\phi}(\Delta^U)$ and the participation constraint (54).

We next describe three natural examples of the relationship $V_i(U_i)$ between the firm's utility and consumer surplus. In each of these examples, suppose the firm's profit in state i is $\pi_i(p_i)$ when it offers the price p_i, and $v_i(p_i)$ is (gross) consumer surplus. Let $w_i(\cdot) \equiv v_i(\cdot) + \pi_i(\cdot)$ denote the total unweighted surplus function, and suppose p_i^* is the price that maximizes welfare $w_i(\cdot)$ in state i. If the regulator requires the firm to offer the price p_i and gives the firm a transfer payment T_i in state i, the rent of the firm is $R_i = \pi_i(p_i) + T_i$.[78]

Case 1: Risk-neutral firm when transfers are employed

When the firm is risk neutral its utility is equal to its rent, and so $U_i = R_i = \pi_i(p_i) + T_i$. Therefore, $V_i(U_i)$, which is the maximum level of (net) consumer surplus $v_i(p_i) - T_i$ that can be achieved for a utility level U_i, is given by

$$V_i(U_i) = w_i(p_i^*) - U_i.$$

[77] Thus, we assume consumers are "risk neutral" in their valuation of consumer surplus. The ensuing analysis is unaltered if the regulator seeks to maximize a weighted average of consumer surplus and utility, $S + \alpha U$, provided the weight α is not so large that the firm's participation constraint does not bind at the optimum.

[78] For ease of exposition, we assume the firm produces a single product. The analysis is readily extended to allow for multiple products.

In this case, the firm's utility and maximized consumer surplus sum to a constant, i.e.,

$$W_i(U_i) \equiv w_i(p_i^*), \tag{57}$$

and the available total surplus is invariant to the rent/utility afforded the firm.

Case 2: Risk-averse firm when transfers are employed

When the firm is risk averse and its rent in state i is $R_i = \pi_i(p_i) + T_i$, its utility U_i can be written as $u(R_i)$ where $u(\cdot)$ is a concave function. Therefore, $V_i(U_i)$ is given by

$$V_i(U_i) = w_i(p_i^*) - u^{-1}(U_i), \tag{58}$$

where $u^{-1}(\cdot)$ is the inverse function of $u(\cdot)$. Here, there is a decreasing and concave relationship between firm utility and consumer surplus. In this case, firm utility and maximized consumer surplus do not sum to a constant, and $W_i(U_i)$ is a concave function. However, the trade-off between the firm's utility and consumer surplus does not depend on the prevailing state. Consequently,

$$V_L'(U) \equiv V_H'(U). \tag{59}$$

Case 3: Risk-neutral firm when no transfers are employed

When the firm is risk neutral and no lump-sum transfers are employed, $U_i = R_i = \pi_i(p_i)$. Therefore, $V_i(U_i)$ is just the level of consumer surplus $v_i(p_i)$ when the price is such that $\pi_i(p_i) = U_i$. Consequently,

$$V_i(U_i) = v_i(\pi_i^{-1}(U_i)). \tag{60}$$

In this case, firm utility and maximized consumer surplus again do not sum to a constant. In the special case where the demand function is iso-elastic with elasticity η,

$$V_i'(U_i) = \frac{-1}{1 - \eta[\frac{p_i - c_i}{p_i}]}, \tag{61}$$

where p_i is the price that yields rent $U_i = \pi_i(p_i)$.

Full-information benchmark Consider the hypothetical setting where the regulator can directly control effort ϕ, so the effort selection constraint, $\phi = \hat{\phi}(\Delta^U)$, can be ignored. If λ is the Lagrange multiplier for the participation constraint (54) in this full-information problem, the optimal choices for U_L and U_H satisfy

$$V_L'(U_L) = V_H'(U_H) = -(1 + \lambda). \tag{62}$$

Expression (62) shows that at the full-information optimum, the regulator should ensure that the marginal rate of substitution between the firm's utility and consumer surplus is the same in the two states. This is just an application of standard Ramsey principles.

Second-best optimum Now return to the setting where the regulator must motivate ϕ, and so the constraint $\phi = \hat{\phi}(\Delta^U)$ is relevant. Let $\hat{\lambda}$ denote the Lagrange multiplier associated with (54) in this second-best problem. Then the first-order conditions for the choice of U_i in expression (56) in this setting are

$$V_L'(U_L) = -(1+\hat{\lambda}) - \frac{\hat{\phi}'}{\hat{\phi}}\Delta^V; \qquad V_H'(U_H) = -(1+\hat{\lambda}) + \frac{\hat{\phi}'}{1-\hat{\phi}}\Delta^V, \tag{63}$$

where $\Delta^V \equiv V_L(U_L) - V_H(U_H)$ is the increment in consumer surplus in the desirable state L at the optimum. Notice that in the extreme case where the firm cannot affect the probability of a favorable outcome, so that $\hat{\phi}' = 0$, expression (63) collapses to the full-information condition in (62), and so the full-information outcome is attained.[79]

In the ensuing sections we consider the special cases of optimal regulation of a risk-neutral firm (case 1 in the preceding discussion) and a risk-averse firm (case 2). The discussion of the case of limited regulatory instruments (case 3) is deferred until Section 3.3.

2.6.1. Regulation of a risk-neutral firm

It is well known that when the firm is risk neutral and can bear unlimited losses ex post, the full-information outcome is attainable. To see why, substitute expression (57) into expected welfare (56). Doing so reveals that the regulator's objective is to maximize

$$W = \phi w_L(p_L^*) + (1-\phi) w_H(p_H^*) - D(\phi), \tag{64}$$

subject to $\phi = \hat{\phi}(\Delta^U)$ and the participation constraint (54). The regulator can structure the two utilities U_L and U_H to meet the firm's participation constraint (54) without affecting the firm's effort incentives. Since there is a one-to-one relationship between the incremental utility Δ^U and the effort level ϕ, the regulator will choose Δ^U to implement the value of ϕ that maximizes expression (64), and the full-information outcome is achieved.

PROPOSITION 8. *The full-information outcome is feasible (and optimal) in the pure moral hazard setting when the firm is risk-neutral and transfers can be employed. The optimal outcomes for the firm and for consumers are*

$$D'(\phi) = U_L - U_H = w_L(p_L^*) - w_H(p_H^*); \qquad V_L(U_L) = V_H(U_H). \tag{65}$$

The conclusion in Proposition 8 parallels the conclusion of the model of regulation under adverse selection when distributional concerns are absent (so $\alpha = 1$), discussed in Section 2.3.1. In both cases, the firm is made the residual claimant for the social surplus and consumers are indifferent about the realized state. In the present moral hazard setting, this requires that the firm face a high-powered incentive scheme. If state i occurs and the firm chooses price p_i, the regulator gives the firm a transfer payment

[79] The two multipliers λ and $\hat{\lambda}$ are equal in this case.

$T_i = v_i(p_i) - K$. Here, the constant K is chosen so that the firm makes zero rent in expectation. Under this policy, the firm has the correct incentives to set prices in each state, so $p_i = p_i^*$ is chosen. In addition, the firm has the correct incentives to choose ϕ to maximize social welfare in expression (64) because the firm has been made the residual claimant for the welfare generated by its actions.

2.6.2. *Regulation of a risk-averse firm*

When the relationship between firm utility and net consumer surplus is as specified in Equation (58), conditions (59) and (62) together imply that if the regulator could directly control the firm's effort ϕ, the outcomes for consumers and the firm would optimally be

$$U_L = U_H; \qquad V_L(U_L) - V_H(U_H) = w_L(p_L^*) - w_H(p_H^*). \tag{66}$$

In words, if the firm's effort could be controlled directly, the risk-averse firm should be given full insurance, so that it would receive the same utility (and rent) in each state. Of course, full insurance leaves the firm with no incentive to achieve the desirable outcome. In contrast, a higher-powered scheme ($U_L > U_H$) provides effort incentives, but leaves the firm exposed to risk.

The second-best policy is given by expression (63) above. In particular, it is still optimal to have the full-information prices p_i^* in each state i, since these prices maximize the available surplus that can be shared between the firm and consumers in any given state i.[80] Assuming that $w_L(p_L^*)$ is greater than $w_H(p_H^*)$, which is implied by the convention that L is the socially desirable state, expression (63) implies that[81]

$$U_L \geqslant U_H; \qquad V_L(U_L) \geqslant V_H(U_H). \tag{67}$$

Therefore, the firm is given an incentive to achieve the desirable outcome, but this incentive is sufficiently small that consumers are better off when the good state is realized. The more pronounced is the firm's aversion to risk, the more important is the need to insure the firm and the lower is the power of the optimal incentive scheme. In the limit as the firm becomes infinitely risk averse so that the firm's utility function in expression (54) becomes

$$U = \min\{R_L, R_H\} - D(\phi),$$

[80] This is another version of the incentive-pricing dichotomy discussed in Laffont and Tirole (1993b): prices are employed to ensure allocative efficiency, while rent is employed to create incentives to increase productive efficiency.

[81] To see this, suppose $\Delta^V \geqslant 0$ at the optimum. Then expression (63) implies $U_L \geqslant U_H$. Suppose by contrast $\Delta^V < 0$. Then expression (63) implies $U_L < U_H$. But since

$$\Delta^V = [w_L(p_L^*) - w_H(p_H^*)] - [u^{-1}(U_L) - u^{-1}(U_H)],$$

it follows that $\Delta^V > [w_L(p_L^*) - w_H(p_H^*)] > 0$ when $U_L < U_H$, which is a contradiction. Therefore, the only configuration consistent with expression (63) is $\Delta^V \geqslant 0$ and $U_L \geqslant U_H$, as claimed.

the firm does not respond to incentives since it cares only about its rent in the worse state. In this case, the firm delivers no effort to attain the desirable outcome, and the regulator does not benefit by setting $R_L > R_H$.

2.6.3. Regulation of a risk-neutral firm with limited liability

The analysis to this point has not considered any lower bounds that might be placed on the firm's returns. In practice, bankruptcy laws and liability limits can introduce such lower bounds. To analyze the effects of such bounds, the model of Section 2.6.1 is modified to incorporate an ex post participation constraint that the firm must receive rent $R_i \geqslant 0$ in each state. Since the firm now cannot be punished when there is a bad outcome, all incentives must be delivered through a reward when there is a good outcome.[82] In this case, the regulator will set $R_H = 0$ and use the rent in the good state to motivate the firm. The firm's overall expected rent is $\phi R_L - D(\phi)$, and it will choose effort ϕ to maximize this expression, so that $D'(\phi) = R_L$. Since the firm will enjoy positive expected rent in this model, the regulator's valuation of rent will be important for the analysis. Therefore, as with the adverse selection analysis, suppose the regulator places weight $\alpha \in [0, 1]$ on the firm's rent. In this case, much as in Section 2.6.1 above, the regulator's objective is to choose R_L to maximize

$$W = \phi\{w_L(p_L^*) - (1-\alpha)R_L\} + (1-\phi)w_H(p_H^*) - \alpha D(\phi),$$

subject to the incentive constraint $D'(\phi) = R_L$. (As before, it is optimal to set the full-information prices p_i^* and to use transfers to provide effort incentives.) Therefore, since $R_L = D'(\phi)$, the regulator should choose ϕ to maximize

$$W = \phi\{w_L(p_L^*) - (1-\alpha)D'(\phi)\} + (1-\phi)w_H(p_H^*) - \alpha D(\phi).$$

The solution to this problem has the first-order condition

$$D'(\phi) = w_L(p_L^*) - w_H(p_H^*) - (1-\alpha)\phi D''(\phi). \tag{68}$$

Comparing expression (68) with expression (65), the corresponding expression from the setting where there is no ex post participation constraint, it is apparent that this constraint produces lower equilibrium effort. (Recall $D''(\cdot) > 0$.) Therefore, the introduction of a binding limited liability constraint reduces the power of the optimal incentive scheme. The reduced power is optimal in the presence of limited liability because the regulator can no longer simply lower the firm's payoff when the unfavorable outcome is realized so as to offset any incremental reward that is promised when the favorable outcome is realized. The only situation where the power of the optimal incentive scheme is not reduced by the imposition of limited liability constraints is when the

[82] The ex ante participation constraint is assumed not to bind in the ensuing analysis. See Laffont and Martimort (2002, Section 3.5) for further discussion of limited liability constraints.

regulator has no strict preference for consumer surplus over firm rent ($\alpha = 1$), just as in the adverse selection paradigm.

Notice that this limited liability setting produces results similar to those obtained under risk aversion in Section 2.6.2. The full-information outcome is not feasible and too little effort is supplied relative to the full-information outcome in both settings. The limited liability setting also provides parallels with the adverse selection analysis in Section 2.3.1. In the limited liability setting, the regulator faces a trade-off between rent extraction and incentives. In the adverse selection settings, the regulator faces a corresponding trade-off.

2.6.4. *Repeated moral hazard*

Three primary additional considerations arise when the moral hazard model is repeated over time. First, the firm can effectively become less averse to risk, since it can pool the risk over time, and offset a bad outcome in one period by borrowing against the expectation of a good future outcome. Second, with repeated observations of the outcome, the regulator has better information about the firm's effort decisions (especially if current effort decisions have long-term effects). Third, the firm can choose from a wide range of possible dynamic strategies. For instance, the firm's managers can choose when to invest in effort, and might respond to a positive outcome in the current period by reducing effort in the future, for example. Consequently, the regulator's optimal inter-temporal policy, and the firm's profit-maximizing response to the policy, can be complicated.[83] In particular, the optimal policy typically will make the firm's reward for a good outcome in the current period depend on the entire history of outcomes, even in a setting where effort only affects the outcome in the current period. The dynamic moral hazard problem is discussed further in Section 3.2.3 below, where the optimal frequency of regulatory review is considered.

2.7. *Conclusions*

Asymmetric information about the regulated industry can greatly complicate the design of regulatory policy. This section has reviewed the central insights provided by the pioneering studies of this issue and by subsequent analyses. The review reveals that the manner in which the regulated firm is optimally induced to employ its superior knowledge in the best interests of consumers varies according to the nature of the firm's

[83] See Rogerson (1985). Holmstrom and Milgrom (1987) examine a continuous time framework in which the optimal inter-temporal incentive scheme is linear in the agent's total production. Bolton and Dewatripont (2005, ch. 11) emphasize the effects of limited commitment on the part of the principal. Also see the analyses of renegotiation by Fudenberg and Tirole (1990), Chiappori et al. (1994), Ma (1994), and Matthews (2001). Laffont and Martimort (2002, Section 8.2) analyze the two-period model with full commitment. Radner (1981, 1985) provides early work on the repeated moral hazard problem.

privileged information and according to the intertemporal commitment powers of the regulator.

The review emphasized five general principles. First, when a regulated firm has privileged information about the environment in which it operates, the firm typically is able to command rent from its superior information. Second, to help limit this rent, a regulator can design options from which the firm is permitted to choose. When designed appropriately, the options induce the firm to employ its superior industry knowledge to realize Pareto gains. Third, the options intentionally induce outcomes that differ from the outcomes the regulator would implement if he shared the firm's knowledge of the industry. These performance distortions serve to limit the firm's rent. Fourth, a benevolent regulator is better able to limit the firm's rent and secure gains for consumers via the careful design of regulatory options when he is endowed with a broader set of regulatory instruments and more extensive commitment powers. Fifth, when the regulator's commitment powers are limited, it may be optimal to limit the regulator's access to information, in order to limit inappropriate use of the information.

The analysis in this section has focused on the design of optimal regulatory policy when there is a single monopoly supplier of regulated services.[84,85] Section 4 reviews some of the additional considerations that arise in the presence of actual or potential competition. First, though, Section 3 discusses several simple regulatory policies, including some that are commonly employed in practice.

3. Practical regulatory policies

The discussion in Section 2 focused on optimal regulatory policy. Such analyses model formally the information asymmetry between the regulator and the firm and then determine precisely how the regulator optimally pursues his goals in the presence of this asymmetry. While this normative approach can provide useful insights for the design

[84] The analysis in this section also has taken as given the quality of the goods and services delivered by the regulated firm. Section 3 discusses policies that can promote increased service quality. Laffont and Tirole (1993b, ch. 4) and Lewis and Sappington (1992) discuss how regulated prices are optimally altered when they must serve both to motivate the delivery of high-quality products and to limit incentives to misrepresent private information. Lewis and Sappington (1991a) note that consumers and the regulated firm can both suffer when the level of realized service quality is not verifiable. In contrast, Dalen (1997) shows that in a dynamic setting where the regulator's commitment powers are limited, consumers may benefit when quality is not verifiable.

[85] The analysis in this section also has taken as given the nature of the information asymmetry between the regulator and the firm. Optimal regulatory policies will differ if, for example, the regulator wishes to motivate the firm to obtain better information about its environment, perhaps in order to inform future investment decisions. [See Lewis and Sappington (1997) and Crémer, Khalil and Rochet (1998a, 1998b), for example.] Iossa and Stroffolini (2002) show that optimal regulatory mechanisms of the type described in Proposition 3 provide the firm with stronger incentives for information acquisition than do price cap plans of the type considered in Section 3. Iossa and Stroffolini (2005) stress the merits of revenue sharing requirements under price cap regulation in this regard.

and evaluation of real-world regulatory policy, the approach has its limitations. In particular: (i) all relevant information asymmetries can be difficult to characterize precisely; (ii) the form of optimal regulatory policies is not generally known when information asymmetries are pronounced and multi-dimensional; (iii) a complete specification of all relevant constraints on the regulator and firm can be difficult to formulate; (iv) some of the instruments that are important in optimal reward structures (such as transfers) are not always available in practice; and (v) even the goals of regulators can be difficult to specify in some situations. Therefore, although formal models of optimal regulatory policy can provide useful insights about the properties of regulatory policies that may perform well in practice, these models seldom capture the full richness of the settings in which actual regulatory policies are implemented.[86]

This has led researchers and policy makers to propose relatively simple regulatory policies that appear to have some desirable properties, even if they are not optimal in any precise sense. The purpose of this section is to review some of these pragmatic policies. The policies are sorted on four dimensions: (1) the extent of pricing flexibility granted to the regulated firm; (2) the manner in which regulatory policy is implemented and revised over time; (3) the degree to which regulated prices are linked to realized costs; and (4) the discretion that regulators themselves have when they formulate policy. These dimensions are useful for expository purposes even though they incorporate substantial overlap.

To begin, it may be helpful to assess how two particularly familiar regulatory policies compare on these four dimensions. Table 27.1 provides a highly stylized interpretation of how price cap and rate-of-return regulation differ along these dimensions, and the broad effects of such policies. Under a common form of price cap regulation, the prices the firm charges for specified services are permitted to increase, on average, at a specified rate for a specified period of time. The specified average rate of price increase often is linked to the overall rate of price inflation, and typically does not reflect the firm's realized production costs or profit. In contrast, rate-of-return regulation specifies an allowed rate of return on investment for the firm, and adjusts the firm's prices as its costs change to ensure the firm a reasonable opportunity to earn the authorized return.

Table 27.1 reflects the idea that, at least under a common caricature of price cap regulation: (i) only the firm's average price is controlled (which leaves the firm free to control the pattern of relative prices within the basket of regulated services); (ii) the rate at which prices can increase over time is fixed for several years, and is not adjusted to reflect realized costs and profits during the time period; (iii) current prices are not explicitly linked to current costs; and (iv) the regulator has considerable discretion over future policy (once the current price control period has expired). Because prices are not directly linked to costs for relatively long periods of time, the firm can have strong incentives to reduce its operating costs. By contrast, under the classic depiction of rate-of-return regulation: (i) the regulator sets prices, and affords the firm little discretion in

[86] See Crew and Kleindorfer (2002) and Vogelsang (2002) for critical views regarding the practical relevance of the recent optimal regulation literature.

Table 27.1
Price cap versus rate-of-return regulation

	Price cap	Rate-of-return
Firm's flexibility over relative prices	Yes	No
Regulatory lag	Long	Short
Sensitivity of prices to realized costs	Low	High
Regulatory discretion	Substantial	Limited
Incentives for cost reduction	Strong	Limited
Incentives for durable sunk investment	Limited	Strong

altering these prices; (ii) prices are adjusted as necessary to ensure that the realized rate of return on investment does not deviate substantially from the target rate; (iii) prices are adjusted to reflect significant changes in costs; and (iv) the regulator is required to ensure that the firm has the opportunity to earn the target rate of return on an ongoing basis. Because the firm is ensured a reasonable opportunity to earn the authorized return on its investments over the long term, the firm has limited concern that its sunk investments will be expropriated by future regulatory policy.

Rate-of-return and price cap regulation can have different effects on unobservable investment (e.g., managerial effort) designed to reduce operating costs and observable infrastructure investment. Because it links prices directly to realized costs, rate-of-return regulation is unlikely to induce substantial unobserved cost-reducing investment. However, rate-of-return regulation can promote observable infrastructure investment by limiting the risk that such investment will be expropriated. In contrast, price cap regulation can provide strong incentives for unobservable cost-reducing effort, especially when the regulatory commitment period (the length of time between regulatory reviews) is relatively long. Therefore, the choice between these two forms of regulation will depend in part on the relative importance of the two forms of investment. In settings where the priority is to induce the regulated firm to employ its existing infrastructure more efficiently, a price cap regime may be preferable. In settings where it is important to reverse a history of chronic under-investment in key infrastructure, a guaranteed rate of return on (prudently incurred) investments may be preferable.[87] The relative performance of price cap and rate-of-return regulation is explored in more detail and in other dimensions in the remainder of Section 3.[88]

[87] Regulatory regimes also differ according to the incentives they provide the firm to modernize its operating technology. In contrast to rate-of-return regulation, for example, price cap regulation can encourage the regulated firm to replace older high-cost technology with newer low-cost technology in a timely fashion. It can do so by severing the link between the firm's authorized earnings and the size of its rate base. See Biglaiser and Riordan (2000) for an analysis of this issue.

[88] For more detailed discussions of the key differences between price cap regulation and rate-of-return regulation, see, for example, Acton and Vogelsang (1989), Cabral and Riordan (1989), Hillman and Braeutigam (1989), Clemenz (1991), Braeutigam and Panzar (1993), Liston (1993), Armstrong, Cowan and Vickers

3.1. Pricing flexibility

In a setting where the regulated firm has no privileged information about its operating environment, there is little reason for the regulator to delegate pricing decisions to the firm. Such delegation would simply invite the firm to implement prices other than those that are most preferred by the regulator. In contrast, if the firm is better informed than the regulator about its costs or about consumer demand, then, by granting the firm some authority to set its tariffs, the regulator may be able to induce the firm to employ its superior information to implement prices that generate higher levels of welfare than the regulator could secure by dictating prices based upon his limited information. A formal analysis of this possibility is presented in Section 3.1.1. Section 3.1.2 compares the merits of two particular means by which the firm might be afforded some flexibility over its prices: *average revenue* regulation and *tariff basket* regulation.

Despite the potential merits of delegating some pricing flexibility to the regulated firm, there are reasons why a regulator might wish to limit the firm's pricing discretion. One reason is that the regulated firm may set prices to disadvantage rivals, as explained in Section 3.1.3. A second reason is the desire to maintain pricing structures that reflect distributional or other political objectives. In practice, regulators often limit a firm's pricing flexibility in order to prevent the firm from unraveling price structures that have been implemented to promote social goals such as universal service (i.e., ensuring that nearly all citizens consume the service in question).

3.1.1. The cost and benefits of flexibility with asymmetric information

The merits of affording the regulated firm some discretion in setting prices vary according to whether the firm is privately informed about its costs or its demand.[89] We assume that transfer payments to or from the firm are not feasible, and the firm's tariff must be designed to cover its costs. As in Section 2, the regulator seeks to maximize a weighted average of expected consumer surplus and profit, where $\alpha \leqslant 1$ is the weight the regulator places on profit.

Asymmetric cost information Suppose first that the firm has superior knowledge of its (exogenous) cost structure, while the regulator and firm are both perfectly informed about industry demand. The regulated firm produces n products. The price for product i is p_i, and the vector of prices that the firm charges for its n products is $\mathbf{p} = (p_1, \dots, p_n)$. Suppose that consumer surplus with prices $\mathbf{p}$ is $v(\mathbf{p})$, where this function is known to all parties. Suppose also that the firm's total profit with prices $\mathbf{p}$ is $\pi(\mathbf{p})$. Since the firm has superior information about its costs in this setting, the regulator is not completely informed about the firm's profit function, $\pi(\cdot)$.

(1994), Blackmon (1994), Mansell and Church (1995), Sappington (1994, 2002), Sappington and Weisman (1996a), and Joskow (2005).

[89] This discussion is based on Armstrong and Vickers (2000).

Some pricing flexibility is always advantageous in this setting. To see why, suppose the regulator instructs the firm to offer the fixed price vector $\mathbf{p}^0 = (p_1^0, \ldots, p_n^0)$. Provided these prices allow the firm to break even, so that the firm agrees to participate, this policy yields welfare $v(\mathbf{p}^0) + \alpha\pi(\mathbf{p}^0)$. Suppose instead, the regulator allows the firm to choose any price vector that leaves consumers in aggregate just as well off as they were with $\mathbf{p}^0$, so that the firm can choose any price vector

$$\mathbf{p} \in \mathcal{P} = \{\mathbf{p} \mid v(\mathbf{p}) \geqslant v(\mathbf{p}^0)\}. \tag{69}$$

By construction, this regulatory policy ensures that consumers are no worse off in aggregate than they are under the fixed pricing policy $\mathbf{p}^0$.[90] Furthermore, the firm will be strictly better off when it can choose a price from the set $\mathcal{P}$, except in the knife-edge case where $\mathbf{p}^0$ happens to be the most profitable way to generate consumer surplus $v(\mathbf{p}^0)$. Therefore, welfare is sure to increase when the firm is granted pricing flexibility in this manner.[91]

Asymmetric demand information The merits of pricing flexibility are less clear cut when the firm has superior knowledge of industry demand. To see why it might be optimal not to grant the firm any authority to set prices when consumer demand is private information, suppose the firm has known, constant marginal costs $\mathbf{c} = \{c_1, \ldots, c_n\}$ for its n products and has no fixed cost of operation. Then, regardless of the form of consumer demand, the full-information outcome is achieved by constraining the firm to offer the single price vector $\mathbf{p} = \mathbf{c}$, so that prices are equal to marginal costs. If the firm is given the flexibility to choose from a wider set of price vectors, it will typically choose prices that deviate from costs, thereby reducing welfare.

More generally, whether the firm should be afforded any pricing flexibility depends on whether the full-information prices are incentive compatible. In many natural cases, a firm will find it profitable to raise price when demand increases. However, welfare considerations suggest that prices should be higher in those markets with relatively inelastic demand, not necessarily in markets with large demand. Thus, if an increase in demand is associated with an increase in the demand elasticity, the firm's incentives are not aligned with the welfare-maximizing policy, and so it is optimal to restrict the firm to offer a single price vector. If, by contrast, an increase in demand is associated with a reduction in the market elasticity, then private and social incentives coincide, and it is optimal to afford the firm some authority to set prices.

This analysis parallels the analysis in Section 2.3.2 of the optimal regulation (with transfers) of a single-product firm that is privately informed about its demand function. In that setting, when the firm has a concave cost function, an increase in demand is

[90] Since some prices will increase under this policy, some individual consumers may be made worse off.

[91] Notice that the profit-maximizing prices for the firm operating under this constraint are closely related to Ramsey prices: profit is maximized subject to a constraint on the level of consumer surplus achieved, or, equivalently, consumer surplus is maximized subject to a profit constraint. However, the prices are not true Ramsey prices since the firm's rent will not be zero in general.

associated with a lower marginal cost. Therefore, the firm's incentives – which typically are to set a higher price in response to greater demand – run counter to social incentives, which are to set a lower price when marginal cost is lower, i.e., when demand is greater. These conflicting incentives make it optimal to give the firm no authority to choose its prices.

In summary, unequivocal conclusions about the merits of granting pricing flexibility to a regulated firm are not available. In practice, a regulated firm typically will be better informed than the regulator about both its demand and its cost structure. Furthermore, the regulator will often be unaware of the exact nature of likely variation in demand. Consequently, the benefits that pricing flexibility will secure in any specific setting may be difficult to predict in advance. However, the foregoing principles can inform the choice of the degree of pricing flexibility afforded the firm.

3.1.2. Forms of price flexibility

The merits of affording the regulated firm some pricing flexibility vary with the form of the contemplated flexibility. To illustrate this point, consider two common variants of average price regulation: average revenue regulation and tariff basket regulation.[92] Suppose consumer demand for product i with the price vector $\mathbf{p}$ is $Q_i(\mathbf{p})$, and $v(\mathbf{p})$ is the corresponding total consumer surplus function. In order to compare outcomes under various regimes, notice that, for any pair of price vectors $\mathbf{p}^1$ and $\mathbf{p}^2$, the following inequality holds[93]

$$v(\mathbf{p}^2) \geqslant v(\mathbf{p}^1) - \sum_{i=1}^{n} (p_i^2 - p_i^1) Q_i(\mathbf{p}^1). \tag{70}$$

Expression (70) states that consumer surplus with price vector $\mathbf{p}^2$ is at least as great as consumer surplus with price vector $\mathbf{p}^1$, less the difference in revenue generated by the two price vectors when demands are $Q_i(\mathbf{p}^1)$. The inequality follows from the convexity of the consumer surplus function.

Average revenue regulation In its simplest form, average revenue regulation limits to a specified level, $\bar{p}$, the average revenue the firm derives from its regulated operations. Formally, the average revenue constraint requires the firm's price vector to lie in the set

$$\mathbf{p} \in \mathcal{P}^{AR} = \left\{ \mathbf{p} \;\middle|\; \frac{\sum_{i=1}^{n} p_i Q_i(\mathbf{p})}{\sum_{i=1}^{n} Q_i(\mathbf{p})} \leqslant \bar{p} \right\}. \tag{71}$$

[92] This section is based on Armstrong and Vickers (1991).

[93] The expression to the right of the inequality in (70) reflects the level of consumer surplus that would arise under prices $\mathbf{p}^1$ if consumers did not alter their consumption when prices changed from $\mathbf{p}^2$ to $\mathbf{p}^1$ (and instead just benefited from the monetary savings permitted by the new prices). Since consumers generally will be able to secure more surplus by altering their consumption in response to new prices, the inequality follows.

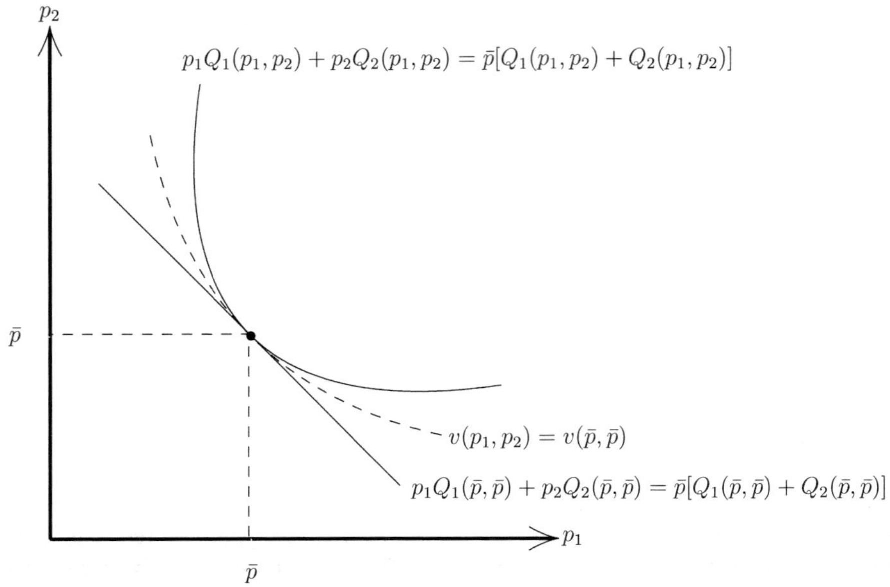

Figure 27.2. Average revenue and tariff basket regulation.

The term to the left of the inequality in expression (71) is average revenue: total revenue divided by total output.[94] Notice that if $\mathbf{p}^2$ is the vector of prices where all services have the same benchmark price, $\bar{p}$, and $\mathbf{p}^1$ is any price vector that satisfies the average revenue constraint in (71) exactly, then inequality (70) implies that $v(\mathbf{p}^1) \leqslant v(\mathbf{p}^2)$. Therefore, regardless of the prices the firm sets under this form of regulation, consumers will be worse off than if the firm were required to set price $\bar{p}$ for each of its products.[95] The reduction in consumer surplus arises because as the firm raises prices, the quantity demanded decreases, which reduces average revenue, and thereby relaxes the average revenue constraint.

This reduction in consumer surplus is illustrated in Figure 27.2 for the case where the firm offers two products. Here the boundary of the set $\mathcal{P}^{AR}$ in (71) lies inside the set of price vectors that make consumers worse off than they are with the uniform price vector $(\bar{p}, \bar{p})$. (Consumer surplus declines with movements to the north-east in Figure 27.2.)

The following result summarizes the main features of average revenue regulation:

[94] Since total output is calculated by summing individual output levels, average revenue regulation in this form is most appropriate in settings where the units of output of the n regulated products are commensurate.

[95] Armstrong, Cowan and Vickers (1995) show that, for similar reasons, allowing non-linear pricing reduces consumer surplus when average revenue regulation is imposed on the regulated firm, compared to a regime where the firm offers a linear tariff.

PROPOSITION 9. (i) *Consumer surplus is lower under binding average revenue regulation when the firm is permitted to set any prices that satisfy inequality* (71) *rather than being required to set each price at* $\bar{p}$.

(ii) *Total welfare (the weighted sum of consumer surplus and profit) could be higher or lower when the firm is permitted to set any prices that satisfy inequality* (71) *rather than being required to set each price at* $\bar{p}$.

(iii) *Consumer surplus can decrease under average revenue regulation when the authorized level of average revenue* $\bar{p}$ *declines.*

Part (ii) of Proposition 9 states that, although consumers are necessarily worse off with average revenue regulation, the effect on total welfare is ambiguous because the pricing discretion afforded the firm leads to increased profit. This increased profit might outweigh the reduction in consumer surplus. Part (iii) of Proposition 9 indicates that a more stringent price constraint is not always in the interests of consumers under average revenue regulation. To see why, consider the firm's incentives as the authorized level of average revenue $\bar{p}$ declines. Clearly, average revenue, as calculated in expression (71), does not vary with production costs. Consequently, a required reduction in average revenue may be achieved with the smallest reduction in profit by reducing the sales of those products that are particularly costly to produce. If consumers value these products highly, then the reduction in consumer welfare due to the reduced consumption of highly-valued products can outweigh any increase in consumer welfare due to the reduction in average prices that accompanies a reduction in $\bar{p}$.[96]

The drawbacks of average revenue regulation can be illustrated in the case where the regulated firm sells a single product using a two-part tariff. This tariff consists of a fixed charge A and a per-unit price p. Suppose the firm is required to keep calculated average revenue below a specified level $\bar{p}$. Then, as long as the number of consumers is invariant to the firm's pricing policy over the relevant range of prices, the regulatory constraint (71) is

$$p + \frac{A}{Q(p)} \leqslant \bar{p}. \tag{72}$$

Inequality (72) makes apparent the type of strategic pricing that could be profitable for the firm under average revenue regulation. By setting a low usage price p, the firm can induce consumers to purchase more of its product. The increased consumption enables the firm to set a higher fixed charge without violating the average revenue constraint. From Proposition 9, this strategic pricing always causes consumer surplus to

[96] See Bradley and Price (1988), Law (1995), and Cowan (1997b), for example. Flores (2005) identifies conditions under which a more stringent price cap constraint can increase a firm's profit by allowing it to credibly commit to a more aggressive pricing, and thereby induce accommodating actions from rivals. Kang, Weisman and Zhang (2000) demonstrate that the impact of a tighter price cap constraint on consumer welfare can vary according to whether the basket of regulated services contains independent, complementary, or substitute products.

fall compared to the case where the firm is required to charge $\bar{p}$ for each unit of output (and set $A = 0$). Moreover, aggregate welfare may fall when two-part pricing is introduced under an average revenue constraint.[97] The profit-maximizing behavior of the firm under the average revenue constraint in inequality (72) is readily calculated in the setting where consumer participation in the market is totally inelastic and the firm has a constant marginal cost c per unit of supply. Since the firm's profit is increasing in A, the average revenue constraint (72) will bind, and so the firm's profit is

$$\pi = (p - c)Q(p) + A = (\bar{p} - c)Q(p).$$

Therefore, assuming $\bar{p} > c$ (as is required for the firm to break even), the firm sets its unit price p to maximize output, so that p is chosen to be as small as possible.[98] Consequently, average revenue regulation in this setting induces a distorted pattern of demand: the unit price is too low (below cost), while consumers pay a large fixed charge (a combination that makes consumers worse off compared to the case where they pay a constant linear price $\bar{p}$). In effect, under average revenue regulation, the firm effectively is allowed a margin $\bar{p} - c$ per unit of its output, and so it has an incentive to expand output inefficiently.[99]

Tariff basket regulation Tariff basket regulation provides an alternative means of controlling the overall level of prices charged by a regulated firm while affording the firm pricing flexibility. One representation of tariff basket regulation specifies reference prices, $\mathbf{p}^0$, and permits the firm to offer any prices that would reduce what consumers have to pay for their preferred consumption at the reference prices $\mathbf{p}^0$. Formally, the firm must choose prices that lie in the set

$$\mathbf{p} \in \mathcal{P}^{TB} = \left\{ \mathbf{p} \;\middle|\; \sum_{i=1}^{n} p_i Q_i(\mathbf{p}^0) \leqslant \sum_{i=1}^{n} p_i^0 Q_i(\mathbf{p}^0) \right\}. \tag{73}$$

Under this form of tariff basket regulation, the weights that are employed to calculate the firm's average price are exogenous to the firm, and are proportional to consumer demands at the reference prices $\mathbf{p}^0$.

Notice that consumers are always better off with this form of regulation than they would be with the reference tariff $\mathbf{p}^0$.[100] This form of tariff basket regulation is a linear

[97] See Sappington and Sibley (1992), Cowan (1997a) and Currier (2005) for dynamic analyses along these lines. The firm's ability to manipulate price cap constraints can be limited by requiring the firm to offer the uniform tariff $(p^0, 0)$ each year in addition to any other tariff (p, A) that satisfies the price cap constraint – see Vogelsang (1990), Sappington and Sibley (1992), and Armstrong, Cowan and Vickers (1995).

[98] That is to say, the price is zero if a zero price results in finite demand.

[99] This conclusion is similar to Averch and Johnson's (1962) finding regarding over-investment under rate-of-return regulation. In their model, the regulated firm earns a return on capital that exceeds the cost of capital. Consequently, the firm employs more than the cost-minimizing level of capital.

[100] This follows from inequality (70) if we let $\mathbf{p}^1$ be the reference price vector $\mathbf{p}^0$ and let $\mathbf{p}^2$ be any vector in the set $\mathcal{P}^{TB}$ defined in expression (73).

approximation to the regulatory policy specified in expression (69). In particular, the set of prices in (73) lies inside the set (69) which, by construction, is the set of prices that make consumers better off than they are with prices $\mathbf{p}^0$. This finding is illustrated in Figure 27.2 for the case where the reference price vector $\mathbf{p}^0$ is $(\bar{p}, \bar{p})$. The boundary of the region of feasible prices $\mathcal{P}^{TB}$ in expression (73) is the straight line in the figure. Since this line lies everywhere below the locus of prices at which consumer surplus is $v(\bar{p}, \bar{p})$, consumers are better off when the regulated firm is given the pricing flexibility reflected in expression (73). Since the firm will also be better off with the flexibility permitted in constraint (73), it follows that welfare is higher under this form of regulation than under the fixed price vector $\mathbf{p}^0$.

The benefits of this form of regulation are evident in the case where the regulated firm sets a two-part tariff, with fixed charge A and unit price p, for the single product it sells. Here, the reference tariff is just the linear tariff where each unit of the product is sold at price p^0. In this case, constraint (73) becomes

$$A + pQ(p^0) \leqslant p^0 Q(p^0).$$

Assuming that consumer participation does not vary with the established prices, this constraint will bind, and so the firm's per-consumer profit with the unit price p is

$$\pi = (p^0 - p)Q(p^0) + (p - c)Q(p),$$

where c is the firm's constant marginal cost of production. It is readily shown that the profit-maximizing price p lies between the reference price and cost: $c < p < p^0$. This outcome generates more consumer surplus and higher welfare than does the linear price p^0.

Although this form of tariff basket regulation can secure increased consumer surplus and welfare, its implementation requires knowledge of demands at the reference prices $\mathbf{p}^0$ even when those prices are not actually chosen. Thus, demand functions must be known in static settings. By contrast, with average revenue regulation – where the weights in the price index reflect actual, not hypothetical, demands – only realized demands at the actual prices offered need to be observed. In dynamic settings, outputs in the previous period might be employed as current period weights when implementing tariff basket regulation, as explained in Section 3.2.1 below.

3.1.3. Price flexibility and entry

The type of pricing flexibility afforded the regulated firm can have important effects on the firm's response to entry by competitors.[101] To illustrate this fact, suppose the incumbent firm operates in two separate markets. Suppose further that if entry occurs at all, it will occur in only one of these markets. There are then four natural pricing regimes to consider:

[101] This discussion is based on Armstrong and Vickers (1993). See Anton, Vander Weide and Vettas (2002) for further analysis.

1. *Laissez-faire*: Here the incumbent can set its preferred prices in the two markets.
2. *Ban on price discrimination*: Here the incumbent can set any prices it desires, as long as the prices are the same in the two markets. (Regulators often implement such policies with the stated aim of bringing the benefits of competition to all consumers, including those who reside in regions where direct competition among firms is limited.) Here, if the incumbent lowers its price in one market in response to entry, it must also lower its price in the other market, even if entry is not a threat in that market.
3. *Separate price caps*: Here the incumbent faces a distinct upper limit on the price it can charge in each market. Because there is a distinct price cap in each market, the price the firm sets in one market does not affect the price it can charge in the other market.
4. *Average price cap*: Here the incumbent operates under a single price cap that limits the average price charged in the two markets. Under such an average price cap, if the incumbent lowers its price in one market in response to entry, it can raise its price in the other market without violating the average price cap. Thus, in contrast to the case where price discrimination is not permitted, feasible prices have an inverse relationship here.

Regimes 1 and 2 here apply to situations where the firm is unregulated, at least in terms of the level of its average tariff, whereas regimes 3 and 4 entail explicit regulation of price levels.

These four policies will induce different responses to entry by the incumbent supplier. To illustrate this fact, suppose there is a sunk cost of entry, so the potential entrant will only enter if it anticipates profit in excess of this sunk cost. Once entry takes place, some competitive interaction occurs. Under regime 2, which bans price discrimination, the incumbent will tend to accommodate entry. This is because any price reduction in the competitive market forces the incumbent to implement the same price reduction in the captive market, which can reduce the incumbent's profit in the captive market. The incumbent's resulting reluctance to cut prices in response to entry can result in higher profit for the entrant. Thus, a restriction on the regulated firm's pricing discretion can act as a powerful form of entry assistance. In particular, a ban on price discrimination can induce entry that would not occur under the *laissez-faire* regime, which, in turn, can cause prices in both markets to fall below their levels in the *laissez-faire* regime.

The average price cap regime induces the opposite effects. The incumbent will react more aggressively to entry under an average price cap regime than under a regime that imposes a separate cap in each market. In particular, the incumbent may reduce the price it charges in the competitive market below its marginal cost because of the high price it can then charge in the captive market. Therefore, an average price cap regime can act as a powerful source of entry deterrence. This observation implies the merits of granting the firm some authority to set its prices – for instance, by regulating the firm under an average price cap instead of separate caps – require careful study when entry is a possibility. This issue is analyzed further in Section 5.2, which considers the regulation of a vertically-integrated supplier.

3.2. Dynamics

Regulatory policies also vary according to their implementation over time. A regulatory policy may be unable to secure substantial surplus for consumers when it is first implemented, but repeated application of the policy may serve consumers well. This section provides a four-part discussion of dynamic elements of regulatory policy. Section 3.2.1 considers different forms of dynamic average price regulation when transfer payments from the regulator to the firm are not permitted. Section 3.2.2 extends the analysis to allow the regulator to make transfers to the firm. Section 3.2.3 examines how frequently a firm's prices should be realigned to match its observed costs. Section 3.2.4 discusses the effect of (exogenous) technological change on prices.

3.2.1. Non-Bayesian price adjustment mechanisms: no transfers

First consider the natural dynamic extension of the tariff basket form of price regulation analyzed in Section 3.1.2. In this dynamic extension, the weights employed in the current regulatory period reflect the previous period's outputs.[102] Call the initial period in this dynamic setting period 0, and label subsequent periods $t = 1, 2, \ldots$. Let $\mathbf{p}^t = (p_1^t, \ldots, p_n^t)$ denote the vector of prices the firm charges for its n regulated products in period t. Let $\mathbf{q}^t = (q_1^t, \ldots, q_n^t)$ denote the corresponding vector of outputs, where $q_i^t = Q_i(\mathbf{p}^t)$. Tariff basket regulation in this dynamic setting states that if the price vector was $\mathbf{p}^{t-1}$ in period $t-1$, the firm can choose any price vector $\mathbf{p}^t$ in period t satisfying

$$\mathbf{p}^t \in \mathcal{P}^t = \left\{ \mathbf{p}^t \,\middle|\, \sum_{i=1}^{n} p_i^t q_i^{t-1} \leqslant \sum_{i=1}^{n} p_i^{t-1} q_i^{t-1} \right\}. \tag{74}$$

For now, assume the initial price vector $\mathbf{p}^0$ is specified exogenously. (This assumption will be revisited shortly.) Notice that the regulator only needs to observe the firm's (lagged) realized sales in order to implement this regulatory policy. In contrast, to implement the static version of tariff basket regulation considered in Section 3.1.2, the regulator needed to know the demand functions themselves (since he needed to know demands at the reference prices $\mathbf{p}^0$). Note that expression (74) can be written as

$$\mathbf{p}^t \in \mathcal{P}^t = \left\{ \mathbf{p}^t \,\middle|\, \sum_{i=1}^{n} \frac{R_i^{t-1}}{R^{t-1}} \left[\frac{p_i^t - p_i^{t-1}}{p_i^{t-1}} \right] \leqslant 0 \right\}, \tag{75}$$

where $R_i^{t-1} = p_i^{t-1} q_i^{t-1}$ is the revenue generated by product i in period $t-1$, and R^{t-1} is total revenue from the n products in period $t-1$. Constraint (75) states that a weighted average of proportional price increases cannot be positive in any period, where the weights are revenue shares in the preceding period.

[102] This discussion is based on Vogelsang (1989).

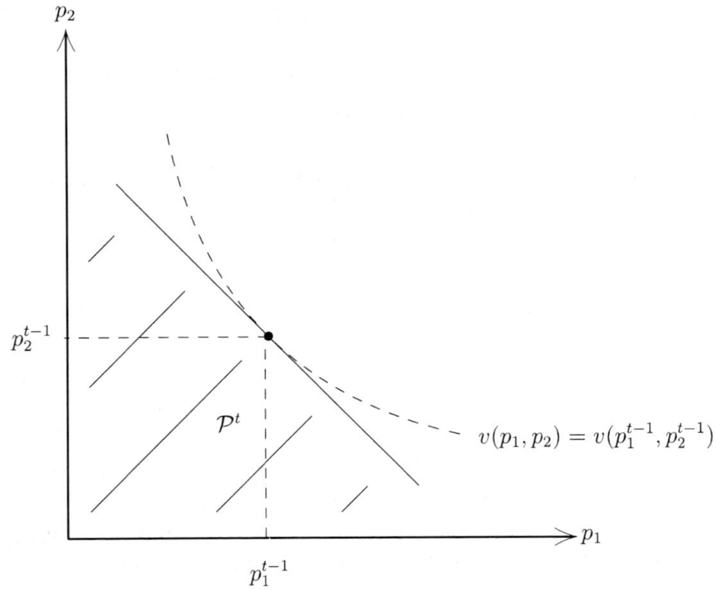

Figure 27.3. Dynamic tariff basket regulation.

Figure 27.3 illustrates how this form of dynamic average price regulation evolves over time. For the reasons explained in Section 3.1.2, any price vector in the set (74) generates at least the level of consumer surplus generated in the previous period, so $v(\mathbf{p}^t) \geqslant v(\mathbf{p}^{t-1})$. In particular, compared to the regime where the firm is forced to charge the same price vector $\mathbf{p}^0$ in each period, this more flexible regime yields higher welfare: consumers are better off (in each period) and, since the firm can implement the same vector $\mathbf{p}^0$ in each period if it chooses to do so, the firm is also better off. This dynamic process converges and the steady-state price vector will have the Ramsey form: profit is maximized subject to consumer surplus exceeding some specified level.[103] However, as in Section 3.1.1, long-run prices may diverge from Ramsey prices because the firm's rent is not necessarily zero.

The regulator might choose the initial price vector $\mathbf{p}^0$ to ensure that the firm makes only small rent in the long term and that total discounted expected welfare is maximized. Such a calculation would require considerable information, however. Alternatively, the firm might set $\mathbf{p}^0$ without constraint, but knowing that it will subsequently be controlled by the regulatory mechanism (74). In this setting, the firm will set its initial prices strategically in order to affect the weights in future constraints. For instance, the firm

[103] In a steady state, the firm's (short-run) profit-maximizing price vector in period t, $\mathbf{p}^t$, must be the same as the previous period's price vector, $\mathbf{p}^{t-1}$. From Figure 27.3, this implies that the firm's profit contour is tangent to the consumer surplus contour.

can set a high price for product i in period 0, and thereby reduce the weight applied to the price of product i in period 1. The net effect of such strategic pricing can be to reduce aggregate welfare below the level achieved in the absence of any regulation.[104]

Tariff basket regulation can also invite strategic pricing distortions when consumer demand and/or production costs are changing over time in predictable ways. To illustrate, the regulated firm will typically find it profitable to raise the price of a product for which consumer demand is increasing over time. Lagged output levels understate the actual losses a price increase imposes on consumers when demand is increasing over time. In this sense, tariff basket regulation does not penalize the firm sufficiently for raising prices on products for which demand is growing, and so induces relatively high prices on these products.[105]

Although this form of dynamic regulation leads to an increase in consumer surplus in every period, it need not lead to a particularly high level of consumer surplus. In particular, the firm may continue to make positive rent in the long run, even if the environment is stationary. One possible way to mitigate this problem, especially when demand is growing exogenously or when costs are falling exogenously, is to require average price reductions over time, so that average prices are required to fall proportionally by a factor X, say, in each period.[106] Formally, constraint (75) is modified to

$$\mathbf{p}^t \in \mathcal{P}^t = \left\{ \mathbf{p}^t \;\middle|\; \sum_{i=1}^{n} \frac{R_i^{t-1}}{R^{t-1}} \left[\frac{p_i^t - p_i^{t-1}}{p_i^{t-1}} \right] \leqslant -X \right\}. \tag{76}$$

The key difficulty in implementing this mechanism, of course, is the choice of X. If X is too small (compared to potential productivity gains), the firm may be afforded substantial, persistent rent. In contrast, if X is too large, the firm may encounter financial difficulties. In a stationary environment, any positive value of X will eventually cause the firm to incur losses.

One possible way to determine an appropriate value for X involves the use of historic data on the firm's expenditures. To illustrate this approach, consider a policy that allows the regulated firm to set any price vector for its products in a given period, as long as the prices generate non-positive accounting profit for the firm when applied to outputs and costs in the previous period.[107] Suppose the firm's observable production expenditures in year t are E^t.[108] Formally, this policy permits the firm to select any vector of prices

[104] See Law (1997). Foreman (1995) identifies conditions under which strategic pricing to relax the price cap constraint is more pronounced when relative revenue weights are employed than when quantity weights are employed.

[105] Brennan (1989), Neu (1993), and Fraser (1995) develop this and related observations.

[106] We will discuss other aspects of this issue in Section 3.2.4.

[107] This policy is proposed and analyzed in Vogelsang and Finsinger (1979).

[108] For simplicity, we abstract from intertemporal cost effects, so that all costs of producing output in period t are incurred in period t.

in period t that lie in the set

$$\mathbf{p}^t \in \mathcal{P}^t = \left\{ \mathbf{p} \,\middle|\, \sum_{i=1}^{n} p_i q_i^{t-1} \leqslant E^{t-1} \right\}. \tag{77}$$

This policy, which we term the *lagged expenditure* policy, differs from the regulatory regime reflected in expression (74) in that last period's expenditure replaces last period's revenue as the cap on the current level of calculated revenue. Letting $\Pi^t = \sum_{i=1}^n p_i^t q_i^t - E^t$ denote the firm's observed profit in period t, constraint (77) can be re-written as

$$\mathbf{p}^t \in \mathcal{P}^t = \left\{ \mathbf{p} \,\middle|\, \sum_{i=1}^{n} p_i q_i^{t-1} \leqslant \sum_{i=1}^{n} p_i^{t-1} q_i^{t-1} - \Pi^{t-1} \right\}.$$

Thus, prices in each period must be such that the amount consumers would have to pay for the bundle of regulated products purchased in the preceding period decreases sufficiently to eliminate the observed profit of the firm in the previous period (and does not simply decrease, as in expression (74)). Expression (70) reveals that $v(\mathbf{p}^t) \geqslant v(\mathbf{p}^{t-1}) + \Pi^{t-1}$. Therefore, any profit the firm enjoys in one period is (more than) transferred to consumers in the next period. Notice that the regulator only needs to observe the firm's realized revenues and costs in order to implement the mechanism. The regulator does not need to know the functional form of the demand or cost functions in the industry.

Even though it can be implemented with very little information, the lagged expenditure policy can induce desirable outcomes under certain (stringent) conditions. In particular, the mechanism can sometimes eventually induce Ramsey prices (i.e., the prices that maximize surplus while securing non-negative rent for the firm). This conclusion is summarized in Proposition 10.

PROPOSITION 10. *Suppose demand and cost functions do not change over time and the firm's technology exhibits decreasing ray average cost.*[109] *Further suppose the regulated firm maximizes profit myopically each period. Then the lagged expenditure policy induces the firm to set prices that converge to Ramsey prices.*

The conditions under which the policy secures Ramsey prices are restrictive. If demand or cost functions shift over time, convergence is not guaranteed, and the regulated firm may experience financial distress. Even in a stationary environment, the non-myopic firm can delay convergence to the Ramsey optimum and reduce welfare substantially in the process. It can do so, for example, by intentionally increasing production costs above their minimum level. This behavior reflects the general proposition

[109] The cost function $C(\mathbf{q})$ exhibits decreasing ray average cost if $rC(\mathbf{q}) \geqslant C(r\mathbf{q})$ for all $r \geqslant 1$ and output vectors $\mathbf{q}$. Decreasing ray average costs ensure the firm can continue to secure non-negative profit under the mechanism as prices decline and outputs increase.

that when the firm's (current or future) permitted prices increase as the firm's current realized costs increase, the firm has limited incentives to control these costs.

To illustrate this last point, suppose the firm produces a single product and has a constant unit cost in each period, which the regulator can observe. If unit cost is c^{t-1} in the previous period, then the policy in expression (77) requires the firm to set a price no higher than c^{t-1} in the current period. Suppose that the firm can simply choose the unit cost, subject only to the constraint that $c^t \geqslant c$, where c is the firm's true (minimum possible) unit cost. Thus, any choice $c^t > c$ constitutes "pure waste". (Note that this inflated cost is actually incurred by the firm, and not simply misreported.) The firm discounts future profit at the rate δ, and its discounted profit in period zero is $\sum_{t=0}^{\infty} \delta^t Q(p^t)(p^t - c^t)$. The regulator chooses the initial price $p^0 > c$, and subsequently follows the rule $p^t = c^{t-1}$. If there were no scope for pure waste, the observed unit cost in period 0 would be c, and the firm would make profit $Q(p^0)(p^0 - c)$ for one period. It would make no profit thereafter, because price would equal unit cost in all subsequent periods. However, when δ is sufficiently large, the firm can increase the present discounted value of its profit by undertaking pure waste. To see why, notice that the firm could choose an inflated cost $c_H > c$ in period 0, and then implement the minimum cost c in every period thereafter. With this strategy, the firm's discounted profit is

$$Q(p^0)(p^0 - c_H) + \delta Q(c_H)(c_H - c). \tag{78}$$

Expression (78) is increasing in c_H at $c_H = c$ when $\delta Q(c) > Q(p^0)$. Consequently, whenever the discount factor is high enough – so the firm cares sufficiently about future profit – the firm will find it profitable to inflate its costs.[110]

These dynamic price regulation mechanisms affect both the pattern of relative prices and the average price level. The tariff-basket adjustment mechanism reflected in constraint (74) performs well on the first dimension. Starting from some initial price vector, consumer surplus rises monotonically over time and converges to a desirable Ramsey-like pattern of relative prices. However, this mechanism may not control adequately the average price level, and the firm may enjoy positive rent indefinitely. The lagged expenditure policy attempts to deliver a desirable equilibrium pattern of relative prices and to eliminate rent over time. However, it is essentially a form of cost-plus (or rate-of-return) regulation, albeit one that gives the firm flexibility over the pattern of its relative prices. When the firm's cost function is exogenous, the scheme works reasonably well. However, when the firm can affect its production costs, the scheme can provide poor incentives to control costs, and so can induce high average prices.

110 Sappington (1980) shows that, because of the pure waste it can induce, the lagged expenditure policy may cause welfare to fall below the level that would arise in the absence of any regulation. Hagerman (1990) shows that incentives for pure waste can be eliminated if the policy is modified to allow the firm to make discretionary transfer payments to the regulator. These transfer payments provide a less costly way for the firm to relax the constraint that the lagged expenditure policy imposes on prices.

3.2.2. Non-Bayesian price adjustment mechanisms: transfers

Although Section 3 focuses on policies in which the regulator has no authority to make transfer payments to the regulated firm, we briefly discuss here some non-Bayesian policies that do permit transfers. When transfers are employed, the relevant benchmark entails marginal-cost prices, rather than the Ramsey (and Ramsey-like) prices that were the focus of Section 3.2.1. There are at least three non-Bayesian policies that can eventually implement marginal-cost pricing under certain conditions. The speed of convergence and the distribution of surplus varies considerably under these three mechanisms.

The first such policy was discussed in Section 2.3.1. If the regulator is perfectly informed about consumer demand for the regulated product, he can induce marginal-cost pricing immediately by offering the firm a transfer payment, T, equal to the level of consumer surplus, $v(p)$, generated by the price, p, the firm sets for its product. (For simplicity, assume the firm produces a single product.) By awarding to the firm the entire surplus generated by its actions, this policy induces the firm to maximize total surplus by setting the price equal to its marginal cost.[111] An obvious drawback to this policy is the highly asymmetric distribution of surplus it implements. To recoup some surplus for consumers without distorting the firm's incentive to establish an efficient price, the regulator might subtract a fixed amount (k) from the transfer payment to the firm (so $T = v(p) - k$). Of course, determining an appropriate value for k can be problematic. If k is too small, the firm will continue to enjoy substantial rent. If k is too large, the firm will refuse to operate, and thereby eliminate all surplus.[112]

In a dynamic context, it is possible to return surplus to consumers over time and still maintain marginal-cost pricing. One way to do so is with the following policy.[113] In each period t the regulated firm is permitted to set any price p^t for its product. The regulator pays the firm a transfer each period equal to the difference between the incremental (not the total) consumer surplus derived from its pricing decisions and the firm's profit in the preceding period. Formally, this transfer in period t, T^t, is defined by

$$T^t = \left[v\left(p^t\right) - v\left(p^{t-1}\right)\right] - \Pi^{t-1}, \tag{79}$$

where $v(\cdot)$ is the (known) consumer surplus function and Π^{t-1} is the firm's actual profit in the previous period $t-1$, which is observed by the regulator. In addition to this transfer, the firm is permitted to keep its profit Π^t in each period.

To illustrate the workings of this policy, termed the *incremental surplus subsidy* policy, suppose there is an exogenous profit function $\pi(p^t)$, the precise form of which is not known to the regulator. (Only actual profit $\Pi^t = \pi(p^t)$ is observed.) In period t,

[111] Loeb and Magat (1979) analyze this regulatory policy.

[112] Section 4.5 discusses how the choice of k may be more straightforward when the regulated firm supplies many products.

[113] This policy is due to Sappington and Sibley (1988).

the firm's pricing decision affects its profit $\pi(p^t)$ in that period, its transfer payment T^t in that period, and its transfer payment in the subsequent period T^{t+1}. In sum, from the perspective of period t, the firm's discounted profit due to its period-t price decision is

$$\pi(p^t) + v(p^t) - \delta[\pi(p^t) + v(p^t)] = (1-\delta)[\pi(p^t) + v(p^t)],$$

where δ denotes the firm's discount factor. Therefore, the firm will choose its price to maximize $[\pi(p^t) + v(p^t)]$, which entails marginal-cost pricing in all periods $t = 1, 2, \ldots$. Moreover, from period 2 onward the firm makes zero rent in each period. (Its price is constant, and the firm's stationary operating profit Π is extracted by the transfer in each period.)

Notice also that, in contrast to the lagged expenditure policy, the incremental surplus subsidy policy does not provide incentives for the firm to distort its observed profit. To see why, suppose that when it takes some (unobserved) action e, the firm's realized profit function is $\pi(p, e)$. (For instance, e could take the form of "pure waste", so that $\Pi = \pi(p) - e$ for some "true" profit function π.) Then in period t the firm will choose p^t and e^t in order to maximize $(1-\delta)[\pi(p^t, e^t) + v(p^t)]$, and so the socially efficient level of e^t will be chosen.

In sum[114]:

PROPOSITION 11. *In a stationary environment the incremental surplus subsidy policy ensures*: (i) *marginal-cost pricing from the first period onwards*; (ii) *the absence of pure waste*; *and* (iii) *zero rent from the second period onwards.*

Despite its potential merit in returning surplus to consumers, the policy has at least four drawbacks. First, it can impose financial hardship on the firm if its costs rise over time.[115] Second, the large subsidy payments that the mechanism initially requires are socially costly when the regulator prefers consumer surplus to rent.[116] Third, the regulator must know consumer demand to implement the policy. Finally, although it avoids pure waste, the policy does not preclude "abuse". Abuse is defined as expenditures in excess of minimal feasible costs that provide direct benefit to the firm's managers or employees. Abuse includes perquisites for the firm's managers and the lower managerial effort required to produce at inefficiently high cost, for example.[117]

[114] Schwermer (1994) and Lee (1997b) provide extensions of the incremental surplus subsidy policy to settings with Cournot and Stackelberg competition. Sibley (1989) modifies the scheme to allow the firm to have private information about consumer demand.

[115] See Stefos (1990) and Sappington and Sibley (1990).

[116] Lyon (1996) presents simulations which suggest that once subsidy costs are accounted for, the lagged expenditure policy [modified as Hagerman (1990) suggests to eliminate incentives for pure waste] often generates higher levels of welfare than the incremental surplus subsidy policy.

[117] Sappington and Sibley (1993) show that the mechanism induces the firm's owners to undertake efficient precautions against abuse by subordinates in the firm. However, abuse by the owners themselves can be problematic under the mechanism.

To understand why the regulated firm may undertake abuse under the incremental surplus subsidy policy, consider a case where the regulator can observe some, but not all, components of the firm's costs. Specifically, suppose unit cost c is observed, while the fixed cost $F(c)$, which represents the managerial effort associated with producing with unit cost c, is not observed. Further suppose the transfer payment in period t is

$$T^t = \left[v(p^t) - v(p^{t-1})\right] - Q(p^{t-1})(p^{t-1} - c^{t-1}). \tag{80}$$

In this setting, the firm will choose p^t and c^t to maximize $(1-\delta)[Q(p^t)(p^t - c^t) + v(p^t)] - F(c^t)$. Price p^t will be set equal to realized cost c^t, but c^t will be set at an inefficiently high level.[118] This is because the firm does not retain the full benefit of a cost reduction, since any profit generated in one period is fully usurped in the next period. (Notice from Equation (80) that if, by incurring a high fixed cost, the firm achieves a low marginal cost c^t in one period, it will receive a lower transfer T^{t+1} in the subsequent period. Consequently, the firm will not appropriate the full benefits of its unobserved cost-reducing activity.)

In more realistic settings where realized consumer demand is observed but the regulator does not know the functional form of the demand curve for the firm's product, the exact incremental surplus element of the transfer (79), $[v(p^t) - v(p^{t-1})]$, might be replaced by the linear approximation $q^{t-1}[p^{t-1} - p^t]$, where q^{t-1} denotes realized consumer demand in period $t-1$.[119] Under this policy, the transfer payment to the firm in period t would be

$$T^t = q^{t-1}\left[p^{t-1} - p^t\right] - \Pi^{t-1}. \tag{81}$$

This policy eventually ensures outcomes similar to those induced by the incremental surplus subsidy policy. Thus, if demand and cost functions do not change over time, this mechanism ultimately achieves the outcome a welfare-maximizing regulator would implement if he shared the firm's private knowledge of its environment. However, the convergence of price to marginal cost and the convergence of rent to zero take place only gradually.[120]

3.2.3. Frequency of regulatory review

Even when regulatory policies do not explicitly link prices to realized costs, such linkage can be effected when the policies are updated.[121] To illustrate, suppose the authorized rate at which prices can rise (i.e., the X factor) in a price cap regulation regime

[118] This distortion parallels the optimal distortion induced in the Laffont–Tirole setting of Proposition 3 above.

[119] Finsinger and Vogelsang (1981, 1982) proposed this policy (before the incremental surplus subsidy policy was proposed). As originally proposed, this policy was designed to motivate public enterprises. The ensuing discussion adapts the original policy to apply to a profit-maximizing regulated firm.

[120] Finsinger and Vogelsang (1981, 1982) prove this convergence result. Vogelsang (1988) proves that pure waste will not occur.

[121] Explicit linkage of prices to costs is discussed in Section 3.3.

is updated periodically to eliminate the firm's expected future profit. Also suppose expectations about future profit are based in part upon the firm's current realized revenues and costs.[122] Even though a regulatory regime of this sort permits the firm to retain all the profit it generates in any given year, the firm recognizes that larger present profits – generated by efficiency gains, for instance – may result in smaller future earnings. Consequently, implicit intertemporal profit sharing of this sort can limit the firm's incentive to reduce its operating costs and expand its revenues, just as explicit profit-sharing requirements can.

The diminution in incentives will be more pronounced the more frequently the regulatory regime is revised to eliminate expected rent. On the other hand, an infrequent revision of the regime could allow prices to diverge from costs for long periods, and thereby reduce allocative efficiency. The optimal choice of "regulatory lag" trades off these two opposing effects.[123] The following extreme settings provide some intuition for the key determinants of the optimal frequency of regulatory review:

- If the firm cannot affect its realized costs, frequent regulatory reviews are optimal. Because there is no need to provide incentives for cost reduction in this case, the only concern is to achieve allocative efficiency. When costs vary over time, this goal is best accomplished through frequent reviews that set prices to match realized costs.
- If consumer demand is inelastic, so there is little deadweight welfare loss when prices depart from costs, reviews should be infrequent. If prices are permitted to diverge from realized costs for long periods of time, the firm will have strong incentives to reduce costs, since the firm keeps most of the extra surplus it generates. And when there is little efficiency gain from ensuring that prices track costs closely, it is optimal to implement long lags between regulatory reviews.

Clearly, any realistic case will fall between these two extremes, and the optimal period between reviews in a price cap regime will depend upon the specifics of the regulatory environment. A key element of this environment is the regulator's ability to implement credible long-term contracts. If formal regulatory reviews are carried out only infrequently, the firm's realized profits can become too large or too small for the regulator

[122] When implemented in this manner, price cap regulation operates much like rate-of-return regulation with a specified regulatory lag. Baumol and Klevorick (1970) and Bailey and Coleman (1971), among others, analyze the effects of regulatory lag on incentives for cost reduction under rate-of-return regulation. Pint (1992) examines the effects of regulatory lag under price cap regulation and demonstrates the importance of basing projections of future costs on realized costs throughout the price cap regime rather than in a single test year. When a test year is employed, the regulated firm can limit its cost-reducing effort in the test year and shift costs to that year in order to relax future regulatory constraints.

[123] This discussion is based on Armstrong, Rees and Vickers (1995). Notice that the choice of an infrequent regulatory review may enable the regulator to commit to remaining partially ignorant of the firm's costs. This ignorance allows the regulator to promise credibly not to link prices too closely to costs, even when he cannot commit to future pricing policies. (Recall the discussion of an analogous strategy in Section 2.5.) Isaac (1991) points out that rate shock (substantial, rapid price changes) may occur if prices are revised to reflect realized operating costs only infrequently.

to refrain from intervening to re-set prices before the scheduled review. In such cases, long regulatory lags are not credible.

The lagged expenditure policy discussed in Section 3.2.1 can be viewed as a regulatory regime with frequent regulatory reviews. With this policy, the firm's prices in each period are required to fall to a level that reflects realized expenditures in the previous period. As noted, this mechanism can provide poor incentives to control costs, even though it serves to implement desirable prices given the realized costs. More generally, the frequency of regulatory review is essentially a choice about how responsive prices will be to realized costs. This issue is explored further in Section 3.3.

3.2.4. *Choice of 'X' in price cap regulation*

Recall from the discussion in Section 3.2.1 that it may be desirable to require the (inflation-adjusted) prices charged by a regulated firm to decline at a specified rate, X. In practice, it can be difficult to determine the most appropriate value of this "X factor". To provide some insight regarding the appropriate choice of an X factor, consider a setting where (in contrast to the preceding discussion of dynamic regulatory policies) the firm invests in durable capacity over time. To simplify the analysis, suppose there is no asymmetric information and the regulated firm produces a single product.[124]

Further suppose that investment, production and consumption all take place in periods $t = 0, 1, \ldots$. Let p_t denote the price for the firm's product in period t. Suppose that consumer surplus and the demand function for the firm's product in period t are, respectively, $v_t(p_t)$ and $Q_t(p_t)$. For simplicity, demand in each period is assumed to depend only on the price set in that period. Over time, the firm invests in the capacity required to deliver its product. For simplicity, one unit of capacity is assumed to be needed to provide one unit of service. Capacity at time t is denoted K_t. Capacity depreciates at the proportional rate d in each period. The cost of installing a unit of capacity in period t is β_t, so there are constant returns to scale in installing capacity. Let I_t be the investment (in money terms) undertaken in period t, so the amount of new capacity installed in period t (in physical units) is I_t/β_t. Therefore, capacity evolves according to the dynamic relation

$$K_{t+1} = (1-d)K_t + \frac{I_{t+1}}{\beta_{t+1}}. \tag{82}$$

All investment can be used as soon as it is installed.

What is the marginal cost of providing an extra unit of service in period t in this setting? Suppose the investment plan is $K_t, K_{t+1}, \ldots, I_t, I_{t+1}, \ldots$, satisfying expression (82). Then if K_t is increased by 1, all subsequent values for K and I are unchanged

[124] The analysis in this section is based on Laffont and Tirole (2000, Section 4.4.1.3). See Kwoka (1991, 1993), Armstrong, Cowan and Vickers (1994, Section 6.3), and Bernstein and Sappington (1999) for further discussions.

if next period's investment I_{t+1} is reduced so as to the keep the right-hand side of expression (82) constant, i.e., if I_{t+1} is reduced by $(1-d)\beta_{t+1}$.[125] If the interest rate is r, so that the firm's discount factor is $\delta = \frac{1}{1+r}$, then the net cost of this modification to the investment plan is

$$C_t = \beta_t - \frac{1-d}{1+r}\beta_{t+1}. \tag{83}$$

Expression (83) specifies the marginal cost of obtaining a unit of capacity for use in period t. If technical progress causes the unit cost of new capacity to fall at the exogenous rate γ every period, then $\beta_{t+1} = (1-\gamma)\beta_t$. With technical progress at the rate γ, formula (83) becomes[126]

$$C_t = \beta_t\left(1 - \frac{(1-d)(1-\gamma)}{1+r}\right). \tag{84}$$

Clearly, this marginal cost of capacity falls (with β_t) at the rate γ.

Suppose it costs the firm an amount c_t to convert a unit of capacity into a unit of the final product. Then the total marginal cost for supplying the final product is $C_t + c_t$, and so the optimal price in period t is $p_t = C_t + c_t$, where C_t is defined in expression (84). Thus, in this setting with constant returns to scale, welfare is maximized if, in each period, price is set equal to the correctly calculated marginal cost of expanding available capacity for one period, C_t, plus the operating cost c_t. If both the cost of capacity β_t and the operating cost c_t fall at the same exogenous rate γ, then this optimal price should also fall at this rate γ, i.e., 'X' should be equal to the exogenous rate of technical progress.

Of course, the cost structure of the regulated firm and the (potential) rate of technical progress are unlikely to be common knowledge in practice.[127] To secure a modest X, the regulated firm may claim that its potential for cost reduction and the rate of technical progress are modest. In contrast, consumer advocates are likely to argue that the firm is capable of achieving pronounced productivity gains. In practice, a regulator is forced to weigh the available evidence, however limited it might be, and make his best judgment about a reasonable value for the X factor.

3.3. The responsiveness of prices to costs

The discussion in Section 3.2 emphasized the importance of the extent to which regulated prices are (implicitly or explicitly) linked to costs. The present section considers

[125] Assume that demand conditions are such that investment in each period is strictly positive, which ensures that this modification is feasible.

[126] If the parameters d, r and γ are reasonably small, this formula is approximated by $C_t \approx \beta_t(r+\gamma+d)$. This is a familiar equation in continuous-time investment models.

[127] In addition, in practice there is considerable uncertainty (for both the regulator and firm) about how consumer demand and technology develop over time. See Dobbs (2004), for instance, for an account of how the principles of dynamic price regulation are altered in the presence of uncertainty. Guthrie (2006) provides a survey of the literature that examines the effects of regulatory policy on investment.

this linkage in more detail, and explores the trade-offs involved in varying the extent to which prices reflect realized costs. The focus in this section is on the trade-off between allocative efficiency and providing incentives for the firm to control its costs. The discussion employs the moral hazard framework of Section 2.6.

Recall from Section 2.6.1 that when transfer payments between the regulator and the firm are possible and the firm is risk neutral, consumers are best served by affording the firm the entire social gains that its unobserved activities secure. The reason is that incentive issues are resolved fully when the firm is the residual claimant for the surplus it generates, and the firm can be required to compensate consumers in advance for the right to retain the incremental surplus it generates, which resolves the distributional issue. This conclusion suggests that high-powered incentive schemes like price cap regulation are better suited for resolving moral hazard problems than are low-powered policies like rate-of-return regulation, at least when risk aversion, limited liability, and asymmetric knowledge of the firm's production technology are not serious concerns. It is useful to examine how this conclusion is modified when transfer payments from the regulator to the firm are not possible.

For simplicity, consider the moral hazard setting where marginal cost can be either high or low, so that the firm's profit function in state i is $\pi_i(p) \equiv Q(p)(p - c_i)$. The equilibrium probability of achieving a low-cost outcome, $\hat{\phi}(\Delta^U)$, is given by expression (55) above. (Recall $\Delta^U = U_L - U_H$ is the difference between the firm's utility in the low state and the high state.) Suppose further that the demand function is iso-elastic, with constant elasticity equal to η.[128] Suppose that transfer payments are prohibitively costly, so the regulator can only dictate the unit price the firm will be allowed to charge given its realized costs.[129]

In this setting, prices are required to perform two tasks. First, they must provide the firm with incentives to reduce costs. To provide such incentives, the firm's profit must be higher when its costs are lower. Second, prices must not depart too far from realized cost in order to promote allocative efficiency. Clearly, ideal incentives and allocative efficiency cannot be achieved simultaneously, and a compromise is required.

It follows from Equations (61) and (62) that the full-information prices in this setting (i.e., the prices the regulator would allow the firm to choose if the regulator could directly control the firm's cost-reducing effort) are

$$\frac{p_L - c_L}{p_L} = \frac{p_H - c_H}{p_H} = \left[\frac{\lambda}{1+\lambda}\right]\frac{1}{\eta}, \tag{85}$$

[128] If demand is inelastic so $\eta \leqslant 1$, suppose that demand goes to zero when price reaches some high "choke price" in order to make consumer surplus well defined. This choke price is assumed to be higher than any of the prices identified in the following discussion.

[129] Implicitly, we rule out both transfer payments from taxpayers to the firm and two-part tariffs. The following discussion is closely related to Schmalensee (1989). His model differs in that a continuum of cost states are possible and he restricts attention to linear incentive schemes. (This restriction is inconsequential when there are just two possible outcomes.) He also models the regulator as being uncertain about the cost of effort function for the firm. See Gasmi, Ivaldi and Laffont (1994) for further analysis of a similar model.

where, recall, λ is the Lagrange multiplier associated with the firm's participation constraint. Thus, the Lerner index $(p_i - c_i)/p_i$ is equal for the two cost realizations, in accordance with standard Ramsey principles. (See expression (2) above.) At this full-information outcome, prices vary proportionally with realized costs. The resulting relationship between profit and the cost realization depends on the demand elasticity: with equal mark-ups, the firm's profit $\pi_i(p_i)$ is higher (respectively lower) when costs are low if $\eta > 1$ (respectively if $\eta < 1$). Thus, when demand is inelastic, the firm makes less profit when its costs are low under the full-information policy. Of course, such a policy provides no incentive for the firm to achieve a low cost.

Turning to the second-best problem where the regulator cannot directly control the firm's cost-reducing effort, expression (63) in the present setting becomes

$$\frac{p_L - c_L}{p_L} = \left[\frac{\hat{\lambda}\hat{\phi} + \Delta^V \hat{\phi}'}{(1+\hat{\lambda})\hat{\phi} + \Delta^V \hat{\phi}'}\right]\frac{1}{\eta},$$
$$\frac{p_H - c_H}{p_H} = \left[\frac{\hat{\lambda}(1-\hat{\phi}) - \Delta^V \hat{\phi}'}{(1+\hat{\lambda})(1-\hat{\phi}) - \Delta^V \hat{\phi}'}\right]\frac{1}{\eta}. \tag{86}$$

Here, $\Delta^V = v(p_L) - v(p_H)$ is the difference in consumer surplus in the two states at the optimum.

As in Section 3.2.3, it is useful to consider two extreme cases:

- If the success probability ϕ is exogenous, there is no need to motivate the firm to achieve lower production costs. (In this case, $\hat{\phi}'(\cdot) = 0$ and expressions (86) reduce to the standard full-information Ramsey formulas (85).) Thus, pure cost-plus regulation is optimal in this setting.
- If demand is perfectly inelastic, there is no welfare loss when price diverges from cost. Consequently, in this setting, it is optimal to provide the maximum incentive for cost reduction. This is accomplished by setting a price that does not vary with realized costs (so $p_L = p_H$). In this case, it is optimal to implement pure price cap regulation, and the full-information outcome is achieved again.[130]

In less extreme cases, departures from the full-information policy are optimal. Expressions (86) imply that[131]

[130] This is essentially an instance of the analysis of optimal regulation with a risk-neutral firm when transfers are used, discussed in Section 2.6.1. When demand is perfectly inelastic, there is no difference between the use of prices and transfers, and a prohibition on the regulator's use of transfers is not restrictive.

[131] If $p_L \leqslant p_H$ then $\Delta^V \geqslant 0$. In this case, expressions (86) imply that

$$\frac{p_L - c_L}{p_L} \geqslant \left[\frac{\hat{\lambda}}{1+\hat{\lambda}}\right]\frac{1}{\eta} \geqslant \frac{p_H - c_H}{p_H},$$

so the Lerner index is higher for the low-cost firm. On the other hand, if $p_L > p_H$, expression (86) implies

$$\frac{p_L - c_L}{p_L} < \frac{p_H - c_H}{p_H},$$

which is clearly inconsistent with $p_L > p_H$. Therefore, the only possible configuration consistent with (86) is as given in expression (87).

$$\frac{p_L - c_L}{p_L} \geqslant \frac{p_H - c_H}{p_H}, \qquad p_L \leqslant p_H \tag{87}$$

and so the Lerner index is higher in the low-cost state than in the high-cost state in order to provide an incentive for cost reduction. In particular, regulated prices do not fully reflect costs, although the regulated price declines as realized cost declines. To provide strong incentives to reduce cost, it can even be optimal to set price below cost when the high cost is realized.

In summary, when the regulator cannot make transfer payments to the firm, prices are required to pursue both allocative efficiency and productive efficiency. The inevitable compromise that ensues results in prices that are higher when realized costs are low than they would be in a full-information world. The higher prices motivate the firm to secure low costs.[132]

This discussion has so far been confined to a pure moral hazard framework, in which the firm has no private information at the time regulatory policy is formulated. A richer framework would allow the firm to possess private information about its ability to obtain low costs, for instance. In such cases, the regulator might offer the firm a choice among regulatory plans. To understand the nature of this choice, consider a benchmark case of pure adverse selection, where the firm knows its probability of achieving a low cost realization, but has no ability to affect this probability. (The firm does not know the actual cost realization at the time the regulatory policy is determined, however.) Suppose the firm is either type L or type H. The type-L firm has a higher probability of achieving low cost than the type-H firm. In this setting where transfer payments are not feasible, the regulator will offer the firm a choice between two pairs of prices, (p_L^L, p_H^L) and (p_L^H, p_H^H), where p_i^j denotes the regulated price when the firm claims to be type j and realized (and observed) cost is c_i. These prices will be designed to ensure the type-H firm enjoys no expected rent while the type-L firm is indifferent between the two pairs of prices. To make the (p_L^H, p_H^H) option less attractive to the type-L firm and thereby to reduce the type-L firm's rent, p_L^H will be reduced below the Ramsey levels identified in expression (85). Because the type-L firm is more likely to achieve cost c_L than the type-H firm, the reduction in p_L^H (and corresponding increase in p_H^H) is differentially unattractive to the type-L firm. The regulator implements no corresponding distortions from Ramsey prices in the (p_L^L, p_H^L) option, because such distortions would not reduce the rent of the type-H firm, which strictly prefers the (p_L^H, p_H^H) option to the (p_L^L, p_H^L) option.[133]

Richer models could incorporate both moral hazard and adverse selection. For instance, the firm might have private information about its ability to reduce costs. As the analysis in Section 2 suggests, a carefully structured choice among regulatory plans can

[132] This analysis is closely related to the analysis in Section 2.6.2, where transfer payments are possible and the firm is risk averse. In both cases, a concave relationship between consumer surplus and the firm's utility makes the optimal regulatory policy less high powered than the full-information policy.

[133] See Armstrong and Vickers (2000, Section IV) for a model along these lines.

limit the regulated firm's incentive to understate its potential to achieve productivity gains. To illustrate, the firm might be afforded the choice between: (1) a pure price cap plan; and (2) a plan where prices reflect realized costs to some extent. When the parameters of these plans are chosen appropriately, the firm can be induced to select: (1) the pure price cap plan when it knows that it has pronounced ability to reduce its operating costs; and (2) the earnings sharing plan when it knows that its ability to reduce operating costs is more limited.[134] The more capable firm is willing to guarantee lower prices to consumers in return for the expanded opportunity to retain more of the relatively high earnings it knows it can generate. The less capable firm is willing to share its (relatively modest) earnings with its customers when doing so allows it to guarantee more modest price reductions.

3.4. Regulatory discretion

The final key element of the design of regulatory policy that will be considered here is the degree of policy discretion afforded the regulator. When the regulator has extensive, ongoing experience in the industry, he will often be well informed about relevant industry conditions, in which case it can be advantageous to afford him considerable latitude in policy design. However, a regulator might employ this latitude inappropriately. In particular, the regulator might behave opportunistically over time, maximizing welfare ex post in such a way as to distort the ex ante incentives of the firm. Alternatively, the regulator might succumb to industry pressure to act in a non-benevolent manner. These two dangers are discussed in turn.

3.4.1. Policy credibility

Section 2.5.3 explained how a regulator's inability to commit to future policy can harm the regulatory process. The key problem in Section 2.5.3 was that the regulator could not refrain from using information revealed early in the process to maximize subsequent welfare. Another fundamental problem arises in the presence of sunk investments.[135] Once the firm has made irreversible investments, a regulator with limited commitment powers may choose not to compensate the firm for those investments, in an attempt to

[134] See Laffont and Tirole (1986) and Lewis and Sappington (1989d) for formal analyses of this issue, and Sappington and Weisman (1996a, pp. 155–165) for further discussion. Rogerson (2003) provides conditions under which a particularly simple regulatory policy secures a large fraction (at least three-quarters in a parameterized example) of the surplus secured by the optimal regulatory policy. The simple regulatory policy consists of only two options: a pure price cap plan and a plan under which the firm's realized costs are fully reimbursed. Bower (1993), Gasmi, Laffont and Sharkey (1999), McAfee (2002), and Chu and Sappington (2007) also analyze settings in which a limited number of options and/or simple contracts secure much of the surplus that a richer set of options can secure.

[135] See Williamson (1975) for a pioneering treatment of the problem, and Newbery (1999, ch. 2) for a detailed discussion of the problem of regulatory commitment. Tirole (1986b) considers both the information and investment aspects of the commitment problem.

deliver the maximum future benefits to consumers. This expropriation might take the form of low mandated future prices. Alternatively, the expropriation might arise in the form of permitting entry into the industry.[136] When it anticipates expropriation of some form, the firm will typically undertake too little investment.[137]

One natural way to overcome the temptation for a regulator to behave opportunistically is to limit the regulator's policy discretion. This might be done, for instance, by imposing a legal requirement that the firm earn a specified rate of return on its assets.[138] The promise of a fair return on investment can provide relatively strong incentives for infrastructure investment in a dynamic setting where the regulator has weak commitment powers. However, a blanket commitment to deliver a specified return on assets can reduce significantly the firm's incentives to control its costs, in part because the commitment rewards inefficient or unnecessary projects in the same way it rewards efficient projects. To limit this problem, the naive rate-of-return commitment could be modified to consider whether the assets are ultimately "used and useful". There are two problems with such a policy, though. First, an investment might ultimately prove to be unnecessary even though it was originally desirable. The merits of a given investment often are difficult to predict precisely, in practice. Second, if the regulator has some discretion in defining which sunk investments are included in the asset base, the problem of limited regulatory commitment resurfaces.[139]

[136] Price cap regulation can encourage the regulator to expropriate the incumbent firm by introducing competition. Recall that under price cap regulation, prices are not linked explicitly to the earnings of the regulated firm. In particular, the regulator is under no obligation to raise prices in the regulated industry if the firm's profit declines. This fact may encourage the regulator to facilitate entry into the industry in order to secure even lower prices for consumers. The regulator may be more reluctant to encourage entry under rate-of-return regulation because he might then be obliged to raise industry prices in order to mitigate any major impact of entry on the profits of the incumbent firm – see Weisman (1994). Lehman and Weisman (2000) provide some empirical support for this effect. Kim (1997) analyzes a model in which a welfare-maximizing regulator decides whether entry should be permitted once the incumbent has made investment decisions. Biglaiser and Ma (1999) find that entry into a regulated industry where the regulator's commitment powers are limited can either enhance or diminish incentives for cost-reducing investment by the incumbent firm. The direction of the effect depends upon how investment affects the distribution of the firm's operating costs.

[137] Spiegel (1994) and Spiegel and Spulber (1994, 1997) demonstrate how the regulated firm may alter its capital structure in order to induce a regulator with limited commitment power to authorize a higher regulated price. Specifically, the firm may choose a high debt-equity ratio in order to make bankruptcy – which involves extra costs that the regulator takes into account when determining future pricing policy – more likely for a given price policy. To avoid the costs of bankruptcy, the regulator implements a more generous pricing policy than he otherwise would.

[138] See Greenwald (1984). Levy and Spiller (1994) and Sidak and Spulber (1997) examine the legal framework governing a regulator's ability to expropriate a firm's sunk investments.

[139] See Kolbe and Tye (1991), Lyon (1991, 1992), Gilbert and Newbery (1994), and Encinosa and Sappington (1995) for analyses of regulatory cost disallowances and "prudence reviews". Sappington and Weisman (1996b) examine how the discretion of the regulator to disallow certain investments affects the firm's investment decisions.

Although limited regulatory commitment can discourage investment, it need not always do so.[140] When the regulator and firm interact repeatedly, mutual threats by the firm and regulator to "punish" one another can sustain desirable investment and compensation levels.[141] To illustrate, in a model where investments last forever – which is where the danger of expropriation is especially great – desired investment levels can ultimately be achieved if the firm gradually builds up its asset base. Here, if the regulator reneges on his implicit promise to deliver a reasonable return on capital, the firm can punish the regulator by refusing to continue its capital expansion program.[142]

Institutional design also can enhance regulatory commitment powers. For instance, a government might intentionally employ a regulator who values industry profit (relative to consumer surplus) more highly than the government. Such a regulator will be relatively unlikely to expropriate industry investment, and so valued investment is relatively likely to be undertaken.[143] The division of regulatory responsibility among multiple regulators, each with a different objective, also may help to enhance regulatory commitment powers. Absent commitment problems, the conflicting objectives of multiple regulators can complicate policy design and implementation.[144] However, the conflicting objectives and dispersed powers can limit the incentive and ability of any single regulator to renege on a promise he has made, and thereby enhance incentives for the firm to undertake valued investment.[145]

[140] Besanko and Spulber (1992) demonstrate that a regulated firm may undertake excessive investment to induce an opportunistic regulator to set a higher price for the firm's product. In the model, the regulator is uncertain about the relationship between the firm's observable capital stock and its unobservable unit operating cost. In equilibrium, higher levels of capital lead the regulator to increase his estimate of the firm's unit cost of operation. Consequently, the firm undertakes more than the cost-minimizing level of capital investment to induce the regulator to revise upward his estimate of the firm's operating cost, and to set a correspondingly higher price for the firm's product.

[141] Of course, this is just an instance of the general theory of dynamic and repeated games. See Fudenberg and Tirole (1991, ch. 5) for an overview. Gilbert and Newbery (1994) and Newbery (1999, ch. 2) compare the abilities of three kinds of regulatory contracts to induce desirable investment in the presence of limited regulatory commitment: (i) naive rate-of-return regulation, (ii) rate-of-return regulation with a "used and useful" requirement, and (iii) price-cap regulation. Consumer demand is uncertain in their model, and so capacity investment that is desirable ex ante may not be required ex post. The authors show that regime (ii) can sustain the desirable rate of investment for a larger range of parameter values than either regime (i) or regime (iii). Lewis and Sappington (1990, 1991b) assess the merits of alternative regulatory charters.

[142] See Salant and Woroch (1992) for a formal analysis of this issue, and see Levine, Stern and Trillas (2005) for a model based on regulatory reputation. Lewis and Yildirim (2002) show that learning-by-doing considerations can limit incentives for regulatory expropriation. When higher present output reduces future operating costs, a regulator may persistently induce greater output from, and thereby provide more rent to, the regulated firm than in settings where present output levels do not affect future costs.

[143] Again, see Levine, Stern and Trillas (2005).

[144] See Baron (1985), for example.

[145] To illustrate this possibility, consider the possible benefits of private versus public ownership of an enterprise as discussed in Laffont and Tirole (1991c) and Laffont and Tirole (1993b, ch. 17). Under public ownership, the government tends to use assets for social goals instead of for profit, and so a commitment problem may arise. With (regulated) private ownership, however, the firm's manager has two bodies con-

A regulator's incentive to expropriate sunk investments also may be tempered by increasing the political cost of such expropriation. This political cost might be increased, for example, by privatizing and promoting widespread ownership of a regulated firm. (The widespread ownership might be accomplished by setting low share prices, restricting the number of shares an individual can own, and providing long-term incentives not to sell the shares.) Such widespread ownership can help to ensure that a large fraction of the population will be harmed financially if the regulator expropriates the firm. Such widespread harm can increase the political cost of expropriation, and thereby limit its attraction to the regulator.[146]

The foregoing discussion presumes regulatory commitment is desirable. The ability to commit generally will be desirable when the regulator naturally pursues long-term social objectives. However, limited commitment may be preferable when the regulator is susceptible to capture or is myopic. To see why, consider a simple dynamic setting in which a regulator is susceptible to capture in each period with some exogenous probability. Suppose the government can decide whether to allow the regulator to write long-term contracts with the firm in this setting, i.e., whether the regulator can commit to future policy. Endowing the regulator with such commitment power involves a trade-off: commitment can enable the regulator to promise credibly not to expropriate the firm's sunk investments (and thereby encourage such investments), but it also allows a captured regulator to commit to policies that harm consumers. Whether commitment is desirable in such a setting can depend in complicated ways on model parameters. For instance, commitment is desirable if the probability of capture is small (as one would expect). However, commitment can also be desirable if capture is very likely.[147,148] Similar considerations arise when the regulator may act myopically. For instance, a regulator might have a relatively short term of office and maximize the welfare only over this term, ignoring the effects of his actions after his term has ended. In this case, the

trolling him: the regulator (who is interested in maximizing future welfare) and shareholders (who seek to maximize profit). These two bodies simultaneously offer the manager an incentive scheme, rewarding him on the basis of his performance. The equilibrium of this game between shareholders and the regulator determines the manager's actions. Joint control can produce a higher level of investment than is secured under unilateral control by government, and so can mitigate the commitment problem that exists under public ownership. See Martimort (1999) for further analysis of how multiple regulators can lessen a regulator's temptation to renegotiate contracts over time.

146 See Vickers (1991), Schmidt (2000) and Biais and Perotti (2002) for formal analyses of this issue.

147 Laffont and Tirole (1993b, ch. 16) analyze this model. The comparative statics with respect to the probability of capture are ambiguous because there are two conflicting effects. To see why, suppose, for simplicity, there are two periods and regulators are short-lived. If capture is unlikely, then it generally is desirable to allow the initial regulator to write long-term contracts in order to induce efficient long-term investment by the firm. However, when capture is unlikely, it is also likely that the second-period regulator will be honest, and will correct any bad policy made in the first period (in the unlikely event that the initial regulator was corrupt). This latter effect tends to make short-term contracts more desirable.

148 Faure-Grimaud and Martimort (2003) show that despite the danger of capture by the regulated firm, a government may grant a regulator some long-term independence in order to limit the influence of future governments (with different political interests) on industry policy.

ability to write long-term contracts may be undesirable because it can allow the regulator to pass excessive costs on to future generations.[149]

3.4.2. Regulatory capture

In the model of regulatory capture analyzed in Section 2.4.2, the optimal response to the danger of collusion was (i) to provide the regulator with countervailing incentives to act in the interests of society, and (ii) to reduce the firm's benefit from capturing the regulator. That model proposed what might be termed a "complete contracting" response to the capture problem, as the "constitution" provided the regulator with explicit monetary incentives to behave appropriately. In practice, such detailed contingencies can be difficult to design and implement. Instead, a constitution may only authorize or preclude certain regulatory actions. In such an "incomplete contracting" setting, a constitution might simply prohibit regulators from future employment in the industries they oversee in order to limit regulatory capture.[150] Alternatively, a constitution might preclude transfer payments between the regulator and firm for the same reason.[151] To see why in a specific setting, suppose the regulated firm's fixed cost initially is unknown. If transfer payments from taxpayers to the firm are possible, then marginal-cost pricing is feasible, which enhances allocative efficiency. If transfers are not possible, then average-cost pricing must be pursued.[152] If the regulator is captured, and thus allows an exaggerated report of the firm's fixed costs to be used as the basis for setting tariffs, then: (i) when transfers are used, the large fixed costs are covered by taxpayers and are not reflected in prices, and so go largely unnoticed by consumers; whereas (ii) when average-cost pricing is used, consumers may be acutely aware of any report of high costs by the firm/regulator, since high costs translate into higher prices. If consumers are better organized (or more observant) than taxpayers, then average-cost pricing may result in greater monitoring of the regulator, and hence act as a more effective impediment to capture. In this case, the beneficial effects of a reduced likelihood of capture could outweigh the allocative inefficiencies introduced by the use of average-cost pricing.

[149] See Lewis and Sappington (1990) for an analysis of this issue.

[150] However, Che (1995) shows that the possibility of future employment at a regulated firm can induce regulators to work more diligently during their tenure as regulators. Che also shows that some collusion between the regulator and firm might optimally be tolerated in order to induce the regulator to monitor the firm's activities more closely (in the hopes of securing a profitable side contract with the firm). Also see Salant (1995) for an analysis of how non-contractible investment could be encouraged when the regulator may later be employed by the firm.

[151] This discussion is based on Laffont and Tirole (1990c) and Laffont and Tirole (1993b, ch. 15). For a theory of why transfers should not be permitted that depends on regulatory failures related to commitment problems, see Laffont and Tirole (1993b, pp. 681–682).

[152] There is therefore a restriction to linear pricing in the no-transfer case.

3.5. Other topics

3.5.1. Service quality

To this point, the discussion of practical regulatory policies has abstracted from service quality concerns. In practice, regulators often devote substantial effort to ensuring that consumers receive high-quality regulated services. Before concluding this section, some practical policies that can help to secure appropriate levels of quality for regulated services are discussed briefly.[153]

To understand the basic nature of many practical policies that might be employed to secure appropriate levels of service quality, consider first the levels of service quality that an unregulated monopolist will supply when it can deliver different levels of quality to different consumers. An unregulated monopolist that sells its products to consumers with heterogeneous valuations of quality will tend to deliver less than the welfare-maximizing level of quality to consumers who have relatively low valuations of quality. This under-supply of quality to low-valuation customers enables the monopolist to extract more surplus from high-valuation customers. It does so by making particularly unattractive to high-valuation customers the variant of the firm's product that low-valuation consumers purchase. Faced with a particularly unattractive alternative, high-valuation customers are willing to pay more for a higher-quality variant of the firm's product.[154]

This pattern of quality supply by an unregulated monopolist suggests regulatory policies that might increase welfare. For example, a minimum quality requirement might increase toward its welfare-maximizing level the quality delivered to low-valuation customers. A price ceiling might also preclude the firm from charging high-valuation customers for the entire (incremental) value that they derive from the high-quality variant of the firm's product. Consequently, the firm's incentive to under-supply quality to low-valuation customers may be reduced.[155] And substantial profit taxes can also limit the financial benefits the firm perceives from under-supplying quality to low-valuation customers in order to secure greater profit from serving high-valuation customers.[156]

Price cap regulation alone generally does not provide the ideal incentives for service quality enhancement. Under price cap regulation, the regulated firm bears the full costs

[153] See Sappington (2005b) for a more detailed review of the literature on service quality regulation.

[154] See Mussa and Rosen (1978) for the seminal work in this area.

[155] See Besanko, Donnenfeld and White (1987, 1988) for analyses of these policies. See Ronnen (1991) for an analysis of the merits of minimum quality requirements in a setting where the prices set by competing firms are not regulated. Crampes and Hollander (1995) and Scarpa (1998) provide related analyses.

[156] Kim and Jung (1995) propose a policy that includes lagged profit taxes, and demonstrate that the policy can induce a firm to deliver the welfare maximizing level of service quality to all consumers, provided the firm does not undertake strategic abuse. (Recall from Section 3.2.2 that abuse entails expenditures in excess of minimum feasible costs that provide direct benefit to the firm.) Lee (1997a) proposes a modified policy with lower tax rates that limits incentives for abuse.

of increasing quality, but the price cap constraint prevents the firm from recovering the full value that consumers derive from the increased quality. Therefore, the firm generally will have insufficient incentive to deliver the welfare-maximizing level of service quality. Consequently, price cap regulation plans often incorporate explicit rewards and penalties to ensure the delivery of desired levels of service quality.[157]

When the regulated firm is privately informed about its costs of providing service quality on multiple dimensions, welfare gains can be secured by presenting the firm with a schedule of financial rewards and penalties that reflect the gains and losses that consumers incur as service quality varies on multiple dimensions.[158] In essence, such a schedule, coupled with a policy like price cap regulation that divorces regulated prices from costs, induces the firm to internalize the social benefits and costs associated with variations in the service quality it delivers.[159] Consequently, the schedule can induce the firm to minimize its costs of delivering service quality and to deliver to customers the levels of service quality on multiple dimensions that they value most highly.

3.5.2. Incentives for diversification

Firms that operate in regulated markets often participate in unregulated markets as well. For example, regulated suppliers of basic local telephone service often supply long distance telephone service and/or broadband Internet services at unregulated rates. Additional policy considerations arise when a firm operates, or has the opportunity to operate, simultaneously in both regulated and unregulated markets.

In particular, regulatory policy can affect the incentives of regulated firms to diversify into unregulated markets. To illustrate, suppose a firm operates under a cost-based regulatory policy (like rate-of-return regulation) in which the prices of the firm's regulated services are set to generate revenue that just covers the firm's costs of producing the regulated services. Suppose further that these costs include a portion of the shared (e.g., overhead) costs that arise from the production of both regulated and unregulated services. If the fraction of shared costs that are allocated to regulated operations declines as the firm's output in non-regulated markets increases, the firm typically will produce less than the welfare-maximizing level of unregulated services. This under-supply of

[157] See Laffont and Tirole (2000, p. 88). Spence (1975) and Besanko, Donnenfeld, and White (1987, 1988) note that price cap regulation may diminish the firm's incentive to deliver service quality relative to rate-of-return regulation when the provision of quality is capital intensive. Weisman (2005) points out that penalties for insufficient service quality that are imposed as reductions in the share of realized revenue to which a firm is entitled can reduce a firm's incentive to deliver service quality.

[158] See Berg and Lynch (1992) and Lynch, Buzas and Berg (1994). De Fraja and Iozzi (2004) demonstrate how a regulator that is well informed about consumers' marginal valuations of quality can modify the lagged expenditure policy discussed in Section 3.2.1 to induce a regulated monopoly to set welfare-maximizing prices and quality levels.

[159] Such a policy thereby acts much like the policy proposed by Loeb and Magat (1979), which provides financial rewards to the firm that reflect the level of consumer surplus its performance generates.

unregulated services arises because the cost allocation procedure effectively taxes the firm's output of unregulated services, which reduces their supply.[160]

In contrast, a regulated firm may undertake excessive expansion into unregulated markets if it is able to engage in cost shifting. Cost shifting occurs when the regulator counts as costs incurred in producing regulated services costs that truly arise solely from the production of unregulated services. Under cost-based regulation, cost shifting forces the customers of regulated services to bear some of the costs of the regulated firm's operation in unregulated markets, which explains the excessive expansion of these operations.[161]

Regulated firms that operate in both regulated and unregulated markets also may adopt inefficient production technologies. Technologies that entail particularly high fixed, shared costs and particularly low incremental costs of producing unregulated services can be profitable for a firm that operates under a form of cost-based regulation that attributes most or all shared costs to regulated operations.[162]

Although operations in unregulated markets can harm consumers of regulated services by admitting cost shifting and encouraging inefficient production technologies, diversification into unregulated markets also can benefit regulated customers. The benefits can flow from cost reductions in regulated markets that arise from economies of scope in producing regulated and unregulated services, for example.[163] The opportunity to pursue profit from unregulated operations may also induce a firm to undertake more research and development than it does absent diversification, to the benefit of customers of regulated services.[164]

A regulator also can secure gains for regulated customers by linking the firm's earnings from diversified operations to the welfare of regulated customers. To illustrate, suppose the regulator allows the firm to share the incremental consumer surplus that its diversified operations generates for consumers of the firm's regulated product. (The incremental surplus may arise from price reductions that are facilitated by economies of scope in the production of regulated and unregulated services, for example.) Such a policy, which is feasible when consumer demand for the regulated service is known, can induce the regulated firm to minimize its production costs and to diversify into a competitive unregulated market only when doing so increases aggregate welfare.[165]

A regulator also can secure gains for regulated customers by controlling directly the level of the regulated firm's participation in unregulated markets. To illustrate this fact, consider a variant of Baron and Myerson's (1982) model in which the regulated firm

[160] See Braeutigam and Panzar (1989), Weisman (1993), and Chang and Warren (1997) for formal analyses of this phenomenon.

[161] See Brennan (1990) and Brennan and Palmer (1994).

[162] See Baseman (1981), Brennan (1990), and Crew and Crocker (1991).

[163] Brennan and Palmer's (1994) investigation of the likely benefits and costs of diversification by regulated firms includes an analysis of the potential impact of scope economies.

[164] See Palmer (1991).

[165] See Braeutigam (1993).

produces a regulated service and may, with the regulator's permission, also produce an unregulated service. The firm is privately informed about its production costs. The regulator values the welfare of consumers of the regulated service more than he values the welfare of consumers of the unregulated service. In this setting, the regulator will optimally restrict the firm's participation in the unregulated market severely when the firm claims to have high costs, but will implement less severe output distortions in the regulated market. This policy serves to mitigate the firm's incentive to exaggerate its production costs without implementing substantial output distortions in the regulated market where the regulator is particularly averse to such distortions because of their impact on the welfare of consumers of the regulated service.[166]

3.6. Conclusions

The simple, practical regulatory policies reviewed in this section complement the optimal regulatory policies reviewed in Section 2. The practical policies provide insight about the gains that regulation can secure even when the regulator's knowledge of the regulated industry is extremely limited. The optimal policies provide further insight about how a regulator can employ any additional information that he may gain about the regulatory environment to refine and improve upon simple regulatory plans.

The analyses of optimal and practical regulatory policies together provide at least four important observations. First, carefully designed regulatory policies often can induce the regulated firm to employ its superior information in the best interests of consumers. Although the objectives of the regulated firm typically differ from those of society at large, the two sets of objectives seldom are entirely incongruent. Consequently, Pareto gains often can be secured. Second, the Pareto gains are secured by delegating some discretion to the regulated firm. The (limited) discretion afforded the firm is the means by which it can employ its superior knowledge to secure Pareto gains. The extent of the discretion that is optimally afforded the firm will depend upon both the congruity of the preferences of the regulator and the firm and the nature and extent of the prevailing information asymmetry.

Third, it generally is not costless to induce the firm to employ its superior information in the best interests of consumers. The firm typically will command rent from its superior knowledge of the regulatory environment. Although the regulator may place little or no value on the firm's rent, any attempt to preclude all rent can eliminate large potential gains for consumers. Consequently, the regulator may further the interests of consumers by credibly promising not to usurp all of the firm's rent. Fourth, the regulator's ability to achieve his objectives is influenced significantly by the instruments at his

[166] See Anton and Gertler (1988). Lewis and Sappington (1989c) also demonstrate how a regulator can secure gains for regulated customers by limiting the firm's participation in an unregulated market severely when it claims to have high operating costs in the regulated market. Sappington (2003) examines the optimal design of diversification rules to prevent a regulated firm from devoting an excessive portion of its limited resources to reducing its operating costs in diversified markets.

disposal. The regulator with fewer instruments than objectives typically will be unable to achieve all of his objectives, regardless of how well informed he is about the regulatory environment. Of course, limited information compounds the problems associated with limited instruments.

This fourth observation, regarding the instruments available to the regulator, is also relevant to the discussion in Section 4. The discussion there explains how a regulator can employ another instrument – potential or actual competition – to discipline the regulated firm and increase social welfare.

4. Optimal regulation with multiple firms

Even though regulation often is implemented in monopoly settings, it frequently is implemented in other settings as well. Consequently, the design of regulatory policy often must account for the influence of competitive forces. The primary purpose of this section is to consider how competitive forces can be harnessed to improve regulatory policy. This section also considers how the presence of competition can complicate the design of regulatory policy.

Competition has many potential benefits.[167] The present discussion focuses on two of these benefits: the *rent-reducing benefit* and the *sampling benefit*. In a competitive setting, the regulator may be able to terminate operations with a supplier who claims to have high costs because the regulator can secure output from an alternative supplier. Consequently, firms may have limited leeway to misrepresent their private information, and so may command less rent from their private information. This is the rent-reducing benefit of competition. The sampling benefit of competition emerges because, as the number of potential suppliers increases, the chosen supplier is more likely to be a particularly capable one. Together, the sampling and rent-reducing benefits of competition can help the regulator to identify a capable supplier and to limit the rent that accrues to the supplier.

The analysis of these benefits of competition and other benefits of competition begins in Section 4.1, which examines the design of yardstick competition. Under yardstick competition, a monopoly supplier in one jurisdiction is disciplined by comparing its activities to the activities of monopolists that operate in other jurisdictions. Section 4.2 analyzes the optimal design of competition *for* a market when competition *in* the market is precluded by scale economies and when yardstick competition is precluded by the absence of comparable operations in other jurisdictions. Section 4.3 examines how the presence of unregulated rivals affects the design of regulatory policy for a dominant supplier.

In contrast to Sections 4.1 through 4.3, which take the industry structure as given and beyond the regulator's control, Sections 4.4 and 4.5 examine the optimal structuring of

167 See Vickers (1995b), for instance, for a survey.

a regulated industry. Section 4.4 analyzes the number of firms that a regulator should authorize to produce a single product. Section 4.5 extends this analysis to settings where there are multiple regulated products, and the regulator can determine which firm supplies which product. Integration of production activities (i.e., choosing a single firm to supply all products) can provide a rent-reducing benefit, unless there is strong correlation between the costs of supplying the various services or unless the products are close substitutes. Section 4.6 considers the additional complications that arise when the quality of the regulated products delivered by multiple (actual or potential) suppliers is difficult for the regulator and/or for consumers to discern. Section 4.7 summarizes key conclusions regarding the interplay between regulation and competition.

4.1. Yardstick competition

In some settings, scale economies render operation by two or more firms within the same market prohibitively costly. However, even when direct competition among firms is not feasible within a market, a regulator may still be able to harness competitive forces to discipline a monopoly provider. He may do so by basing each firm's compensation on its performance (or report) relative to the performance (or reports) of firms that operate in other markets. When the firms are known to operate in similar environments, yardstick competition can produce a powerful rent-reducing benefit. The benefit can be so pronounced as to ensure the full-information outcome. We develop this conclusion in two distinct settings, which we refer to as the "yardstick performance" setting and the "yardstick reporting" setting. The sampling benefit of competition does not arise in either of these settings because, by assumption, there is only a single firm that is available to operate in each market.

4.1.1. Yardstick performance setting

To illustrate the potential value of yardstick competition, consider the following simple yardstick performance setting.[168] Suppose there are n identical and independent markets, each served by a separate monopolist. The local monopolists all face the same demand curve, $Q(p)$, and have identical opportunities to reduce marginal costs. Specifically, suppose $F(c)$ is the fixed cost that a firm must incur to achieve marginal cost c. The regulator is assumed to have no knowledge of the functional form of either $Q(\cdot)$ or $F(\cdot)$. However, the regulator can observe a firm's realized marginal cost of production c_i and its cost-reducing expenditures F_i in each market $i = 1, \dots, n$. The regulator specifies the price p_i that firm i must set and the transfer payment T_i that will be awarded to firm i. The regulator seeks to maximize the total surplus generated in the n markets, while ensuring that each producer makes non-negative profit. After observing the prices and transfer payments specified by the regulator, the firms choose cost-reducing expenditure levels simultaneously and independently. Each firm acts to maximize its profit,

[168] The following discussion is based on Shleifer (1985).

taking as given the predicted actions of the other firms. Collusion is assumed not to occur in this yardstick performance setting.

Proposition 12 reveals how, despite his limited knowledge, the regulator can exploit the symmetry of the environments to achieve the full-information outcome. In the full-information outcome, the price in each market equals the realized marginal cost of production ($p_i = c_i$) and each firm undertakes cost-reducing expenditures up to the point at which the marginal expenditure and the associated marginal reduction in operating costs are equal (i.e., $Q(c_i) + F'(c_i) = 0$, as in expression (11) above).

PROPOSITION 12. *The regulator can ensure the full-information outcome as the unique symmetric Nash equilibrium among the monopolists in the yardstick performance setting by setting each firm's price equal to the average of the marginal costs of the other firms and providing a transfer payment to each firm equal to the average cost-reducing expenditure of the other firms. Formally,*

$$p_i = \frac{1}{n-1} \sum_{j \neq i} c_j; \qquad T_i = \frac{1}{n-1} \sum_{j \neq i} F_j \quad \textit{for } i = 1, \ldots, n.$$

Since each firm's compensation is independent of its own actions under the reward structure described in Proposition 12, each firm acts to minimize its own production costs ($c_i Q(p_i) + F(c_i)$). The requirement to price at the average realized marginal cost of other producers then ensures prices that maximize total surplus. The authorized prices and transfer payments provide zero rent to all producers in this symmetric setting.

Proposition 12 illustrates vividly the potential gains from yardstick competition. Even when the regulator has little knowledge of the operating environment in each of the symmetric markets, he is able to ensure the ideal outcome in all markets.[169] In principle, corresponding results could be achieved if the producers faced different operating environments. In this case, though, the regulator would require detailed knowledge of the differences in the environments in order to ensure the full-information outcome.[170] Failure to adjust adequately for innate differences in operating environments could lead to financial hardship for some firms, significant rents for others, and suboptimal levels of cost-reducing expenditures.[171]

[169] Notice, in particular, that the regulator does not have well defined Bayesian prior beliefs about the functional form of each firm's technological capabilities, just as in the non-Bayesian models of regulation reviewed in Section 3. The regulator's ability to ensure the full-information outcome here is reminiscent of his ability to induce Ramsey prices with the lagged expenditure policy discussed in Section 3.2.1. There, the repeated observation of the performance of a single myopic monopolist in a stationary environment plays the same role that the observation of the performance of multiple monopolists in symmetric environments plays in the current context.

[170] See Shleifer (1985) for a discussion of how the regulatory policy might be modified when different firms produce in different operating environments.

[171] See, for example, Nalebuff and Stiglitz (1983).

A crucial simplifying feature of the yardstick performance setting is that the firms face no uncertainty.[172] If uncertainty is introduced into the production functions, then the full-information outcome typically is not possible when firms are risk averse. This is because the regulator must consider the firms' aversion to risk when determining the optimal power of the incentive scheme (as discussed in Section 2.6.2). The policy proposed in Proposition 12 is high powered and would expose risk-averse firms to excessive risk. Nevertheless, even when there is uncertainty and when firms are risk averse, it is generally optimal to condition each firm's reward on the performance of other firms, thereby incorporating yardstick competition to some degree.[173]

Despite the pronounced gains it can secure in some settings, yardstick competition can discourage innovative activity when spillovers are present or when the regulator's commitment powers are limited. To illustrate, suppose the cost-reducing expenditure of each firm in the yardstick performance setting serves to reduce both its own costs and (perhaps to a lesser extent) the costs of other firms. Then a reward structure like the one described in Proposition 12 will not induce the full-information outcome because it does not reward each firm fully for the beneficial impacts of its expenditures on the costs of other firms. Indeed, the price a firm is permitted to charge would decline as its cost-reducing expenditure increased, since the increased expenditure would reduce the operating costs of the other firms. More generally, when externalities of this sort are present and when the regulator cannot commit in advance to limit his use of yardstick regulation to extract rent from the regulated firms, social welfare can be lower when the regulator is empowered to employ yardstick regulation than when he is precluded from doing so.[174]

4.1.2. Yardstick reporting setting

Yardstick competition also can admit a powerful rent-reducing benefit simply by comparing the cost reports of actual or potential competitors. To illustrate this fact, consider the following yardstick reporting setting, which parallels the setting considered in Section 2.4.1.[175] There are two firms, A and B, that operate in correlated environments. Firm A has exogenous marginal cost $c^A \in \{c_L^A, c_H^A\}$ and fixed cost F^A. Firm B has

[172] The yardstick performance setting also abstracts from potential collusion among producers. Potters et al. (2004) present an experimental study of the extent of collusion under different yardstick competition policies.

[173] See Mookherjee (1984) for an analysis of the moral hazard problem with several agents. Mookherjee shows that, except in the special case where the uncertainty faced by the agents is perfectly correlated, the full-information outcome is not possible when agents are risk averse. He also shows that the optimal incentive scheme for one agent should depend on the performance of other agents whenever uncertainty is correlated. Also see Armstrong, Cowan and Vickers (1994, Section 3.4) for a simplified analysis in which regulatory policy is restricted to linear schemes.

[174] Dalen (1998) and Sobel (1999) prove this observation. Meyer and Vickers (1997) provide related insights in their analysis of implicit rather than explicit relative performance comparisons.

[175] This discussion is based on the analysis in Demski and Sappington (1984) and Crémer and McLean (1985).

marginal cost $c^B \in \{c_L^B, c_H^B\}$ and fixed cost F^B. Fixed costs are common knowledge, but each firm is privately informed about its realized marginal cost.

Initially, suppose that firm B can be relied upon to report its cost truthfully, and consider the optimal policy towards firm A. Let ϕ_i^A denote the probability that firm B has a low-cost realization c_L^B when firm A's marginal cost is c_i^A, for $i = L, H$. To capture the fact that the two firms operate in correlated environments, assume $\phi_L^A > \phi_H^A$. Just as in Section 2.4.1, the regulator can ensure marginal-cost pricing for firm A without ceding any rent if there are no bounds on the penalties that can be imposed on the risk-neutral firm. He can do so by conditioning the transfer payment to firm A on its report of its own cost and on the cost report of firm B.

Specifically, let T_{ij}^A be the transfer payment to firm A when it claims its cost is c_i^A and when firm B claims its cost to be c_j^B. If firm A claims to have a high cost, it is permitted to charge the unit price $p_H^A = c_H^A$. In addition, firm A receives a generous transfer payment when firm B also claims to have high costs, but is penalized when firm B claims to have low costs. These transfer payments can be structured to provide an expected transfer of F^A to firm A when its marginal cost is indeed c_H^A, so that

$$\phi_H^A T_{HL}^A + (1 - \phi_H^A) T_{HH}^A = F^A.$$

At the same time, the payments can be structured to provide an expected return to firm A when it has low costs that is sufficiently far below F^A that it eliminates any rent firm A might anticipate from being able to set the relatively high price ($p_H^A = c_H^A$), so that

$$\phi_L^A T_{HL}^A + (1 - \phi_L^A) T_{HH}^A \ll F^A.$$

The transfers T_{HL}^A and T_{HH}^A can always be set to satisfy this pair of expressions except when the costs of the two firms are independently distributed ($\phi_L^A = \phi_H^A$). When firm A reports it has low cost, it is simply offered its (deterministic) full information contract, with price equal to c_L^A and transfer payment equal to F^A. Consequently, provided that firm B reports its cost truthfully, the full-information outcome can be implemented for firm A with this pair of contracts. Firm B's cost report serves precisely the same role that the audit did in Section 2.4.1.

Of course, an identical argument can be applied to the regulation of firm B. In particular, if firm A can be induced to report its cost truthfully, then the full-information outcome can be implemented for firm B. Consequently, a yardstick reporting policy can implement the full-information outcome in both markets as a Nash equilibrium. Thus, even a very limited correlation among firms' costs can constitute a powerful regulatory instrument when feasible payments to firms are not restricted and when firms are risk neutral. This is because a firm with a low cost knows that other firms are also likely to have low costs. Consequently, cost exaggeration poses considerable risk of a severe penalty.

When the firms' costs are not highly correlated, extreme penalties may be required to eliminate a firm's unilateral incentive for cost exaggeration. Just as in Section 2.4.1, this can be problematic if firms are risk averse or if feasible payoffs to firms are bounded.[176] Another potential complication with a yardstick reporting policy of this type is that it might encourage the firms to coordinate their behavior. Although there is an equilibrium where the two firms truthfully report their private cost information, other equilibria can arise in which the firms systematically exaggerate their costs, leading to high prices and rent for the firms. More generally, when firms are rewarded according to how their performance or their reports compare to the performance or reports of their peers, the firms typically can coordinate their actions or reports and thereby limit the regulator's ability to implement effective yardstick competition.[177]

4.2. Awarding a monopoly franchise

Yardstick regulation relies upon the operation of monopolists in distinct markets. In contrast, franchise bidding creates competition among multiple potential suppliers for the right to serve as a monopolist in a single market.[178] Such competition can promote both sampling and rent-reducing benefits.

4.2.1. A static model

To illustrate how a regulator might employ franchise bidding to discipline a monopoly supplier, consider the following setting based on the Baron–Myerson model described in Section 2.3.1. Suppose there are $N \geqslant 1$ firms that are qualified to serve as a monopoly provider in a particular market.[179] Each firm has either low marginal cost (c_L) or high marginal cost (c_H). Let ϕ denote the probability that a given firm has a low-cost realization, and suppose the costs of the N firms are distributed independently.[180] The firm

[176] Demski and Sappington (1984) analyze a setting where firms are risk averse. Demski, Sappington and Spiller (1988), Dana (1993) and Lockwood (1995), among others, consider settings where feasible rewards and penalties are bounded.

[177] Ma, Moore and Turnbull (1988), Glover (1994), and Kerschbamer (1994) show how reward structures can be modified in adverse selection settings to rule out undesired equilibria in which firms systematically misreport their private cost information. Laffont and Martimort (1997) and Tangerås (2002) analyze the additional insights that arise when regulated firms are able to coordinate their actions explicitly. For instance, Tangerås (2002) shows that the value of yardstick competition becomes negligible as the firms' private cost information becomes perfectly correlated.

[178] Demsetz (1968) provides a pioneering discussion of the merits of franchise bidding.

[179] See Kjerstad and Vagstad (2000) for an analysis of the case where the number of participating bidders depends on the expected rents from the auction. Taylor (1995), Fullerton and McAfee (1999), and Che and Gale (2003) demonstrate the merits of limiting the number of firms that are permitted to compete for the right to supply a product. The entry restrictions increase the likelihood that any particular firm will be selected to produce, and thereby increase each firm's incentive to incur sunk development costs that improve its performance.

[180] The regulator can achieve the full-information outcome in this setting if the firms' costs are correlated by making use of the yardstick reporting mechanism discussed in Section 4.1.2.

that actually produces incurs the known fixed cost F. When F is sufficiently large, the regulator will optimally authorize the operation of only one producer.[181]

The optimal regulatory policy in this setting is readily shown to take the following form. After the regulator announces the terms of the regulatory policy, the firms simultaneously announce their cost realizations. If at least one firm claims to have low costs, one of these firms is selected at random to serve as the monopoly supplier. If all N firms report high costs, one of the firms is selected at random to be the monopoly supplier. The regulatory policy specifies that when a firm is selected to produce after reporting cost c_i, the firm must charge price p_i for its product and receive a transfer payment T_i from the regulator.[182] When a firm that truthfully announces cost c_i is selected to produce, it will receive rent $R_i = Q(p_i)(p_i - c_i) - F + T_i$. A firm that announces cost c_i will be selected to produce with probability ρ_i. In the equilibrium where all firms announce their costs truthfully (which can be considered without loss of generality if there is no collusion between firms), a firm that announces it has high costs will only win the contract when all other firms have high costs, and in that case only with probability $1/N$. Therefore,

$$\rho_H = \frac{(1-\phi)^{N-1}}{N}$$

is the probability that a firm that announces it has high costs will win the auction. Similarly, if a firm announces it has low costs, it will win the contest with the (if $N > 1$) higher probability[183]

$$\rho_L = \frac{1-(1-\phi)^N}{N\phi}.$$

Therefore, taking into account its probability of winning, the equilibrium expected rent of a firm with cost c_i is $\rho_i R_i$.

Now consider the incentive compatibility constraints that must be satisfied. As with expression (4), if a low-cost firm claims to have high costs and wins the contest, it will earn rent $R_H + \Delta^c Q(p_H)$. However, cost exaggeration reduces the equilibrium probability of winning the franchise from ρ_L to ρ_H. Consequently, a truthful report of low cost is ensured if $\rho_L R_L \geqslant \rho_H[R_H + \Delta^c Q(p_H)]$, or

$$R_L \geqslant \frac{\rho_H}{\rho_L}\big[R_H + \Delta^c Q(p_H)\big]. \tag{88}$$

Comparing expression (88) with expression (4), the corresponding constraint when there is only one potential supplier, it is apparent that competition relaxes the rele-

[181] The possibility of simultaneous production by multiple producers is considered below in Section 4.4, as is the possibility of an endogenous number of active producers.

[182] In principle, p_i and T_i might vary with the costs reported by the firms that are not selected to operate. However, such variation provides no strict gains when the costs of all potential suppliers are independent.

[183] For instance, see Lemma 1 in Armstrong (2000).

vant incentive compatibility constraint.[184] This is the rent-reducing benefit of franchise bidding.

As in expression (15), social welfare when a firm with cost c_i is selected to produce is $w_i(p_i) - (1-\alpha)R_i$, where $w_i(p_i)$ is total surplus when price is p_i and $\alpha \leqslant 1$ is the weight the regulator places on rent. Since the probability that a low-cost firm is selected to produce is $1-(1-\phi)^N$, total expected welfare is

$$W = \left(1-(1-\phi)^N\right)\left\{w_L(p_L) - (1-\alpha)R_L\right\} \\ + (1-\phi)^N\left\{w_H(p_H) - (1-\alpha)R_H\right\}. \tag{89}$$

Comparing expression (89) with expression (16), the corresponding expression when there is only one potential producer, reveals the sampling benefit of competition: the probability that the monopoly producer has low cost increases.

Standard arguments show that $R_H = 0$ and $p_L = c_L$ under the optimal policy. Also, the incentive constraint (88) will bind, and so p_H is chosen to maximize

$$(1-\phi)^N w_H(\cdot) - \left(1-(1-\phi)^N\right)\frac{\rho_H}{\rho_L}(1-\alpha)\Delta^c Q(\cdot).$$

Therefore, the price charged by the high-cost firm is

$$p_H = c_H + \frac{\phi}{1-\phi}(1-\alpha)\Delta^c,$$

which does not depend on N, and is exactly the optimal price specified in expression (5) that prevails in the absence of competition for the market.

It may be surprising that (conditional on the realized cost) the prices ultimately charged by the selected supplier do not vary with the number of firms that compete to serve as the monopoly supplier.[185] This invariance holds because two conflicting effects offset each other. The first effect arises because a low-cost firm that faces many competitors for the franchise is less tempted to exaggerate its cost, since the exaggeration reduces the probability (from ρ_L to ρ_H) that it will be selected to operate the franchise. Consequently, a smaller output distortion for a high-cost firm is needed to deter cost exaggeration, and so p_H can be reduced toward c_H. The second effect arises because the likelihood that a low-cost firm will be awarded the franchise increases as N increases. Therefore, it becomes more important to reduce the rent of the low-cost firm by raising p_H above c_H. These two effects turn out to offset each other exactly in this setting with risk-neutral firms and independently distributed costs.

Expression (88) reveals that the equilibrium rent of a low-cost firm that wins the contest is $R_L = \frac{\rho_H}{\rho_L}\Delta^c Q(p_H)$. Since ρ_H/ρ_L is decreasing in the number of bidders and

[184] As usual, the only binding incentive compatibility constraint is the one that ensures the low-cost firm will not exaggerate its cost.

[185] This result is not an artifact of the particular framework we use here (involving exogenous costs and binary realizations). Laffont and Tirole (1987) term the result the 'separation property'.

the high-cost price p_H is independent of the number of bidders, this rent decreases with the number of bidders.[186] Furthermore, since the probability that a low-cost firm wins is $[1-(1-\phi)^N]$, the aggregate expected rent of all bidders is

$$\left[1-(1-\phi)^N\right]\frac{\rho_H}{\rho_L}\Delta^c Q(p_H)=\phi(1-\phi)^{N-1}\Delta^c Q(p_H). \tag{90}$$

This expected industry rent is decreasing in N. These key features of the optimal regulatory policy in this setting are summarized in Proposition 13.[187]

PROPOSITION 13. *The optimal franchise auction in this static setting with independent costs has the following features*:
- (i) *The franchise is awarded to the firm with the lowest cost.*
- (ii) *A high-cost firm makes zero rent.*
- (iii) *The rent enjoyed by a low-cost firm that wins the contest decreases as the number of bidders increases.*
- (iv) *The total expected rent of the industry decreases as the number of bidders increases.*
- (v) *The prices that the winning firm charges do not depend on the number of bidders, and are the optimal prices in the single-firm setting, as specified in expression* (5).

This static analysis of franchise auctions has assumed that all potential operators are identical ex ante. When some operators are known to have higher expected costs than others, it can be advantageous to favor these operators by awarding the franchise to them with higher probability than it is awarded to operators with lower expected cost, ceteris paribus. Doing so can induce the operators with lower expected costs to bid more aggressively than they would in the absence of such handicapping.[188,189] Because such a policy may not award the franchise to the least-cost supplier, the policy intentionally sacrifices some productive efficiency in order to reduce the rent enjoyed by low-cost firms.

[186] When potential operators have limited resources, more capable operators cannot necessarily outbid their less capable rivals. Consequently, Lewis and Sappington (2000) show that the potential operators may resort instead to sharing larger fractions of realized profit with consumers. See Che and Gale (1998, 2000) for related analyses.

[187] Parallel results are obtained by Riordan and Sappington (1987a), Laffont and Tirole (1987), and McAfee and McMillan (1987b). Riordan and Sappington (1987a) analyze a model where the firm has only imperfect information about its eventual cost at the time of bidding. The other two studies examine settings where realized production costs are endogenous and observable.

[188] For instance, see the discussion in McAfee and McMillan (1987a, Section VII).

[189] We have not discussed the possibility of collusion between the regulator and one or more bidders, which is another kind of "favoritism". For discussions of this point, see Laffont and Tirole (1991a) and Celentani and Ganuza (2002).

4.2.2. Dynamic considerations

Although franchise bidding admits the rent-reducing and sampling benefits of competition, it is not without its potential drawbacks. These drawbacks include the following three.[190] First, it may be difficult to specify fully all relevant dimensions of performance, particularly if the franchise period is long. Therefore, actual performance may fall short of ideal performance on many dimensions, as the firm employs unavoidable contractual incompleteness to its own strategic advantage. Second, a franchise operator may be reluctant to incur sunk investment costs if there is a substantial chance that its tenure will end before the full value of the investment can be recovered. Consequently, the supplier may not operate with the least-cost technology. Third, incumbency advantages (such as superior knowledge of demand and cost conditions or substantial consumer loyalty) can limit the intensity of future competition for the right to serve as the franchise operator, as new potential operators perceive their chances of winning the contract on profitable terms to be minimal.[191]

To overcome the first of these potential drawbacks (contractual incompleteness), it may be optimal to award the monopoly franchise for a relatively short period of time. In contrast, the second potential drawback (limited investment incentives) may be best mitigated by implementing a relatively long franchise period, thereby providing a relatively long period of time over which the incumbent can benefit from its investments. To alleviate the tension introduced by these two counteracting effects, it may be optimal to award a franchise contract for a relatively short period of time, but to bias subsequent auctions in favor of the incumbent. Of course, such a policy can aggravate the third potential drawback to franchise bidding (incumbency advantages).

Although biasing franchise renewal auctions in favor of the incumbent can aggravate the potential problems caused by incumbency advantages, such biasing can be optimal when non-contractible investments by the incumbent reduce operating costs or enhance product quality substantially and when the benefits of these investments flow naturally to future franchise operators. Increasing the likelihood that the incumbent will be selected to operate the franchise in the future can increase the incumbent's expected return from such transferable, sunk investments. Consequently, such a bias can enhance incentives for the incumbent to undertake these valuable investments.[192] By contrast, when its investments are not transferable to rivals, the incumbent has stronger incentives to undertake such investments. In such a case, because the incumbent is expected to have

[190] Williamson (1976) discusses these potential drawbacks in more detail. Prager (1989), Zupan (1989b, 1989a) and Otsuka (1997) assess the extent to which these potential problems arise in practice.

[191] If incumbent suppliers acquire privileged information about the profitability of serving the franchise area, non-incumbent potential suppliers may not bid aggressively for the right to serve the franchise area, for fear of winning the franchise precisely when they have over-estimated its value.

[192] An examination of the optimal policy to motivate transferable investment by an incumbent would naturally include a study of the optimal length of the monopoly franchise, as discussed in Section 3.2.3.

lower operating costs than its rivals in subsequent auctions, it can be optimal to bias the subsequent auctions against the incumbent.[193]

Second sourcing in procurement settings is similar to franchise renewal in regulatory settings. Under second sourcing, the regulator may transfer operating rights from an incumbent to an alternative supplier. The second source might be a firm that presently serves other markets, or it might be a potential supplier that does not presently operate elsewhere. Second sourcing can increase welfare: (1) by shifting production from the incumbent to the second source when the latter has lower operating costs than the former (the sampling benefit); and (2) by reducing the rent the supplier secures from its privileged knowledge of its operating environment. This rent-reducing effect can arise for two reasons. First, as reflected in expression (88) above, the incumbent will be less inclined to exaggerate its operating costs when the probability that it is permitted to operate declines as its reported costs increase.[194] Second, when the incumbent's production technology can be transferred to the second source, the technology may generate less rent for the second source than it does for the incumbent. This will be the case if cost variation under the incumbent's technology is less sensitive to variations in the innate capability of the second source than it is to the corresponding variation in the incumbent's ability.[195]

When the operating costs of the incumbent and the second source are correlated, the optimal second-sourcing policy can share some features of the auditing and yardstick policies described in Sections 2.4.1 and 4.1.2. In particular, an incumbent that reports high cost can be punished (by terminating its production rights) when the second source reports low cost. In contrast, the incumbent can be rewarded when the second source corroborates the incumbent's report by reporting high cost also. However, an optimal second sourcing policy differs from an optimal auditing policy in at least two respects. First, cost reports by the second source are endogenous and are affected by the prevailing regulatory policy. Second, a second source enables the regulator to alter the identity of the producer while an audit in a monopoly setting does not change the producer's identity. These differences can lead the regulator to solicit a costly report from the second source more or less frequently than he will undertake an equally costly audit, and to set different prices in the regulated industry in response to identical reports from an audit and a second source. To best limit the rent of the incumbent, it can be optimal

[193] Laffont and Tirole (1988b) analyze these effects in detail. See also Luton and McAfee (1986) for a model without investment.

[194] Sen (1996) demonstrates the useful role that the threat of termination can play in adverse selection settings. He shows that when a regulator can credibly threaten to replace an incumbent with a second source, the quantity distortions that are implemented to limit information rents may be reduced. Also see Dasgupta and Spulber (1989/1990). Anton and Yao (1987) demonstrate the benefits of being able to shift production to a second source even when doing so can increase industry costs by foregoing valuable learning economies.

[195] For example, when it operates with the incumbent's technology, the second source's marginal cost of production may be a weighted average of its own innate cost and that of the incumbent. See Stole (1994).

to use the second source even when it is known to have a higher cost than the incumbent.[196]

Although second sourcing may increase welfare, second sourcing (like auditing) does not necessarily do so when the regulator has limited commitment powers. Second sourcing can reduce welfare by enabling the regulator to limit severely the rent the incumbent earns when its operating costs are low. When it anticipates little or no rent from realizing low production costs, the incumbent will not deliver substantial unobservable cost-reducing effort. Therefore, in settings where substantial cost-reducing effort is desirable and where limited commitment powers force the regulator to implement the policy that is best for consumers after the incumbent has delivered its cost-reducing effort, welfare can be higher when second sourcing is not possible. In essence, eliminating the possibility of second sourcing helps to restore some of the commitment power that is needed to motivate cost-reducing effort.[197]

4.3. Regulation with unregulated competitive suppliers

Situations often arise where a dominant firm and a number of smaller firms serve the market simultaneously, and the regulator only controls directly the activities of the dominant firm.[198] In these settings, the presence of alternative unregulated suppliers can affect both the optimal regulation of the dominant firm and overall welfare in a variety of ways. Competition can enhance or reduce welfare. While competition can introduce the rent-reducing and sampling benefits, unregulated competitors may undermine socially desirable tariffs that have been imposed on the regulated firm.

To analyze these effects formally, consider the following simple example which extends the Baron–Myerson model summarized in Section 2.3.1. Suppose the dominant firm's marginal cost is either low c_L or high c_H. In the absence of competition, the optimal regulatory policy would be as specified in Proposition 1. Suppose now there are a large number of rivals, each of which supplies exactly the same product as the dominant firm and each of which has the (known) unit cost of supply, c^R. Competition within this "competitive fringe" ensures the fringe always offers the product at price c^R. (For simplicity, we abstract from fixed costs of production for the fringe and the regulated dominant firm.)

There are four cases of interest, depending on the level of the fringe's cost c^R. First, suppose $c^R < c_L$. The fringe will increase welfare in this case because the industry

[196] See Demski, Sappington and Spiller (1987) for details.

[197] See Riordan and Sappington (1989) for a formal analysis of this effect. Notice that the decision to eliminate a second source here serves much the same role that favoring the incumbent supplier plays in the franchise bidding setting analyzed by Laffont and Tirole (1988b). Of course, as Rob (1986) and Stole (1994) demonstrate, if the regulator's commitment powers are unimpeded, second sourcing typically will improve welfare even when substantial unobservable cost-reducing effort is socially desirable.

[198] In contrast, in the models of second sourcing discussed in the previous section, the regulator could choose when to allow entry, and on what terms.

price and production costs are always lower when the fringe is active. Second, suppose $c_L < c^R < c_H$. Here too, the fringe increases welfare. The optimal regulatory policy in this case requires the dominant firm to set the price $p = c_L$. The firm will reject this contract if its cost is high, in which case the market is served by the fringe. This policy ensures the full-information outcome: the least-cost provider supplies the market, price is equal to marginal cost, and no firm receives any rent. Thus, the competitive fringe provides both a sampling and a rent-reducing benefit in this setting. The sampling benefit arises because the fringe supplies the market at lower cost than can the high-cost dominant firm. The rent-reducing effect arises because the low-cost dominant firm has no freedom to exaggerate its costs. Third, suppose $c^R > p_H$, where p_H is given in expression (5). In this case, the fringe has no impact on regulatory policy. The fringe's cost is so high that it cannot undercut even the inflated price of the high-cost firm, and so the policy recorded in Proposition 1 is again optimal.

The final (and most interesting) case arises when $c_H < c^R < p_H$. In this case, the marginal cost of the fringe always exceeds the marginal cost of the dominant firm. However, the cost disadvantage of the fringe is sufficiently small that it can profitably undercut the price (p_H) that the high-cost dominant firm is optimally induced to set in the absence of competition. Therefore, the presence of the fringe admits two regulatory responses: (i) reduce the regulated price from p_H to c^R for the high-cost dominant firm, thereby precluding profitable operation by the fringe; or (ii) allow the fringe to supply the entire market (at price c^R) when the dominant firm has high cost. Policy (ii) is implemented by requiring the dominant firm to charge the price equal to c_L if it wishes to supply the market.

Policy (i) offers the potential advantages of ensuring production by the least-cost supplier and moving price closer to marginal cost when the dominant firm has high costs. However, these potential gains are more than offset by the additional rent that policy (i) affords the dominant firm. Recall from Equations (28) and (29) that once the rent of the dominant firm is accounted for, expected welfare is the welfare derived from the setting in which the regulator is fully informed about the firm's cost but where the high cost is inflated to p_H. Because the fringe has a lower marginal cost than the adjusted cost of the high-cost dominant firm ($c^R < p_H$), expected welfare is higher when the fringe operates in place of the high-cost dominant firm.[199]

Proposition 14 summarizes these observations.

PROPOSITION 14. *Consumer surplus and welfare are higher, and the rent of the dominant firm is lower, in the competitive fringe setting than in the corresponding setting where the fringe does not operate.*

Notice that competition does not undermine socially desirable prices or otherwise reduce welfare in this simple setting. The same is true in similar settings, where the

[199] This same logic explains why a regulator might favor a less efficient bidder in a franchise auction, as discussed in Section 4.2.

fringe's cost is uncertain and may be correlated with the dominant firm's cost.[200,201] However, competition can reduce welfare in some settings. It might do so, for example, by admitting "cream-skimming", which occurs when competitors attempt to attract only the most profitable customers, leaving the incumbent regulated supplier to serve the less profitable (and potentially unprofitable) customers. To illustrate this possibility, consider the following simple setting. Suppose the incumbent regulated firm has no private information about its cost of operation. The friction in this setting arises because (in contrast to most of the other settings considered in this survey) there is a social cost of public funds $\Lambda > 0$.[202] (See Section 2.1 above.) The firm offers n products at prices $\mathbf{p} = (p_1, \ldots, p_n)$. At these prices, the firm's profit is $\pi(\mathbf{p})$ and consumer surplus is $v(\mathbf{p})$. In this setting, as in expression (1), welfare is $v(\mathbf{p}) + (1 + \Lambda)\pi(\mathbf{p})$. In the absence of competition, optimal (Ramsey) prices $\mathbf{p}^*$ maximize this expression.

Now suppose there is a competitive fringe that supplies a single product (product i) at price (and cost) equal to c_i^R. If $c_i^R > p_i^*$, the fringe does not interfere with the Ramsey prices. However, if $c_i^R < p_i^*$, the fringe will undercut the Ramsey price for product i. The lower price could increase welfare if the fringe's cost is sufficiently small relative to the corresponding cost of the regulated firm. However, if the fringe's cost advantage is sufficiently limited, welfare will decline. This is most evident when the two marginal costs are identical. In this case, the fringe does not reduce industry operating costs, but its presence forces a price for product i below the Ramsey price, p_i^*. When the fringe has higher costs than the regulated firm but can still operate profitably at price p_i^*, the operation of the fringe will both raise industry costs and divert prices from their Ramsey levels. Consequently, an unregulated competitive fringe can limit the options available to the regulator without offering offsetting benefits, such as those that arise from the rent-reducing or sampling benefits of competition.[203,204]

200 See Caillaud (1990). Caillaud shows that when the costs of the regulated firm and the fringe are positively correlated, smaller output distortions will be implemented when the competitive fringe is present. When costs are positively correlated, the regulated firm is less tempted to exaggerate costs, ceteris paribus, because it anticipates that the fringe will have low cost when the regulated firm does. Consequently, the reduced output that the regulated firm will be authorized to produce when it exaggerates cost will induce the fringe to supply a particularly large output level, resulting in a low market price and low profit for the regulated firm. The regulator responds to the firm's reduced incentive for cost exaggeration by imposing smaller output distortions.

201 Biglaiser and Ma (1995) show that when firms supply differentiated products and have superior knowledge of market demand, the presence of an unregulated producer can have different qualitative effects on optimal regulatory policy. Prices can be distorted above or below marginal cost, in part to induce a preferred allocation of customers among producers.

202 If $\Lambda = 0$ the regulator could ensure the ideal full-information outcome simply by requiring marginal-cost prices and delivering the transfer required to ensure the firm's participation. Competition would be beneficial in such a setting.

203 Baumol, Bailey and Willig (1977) and Baumol, Panzar and Willig (1982) identify (restrictive) conditions under which Ramsey prices are not vulnerable to such competitive entry.

204 Laffont and Tirole (1990b) analyze a variant of this model that involves second-degree price discrimination. There are two groups of consumers, high- and low-volume users, and the fringe has a technology that is

Such undesirable entry also can occur when the regulator has distributional objectives, and favors the welfare of one group of consumers over another.[205] (For instance, telecommunications regulators often try to keep basic local service rates low, but allow relatively high rates for long distance and international calls.) The relatively high prices that the regulator would like to set on certain services may enable competitors to provide the services profitably, even if they have higher production costs than the regulated firm. Consequently, unfettered competition can both undermine Ramsey prices and prices that reflect distributional concerns, and increase industry costs.

The mark-ups of prices above marginal costs that can arise under Ramsey pricing or in the presence of distributional concerns can be viewed as taxes that consumers must pay when they purchase products from the regulated firm. These taxes are used either to fund the firm's fixed costs or to subsidize consumption by favored consumer groups. In contrast, consumers pay no such taxes when they purchase products from an unregulated competitive fringe. Consequently, the effect of unfettered competition can be to undermine the tax base. This perspective suggests an obvious solution to the problem caused by unregulated competition: consumers should be required to pay the same implicit tax whether they purchase a product from the regulated firm or from the competitors. Such a policy, which entails regulation of the competitors, can ensure that entry occurs only when the an entrant is the least-cost supplier of a product. It can also ensure that entry does not undermine policies designed to recover fixed costs most efficiently or to achieve distributional objectives. Consequently, entry will occur only when it enhances welfare.

This policy can be illustrated using the Ramsey pricing example considered just above. If the incumbent's marginal cost for product i is c_i, the implicit tax on this product under the Ramsey prices $\mathbf{p}^*$ is $t_i = p_i^* - c_i$. If consumers must also pay this tax t_i when they buy the product from a rival firm, then entry is profitable only if the entrant has lower marginal cost than the incumbent supplier.[206] Moreover, if entry does take place, the proceeds of the tax paid by the consumers of the entrant's service can

attractive only to the high-volume consumers. Competition can force the regulator to lower the tariff offered to the high-volume users in order to induce them to purchase from the regulated firm and thereby help to finance the firm's fixed costs. But when the competitive threat is severe, the reduction in the high-volume tariff may be so pronounced that low-volume customers will also find it attractive to purchase on this tariff. To deter the low-volume customers from doing so, the usage charge on the tariff is reduced below marginal cost and the fixed charge is raised just enough to leave unchanged the surplus that the tariff provides to high-volume customers. Nevertheless, the low-volume customers benefit from the opportunity to purchase on the attractive tariff that is selected by high-volume customers, and so the welfare of all users can increase in the presence of bypass competition. Aggregate welfare can decline, though, once the costs of transfer payments to the regulated firm are taken into account. See Einhorn (1987) and Curien, Jullien and Rey (1998) for further analysis of this issue.

[205] See Laffont and Tirole (1993b, ch. 6) and Riordan (2002) for discussions of this issue, and for further references.

[206] If the entrant's unit cost for this product is c_i^R, it will find it profitable to serve consumers if and only if $c_i^R + t_i \leqslant p_i^*$, i.e., if $c_i^R \leqslant c_i$.

be used to cover the incumbent's fixed costs. In practice, though, it is often impractical to levy taxes directly on the products supplied by competitors, although access charges can sometimes be employed to levy such taxes indirectly.[207]

In summary, competition can enhance welfare, in part by introducing rent-reducing and sampling benefits. However, unfettered competition also can complicate regulatory policy by undermining preferred pricing structures.

4.4. Monopoly versus oligopoly

The preceding discussion of the interaction between regulation and competition has taken as given the configuration of the regulated industry. In practice, regulators often have considerable influence over industry structure. For example, regulators typically can authorize or deny the entry of new producers into the regulated industry. This section and the next consider the optimal structuring of a regulated industry. This section analyzes the desirable number of suppliers of a single product. Section 4.5 explores multiproduct industries, and considers whether a single firm should provide all products or whether the products should be supplied by separate firms.[208]

When choosing the number of firms to operate in an industry, a fundamental trade-off often arises. Although additional suppliers can introduce important benefits (such as increased product variety and quality, and the rent-reducing and sampling benefits of competition), industry production costs can increase when production is dispersed among multiple suppliers. The trade-off between monopoly regulation and duopoly competition is illustrated in Section 4.4.1. The optimal number of industry participants is considered in Section 4.4.2 for a simple setting in which the regulator's powers are limited.

4.4.1. Regulated monopoly versus unregulated duopoly

Consider an extension of the Baron–Myerson setting of Section 2.3.1 in which the regulator can allow a rival firm to operate in the market. We will compare the performance of two regimes in this setting: the regulated monopoly regime and the unregulated duopoly regime. Monopoly regulation imposes a fixed cost $G \geqslant 0$ on society. G might include the salaries of the regulator and his staff, as well as all associated support costs for example. If the rival enters the market, the two firms engage in Bertrand price competition.

Initially, suppose the rival's marginal cost is always the same as the incumbent's marginal cost.[209] Consequently, there is no need to regulate prices if entry occurs, since competition will drive the equilibrium price to the level of the firms' marginal cost of production. Eliminating the need for regulation saves the ongoing cost of funding the regulator, G. Of course, anticipating the intense competition that will ensue, the rival

[207] See Armstrong (2001) for further discussion. Related issues are considered in Sections 5.1.2 and 5.1.3.

[208] Regulators sometimes determine whether a regulated supplier of an essential input can integrate downstream and supply a retail service in competition with other suppliers. This issue is discussed in Section 5.2.

[209] This discussion of the case of perfect cost correlation is based on Armstrong, Cowan and Vickers (1994, Section 4.1.1).

will only enter the industry if the regulator provides a subsidy that is at least as large as the rival's fixed cost of operation, F. In this setting, the regulator effectively has the opportunity to purchase an instrument (the rival's operation) that eliminates both the welfare losses that arise from asymmetric information about the incumbent firm's operating costs and the ongoing regulatory costs, G. The regulator will purchase this instrument only if the benefits it provides outweigh its cost, which is the rival's fixed operating cost F. If F is sufficiently small, the regulator will induce the rival to operate.

Of course, the costs of an incumbent supplier and a rival are unlikely to be perfectly correlated. To examine the effects of imperfect cost correlation, consider the following setting.[210] Suppose that if the regulator authorizes entry by a rival producer, the rival and incumbent produce identical products and engage in Bertrand price competition. For simplicity, suppose the two firms have the same fixed cost F of production, but their marginal costs $c \in \{c_L, c_H\}$ may differ. Each firm has the low marginal cost c_L with probability $\frac{1}{2}$. The parameter $\rho \in [\frac{1}{2}, 1]$ is the probability that the two firms have the same cost.[211] The firms' costs are uncorrelated when $\rho = \frac{1}{2}$ and perfectly correlated when $\rho = 1$. Suppose each firm knows its own marginal cost and its rival's marginal cost when it sets its price. No transfer payments to or from the firms in the industry are possible in this duopoly setting. Initially, suppose the two firms find it profitable to operate in the industry.

Bertrand price competition ensures the equilibrium price will be c_H except when both firms have low cost, which occurs with probability $\frac{1}{2}\rho$. A firm's operating profit is zero unless it has the low marginal cost and its rival has the high marginal cost. The low-cost firm in this case secures profit $\Delta^c Q(c_H)$.[212] This positive profit is realized with probability $(1 - \rho)$. Consequently, expected industry profit in this unregulated duopoly setting is $(1 - \rho)\Delta^c Q(c_H)$, which declines as the firms' costs become more highly correlated. Notice that the probability that the industry supplier has low marginal cost is $(1 - \frac{1}{2}\rho)$. This probability decreases as ρ increases, because the sampling benefit of competition is diminished when costs are highly correlated. In contrast, the probability that the industry price will be c_L is $\frac{1}{2}\rho$, which increases as ρ increases. If α is the relative weight on industry profit in the welfare function, expected welfare in this unregulated duopoly setting is

$$\frac{1}{2}\rho v(c_L) + \left(1 - \frac{1}{2}\rho\right) v(c_H) + \alpha(1 - \rho)\Delta^c Q(c_H), \tag{91}$$

where the fixed cost incurred with duopoly supply $(2F)$ has been ignored for now.

210 This discussion is based on Section 3 of Armstrong and Sappington (2006). See Auriol and Laffont (1992) and Riordan (1996) for related analysis. Anton and Gertler (2004) show how a regulator can define the boundaries of local monopoly jurisdictions according to the costs reported by two local monopolists.

211 The probability that both firms have high cost is $\rho/2$, the probability that both firms have low cost is $\rho/2$, and the probability that a given firm has low cost while its rival has high cost is $(1 - \rho)/2$.

212 The profit-maximizing price for a firm with the low marginal cost is assumed to exceed c_H. Consequently, when only one firm has the low marginal cost, it will serve the entire market demand at price c_H in equilibrium.

If monopoly regulation is chosen, it proceeds as in the Baron and Myerson framework of Section 2.3.1. As discussed in Section 2.3.3 (see expressions (28) and (29)), the maximum expected welfare in the regulated monopoly regime is

$$\frac{1}{2}v(c_L) + \frac{1}{2}v\big(c_H + (1-\alpha)\Delta^c\big), \tag{92}$$

abstracting from the fixed cost of monopoly supply (F) and the fixed cost of monopoly regulation (G) for now.

Regulated monopoly offers three potential advantages over unregulated duopoly in this simple setting: (1) industry prices can be controlled directly; (2) transfer payments can be made to the firm to provide desired incentives; (3) economies of scale in supply are preserved because there is only one industry supplier.[213] Unregulated duopoly also offers three potential advantages in this setting. First, the likelihood that the industry producer has the low marginal cost is higher under duopoly than under monopoly (unless $\rho = 1$) due to the sampling benefit of competition: if one firm fails to secure the low cost, its rival may do so. Second, the presence of a rival with correlated costs reduces the information advantage of the industry producer. This is the rent-reducing benefit of competition. Third, the cost of ongoing regulation, G, is avoided in the unregulated duopoly regime.

A formal comparison of these potential benefits of regulated monopoly and unregulated duopoly is facilitated initially by considering the case where $G = F = 0$. A comparison of expressions (91) and (92) provides three insights regarding the relative performance of regulated monopoly and unregulated duopoly.

First, as noted above, unregulated duopoly delivers a higher level of expected social welfare than does regulated monopoly when the duopolists' costs are perfectly correlated (so $\rho = 1$).[214] When costs are perfectly correlated, the industry producer never has a cost advantage over its rival, and so commands no rent in the duopoly setting. Furthermore, competition drives the industry price to the level of realized marginal cost. Therefore, the ideal full-information outcome is achieved under duopoly, but not under monopoly, where regulated prices diverge from marginal cost in order to limit the rent the monopolist commands from its privileged knowledge of cost. In this case, then, unregulated duopoly is preferred to regulated monopoly, even though the former offers no sampling benefit. The benefits of competition arise entirely from rent reduction in this case.

Second, when demand is perfectly inelastic, unregulated duopoly produces a higher level of expected welfare than does regulated monopoly.[215] When demand is perfectly inelastic, price distortions do not change output levels, and therefore do not affect the

[213] In addition, when there is a social cost of public funds ($\Lambda > 0$), the firm's profit can be taxed to reduce the overall public tax burden. This benefit is not available in the case of unregulated duopoly.

[214] If $\alpha = 1$, the two regimes provide the same expected social welfare.

[215] When demand is perfectly inelastic (so $Q(p) \equiv 1$, for example), expression (91) is weakly greater than (92) whenever $\frac{1}{2}\rho \geqslant (\rho - \frac{1}{2})\alpha$, which is always the case.

firm's rent or total surplus. Consequently, only the probability of obtaining a low-cost supplier affects expected welfare, and this probability is higher under duopoly than under monopoly because of the sampling benefit of competition.[216]

Third, when demand is sufficiently elastic (and $\rho < 1$), regulated monopoly will generate a higher level of expected welfare than unregulated duopoly. When demand is elastic, prices that do not track costs closely entail substantial losses in surplus. Prices track costs more closely under regulated monopoly than under unregulated duopoly.[217]

The discussion to this point has abstracted from fixed costs of supply. When the fixed cost F is sufficiently large, regulated monopoly will outperform unregulated duopoly in the simple model analyzed here because monopoly avoids the duplication of the fixed cost.[218] The analysis to this point also has assumed that both firms find it profitable to operate in the unregulated duopoly setting. If their marginal costs are highly correlated, two unregulated suppliers of a homogeneous product may not find it profitable to operate in the industry, even if fixed costs are not particularly large. This is because the firms earn no profit when their costs are identical, and so expected profit will be meager when costs are likely to be identical. Consequently, financial subsidies will be necessary to attract competing suppliers of homogeneous products when their costs are highly correlated. This situation can provide a coherent argument for assisting entry into the market.[219] The requisite subsidies will tend to be smaller when industry price competition is less intense, as it can be when the firms' products are not homogeneous, for example.

Obviously, this simple, illustrative comparison of the relative performance of regulation and competition is far from complete. A complete comparison would need to consider more carefully the policy instruments available to the regulator, for example.[220] The foregoing discussion presumes the regulator can tax consumers to finance transfer payments to the firm. In practice (as emphasized throughout Section 3), regulators are not always able to make transfer payments to the firms they regulate. Absent this ability, a regulator who wishes to ensure the monopolist never terminates its operations in the present setting can do no better than to set a single price equal to the high

[216] A similar insight is that unregulated duopoly outperforms regulated monopoly when Δ^c, the difference between the high and the low marginal cost, is close to zero. Monopoly rent and duopoly profit are both negligible in this case, and so the choice between monopoly and duopoly depends upon which regime produces the low marginal cost more frequently.

[217] The convexity of $v(\cdot)$ implies that welfare in (92) is no lower than $\frac{1}{2}v(c_L)+\frac{1}{2}v(c_H)-\frac{1}{2}(1-\alpha)\Delta^c Q(c_H)$. Hence, the difference between (92) and (91) is at least $\frac{1}{2}(1-\rho)(v(c_L)-v(c_H))-[\frac{1-\alpha}{2}+\alpha(1-\rho)]\Delta^c Q(c_H)$. Since this expression is increasing in α, it is at least $\frac{1}{2}(1-\rho)(v(c_L)-v(c_H))-\frac{1}{2}\Delta^c Q(c_H)$. Therefore, welfare is higher with regulated monopoly whenever $v(c_L) \geqslant v(c_H)+\Delta^c Q(c_H)/(1-\rho)$. This inequality will hold if demand is sufficiently elastic.

[218] In contrast, if the fixed cost of regulation, G, is sufficiently large, unregulated duopoly will outperform regulated monopoly.

[219] See Armstrong and Sappington (2006) for additional discussion of the merits and drawbacks to various forms of entry assistance.

[220] A complete analysis also should consider the social cost of public funds (Λ). When Λ is large, the taxable profit generated under regulated monopoly can increase welfare substantially.

marginal cost $p = c_H$ (assuming fixed costs are zero). This policy generates expected welfare

$$v(c_H) + \frac{1}{2}\alpha \Delta^c Q(c_H). \tag{93}$$

The level of expected welfare in expression (93) is lower than the corresponding level for duopoly in expression (91).[221] Consequently, unregulated duopoly is always preferred to this restricted form of monopoly regulation (when fixed costs of supply are not significant). More generally, the relative benefits of monopoly regulation may be diminished by important practical limitations such as the possibility of regulatory capture, imperfect regulatory commitment powers, and more severe information asymmetries, for example.

Finally, in the simple static setting analyzed here, franchise bidding can secure the benefits of both regulated monopoly and unregulated duopoly, and thereby outperform both regimes. To prove this conclusion formally, return to the setting of Section 4.2. For simplicity, suppose there are two potential bidders and the two possible cost realizations are equally likely for each firm. In addition, suppose the two firms' cost realizations are independent, so that $\rho = \frac{1}{2}$. (Otherwise, the full-information outcome is possible by making use of the yardstick reporting schemes discussed in Section 4.2.2.) Consequently, a firm with the low marginal cost will be selected to serve as the monopoly supplier with probability $\frac{3}{4}$. From Proposition 13, the maximum expected welfare in the franchise bidding setting is

$$\frac{3}{4}v(c_L) + \frac{1}{4}v\big(c_H + (1-\alpha)\Delta^c\big), \tag{94}$$

where the fixed cost of supply (F) and any costs of awarding and enforcing the franchise auction have been ignored. It is apparent that expression (94) exceeds expression (92) due to the sampling benefit of competition. Expression (94) also exceeds expression (91) when $\rho = \frac{1}{2}$.[222]

In summary, franchise bidding outperforms monopoly regulation and duopoly competition in this simple setting by securing the key benefits of both regimes. Franchise bidding permits transfer payments and price regulation to pursue social goals. It also ensures the benefit of scale economies by selecting a single supplier. In addition, franchise bidding secures the sampling and rent-reducing benefits of competition. Of course, this simple model has abstracted from several of the important potential drawbacks to franchise bidding discussed in Section 4.2. These problems include the practical difficulties associated with specifying all relevant contingencies in a franchise contract and with motivating incumbent suppliers to undertake sunk investments when regulatory expropriation is a concern.

[221] The difference between expressions (91) and (93) is $\frac{\rho}{2}(v(c_L) - v(c_H)) + \alpha(\frac{1}{2} - \rho)\Delta^c Q(c_H)$. From the convexity of $v(\cdot)$, this difference is at least $[\frac{\rho}{2} - (\rho - \frac{1}{2})\alpha]\Delta^c Q(c_H) \geqslant 0$.

[222] The convexity of $v(\cdot)$ implies that welfare in (94) is no lower than $\frac{3}{4}v(c_L) + \frac{1}{4}v(c_H) - \frac{1}{4}(1-\alpha)\Delta^c Q(c_H)$. Consequently, the difference between (94) and (91) is at least $\frac{1}{2}(v(c_L) - v(c_H)) - \frac{1}{4}(1+\alpha)\Delta^c Q(c_H) \geqslant 0$. The final inequality arises from the convexity of $v(\cdot)$.

4.4.2. The optimal number of industry participants

To consider the optimal number of industry participants more generally, consider a different setting where the only form of industry regulation is a determination of the number of operating licenses that are awarded. It is well known that a *laissez-faire* policy toward entry will often induce too many firms to enter, and so, in principle, entry restrictions could increase welfare.[223] In practice, of course, it is an informationally demanding task to assess both the optimal number of competitors and the identity of the "best" competitors. The latter problem may be resolved in some settings by auctioning to the highest bidders a specified number of operating licenses.[224]

In some circumstances, the regulator will choose to issue fewer licenses than he would in the absence of asymmetric knowledge of operating costs. The reason for doing so is to encourage more intense bidding among potential operators. When potential operators know that a large number of licenses will be issued, they have limited incentive to bid aggressively for a license for two reasons. First, when many licenses are available, a potential supplier is relatively likely to be awarded a license even if it does not bid aggressively for a license. Second, the value of a license is diminished when many other licenses are issued because the increased competition that results when more firms operate in the industry reduces the rent that accrues to each firm. Therefore, to induce more aggressive bidding for the right to operate (and thereby secure greater payments from potential operators that can be distributed to taxpayers), a regulator may restrict the number of licenses that he issues, thereby creating a relatively concentrated industry structure.[225]

Entry policy also can affect the speed with which consumers are served. Consider, for example, a setting where firms must incur sunk costs in order to operate, and where

[223] As Mankiw and Whinston (1986) demonstrate, excess entry can arise because an individual firm does not internalize the profit reductions that its operation imposes on other firms when it decides whether to enter an industry. The authors also show that excess entry may not arise when firms supply differentiated products. Vickers (1995b) shows that excess entry may not arise when firms have different operating costs. In this case, market competition generally affords larger market shares to the least-cost suppliers (which is related to the sampling benefit of competition). The inability of firms to capture the entire consumer surplus derived from their operation in retail markets can result in an inefficiently small amount of entry. Ghosh and Morita (2004) show that less than the socially efficient level of entry may occur in a wholesale (as opposed to a retail) industry, even when all inputs and outputs are homogeneous. Upstream entry generates downstream profit, which is not internalized by the upstream entrant in the authors' model.

[224] McMillan (1994), McAfee and McMillan (1996), Cramton (1997), Milgrom (1998), Salant (2000), and Hoppe, Jehiel and Moldovanu (2006) discuss some of the complex issues that arise in designing auctions of spectrum rights. Fullerton and McAfee (1999) analyze how best to auction rights to participate in an R&D contest. They find that it is often optimal to auction licenses to two firms, who subsequently compete to innovate.

[225] This basic conclusion arises in a variety of settings, including those analyzed by Auriol and Laffont (1992), Dana and Spier (1994), and McGuire and Riordan (1995). Also see Laffont and Tirole (2000, pp. 246–250). Wilson (1979) and Anton and Yao (1989, 1992) identify a related, but distinct, drawback to allowing firms to bid for portions of a project rather than the whole project. When split awards are possible, firms can implicitly coordinate their bids and share the surplus they thereby extract from the procurer.

firms have different marginal costs of production. If a regulator were simply to authorize a single, randomly-selected firm to operate, duplication of sunk costs would be avoided and consumers could be served immediately. However, the least-cost supplier might not be chosen to operate under this form of regulated monopoly. Under a *laissez-faire* policy regarding entry, firms may be reluctant to enter the industry for fear of facing intense competition from lower-cost rivals. Under plausible conditions, there is an equilibrium in this setting in which a low-cost firm enters more quickly than does a high-cost firm. Consequently, if all potential operators have high costs, entry may be delayed. Therefore, monopoly may be preferred to unfettered competition when immediate production is highly valued.[226]

In concluding this section, we note that the discussion to this point has abstracted from the possibility of regulatory capture. This possibility can introduce a bias toward competition and away from monopoly. To see why, consider a setting where a political principal relies on advice from a (better informed) regulator to determine whether additional competition should be admitted into the regulated industry. Because increased competition typically reduces the rent a regulated firm can secure, the firm will have an incentive to persuade the regulator to recommend against allowing additional competition. To overcome this threat of regulatory capture, it can be optimal to bias policy in favor of competition by, for example, introducing additional competition even when the regulator recommends against doing so.[227]

4.5. *Integrated versus component production*

In multiproduct industries, regulators often face the task of determining which firms will supply which products. In particular, the regulators must assess the advantages and disadvantages of integrated production and component production. Under integrated production, a single firm supplies all products. Under component production, different firms supply the different products.

One potential advantage of component production is that it may admit yardstick competition which, as indicated in Section 4.1, can limit substantially the rent of regulated suppliers. One obvious potential advantage of integrated production is that it may allow technological economies of scope to be realized. Integrated production can also give rise to *informational* economies of scope in the presence of asymmetric information. To illustrate the nature of these informational economies of scope, first consider the following simple setting with independent products.

[226] See Bolton and Farrell (1990). The authors do not consider the possibility of auctioning the monopoly franchise. When franchise auctions are feasible, their use can increase the benefits of monopoly relative to oligopoly.

[227] See Laffont and Tirole (1993a) for a formal analysis of this effect. Thus, although the possibility of capture might be expected to reduce the likelihood of entry, it acts to increase the likelihood of entry once the political principal has responded appropriately to the threat. Recall the corresponding observation in Section 2.4.2.

4.5.1. Independent products

In the setting with independent products, consumer demand for each product does not depend on the prices of the other products. To illustrate most simply how informational economies of scope can arise under integrated production in this setting, suppose there are many independent products.[228] Suppose further that each product is produced with a constant marginal cost that is observed by the producer, but not by the regulator. In addition, it is common knowledge that the cost realizations are independently distributed across the products. In this setting, the full-information outcome can be closely approximated when a single firm produces all of the regulated products. To see why, suppose the single integrated firm is permitted to choose its prices for the products it supplies. Further suppose the firm is awarded (as a transfer payment) the entire consumer surplus its prices generate. For the reasons identified in Section 2.3.1, the firm will set prices equal to marginal costs under this regulatory policy.[229] Of course, the firm will enjoy significant rent under the policy. The rent is socially costly when the regulator places more weight on consumer surplus than on rent. However, the aggregate realized rent is almost independent of the firm's various cost realizations when there are many products, each produced with an independent marginal cost. Consequently, the regulator can recover this rent for consumers by imposing a lump-sum tax on the firm (almost) equal to its expected rent, thereby approximating the full-information outcome.

In this simple setting, no role for yardstick competition arises because cost realizations are not correlated. To examine the comparison between integrated and component production when yardstick effects are present, recall the two-product framework discussed in Section 2.4.3.[230] The analysis in that section derived the optimal regulatory regime under integrated production. Now consider the optimal regime under component production. First, consider the benchmark case in which the cost realizations for the two products are independently distributed. Absent cost correlation, there is no role for yardstick competition, and the optimal regulatory regime is just the single-product regime specified in Proposition 1, applied separately to the supplier of each product. It is feasible for the regulator to choose this regime under integrated production as well. However, part (iii) of Proposition 5 indicates that the regulator can secure a higher level of welfare with a different regime. Therefore, when costs are independently distributed, integrated production is optimal.

Now suppose there is some correlation between the costs of producing the two products. If the firms are risk neutral and there are no restrictions on the losses a firm can bear, the discussion in Section 4.1.2 reveals that the full-information outcome is possible with yardstick competition, and so component production is optimal, provided the two producers do not collude. In contrast, the full-information outcome will not be attainable

[228] The following discussion, found in Dana (1993), also applies naturally to the subsequent discussion about complementary products.

[229] See Loeb and Magat (1979).

[230] The following discussion is based on Dana (1993).

if the firms must receive non-negative rent for all cost reports (due to limited liability concerns, for example). However, when the correlation between the two costs is strong, the penalties required to achieve a desirable outcome are relatively small. Consequently, limits on feasible penalties will not prevent the regulator from securing a relatively favorable outcome when the firms' costs are highly correlated. In contrast, when costs are nearly independently distributed, bounds on feasible penalties will preclude the regulator from achieving a significantly higher level of welfare under yardstick regulation than he can secure by regulating each firm independently. It is therefore intuitive (and can be shown formally) that component production is preferable to integrated production only when the correlation between cost realizations is sufficiently high.[231,232] When the correlation between costs is high, part (ii) of Proposition 5 reveals that the best policy under integrated production is to treat each firm as an independent single-product monopolist. Yardstick competition can secure a higher level of expected welfare, even when there are limits on the losses that firms can be forced to bear.

The relative merits of integrated and component production can also be investigated in a franchise auction context. For instance, suppose there are two independent franchise markets, 1 and 2, and the regulator must decide whether to auction access to the two markets in separate auctions or to "bundle" the markets together in a single franchise auction. Suppose there are two potential operators, A and B, each of which can operate in one or both markets. Suppose the cost of providing the specified service in market m is c_i^m for firm i, where $m = 1, 2$ and $i = A, B$. Further, suppose there are no economies (or diseconomies) of scope in joint supply, so that firm i's cost of supplying both markets is $c_i^1 + c_i^2$. Suppose the regulator wishes to ensure production in each market, and so imposes no reserve price in the auction(s).

If the regulator awards the franchise for the two markets by means of two separate second-price auctions, he will have to pay the winner(s)

$$\max\{c_A^1, c_B^1\} + \max\{c_A^2, c_B^2\}. \tag{95}$$

[231] Ramakrishnan and Thakor (1991) provide a related analysis in a moral hazard setting. In moral hazard settings, integrated production can provide insurance to the risk averse agent, particularly when the cost realizations are not too highly correlated. Thus, as in Dana's (1993) model of adverse selection, a preference for integrated production tends to arise in moral hazard settings when the cost realizations are not too highly correlated. The reason for the superiority of integrated production is similar in the two models: the variability of the uncertainty is less pronounced under integrated production.

[232] Riordan and Sappington (1987b) provide related findings in a setting where production proceeds sequentially, and the supplier of the second input does not learn the cost of producing the second input until after production of the first input has been completed. When costs are positively correlated, integrated production increases the agent's incentive to exaggerate his first-stage cost. This is because a report of high costs in the first stage amounts to a prediction of high costs in the second stage. Since integrated production thereby makes it more costly for the regulator to induce truthful reporting of first-stage costs, the regulator prefers component production. In contrast, integrated production can reduce the agent's incentives to exaggerate first-stage costs when costs are negatively correlated. The countervailing incentives that ensue can lead the regulator to prefer integrated production when costs are negatively correlated.

If the regulator awards the two markets by means of a second-price single auction, he will have to pay the winner

$$\max\{c_A^1 + c_A^2, c_B^1 + c_B^2\},$$

which is always (weakly) less than the amount in expression (95). Therefore, the regulator will pay less when he bundles the two franchise markets in a single auction than when he conducts two separate auctions (with potentially two different winners). This conclusion reflects the rent-reducing benefit of integrated production.[233]

4.5.2. Complementary products

Now, suppose there is a single final product that is produced by combining two essential inputs.[234] For simplicity, suppose the inputs are perfect complements, so one unit of each input is required to produce one unit of the final product. Consumer demand for the final product is perfectly inelastic at one unit up to a known reservation price, so the regulator procures either one unit of the final product or none of the product. The cost of producing a unit of the final product is the sum of the costs of producing a unit of each of the inputs, so again there are no technological economies of scope. The cost of producing each input is the realization of an independently distributed random variable. Therefore, there is no potential for yardstick competition under component production in this setting.[235]

In this setting, the regulator again prefers integrated production to component production. To see why most simply, suppose the cost for each input can take on one of two values, c_L or c_H, where $c_L < c_H$. Also suppose the probability of obtaining a low-cost outcome is ϕ, and the costs of producing the two inputs are independently distributed. Further suppose it is optimal to supply one unit of the final product except when both inputs have a high cost.[236]

First consider integrated production, and let R_{ij} denote the rent of the integrated firm when it has cost c_i for the first input and cost c_j for the second input. Since the

[233] This discussion is based on Palfrey (1983), who shows that the ranking between integrated and component production may be reversed when there are more than two bidders. Notice that when the two markets are awarded as a bundle, inefficient production may occur because the firm with the lowest total cost is not necessarily the firm with the lowest cost in each market. For additional analysis of the optimal design of multiproduct auctions, see Armstrong (2000), for example.

[234] The following discussion is based on Baron and Besanko (1992) and Gilbert and Riordan (1995).

[235] See Jansen (1999) for an analysis of the case where the costs of the two inputs are correlated and when, as in Dana (1993), limited liability constraints bound feasible penalties. Jansen, like Dana, concludes that when the extent of correlation is high, the benefits of yardstick competition outweigh the informational economies of scope of integrated production.

[236] It is straightforward to show that if it is optimal to ensure production for all cost realizations, the regulator has no strict preference between component production and integrated production. When supply is essential, the regulator must pay the participants the sum of the two highest possible cost realizations under both industry structures. (The same is true if production is desirable only when both components are produced with low cost.)

regulator optimally terminates operations when both costs are c_H, he can limit the firm's rent to zero when it has exactly one high-cost realization, so $R_{LH} = R_{HL} = 0$. Then, as in expression (42), the incentive constraint that ensures the firm does not claim to have exactly one high-cost realization when it truly has two low-cost realizations is $R_{LL} \geqslant \Delta^c \equiv c_H - c_L$. Since the probability of having low costs for both products is ϕ^2, the regulator must allow the integrated firm an expected rent of

$$R_{INT} = \phi^2 \Delta^c.$$

Now consider component production. Suppose a firm receives the expected transfer T_i when it claims to have $c = c_i$. If one firm reports that it has low costs, then production definitely takes place since the regulator is prepared to tolerate one high-cost realization. Consequently, the expected rent of a low-cost firm is $R_L = T_L - c_L$. If a firm reports that it has a high cost, then production takes place only with probability ϕ (i.e., when the other firm reports a low cost), and so that firm's expected rent is $R_H = T_H - \phi c_H$. The regulator will afford no rent to a firm when it has high cost, so $R_H = 0$. The incentive compatibility constraint for the low-cost firm is $R_L \geqslant T_H - \phi c_L = R_H + \phi \Delta^c = \phi \Delta^c$. Therefore, the regulator must deliver an expected rent of $\phi^2 \Delta^c$ to each firm under component production, yielding a total expected industry rent of

$$R_{COMP} = 2\phi^2 \Delta^c.$$

Thus, the regulator must deliver twice as much rent under component production than he delivers under integrated production, and so integrated production is the preferred industry structure.[237]

The regulator's preference for integrated production in this setting arises because integration serves to limit a firm's incentive to exaggerate its cost. It does so by forcing the firm to internalize an externality. The regulator disciplines the suppliers in this setting by threatening to terminate their operation if total reported cost is too high. Termination reduces the profit that can be generated on both inputs. Under component production, a firm that exaggerates its cost risks only the profit it might secure from producing a single input. Each supplier ignores the potential loss in profit its own cost exaggeration may impose on the other supplier, and so is not sufficiently reticent about cost exaggeration. In contrast, under integrated production, the single supplier considers the entire loss in profit that cost exaggeration may engender, and so is more reluctant to exaggerate costs.[238]

[237] Baron and Besanko (1992) and Gilbert and Riordan (1995) show that the regulator's preference for integrated production persists in some settings where consumer demand for the final product is not perfectly inelastic. However, Da Rocha and de Frutos (1999) report that the regulator may prefer component production to integrated production when the supports of the independent cost realizations are sufficiently disparate.

[238] This result might be viewed as the informational analogue of the well-known conclusion that component production of complementary products results in higher (unregulated) prices and lower welfare than integrated production – see Cournot (1927). As such, the result for complementary products is perhaps less surprising than the corresponding result for independent products.

4.5.3. Substitute products

To identify a setting in which component production is preferred to integrated production, suppose consumers view the two products as perfect substitutes.[239] Further suppose that consumers wish to consume at most one unit of the product. The cost of producing this unit can be either low (c_L) or high (c_H). The probability of a low cost realization is ϕ, and the production costs for the two versions of the product are independently distributed. The regulator wishes to ensure supply of the product, and is considering whether to mandate integrated production (where a single firm supplies both versions of the product) or component production.

Under integrated production, the regulator must deliver transfer payment c_H to the single firm to ensure the product is supplied. Consequently, the firm secures rent Δ^c unless its cost of producing each version of the product is c_H, which occurs with probability $(1-\phi)^2$. The integrated firm's expected rent is therefore

$$R_{INT} = \big(1 - (1-\phi)^2\big)\Delta^c.$$

Under component production, the regulator can ensure the supply of the product by employing the auction mechanism described in Section 4.2 (specialized to the case of inelastic demand). Expression (90) shows that the industry rent with component production is

$$R_{COMP} = \phi(1-\phi)\Delta^c.$$

Rent is clearly lower under component production than under integrated production. Thus, the rent-reducing benefit of competition provides a strict preference for component production (i.e., for competition) over integrated production when products are close substitutes.

4.5.4. Conclusion

The simple environments considered in this section suggest two broad conclusions regarding the optimal structure of a regulated industry. First, component production will tend to be preferred to integrated production when the costs of producing inputs are highly correlated, since the yardstick competition that component production admits can limit rent effectively. Second, integrated production will tend to be preferred to component production when the components are better viewed as complements than

[239] The following discussion is closely related to the discussion in Section 4.4.1, where demand is inelastic. The differences are that here: (i) the integrated monopoly firm has two chances to obtain a low cost realization (so there is no sampling benefit of competition); (ii) the duopoly is regulated; and (iii) the duopoly firms do not know each other's cost realization.

as substitutes. In this case, integrated production can avoid what might be viewed as a double marginalization of rents that arises under component production.[240,241]

4.6. *Regulating quality with competing suppliers*

When a firm's service quality is verifiable, standard auction procedures for monopoly franchises can be modified to induce the delivery of high quality services. For example, the regulator can announce a rule that specifies how bids on multiple dimensions of performance (e.g., price and service quality) will be translated into a uni-dimensional score. The regulator can also announce the privileges and obligations that will be assigned to the firm that submits the winning score. For example, the winning bidder might be required to implement either the exact performance levels that he bid or the corresponding performance promised by the bidder with the second-highest score. The optimal scoring rule generally does not simply reflect customers' actual valuations of the relevant multiple performance dimensions. Different implicit valuations are employed to help account for the different costs of motivating different performance levels. These costs include the rents that potential producers can command from their superior knowledge of their ability to secure performance on multiple dimensions.[242]

The regulator's task is more difficult when a firm's performance on all relevant dimensions of service quality is not readily measured. In this case, financial rewards and penalties cannot be linked directly to the levels of delivered service quality. When quality is not verifiable, standard procedures such as competitive bidding that work well to select least-cost providers may not secure high levels of service quality. A competitive bidding procedure may award a monopoly franchise to a producer not because the producer is more able to serve customers at low cost, but because the producer's low costs reflect the limited service quality it delivers to customers. Consequently, when quality is not verifiable, consumers may be better served when the regulator engages in individual negotiations with a randomly chosen firm than when he implements a competitive bidding process.[243]

[240] See Severinov (2003) for a more detailed analysis of the effects of substitutability or complementarity on the relative merits of component and integrated production. Cost information is assumed to be uncorrelated across the two activities, so there is no potential for yardstick comparisons. The paper also discusses an industry configuration in which the regulator deals with one firm, which sub-contracts with the second firm.

[241] Iossa (1999) analyzes a model where the information asymmetries concern consumer demand rather than cost and where only one firm has private information under component production. In this framework, integrated production tends to be preferred when the products are substitutes whereas component production tends to be preferred when the products are complements.

[242] See Che (1993), Cripps and Ireland (1994) and Branco (1997) for details. Asker and Cantillon (2005) consider a setting where firms have multi-dimensional private information about their costs of supply.

[243] Manelli and Vincent (1995) derive this conclusion in a setting where potential suppliers are privately informed about the exogenous quality of their product. Their conclusion that it is optimal to assign the same probability of operation to all potential suppliers is related to the conclusion in Section 2.3.3 regarding the optimality of pooling. In Manelli and Vincent's model, incentive compatibility considerations imply that a

Unverifiable quality need not be as constraining when production by multiple suppliers is economical. In this case, if consumers can observe the level of quality delivered by each supplier (even though quality is unverifiable), market competition can help to ensure that reasonably high levels of quality and reasonably low prices arise in equilibrium.[244,245]

4.7. Conclusions

The discussion in this section has delivered two key messages. First, actual or potential competition can greatly assist a regulator in his attempts to secure a high level of consumer surplus. Competition can serve to reduce industry operating costs and reduce the rents of industry operators. Second, competition can complicate the design of regulatory policy considerably. For example, unregulated competitors may undermine pricing structures that are designed to recover fixed operating costs efficiently or to pursue distributional objectives. The presence of multiple potential operators also introduces complex considerations with regard to the design of industry structure.[246] The optimal design of regulatory policy in the presence of potential or actual competition can entail many subtleties and can require significant knowledge of the environments in which regulated and unregulated suppliers operate. An important area for future research is the design of regulatory policy when the regulator has little information about the nature and extent of competitive forces.

firm with a low-quality product, and thus low operating costs, must be selected to operate at least as often as is a firm with a high-quality product, and thus high operating costs. However, welfare is higher when high-quality products are produced. This fundamental conflict between what incentive compatibility concerns render feasible and what is optimal is resolved by a compromise in which all potential suppliers have the same probability of being selected to operate, regardless of their costs (and thus the quality of their product). Hart, Shleifer and Vishny (1997) provide the related observation that when key performance dimensions are not contractible, supply by a public enterprise may be preferable to supply by a private enterprise. The public enterprise's reduced focus on profit can lead it to supply a higher level of the costly non-contractible performance dimension (e.g., quality) than the private enterprise.

[244] Because imperfect competition generally directs too few consumers to the most efficient producer, a regulator with substantial knowledge of firms' costs and consumers' preferences may prefer to set market boundaries for individual producers rather than allow market competition to determine these boundaries. [See Anton and Gertler (2004).] When the regulator's information is more limited, he may prefer to allow competitive forces to determine the customers that each firm serves. (See Wolinsky (1997).)

[245] In network settings where the final quality delivered to consumers depends on the quality of all network components, producers of some network components may "free-ride" on the quality delivered by the producers of other network components. Consequently, realized quality may fall below the ideal level of quality, and a regulator may optimally allow monopoly supply of all network components in order to overcome the free-rider problem. See Auriol (1998) for further details.

[246] Industry structure, in turn, can affect realized service quality. In the electric power industry, for example, recent trends toward vertical disintegration and reduced horizontal concentration have led to concerns about system reliability. See Joskow (1997, 2004), for example.

5. Vertical relationships

Regulated industries rarely take the simple form that has been assumed throughout much of the preceding discussion. Regulated industries often encompass several complementary segments that differ in their potential for competition.[247] For instance, an industry might optimally entail monopolistic supply of essential inputs (e.g., network access) but admit competitive supply of retail services. In such a setting, competitors will require access to the inputs produced in the monopolistic sector if they are to offer retail services to consumers.

Figure 27.4 illustrates two important policy issues that arise in such a setting. The first question, addressed in Section 5.1, concerns the terms on which rivals should be afforded access to the inputs supplied by the monopolist. A key consideration is how these terms should vary according to the extent of the monopolist's participation in the retail market, whether the monopolist's retail tariff is regulated, whether rivals can operate using inputs other than the input supplied by the monopolist, and whether the rivals are regulated. The second question, addressed in Section 5.2, is whether the monopolist should be permitted to operate in the potentially competitive retail market. Section 5.3 extends the discussion of access pricing to a setting where competing firms wish to purchase essential inputs from each other.

The discussion in most of this section presumes the regulator is fully informed about industry demand and cost conditions. This departure from preceding discussions reflects both the focus in the literature and the complexity of the issues raised by vertical relationships even in the presence of complete information.

5.1. One-way access pricing

Before analyzing (in Section 5.1.2) the optimal access pricing policy when the monopolist is vertically integrated, consider the simpler case where the input supplier does not operate downstream.[248] If the downstream industry is competitive in the sense that there is a negligible markup of the retail price over marginal cost, then pricing access at cost is approximately optimal. The reason is that the markup of the retail price over the total cost of providing the end-to-end service will be close to zero in this setting. In contrast, if the downstream market is not perfectly competitive, it may be optimal (if feasible) to price access below cost in order to induce lower downstream prices, which exceed marginal costs due to the imperfect competition.

[247] For an account of the theory of vertical relationships in an unregulated context, see Rey and Tirole (2007).

[248] See, for instance, Armstrong, Cowan and Vickers (1994, Section 5.2.1) and Laffont and Tirole (2000, Section 2.2.5). See Armstrong (2002, Section 2) for a more detailed account of the theory of access pricing, from which Section 5.1 is taken. See Vogelsang (2003) for a complementary review of the recent literature on access pricing in network industries. Section 5.1 abstracts from the possibility that the monopolist may try to disadvantage downstream rivals using various non-price instruments. Section 5.2 considers this possibility.

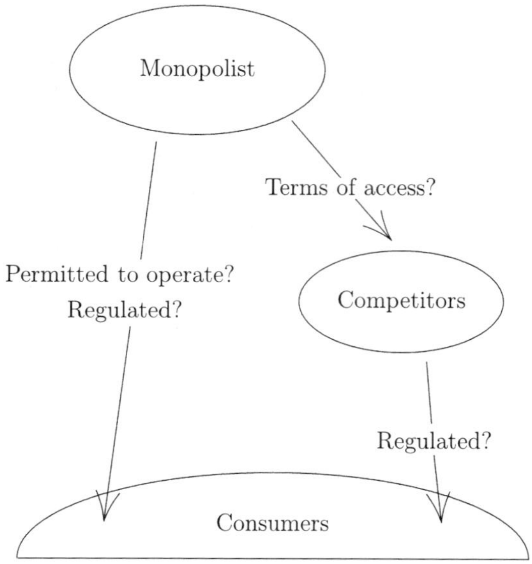

Figure 27.4. Vertical relationships.

5.1.1. *The effect of distorted retail tariffs*

The retail prices charged by regulated firms often depart significantly from underlying marginal costs. Section 4.3 suggested two reasons for such divergence. First, marginal-cost prices will generate negative profit for a firm that operates with increasing returns to scale. Second, regulated retail tariffs may be set to promote universal service or to redistribute income. The ensuing discussion in this section considers the impact on welfare and entry of regulated prices that diverge from cost.

The interaction between distorted tariffs and entry is illustrated most simply by abstracting from vertical issues. Therefore, suppose initially that the regulated firm's rivals do not need access to any inputs supplied by the regulated firm to provide their services. As in Section 4.3, consider a competitive fringe model in which the same service is offered by a group of rivals. Competition within the fringe means that the competitors' prices reflect their operating costs, and the fringe makes no profit.[249]

Suppose the fringe and the regulated firm offer differentiated products to final consumers. Let P and p denote the regulated firm's price and the fringe's price for their respective retail services. (Throughout this section, variables that pertain to the regulated firm will be indicated by upper-case letters. Variables that pertain to the fringe

[249] If entrants had market power, access charges should be chosen with the additional aim of controlling the retail prices of entrants. This would typically lead to a reduction in access charges. The lower input costs reduce equilibrium prices, thereby counteracting the entrants' market power. See Laffont and Tirole (2000, Section 3.3.1) for a discussion of this issue.

will be denoted by lower-case letters.) Let $V(P, p)$ be total consumer surplus when prices P and p are offered. The consumer surplus function satisfies the envelope conditions $V_P(P, p) = -X(P, p)$ and $V_p(P, p) = -x(P, p)$, where $X(\cdot,\cdot)$ and $x(\cdot,\cdot)$ are, respectively, the demand functions for the services of the regulated firm and the fringe. (Subscripts denote partial derivatives.) Assume the two services are substitutes, so $X_p(\cdot, \cdot) \equiv x_P(\cdot, \cdot) \geqslant 0$. The regulated firm has constant marginal cost C_1 and the fringe has marginal (and average) cost c. To implement the optimal output from the fringe, suppose the regulator levies a per-unit output tax t on the fringe's service. Then competition within the fringe ensures the fringe's equilibrium price is $p = c + t$. Suppose the regulated firm's price is fixed exogenously at P. Also suppose the regulator seeks to maximize total unweighted surplus (including tax revenue).[250] Total surplus in this setting is

$$W = \underbrace{V(P, c+t)}_{\text{consumer surplus}} + \underbrace{tx(P, c+t)}_{\text{tax revenue}} + \underbrace{(P - C_1)X(P, c+t)}_{\text{regulated firm's profits}}. \tag{96}$$

Maximizing W with respect to t reveals the optimal output tax for the fringe is

$$t = \sigma_d(P - C_1), \tag{97}$$

where

$$\sigma_d = \frac{X_p}{-x_p} \geqslant 0 \tag{98}$$

is a measure of the substitutability of the two retail services. In particular, σ_d measures the reduction in the demand for the regulated firm's service when the fringe supplies one additional unit of its service (and where this increase in fringe supply is caused by a corresponding reduction in its price p). If increased fringe supply comes primarily from reduced sales by the regulated incumbent, then $\sigma_d \approx 1$. If increased fringe supply largely reflects an expansion of total output with little reduction in the regulated firm's output, then $\sigma_d \approx 0$. Equation (97) implies that when sales are profitable for the regulated firm ($P > C_1$) it is optimal to raise the fringe's price above cost as well ($t > 0$). This is because profits are socially valuable, and when $P > C_1$ it is optimal to stimulate demand for the regulated firm's service in order to increase its profit. This stimulation is achieved by increasing the fringe's price. A *laissez-faire* policy towards entry ($t = 0$) would induce excessive fringe supply if the market is profitable for the regulated firm and insufficient fringe supply if the regulated firm incurs a loss in the market. Of course, if the regulated firm's price reflects its cost ($P = C_1$), then there is no need to impose an output tax on the fringe.

In expression (97), the tax t is set equal to the profit the regulated firm foregoes when fringe supply increases by a unit. This lost profit (or "opportunity cost") is the product

[250] Because there is no asymmetric information in this analysis, there is no reason to leave the regulated firm with rent. Consequently, maximization of total surplus is an appropriate objective.

of: (1) the regulated firm's unit profit $(P - C_1)$ from the sale of its product; and (2) σ_d, the reduction in the regulated firm's final sales caused by increasing fringe output by one unit. If the services are not close substitutes (σ_d is close to zero), this optimal tax should also be close to zero, and a *laissez-faire* policy towards rivals is nearly optimal. This is because a tax on the fringe's sales has little impact on the welfare associated with the sales of the regulated firm, and therefore there is little benefit from causing the fringe's price to diverge from cost.[251]

5.1.2. *Access pricing with exogenous retail prices for the monopolist*

Now return to our primary focus on vertically-related markets where the fringe requires access to inputs supplied monopolistically by the regulated firm. This section considers how best to set access prices, given the prevailing tariff for the monopolist's retail products. Ideally, a regulator would set retail prices and access prices simultaneously. (See Section 5.1.3.) However, in practice, retail tariffs often are dictated by historical, political, or social considerations, and regulators are compelled to set access prices, taking retail tariffs as given.

Suppose the monopolist supplies its retail service at constant marginal cost C_1, and supplies its access service to the fringe at constant marginal cost C_2. Let P denote the (exogenous) price for the monopolist's retail service and a denote the per-unit price paid by the fringe for access to the monopolist's input. Suppose that when it pays price a for access the fringe has the constant marginal cost $\psi(a)$ for producing a unit of its own retail service. (The cost $\psi(a)$ includes the payment a per unit of access to the monopolist.) If the fringe cannot bypass the monopolist's access service, so that exactly one unit of access is needed for each unit of its final product, then $\psi(a) \equiv a + c$, where c is the fringe's cost of converting the input into its retail product. If the fringe can substitute away from the access service, then $\psi(a)$ is a concave function of a. Note that $\psi'(a)$ is the fringe's demand for access per unit of its retail service (by Shephard's lemma). Therefore, when it supplies x units of service to consumers, the fringe's demand for access is $\psi'(a)x$. Note also that the end-to-end marginal cost of supplying one unit of the fringe's output when the price for access is a is[252]

$$\hat{c}(a) \equiv \psi(a) - (a - C_2)\psi'(a). \tag{99}$$

[251] Given the welfare function (96), it makes little difference whether the proceeds from the tax t are passed directly to the regulated firm, to the government, or into an industry fund. If the regulated firm has historically used the proceeds from a profitable activity to finance loss-making activities or to cover its fixed costs, then the firm will not face funding problems as a result of the fringe's entry if the fringe pays the tax to the firm. A more transparent mechanism would be to use a "universal service" fund to finance loss-making services. See Armstrong (2002, Section 2.1) for details. More generally, see Braeutigam (1979, 1984) and Laffont and Tirole (1993b, ch. 5) for discussions of Ramsey pricing in the presence of competition, including cases where rivals are regulated.

[252] The fringe incurs the per-unit cost $\psi(a)$, while for each unit of fringe supply the monopolist receives revenue from the fringe equal to $a\psi'(a)$ and incurs the production cost $C_2\psi'(a)$.

Whenever the fringe has some ability to substitute away from the monopolist's input, i.e., when $\psi'' \neq 0$, the access pricing policy that minimizes the fringe supply cost $\hat{c}(a)$ entails marginal-cost pricing of access: $a = C_2$. Only in this case will the fringe make the efficient input choice. In the special case where the fringe cannot substitute away from the monopolist's input ($\psi(a) \equiv a + c$), the choice of a has no impact on productive efficiency and $\hat{c}(a) \equiv C_2 + c$.

The following analysis proceeds in two stages. First, the optimal policy is derived in the case where the regulator has a full range of policy instruments with which to pursue his objectives. Second, the optimal policy is analyzed in the setting where the regulator's sole instrument is the price of access.

Regulated fringe price Suppose the regulator can control both the price of access and the fringe's retail price. When the regulator levies a per-unit output tax t on the fringe, its retail price is $p = t + \psi(a)$. Then, much as in expression (96), total welfare is

$$W = \underbrace{V\big(P, t + \psi(a)\big)}_{\text{consumer surplus}} + \underbrace{(P - C_1)X\big(P, t + \psi(a)\big)}_{\text{monopoly's profits from retail}} + \underbrace{(a - C_2)\psi'(a)x\big(P, t + \psi(a)\big)}_{\text{monopoly's profits from access}} + \underbrace{tx\big(P, t + \psi(a)\big)}_{\text{tax revenue}}. \tag{100}$$

Since $p = t + \psi(a)$, the regulator can be viewed as choosing p and a rather than t and a. In this case, expression (100) simplifies to

$$W = V(P, p) + (P - C_1)X(P, p) + \big(p - \hat{c}(a)\big)x(P, p), \tag{101}$$

where $\hat{c}(\cdot)$ is given in expression (99). Since a does not affect any other aspect of welfare in expression (101), a should be chosen to minimize $\hat{c}(\cdot)$. In particular, whenever the fringe can substitute away from the monopolist's input ($\psi''(a) \neq 0$), it is optimal to set $a = C_2$. Also, maximizing expression (101) with respect to $p = t + \psi(a)$ yields formula (97) for the output tax t. In sum, the optimal policy involves

$$a = C_2; \qquad t = \sigma_d(P - C_1). \tag{102}$$

When the regulator can utilize an output tax to control the fringe's supply, access should be priced at cost, and the fringe's output tax should be equal to the monopolist's opportunity cost of fringe supply, as given in (97). In contrast, if the fringe had access to the monopolist's input at cost but did not have to pay an output tax, then (just as in Section 5.1.1) there would be excess fringe supply if $P > C_1$ and insufficient fringe supply if $P < C_1$. There would, however, be no productive inefficiency under this policy, and the fringe's service would be supplied at minimum cost. As before, if the monopolist's retail price is equal to its cost ($P = C_1$), there is no need to regulate the fringe and a policy to allow entrants to purchase access at marginal cost is optimal.

Provided the regulator has enough policy instruments to pursue all relevant objectives, there is no need to sacrifice productive efficiency even when the monopolist's retail price differs from its cost. An output tax on rivals can be used to counteract incumbent retail tariffs that diverge from cost, while pricing access at marginal cost can ensure productive efficiency in rival supply.

Unregulated fringe price Now consider the optimal policy when the access price is the sole instrument available to the regulator.[253] In this case, $t = 0$ in (100), and welfare when the price for access is a is

$$W = \underbrace{V\big(P, \psi(a)\big)}_{\text{consumer surplus}} + \underbrace{(P - C_1)X\big(P, \psi(a)\big)}_{\text{monopoly's profits from retail}} + \underbrace{(a - C_2)\psi'(a)x\big(P, \psi(a)\big)}_{\text{monopoly's profits from access}}. \quad (103)$$

Notice that in this setting, the only way the regulator can ensure a high price for the fringe's output (perhaps because he wishes to protect the monopolist's socially valuable profit as outlined in Section 5.1.1) is to set a high price for access. The high access price typically will cause some productive inefficiency in fringe supply.

Maximizing expression (103) with respect to a reveals that the optimal price of access is

$$a = C_2 + \sigma(P - C_1), \quad (104)$$

where

$$\sigma = \frac{X_p \psi'(a)}{-z_a} \geqslant 0 \quad (105)$$

and $z(P, a) \equiv \psi'(a)x(P, \psi(a))$ is the fringe's demand for access. The "displacement ratio" σ measures the reduction in demand for the monopolist's retail service caused by supplying the marginal unit of access to the fringe.[254] Therefore, expression (104) states that the price of access should be equal to the cost of access, C_2, plus the monopolist's foregone profit (opportunity cost) caused by supplying a unit of access to its rivals. This rule is sometimes known as the "efficient component pricing rule" (or ECPR).[255]

Considerable information is required to calculate the displacement ratio σ. In practice, a regulator may have difficulty estimating this ratio accurately. The social costs of the estimation errors can be mitigated by bringing the monopolist's retail price P closer to its cost, C_1. From expression (104), doing so lessens the dependence of the access price on σ. As before, if $P = C_1$, it is optimal to price access at cost.

In the special case where consumer demands for the two retail services are approximately independent (so $X_p(\cdot,\cdot) \approx 0$), formula (104) states that the access price

[253] This discussion is based on Armstrong, Doyle and Vickers (1996).

[254] The access charge a must fall by $1/z_a$ to expand the fringe demand for access by one unit. This reduction in a causes X to decline by $X_p\psi'/z_a$.

[255] This rule appears to have been proposed first in Willig (1979). See Baumol (1983), Baumol and Sidak (1994a, 1994b), Baumol, Ordover and Willig (1997), Sidak and Spulber (1997), and Armstrong (2002, Section 2.3.1) for further discussions of the ECPR.

should involve no mark-up over the cost of providing access, even if $P \neq C_1$. In other cases, however, the optimal price for access is not equal to the associated cost. Consequently, there is productive inefficiency whenever there is some scope for substitution ($\psi''(a) \neq 0$). The inefficiency arises because a single instrument, the access price, is forced to perform two functions – to protect the monopolist's socially valuable profit, and to induce fringe operators to employ an efficient mix of inputs – and the regulator must compromise between these two objectives.

This analysis is simplified in the special case where the fringe cannot substitute away from the monopolist's input, so $\psi(a) \equiv c + a$. In this case, expression (104) becomes

$$a = C_2 + \sigma_d(P - C_1), \tag{106}$$

where σ_d is the demand substitution parameter given in expression (98). Expression (106) states that the optimal access price is the sum of the cost of providing access and the optimal output tax given in expression (97). Thus, an alternative way to implement the optimum in this case would be to price access at cost (C_2) and simultaneously levy a tax on the output of rivals, as in expression (102). When exactly one unit of access is needed to produce one unit of fringe output (so there is no scope for productive inefficiency), this output tax could also be levied on the input. In this case, the regulator's lack of policy instruments is not constraining. More generally, however, the regulator can achieve a strictly higher level of welfare if he can choose both an output tax and an access price.

5.1.3. Ramsey pricing

Now consider the optimal simultaneous choice of the monopolist's retail and access prices.[256] The optimal policy will again depend on whether rivals can substitute away from the input, and, if they can, on the range of policy instruments available to the regulator.

Regulated fringe price Suppose first that the regulator can set the price for the monopolist's retail product P, impose a per-unit output tax t on the fringe, and set price a for the input. Also suppose the proceeds of the output tax are used to contribute to the financing of the monopolist's fixed costs. As before, the price of the fringe's product is equal to the perceived marginal cost, so $p = t + \psi(a)$. The regulator can again be considered to choose p rather than t. Letting $\lambda \geqslant 0$ be the Lagrange multiplier on the monopolist's profit constraint, the regulator's problem is to choose P, p and a to maximize

$$W = V(P, p) + (1 + \lambda)\big[(P - C_1)X(P, p) + \big(p - \hat{c}(a)\big)x(P, p)\big]. \tag{107}$$

[256] See Laffont and Tirole (1994) and Armstrong, Doyle and Vickers (1996).

For any retail prices, P and p, the access price a affects only the production cost of the fringe. Consequently, a should be chosen to minimize the cost of providing the fringe's service, $\hat{c}(a)$. As before, whenever the fringe can substitute away from the input ($\psi'' \neq 0$), the optimal policy is to price access at cost (so $a = C_2$).[257] The two retail prices, P and p, are then chosen to maximize total surplus subject to the monopolist's profit constraint.

Unregulated fringe price Now suppose the regulator cannot impose an output tax on the fringe. In this case, $p = \psi(a)$, and the access price takes on the dual role of attempting to ensure the fringe employs an efficient input mix and influencing the fringe retail price in a desirable way. Following the same logic that underlies expressions (103) and (107), welfare in this setting can be written as

$$\begin{aligned} W = V\big(P, \psi(a)\big) + (1+\lambda)\big[(P - C_1)X\big(P, \psi(a)\big) \\ + (a - C_2)\psi'(a)x\big(P, \psi(a)\big)\big]. \end{aligned} \tag{108}$$

The first-order condition for maximizing expression (108) with respect to a is

$$a = \underbrace{C_2 + \sigma(P - C_1)}_{\text{ECPR price}} + \left[\frac{\lambda}{1+\lambda}\right]\frac{a}{\eta_z}, \tag{109}$$

where σ is given in expression (105), $\eta_z = -az_a/z > 0$ is the own-price elasticity of demand for access, and P is the Ramsey price for the monopolist's retail service. Expression (109) states that the optimal access price is given by the ECPR expression (104), which would be optimal if the monopolist's retail price were exogenously fixed at P, plus a Ramsey markup that is inversely related to the elasticity of fringe demand for access. This Ramsey markup reflects the benefits (in terms of a reduction in P) caused by increasing the revenue generated by selling access to the fringe. One can show that the Ramsey pricing policy entails $P > C_1$ and $a > C_2$, and so access is priced above marginal cost. Thus, a degree of productive inefficiency arises whenever the fringe can substitute away from the monopolist's input. As in Section 5.1.2, when the access price is called upon to perform multiple tasks, a compromise is inevitable.

5.1.4. Unregulated retail prices

Now consider how best to price access when the access price is the regulator's only instrument. Suppose the monopolist can set its preferred retail price P.[258] In addition,

[257] This is just an instance of the general principle that productive efficiency is optimally induced when the policy maker has a sufficient number of control instruments at his disposal. See Diamond and Mirrlees (1971).
[258] This discussion is adapted from Laffont and Tirole (1994, Section 7) and Armstrong and Vickers (1998). For other analyses of access pricing with an unregulated downstream sector, see Economides and White (1995), Lewis and Sappington (1999), Lapuerta and Tye (1999), and Sappington (2005a), for example.

suppose the fringe's price is unregulated, and the regulator cannot impose an output tax on the fringe. As before, if the regulator sets the access price a, the fringe's price is $p = \psi(a)$. Given a, the monopolist will set its retail price P to maximize its total profit

$$\Pi = (P - C_1)X\big(P, \psi(a)\big) + (a - C_2)\psi'(a)x\big(P, \psi(a)\big).$$

Let $\bar{P}(a)$ denote the monopolist's profit-maximizing retail price given access price a. The firm generally will set a higher retail price when the price of access is higher (so $\bar{P}'(a) > 0$). This is the case because the more profit the monopolist anticipates from selling access to its rivals, the less aggressively the firm will compete with rivals at the retail level. Social welfare is given by expression (103), where the monopolist's price P is given by $\bar{P}(a)$. The welfare-maximizing access price in this setting satisfies

$$a = \underbrace{C_2 + \sigma\big(\bar{P}(a) - C_1\big)}_{\text{ECPR price}} - \frac{X\bar{P}'}{-z_a}, \tag{110}$$

where σ is given in expression (105). Equation (110) reveals that the optimal access price in this setting is below the level in the ECPR expression (104), which characterizes the optimal access price in the setting where the monopolist's retail price was fixed at $\bar{P}(a)$. The lower access charge is optimal here because a reduction in a causes the retail price P to fall towards cost, which increases welfare.[259]

In general, it is difficult to determine whether the price of access, a, is optimally set above, at, or below the marginal cost of providing access, C_2. However, there are three special cases where the price of access should equal cost: (1) when the fringe has no ability to substitute away from the input ($\psi(a) \equiv a + c$) and the demand functions $X(\cdot,\cdot)$ and $x(\cdot,\cdot)$ are linear; (2) when the monopolist and fringe operate in separate retail markets, with no cross-price effects[260]; and (3) when the fringe and the monopolist offer the same homogeneous product, i.e., when the retail market is potentially perfectly competitive. To understand the third (and most interesting) of these cases, consider a setting where consumers purchase from the supplier that offers the lowest retail price. If the price of access is a, the fringe will supply consumers whenever the monopolist offers a retail price greater than the fringe's cost, $\psi(a)$. Therefore, given a, the monopolist has two options. First, it can preclude fringe entry by setting a retail price just below $\psi(a)$. Doing so ensures it a profit of $\psi(a) - C_1$ per unit of retail output. Second, the monopolist can choose not to supply the retail market itself, and simply sell access to the fringe. By following this strategy, the monopolist secures profit $(a - C_2)\psi'(a)$ per unit of retail output. The monopolist will choose to accommodate entry if and only if the

[259] By contrast, it was optimal to raise the access charge above (104) in the Ramsey problem – see expression (109) above. This is because an increase in the access charge allowed the incumbent's retail price to fall, since the access service then financed more of the regulated firm's costs.

[260] The profit-maximizing retail price $\bar{P}$ does not depend on a in this case. Also, since $\sigma = 0$, expression (110) implies that marginal-cost pricing of access is optimal.

latter profit margin exceeds the former, i.e., if

$$C_1 \geqslant \hat{c}(a),$$

where $\hat{c}(\cdot)$ is given in expression (99). Therefore, the monopolist will allow entry by the fringe if and only if retail supply by the fringe is less costly than supply by the monopolist (when the access price is a). Perhaps surprisingly, then, the choice of access price does not bias competition for or against the fringe in this setting. The reason is that, although the monopolist's actual cost of supplying consumers is C_1, its opportunity cost of supplying consumers is $\hat{c}(a)$, since it then foregoes the profits from selling access to the fringe.[261] However, the choice of access price has a direct effect on the equilibrium retail price, which is $\psi(a)$ regardless of which firm supplies consumers. Consequently, when the fringe firms are the more efficient suppliers (i.e., $\psi(C_2) \leqslant C_1$), it is optimal to provide access to the fringe at cost. Doing so will ensure a retail price equal to the minimum cost of production and supply by the least-cost supplier.[262]

More generally, when the monopolist has some market power in the retail market, the optimal access price will equal marginal cost only in knife-edge cases. Clear-cut results are difficult to obtain in this framework because the access price is called upon to perform three tasks. It serves: (i) to control the market power of the monopolist (a lower value of a induces a lower value for the monopolist's retail price P); (ii) to protect the monopolist's socially valuable profit (as discussed in Section 5.1.1); and (iii) to pursue productive efficiency for the fringe (which requires $a = C_2$) whenever there is a possibility for substituting away from the input. In general, tasks (i) and (iii) argue for an access price no higher than cost. (When $a = C_2$ the monopolist will choose $P > C_1$. Setting $a < C_2$ will reduce its retail price towards cost. Task (iii) will mitigate, but not reverse, this incentive.) However, unless a is chosen to be so low that $P < C_1$, task (ii) will give the regulator an incentive to raise a above cost – see expression (104). These counteracting forces preclude unambiguous conclusions regarding the relative magnitudes of the optimal price of access and the cost of providing access in unregulated retail markets.

5.1.5. Discussion

Setting access prices equal to the cost of providing access offers two primary advantages. First, at least in settings where the monopolist's costs are readily estimated, this

[261] Sappington (2005a) presents a model where, given the price of access, an entrant decides whether to purchase the input from the monopolist before the two firms compete to supply consumers. The entrant's "make-or-buy" decision is shown not to depend on the price of access, as the entrant chooses to buy the input from the monopolist whenever this is the efficient choice. Therefore, the access price does not affect productive efficiency, but does affect equilibrium retail prices.

[262] If industry costs are lower when the monopolist serves the market even when the fringe can purchase access at cost (i.e., if $\psi(C_2) > C_1$), then it is optimal to subsidize access (to be precise, to set the access charge to satisfy $\psi(a) = C_1$) so that competition forces the monopolist to price its retail service at its own cost.

policy is relatively simple to implement. In particular, no information about consumer demand or rivals' characteristics is needed to calculate these prices (at least in the simple models presented above).[263] Of course, it can be difficult to measure the monopolist's costs accurately in practice, especially when the firm produces multiple products and makes durable investments.[264] Second, pricing access at cost can help to ensure that rivals adopt cost-minimizing production policies. If access is priced above cost, an entrant may construct its own network rather than purchase network services from the regulated firm, even though the latter policy entails lower social cost.[265]

In simple terms, cost-based access prices are appropriate when access prices do not need to perform the role of correcting for distortions in the monopolist's retail tariff. There are three main settings in which such a task may not be necessary:

1. If the monopolist's retail tariff reflects its marginal costs, no corrective measures are needed. In particular, access prices should reflect the marginal costs of providing access. Thus, a complete rebalancing of the monopolist's tariff (so retail prices reflect costs) can greatly simplify input pricing policies, and allow access prices to focus on the task of ensuring productive efficiency.
2. If there are distortions in the regulated tariff, but corrections to this are made by using another regulatory instrument (such as output taxes levied on rivals), then access prices should reflect costs.
3. When the monopolist operates in a vigorously competitive retail market and is free to set its own retail tariff, pricing access at cost can be optimal.

In settings other than these, pricing access at cost generally is not optimal.

5.2. Vertical structure

The second important policy issue is whether to allow the monopoly supplier of a regulated input to integrate downstream to supply a final product to consumers in com-

[263] See Hausman and Sidak (2005) for a more general treatment of this issue.

[264] Sidak and Spulber (1997), Hausman (1997), and Hausman and Sidak (1999, 2005), among others, discuss how the cost of capital and the irreversibility of capital investment affect the cost of providing access. They note that the cost of capital tends to increase in competitive settings, since an incumbent's capital investment may be stranded in a competitive environment. Hausman also emphasizes the asymmetric advantage an entrant may be afforded when it can purchase access at a cost that does not fully reflect the risk an incumbent supplier faces. While the incumbent must invest before all the relevant uncertainty is resolved, the entrant often can wait to decide whether to make or buy the input until after the uncertainty is resolved. Also see Laffont and Tirole (2000, Section 4.4).

[265] A bias in the opposite direction has been alleged when regulators use forms of forward-looking cost-based access pricing. In the United States, the Federal Communications Commission has decided that the major incumbent suppliers of local exchange services must unbundle network elements and make these elements available to competing suppliers at prices that reflect the incumbent's total element long-run incremental cost (TELRIC). Mandy (2002) and Mandy and Sharkey (2003), among others, explore the calculation of TELRIC prices. Hausman (1997), Kahn, Tardiff and Weisman (1999), and Weisman (2002), among others, criticize TELRIC pricing of network elements, arguing that TELRIC prices provide little incentive for competitors to build their own networks and that, in practice, regulators do not have the information required to calculate appropriate TELRIC prices.

petition with other suppliers.[266] Downstream integration by a monopoly input supplier can alter industry performance in two main ways. First, it can influence directly the welfare generated in the retail market by changing the composition of, and the nature of competition in, the retail market. Second, downstream integration can affect the incentives of the monopolist, and thereby influence indirectly the welfare generated in both the upstream and downstream industries.

First consider the effects of altering the composition of the retail sector. If retail competition is imperfect, retail supply by the input monopolist can enhance competition, thereby reducing price and increasing both output and welfare in the retail market.[267] The welfare increase can be particularly pronounced if the monopolist can supply the retail service at lower cost than other retailers.[268] Furthermore, downstream production by the input monopolist can deter some potential suppliers from entering the industry and thereby avoid duplicative fixed costs of production.[269]

Now consider how the opportunity to operate downstream can affect the incentives of the input monopolist. When it competes directly in the retail market, the monopolist generally will anticipate greater profit from its retail operations as the costs of its rivals increase. Therefore, the integrated firm may seek to increase the costs of its retail rivals. It can do this in at least two ways. First, if the regulator is uncertain about the monopolist's cost of supplying the input, the monopolist may seek to raise the costs of downstream rivals by exaggerating its input cost. If the monopolist can convince the regulator that its upstream production costs are high, the regulator may raise the price of the input, thereby increasing the operating costs of downstream competitors.[270] By increasing the incentive of the monopolist to exaggerate its access costs in this manner, vertical integration can complicate the regulator's critical control problem.[271]

Second, the integrated firm may be able to raise its rivals' costs by degrading the quality of the input it supplies, by delaying access to its input, or by imposing burdensome purchasing requirements on downstream producers, for example.[272] The regulator can affect the monopolist's incentive to raise the costs of its downstream rivals through the

[266] Section 3.5.2 discusses the merits of allowing a regulated supplier to diversify into horizontally related markets.

[267] See Hinton et al. (1998) and Weisman and Williams (2001) for assessments of this effect in the United States telecommunications industry.

[268] See Lee and Hamilton (1999).

[269] See Vickers (1995a).

[270] Bourreau and Dogan (2001) consider a dynamic model in which an incumbent vertically-integrated supplier may wish to set an access charge that is unduly low. The low access charge induces retail competitors to employ the incumbent's old technology rather than invest in a more modern, superior technology.

[271] Vickers (1995a) analyzes this effect in detail. Lee and Hamilton (1999) extend Vickers' analysis to allow the regulator to condition his decision about whether to allow integration on the monopolist's reported costs.

[272] Economides (1998) examines a setting in which the incentives for raising rivals' costs in this manner are particularly pronounced. Also see Reiffen, Schumann and Ward (2000), Laffont and Tirole (2000, Section 4.5), Mandy (2000), Beard, Kaserman and Mayo (2001), Crandall and Sidak (2002), Bustos and Galetovic (2003), Sappington and Weisman (2005), and Crew, Kleindorfer and Sumpter (2005).

regulated price for access. When the monopolist enjoys a substantial profit margin on each unit of access it sells to downstream producers, the monopolist will sacrifice considerable upstream profit if it raises the costs of downstream rivals and thereby reduces their demand for access. Therefore, the regulator may reduce any prevailing incentive to degrade quality by raising the price of access.[273] A complete assessment of optimal regulatory policy in this regard awaits further research.

The input monopolist's participation in the retail market can complicate the design of many simple, practical regulatory policies, including price cap regulation. To understand why, recall from Section 3.1.3 that price cap regulation often constrains the average level of the regulated firm's prices. An aggregate restriction on overall price levels can admit a substantial increase in the price of one service (e.g., the input sold to downstream competitors), as long as this increase is accompanied by a substantial decrease in the price of another service (e.g., the monopolist's retail price). Consequently, price cap regulation that applies to all of the prices set by an integrated monopolist could allow the firm to exercise a price squeeze. An integrated monopolist exercises a price squeeze when the margin between its retail price and its access price is not sufficient to allow an equally efficient entrant to operate profitably. As discussed in Section 3.1.3, additional restrictions on the pricing flexibility of vertically integrated firms that operate under price cap regulation often are warranted to prevent price squeezes that force more efficient competitors from the downstream market.[274]

In summary, downstream integration by a monopoly supplier of an essential input generally entails both benefits and costs. Either the benefits or the costs can predominate, depending upon the nature of downstream competition, the relevant information asymmetries, and the regulator's policy instruments. Appropriate policy, therefore, will generally vary according to the setting in which it is implemented.

5.3. Two-way access pricing

Different issues can arise when two established firms need to buy inputs from each other. Such a need can arise, for example, when competing communications networks require mutual interconnection to allow customers on one network to communicate with customers on the other network.[275] Even though competition for customers may be sufficiently vigorous to limit the need for explicit regulation of retail tariffs, regulation may still be needed to ensure interconnection agreements that are in the public interest.

[273] Thus, one advantage of the ECPR policy discussed in Section 5.1.2 (which can involve a significant markup of the access charge above cost) is that the firm's incentive to degrade quality is lessened, relative to a cost-based policy. See Weisman (1995, 1998), Reiffen (1998), Sibley and Weisman (1998), Beard, Kaserman and Mayo (2001), and Sand (2004) for related analyses.

[274] See Laffont and Tirole (1996) and Bouckaert and Verboven (2004).

[275] Interconnection is one aspect of the general issue of compatibility of services between rival firms. See Farrell and Klemperer (2007) for a survey which includes a discussion of this issue.

Suppose for simplicity there are two symmetric networks, A and B, and consumers wish to subscribe to one of these networks (but not both).[276] If the two firms set the same retail tariff they will attract an equal number of subscribers. In this case, suppose a subscriber on network A, say, makes half her telephone calls to subscribers on network A and half to subscribers on network B. To complete these latter calls, A will need to arrange for B to deliver the calls destined for B's subscribers that originate on A's network. Similarly, B will need to arrange for A to deliver calls to A's subscribers initiated by B's subscribers.

Consider the following timing. Suppose the network operators first negotiate their mutual access prices and then compete non-cooperatively in the retail market for subscribers, taking as given the negotiated access prices. In a symmetric setting, the negotiated prices for access will be reciprocal, so that the payment A makes to B for each of A's calls that B delivers is the same as the corresponding payment from B to A. Moreover, the two firms will have congruent preferences regarding the ideal reciprocal access price.[277] Of course, a regulator will want to know if the firms might employ interconnection arrangements to distort retail competition, and, if so, whether the negotiated access prices will exceed or fall below the access prices that are ideal from the social perspective.[278]

The answers to these questions turn out to be subtle, and to depend in part on the kinds of retail tariffs firms employ. Consider the following three types of tariff.

Linear pricing First suppose the two network operators employ linear pricing, so that they charge a single per-minute price for calls with no additional fixed (e.g., monthly) charge. In this case, firms will be tempted to choose high payments for access in order to relax competition for subscribers. The mutual benefit of a high reciprocal access price is apparent. Because firm A's customers make a fraction of their calls to customers on firm B's network, a high access charge paid to B will increase A's effective cost of providing calls to its subscribers. In equilibrium, this inflated cost induces a high equilibrium retail price. Therefore, in this setting, firms may try to negotiate a high reciprocal access price in order to implement high retail prices and thereby increase their joint profits. (Of course, in a symmetric equilibrium, firms receive access revenue from their rival exactly equal to the access payments they deliver to the rival. Consequently, the only effect of high access payments on profit is the beneficial effect of higher induced retail prices.) Therefore, an active role for regulation may persist in this setting to ensure firms do not agree to set access payments that are unduly high.

[276] The following discussion is based on Armstrong (1998), Laffont, Rey and Tirole (1998a), and Carter and Wright (1999). See Laffont and Tirole (2000, ch. 5) and Armstrong (2002, Section 4.2) for more comprehensive reviews of the literature on two-way access pricing.

[277] Carter and Wright (2003) and Armstrong (2004) demonstrate that such congruence is not ensured when firms are asymmetric.

[278] In benchmark models where network and call externalities are unimportant, for example, the socially optimal price for access is the marginal cost of providing access, because that access price induces a unit call price equal to the cost of making a call.

Two-part pricing Now consider the (more realistic) case where firms compete for subscribers using two-part tariffs (that consist of a per-minute price and a monthly fixed charge, for example). As with linear pricing, the access price affects each firm's perceived marginal cost of providing calls. Consequently, a high access price will induce a high per-minute price in equilibrium, which, in turn, will generate high profits from supplying calls. However, firms now have an additional instrument with which to compete for subscribers – the monthly fixed charge. Since high access payments ensure a high (per-subscriber) profit from providing calls, firms will compete vigorously to attract additional subscribers to their network. They will do so by setting a low fixed charge. In simple models of subscriber demand for networks (e.g., a Hotelling market for subscribers), equilibrium profit turns out to be independent of the established access price.[279] Consequently, firms have no strict preference among access prices, and so are likely to be amenable to setting socially desirable prices for access.

Price discrimination Finally, consider the case where firms can set a different price for a call depending on whether the call is made to a subscriber on the same network (an "on-net" call) or to a subscriber on the rival network (an "off-net" call).[280] (Firms continue to set a fixed monthly charge as well.) Such discriminatory tariffs can introduce important network size effects. To illustrate, suppose firms charge a higher price for off-net calls than for on-net calls. This pricing structure will induce subscribers to prefer the network with the larger number of subscribers, all else equal. This preference reflects the fact that a subscriber on the larger network can make more calls at a relatively low price. This preference gives rise to a positive network size effect, as larger firms are better able to attract subscribers than smaller firms. In contrast, suppose the price of an off-net call is lower than the price of an on-net call. A negative network size effect arises in this case, as subscribers prefer to subscribe to the smaller network, all else equal. When two established firms vie for subscribers (with no scope for market entry or exit), competition is less intense (in the sense that equilibrium prices are higher) in settings with negative network size effects than in settings with positive network size effects. Competition is less intense in the former case because a unilateral price reduction does not attract many new subscribers, since subscribers prefer not to join the larger network.

Firms can determine whether positive or negative network size effects arise through the access tariffs they set. When the firms establish a reciprocal access price in excess of the marginal cost of delivering a call, the equilibrium price for an off-net call will exceed the equilibrium price for an on-net call and a positive network size effect will arise. This effect will intensify competition for subscribers. In contrast, if the firms

[279] Dessein (2003) and Hahn (2004) show that this "profit neutrality" result extends to settings where subscribers have heterogeneous demands for calls and where firms can offer different tariffs to different consumer types. Dessein shows that the profit neutrality result does not extend to cases where the total number of subscribers is affected by the prevailing retail tariffs.

[280] Laffont, Rey and Tirole (1998b) and Gans and King (2001) analyze this possibility.

set the access price below marginal cost, the equilibrium price for an on-net call will exceed the equilibrium for an off-net call. The resulting negative network size effect will induce relatively weak competition for subscribers, and thereby increase the profit of established competitors. Therefore, in this setting, the firms will wish to price access below the socially desirable access price. The regulator's task in this setting, then, will be to ensure the firms do not negotiate access payments that are unduly low.[281,282]

In sum, the developing literature on two-way access pricing suggests a number of continuing roles for regulation, even when competition for subscribers is sufficiently vigorous to limit the need for explicit retail tariff regulation.

5.4. Conclusions

The discussion in this section has reviewed some of many subtleties that arise when a regulated firm operates at multiple stages of the production process. The discussion emphasized the standard theme that a regulator generally is better able to achieve social goals the more instruments he has at his disposal. In particular, a well-informed regulator generally can secure greater industry surplus when he can set access prices and retail prices simultaneously and when he can control the activities of all industry competitors. The discussion also emphasized the fact that even after substantial competition develops among facilities-based network operators, regulatory oversight of the interconnection agreements between these operators may be warranted.

The discussion in this section has followed the literature in focusing on settings in which the regulator is fully informed about the regulated industry. Further research is warranted on the design of regulatory policy in vertically-integrated industries where regulators are less omniscient. Additional directions for future research are suggested in Section 6.

6. Summary and conclusions

This chapter has reviewed recent theoretical studies of the design of regulatory policy, focussing on studies in which the regulated firm has better information about its environment than does the regulator. The regulator's task in such settings often is to try to

[281] "Bill-and-keep" is a common policy that implements access charges below cost. Under a bill-and-keep policy, each network agrees to complete the calls initiated on other networks without charge. While such a policy can reduce the intensity of competition, it may have a more benign effect, which is to reduce the price for making calls so that call externalities – the (often) beneficial effect of a call on the recipient of a call – are internalized. [See Hermalin and Katz (2004) and Jeon, Laffont and Tirole (2004), for example.] The presence of significant call externalities can render bill-and-keep a desirable policy. [See DeGraba (2003, 2004) and Berger (2005), for example.]

[282] Laffont, Rey and Tirole (1998b) argue that when network-based price discrimination is practiced, high access charges (and hence high off-net call charges) by incumbents can be used as an instrument to deter entry.

induce the firm to employ its superior information in the broader social interest. One central message of this chapter is that this regulatory task can be a difficult and subtle one. The regulator's ability to induce the firm to use its privileged information to pursue social goals depends upon a variety of factors, including the nature of the firm's private information, the environment in which the firm operates, the regulator's policy instruments, and his commitment powers.

Recall from Section 2, for example, that despite having limited knowledge of consumer demand, a regulator may be able to secure the ideal outcome for consumers when the regulated firm operates with decreasing returns to scale. In contrast, a regulator generally is unable to secure the ideal outcome for consumers when the regulated firm has privileged knowledge of its cost structure. However, even in this setting, a regulator with strong commitment powers typically can ensure that consumers and the firm both gain as the firm's costs decline. The regulator can do so by providing rent to the firm that admits to having lower costs. But when a regulator cannot make long-term commitments about how he will employ privileged information revealed by the firm, the regulator may be unable to induce the firm to employ its superior information to achieve Pareto gains. Thus, the nature of the firm's superior knowledge, the firm's operating technology, the regulator's policy instruments, and his commitment powers are all of substantial importance in the design of regulatory policy.

The fact that information, technology, instruments, and institutions all matter in the design of regulatory policy implies that the best regulatory policy typically will vary across industries, across countries, and over time. Thus, despite our focus in this chapter on generic principles that apply in a broad array of settings, institutional details must be considered carefully when designing regulatory policy for a specific institutional setting. Future research that transforms the general principles reviewed above to concrete regulatory policies in particular settings will be of substantial value.

Another central message of this chapter is that options constitute important policy instruments for the regulator. It is through the careful structuring of options that the regulator can induce the regulated firm to employ its privileged information to further social goals. As noted above, the options generally must be designed to cede rent to the regulated firm when it reveals that it has the superior ability required to deliver greater benefits to consumers. Consequently, it is seldom costless for the regulator to induce the regulated firm to employ its privileged information in the social interest. However, the benefits of providing discretion to the regulated firm via carefully-structured options generally outweigh the associated costs, and so such discretion typically is a component of optimal regulatory policy in the presence of asymmetric information.

This chapter has reviewed two distinct strands of the literature. Section 2 reviewed studies of the optimal design of regulatory policy in Bayesian settings. Section 3 reviewed non-Bayesian analyses of simple, practical regulatory policies and policies that have certain desirable properties in specified settings. Bayesian analyses of the optimal design of regulatory policy typically entail the structuring of options for the regulated firm. As noted above, in such analyses, the regulator employs his limited knowledge of the regulatory environment to construct a set of options, and then permits the firm to choose one of the specified options. In contrast, non-Bayesian analyses often consider the implementation of a single regulatory policy that does not present the firm with an explicit choice among options.[283] One interpretation of the non-Bayesian approach may be that regulatory plans that encompass options are "complicated", and therefore prohibitively costly to implement.[284] A second interpretation might be that the regulator has no information about the regulatory environment that he can employ to structure options for the firm. To assess the validity of this interpretation, future research might analyze the limit of optimal Bayesian regulatory policies as the regulator's knowledge of the regulatory environment becomes less and less precise. It would be interesting to determine whether any of the policies reviewed in Section 3 emerge as the limit of optimal regulatory policies in such an analysis.

Future research might also analyze additional ways to harness the power of competition to complement regulatory policy. As emphasized in Section 4, even though competition can complicate the design and implementation of regulatory policy, it can also provide pronounced benefits for consumers. The best manner in which to capture these benefits without sacrificing unduly the benefits that regulation can provide merits additional consideration, both in general and in specific institutional settings. The analysis in this chapter has focused on the substantial benefits that competition can deliver in static settings, where products and production technologies are immutable. In dynamic settings, competition may deliver better products and superior production techniques, in addition to limiting the rents of incumbent suppliers. Reasonable, if not optimal, policies to promote and harness these potential benefits of competition merit additional research, particularly in settings where the regulator's information about key elements of the regulated industry is severely limited.

In addition to examining how competition can best complement regulatory policy, future research might analyze the conditions under which competition can replace regulatory oversight. Broad conclusions regarding the general merits of deregulation and specific findings regarding the merits of deregulation in particular institutional settings would both be valuable. Most of the analyses reviewed in this chapter have taken as given the fact that a regulator will dictate the prices that a monopoly provider can charge. Two related questions warrant further study. First, how can a regulator determine when sufficient (actual or potential) competition has developed in an industry so that ongoing price regulation is no longer in the social interest? Second, when direct price regulation is no longer warranted, are other forms of regulatory oversight and control useful? For example, might ongoing monitoring of industry prices, service quality, and the state of competition usefully supplement standard antitrust policy immediately following industry deregulation?[285]

[283] Of course, the regulator provides the firm with meaningful options whenever he offers the firm some discretion over its prices, as in Section 3.1.

[284] Ideally, the costs of complexity should be modeled explicitly, and the costs of more complicated regulatory plans should be weighed against their potential benefits.

[285] Armstrong and Sappington (2006) and Gerardin and Sidak (2006), among others, discuss the interaction between regulatory and antitrust policy.

In closing, we emphasize the importance of empirical work as a complement to both the theoretical work reviewed in this chapter and future theoretical work on the design of regulatory policy.[286] Theoretical research typically models the interplay among conflicting economic forces, and specifies conditions under which one force outweighs another force. Often, though, theoretical analysis cannot predict unambiguously which forces will prevail in practice. Carefully structured empirical research can determine which forces prevailed under particular circumstances, and can thereby provide useful insight about the forces that are likely to prevail in similar circumstances. Thus, despite our focus on theoretical work in this chapter, it is theoretical work and empirical work together that ultimately will provide the most useful guidance to policy makers and the greatest insight regarding the design of regulatory policy.

Acknowledgements

We are grateful to Carli Coetzee, Simon Cowan, Ernesto Dal Bó, Jos Jansen, Paul Joskow, Rob Porter, Ray Rees, Michael Riordan, Jean Tirole, and Ingo Vogelsang for helpful comments.

References

Acton, J., Vogelsang, I. (1989). "Introduction to the symposium on price cap regulation". RAND Journal of Economics 20 (3), 369–372.

Anton, J., Gertler, P. (1988). "External markets and regulation". Journal of Public Economics 37 (2), 243–260.

Anton, J., Gertler, P. (2004). "Regulation, local monopolies and spatial competition". Journal of Regulatory Economics 25 (2), 115–142.

Anton, J., Yao, D. (1987). "Second sourcing and the experience curve: Price competition in defense procurement". RAND Journal of Economics 18 (1), 57–76.

Anton, J., Yao, D. (1989). "Split awards, procurement and innovation". RAND Journal of Economics 20 (4), 538–552.

Anton, J., Yao, D. (1992). "Coordination in split award auctions". Quarterly Journal of Economics 97 (2), 681–707.

Anton, J., Vander Weide, J., Vettas, N. (2002). "Entry auctions and strategic behavior under cross-market price constraints". International Journal of Industrial Organization 20 (5), 611–629.

Armstrong, M. (1998). "Network interconnection in telecommunications". Economic Journal 108 (448), 545–564.

Armstrong, M. (1999). "Optimal regulation with unknown demand and cost functions". Journal of Economic Theory 84 (2), 196–215.

Armstrong, M. (2000). "Optimal multi-object auctions". Review of Economic Studies 67 (3), 455–481.

Armstrong, M. (2001). "Access pricing, bypass and universal service". American Economic Review 91 (2), 297–301.

[286] Sappington (2002) provides a review of recent empirical work that examines the effects of incentive regulation in the telecommunications industry. Also see Kridel, Sappington and Weisman (1996).

Armstrong, M. (2002). "The theory of access pricing and interconnection". In: Cave, M., Majumdar, S., Vogelsang, I. (Eds.), Handbook of Telecommunications Economics, vol. I. North-Holland, Amsterdam.

Armstrong, M. (2004). "Network interconnection with asymmetric networks and heterogeneous calling patterns". Information Economics and Policy 16 (3), 375–390.

Armstrong, M., Rochet, J.-C. (1999). "Multi-dimensional screening: A user's guide". European Economic Review 43 (4), 959–979.

Armstrong, M., Sappington, D. (2004). "Toward a synthesis of models of regulatory policy design with limited information". Journal of Regulatory Economics 26 (1), 5–21.

Armstrong, M., Sappington, D. (2006). "Regulation, competition and liberalization". Journal of Economic Literature 44 (2), 325–366.

Armstrong, M., Vickers, J. (1991). "Welfare effects of price discrimination by a regulated monopolist". RAND Journal of Economics 22 (4), 571–580.

Armstrong, M., Vickers, J. (1993). "Price discrimination, competition and regulation". Journal of Industrial Economics 41 (4), 335–360.

Armstrong, M., Vickers, J. (1998). "The access pricing problem with deregulation: A note". Journal of Industrial Economics 46 (1), 115–121.

Armstrong, M., Vickers, J. (2000). "Multiproduct price regulation under asymmetric information". Journal of Industrial Economics 48 (2), 137–160.

Armstrong, M., Cowan, S., Vickers, J. (1994). Regulatory Reform: Economic Analysis and British Experience. MIT Press, Cambridge, MA.

Armstrong, M., Cowan, S., Vickers, J. (1995). "Nonlinear pricing and price cap regulation". Journal of Public Economics 58 (1), 33–55.

Armstrong, M., Doyle, C., Vickers, J. (1996). "The access pricing problem: A synthesis". Journal of Industrial Economics 44 (2), 131–150.

Armstrong, M., Rees, R., Vickers, J. (1995). "Optimal regulatory lag under price cap regulation". Revista Espanola De Economia 12, 93–116.

Asker, J., Cantillon, E. (2005). "Optimal procurement when both price and quality matter". Mimeo.

Auriol, E. (1998). "Deregulation and quality". International Journal of Industrial Organization 16 (2), 169–194.

Auriol, E., Laffont, J.-J. (1992). "Regulation by duopoly". Journal of Economics and Management Strategy 1 (3), 507–533.

Averch, H., Johnson, L. (1962). "Behavior of the firm under regulatory constraint". American Economic Review 52 (5), 1053–1069.

Bailey, E., Coleman, R. (1971). "The effect of lagged regulation in an Averch–Johnson model". Bell Journal of Economics 2 (1), 278–292.

Baron, D. (1985). "Noncooperative regulation of a nonlocalized externality". RAND Journal of Economics 16 (4), 553–568.

Baron, D. (1988). "Regulation and legislative choice". RAND Journal of Economics 29 (3), 457–477.

Baron, D. (1989). "Design of regulatory mechanisms and institutions". In: Schmalensee, R., Willig, R. (Eds.), Handbook of Industrial Organization, vol. II. North-Holland, Amsterdam.

Baron, D., Besanko, D. (1984a). "Regulation and information in a continuing relationship". Information Economics and Policy 1 (4), 267–302.

Baron, D., Besanko, D. (1984b). "Regulation, asymmetric information, and auditing". RAND Journal of Economics 15 (4), 447–470.

Baron, D., Besanko, D. (1987a). "Commitment and fairness in a dynamic regulatory relationship". Review of Economic Studies 54 (3), 413–436.

Baron, D., Besanko, D. (1987b). "Monitoring, moral hazard, asymmetric information, and risk sharing in procurement contracting". RAND Journal of Economics 18 (4), 509–532.

Baron, D., Besanko, D. (1992). "Information, control, and organizational structure". Journal of Economics and Management Strategy 1 (2), 237–275.

Baron, D., Myerson, R. (1982). "Regulating a monopolist with unknown costs". Econometrica 50 (4), 911–930.

Baseman, K. (1981). "Open entry and cross-subsidization in regulated markets". In: Fromm, G. (Ed.), Studies in Public Regulation. MIT Press, Cambridge, MA.
Baumol, W. (1983). "Some subtle issues in railroad regulation". International Journal of Transport Economics 10 (1–2), 341–355.
Baumol, W., Klevorick, A. (1970). "Input choices and rate-of-return regulation: An overview of the discussion". Bell Journal of Economics 1 (2), 162–190.
Baumol, W., Sidak, G. (1994a). "The pricing of inputs sold to competitors". Yale Journal on Regulation 11 (1), 171–202.
Baumol, W., Sidak, G. (1994b). Toward Competition in Local Telephony. MIT Press, Cambridge, MA.
Baumol, W., Bailey, E., Willig, R. (1977). "Weak invisible hand theorems on the sustainability of prices in a multiproduct monopoly". American Economic Review 67 (3), 350–365.
Baumol, W., Ordover, J., Willig, R. (1997). "Parity pricing and its critics: A necessary condition for efficiency in the provision of bottleneck services to competitors". Yale Journal on Regulation 14 (1), 145–164.
Baumol, W., Panzar, J., Willig, R. (1982). Contestable Markets and the Theory of Industry Structure. Harcourt Brace Jovanovich, Inc., New York.
Beard, R., Kaserman, D., Mayo, J. (2001). "Regulation, vertical integration, and sabotage". Journal of Industrial Economics 46 (3), 319–333.
Berg, S., Lynch, J. (1992). "The measurement and encouragement of telephone service quality". Telecommunications Policy 16 (3), 210–224.
Berger, U. (2005). "Bill-and-keep vs. cost-based access pricing revisited". Economics Letters 86 (1), 107–112.
Bernstein, J., Sappington, D. (1999). "Setting the X factor in price cap regulation plans". Journal of Regulatory Economics 16 (1), 5–25.
Besanko, D. (1985). "On the use of revenue requirements regulation under imperfect information". In: Crew, M. (Ed.), Analyzing the Impact of Regulatory Change in Public Utilities. Lexington Books, Lexington, MA.
Besanko, D., Spulber, D. (1992). "Sequential-equilibrium investment by regulated firms". RAND Journal of Economics 23 (2), 153–170.
Besanko, D., Donnenfeld, S., White, L. (1987). "Monopoly and quality distortion: Effects and remedies". Quarterly Journal of Economics 102 (4), 743–767.
Besanko, D., Donnenfeld, S., White, L. (1988). "The multiproduct firm, quality choice, and regulation". Journal of Industrial Economics 36 (4), 411–429.
Bester, H., Strausz, R. (2001). "Contracting with imperfect commitment and the revelation principle: The single agent case". Econometrica 69 (4), 1077–1098.
Biais, B., Perotti, E. (2002). "Machiavellian privatization". American Economic Review 92 (1), 240–258.
Biglaiser, G., Ma, C.-T.A. (1995). "Regulating a dominant firm: Unknown demand and industry structure". RAND Journal of Economics 26 (1), 1–19.
Biglaiser, G., Ma, C.-T.A. (1999). "Investment incentives of a regulated dominant firm". Journal of Regulatory Economics 16 (3), 215–236.
Biglaiser, G., Riordan, M. (2000). "Dynamics of price regulation". RAND Journal of Economics 31 (4), 744–767.
Blackmon, G. (1994). Incentive Regulation and the Regulation of Incentives. Kluwer Academic Publishers, Norwell, MA.
Boiteux, M. (1956). "Sur la gestion des monopoles publics astreints à l'équilibre budgétaire". Econometrica 24 (1), 22–40.
Bolton, P., Dewatripont, M. (2005). Contract Theory. MIT Press, Cambridge, MA.
Bolton, P., Farrell, J. (1990). "Decentralization, duplication, and delay". Journal of Political Economy 98 (4), 803–826.
Bouckaert, J., Verboven, F. (2004). "Price squeezes in a regulatory environment". Journal of Regulatory Economics 26 (3), 321–351.
Bourreau, M., Dogan, P. (2001). "Regulation and innovation in the telecommunications industry". Telecommunications Policy 25 (3), 167–184.

Bower, A. (1993). "Procurement policy and contracting efficiency". International Economic Review 34 (4), 873–901.
Bradley, I., Price, C. (1988). "The economic regulation of private industries by price constraints". Journal of Industrial Economics 37 (1), 99–106.
Braeutigam, R. (1979). "Optimal pricing with intermodal competition". American Economic Review 69 (1), 38–49.
Braeutigam, R. (1984). "Socially optimal pricing with rivalry and economies of scale". RAND Journal of Economics 15 (1), 127–134.
Braeutigam, R. (1989). "Optimal policies for natural monopolies". In: Schmalensee, R., Willig, R. (Eds.), Handbook of Industrial Organization, vol. II. North-Holland, Amsterdam.
Braeutigam, R. (1993). "A regulatory bargain for diversified enterprises". International Journal of Industrial Organization 11 (1), 1–20.
Braeutigam, R., Panzar, J. (1989). "Diversification incentives under 'price-based' and 'cost-based' regulation". RAND Journal of Economics 20 (3), 373–391.
Braeutigam, R., Panzar, J. (1993). "Effects of the change from rate-of-return regulation to price cap regulation". American Economic Review 83 (2), 191–198.
Branco, F. (1997). "The design of multidimensional auctions". RAND Journal of Economics 28 (1), 63–81.
Brennan, T. (1989). "Regulating by 'capping prices' ". Journal of Regulatory Economics 1 (2), 133–147.
Brennan, T. (1990). "Cross-subsidization and cost misallocation by regulated monopolists". Journal of Regulatory Economics 2 (1), 37–52.
Brennan, T., Palmer, K. (1994). "Comparing the costs and benefits of diversification by regulated firms". Journal of Regulatory Economics 6 (1), 115–136.
Bustos, A., Galetovic, A. (2003). "Vertical integration and sabotage in regulated industries". Mimeo.
Cabral, L., Riordan, M. (1989). "Incentives for cost reduction under price cap regulation". Journal of Regulatory Economics 1 (2), 93–102.
Caillaud, B. (1990). "Regulation, competition, and asymmetric information". Journal of Economic Theory 52 (1), 87–110.
Caillaud, B., Guesnerie, R., Rey, P. (1992). "Noisy observation in adverse selection models". Review of Economic Studies 59 (3), 595–615.
Caillaud, B., Guesnerie, R., Rey, P., Tirole, J. (1988). "Government intervention in production and incentives theory: A review of recent contributions". RAND Journal of Economics 19 (1), 1–26.
Carter, M., Wright, J. (1999). "Interconnection in network industries". Review of Industrial Organization 14 (1), 1–25.
Carter, M., Wright, J. (2003). "Asymmetric network interconnection". Review of Industrial Organization 22 (1), 27–46.
Celentani, M., Ganuza, J.-J. (2002). "Corruption and competition in procurement". European Economic Review 46 (7), 1273–1303.
Chang, Y.-M., Warren, J. (1997). "Allocative efficiency and diversification under price-cap regulation". Information Economics and Policy 9 (1), 3–17.
Che, Y.-K. (1993). "Design competition through multidimensional auctions". RAND Journal of Economics 24 (4), 668–680.
Che, Y.-K. (1995). "Revolving doors and the optimal tolerance for agency collusion". RAND Journal of Economics 26 (3), 378–397.
Che, Y.-K., Gale, I. (1998). "Standard auctions with financially constrained bidders". Review of Economic Studies 65 (1), 1–22.
Che, Y.-K., Gale, I. (2000). "The optimal mechanism for selling to budget-constrained consumers". Journal of Economic Theory 92 (2), 198–233.
Che, Y.-K., Gale, I. (2003). "Optimal design of research contests". American Economic Review 93 (3), 64–671.
Chiappori, P., Macho, I., Rey, P., Salanié, B. (1994). "Repeated moral hazard: The role of memory, commitment and the access to credit markets". European Economic Review 38 (8), 1527–1553.

Chu, L.Y., Sappington, D. (2007). "Simple cost-sharing contracts". American Economic Review 97 (1), 419–428.

Clemenz, G. (1991). "Optimal price cap regulation". Journal of Industrial Economics 39 (4), 391–408.

Cooper, R. (1984). "On the allocative distortions in problems of self-selection". RAND Journal of Economics 15 (4), 568–577.

Cournot, A. (1927). Researches into the Mathematical Principles of the Theory of Wealth. Macmillan, New York.

Cowan, S. (1997a). "Price-cap regulation and inefficiency in relative pricing". Journal of Regulatory Economics 12 (1), 53–70.

Cowan, S. (1997b). "Tight average revenue regulation can be worse than no regulation". Journal of Industrial Economics 45 (1), 75–88.

Cowan, S. (2004). "Optimal risk allocation for regulated monopolies and consumers". Journal of Public Economics 88 (1), 285–303.

Crampes, C., Hollander, A. (1995). "Duopoly and quality standards". European Economic Review 39 (1), 71–82.

Cramton, P. (1997). "The FCC spectrum auctions: An early assessment". Journal of Economics and Management Strategy 6 (3), 431–495.

Crandall, R., Sidak, J.G. (2002). "Is structural separation of incumbent local exchange carriers necessary for competition?". Yale Journal on Regulation 19 (2), 335–411.

Crew, M., Crocker, K. (1991). "Diversification and regulated monopoly". In: Crew, M. (Ed.), Competition and the Regulation of Utilities. Kluwer Academic Publishers, Boston, MA.

Crew, M., Kleindorfer, P. (2002). "Regulatory economics: Twenty years of progress?". Journal of Regulatory Economics 21 (1), 5–22.

Crew, M., Kleindorfer, P., Sumpter, J. (2005). "Bringing competition to telecommunications by divesting the RBOCs". In: Crew, M., Spiegel, M. (Eds.), Obtaining the Best from Regulation and Competition. Kluwer Academic Publishers, Norwell, MA.

Cripps, M., Ireland, N. (1994). "The design of auctions and tenders with quality thresholds: The symmetric case". Economic Journal 104 (423), 316–326.

Crémer, J., Khalil, F., Rochet, J.-C. (1998a). "Contracts and productive information gathering". Games and Economic Behavior 23 (2), 174–193.

Crémer, J., Khalil, F., Rochet, J.-C. (1998b). "Strategic information gathering before a contract is offered". Journal of Economic Theory 81 (1), 163–200.

Crémer, J., McLean, R. (1985). "Optimal selling strategies under uncertainty for a discriminating monopolist when demands are interdependent". Econometrica 53 (2), 345–361.

Curien, N., Jullien, B., Rey, P. (1998). "Pricing regulation under bypass competition". RAND Journal of Economics 29 (2), 259–279.

Currier, K. (2005). "Strategic firm behavior under average-revenue-lagged regulation". Journal of Regulatory Economics 27 (1), 67–80.

Da Rocha, J., de Frutos, M.A. (1999). "A note on the optimal structure of production". Journal of Economic Theory 89 (2), 234–246.

Dalen, D.M. (1997). "Regulation of quality and the ratchet effect: Does unverifiability hurt the regulator?". Journal of Regulatory Economics 11 (2), 139–155.

Dalen, D.M. (1998). "Yardstick competition and investment incentives". Journal of Economics and Management Strategy 7 (1), 105–126.

Dana, J. (1993). "The organization and scope of agents: Regulating multiproduct industries". Journal of Economic Theory 59 (2), 288–310.

Dana, J., Spier, K. (1994). "Designing a private industry: Government auctions with endogenous market structure". Journal of Public Economics 53 (1), 127–147.

Dasgupta, S., Spulber, D. (1989/1990). "Managing procurement auctions". Information Economics and Policy 4 (1), 5–29.

De Fraja, G., Iozzi, A. (2004). "Bigger and better: A dynamic regulatory mechanism for optimum quality". Mimeo.

DeGraba, P. (2003). "Efficient intercarrier compensation on competing networks when customers share the value of a call". Journal of Economics and Management Strategy 12 (2), 207–230.

DeGraba, P. (2004). "Reconciling the off-net pricing principle with efficient network utilization". Information Economics and Policy 16 (3), 475–494.

Demougin, D., Garvie, D. (1991). "Contractual design with correlated information under limited liability". RAND Journal of Economics 22 (4), 477–489.

Demsetz, H. (1968). "Why regulate utilities?". Journal of Law and Economics 11 (1), 55–65.

Demski, J., Sappington, D. (1984). "Optimal incentive contracts with multiple agents". Journal of Economic Theory 33 (1), 152–171.

Demski, J., Sappington, D. (1987). "Hierarchical regulatory control". RAND Journal of Economics 18 (3), 369–383.

Demski, J., Sappington, D., Spiller, P. (1987). "Managing supplier switching". RAND Journal of Economics 18 (1), 77–97.

Demski, J., Sappington, D., Spiller, P. (1988). "Incentive schemes with multiple agents and bankruptcy constraints". Journal of Economic Theory 44 (1), 156–167.

Dessein, W. (2003). "Network competition in nonlinear pricing". RAND Journal of Economics 34 (4), 593–611.

Diamond, P., Mirrlees, J. (1971). "Optimal taxation and public production. I. Production efficiency". American Economic Review 61 (1), 8–27.

Dobbs, I. (2004). "Intertemporal price cap regulation under uncertainty". Economic Journal 114 (495), 421–440.

Eckel, C., Lutz, N. (2003). "Introduction: What role can experiments play in research on regulation?". Journal of Regulatory Economics 23 (2), 103–108.

Economides, N. (1998). "The incentive for non-price discrimination by an input monopolist". International Journal of Industrial Organization 16 (3), 271–284.

Economides, N., White, L. (1995). "Access and interconnection pricing: How efficient is the efficient component pricing rule?". The Antitrust Bulletin 40 (3), 557–579.

Einhorn, M. (1987). "Optimality and sustainability: Regulation and intermodal competition in telecommunications". RAND Journal of Economics 18 (4), 550–563.

Encinosa, W., Sappington, D. (1995). "Toward a benchmark for optimal prudency policy". Journal of Regulatory Economics 7 (2), 111–131.

Farrell, J., Klemperer, P. (2007). "Coordination and lock-in: Competition with switching costs and network effects". In: Armstrong, M., Porter, R. (Eds.), Handbook of Industrial Organization, vol. 3. North-Holland, Amsterdam (this volume).

Faure-Grimaud, A., Martimort, D. (2003). "Regulatory inertia". RAND Journal of Economics 34 (3), 413–437.

Finsinger, J., Vogelsang, I. (1981). "Alternative institutional frameworks for price incentive mechanisms". Kyklos 34 (3), 338–404.

Finsinger, J., Vogelsang, I. (1982). "Performance indices for public enterprises". In: Jones, L. (Ed.), Public Enterprise in Less Developed Countries. Cambridge Univ. Press, Cambridge.

Flores, D. (2005). "Price cap regulation in the Mexican telephone industry". Information Economics and Policy 17 (2), 231–246.

Foreman, D. (1995). "Pricing incentives under price-cap regulation". Information Economics and Policy 7 (4), 331–351.

Fraser, R. (1995). "The relationship between the costs and the prices of a multi-product monopoly: The role of price-cap regulation". Journal of Regulatory Economics 8 (1), 23–32.

Freixas, X., Guesnerie, R., Tirole, J. (1985). "Planning under incomplete information and the ratchet effect". Review of Economic Studies 52 (2), 173–191.

Fudenberg, D., Tirole, J. (1990). "Moral hazard and renegotiation in agency contracts". Econometrica 58 (6), 1279–1320.

Fudenberg, D., Tirole, J. (1991). Game Theory. MIT Press, Cambridge, MA.

Fullerton, R., McAfee, P. (1999). "Auctioning entry into tournaments". Journal of Political Economy 107 (3), 573–605.

Gans, J., King, S. (2001). "Using 'bill and keep' interconnect agreements to soften network competition". Economics Letters 71 (3), 413–420.

Gary-Bobo, R., Spiegel, Y. (2006). "Optimal state-contingent regulation under limited liability". RAND Journal of Economics 37 (2), 431–448.

Gasmi, F., Ivaldi, M., Laffont, J.-J. (1994). "Rent extraction and incentives for efficiency in recent regulatory proposals". Journal of Regulatory Economics 6 (2), 151–176.

Gasmi, F., Laffont, J.-J., Sharkey, W. (1999). "Empirical evaluation of regulatory regimes in local telecommunications markets". Journal of Economics and Management Strategy 8 (1), 61–93.

Gerardin, D., Sidak, J.G. (2006). "European and American approaches to antitrust remedies and the institutional design of regulation in telecommunications". In: Majumdar, S., Vogelsang, I., Cave, M. (Eds.), In: Handbook of Telecommunications Economics, vol. II. North-Holland, Amsterdam.

Ghosh, A., Morita, H. (2004). "Free entry and social efficiency under vertical oligopoly". Mimeo.

Gilbert, R., Newbery, D. (1994). "The dynamic efficiency of regulatory constitutions". RAND Journal of Economics 25 (4), 538–554.

Gilbert, R., Riordan, M. (1995). "Regulating complementary products: A comparative institutional approach". RAND Journal of Economics 26 (2), 243–256.

Glover, J. (1994). "A simpler method that stops agents from cheating". Journal of Economic Theory 62 (1), 221–229.

Greenwald, B. (1984). "Rate base selection and the structure of regulation". RAND Journal of Economics 15 (1), 85–95.

Guesnerie, R., Laffont, J.-J. (1984). "A complete solution to a class of principle-agent problems with an application to the control of a self-managed firm". Journal of Public Economics 25 (3), 329–369.

Guthrie, G. (2006). "Regulating infrastructure: The impact on risk and investment". Journal of Economic Literature 44 (4), 925–972.

Hagerman, J. (1990). "Regulation by price adjustment". RAND Journal of Economics 21 (1), 72–82.

Hahn, J.-H. (2004). "Network competition and interconnection with heterogeneous subscribers". International Journal of Industrial Organization 22 (1), 611–631.

Harris, M., Townsend, R. (1981). "Resource allocation under asymmetric information". Econometrica 49 (1), 33–64.

Hart, O., Shleifer, A., Vishny, R. (1997). "The proper scope of government: Theory and an application to prisons". Quarterly Journal of Economics 113 (4), 1127–1161.

Hausman, J. (1997). "Valuing the effect of regulation on new services in telecommunications". In: Brookings Papers on Economic Activity: Microeconomics, pp. 1–38.

Hausman, J., Sidak, J.G. (1999). "A consumer-welfare approach to the mandatory unbundling of telecommunications networks". Yale Law Journal 109 (3), 417–505.

Hausman, J., Sidak, J.G. (2005). "Telecommunications regulation: Current approaches with the end in sight". Mimeo.

Hermalin, B., Katz, M. (2004). "Sender or receiver: Who should pay to exchange an electronic message?". RAND Journal of Economics 35 (3), 423–447.

Hillman, J., Braeutigam, R. (1989). Price Level Regulation for Diversified Public Utilities. Kluwer Academic Publishers, Boston, MA.

Hinton, P., Zona, J.D., Schmalensee, R., Taylor, W. (1998). "An analysis of the welfare effects of long-distance market entry by an integrated access and long-distance provider". Journal of Regulatory Economics 13 (2), 183–196.

Holmstrom, B., Milgrom, P. (1987). "Aggregation and linearity in the provision of intertemporal incentives". Econometrica 55 (2), 303–328.

Hoppe, H., Jehiel, P., Moldovanu, B. (2006). "License auctions and market structure". Journal of Economics and Management Strategy 15 (2), 371–396.

Inderst, R. (2002). "Contract design and bargaining power". Economics Letters 74 (2), 171–176.

Iossa, E. (1999). "Informative externalities and pricing in regulated multiproduct industries". Journal of Industrial Economics 47 (2), 195–220.
Iossa, E., Stroffolini, F. (2002). "Price cap regulation and information acquisition". International Journal of Industrial Organization 20 (7), 1013–1036.
Iossa, E., Stroffolini, F. (2005). "Price cap regulation, revenue sharing and information acquisition". Information Economics and Policy 17 (2), 217–230.
Isaac, R.M. (1991). "Price cap regulation: A case study of some pitfalls of implementation". Journal of Regulatory Economics 3 (2), 193–210.
Jansen, J. (1999). "Regulating complementary input supply: Cost correlation and limited liability". Mimeo. Berlin.
Jeon, D.-S., Laffont, J.-J., Tirole, J. (2004). "On the receiver pays principle". RAND Journal of Economics 35 (1), 85–110.
Joskow, P. (1997). "Restructuring, competition and regulatory reform in the U.S. electricity sector". Journal of Economic Perspectives 11 (3), 119–138.
Joskow, P. (2004). "The difficult transition to competitive electricity markets in the U.S.". In: Griffin, J., Puller, S. (Eds.), Electricity Deregulation: Where to Go from Here? University of Chicago Press, Chicago.
Joskow, P. (2005). "Incentive regulation in theory and practice: Electricity and distribution networks". Mimeo.
Jullien, B. (2000). "Participation constraints in adverse selection models". Journal of Economic Theory 93 (1), 1–47.
Kahn, A., Tardiff, T., Weisman, D. (1999). "The 1996 Telecommunications Act at three years: An economic evaluation of its implementation by the FCC". Information Economics and Policy 11 (4), 319–365.
Kang, J., Weisman, D., Zhang, M. (2000). "Do consumers benefit from tighter price cap regulation?". Economics Letters 67 (1), 113–119.
Kerschbamer, R. (1994). "Destroying the "pretending" equilibria in the Demski–Sappington–Spiller model". Journal of Economic Theory 62 (1), 230–237.
Khalil, F. (1997). "Auditing without commitment". RAND Journal of Economics 28 (4), 629–640.
Kim, J. (1997). "Inefficiency of subgame optimal entry regulation". RAND Journal of Economics 28 (1), 25–36.
Kim, J.-C., Jung, C.-Y. (1995). "Regulating a multi-product monopolist". Journal of Regulatory Economics 8 (3), 299–307.
Kjerstad, E., Vagstad, S. (2000). "Procurement auctions with entry of bidders". International Journal of Industrial Organization 18 (8), 1243–1257.
Kofman, F., Lawarrée, J. (1993). "Collusion in hierarchical agency". Econometrica 61 (3), 629–656.
Kolbe, L., Tye, W. (1991). "The Duquesne opinion: How much 'hope' is there for investors in regulated firms". Yale Journal of Regulation 8 (1), 113–157.
Kridel, D., Sappington, D., Weisman, D. (1996). "The effects of incentive regulation in the telecommunications industry: A survey". Journal of Regulatory Economics 9 (3), 269–306.
Kwoka, J. (1991). "Productivity and price caps in telecommunications". In: Einhorn, M. (Ed.), Price Caps and Incentive Regulation in Telecommunications. Kluwer Academic Publishers, Boston.
Kwoka, J. (1993). "Implementing price caps in telecommunications". Journal of Policy Analysis and Management 12 (4), 726–752.
Laffont, J.-J. (2005). Regulation and Development. Cambridge Univ. Press, Cambridge, UK.
Laffont, J.-J., Martimort, D. (1997). "Collusion under asymmetric information". Econometrica 65 (4), 875–912.
Laffont, J.-J., Martimort, D. (1999). "Separation of regulators against collusive behavior". RAND Journal of Economics 30 (2), 232–262.
Laffont, J.-J., Martimort, D. (2002). The Theory of Incentives: The Principal–Agent Model. Princeton Univ. Press, Princeton, NJ.
Laffont, J.-J., Rochet, J.-C. (1998). "Regulation of a risk averse firm". Games and Economic Behavior 25 (2), 149–173.
Laffont, J.-J., Tirole, J. (1986). "Using cost observation to regulate firms". Journal of Political Economy 94 (3), 614–641.

Laffont, J.-J., Tirole, J. (1987). "Auctioning incentive contracts". Journal of Political Economy 95 (5), 921–937.

Laffont, J.-J., Tirole, J. (1988a). "The dynamics of incentive contracts". Econometrica 56 (5), 1153–1176.

Laffont, J.-J., Tirole, J. (1988b). "Repeated auctions of incentive contracts, investment, and bidding parity with an application to takeovers". RAND Journal of Economics 19 (4), 516–537.

Laffont, J.-J., Tirole, J. (1990a). "Adverse selection and renegotiation in procurement". Review of Economic Studies 57 (4), 597–626.

Laffont, J.-J., Tirole, J. (1990b). "Optimal bypass and cream skimming". American Economic Review 80 (4), 1041–1051.

Laffont, J.-J., Tirole, J. (1990c). "The politics of government decision-making: Regulatory institutions". Journal of Law, Economics, and Organization 6 (1), 1–32.

Laffont, J.-J., Tirole, J. (1991a). "Auction design and favoritism". International Journal of Industrial Organization 9 (1), 9–42.

Laffont, J.-J., Tirole, J. (1991b). "The politics of government decision-making: A theory of regulatory capture". Quarterly Journal of Economics 106 (4), 1089–1127.

Laffont, J.-J., Tirole, J. (1991c). "Privatization and incentives". Journal of Law, Economics, and Organization 7 (3), 84–105.

Laffont, J.-J., Tirole, J. (1993a). "Cartelization by regulation". Journal of Regulatory Economics 5 (2), 111–130.

Laffont, J.-J., Tirole, J. (1993b). A Theory of Incentives in Procurement and Regulation. MIT Press, Cambridge, MA.

Laffont, J.-J., Tirole, J. (1994). "Access pricing and competition". European Economic Review 38 (9), 1673–1710.

Laffont, J.-J., Tirole, J. (1996). "Creating competition through interconnection: Theory and practice". Journal of Regulatory Economics 10 (3), 227–256.

Laffont, J.-J., Tirole, J. (2000). Competition in Telecommunications. MIT Press, Cambridge, MA.

Laffont, J.-J., Rey, P., Tirole, J. (1998a). "Network competition. I. Overview and nondiscriminatory pricing". RAND Journal of Economics 29 (1), 1–37.

Laffont, J.-J., Rey, P., Tirole, J. (1998b). "Network competition. II. Price discrimination". RAND Journal of Economics 29 (1), 38–56.

Lapuerta, C., Tye, W. (1999). "Promoting effective competition through interconnection policy". Telecommunications Policy 23 (2), 129–145.

Law, P. (1995). "Tighter average revenue regulation can reduce consumer welfare". Journal of Industrial Economics 42 (4), 399–404.

Law, P. (1997). "Welfare effects of pricing in anticipation of Laspeyres price cap regulation: An example". Bulletin of Economic Research 49 (1), 17–27.

Lee, S.-H. (1997a). "A note on regulating a multiproduct monopolist". Journal of Regulatory Economics 12 (3), 311–318.

Lee, S.-H. (1997b). "A note on regulating oligopolistic industries". Journal of Regulatory Economics 12 (1), 91–97.

Lee, S.-H., Hamilton, J. (1999). "Using market structure to regulate a vertically integrated monopolist". Journal of Regulatory Economics 15 (3), 223–248.

Lehman, D., Weisman, D. (2000). "The political economy of price cap regulation". Review of Industrial Organization 16 (4), 343–356.

Levine, P., Stern, J., Trillas, F. (2005). "Utility price regulation and time inconsistency: Comparisons with monetary policy". Oxford Economic Papers 57 (3), 447–478.

Levy, B., Spiller, P. (1994). "The institutional foundations of regulatory commitment: A comparative analysis of telecommunications". Journal of Law and Economics and Organization 10 (2), 201–246.

Lewis, T., Sappington, D. (1988a). "Regulating a monopolist with unknown demand". American Economic Review 78 (5), 986–998.

Lewis, T., Sappington, D. (1988b). "Regulating a monopolist with unknown demand and cost functions". RAND Journal of Economics 18 (3), 438–457.

Lewis, T., Sappington, D. (1989a). "Countervailing incentives in agency problems". Journal of Economic Theory 49 (2), 294–313.
Lewis, T., Sappington, D. (1989b). "Inflexible rules in incentive problems". American Economic Review 79 (1), 69–84.
Lewis, T., Sappington, D. (1989c). "An informational effect when regulated firms enter unregulated markets". Journal of Regulatory Economics 1 (1), 35–46.
Lewis, T., Sappington, D. (1989d). "Regulatory options and price cap regulation". RAND Journal of Economics 20 (3), 405–416.
Lewis, T., Sappington, D. (1990). "Sequential regulatory oversight". Journal of Regulatory Economics 2 (4), 327–348.
Lewis, T., Sappington, D. (1991a). "Incentives for monitoring quality". RAND Journal of Economics 22 (3), 370–384.
Lewis, T., Sappington, D. (1991b). "Oversight of long-term investment by short-lived regulators". International Economic Review 32 (3), 579–600.
Lewis, T., Sappington, D. (1992). "Incentives for conservation and quality improvement by public utilities". American Economic Review 82 (5), 1321–1340.
Lewis, T., Sappington, D. (1997). "Information management in incentive problems". Journal of Political Economy 105 (4), 796–821.
Lewis, T., Sappington, D. (1999). "Access pricing with unregulated downstream competition". Information Economics and Policy 11 (1), 73–100.
Lewis, T., Sappington, D. (2000). "Motivating wealth-constrained actors". American Economic Review 90 (4), 944–960.
Lewis, T., Yildirim, H. (2002). "Learning by doing and dynamic regulation". RAND Journal of Economics 33 (1), 22–36.
Liston, C. (1993). "Price-cap versus rate-of-return regulation". Journal of Regulatory Economics 5 (1), 25–48.
Lockwood, B. (1995). "Multi-firm regulation without lump-sum taxes". Journal of Public Economics 56 (1), 31–53.
Loeb, M., Magat, W. (1979). "A decentralized method for utility regulation". Journal of Law and Economics 22 (2), 399–404.
Luton, R., McAfee, P. (1986). "Sequential procurement auctions". Journal of Public Economics 31 (2), 181–195.
Lynch, J., Buzas, T., Berg, S. (1994). "Regulatory measurement and evaluation of telephone service quality". Management Science 40 (2), 169–194.
Lyon, T. (1991). "Regulation with 20–20 hindsight: 'Heads I win, tails you lose' ". RAND Journal of Economics 22 (4), 581–595.
Lyon, T. (1992). "Regulation with 20–20 hindsight: Least-cost rules and variable costs". Journal of Industrial Economics 40 (3), 277–289.
Lyon, T. (1996). "A model of sliding-scale regulation". Journal of Regulatory Economics 9 (3), 227–247.
Ma, C.-T.A. (1994). "Renegotiation and optimality in agency contracts". Review of Economic Studies 61 (1), 109–130.
Ma, C.-T.A., Moore, J., Turnbull, S. (1988). "Stopping agents from 'cheating' ". Journal of Economic Theory 46 (2), 335–372.
Maggi, G., Rodriguez-Clare, A. (1995). "On countervailing incentives". Journal of Economic Theory 66 (1), 238–263.
Mandy, D. (2000). "Killing the goose that laid the golden egg: Only the data know whether sabotage pays". Journal of Regulatory Economics 17 (2), 157–172.
Mandy, D. (2002). "TELRIC pricing with vintage capital". Journal of Regulatory Economics 22 (3), 215–249.
Mandy, D., Sharkey, W. (2003). "Dynamic pricing and investment from static proxy models". Review of Network Economics 2 (4), 403–439.
Manelli, A., Vincent, D. (1995). "Optimal procurement mechanisms". Econometrica 63 (3), 591–620.
Mankiw, N.G., Whinston, M. (1986). "Free entry and social inefficiency". RAND Journal of Economics 17 (1), 48–58.

Mansell, R., Church, J. (1995). Traditional and Incentive Regulation: Applications to Natural Gas Pipelines in Canada. The Van Horne Institute, Calgary.
Martimort, D. (1999). "Renegotiation design with multiple regulators". Journal of Economic Theory 88 (2), 261–293.
Matthews, S. (2001). "Renegotiating moral hazard contracts under limited liability and monotonicity". Journal of Economic Theory 97 (1), 1–29.
McAfee, R.P. (2002). "Coarse matching". Econometrica 70 (5), 2025–2034.
McAfee, R.P., McMillan, J. (1987a). "Auctions and bidding". Journal of Economic Literature 25 (2), 699–738.
McAfee, R.P., McMillan, J. (1987b). "Competition for agency contracts". RAND Journal of Economics 18 (2), 296–307.
McAfee, R.P., McMillan, J. (1996). "Analyzing the airwaves auction". Journal of Economic Perspectives 10 (1), 159–175.
McGuire, T., Riordan, M. (1995). "Incomplete Information and optimal market structure: Public purchases from private producers". Journal of Public Economics 56 (1), 125–141.
McMillan, J. (1994). "Selling spectrum rights". Journal of Economic Perspectives 8 (3), 145–162.
Meyer, M., Vickers, J. (1997). "Performance comparisons and dynamic incentives". Journal of Political Theory 105 (3), 547–581.
Milgrom, P. (1998). "Game theory and the spectrum auctions". European Economic Review 42 (3–5), 771–778.
Mirrlees, J. (1976). "Optimal tax theory: A synthesis". Journal of Public Economics 6, 327–358.
Mookherjee, D. (1984). "Optimal incentive schemes with many agents". Review of Economic Studies 51 (3), 433–446.
Mussa, M., Rosen, S. (1978). "Monopoly and product quality". Journal of Economic Theory 18 (2), 301–317.
Myerson, R. (1979). "Incentive compatibility and the bargaining problem". Econometrica 47 (1), 61–73.
Nalebuff, B., Stiglitz, J. (1983). "Prizes and incentives: Towards a general theory of compensation and competition". Bell Journal of Economics 14 (1), 21–43.
Neu, W. (1993). "Allocative inefficiency properties of price-cap regulation". Journal of Regulatory Economics 5 (2), 159–182.
Newbery, D. (1999). Privatization, Restructuring, and Regulation of Network Utilities. MIT Press, Cambridge, MA.
Otsuka, Y. (1997). "A welfare analysis of local franchises and other types of regulation: Evidence from the cable TV industry". Journal of Regulatory Economics 11 (2), 157–180.
Palfrey, T. (1983). "Bundling decisions by a multiproduct monopolist with incomplete information". Econometrica 51 (2), 463–484.
Palmer, K. (1991). "Diversification by regulated monopolies and incentives for cost-reducing R&D". American Economic Review 81 (2), 266–270.
Pint, E. (1992). "Price-cap versus rate-of-return regulation in a stochastic-cost model". RAND Journal of Economics 23 (4), 564–578.
Potters, J., Rockenbach, B., Sadrieh, A., van Damme, E. (2004). "Collusion under yardstick competition: An experimental study". International Journal of Industrial Organization 22 (7), 1017–1038.
Prager, R. (1989). "Franchise bidding for natural monopoly: The case of cable television in Massachusetts". Journal of Regulatory Economics 1 (2), 115–132.
Radner, R. (1981). "Monitoring cooperative agreements in a repeated principal–agent relationship". Econometrica 49 (5), 1127–1148.
Radner, R. (1985). "Repeated principal–agent relationships with discounting". Econometrica 53 (5), 1173–1198.
Ramakrishnan, R.T.S., Thakor, A.V. (1991). "Cooperation versus competition in agency". Journal of Law, Economics and Organization 7 (2), 248–283.
Ramsey, F. (1927). "A contribution to the theory of taxation". Economic Journal 37 (145), 47–61.
Reiffen, D. (1998). "A regulated firm's incentive to discriminate: A reevaluation and extension of Weisman's result". Journal of Regulatory Economics 14 (1), 79–86.

Reiffen, D., Schumann, L., Ward, M. (2000). "Discriminatory dealing with downstream competitors: Evidence from the cellular industry". Journal of Industrial Economics 48 (3), 253–286.
Rey, P., Salanié, B. (1996). "On the value of commitment with asymmetric information". Econometrica 64 (6), 1395–1414.
Rey, P., Tirole, J. (2007). "A primer on foreclosure". In: Armstrong, M., Porter, R. (Eds.), Handbook of Industrial Organization, vol. 3. North-Holland, Amsterdam (this volume).
Riordan, M. (1984). "On delegating price authority to a regulated firm". RAND Journal of Economics 15 (1), 108–115.
Riordan, M. (1996). "Contracting with qualified suppliers". International Economic Review 37 (1), 115–128.
Riordan, M. (2002). "Universal residential telephone service". In: Cave, M., Majumdar, S., Vogelsang, I. (Eds.), Handbook of Telecommunications Economics, vol. I. North-Holland, Amsterdam.
Riordan, M., Sappington, D. (1987a). "Awarding monopoly franchises". American Economic Review 77 (3), 375–387.
Riordan, M., Sappington, D. (1987b). "Information, incentives, and organizational mode". Quarterly Journal of Economics 102 (2), 243–263.
Riordan, M., Sappington, D. (1988). "Optimal contracts with public ex post information". Journal of Economic Theory 45 (1), 189–199.
Riordan, M., Sappington, D. (1989). "Second sourcing". RAND Journal of Economics 20 (1), 41–58.
Rob, R. (1986). "The design of procurement contracts". American Economic Review 76 (3), 378–389.
Rochet, J.-C., Stole, L. (2003). "The economics of multidimensional screening". In: Dewatripont, M., Hansen, L.P., Turnovsky, S. (Eds.), Advances in Economics and Econometrics: Theory and Applications, Eighth World Congress. Cambridge Univ. Press, Cambridge, UK.
Rogerson, W. (1985). "Repeated moral hazard". Econometrica 53 (1), 69–76.
Rogerson, W. (2003). "Simple menus of contracts in cost-based procurement and regulation". American Economic Review 93 (3), 919–926.
Ronnen, U. (1991). "Minimum quality standards, fixed costs, and competition". RAND Journal of Economics 22 (4), 490–504.
Salant, D. (1995). "Behind the revolving door: A new view of public utility regulation". RAND Journal of Economics 26 (3), 362–377.
Salant, D. (2000). "Auctions and regulation: Reengineering of regulatory mechanisms". Journal of Regulatory Economics 17 (3), 195–204.
Salant, D., Woroch, G. (1992). "Trigger price regulation". RAND Journal of Economics 23 (1), 29–51.
Sand, J. (2004). "Regulation with non-price discrimination". International Journal of Industrial Organization 22 (8), 1289–1307.
Sappington, D. (1980). "Strategic firm behavior under a dynamic regulatory adjustment process". Bell Journal of Economics 11 (1), 360–372.
Sappington, D. (1982). "Optimal regulation of research and development under imperfect information". Bell Journal of Economics 13 (2), 354–368.
Sappington, D. (1983). "Limited liability contracts between principal and agent". Journal of Economic Theory 29 (1), 1–21.
Sappington, D. (1986). "Commitment to regulatory bureaucracy". Information Economics and Policy 2 (4), 243–258.
Sappington, D. (1994). "Designing incentive regulation". Review of Industrial Organization 9 (3), 245–272.
Sappington, D. (2002). "Price regulation and incentives". In: Cave, M., Majumdar, S., Vogelsang, I. (Eds.), Handbook of Telecommunications Economics, vol. I. North-Holland, Amsterdam.
Sappington, D. (2003). "Regulating horizontal diversification". International Journal of Industrial Organization 21 (3), 291–315.
Sappington, D. (2005a). "On the irrelevance of input prices for make-or-buy decisions". American Economic Review 95 (5), 1631–1638.
Sappington, D. (2005b). "Regulating service quality: A survey". Journal of Regulatory Economics 27 (2), 123–154.

Sappington, D., Sibley, D. (1988). "Regulating without cost information: The incremental surplus subsidy scheme". International Economic Review 29 (2), 297–306.
Sappington, D., Sibley, D. (1990). "Regulating without cost information: Further observations". International Economic Review 31 (4), 1027–1029.
Sappington, D., Sibley, D. (1992). "Strategic nonlinear pricing under price cap regulation". RAND Journal of Economics 23 (1), 1–19.
Sappington, D., Sibley, D. (1993). "Regulatory incentive policies and abuse". Journal of Regulatory Economics 5 (2), 131–141.
Sappington, D., Weisman, D. (1996a). Designing Incentive Regulation for the Telecommunications Industry. MIT Press, Cambridge, MA.
Sappington, D., Weisman, D. (1996b). "Revenue sharing in incentive regulation plans". Information Economics and Policy 8 (3), 229–248.
Sappington, D., Weisman, D. (2005). "Self-sabotage". Journal of Regulatory Economics 27 (2), 155–175.
Scarpa, C. (1998). "Minimum quality standards with more than two firms". International Journal of Industrial Organization 16 (5), 665–676.
Schmalensee, R. (1989). "Good regulatory regimes". RAND Journal of Economics 20 (3), 417–436.
Schmidt, K. (2000). "The political economy of mass privatization and the risk of expropriation". European Economic Review 44 (2), 393–421.
Schwermer, S. (1994). "Regulating oligopolistic industries: A generalized incentive scheme". Journal of Regulatory Economics 6 (1), 97–108.
Sen, A. (1996). "Termination clauses in long-term contracts". Journal of Economics and Management Strategy 5 (4), 473–496.
Severinov, S. (2003). "Optimal organization: Centralization, decentralization or delegation?" Mimeo. Duke University.
Shleifer, A. (1985). "A theory of yardstick competition". RAND Journal of Economics 16 (3), 319–327.
Sibley, D. (1989). "Asymmetric information, incentives, and price cap regulation". RAND Journal of Economics 20 (3), 392–404.
Sibley, D., Weisman, D. (1998). "Raising rivals' costs: The entry of an upstream monopolist into downstream markets". Information Economics and Policy 10 (4), 451–470.
Sidak, G., Spulber, D. (1997). Deregulatory Takings and the Regulatory Contract. Cambridge Univ. Press, Cambridge, UK.
Sobel, J. (1999). "A reexamination of yardstick regulation". Journal of Economics and Management Strategy 8 (1), 33–60.
Spence, M. (1975). "Monopoly, quality, and regulation". Bell Journal of Economics 6 (2), 417–429.
Spiegel, Y. (1994). "The capital structure and investment of regulated firms under alternative regulatory regimes". Journal of Regulatory Economics 6 (3), 297–320.
Spiegel, Y., Spulber, D. (1994). "The capital structure of regulated firms". RAND Journal of Economics 25 (3), 424–440.
Spiegel, Y., Spulber, D. (1997). "Capital structure with countervailing incentives". RAND Journal of Economics 28 (1), 1–24.
Spiller, P. (1990). "Politicians, interest groups, and regulators: A multiple-principals agency theory of regulation (or "let them be bribed")". Journal of Law and Economics 33 (1), 65–101.
Stefos, T. (1990). "Regulating without cost information: A comment". International Economic Review 31 (4), 1021–1026.
Stole, L. (1994). "Information expropriation and moral hazard in optimal second-source auctions". Journal of Public Economics 54 (3), 463–484.
Tangerås, T. (2002). "Collusion-proof yardstick competition". Journal of Public Economics 83 (2), 231–254.
Taylor, C. (1995). "Digging for golden carrots: An analysis of research tournaments". American Economic Review 85 (4), 872–890.
Tirole, J. (1986a). "Hierarchies and bureaucracies: On the role of collusion in organizations". Journal of Law, Economics and Organization 2 (2), 181–214.

Tirole, J. (1986b). "Procurement and renegotiation". Journal of Political Economy 94 (2), 235–259.

Vickers, J. (1991). "Privatization and the risk of expropriation". Rivista Di Politica Economica 11, 115–146.

Vickers, J. (1995a). "Competition and regulation in vertically related markets". Review of Economic Studies 62 (1), 1–17.

Vickers, J. (1995b). "Concepts of competition". Oxford Economic Papers 47 (1), 1–23.

Vogelsang, I. (1988). "A little paradox in the design of regulatory mechanisms". International Economic Review 29 (3), 467–476.

Vogelsang, I. (1989). "Price cap regulation of telecommunications services: A long-run approach". In: Crew, M. (Ed.), Deregulation and Diversification of Utilities. Kluwer Academic Publishers, Boston, MA.

Vogelsang, I. (1990). "Optional two-part tariffs constrained by price caps". Economics Letters 33 (3), 287–292.

Vogelsang, I. (2002). "Incentive regulation and competition in public utility markets: A 20-year perspective". Journal of Regulatory Economics 22 (1), 5–28.

Vogelsang, I. (2003). "Price regulation of access to telecommunications networks". Journal of Economic Literature 41 (3), 830–862.

Vogelsang, I., Finsinger, J. (1979). "A regulatory adjustment process for optimal pricing by multiproduct monopoly firms". Bell Journal of Economics 10 (1), 151–171.

Weisman, D. (1993). "Superior regulatory regimes in theory and practice". Journal of Regulatory Economics 5 (4), 355–366.

Weisman, D. (1994). "Why more may be less under price-cap regulation". Journal of Regulatory Economics 6 (4), 339–362.

Weisman, D. (1995). "Regulation and the vertically integrated firm: The case of RBOC entry into InterLATA long distance". Journal of Regulatory Economics 8 (3), 249–266.

Weisman, D. (1998). "The incentive to discriminate by a vertically-integrated firm: A reply". Journal of Regulatory Economics 14 (1), 87–91.

Weisman, D. (2002). "Did the High Court reach an economic low in Verizon v. FCC?". Review of Network Economics 1 (2), 90–105.

Weisman, D. (2005). "Price regulation and quality". Information Economics and Policy 17 (2), 165–174.

Weisman, D., Williams, M. (2001). "The costs and benefits of long-distance entry: Regulation and non-price discrimination". Review of Economic Organization 18 (3), 275–282.

Williamson, O. (1975). Markets and Hierarchies: Analysis and Antitrust Implications. Free Press, New York.

Williamson, O. (1976). "Franchise bidding for natural monopolies – In general and with respect to CATV". Bell Journal of Economics 7 (1), 73–104.

Willig, R. (1979). "The theory of network access pricing". In: Trebing, H. (Ed.), Issues in Public Utility Regulation. Michigan State Univ. Press, East Lansing, MI.

Wilson, R. (1979). "Auctions of shares". Quarterly Journal of Economics 93 (4), 675–689.

Wolinsky, A. (1997). "Regulation of duopoly: Managed competition vs. regulated monopolies". Journal of Economics and Management Strategy 6 (4), 821–847.

Zupan, M. (1989a). "Cable franchise renewals: Do incumbent firms behave opportunistically?". RAND Journal of Economics 20 (4), 473–482.

Zupan, M. (1989b). "The efficacy of franchise bidding schemes in the case of CATV: Some systematic evidence". Journal of Law and Economics 32 (2), 401–456.

Chapter 28

THE ECONOMIC ANALYSIS OF ADVERTISING

KYLE BAGWELL
Columbia University

Contents

Handbook of Industrial Organization, Volume 3
Edited by M. Armstrong and R. Porter

DOI: 10.1016/S1573-448X(06)03028-7

Abstract

This chapter offers a comprehensive survey of the economic analysis of advertising. A first objective is to organize the literature in a manner that clarifies what is known. A second objective is to clarify how this knowledge has been obtained. The chapter begins with a discussion of the key initial writings that are associated with the persuasive, informative and complementary views of advertising. Next, work that characterizes empirical regularities between advertising and other variables is considered. Much of this work is conducted at the inter-industry level but important industry studies are also discussed. The chapter then offers several sections that summarize formal economic theories of advertising. In particular, respective sections are devoted to positive and normative theories of monopoly advertising, theories of price and non-price advertising, theories of advertising and product quality, and theories that explore the potential role for advertising in deterring entry. At this point, the chapter considers the empirical support for the formal economic theories of advertising. A summary is provided of empirical work that evaluates the predictions of recent theories of advertising, including work that specifies and estimates explicitly structural models of firm and consumer conduct. This work is characterized by the use of industry (or brand) and even household-level data. The chapter then considers work on endogenous and exogenous sunk cost industries. At a methodological level, this work is integrative in nature: it develops new theory that delivers a few robust predictions, and it then explores the empirical relevance of these predictions at both inter-industry and industry levels. Finally, the chapter considers new directions and other topics. Here, recent work on advertising and media markets is discussed, and research on behavioral economics and neuroeconomics is also featured. A final section offers some concluding thoughts.

Keywords

Advertising, Survey, Theory, Empirical analysis

JEL classification: M300, L100, D800

"What makes the advertising issue fascinating . . . is that it is fundamentally an issue in how to establish truth in economics." (Phillip Nelson, 1974a)

1. Introduction

By its very nature, advertising is a prominent feature of economic life. Advertising reaches consumers through their TV sets, radios, newspapers, magazines, mailboxes, computers and more. Not surprisingly, the associated advertising expenditures can be huge. For example, Advertising Age (2005) reports that, in 2003 in the U.S., General Motors spent $3.43 billion to advertise its cars and trucks; Procter and Gamble devoted $3.32 billion to the advertisement of its detergents and cosmetics; and Pfizer incurred a $2.84 billion advertising expense for its drugs. Advertising is big business indeed.

From the current perspective, it is thus surprising to learn that the major economists of the 19th century and before paid little attention to advertising. The economic analysis of advertising is almost entirely a 20th-century project. Why did not 19th-century economists analyze advertising? Two reasons stand out.

First, 19th-century economic research is devoted largely to the development of the theory of perfect competition, and this theory does not immediately suggest a role for advertising. As Pigou (1924, pp. 173–174) remarks, "Under simple competition there is no purpose in this advertisement, because, *ex hypothesi*, the market will take, at the market price, as much as any one small seller wants to sell". Of course, whether a firm is competitive (i.e., price-taking) or not, it might advertise if it were thereby able to shift its demand curve upward so that a higher price could be obtained. But here a more basic problem arises: under the conventional assumptions that consumers have fixed preferences over products and perfect information with regard to prices and qualities, there is no reason for consumers to respond to advertising, and so the posited demand shift is unjustified.[1]

Second, while advertising has long been used by merchants, its transition to "big business" is more modern. In the late 19th and early 20th centuries, following significant advances in transportation (railroads) and communication (telegraph) networks, manufacturers were motivated to pursue innovations in the machinery of production and distribution, so that economies of scale could be reaped. These economies, however, could be achieved only if demand were appropriately stimulated. The turn-of-the-century technological innovations that are associated with mass production and

[1] As Braithwaite (1928, p. 28) explains: "Under conditions of perfect competition producers would gain nothing by spending money on advertisement, for those conditions assume two things – (1) that the demand curve is fixed and cannot be altered directly by producers, and (2) that since producers can sell all that they can produce at the market price, none of them could produce (at a given moment) more at that price than they are already doing".

distribution thus gave significant encouragement to large-scale brand advertising and mass marketing activities.[2]

At the beginning of the 20th century, advertising was thus a ripe topic for economic research. The economic analysis of advertising begins with Marshall (1890, 1919), who offers some insightful distinctions, and then gathers momentum with Chamberlin's (1933) integration of selling costs into economic theory. Over the second half of the century, the economic analysis of advertising has advanced at a furious pace. Now, following the close of the 20th century, a substantial literature has emerged. My purpose here is to survey this literature.

In so doing, I hope to accomplish two objectives. A first objective is to organize the literature in a manner that clarifies *what* is known.[3] Of course, it is impossible to summarize all of the economic studies of advertising. Following a century of work, though, this seems a good time to bring to the surface the more essential contributions and take inventory of what is known. Second, I hope to clarify *how* this knowledge has been obtained. The economic implications of advertising are of undeniable importance; however, the true nature of these implications has yielded but slowly to economic analysis. There is a blessing in this. With every theoretical and empirical methodological innovation in industrial organization, economists have turned to important and unresolved issues in advertising, demonstrating the improvements that their new approach offers. Advertising therefore offers a resilient set of issues against which to chart the progress gained as industrial organization methods have evolved.

It is helpful to begin with a basic question: Why do consumers respond to advertising? An economic theory of advertising can proceed only after this question is confronted. As economists have struggled with this question, three views have emerged, with each view in turn being associated with distinct positive and normative implications.

The first view is that advertising is *persuasive*. This is the dominant view expressed in economic writings in the first half of the 20th century. The persuasive view holds that advertising alters consumers' tastes and creates spurious product differentiation and brand loyalty. As a consequence, the demand for a firm's product becomes more inelastic, and so advertising results in higher prices. In addition, advertising by established firms may give rise to a barrier to entry, which is naturally more severe when there are economies of scale in production and/or advertising. The persuasive approach therefore suggests that advertising can have important anti-competitive effects, as it has no "real"

[2] The emergence of large-scale advertising is also attributable to income growth, printing and literacy advances, and urbanization. See also Borden (1942), Chandler (1990), Harris and Seldon (1962), Pope (1983), Simon (1970) and Wood (1958).

[3] Surprisingly, there does not appear to exist another contemporary and comprehensive survey of the economic analysis of advertising. Various portions of the literature are treated in other work. For example, Ekelund and Saurman (1988) offer an interesting discussion of early views on advertising by economists, and Comanor and Wilson (1979) and Schmalensee (1972) provide valuable surveys of early empirical analyses. Tirole (1988) discusses in detail a few of the recent theories of advertising. Finally, in Volumes 1 and 2 of the Handbook of Industrial Organization, Schmalensee (1989) provides further discussion of empirical findings, while Stiglitz (1989) offers some brief reflections on the theory of advertising.

value to consumers, but rather induces artificial product differentiation and results in concentrated markets characterized by high prices and profits.

The second view is that advertising is *informative*. This view emerged in force in the 1960s, under the leadership of the Chicago School. According to this approach, many markets are characterized by imperfect consumer information, since search costs may deter a consumer from learning of each product's existence, price and quality. This imperfection can lead to market inefficiencies, but advertising is not the cause of the problem. Instead, advertising is the endogenous response that the market offers as a solution. When a firm advertises, consumers receive at low cost additional direct (prices, location) and/or indirect (the firm is willing to spend on advertising) information. The firm's demand curve becomes more elastic, and advertising thus promotes competition among established firms. As well, advertising can facilitate entry, as it provides a means though which a new entrant can publicize its existence, prices and products. The suggestion here, then, is that advertising can have important pro-competitive effects.

A third view is that advertising is *complementary* to the advertised product. According to this perspective, advertising does not change consumers' preferences, as in the persuasive view; furthermore, it may, but need not, provide information. Instead, it is assumed that consumers possess a stable set of preferences into which advertising enters directly in a fashion that is complementary with the consumption of the advertised product. For example, consumers may value "social prestige", and the consumption of a product may generate greater prestige when the product is (appropriately) advertised. An important implication is that standard methods may be used to investigate whether advertising is supplied to a socially optimal degree, even if advertising conveys no information.

These views are all, at some level, plausible. But they have dramatically different positive and normative implications. The persuasive and informative views, in particular, offer conflicting assessments of the social value of advertising. It is of special importance, therefore, to subject these views to rigorous empirical and theoretical evaluation. Over the past fifty years, the economic analysis of advertising, like the field of industrial organization itself, can be described in terms of a sequence of empirical, theoretical and again empirical evaluative phases.

The empirical analysis of advertising was at center stage from the 1950s through the 1970s. Over this period, a voluminous literature investigated general empirical relationships between advertising and a host of other variables, including concentration, profit, entry and price. Much of this work employs regression methods and uses inter-industry data, but important studies are also conducted at the industry, firm and even brand levels. This period is marked by vigorous and mostly edifying debates between advocates of the persuasive and informative views. The debates center on both the robustness and the interpretation of empirical findings, and they identify some of the limitations of regression analyses, particularly at the inter-industry level. While the inter-industry analyses are often inconclusive, defensible empirical patterns emerge within particular industries or narrow industry categories. The evidence strongly suggests that no single view of advertising is valid in all settings.

The empirical studies suggest important roles for advertising theory. First, theoretical work might make progress where empirical work has failed. A general theoretical argument might exist, for example, that indicates that advertising is always excessively supplied by the market. Likewise, a theoretical model might assess the validity of the persuasive-view hypothesis that advertising deters entry. Second, advances in the theory of advertising might generate new predictions as to the relationships between advertising and market structure. In turn, these predictions could motivate new empirical work. Third, and relatedly, theoretical work might provide a foundation from which to appropriately specify the supply side of more sophisticated econometric analyses, in which the endogeneity of consumer and firm conduct is embraced. Utilizing recent advances in game theory, economists thus began in the late 1970s to advance formal theories of advertising. This work is vital and ongoing.

Beginning in the 1980s, economists approached the empirical analyses of advertising with renewed interest. For the purposes of this survey, it is useful to organize the modern work in three broad groups. Studies in the first group often use new data sources and further evaluate the empirical findings of the earlier empirical work. These studies are not strongly influenced by the intervening theoretical work. Studies in the second group also draw on new data sets, sometimes constructed at the brand and even household levels, and reflect more strongly the influence of the intervening theoretical work. The conduct of firms and consumers in particular industries is emphasized. Studies in this group evaluate the predictions of strategic theories of advertising, and may even specify and estimate explicit structural models of consumer and firm conduct. Finally, following Sutton (1991), a third group of studies culls from the intervening theoretical work a few robust predictions that might apply across broad groups of industries. Studies in the third group thus sometimes return to the inter-industry focus that characterized much of the earlier empirical work; however, the empirical analysis is now strongly guided by general theoretical considerations.

This historical description provides a context in which to understand the organization of this survey. In Section 2, I describe the work of Marshall (1890, 1919) and Chamberlin (1933), and I review the key initial writings that are associated with each of the three views. This discussion is developed at some length, since these writings contain the central ideas that shape (and are often re-discovered by) the later literature. Section 3 contains a summary of the findings of the initial and modern (first-group) empirical efforts.[4] In Sections 4 through 7, I present research on advertising theory. Next, in Section 8, I describe the modern (second-group) empirical efforts. The modern (third-group) work is discussed in Section 9. Section 10 identifies new directions and omitted topics, and Section 11 concludes.

The survey is comprehensive and thus long. The sections are organized around topics, however, making it easy to locate the material of greatest interest. For teaching purposes,

[4] It is not always clear whether a study belongs in the first or second group. When there is any ambiguity, I place the study in the first group, so that the topic treatments found in Section 3 may be more self contained.

if a thorough treatment of advertising is planned, then the survey may be assigned in full. Alternatively, if the plan is to focus on a particular topic within advertising, then Section 2 and the section that covers the corresponding topic may be assigned. Section 2 provides a general context in which to understand any of the topic treatments found in later sections.

2. Views on advertising

In this section, I discuss the key initial writings that led to each of the three main views (persuasive, informative, complementary) of advertising. The assignment of economists to views is, to some degree, arbitrary, as it is commonly recognized that advertising can influence consumer behavior for different reasons. There are, however, important differences in emphasis among many of the key contributors. I begin with Marshall (1890, 1919) and especially Chamberlin (1933), who set the stage by identifying some of the possible views and implications of advertising. I then review the key contributions that emphasize more forcefully the development of one view over another. The section concludes with a general discussion that inventories the potential social benefits and costs of advertising.

2.1. Setting the stage

Some initial reflections on advertising are offered by Marshall (1890, 1919). As Marshall (1919) explains, advertising can play a *constructive role* by conveying information to consumers. Constructive advertising can alert consumers to the existence and location of products, and it can also convey (pre-purchase) information concerning the functions and qualities of products. But Marshall (1890, 1919) also emphasizes that some kinds of advertising can be socially wasteful. In particular, some advertising involves repetitive messages, and such advertising plays a *combative role*, as its apparent purpose is to redistribute buyers from a rival firm to the advertising firm.[5]

Unfortunately, Marshall did not pursue a formal integration of advertising into economic theory. With the development of his theory of monopolistic competition, however, Chamberlin (1933) embraces this integration. Fundamental to Chamberlin's approach is the assumption that, within a given industry, firms sell differentiated products.

[5] Along with Marshall (1890, 1919), other early contributors to the economic analysis of advertising include Fogg-Meade (1901), Pigou (1924), Shaw (1912), Sherman (1900) and Shryer (1912). Fogg-Meade argues that advertising is a positive force for society, since it educates consumers by bringing new goods to their attention. Pigou emphasizes that much advertising is combative and thus socially wasteful. Shaw argues that advertising enables manufacturers to by-pass the middleman and establish their brand names with consumers. Advertising thus gives manufacturers incentive to maintain reputations for high quality. Sherman details the extent and nature of advertising in the U.S. in the 19th century. He also observes that advertising can play constructive and combative roles. Shryer offers one of the first quantitative studies of advertising. Using mail-order data, he argues that the effect of advertising on sales exhibits decreasing returns.

As a consequence, each firm faces a downward-sloping demand curve and thus possesses some monopoly power. Chamberlin argues additionally that a firm can use advertising and other promotional activities to further differentiate its product from those of its rivals. Advertising-induced product differentiation is beneficial to a firm as a means of expanding its market; in graphical terms, by advertising, a firm generates an outward shift in its demand curve. When a firm considers increasing its advertising, it thus balances this market-expansion benefit against the additional "selling costs" that such an increase would entail.

Chamberlin does not model consumer behavior explicitly, and he takes as given that consumers respond to advertising. He does, however, offer two explanations for the presumed responsiveness. Chamberlin (1933, pp. 118–120) argues that advertising affects demand, because it (i) conveys information to consumers, with regard to the existence of sellers and the price and qualities of products in the marketplace, and (ii) alters consumers' "wants" or tastes. When advertising communicates information that concerns the existence of the firm's product, the effect is to expand the firm's market with an outward shift in demand. If advertising conveys price information as well, then the firm's expanded demand curve also may be more elastic, as more consumers then can be informed of a price reduction. But if advertising serves its second general purpose – that of creating wants through brand development and the like – then the advertising firm's demand curve shifts out and may be made more inelastic. Chamberlin thus identifies the informative and persuasive roles for advertising.

Scale economies figure prominently in Chamberlin's approach. First, Chamberlin assumes that a firm's production technology is characterized by increasing returns to scale up to a critical level of output. Second, Chamberlin (1933, pp. 133–136) stresses as well that there may be an economy of scale in advertising. To motivate this scale economy, Chamberlin argues that (i) a consumer's responsiveness to advertising messages may be "fortified by repetition", and (ii) there may be improvement in the organization of advertising expenditures at higher levels, as gains from specialization in selling are realized and as more effective media (which may be accessible only at higher expenditures) are used. At the same time, beyond a critical sales volume, diminishing returns are inevitable, since additional advertising becomes less effective once the most responsive buyers are already reached. In total, Chamberlin concludes that the unit costs of production and selling are each U-shaped, and on this basis he argues that a firm's combined unit cost curve is U-shaped as well.

Using these ingredients, Chamberlin describes a monopolistic–competition equilibrium, in which each firm sets its monopoly price and yet earns zero profit. As the standard textbook diagram depicts, at the firm's monopoly price, its downward-sloping demand curve is just tangent to its combined unit cost curve. Chamberlin argues that this tangency is a necessary consequence of the competitive forces of entry. In this general manner, Chamberlin reconciles monopolistic and competitive forces, by introducing a modeling paradigm that emphasizes product differentiation, scale economies and advertising.

In an important application of his framework, Chamberlin (1933, pp. 165–167) considers the possible price effects of advertising. He compares the monopolistic-competition equilibrium when advertising is allowed with the corresponding equilibrium that would emerge if advertising were not allowed. On the one hand, the demand-expanding effect of advertising enables firms to better achieve economies of scale in production, and this *scale effect* works to reduce prices.[6] On the other hand, advertising entails selling costs, and so a firm's combined unit cost is higher when advertising is permitted. In a zero-profit equilibrium, this *cost effect* works to increase prices. Finally, advertising affects pricing as well through an *elasticity effect*. When advertising increases the elasticity of a firm's demand, as advertising might when it contains price information, there is further support for the suggestion that advertising reduce prices. Of course, the opposite suggestion is given further credence, if advertising makes the firm's demand less elastic, as advertising might when it creates wants and encourages brand loyalty.

In light of these conflicting effects, Chamberlin (1933, p. 167) concludes that the net effect of advertising on prices cannot be resolved by theory alone: "The effect of advertising in any particular case depends upon the facts of the case." Among these facts, Chamberlin's discussion clearly suggests that the purpose of advertising (persuasive or informative) and the extent of scale economies (in production and advertising) warrant greatest attention. This is a balanced and penetrating suggestion. It also serves to provide a general context in which to understand subsequent research, wherein economists debate the purpose of advertising and the probable extent of scale economies.

2.2. *The persuasive view*

In the writings that initially followed Chamberlin's effort, advertising's persuasive powers are given primary emphasis. These writings acknowledge a role for scale economies, under which advertising may exert a price-reducing influence, but the conclusion that emerges is that advertising may have important anti-competitive consequences. In arriving at this conclusion, the persuasive-view advocates go beyond Chamberlin to emphasize that advertising has an *entry-deterrence effect*: when advertising creates brand loyalty, it also creates a barrier to entry, since established firms are then able to charge high prices and earn significant profits without facing entry. As I describe below, the persuasive view is developed through an increasingly sophisticated set of conceptual and empirical arguments.

In fact, the first advocates of the persuasive view were contemporaries of Chamberlin's. In her development of the theory of imperfect competition, Robinson (1933, p. 5) includes some brief discussion of advertising, in which she argues that "the customer will be influenced by advertisement, which plays upon his mind with studied skill, and

[6] Marshall (1890, ch. XIV) also briefly discusses the possibility that advertising induces a beneficial scale effect.

makes him prefer the goods of one producer to those of another because they are brought to his notice in a more pleasing and forceful manner". Likewise, in considering the potential anti-competitive implications of advertising, Robinson (1933, p. 101) claims that if "a firm finds the market becoming uncomfortably perfect (i.e., more competitive) it can resort to advertisement and other devices which attach customers more firmly to itself". In total, Robinson suggests that advertising has strong anti-competitive consequences, since it deters entry and sustains monopoly power in a market where the conduct of established firms otherwise would be suitably disciplined by competitive pressures.

In a perceptive paper that, unaccountably, now seems largely forgotten, Braithwaite (1928) contributes significantly toward a conceptual foundation for the persuasive view.[7] Braithwaite regards advertising as a "selling cost", the purpose of which is to re-arrange consumers' valuations, so that they are persuaded to value more greatly the advertised product. Advertising shifts out a consumer's demand for the advertised product, and it thus distorts the consumer's decisions as compared to those that reflect his "true" preferences (as captured in his pre-advertising demand). The real economic resources that are expended through advertising activities thus may be wasted, since advertising's effect is to induce consumers to purchase the wrong quantities of goods that are not well adapted to their true needs at prices that are swollen from the cost effect of advertising. On the other hand, Braithwaite recognizes that advertising may also induce a scale effect that exerts a downward pressure on price.

In light of these competing influences, Braithwaite (1928, p. 35) establishes the following result: if a monopolist's advertising shifts out the demand for its product, and if consumer surplus is evaluated relative to the initial (pre-advertising) demand, then advertising increases consumer surplus *only if* it is accompanied by a strict reduction in price. Figure 28.1 illustrates that consumer surplus may fall, even if there is a strict reduction in price. The consumer surplus gain from a lower price is marked as G, while the consumer surplus loss that comes from distorted consumption is marked as L. Certainly, L can exceed G if the price decrease is modest, and L necessarily exceeds G if price is unaltered.

Braithwaite also advances the entry-deterrence effect of advertising. She argues that, by advertising, an established firm creates a "reputation" for its brand among consumers. New entrants can then succeed only by developing their own reputation through advertising, and Braithwaite (1928, p. 32) claims that for them the necessary expenditures may be even higher: "But, since they have to create reputation in the face of one already established, the probability is that their advertisement costs will be heavier than those of the original manufacturer". Advertising thus may result in the creation of "reputational monopolies". This entry-deterrence effect offers further support for the belief that advertising causes higher prices and lower welfare.

[7] Braithwaite (1928) and Chamberlin (1933) cover some similar terrain, and the contributions appear to be independent [see Chamberlin (1933, p. 126)].

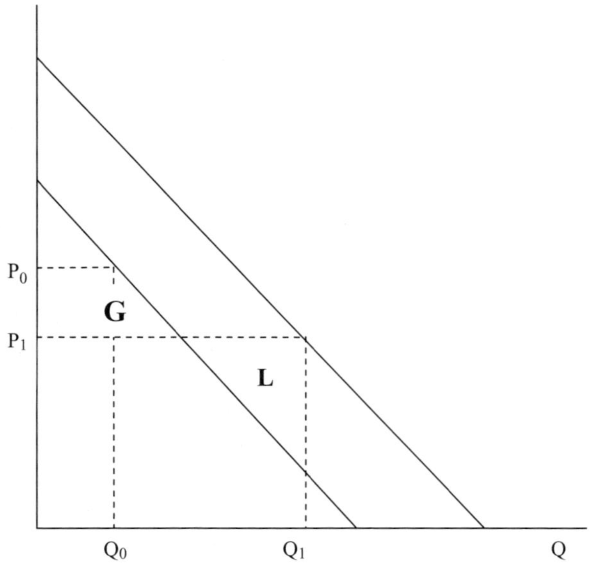

Figure 28.1. Consumption distortion.

Finally, Braithwaite (1928, p. 36) considers whether reputation itself may confer some possible benefit to the consumer. She states one possibility: "Advertisers maintain that their reputation is a guarantee of quality. For they say that it is not worth a manufacturer's while to stake his name and spend his money on advertising an article of poor quality." In the end, she argues that the *quality-guarantee effect* is modest.[8] Her reasons are that: (i) factually, reputations are sometimes created for inferior goods which enjoy short-lived profits, (ii) consumers can be poor judges of quality, and they may linger with an inferior product, and (iii) any such guarantee is to some degree redundant, since a reliable retailer already offers an implicit guarantee as to the quality of products sold in his store. In view of these considerations, Braithwaite (1928, p. 37) concludes that reputation does not offer advantages to consumers that are sufficient to compensate for the harmful effects of advertisement that she otherwise identifies.

The persuasive view of advertising is further advanced by Kaldor (1950). He draws a distinction between the direct and indirect effects of advertising on social welfare. The direct effect of advertising is associated with its role in the provision of price and product-quality information to consumers, while the indirect effects of advertising include any consequent scale economies in production and distribution.

[8] Fogg-Meade (1901), Marshall (1919) and Shaw (1912) are early proponents of the quality-guarantee effect. In contrast to Braithwaite (1928), they suggest that advertising and trademarks can greatly enhance the incentive for manufacturers to offer high-quality products.

Kaldor begins with the direct effect. Observing that the "price" of advertising to the buyer is typically zero, Kaldor regards advertising as a subsidized commodity (i.e., a commodity sold below marginal cost) that is sold jointly with the advertised product. Advertising is then profitable to the seller, because it is "complementary" to the advertised product (i.e., advertising increases the demand for the advertised product). As Kaldor explains, given the absence of a separate market for advertising and the associated divergence between price and marginal cost, there can be no presumption that the amount of advertising is efficient. Moreover, while advertising can convey information, this information is offered by an interested party. Kaldor (1950, p. 7) thus argues that the majority of advertising is persuasive in nature. After considering the direct effect of advertising, Kaldor suggests that advertising is a wasteful means of conveying a modest degree of information.

If advertising is to be justified, then the justification must come from its indirect effects. Here, the core of Kaldor's argument is that advertising promotes greater concentration; hence, the primary indirect effects of advertising are the same as those that are associated with increased concentration. The indirect effects thus can cut both ways. On the one hand, there may be a detrimental elasticity effect: greater advertising may lead through greater concentration to enhanced monopoly power and the loss in efficiency that such power brings. On the other hand, there may be a beneficial scale effect: greater advertising and the increased concentration that it implies may give rise to an efficiency gain, due to achievement of scale economies in production and/or distribution.

On what basis does Kaldor conclude that advertising promotes greater concentration? To develop this position, Kaldor assumes that an economy of scale to advertising exists and that larger, more profitable firms are better able to finance larger advertising expenditures. Kaldor (1950, p. 13) then argues that advertising introduces an instability in the initial distribution of market shares, "with the consequence (a) that the larger firms are bound to gain at the expense of the smaller ones; (b) if at the start, firms are more or less of equal size, those that forge ahead are bound to increase their lead, as the additional sales enable them to increase their outlay still further". This *concentration effect* of advertising continues until an oligopolistic structure emerges. According to Kaldor, there are two reasons that the process halts before a monopoly structure is achieved. First, advertising eventually becomes subject to diminished returns. Second, at some point, each firm resists any intrusion into its market, being prepared to increase its own advertising in response to any increase in advertising by another firm.

I return now to Kaldor's comparison of indirect effects. Given that these effects are competing, Kaldor reaches the same conclusion as did Chamberlin before him: the net social consequence of advertising cannot be decided on the basis of economic theory alone. To gain further insight, Kaldor considers the role of advertising in Britain in the late 19th century. In Kaldor's view, the advent of large-scale advertising contributed to the emergence of a new organizational structure, which he calls "manufacturers' domination". Manufacturers used advertising to establish brand names and position those names in the foreground of the consumers' consciousness, so that consumers would be persuaded to seek these brands. In this way, large-scale advertising enabled manufacturers to leap over middlemen and establish a direct connection with final consumers.[9] The manufacturing sector then became more concentrated, and additional scale economies (associated with mass-production techniques) were realized. The manufacturers' domination structure is thus characterized by low production costs and high selling costs. As Kaldor acknowledges, his informal study does not afford a conclusive assessment as to advertising's indirect effects. In the main, though, he seems skeptical that manufacturer advertising can be justified by its indirect effects.

The persuasive view next proceeds along two tracks. One set of work embarks on a broad assessment of the social consequences of advertising. Notably, Galbraith (1958, 1967) and Packard (1957, 1969) propose a very negative view of advertising, wherein the institution of modern advertising arises with the purpose of creating wants among a population of passive consumers. I emphasize here a second set of work. This work offers an empirical assessment of the implications of the persuasive view. Persuasive advertising instills brand loyalty and is thus expected to exert an indirect influence on other market variables that correspond to entry barriers, profit rates, concentration ratios and pricing levels. The persuasive view thus may be indirectly evaluated by checking the consistency of its implications with cross-sectional data. The primary initial efforts of this kind are by Bain (1956) and Comanor and Wilson (1967, 1974).

On the basis of extensive interviews and a questionnaire survey, Bain offers a qualitative assessment of the relative importance of specific entry barriers in a sample of 20 large U.S. manufacturing industries. Bain (1956, p. 14) considers four structural forms that an entry barrier may take: absolute cost advantages of established sellers, product differentiation advantages of established sellers, scale economies and capital requirements. From this study, Bain (1956, p. 216) famously concludes that product differentiation is probably the most important entry barrier. Using profit rate data from 1936–1940 and 1947–1951, Bain (1956, pp. 196, 201) further reports that the average profit rates for dominant firms are significantly greater in high than moderate-to-low concentration industries; in addition, among highly concentrated industries, profit rates are significantly higher for those that are categorized as having very high barriers to entry than for those with lesser entry barriers. Bain thus suggests that concentration and barriers to entry are two of the major determinants of profitability.

Where does advertising fit in? As a general matter, Bain (1956, p. 143) does not conclude that advertising per se is the primary source of product differentiation. But drawing on his interviews, questionnaires and estimates of "traceable" advertising expenditures, Bain (1956, pp. 114–115, 125) clearly argues that an incumbent firm may use advertising to contribute importantly toward a preference for its established products in comparison to new-entrant products. This possibility is of particular significance in consumer-goods industries; in fact, Bain (1956, p. 125) concludes that the "single most important basis of product differentiation in the consumer-good category is apparently advertising". On the whole, Bain's pioneering analysis suggests that

[9] Similar observations are made in other early efforts. See Borden (1942), Braithwaite (1928), Chamberlin (1933), Fogg-Meade (1901), Marshall (1919), Shaw (1912) and Tosdal (1918).

advertising-induced product differentiation may constitute an important entry barrier that helps established manufacturers (especially in highly concentrated and consumer-goods industries) to set prices above costs and earn considerable profits. His work thus offers early empirical support for the hypothesis that advertising has significant anti-competitive effects.

As Bain acknowledges, his analysis is not conclusive. It is useful here to note two limitations. First, Bain does not explain the process through which advertising leads to a preference for established products and creates an entry barrier. Second, Bain's empirical analysis relies upon qualitative classifications of industries with respect to market-structure variables.

These limitations motivate Comanor and Wilson (1967, 1974). Echoing the "reputational" reasoning of Braithwaite (1928), they explain that advertising-induced product differentiation can generate an entry barrier, if high prevailing levels of advertising create additional costs for new entrants above those experienced by established firms. In support of this possibility, they emphasize that a new entrant may face greater market-penetration costs than originally did the pioneering firm, since the new entrant must induce consumers to *switch* from an established and familiar product to a new and unknown product. As Comanor and Wilson (1974, pp. 48–49) explain, high prevailing advertising levels then may constitute a barrier to entry, if they "reinforce the experience that consumers have with established products" so as to enhance brand loyalty and exacerbate the differential advertising costs that await new entrants. They stress, too, that a new (small-scale) entrant is at cost disadvantage relative to an established (large-scale) firm, if an advertising scale economy is present.

Comanor and Wilson also respond to the empirical limitations of Bain's analysis. While Bain creates qualitative industry rankings for hard-to-measure market-structure variables, Comanor and Wilson proxy for these variables with alternative variables for which quantitative data are available. They are thus able to perform multi-variate regression analyses on measurable variables. Seeking to explain profit averaged over the period 1954–1957 for manufacturers in 41 consumer-goods industries, they allow for a variety of explanatory variables, including the advertising/sales ratio, the four-firm concentration ratio and measurements that proxy for demand growth, scale economies and capital requirements. The advertising/sales data are taken at the industry level from IRS statistics and proxy for product differentiation. The rate of profit is measured at the industry level as the after-tax rate of return on shareholder equity. As their main finding, Comanor and Wilson report a positive and significant relationship between the rate of profit and the advertising/sales ratio.

Comanor and Wilson's finding is consistent with the hypothesis that advertising causes profitability. But advertising is in fact an endogenous variable, and it thus inappropriate to treat industry advertising intensity as an independent structural variable. Indeed, if firms re-invest a certain percentage of their profit or sales in advertising, then their finding also may be interpreted in support of the reverse hypothesis that profitability causes advertising. Relatedly, there may be underlying influences (inelastic demand, low marginal cost) that result in larger price–cost profit margins. Influences of this kind may generate both higher profit and larger advertising, since firms have greater incentive to advertise when mark-ups are large. If the corresponding variables are omitted from the regression, then the relationship between advertising and profitability may be spurious.[10]

In response to the endogeneity concern, Comanor and Wilson (1974) extend their analysis to include a profitability equation and a second equation in which the advertising/sales ratio is influenced by profit margins and other variables. They find that advertising intensity continues to affect profitability. They also supply some empirical support for the existence of important advertising scale economies. On the basis of these and other findings, Comanor and Wilson (1974, p. 239) interpret their study as offering "empirical support for the conclusion that the heavy volume of advertising expenditures in some industries serves as an important barrier to new competition in the markets served by these industries".

Comanor and Wilson's work marks a significant step forward, but it also has important limitations. First, while their emphasis on the experience-based demand asymmetry between established and new firms is well placed, they do not endogenize the manner in which advertising interacts with consumers' experiences, so as to "reinforce" past experiences and differentially reward established firms. Second, profitability may derive less from advertising itself than from the underlying product and market characteristics that determine advertising as well. The endogeneity concern is fundamental and calls for simultaneous-equation methods; however, in an inter-industry study, the identification of any structural equation is difficult, since most right-hand side variables are endogenous. Third, if advertising generates brand loyalty, then measurement concerns arise: while accounting profit treats advertising as a current expense, a true measure of profit would treat advertising as (intangible) capital that depreciates at some rate. Fourth, inter-industry studies leave unexposed important relationships that may be associated with the particular features of the industry, product or advertising media mix. These and other issues motivate much subsequent research, which I describe in the sections that follow.

2.3. *The informative view*

Under the informative view, advertising is attractive to firms as a means through which they may convey information to consumers. An important implication of this view is that advertising may have pro-competitive consequences. As noted above, elements of this view appear in the writings of Marshall and Chamberlin. But the informative view

[10] The endogeneity concern is defined and thoroughly explored by Schmalensee (1972). As noted below, Telser (1964, p. 551) offers an early statement of this concern. See also Sherman and Tollison (1971). As I detail in Section 3, similar endogeneity problems arise with regard to the relationships between advertising and sales as well as concentration. The endogeneity concern is also suggested by the optimal advertising literature that derives from the work of Dorfman and Steiner (1954). I discuss this literature in Section 4.1.

really took flight in the 1960s, largely under the leadership of a group of "Chicago School" economists.

The formal foundation for the information view is laid by Ozga (1960) and Stigler (1961). Stigler interprets price dispersion as a reflection of consumer ignorance, where this ignorance in turn derives from the costs to consumers of obtaining information as to the existence, location and prices of products. He then constructs a model of optimal consumer search behavior, in which advertising effectively reduces consumers' search costs, since it conveys such information. Stigler thus argues that advertising is a valuable source of information for consumers that results in a reduction in price dispersion. Ozga develops similar themes, although in his analysis consumers passively receive information (from social contacts and/or advertising) and do not search for it. As well, Ozga (1960, p. 40) goes beyond Chamberlin and offers for informative advertising a new rationale for diminishing returns: "as more and more of the potential buyers become informed of what is advertised, more and more of the advertising effort is wasted, because a greater and greater proportion of people who see the advertisements are already familiar with the object".

In Telser's (1964) influential effort, the theoretical and empirical foundations for the informative view are significantly advanced. Telser's explores the following question: Is advertising compatible with competitive (i.e., price-taking) behavior among firms? Telser (1964, p. 558) concludes with a positive answer: "Advertising is frequently a means of entry and a sign of competition. This agrees with the view that advertising is an important source of information."

How does Telser arrive at this conclusion? He begins by considering the theoretical compatibility between advertising and competition. Like Chamberlin and Kaldor before him, Telser concludes that this issue cannot be resolved on the basis of theory alone. In reaching this decision, Telser notes that, on the one hand, some kinds of advertising are compatible with, and even essential to, competition. For example, a certain fixed expenditure on advertising may be necessary to inform consumers of a firm's existence before any sales can be made. In the competitive framework, it then can be understood that price is determined to match average costs, inclusive of advertising expenditures (the cost effect). On the other hand, there are two reasons that advertising may be associated with monopoly power. First, in an early statement of the endogeneity concern, Telser (1964, p. 551) observes that "firms that have some monopoly power are more likely to advertise because they can obtain most of the increased sales stimulated by their advertising". Second, Telser (1964, p. 541) allows that some advertising may be persuasive and thereby give rise to monopoly power.

Given the lack of theoretical resolution, Telser pursues an empirical assessment of the cross-sectional relationship between advertising intensity and other market variables. Methodologically, Telser's analysis is a natural intermediate step between the earlier analysis of Bain and the subsequent analyses of Comanor and Wilson. Telser computes advertising/sales ratios from IRS data and performs simple regression analysis. He offers two kinds of indirect evidence.

First, Telser considers the relationship between advertising and concentration. Recall that Kaldor posits a positive relationship. Telser (1964, p. 542) takes the following perspective: "If advertising fosters monopoly, then concentration and advertising should be positively correlated." For 42 consumer-goods industries, Telser calculates (four-firm) concentration and advertising–sales ratios for three different census years. He then considers a linear regression of concentration on advertising intensity, and he reports a positive but very weak relationship. Telser (1964, p. 544) concludes that "the correlation between concentration and advertising is unimpressive".

Second, Telser examines the relationship between advertising and market-share stability. Telser (1964, p. 547) reasons that if "advertising succeeds in sheltering a firm's products from competitive inroads, this should be reflected in more stable market shares of the more advertised goods". To explore this possibility, he considers the market-share and advertising patterns of products in three consumer-goods classes: food, soap and cosmetics. Using various measures, Telser finds that market-share stability appears inversely related to advertising intensity. Telser (1964, p. 550) thus argues that his findings "refute the view that advertising stabilizes market shares". The apparent implication is that advertising facilitates entry and new-product introductions.

Telser's analysis countered the then-prevailing persuasive view and offered an empirical legitimacy to the alternative view that advertising is an important source of information that promotes competition. His work also spawned an on-going empirical literature that explores the competitive effects of advertising. In this literature, some important limitations of Telser's analysis are noted. Most importantly, Comanor and Wilson (1967, 1974) question Telser's use of concentration as a measure of market power. Like Bain, they contend that profitability is a better measure of market power, and they argue that concentration and entry barriers (such as advertising) are key explanatory variables for profitability.

I turn next to a pair of insightful papers by Nelson (1970, 1974b).[11] He begins with a simple question: How, exactly, does advertising provide information to consumers? The informative content of advertising is clear, when the advertisement contains direct information as to the existence, location, function or price of a product. But what about all of the advertising that does not contain direct information of this kind? Is it persuasive? Nelson argues rather that such advertising still plays an informative role, although the role is indirect. To develop this argument, Nelson (1970) makes a distinction between *search* and *experience goods*. A search good is one whose quality can be determined prior to purchase (but perhaps after costly search), whereas the quality of an experience good can be evaluated only after consumption occurs. Building on this distinction, Nelson (1974b) argues that the indirect information contained in advertising is especially important for experience goods.

Nelson (1974b, pp. 732–734) gives three reasons why advertising may provide indirect information to consumers of experience goods. First, there is a *signaling-efficiency*

[11] As I discuss in Section 3, Nelson (1975) offers additional evidence concerning the consequences of advertising. Nelson (1974a, 1978) elaborates on some of the basic insights.

effect. The demand expansion that advertising induces is most valuable to efficient firms, and these low-cost firms are also inclined to seek demand expansion through other means, such as with lower prices and higher qualities. Thus, by advertising, a firm signals that it is efficient, which implies in turn that it offers good deals.[12] Second, consumers may have heterogeneous tastes, and it may be difficult to efficiently match products and buyers. A seemingly uninformative advertisement can assist in this process, since a firm has the incentive to direct its advertising toward the consumers that value its product the most. This is the *match-products-to-buyers effect*. Third, advertising may remind consumers of their previous experience with the product, and such recollections are of more value to sellers of high-quality goods. Given this *repeat-business effect*, even new consumers may draw a positive association between advertising and quality, and advertising thus may signal quality.[13]

What about search goods? Certainly, advertising can provide indirect information here as well. For example, even if a search-good advertisement contains no direct information, the fact that the good is advertised may suggest that the seller is efficient and thus that the good is aggressively priced. Due to the signaling-efficiency effect, therefore, consumers may be encouraged to search for the advertised good. In comparison to experience goods, though, search goods offer greater potential for direct information transmission through advertising. Nelson (1974b, p. 734) thus adopts the hypothesis that "advertising for experience qualities is dominantly indirect information and advertising for search qualities is dominantly direct information".

Nelson (1970, 1974b) presents a variety of empirical evidence in support of this hypothesis. First, he offers evidence that advertising intensity is higher for experience goods. This is consistent with the idea that the act of advertising itself is the indirect means through which a seller of an experience good provides information to consumers. Second, Nelson presents evidence that the ratio of TV to magazine advertising is significantly higher for experience goods. This supports his contention that search goods are especially conducive to the transfer of direct information. Third, Nelson reports evidence for experience goods that advertising intensity is higher for non-durable and lower-priced goods. These findings are consistent with the general idea that, for major (durable and high-priced) purchases, a consumer relies on the information of friends and

[12] The signaling-efficiency effect appears to have been missed by earlier contributors. In fact, Pigou (1924, p. 177) raises the general issue and reasons toward the opposite conclusion: "There is, however, some slight ground for believing that firms of low productive efficiency tend to indulge in advertisement to a greater extent than their productively more efficient rivals. For, clearly, they have greater inducements to expenditure on devices, such as special packages, designed to obviate comparison of the bulk of commodity offered by them and by other producers at a given price."

[13] Nelson (1974b, p. 734) summarizes the argument as follows: "Advertising increases the probability of a consumer's remembering the name of a brand. Those brands with the highest probability of repeat purchase have the greatest payoff to improved consumer memory. In consequence, brands which provide the highest utility have the greatest incentive to advertise."

family, whereas for more frequent (non-durable and low-priced) purchases, a consumer relies on advertising as a source of indirect information.[14]

Nelson's approach seems to assume that consumers make thoughtful inferences in response to advertising. This is disquieting, since it seems rather that consumers often devote little thought to advertising. But as Nelson stresses, his approach in fact does not require that consumers make such careful judgments. If consumers are responsive to advertising, whether thoughtfully or not, then this can induce a positive relationship between advertising and consumer utility, since it is then the most-efficient and best-deal firms that gain the most from advertising. Thus, when consumers naively respond to advertising, firm behavior is generated that confirms the initial responsiveness.[15]

Nelson's work enriches considerably the informative view of advertising. His work also offers support for the position that the advertising–profitability relationship is spurious, since more efficient firms both earn greater profit and, as Nelson (1974b) argues, advertise more heavily. There are, however, important limitations. First, as Nelson (1974b, p. 749) acknowledges, the empirical distinction between search and experience goods is somewhat arbitrary, and so his empirical findings are not conclusive. Second, Nelson (1974b) reasons that high-quality firms are especially attracted to demand-expanding advertising, but he does not provide a formal model that delivers this prediction. As Schmalensee (1978) emphasizes, if lower-quality goods have lower marginal costs, then it is possible that low-quality firms gain differentially from demand expansion. It is also possible that a high-quality firm might prefer to relay indirect information to consumers through its price choice rather than its advertising outlay. These concerns are featured in subsequent formal research, as I discuss in Section 6.

2.4. *The complementary view*

Under the complementary view of advertising, consumers possess stable preferences, and advertising directly enters these preferences in a manner that is complementary to the consumption of the advertised product. This view is logically distinct from the persuasive view (wherein advertising changes the utility function) and the informative view (wherein advertising directly affects utility only if it contains information). The complementary view allows that advertising may contain information and influence consumer behavior for that reason. But there are other possibilities as well. For example, the consumer may value "social prestige", and advertising by a firm may be an input that contributes toward the prestige that is enjoyed when the firm's product is consumed.

[14] For other early studies in which advertising intensity varies with the nature of the product, see Borden (1942), Doyle (1968a, 1968b), Else (1966) and Telser (1961).

[15] As Nelson (1974b, p. 751) puts it: "Many economists have felt that other consumers think quite imprecisely about advertising – and well they might. But this superficial observation has led economists, but not consumers, astray. Economists have failed to see that consumers' response to advertising persists because of the underlying information role of advertising." See also Nelson (1974a, pp. 50–51).

The complementary view is also associated with the Chicago School. Important elements of this view are found in Telser's (1964) work, but Stigler and Becker (1977) offer a more complete statement of the central principles. Under their approach, consumer utility derives from the consumption of various commodities. These commodities, however, are not sold or purchased on the market; rather, they are produced through a household production technology that uses market goods, advertising and other variables (e.g., time) as inputs. In the simplest representation, a consumer buys a market good in quantity X at some per-unit price P_x, and the market good and its associated advertising expenditures A are then inputs that jointly produce an amount Z of the commodity. The consumption of Z then implies a utility level U for the consumer. For example, if Y represents the level of some composite good, then these relationships might be captured as follows: $U = U(Z, Y)$ and $Z = g(A)X$, where $(U_z, U_y, g(A), g'(A), X, Y) > 0$.

Importantly, this structure implies a complementarity between A and X in the production of Z. As Stigler and Becker (1977, p. 84) put it, when a firm advertises more, its product becomes more attractive to the consumer, since "the household is made to believe – correctly or incorrectly – that it gets a greater output of the commodity from a given input of the advertised product".[16] Using this approach, Stigler and Becker show that even a perfectly competitive firm may advertise. Intuitively, a price-taking firm may be willing to incur an advertising expense, because the derived demand for its product then shifts up, enabling it to "take" a higher price. An implication is that firms may compete in the same commodity (e.g., prestige) market even though they produce different market goods (e.g., jewelry and fashion) and advertise at different levels.

The welfare implications of the complementary approach are explored by Nichols (1985).[17] Drawing on Lancaster's (1966) characteristic approach to consumer behavior, Nichols interprets Z as the level at which a characteristic is enjoyed, when the market good is consumed at level X and advertised at level A. Consumer welfare is then given by $U = U(g(A)X, Y)$, where Y is again a composite non-advertised good. For any given A, the consumer chooses X and Y to maximize U subject to the budget constraint $I = P_x X + P_y Y$, where I is income and P_y is the price of good Y. A profit-maximizing

[16] Bridging the informative and complementary views, Verma (1980) posits that advertising contains information and thereby enables consumers to produce information at lower cost, so that they can more effectively convert market goods and time into valued commodities. Verma describes specifications for the underlying information and commodity household production functions under which it may be *derived* that advertising exerts a complementary influence on the demand for the advertised product. An implication is that advertising should be highest, when the consumers' time cost is high and/or alternative information gathering methods are relatively ineffective. See also Ehrlich and Fisher (1982) and Sauer and Leffler (1990).

[17] See also Hochman and Luski (1988), who reconsider Nichols's (1985) analysis of perfectly competitive commodity markets with advertising, and Fisher and McGowan (1979), who propose that the direct effect of advertising on consumer surplus be included when the welfare effects of advertising are considered. Adams and Yellen (1977) take the same position. As discussed further in Section 4.2, the Fisher–McGowan (1979) paper is written in response to a formalization of the persuasive view offered by Dixit and Norman (1978). See also Wernerfelt (1990), who argues that brand advertising creates value for consumers, since it enables them to signal through brand choice their types to one another.

monopolist chooses A and P_x, where $P_M(A)$ denotes the monopoly price of X for a given level of advertising, A. Nichols then considers a slight increase in advertising from the profit-maximizing level. As this change has no first-order effect on the monopolist's profit, social welfare rises if and only if consumer welfare rises. The consumer experiences a direct gain from the increase in A, but there also may be a harmful effect of a higher price (if $P_M'(A) > 0$). I formally analyze a related model in Section 4.2, but one conclusion is already suggested: the consumer gains – and thus a monopolist undersupplies advertising – when an increase in advertising would not cause an increase in price (i.e., when $P_M'(A) \leqslant 0$).[18]

A related but distinct analysis is developed by Becker and Murphy (1993). Under their approach, the level of advertising A for a good X enters directly into the utility function: $U = U(A, X, Y)$. Over the relevant range, the marginal utility of advertising may be positive ($U_A > 0$), in which case advertising is a "good", or it may be negative ($U_A < 0$), so that advertising is a "bad", but in either event the marginal utility of the advertised product rises with advertising ($U_{AX} > 0$). Advertising is thus complementary to the advertised product and serves to shift out the demand for this product. The existence of a stable preference function ensures that the normative implications of advertising can be explored, once it is explained how the quantity of advertising consumed is determined.

As Becker and Murphy note, it is often infeasible to separately and directly sell advertising to consumers.[19] Instead, advertisements may be given away (e.g., direct mail ads are "free" to receive) or sold jointly with the other products (e.g., newspaper/TV ads are sold jointly with newspapers/TV programs). The former case may be understood as a situation in which advertising is a good (or at least not a bad) that is given away, the quantity of advertising is determined by the producers, and each consumer simply accepts (consumes) all of the advertising that is received. This is the conventional modeling approach. The latter case is more novel. It corresponds to a situation in which each consumer determines his consumption quantity of the joint good, given the price of the joint good. As advertising is complementary, it may be sold at a subsidized implicit price. Indeed, if advertising is a bad (e.g., TV ads may lower utility), then its implicit price is negative (advertisers include free and enjoyable programs to compensate the viewer for watching the ads).[20] Thus, while Becker and Murphy acknowledge

[18] Observe that this implication is incompatible with Braithwaite's (1928) (taste-changing) result that monopoly advertising diminishes consumer surplus unless price is *strictly* reduced.

[19] Consider a separate market for TV advertisements. If the ads were "goods", then consumers would pay for them; and if they were "bads", then consumers would be paid to watch them. Either way, important monitoring problems could arise: it could be difficult to ensure that all watching consumers pay, and that all paid consumers watch. As noted above, the joint-supply nature of advertising is observed also by Kaldor (1950), who concludes that advertising thus may be excessively supplied. By contrast, Telser (1964, 1966) stresses that there may be joint-supply economies, since the transactions (e.g., monitoring) costs associated with a separate advertising market might be considerable. See also Steiner (1966) for a rejoinder.

[20] See also Barnett (1966) and Telser (1978).

that the advertising market has special properties, they conclude that these properties do not prohibit the assimilation of advertising into consumer choice theory.

The welfare analysis of advertising may now proceed using standard techniques. In line with Nichols's finding, Becker and Murphy show that a monopolist undersupplies advertising, when advertising is a good and increased advertising does not raise price. The key point is that a monopolist cannot appropriate all of the consumer-surplus benefits that are associated with advertising.

It is interesting to contrast the complementary view with the other views. In response to the anti-competitive interpretation of advertising under the persuasive view, Nelson (1974b) makes the pro-competitive argument that advertising, when properly understood, is informative. Advocates of the complementary view, by contrast, circle back and agree with the persuasive view that advertising often provides little information. Their response is rather that even uninformative advertising can be beneficial, since consumers may value it directly.

The main advantage of the complementary view is that it offers a framework within which to conduct the welfare analysis of seemingly persuasive advertising, without positing that such advertising embodies indirect information. Surprisingly, the apparent implication is that such ads may be undersupplied, at least in monopoly markets. This view also has important limitations. First, the restrictions that are imposed upon the data may be weak, since the specific predictions are often sensitive to assumptions placed upon unobservable household production or utility functions. Second, the assumption that consumers interact with advertising on a voluntary basis may be challenged. Under the complementary approach, a consumer tolerates an ad that is a bad, since the consumer receives compensation through some joint consumption experience. But there are also ads that lower utility and cannot be avoided. For example, a consumer may find an ad on a passing city bus objectionable but unavoidable.[21] This kind of advertising, like pollution, may be excessively supplied. A complete argument in favor of this suggestion, however, must explain why a firm chooses to supply such an ad. One possibility is that the ad is not a bad to all consumers, and "innocent bystanders" may suffer as the ad makes its journey to the intended audience.

2.5. *Summary*

The discussion above describes the insightful reasoning that led to the formation of each of the three conceptual views of advertising. These views identify the main considerations that govern the impact of advertising on social welfare. Four (not entirely exclusive) considerations are identified:

[21] As Fogg-Meade (1901, pp. 231–232) put it more than a century ago, "The successful advertisement is obtrusive. It continually forces itself upon the attention. It may be on sign boards, in the street-car, on the page of a magazine, or on a theatre program. Everyone reads it involuntarily, and unconsciously it makes an impression. It is a subtle, persistent, unavoidable presence that creeps into the reader's inner consciousness."

2.5.1. Combative advertising

As Marshall explains, some advertising is combative, acting to redistribute consumers among brands. If the real differences between brands are modest, then combative advertising may be excessive. Under the informative view (Ozga, Stigler, Telser, Nelson), also acknowledged by Marshall, advertising is mainly constructive and corresponds to a necessary competitive cost that is associated with the provision of information to consumers.

2.5.2. Persuasion and consumption distortions

As Braithwaite argues, advertising may change tastes and distort consumption quantities. This results in a loss in consumer surplus relative to the pre-advertising benchmark. Informative-view advocates counter that much advertising is informative, either directly or indirectly, and there is no taste-changing consumption distortion. For a given product, complementary-view advocates (Stigler, Becker, Nichols, Murphy) argue further that the post-advertising demand curve is the relevant benchmark, even for non-informative advertising.

2.5.3. Joint supply

As Kaldor stresses, advertising is often jointly supplied, and so there is no separate market for advertising in which consumers may directly register their willingness to pay. Given that the suppliers of advertising value its complementary effects, the supply of advertising may be excessive. Complementary-view advocates counter that consumers make choices as to bundles that include advertising; furthermore, any social welfare analysis should include the manner in which consumers directly value advertising. Advertising may be undersupplied.

2.5.4. Brand loyalty, advertising scale economies and market power

Persuasive-view advocates (Braithwaite, Robinson, Kaldor, Bain, Comanor, Wilson) argue that advertising creates brand loyalty (reputations) and may be subject to increasing returns to scale. Advertising thus results in greater market power for established firms, and market performance suffers: advertising deters entry and leads to higher prices. Informative-view advocates counter that advertising provides price and quality information and facilitates entry. Market performance is enhanced: advertising encourages entry, efficient production, lower prices and higher-quality products.

The key initial writings offer conceptual frameworks with which to identify the main considerations that govern advertising's social value. As well, some initial evidence is presented. At the same time, the arguments have important limitations, as I have noted. There is more to be done. In the remainder of this survey, I describe further progress in the economic analysis of advertising. I begin in the next section, with a description of empirical research that further evaluates the effects of advertising.

3. Empirical regularities

Beginning in the 1960s and 1970s, as the distinctions between the persuasive and informative views became clear, a huge volume of empirical work emerged that evaluates the predictions of these two views. Much of the initial work follows the lead of Bain (1956) and Comanor and Wilson (1967, 1974) and seeks empirical regularities at the inter-industry level. But many of the earlier efforts also search for regularities using data at the industry, firm or even brand level. As I discuss in the Introduction, in the modern empirical literature, studies are increasingly conducted at such levels. In the present section, I review the initial and (first-group) modern empirical analyses of advertising.

The studies are organized by topic. Each subsection treats a separate topic and then wraps up with a summary of the main conclusions coming from research on that topic. By organizing the section in this way, I hope to provide convenient and self-contained treatments of several topics, while enabling a casual reader to simply read the associated summary and then move on to a topic of greater interest. The review is non-technical. I direct the reader to other surveys and books that treat some of these topics in greater detail than is possible here.[22]

At the outset, it is important to emphasize two of the many obstacles with which an empirical analysis of advertising must contend. First, the relationships between advertising and other variables are beset with endogeneity concerns. Advertising may be associated with higher sales, because firms respond to greater sales with greater advertising; advertising may be associated with inelastic demand, since advertising firms are attracted to markets in which consumers are poorly informed; advertising may be associated with greater profitability, because advertising firms are more efficient or operate in markets with inelastic demands; and so on. Second, fundamental measurement problems may arise. For example, a firm's sales and profit may be influenced by its current advertising and its past advertising (due to "goodwill" effects). The proper treatment of advertising (current expense or intangible capital?) in the measured profit rate then becomes an important consideration.

In light of these and other obstacles, it is natural to question the relevance of the empirical studies reviewed here. These studies, however, play a valuable descriptive role. If one view on advertising is generally true, then the implications of that view should be confirmed in the studies reviewed here. Likewise, if the effects of advertising are rather found to vary across circumstances, then the studies reviewed here may suggest empirical regularities for certain groups of industries or among particular variables. Such findings can guide subsequent theory construction, ultimately leading to more successful empirical efforts that use new data sets and obtain consistent estimates of structural parameters. Finally, several of the studies reviewed here confront the endogeneity of

[22] For other reviews of aspects of the material covered here, see Albion and Farris (1981), Berndt (1991), Comanor and Wilson (1979), Ekelund and Saurman (1988), Hay and Morris (1991), Ornstein (1977), Scherer and Ross (1990), Schmalensee (1972, 1989) and Simon (1970).

advertising. Some studies attempt to estimate structural parameters using simultaneous-equation methods, while other studies seek exogenous variation in advertising through laboratory or natural experiments.

3.1. The direct effects of advertising

I begin by considering the direct effects of advertising. Evidence is described that concerns the effect of a firm's advertising on its current and future sales, the sales of other firms and the brand loyalty of its consumers. I also discuss evidence as to the presence or absence of advertising scale economies.

3.1.1. Sales

I review here empirical studies of advertising and sales. Two questions are emphasized. First, is there a positive association between current advertising and current and future sales? If a significant association with future sales is detected, this would support a goodwill effect and thus the contention of Braithwaite (1928) that advertising can have long-lasting reputational effects. Second, does advertising influence overall industry demand, or is it more combative, as Marshall (1890, 1919) suggests, tending to redistribute sales within the industry?

By the start of the 1970s, there existed a number of statistical studies that explain sales or market shares with advertising and other variables. As Schmalensee (1972, ch. 4) details, however, most these studies suffer from serious limitations. With important exceptions, the earlier studies fail to include lagged measures that would permit identification of a goodwill effect and measures that would assess the effect of rival-firm advertising on own sales. In addition, while some early work acknowledges that advertising is endogenous, a simultaneous-equation analysis of advertising and sales did not appear until the late 1960s.[23]

The empirical analysis of the advertising–sales relationship takes a step forward with Lambin's (1976) ambitious effort. Lambin uses various sales, quality, price and advertising data for 107 individual brands from 16 product classes and 8 different Western European countries, where the observations are mainly drawn from the 1960–1970 period. With these data, he can consider how changes in the advertising outlay for one brand may affect the current sales of that brand and rival brands. As well, he can look over time and evaluate goodwill effects and the rival-brand response that an advertising outlay may induce. Further, Lambin offers estimates based on simultaneous-equation methods and concludes that the risk of simultaneity bias in his sample is limited.

[23] Jastram (1955) offers an early discussion of the goodwill effect. Roberts (1947) presents an early analysis of the effect of rival advertising on own sales. The reverse-causality possibility between advertising and sales is acknowledged by Borden (1942) and Berreman (1943), but it appears that the first simultaneous-equation analysis is offered by Bass (1969).

Some of Lambin's findings are as follows. He finds that brand advertising has a significant and positive effect on the brand's current sales and market share. Further, using a distributed-lag model, in which a brand's current sales are explained by current advertising and a constant fraction of previous-period sales, Lambin interprets the lagged-sales coefficient as a measure of advertising's goodwill effect and reports evidence of a goodwill effect for advertising.[24] But the quantitative impact of advertising on (current and future) sales is limited: sales appear more responsive to price and product-quality selections. Lambin also reports that a firm's sales and market share are negatively related to rival advertising. Going further, he indicates that advertising reaction elasticities are often positive over time, so that an increase in brand advertising appears to induce rivals to respond with more advertising. In fact, Lambin offers only limited support for the view that advertising increases industry demand, suggesting instead that the competing effects of own and rival advertising on own sales tend to cancel. Lambin's study thus offers some support for the notion that advertising is combative.

These relationships are explored further in other studies. First, a number of studies explore the goodwill effect of advertising. One group of studies posits a distributed-lag relationship between current sales and advertising expenditures and then estimates the rate at which advertising's effect depreciates through time. In influential early studies, Palda (1964), Peles (1971b) and Telser (1962) suggest that the goodwill effect of advertising may be substantial. For certain industries, they report that the firm-level depreciation rates are in the range of 15 to 50% per year.[25] Lambin's (1976, p. 96) depreciation-rate estimates for brand advertising vary widely across product groups but take an average of around 50% per year. Likewise, in a study of the cigarette industry, Brown (1978) reports brand-level depreciation rates in the 60% range.

In an important survey, Clarke (1976) considers the various distributed-lag studies and identifies a "data-interval-bias" problem. The use of annual advertising data when the effects of advertising on sales depreciate over a shorter period of time can lead to biased estimates of the depreciation rate. On the basis of studies using data for shorter periods, Clarke (1976, p. 355) concludes that "the duration of cumulative advertising effect on sales is between 3 and 15 months; thus this effect is a short-term (about a year or less) phenomenon". More recently, several studies offer further support for this conclusion. Using various data and specifications for the advertising–sales relationship,

[24] Like other distributed-lag studies described below, Lambin follows Koyck (1954) and posits a constant depreciation rate. The formalization involves two steps. First, specify that a brand's current-period sales (S_t) are determined as a function of current (A_t) and past (A_τ, for $\tau < t$) advertising levels: $S_t = \alpha + \theta \sum_{\tau=0}^{t} \beta^{t-\tau} A_\tau + \varepsilon_t$. Second, take differences and derive that $S_t = \alpha(1-\beta) + \beta S_{t-1} + \theta A_t + \upsilon_t$, where $\upsilon_t \equiv \varepsilon_t - \beta\varepsilon_{t-1}$. The weight on previous-period sales now captures the goodwill effect of advertising. A goodwill effect is present when $\beta > 0$, and $1 - \beta$ is the constant rate of depreciation for past advertising. Notice that this approach assumes that persistence in sales derives only from advertising. As I discuss below, some recent research includes the possibility that firm-specific factors (like product quality) generate sales persistence. See also Berndt (1991) for a discussion of alternative formulations.

[25] Other early studies also suggest a low rate of depreciation. Comanor and Wilson (1979), Schmalensee (1972) and Weiss (1969) evaluate a number of the early efforts.

Ashley, Granger and Schmalensee (1980), Boyd and Seldon (1990) and Seldon and Doroodian (1989) all offer evidence that the effect of advertising on sales is often largely depreciated within a year (if not less). Leone's (1995) survey is of particular interest. He provides a theoretical explanation for the data-interval bias and then presents empirical support for the generalization that on average the effect of advertising on sales is largely depreciated within six to nine months.

When assessing the goodwill impact of advertising, it is important that firm-specific factors not be omitted. As Nelson's (1974b) theory suggests, it may be that advertising affects initial sales but that long-term sales are driven by firm-specific factors, like product quality. Given that higher-quality firms may advertise more, the effects of advertising on future sales may be overstated in an empirical analysis that omits product quality. Using CompuStat data for 417 firms for the years 1982 to 1986, Landes and Rosenfield (1994) show that the distributed-lag approach indeed overstates the durability of advertising when firm-specific dummies are not used to control for omitted firm-specific factors.[26] The role of brand-specific factors is also stressed by Thomas (1989), who offers a brand-loyalty specification and reports depreciation rates of 80% and above for brands of soft drinks and cigarettes. Likewise, Kwoka (1993) examines the determinants of model sales in the U.S. auto industry, finding that the effect of advertising is short-lived while product styling has a much longer impact.

Second, a number of studies explore the effect of advertising on industry versus firm or brand sales. In an important early study, Borden (1942) makes a distinction between advertising that increases "selective" (i.e., firm/brand) and "primary" (i.e., industry) demands. His case studies of U.S. industries suggest that advertising is often combative, exerting a strong effect on selective demand. He argues that trends in primary demand derive from underlying social and environmental considerations, with advertising serving to reinforce these trends.

The combative nature of advertising is further explored in more recent work. One strand of work emphasizes advertising reactions. In studies of leading brands in certain Australian markets, Metwally (1975, 1976) reports that advertising reaction elasticities are positive over time and detects a substantial cancellation effect. As with Lambin's study, this work suggests that advertising is often characterized over time by reciprocal cancellation.[27] Some additional support for this suggestion emerges from studies that consider the response of incumbent firms to entry. For example, Alemson's (1970) study

[26] There is also another group of studies, in which the depreciation rate for advertising is inferred as the rate that best accounts for observed relationships between current advertising expenses and market values. Studies of this general nature are offered by Ayanian (1975, 1983), Bloch (1974) and Hirschey (1982). As Landes and Rosenfield (1994) argue, the market-value studies make strong "steady-state" assumptions and (like distributed-lag studies) overstate the durability of advertising when controls are not used for firm-specific factors.

[27] See also Telser (1962) and Brown (1978) for descriptions of competitive advertising among U.S. cigarette manufacturers. Related evidence is offered by Kelton and Kelton (1982) for the U.S. brewery industry. See also Tremblay and Tremblay (2005).

of the Australian cigarette industry suggests a reciprocal cancellation effect, whereby new entrants advertise to gain market share and thereby induce increased advertising by incumbents, who seek to maintain market share. Likewise, Thomas (1999) studies the ready-to-eat cereal industry and reports that incumbent firms often respond to entry with advertising, in order to limit the sales of new entrants. Finally, in cross-sectional work, Cubbin and Domberger (1988) examine 42 consumer-goods industries and report evidence that dominant incumbent firms in static (slow-growth) markets often respond to entry with an increase in advertising.

Another strand of studies emphasizes the relationship between industry advertising and sales. These studies suggest that advertising may increase primary demand in some industries but not others. For example, positive relationships between industry advertising and sales are reported for the UK cigarette industry [Cowling et al. (1975)], the U.S. cigarette industry [Seldon and Doroodian (1989)], the U.S. orange market [Nerlove and Waugh (1961)] and the U.S. auto industry [Kwoka (1993)], but other studies report little evidence of a primary demand effect for the U.S. cigarette market [Baltagi and Levin (1986), Hamilton (1972), Schmalensee (1972)], U.S. beer market [Nelson (2004), Tremblay and Tremblay (2005)], or UK instant-coffee market [Cowling et al. (1975)].

In summary, the studies discussed above suggest three main conclusions. First, a firm's current advertising is associated with an increase in its sales, but this effect is usually short lived. Second, advertising is often combative in nature. An increase in advertising by one firm may reduce the sales of rival firms, and rivals may then react with a reciprocal increase in their own advertising efforts. Third, the overall effect of advertising on primary demand is difficult to determine and appears to vary across industries.

3.1.2. Brand loyalty and market-share stability

According to the persuasive view, the direct effect of advertising is that brand loyalty is created and the demand for the advertised product becomes less elastic. Ideally, a direct empirical assessment of this effect would draw from a longitudinal data set that includes household-level advertising-exposure and brand-purchase data as well as the advertising and pricing behaviors of rival firms. As I discuss in Section 8, with the advent of supermarket scanner data, empirical assessments of this kind have recently appeared. At this point, however, I focus on the earlier empirical investigations of advertising and brand loyalty. These studies pursue two indirect assessments. First, it may be possible to estimate demand functions for individual brands, in order to see if consumers exhibit more "inertia" in highly advertised markets, or if the estimated price elasticities are lower in magnitude in product groups with high advertising intensity. Second, following Telser (1964), it may be possible to infer the extent of brand loyalty, by further examining the relationship between advertising and market-share stability.

In the first category, Lambin captures brand loyalty with a measure of consumer inertia. For the distributed-lag model, Lambin (1976, pp. 72, 115–118) observes that the lagged-sales coefficient may be generally interpreted as a measure of consumer inertia.

He finds significant inertia effects in most markets. Using various measurements of advertising intensity, however, Lambin fails to find a positive and significant relationship between brand inertia rates and brand advertising intensity. Apparently, consumer inertia is important, but the cause of inertia more likely rests with price and quality than with advertising.[28] In a separate approach, Lambin estimates the elasticities of demand for several brands, and he then regresses the absolute value of estimated elasticity alternatively on different measurements of advertising intensity. The regression coefficients are negative, though the statistical significance of the estimates are mostly weak. As Lambin (1976, pp. 138–140) notes, this gives modest support to the position that advertising reduces the elasticity of demand.

In a number of marketing studies from the late 1970s, the effect of advertising on demand elasticity is further examined. As Boulding, Lee and Staelin (1994) explain, however, many of these studies have important limitations. Boulding, Lee and Staelin use longitudinal and cross-section PIMS (Profit Impact of Market Strategies) data, in order to assess at the business-unit level the effect of advertising on demand elasticity. They report evidence that current advertising reduces future demand elasticity for firms that price above the industry average.

The second empirical strategy is to explore the relationship between advertising and market-share stability. A number of studies agree with Telser (1964) that advertising is associated with market-share instability. Support for this conclusion can be found in Ferguson's (1967) study of the liquor industry, Backman's (1967) analysis of consumer non-durable sectors, Alemson's (1970) study of the Australian cigarette industry, and Reekie's (1974) examination of specific UK sectors (particularly, foodstuffs and toiletries). In addition, Lambin offers modest empirical support for the proposition that increased advertising intensity destabilizes market shares.

On the other hand, Gort (1963) examines the market shares of the largest firms in U.S. manufacturing sectors in 1947 and 1954, and he reports that market shares are more stable in industries in which product differentiation is greater. Caves and Porter (1978) attempt to reconcile these divergent findings, by distinguishing between advertising's roles as a conduct variable that is associated with non-price competition and the disturbance of market shares and as a structural variable that is associated with product differentiation and the insulation of market shares. Using PIMS data, Caves and Porter (1978, p. 309) report that structural product differentiation (as measured by advertising intensity) exerts a stabilizing influence on market shares, whereas non-price competition itself (as measured by product R&D) works to destabilize market shares.

Finally, more recent work offers further evidence in support of Telser's (1964) view. In an inter-industry study, Hirschey (1981) considers a large cross-section of U.S. industries over the 1947–1972 period and finds that advertising is positively and significantly

[28] In this context, it is useful to recall the studies by Kwoka (1993), Landes and Rosenfield (1994) and Thomas (1989), which offer evidence in support of the view that brand loyalty is associated more with brand-specific factors (like product quality) than with advertising per se.

associated with entry (over 1963–1972) and the growth of established non-leading firms (over 1947–1963). Similarly, Eckard (1987) looks at the 1963–1982 period and finds no evidence that the market-share instability of leading firms is lower in high-advertising industries. In an industry study, Eckard (1991) considers the effect of the 1970 U.S. ban on TV advertising for cigarettes. He finds that brand and firm market shares are more stable in the period after the ban; furthermore, leading-brand shares were declining before the ban and are stable after the ban. Likewise, Sass and Saurman (1995) conduct an industry analysis of the malt beverage market. They report evidence that large national brewers gain market share at the expense of smaller brewers, in states where (retail) price advertising is restricted.

What conclusions emerge? Given the data limitations, any conclusions must be tentative. That said, it is perhaps most relevant to remark that the studies do not provide strong evidence that advertising consistently increases brand loyalty or stabilizes market shares.

3.1.3. Advertising scale economies

I consider here empirical studies that evaluate the possibility of an advertising scale economy. It may be recalled that Kaldor's concentration effect derives from an assumed economy of this kind. Broadly, the empirical studies stress that an advertising scale economy may arise for two reasons: (i) the marginal effectiveness of advertising messages in generating sales may be greater, when the number of messages is already large, and (ii) the advertising expenditure per message (the price per message) may fall as more messages are sent.

Consider first the effectiveness of advertising on sales. As Chamberlin (1933, pp. 133–136) and Ozga (1960, p. 40) suggest, there are conflicting effects. Intuitively, an advertising scale economy may appear (i) if advertising expenditures must pass a threshold level before they command the consumer's attention, or (ii) if, beyond any such threshold level, the marginal benefit to sales of advertising messages is increasing, due to the increased control that the advertised product exercises over the consumer's consciousness. At high levels of advertising, however, a decreasing return to scale may arise (i) as less responsive consumers are reached, or (ii) as an increasing number of messages must be sent in order to reach a consumer that has not yet been exposed to the advertisement. This intuitive discussion suggests that an advertising scale economy may emerge at low sales volumes (due to the threshold effect), but it does not offer a clear suggestion as to the presence of such an economy at higher sales volumes. A role for empirical study is thus suggested.

Using various (e.g., logarithmic) measures, a number of studies regress sales on advertising and offer evidence that advertising's effectiveness is subject to diminishing returns. In essence, these studies hold other inputs constant and argue that doubled advertising results in less than doubled sales. Simon (1970, p. 21) offers a summary of the advertising studies of this kind. He concludes that "there is not one single piece of strong evidence to support the general belief that increasing returns exist in advertising".[29] Simon (1970) also presents evidence for direct-mail and clip-out coupon advertising methods that decreasing returns set in even at low sales volumes. Lambin (1976, pp. 95–98) presents further evidence consistent with decreasing returns, as his estimated advertising–sales elasticity coefficients are less than unity. But Lambin's (1976, pp. 127–129) findings also suggest a possible threshold effect, since he finds that small brands keep a higher ratio of advertising share to market share than do large brands.

As Comanor and Wilson (1974, 1979) emphasize, scale economies are normally defined with reference to a proportional increase in *all* inputs. This is potentially important, since economies may be achieved only when advertising is increased in unison with other marketing and production inputs. Under some circumstances, however, the costs of advertising and production are plausibly separable, in which case an important consideration is that advertising in all media be increased in the same proportion. Brown (1978) conducts an interesting study of this kind for the cigarette industry. Using a distributed-lag, simultaneous-equation model of advertising and sales, Brown (1978, p. 433) uses his estimates to calculate the "amount of advertising capital required per unit of sales for any chosen level of sales". The estimated average cost function is decreasing over a large volume of sales, and higher for new brands, suggesting a cost disadvantage for new entrants. Seldon, Jewell and O'Brien (2000) offer a related analysis of the beer industry, but their estimates suggest diseconomies of scale.[30]

In other recent work, heterogeneity across brands is emphasized. Much of this work also reports evidence of diseconomies of scale in advertising. In a study of 174 brands in 11 categories of small, packaged consumer goods, Boyer and Lancaster (1986, p. 515) find "little support for the proposition that large brands support their market shares with a disproportionately small share of advertising expenditure". Likewise, Thomas (1989) specifies a brand-loyalty model that allows for heterogeneous brand quality. He reports evidence of advertising scale diseconomies in the cigarette and soft drink industries. On the other hand, Dube, Hitsch and Manchanda (2005) specify a model in which advertising must exceed a threshold level in order to contribute to the goodwill stock. Studying the major brands in the Frozen Entree Category, they find strong evidence of a positive threshold level. As they argue, this finding also provides an interpretation of observed "pulsing" strategies, whereby a company rotates between positive-advertising and no-advertising phases.

Consider now the possibility that advertising scale economies are generated through a reduction in the advertising expenditure per message as more messages are sent. One

[29] Early advertising studies that find evidence of diminishing returns include Palda (1964), Peles (1971a), Roberts (1947), Shryer (1912) and Telser (1962). Schmalensee (1972) reviews the early studies. More recent reviews are offered by Albion and Farris (1981), Arndt and Simon (1983), Berndt (1991) and Simon and Arndt (1980).

[30] See also Bresnahan (1984), who reports some evidence in support of advertising scale economies in his study of the beer industry. Seldon, Jewell and O'Brien (2000) explain the differences between their methodology and that used by Bresnahan (1984). For further discussion of advertising in the beer industry, see Fare et al. (2004), Nelson (2004) and Tremblay and Tremblay (2005).

possibility is that the advertising rate schedule favors large advertisers. In this context, a vigorous debate has emerged with respect to the rates charged by TV networks, particularly in the early 1960s.[31] Blake and Blum (1965) observe that published rate schedules for network television advertising were characterized by significant quantity discounts. In a comprehensive response, Blank (1968) emphasizes the distinction between published price lists and the prices that were actually paid. Over the relevant time period, the cost per minute of advertising varied with cumulative purchases, but it also varied importantly with the program to which the advertisement was joined. Using data for 1965 and 1966, Blank finds that larger advertisers actually paid higher prices per unit of time (i.e., per minute), since they advertised in more popular programs. Furthermore, he notes that price per unit of time is not the relevant measure: the real issue is whether larger advertisers paid less per "unit of audience". To operationalize this idea, he considers the cost per thousand homes reached per commercial minute. Blank (1968, p. 28) finds "*no* consistent relationship between cost per thousand and size of the advertiser".[32]

A second possibility is that large advertisers are favored in that there are benefits to national versus local TV advertising. In line with Chamberlin's (1933, p. 134) general discussion, national advertising may be a more effective medium that is available only at high levels of advertising expenditure. Porter (1976a) argues that there is a distinct cost advantage from national (network) TV advertising as compared to achieving the same coverage through local (spot) TV advertising. But Peterman (1979) presents evidence that differences between network and spot rates are far smaller than Porter's (1976a) discussion suggests. In addition, as Scherer and Ross (1990, p. 135) observe, even if network advertising has a cost advantage, there is also an offsetting consideration: network advertising is less flexible than spot advertising, since spot advertising can be better adapted to the conditions of the local market.

Finally, a different approach is to seek indirect evidence of an advertising scale economy, while remaining agnostic as to the reason that this scale economy exists. In this context, it may be noted that Porter (1976a) offers indirect evidence of a scale economy that is associated with TV advertising. Like Comanor and Wilson (1967, 1974), he considers U.S. industries that manufacture consumer goods, and he regresses industry

[31] This period is of special interest, because of a 1963 decision by the FTC not to allow a merger between Clorox and Procter & Gamble. It was feared that the merger would enable the Clorox brand to enjoy quantity discounts in advertising, which would put it at an advantage relative to other liquid bleaches. Blank (1968) and Peterman (1968) state that the networks ceased to offer quantity discounts in 1966.

[32] In a subsequent study, Peterman (1968) considers the 1960–1963 period and affirms that there is little empirical support for actual discrimination in favor of large advertisers. Comanor and Wilson (1974, pp. 53–61), however, distinguish between discounts associated with the total number of messages purchased from a network and those purchased on specific programs. They report evidence that supports the presence of discounts within programs. But Peterman and Carney (1978) re-examine the estimates once more, and they conclude that the estimated discounts are much smaller than those reported by Comanor and Wilson (1974). Further support for Blank's (1968) conclusions is offered by Schmalensee (1972) and Riesz (1973). The latter study finds that the extent to which firms concentrate their advertising expenditures among the networks is generally stable across firms of differing sizes.

profits on advertising measures and other variables. When he replaces industry advertising intensity with industry TV advertising intensity, he discovers an increase in the size and significance of the coefficient on advertising.[33] Similar indirect evidence is offered by Mueller and Rogers (1980, 1984), who find an important role for TV advertising in explaining increases in concentration for U.S. consumer-goods industries. On the other hand, Lynk (1981) offers evidence that TV advertising is associated with reductions in concentration. These studies are discussed in greater detail below.

What tentative conclusions are suggested? On the whole, the studies that evaluate the effectiveness of advertising suggest that advertising often entails diminishing returns beyond a threshold level, where the threshold level varies across circumstances and may be small. Turning to the studies that evaluate the TV advertising rate schedule, the evidence appears to suggest that any historic discrimination in favor of large advertisers is small. There is, however, some indirect evidence of a scale economy that is associated with TV advertising.

3.2. The indirect effects of advertising

I consider now the indirect effects of advertising on market outcomes. Specifically, I examine the associations between advertising and concentration, profit, entry, prices and quality.

3.2.1. Concentration

According to Kaldor, advertising scale economies exist and big firms are better able to finance large advertising expenditures; as a consequence, advertising promotes greater concentration and leads to an oligopolistic structure. I discuss above the studies that examine the existence of scale economies in advertising. Here, I consider further empirical analyses of the association between advertising and concentration.

The first empirical examination of the advertising–concentration relationship was offered by Kaldor and Silverman (1948). For 118 English industries in 1938, they measure (advertising) concentration by the number of firms needed to account for 80% of industry advertising, and they then calculate the mean advertising intensity for each concentration category. Kaldor and Silverman find that advertising intensity is highest in the eight-firm concentration category, with the advertising intensity declining substantially when the concentration measure exceeds 9 firms or falls below 4 firms. Advertising intensity thus is related to this measure of concentration in an inverted-U fashion. Evidently, large-scale advertising is associated with oligopolistic industries.[34]

[33] Related findings, using different measures of profitability, are provided by Hirschey (1978, 1982) and Connor and Peterson (1992).

[34] See Schnabel (1970) for a re-examination of the Kaldor–Silverman data. Else (1966) and Doyle (1968b) also use UK data to relate (advertising) concentration to advertising intensity.

The next set of work explored the possibility of a linear relationship from advertising intensity to concentration, using inter-industry data, regression analysis and standard (e.g., four-firm) measures of concentration. As discussed in Section 2.3, Telser (1964) offered the first test of this kind. For 42 three-digit consumer-product groups, he finds that the relationship is weak and unimpressive. No significant relationship is also observed by Comanor and Wilson (1974), Guth (1971), Lambin (1976) and Schnabel (1970), while Ornstein and Lustgarten (1978) report a significant but weak positive relationship in the 1960s (but none in the 1940s). Examining Telser's (1964) data, Nelson (1975) likewise finds no significant correlation between advertising intensity and concentration for non-durable experience goods and durable goods; however, he reports a significant correlation between advertising intensity and concentration for search goods.[35]

A related set of studies explores a linear relationship from advertising intensity to concentration, using data for a given industry that varies across different markets (brands, regions, etc.). For example, Vernon (1971) examines 18 therapeutic product classes in the U.S. ethical pharmaceutical industry. In a multi-variate analysis, he finds no evidence that high promotion results in high concentration; indeed, he suggests that high promotion may be associated with less concentration (and thus, perhaps, greater entry). Likewise, Edwards (1973) regresses concentration on advertising intensity for 36 large banks from 23 distinct metropolitan areas, where concentration is measured by the ratio of deposits of the three largest banks in the area to the total deposits in the area. A multi-variate analysis again reveals no significant relationship between advertising intensity and concentration. Finally, utilizing cross-state variation in the legal restrictions on beer advertising, Sass and Saurman (1995) report evidence that (retail) price advertising reduces state-level concentration for brewers.

Some studies use inter-industry data over different time periods to consider advertising as a determinant of changes in concentration. Various studies report evidence that post-war U.S. concentration levels have increased over time in industries that manufacture consumer goods and that the rate of increase is positively associated with advertising intensity.[36] For example, Mueller and Hamm (1974) look at 166 U.S. industries over the period 1947–1970. For consumer-goods industries, they report a significant positive relationship between advertising intensity and changes in four-firm concentration, when the advertising-intensity dummy variable is medium or high. In comprehensive efforts that use a continuous measure of advertising intensity and differentiate between alternative types of media advertising, Mueller and Rogers (1980, 1984) offer multiple-regression analyses and report a large and significant role for TV advertising in explaining changes in four-firm concentration ratios for U.S. manufacturers in consumer-goods industries between 1947 and 1977. From this evidence, it appears that

[35] Other influential studies include Mann, Henning and Meehan Jr. (1967) and Telser (1969b). See Ornstein (1977) for a survey of early empirical investigations of advertising and concentration.

[36] See Ornstein (1977) for a survey of early empirical studies of this kind.

the emergence of TV advertising in the 1950s created a structural disequilibrium that resolved over time with a growth in concentration levels for consumer-goods industries.

Going further, this evidence might be interpreted as support for the persuasive view that (TV) advertising confers market power. But this interpretation may not be valid. First, the empirical relationship may be challenged. Lynk (1981) observes that concentration tended to fall for those U.S. industries that most increased the fraction of advertising in TV. Lynk's interpretation is that an exogenous reduction in the cost of transmitting information (i.e., the emergence of TV) promotes entry and reduces concentration, much as informative-view advocates suggest. Likewise, in his time-series analysis of the 1970 U.S. TV ban on cigarette advertising, Eckard (1991) reports that industry concentration was declining prior to the ban and that this trend reversed after the ban. Second, even if it is accepted that TV advertising is positively associated with concentration, this does not imply that TV advertising is associated with greater market power. TV advertising may facilitate the entry of more efficient firms or the realization of scale economies in production, distribution or advertising. Complementing the Mueller–Rogers (1980, 1984) data set with additional industry price and output data between 1963 and 1977, Eckard (1987) finds that prices grew more slowly and output grew more quickly in industries that used TV advertising.

Beginning in the 1970s, economists emphasized that the causality between advertising and concentration might run both ways, with concentration also influencing advertising. This suggests a more complex, non-linear relationship, such as the quadratic, inverted-U pattern reported by Kaldor and Silverman. Significant non-linear relationships are reported in many studies [Cable (1972), Cowling et al. (1975), Greer (1971, 1973), Martin (1979a, 1979b), Sutton (1974), Strickland and Weiss (1976), Weiss, Pascoe and Martin (1983)]. But other studies offer little support for a quadratic relationship [Brush (1976), Mann, Henning and Meehan Jr. (1973), Ornstein (1977), Ornstein and Lustgarten (1978)], present mixed findings [Rees (1975)] or provide little evidence of a positive relationship [Reekie (1975)]. More recent work, however, emphasizes industries in which a large share of sales go to final consumers and offers evidence of a quadratic, inverted-U pattern. Buxton, Davies and Lyons (1984) distinguish between 51 UK (3-digit) manufacturing industries on the basis of the proportion of sales that go to final consumers. With advertising intensity as the dependent variable, they find a significant quadratic relationship between advertising intensity and concentration, especially for industries of less-than-average concentration and with a greater proportion of sales to final consumers. Likewise, Uri (1987) considers 301 U.S. (4-digit) industries and reports evidence of an inverted-U pattern for industries with a high share of sales to final consumers.

The interpretation of an inverted-U relationship is not clear. Greer (1971) suggests one perspective: in less concentrated markets, competitive escalations in advertising may induce greater concentration, much as Kaldor originally argued; whereas, in highly concentrated markets, collusion among firms and decreasing returns to scale in advertising may limit combative advertising. Rivalrous advertising may thus be most acute in oligopolistic markets. Building on themes suggested by Demsetz (1973, 1974), Nelson (1974b, 1975) and Telser (1964), however, an alternative interpretation also might be advanced: advertising is an instrument of competition, used with particular vigor by low-cost firms in oligopolistic markets, that increases concentration by directing sales to the most efficient firms.

In summary, the relationship between advertising and concentration is complex. As Telser (1964) initially argued, the hypothesis of a linear and positive relationship between advertising and concentration receives little support. Some support does emerge, however, for an inverted-U relationship, especially in industries that direct sales largely to final consumers. Some support also can be found for an association between the emergence of TV advertising and the subsequent increase in concentration rates for industries that manufacture consumer goods. The appropriate interpretation of these relationships, however, is not clear.[37]

3.2.2. *Profit*

Under the persuasive view, advertising creates brand loyalty and works to deter entry. As Bain (1956) and Comanor and Wilson (1967, 1974) argue, this conclusion may be indirectly evaluated by examining the inter-industry association between advertising intensity and profitability. I consider here further work that evaluates the effects of advertising on profits.

The main finding of Comanor and Wilson (1967, 1974) is that a strong and positive relationship exists between advertising intensity and profitability (measured under accounting procedures as the after-tax rate of return on equity) for U.S. manufacturing industries that produce consumer goods. As Comanor and Wilson (1967, 1974) demonstrate, this finding emerges in multi-variate regressions when single- or multiple-regression techniques are used. And related results arise also in other studies, using Canadian, Japanese, U.S. and UK data.[38] Arguably, this finding may be accepted as a "stylized fact". I consider here two further questions. First, does the relationship between advertising intensity and profit vary with the nature of the industry? Second, are

[37] As I discuss in Section 9, recent work by Sutton (1991) draws on the intervening game-theoretic models and offers an interpretation of the relationship between advertising, concentration and market size.

[38] The literature is vast, and I provide here only a sample. Supportive studies using U.S. data include those by Backman (1967), Boyer (1974), Connolly and Hirschey (1984), Connor and Peterson (1992), Domowitz, Hubbard and Petersen (1986a, 1986b), Esposito and Esposito (1971), Gomes (1986), Hirschey (1978, 1985), Jones, Laudadio and Percy (1977), Kwoka and Ravenscraft (1986), Mann (1966), Martin (1979a, 1979b), Miller (1969), Porter (1974, 1976a, 1976b, 1979), Ravenscraft (1983), Vernon and Nourse (1973) and Weiss (1974). Likewise, Cowling et al. (1975), Geroski (1982) and Nickell and Metcalf (1978) use UK data and report evidence of a positive relationship between advertising and profitability. Similar findings are reported by Jones, Laudadio and Percy (1973, 1977) and Orr (1974b) for Canadian data and by Caves and Uekusa (1976) and Nakao (1979) for Japanese data. There are also some dissenting studies. For example, Salinger (1984) finds that advertising interacted with concentration fails to exert a significant and positive influence on profitability measures; Eckard (1991) reports that cigarette-industry profit margins increased after the 1970 U.S. ban on TV advertising; and Landes and Rosenfield (1994) offer evidence that the relationship may reflect the omission of firm-specific variables (like product quality).

there measurement and/or endogeneity concerns that confound the interpretation of this finding as evidence that advertising deters entry?

Consider first the nature of the industry. As Telser (1964) observes, in industries that manufacture producer goods, advertising may play a less central role in the selling costs of the firm. Selling costs may reflect more the expenses that are associated with salesmen and so on. Some empirical support for a diminished role of advertising for manufacturers of producer goods is offered by Weiss, Pascoe and Martin (1983). It therefore might be expected that the relationship between advertising intensity and profitability would be weaker in producer-goods industries. Domowitz, Hubbard and Petersen (1986a, 1986b) provide evidence that is consistent with this expectation. They find that the positive relationship between advertising intensity and profitability is weakened in manufacturing industries that supply producer goods.[39]

The nature of the industry may be important, even among industries that manufacture consumer goods. Following Copeland (1923) and Chamberlin (1933, ch. VI), Porter (1974, 1976b) draws a distinction between *convenience* and *non-convenience goods*. Convenience goods are low-priced, frequently purchased consumer goods, such as soft drinks, toothpaste and soap, that are widely available at retail outlets. By contrast, non-convenience goods are high-priced, infrequently purchased consumer goods, such as furniture, televisions, and motor vehicles, that are available at more specialized retail outlets. For the consumer, the purchase of a convenience good is a relatively unimportant event, and brand choice may be made on the basis of vague information that is available at low cost. Manufacturer brand advertising may then influence the consumer and thereby represent a key source of product differentiation. By contrast, for non-convenience goods, the consumer's purchase decision is more important. The consumer is then willing to incur meaningful search costs in order to obtain better information. Consequently, competing brands may be differentiated on the basis of point-of-service information provided by sales personnel at retail outlets. In short, consumer choice may be more responsive to advertising by manufacturers of convenience than non-convenience goods.[40]

An important implication is that the role of manufacturer advertising in shaping the bilateral power relationship between manufacturers and retailers may vary with the type of good.[41] A convenience-good outlet is pressured by its consumers to carry heavily advertised goods, and the manufacturer of a convenience good thus may advertise over

[39] See also Esposito and Esposito (1971), Jones, Laudadio and Percy (1977) and Miller (1969).

[40] Similar themes are advanced by Doyle (1968a, 1968b). As I describe in Section 2, Nelson (1970, 1974b) offers the related finding that advertising intensity tends to be higher for frequently purchased, lower-priced and non-durable goods. He interprets advertising as representing a source of indirect information. See also Ehrlich and Fisher (1982) and Verma (1980), who emphasize that advertising provides information that reduces time costs. Advertising intensity then may be lower in market settings for which other forms of information transmission (e.g., personal selling) are more efficient. Laband (1986) offers evidence that supports this conclusion. See also Sauer and Leffler (1990).

[41] For related points in earlier work, see Kaldor (1950) and the references cited in footnote 9. See also the discussion in Section 3.2.4 of Steiner's (1973, 1978, 1984, 1993) work.

the head of retailers to reach final consumers and thereby improve its bargaining position with retailers. On the other hand, for non-convenience goods, retailers are in a powerful position, as a retailer can always stock and push alternative brands. The manufacturer of a non-convenience good is thus less able to use advertising to improve its terms of trade with retailers.

As Porter (1974, p. 425) puts it, the broad point here is that "advertising is a more powerful influence on the rate of return for products sold through convenience outlets than for those sold through non-convenience outlets due to the differential importance of advertising on consumer choice and on the rate-of-return bargain between manufacturer and retailer". To test this hypothesis, Porter (1974, 1976b) follows Comanor and Wilson (1967) and considers 42 U.S. consumer-goods industries, which he then subdivides into convenience and non-convenience industries. The empirical findings support Porter's (1974) hypothesis. For the convenience-good category, advertising intensity emerges as a powerful and significant determinant of profitability. The role of advertising in explaining profitability is substantially diminished for non-convenience goods.

A further distinction can be made between industries that manufacture consumer goods and the retail and service industries that deal directly with the public. Advertising by retailers is expected to have greater information content, whereas advertising by manufacturers may reflect a greater persuasive orientation. This distinction is embraced by Boyer (1974), who examines the impact of advertising intensity on profitability for 41 consumer-goods manufacturers and also for consumer retail and service sectors. He finds that the association between advertising intensity and profitability is again strong and positive for consumer-goods manufacturing industries. But his novel finding is that there is a weak and negative association between advertising and profitability in retailing and service industries. Boyer interprets this finding as indicating that retailers, who often advertise in print media as opposed to TV, provide informative advertisements that lead to lower prices.[42]

I consider next the interpretation of the positive relationship between advertising and profitability. A first issue is whether this relationship reflects a measurement problem in the treatment of profit rates. The empirical studies of this relationship commonly measure the rate of profit as reported after tax profit divided by net worth (assets or equity), where both the numerator and denominator are measured according to accounting procedures under which advertising outlays are treated as current expenses. But this "accounting profit rate" may be a biased measure of the "true profit rate", if advertising has a goodwill effect. This is because advertising expenditures are then in truth investments that generate "intangible capital". The accounting profit rate may be biased in either direction, since it may understate the numerator (the firm's advertising outlay may exceed the true current depreciation in its advertising capital) and the denominator (the firm's stock of advertising capital should be included in its total asset value).[43]

[42] This is also consistent with Nelson's (1975) finding that the relationship between advertising and profitability is negative for search goods, though the relationship is not significant.

[43] Following Telser (1969a) and Demstez (1979), it may be shown that the accounting profit rate overstates the true profit rate if the accounting profit rate exceeds the growth rate of advertising capital. To see this, let

This raises the possibility that the positive advertising–profitability relationship is spurious, being derived from a measurement approach that biases the profit rate upward in the presence of heavy advertising. This possibility was first noted by Backman (1967), Telser (1968, 1969a) and Weiss (1969).

The two profit rates differ only in the presence of a goodwill effect. An investigation of this bias thus requires some estimate of the depreciation rate for advertising capital. Weiss (1969) concludes that the relationship between advertising intensity and profit rates remains positive, as in the original Comanor–Wilson (1967) regressions, when the profit rate is recomputed under the assumption that advertising has a durable effect that depreciates at a rate of 33% per year. Comanor and Wilson (1974) confirm this conclusion, after using higher depreciation rates derived from their industry demand estimates. On the other hand, using an advertising depreciation rate of 5% rate per year for all firms, Bloch (1974) argues that advertising does not have a statistically significant effect on the true rate of profit; and Ayanian (1975) reports a similar finding, using somewhat higher depreciation rates that vary across industries.[44] Yet, as I discuss in Section 3.1.1, more recent studies suggest that the depreciation rate is often quite high. This suggests that any bias may be small in magnitude.

A second interpretative issue is whether the advertising–profitability relationship reflects the fact that advertising and profitability are jointly determined. As Schmalensee (1972, 1976a, 1989) emphasizes, advertising intensity and profitability may be positively associated, because they are endogenous and positively related to omitted variables that induce large mark ups. In particular, and in line with arguments by Demsetz (1973, 1974) and Nelson (1974b, 1975), firms of superior efficiency may advertise more and earn more. Following this line of reasoning, it may be possible to disentangle the causal possibilities somewhat by looking at how the relationship between advertising and profitability varies within an industry between large and small firms. If advertising deters entry, then small and large firms may both benefit from this "shared asset", in which case a positive advertising–profitability association for all firms may be expected. But, if advertising facilitates the entry of efficient, large firms, then the advertising–profitability association may be much stronger for large firms. Gomes (1986), Kwoka and Ravenscraft (1986) and Porter (1979) provide inter-industry evidence that the advertising–profitability association indeed is significantly greater for large firms. This finding offers some support for the informative view. It is also possible, however, that persuasive advertising insulates large, pioneering firms from competitive incursions, even though recent entrants would be more efficient yet were they to operate at large scale.

π/E (π^*/E^*) denote the accounting (true) profit on equity. Then $\pi/E \equiv [R - VC - a - d_k K]/K$ and $\pi^*/E^* \equiv [R - VC - d_a A - d_k K]/[A + K]$, where $R - VC$ is revenue less variable costs, a is current advertising outlay, K is tangible capital which depreciates at rate d_k, and A is advertising capital which depreciates at rate d_a. The bias is then characterized as $\pi/E - \pi^*/E^* = [\pi/E - A'/A][A/(A + K)]$, where $A' \equiv a - d_a A$ is the net advertising investment.

[44] Further studies include Ayanian (1983), Comanor and Wilson (1979), Demsetz (1979), Grabowski and Mueller (1978), Hirschey (1982), Landes and Rosenfield (1994) and Nakao (1979).

Clearly, the endogeneity concern is formidable. Furthermore, simultaneous-equation methods are unlikely to fully resolve this concern. As Schmalensee (1989) explains, in the long run essentially all conduct and structure variables are endogenous; as a consequence, there may be a shortage of exogenous variables that can be used as valid instruments.[45]

In summary, there is evidence that advertising intensity is positively associated with (accounting) profitability for manufacturers of consumer goods. Within the consumer-goods category, this association is strongest for convenience goods. The advertising–profitability association is weaker for producer goods, and the association appears negative for retail and service sectors. These patterns admit plausible economic interpretations. But it is difficult to draw general inferences as to the association between advertising and entry, due to measurement and endogeneity concerns.

3.2.3. Entry

It is also possible to examine the entry-deterrence effect of advertising by exploring the direct relationship between advertising and entry. I consider empirical research of this kind next.

One group of studies suggests that advertising indeed deters entry. For example, Orr (1974a) obtains data on entry for 71 Canadian manufacturing industries in each year from 1963 to 1967, where entry is measured by the increase in the number of corporations in the industry. Orr then regresses entry on a number of variables, and he finds that advertising intensity exerts a significant and negative influence on entry in consumer-goods but not producer-goods manufacturing industries. Related findings are also offered by Duetsch (1975), Gorecki (1976), Harris (1976), Masson and Shannon (1982), Schwalbach (1987) and Shapiro and Khemani (1987). In the market for physician services, Rizzo and Zeckhauser (1990) find that the potential returns from advertising are greatest for experienced physicians, which suggests that advertising may inhibit entry in this industry.

A second group of studies, however, suggests that advertising may facilitate entry. Alemson (1970), Ferguson (1967), Hirschey (1981), MacDonald (1986) and Telser (1962) report evidence that is consistent with the view that advertising facilitates entry and new-product innovations. Backman (1967), Eckard (1991), Farris and Buzzell (1979), Lambin (1976) and Leffler (1981) also report evidence for various industries and product classes that advertising intensity is positively correlated with new-product innovations. Porter (1978) observes further that a firm's use of network TV advertising is strongly and positively associated with its rate of new introductions to the product line and its overall sales volume.[46] Finally, in an inter-industry study, Kessides (1986)

[45] Studies that use simultaneous-equation methods include Comanor and Wilson (1974), Connolly and Hirschey (1984), Geroski (1982), Martin (1979a, 1979b) and Strickland and Weiss (1976).

[46] The interpretation of a positive relationship between new-product innovations and advertising is not straightforward: such innovations might reflect entry (a new product from a new firm) or entry deterrence

seeks to explain net entry in 266 U.S. manufacturing industries between 1972 and 1977. He concludes that, in most industries, advertising facilitates entry.[47]

Questionnaire studies offer further insight. In a survey of nearly 300 U.S. product managers in a variety of product groups, Smiley (1988) and Bunch and Smiley (1992) consider the strategies that are most commonly used by firms that seek to deter entry. They find that the creation of product loyalty through advertising is one of the most frequently used entry-deterrence strategies. Limit pricing and capacity expansion, for example, are less popular. In a related study of U.K. product/brand managers, Singh, Utton and Waterson (1998) report that a modest fraction of managers regard advertising as an important variable with which to slow down or dissuade new rival products. In their study, advertising appears most important as a means for launching new products. Together, these studies suggest two lessons. First, advertising is an important strategic variable. Second, managers both use advertising to deter (or restrain) the entry of new products by rivals and to promote the entry of their own new products.[48]

The U.S. pharmaceutical industry is an especially well-suited industry in which to search for an entry-deterrence effect of advertising. In this industry, an incumbent firm enjoys a long period of monopoly power followed by a specific patent-expiration date after which generic-firm entry is possible. The data thus may be divided into "pre-entry" and "post-entry" periods, and it is possible to explore the effect of incumbent pre-entry advertising on entry. As Scott Morton (2000) explains, many studies treat incumbent pre-entry advertising as exogenous to the entry decision.[49] Under this hypothesis, and for a sample of 98 drugs that lost patent protection between 1986 and 1992, she finds that advertising may exert a very slight effect on generic entry, where the sign of the effect depends on the type of advertising. The exogeneity hypothesis, however, is suspect: incumbent pre-entry advertising and entry both depend on unobserved expectations as to the profitability of the post-entry market. Scott Morton thus instruments for incumbent pre-entry advertising in an equation that explains generic entry. The coefficient on advertising is then insignificantly different from zero. Scott Morton (2000, p. 1103) concludes "that brand advertising is not a barrier to entry in the US pharmaceutical industry".

(product proliferation by an established firm). Henning and Mann (1978) offer evidence in support of the latter interpretation. Clearly, though, advertising can complement innovation, if it enables firms to establish trademarks and develop reputations. See Shaw (1912) for an early statement.

47 See also Highfield and Smiley (1987). They report no significant relationship between advertising intensity and new firm creation for four-digit U.S. industries over the 1976–1981 period.

48 The association between advertising and entry also may be guaged by examining the manner in which incumbent firms adjust advertising following entry. As observed in Section 3.1.1, Alemson (1970), Cubbin and Domberger (1988) and Thomas (1999) describe situations in which incumbents respond to entry with advertising. Further studies of this behavior are reported in Section 8. But it is also often true that entry meets with little incumbent response. See Bunch and Smiley (1988), Geroski (1995), Grabowski and Vernon (1992), Leffler (1981), Robinson (1988), Singh, Utton and Waterson (1998) and Smiley (1988).

49 See Grabowski and Vernon (1992), Hurwitz and Caves (1988) and Leffler (1981).

In total, the direct evidence of the association between advertising and entry is somewhat mixed. Advertising may be used to raise the cost of entry, but it also may be the means of effective entry. The appropriate interpretation of the advertising–entry relationship is subtle and seems to vary across industries.

3.2.4. Price

As Chamberlin (1933) explains, advertising has conflicting effects on price, and the overall relationship cannot be deduced on theoretical grounds alone. I review next the empirical research that addresses the advertising–price relationship.

Consider first the impact of *manufacturer* advertising on the retail price. A variety of evidence suggests that heavily advertised brands are more expensive for final consumers than are less-advertised goods within the same product class. See, for example, Borden (1942), Backman (1967, p. 125), Nickell and Metcalf (1978), Scherer and Ross (1990, pp. 581–592), Telser (1964, p. 542) and Tremblay and Tremblay (1995). This evidence is consistent with the persuasive view. But, as information- and complementary-view advocates might argue, it is also possible that heavily advertised goods have higher prices, because they have higher (or less variable) quality or embody prestige effects that consumers directly value. Moreover, even if the *relative* prices of advertised products are higher, there remains the question of whether on average *absolute* prices are higher when advertising is present than when it is not. This is a difficult question, to which I now turn.[50]

In a series of papers, Steiner (1973, 1978, 1984, 1993) considers the relationship between manufacturer advertising and retailer margins and prices. Like Kaldor, Steiner argues that manufacturer advertising shifts power to the manufacturer.[51] Retail margins may fall for two reasons. First, when a brand is heavily advertised, retailers are more attracted to a reduced retail price for the brand. Intuitively, a heavily advertised brand is "identifiable" and serves as a benchmark by which consumers may compare prices across retailers; thus, a retailer's reputation for low pricing is particularly sensitive to the price that it sets for the advertised brand. Extending this argument, a retailer may regard a heavily advertised brand as an especially attractive candidate for "specials" and loss-leader promotions. Second, when a brand is heavily advertised and thus of particular value to retailers, the manufacturer may be tempted to raise the wholesale price. For these reasons, a negative relationship between manufacturer advertising and retail margins is implied.[52] The overall effect of manufacturer advertising on the final retail price is less clear and depends on the extent to which the manufacturer raises its

[50] For other approaches to this question, see Eckard (1987), Gallet (1999) and Leahy (1991). They provide evidence that manufacturer advertising may be associated with lower prices.

[51] Similar arguments appear also in earlier work, as observed in footnote 9. Albion and Farris (1981) and Farris and Albion (1980) discuss some of Steiner's arguments in further detail.

[52] Marshall (1919, pp. 301–302) also argues that branded goods are often used as "leaders" and that wholesale prices are often high.

wholesale price. Retailers set a lower retail price on the advertised brand *if* any increase in the wholesale price is small.

In support of this argument, Steiner (1973) considers the toy industry and reports evidence that the emergence of large-scale TV advertising in the late 1950s precipitated a substantial drop in retail margins. In cross-sectional work, Albion (1983), Reekie (1979), Farris and Albion (1987) and Nelson (1978) offer evidence that manufacturers' advertising and retailer margins are inversely related, while Steiner (1993) provides anecdotal support of this relationship in particular industries. In a related study, Nelson, Siegfried and Howell (1992) consider the relationship between market share and the wholesale price for the Maxwell House coffee brand in different regions. They find that the wholesale price is higher in regions for which market share is higher. In their suggested interpretation, well-known brands are attractive to retailers as items on which to run specials, since such brands are used as benchmarks for cross-store price comparisons, and manufacturers of such brands are thus able to charge higher wholesale prices.[53]

Manufacturer advertising also may impact retail pricing by influencing the scale and function of retail firms. This argument builds from the observation that manufacturer brand advertising and point-of-sale retail service are substitute sources of pre-purchase information for consumers. Brand advertising provides consumers with an implicit quality guarantee, due to the reputational capital that the brand embodies, and a retailer provides a similar implicit guarantee when it elects to carry a brand. In addition, retailer service can improve consumers' information with regard to specific product features. Suppose now that some underlying change were to occur that occasioned a substantial increase in manufacturer brand advertising. Time-constrained consumers might then demand less information from retailers, and retail competition could then focus more on price and less on service. Discount chains carrying brand goods might emerge.

Evidence of this pattern is reported in some industries. In particular, Steiner (1978) argues that this pattern describes the U.S. toy industry, and Pashigian and Bowen (1994) report supportive evidence from the mid-1970s for the U.S. apparel and toy industries. But what is the underlying change? As Steiner (1978) argues, one possibility is that the emergence of TV advertising in the 1950s lowered the cost to manufacturers of providing brand information.[54] Pashigian and Bowen propose a second possibility: the growth in (relative) earnings by females in the mid-1970s implied an increased cost to shopping time, this instigated a growth in branding, and brand advertising eventually substituted for retail service. Under both interpretations, greater manufacturer advertising is associated with the emergence of large-scale retailers that offer modest service and low prices.

[53] Some related themes emerge in a recent study by Chevalier, Kashyap and Rossi (2003). Using scanner data from a large supermarket chain, they find that retail prices and margins tend to be lower for an item over periods for which the item is in peak demand (e.g., tuna at Lent). This is also the time at which the item is more likely to be advertised by the retailer.

[54] See also Bresnahan (1984).

Consider second the impact of *retail* advertising on the retail price. The classic study on this topic is offered by Benham (1972). In the 1960s, considerable variation existed across states in the U.S. with respect to the legal treatment of advertising in the eyeglass industry. Broadly, states fell into three groups: some states prohibited all advertising, some states prohibited price advertising but allowed non-price advertising, and some states had no restrictions. This variation provides a natural experiment with which to assess the effect of retail advertising on retail pricing. Benham reports that eyeglass prices were substantially higher in states that prohibited all advertising than in states that had no restrictions; furthermore, prices were only slightly higher in states that allowed only non-price advertising than in states with no restrictions. The association between price advertising and lower prices is striking and directly supports the informative view. The association between non-price advertising and low prices is also striking. It appears to reflect the entry of large-scale retail firms into markets that permit non-price advertising.[55]

Similar findings are reported in studies of other industries. Cady (1976) considers the U.S. retail market for prescription drugs in 1970, when legal restrictions on retail advertising varied across states. He finds that retail prices are significantly and positively related to advertising restrictions, and he also reports a price-reducing influence for non-price advertising. Maurizi and Kelly (1978) compare retail gasoline prices across major cities. They find that both the mean and variance of prices are lower in states where price advertising is allowed. The same finding is reported by Feldman and Begun (1978, 1980), who study the price of examinations performed by optometrists. The optometry industry is also the subject of an important FTC (1980) study. Using FTC data, Kwoka (1984) finds that non-advertising and especially advertising firms reduce the price of examinations in markets for which advertising is allowed.[56] Using survey data for the routine legal service market in 17 U.S. metropolitan areas, Schroeter, Smith and Cox (1987) report evidence that price–cost ratios are lower when area-wide advertising intensity is greater. These studies all support the informative view.

As Benham acknowledges, it is possible that advertising restrictions and prices are both endogenous variables that reflect some underlying influence; for example, if sellers are well organized in a given region, then they may be able to secure legislation (advertising restrictions) that facilitates their collusive conduct (high prices). This concern motivates two longitudinal efforts. First, Glazer (1981) compares supermarket food prices in Queens, New York and Long Island, over a two-month period in 1978 when a newspaper strike limited the price information that could be communicated through advertising in Queens. The newspaper strike is clearly an exogenous source of variation

[55] Benham and Benham (1975), Haas-Wilson (1986) and an FTC (1980) study consider the impact of a range of commercial practice restrictions in the optometry industry. These studies suggest that restrictions impede the flow of information from firms to consumers and thus deter the entry of large-scale ("commercial") firms that offer low prices.

[56] An important issue is whether the quality-adjusted price is also lower at advertising firms. For different perspectives, see Kwoka (1984) and Parker (1995).

in advertising restrictions. For a few commonly advertised grocery items, Glazer reports that relative prices rose in Queens during the strike, before returning to normal levels at the end of the strike. Second, Milyo and Waldfogel (1999) consider the liquor industry and make use of an exogenous shock: the 1996 Supreme Court ruling that overturned Rhode Island's ban on advertising prices of alcoholic beverages.[57] Using data for 33 alcoholic beverage products at 115 stores between 1995 and 1997, they find that advertising stores substantially cut the prices of advertised products and have lower prices on average than other stores. In contrast to Stigler's (1961) predictions, however, the introduction of price advertising has little effect on the prices of non-advertised products and is not associated with a reduction in price dispersion across stores.

In summary, the impact of manufacturer advertising on retail prices is complex. There is some evidence, though, that manufacturer advertising may encourage loss-leaders featuring the advertised item and facilitate the growth of low-price discount outlets. For many industries, there is also substantial evidence that retail advertising leads to lower retail prices. Recent work, however, suggests that the distinction between the effect of advertising on the prices of advertised and non-advertised products warrants greater attention.

3.2.5. *Quality*

According to Nelson (1974b), when a product is heavily advertised, it is more likely that the quality of the product is high. I summarize now empirical work that examines further the relationship between advertising and quality.

In most empirical studies, a positive relationship between advertising and product quality is observed in some circumstances, but the relationship fails (or weakens) in other circumstances. For example, Archibald, Haulman and Moody Jr. (1983) examine the market for running shoes for 178 brands. They consider the correlation between advertising levels and product quality, where quality is measured by published rankings in the magazine *Runners' World*. The correlation between advertising and quality is found to strengthen significantly after the publication of ratings. Caves and Greene (1996) consider 196 product categories and evaluate the rank correlations between brands' product-quality rankings and advertising outlays, where quality rankings are measured using *Consumer Reports* data. They find that advertising and quality are generally uncorrelated among brands. The advertising–quality relationship is positive, however, for innovative goods and also goods for which buyers' experience and search are both useful in making the brand choice. Finally, Tellis and Fornell (1988) explore the advertising–quality relationship over the product life cycle. Using PIMS data for a sample of 749 consumer businesses for the period 1970–1983, wherein a firm's product quality is measured on the basis of a (confidential) self-assessment, they find that advertising, market

[57] For an earlier longitudinal study of the liquor industry, see Luksetich and Lofgreen (1976), who argue that legislation that relaxed restrictions against price advertising in Minnesota resulted in lower retail prices.

share and profitability are all positively associated with product quality. They observe further that these relationships are especially strong at later stages in the product life cycle.[58]

A common theme in these studies is that consumers are responsive to advertising that contains direct information as to product quality. This suggests that a positive advertising–quality relationship often may reflect the differential benefit that firms with high-quality products enjoy from providing direct product-quality information through their advertisements.[59] The study by Archibald, Haulman and Moody Jr., for instance, suggests that firms with high rankings are eager to communicate this information to consumers through advertising. Likewise, Caves and Greene (1996, p. 50) explain that their findings are "consistent with advertising as information, if higher quality goods have more features or capabilities (which buyers learn from verifiable advertised information)". The findings of Tellis and Fornell can be viewed in this way, as well. To interpret the strengthening of the relationship over the product life cycle, Tellis and Fornell explain that it is less tempting for a low-quality firm to advertise once the product matures, in part because consumers are then better informed.

This discussion highlights the distinction between direct and indirect product-quality information. In fact, this distinction becomes ambiguous, once it is allowed that consumers have imperfect memories. As Nelson (1974b) argues in his discussion of the repeat-business effect, a firm with a high-quality product gains more from rekindling the memories of its old consumers, and the fact that the firm advertises therefore represents a source of indirect information to new consumers. But advertising is then also a means by which old consumers gain access to direct information that concerns the product's quality and attributes. From this perspective, an advertisement that provides indirect information to new consumers simultaneously provides direct information to old consumers. The "memory-activation" role for advertising may be of special value for firms with high-quality goods that are in the later stages of the product life cycle. This suggests that the life-cycle pattern observed by Tellis and Fornell might emerge, even if the content of advertisements for mature, high-quality products is not more informative in some literal sense.[60]

Experimental work offers a means by which a researcher might gain direct evidence as to the manner in which advertising influences consumers' perceptions. The experiments conducted by Homer (1995), Kirmani and Wright (1989) and Kirmani (1990, 1997) are of particular interest. These studies examine how subjects' expectations about product quality are affected by perceived advertising expenditures. An

[58] For additional studies that report evidence of a positive advertising–quality relationship, see Marquardt and McGann (1975) and Rotfeld and Rotzoll (1976). Kirmani and Rao (2000) offer a recent survey.

[59] A related point is that firms may have greater incentive to select high-quality products when consumers possess greater direct product-quality information. Jin and Leslie (2003) offer striking evidence in support of this point.

[60] This suggestion is of particular relevance, in light of work by Arterburn and Woodbury (1981) and Resnik and Stern (1978) that studies the content of magazine and TV advertising. Their studies suggest that often little "hard" information is supplied through these media. See Abernethy and Franke (1996) for further discussion.

inverted-U relationship is suggested. Provided that advertising expenditures are not unreasonably high, consumers perceive higher advertising expenditures as indicating that the manufacturer has greater confidence in the quality of the product. When advertising levels reach excessive levels, however, consumers may infer that the manufacturer lacks confidence in the product's quality and is desperate. These studies provide some evidence that consumers infer a positive relationship between advertising expenditures and product quality. This inference is broadly consistent with Nelson's (1974b) reasoning.

There exists also a small literature that examines the advertising–quality relationship in the retail sector. Utilizing state-level variation in advertising restrictions for the optometry industry, Kwoka (1984) considers whether the ability to advertise results in a deterioration in quality of eye examinations, where quality is measured as time spent in the examination. In comparison to firms in states that restrict advertising, advertising firms offer lower quality but non-advertising firms select higher quality. In total, Kwoka's work thus suggests that the presence of advertising serves to (i) reduce prices and lower quality at advertising firms, and (ii) reduce (to a smaller extent) prices and raise quality at non-advertising firms. Kwoka also suggests that average quality is higher in markets for which advertising is allowed than in markets for which it is not.[61] This suggestion, however, is disputed by Parker (1995), who considers alternative measures of quality.

What are the main lessons? Perhaps the main finding is a negative one: the studies described here do not offer strong support for the hypothesis of a systematic positive relationship between advertising and product quality. The studies do suggest, however, that a positive relationship is more likely when advertising conveys direct information (broadly defined) to consumers. Finally, when advertising is allowed in retail service industries, there is some evidence that advertising firms may have lower product quality and non-advertising firms may have higher product quality than they would were advertising not allowed.

3.3. Summary

At a broad level, the empirical research described here offers progress on three fronts. First, it indicates clearly that no single view of advertising is valid in all circumstances. This in itself is progress, and especially so when compared to the absolutist tone adopted in many of the initial discussions of advertising.[62] Second, progress is also achieved at a more constructive level: a number of important regularities are identified that hold within particular industries or narrow industry categories. Finally, progress is also apparent at a methodological level. While some of the earlier empirical work regards

[61] Similarly, Haas-Wilson (1986) studies the price of an eye examination bundled with a pair of glasses, where quality is measured by the thoroughness of the eye examination and the accuracy of the eyeglass prescription. She finds that commercial practice restrictions raise price without increasing quality.

[62] As Lambin (1976, p. 99) puts it: "The feeling that emerges is that the economic power of advertising has been overstated by critics and apologists of advertising."

advertising as a structural variable that proxies for product differentiation, subsequent work is increasingly attentive to the endogeneity of advertising and the interpretive as well as econometric issues that endogeneity implies.

As mentioned in the Introduction, the empirical studies suggest important roles for advertising theory. Theoretical work might offer important insight into questions – Is advertising excessively supplied? Does it deter entry? – that the empirical analyses fail to resolve. In addition, theoretical work may provide novel interpretations of some of the constructive findings that the empirical analyses offer for different market structures. New predictions may also emerge. Finally, with advances in advertising theory, a foundation may be provided on which to specify the endogenous determination of advertising, so that future empirical analyses might proceed at a more structural level. With these roles in mind, I present in the next four sections a review of the economic theory of advertising.

4. Monopoly advertising

In this section, I focus on positive and normative theories of monopoly advertising. The monopoly case is of interest in its own right, and it also represents a simple setting within which to begin the formal analysis of advertising. In subsequent sections, I consider more advanced topics, including multi-firm markets and monopoly advertising that signals product quality.

4.1. The positive theory of monopoly advertising

In the preceding two sections, it is emphasized that any observed relationship between advertising and other variables (e.g., profit) must be interpreted with great care, since advertising is endogenous. At a broad level, the significance of this idea can be appreciated without the aid of a formal model, and indeed I have proceeded on this assumption. The development of a formal theory, however, does make possible important additional insights. In a classic paper, Dorfman and Steiner (1954) offer one of the first formal theories of optimal monopoly advertising.[63] This theory identifies the key structural features on which endogenous monopoly advertising depends, and it also offers a general framework within which specific theories of monopoly advertising may be developed.

4.1.1. The Dorfman–Steiner model

The Dorfman–Steiner model takes the following form. Suppose that a monopolist chooses the price of its product, P, and a level of advertising, A, where A may denote the number of fliers sent, minutes of TV or radio time bought, etc. The cost

[63] See also Rasmussen (1952), who presents a formal analysis of optimal advertising but imposes the assumption that price is fixed. See Schmalensee (1972) for further discussion.

per advertisement is assumed constant and is given by κ. The market demand function is represented as $D(P, A)$, where attention is restricted to $(P, A) \geqslant 0$ for which $D > 0$ and $D_A > 0 > D_P$. The monopolist's variable cost of production is given by $C(D(P, A))$, where $C' > 0$. Under these assumptions, the monopolist's profit function is defined as $\Pi(P, A) \equiv PD(P, A) - C(D(P, A)) - \kappa A$. This model assumes that consumers respond to advertising, but it does not explain why. The model is therefore not yet suitable for normative analysis. It is, however, now possible to derive a positive theory of monopoly pricing and advertising.

To this end, it is useful to examine the first-order conditions for profit maximization. Assuming throughout that second-order conditions hold, the monopolist maximizes profit if and only if its price and advertising selections satisfy the following first-order conditions:

$$\Pi_P = (P - C')D_P + D = 0, \tag{4.1}$$

$$\Pi_A = (P - C')D_A - \kappa = 0. \tag{4.2}$$

Let $P_M(A)$ denote that price that satisfies (4.1). This is the profit-maximizing price for any given level of advertising. Similarly, for any given price, let $A_M(P)$ denotes the advertising level that satisfies (4.2). The monopolist maximizes profit with its joint selection of price and advertising when it picks a pair (P_M, A_M) such that $(P_M, A_M) = (P_M(A_M), A_M(P_M))$.

To interpret the first-order conditions, let $\varepsilon_P \equiv -PD_P/D$ and $\varepsilon_A \equiv AD_A/D$ denote the price and advertising elasticities of demand, respectively. Manipulation of (4.1) yields the familiar markup rule:

$$\frac{(P - C')}{P} = \frac{1}{\varepsilon_P}. \tag{4.3}$$

Substituting (4.3) into (4.2), it follows that the marginal revenue from a dollar increase in advertising expenditure must equal the price-elasticity of demand:

$$\frac{PD_A}{\kappa} = \varepsilon_P. \tag{4.4}$$

The ratio of advertising expenditures to sales revenue, or the advertising intensity, is $\kappa A/PD$. Using (4.4), the advertising intensity must equal the ratio of elasticities of demand with respect to advertising and price:

$$\frac{\kappa A}{PD} = \frac{\varepsilon_A}{\varepsilon_P}. \tag{4.5}$$

The proportion of sales revenue that a profit-maximizing monopolist spends on advertising is thus determined by a simple elasticity ratio.[64]

[64] Related rules may be derived in dynamic settings with goodwill effects. See Nerlove and Arrow (1962), Friedman (1983), Gould (1970) and Schmalensee (1972).

Dorfman and Steiner provide a formal expression for some of the reverse-causality concerns raised in Sections 2 and 3. For example, consider the persuasive-view hypothesis that a high advertising intensity makes the demand function more price inelastic and thereby leads to a large markup. Dorfman and Steiner provide a formal basis under which the reverse causal pattern also may be advanced: all else equal, when the demand function is more price inelastic (i.e., when ε_P is smaller), a monopolist chooses a high advertising intensity and a large markup.

4.1.2. Two examples

This general framework places little restriction on the manner in which advertising impacts demand. By imposing further structure, it is possible to capture some of the effects emphasized under alternative views of advertising. I consider two examples.[65] In the first example, monopoly advertising raises the willingness of consumers to pay and thereby generates an upward shift in the monopolist's demand function. This example is illustrative of the persuasive view. In the second example, monopoly advertising informs new consumers that the product exists and thereby generates an outward shift in the monopolist's demand function. This example is illustrative of the informative view. At a positive level, both examples are compatible with the complementary view.

In the first example, each consumer considers whether to buy a unit of the monopolist's product, where the consumer's valuation for this product may be influenced by the monopolist's advertising. Consumers are "vertically differentiated" with respect to the influence of advertising on their valuations. Formally, when the monopolist advertises at level A and sets the price P, a consumer of type θ enjoys utility $\theta g(A) - P$ if the consumer buys one unit of the monopolist's product, where $g(0) = 1$ and $g'(A) > 0$. The consumer receives zero utility otherwise. There is a mass of consumers of size $N > 0$, and θ is uniformly distributed over $[0, 1]$. A consumer of type θ thus buys the monopolist's product if and only if $\theta \geqslant P/g(A)$, and so the market demand function is $D(P, A) = N[1 - P/g(A)]$.

As the persuasive view suggests, when advertising is increased, the demand function becomes more inelastic. Formally, it is easily derived that $\varepsilon_P = P/(g(A) - P)$, so that the elasticity effect is $\frac{\mathrm{d}\varepsilon_P}{\mathrm{d}A} < 0$. The persuasive view also holds that the profit-maximizing price, $P_M(A)$, rises when the level of advertising is raised, provided that no offsetting scale effect is present. Using (4.1), it may be confirmed that $\Pi_{PA} = N[g' + C'' D_A]/g$ when evaluated at $P = P_M(A)$. It follows that

$$\mathrm{sign}\{P'_M(A)\} = \mathrm{sign}\{g' + C'' D_A\}. \tag{4.6}$$

Therefore, if marginal cost is constant or increasing, then the monopoly price indeed does rise when advertising is increased. On the other hand, if there is a significant scale effect, then greater advertising could lower the monopoly price.

[65] See also Pepall, Richards and Norman (1999, ch. 10) for a similar presentation.

Further insight can be developed using the inverse demand function. This function is represented here as $P(A, Q) = g(A)(1 - Q/N)$, where Q denotes the quantity of units sold. Observe that $P_{AQ} = -g'/N < 0$, which indicates that advertising shifts up the demand function by more at lower quantities. Intuitively, the marginal consumer has a lower θ and thus gets a smaller valuation gain from an advertising increase than do the inframarginal consumers who have higher θ's.

The second example builds on an approach suggested by Butters (1977). Suppose there are N consumers, each of whom possesses the same individual demand function, $d(P)$, for the monopolist's product, where d is positive and decreasing below a reservation price: $d'(P) < 0$ for $P \in [0, R]$ and $d(R) = 0$. The monopolist chooses the number of advertising messages, A, that are sent. Each "ad" is received by exactly one consumer, and each consumer is equally likely to receive any given ad. A consumer becomes aware of the monopolist's product only by receiving an ad. The probability that a consumer receives no ad is then $[1 - 1/N]^A \approx e^{-A/N}$ for N large. The market demand function is thus $D(P, A) = N[1 - e^{-A/N}]d(P) \equiv G(A)d(P)$. Observe that $G' > G(0) = 0 > G''$.

As the informative view suggests, when advertising is increased, the demand function does not become more inelastic. In fact, advertising here has no elasticity effect: $\frac{\mathrm{d}\varepsilon_P}{\mathrm{d}A} = 0$.[66] Consider next the impact of an increase in the level of advertising upon the profit-maximizing price, $P_M(A)$. Using (4.1), it is readily shown that $\Pi_{PA} = -D_P C'' D_A$ when evaluated at $P = P_M(A)$. Therefore, for $A > 0$, the effect of advertising on the monopoly price is entirely dictated by the scale effect:

$$\operatorname{sign}\{P_M'(A)\} = \operatorname{sign}\{C''\}. \tag{4.7}$$

In contrast to the first example above, if marginal cost is constant, then advertising has no effect on the monopoly price.

The inverse demand function is now $P(A, Q) = d^{-1}(Q/G(A))$, where d^{-1} is a strictly decreasing function. Calculations reveal that $P_{AQ} > 0$ provided that a demand-curvature condition, $dd'' - (d')^2 < 0$, is satisfied. Under this condition, advertising shifts up the demand function by more at higher quantities. Intuitively, at a given level of advertising, if the quantity is high, then the individual demand, $d(P)$, must be high, and so a low price is implied. From this starting point, an increase in advertising would lead to a significant volume increase, as new consumers would bring forth large individual demands at the low price. To maintain the original volume, a significant price increase is then required.

Finally, it is interesting to link these examples back to the earlier literature. Two points warrant emphasis. First, the examples confirm Chamberlin's insight: the effect of advertising on price is determined by the elasticity and scale effects of advertising, where the former is itself determined by the purpose (persuasion or information) of advertising.

[66] The informative view in fact holds that advertising *increases* the price-elasticity of demand. This effect arises in differentiated-goods markets with multiple firms, as I discuss in Section 5.2.

The second point concerns the market demand function D under the informative view. This function is strictly increasing and concave in A, and it captures formally Ozga's rationale for diminishing returns. In particular, at a higher level of advertising, the benefit of additional advertising is lower, since it becomes less likely that a new ad reaches a consumer who has not already learned of the product's existence.

4.2. The normative theory of monopoly advertising

Does a monopolist advertise to an extent that is socially excessive, inadequate or optimal? Many of the earliest commentators on advertising offer unequivocal answers, but the theoretical frameworks on which their answers are based are rarely clarified. Empirical efforts also fail to offer a conclusive answer. Perhaps advances in theory might provide a means by which to answer this question with guarded confidence. Motivated by this prospect, I offer here a formal discussion of the recent development of the normative theory of monopoly advertising. Under the assumption that advertising is utility increasing (a good), this work suggests that a profit-maximizing monopolist may advertise to an extent that is socially inadequate. To develop this suggestion, I use the model and two examples presented just above. They constitute a unifying framework in which to present recent developments in the persuasive, informative and complementary views.

4.2.1. The persuasive view

Under the persuasive view, advertising changes the preferences of consumers. An issue thus arises as to the standard by which consumer welfare should be assessed. Braithwaite offers the first analysis of this kind. As discussed in Section 2.2, she measures consumer welfare relative to pre-advertising tastes, and she establishes that monopoly advertising lowers consumer welfare if the monopoly price rises or remains unchanged when advertising occurs. As Figure 28.1 illustrates, consumer surplus may (but need not) increase if advertising is coupled with a decrease in the monopoly price. Intuitively, advertising induces a consumption distortion: consumers purchase additional units at a price that exceeds what those units are "truly" worth. This consumer-welfare loss, L, due to advertising can be offset only if the price falls, so that there is a consumer-welfare gain, G, from the purchase of truly desirable units at a lower price.

But a complete welfare analysis requires as well that the impact of advertising on profit be considered. This step is taken by Dixit and Norman (1978). To understand their argument, consider Figure 28.2, in which an increase in advertising from A_0 to A_1 results in an outward shift in demand from $D(P, A_0)$ to $D(P, A_1)$. As depicted, Dixit and Norman assume that the additional advertising increases price from P_0 to P_1 and quantity sold from $D(P_0, A_0)$ to $D(P_1, A_1)$. Let $\Delta A \equiv A_1 - A_0 > 0$ and $\Delta P \equiv P_1 - P_0 > 0$. For simplicity, they suppose that the marginal cost of production, C', is constant.

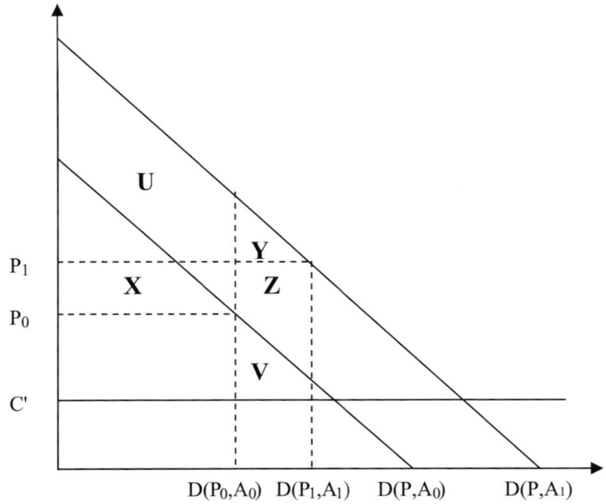

Figure 28.2. Welfare and persuasive advertising.

Two interpretations are possible. First, if $A_0 = 0$, then the initial demand curve, $D(P, A_0)$, corresponds to a market without advertising, so that the subsequent demand curve, $D(P, A_1)$, reflects the level of demand once advertising is allowed. Second, if $A_0 > 0$, then the demand shift describes a market with an initial level of advertising that is subsequently increased. Allowing for either interpretation, I refer to $D(P, A_0)$ as the *initial demand curve* and to $D(P, A_1)$ as the *subsequent demand curve*. Dixit and Norman are flexible when it comes to the precise standard by which consumer welfare is measured; however, they do require that the same standard be used before and after advertising is increased. I define the *initial* (*subsequent*) *standard* as the consumer surplus associated with the initial (subsequent) demand curve.

Consider first the case in which the initial standard is used. As Braithwaite observes, under the assumption that advertising leads to a higher price, consumer welfare is then decreased by advertising, due to the induced consumption distortion: consumers pay more for additional units than those units are truly worth, as depicted by the area Z, and pay more now for units that were desirable even before the change in advertising, as captured by the area X.[67] The change in consumer surplus under the initial standard is thus $\Delta CS_0 \equiv -[X+Z] < 0$. But the monopolist enjoys an increase in producer surplus in amount $X + Z + V > 0$. The change in the monopolist's profit, $\Delta\Pi \equiv \Pi(P_1, A_1) - \Pi(P_0, A_0)$, balances the increase in producer surplus against the additional advertising expenditure: $\Delta\Pi = X + Z + V - \kappa\Delta A$. Under the assumption that the advertising industry operates at constant cost and earns zero rents, the resource cost of advertising,

[67] In Figure 28.2, the unlabeled triangle that is southwest of the area Y is understood to rest in both region X and region U.

$\kappa\Delta A$, is the same for the monopolist as for society. The change in welfare under the initial standard, $\Delta W_0 \equiv \Delta CS_0 + \Delta\Pi$, is thus determined as $\Delta W_0 = V - \kappa\Delta A$.

While the monopolist and a social planner agree on the cost of advertising, they disagree on the size of the benefit that additional advertising implies. Consider a small increase in advertising. Then, quantity and price both change little, and so Z is second order in size. The following relationship is apparent:

$$\Delta W_0 \approx \Delta\Pi - D(P_0, A_0)\Delta P. \tag{4.8}$$

The disagreement thus emerges because consumers must pay a higher price on units that were purchased even in the initial situation. The transfer has no welfare significance, but it does increase monopoly profit. Under the initial standard, therefore, the private benefit to the monopolist of small expansion in advertising that results in a higher price exceeds the social benefit.

Consider second the case in which the subsequent standard is adopted. The same logic applies. To see this, observe that the change in consumer surplus, ΔCS_1, is now captured in Figure 28.2 as $\Delta CS_1 = Y - X$, where Y reflects the new consumer surplus that is enjoyed under the subsequent standard when additional units are consumed at the price P_1. The monopolist's change in profit remains $\Delta\Pi = X + Z + V - \kappa\Delta A$. The change in welfare under the subsequent standard, $\Delta W_1 \equiv \Delta CS_1 + \Delta\Pi$, is thus determined as $\Delta W_1 = Y + Z + V - \kappa\Delta A$. As before, for a small increase in advertising, quantity and price both change little, and so Z and now Y are second order in size. But this means that the welfare difference under the two standards, $\Delta W_1 - \Delta W_0$, is second order. Indeed, for small changes, we obtain the same formula

$$\Delta W_1 \approx \Delta\Pi - D(P_0, A_0)\Delta P. \tag{4.9}$$

Thus, even under the subsequent standard, the private benefit to the monopolist of a small expansion in price-increasing advertising exceeds the social benefit.

Using (4.8) and (4.9), two findings are obtained. First, for a small increase in advertising, whether the initial or subsequent standard is used, the monopolist will not undersupply and may oversupply price-increasing advertising. Put differently, for a small amount of price-increasing advertising, private profitability is necessary, but not sufficient, for social desirability. Next, suppose that (i) the initial and subsequent advertising levels are given as $A_0 = A_M - \Delta A < A_M = A_1$, and (ii) for any advertising level A, the monopolist chooses its profit-maximizing price, $P_M(A)$. Given the assumption that advertising is price-increasing, it follows that $P_0 = P_M(A_M - \Delta A) < P_M(A_M) = P_M = P_1$. An envelope argument is now available: under (4.1) and (4.2), when the price–advertising pair is increased slightly from (P_0, A_0) to (P_1, A_1), there is no first-order effect on monopoly profits and hence $\Delta\Pi = 0$. According to (4.8) and (4.9), social welfare would rise under either standard if the monopolist were to slightly reduce its advertising and price from their profit-maximizing levels, (P_M, A_M). A second finding is thus established: monopoly advertising that increases price is excessive.[68]

[68] It is also possible to evaluate the increase in advertising from $A_0 = A_M - \Delta$ to $A_1 = A_M$ using the pre-advertising standard (i.e., the consumer surplus associated with the demand curve $D(P, 0)$). As Dixit and

These are striking findings. But important concerns may be raised. A first concern is the assumption that advertising increases price. As discussed in Section 3.2.4, in multi-firm markets at least, the empirical support for the price-increasing assumption is mixed. Likewise, in the positive models of advertising, the price-increasing assumption finds mixed theoretical support: under constant marginal costs, the assumption holds in the first but not the second example. A second concern is the manner in which Dixit and Norman measure consumer welfare. This concern is more subtle, and I turn to it next.

4.2.2. An alternative approach

Under the Dixit–Norman approach, the impact of advertising on consumer welfare is measured relative to a fixed standard. Price-increasing monopoly advertising is then excessive, since the monopolist is motivated by the prospect of obtaining a higher price on those units that are initially purchased. This accounts for the term $D(P_0, A_0)\Delta P$ in (4.8) and (4.9). As Dixit and Norman acknowledge, an important feature of their approach is that the area between the initial and subsequent demand curves on infra-marginal units (i.e., units below $D(P_0, A_0)$) plays no part in the calculations. In Figure 28.2, this is depicted by the area U.

An alternative perspective is that the right comparison is rather between the consumer surplus under the initial demand curve at the price–quantity pair $(P_0, D(P_0, A_0))$ with the consumer surplus under the subsequent demand curve at the price–quantity pair $(P_1, D(P_1, A_1))$. For small changes, this amounts to a comparison between consumer surplus under $D(P, A_0)$ at the price–quantity pair $(P_0, D(P_0, A_0))$ with the consumer surplus under $D(P, A_1)$ at the price–quantity pair $(P_1, D(P_0, A_0))$. Intuitively, the "Dixit–Norman term", $D(P_0, A_0)\Delta P$, would enter into this comparison and again provide an influence toward excessive price-increasing monopoly advertising. But a new "infra-marginal term", corresponding to the area U, would also arise. The latter term would account for the additional consumer surplus that advertising generates on the initial units as demand shifts from $D(P, A_0)$ to $D(P, A_1)$. This additional surplus arises regardless of the direction of the change in price, and it represents a social benefit from advertising that the monopolist cannot appropriate. Accordingly, the infra-marginal term provides an influence toward inadequate monopoly advertising.

The Dixit–Norman and alternative approaches can be understood with reference to the two examples presented above. The Dixit–Norman approach may be associated with the first example, if it is assumed that an existing consumer of type θ does not experience a "real" gain in utility when advertising is increased. The alternative approach is founded on the informative and the complementary views. First, in line with the second example presented above and as Kotowitz and Mathewson (1979a) and Shapiro (1980) explain, the upward shift in demand might reflect informative advertising that brings

Norman show, the case for excessive advertising is then even greater, since advertising induces a (first-order) consumption–distortion cost.

new consumers into the market. Surely, the surplus enjoyed by these consumers should enter into the welfare calculation. Second, as Fisher and McGowan (1979) emphasize, even in the first example, it is possible that consumers value the social prestige that an advertised product may facilitate.

Two conclusions of the alternative approach may now be anticipated. First, monopoly advertising is inadequate if advertising does not raise price. Intuitively, in the case of price-maintaining or price-decreasing advertising, the Dixit–Norman term is neutral or reinforces the infra-marginal term. Second, monopoly advertising may be inadequate, even if advertising raises price. In this case, the Dixit–Norman and infra-marginal terms pull in opposite directions, but the latter may dominate if the price increase is not too great. This second conclusion, of course, contrasts with the implication under the persuasive view (as formalized by Dixit and Norman) that a monopolist always supplies price-increasing advertising to a socially excessive extent.

With the central ideas now in place, I now formalize the alternative approach and develop its two main conclusions. Drawing on the two examples, I also develop the informative and complementary foundations for the alternative approach in some further detail.

4.2.3. Price-maintaining and price-decreasing monopoly advertising

For a given price and advertising level, let social welfare be defined as

$$W(P, A) = \Pi(P, A) + \int_{P}^{R(A)} D(P, A)\,\mathrm{d}P, \tag{4.10}$$

where $R(A)$ satisfies $D(R(A), A) = 0$ and may vary with A. Notice that this formulation captures the alternative approach: under (4.10), when the price–advertising pair changes from (P_0, A_0) to (P_1, A_1), the change in consumer welfare is calculated by comparing the consumer surplus under $D(P, A_0)$ at the price–quantity pair $(P_0, D(P_0, A_0))$ with the consumer surplus under $D(P, A_1)$ at the price–quantity pair $(P_1, D(P_1, A_1))$.

In line with the Dixit–Norman analysis, suppose now that (i) the monopolist begins at its monopoly solution, (P_M, A_M), and (ii) when advertising is changed to some nearby level A, the monopolist responds with its profit-maximizing price, $P_M(A)$. Using (4.10), it then follows that

$$\begin{aligned}
&\left.\frac{\mathrm{d}W(P_M(A), A)}{\mathrm{d}A}\right|_{A=A_M} \\
&\quad = \left\{\frac{\mathrm{d}\Pi(P_M(A), A)}{\mathrm{d}A} + D\big(R(A), A\big)R'(A)\right. \\
&\qquad \left.\left. - D\big(P_M(A), A\big)P_M'(A) + \int_{P_M(A)}^{R(A)} D_A(P, A)\,\mathrm{d}P\right\}\right|_{A=A_M}.
\end{aligned} \tag{4.11}$$

Under (4.1) and (4.2), advertising does not have a first-order effect on profit. Given that $D(R(A), A) = 0$, (4.11) thus may be re-written as

$$\left.\frac{\mathrm{d}W(P_M(A), A)}{\mathrm{d}A}\right|_{A=A_M} = -D(P_M, A_M)P_M'(A_M) + \int_{P_M}^{R(A_M)} D_A(P, A_M)\,\mathrm{d}P. \tag{4.12}$$

As the discussion above anticipates, there are two terms. The first term in (4.12) is the Dixit–Norman term. The sign of this term is dictated by the impact of advertising on price. The second term in (4.12) is the new infra-marginal term. The sign of this term is positive.

The first conclusion is now established: if additional advertising would not cause the monopolist to raise its price (i.e., if $P_M'(A_M) \leqslant 0$), then welfare would be increased were the monopolist to raise its advertising above the monopoly level. Put differently, the monopoly supply of price-decreasing and price-maintaining advertising is inadequate. Intuitively, in the absence of a price increase, additional monopoly advertising induces a consumer-surplus gain that the monopolist cannot appropriate; therefore, the monopolist advertises to an inadequate extent.

To see this conclusion in action, consider the case of informative monopoly advertising, as captured in the second example above. The appropriate measure of welfare is then given by (4.10), where $D(P, A) = G(A)d(P)$ and $R(A) \equiv R$. Using (4.7), the first conclusion now may be stated at a structural level: when advertising is informative, monopoly advertising is inadequate if marginal cost is constant or decreasing. Kotowitz and Mathewson (1979a) and Shapiro (1980) offer early statements of this result for the case of constant marginal costs.

Consider next the case of complementary advertising. The first conclusion is of course valid for this case as well, and indeed Nichols (1985) and Becker and Murphy (1993) offer general derivations of this conclusion. But when advertising has a social-prestige component, the possibility that advertising is price-increasing is of special relevance. In the first example above, consumers directly value advertising, and greater monopoly advertising generates a higher monopoly price when marginal cost is constant or increasing. In this case, it cannot be concluded from (4.12) that complementary monopoly advertising is inadequate. The possibility of price-increasing advertising thus requires further consideration.

4.2.4. Price-increasing monopoly advertising

When advertising increases price, the Dixit–Norman and infra-marginal effects are conflicting. In the presence of conflicting effects, one strategy is to directly calculate the net welfare effects of advertising for the problem at hand. Another strategy is to look for a new sufficient condition under which one effect dominates the other. Both strategies are illustrated here.

I start with a net welfare calculation. Consider the first example above, under which welfare is given by (4.10) when $D(P, A) = N[1-P/g(A)]$ and $R(A) = g(A)$. Suppose further that marginal cost is constant at some level c, where $0 < c < g(0)$. Then (4.1) may be solved, yielding $P_M(A) = [g(A) + c]/2$, so that $P'_M(A_M) = g'(A_M)/2 > 0$. Notice that $D(P_M, A_M) = N[g(A_M) - P_M]/g(A_M) > 0$ and $D_A = NPg'/g^2 > 0$. Using (4.12), it can be shown that

$$\left.\frac{\mathrm{d}W(P_M(A), A)}{\mathrm{d}A}\right|_{A=A_M} = D_A(P_M, A_M)D(P_M, A_M)g(A_M)/2N > 0.$$

Thus, even though advertising raises price and induces a welfare-reducing Dixit–Norman effect, it also shifts out demand and generates a welfare-enhancing infra-marginal effect. In the first example, the latter effect dominates, so that even price-increasing advertising is inadequately supplied by a monopolist.

The second strategy is to look for a new sufficient condition that allows for price-increasing advertising. To this end, I borrow from the product-quality analysis offered by Spence (1975) and Tirole (1988, Section 2.2.1), with advertising now substituting for product quality. The analysis is conducted with reference to the inverse-demand function, $P(Q, A)$, where $P_A > 0 > P_Q$. In this context, the monopolist's profit function is given as $\pi(Q, A) = P(Q, A)Q - C(Q) - \kappa A$. The first-order conditions for profit maximization are then

$$\pi_Q = P - C' + QP_Q = 0, \tag{4.13}$$

$$\pi_A = QP_A - \kappa = 0. \tag{4.14}$$

Let $Q_M(A)$ denote the solution to (4.13), and let $A_M(Q)$ represent the solution to (4.14). The monopoly solution, (Q_M, A_M), is then defined by $Q_M = Q_M(A_M)$ and $A_M = A_M(Q_M)$.

Social welfare may be represented as

$$W(Q, A) = \int_0^Q P(X, A)\,\mathrm{d}X - C(Q) - \kappa A. \tag{4.15}$$

Suppose now that (i) the monopolist begins at its monopoly solution, (Q_M, A_M), and (ii) when advertising is changed to some nearby level A, the monopolist responds with its profit-maximizing quantity, $Q_M(A)$. Then, using (4.15),

$$\left.\frac{\mathrm{d}W(Q_M(A), A)}{\mathrm{d}A}\right|_{A=A_M} = \left[P(Q_M, A_M) - C'(Q_M)\right]Q'_M(A_M) + \int_0^{Q_M} P_A(X, A_M)\,\mathrm{d}X - k. \tag{4.16}$$

This expression can be signed under two conditions. Assume first that the value of advertising is greater for infra-marginal than marginal consumers: $P_{AQ} < 0$. Assume second that advertising beyond the monopoly level does not decrease the profit-maximizing level of output: $Q'_M(A_M) \geqslant 0$. Then, by (4.16),

$$\left.\frac{\mathrm{d}W(Q_M(A), A)}{\mathrm{d}A}\right|_{A=A_M} > \left[P(Q_M, A_M) - C'(Q_M)\right]Q'_M(A_M) + Q_M P_A(Q_M, A_M) - k = -Q_M P_Q(Q_M, A_M)Q'_M(A_M) \geqslant 0,$$

where the first inequality uses $P_{AQ} < 0$, the equality uses (4.13) and (4.14), and the second inequality uses $Q'_M(A_M) \geqslant 0$. With this, a second conclusion is now established: if $P_{AQ} < 0$ and $Q'_M(A_M) \geqslant 0$, then advertising is supplied by a monopoly to an extent that is socially inadequate.[69]

The key intuition can be easily summarized. As (4.14) reveals, when the monopolist chooses advertising while holding quantity fixed, it balances the cost of additional advertising against the benefit of selling the fixed quantity at a higher price. The extent to which price rises is in turn measured by the benefit that additional advertising brings to the marginal consumer. On the other hand, as (4.15) suggests, a social planner balances the cost of additional advertising against the benefit it brings to all of the monopolist's consumers. If $P_{AQ} < 0$, then the marginal consumer gets the least benefit from additional advertising; thus, for a given quantity, the monopolist provides too little advertising. As is standard, for any given level of advertising, the monopolist also provides too little quantity. It follows that welfare would rise if the monopolist were to increase advertising without decreasing quantity.

This analysis dovetails nicely with the first example. Under constant marginal costs, this example satisfies both of the two conditions: $P_{AQ} < 0$ is established above, and $Q'_M(A_M) \geqslant 0$ is easily confirmed.[70] Thus, the first example offers a concrete illustration of the sufficient conditions just derived. At the same time, the analysis clarifies the general features that are embodied in the example and that underlie the finding of inadequate advertising. Of course, the second conclusion holds as stated whether advertising is complementary due to the information it conveys or the social prestige that it facilitates. The former case is captured by the second example, but in this example $P_{AQ} > 0$ when individual demands are not too convex. The second conclusion appears most relevant for advertising that facilitates social prestige.

Nichols (1985) presents a related sufficient condition that applies when consumer welfare is the maximized value of $U(g(A)X, Y)$, where X and Y are chosen subject to a budget constraint: $P_x X + P_y Y = I$. Nichols derives that consumer welfare rises with greater advertising if and only if $[g'A/g - P'_M(A)A/P_M(A)] > 0$, where $P_M(A)$ is the monopoly price of good X when A is given. Thus, social welfare rises when

[69] Becker and Murphy (1993) also discuss the case of price-increasing advertising, and they derive an expression corresponding to (4.16). I add here two conditions ($P_{AQ} < 0$ and $Q'_M(A_M) \geqslant 0$) that suffice for inadequate price-increasing monopoly advertising. As I discuss below, Nichols (1985) derives a related sufficient condition for the characteristic approach that he adopts.

[70] In particular, $\left.\frac{\mathrm{d}D(P_M(A), A)}{\mathrm{d}A}\right|_{A=A_M} = \frac{Ncg'(A_m)}{2[g(A_M)]^2} > 0$.

the monopolist increases advertising above the monopoly level if and only if additional advertising increases "prestige productivity" (i.e., g) in a greater percentage than it increases the price of the advertised product. This requirement is automatically satisfied if advertising is price-maintaining or price-decreasing. A limitation of this approach is that g is not easily observed.

Finally, it is important to remark on the possibility raised in Section 2.4 that advertising is a bad that is sold jointly with some other good (e.g., TV programs may compensate viewers for watching TV ads). This possibility is not included in the analysis above, where I follow the conventional modeling approach and assume that advertising is a good whose quantity is determined by the monopolist. But Becker and Murphy argue that the first conclusion above continues to hold when advertising is a bad that is jointly sold. Intuitively, if the consumer voluntarily accepts additional advertising and the price of the good does not rise, then additional monopoly advertising again induces a consumer surplus gain that the monopolist is unable to appropriate.

4.3. Summary

In this section, I summarize research on the positive and normative theory of monopoly advertising. The Dorfman–Steiner model offers a positive theory of a monopolist's price and advertising selections, and the first-order conditions provide a formal interpretation for some of the endogeneity concerns raised in the previous section. Two examples are also examined. These examples confirm Chamberlin's insight that advertising's effect on price is related to the elasticity and scale effects of advertising, where the elasticity effect is determined by the purpose of advertising. The second (informative) example also captures Ozga's rationale for diminishing returns to advertising.

Dixit and Norman provide a foundation for the normative theory of persuasive advertising. They argue that, if the consumer welfare that advertising renders is measured relative to a standard that remains fixed as advertising changes, then a monopolist provides price-increasing advertising to an extent that is socially excessive. Proponents of the informative and complementary views, however, argue that the fixed-standard approach ignores consumer-welfare gains from advertising that are associated with information and social prestige. Under the alternative approach that their work suggests, a monopolist provides price-maintaining and price-decreasing advertising to an extent that is socially inadequate. Furthermore, under conditions that are plausible when advertising facilitates social prestige, a monopolist provides even price-increasing advertising to an extent that is socially inadequate. On the whole, the research described above suggests that a profit-maximizing monopolist may advertise to an extent that is socially inadequate.

At the same time, it is important to highlight two assumptions of the models presented here. First, as mentioned in Section 2.4, the models do not include ads that are utility reducing (bads) and unavoidable. For example, an objectionable ad on a city bus, streetcar or taxi is difficult to avoid, and Internet "pop-up" ads are also intrusive. If a monopolist can profit from ads that are objectionable and unavoidable, then the possibility of excessive monopoly advertising would gain renewed credibility. Second, the models assume that the monopolist is unable to segment the market by targeting its ads to certain groups and then practicing price discrimination. If a monopolist can segment its consumers, then it may be able to appropriate the increase in surplus that its advertising creates. It then becomes more likely that the monopolist advertises at a socially optimal level.[71]

5. Advertising and price

Monopoly advertising may be inadequate, since the monopolist cannot appropriate the consumer surplus that additional advertising creates. But in markets with multiple firms advertising is also an important instrument of competition. The advertising of one firm may steal the business and thus diminish the profit of another. This business-stealing externality raises the possibility that advertising may be excessive. In multi-firm markets, it is thus unclear, a priori, whether advertising is inadequate, excessive or optimal.

This tension is recognized by Marshall (1919), who acknowledges both the beneficial constructive and wasteful combative roles that informative advertising may play. In the context of persuasive advertising, an early formalization is offered by Dixit and Norman (1978), who consider not just monopoly but also multi-firm markets. Due to the business-stealing externality, they find that advertising then may be excessive even when it results in a lower price. With important exceptions, however, the recent theoretical literature emphasizes informative advertising.[72] I summarize here recent theoretical analyses of multi-firm markets in which advertising provides price information.

5.1. *Homogeneous products*

In a classic paper, Butters (1977) offers the first equilibrium analysis of informative advertising in a multi-firm model. In Butters's model, firms produce a homogeneous product at a constant unit cost c. There are N consumers. As in the second example above, a consumer can learn of a firm's existence and price only by receiving an ad from that firm, and ads are distributed randomly across consumers at a cost of κ per ad. Finally, and in contrast to the second example, consumers have symmetric unit-demand functions, so that $R - P$ is the surplus that a consumer enjoys when a unit is purchased at price P. To ensure that production has social value, assume that $R > c + \kappa$.

[71] For further discussion, see Adams and Yellen (1977) and Lewis and Sappington (1994).

[72] For example, see Friedman (1983) and Schmalensee (1972, 1976b) for positive theories of oligopolistic advertising competition, under the general assumption that a firm's advertising increases the demand for its product. For other models in which advertising plays a persuasive role, see Banerjee and Bandyopadhyay (2003), Baye and Morgan (2004), Bloch and Manceau (1999), Chioveanu (2005), Doraszelski and Markovich (in press), Kotowitz and Mathewson (1979b), Von der Fehr and Stevik (1998) and Tremblay and Martins-Filho (2001). Becker and Murphy (1993), Hochman and Luski (1988), Nichols (1985) and Stigler and Becker (1977) consider complementary advertising in perfectly competitive markets.

In this multi-firm setting, there are three kinds of consumers. Some consumers are *uninformed*: they receive no ads. Uninformed consumers never learn of any firm, make no purchase and receive zero utility. Other consumers are *captive*: they receive ads from only one firm. A captive consumer knows of one firm and thus buys from that firm, provided that the price does not exceed R. Finally, some consumers are *selective*: they receive ads from more than one firm. A selective consumer buys from the lowest-priced known firm, if that price does not exceed R. If there is more than one such firm, a selective consumer picks one at random.

The number of uninformed consumers is determined by the total number of ads, A, that firms send. Let Φ denote the probability that a consumer receives at least one ad. The probability that the consumer is uninformed is then $1 - \Phi = (1 - 1/N)^A \approx e^{-A/N}$ for N large. If a proportion Φ of consumers are to receive at least one ad, then a total of $A = N \cdot \ln[1/(1 - \Phi)]$ ads must be sent. The social cost of advertising so that a proportion Φ of consumers are not uninformed is thus

$$A(\Phi) = \kappa N \cdot \ln\bigl[1/(1 - \Phi)\bigr]. \tag{5.1}$$

Each firm chooses which price (or prices) to advertise and the number of ads to send out at each such price. As Butters shows, when the number of firms is finite, firms adopt mixed strategies in any Nash equilibrium. To see the forces at hand, hypothesize an equilibrium in which all firms advertise the same price. If this price were to exceed $c + \kappa$, then a firm could do better by sending the same number of ads but deviating to a slightly lower price. The firm then increases its expected profit, since it wins its selective consumers with probability one. On the other hand, if the candidate equilibrium price is $c + \kappa$ or lower, then a firm earns negative profit, since some recipients are selective and choose a different firm. The sunk cost of sending an ad, κ, is then not covered, and a firm would do better by sending no ads.

It is possible, however, to describe simply the limiting behavior that obtains when the numbers of firms and consumers are sufficiently large. Each seller is then negligible relative to the market. The behavior of any individual seller is indeterminant, but equilibrium does constrain market behavior. Butters shows that every $P \in [c + \kappa, R]$ must be advertised by some firm and that every such price must generate zero expected profit. For $P \in [c + \kappa, R]$, let $x(P)$ denote the equilibrium probability that an ad with price P would be accepted by the consumer that receives it. Then $x(P)$ is the probability that a consumer does not receive an ad with a price below P. It follows that $x(P)$ is strictly decreasing. In fact, since every $P \in [c + \kappa, R]$ earns zero profit, $x(P)$ is defined by $(P - c)x(P) - \kappa = 0$. This implies that $x(c + \kappa) = 1 > \kappa/(R - c) = x(R)$.

In effect, $x(P)$ is a downward-sloping demand curve that confronts each firm in equilibrium. The firms compete with one another, but each firm also possesses some monopoly power, due to the informational product differentiation that advertising creates. The demand curve is thus not perfectly elastic. But firms earn zero profit, once the cost of advertising is included. Butters thus offers a first equilibrium model of monopolistic competition with informative advertising.

What are the normative implications? Given that consumers possess identical unit demands, price plays no welfare role. A social inefficiency occurs only if the advertising choice is excessive or inadequate, so that too few or many consumers are uninformed. In the market equilibrium, the probability $x(R)$ that a consumer purchases when the highest possible price is received must equal the probability $1 - \Phi^e$ that the consumer does not receive any other ad. Hence, $1 - \Phi^e = x(R) = \kappa/(R - c)$. Consider now the social planner's choice. When an additional consumer learns of the existence of some firm, the social benefit is $R - c$. But there is also a cost to reaching a previously uninformed consumer. Using (5.1), the advertising cost per-consumer is $A(\Phi)/N = \kappa \cdot \ln[1/(1 - \Phi)]$, which is increasing in Φ. Balancing these considerations, a social planner chooses Φ^* to solve

$$\max_{\Phi}\left\{\Phi(R - c) - \kappa \cdot \ln\left[1/(1 - \Phi)\right]\right\}.$$

The first-order condition is $R - c - \kappa/(1 - \Phi^*) = 0$, which implies that the market equilibrium level of advertising is socially optimal: $\Phi^e = \Phi^*$.

This is a striking finding. To see the intuition, consider the private benefit to a firm of sending an ad at the price R.[73] This benefit equals $(R - c)$ times the probability that the consumer receives no other ad. But this is also the social benefit from sending an ad, since the ad increases social surplus (in amount $R - c$) only when the consumer receives no other ad. Put differently, the highest-priced firm appropriates all consumer surplus and steals no business from rivals; therefore, it advertises at the socially optimal rate. Now consider the private benefit to a firm from sending an ad at a lower price, $P < R$. Such an ad generates consumer surplus that the firm does not appropriate, and it also may steal business. Given that every $P \in [c + \kappa, R]$ earns zero profit, however, the private benefit to a firm from sending an ad is the same whether $P < R$ or $P = R$. Private and social benefits thus agree even for ads with $P < R$.

Butters's model has been extended in many interesting directions. Stegeman (1991) assumes that the numbers of consumers and firms are large, and then modifies Butters's model with the assumption that consumer valuations are heterogeneous. He shows that informative advertising is then inadequate. Intuitively, in equilibrium, the highest-priced firm sets its price strictly below the highest consumer reservation value; therefore, a firm that advertises the highest price no longer captures all of the surplus from the new sales that it creates. Since such a firm does not steal business from any other, it advertises at a socially inadequate rate. Additional ads at lower prices would increase social surplus by at least as much, and so an increase in advertising at any advertised price would increase welfare. Likewise, Stahl (1994) reports that equilibrium advertising is inadequate, when the Butters model with a finite number of firms is extended to allow for downward-sloping individual demand curves (as in the second example above) and

[73] Butters does not offer an intuition for his welfare finding. My discussion here draws on Tirole (1988, Section 7.3.2) and Stegeman (1991).

general advertising technologies. Stahl shows that the unique mixed-strategy Nash equilibrium is symmetric, and he finds that sellers choose a common advertising level while mixing over prices.

The Butters model also may be extended to allow a more active role for consumers. Suppose that consumers are aware of the existence of firms and seek only price information. This is plausible in an established industry. Ads are one source of price information, but a consumer might also obtain price information through costly search. In comparison to the work described above, an important new feature is that uninformed consumers may search for firms and make purchases. Robert and Stahl (1993) provide an analysis of price advertising in an optimal search model.[74] Assuming that firms make simultaneous advertising and pricing choices, Robert and Stahl characterize a unique and symmetric price-dispersion equilibrium, in which a firm either charges a high price that is not advertised or selects from an interval of lower prices that are advertised. The high price may be interpreted as a "list price". Firms that charge this price sell only to uninformed consumers, and the list price is set at a level that dissuades such consumers from further search. In the interval of advertised "sales", an interesting prediction is that advertising intensity is greater at lower prices. Intuitively, the marginal benefit of advertising is greater at lower prices, since such prices are more likely to attract the recipient (who may be selective).[75]

Interesting findings also arise when the model is extended to allow for sequential choices by firms. McAfee (1994) posits that firms first choose their advertising rates and then choose their prices. A firm's advertising rate determines the probability that a consumer obtains its price offer. An asymmetric equilibrium then exists, wherein one firm advertises more than do other firms, who all advertise equally. Prices are mixed, and now the firm with the higher advertising rate charges *higher* prices (in the sense of first-order stochastic dominance). The reason is that such a firm has a greater stock of captive consumers. Roy (2000) also considers a sequential-choice game, and he allows further that firms may "target" the individual consumers to whom their respective ads are delivered.[76] Working with a duopoly model, he finds that the two firms divide

[74] Butters considers an extended model with search, but he does not analyze optimal search. Baye and Morgan (2001) also examine a model of price advertising in which the information-gathering activities of consumers are endogenized. In their model, a "gatekeeper", such as a magazine or an Internet site, charges fees to firms that advertise prices and to consumers who choose to access the list of advertised prices. Baye and Morgan (2004) extend the model to allow that firms may also engage in brand advertising, where brand advertising by a firm increases the number of consumers that are loyal to the firm's product.

[75] Bester (1994) conducts a related analysis in a monopoly model. Consumers must sink a search cost in order to visit the monopolist's store, and the monopolist thus seeks a device through which to commit to low prices. Price advertising is such a device. A mixed-strategy equilibrium is constructed, in which the monopolist advertises only low prices. Modifying the model to allow that the monopolist is privately informed as to its costs of production, Caminal (1996) constructs a pure-strategy equilibrium, in which the monopolist advertises low prices when its costs are low.

[76] For other studies of targeted advertising, see Adams and Yellen (1977), Esteban, Gil and Hernandez (2001), Esteban, Hernandez and Moraga-Gonzalez (2006), Galeotti and Moraga-Gonzales (2004), Hernandez-Garcia

the entire market into mutually exclusive captive segments within which each firm operates as a local monopolist. Under the assumption that consumers have identical unit demands, the resulting equilibria are socially efficient: firms appropriate all consumer surplus by pricing at R, and the social cost of informing consumers is minimized (every consumer receives exactly one ad).

5.2. *Differentiated products*

Grossman and Shapiro (1984) extend the Butters model to include horizontal product differentiation. In their model, firms are located around a circle, and the number of firms may be endogenous. Following Tirole (1988, Section 7.3.2), I focus here on a duopoly model in which firms are located on a line. Even when simplified in this way, the Grossman–Shapiro model offers novel insights, and at the same time provides a unified framework within which to interpret a broad range of issues that arise in earlier writings and empirical efforts.

Consider then the following model. A unit mass of consumers are uniformly distributed along a line of unit length. Each consumer has reservation value R for a single unit of an ideal product, and suffers a transportation cost t per unit of distance from the ideal. There are two firms, located at opposite endpoints. Advertising operates as in Butters's model: a consumer can learn of a firm's existence and price only by receiving an ad from that firm, and each ad is distributed randomly over consumers. The cost of reaching a fraction Φ_i of consumers is denoted $A(\Phi_i)$. Grossman and Shapiro allow for general advertising technologies (of which the Butters's technology given in (5.1) is a special case), and I specify here a quadratic relationship: $A(\Phi_i) = a(\Phi_i)^2/2$, where $a > t/2$.

There are again three kinds of consumers. If firms 1 and 2 advertise at levels so that fractions Φ_1 and Φ_2 of consumers are reached, respectively, then a fraction $[1-\Phi_1][1-\Phi_2]$ of consumers receive no ad and are uninformed. A fraction $\Phi_1[1-\Phi_2]$ receive only firm 1's ads and are thus captive to firm 1; likewise, a fraction $\Phi_2[1-\Phi_1]$ are captive to firm 2. Finally, a fraction $\Phi_1\Phi_2$ consumers receive ads from both firms and are thus selective. Suppose that R is sufficiently large that a consumer purchases if any ad is received. Suppose also that the number of selective consumers is of sufficient size that the firms compete for this common demand. This is the case if the cost of advertising is not too great.

What demand function does firm 1 confront? If the firms choose prices P_1 and P_2, respectively, then the marginal selective consumer is located at $x = (P_2 - P_1 + t)/2t$. When a firm chooses its advertising expenditure, it equivalently chooses its reach. Firm 1's demand function thus may be written as follows:

$$D_1(P_1, P_2, \Phi_1, \Phi_2) = \Phi_1\big[(1 - \Phi_2) + \Phi_2(P_2 - P_1 + t)/2t\big].$$

(1997) and Manduchi (2004). The related possibility of coupon targeting is considered by Bester and Petrakis (1996), Moraga-Gonzalez and Petrakis (1999) and Shaffer and Zhang (1995), for example.

The informative view holds that a firm faces a more price-elastic demand in markets with greater advertising. This elasticity effect is confirmed here. Firm 1's elasticity of demand when evaluated at $P_1 = P_2 = P$ and $\Phi_1 = \Phi_2 = \Phi$ is easily shown to be $[\Phi P/(2 - \Phi)t]$, which is increasing in Φ and thus in the market level of advertising.

Consider now a game in which the two firms simultaneously choose their prices and advertising levels. If the marginal costs of production are constant, firm 1 thus chooses P_1 and Φ_1 to maximize $[P_1 - c]D_1(P_1, P_2, \Phi_1, \Phi_2) - A(\Phi_1)$. It is now straightforward to derive price and advertising reaction curves and then solve for a symmetric equilibrium, $P_1^e = P_2^e = P^e$ and $\Phi_1^e = \Phi_2^e = \Phi^e$. The equilibrium is characterized as follows:

$$P^e = c + t \cdot \frac{2 - \Phi^e}{\Phi^e} = c + \sqrt{2at}, \tag{5.2}$$

$$\Phi^e = \frac{2}{1 + \sqrt{2a/t}}, \tag{5.3}$$

$$\Pi^e = \frac{2a}{(1 + \sqrt{2a/t})^2}, \tag{5.4}$$

where Π^e is the equilibrium profit earned by a single firm.

At a positive level, these equations yield a number of important implications. Consider first the equilibrium price. As (5.2) reveals, it is higher than $c+t$, which is the price that would emerge were consumers informed of all prices. The reason is that demand is less elastic in the presence of informational product differentiation. This does not mean that advertising increases prices; indeed, the market would close in the absence of advertising. As Stigler (1961) and Ozga (1960) suggest, it is consumer ignorance that leads to higher prices, while advertising provides information and lowers prices. This may be confirmed by noting that the equilibrium price falls when the cost of advertising falls (i.e., when a decreases). Second, using (5.3), the equilibrium advertising level is higher when advertising is less costly and when products are more differentiated (i.e., when t is greater). The latter effect suggests that greater product differentiation leads to more advertising. This contrasts with the empirical interpretations offered by Comanor and Wilson (1967, 1974), who posit that advertising induces product differentiation. In the Grossman–Shapiro model, where advertising is endogenized, product differentiation induces advertising.

As (5.4) shows, equilibrium profit is increasing in product differentiation and, more surprisingly, the cost of advertising. When a increases, the direct effect is that each firm experiences a cost increase, but the resulting decrease in advertising also gives rise to a strategic effect: each firm faces a less elastic demand and thus charges a higher price. The strategic effect dominates here, and firms benefit overall when advertising is more costly (but not prohibitively so). This finding provides a formal interpretation of work by Benham (1972) and others (see Section 3.2.4) suggesting that some professions encourage legal restrictions on advertising.[77] It also offers a formal interpretation of the

[77] But see also Peters (1984), who considers a model in which firms sell a homogeneous good, face capacity constraints, and are privately informed as to their respective costs of production. He argues that advertising

profit-advertising relationship described by Comanor and Wilson (1967, 1974) and others (see Section 3.2.2). In the Grossman–Shapiro model, advertising does not cause profit, nor does profit cause advertising. Instead, as (5.3) and (5.4) confirm, advertising and profit are both endogenous variables that are jointly determined from exogenous variables corresponding to the extent of product differentiation and the cost of advertising. In a given sample of industries, as the extent of product differentiation varies, advertising and profit move together; however, as the cost of advertising varies, advertising and profit may move in opposite directions. From this perspective, the sign of an observed correlation between advertising and profit simply reflects which of the exogenous variables varies most in the sample at hand.

The key normative finding in this model is that advertising may be inadequate or excessive.[78] To understand the various effects, consider first additional advertising by a firm that reaches a consumer who otherwise would be uninformed. The social benefit of such advertising exceeds the private benefit, since the firm is unable to appropriate the resulting consumer surplus. This suggests that advertising is inadequate. Consider next the effect of additional advertising by a firm that reaches a consumer that also receives an ad from the other firm. Social surplus is created if the consumer is located closer to the firm that undertakes the additional advertising. The advertising firm does not internalize this matching benefit, and so the matching effect also suggests that market advertising is inadequate. But the firm is motivated by the profit margin that it would enjoy on the "stolen" consumer, while social welfare is not impacted by the re-distribution of margins from one firm to another. This business-stealing externality parallels Marshall's (1919) notion of combative advertising and suggests that the market advertising may be excessive.

Bester and Petrakis (1995) offer an interesting extension. In their model, consumers live in one of two regions, where each region has a single firm. All consumers are informed of the existence of both firms, and every consumer also knows the price of the "local" firm. A consumer forms an expectation as to the price charged by the distant firm, and a consumer learns the actual price if an ad is received from the distant firm. In this setting, Bester and Petrakis characterize a symmetric mixed-strategy equilibrium. Their findings share features with those of Robert and Stahl and also Grossman and Shapiro. In equilibrium, with some probability a firm posts a "list price" and attracts only local consumers and with the remaining probability a firm advertises a low "sale" price and tries to attract distant consumers.[79] Moreover, firms gain from an increase in the cost of advertising, and market advertising may be inadequate or excessive.

Finally, Rogerson (1988) considers a model in which firms advertise prices and also select product qualities. Each consumer observes the advertised prices, selects a firm, observes the product quality offered by this firm, and then decides whether to purchase

restrictions may benefit high-cost (harm low-cost) producers, and it can happen that prices are lower when advertising is restricted. See also LeBlanc (1998).

[78] See Tirole (1988, p. 294) for a formal confirmation of this finding.

[79] See also Bester (1994) and Caminal (1996), as discussed in footnote 75.

or engage in sequential search. Consumers have heterogeneous search costs and differ also in their willingness to pay for quality. Rogerson characterizes a monopolistically competitive equilibrium, in which firms that offer higher-quality products also enjoy larger markups. Consumers infer quality from the advertised price, and those that are more willing to pay for quality select firms that advertise higher prices. Intuitively, a firm will not "rip off" its consumers with a lower quality, if the implied cost savings on those consumers that remain would be small in comparison to the markup that would be lost on those consumers that search again. At higher quality, the potential cost savings are greater, and a higher markup is needed to dissuade the firm from cheating. With U-shaped average costs and a zero-profit requirement, larger markups must be paired with lower sales; thus, Rogerson finds that higher-quality firms are smaller. Rogerson also examines a no-advertising benchmark, finding that social welfare is higher when advertising is allowed.

5.3. Non-price advertising

Bagwell and Ramey (1994a) emphasize two features of the modern retail market. First, in many retail categories, large-scale discount firms co-exist with small firms, and the large firms share a common set of attributes: high sales volumes, heavy advertising expenditures, low prices and large investments in advanced selling technologies. Second, competition between retail firms often occurs through non-price advertising. The typical TV or radio retail ad, for example, contains little or no direct ("hard") information. Motivated by these features, Bagwell and Ramey develop a new model of the retail firm and offer an equilibrium interpretation of non-price advertising by retailers.[80]

The retail-firm model is easily described with reference to a monopolist that expects $N > 0$ consumers, where each consumer possesses the positive and downward-sloping individual demand function, $d(P)$. The monopolist chooses a price $P \geqslant 0$ and a level of investment $K \geqslant 0$. The cost of investment is $r > 0$ per unit, and the benefit of greater investment is that the marginal cost of selling is thereby reduced: $c'(K) < 0$. The firm's net revenue is thus $R(P, K, N) \equiv [P - c(K)]Nd(P) - rK$. For given N, let $P_M(N)$ and $K_M(N)$ be the price and investment levels that jointly maximize R. Assuming that second-order conditions are satisfied, these monopoly values satisfy $R_P = R_K = 0$. Let $\Pi^*(N) \equiv R(P_M(N), K_M(N), N)$ denote the maximized value of net revenue.

Bagwell and Ramey establish a "coordination economy" that is enjoyed by a firm and its consumers when the firm gets larger. First, using a standard envelope argument, it follows that a firm does better when it expects more consumers: $\Pi^{*\prime}(N) > 0$. Second,

[80] Advanced selling technologies include advanced information systems (electronic-scanner checkout systems, privately owned satellites) and superior delivery systems (privately owned warehouses and trucks). Bagwell and Ramey observe, too, that large firms offer greater product variety, and their retail-firm model accounts for this attribute as well. I present a simplified single-product model below. It is, however, useful to keep the multi-product version in mind, since the focus on non-price advertising is most compelling for a retailer with many products.

a consumer also does better when a firm expects more consumers. To see this, observe that $R_{PN} = 0$ at the monopoly values (since $R_P = 0$), $R_{KN} = -c'd > 0$ and $R_{KP} = -c'Nd' < 0$. It follows that $K'_M(N) > 0$ and $P'_M(N) < 0$: a monopolist invests more and prices lower when more consumers are expected. Intuitively, an investment that reduces marginal cost is more attractive when a higher sales volume is anticipated, and the reduction in marginal cost in turn makes a lower price more attractive.

At a general level, it is now possible to anticipate a role for non-price advertising. Imagine that consumers do not observe the firm's price until after a search cost is incurred. Consumers do, however, observe the firm's non-price advertising. Suppose now that advertising attracts consumers: $N'(A) > 0$. Then, a higher advertising level leads to greater expected sales, which in turn induces greater investment and thereby a lower price. Therefore, if it is supposed that consumers respond to advertising, then a firm that advertises heavily also adopts a low price, and so the supposed responsiveness of consumers to advertising becomes justified. From this perspective, it is entirely rational for consumers to respond to non-price advertising. This conclusion holds as well in multi-firm markets, if a firm expects greater market share when it advertises more heavily.

To go further, an equilibrium model of retail advertising is required. Consider a three-stage game. In the first stage, firms decide whether to enter. Entry entails a sunk cost, $\sigma > 0$. In the second stage, the firms simultaneously make price, investment and advertising selections. Finally, in the third stage, each consumer picks a firm from which to buy, based on the information that the consumer possesses. There are two kinds of consumers. Informed consumers observe the firm that makes the greatest advertising expenditure.[81] Uninformed consumers do not observe advertising efforts. There is a unit mass of consumers in total. Let I and U denote the exogenous proportions of informed and uninformed consumers, respectively, where $I + U = 1$ and $U \in (0, 1)$. No consumer observes a firm's price and investment selections prior to picking a firm. The firms thus select their monopoly price and investment levels, given the number of consumers that they respectively expect.

As a benchmark, consider the *random equilibrium* that obtains when consumers are not responsive to advertising and thus pick firms at random. Entering firms then choose zero advertising and divide the market. Thus, if n firms enter, each firm expects $N = 1/n$ consumers. Ignoring integer constraints, the equilibrium number of firms is the value n_r that satisfies $\Pi^*(1/n_r) = \sigma$. Each firm adopts the price $P_M(1/n_r)$.

Now consider an *advertising equilibrium*, in which informed consumers adopt the rule of thumb of buying from the firm that advertises the most. As Bagwell and Ramey show, for any $n \geqslant 2$, a mixed-strategy equilibrium is induced. This equilibrium is characterized by a distribution function $F(A)$ that ensures for each firm that the higher

81 Bagwell and Ramey thus posit a different advertising technology than do Butters (1977) and Grossman and Shapiro (1984). In the latter work, an individual consumer that receives an ad (or ads) has no further information as to the respective advertising expenditures of firms.

cost of additional advertising is balanced against the benefit of a higher expected sales volume. In an advertising equilibrium, when a firm advertises at level A, it expects to win the informed consumers with probability $F(A)^{n-1}$. Therefore, when a firm advertises at level A, it expects $N(A) = F(A)^{n-1}I + U/n$ consumers, which is indeed an increasing function. The distribution function is formally defined by $\Pi^*(F(A)^{n-1}I + U/n) - \kappa A = \Pi^*(U/n)$, where $\Pi^*(U/n)$ is the profit that is enjoyed by a firm that chooses zero advertising. Observe that the simple rule used by informed consumers is rational. When a firm advertises at level A, it sets the price $P_M(F(A)^{n-1}I + U/n)$, and so higher-advertising firms indeed offer lower prices. This is consistent with the general discussion above. Finally, ignoring integer constraints, entry occurs until expected profit is zero. Since a firm is indifferent over all advertising selections in the support, the equilibrium number of firms is the value n_a that generates zero profit when a firm selects zero advertising: $\Pi^*(U/n_a) = \sigma$.

The random equilibrium would obtain, for example, if advertising were prohibited, while the advertising equilibrium might be predicted when advertising is legal. It is thus interesting to compare these two equilibria. Observe first that the market with advertising has fewer firms that are on average larger: $n_r > n_a$. This observation follows, since $\Pi^*(1/n_r) = \sigma = \Pi^*(U/n_a)$ and $\Pi^{*\prime} > 0$ imply that $1/n_r = U/n_a$. Observe second that, with probability one, in a market with advertising every firm offers a lower price than in a market without advertising. To see this, observe that the highest possible price in the advertising equilibrium occurs when a firm does not advertise, and the price then charged equals the price that is always offered in the random equilibrium: $P_M(U/n_a) = P_M(1/n_r)$. Therefore, expected consumer welfare is higher when advertising is allowed. Since firms make zero expected profit either way, social welfare is higher when advertising is allowed than when it is not.

Bagwell and Ramey capture and build upon a number of themes from earlier work. In line with Chamberlin's (1933) work, they construct a monopolistically competitive equilibrium, in which profits are dissipated through advertising expenditures and entry, and advertising operates through a scale effect to facilitate lower prices. But the scale effect that they utilize is a "long-run" effect, under which greater expected sales volume leads to additional cost-reducing investments.[82] In addition, their advertising equilibrium exhibits endogenous firm heterogeneity: some firms advertise heavily, enjoy high expected sales, choose low prices and make large investments, while other firms advertise less but expect low sales and set high prices while making small investments. Bagwell and Ramey also provide a formalization of Nelson's (1974b) signaling-efficiency effect. In particular, they find that a choice of heavy advertising is paired with a selection of large investment, and so rational consumers indeed can use ostensibly uninformative advertising expenditures as an indication of low costs and thus low prices. Finally, they

[82] Bagwell and Ramey show that a short-run scale effect, corresponding to marginal costs that decline with output, would reinforce their findings. Declining marginal costs may be relevant when large retailers receive quantity discounts.

offer an equilibrium interpretation for the empirical finding of Benham (1972) and others (see Section 3.2.4) that the introduction of even non-price advertising leads to the entry of large-scale firms and lower prices.

Bagwell and Ramey (1994b) offer an alternative formulation. In a first model, where one firm is known to be more efficient than a second, they show that the possibility of advertising ensures that all consumers coordinate on the efficient firm. If another equilibrium were posited, then the efficient firm could break this equilibrium by advertising heavily. Sophisticated consumers would understand that the efficient firm could then possibly profit, only if it were to receive a large number of consumers and price at the associated low monopoly price. Advertising is not required on the equilibrium path, though, once consumers are coordinated on the efficient firm. In a second model, a firm is privately informed as to whether it is more efficient than its rival. In the (refined) separating equilibrium, when this firm is more efficient, it advertises a positive amount on the equilibrium path, in order to signal its low costs and the associated low monopoly price. This prediction confirms Nelson's (1974b) signaling-efficiency effect, when a firm's level of efficiency is exogenous and privately known.

In the Bagwell–Ramey (1994a, 1994b) models, a consumer desires to visit a firm that expects a large number of other consumers. In this sense, an "indirect" network externality exists between consumers. Chwe (2001), Clark and Horstmann (2005) and Pastine and Pastine (2002) consider the related but distinct case of a "direct" network externality among consumers, whereby a consumer enjoys the social prestige that is associated with purchasing from a firm that actually sells to a large number of other consumers.[83] Under both approaches, advertising may promote improved coordination and welfare gains.

5.4. *Loss leaders*

The discussion above emphasizes extreme cases, in which a firm can advertise all or none of the prices of its products. In many categories, retailers carry thousands of items, and it is clearly not realistic to assume that all prices can be meaningfully advertised. As mentioned in Section 3.2.4, however, a firm may then advertise the price of particular "loss-leader" products.

I describe here the "commitment" and "signaling" theories of loss-leader pricing. The commitment theory is advanced by Lal and Matutes (1994).[84] In their duopoly model, one firm is located at each endpoint of the Hotelling line, each firm offers two products and each firm can advertise the price of just one product. For any firm, consumers observe one advertised price at zero cost and must pay a search cost to observe the other,

[83] For further discussion of research on network externalities, see the contribution to this volume by Farrell and Klemperer.

[84] See also Lal and Rao (1997) and Wernerfelt (1994). Gerstner and Hess (1990) and Hess and Gerstner (1987) offer related analyses that feature loss-leader pricing, bait-and-switch tactics and rain checks.

unadvertised price. Except for their locations, consumers are identical and have independent unit demands for both goods. For simplicity, suppose that consumers have a common reservation price R for each good. A firm then faces a commitment problem: it is unable to credibly promise that it will charge a price below R on an unadvertised good. In the absence of any advertising, therefore, consumers would foresee that all products are priced at R and choose not to visit any firm, thus saving the search cost. In the presence of advertising, however, a firm can use an advertised loss-leader price to guarantee sufficient consumer surplus to justify costly search, even though the unadvertised good is priced at R. Notice that consumers rationally expect that the price of the unadvertised product is independent of the advertised loss-leader price.[85]

Lal and Narasimhan (1996) extend the commitment theory to include a preceding stage in which the manufacturer of the loss-leader good selects a wholesale price and a level of advertising. Manufacturer advertising raises the demand for the manufacturer's good; specifically, it increases the reservation value that consumers have for a second unit of the loss-leader good. Lal and Narasimhan argue that manufacturer advertising may lower the retail price and raise the wholesale price of the loss-leader good, so that the retail margin is reduced and the wholesale margin is increased. This theory provides a formal foundation for work by Steiner (1973, 1978, 1984, 1993) and others, as discussed in Section 3.2.4.

Building on Nelson's (1974b) signaling-efficiency effect, the signaling theory holds that a firm uses an advertised low price to signal low costs. Consumers then rationally expect the price of the unadvertised product to be relatively low as well. Bagwell (1987) offers a formalization of this general idea. He considers a two-period model, in which demand is downward-sloping, consumers must pay a search cost to observe the current price and a firm is privately informed as to whether its costs are high or low. A low-cost firm may signal its costs with an "introductory sale". The firm then obtains greater repeat business, since consumers rationally expect the firm to charge a low price in the future. As Bagwell (1987, p. 384) notes, his two-period, single-good model may be reinterpreted as a single-period, two-good model, in which an advertised loss-leader price signals low costs and thus a low price on the unadvertised product. Simester (1995) develops this loss-leader model in detail and records a number of interesting predictions.[86]

5.5. Summary

The multi-firm models described above yield a striking set of predictions. Some of these predictions confirm and extend ideas found in earlier writings. The formal models also offer a number of new predictions. At a normative level, this work offers support for

[85] In their contribution to this volume, Farrell and Klemperer discuss a related "bargains-then-ripoffs" theme that arises in dynamic models with switching costs. For interesting recent contributions to the commitment theory, see Ellison (2005), Konishi and Sandfort (2002) and Rao and Syam (2001).

[86] See also Bagwell and Ramey (1994b). They provide an extended model in which loss-leader pricing is used to ensure that consumers coordinate on the most efficient firm.

the presumption that retail markets perform better when advertising is possible. This is true for both price and non-price advertising. At the same time, there is no presumption that the level of advertising is optimal. As in the normative theory of monopoly advertising, inadequate advertising may arise, since a firm does not internalize the consumer surplus that an additional ad may generate. Furthermore, when there are multiple firms, excessive advertising may occur, since a firm privately benefits from the sale that an additional ad may generate, even when this sale is "stolen" from another firm and offers no or modest social benefit. Finally, in many retail categories, large retailers sell thousands of products. The amount of direct price information that advertising can convey is then necessarily limited. Important future work might consider further the role of price and non-price advertising activities by multi-product retailers.

6. Advertising and quality

Nelson (1974b) predicts a positive relationship between advertising and product quality, especially for experience goods. In support of this prediction, he identifies the signaling-efficiency, repeat-business and match-products-to-buyers effects. As discussed in Section 3.2.5, however, the empirical literature offers mixed support for this prediction. I consider now recent theoretical analyses of advertising and quality. I organize this discussion around the three effects that Nelson (1974b) identifies. The signaling-efficiency effect is formalized using a static model. A related dynamic model is then presented, so that the repeat-business effect may be examined. This is followed by a short discussion of the match-products-to-buyers effect. Finally, I also discuss research that considers advertising in the context of the quality-guarantee effect.

6.1. Signaling-efficiency effect

Nelson (1974b) argues that demand expansion is most attractive to efficient firms. Such firms may enhance demand by advertising heavily, setting low prices and providing high quality; consequently, consumers may draw inferences as to the deal that a firm offers after observing its advertising. Above, I discuss the manner in which observed advertising may signal efficiency and thereby price for a retailer that offers search goods. I consider now how observed advertising and price may signal efficiency and thereby the (exogenous) quality of an experience good. This analysis may be most relevant for the manufacturer of a new product.

My approach is to draw on techniques developed by Bagwell and Ramey (1988) for signaling games with multiple signals. They analyze price and advertising as signals of cost in an entry-deterrence model (see Section 7.2 below). As Bagwell (1992) and Overgaard (1991) observe, these techniques also can be used to analyze how a high-quality monopolist best uses multiple signals to signal its quality.[87] In particular, Overgaard examines the static model that I now summarize.[88]

Formally, suppose a monopolist privately observes whether its product-quality type is low or high, $t \in \{L, H\}$, and then selects a price $P \geqslant 0$ and an advertising level $A \geqslant 0$. Consumers observe P and A, form some belief $b = b(P, A) \in [0, 1]$ as to the likelihood of high quality, and then demand $D(P, A, b) > 0$ units, where $D_P < 0 < D_b$ and $D_A \geqslant 0$. Advertising may be dissipative ($D_A = 0$), or it may contain information and/or induce social prestige and thus be demand-enhancing ($D_A > 0$). Let $c(t)$ denote the constant marginal cost of production when quality is type t. If $c(H) < c(L)$, then the high-quality monopolist is also the efficient (low-cost) monopolist. This is the case to which Nelson's (1974b) signaling-efficiency effect refers. As Schmalensee (1978) emphasizes, however, it may be more plausible to assume that a high-quality product has a higher marginal cost: $c(H) > c(L)$. Both cases are considered here.[89]

A monopolist of type t makes profit $\Pi(P, A, b, t) \equiv (P - c(t))D(P, A, b) - \kappa A$. For fixed t and b, assume $\Pi(P, A, b, t)$ has unique maximizers, $P_m(t, b)$ and $A_m(t, b)$, and is strictly concave in P. In the complete-information benchmark, the monopoly selections are $(P_M(H), A_M(H)) \equiv (P_m(H, 1), A_m(H, 1))$ and $(P_M(L), A_M(L)) \equiv (P_m(L, 0), A_m(L, 0))$. The complete-information monopoly profits are $\pi_M(H) = \Pi(P_M(H), A_M(H), 1, H)$ and $\pi_M(L) = \Pi(P_M(L), A_M(L), 0, L)$. Assume $\pi_M(t) > 0$ for $t \in \{L, H\}$, so that both quality types are profitable.

A *Perfect Bayesian Equilibrium* is a set of strategies, $\{P(t), A(t)\}_{t=L,H}$, and beliefs, $b(P, A)$, such that: (i) for each $t \in \{L, H\}$, $(P(t), A(t))$ maximizes $\Pi(P, A, b(P, A), t)$, and (ii) $b(P, A)$ is derived from the equilibrium strategies using Bayes' rule whenever possible. I focus here on *separating equilibria*, in which $(P(H), A(H)) \neq (P(L), A(L))$ and thus $b(P(H), A(H)) = 1 > 0 = b(P(L), A(L))$. In a separating equilibrium, the low-quality monopolist is "found out". It can do no better than to make its complete-information selections, $(P(L), A(L)) = (P_M(L), A_M(L))$, and earn the corresponding profit, $\pi_M(L)$.[90] Thus, if the high-quality monopolist is to separate, then

[87] Here and in Section 7.2 below, I illustrate these techniques using a simple Lagrangian argument. A more general treatment is available in the original papers.

[88] See also Zhao (2000), who places additional structure on the demand function and derives a related set of findings. For models in which a high-quality monopolist signals its quality using only price, see Bagwell and Riordan (1991) and Bagwell (1991, 1992). Under the assumption that a higher-quality product entails a higher marginal cost, they show that the high-quality monopolist adopts a high (supra-monopoly) price. This prediction is maintained below, when the model is expanded to include advertising as a signal.

[89] While it is plausible that unit costs tend to be higher for higher-quality products, this relationship may fail if higher-quality products achieve greater market share and thereby enjoy scale economies. Phillips, Chang and Buzzell (1983) use PIMS data and report that businesses with higher relative quality often have higher market shares and lower relative unit costs.

[90] Suppose $(P(L), A(L)) \neq (P_M(L), A_M(L))$. Then the low-quality monopolist could deviate to $(P_M(L), A_M(L))$ and earn strictly higher profit, since

$$\Pi\big(P(L), A(L), 0, L\big) < \Pi\big(P_M(L), A_M(L), 0, L\big) \leqslant \Pi\big(P_M(L), A_M(L), b(\cdot), L\big),$$

it must choose some pair (P, A) that the low-quality monopolist would not mimic:

$$\Pi(P, A, 1, L) \leqslant \pi_M(L). \tag{6.1}$$

To make the problem interesting, assume that signaling is costly for the high-quality monopolist: $(P_M(H), A_M(H))$ does not satisfy (6.1).

In the *least-cost separating equilibrium*, the high-quality monopolist separates in the way that it finds most profitable. The least-cost separating equilibrium is of particular interest, and it is also selected when standard refinements are employed. Formally, define (P^*, A^*) as the price–advertising pair that solves

$$\text{Max}_{P,A}\ \Pi(P, A, 1, H) \quad \text{subject to} \quad (6.1). \tag{6.2}$$

In a least-cost separating equilibrium, $(P(H), A(H)) = (P^*, A^*)$. Following arguments by Bagwell (1992) and Overgaard (1991), the existence of the least-cost separating equilibrium may be established. Here, I focus on the characterization of this equilibrium.

To gain some intuition, consider any two price–advertising pairs, (P_1, A_1) and (P_2, A_2), that yield the same profit for a mimicking low-quality monopolist: $\Pi(P_1, A_1, 1, L) = \Pi(P_2, A_2, 1, L)$. Observe that

$$\begin{aligned}
&\Pi(P_2, A_2, 1, H) - \Pi(P_1, A_1, 1, H) \\
&\quad = \big[\Pi(P_2, A_2, 1, H) - \Pi(P_1, A_1, 1, H)\big] \\
&\qquad - \big[\Pi(P_2, A_2, 1, L) - \Pi(P_1, A_1, 1, L)\big] \\
&\quad = \big[c(H) - c(L)\big]\big[D(P_1, A_1, 1) - D(P_2, A_2, 1)\big].
\end{aligned} \tag{6.3}$$

Suppose that $c(H) > c(L)$, and consider a change from (P_1, A_1) to (P_2, A_2) that leaves the low-quality monopolist indifferent. According to (6.3), if demand is lower at the new price–advertising pair, then the high-quality monopolist gains from the change. The key idea is that demand-reducing changes are more attractive to the high-quality monopolist when marginal costs increase with quality, since the demand reduction then offers a greater cost savings. Similarly, if $c(H) < c(L)$, then a change that leaves the mimicking low-quality monopolist indifferent and enhances demand is preferred by the high-quality monopolist.

Further insight may be gained by analyzing the program given in (6.2). The Lagrangian is $L(P, A, \lambda) \equiv \Pi(P, A, 1, H) + \lambda[\pi_M(L) - \Pi(P, A, 1, L)]$. Using (6.3), it may be verified that $\lambda \in (0, 1)$ at the optimum.[91] The Lagrangian may be rewrit-

where $b(\cdot) \equiv b(P_M(L), A_M(L))$. The final inequality follows since $D_b > 0$ and $\pi_M(L) > 0$, with the latter implying that $P_M(L) > c(L)$.

[91] The costly-signaling assumption implies that $\lambda > 0$. Given A^*, the first-order condition $L_P = 0$ determines P^* as the solution to

$$\Pi_P(P, A^*, 1, H) - \Pi_P(P, A^*, 1, L) = (\lambda - 1)\Pi_P(P, A^*, 1, L).$$

ten as

$$L(P, A, \lambda) = (1-\lambda)\left\{\left(P - \frac{c(H) - \lambda c(L)}{1-\lambda}\right)D(P, A, 1) - \kappa A\right\} + \lambda \pi_M(L). \tag{6.4}$$

As the bracketed term in (6.4) reveals, in the least-cost separating equilibrium, the high-quality monopolist makes the same price–advertising selection as it would were it to produce at constant marginal cost $c_o \equiv [c(H) - \lambda c(L)]/(1-\lambda)$ and offer a product of known high quality. Observe that $\lambda \in (0, 1)$ implies $\text{sign}\{c_o - c(H)\} = \text{sign}\{c(H) - c(L)\}$.

Consider first the case in which a high-quality product entails a greater marginal cost: $c(H) > c(L)$. In the least-cost separating equilibrium, the high-quality monopolist then undertakes a "cost-increasing distortion", in that it sets the same price–advertising pair as it would were its quality known but its marginal costs higher ($c_o > c(H)$). It is natural to assume that under complete information a monopolist would choose a higher price and less demand-enhancing advertising were its constant marginal costs increased.[92] Under this assumption, in the least-cost separating equilibrium, the high-quality monopolist distorts its price upward ($P^* > P_M(H)$) and its demand-enhancing advertising downward ($A^* < A_M(H)$). A high-quality monopolist thus best signals its quality with a high price and a low level of demand-enhancing advertising. In essence, the high-quality monopolist is signaling that it has high costs and is willing to reduce demand.

Consider second the case in which a high-quality product entails a lower marginal cost: $c(H) < c(L)$. Then, in the least-cost separating equilibrium, the high-quality monopolist undertakes a "cost-reducing distortion" ($c_o < c(H)$). The result is a downward pricing distortion ($P^* < P_M(H)$) and an upward distortion in the level of demand-enhancing advertising ($A^* > A_M(H)$). As Nelson (1974b) predicts, the high-quality monopolist best signals its quality with a low price and high level of demand-enhancing advertising. Fundamentally, the high-quality monopolist is signaling that it has low costs and welcomes an expansion in demand.

What if advertising is dissipative? Whether marginal cost rises or falls with product quality, dissipative advertising would not be used by a monopolist with a known

Take the case in which $c(H) > c(L)$. The left-hand side is then positive. Consider the right-hand side. Let $\tilde{P}_m(t)$ maximize $\Pi(P, A^*, 1, t)$. Suppose first that $P^* < \tilde{P}_m(L)$. Then let $(P_1, A_1) = (P^*, A^*)$ and $(P_2, A_2) = (\bar{P}^*, A^*)$, where $\bar{P}^* > \tilde{P}_m(L)$ satisfies $\Pi(P^*, A^*, 1, L) = \Pi(\bar{P}^*, A^*, 1, L)$. $\bar{P}^* > P^*$ implies $D(P^*, A^*, 1) > D(\bar{P}^*, A^*, 1)$. Using $c(H) > c(L)$ and (6.3), the high-quality monopolist strictly prefers $(\bar{P}^*, A^*)$, which contradicts that (P^*, A^*) solves (6.2). Suppose second that $P^* = \tilde{P}_m(L)$. It follows from $c(H) > c(L)$ that $\tilde{P}_m(L) < \tilde{P}_m(H)$. Starting at (P^*, A^*), consider a small price increase, so that the new pair, $(P^* + \varepsilon, A^*)$, satisfies $P^* + \varepsilon \leqslant \tilde{P}_m(H)$. Given the strict concavity of profit in price, the high-quality (low-quality) monopolist strictly prefers the new (old) pair, and again a contradiction is reached. It must be that $P^* > \tilde{P}_m(L)$. This implies that $\Pi_P(P, A^*, 1, L) < 0$ at P^*; hence, the right-hand side is positive if and only if $\lambda < 1$. A similar argument applies when $c(H) < c(L)$.

92 For instance, it may be verified that this assumption is satisfied when demand is described by either of the two examples considered in Section 4.1.2.

high-quality product; thus, such advertising is not used as a signal.[93] In this model, advertising is used as a signal of quality only if it is demand-enhancing.

While the model is static, the findings suggest a dynamic perspective. In particular, once the monopolist's product is sufficiently mature, consumers are presumably informed about its quality, and so the high-quality monopolist then sets its price and advertising at their complete-information levels ($P_M(H)$ and $A_M(H)$). Over the long run, the model thus predicts that the high-quality product's price declines and its demand-enhancing advertising increases, if marginal cost rises with quality. The opposite prediction (rising price, declining advertising) applies when marginal cost falls with quality. Whether its product is new or mature, the monopolist would never use dissipative advertising.

A further prediction is that the correlation between advertising and quality fluctuates across market settings. Suppose that marginal cost rises with quality and consider a new product. Relative to the complete-information benchmark, a high-quality monopolist distorts its advertising downward ($A(H) = A^* < A_M(H)$), while a low-quality monopolist does not distort its advertising ($A(L) = A_M(L)$). But it is not clear whether the level of complete-information advertising is greater when quality is high or low. Intuitively, complete-information advertising is expected to be greater when quality is high, if marginal cost rises slowly with quality and the marginal impact of advertising on demand rises quickly with quality. Pulling these themes together, it is possible that the advertising–quality correlation is positive under complete information and thus for a mature product, and yet the correlation is negative for a new product ($A^* < A_M(L) < A_M(H)$).[94] More generally, when $c(H) > c(L)$, the advertising–quality correlation is stronger (more positive, less negative) for a mature product. These findings offer a possible interpretation for empirical efforts (see Section 3.2.5) that report a generally weak advertising–quality correlation that is stronger for established products.

The model may be extended to consider a monopolist of intermediate age, so that some but not all consumers are informed of quality. If ζ represents the fraction of uninformed consumers, then the profit for a monopolist now depends upon its type through its marginal cost *and* the demand of informed consumers. For example, the profit for a high-quality monopolist becomes $\zeta\Pi(P, A, b, H) + (1 - \zeta)\Pi(P, A, 1, H)$. Linnemer (2002) develops a static model of this kind. When $c(H) > c(L)$ and an intermediate number of informed consumers exists, he shows that dissipative advertising may be used along with a high (supra-monopoly) price to signal high quality. Linnemer's model shares important formal features with the Milgrom–Roberts (1986) model, as I explain below.

[93] Formally, if advertising is dissipative, then $L_A(P, A, \lambda) = \kappa[\lambda - 1] < 0$, where the inequality follows since $\lambda < 1$ (as shown in footnote 91). Thus, when advertising is dissipative, it is optimally set at a boundary: $A^* = 0$.

[94] For further discussion, see Orzach, Overgaard and Tauman (2002) and Zhao (2000).

It is also possible to extend the model to allow for multiple sellers. Under the assumption that advertising is dissipative, Kihlstrom and Riordan (1984) explore a model in which quality is high or low and firms are competitive price takers, where the price that is "taken" may differ depending upon whether a firm is perceived to offer a high- or low-quality product. In this context, advertising can be understood as an "entry fee" that is necessary to enter the high-quality market. They show that dissipative advertising can signal high quality even in a static model, if marginal cost is sufficiently lower when quality is high. The idea is that a high-quality firm then enjoys a larger mark-up from a sale in the high-quality market, and so the advertising expenditure can fall in a range that only a high-quality firm would be willing to incur.[95]

As Fluet and Garella (2002) and Hertzendorf and Overgaard (2001) demonstrate, dissipative advertising may also signal high quality in a static duopoly model. In the Hertzendorf–Overgaard model, exactly one seller offers a high-quality product, but consumers do not know the identity of this seller. A key feature of this model is that the sellers share private information as to the identity of the high-quality firm. As a consequence, one seller's price–advertising selection provides potential information concerning the other seller's quality. This enriches the set of signaling possibilities.[96] Under the assumption that marginal cost is independent of quality, dissipative advertising is sometimes used as a signal of quality, and the correlation between advertising and quality is highest when the quality difference is intermediate in size. Allowing that marginal cost increases with quality, Fluet and Garella conduct a related analysis and find that any separating equilibrium entails positive advertising by the high-quality firm, provided that the quality difference is not too great.

6.2. Repeat-business effect

Nelson (1974b) argues that advertising rekindles memories of experiences with the advertised product. As recollections are more likely to prompt repeat business when the quality of product is high, a high-quality product may be advertised to a greater extent, and even new consumers may thus infer high quality from heavy advertising. I now summarize several recent efforts that use explicit dynamic models in order to capture a repeat-business effect. These efforts differ somewhat from Nelson's conception, in that a memory-activation process is not modeled; instead, the repeat-business effect emerges in the following sense: the return from advertising and thereby achieving an initial sale

[95] Wiggins and Lane (1983) also consider the manner in which advertising may signal quality when prices are fixed. In their model, consumers are risk averse, and advertised products are of more uniform quality. Horstmann and Moorthy (2003) examine a model in which competitive firms face uncertain demand. Advertising by a firm can improve its capacity utilization in low-demand states, by attracting consumers who otherwise would be uninformed. Since lower-quality firms may have greater excess capacity in low-demand states, this particular benefit from advertising can be greater for low-quality firms.

[96] For other multi-sender signaling models, see Bagwell and Ramey (1991), de Bijl (1997) and Matthews and Fertig (1990).

may be greater for a high-quality product, due to the greater repeat purchases that come from satisfied customers.

Schmalensee (1978) offers a first formal investigation. As noted above, he argues that the marginal cost of production is greater when a high-quality good is produced. Under the assumption that all sellers must charge the same price, the value of an initial sale may be greater when a low-quality good is sold, as then the mark-up is larger. This "reverse" signaling-efficiency effect favors low-quality firms and can counter the repeat-business effect that favors high-quality firms. Indeed, Schmalensee demonstrates that low-quality products are more heavily advertised, if consumers are responsive to advertising and marginal cost is sufficiently greater for a high-quality product.

As Schmalensee acknowledges, a weakness of his model is that consumer behavior is irrational: consumers are responsive to advertising, even though advertising is associated with low-quality products. This weakness is addressed by Kihlstrom and Riordan. I discuss above their finding for a static model, but they also consider a two-period formulation that allows for a repeat-business effect. Due to this effect, the value of an initial (first-period) sale is greater for a high-quality firm, and so dissipative advertising can signal high quality even if low-quality firms enjoy a modest marginal-cost advantage. The precise extent of the critical advantage varies with the particular assumption that is made as to the information held by second-period consumers.

Working with a monopoly model, Milgrom and Roberts (1986) allow that consumers may draw product–quality inferences from advertising and price. In effect, they extend the static model with dissipative advertising from Section 6.1 to include a second period. The product is non-durable, and consumers have unit demands in each period and heterogeneous reservation values. When a product is consumed, the consumer discovers whether he is satisfied with the product. A satisfied consumer enjoys the gross surplus (measured by the reservation value) that the product offers, while an unsatisfied consumer receives zero gross surplus. Product quality is operationalized as the probability that a randomly selected consumer finds the product satisfactory. If the product is satisfactory for a consumer in the first period, then it will remain so for this consumer in the second period. In the second period, the monopolist sells only to consumers that purchased in the first period and had a satisfactory experience.

The main features of their analysis may be understood with reference to a two-period profit function, $V(P, A, b, t) = \Pi(P, A, b, t) + \delta\tilde{\pi}(P, b, t)$, where $\delta \in (0, 1)$ is the discount factor, $\Pi(P, A, b, t)$ is the profit function used above in the static model and $\tilde{\pi}$ is a reduced-form profit function for the second period. As above, the consumers' belief b derives from first-period price and advertising observations: $b = b(P, A)$. I assume that $\tilde{\pi}$ is decreasing in P and increasing in b, since a firm can earn greater second-period profit if it sold to a larger number of consumers in the first period. More importantly, I assume that $\tilde{\pi}$ embodies a repeat-business effect in the following sense: $\tilde{\pi}_P$ is higher when $t = L$ than when $t = H$.

The intuition for the repeat-business effect is as follows. For any given belief, when the monopolist raises its first-period price, some consumers elect not to buy. Consider whether these "lost" consumers are of greater value to a low- or high-quality monopolist in the second period. There are two considerations. First, lost consumers might be more painful for the high-quality monopolist, since a greater fraction then would have been satisfied and thus given repeat business. Second, if marginal cost increases with quality, then lost consumers might be less painful for the high-quality monopolist, since a smaller markup then would be enjoyed on those lost consumers that did offer repeat business. The first (second) consideration works in favor of (against) the assumption made above. The assumption therefore holds if the high-quality monopolist has a weak cost advantage ($c(H) \leqslant c(L)$) or if any cost disadvantage of high-quality production is sufficiently modest.

Consider now the implications of the assumption that advertising is dissipative. First, the first-period profit function, $\Pi(P, A, b, t)$, depends directly upon advertising only through the cost of advertising: $\Pi_A = -\kappa$. A second implication, already reflected in the notation, is that $\tilde{\pi}$ depends on A only through the belief function $b(P, A)$. Third, advertising occurs (if at all) only in the introductory period. The monopolist would not advertise in the second period, since advertising does not directly alter demand and no opportunities for signaling remain (for all second-period consumers the product is already known to be satisfactory). Finally, in a separating equilibrium, if the monopolist offers a low-quality product, then it selects zero advertising. In analogy with the discussion above, in a separating equilibrium, the low-quality monopolist picks its complete-information monopoly price–advertising pair. When advertising is dissipative, the complete-information solution entails zero advertising.

In the least-cost separating equilibrium, is it possible that the high-quality monopolist picks positive advertising? Let $v_M(L)$ denote the discounted two-period profit that the low-quality monopolist earns in a separating equilibrium. In the least-cost separating equilibrium, the price–advertising pair selected by the high-quality monopolist solves the following program:

$$\text{Max}_{P,A}\, V(P, A, 1, H) \quad \text{subject to} \quad V(P, A, 1, L) \leqslant v_M(L). \tag{6.5}$$

Suppose that the solution to (6.5) entails positive advertising. Then the first-order condition for advertising is $V_A(P, A, 1, H) = \lambda V_A(P, A, 1, L)$. Given that advertising is dissipative, this condition reduces to $\lambda = 1$. Consider next the first-order condition for price. Using $\lambda = 1$, this can be written as

$$\Pi_P(P, A, 1, H) - \Pi_P(P, A, 1, L) = \delta\big[\tilde{\pi}_P(P, 1, L) - \tilde{\pi}_P(P, 1, H)\big]. \tag{6.6}$$

Thus, if the high-quality monopolist chooses a positive amount of dissipative advertising, then the high-quality price must satisfy (6.6).

Consider first the case in which $c(H) > c(L)$. Then the left-hand side of (6.6) is positive. The right-hand side of (6.6) is also positive, due to the repeat-business effect. In this case, therefore, it is possible that a high-quality monopolist signals its quality with a positive level of dissipative advertising along with a distorted price. Milgrom and Roberts discuss the specific circumstances under which such a separating equilibrium occurs.

Consider second the case in which $c(H) \leqslant c(L)$.[97] Then the left-hand side of (6.6) is non-positive. Given that the right-hand side is positive under the repeat-business effect, (6.6) cannot be satisfied. A main conclusion is now apparent: in the least-cost separating equilibrium, the high-quality monopolist uses dissipative advertising to signal its quality only if the marginal cost of production is greater for a high-quality product.

The underlying intuition is as follows. When the monopolist raises its first-period price, sales for the first period are reduced. If a high-quality product entails a higher marginal cost, this first-period effect is less painful for a high-quality monopolist. The price hike also reduces sales in the second period, since there are then fewer satisfied consumers that emerge from the first period. Under the repeat-business effect, this second-period effect is more painful for a high-quality monopolist, as a greater fraction of its first-period consumers would have had a satisfactory experience. Due to these offsetting effects, the cost of a price increase can be equalized across the low- and high-quality types of monopolists (i.e., (6.6) can hold). As both types also experience the same cost from dissipative advertising, the monopolist may have no better option than to use both a distorted price and a positive advertising expenditure when signaling high quality. By contrast, if marginal cost (weakly) falls with quality, then the cost of a price hike is (weakly) greater for a high-quality monopolist. The high-quality product is then best signaled with a low price and no advertising.

It is interesting to compare the predictions of the Milgrom–Roberts model with those of the static model. In the static model, dissipative advertising is not used as a signal. Furthermore, when advertising is demand-enhancing and $c(H) > c(L)$, a high-quality monopolist distorts its advertising downward, with advertising rising in the future (once consumers are informed) to its undistorted level. By contrast, in the dynamic model, if $c(H) > c(L)$, then a high-quality monopolist may use dissipative advertising as a signal, with advertising falling in the future to its undistorted level of zero. The inclusion of the repeat-business effect thus generates novel predictions, illustrating further the complex relationship between advertising and product quality. Finally, recall Linnemer's (2002) extension of the static model. In his model, the profit earned on informed consumers plays a role similar to that played by second-period profit in the Milgrom–Roberts model.[98]

Hertzendorf (1993) offers an interesting extension. He supposes that consumers observe the monopolist's advertising expenditure with error. By contrast, the monopolist's price is perfectly observed. If no advertising is observed, it may be unclear whether the firm failed to advertise or the consumer failed to observe the advertising. In this setting, if the monopolist's price reveals quality, then the monopolist will not use advertising as a signal. Intuitively, if the monopolist were to use advertising, then it could deviate to

[97] In the two-period model, future demand depends directly upon actual quality, and it is possible that a separating equilibrium exists even when $c(H) = c(L)$.

[98] In Linnemer's model, the formal analog of the repeat-business effect emerges as follows: over the range of prices that a high-quality monopolist might choose, a price increase diminishes the profit earned on informed consumers by a greater amount for a high-quality monopolist.

a lower advertising level, without being detected and without altering the consumers' belief (since price already reveals quality). Advertising may be used, however, when the monopolist's price is independent of product quality.[99] In this case, if repeat-business effects are sufficiently large and/or marginal cost does not rise too swiftly with quality, then the high-quality monopolist advertises to a greater extent.

Horstmann and MacDonald (1994) consider a different kind of noise. In their model, consumers observe price and advertising perfectly, but the consumption experience generates only an imperfect indication of quality. Specifically, they consider a two-period model in which a monopolist privately observes whether the quality of its product is high or low, where the marginal cost of production is independent of quality and in each period a higher-quality product yields a satisfactory experience with a higher probability. A consumer's experience with the product is then not fully informative: a product may offer a satisfactory experience in the first period and fail to do so in the second period. In the first period, there is no basis for the monopolist to use price and advertising as signals of quality. Imperfect signaling is possible in the second period, however, since this period has a greater expected number of satisfied consumers when quality is high. In a refined equilibrium, second-period play takes the following form: the high-quality monopolist prices high and advertises, while the low-quality monopolist sometimes adopts this behavior and otherwise sets a low price and does not advertise. The high price is such that a consumer purchases in period two only if the product yielded a satisfactory experience in period one. Two predictions follow. First, advertising does not signal the quality of newly introduced goods. Second, advertising can signal the quality of an established good, but even then the signal is imperfect. These predictions offer further interpretations for empirical efforts (see Section 3.2.5) that report a generally weak advertising–quality correlation that is stronger for established products.[100]

6.3. *Match-products-to-buyers effect*

I consider next Nelson's (1974b) match-products-to-buyers effect, whereby even seemingly uninformative advertising can provide indirect information that improves the match between product and buyer, since a firm has greater incentive to send its ads to those consumers that value its product the most. Aspects of this effect appear in some of the preceding discussion. In particular, Grossman and Shapiro (1984) provide conditions under which advertising that contains direct information as to a product's existence, attributes and price serves to increase consumer surplus by generating improved matches and expanded sales. In the following, I consider work in which the matching effect operates in markets for which consumers are already informed of the

[99] Moraga-Gonzalez (2000) offers a related finding in a model in which advertising provides direct information about product quality but not all consumers observe advertising efforts.

[100] For other interpretations, see Orzach, Overgaard and Tauman (2002), Zhao (2000) and the discussion above in Section 6.1.

existence of products. This work emphasizes advertising that provides information as to the attributes of the advertised product, where the information may be direct or indirect.

Meurer and Stahl (1994) offer a model in which advertising provides direct information as to horizontal attributes. In their model, there are two firms, and each consumer desires one unit of the product. For a given consumer, one product is a good match and offers gross utility V, while the other product is a bad match and offers zero gross utility. In the first stage of the game, firms simultaneously choose advertising levels. An ad provides direct and truthful information as to the attributes of the advertised product. A recipient of an ad thus knows whether the advertised product offers a good match. If it does not, then the other product must. For a consumer that receives no ad, the two products are homogeneous and each provide an expected gross utility of $V/2$. Advertising therefore induces product differentiation. This is consistent with some of the arguments advanced by proponents of the persuasive view, although here advertising-induced product differentiation derives not from a change in tastes but from the information that advertising provides. In the second stage of the game, each firm sets its (publicly observed) price. The marginal cost of production is $c < V/2$.

As Meurer and Stahl show, the effects of advertising on social surplus are non-monotonic. The equilibrium characterization entails mixed strategies, but the key ideas are easily related. One the one hand, as advertising increases, more consumers are "informed" (i.e., receive an ad) and thus obtain a good match. On the other hand, at higher levels of advertising, the extent of product differentiation is greater and each firm has more market power. In particular, each firm is then especially tempted to raise price to V and profit on those informed consumers for which its product offers a good match. But expected sales are then reduced, since uninformed consumers are unwilling to purchase at this price. The better-matching and reduced-sales effects of advertising are conflicting. The result is a non-monotonic relationship between advertising and social surplus. Building on these themes, Meurer and Stahl show further that the Nash advertising level may be excessive or inadequate.

A tension between the better-matching and reduced-sales effects of advertising also arises in the monopoly models analyzed by Lewis and Sappington (1994) and Johnson and Myatt (2006). Lewis and Sappington consider a monopolist that may use advertising to supply pre-purchase information to buyers. Advertising provides direct but possibly noisy information about product attributes and thus raises the expected value of the product for some consumers while lowering it for others. As Johnson and Myatt emphasize, advertising then induces greater dispersion in consumers' expected valuations and thereby generates a clockwise rotation of the demand curve. In these models, the monopolist can vary the precision of the information, by varying the content of the ads. At one extreme, if the monopolist provides no information, then each consumer regards himself as an "average type", and the monopolist selects the monopoly price for that type. At the other extreme, if the monopolist provides perfect information, then consumers learn their respective valuations, and the monopolist then sets a higher price that is attractive only to consumers with above-average valuations. This latter strategy facilitates better matching but also entails reduced sales. The main finding in this work is that the monopolist's expected profit often achieves its maximum at one of the extremes; thus, a profit-maximizing monopolist either provides no or perfect information about product attributes. Further, the latter option is more attractive when consumer valuations are heterogeneous and costs are high.

Anderson and Renault (2006) also analyze a model of monopoly advertising. In their model, however, search costs play an important role, and advertising may provide direct information as to product attributes *and* price. The basic model has a single consumer, who seeks one unit of the monopolist's product. The consumer can learn the product's price and his "match" (reservation) value for the product by incurring a search cost. The monopolist is also uncertain of the match value. When the search cost is sufficiently low, the consumer is willing to incur the cost, even though the monopoly price is anticipated, since he will enjoy positive consumer surplus if a high match value is realized. If the search cost is higher, however, the consumer is unwilling to incur the cost, unless the monopolist provides some information that raises the expected benefit from search. In line with the discussion in Section 5.4, if the monopolist could use advertising to transmit price information only, then it would raise the benefit of search by advertising its commitment to a sub-monopoly price. Anderson and Renault go further, however, and allow that the monopolist may use advertising to transmit price and/or attribute information. The consumer's match value may be determined by several product attributes, and the monopolist may elect to offer partial match information. Importantly, such information may raise the expected benefit of search for the consumer, by reassuring the consumer that the match value is not too low. Building from these points, Anderson and Renault find that the monopolist uses advertising to transmit partial match information for intermediate levels of the search cost, and uses advertising to transmit price and partial match information when the search cost is higher.

Bagwell and Ramey (1993) present a multi-firm model in which advertising offers indirect information as to vertical attributes.[101] In their model, marginal cost is increasing in quality, and consumers possess downward-sloping demands. Some consumers prefer high-quality, high-priced goods, while others prefer low-quality, low-priced goods. Advertising may then provide information that better enables buyers to match with their respective preferred products. Formally, they consider a three-stage game. In the first stage, firms choose whether to enter. If a firm enters, then at the same time if chooses its price, quality level and advertising activities (i.e., claims and expenditures). In the second stage, each consumer observes advertising activities, but not price and quality

[101] For an early discussion in which advertising plays a matching role in a market with vertically differentiated products, see Rosen (1978). He proceeds under the assumption that advertised claims are truthful. For another model in which advertising provides indirect information, see Anand and Shachar (2004a). They explore a duopoly model in which advertising content provides direct but noisy information; furthermore, the fact that a firm chooses to target its ad to particular media channels provides indirect information that the firm's product may be a good match for consumers that are exposed to those channels.

choices, and picks a single firm to visit. Finally, in the third stage, each consumer observes the price and quality at the selected firm and chooses a purchase quantity.[102]

Advertising claims need not be truthful. A firm that offers one quality of product may mimic the advertised claims and expenditures of firms that offer the other quality of product. The benefit of misrepresentation is that a firm thereby "tricks" consumers that prefer the alternative price–quality offering into visiting its store. But there is also a cost: the misrepresenting firm loses those consumers that prefer its (true) price–quality offering and to whom it otherwise would have sold. The net gain from misrepresentation hinges upon the differences in market share that accrue to firms offering the different qualities. An equilibrium in which advertising provides information is thus possible only if prices, advertising activities, and market shares satisfy incentive-compatibility and free-entry conditions. Fortunately, a sorting condition is available: a quality-sensitive consumer may yield more profit to a high-quality firm, since the demand expansion that ensues is sufficient to overwhelm the higher marginal cost. If the market shares are sufficiently similar across qualities, then costless advertising claims ("cheap talk") are credible, as under the sorting condition a firm does not gain from trading consumers that prefer its product for a similar number of consumers that do not. But if market shares differ sufficiently across qualities, then firms that offer the low-market-share quality are tempted to misrepresent, and so firms that provide the high-market-share quality must use dissipative advertising expenditures to discourage mimicry and signal quality. In a free-entry equilibrium, high market shares are associated with high fixed costs. Thus, if fixed costs are roughly constant across quality levels, then cheap talk credibly communicates quality. But if fixed costs vary significantly with quality, then dissipative advertising is used by firms offering the quality of product that has the higher fixed costs.

6.4. *Quality-guarantee effect*

Up to this point, I have emphasized the extent to which advertising signals product quality, when quality is exogenous or determined by a once-and-for-all choice. In many markets, however, firms offer experience goods and must be given incentive to provide a high-quality good in each period. An intertemporal tradeoff is suggested. On the one hand, a firm's short-run incentive is to save costs and offer unsuspecting consumers a low-quality product. Balanced against this short-term benefit, however, is the long-run cost of a lost reputation for quality. A firm that saves costs and provides a low-quality good today foresakes its reputation and thus the profit that it could earn on repeat sales tomorrow.

Where does advertising fit in? The reputational argument just advanced presumes that the firm is not anonymous. Clearly, a firm must be identifiable if it is to be rewarded with

[102] In this game, the product is a search good. Bagwell and Ramey also analyze the possibility of an experience good, in which case quality is not observed at the time of purchase.

repeat business only when it provides high-quality products. In turn, a firm may acquire a "name" by advertising its brand. From this perspective, advertising is associated with higher-quality products, since a "known" firm is reluctant to lose its reputation by offering a shoddy product. Advertising thus has a quality-guarantee effect that is reassuring even to first-time buyers.

The quality-guarantee effect is emphasized by early writers. Fogg-Meade (1901), Marshall (1919) and Shaw (1912) all argue that the advent of large-scale advertising gave manufacturers a significantly greater incentive to provide high-quality products. As observed in Section 2.2, Braithwaite (1928) takes an opposing view and argues that the quality-guarantee effect is modest, while Galbraith (1958, 1967) and Packard (1957, 1969) go further and suggest that brand advertising has powerful and negative social consequences. The same debate continues in the modern era, perhaps with even greater intensity, as the effects of "globalization" are scrutinized. The Economist (2001), for example, argues that a brand name removes the curtain of anonymity and makes a firm accountable for the quality of its product and the working conditions of its laborers. But Klein (2001) contends that persuasive (life-style) advertising is an important means by which brand-name multinationals influence media, shape culture and generally distort the economic and social aspirations of individuals.

This on-going debate is not resolved here. Accommodating aspects of both views, I assume that a monopolist's brand is known to consumers by name and that advertising is demand-enhancing (perhaps due to its persuasive powers). In this general context, my goal is to investigate the theoretical underpinnings of the quality-guarantee effect. Two questions are asked. First, in what manner must the monopolist distort its price and/or advertising selections, in order to provide a quality-guarantee effect? Second, among those price–advertising selections that do guarantee a high-quality product, which selection is preferred by the monopolist? By answering these questions, I hope to determine whether advertising may play a quality-guarantee role, even when consumers already know the brand name and the monopoly can also provide quality assurances with its price.

Formally, I consider an infinitely repeated game. In each period, the monopolist chooses a price P, an advertising level A and a quality level t, where quality is either low or high: $t \in \{L, H\}$. Consumers observe P and A but not t, form a belief b as to the probability that the monopolist has selected a high-quality product, and then demand a quantity $D(P, A, b)$. After any consumption experience is concluded, the monopolist earns profit $\Pi(P, A, b, t) \equiv (P - c(t))D(P, A, b) - \kappa A$ and consumers observe the chosen quality t. Assume that a high-quality product involves a higher marginal cost of production ($c(H) > c(L)$). Departing from the structure developed above, assume further that a consumer would never knowingly purchase a low-quality product ($D(P, A, 0) = 0$). The stage game is then repeated. I focus on stationary subgame perfect equilibria. In a stationary equilibrium, along the equilibrium path, the monopolist makes the same price, advertising and quality choices in every period.

To fix ideas, suppose for the moment that the stage game is *not* infinitely repeated. In a static model, for any given price and advertising expenditure, if consumers were to form a belief that results in a positive demand, then the monopolist would surprise consumers with a low-quality product, as it would thereby save costs without affecting demand. This logic also carries through in any finite-horizon game. The firm would "cheat" and provide low-quality in the last period. Using backward induction, it follows that no transaction ever occurs.

In the infinitely repeated game, however, the short-run cost savings that accompany a low-quality selection can be balanced against an associated long-run reputational cost. Suppose that consumers believe that the monopolist will provide a high-quality product if and only if it has always done so before and the price and advertising selections fall in a range that guarantees quality. Formally, quality is guaranteed for a reputable firm when the price and advertising selections fall in the range for which

$$\Pi(P, A, 1, L) - \Pi(P, A, 1, H) \leqslant \sum_{t=1}^{\infty} \delta^t \Pi(P, A, 1, H), \tag{6.7}$$

where $\delta \in (0, 1)$ is the discount factor. The left-hand side represents the short-run cost savings that the monopolist enjoys when it cheats and surprises consumers with a low-quality selection. The right-hand side captures the long-run reputational cost that the monopolist incurs, if it cheats in the current period and thus sacrifices its reputation and the prospect of repeat purchases at all later dates.[103]

Recalling the first question raised above, I now characterize the price and advertising selections that guarantee quality. The incentive constraint captured in (6.7) may be re-written as follows:

$$\big(c(H) - c(L)\big)D(P, A, 1) \leqslant \frac{\delta}{1-\delta}\big\{\big(P - c(H)\big)D(P, A, 1) - \kappa A\big\}. \tag{6.8}$$

Let the interest rate r be defined by $\delta = 1/(1+r)$. It is now straightforward to re-write (6.8) as

$$\big[P - \big(c(H) + r\big(c(H) - c(L)\big)\big)\big]D(P, A, 1) - \kappa A \geqslant 0. \tag{6.9}$$

As (6.9) reveals, the monopolist has the incentive to provide a high-quality product if and only if its price and advertising selections would generate non-negative profit, under a hypothetical situation in which the firm's marginal cost is $c(H) + r(c(H) - c(L))$ and consumers believe that product quality is high.

An important implication is that the monopolist provides a high-quality product only if the price strictly exceeds the true marginal cost, $c(H)$. Intuitively, the monopolist will forego the current-period opportunity to cheat consumers only if profitable repeat business then would be lost in the future. Notice that advertising is not essential for the quality-guarantee effect (once the name of the product is known). To see this, put $A = 0$

[103] If the monopolist cheats, then in all future periods play reverts to the Nash equilibrium of the static game, whereby the monopolist does not advertise and offers a low-quality product while consumers do not purchase. The monopolist then earns zero profit.

and observe that (6.9) holds if and only if

$$P \geqslant c(H) + r\bigl(c(H) - c(L)\bigr). \tag{6.10}$$

When price exceeds this critical level, the quality-guarantee effect is achieved through price alone.

Consider now the second question raised above. Among those price–advertising selections that guarantee quality, which one maximizes the monopolist's profit? The profit-maximizing selection solves the following program:

$$\max_{P,A} \Pi(P, A, 1, H) \quad \text{subject to} \quad (6.9). \tag{6.11}$$

The associated Lagrangian can be expressed as

$$\begin{aligned} &L(P, A, \lambda) \\ &\quad = (1+\lambda)\left\{\left[P - \left(c(H) + \frac{\lambda}{1+\lambda} r\bigl(c(H) - c(L)\bigr)\right)\right] D(P, A, 1) - \kappa A\right\}, \end{aligned} \tag{6.12}$$

where λ is the Lagrange multiplier. As the bracketed term in (6.12) reveals, in the most-profitable stationary equilibrium the monopolist offers a high-quality product and makes the same price–advertising selection as it would were it to produce at constant marginal cost $c_1 \equiv c(H) + \frac{\lambda}{1+\lambda} r(c(H) - c(L))$ and offer a product of known high quality.

The reputation model exhibits a surprising similarity to the static signaling model of Section 6.1. As in the static model, a cost-increasing distortion is implied: the high-quality monopolist does best when it sets the same price–advertising pair as it would were its quality of product known but its marginal costs higher ($c_1 > c(H)$). In comparison to the complete-information and high-quality monopoly price and advertising selections, an upward distortion in price and a downward distortion in demand-enhancing advertising is again predicted. Intuitively, the upward distortion in price and downward distortion in advertising contribute to a *downward* distortion in demand, thereby reducing the short-run cost savings that would be gained if the monopolist were to cheat.[104]

Klein and Leffler (1981) offer an early formalization of some of these themes. They establish that a competitive firm has incentive to offer a high-quality product only if price exceeds marginal cost for the high-quality product (so that repeat business has value). Their expression for the "quality-assuring price" is analogous to (6.10).[105] They also introduce advertising as an investment in brand-name capital that is forfeited if a firm degrades its reputation. In light of such advertising expenses, they argue that the zero-profit requirement of competitive markets may be reconciled with a positive

[104] Likewise, if advertising were dissipative, then the high-quality monopolist would guarantee quality most profitably by not advertising (i.e., setting $A = 0$).

[105] The formal expression in (6.10) is first derived by Shapiro (1983). See also Telser (1980) for related themes and Stiglitz (1989) for further discussion.

markup. An implication is that an observed correlation between advertising and profit (see Section 3.2.2) may reflect the rents that are necessary for high-quality performance rather than the presence of market power that is brought forth by an advertising-induced barrier to entry.

The reputation model presented above may be modified to illustrate the investment interpretation of advertising that Klein and Leffler advance. In particular, consider an equilibrium in which the monopolist does not advertise through time (i.e., $A = 0$), but does advertise at the time of entry. Suppose further that the initial advertising A_0 creates actual brand-name capital, in that it causes a (reputable) monopolist's demand to grow through time, where the (constant) rate of growth increases with the initial advertising outlay. Two implications follow. First, if the initial advertising outlay is increased, then the monopolist faces a greater long-term loss from cheating (since a faster-growing consumer demand is forfeited), and so a lower quality-guaranteeing price can be achieved. Importantly, advertising that creates brand-name capital may thus represent a means through which a firm can offer a more competitive price while maintaining its incentive to offer a high-quality product. Second, if consumers require a sufficient up-front investment in advertising, it remains possible to reconcile a positive markup with a zero-profit condition.[106] Interesting future work might expand this framework to allow for multiple firms that can choose to invest in advertising at any date.

Klein and Leffler also discuss the possibility that consumers may be uninformed as to firms' costs. They introduce the provocative idea that a firm's dissipative advertising expenditure may signal its cost type and thereby influence consumers' quality perceptions. Intuitively, a firm benefits if consumers believe it to have low costs (where a firm has "low costs" if for that firm $c(H) + r(c(H) - c(L))$ is low), since it can then offer a lower quality-guaranteeing price. While the idea is simple and intuitive, the appropriate formalization is non-trivial, as it involves dynamic signaling in a rivalrous environment. Rogerson (1986) offers a formal investigation of this kind. This area, too, represents a promising direction for further work.

Finally, consider the implications of the reputation theory for multiproduct firms. Suppose that the framework above is extended to allow that the monopolist carries two products. If the products do not have the same brand name, then consumers may be unaware that the products are linked. The quality-guaranteeing price for each product might then be determined by the product-by-product application of the incentive constraint captured in (6.9). Now suppose that the products have a common brand name. They are then linked in the consumers' minds, and the monopolist may lose

[106] Formally, suppose that demand at time t is given as $g(A_0)^t d(P, 1)$, where $g(A_0) - 1$ is the demand growth rate, P is the stationary price selection and $b = 1$ is the belief. Suppose that $g(0) = 1$, $g' > 0$, and $\delta g(A_0)$ is bound below unity. Then δ in (6.8) is replaced by the effective (growth-included) discount factor, $\delta_e \equiv \delta g(A_0)$. The quality-guaranteeing price is again given by (6.10), when r is replaced by the effective interest rate, $r_e \equiv [1 + r - g(A_0)]/g(A_0)$. Observe that $\text{sign}\{r - r_e\} \equiv \text{sign}\{g(A_0) - 1\} > 0$ for $A_0 > 0$. Finally, the monopolist earns discounted profit in amount $\Pi(P, 0, 1, H)/(1 - \delta_e) - \kappa A_0$, which is driven to zero at a finite and positive level for A_0.

repeat business on both products if it cheats on either. In the relevant incentive constraint, the product-by-product incentive constraints are pooled (i.e., added together): the gains from cheating on both products must be no greater than the loss in profits on both products that cheating would imply. It is possible that the monopolist can be induced to supply high-quality products, even when the price–advertising selection for one product would fail the incentive constraint for that product alone. Branding may thus benefit a firm by expanding the set of quality-guaranteeing price–advertising selections.[107] This discussion reinforces the argument that advertising can motivate high-quality choices by reducing anonymity and making brand names known.

6.5. Summary

A huge theoretical literature analyzes the relationship between advertising and product quality. The relationship is subtle, and it varies across circumstances. One set of work analyzes the manner in which advertising may signal quality. In this context, the advertising–quality relationship can be understood with reference to the three effects that Nelson (1974b) identifies. These effects provide a basis for a positive relationship between advertising and product quality. But the signaling-efficiency effect may be reversed in a number of environments, since higher-quality goods may use more expensive materials and thus have higher marginal costs. In such environments, greater advertising may be associated with higher quality *if* Nelson's other effects are prominent. The main empirical implication is that no systematic correlation between advertising and quality is expected, since the relationship reflects market circumstances and the simultaneous use of price and advertising as signals of quality. This implication is consistent with the empirical work summarized in Section 3.2.5. It also motivates new empirical work (as discussed in Section 8) that considers price and advertising as joint signals.

A second set of work investigates the extent to which advertising may provide an incentive for the continued selection of high-quality products. As early writers argue, advertising can play an important role by making brands known and identifiable, so that brand reputations can be forged and maintained. Once brands are known, however, if advertising enhances current demand, then the quality-guarantee effect is most profitably generated when price is distorted up and advertising is distorted down. If advertising also creates brand-name capital by enhancing future demand, then it appears possible that a firm may distort its advertising upward, in order to be able to offer a lower quality-guaranteeing price.

[107] For further formal analyses of branding, see Bagwell (1992), Cabral (2000), Choi (1998), Montgomery and Wernerfelt (1992) and Wernerfelt (1988). The general idea that incentive constraints are relaxed when pooled is also exploited in the collusion literature. See Telser (1980) for a first formalization. Further analysis is offered by Bernheim and Whinston (1990).

7. Advertising and entry deterrence

With a few exceptions, the theory summarized above does not address the relationship between advertising and entry. This is an important omission, since the persuasive view hypothesizes that advertising exerts an entry-deterrence effect. As discussed in Section 3, the empirical support for this hypothesis is mixed. In the absence of an empirical resolution concerning the relationship between advertising and entry, theoretical analyses may be of special value.

In the tradition of Bain's (1949) limit-pricing model, many of the first models of advertising as an entry barrier employ the assumption that the incumbent can credibly commit to maintain its pre-entry advertising expenditures if entry occurs.[108] A high pre-entry advertising expenditure may then imply a hostile environment for a potential entrant, in which case such advertising may deter entry. But the credibility of this commitment is questionable. As Needham (1976) argues, in the absence of such a commitment, an incumbent's pre-entry advertising influences the entry decision only if there is some link between pre-entry advertising and the entrant's post-entry expected profit.[109]

I consider here two possible links. First, advertising may have a goodwill effect, so that some consumers favor the incumbent in the post-entry period when the incumbent advertises heavily in the pre-entry period. While the empirical studies reviewed in Section 3.1.1 suggest that the goodwill effect of advertising is often modest, the effect may be pronounced in certain industries. Second, the incumbent's pre-entry advertising behavior may signal the incumbent's private information and thereby affect the entrant's expected profit from entry.

7.1. Advertising and goodwill

If advertising generates goodwill for the incumbent, then it is natural to expect that an incumbent could deter entry by engaging in heavy pre-entry advertising. But is this expectation confirmed in an equilibrium model? To answer this question, the source of the goodwill effect must be specified. An "informational goodwill effect" is present, if an incumbent's pre-entry advertising provides consumers with hard information of durable value concerning the incumbent's existence and prices. The incumbent might include its location and phone number on the ads, for instance. Alternatively, as persuasive-view advocates emphasize (see Section 2.2), the incumbent's pre-entry advertising generates a "reputational goodwill effect", if in some general sense it reinforces consumers' past experiences so as to differentially reward an established firm. For example, the incumbent's advertising efforts may reinforce any reputation that it has for providing reliable and high-quality products.

[108] See, for example, Salop (1979), Spence (1980) and Williamson (1963).
[109] See also Cubbin (1981).

In Schmalensee's (1983) model, an informational goodwill effect is posited. He considers a homogeneous-products market served by an incumbent and potentially an entrant. Consumers learn of a firm's existence and price through an advertising technology of the kind proposed by Butters (1977). The three-stage game proceeds as follows. In the first (pre-entry) stage, the incumbent sends out ads to consumers. A consumer who receives such an ad is informed of the incumbent's existence and can learn the incumbent's (eventual) price at zero cost. In the second stage, after observing the incumbent's advertising behavior, the entrant considers whether to incur a sunk cost and enter. If entry occurs, then the entrant sends out its own ads. In this event, each firm then has a set of captive consumers, and there is also a set of selective consumers. Finally, in the third (post-entry) stage, active firms play some simultaneous-move oligopoly game. As Schmalensee observes, if entry occurs and firms choose prices, then a pure-strategy Nash equilibrium does not exist. He thus supposes that the firms compete in quantities.

In this model, advertising is a durable investment and entry entails a sunk cost. It is thus tempting to reason by analogy with Dixit's (1980) entry-deterrence model and conclude that the incumbent strategically overinvests in advertising in order to deter entry. But this analogy is false. As Schmalensee shows, the incumbent can deter entry, but it does so with a *reduced* advertising expenditure. Intuitively, if the incumbent were to advertise heavily, then it would have many captive consumers. The incumbent would then be tempted to set a low output, so as to sell only to these consumers at a high price. A rational entrant would thus perceive that the incumbent would be a "soft" competitor. Consequently, if the incumbent seeks to deter entry, it should underinvest in advertising, thereby ensuring that it has few captive consumers and would respond to entry with vigorous competition for selective consumers.

Ishigaki (2000) modifies this three-stage game to allow that post-entry competition occurs in prices. After characterizing the mixed-strategy pricing equilibria that entry induces, Ishigaki finds that the entry is either blockaded (the incumbent deters entry when it behaves as it would were there no entrant) or accommodated (the incumbent optimally allows entry and sets its Stackelberg advertising level). There is no parameter region for which the incumbent strategically distorts its advertising choice in order to deter entry. Together, the models of Schmalensee and Ishigaki suggest the following striking conclusion: in homogeneous-products markets, when the goodwill effect of advertising is informational, a profit-maximizing incumbent does not deter entry by investing more in advertising than it would were there no entry threat. These models therefore provide no formal support for the entry-deterrence effect.

As Fudenberg and Tirole (1984) establish, a similar conclusion may obtain when the incumbent and entrant sell differentiated products. They consider a simple two-period model that captures some of the central themes raised above. In the first (pre-entry) period, the incumbent (firm 1) chooses a fraction Φ_1 of consumers to inform of its existence and price. As in the Grossman–Shapiro (1984) model, the cost to the incumbent of informing a fraction Φ_1 is $A(\Phi_1)$, where $A(\Phi_1)$ is positive, increasing and convex for $\Phi_1 > 0$. Assume further that initially it is prohibitively costly to reach all consumers: $A(1) = \infty$. The informational goodwill effect is captured with a strong assumption: consumers who receive an ad in the first period do not bother to read any ads that they may receive in the second (post-entry) period, and they thus remain captive consumers for the incumbent throughout the game. The incumbent selects its monopoly price in the pre-entry period and achieves a net revenue of $R_M > 0$ per consumer. The incumbent's pre-entry profit is thus $\Phi_1 R_M - A(\Phi_1)$.

In the second period, the incumbent and the entrant (firm 2) make advertising and pricing selections. Under the goodwill assumption, $1 - \Phi_1$ consumers remain in the second period that are not captive to the incumbent. Fudenberg and Tirole assume that the firms advertise so as to cover the remaining market. Let $\bar{A}$ denote the second-period advertising expenditure incurred by each firm in the course of creating $1 - \Phi_1$ selective consumers. The second-period prices of the incumbent and entrant, respectively, are denoted as P_1 and P_2. In the second period, the incumbent enjoys per-customer net revenues of $R_1(P_1, P_2)$ from a selective consumer and $R_1(P_1, \infty)$ from a captive consumer. The entrant sells only to selective consumers and enjoys a per-customer net revenue of $R_2(P_1, P_2)$. Assume that the net revenue functions are differentiable, concave in own prices, increasing in rival prices and characterized by positive cross-partials (i.e., for $i = 1, 2$, $\frac{\partial^2 R_i}{\partial P_1 P_2} > 0$). The final assumption indicates that prices are strategic complements.

For this two-period game, payoff functions are defined as follows:

$$\Pi_1(\Phi_1, P_1, P_2) = \left[\Phi_1 R_M - A(\Phi_1)\right] + \delta\left[\Phi_1 R_1(P_1, \infty) + (1 - \Phi_1) R_1(P_1, P_2) - \bar{A}\right], \tag{7.1}$$

$$\Pi_2(\Phi_1, P_1, P_2) = \delta\left[(1 - \Phi_1) R_2(P_1, P_2) - \bar{A}\right], \tag{7.2}$$

where $\delta \in (0, 1)$ is the common discount factor. Assume a Nash equilibrium (P_1^*, P_2^*) for the second-stage subgame exists and satisfies the first-order conditions:

$$\frac{\partial \Pi_1(\Phi_1, P_1, P_2)}{\partial P_1} = \delta\left[\Phi_1 \frac{\partial R_1(P_1, \infty)}{\partial P_1} + (1 - \Phi_1)\frac{\partial R_1(P_1, P_2)}{\partial P_1}\right] = 0, \tag{7.3}$$

$$\frac{\partial \Pi_2(\Phi_1, P_1, P_2)}{\partial P_2} = \delta(1 - \Phi_1)\frac{\partial R_2(P_1, P_2)}{\partial P_2} = 0. \tag{7.4}$$

Throughout, the dependence of P_i^* on Φ_1 is suppressed.

Given that prices are strategic complements, (7.3) implies that

$$\frac{\partial R_1(P_1^*, \infty)}{\partial P_1} > 0 > \frac{\partial R_1(P_1^*, P_2^*)}{\partial P_1}. \tag{7.5}$$

In the second period, the incumbent thus would like to raise its price on captive consumers and lower the price that it offers to selective consumers. The incumbent thus picks a second-period price that optimally balances these considerations.

The following relationships are now direct from (7.3), (7.4) and (7.5):

$$\frac{\partial^2 \Pi_1(\Phi_1, P_1^*, P_2^*)}{\partial P_1 \partial \Phi_1} > 0, \tag{7.6}$$

$$\frac{\partial^2 \Pi_2(\Phi_1, P_1^*, P_2^*)}{\partial P_2 \partial \Phi_1} = 0, \tag{7.7}$$

$$\frac{\partial^2 \Pi_1(\Phi_1, P_1^*, P_2^*)}{\partial P_1 \partial P_2} > 0, \tag{7.8}$$

$$\frac{\partial^2 \Pi_2(\Phi_1, P_1^*, P_2^*)}{\partial P_2 \partial P_1} > 0. \tag{7.9}$$

According to (7.6), and as in Schmalensee's model, when the incumbent's pre-entry advertising is greater, it becomes more attracted to higher post-entry prices. In the formulation considered here, as (7.7) confirms, the incumbent's pre-entry advertising does not directly alter the entrant's preferred price. But, as (7.9) indicates, if greater pre-entry advertising leads the incumbent to price higher, then the entrant becomes attracted to higher prices for this reason.

Under a standard stability condition, it is now easy to confirm that (7.6)–(7.9) yield the anticipated conclusion:

$$\frac{\partial P_1^*}{\partial \Phi_1} > 0 \quad \text{and} \quad \frac{\partial P_2^*}{\partial \Phi_1} > 0.^{110} \tag{7.10}$$

Thus, as the incumbent advertises more heavily in the pre-entry period, a greater number of captive consumers are created, and so the incumbent prices higher in the post-entry period. Given that prices are strategic complements, the entrant prices higher as well.

Consider now the advertising level at which the incumbent accommodates the entrant in the most profitable manner. Assuming that the second-order condition is satisfied, the incumbent maximizes its payoff when it chooses in the pre-entry period the value Φ_1^* that satisfies the first-order condition $\frac{\mathrm{d}\Pi_1(\Phi_1, P_1^*, P_2^*)}{\mathrm{d}\Phi_1} = 0$. Using (7.3), this condition may be re-stated as

$$R_M + \delta\big[R_1(P_1^*, \infty) - R_1(P_1^*, P_2^*)\big] + \delta(1 - \Phi_1)\frac{\partial R_1(P_1^*, P_2^*)}{\partial P_2}\frac{\partial P_2^*}{\partial \Phi_1} = A'(\Phi_1). \tag{7.11}$$

On the left-hand side of (7.11), the first two terms are positive and capture the direct effect of greater pre-entry advertising on first- and second-period net revenue. The third term is also positive. This term represents the strategic effect of greater pre-entry advertising. As established in (7.10), when the incumbent advertises more heavily, the entrant prices higher. The incumbent thereby earns greater profit in the post-entry period. Finally, the term on the right-hand side captures the cost of additional advertising.

It is interesting to compare Φ_1^* with the value that would occur if the entrant's post-entry price were unresponsive to the incumbent's pre-entry advertising. In the absence of the strategic effect, the left-hand side would be smaller. Given the convexity of the

[110] With P_1 on the y-axis, the stability condition indicates that the second-period pricing reaction function of the incumbent is flatter than that of the entrant.

function $A(\Phi_1)$, it follows that the optimal value for Φ_1 would then fall below Φ_1^*. It thus may be concluded that the incumbent overinvests in pre-entry advertising, in order to create a larger captive group of consumers and thereby commit itself to a higher post-entry price, so that the entrant will respond with a higher price of its own. As Fudenberg and Tirole put it, the incumbent best accommodates the entrant by overinvesting so as to become a "fat cat".[111]

Suppose now that the entrant must incur a sunk cost if it chooses to enter. Rather than accommodate the entrant, the incumbent might then choose to deter entry. But how is this achieved? Intuitively, if the incumbent seeks to deter entry, then it may achieve an indirect benefit by underinvesting in advertising, so as to create a small group of captive consumers and thereby commit itself to a low price in the event of entry. Fudenberg and Tirole refer to this as the "lean-and-hungry look". But an argument also can be made that the incumbent should overinvest in advertising, since it thereby achieves the direct benefit of reducing the entrant's possible market. To see these competing effects more clearly, use (7.4) and note that the overall effect of pre-entry incumbent advertising on post-entry profit to the entrant is given as follows:

$$\frac{\mathrm{d}\Pi_2(\Phi_1, P_1^*, P_2^*)}{\mathrm{d}\Phi_1} = \delta\left[(1-\Phi_1)\frac{\partial R_2(P_1^*, P_2^*)}{\partial P_1}\frac{\partial P_1^*}{\partial \Phi_1} - R_2(P_1^*, P_2^*)\right]. \tag{7.12}$$

The first term is positive under (7.10) and captures the indirect benefit to the incumbent of reduced pre-entry advertising, but the second term is negative and reflects the direct benefit to the incumbent of increased pre-entry advertising. As Fudenberg and Tirole observe, in an important set of environments, the indirect benefit of reduced pre-entry advertising dominates, and entry deterrence again requires underinvestment in advertising.[112]

The models developed above, however, all posit an informational goodwill effect. What if instead advertising induces a reputational goodwill effect? To begin, it is useful to distinguish between two issues.[113] A first issue is whether an incumbent with an existing reputation for reliable and high-quality products has an advantage relative to an

[111] Boyer and Moreaux (1999) consider a different demand specification, under which the entrant also has captive consumers. In their formulation, the incumbent's advertising level exerts a strategic effect through its impact on the *entrant's* price reaction curve. For example, when the incumbent and entrant sell substitute products and prices are strategic complements, if the incumbent advertises more heavily, then the entrant has a smaller set of captive consumers, and so the entrant's price reaction curve shifts downward. In contrast to Fudenberg and Tirole, Boyer and Moreaux argue that the incumbent best accommodates entry by underinvesting in advertising. Furthermore, this finding holds for a variety of sequential-move games and whether the products are substitutes or complements. See Fershtman and Muller (1993) for an earlier discussion of the underinvestment finding when products are substitutes.

[112] In recent work, Doraszelski and Markovich (in press) use numerical methods to compute the Markov-perfect equilibria for a dynamic game with an informational goodwill effect. In their model, an incumbent may deter entry by *overinvesting* in advertising, while the optimal accommodation strategy can vary with market characteristics.

[113] This distinction is explored in Section 2.2. It is also emphasized by Demsetz (1982).

entrant with no existing reputation. Undeniably, this is often the case. Consumers are naturally willing to pay a premium for a product from a reputable firm relative to that which they would pay for a product from an unknown firm. This suggests that informational product differentiation may be a barrier to entry. As Bagwell (1990), de Bijl (1997), Farrell (1986) and Schmalensee (1982) demonstrate, this suggestion is readily confirmed in formal models.[114] A second issue concerns the extent to which advertising is the source of this entry barrier. With respect to this issue, it is noteworthy that the incumbent is not allowed to advertise in the formal entry-deterrence models just mentioned. In these models at least, there is clearly no formal sense in which advertising is necessary for informational product differentiation to act as an entry barrier.

But might advertising somehow reinforce consumers' past experiences with the established product and thereby exacerbate the informational barrier to entry? It is, of course, possible to assume that advertising is more effective when consumers have greater experience with the advertised product.[115] But a more compelling model would yield the reinforcement effect as an implication of optimizing behavior. I am not aware of a model of this kind.

Drawing on the earlier writings, let me highlight one approach that may warrant formalization. As Braithwaite (1928, p. 32), Marshall (1919, p. 307) and Comanor and Wilson (1974, ch. 4) explain, a firm's ad must bid for the consumer's attention, and it may be more costly for a new firm to get the consumer's attention when the consumer is already overloaded with related ads from established firms. As Comanor and Wilson (1974, p. 47) put it:

> "To the extent that the advertising of others creates 'noise' in the market, one must 'shout' louder to be heard, so that the effectiveness of each advertising message declines as the aggregate volume of industry advertising increases. In this case, it will be necessary for new entrants to spend more today to gain an established market position than existing firms spent yesterday, when aggregate industry advertising was probably far less. From these circumstances also, new entrants may have differentially higher advertising costs than did established firms at their entry into the market."

[114] Schmalensee (1982) offers a first formalization of the brand loyalty that consumers exhibit toward pioneering brands of known quality. He shows that a high-quality incumbent can earn positive profit without inducing the entry of an equally efficient, high-quality entrant. Bagwell (1990) extends this model to allow that consumers rationally infer quality from price and that the entrant may offer a superior product. The key finding is that a low-quality incumbent may deter entry, even when the entrant actually offers a high-quality (and socially efficient) product. de Bijl (1997) establishes a similar finding for search goods when search costs are high, and shows as well that the entry barrier may be diminished if the incumbent is informed of the entrant's quality. Farrell (1986) extends the analysis to consider the manner in which the incumbent's behavior affects the entrant's incentive to choose a high-quality product. See also Schmalensee (1979) for a detailed discussion of the product-differentiation advantages that accrued to pioneering brands in the market for lemon juice.

[115] See Comanor and Wilson (1974, chs. 3 and 4) for a model in which it is assumed that advertising's effectiveness varies with consumers' experience with the advertised product.

This "noise effect" suggests that the incumbent may strategically overinvest in advertising, in order to jam the message space and force the entrant to be more stentorian with its advertising efforts. Incumbent advertising would then raise the entrant's advertising costs and exacerbate the entry barrier. This cost-raising strategy is informally discussed by Hilke and Nelson (1984), who provide evidence in the U.S. coffee market that Maxwell House used such a strategy when facing entry by Folgers. Future work might revisit this noise effect, in a model that endogenizes the manner in which consumers with finite information-storage capabilities manage (as possible) their exposure to advertising.

7.2. Advertising and signaling

I consider now the possibility that the incumbent's pre-entry behavior may signal its private information. This information may be relevant for the entrant's calculation of the expected profit from entry. In this case, an informational link connects the incumbent's pre-entry behavior and the entrant's post-entry expected profit.

Milgrom and Roberts (1982) establish that a low-cost incumbent may distort its pre-entry price downward in order to signal its costs and thereby deter entry. Bagwell and Ramey (1988) extend the Milgrom–Roberts analysis to allow that the low-cost incumbent may signal its costs by distorting its pre-entry price and/or advertising. As I explain below, they find that the low-cost incumbent deters entry most profitably, when its pre-entry price is distorted downward and its demand-enhancing advertising is distorted upward.[116] They thus provide a theory in which an incumbent overinvests in advertising in order to deter entry.[117]

Bagwell and Ramey consider a signaling game with two periods. In the pre-entry period, an incumbent of cost type $t \in \{L, H\}$ selects its pre-entry price $P \geqslant 0$ and advertising level $A \geqslant 0$. The incumbent earns pre-entry profit $\Pi(P, A, t) \equiv (P - c(t))D(P, A) - \kappa A$, where $D > 0$, $D_P < 0$, $D_A \geqslant 0$ and $c(H) > c(L)$. Advertising may be demand-enhancing ($D_A > 0$) or dissipative ($D_A = 0$). For $t \in \{L, H\}$, assume further that $\Pi(P, A, t)$ is strictly concave in P, with a unique maximizing pair, $(P_M(t), A_M(t))$. This pair denotes the monopoly price–advertising selection. The corresponding monopoly profit is $\pi_M(t) \equiv \Pi(P_M(t), A_M(t), t)$.

At the start of the post-entry period, a single entrant observes the pre-entry price and advertising level, but not the incumbent's type, and forms some belief $b = b(P, A) \in [0, 1]$ as to the probability that the incumbent has high costs. The entrant then enters

[116] Methodologically, the analysis presented below is closely related to that presented above in Section 6.1. Notice, though, that the incumbent now uses price and advertising to signal its cost to an entrant, whereas in Section 6.1 the monopolist uses price and advertising to signal quality to consumers.

[117] Milgrom and Roberts offer an information-theoretic foundation for Bain's (1949) prediction that an incumbent can deter entry by limit pricing. Likewise, Bagwell and Ramey provide a theoretical counterpart to an interesting extension of Bain's approach that is offered by Williamson (1963). In Williamson's model, the incumbent deters entry, by making a pre-entry commitment to a low price and a high level of advertising.

or not, where $E = 1$ ($E = 0$) denotes (no) entry. If entry does not occur, then the incumbent earns monopoly profit $\pi_M(t)$ in the post-entry period. If entry does occur, then the entrant learns the incumbent's type, and the incumbent and entrant play some post-entry duopoly game, earning $\pi_D(t)$ and $\pi_D^e(t)$, respectively. The sunk cost of entry is included in $\pi_D^e(t)$.

For a given price P, advertising level A, entry decision E and incumbent type t, the incumbent and entrant payoffs are

$$V(P, A, E, t) = \Pi(P, A, t) + \delta\big[E\pi_D(t) + (1 - E)\pi_M(t)\big], \tag{7.13}$$

$$u(E, t) = \delta E\pi_D^e(t), \tag{7.14}$$

respectively, where δ is the common discount factor. At the time of the entry decision, the entrant's expected profit from entry is

$$U(P, A, E, b) \equiv \big[bu(E, H) + (1 - b)u(E, L)\big]/\delta. \tag{7.15}$$

Using (7.14) and (7.15), it follows that $U(P, A, 0, b) = 0$ and $U(P, A, 1, b) = b\pi_D^e(H) + (1 - b)\pi_D^e(L)$.

Further structure is provided by three key assumptions. First, whatever its type, the incumbent prefers that entry not occur: $\pi_M(t) > \pi_D(t)$. Second, the entrant earns positive profit from entry if and only if the incumbent has high costs: $\pi_D^e(H) > 0 > \pi_D^e(L)$. Third, the incumbent gains at least as much from entry deterrence when its costs are low as when its costs are high: $\pi_M(L) - \pi_D(L) \geqslant \pi_M(H) - \pi_D(H)$. The first assumption is unobjectionable, the second assumption holds in standard duopoly models if the sunk cost of entry falls in an intermediate range, and the third assumption reflects the differential benefit of greater sales to a lower-cost firm and holds in many popular duopoly models.

A Perfect Bayesian Equilibrium is a set of strategies $\{P(t), A(t), E(P, A)\}_{t=L,H}$ and beliefs $b(P, A)$ such that: (i) for each $t \in \{L, H\}$, $(P(t), A(t))$ maximizes $V(P, A, E(P, A), t)$, (ii) for all $(P, A) \geqslant 0$, $E(P, A)$ maximizes $U(P, A, E, b(P, A))$, and (iii) $b(P, A)$ is derived from the equilibrium strategies whenever possible. I again focus on separating equilibria. For such equilibria, $(P(H), A(H)) \neq (P(L), A(L))$ and thus $b(P(H), A(H)) = 1 > 0 = b(P(L), A(L))$. The entrant infers the incumbent's type and enters if and only if the incumbent has high costs. As the high-cost incumbent is "found out", it can do no better than to make its monopoly selection, $(P(H), A(H)) = (P_M(H), A_M(H))$, and then face entry.[118] The high-cost incumbent thus receives the payoff $V(P_M(H), A_M(H), 1, H) \equiv V_M(H)$. Separation then

[118] Suppose $(P(H), A(H)) \neq (P_M(H), A_M(H))$. Then the high-cost incumbent could achieve a strict gain with a deviation to $(P_M(H), A_M(H))$, since

$$V\big(P(H), A(H), 1, H\big) < V\big(P_M(H), A_M(H), 1, H\big) \leqslant V\big(P_M(H), A_M(H), E(\cdot), H\big),$$

where $E(\cdot) \equiv E(P_M(H), A_M(H))$. The final inequality follows, since $\pi_M(H) > \pi_D(H)$.

requires that the low-cost incumbent choose some pair (P, A) that the high-cost incumbent would not mimic:

$$V(P, A, 0, H) \leqslant V_M(H). \tag{7.16}$$

To ensure that separation is costly, I assume that the low-cost incumbent's monopoly selection $(P_M(L), A_M(L))$ does not satisfy (7.16).

In the least-cost separating equilibrium, the low-cost incumbent makes the selection $(P(L), A(L)) = (P^*, A^*)$, where (P^*, A^*) is the price–advertising selection that solves the following program:

$$\text{Max}_{P,A}\ V(P, A, 0, L) \quad \text{subject to} \quad (7.16). \tag{7.17}$$

Bagwell and Ramey (1988) establish that the least-cost separating equilibrium exists. I focus here on the characterization of such an equilibrium.

To gain intuition, consider any two price–advertising pairs, (P_1, A_1) and (P_2, A_2), that leave the mimicking high-cost incumbent indifferent. Since each pair deters entry, indifference means that $\Pi(P_1, A_1, H) = \Pi(P_2, A_2, H)$. Thus

$$\begin{aligned} &\Pi(P_2, A_2, L) - \Pi(P_1, A_1, L) \\ &\quad = \big[\Pi(P_2, A_2, L) - \Pi(P_1, A_1, L)\big] - \big[\Pi(P_2, A_2, H) - \Pi(P_1, A_1, H)\big] \\ &\quad = \big[c(H) - c(L)\big]\big[D(P_2, A_2) - D(P_1, A_1)\big]. \end{aligned} \tag{7.18}$$

As (7.18) reveals, given that $c(H) > c(L)$, the low-cost incumbent prefers the pair at which demand is highest. Intuitively, a demand-increasing change is more attractive to a low-cost incumbent, since the demand increase then translates into a smaller cost increase.

For further insight, consider the program given in (7.17). The Lagrangian is $L(P, A, \lambda) \equiv V(P, A, 0, L) + \lambda[V_M(H) - V(P, A, 0, H)]$. It may be verified that $\lambda \in (0, 1)$ at the optimum.[119] Using (7.13), the Lagrangian may be re-written as

$$L(P, A, \lambda) = (1 - \lambda)\left\{\left(P - \frac{c(L) - \lambda c(H)}{1 - \lambda}\right)D(P, A) - \kappa A\right\} + K(\lambda, \delta), \tag{7.19}$$

where $K(\lambda, \delta)$ is independent of P and A. As the bracketed term in (7.19) reveals, in the least-cost separating equilibrium, the low-cost incumbent makes the same price–advertising selection as it would were its constant marginal cost known to be $c_2 \equiv [c(L) - \lambda c(H)]/(1 - \lambda)$. Observe that $\lambda \in (0, 1)$ implies $c_2 < c(L)$.

In the least-cost separating equilibrium, the low-cost incumbent thus undertakes a "cost-reducing distortion", in that it selects the same price–advertising pair as it would were its costs known and lower than they truly are. Put differently, the low-cost incumbent behaves as it would were it a monopolist operating in a single-period setting with

[119] The proof is analogous to that given in footnote 91 for the product-quality signaling model.

constant marginal cost $c_2 < c(L)$. It is natural to assume that a single-period monopolist would lower its price and raise its demand-enhancing advertising were its constant marginal cost of production reduced.[120] Under this assumption, the low-cost incumbent distorts downward its price ($P^* < P_M(L)$) and upward its demand-enhancing advertising ($A^* > A_M(L)$). Intuitively, the low-cost incumbent undertakes these distortions in order to demonstrate its willingness to increase demand. Finally, dissipative advertising is not used as a signal, since it would never be used by an incumbent with known costs.

As in the Milgrom–Roberts model, profitable entry is not deterred in a separating equilibrium. The entrant infers the incumbent's cost type and resists entry exactly when entry would be unprofitable (i.e., when the incumbent has low costs). The incumbent's pre-entry behavior credibly reveals its cost type, however, only when the low-cost incumbent distorts its pre-entry selection. In the least-cost separating equilibrium, the low-cost incumbent deters (unprofitable) entry by limit pricing and overinvesting in demand-enhancing advertising.

With these predictions at hand, it is interesting to revisit the relationships between advertising, profitability and entry (see Sections 3.2.2 and 3.2.3). The Bagwell–Ramey model predicts that greater incumbent advertising is associated with higher profitability and lower rates of entry. These predictions match closely those suggested by Comanor and Wilson (1967, 1974) and other persuasive-view advocates. The predictions, however, are not attributable to advertising-induced brand loyalty; instead, they arise because an efficient incumbent advertises more, earns more and faces less entry than would an inefficient incumbent. The Bagwell–Ramey model thus offers some support for the "superior efficiency" interpretation advanced by Demsetz (1973, 1974) and Nelson (1974b, 1975).

The basic model can be extended in several directions. Bagwell and Ramey (1990) suppose that the incumbent's private information concerns the level of industry demand. The incumbent now deters entry by signaling that demand is low. They establish that a "demand-reducing distortion" occurs: the low-demand incumbent behaves as if it were a single-period monopolist but demand is lower than it truly is. Under natural assumptions, in the least-cost separating equilibrium, the low-demand incumbent's price and demand-enhancing advertising are both distorted downward. Thus, entry deterrence entails limit pricing, whether the incumbent is privately informed of its costs or the level of industry demand; however, entry deterrence results in an underinvestment in demand-enhancing advertising when the incumbent is privately informed as to the level of industry demand. Bagwell and Ramey also consider the possibility that the incumbent may wish to signal that demand is high, so as to influence the entrant's beliefs and accommodate entry in the most profitable manner possible. In this case, a "demand-increasing distortion" occurs, with the implication that the high-demand incumbent distorts upward both price and demand-enhancing advertising.[121]

[120] As observed in footnote 92, this assumption holds in each of the two examples discussed in Section 4.1.2.

[121] Bagwell and Ramey also provide propositions that characterize necessary features of refined pooling equilibria. But Albaek and Overgaard (1992a) show that, in fact, refined pooling equilibria fail to exist in this model.

The work described here also can be extended to analyze manufacturer–retailer relations. Suppose that a manufacturer has private information concerning the eventual demand for its new product. The retailer may wish to carry the manufacturer's product only if the retailer believes that there is a high demand for this product. The manufacturer thus may wish to use its advertising expenditure and (wholesale) price to signal to the retailer that demand is high. Following the logic just described, the manufacturer signals that it offers a high-demand product by engaging in a demand-increasing distortion, whereby it distorts upward both price and demand-enhancing advertising.[122] This discussion provides a formal counterpart to a common argument expressed in earlier writings that a manufacturer uses heavy advertising to communicate its confidence in the new product to retailers. See, for example, Berreman (1943) and Chamberlin (1933, p. 121).

Finally, Linnemer (1998) offers an interesting extension, in which an incumbent firm has private information with respect to its product quality *and* production costs. He considers a two-period model, in which the incumbent's first-period price and dissipative advertising outlays are used by consumers to infer quality and by a potential entrant to infer costs. Specifically, the incumbent either has a low-quality product and low costs, a high-quality product and medium costs, or a high-quality product and high costs. Consumers know product quality in the second period, but they must infer it in the first period. The entrant knows the incumbent's product quality; however, the entrant does not know whether a high-quality incumbent has medium or high costs. The entrant wants to enter, unless the incumbent has a high-quality product that it produces at medium cost. The interesting point is that the high-quality incumbent with medium costs has a conflict. As in the static signaling model presented in Section 6.1, it is tempted to distort price upward in order to signal quality to consumers. But, as in the limit-pricing literature discussed just above, it is also tempted to distort price downward in order to signal that its costs are not high and thus that entry would not be profitable. In rough analogy with the Milgrom–Roberts (1986) model, given these conflicting considerations, the high-quality medium-cost incumbent may have no better option than to use a distorted price and a positive dissipative advertising expenditure when signaling its type. As in the Bagwell–Ramey (1988) model, the consequent overinvestment in advertising deters entry that is unprofitable.

7.3. Summary

In summary, when the goodwill effect of advertising is informational, the theoretical literature emphasizes that an incumbent firm that seeks to deter entry may underinvest in pre-entry advertising. It is also possible that advertising generates a reputational

[122] See Chu (1992) for a formalization of this extension, wherein the retailer learns demand if it decides to carry the incumbent's product. Albaek and Overgaard (1992b) suppose that the retailer carries the product but does not learn demand prior to setting the retail price. The retailer's beliefs then impact its price choice. Now, a manufacturer may undertake a demand-reducing distortion in order to signal that demand is low, as it thereby encourages the retailer to set a low price and hence mitigates the double-marginalization problem.

goodwill effect, by reinforcing consumers' experiences with the established product and exacerbating informational product differentiation. I am not aware, however, of an equilibrium model of this kind. On the whole, the entry-deterrence effect of advertising is not strongly supported by the existing theoretical models that emphasize advertising's possible goodwill effects. Future work might endogenize the "noise effect" that is emphasized in earlier writings.

I also consider the possibility that the incumbent's pre-entry pricing and advertising behavior may signal its private information and thereby affect the entrant's expected profit from entry. When the incumbent has private information about its costs, a low-cost incumbent may limit price and overinvest in advertising, in order to signal its costs and thereby deter entry. On the other hand, if the incumbent has private information as to the level of industry demand, a low-demand incumbent may limit price and underinvest in advertising, in order to signal demand and thereby deter entry. The overinvestment finding provides some support for the entry-deterrence effect of advertising; however, it must be noted that entry is deterred only when it is intrinsically unprofitable. In other words, the low-cost incumbent's heavy advertising does not make entry unprofitable; rather, it reveals that entry would be unprofitable.

8. Empirical analyses

While inter-industry studies offer useful descriptions of economy-wide empirical regularities, they often suffer from important endogeneity and measurement concerns (as detailed in Section 3) and ultimately fail to identify the underlying structural parameters that describe how individual markets work. As mentioned in the Introduction, the modern (second-group) empirical analyses of advertising increasingly use new data sets, which are often constructed at remarkably disaggregated levels, and emphasize consumer and firm conduct. Strategic theories of advertising (as reviewed in Sections 4–7) influence the specification of demand functions and supply relationships in these analyses. In this section, I offer a brief and non-technical review of this empirical literature.

8.1. Advertising and the household

I begin with a group of empirical studies that examine the impact of advertising on brand purchase decisions. The studies utilize household brand purchase panel data and often household advertising exposure data. With such disaggregated data, it is possible to gain insight into the respective roles of advertising and experience in explaining household brand purchase behavior. Likewise, it is possible to better distinguish between the informative, persuasive and complementary effects of advertising.

How are such data obtained and analyzed? One approach is to use a controlled field experiment. In this way, Krishnamurthi and Raj (1985) examine the effect of an increase in advertising on the elasticity of demand for an unnamed frequently purchased brand.

Household brand purchase data are obtained through panel diaries maintained by households in a test city over a 52-week pre-test period and a 24-week test period. Advertising exposure is controlled through a split-cable TV experiment: a test panel of families is connected to one cable while a control panel of families in connected to another cable, and then the level of (non-price) advertising for the brand is increased in the test period for the test panel. At the family-panel level, Krishnamurthi and Raj specify a log-linear demand for the brand, where the log of the (relative) price of the brand is interacted with a time (pre-test, test) dummy variable. They report that demand for the brand becomes significantly more inelastic in the test panel of families once advertising is increased.

Guadagni and Little (1983) advance an alternative approach. They obtain household brand purchase data through supermarket scanner data. These data include individual item sales and prices by store by week, promotional activities within the store, and histories of purchases for samples of households. The multinomial logit choice model of brand choice is well suited for the analysis of such data. Guadagni and Little illustrate the power of this approach, by using scanner data on 32 weeks of purchases of coffee by 100 households and estimating the parameters that govern consumers' optimal brand-size choices.

In the multinomial logit model, consumer i enjoys utility u_k^i from alternative k (i.e., a brand-size choice), where utility consists of deterministic and random components: $u_k^i = v_k^i + \epsilon_k$. Under an appropriate (extreme value) distributional assumption for ϵ_k, consumer i optimally chooses alternative k with probability

$$p_k^i = e^{v_k^i} \Big/ \sum_{j \in S^i} e^{v_j^i},$$

where S^i is the set of alternatives under consideration by consumer i.[123] Next, the deterministic term is decomposed into a linear combination of attributes that are associated with alternative k:

$$v_k^i = \sum_{j \in T} b_j x_{jk}^i,$$

where x_{jk}^i denotes the value of attribute j for consumer i under alternative k. The set T of attributes includes price, promotion and also brand and size experience measures.[124] The econometrican observes consumer choices and attribute values and then estimates the b_j parameters using maximum likelihood methods.

How is brand experience measured? At the time of the nth coffee purchase of consumer i, the experience that this consumer has with the brand associated with brand-size alternative k is an attribute of this alternative that is measured as a weighted average

[123] See McFadden (1974).

[124] Measurements of past purchase behavior are also sometimes referred to as indicating brand (or size) loyalty.

of past purchases of the brand, where past purchases are treated as 0–1 variables.[125] The experience variables are then initialized using household purchase observations for previous weeks. Using this approach, Guadagni and Little report that brand and size experience are the most important attributes in explaining consumer brand-size choice. Guadagni and Little do not have household advertising exposure data, however, and so their analysis leaves open an important question: What are the respective roles of advertising and experience in explaining household brand purchase behavior?

This question is the focus of subsequent work. For 251 households in a test city, Tellis (1988) obtains scanner data for purchases of 10 brands of toilet tissues over a 52-week period, and he also obtains TV meter records of household exposure to brand advertising. Tellis seeks to explain both brand choice and volume, where explanatory variables include brand experience, volume experience, advertising exposure and price. Like Guadagni and Little, Tellis uses purchase behavior in a pre-test period to develop experience measures. Using advertising exposure data, he is also able to assess the impact of advertising on brand choice and volume, both directly and interacted with experience. In line with Lambin's (1976) work, Tellis reports that experience is the strongest determinant of purchase behavior, and that other marketing variables like price are more important than advertising. Advertising appears to have only a small effect on brand choice.[126] According to this evidence, pioneering firms may enjoy important experience-based advantages; however, advertising itself is not one of the more important determinants of purchase behavior.

These findings are evaluated in further work that uses scanner and advertising exposure data and multinomial logit models to explain household brand-choice behavior. Kanetkar, Weinberg and Weiss (1992), for example, consider the product categories of aluminum foil and dry dog food. Their explanatory variables include brand experience, advertising exposure and price. They also find that the direct impact of advertising appears small in comparison to other marketing variables like price. Examining the interaction of price with advertising exposure, they further report that increased advertising exposure is associated with greater brand choice price sensitivity. One interpretation is that advertising increases the "identifiability" of different brands and thereby promotes price comparisons.[127] Deighton, Henderson and Neslin (1994) consider ketchup and detergent. They find a large inertia (loyalty) effect, in that a buyer is likely to purchase the same brand as was bought on the previous shopping trip. Allowing for interactions between previous purchase and advertising, they find that advertising does little

[125] Let $x^i_{bk}(n)$ denote the brand experience that consumer i has at the time of the nth purchase occasion for the brand associated with the brand-size alternative k. Then $x^i_{bk}(n) = \alpha_b x^i_{bk}(n-1) + (1-\alpha_b)d^i_k(n-1)$, where $d^i_k(n-1)$ is a 0–1 dummy variable that takes value 1 if consumer i bought the brand associated with brand-size k at purchase occasion $(n-1)$. The smoothing constant α_b is selected by trial and then refined. Size experience is measured similarly.

[126] Pedrick and Zufryden (1991) consider the yogurt product category. In comparison to Tellis's (1988) study, they report a stronger direct effect of advertising exposure on brand choice.

[127] This is in the spirit of Steiner's (1973, 1978, 1984, 1993) work. See Section 3.2.4.

to change the repeat-purchase probabilities of consumers that have just purchased the brand. Advertising can be effective, however, in attracting consumers who have not recently purchased the brand.

The studies above are published in marketing journals, but economists are now also conducting related analyses. Ackerberg (2001) constructs a binary logit model to explain the household choice of whether to purchase a newly introduced yogurt product, Yoplait 150. Explanatory variables include previous purchase measures, advertising exposure, price and time. Advertising is also interacted with an experience variable, where a consumer is experienced (inexperienced) if he has (never) purchased Yoplait 150 in the past. Advertising's effect on inexperienced consumers is positive and significant, whereas advertising has only a small and insignificant effect on experienced consumers. Ackerberg also considers a specification in which experience is measured in terms of the number of previous purchases. He finds that the effectiveness of advertising declines as the consumer becomes more experienced (i.e., as the number of previous purchases increases).[128]

The models described above endogenize consumers' current brand choices but are nevertheless "reduced form". Consumers' past purchases are regarded as exogenous data that generate a brand experience attribute with which to better explain current brand choices. On the other hand, in a "structural" empirical model, the consumers' dynamic choice problem is fully specified, and the parameters of the consumers' utility function and/or constraints are estimated. A structural model thus may offer greater insight into the process through which advertising affects consumer purchase behavior.

In Erdem and Keane's (1996) structural model, the utility that a consumer derives from the purchase of a brand is a function of the brand's attributes and a random component; however, for each brand there is now an attribute ("quality") whose value is uncertain and experienced with noise. The utility function is parameterized to allow that the consumer may be risk averse with respect to the experienced value of this attribute. The consumer seeks to learn the mean value of a brand's attribute, and the precision of the consumer's information may be improved by direct experience with the brand and observation of brand advertising messages. A forward-looking consumer thus may experiment and purchase a brand today, in order to acquire information. The method of simulated maximum likelihood is used to estimate parameters that describe the utility function and the precision of experience and advertising exposure signals, so as to best explain brand choices. Using scanner data and household advertising exposure data for different brands of laundry detergent, Erdem and Keane report that consumers are risk averse and that experience is much more informative than advertising. The model thus provides insight into *how* brand loyalty is formed: due to risk aversion, consumers are loyal to brands that have delivered positive use experiences.

[128] Shum (2004) reports similar findings in his study of household brand choice in the breakfast cereal category. His investigation uses scanner data for 50 brands of breakfast cereal combined with an aggregate measure of advertising exposure (namely, quarterly brand-level national advertising expenditures).

Ackerberg (2003) offers a related structural model of brand choice. In his utility specification, however, the consumer may be interested in observed advertising for two reasons. First, if a consumer's prior belief is that a brand's advertising intensity is positively associated with the value of its attribute, then observed brand advertising provides indirect (signaling) information as to the brand's attribute value. Second, if a consumer directly values the prestige effect that higher brand advertising intensity is perceived to imply, then greater observed brand advertising is indicative of a higher direct utility from brand purchase. Using scanner data and advertising exposure data for Yoplait 150, Ackerberg conducts a structural estimation. Identification of the informative and prestige effects is possible, since the informative effect suggests that advertising affects the purchase probabilities of inexperienced consumers only whereas the prestige effect implies that advertising also affects the purchase probabilities of experienced consumers. Ackerberg reports that advertising has a large and significant informative effect and an insignificant prestige effect.[129]

Finally, as Ippolito and Mathios (1990) illustrate, the effect of advertising on household purchase behavior also may be examined using event studies. They focus on the ready-to-eat cereal market. In response to growing evidence of fiber's potential cancer-preventing benefit, a regulatory ban in the U.S. on health-claim advertising by cereal producers was lifted in 1985. Using brand-level cereal consumption data, Ippolito and Mathios find that fiber cereal consumption increased significantly, once the ban on health-claim advertising was removed. They also use brand-level cereal consumption data for samples of individuals in 1985 (prior to most health-claim advertising) and 1986 (more than a year after health-claim advertising began). The household data suggest that advertising lowered the cost of acquiring health-related information for individuals who were not well reached by other health information sources.

In broad terms, the studies described above point toward a number of striking conclusions. For a set of frequently purchased consumer goods: (1) experience is a very important determinant of household purchase behavior; (2) advertising also influences household purchase behavior, but experience is the more powerful input; (3) advertising and experience are substitutes, in that advertising is less effective in influencing purchase behavior for households that have recent experience with the brand; and (4) much

[129] The studies above emphasize the effect of advertising on household purchase behavior for various consumer goods. By contrast, Shachar and Anand (1998) consider the effect of "tune-in" ads (i.e., TV ads in which a network advertises one of its own shows) on the TV viewing decisions of individuals. Viewers are assumed to possess greater prior information about the existence and attributes of regular shows than specials; thus, a differential effect of tune-in ads on viewing decisions across the two show categories may suggest that advertising has informational content. Using a Neilsen data set that records individual characteristics and viewing behavior, Shachar and Anand specify a nested multinomial logit model and report estimates indicating that a differential effect is indeed present. Anand and Shachar (2004b) provide further support for the informative content of tune-in ads. Consistent with the models reviewed in Section 6.3, they provide evidence that advertising enables buyers to better match their respective tastes with the product attributes offered by different shows. Finally, Byzalov and Shachar (2004) also study TV viewing decisions and report that advertising has a negligible direct effect on utility; instead, advertising provides information and thereby reduces the uncertainty that risk-averse consumers face when contemplating purchase of the advertised product.

of advertising's effect derives from the information that it contains or implies. On the whole, the studies provide support for the informative view of advertising.

The studies are of particular interest in light of the long-standing debate as to whether advertising deters entry. As discussed in Section 7.1, existing theory demonstrates that informational product differentiation may be a barrier to entry; however, the theoretical literature to this point does not clearly identify a sense in which advertising "reinforces" consumers' experience and exacerbates the informational barrier to entry. Likewise, the studies described above support the idea that consumer experience is an important asset for pioneering brands; however, they suggest that advertising itself does little to reinforce experience.

At the same time, it must be emphasized that the studies have important limitations. First, they focus on a narrow set of consumer goods. An important task of future work is to determine the extent to which the conclusions of these studies extend to other goods. Second, the studies treat price and advertising exposure as exogenous variables. This is a concern, since brand choice may depend upon attributes that are observable to market participants but unobservable to the econometrician. In this case, price and advertising exposure may be correlated with the error term.[130] The possibility of endogeneity bias thus motivates a structural approach that jointly estimates demand function parameters along with parameters that determine firm behavior. Work of this kind is considered in the next subsection.

8.2. *Advertising and firm conduct*

I consider next empirical studies that reflect the strong influence of the intervening theoretical work and emphasize firm conduct. Some studies adopt a reduced-form approach and evaluate the predictions of strategic theories of advertising, while others adopt a more structural approach and specify demand functions, cost functions and supply relationships.

Consider first the reduced-form studies that assess the predictions of strategic advertising theories. While some recent papers discussed in Section 3 report evidence that is relevant for the descriptive validity of intervening theoretical work, I illustrate this style of analysis here using papers by Thomas, Shane and Weiglet (1998), Horstmann and MacDonald (2003) and Ellison and Ellison (2000). I do this for two reasons. First, these papers identify and assess predictions that are tightly linked with the intervening theoretical work. Second, it is useful to collect as many papers as possible in Section 3, so that the topic treatments found there may be more self contained.

Using auto industry data, Thomas, Shane and Weiglet assess the advertising–quality relationship. They provide evidence that models priced higher than the full-information price tend to have higher advertising levels. Referring to the Milgrom–Roberts (1986) model, the authors emphasize that this behavior is consistent with the hypothesis that

130 For further discussion, see Berry (1994), Villas-Boas and Winer (1999) and Nevo (2001).

manufacturers of high-quality models signal unobservable quality attributes by setting prices above full-information levels and advertising expenditures beyond those incurred by manufacturers of low-quality models.[131] The signaling interpretation is further supported by the finding that these relationships are weaker for older models. Finally, as the repeat-business effect suggests, they find that automobiles that experience higher sales five years after introduction are characterized by greater advertising in the introductory period. These findings are broadly consistent with Nelson's (1974b) reasoning, but he does not address the possibility that price and advertising serve as joint signals of quality. The predicted relationships between price and advertising are thus strongly influenced by the intervening theoretical work.

Horstmann and MacDonald (2003) provide a related analysis that focuses on the compact disc player market. Using panel data on advertising and pricing during 1983–1992 and controlling for product features, firm heterogeneity and aggregate effects, they provide evidence that advertising increases after a player is introduced and price falls from the outset. As Horstmann and MacDonald observe, this pattern is not easily reconciled with signaling models in which advertising is dissipative. A possible interpretation of this pattern is provided by the static signaling model of Section 6.1, however, when advertising is demand-enhancing and a higher-quality product has a higher marginal cost. The high-quality monopolist then best signals its quality by distorting its demand-enhancing advertising downward and its price upward. In the dynamic perspective suggested by that model, the high-quality product's demand-enhancing advertising increases over time and its price falls over time.

Ellison and Ellison (2000) consider the behavior of pharmaceutical incumbents in the period of time that precedes the loss of patent protection. The incentive to deter entry is greatest in intermediate-sized markets, since entry deterrence is unnecessary (impossible) in markets that are sufficiently small (large). For prescription drugs, incumbent advertising has a public-good aspect, in that some of the benefits may accure to generic entrants; thus, an incumbent operating in an intermediate-sized market has a potential incentive to reduce advertising and thereby reduce the profitability of entry. This rationale for diminished advertising is weakened in larger markets, as the incumbent's focus switches from deterrence to accommodation. Arguing in this way, Ellison and Ellison build on intervening theoretical work [e.g., Fudenberg and Tirole (1984)] and offer a novel prediction: advertising may be reduced most rapidly in years prior to patent expiration in markets of intermediate size. Using data on 63 drugs that faced patent expirations over 1986–1992, they also report evidence that supports this prediction.

[131] Specifically, the authors first regress model i's price at time t on the model's observable quality attributes (horsepower, etc.) and other variables. The residual is interpreted as capturing deviations from the full-information price that are due to unobservable quality attributes. Second, they regress the advertising level for model i at time t on the corresponding price residual (and other variables). A positive coefficient is consistent with the described hypothesis.

Consider next empirical studies that follow the methodology of the "new empirical industrial organization" (NEIO) and adopt a more structural approach. It is instructive to contrast the NEIO approach with the earlier structure-conduct-performance paradigm (SCPP) that underlies the inter-industry studies of Bain (1956), Comanor and Wilson (1967, 1974) and followers. In broad terms, the SCPP makes two assumptions: (1) across large groups of industries, a stable and causal relationship runs from exogenous structural characteristics through conduct to performance; and (2) market-power measurements of performance may be calculated from available (e.g., accounting profit) data. As Bresnahan (1989) explains, the NEIO is distinguished from the SCPP in several respects. Among these are: (1) the assumption of symmetry across industries is abandoned, and instead an econometric model of a single industry (or a closely related set of markets) is developed; (2) market power is not treated as observable, and instead the analyst infers marginal cost from firm behavior; and (3) firm and industry conduct are not treated as simple implications of market-structure variables, and instead the analyst specifies behavioral equations that are based on theoretical models and uses estimates to test between models.

The standard NEIO analysis has three basic ingredients.[132] First, demand functions are specified. For example, a firm's output may be a linear function of own and rival prices as well as exogenous demand variables like income. Second, marginal cost functions are specified. A firm's marginal cost might be a linear function of its output and exogenous cost variables like input prices, for instance. Third, supply relationships are specified. A firm's supply relationship corresponds to a first-order condition for optimizing behavior. Once the marginal cost functions are substituted into the firms' respective supply relationships, the demand functions and supply relationships constitute an econometric system of equations, in which outputs and prices are endogenous variables, and the demand, marginal cost and any conduct parameters may be estimated.

How are the supply relationships specified? Under one approach, the supply relationships include a conjectural variations or conduct parameter that is estimated as a continuous variable. Under appropriate conditions, the conduct parameter can be identified and a performance inference thereby obtained.[133] The conjectural variations approach includes as special cases a number of hypotheses as to firm behavior. The analyst may then test among these hypotheses using nested methods. But the approach also has limitations: the estimated conduct parameter may not correspond to any particular model of firm behavior, and some interesting types of behavior (such as asymmetric collusion) may not be included as special cases. An alternative approach is to consider a menu of models. For example, the Bertrand, Stackelberg and Collusive models imply distinct supply relationships that may be individually considered. Under the menu approach, the analyst may test among models using non-nested methods and then emphasize parameter estimates for the preferred model.

[132] See Bresnahan (1989), Church and Ware (1999) and Kadiyali, Sudhir and Rao (2001).

[133] The conjectural variations approach is pioneered by Iwata (1974). See Nevo (1998) and Corts (1999) for discussion of identification problems under the conjectural variations approach.

Some recent NEIO studies include advertising as an endogenous variable. The models are then more complex. Each firm may have multiple choice variables; furthermore, if a goodwill effect is allowed, then the demand functions and supply relationships must be dynamic. If the conjectural variations approach is adopted, then dynamic conduct parameters may be specified and estimated, where such parameters indicate a firm's perception as to how a change in its current behavior would alter rival behavior in the future. The identification of structural parameters then requires that some restrictions be placed on the dynamic conduct parameters. Finally, it is desirable that the specification of demand functions be sufficiently flexible to include the primary (market-size) and selective/combative (market-share) effects of advertising.

Roberts and Samuelson (1988) offer an early study of this general nature. They develop an analysis of dynamic non-price rivalry among U.S. cigarette manufacturers in high- and low-tar cigarette markets over the 1971–1982 period.[134] The demand functions are specified in a multiplicatively separable fashion that facilitates the identification of the market-size and market-share effects of advertising. Making use of factor demand data, Roberts and Samuelson estimate marginal costs directly.[135] Finally, the supply relationships are captured as dynamic first-order conditions for firms' goodwill choices, where a firm's dynamic conduct parameter is restricted to describe the extent to which an increase in the firm's goodwill stock at date t would induce rivals to increase their goodwill stocks in period $t + 1$. Their estimates suggest that advertising is not combative; in fact, advertising in new-product categories (i.e., in the low-tar market) appears to expand market sizes and constitute a public good among firms. They further report that the estimated dynamic conduct parameters are negative. Evidently, firms are not naive: each recognizes that an increase in its own advertising would encourage less (market-size-expanding) advertising from rivals in the future.

Using data on the Coca-Cola and Pepsi-Cola markets over the 1968–1986 period, Gasmi, Laffont and Vuong (1992) illustrate the menu approach. They specify a demand function for each product, where sales depend on own and rival price and advertising selections. The demand specification presumes that advertising has no goodwill effect. Marginal cost is constant at a value that is specified to be linear in input prices. Using the demand and cost specifications, they then turn to the supply relationships and derive first order conditions for each firm in price and advertising, where the parameters of these conduct equations take different restrictions as different oligopoly games (Nash in prices and advertising, Nash in prices and collusion in advertising, etc.) are

[134] Cigarette advertising was banned from TV and radio over this period, but substantial advertising expenditures were made in magazines, newspapers and outdoor media.

[135] The approach here is to specify a total cost function, use Shephard's lemma to derive a system of factor demands and then estimate the parameters of this system. With the cost parameters thus estimated, the estimated value of marginal cost can be determined as a function of input prices and output volumes. See Bresnahan (1989, pp. 1039–1040) for discussion of the strengths and weaknesses of this approach relative to the alternative approach mentioned previously, whereby marginal cost is inferred from the supply behavior of firms.

considered. For any given game, the two demand and four conduct equations can be simultaneously estimated, where the six endogenous variables are the prices, advertising levels and quantities of the two firms. After determining the best-fitting game, the authors then emphasize the associated parameter estimates. Their analysis suggests that Coca-Cola was a Stackelberg leader in price and advertising until a mid-sample period (1976). After this period, duopoly conduct is characterized by collusion in advertising and possibly price. In this context, their estimates suggest that advertising in the cola market is largely combative.

This approach is also used by Kadiyali (1996), who analyzes the U.S. photographic film industry. In the 1970s, Kodak had a virtual monopoly of this industry; however, Kodak accommodated entry by Fuji in the 1980s. Kadiyali refers to 1970–1980 (1980–1990) as the pre-entry (post-entry) period. She specifies a demand function and a constant marginal cost for each firm, and then considers the two periods separately. In the pre-entry period, only Kodak is active, and the supply relationship is described by Kodak's pricing and advertising first-order conditions. In the post-entry period, the supply relationship is described by pricing and advertising first-order conditions for both firms, where the parameters of these conditions assume different restrictions as different post-entry games are considered. Kadiyali's parameter estimates for the pre-entry period indicate that Kodak maintained its monopoly position by using limit pricing and high advertising. As in the Bagwell–Ramey (1988) model, a possible interpretation is that Kodak reduced price and raised advertising in order to signal low costs. Kadiyali's estimates for the post-entry period suggest several conclusions, including: (1) Kodak was compelled to accommodate Fuji by 1980, since Fuji enjoyed demand and cost advantages; (2) Kodak and Fuji then colluded in price and advertising, putting a large weight on Fuji's profit; and (3) advertising expanded market size and constituted a public good across firms.

Finally, Slade (1995) develops a dynamic "state-space" approach with which to study price and advertising brand rivalry. In this formulation, firms adopt Markov strategies that determine price and advertising behavior, given the current state of play. The empirical model is described by demand and strategy equations. The endogenous variables of the strategy equations are the size and probability of price and advertising changes, while the exogenous variables include factor prices (costs) and past endogenous choices (goodwill). Using weekly price, sales and advertising data for four brands of saltine crackers sold in grocery stores in a small town, Slade obtains estimates suggesting that a brand's sales are decreasing (increasing) in own price (advertising) and increasing (decreasing) in rival-brand price (advertising). Advertising is thus combative, but it has an overall positive effect on market size. Given the specification of linear demand and costs, the demand coefficient estimates may be used to draw inferences about the strategic environment. Slade reports cross-brand evidence that advertising efforts are strategic substitutes, prices are strategic complements, and low prices and high advertising make a brand "tough" (i.e., reduce rival-brand profits). In the dynamic game, firms thus compete aggressively in advertising and accommodate when setting prices, but the resulting high prices do not reflect collusive behavior.[136] A further implication is that entry-deterring behavior would involve limit pricing and high advertising.

Placing firm conduct at centerstage, the empirical studies reviewed here are strongly influenced by the intervening theoretical work. While the NEIO analysis of advertising is just getting underway, it is already clear that one conclusion of the earlier empirical work is retained: the effects of advertising vary importantly across markets. The recent work also generates some interesting specific findings. First, in some markets, there is evidence that firms choose advertising in a collusive manner. This contrasts with a common view that firms compete aggressively in non-price variables, although support for the common view is found in other markets. Second, while advertising is often combative, there is also some support for the market-size effect (e.g., in new-product categories). Finally, some studies offer new evidence that limit pricing and high advertising may deter entry. While these are interesting findings, the primary contribution of the existing NEIO advertising studies is methodological.[137] The studies reviewed here pave the way for what should be an active and valuable research area in the coming years.

8.3. Summary

The research described here constitutes an important advance in the empirical analysis of advertising. While the earlier inter-industry analyses searched for evidence of general causal relationships from structure to performance, the studies reviewed above emphasize the limitations of the inter-industry approach and instead use new disaggregated data sources to explore household and firm conduct. One set of studies examine purchase decisions, using household-level brand-purchase and advertising-exposure panel data. These data offer a remarkable opportunity to study a long-standing and fundamental question in the economic analysis of advertising: Does advertising reinforce consumer experience and insulate pioneering firms from entry? A second set of studies integrate game-theoretic models of advertising into the empirical investigation. Some studies examine the descriptive validity of the models, while others implant a model of the supply relationship into the system of equations that is to be estimated. These studies offer a window into the strategic conduct of firms.

9. Sunk costs and market structure

As Sections 5 through 7 reveal, an important lesson of game-theoretic models in industrial organization is that details may matter. Empirical efforts that follow the SCPP and

[136] Nevo (2001) draws a similar conclusion in his analysis of the ready-to-eat cereal industry. See also Vilcassim, Kadiyali and Chintagunta (1999).

[137] The work described above highlights two advantages of the structural methodology: it may be used to estimate unobserved economic parameters and to compare the predictive power of alternative theories. A further advantage is that an estimated structural model may be used to make policy recommendations. Dube, Hitsch and Manchanda (2005) perform an analysis of this kind.

seek inter-industry confirmation of sweeping causal hypotheses are thus too ambitious. But what are the alternatives? As illustrated by the NEIO studies reviewed in the previous section, one alternative empirical strategy is to focus on a particular industry, where more details are observed and the theory imposes tighter restrictions. As Sutton (1991) emphasizes, a second strategy is to cull from the game-theoretic models a few robust implications and then examine those implications at inter-industry and industry levels. In this section, I provide a brief review of work by Sutton and others that follows this second strategy.[138]

9.1. Main ideas

Sutton develops robust predictions that concern the manner in which the endogeneity of sunk costs and the "toughness of price competition" influence the relationship between market size and concentration.[139] To this end, he models industry equilibrium in terms of a multi-stage game, in which firms enter, sink costs, and then compete (e.g., in prices) in the product market. Considerable latitude is allowed as to whether firms sell horizontally or vertically differentiated products, move sequentially or simultaneously within given stages of the game, sell single or multiple products, or choose prices or outputs.

Sutton distinguishes between two categories of industries. In an *exogenous sunk cost industry*, the only sunk costs are exogenous setup costs. These are the costs of acquiring a single plant of minimum efficient scale and perhaps advertising at some threshold level. An exogenous sunk cost industry may be an industry with homogeneous or horizontally differentiated goods, for example. In an *endogenous sunk cost industry*, by contrast, a firm incurs advertising (or R&D) outlays which result in an enhanced demand for that firm's product in the subsequent stage of product–market competition.[140] As in the first example described in Section 4, an industry is characterized by endogenous sunk costs if products are vertically differentiated as a consequence of brand-image advertising, for instance. Sutton is not concerned with the reason that advertising works in such an industry; rather, he assumes that it does and then examines the implications.

Consider first the case of an exogenous sunk cost industry. To illustrate the key predictions, imagine that firms sell products that are differentiated in a symmetric sense, so that the equilibrium price when N firms enter may be represented as $p(N \mid \theta)$, where θ denotes the toughness of price competition.[141] For example, θ may correspond to transportation costs or competition policy. A firm's cost function is $C(q) = cq + \sigma$, where

[138] For further discussion, see Bresnahan (1992), Schmalensee (1992), Sutton (1997a) and Sutton's contribution to this volume.

[139] Sutton's analysis builds on that in Shaked and Sutton (1983, 1987, 1990).

[140] The analysis is extended to include endogenous R&D sunk costs in Sutton (1997b, 1998). For an early analysis of this kind, see Dasgupta and Stiglitz (1980).

[141] For example, Dixit and Stiglitz (1977), Shubik and Levitan (1980) and Sutton (1997a, 1998) provide models of this kind. My discussion here follows that in Sutton (1997a).

$\sigma > 0$ denotes the exogenous setup costs that are associated with entry. An increase in the market size $S > 0$ is accomplished through successive replications of the consumer population. This ensures that the distribution of tastes is not altered, so that the equilibrium price does not depend directly upon market size. Ignoring the setup cost σ, it is then possible to denote a firm's equilibrium gross profit function as $S\Pi(N \mid \theta)$. In most such models, $p(N \mid \theta)$ is non-increasing in N and $p(N \mid \theta) > c$ for all N.[142] Assume then that $\Pi(N \mid \theta)$ is positive and decreasing in N, with $\Pi(N \mid \theta) \to 0$ as $N \to \infty$. The equilibrium level of entry is determined by $S\Pi(N \mid \theta) = \sigma$.

Using this example, two predictions can be described. First, as market size S increases indefinitely relative to the setup cost σ, the equilibrium concentration, measured as $1/N$, converges monotonically to zero. Intuitively, an increase in market size always raises profit and invites further entry, where the additional entry restores the zero-profit requirement by reducing each firm's market share without increasing its markup. Economies of scale thus become unimportant as a barrier to entry in markets that are sufficiently large. The second prediction concerns the effect of an increase in the toughness of price competition. An increase in θ is associated with a reduction in $p(N \mid \theta)$. Assume then that $\Pi(N \mid \theta)$ is decreasing in θ. Under this assumption, a second prediction follows: an increase in the toughness of price competition shifts the equilibrium concentration upward. This simply reflects the familiar intuition that fewer firms can enter in a zero-profit equilibrium, when price competition is more vigorous.

As Sutton discusses, the main features of this example generalize across a wide range of models. In some of these models, multiple equilibria may arise. For example, if products are horizontally differentiated, then there may exist many single-product firms or a smaller number of multi-product firms. The functional relationship just described between concentration and market size is thus replaced by a lower bound relation. More generally, as Sutton (1991, p. 308) states, the two robust predictions for exogenous sunk cost industries are: (i) the function that gives the lower bound to equilibrium concentration converges monotonically to zero as market size increases; and (ii) this lower bound shifts upward, in response to an increase in the toughness of price competition. These predictions are illustrated in Figure 28.3a.

Consider second the case of an endogenous sunk cost industry. As Sutton (1991, p. 47) puts it, the main point is then as follows:

> "If it is possible to enhance consumers' willingness-to-pay for a given product to some minimal degree by way of a proportionate increase in *fixed* cost (with either no increase or only a small increase in unit variable costs), then the industry will not converge to a fragmented structure, however large the market becomes."

As this quotation suggests, in endogenous sunk cost industries, the negative relationship between concentration and market size breaks down.

142 An exception is the case of Bertrand competition with homogeneous goods. In this case, only one firm enters, regardless of market size.

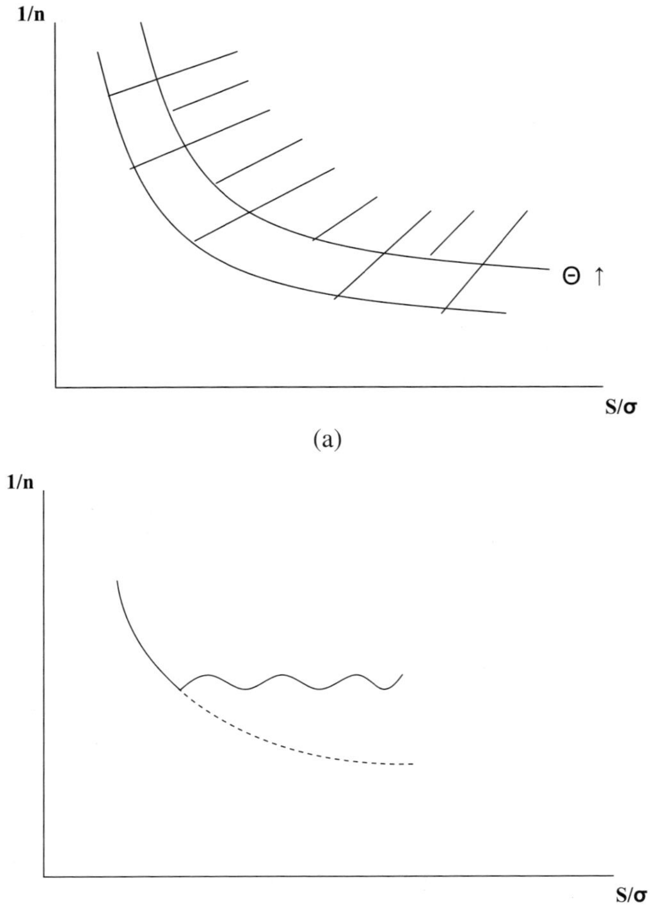

Figure 28.3. Concentration and market size.

Formally, suppose that a firm's product is described in terms of a single vertical attribute, u, where the willingness-to-pay of all consumers is increasing in u. In an endogenous sunk cost industry, a firm's advertising expenditures may affect its brand image and thus u; therefore, let the advertising response function, $A(u)$, indicate the sunk expenditure that a firm must incur in order to achieve u, where $A(u)$ is non-negative and increasing. A firm's total fixed cost expenditure is then $F(u) = A(u) + \sigma$. Let $c(u) \geqslant 0$ denote the firm's unit cost of production. Now, assume that there exist constants $\alpha > 0$ and $K > 1$ such that by incurring K times more fixed costs than any of its rivals, a firm will achieve a final stage (i.e., gross) profit that is no less than αS, where S corresponds to total consumer expenditure in the market. This assumption can be understood as embodying two features: (i) a sufficiently high attribute implies a certain minimal level of profit in the final stage (i.e., $c(u)$ does not increase too quickly with u), and (ii) a certain large increase in fixed advertising expenditures translates into a sufficiently high attribute (i.e., $F(u)$ is increasing and continuous, with an elasticity that is bounded above). Under this assumption, as Sutton (1991, pp. 73–74) establishes, a non-convergence property is implied: there exists some $B > 0$ such that some firm must enjoy at least a fraction B of total industry sales at any subgame perfect equilibrium, independent of the size of the market.[143]

The proof is instructive and simple. For a given equilibrium, let $\bar{u}$ denote the highest value of u offered by any firm, and let $\bar{m}$ denote the highest share of industry sales enjoyed by any firm. The profit in the final stage to any firm clearly cannot exceed $\bar{m}S$. Hence, if the firm that offers $\bar{u}$ is to earn non-negative profit in the game, then it is necessary that

$$\bar{m}S \geqslant F(\bar{u}). \tag{9.1}$$

Now suppose a firm were to deviate and advertise to such an extent as to incur fixed costs $KF(\bar{u})$. Using the assumption stated above, the deviant firm enjoys net profit that is at least

$$\alpha S - KF(\bar{u}). \tag{9.2}$$

Using (9.1) and (9.2), it follows that the deviant firm earns at least $\alpha S - K\bar{m}S = [\alpha - K\bar{m}]S$. Of course, in equilibrium, a firm cannot earn net profit in excess of $\bar{m}S$. Therefore, an equilibrium exists only if $\bar{m}S \geqslant [\alpha - K\bar{m}]S$, or equivalently,

$$\bar{m} \geqslant \frac{\alpha}{1+K} \equiv B. \tag{9.3}$$

Thus, as (9.3) confirms, regardless of the size of the market, in any equilibrium the maximal market share must exceed the constant B.

Intuitively, under the assumption that a given proportionate increase in a firm's advertising outlay relative to that of rivals can induce some fixed fraction of consumers to purchase that firm's product at a price that exceeds the firm's unit variable cost, a fragmented market structure cannot stand: some firm would deviate with a large advertising outlay and earn greater profit. In equilibrium, as market size increases, the tendency toward fragmentation is offset by a competitive escalation in advertising outlays. This suggests that the relationship between market size and concentration may be non-monotonic. Sutton provides some examples in support of this suggestion. In

[143] The proof below is developed for a three-stage game between single-product firms, in which firms enter, sink costs and then compete, with simultaneous moves in each stage. In some settings, equilibria may fail to exist, and so only the necessary features of equilibria are characterized. As Sutton explains, the proof may be applied to a variety of related games. For example, if firms sink costs sequentially within the second stage of the game, then the proof applies once the deviant firm is identified as the firm that comes last in the sequence. See Sutton (1997b, 1998) for further discussion of such games.

summary, two robust predictions for endogenous sunk cost industries are that the lower bound to equilibrium concentration (i) is bounded away from zero as market size increases, and (ii) is not necessarily monotonic in market size.[144] Figure 28.3b illustrates.

9.2. *Econometric tests and industry histories*

Sutton (1991) next confronts the predictions of the theoretical analysis with a careful analysis of twenty narrowly defined food and drink manufacturing industries across six countries.[145] He divides the industries into two groups. In the first group, firms sell homogeneous products, and advertising outlays are very low. The homogeneous-goods industries are examined in light of the theoretical predictions for exogenous sunk cost industries. In the second industry group, advertising outlays are moderate to high. The advertising-intensive industries are thus analyzed with reference to the theoretical predictions for endogenous sunk cost industries. Cross-country comparisons afford the necessary variation in market size.

The empirical effort begins with a cross-sectional econometric analysis of observed concentration levels. The empirical regularities that Sutton uncovers are consistent with the predictions of the theory. In the group of homogeneous-goods industries, he reports a strong negative correlation between (four-firm) concentration and the ratio of market size to setup cost, S/σ. He observes further that the lowest levels of concentration found at large values of S/σ are very small (below 5%). By contrast, in the advertising-intensive group, the lowest level of concentration is 25%. Several of these industries also have large values of S/σ. Bounds regression analysis offers further support for the predictions of the theory.

With the inter-industry statistics in place, Sutton next presents a remarkable set of industry studies. Interesting on their own, these studies offer further opportunities for assessing the theory. For example, in his discussion of homogeneous-goods industries, Sutton considers the salt and sugar industries and identifies international differences in competition policy that suggest variation in the toughness of price competition. This variation facilitates an examination of the prediction that, for exogenous sunk cost industries, tougher price competition is associated with more concentrated markets. Broadly, the industry experiences are consistent with this prediction. Likewise, within the group of advertising-intensive industries, Sutton offers convincing qualitative support for the main theoretical ideas. For example, consistent with the hypothesis of a lower bound, in the frozen food industry, a wave of new entry resulted in a fragmentation of the market that sparked a competitive escalation in advertising outlays by leading firms, leading back to a more consolidated structure. Finally, Sutton's case studies also confirm that details matter. Above the lower bound, a rich array of strategic interaction is observed.

[144] Sutton (1991, p. 308) mentions further the robust prediction that an increase in setup cost (σ) results in an increase in the lower bound for concentration.

[145] The six countries are France, Germany, Italy, Japan, the UK and the U.S.

9.3. Related work

Sutton's research is related to several strands of work that are discussed above. I describe here four such relationships. I then mention some recent work that extends Sutton's theoretical and empirical analyses.

Consider first the inter-industry studies of advertising and concentration. As discussed in Section 3.2.1, while the advertising–concentration relationship is central to Kaldor's arguments and the focus of a number of inter-industry studies, the relationship has defied a simple characterization. Sutton (1991, pp. 125–128) explains that his work encompasses a possible interpretation: if the relationship between market size and concentration varies in kind between homogeneous goods and advertising-intensive industries, then the earlier studies, which use pooled data and ignore this switch of regime problem, are misspecified. This interpretation explains further why such studies occasionally report a positive and significant relationship between advertising intensity and concentration. Consistent with Sutton's theory, suppose that (i) a negative (null) relationship exists between concentration and market size for the homogeneous goods (advertising-intensive) group, and (ii) the mean level of concentration is higher in the advertising-intensive group. Under this supposition, if pooled data are used and concentration is regressed on the market size/setup cost ratio and advertising intensity, then a positive coefficient is expected on the advertising intensity variable.

Second, while Sutton studies manufacturing industries, similar relationships may also emerge in retail industries. As discussed in Section 3.2.4, some evidence suggests an association between advertising and the growth of large-scale retail firms. Consider the retail eyeglass industry. In the 1960s, considerable variation existed across states in the U.S. with respect to the legal restrictions imposed on advertising in the retail eyeglass industry. Depending on the scope of other sunk cost outlays, it may be appropriate to regard a retail eyeglass market as characterized by exogenous (endogenous) sunk costs when advertising is (not) restricted in the corresponding state. Interestingly, work by Benham (1972) and others (see footnote 55) suggests that large-scale retail firms operated in states that permitted advertising. Likewise, as Steiner (1978) and Pashigian and Bowen (1994) argue, the growth in manufacturer brand advertising, instigated by the emergence of TV and the growth in (relative) earnings by females, may have substituted for retail service and facilitated the emergence of a more concentrated retail market structure.

In this context, it is also interesting to compare Sutton's theoretical approach with that of Bagwell and Ramey (1994a). As discussed in Section 5.3, Bagwell and Ramey explore a multi-stage model of retail competition, in which firms first enter and then make their advertising, pricing and (cost-reduction) investment decisions. It is straightforward to extend their model to include a market size variable, S, corresponding to the total mass of consumers. If advertising is banned, a zero-profit "random" equilibrium obtains, in which each of the n entering firms sells to S/n consumers. As in Sutton's exogenous sunk cost industries, the market fragments as S gets large. On the other hand, when advertising is endogenous, a zero-profit "advertising" equilibrium obtains, in which entering firms make heterogeneous decisions. As in Sutton's endogenous sunk cost industries, the market does not fragment as S gets large.[146]

Third, Sutton's multi-stage approach, in which advertising outlays are sunk prior to price competition, may be questioned in light of the empirical studies discussed in Section 3.1.1, which find that the effects of advertising on sales are often brief. While this concern has some merit, it should be noted that the no-fragmentation prediction for advertising-intensive industries may also hold when advertising outlays do not precede price choices. Using a variant of the Schmalensee (1976b) model of advertising competition, Schmalensee (1992, pp. 130) suggests that this prediction may be maintained whenever market share is "sufficiently sensitive to variations in *fixed* costs, so that rivalry is both tough and focused on fixed outlays, not on per-unit price–cost margins".[147]

Fourth, it is interesting to compare Sutton's theoretical findings with the persuasive-view (see Section 2) and game-theoretic (see Section 7) examinations of advertising's entry-deterrence effect. Sutton offers some support for the entry-deterrence effect, in that the scope for profitable entry is limited when advertising expenditures escalate. At the same time, it must be noted that Sutton does not offer a theory in which an incumbent firm strategically advertises at a high level in order to deter subsequent entry. In fact, advertising follows the entry choice in Sutton's basic model, so that it is the expectation of future advertising rivalry that restrains entry.

Sutton's theoretical and empirical analyses has been extended in several recent efforts. Symeonidis (2000a) considers the theoretical effect of tougher price competition on concentration in endogenous sunk cost industries. When price competition is tougher, final-stage profits are reduced, giving firms less incentive to sink advertising expenditures in the penultimate stage. As both gross profit and sunk costs are then lower, the overall effect on net profit may be ambiguous. As a general matter, then, in industries with endogenous sunk costs, an increase in the toughness of price competition has a theoretically indeterminant effect on concentration. In recent empirical work, Symeonidis (2000b) examines the evolution of concentration in UK manufacturing industries following a change in competition law that prohibited price-fixing agreements. The resulting increase in the toughness of price competition is associated with greater concentration in exogenous and even endogenous sunk cost industries. The relationship between concentration and market size is negative in exogenous sunk cost industries, and the relationship breaks down in industries with high advertising. These findings are consistent with Sutton's predictions. Other supportive empirical studies of manufacturers are offered by Bronnenberg, Dhar and Dube (2005), who study the geographic distribution of brand market shares across U.S. metropolitan markets for several

[146] In particular, the highest-advertising firm achieves a share of industry sales that is bounded from below by the fraction of informed (i.e., advertising-responsive) consumers, I. See also Bagwell, Ramey and Spulber (1997), who offer a related dynamic model of price competition that describes the evolution of a concentrated retail market structure.

[147] Likewise, in the Bagwell–Ramey (1994a) model, a no-fragmentation prediction occurs, even though advertising and pricing decisions are simultaneously made.

consumer package goods industries, Matraves (1999), who examines the global pharmaceutical industry, and Robinson and Chang (1996), who use PIMS data. Looking across U.S. metropolitan areas, Berry and Waldfogel (2004) study the newspaper industry and offer evidence consistent with Sutton's predictions for endogenous sunk cost industries. Finally, Ellickson (2001a, 2001b) considers the retail supermarket industry. He reports that endogenous sunk costs associated with investments in store size and information and distribution networks are an important source of concentration in this retail market.

9.4. Summary

Sutton's innovative effort contributes importantly at both methodological and substantive levels. Methodologically, Sutton demonstrates an eclectic approach that evaluates game theoretic models by employing traditional inter-industry (SCPP) and recent industry-study (NEIO) empirical methods. This approach invites theorists to explicitly distinguish between the robust and particular implications of their models. Robust implications, such as those associated with the lower bound, may be examined using traditional inter-industry regressions. But there is also a rich set of observed behaviors that occur above the lower bound. The specific experiences of a given industry can be further interpreted using particular strategic models, historical analyses and recent industry-study methods. At the substantive level, Sutton convincingly makes the fundamental point that endogenous sunk costs in the form of advertising outlays often play a critical role in the evolution of market structure. The role of (brand and retail) advertising in the evolution of concentrated retail structures represents a promising direction for future research.

10. New directions and other topics

In this section, I briefly discuss two new directions for advertising research. The first direction concerns the use of advertising in media markets. This is a long-standing research topic that has enjoyed renewed attention in the past few years. The second direction is at an earlier stage and concerns the potential implications of findings in the fields of behavioral economics and neuroeconomics for advertising research. Finally, despite the length of this survey, many topics remain untreated. At the end of the section, I mention a few such topics and identify some research for further reading.

10.1. Advertising and media markets

In the research reviewed above, sellers choose advertising levels and incur a cost when delivering advertising messages to consumers. The models, however, generally treat the cost of advertising as exogenous.[148] How is the price of an advertising message de-

[148] Baye and Morgan (2001) offer a notable exception. As discussed in footnote 74, they focus on a single information gatekeeper (i.e., a "monopoly platform") that sells advertising to firms and information to

termined? As emphasized by Kaldor (1950), advertising and entertainment are often jointly supplied to the consumer: much advertising reaches consumers through media markets. A viewer of a commercial TV broadcast, for example, encounters frequent advertisements, and advertisements are also prominent in magazines, newspapers and radio broadcasts. Advertising revenue is a major source of income for media companies, and such companies naturally have some control over the price of an advertising message. But an advertiser is willing to pay only so much for a message, and the advertiser's willingness-to-pay is driven by the number of potential consumers that the message might reach.

It is useful to think of the media market as a *two-sided market*.[149] In a two-sided market, two groups interact through an intermediary or platform, and inter-group network externalities are present in that members of one group are directly affected by the number from the other group that use the same platform. In the commercial TV market, for example, the two groups that interact are consumers and advertisers, and the platform is the broadcast company. Advertisers benefit when the broadcast has more viewers, since those viewers represent potential consumers for the advertised products. Thus, for a given broadcast, a positive network externality flows from viewers to advertisers. At the same time, viewers may regard ads as a nuisance; and if the nuisance cost outweighs any other benefit that is associated with the ad, then a negative network externality flows from advertisers to viewers. The broadcast company must then ensure that consumers stay on board, by bundling the ads with entertainment.[150]

Anderson and Coate (2005) provide a theory of commercial broadcasting and advertising that captures many of these features.[151] In particular, their model permits a welfare analysis concerning how well the commercial broadcast market fulfills its two-sided role of delivering programming to viewers and enabling advertisers to contact potential consumers. Advertising has a social benefit in their model, since it is the means through which firms inform consumers of the existence of their respective products. But advertising also has a social cost; namely, a viewer incurs a nuisance cost when an ad is viewed. In this general setting, when a broadcaster chooses a level of advertising, it determines the number of viewers and thereby induces a price for advertising at which firms are willing to demand the chosen level of advertising.

The basic model has two channels, where each channel carries one program and a program can be of two possible types (e.g., news or sports). A given viewer can watch

consumers. My focus below is on research that characterizes the price of advertising when multiple media companies exist and compete for firms' advertising messages.

[149] For more on two-sided markets, see Armstrong (2006), Caillaud and Jullien (2003) and Rochet and Tirole (2003).

[150] As noted in Section 2.4, some similar themes appear in work by Barnett (1966), Becker and Murphy (1993) and Telser (1978).

[151] See Armstrong (2006), Dukes (2004), Kind, Nilssen and Sorgard (2003) and Nilssen and Sorgard (2001) for related efforts. Berry and Waldfogel (1999) provide a related empirical analysis of the radio broadcasting market. I do not provide an extensive survey of work on advertising and the media here. Instead, I refer the reader to Anderson and Gabszewicz (2006), who provide a comprehensive and recent review of such work.

only one program, and viewers have different preferences over program types. Viewers are distributed along a Hotelling line, with a viewer's location defining that viewer's ideal program type; and the two possible program types are located at the respective endpoints of that line.[152] A viewer's benefit from viewing one of the possible program types decreases with the distance of this type from the viewer's ideal type. All viewers also suffer a (common) nuisance cost from watching ads. Ads are placed by firms with new goods and inform viewers of the existence and nature of these goods. Firms are differentiated with regard to their desire to advertise: one firm may offer a product that is more likely to be satisfactory to consumers than is the product of another firm. Each firm is a monopoly in its product market, facing consumers who each desire at most one unit and have a common reservation value for a satisfactory product. Once a firm advertises, it therefore prices at the reservation value, sells to those consumers who regard the product as satisfactory, and collects all social surplus associated with the introduction of the new good. Under the assumption that a viewer can watch only one program, each broadcaster has monopoly control over the access by firms to its viewers.[153] When the broadcaster chooses a level of advertising for its program, a price for advertising is induced, and those firms with products that are more often satisfactory elect to advertise.

Anderson and Coate show that the equilibrium level of advertising is below (above) the socially optimal level if the nuisance cost of advertising is low (high). Intuitively, broadcasters determine the level of advertising with the objective of maximizing advertising revenue; thus, the nuisance cost of advertising affects the level of advertising provided by the market only insofar as a broadcaster perceives that additional advertising would induce a marginal viewer to switch off or over to the other program. It is particularly interesting that the market may provide programs that have too few ads. This finding reflects two considerations. First, broadcasters compete for viewers, and they can do so only by lowering advertising levels. Second, for any given set of viewers, each broadcaster has a monopoly in delivering those viewers to advertisers. A broadcaster may thus hold down advertising levels, in order to drive up the price of advertising. A further and related finding is that the level of advertising would be higher if the two programs were operated by a monopoly. The key intuition is that a monopoly broadcaster does not reduce advertising levels in order to compete for viewers; instead,

[152] Anderson and Coate also discuss the endogenous determination of programs. I focus here on their analysis of advertising when programming decisions are given.

[153] In terms of the literature on two-sided markets, each viewer can use only one platform (i.e., watch only one program) and thus *single-homes*. By contrast, a firm can use both platforms (i.e., advertise on both programs) and may thus *multi-home*. As Armstrong (2006) shows, in such a situation a "competitive bottleneck" arises: platform competition is more intense over the party that single-homes. See also Caillaud and Jullien (2003) and Rochet and Tirole (2003). In an extension of their advertising model, Anderson and Coate allow that viewers may be charged subscription fees. Consistent with the literature on two-sided markets, they find that competition often drives such fees to zero (when subsidies for viewing are infeasible; see also footnote 19). Focusing on newspapers, Gabszewicz, Laussel and Sonnac (2001) establish a similar finding. The single-homing assumption is perhaps more natural with respect to newspapers than with TV channels, since with the latter consumers may switch platforms more frequently.

the monopolist is concerned only that greater advertising might cause some viewers to watch no program.

The basic model can be extended in a variety of directions. For example, the assumption that advertising generates a nuisance cost is more plausible in some media markets than in others. Rysman (2004) offers an empirical analysis of the market for Yellow Pages directories. His estimates indicate that consumers value advertising; thus, the nuisance cost of advertising is negative. This is consistent with the idea that consumers visit the Yellow Pages platform to obtain information that is embodied in ads. Similarly, Gabszewicz, Laussel and Sonnac (2001) focus on newspapers, where ads are easily avoided. They make the plausible assumption that ads do not generate a nuisance cost in this context.

At this point, it is useful to remark on some recent trends in the advertising and media industries. Several commentators argue that, over the past several years, firms have increasingly opted for ads that target specific consumer groups.[154] At a broad level, the greater emphasis on targeted advertising seems to reflect two related considerations. First, the returns from mass-audience advertising may be lower due to an underlying fragmentation of media platforms. The commercial TV platform is now a less dominant means of reaching potential consumers, since such consumers increasingly enjoy a range of alternative media platforms, including Internet sites, cable-TV programs and specialty magazines. Second, the relative returns from targeted advertising may be higher due to advances in digital technology. For example, personal video recorder devices, such as TIVO, enable consumers to rapidly skip through TV ads and thus reduce the effectiveness of some mass-audience advertising. At the same time, Internet ads that are affiliated with keywords on search engines better enable firms to target their ads to interested consumers and then measure the impact of these ads.

If the reported trends are accurate, what might they suggest for future research on advertising? First, research on targeted advertising and price discrimination is of special importance. Several recent studies of this kind are mentioned briefly in Section 5 (footnote 76). Second, empirical studies of the substitutability across different media of the demand for advertising may be of particular value. For recent work of this kind, see Fare et al. (2004), Seldon, Jewell and O'Brien (2000), and Silk, Klein and Berndt (2002). Third, the described patterns suggest a greater role for ads that offer information. Consumers are more likely to view such ads, and relevant information may be more easily transmitted using digital media platforms. Theoretical work that further analyzes Nelson's (1974b) match-products-to-buyers effect may be especially relevant. Some recent work on this topic is described in Section 6.3. Finally, as the nature of advertising evolves, so, too, will the industry that "produces" advertising content. Silk and Berndt (1993, 1995, 2004) study the production of advertising and estimate the cost structure of advertising agencies. Interesting future work might further study the on-going evolution of this industry.

[154] See, e.g., Bianco (2004), Delaney (2005), Lewis (2000) and *The Economist* (2005).

10.2. Advertising, behavioral economics and neuroeconomics

As discussed in Section 2, some of the early proponents of the persuasive view, such as Braithwaite (1928) and Robinson (1933), emphasize that advertising alters consumers' tastes and creates brand loyalty. As detailed in Section 3, the empirical implications of this view have been extensively assessed; however, much less attention has been given to the process by which advertising distorts tastes. According to the complementary view, for example, advertising does not change tastes and instead enters as an argument in a stable utility function. As discussed in Section 4, Dixit and Norman (1978) offer a sophisticated normative treatment of persuasive advertising, but they remain somewhat agnostic as to the underlying mechanism through which advertising shifts tastes.

Given this state of affairs, it is natural that economists would seek insights from other disciplines. Two related approaches stand out. First, over the past two decades, behavioral decision research in psychology has contributed to the field of behavioral economics. Work in this field is motivated by the desire to increase the psychological realism of economic models by imposing assumptions that are rooted in psychological regularity. Thus, preference functions or associated behavioral rules that have experimental support are embedded in theoretical models, in order to achieve new theoretical insights and better predictions. Second, in recent years, neuroscience research has used imaging of brain activity and other methods to gather insight into the way that the brain works. This works informs the new and emerging field of neuroeconomics, which seeks to understand economic decision making at a more foundational level.[155]

Recent work by Gabaix and Laibson (2004) illustrates the behavioral approach.[156] They endow some consumers with a behavioral bias by assuming that these consumers are naïve and fail to foresee "shrouded attributes", such as maintenance costs, expensive add-ons and hidden fees. For example, when a guest checks into a hotel, the guest pays a room charge but may not fully anticipate the additional expenses attributable to large markups on extra services (parking, meals, minibar, phone, etc.). In a standard model of price competition between firms, if price advertising were costless, firms would reveal all expenses and compete over the total price. Information revelation may break down in the presence of naïve consumers, however. Firms will not compete by publicly undercutting their competitors' add-on prices, even when advertising is costless, if add-ons have close substitutes that are only exploited by sophisticated consumers and many naïve consumers would drop out of the market altogether once the add-on expenses were made more salient.

The model suggests some novel predictions for advertising theory. First, the competitive pressure that is normally associated with price advertising may be suppressed when

[155] For overviews of behavioral economics and neuroeconomics, respectively, see Camerer and Loewenstein (2004) and Camerer, Loewenstein and Prelec (2005).

[156] See also Brekke and Rege (2004) and Krahmer (2004). The former paper considers how advertising may impact consumers' assessments as to the popularity of a brand, while the latter paper offers a formalization of Nelson's (1974b) memory-activation role for advertising (see footnote 13 and Section 6.2).

pricing is complex and some consumers are thus naïve. Second, in markets with naïve consumers, advertising content is more likely to shroud negative product information. Finally, in comparison to the loss-leader literature reviewed in Section 5.4, a new prediction is that loss-leader behavior (e.g., a low room rate with large markups on extra services) is used by profit-maximizing firms, even when it is costless for firms to make commitments as to add-on prices.

Recent work in neuroscience suggests that human behavior is the outcome of an interaction between distinct neural systems. McClure et al. (2004a) use functional magnetic resonance imaging and report evidence that parts of the limbic system are activated by decisions involving immediately available rewards while regions of the prefrontal cortex are engaged by intertemporal choices. This work provides neurological support for models in which decision makers use a hyperbolic discounting function. More generally, as McClure et al. (2004a, p. 506) explain, recent imaging studies "suggest that human behavior is often governed by a competition between lower level, automatic processes that may reflect evolutionary adaptations to particular environments, and the more recently evolved, uniquely human capacity for abstract, domain-general reasoning and future planning".

The imaging studies motivate new two-system models of decision making. Loewenstein and O'Donoghue (2004) develop a model in which decisions reflect an interaction between a deliberative system that assesses options using a goal-based perspective and an affective system that encompasses emotions and motivational drives. Environmental stimuli might activate one or both systems. With the exertion of willpower (cognitive effort), which is a scarce neural resource, the deliberative system may partially override the affective system. Formally, Loewenstein and O'Donoghue represent the decision-making process as a kind of principal-agent model. The deliberative system (the principal) chooses behavior to maximize its objective function subject to the constraint that it must incur the cost of exerting the willpower that is required to get the affective system (the agent) to carry out the chosen behavior.[157] Focusing on addiction, Bernheim and Rangel (2004) develop a related model in which the brain can operate in a "cold mode" or a "hot mode". At a broad level, the cold (hot) mode is analogous to the deliberative (affective) system. In the Bernheim–Rangel model, however, at any given point in time, either the cold mode or the hot mode is in total control. The model is also dynamic: when an individual makes a decision in the cold mode, he takes into account the associated probability that cues will be encountered that trigger hot modes in the future.

In such two-system models, what is the appropriate measure of decision-maker welfare? Loewenstein and O'Donoghue suggest that the deliberative system objective function guide welfare calculations, but they offer arguments for and against including the cost of exerting willpower. Bernheim and Rangel, on the other hand, unambiguously

[157] For further discussion of self-control and willpower, see Benabou and Tirole (2004).

recommend that welfare be measured using cold-state preferences. In their view, hot-mode decisions are cue-triggered errors that correspond to imperfections in the process by which the brain delivers choices.

What has this to do with advertising? As Braithwaite, Robinson and other persuasive-view advocates argued long ago, advertising is often designed to elicit emotions and motivational drives. In other words, advertising content may be designed to serve as an environmental cue that activates the affective/hot-mode system. If advertising indeed plays this role, then it may be possible to use models similar to those just described and reconsider the welfare effects of persuasive advertising. For example, in the Dixit–Norman (1978) model reviewed in Section 4, the pre-advertising (post-advertising) demand curve may be broadly associated with the deliberative system or the cold mode (the affective system or the hot mode). These models may also give rise to new rationales for bans on advertising of addictive products. More generally, as further advances are achieved in the analysis of two-system models, important new tools may be created for positive and normative analyses of advertising.

Neurological studies may also provide insight into the elusive concept of brand loyalty. McClure et al. (2004b) offer a first study of this kind. In a blind taste test, they find that subjects split equally in their preferences for Coke and Pepsi. When one cup was labeled "Coke", however, individuals showed a significant bias for the labeled cup (even though the unlabeled cup also contained Coke); further, when the subjects were informed that they were drinking Coke, brain regions associated with memory were activated. By contrast, brand knowledge of Pepsi did not have similar effects on choice or brain activity. This study gives striking neurophysiological evidence that is consistent with the hypothesis that some consumers exhibit brand loyalty toward Coke. The full implications of this study are not yet clear; however, it does at least raise the possibility that future neurological studies may provide important and novel insight as to when and how advertising may instill brand loyalty.

10.3. Other topics

Advertising is a huge research area, with key contributions from various disciplines including economics, marketing, psychology, neuroscience and political science. Clearly, it is not possible to summarize all of this work in one survey. Here, I simply mention a few omitted topics and offer suggestions for further reading.

First, I largely ignore the literature that considers the economic consequences of laws against deceptive advertising. Pitofsky (1978) describes the rationale behind the government regulation of truth-in-advertising. Sauer and Leffler (1990) provide an empirical assessment of the implications of such regulation for advertising content. In a recent effort, Barigozzi, Garella and Peitz (2002) show that laws concerning the veracity of comparative advertisements can enhance the signaling potential of advertising. Second, I ignore many aspects of advertising that are emphasized in other social sciences. Advertising plays an important role in political contests, for example. For recent work of this kind, see Coate (2004) and Prat (2002). Finally, the success of a given ad depends in part on the associations that it triggers in consumers' minds and thus hinges on specific psychological considerations that are not considered here. For research of this kind, see Kardes (2002).

10.4. Summary

I discuss in this section two new directions for advertising research. First, recent work returns to a long-standing research topic and analyzes the role of advertising in media markets. This work highlights the two-sided nature of the media market, and provides novel insights regarding the endogenous determination of the price of advertising and the potential welfare consequences of advertising. Second, recent work also considers the implications of findings in the fields of behavioral economics and neuroeconomics for advertising research. This work is just getting underway but already offers striking new perspectives on persuasive advertising and brand loyalty.

11. Conclusion

This survey is written with two objectives in mind. A first objective is to summarize the economic analysis of advertising in a way that brings to the surface the more essential contributions and thereby clarifies *what* is known. To this end, I describe these contributions and summarize the main theoretical and empirical findings. These summaries are found at the close of the various sections (and subsections) above.

The second objective is to clarify *how* this knowledge has been obtained. Throughout the last century, advertising has provided the field with a number of important and difficult questions, including: Why do consumers respond to advertising? Does advertising reinforce consumer experiences and deter entry? What is the relationship between advertising and concentration, profit, price and quality? Does the market provide too much advertising? With every methodological innovation in the field of industrial organization, economists have turned to these and other questions, demonstrating the additional insight that their new approach affords. In effect, advertising represents a case study with which to assess the progress gained as industrial organization methods have evolved.

But has progress been achieved? As a body, the research summarized in this survey makes a strong case for an affirmative answer. The progress achieved takes several forms. In some cases, progress is destructive in nature, as when recent studies reject the simplistic and often absolutist conclusions put forth by some key early contributors. In other cases, progress is constructive and reflects the discovery of new evidence and the generation of novel insights. Finally, with the development of new data sets and advances in econometric techniques and theoretical models, substantial progress is evident at a methodological level. At the same time, one must not get carried away. While much has been learned, the economic implications of advertising are subtle and controversial, and many of the most important questions remain unresolved.

Acknowledgements

I thank Susan Athey, Alberto Martin, Martin Peitz, Per Baltzer Overgaard, Michael Riordan, Victor Tremblay, Ting Wu and especially Mark Armstrong and Rob Porter for helpful comments. Discussions with Andrew Pyo and Laura Silverman are also gratefully acknowledged.

References

Abernethy, A.M., Franke, G.R. (1996). "The information content of advertising: A meta-analysis". Journal of Advertising 25, 1–17.
Ackerberg, D.A. (2001). "Empirically distinguishing informative and prestige effects of advertising". RAND Journal of Economics 32, 316–333.
Ackerberg, D.A. (2003). "Advertising, learning, and consumer choice in experience good markets: A structural empirical examination". International Economic Review 44, 1007–1040.
Adams, W.J., Yellen, J.L. (1977). "What makes advertising profitable?". Economic Journal 87, 427–449.
Advertising Age: Fact Pack Supplement (2005). February 28.
Albaek, S., Overgaard, P. (1992a). "Advertising and pricing to deter or accommodate entry when demand is unknown: Comment". International Journal of Industrial Organization 12, 83–87.
Albaek, S., Overgaard, P. (1992b). "Upstream pricing and advertising signal downstream demand". Journal of Economics and Management Strategy 1, 677–698.
Albion, M.S. (1983). Advertising's Hidden Effects: Manufacturers' Advertising and Retail Pricing. Auburn House Publishing Company, Boston, MA.
Albion, M.S., Farris, P.W. (1981). The Advertising Controversy: Evidence on the Economic Effects of Advertising. Auburn House Publishing Company, Boston, MA.
Alemson, M.A. (1970). "Advertising and the nature of competition in oligopoly over time: A case study". The Economic Journal 80, 282–306.
Anand, B.N., Shachar, R. (2004a). "The message supports the medium". Mimeo.
Anand, B.N., Shachar, R. (2004b). "Advertising, the matchmaker". Mimeo.
Anderson, S.P., Coate, S. (2005). "Market provision of broadcasting: A welfare analysis". Review of Economic Studies 72, 947–972.
Anderson, S.P., Gabszewicz, J.J. (2006). "The media and advertising: A tale of two-sided markets". In: Ginsburgh, V., Throsby, D. (Eds.), Handbook of the Economics of Art and Culture. Elsevier, Amsterdam.
Anderson, S.P., Renault, R. (2006). "Advertising content". American Economic Review 96, 93–113.
Archibald, R.B., Haulman, C.H., Moody Jr., C.E. (1983). "Quality, price, advertising and published quality ratings". Journal of Consumer Research 9, 347–356.
Armstrong, M. (2006). "Competition in two-sided markets". RAND Journal of Economics 37, 668–691.
Arndt, J., Simon, J. (1983). "Advertising and economies of scale: Critical comments on the evidence". Journal of Industrial Economics 32, 229–242.
Arterburn, A., Woodbury, J. (1981). "Advertising, price competition and market structure". Southern Economic Journal 47, 763–775.
Ashley, R., Granger, C.W.J., Schmalensee, R. (1980). "Advertising and aggregate consumption: An analysis of causality". Econometrica 48, 1149–1168.
Ayanian, R. (1975). "Advertising and rate of return". Journal of Law and Economics 18, 479–506.
Ayanian, R. (1983). "The advertising capital controversy". Journal of Business 56, 349–364.
Backman, J. (1967). Advertising and Competition. New York Univ. Press, New York.
Bagwell, K. (1987). "Introductory price as a signal of cost in a model of repeat business". Review of Economic Studies 54, 365–384.

Bagwell, K. (1990). "Informational product differentiation as a barrier to entry". International Journal of Industrial Organization 8, 207–223.
Bagwell, K. (1991). "Optimal export policy for a new-product monopoly". American Economic Review 81, 1156–1169.
Bagwell, K. (1992). "Pricing to signal product line quality". Journal of Economics and Management Strategy 1, 151–174.
Bagwell, K., Ramey, G. (1988). "Advertising and limit pricing". RAND Journal of Economics 19, 59–71.
Bagwell, K., Ramey, G. (1990). "Advertising and pricing to deter or accommodate entry when demand is unknown". International Journal of Industrial Organization 8, 93–113.
Bagwell, K., Ramey, G. (1991). "Oligopoly limit pricing". RAND Journal of Economics 22, 155–172.
Bagwell, K., Ramey, G. (1993). "Advertising as information: Matching products to buyers". Journal of Economics and Management Strategy 2, 199–243.
Bagwell, K., Ramey, G. (1994a). "Coordination economies, advertising, and search behavior in retail markets". American Economic Review 84, 498–517.
Bagwell, K., Ramey, G. (1994b). "Advertising and coordination". Review of Economic Studies 61, 153–172.
Bagwell, K., Riordan, M.H. (1991). "High and declining prices signal product quality". American Economic Review 81, 224–239.
Bagwell, K., Ramey, G., Spulber, D. (1997). "Dynamic retail price and investment competition". RAND Journal of Economics 28, 207–227.
Bain, J.S. (1949). "A note on pricing in monopoly and oligopoly". American Economic Review 39, 448–464.
Bain, J.S. (1956). Barriers to New Competition: Their Character and Consequences in Manufacturing Industries. Harvard Univ. Press, Cambridge, MA.
Baltagi, B.H., Levin, D. (1986). "Estimating dynamic demand for cigarettes using panel data: The effects of bootlegging, taxation and advertising reconsidered". The Review of Economics and Statistics 68, 148–155.
Banerjee, B., Bandyopadhyay, S. (2003). "Advertising competition under consumer inertia". Marketing Science 22, 131–144.
Barigozzi, F., Garella, P.G., Peitz, M. (2002). "With a little help from my enemy: Comparative advertising". Mimeo.
Barnett, H.J. (1966). "Discussion of the economics of advertising and broadcasting". American Economic Review Paper and Proceedings 56, 467–470.
Bass, F.M. (1969). "A simultaneous equation regression study of advertising and sales of cigarettes". Journal of Marketing Research 6, 291–300.
Baye, M.R., Morgan, J. (2001). "Information gatekeepers on the Internet and the competitiveness of homogeneous product markets". American Economic Review 91, 454–474.
Baye, M.R., Morgan, J. (2004). "Brand and price advertising in online markets". Mimeo.
Becker, G.S., Murphy, K.M. (1993). "A simple theory of advertising as a good or bad". Quarterly Journal of Economics 108, 942–964.
Benabou, R., Tirole, J. (2004). "Willpower and personal rules". Journal of Political Economy 112, 848–886.
Benham, L. (1972). "The effect of advertising on the price of eyeglasses". Journal of Law and Economics 15, 337–352.
Benham, L., Benham, A. (1975). "Regulating through the professions: A perspective on information control". Journal of Law and Economics 18, 421–447.
Berndt, E.R. (1991). "Causality and simultaneity between advertising and sales". In: Berndt, E.R. (Ed.), The Practice of Econometrics: Classic and Contemporary. Addison–Wesley, Reading. Chapter 8.
Bernheim, B.D., Rangel, A. (2004). "Addication and cue-triggered decision processes". American Economic Review 94, 1558–1590.
Bernheim, B.D., Whinston, M. (1990). "Multimarket contact and collusive behavior". RAND Journal of Economics 21, 1–26.
Berreman, J.V. (1943). "Advertising and the sale of novels". Journal of Marketing 7, 234–240.
Berry, S. (1994). "Estimating discrete choice models of product differentiation". RAND Journal of Economics 25, 242–262.

Berry, S., Waldfogel, J. (1999). "Free entry and social inefficiency in radio broadcasting". RAND Journal of Economics 30, 397–420.
Berry, S., Waldfogel, J. (2004). "Product quality and market size". Mimeo.
Bester, H. (1994). "Random advertising and monopolistic price dispersion". Journal of Economics and Management Strategy 3, 545–560.
Bester, H., Petrakis, E. (1995). "Price competition and advertising in oligopoly". European Economic Review 39, 1075–1088.
Bester, H., Petrakis, E. (1996). "Coupons and oligopolistic price discrimination". International Journal of Industrial Organization 14, 227–242.
Bianco, A. (2004). "The vanishing mass market: New technology. Product proliferation. Fragmented media. Get ready: It's a whole new world". Business Week 12 (July), 60–68.
Blake, H.M., Blum, J.A. (1965). "Network television rate practices: A case study in the failure of social control of price discrimination". Yale Law Journal 74, 1339–1401.
Blank, D.M. (1968). "Television advertising: The great discount illusion, or Tonypandy revisited". Journal of Business 41, 10–38.
Bloch, H. (1974). "Advertising and profitability: A reappraisal". Journal of Political Economy 82, 267–286.
Bloch, F., Manceau, D. (1999). "Persuasive advertising in hotelling's model of product differentiation". International Journal of Industrial Organization 17, 557–574.
Borden, N.H. (1942). The Economic Effects of Advertising. Richard D. Irwin, Inc., Chicago.
Boulding, W., Lee, O.-K., Staelin, R. (1994). "Marketing the mix: Do advertising, promotions and sales force activities lead to differentiation?". Journal of Marketing Research 31, 159–172.
Boyd, R., Seldon, B.J. (1990). "The fleeting effect of advertising: Empirical evidence from a case study". Economics Letters 34, 375–379.
Boyer, K.D. (1974). "Informative and goodwill advertising". The Review of Economics and Statistics 56, 541–548.
Boyer, K.D., Lancaster, K.M. (1986). "Are there scale economies in advertising?". Journal of Business 59, 509–526.
Boyer, M., Moreaux, M. (1999). "Strategic underinvestment in informative advertising: The cases of substitutes and complements". Canadian Journal of Economics 22, 654–672.
Braithwaite, D. (1928). "The economic effects of advertisement". Economic Journal 38, 16–37.
Brekke, K.A., Rege, M. (2004). "Advertising as a distortion of social learning". Mimeo.
Bresnahan, T.F. (1984). "The demand for advertising by medium: Implications for the economies of scale in advertising". In: Ippolito, P.M., Scheffman, D.T. (Eds.), Empirical Approaches to Consumer Protection Economics. Federal Trade Commission, Washington, DC, pp. 135–163.
Bresnahan, T.F. (1989). "Empirical studies of industries with market power". In: Schmalensee, R., Willig, R. (Eds.), Handbook of Industrial Organization. vol. 2. North-Holland, Amsterdam, pp. 1011–1057.
Bresnahan, T.F. (1992). "Sutton's sunk costs and market structure: Price competition, advertising, and the evolution of concentration". RAND Journal of Economics 23, 137–152.
Bronnenberg, B.J., Dhar, S.K., Dube, J.-P. (2005). "Endogenous sunk costs and the geographic distribution of brand shares in consumer package goods industries". Mimeo.
Brown, R.S. (1978). "Estimating advantages to large-scale advertising". The Review of Economics and Statistics 60, 428–437.
Brush, B. (1976). "Influence of market structure on industry advertising intensity". Journal of Industrial Economics 25, 55–67.
Bunch, D.S., Smiley, R. (1992). "Who deters entry? Evidence on the use of strategic entry deterrents". The Review of Economics and Statistics 74, 509–521.
Butters, G. (1977). "Equilibrium distributions of sales and advertising prices". Review of Economic Studies 44, 465–491.
Buxton, A.J., Davies, S.W., Lyons, B.R. (1984). "Concentration and advertising in consumer and producer markets". Journal of Industrial Economics 32, 451–464.
Byzalov, D., Shachar, R. (2004). "The risk reduction role of advertising". Quantitative Marketing and Economics 2, 283–320.

Cable, J. (1972). "Market structure, advertising policy, and intermarket differences in advertising intensity". In: Cowling, K. (Ed.), Market Structure and Corporate Behavior. Gray-Mills Publishing, London, pp. 107–124.
Cabral, L. (2000). "Stretching firm and brand reputation". RAND Journal of Economics 31, 658–673.
Cady, J.F. (1976). "An estimate of the price effects of restrictions on drug price advertising". Economic Inquiry 14, 493–510.
Caillaud, B., Jullien, B. (2003). "Chicken and egg: Competition among intermediation service providers". RAND Journal of Economics 34, 309–328.
Camerer, C.F., Loewenstein, G. (2004). "Behavioral economics: Past, present, and future". In: Camerer, C.F., Loewenstein, G., Rabin, M. (Eds.), Advances in Behavioral Economics. Russell Sage Foundation, New York.
Camerer, C., Loewenstein, G., Prelec, D. (2005). "Neuroeconomics: How neuroscience can inform economics". Journal of Economic Literature 43, 9–64.
Caminal, R. (1996). "Price advertising and coupons in a monopoly model". Journal of Industrial Economics 44, 33–52.
Caves, R.E., Greene, D.P. (1996). "Brands' quality levels, prices and advertising outlays: Empirical evidence on signals and information costs". International Journal of Industrial Organization 14, 29–52.
Caves, R.E., Porter, M.E. (1978). "Market structure, oligopoly and stability of market shares". Journal of Industrial Economics 27, 289–312.
Caves, R.E., Uekusa, M. (1976). Industrial Organization in Japan. Brookings Institute, Washington, DC.
Chamberlin, E. (1933). The Theory of Monopolistic Competition. Harvard Univ. Press, Cambridge, MA.
Chandler, A.D. (1990). Scale and Scope: The Dynamics of Industrial Capitalism. Harvard Univ. Press, Cambridge, MA.
Chevalier, J., Kashyap, A., Rossi, P. (2003). "Why don't prices rise during periods of peak demand? Evidence from scanner data". American Economic Review 93, 15–37.
Chioveanu, I. (2005). "Advertising, brand loyalty and pricing". Mimeo.
Choi, J.P. (1998). "Brand extension as informational leverage". The Review of Economic Studies 65, 655–669.
Chu, W. (1992). "Demand signalling and screening in channels of distribution". Marketing Science 11, 327–347.
Church, J.R., Ware, R. (1999). Industrial Organization: A Strategic Approach. McGraw–Hill, New York.
Chwe, M. (2001). Rational Ritual: Culture, Coordination, and Common Knowledge. Princeton Univ. Press, Princeton, NJ.
Clark, C., Horstmann, I. (2005). "Advertising and coordination in markets with consumption scale effects". Journal of Economics and Management Strategy 14, 377–401.
Clarke, D.G. (1976). "Econometric measurement of the duration of advertising effect on sales". Journal of Marketing Research 13, 345–357.
Coate, S. (2004). "Political competition with campaign contributions and informative advertising". Journal of the European Economic Association 2, 772–804.
Comanor, W.S., Wilson, T.A. (1967). "Advertising, market structure and performance". The Review of Economics and Statistics 49, 423–440.
Comanor, W.S., Wilson, T.A. (1974). Advertising and Market Power. Harvard Univ. Press, Cambridge, MA.
Comanor, W.S., Wilson, T.A. (1979). "The effect of advertising on competition: A survey". Journal of Economic Literature 42, 453–476.
Connolly, R.A., Hirschey, M. (1984). "R&D, market structure and profits: A value-based approach". The Review of Economics and Statistics 66, 682–686.
Connor, J.M., Peterson, E.B. (1992). "Market-structure determinants of national brand-private label price differences of manufactured food products". Journal of Industrial Economics 40, 151–172.
Copeland, M.T. (1923). "Relation of consumers' buying habits to marketing methods". Harvard Business Review 1, 282–289.
Corts, K.S. (1999). "Conduct parameters and the measurement of market power". Journal of Econometrics 88, 227–250.

Cowling, K., Cable, J., Kelly, M., McGuinness, T. (1975). Advertising and Economic Behavior. The Macmillan Press, Ltd., London.
Cubbin, J. (1981). "Advertising and the theory of entry barriers". Economica 48, 289–298.
Cubbin, J., Domberger, S. (1988). "Advertising and post-entry oligopoly behavior". Journal of Industrial Economics 37, 123–140.
Dasgupta, P., Stiglitz, J. (1980). "Industrial structure and the nature of innovative activity". Economic Journal 90, 266–293.
de Bijl, P.W.J. (1997). "Entry deterrence and signaling in markets for search goods". International Journal of Industrial Organization 16, 1–19.
Deighton, J., Henderson, C.M., Neslin, S.A. (1994). "The effect of advertising on brand switching and repeat purchasing". Journal of Marketing Research 31, 28–43.
Delaney, K.J. (2005). "Google to buy Urchin software, provider of data for advertisers. In battle with Microsoft, tracking ads' effectiveness is seen as competitive key". The Wall Street Journal March 29, B4.
Demsetz, H. (1973). "Industry structure, market rivalry, and public policy". Journal of Law and Economics 16, 1–9.
Demsetz, H. (1974). "Two systems of belief about monopoly". In: Goldschmid, H.J., Mann, H.M., Weston, J.F. (Eds.), Industrial Concentration: The New Learning. Little, Brown, Boston, pp. 164–184.
Demsetz, H. (1979). "Accounting for advertising as a barrier to entry". Journal of Business 52, 345–360.
Demsetz, H. (1982). "Barriers to entry". American Economic Review 72, 47–57.
Dixit, A. (1980). "The role of investment in entry deterrence". Economic Journal 90, 95–106.
Dixit, A., Norman, V. (1978). "Advertising and welfare". The Bell Journal of Economics 9, 1–17.
Dixit, A., Stiglitz, J. (1977). "Monopolistic competition and optimum product diversity". American Economic Review 67, 297–308.
Domowitz, I., Hubbard, R.G., Petersen, B.C. (1986a). "Business cycles and the relationship between concentration and price–cost margins". RAND Journal of Economics 17, 1–17.
Domowitz, I., Hubbard, R.G., Petersen, B.C. (1986b). "The intertemporal stability of the concentration–margins relationship". Journal of Industrial Economics 35, 13–34.
Doraszelski, U., Markovich, S. (in press). "Advertising dynamics and competitive advantage". RAND Journal of Economics.
Dorfman, R., Steiner, P.O. (1954). "Optimal advertising and optimal quality". American Economic Review 44, 826–836.
Doyle, P. (1968a). "Economic aspects of advertising: A survey". Economic Journal 78, 570–602.
Doyle, P. (1968b). "Advertising expenditure and consumer demand". Oxford Economic Papers 20, 394–415.
Dube, J.-P., Hitsch, G.J., Manchanda, P. (2005). "An empirical model of advertising dynamics". Quantitative Marketing and Economics 3, 107–144.
Duetsch, L.L. (1975). "Structure, performance, and the net rate of entry into manufacturing industries". Southern Economic Journal 41, 450–456.
Dukes, A. (2004). "The advertising market in a product oligopoly". Journal of Industrial Economics 52, 327–348.
Eckard Jr., E.W. (1987). "Advertising, competition, and market share instability". Journal of Business 60, 539–552.
Eckard Jr., E.W. (1991). "Competition and the cigarette TV advertising ban". Economic Inquiry 29, 119–133.
The Economist (2001). "Pro logo: Why brands are good for you". 360.8238, September 8–14, 11, 26–28.
The Economist (2005). "Crowned at last: A survey of consumer power". April 2, 1–16.
Edwards, F.R. (1973). "Advertising and competition in banking". Antitrust Bulletin 18, 23–32.
Ehrlich, I., Fisher, L. (1982). "The derived demand for advertising: A theoretical and empirical investigation". American Economic Review 72, 366–388.
Ekelund Jr., R.B., Saurman, D.S. (1988). Advertising and the Market Process: A Modern Economic View. Pacific Research Institute for Public Policy, San Francisco, CA.
Ellickson, P. (2001a). "Supermarkets as a natural oligopoly". Mimeo.
Ellickson, P. (2001b). "Competition in the supermarket industry: Sunk costs and market structure". Mimeo.

Ellison, G. (2005). "A model of add-on pricing". Quarterly Journal of Economics 120, 585–637.
Ellison, G., Ellison, S.F. (2000). "Strategic entry deterrence and the behavior of pharmaceutical incumbents prior to patent expiration". Mimeo.
Else, P.K. (1966). "The incidence of advertising in manufacturing industries". Oxford Economic Papers 18, 88–105.
Erdem, T., Keane, M. (1996). "Decision-making under uncertainty: Capturing dynamic brand choice processes in turbulent consumer goods markets". Marketing Science 15, 1–20.
Esteban, L., Gil, A., Hernandez, J.M. (2001). "Informative advertising and optimal targeting in a monopoly". The Journal of Industrial Economics 49, 161–180.
Esteban, L., Hernandez, J.M., Moraga-Gonzalez, J.L. (2006). "Customer directed advertising and product quality". Journal of Economics and Management Strategy 15, 943–968.
Esposito, L., Esposito, F. (1971). "Foreign competition and domestic industry profitability". The Review of Economics and Statistics 53, 343–353.
Fare, R., Grosskopf, S., Seldon, B.J., Tremblay, V.J. (2004). "Advertising efficiency and the choice of media mix: A case of beer". International Journal of Industrial Organization 22, 503–522.
Farrell, J. (1986). "Moral hazard as an entry barrier". RAND Journal of Economics 17, 440–449.
Farris, P.W., Albion, M.S. (1980). "The impact of advertising on the price of consumer products". Journal of Marketing 44, 17–35.
Farris, P.W., Albion, M.S. (1987). "Manufacturer advertising and retail gross margins". Advances in Marketing and Public Policy 1, 107–136.
Farris, P.W., Buzzell, R.D. (1979). "Why advertising and promotional costs vary: Some cross-sectional analyses". Journal of Marketing 43, 112–122.
Federal Trade Commission (1980). Staff Report: Effects of Restrictions, on Advertising and Commercial Practice in the Professions: The Case of Optometry. U.S. Government Printing Office, Washington, DC.
Feldman, R.D., Begun, J.W. (1978). "The effects of advertising – Lessons from optometry". Journal of Human Resources 13, 247–262.
Feldman, R.D., Begun, J.W. (1980). "Does advertising of prices reduce the mean and variance of prices?". Economic Inquiry 18, 487–492.
Ferguson, J.M. (1967). "Advertising and liquor". Journal of Business 40, 414–434.
Fershtman, C., Muller, E. (1993). "The benefits of being small: Duopolistic competition with market segmentation". Review of Industrial Organization 8, 101–111.
Fisher, F.M., McGowan, J.J. (1979). "Advertising and welfare: Comment". The Bell Journal of Economics 10, 726–727.
Fluet, C., Garella, P.G. (2002). "Advertising and prices as signals of quality in a regime of price rivalry". International Journal of Industrial Organization 20, 907–930.
Fogg-Meade, E. (1901). "The place of advertising in modern business". Journal of Political Economy 9, 218–242.
Friedman, J. (1983). Oligopoly Theory. Cambridge Univ. Press, Cambridge.
Fudenberg, D., Tirole, J. (1984). "The fat-cat effect, the puppy-dog ploy, and the lean and hungry look". American Economic Review, Papers and Proceedings 74, 361–366.
Gabaix, X., Laibson, D. (2004). "Shrouded attributes and information suppression in competitive markets". Mimeo.
Gabszewicz, J.J., Laussel, D., Sonnac, N. (2001). "Press advertising and the ascent of the 'pensee unique' ". European Economic Review 45, 645–651.
Galbraith, J.K. (1958). The Affluent Society. Houghton-Mifflin, Co., Boston, MA.
Galbraith, J.K. (1967). The New Industrial State. Houghton-Mifflin, Co., Boston, MA.
Galeotti, A., Moraga-Gonzalez, J.L. (2004). "A model of strategic targeted advertising". Mimeo.
Gallet, C.A. (1999). "The effect of the 1971 advertising ban on behavior in the cigarette industry". Managerial and Decision Economics 20, 299–303.
Gasmi, F., Laffont, J.J., Vuong, Q. (1992). "Econometric analysis of collusive behavior in a soft-drink market". Journal of Economics and Management Strategy 1, 277–311.

Geroski, P. (1982). "Simultaneous-equations models of the structure-performance paradigm". European Economic Review 19, 145–158.
Geroski, P. (1995). "What do we know about entry?". International Journal of Industrial Organization 13, 421–440.
Gerstner, E., Hess, J. (1990). "Can bait and switch benefit consumers?". Marketing Science 9, 114–124.
Glazer, A. (1981). "Advertising, information, and prices – A case study". Economic Inquiry 19, 661–671.
Gomes, L.J. (1986). "The competitive and anticompetitive theories of advertising: An empirical analysis". Applied Economics 18, 599–613.
Gorecki, P.K. (1976). "The determinants of entry by domestic and foreign enterprises in Canadian manufacturing". The Review of Economics and Statistics 58, 485–488.
Gort, M. (1963). "Analysis of stability and change in market shares". Journal of Political Economy 71, 51–61.
Gould, J.P. (1970). "Diffusion processes and optimal advertising policy". In: Phelps, E.S. (Ed.), Microeconomic Foundations of Employment and Inflation Theory. Norton, New York, pp. 338–368.
Grabowski, H.G., Mueller, D.C. (1978). "Industrial research and development, intangible capital stocks, and firm profit rates". The Bell Journal of Economics 9, 328–343.
Grabowski, H.G., Vernon, J. (1992). "Brand loyalty, entry, and price competition in pharmaceuticals after the 1984 drug act". Journal of Law and Economics 35, 331–350.
Greer, D.F. (1971). "Advertising and market concentration". Southern Economic Journal 38, 19–32.
Greer, D.F. (1973). "Advertising and market concentration: A reply". Southern Economic Journal 39, 451–453.
Grossman, G.M., Shapiro, C. (1984). "Informative advertising with differentiated products". The Review of Economic Studies 51, 63–81.
Guadagni, P.M., Little, J.D.C. (1983). "A logit model of brand choice calibrated on scanner data". Marketing Science 2, 203–238.
Guth, L. (1971). "Advertising and market structure: Revisited". Journal of Industrial Economics 19, 179–198.
Haas-Wilson, D. (1986). "The effect of commercial practice restrictions: The case of optometry". Journal of Law and Economics 29, 165–186.
Hamilton, J.L. (1972). "The demand for cigarettes: Advertising, the health scare, and the cigarette advertising ban". The Review of Economics and Statistics 54, 401–411.
Harris, M.N. (1976). "Entry and long-term trends in industry performance". Antitrust Bulletin 21, 295–314.
Harris, R., Seldon, A. (1962). Advertising and the Public. The Institute of Economic Affairs, London.
Hay, D.A., Morris, D. (1991). Industrial Economics and Organization: Theory and Evidence, second ed. Oxford Univ. Press, New York.
Henning, J.A., Mann, H.M. (1978). "Advertising and oligopoly: Correlations in search of understanding". In: Tuerck, D.G. (Ed.), Issues in Advertising: The Economics of Persuasion. American Enterprise Institute for Public Policy Research, Washington, DC, pp. 253–266.
Hernandez-Garcia, J.M. (1997). "Informative advertising, imperfect targeting and welfare". Economic Letters 55, 131–137.
Hertzendorf, M. (1993). "I'm not a high-quality firm – But I play one on TV". RAND Journal of Economics 24, 236–247.
Hertzendorf, M., Overgaard, P.B. (2001). "Price competition and advertising signals – Signaling by competing senders". Journal of Economics and Management Strategy 10, 621–662.
Hess, J., Gerstner, E. (1987). "Loss leader pricing and rain check policy". Marketing Science 6, 358–374.
Highfield, R., Smiley, R. (1987). "New business starts and economic activity". International Journal of Industrial Organization 5, 51–66.
Hilke, J.C., Nelson, P.B. (1984). "Noisy advertising and the predation rule in antitrust analysis". American Economic Review, Papers and Proceedings 74, 367–371.
Hirschey, M. (1978). "Television advertising and profitability". Economic Letters 1, 259–264.
Hirschey, M. (1981). "The effect of advertising on industrial mobility, 1947–72". Journal of Business 54, 329–339.
Hirschey, M. (1982). "Intangible capital aspects of advertising and R&D expenditures". Journal of Industrial Economics 34, 375–390.

Hirschey, M. (1985). "Market structure and market value". Journal of Business 58, 89–98.
Hochman, O., Luski, I. (1988). "Advertising and economic welfare: Comment". American Economic Review 78, 290–296.
Homer, P.M. (1995). "Ad size as an indicator of perceived advertising costs and effort: The effects on memory and perceptions". Journal of Advertising 24, 1–12.
Horstmann, I.J., MacDonald, G.M. (1994). "When is advertising a signal of quality?". Journal of Economics and Management Strategy 3, 561–584.
Horstmann, I.J., MacDonald, G.M. (2003). "Is advertising a signal of product quality? Evidence from the compact disc player market, 1983–92". International Journal of Industrial Organization 21, 317–345.
Horstmann, I.J., Moorthy, S. (2003). "Advertising spending and quality for services: The role of capacity". Quantitative Marketing and Economics 1, 337–365.
Hurwitz, M., Caves, R. (1988). "Persuasion or information? Promotion and the shares of brand name and generic pharmaceuticals". Journal of Law and Economics 31, 299–320.
Ippolito, P.M., Mathios, A.D. (1990). "Information, advertising and health choices: A study of the cereal market". RAND Journal of Economics 21, 459–480.
Ishigaki, H. (2000). "Informative advertising and entry deterrence: A Bertrand model". Economic Letters 67, 337–343.
Iwata, G. (1974). "Measurement of conjectural variations in oligopoly". Econometrica 42, 947–966.
Jastram, R.W. (1955). "A treatment of distributed lags in the theory of advertising expenditures". Journal of Marketing 20, 36–46.
Jin, G.Z., Leslie, P. (2003). "The effect of information on product quality: Evidence from restaurant hygiene grade cards". Quarterly Journal of Economics 118, 409–451.
Johnson, J.P., Myatt, D.P. (2006). "On the simple economics of advertising, marketing, and product design". American Economic Review 96, 756–784.
Jones, J.C.H., Laudadio, L., Percy, M. (1973). "Market structure and profitability in Canadian manufacturing industry: Some cross-section results". Canadian Journal of Economics 6, 356–368.
Jones, J.C.H., Laudadio, L., Percy, M. (1977). "Profitability and market structure: A cross-section comparison of Canadian and American manufacturing industry". Journal of Industrial Economics 25, 195–211.
Kadiyali, V. (1996). "Entry, its deterrence, and its accommodation: A study of the U.S. photographic film industry". RAND Journal of Economics 27, 452–478.
Kadiyali, V., Sudhir, K., Rao, V.R. (2001). "Structural analysis of competitive behavior: New empirical industrial organization methods in marketing". International Journal of Research in Marketing 18, 161–186.
Kaldor, N.V. (1950). "The economic aspects of advertising". Review of Economic Studies 18, 1–27.
Kaldor, N., Silverman, R. (1948). A Statistical Analysis of Advertising Expenditure and of the Revenue of the Press. University Press, Cambridge, UK.
Kanetkar, V., Weinberg, C.B., Weiss, D.L. (1992). "Price sensitivity and television advertising exposures: Some empirical findings". Marketing Science 11, 359–371.
Kardes, F.R. (2002). Consumer Behavior and Managerial Decision Making. Prentice Hall, Upper Saddle River, NJ.
Kelton, C.M.L., Kelton, W.D. (1982). "Advertising and intraindustry brand shift in the U.S. brewing industry". Journal of Industrial Economics 30, 293–303.
Kessides, I.N. (1986). "Advertising, sunk costs, and barriers to entry". The Review of Economics and Statistics 68, 84–95.
Kihlstrom, R.E., Riordan, M.H. (1984). "Advertising as a signal". Journal of Political Economy 92, 427–450.
Kind, H.J., Nilssen, T., Sorgard, L. (2003). "Advertising on TV: Under- or overprovision?". Mimeo.
Kirmani, A. (1990). "The effect of perceived advertising costs on brand perceptions". Journal of Consumer Research 17, 160–171.
Kirmani, A. (1997). "Advertising repetition as a signal of quality: If it's advertised so often, something must be wrong". Journal of Advertising 26, 77–86.
Kirmani, A., Rao, A.R. (2000). "No pain, no gain: A critical review of the literature on signaling unobservable product quality". Journal of Marketing 64, 66–79.

Kirmani, A., Wright, P. (1989). "Money talks: Perceived advertising expense and expected product quality". Journal of Consumer Research 16, 344–353.
Klein, N. (2001). No Logo. Picador USA, New York.
Klein, B., Leffler, K.B. (1981). "The role of market forces in assuring contractual performance". Journal of Political Economy 89, 615–641.
Konishi, H., Sandfort, M.T. (2002). "Expanding demand through price advertisement". International Journal of Industrial Organization 20, 965–994.
Kotowitz, Y., Mathewson, F. (1979a). "Informative advertising and welfare". American Economic Review 69, 284–294.
Kotowitz, Y., Mathewson, F. (1979b). "Advertising, consumer information, and product quality". The Bell Journal of Economics 10, 566–588.
Koyck, I.M. (1954). Distributed Lags and Investment Analysis. North-Holland, Amsterdam.
Krahmer, D. (2004). "Advertising and consumer memory". Mimeo.
Krishnamurthi, L., Raj, S.P. (1985). "The effect of advertising on consumer price sensitivity". Journal of Marketing Research 22, 119–129.
Kwoka Jr, J.E. (1984). "Advertising and the price and quality of optometric services". American Economic Review 74, 211–216.
Kwoka Jr., J.E. (1993). "The sales and competitive effects of styling and advertising practices in the U.S. auto industry". The Review of Economics and Statistics 75, 649–656.
Kwoka Jr., J.E., Ravenscraft, D. (1986). "Cooperation V. Rivalry: Price–cost margins by line of business". Economica 53, 351–363.
Laband, D.N. (1986). "Advertising as information: An empirical note". The Review of Economics and Statistics 68, 517–521.
Lal, R., Matutes, C. (1994). "Retail pricing and advertising strategies". Journal of Business 67, 345–370.
Lal, R., Narasimhan, C. (1996). "The inverse relationship between manufacturer and retailer margins: A theory". Marketing Science 15, 132–151.
Lal, R., Rao, R.C. (1997). "Supermarket competition: The case of every day low pricing". Marketing Science 16, 60–80.
Lambin, J.J. (1976). Advertising, Competition and Market Conduct in Oligopoly Over Time. North-Holland, Amsterdam.
Lancaster, K.J. (1966). "A new approach to consumer theory". Journal of Political Economy 74, 132–157.
Landes, E.M., Rosenfield, A.M. (1994). "The durability of advertising revisited". Journal of Industrial Economics 42, 263–274.
Leahy, A.S. (1991). "The effect of television advertising on prices". In: Rhodes, G.F. (Ed.), Advances in Econometrics, vol. 9. JAI Press, Inc., Greenwich, CT.
LeBlanc, G. (1998). "Informative advertising competition". Journal of Industrial Economics 46, 63–77.
Leffler, K.B. (1981). "Persuasion or information? The economics of prescriptive drug advertising". Journal of Law and Economics 24, 45–74.
Leone, R.P. (1995). "Generalizing what is known about temporal aggregation and advertising carryover". Marketing Science 14, 141–150.
Lewis, M. (2000). "Boom box". The New York Times Magazine August 13, 36–41, 51, 65–67.
Lewis, T.R., Sappington, D.E.M. (1994). "Supplying information to facilitate price discrimination". International Economic Review 35, 309–327.
Linnemer, L. (1998). "Entry deterrence, product quality: Price and advertising as signals". Journal of Economics and Management Strategy 7, 615–645.
Linnemer, L. (2002). "Price and advertising as signals of quality when some consumers are informed". International Journal of Industrial Organization 20, 931–947.
Loewenstein, G., O'Donoghue, T. (2004). "Animal spirits: Affective and deliberative processes in economic behavior". Mimeo.
Luksetich, W., Lofgreen, H. (1976). "Price advertising and liquor prices". Industrial Organization Review 4, 13–25.

Lynk, W.J. (1981). "Information, advertising and the structure of the market". Journal of Business 54, 271–303.
MacDonald, J.M. (1986). "Entry and exit on the competitive fringe". Southern Economic Journal 52, 640–652.
Manduchi, A. (2004). "Price discrimination of buyers with identical preferences and collusion in a model of advertising". Journal of Economic Theory 116, 347–356.
Mann, H.M. (1966). "Seller concentration, barriers to entry, and rates of return in thirty industries, 1950–60". The Review of Economics and Statistics 48, 296–307.
Mann, H.M., Henning, J.A., Meehan Jr., J.W. (1967). "Advertising and concentration: An empirical investigation". Journal of Industrial Economics 16, 34–45.
Mann, H.M., Henning, J.A., Meehan Jr., J.W. (1973). "Advertising and market concentration: Comment". Southern Economic Journal 39, 448–451.
Marquardt, R.A., McGann, A.F. (1975). "Does advertising communicate product quality to consumers? Some evidence from consumer reports". Journal of Advertising 4, 27–31.
Marshall, A. (1890). Principles of Economics. MacMillan and Co., London.
Marshall, A. (1919). Industry and Trade: A Study of Industrial Technique and Business Organization; and of Their Influences on the Conditions of Various Classes and Nations. MacMillan and Co., London.
Martin, S. (1979a). "Advertising, concentration and profitability: The simultaneity problem". Bell Journal of Economics 10, 639–647.
Martin, S. (1979b). "Entry barriers, concentration and profits". Southern Economic Journal 46, 471–488.
Masson, R.T., Shaanan, J. (1982). "Stochastic-dynamic limit pricing: An empirical test". The Review of Economics and Statistics 64, 413–422.
Matraves, C. (1999). "Market structure, R&D and advertising in the pharmaceutical industry". Journal of Industrial Economics 47, 169–194.
Matthews, S., Fertig, D. (1990). "Advertising signals of product quality". Northwestern University CMSEMS Discussion Paper No. 881.
Maurizi, A.R., Kelley, T. (1978). Prices and Consumer Information. American Enterprise Institute for Public Policy Research, Washington, DC.
McAfee, R.P. (1994). "Endogenous availability, cartels, and merger in an equilibrium price dispersion". Journal of Economic Theory 62, 24–47.
McClure, S.M., Laibson, D.I., Loewenstein, G., Cohen, J.D. (2004a). "Separate neural systems value immediate and delayed monetary rewards". Science 306, 503–507.
McClure, S.M., Li, J., Tomlin, D., Cypert, K.S., Montague, L.M., Montague, P.R. (2004b). "Neural correlates of behavioral preference for culturally familiar drinks". Neuron 44, 379–387.
McFadden, D. (1974). "Conditional logit analysis of qualitative choice behavior". In: Zarembka, P. (Ed.), Frontiers in Econometrics. MIT Press, Cambridge, MA, pp. 105–142.
Metwally, M.M. (1975). "Advertising and competitive behavior of selected Australian firms". The Review of Economics and Statistics 57, 417–427.
Metwally, M.M. (1976). "Profitability of advertising in Australia: A case study". Journal of Industrial Economics 24, 221–231.
Meurer, M., Stahl II, D.O. (1994). "Informative advertising and product match". International Journal of Industrial Organization 12, 1–19.
Milgrom, P., Roberts, J. (1982). "Limit pricing and entry under incomplete information: An equilibrium analysis". Econometrica 50, 443–460.
Milgrom, P., Roberts, J. (1986). "Price and advertising signals of product quality". Journal of Political Economy 94, 796–821.
Miller, R.A. (1969). "Market structure and industrial performance: Relation of profit rates to concentration, advertising intensity, and diversity". Journal of Industrial Economics 17, 104–118.
Milyo, J., Waldfogel, J. (1999). "The effect of price advertising on prices: Evidence in the wake of 44 liquormart". American Economic Review 89, 1081–1096.
Montgomery, C., Wernerfelt, B. (1992). "Risk reduction and umbrella branding". Journal of Business 65, 31–50.

Moraga-Gonzalez, J.L. (2000). "Quality uncertainty and informative advertising". International Journal of Industrial Organization 18, 615–640.
Moraga-Gonzalez, J.L., Petrakis, E. (1999). "Coupon advertising under imperfect price information". Journal of Economics and Management Strategy 8, 523–544.
Mueller, W.F., Hamm, L.G. (1974). "Trends in industrial market concentration, 1947 to 1970". The Review of Economics and Statistics 56, 511–520.
Mueller, W.F., Rogers, R.T. (1980). "The role of advertising in changing concentration of manufacturing industries". The Review of Economics and Statistics 62, 89–96.
Mueller, W.F., Rogers, R.T. (1984). "Changes in market concentration of manufacturing industries". Review of Industrial Organization 1, 1–14.
Nakao, T. (1979). "Profit rates and market shares of leading industrial firms in Japan". Journal of Industrial Economics 27, 371–383.
Needham, D. (1976). "Entry barriers and non-price aspects of firms' behavior". Journal of Industrial Economics 25, 29–43.
Nelson, P. (1970). "Information and consumer behavior". Journal of Political Economy 78, 311–329.
Nelson, P. (1974a). "The economic value of advertising". In: Brozen, Y. (Ed.), Advertising and Society. New York Univ. Press, New York, pp. 43–66.
Nelson, P. (1974b). "Advertising as information". Journal of Political Economy 82, 729–754.
Nelson, P. (1975). "The economic consequences of advertising". Journal of Business 48, 213–241.
Nelson, P. (1978). "Advertising as information once more". In: Tuerck, D.G. (Ed.), Issues in Advertising: The Economics of Persuasion. American Enterprise Institute for Public Policy Research, Washington, DC, pp. 133–160.
Nelson, J.P. (2004). "Beer advertising and marketing update: Structure, Conduct, and Social Costs". Mimeo.
Nelson, P., Siegfried, J., Howell, J. (1992). "A simultaneous equations model of coffee brand pricing and advertising". The Review of Economics and Statistics 74, 54–63.
Nerlove, M., Waugh, F. (1961). "Advertising without supply control: Some implications of a study of the advertising of oranges". Journal of Farm Economics 43, 813–837.
Nerlove, M., Arrow, K.J. (1962). "Optimal advertising policy under dynamic conditions". Economica 29, 129–142.
Nevo, A. (1998). "Identification of the oligopoly solution concept in a differentiated products industry". Economics Letters 59, 391–395.
Nevo, A. (2001). "Measuring market power in the ready-to-eat cereal industry". Econometrica 69, 307–342.
Nickell, S., Metcalf, D. (1978). "Monopolistic industries and monopoly profits or, are Kellogg's cornflakes overpriced?". Economic Journal 88, 254–268.
Nichols, L.M. (1985). "Advertising and economic welfare". American Economic Review 75, 213–218.
Nilssen, T., Sorgard, L. (2001). "The TV Industry: Advertising and programming". Mimeo.
Ornstein, S.I. (1977). Industrial Concentration and Advertising Intensity. American Enterprise Institute for Public Policy Research, Washington, DC.
Ornstein, S.I., Lustgarten, S. (1978). "Advertising intensity and industrial concentration – An empirical inquiry, 1947–1967". In: Tuerck, D.G. (Ed.), Issues in Advertising: The Economics of Persuasion. American Enterprise Institute for Public Policy Research, Washington, DC, pp. 217–252.
Orr, D. (1974a). "The determinants of entry: A study of the Canadian manufacturing industries". The Review of Economics and Statistics 56, 58–66.
Orr, D. (1974b). "An index of entry barriers and its application to the market structure performance relationship". Journal of Industrial Economics 23, 39–49.
Orzach, R., Overgaard, P.B., Tauman, Y. (2002). "Modest advertising signals strength". RAND Journal of Economics 33, 340–358.
Overgaard, P.B. (1991). "Product quality uncertainty". Unpublished Ph.D. Thesis. CORE, Universite Catholique de Louvain.
Ozga, S.A. (1960). "Imperfect markets through lack of knowledge". Quarterly Journal of Economics 74, 29–52.

Packard, V. (1957). Hidden Persuaders. D. McKay Co., New York.
Packard, V. (1969). The Waste Makers. D. McKay Co., New York.
Palda, K.S. (1964). The Measurement of Cumulative Advertising Effects. Prentice-Hall, Englewood Cliffs, NJ.
Parker, P.M. (1995). "'Sweet lemons': Illusory quality, self-deceivers, advertising, and price". Journal of Marketing Research 32, 291–307.
Pashigian, B.P., Bowen, B. (1994). "The rising cost of time of females, the growth of national brands and the supply of retail services". Economic Inquiry 32, 33–65.
Pastine, I., Pastine, T. (2002). "Consumption externalities, coordination and advertising". International Economic Review 43, 919–943.
Pedrick, J.H., Zufryden, F.S. (1991). "Evaluating the impact of advertising media plans: A model of consumer purchase dynamics using single-source data". Marketing Science 10, 111–130.
Peles, Y. (1971a). "Economies of scale in advertising beer and cigarettes". Journal of Business 44, 32–37.
Peles, Y. (1971b). "Rates of amortization of advertising expenditures". Journal of Political Economy 79, 1032–1058.
Pepall, L., Richards, D.J., Norman, G. (1999). Industrial Organization: Contemporary Theory and Practice. South-Western College Publishing, United States.
Peterman, J.L. (1968). "The Clorox case and the television rate structures". Journal of Law and Economics 11, 321–422.
Peterman, J.L. (1979). "Differences between the levels of spot and network television advertising rates". Journal of Business 52, 549–562.
Peterman, J.L., Carney, M. (1978). "A comment on television network price discrimination". Journal of Business 51, 343–352.
Peters, M. (1984). "Restrictions on price advertising". Journal of Political Economy 92, 472–485.
Phillips, L.W., Chang, D.R., Buzzell, R.D. (1983). "Product quality, cost position and business performance: A test of some key hypotheses". Journal of Marketing 47, 26–43.
Pigou, A.C. (1924). Economics of Welfare, second ed. MacMillan and Co., London.
Pitofsky, R. (1978). "Advertising regulation and the consumer movement". In: Tuerck, D.G. (Ed.), Issues in Advertising: The Economics of Persuasion. American Enterprise Institute for Public Policy Research, Washington, DC, pp. 27–44.
Pope, D. (1983). The Making of Modern Advertising. Basic Books, New York.
Porter, M.E. (1974). "Consumer behavior, retailer power and market performance in consumer goods industries". The Review of Economics and Statistics 56, 419–436.
Porter, M.E. (1976a). "Interbrand choice, media mix and market performance". American Economic Review 66, 398–406.
Porter, M.E. (1976b). Interbrand Choice, Strategy and Bilateral Market Power. Harvard Univ. Press, Cambridge, MA.
Porter, M.E. (1978). "Optimal advertising: An intra-industry approach". In: Tuerck, D.G. (Ed.), Issues in Advertising: The Economics of Persuasion. American Enterprise Institute for Public Policy Research, Washington, DC, pp. 91–114.
Porter, M.E. (1979). "The structure within industries and companies' performance". The Review of Economics and Statistics 61, 214–227.
Prat, A. (2002). "Campaign advertising and voter welfare". The Review of Economic Studies 69, 999–1017.
Rao, R.C., Syam, N. (2001). "Equilibrium price communication and unadvertised specials by competing supermarkets". Marketing Science 20, 61–81.
Rasmussen, A. (1952). "The determination of advertising expenditure". Journal of Marketing 16, 439–446.
Ravenscraft, D. (1983). "Structure–profit relationships at the line of business and industry level". The Review of Economics and Statistics 65, 22–31.
Reekie, W.D. (1974). "Advertising and market share mobility". Scottish Journal of Political Economy 21, 143–158.
Reekie, W.D. (1975). "Advertising and market structure: Another approach". Economic Journal 85, 165–174.

Reekie, W.D. (1979). Advertising and Price. The Advertising Association, London.
Rees, R.D. (1975). "Advertising, concentration, and competition: A comment and further results". Economic Journal 85, 156–164.
Resnik, A., Stern, B. (1978). "An analysis of the information content in television advertising". Journal of Marketing 41, 50–53.
Riesz, P.C. (1973). "Size versus price, or another vote for Tonypandy". Journal of Business 46, 396–403.
Rizzo, J.A., Zeckhauser, R.J. (1990). "Advertising and entry: The case of physician services". Journal of Political Economy 98, 476–500.
Robert, J., Stahl II, D.O. (1993). "Informative price advertising in a sequential search model". Econometrica 61, 657–686.
Roberts, H.V. (1947). "The measurement of advertising results". Journal of Business 20, 131–145.
Roberts, M.J., Samuelson, L. (1988). "An empirical analysis of dynamic, nonprice competition in an oligopolistic industry". RAND Journal of Economics 19, 200–220.
Robinson, J. (1933). Economics of Imperfect Competition. MacMillan and Co., London.
Robinson, W.T. (1988). "Marketing mix reactions to entry". Marketing Science 7, 368–385.
Robinson, W.T., Chang, J. (1996). "Are Sutton's predictions robust? Empirical insights into advertising, R&D, and concentration". Journal of Industrial Economics 44, 389–408.
Rochet, J.-C., Tirole, J. (2003). "Platform competition in two-sided markets". Journal of the European Economic Association 1, 990–1029.
Rogerson, W.P. (1986). "Advertising as a signal when price guarantees quality". Northwestern University CMSEMS Discussion Paper No. 704.
Rogerson, W.P. (1988). "Price advertising and the deterioration of product quality". Review of Economic Studies 55, 215–229.
Rosen, S. (1978). "Advertising, information, and product differentiation". In: Tuerck, D.G. (Ed.), Issues in Advertising: The Economics of Persuasion. American Enterprise Institute for Public Policy Research, Washington, DC, pp. 161–191.
Rotfeld, H.J., Rotzoll, T.B. (1976). "Advertising and product quality: Are heavily advertised products better?". Journal of Consumer Affairs 10, 33–47.
Roy, S. (2000). "Strategic segmentation of a market". International Journal of Industrial Organization 18, 1279–1290.
Rysman, M. (2004). "Competition between networks: A study of the market for yellow pages". Review of Economic Studies 71, 483–512.
Salinger, M. (1984). "Tobin's q, unionization and the concentration–profits relationship". RAND Journal of Economics 15, 159–170.
Salop, S. (1979). "Strategic entry deterrence". American Economic Review 69, 335–338.
Sass, T.R., Saurman, D.S. (1995). "Advertising restrictions and concentration: The case of malt beverages". The Review of Economics and Statistics 77, 66–81.
Sauer, R.D., Leffler, K.B. (1990). "Did the Federal Trade Commission's advertising substantiation program promote more credible advertising?". American Economic Review 80, 191–203.
Scherer, F.M., Ross, D. (1990). Industrial Market Structure and Economic Performance, third ed. Houghton-Mifflin Co., Boston, MA.
Schmalensee, R. (1972). The Economics of Advertising. North-Holland, Amsterdam.
Schmalensee, R. (1976a). "Advertising and profitability: Further implications of the null hypothesis". Journal of Industrial Economics 25, 45–54.
Schmalensee, R. (1976b). "A model of promotional competition in oligopoly". Review of Economic Studies 43, 493–507.
Schmalensee, R. (1978). "A model of advertising and product quality". Journal of Political Economy 86, 485–503.
Schmalensee, R. (1979). "On the use of economic models in antitrust: The ReaLemon case". University of Pennsylvania Law Review 127, 994–1050.
Schmalensee, R. (1982). "Product differentiation advantages of pioneering brands". American Economic Review 72, 349–365.

Schmalensee, R. (1983). "Advertising and entry deterrence: An exploratory model". Journal of Political Economy 91, 636–653.
Schmalensee, R. (1989). "Inter-industry studies of structure and performance". In: Schmalensee, R., Willig, R. (Eds.), Handbook of Industrial Organization, vol. 1. North-Holland, Amsterdam, pp. 475–535.
Schmalensee, R. (1992). "Sunk costs and market structure: A review article". Journal of Industrial Economics 40, 125–134.
Schnabel, M. (1970). "A note on advertising and industrial concentration". Journal of Political Economy 78, 1191–1194.
Schroeter, J.R., Smith, S.L., Cox, S.R. (1987). "Advertising and competition in routine legal service markets: An empirical investigation". Journal of Industrial Economics 36, 49–60.
Schwalbach, J. (1987). "Entry by diversified firms into German industries". International Journal of Industrial Organization 5, 43–49.
Scott Morton, F.M. (2000). "Barriers to entry, brand advertising, and generic entry in the U.S. pharmaceutical industry". International Journal of Industrial Organization 18, 1085–1104.
Seldon, B.J., Doroodian, K. (1989). "A simultaneous model of cigarette advertising: Effects of demand and industry response to public policy". The Review of Economics and Statistics 71, 673–677.
Seldon, B.J., Jewell, R.T., O'Brien, D.M. (2000). "Media substitution and economies of scale in advertising". International Journal of Industrial Organization 18, 1153–1180.
Shachar, R., Anand, B.N. (1998). "The effectiveness and targeting of television advertising". Journal of Economics and Management Strategy 7, 363–398.
Shaffer, G., Zhang, Z.J. (1995). "Competitive coupon targeting". Marketing Science 14, 395–416.
Shaked, A., Sutton, J. (1983). "Natural oligopolies". Econometrica 51, 1469–1484.
Shaked, A., Sutton, J. (1987). "Product differentiation and industrial structure". Journal of Industrial Economics 36, 131–146.
Shaked, A., Sutton, J. (1990). "Multiproduct firms and market structure". RAND Journal of Economics 21, 45–62.
Shapiro, C. (1980). "Advertising and welfare: Comment". The Bell Journal of Economics 11, 749–752.
Shapiro, C. (1983). "Premiums for high quality products as returns to reputations". Quarterly Journal of Economics 98, 659–679.
Shapiro, D., Khemani, R.S. (1987). "The determinants of entry and exit reconsidered". International Journal of Industrial Organization 5, 15–26.
Shaw, A.W. (1912). "Some problems in market distribution". Quarterly Journal of Economics 26, 703–765.
Sherman, S.A. (1900). "Advertising in the United States". Publications of the American Statistical Association 7, 1–44.
Sherman, R., Tollison, R. (1971). "Advertising and profitability". The Review of Economics and Statistics November 53, 397–407.
Shryer, W.A. (1912). Analytical Advertising. Business Service Corporation, Detroit.
Shubik, M., Levitan, R. (1980). Market Structure and Behavior. Harvard Univ. Press, Cambridge, MA.
Shum, M. (2004). "Does advertising overcome brand loyalty? Evidence from the breakfast-cereals markets". Journal of Economics and Management Strategy 13, 241–271.
Silk, A.J., Berndt, E.R. (1993). "Scale and scope effects on advertising agency costs". Marketing Science 12, 53–72.
Silk, A.J., Berndt, E.R. (1995). "Costs, institutional mobility barriers, and market structure: Advertising agencies as multiproduct firms". Journal of Economics and Management Strategy 3, 437–480.
Silk, A.J., Berndt, E.R. (2004). "Holding company cost economies in the global advertising and marketing services business". Review of Marketing Science 2. Article 5.
Silk, A.J., Klein, L.R., Berndt, E.R. (2002). "Intermedia substitutability and market demand by national advertisers". Review of Industrial Organization 20, 323–348.
Simester, D. (1995). "Signalling price image using advertised prices". Marketing Science 14, 166–188.
Simon, J. (1970). Issues in the Economics of Advertising. University of Illinois Press, Urbana.
Simon, J., Arndt, J. (1980). "The shape of the advertising response function". Journal of Advertising Research 20, 11–28.

Singh, S., Utton, M., Waterson, M. (1998). "Strategic behavior of incumbent firms in the UK". International Journal of Industrial Organization 16, 229–251.
Slade, M.E. (1995). "Product rivalry with multiple strategic weapons: An analysis of price and advertising competition". Journal of Economics and Management Strategy 4, 445–476.
Smiley, R.H. (1988). "Empirical evidence on strategic entry deterrence". International Journal of Industrial Organization 6, 167–180.
Spence, M. (1975). "Monopoly, quality and regulation". Bell Journal of Economics 6, 417–429.
Spence, M. (1980). "Notes on advertising, economies of scale, and entry barriers". Quarterly Journal of Economics 95, 493–507.
Stahl II, D.O. (1994). "Oligopolistic pricing and advertising". Journal of Economic Theory 64, 162–177.
Stegeman, M. (1991). "Advertising in competitive markets". American Economic Review 81, 210–223.
Steiner, P.O. (1966). "Discussion of the economics of broadcasting and advertising". American Economic Review Papers and Proceedings 56, 472–475.
Steiner, R.L. (1973). "Does advertising lower consumer prices?". Journal of Marketing 37, 19–26.
Steiner, R.L. (1978). "Marketing productivity in consumer goods industries – A vertical perspective". Journal of Marketing 42, 60–70.
Steiner, R.L. (1984). "Basic relationships in consumer goods industries". Research in Marketing 7, 165–208.
Steiner, R.L. (1993). "The inverse association between margins of manufacturers and retailers". Review of Industrial Organization 8, 717–740.
Stigler, G.J. (1961). "The economics of information". Journal of Political Economy 69, 213–225.
Stigler, G.J., Becker, G.S. (1977). "De gustibus non est disputandum". American Economic Review 67, 76–90.
Stiglitz, J.E. (1989). "Imperfect information in the product market". In: Schmalensee, R., Willig, R. (Eds.), Handbook of Industrial Organization, vol. 1. North-Holland, Amsterdam, pp. 769–847.
Strickland, A.D., Weiss, L.W. (1976). "Advertising, concentration, and price–cost margins". Journal of Political Economy 84, 1109–1122.
Sutton, J. (1974). "Advertising, concentration, and competition". Economic Journal 84, 56–69.
Sutton, J. (1991). Sunk Costs and Market Structure. MIT Press, Cambridge, MA.
Sutton, J. (1997a). "Game-theoretic models of market structure". In: Kreps, D.M., Wallis, K.F. (Eds.), Advances in Economics and Econometrics: Theory and Applications, Seventh World Congress, vol. 1. Cambridge Univ. Press, Cambridge, pp. 66–86.
Sutton, J. (1997b). "One smart agent". RAND Journal of Economics 28, 605–628.
Sutton, J. (1998). Technology and Market Structure: Theory and History. MIT Press, Cambridge, MA.
Symeonidis, G. (2000a). "Price and nonprice competition with endogenous market structure". Journal of Economics and Management Strategy 9, 53–83.
Symeonidis, G. (2000b). "Price competition and market structure: The impact of cartel policy on concentration in the UK". Journal of Industrial Economics 48, 1–26.
Tellis, G.J. (1988). "Advertising exposure, loyalty, and brand purchase: A two-state model of choice". Journal of Marketing Research 25, 134–144.
Tellis, G.J., Fornell, C. (1988). "The relationship between advertising and product quality over the product life cycle: A contingency theory". Journal of Marketing Research 25, 64–71.
Telser, L.G. (1961). "How much does it pay whom to advertise?". American Economic Review 50, 194–205.
Telser, L.G. (1962). "Advertising and cigarettes". Journal of Political Economy 70, 471–499.
Telser, L.G. (1964). "Advertising and competition". Journal of Political Economy 72, 537–562.
Telser, L.G. (1966). "Supply and demand for advertising messages". American Economic Review Paper and Proceedings 56, 457–466.
Telser, L.G. (1968). "Some aspects of the economics of advertising". Journal of Business 41, 166–173.
Telser, L.G. (1969a). "Theory of the firm – Discussion". American Economic Review Papers and Proceedings 59, 121–123.
Telser, L.G. (1969b). "Another look at advertising and concentration". Journal of Industrial Economics 18, 85–94.

Telser, L.G. (1978). "Towards a theory of the economics of advertising". In: Tuerck, D.G. (Ed.), Issues in Advertising: The Economics of Persuasion. American Enterprise Institute for Public Policy Research, Washington, DC, pp. 71–89.
Telser, L.G. (1980). "A theory of self-enforcing agreements". Journal of Business 53, 27–44.
Thomas, L.G. (1989). "Advertising in consumer good industries: Durability, economies of scale, and heterogeneity". Journal of Law and Economics 32, 164–194.
Thomas, L.A. (1999). "Incumbent firms' response to entry: Price, advertising and new product introduction". International Journal of Industrial Organization 17, 527–555.
Thomas, L., Shane, S., Weiglet, K. (1998). "An empirical examination of advertising as a signal of quality". Journal of Economic Behavior and Organization 37, 415–430.
Tirole, J. (1988). The Theory of Industrial Organization. MIT Press, Cambridge, MA.
Tosdal, H.R. (1918). "Price maintenance". American Economic Review 8, 283–305.
Tremblay, V.J., Martins-Filho, C. (2001). "A model of vertical differentiation, brand loyalty, and persuasive advertising". In: Baye, M., Nelson, J. (Eds.), Advances in Applied Microeconomics: Advertising and Differentiated Products, vol. 10. JAI Press, New York, pp. 221–238.
Tremblay, C.H., Tremblay, V.J. (1995). "Advertising, price and welfare: Evidence from the U.S. brewing industry". Southern Economic Journal 62, 367–381.
Tremblay, C.H., Tremblay, V.J. (2005). The U.S. Brewing Industry: Data and Economic Analysis. MIT Press, Cambridge, MA.
Uri, N.D. (1987). "A re-examination of the advertising and industrial concentration relationship". Applied Economics 19, 427–435.
Verma, V.K. (1980). "A price theoretic approach to the specification and estimation of the sales-advertising function". Journal of Business 53, S115–S137.
Vernon, J.M. (1971). "Concentration, promotion, and market share stability in the pharmaceutical industry". Journal of Industrial Economics 19, 246–266.
Vernon, J.M., Nourse, R.E.M. (1973). "Profit rates and market structure of advertising intensive firms". Journal of Industrial Economics 22, 1–20.
Vilcassim, N.J., Kadiyali, V., Chintagunta, P.K. (1999). "Investigating dynamic multifirm market interactions in price and advertising". Management Science 45, 499–518.
Villas-Boas, J.M., Winer, R.S. (1999). "Endogeneity in brand choice models". Management Science 45, 1324–1338.
Von der Fehr, N.-H.M., Stevik, K. (1998). "Persuasive advertising and product differentiation". Southern Economic Journal 65, 113–126.
Weiss, L.W. (1969). "Advertising, profits, and corporate taxes". The Review of Economics and Statistics 51, 421–430.
Weiss, L.W. (1974). "The concentration–profits relationship and antitrust". In: Goldschmid, H.J., Mann, H.M., Weston, J.F. (Eds.), Industrial Concentration: The New Learning. Little, Brown, Boston, pp. 184–233.
Weiss, L.W., Pascoe, G., Martin, S. (1983). "The size of selling costs". The Review of Economics and Statistics 65, 668–672.
Wernerfelt, B. (1988). "Umbrella branding as a signal of new product quality: An example of signalling by posting a bond". RAND Journal of Economics 19, 458–466.
Wernerfelt, B. (1990). "Advertising content when brand choice is a signal". Journal of Business 63, 91–98.
Wernerfelt, B. (1994). "Selling formats for search goods". Marketing Science 13, 298–309.
Wiggins, S.N., Lane, W.J. (1983). "Quality uncertainty, search and advertising". American Economic Review 73, 881–894.
Williamson, O.E. (1963). "Selling expense as a barrier to entry". Quarterly Journal of Economics 77, 112–128.
Wood, J.P. (1958). The Story of Advertising. Ronald Press Co., New York.
Zhao, H. (2000). "Raising awareness and signaling quality to uninformed consumers: A price advertising model". Marketing Science 19, 390–396.

Chapter 29

EMPIRICAL MODELS OF ENTRY AND MARKET STRUCTURE

STEVEN BERRY

Yale University and NBER
e-mail: steven.berry@yale.edu

PETER REISS

Stanford University and NBER
e-mail: preiss@optimum.stanford.edu

Contents

Handbook of Industrial Organization, Volume 3
Edited by M. Armstrong and R. Porter

DOI: 10.1016/S1573-448X(06)03029-9

Abstract

This chapter surveys empirical models of market structure. We pay particular attention to equilibrium models that interpret cross-sectional variation in the number of firms or firm turnover rates. We begin by discussing what economists can in principle learn from models with homogeneous potential entrants. We then turn to models with heterogeneous firms. In the process, we review applications that analyze market structure in airline, retail, professional, auction, lodging, and broadcasting markets. We conclude with a summary of more recent models that incorporate incomplete information, "set identified" parameters, and dynamics.

Keywords

Entry, Exit, Market structure, Fixed costs, Discrete games, Multiple equilibria

JEL classification: D40, D43

1. Introduction

Industrial organization (IO) economists have devoted substantial energy to understanding market structure and the role that it plays in determining the extent of market competition.[1] In particular, IO economists have explored how the number and organization of firms in a market, firms' sizes, potential competitors, and the extent of firms' product lines affect competition and firm profits. This research has shaped the thinking of antitrust, regulatory and trade authorities who oversee market structure and competition policies. For example, antitrust authorities regularly pose and answer the question: How many firms does it take to sustain competition in this market? Others ask: Can strategic investments in R&D, advertising and capacity deter entry and reduce competition? Firms themselves are interested in knowing how many firms can 'fit' in a market.

Not too surprisingly, economists' thinking about the relationship between market structure and competition has evolved considerably. Theoretical and empirical work in the 1950s, 1960s and early 1970s examined how variables such as firm profits, advertising, R&D, and prices differed between concentrated and unconcentrated markets. Much of this work implicitly or explicitly assumed market structure was exogenous. Early efforts at explaining why some markets were concentrated, and others not, relied on price theoretic arguments that emphasized technological differences and product market differences [e.g., Bain (1956)]. In the 1970s and 1980s, IO models focused on understanding how strategic behavior might influence market structure. Much of this work treated market structure as the outcome of a two-stage game. In a first stage, potential entrants would decide whether to operate; in a second stage, entering firms would compete along various dimensions. Although these two-stage models underscored the importance of competitive assumptions, the predictions of these models sometimes were sensitive to specific modeling assumptions.

During the 1970s and 1980s, the increased availability of manufacturing census and other firm-level datasets led to a variety of studies that documented rich and diverse patterns in firm turnover and industry structure. For example, Dunne, Roberts and Samuelson (1988) found considerable heterogeneity in firm survival by type of entrant and significant cross-industry correlations in entry and exit rates. The richness of these empirical findings furthered the need for empirical models that could distinguish among competing economic models of market structure.

In this chapter, we describe how empirical IO economists have sought to use game-theoretic models to build structural econometric models of entry, exit and market concentration. Our discussion emphasizes that predictions about market structure depend on observable and unobservable economic variables, including:

- the size and sunkness of set-up costs;
- the sensitivity of firm profits to the entry and exit of competitors;

[1] The term market structure broadly refers to the number of firms in a market, their sizes and the products they offer.

- the extent of product substitutability and product lines;
- potential entrants' expectations about post-entry competition;
- the prevalence and efficiency of potential entrants; and
- the endogeneity of fixed and sunk costs.

Because not all of these economic quantities are observable, empirical models will typically have to be tailored to the type of industry or firm-level data available.

We begin our chapter by outlining a general econometric framework for analyzing cross-section data on the number and sizes of firms in different, yet related, markets. This framework treats the number and identity of firms as endogenous outcomes of a two-stage oligopoly game. In the first stage, firms decide whether to operate and perhaps some product characteristics, such as quality; in the second stage, the entering firms compete. The nature of the competition may be fully specified, or may be left as a kind of "reduced form". This simple framework allows us to consider various economic questions about the nature of competition and sources of firm profitability.

We next discuss more specific models and studies of market structure in the IO literature. We should note that we do not attempt to survey papers that summarize turnover patterns in different industries or sectors. Several excellent surveys of these literatures already exist, including Geroski (1995) and Caves (1998). Instead, we review and interpret existing structural econometric models. Most of the papers we discuss estimate the parameters of static two-stage oligopoly models using cross-section data covering different geographic markets. In this sense, these models are more about modeling long-run equilibria. Although there are a few studies that analyze the structure of the same market through time, these typically do not model the endogenous timing of entry and exit decisions. Later in this chapter, we discuss special issues that time-series data and dynamic models pose for modeling market structure and changes in market structure. As the chapter in this volume by Ulrich Doraszelski and Ariel Pakes suggests, however, dynamic, strategic models often raise difficult econometric and computational issues. Thus, while these models are more theoretically appealing, they are not easily applied to commonly available data. To date, there have been relatively few attempts at estimating such models.

1.1. Why structural models of market structure?

The primary reason we focus on structural models of market structure, entry or exit is that they permit us to estimate unobservable economic quantities that we could not recover using descriptive models. For instance, to assess why a market is concentrated, IO economists must distinguish between fixed and variable cost explanations. Unfortunately, IO economists rarely, if ever, have the accounting or other data necessary to construct accurate measures of firms' fixed or variable costs. This means that IO economists must use other information, such as prices, quantities and the number of firms in a market to draw inferences about demand, variable costs and fixed costs. As we shall see, in order to use this other information, researchers must often make stark modeling assumptions. In some cases, small changes in assumptions, such as the timing of firms' moves or the game's solution concept, can have a dramatic effect on inferences. In the framework that follows, we illustrate some of these sensitivities by comparing models that use plausible alternative economic assumptions. Our intent in doing so is to provide a feel for which economic assumptions are crucial to inferences about market structure and economic quantities such as fixed costs, variable costs, demand, and strategic interactions.

When exploring alternative modeling strategies, we also hope to illustrate how practical considerations, such data limitations, can constrain what economists can identify. For example, ideally the economist would know who is a potential entrant, firms' expectations about competitors, entrants' profits, etc. In practice, IO researchers rarely have this information. For instance, they may only observe who entered and not who potentially could have. In general, the less the IO economist knows about potential entrants, firms' expectations, entrants' profits, etc., the less they will be able to infer from data on market structure, and the more the researcher will have to rely on untestable modeling assumptions.

Many of these general points are not new to us. Previously Bresnahan (1989) reviewed ways in which IO researchers have used price and quantity data to draw inferences about firms' unobserved demands and costs, and competition among firms. Our discussion complements his and other surveys of the market power literature in that most static entry models are about recovering the same economic parameters. There are some key differences however. First, the market power literature usually treats market structure as exogenous. Second, the market power literature does not try to develop estimates of firms' fixed, sunk, entry or exit costs. Third, researchers studying market structure may not have price and quantity information.

From a methodological point of view, market structure models improve on market power models in that they endogenize the number of firms in a market. They do this by simultaneously modeling potential entrants (discrete) decisions to enter or not enter a market. These models rely on the insight that producing firms expect non-negative economic profits, conditional on the expectations or actions of competitors, including those who did not enter. This connection is analogous to revealed preference arguments that form the basis for discrete choice models of consumer behavior. As in the consumer choice literature, firms' discrete entry decisions are interpreted as revealing something about an underlying latent profit or firm objective function. By observing how firms' decisions change, as their choice sets and market conditions change, IO economists can gain insight into the underlying determinants of firm profitability, including perhaps the role of fixed (and/or sunk) costs, the importance of firm heterogeneity, and the nature of competition itself.

If firms made entry decisions in isolation, it would be a relatively simple matter to adapt existing discrete-choice models of consumer choice to firm entry choices. In concentrated markets, however, firms entry decisions are interdependent – both within and sometimes across product markets. These interdependencies considerably complicate the formulation and estimation of market structure models. In particular, the interdependence of discrete entry decisions can pose thorny identification and estimation problems. These problems generally cannot be assumed away without altering the realism of the firm decision making model. For example, simultaneous discrete-choice models are known to have "coherency" problems [e.g., Heckman (1978)] that can only be fixed by strong statistical assumptions. The industrial organization literature that we describe in this chapter has adopted the alternative approach of asking what combinations of economic and statistical assumptions can ameliorate these problems. Similar approaches arise and are being tried in household labor supply models. [See, for example, Bjorn and Vuong (1984), Kooreman (1994) and Bourguignon and Chiappori (1992).] In what follows, we start with simple illustrative models and build toward more complex models of market structure.

2. Entry games with homogeneous firms

This section outlines how IO economists have used the number of firms in a market to recover information about market demand and firms' costs. It does so under the assumption that all potential entrants are the same. The advantage of this assumption is that it allows us to isolate general issues that are more difficult to appreciate in complicated models. The section that follows relaxes the stylized homogeneous firm assumption.

2.1. A simple homogeneous firm model

Our goal is to develop an empirical model of N, the number of homogeneous firms that choose to produce a homogeneous good. To do this, we develop a two-period oligopoly model in which M potential entrants first decide whether to enter and then how much to produce. When developing the empirical model, we limit ourselves to the all too common situation where the empiricist observes N but not firm output q.

The empirical question we seek to address with this model is: What can we learn about economic primitives, such as demand, cost and competitive behavior, from observations on the number of firms $N_1, \ldots, N_T$ that entered T different markets. To do this, we need to relate the observed N_i to the unobserved profits of firms in market i. Given N_i entrants in market i, each entrant earns

$$\pi(N_i) = V(N_i, x_i, \theta) - F_i. \tag{1}$$

Here, $V(\cdot)$ represents a firm's variable profits and F is a fixed cost. Under our homogeneity assumption, all firms in market i have the same variable profit function and fixed cost F_i. The vector x_i contains market i demand and cost variables that affect variable profits. The vector θ contains the demand, cost and competition parameters that we seek to estimate. To relate this profit function to data on the number of firms, we assume that in addition to observing N_i, we observe x_i but not θ or fixed costs F_i. While in principle x_i could include endogenous variables such as prices or quantities, we simplify matters for now by assuming that the only endogenous variable is the number of firms that entered N_i.

Before estimation can proceed, the researcher must specify how variable profits depend on N and what is observable to the firms and researcher. These two decisions typically cannot be made independently, as we shall see in later subsections. The purpose of explicitly introducing variables that the econometrician does not observe is to rationalize why there is not an exact relation between x_i and N_i. As is common in much of the literature, we initially assume that firms have complete information about each other's profits, and that the researcher does not observe firms' fixed costs. Additionally, we assume that the fixed costs the econometrician does not observe are independently distributed across markets according to the distribution $\Phi(F \mid x, \omega)$. As the sole source of unobservables, the distribution $\Phi(F \mid x, \omega)$ describes not only the distribution of F_i, but firm profits $\pi(N_i)$ as well.

Once the profit function is in place, the researcher's next task is to link firms' equilibrium entry decisions to N. Because firms are symmetric, have perfect information and their profits are a non-increasing function of N, we only require two inequalities to do this. For the N^* firms that entered

$$V(N^*, x, \theta) - F \geqslant 0, \tag{2}$$

and for any of the other potential entrants

$$V(N^* + 1, x, \theta) - F < 0. \tag{3}$$

When combined, these two equilibrium conditions place an upper and lower bound on the unobserved fixed costs

$$V(N^*, x, \theta) \geqslant F > V(N^* + 1, x, \theta). \tag{4}$$

These bounds provide a basis for estimating the variable profit and fixed cost parameters θ and ω from information on x_i and N_i. For example, we use the probability of observing N^* firms:

$$\begin{aligned}\operatorname{Prob}\bigl(V(N^*, x) \geqslant F \mid x\bigr) &- \operatorname{Prob}\bigl(V(N^* + 1, x) > F \mid x\bigr) \\ &= \Phi\bigl(V(N^*, x, \theta) \mid x\bigr) - \Phi\bigl(V(N^* + 1, x, \theta) \mid x\bigr)\end{aligned} \tag{5}$$

to construct a likelihood function for N^*. Under the independent and identical sampling assumptions we adopted, this likelihood has an "ordered" dependent variable form

$$\mathcal{L}\bigl(\theta, \omega \mid \{x, N^*\}\bigr) = \sum_i \ln\Bigl(\Phi\bigl(V(N_i^*, x_i)\bigr) - \Phi\bigl(V(N_i^* + 1, x_i)\bigr)\Bigr) \tag{6}$$

where the sum is over the cross-section or time-series of independent markets in the sample. It is essential to note that besides maintaining that firms' unobserved profits are *statistically* independent across markets, this likelihood function presumes that firms' profits are *economically* independent across markets. These independence assumptions are much more likely to be realistic if we are modeling a cross section of different firms in different markets, and not the same firms over time or in different markets.

The simplicity of this likelihood function, and its direct connection to theory, is extremely useful despite the stringent economic assumptions underlying it. Most important, we learn that if we only have discrete data on the number of firms in different markets, we will be forced to impose distributional assumptions on unobserved profits in order to estimate θ and ω. For example, if we assume that unobserved fixed costs have an independent and identically distributed (i.i.d.) normal (logit) distribution, then (6) is an ordered probit (logit) likelihood function. But this structure begs the questions: How did we know profits had a normal (logit) distribution? And, how did we know that fixed costs were i.i.d. across markets? In general, economics provides little guidance about the distribution of fixed costs. Thus, absent some statistical (or economic) structure, we will be unable to recover much from observations on N^* alone.

Given the potential arbitrariness of the assumptions about fixed costs, it seems imperative that researchers explore the sensitivity of estimates to alternative distributional assumptions. Toward this end, recent work on semiparametric estimators by Klein and Sherman (2002), Lewbel (2002) and others may prove useful in estimating models that have more flexible distributions of unobserved profits. These semiparametric methods, however, typically maintain that $V(\cdot)$ is linear in its parameters and they require large amounts of data in order to recover the distribution of unobserved fixed costs.

To summarize our developments to this point, we have developed an econometric model of the number of firms in a market from two equilibrium conditions on homogeneous firms' unobserved profits. One condition is based on the fact that N^* chose to enter. The other is based on the fact that $M - N^*$ chose not to enter. The resulting econometric threshold models bear a close relation to conventional ordered dependent variable models, and thus provide a useful reference point for modeling data on the number of firms. Our discussion also emphasized that to draw information from the number of firms alone, researchers will have to make strong economic and statistical assumptions. In what follows, we show how many of these assumptions can be relaxed, but not without some cost to the simplicity of the econometric model. The next section discusses, following Bresnahan and Reiss (1991b), how one might make inferences about competition in the context of specific models for V. We then discuss how to combine information on post-entry outcomes with information on entry.

2.2. Relating V to the strength of competition

We now take up the question of how to specify the variable profit function $V(N, x, \theta)$ and the fixed cost function $F(x, \omega)$.

There are two main approaches to specifying how $V(\cdot)$ depends on N and x. The first is to pick a parameterization of $V(\cdot)$ that makes estimation simple and yet obeys the restriction that $V(\cdot, x)$ is non-increasing in N. For example, the researcher might assume that x and $1/N$ enter V linearly with constant coefficients, and that the coefficient on $1/N$ is constrained to be positive. The advantage of this descriptive approach is that it yields a conventional probit model. The disadvantage is that it is unclear what economic quantities the θ parameters represent.

A second approach is to derive $V(\cdot)$ directly from specific assumptions about the functional forms of demand and costs, and assumptions about the post-entry game. This approach has the advantage of making it clear what economic assumptions motivate the researcher's choice of $V(\cdot)$ and what the θ parameters represent. A potential disadvantage of this approach is that, even with strong functional form restrictions, the profit specifications can quickly become econometrically challenging.

To see some of the issues involved, consider the market for a homogeneous good with M potential entrants. Suppose each potential entrant j has the variable cost function $C_j(q_j)$ and that demand in market i has the form

$$Q_i = S_i q(P_i), \tag{7}$$

where S is market size (an exogenous "x"), q is per-capita demand and P is price. In a standard Cournot model, each entering firm maximizes profits by choosing output so that in market i

$$P_i = \frac{\eta_i}{\eta_i - s_j} MC_j \quad \text{for } j = 1, \ldots, N \leqslant M, \tag{8}$$

where MC_j is entrant j's marginal cost of production, s_j is firm j's market share (equal to $1/N$ in the symmetric case) and η_i equals minus the market i elasticity of demand.[2]

As Equation (8) stands, it is hard to see how prices (and hence firm-level profits) vary with the number of firms in a market. To explore the effect of N on prices, it is useful to aggregate the markup equations across firms to give the price equation:

$$P = \frac{N\eta}{N\eta - 1} \overline{MC}, \tag{10}$$

where $\overline{MC}$ is the average of the N entrants' marginal cost functions. This equation shows that industry price depends not just on the number of firms N that enter the market, but also on the average of the firms' marginal costs. Alternatively, if interest centers on the size distribution of entrants, we can aggregate (8) using market share weights to obtain

$$P = \frac{\eta}{\eta - H} \overline{MC}^{w}, \tag{11}$$

[2] We could extend this to incorporate different possible equilibrium notions in the "usual" way by writing the pricing equation as

$$P_i = \frac{\eta_i}{\eta_i - \omega_j s_j} MC_j \quad \text{for } j = 1, \ldots, N \leqslant M, \tag{9}$$

where the variable ω_j is said to describe firm j's "beliefs" about the post-entry game. The usual values are $\omega_j = 0$ (competition) and $\omega_j = 1$ (Cournot). Current practice is to not think of ω_j as an arbitrary conjectural parameter. One could also embed monopoly outcomes within this framework provided we resolve how the cartel distributes production.

which links the industry Herfindahl index H to prices and a market-share weighted average of firms' marginal costs.

It is tempting to do comparative statics on Equations (10) and (11) to learn how entry affects price and variable profits. For example, if we specialize the model to the case where firms: have constant marginal costs, face a constant elasticity of demand and are Cournot competitors, then we obtain the usual "competitive" pattern where prices and variable profits are convex to the origin and asymptote to marginal cost. At this level of generality, however, it is unclear precisely how $V(\cdot)$ depends on the number of firms. To learn more, we have to impose more structure.

Suppose, for example, that we assumed demand was linear in industry output

$$Q = S(\alpha - \beta P). \tag{12}$$

Additionally, suppose costs are quadratic in output and the same for all firms

$$F + C(q) = F + cq - dq^2. \tag{13}$$

With these demand and cost assumptions, and assuming firms are Cournot–Nash competitors, we can derive an expression for equilibrium price

$$P = a - N^* \frac{(a - c)}{(N^* + 1 + 2Sd/b)}. \tag{14}$$

Here, $a = \alpha/\beta$ and $b = 1/\beta$. Substituting this expression back into demand, we obtain an expression for firm profits

$$\pi_i(N_i^*, S_i) = V(N_i^*, S_i, \theta) - F_i = \theta_1^2 S_i \frac{(1 + \theta_2 S_i)}{(N_i^* + 1 + 2\theta_2 S_i)^2} - F_i, \tag{15}$$

where $\theta_1 = (a - c)/\sqrt{b}$ and $\theta_2 = d/b$. Expression (15) can now be inserted into the inequalities (4) to construct an ordered dependent variable for the number of firms. For example, setting $d = 0$ we can transform Equation (4) into

$$\ln(N_i^* + 2) > \frac{1}{2}\left(\ln\left(\theta_1^2 S_i\right) - \ln F_i\right) \geqslant \ln(N_i^* + 1). \tag{16}$$

The identification of the demand and cost parameters (up to the scale of unobserved profits or fixed costs) then rests on what additional assumptions we make about whether the demand and cost parameters vary across markets, and what we assume about the observed distribution of fixed costs.

As should be clear from this discussion, changes in the demand and cost specifications will change the form of the bounds. For example, if we had assumed a unit constant-elasticity demand specification $P = \theta_1 \frac{S}{Q}$ and $d = 0$, then we would obtain

$$V(N_i, S_i) = \frac{\theta_1 S_i}{N_i^2},$$

which is similar to that in Berry (1992), and has bounds linear in the natural logarithm of N

$$\ln(N^* + 1) > \frac{1}{2}\big(\ln(\theta_1 S) - \ln F\big) \geqslant \ln(N^*). \tag{17}$$

In this case, knowledge of F and N would identify the demand curve. This, however, is not the case in our previous example (16). More generally, absent knowledge of F, knowledge of N alone will be insufficient to identify separate demand and cost parameters.

These examples make three important points. First, absent specific functional form assumptions for demand and costs, the researcher will not in general know how unobserved firm profits depend on the number of homogeneous firms in a market. Second, specific functional form assumptions for demand, costs and the distribution of fixed costs will be needed to uncover the structure of $V(N^*, x, \theta)$. In general, the identification of demand and cost parameters in θ (separately from F) will have to be done on a case-by-case basis. Finally, apart from its dependence on the specification of demand and costs, the structure of $V(N^*, x, \theta)$ will depend on the nature of firm interactions. For example, the analysis above assumed firms were Cournot–Nash competitors. Suppose instead we had assumed firms were Bertrand competitors. With a homogeneous product, constant marginal costs and symmetric competitors, price would fall to marginal cost for $N \geqslant 2$. Variable profits would then be independent of N. With symmetric colluders and constant marginal costs, price would be independent of N, and $V(N)$ would be proportional to $1/N$.

Our emphasis on deriving how $V(\cdot)$ depends on the equilibrium number of firms is only part of the story. Ultimately, N is endogenous and this then raises an "identification" issue. To see the identification issue, imagine that we do not have sample variation in the exogenous variables x (which in our examples is S, the size of the market). Without variation in x, we will have no variation in N^*, meaning that we can at best place bounds on θ and fixed costs. Thus, x plays a critical role in identification by shifting variable profits independently of fixed costs. In our example, it would thus be important to have meaningful variation in the size of the market S. Intuitively, such variation would reveal how large unobserved fixed costs are relative to the overall size of the market. In turn, the rate at which N changes with market size allows us to infer how quickly V falls in N.

We should emphasize that so far our discussion and example have relied heavily on the assumption that firms are identical. Abandoning this assumption, as we do later, can considerably complicate the relationship between V, x and N. For example, with differentiated products, a new good may "expand the size of the market" and this may offset the effects of competition on variable profits. With heterogeneous marginal costs, the effects of competition on V are also more difficult to describe.

The fact that there are a multitude of factors that affect N is useful because it suggests that in practice information on N alone will be insufficient to identify behavioral, demand and cost conditions that affect N. In general, having more information, such as information on individual firm prices and quantities, will substantially improve what one can learn about market conditions.

2.2.1. Application: entry in small markets

In a series of papers, Bresnahan and Reiss model the entry of retail and professional service businesses into small isolated markets in the United States.[3] The goal of this work is to estimate how quickly entry appears to lower firms' variable profits. They also seek to gauge how large the fixed costs of setting up a business are relative to variable profits. To do this, Bresnahan and Reiss estimate a variety of models, including homogeneous and heterogeneous firm models. In their homogeneous firm models, the number of firms flexibly enters variable profits. Specifically, because their "small" markets have at most a few firms, they allow $V(\cdot)$ to fall by (arbitrary) amounts as new firms enter. While there are a variety of ways of doing this, Bresnahan and Reiss assume variable profits have the form

$$V(N_i^*, S_i, \theta) = S_i\left(\theta_1 + \sum_{k=2}^{M} \theta_k D_k + x_i \theta_{M+1}\right), \tag{18}$$

where the D_k are zero-one variables equal to 1 if at least k firms have entered and θ_{M+1} is a vector of parameters multiplying a vector of exogenous variables x.

The size of the market, S, is a critical variable in Bresnahan and Reiss' studies. Without it, they could not hope to separate out variable profits from fixed costs. In their empirical work, Bresnahan and Reiss assume S is itself an estimable linear function of market population, population in nearby areas and population growth. The multiplicative structure of $V(N_i^*, S_i, \theta)$ in S_i can easily be rationalized following our previous examples (and assuming constant marginal costs). What is less obvious is the economic interpretation of the θ parameters. The $\theta_2, \ldots, \theta_M$ parameters describe how variable profits change as the number of entrants increases from 2 to M. For example, θ_2 is the change in a monopolist's variable profits from having another firm enter. For the variable profit function to make economic sense, $\theta_2, \ldots, \theta_M$ must all be less than or equal to zero, so that variable profits do not increase with entry. Under a variety of demand, cost and oligopoly conduct assumptions, one might also expect the absolute values of $\theta_2, \ldots, \theta_M$ to decline with more entry. Bresnahan and Reiss say less about what the parameters in the vector θ_{M+1} represent. The presumption is that they represent the combined effects of demand and cost variables on (per capita) variable profits.

Besides being interested in how $\theta_2, \ldots, \theta_M$ decline with N, Bresnahan and Reiss also are interested in estimating what they call "entry thresholds": S_N^*. The entry threshold S_N^* is the smallest overall market size S that would accommodate N potential entrants. That is, for given N and fixed costs $\bar{F}$, $S_N^* = \bar{F}/V(N)$.[4] Since S is overall market size, and larger markets are obviously needed to support more firms, it is useful to

[3] See Bresnahan and Reiss (1988, 1990, 1991b).

[4] Bresnahan and Reiss have extended their models to allow F to vary with the number of entrants. They also explore whether profits are linear in S.

standardize S in order to gauge how much additional population (or whatever the units of S) is needed to support a next entrant. One such measure is the fraction of the overall market S that a firm requires to just stay in the market. In the homogeneous firm case this is captured by the "per-firm" threshold is $s_N = \frac{S_N^*}{N}$.[5] These population thresholds can then be compared to see whether firms require increasing or decreasing numbers of customers to remain in a market as N increases. Alternatively, since the units of s_N may be hard to interpret, Bresnahan and Reiss recommend constructing entry threshold ratios such as S_{N+1}/S_N.

To appreciate what per-firm entry thresholds or entry threshold ratios reveal about demand, costs and competition, it is useful to consider the relationship between the monopoly entry threshold and per-firm thresholds for two or more firms. Casual intuition suggests that if it takes a market with 1000 customers to support a single firm, that it should take around 2000 customers to support two firms. In other words, the per-firm entry thresholds are around 1000 and the entry-threshold ratios are close to one. Indeed, in the homogeneous good and potential entrant case, it is not to difficult to show that the entry threshold ratios will be one in competitive and collusive markets. Suppose, however, that we found that it took 10,000 customers to support a second firm (or that the entry threshold ratio was 10). What would we conclude? If we were sure that firms' products and technologies were roughly the same, we might suspect that the first firm was able to forestall the entry of the second competitor. But just how large is an entry threshold ratio of 10? The answer is we do not know unless we make further assumptions. Bresnahan and Reiss (1991b) provide some benchmark calculations to illustrate potential ranges for the entry threshold ratios. Returning to the Cournot example profit function (15) with $d = 0$, we would find $S_{N+1}/S_N = \frac{(N+2)^2}{(N+1)^2}$. Thus, the entry threshold ratio under these assumptions is a convex function of N, declining from 2.25 (duopoly/monopoly) to 1.

As we have emphasized previously, to the extent that additional data, such as prices and quantities, are available it may be possible to supplement the information that entry thresholds provide. Additionally, such information can help evaluate the validity of any maintained assumptions. For example, it may not be reasonable to assume potential entrants and their products are the same, or that all entrants have the same fixed costs.

Bresnahan and Reiss (1991b) argue on a priori grounds that firms' fixed costs are likely to be nearly the same and that their entry threshold rations thus reveal something about competition and fixed costs. Table 29.1 revisits their estimates of these ratios for various retail categories. Recalling the contrast between the Cournot and perfectly collusive and competitive examples above, here we see that the ratios fall toward one as the number of entrants increases. The ratios are generally small and they decline dramatically when moving from one to two doctors, tire dealers or dentists. Plumbers are the closest industry to the extremes of perfect competition or coordination. Absent more

[5] Another way of understanding this standardization is to observe that the Nth firm just breaks even when $V(N)S = F$. Thus, $s_n = F/(NV(N))$.

Table 29.1
Per firm entry thresholds from Bresnahan and Reiss (1991b, Table 5)

Profession	S_2/S_1	S_3/S_2	S_4/S_3	S_5/S_4
Doctors	1.98	1.10	1.00	0.95
Dentists	1.78	0.79	0.97	0.94
Druggists	1.99	1.58	1.14	0.98
Plumbers	1.06	1.00	1.02	0.96
Tire dealers	1.81	1.28	1.04	1.03

information, Bresnahan and Reiss cannot distinguish between these two dramatically different possibilities.

In an effort to understand the information in entry thresholds, Bresnahan and Reiss (1991b) collected additional information on the prices of standard tires from tire dealers in both small and large markets. They then compared these prices to their entry threshold estimates. Consistent with Table 29.1, tire dealers' prices did seem to fall with the first few entrants; they then leveled off after five entrants. Curiously, however, when they compared these prices to those in urban areas they found that prices had in some cases leveled off substantially above those in urban areas where there are presumably a large number of competitors.

2.3. *Observables and unobservables*

So far we have focused on deriving how observables such as x, S, N and P affect entry decisions and said little about how assumptions about unobservables affect estimation. Already we have seen that empirical models of market structure are likely to rest heavily on distributional assumptions. This subsection considers what types of economic assumptions might support these assumptions.

To derive the stochastic distribution of unobserved profits, we can proceed in one of two ways. One is to make assumptions about the distribution of underlying demand and costs. From these distributions and a model of firm behavior, we can derive the distribution of firms' unobserved profits. The second way is to assume distributions for variable profits and fixed costs that appear economically plausible and yet are computationally tractable. The strength of the first of these approaches is that it makes clear how unobserved demand and cost conditions affect firm profitability and entry; a disadvantage of this approach, which is anticipated in the second approach, is that it can lead to intractable empirical models.

To implement the first approach, we must impose specific functional forms for demand and cost. Suppose, for example, the researcher observes inverse market demand up to an additive error and unknown coefficients θ^d

$$P = D\left(x, Q, \theta^d\right) + \epsilon^d \tag{19}$$

and total costs are linear in output

$$TC(q) = F(w) + \epsilon^F + \left(c\left(w, \theta^c\right) + \epsilon^c\right)q. \tag{20}$$

In these equations, the firm observes the demand and cost unobservables ϵ^d and ϵ^c, the w are x are exogenous variables and q is firm output. Suppose in addition firms are symmetric and each firm equates its marginal revenue to marginal cost. The researcher then can calculate the "mark-up" equation

$$P = b(x, q, Q, \theta^d) + c(w, \theta^c) + \epsilon^c. \tag{21}$$

Here, b is minus the derivative of D with respect to firm output multiplied by q. Notice that because we assumed the demand and cost errors are additive, they do not enter the $b(\cdot)$ and $c(\cdot)$ directly. (The errors may enter $b(\cdot)$ indirectly if the firms' output decisions depend on the demand and cost errors.)

This additive error structure has proven convenient in the market power literature [see Bresnahan (1989)]. It permits the researcher to employ standard instrumental variable or generalized method of moment techniques to estimate demand and cost parameters from observations on price and quantity. This error structure, however, complicates estimation methods based on the number of firms. To see this, return to the profit function expression (15) in the linear demand example. If we add ϵ_d to the demand intercept and ϵ_c to marginal cost we obtain

$$\pi_i(N_i^*, S_i) = V(N_i^*, S_i, \theta) - F_i = (\theta_1 + \epsilon_m)^2 S_i \frac{(1 + \theta_2 S_i^2)}{(N_i^* + 1 + 2\theta_2 S_i)^2} - F_i - \epsilon^F,$$

where $\epsilon^m = \epsilon^d - \epsilon^c$. That is, profits are linear in the fixed cost error but quadratic in the demand and marginal cost errors. Consequently, if we assumed the demand and cost errors were i.i.d., profits would be independent but not identically distributed across markets that varied in size (S).

It should perhaps not be too surprising that the reduced form distribution of firms' unobserved profits can be a non-linear function of unobserved demand and cost variables. While these non-linearities complicate estimation, they do not necessarily preclude it. For example, to take the above profit specification to data, one might assume the fixed costs have an additive normal or logit error, or a multiplicative log-normal error. These assumptions lead to tractable expressions for the likelihood function expressions (such as (6)) conditional on values of ϵ^d and ϵ^c. The researcher could then in principle attempt estimation by integrating out the demand and cost errors using either numerical methods or simulation techniques.[6]

2.4. *Demand, supply and endogenous N*

So far we have only considered models based on the number of firms in a market, and not price or quantity. In some applications, researchers are fortunate enough to have price and quantity information in addition to information on market structure. This

[6] To our knowledge this approach has not been attempted. This is perhaps because a proof that such an approach would work and its econometric properties remain to be explored.

subsection asks what the researcher gains by modeling market structure in addition to price and quantity.

It might seem at first that there is little additional value to modeling market structure. Following the literature on estimating market power in homogeneous product markets, one could use price and quantity information alone to estimate industry demand and supply (or markup) equations such as

$$Q = Q(P, X, \theta^d, \epsilon^d)$$

and

$$P = P(q, N, W, \theta^c, \epsilon^c).$$

In these equations, Q denotes industry quantity, q denotes firm quantity, P is price, X and W are exogenous demand and cost variables, and ϵ^d and ϵ^c are demand and supply unobservables. The parameter vectors θ^d and θ^c represent industry demand and cost parameters, such as those found in the previous subsection.

Provided X and W contain valid instruments for price and quantity, it would appear an easy matter to use instrumental variables to estimate θ^d and θ^c. Thus, the only benefit to modeling model market structure would seem to be that it allows the researcher to estimate fixed costs (which do not enter the demand and supply equations above). This impression overlooks the fact that N (or some other measure of industry concentration) may appear separately in the supply equation and thus require instruments.

The examples in previous subsections illustrate why the endogeneity of N can introduce complications for estimating θ^d and θ^c. They also suggest potential solutions and instruments. In previous examples, the number of firms N was determined by a threshold condition on firm profits. This threshold condition depended (non-linearly) on the exogenous demand (x) and variable cost (w) variables, and the demand and total cost unobservables that make up the demand and supply errors. Thus, to estimate the parameters of demand and supply equations consistently, we have to worry about finding valid instruments for the number of firms. The most compelling instruments for the number of firms (or other market concentration measures) would be exogenous variables that affect the number of firms but not demand or supply. One such source are observables that only enter fixed costs. Examples might include the prices of fixed factors of production or measures of opportunity costs.

In some applications, it may be hard to come by exogenous variables that affect fixed costs, but not demand and variable costs. In such cases, functional form or error term restrictions might justify a specific choice of instrument or estimation method. For instance, in the linear demand and marginal cost example of Section 2.2, if we assume $d = 0$ (constant marginal costs), then we can use market size S as an instrument for the number of firms.[7] This is essentially the logic of Bresnahan and Reiss, who note for

[7] Notice that per capita total quantity Q and per capita firm quantity q are independent of S. Thus, S does not enter the per capita demand function or the firm's supply equation.

the markets they study that market size is highly correlated with the number of firms in a market. Market size also is used explicitly as an instrument in Berry and Waldfogel (1999).

2.4.1. Application: market structure and competition in radio

Berry and Waldfogel (1999) examine the theoretical hypothesis that entry can be socially inefficient. They do this by comparing advertising prices, listening shares and numbers of stations in different radio broadcasts markets. Specifically, they ask whether the fixed costs of entry exceed the social benefits of new programming (greater listening) and more competitive advertising prices.[8]

To compute private and social returns to entry, Berry and Waldfogel must estimate: (1) the fixed costs of entrants; (2) by how much new stations expand listening; and (3) by how much entry changes advertising prices. They do all this by developing an empirical model in which homogeneous stations "produce" listeners and then "sell" them to advertisers. The economic primitives of the model include: a listener choice function; an advertiser demand function; and a specification for station fixed costs.

Berry and Waldfogel model radio listeners within a market as having correlated extreme value preferences for homogeneous stations; an outside good (not listening) also is included. Under their station homogeneity and stochastic assumptions, what varies across markets is the fraction of listeners and non-listeners, which are in turn affected by the number of entrants. Specifically, under their assumptions, listener L_i relative to non-listener $(1 - L_i)$ shares in market i are related by

$$\ln\left(\frac{L_i}{1 - L_i}\right) = x_i\beta + (1 - \sigma)\ln(N_i) + \xi_i. \tag{22}$$

That is, the odds for listening depend on a set of market demographics, x_i, the number of (homogeneous) stations in the market, N_i, and a market-specific unobservable, ξ_i. The parameter σ controls the correlation of consumers' idiosyncratic preferences for stations. When $\sigma = 1$, consumers' unobserved preferences for the homogeneous stations are perfectly correlated and thus the entry of new stations does not expand the number of listeners. When $\sigma = 0$, as in the case in a conventional logit model, the entry of an otherwise identical station expands the size of the market because some consumers will have an idiosyncratic preference for it (relative to other stations and not listening).

As a demand equation, (22) is linear in its parameters and thus easily estimated by linear estimation techniques. As we pointed out in the beginning of this subsection, having N on the right-hand side poses a problem – the number of radio stations in a market, N_i, will be correlated with the market demand unobservable ξ. Thus, Berry and Waldfogel must find an instrument for N_i. For the reasons outlined earlier, the

[8] Rysman (2004) studies the welfare effects of entry in the market for telephone Yellow Pages and also considers possible network effects.

population or potential listening audience of a radio market provides a good instrument for the number of stations. It does not enter consumer preferences directly and yet is something that affects total demand.

Next, Berry and Waldfogel introduce advertisers' demand for station listeners. Specifically, they assume that demand has the constant elasticity form

$$\ln(p_i) = x_i\gamma - \eta\ln(L_i) + \omega_i, \tag{23}$$

where p_i is the price of advertising, and ω_i is the demand error. Once again, market size is a good instrument for listening demand, which may be endogenous. Together, the listening share and pricing equations give the revenue function of the firm.

Since the marginal cost of an additional listener is literally zero, Berry and Waldfogel model all costs as fixed costs.[9] The fixed costs must be estimated from the entry equation. As in our earlier discussions, with a homogeneous product and identical firms, N_i firms will enter if

$$R(N_i + 1, x_i, \theta) < F_i < R(N_i, x_i, \theta), \tag{24}$$

where $R(\cdot)$ is a revenue function equal to $p_i(N_i, \gamma, \eta)M_i L_i(N_i, \beta, \sigma)/N_i$, and M_i is the population of market i. Thus, with appropriate assumptions about the distribution of unobserved costs and revenues across markets, Berry and Waldfogel can use ordered dependent variable models to learn the distribution of F across markets. Knowing this distribution, Berry and Waldfogel compare the welfare consequences of different entry regimes. Taking into account only station and advertiser welfare, they find that there appears to be too much entry relative to the social optimum. This is because in many markets the incremental station generates a small number of valued listeners. Berry and Waldfogel note that their welfare analysis does not take into account any external benefits that listeners may receive from having more radio stations. They also do not explore whether their results are sensitive to their homogeneous-firm assumption.

3. Firm heterogeneity

We have so far explored models with identical firms. In reality, firms have different costs, sell different products, and occupy different locations. It is therefore important to explore how entrant heterogeneities might affect estimation. Firm heterogeneities can be introduced in a variety of ways, including observed and unobserved differences in: firms' fixed and variable costs, product attributes, and product distribution. A first important issue to consider is how these differences arose. In some cases, the differences might reasonably be taken as given and outside the firms' control. In other cases, such

[9] More realistically, this fixed cost would be endogenously chosen and would affect the quality of the station, which Berry and Waldfogel do not model.

as product quality, the differences are under a firm's control and thus have to be modeled along with market structure. Almost all empirical models to date have adopted the approach that differences among firms are given. Although we too adopt this approach in much of what follows, the modeling of endogenously determined heterogeneities is ripe for exploration.

As we shall see shortly, empirical models with heterogeneous potential entrants pose thorny conceptual and practical problems for empirical researchers. Chief among them are the possibility that entry models can have multiple equilibria, or worse, no pure-strategy equilibria. In such cases, standard approaches to estimating parameters may break down, and indeed key parameters may no longer be identified.

Although we did not note these problems in our discussion of homogeneous firm models, they can occur there as well. We discuss them here because they pose easier to grasp problems for researchers trying to match firm identities or characteristics to a model's predictions about who will enter. As noted by Sutton (2007) and others, the problems of non-existence and non-uniqueness have traditionally been treated as nuisances – something to be eliminated by assumption if at all possible. We will provide several different examples of this approach in this section. We should remark, however, that multiplicity or non-existence issues may be a fact of markets. For this reason we will consider alternative solutions in the following section.

Here, we emphasize that heterogeneous firm entry models differ along two important dimensions: (1) the extent to which heterogeneities are observable or unobservable to the econometrician; and (2) the extent to which firms are assumed to be uncertain about the actions or payoffs of other firms. Both of these dimensions critically affect the identification and estimation of entry models. For example, McKelvey and Palfrey (1995) and Seim (2006) have shown how introducing asymmetric information about payoffs can mitigate multiple equilibrium problems. Others [e.g., Bresnahan and Reiss (1990), Berry (1992) and Mazzeo (2002)] have explored how observing the timing of firms' decisions can eliminate non-existence and non-uniqueness problems.

To illustrate these economic and econometric issues and solutions, we begin with the simplest form of heterogeneity – heterogeneity in unobserved fixed costs. We first discuss problems that can arise in models in which this heterogeneity is known to the firms but not the researcher. We also discuss possible solutions. We then discuss how entry models change when firms have imperfect information about their differences.

3.1. Complications in models with unobserved heterogeneity

To start, consider a one-play, two-by-two entry game in which there are two potential entrants, each with two potential strategies. Suppose firms 1 and 2 have perfect information about each other and earn $\pi_1(D_1, D_2)$ and $\pi_2(D_1, D_2)$ respectively from taking actions (D_1, D_2), where an action is either 0 ("Do Not Enter") or 1 ("Enter").

Following our earlier derivations, we would like to derive equilibrium conditions linking the firms' observed actions to inequalities on their profits. A natural starting point is to examine what happens when the firms are simultaneous Nash competitors –

Table 29.2
Two-firm market structure outcomes for a simultaneous-move game

Market outcome	N	Conditions on profits
No firms	0	$\pi_1^M < 0 \quad \pi_2^M < 0$
Firm 1 monopoly	1	$\pi_1^M > 0 \quad \pi_2^D < 0$
Firm 2 monopoly	1	$\pi_2^M > 0 \quad \pi_1^D < 0$
Duopoly	2	$\pi_2^D > 0 \quad \pi_1^D > 0$

that is, they make their entry decisions simultaneously and independently. Additionally, we assume that entry by a competitor reduces profits and that a firm earns zero profits if it does not enter.[10] Under these conditions, the threshold conditions supporting the possible entry outcomes are as shown in Table 29.2. Here, the notation π_j^M and π_j^D denote the profits firm i earns as a monopolist and duopolist, respectively.

Following our earlier discussions, the researcher would like to use observations on (D_1, D_2) to recover information about the π_j^M and π_j^D. To do this, we have to specify how firms' profits differ in observable and unobservable ways. In what follows we decompose firms' profits into an observable (or estimable) component and an additively separable unobserved component. Specifically, we assume

$$\pi_j = \begin{cases} 0 & \text{if } D_j = 0, \\ \bar{\pi}_j^M(x, z_j) + \epsilon_j & \text{if } D_j = 1 \text{ and } D_k = 0, \\ \bar{\pi}_j^D(x, z_j) + \epsilon_j & \text{if } D_j = 1 \text{ and } D_k = 1. \end{cases}$$

In these equations, the $\bar{\pi}$ terms represent observable profits. These profits are functions of observable market x and firm-specific z_j variables. The ϵ_j represent profits that are known to the firms but not to the researcher. Notice that this additive specification presumes that competitor k's action only affects competitor j's profits through observed profits; k's action does not affect that part of profits the researcher cannot observe. This special assumption simplifies the analysis. One rationale for it is that the error ϵ_j represents firm j's unobservable fixed costs, and competitor k is unable to raise or lower their rival's fixed costs by being in or out of the market.

The restrictions in Table 29.2, along with assumptions about the distribution of the ϵ_j, link the observed market structures to information about firms' demands and costs. Figure 29.1 displays the values of firms' monopoly profits that lead to the four distinct entry outcomes. Following the rows of Table 29.2, the white area to the southwest represents the region where both firms' monopoly profits are less than zero and neither firm enters. Firm 1 has a monopoly in the area to the southeast with horizontal gray

[10] Bresnahan and Reiss (1991a) discuss the significance of these assumptions.

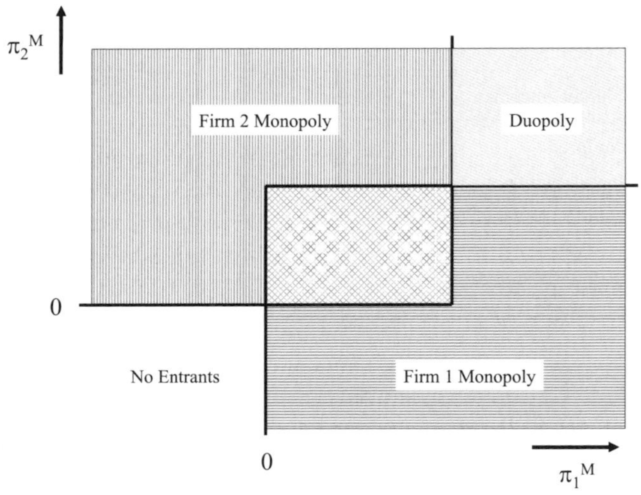

Figure 29.1. Monopoly and duopoly entry thresholds.

stripes. There, firm 1's monopoly profits are positive and yet firm 2's duopoly profits (by assumption less than monopoly profits) are still negative. Similarly, firm 2 has a monopoly in the northeast area with vertical gray stripes. There, firm 2's monopoly profits are positive and firm 1's duopoly profits negative. Finally, the solid gray region to the northeast corresponds to the last row of Table 29.2 in which both firms enter.

The shading of the figure shows that given our assumptions there always is at least one pure-strategy Nash equilibrium. The center cross-hatched region, however, supports two pure-strategy equilibria: one in which firm 1 is a monopolist and one where firm 2 is a monopolist. Absent more information, the conditions in Table 29.2 do not provide an unambiguous mapping from equilibria to inequalities on profits. This causes problems for constructing likelihood functions [see Bresnahan and Reiss (1991a)]. In a moment, we will discuss potential fixes for this problem.

Besides illustrating what problems can arise when relating discrete entry outcomes to equilibrium conditions on profits, Figure 29.1 also shows why conventional probit or logit models are inadequate for modeling heterogeneous firms' entry decisions. A standard probit would presume j would enter whenever $\bar{\pi}_j > -\epsilon_j$. Notice, however, that in the region to the north of the center cross-hatched rectangle firm 2 has positive duopoly profits and firm 1 has negative duopoly profits. Thus, if firm 1 were to have a monopoly here, firm 2 could enter and force firm 1 out. In essence, in this region firm 2 can preempt firm 1. A properly specified model of simultaneous entry decisions needs to recognize this possibility.

Finally, we have thus far focused on what happens when there are two potential entrants. The points made in this duopoly example continue to hold as one moves to larger concentrated oligopolies. In general, the researcher will have conditions that relate firms' latent profits to their discrete decisions. To illustrate, a Nash equilibrium

$D^*\{D_1^*, \ldots, D_N^*\}$ requires

$$D^* \cdot \pi(D^*) > 0, \qquad (1 - D^*) \cdot \pi\big(D^* + S_j \cdot (1 - D^*)\big) \leqslant 0$$

for all S_j, where π is an N-vector of firm profit functions, $\cdot$ is element-by-element multiplication, and S_j is a unit vector with a one in the jth position. The first condition requires that all entrants found it profitable to enter. The second condition requires that no potential entrant finds it profitable to enter.[11] This extended definition again does not rule out multiple equilibria. In general, if several firms have similar ϵ's then there may be values of firm profits (such as in the center of Figure 29.1) which would simultaneously support different subsets of firms entering.

3.2. Potential solutions to multiplicity

A variety of authors have proposed solutions to the multiplicity problem, beginning with Bjorn and Vuong (1984), Bresnahan and Reiss (1991a, 1991b) and Berry (1992). These solutions include (individually or in combination) changing what is analyzed, changing the economic structure of the underlying game, and changing assumptions about firm heterogeneities.

One strategy is to model the probabilities of aggregated outcomes that are robust to the multiplicity of equilibria. A second strategy is to place additional conditions on the model that guarantee a unique equilibrium. A third strategy is to include in the estimation additional parameters that "select" among multiple equilibria. Finally, a recently proposed alternative is to accept that some models with multiple equilibria are not exactly identified, and yet to note that they nevertheless do generate useful restrictions on economic quantities. We consider examples of each of these approaches in the following subsections.[12]

3.2.1. Aggregating outcomes

Bresnaham and Reiss (1988, 1991a) observe that although the threshold inequalities in Table 29.2 describing firms' decisions are not mutually exclusive, the inequalities describing the number of firms are mutually exclusive. In other words, the model uniquely predicts the number of firms that will enter, but not their identities. To see this, return to Figure 29.1. There, the number of firms is described by the following mutually exclusive and exhaustive regions: the white region (no firms), the solid gray region (duopoly) and the region with gray lines (monopoly). Given assumptions about the distribution of

[11] Because entry reduces competitor profits, if the second condition holds for all potential entrants individually, it holds for all combinations of potential entrants.

[12] Sweeting (2005) notes that there may be cases where the existence of multiple equilibrium actually helps in estimation. The reason is that multiple equilibrium can create variance in data that otherwise would not be present and this variance can potentially help to estimate a model.

Table 29.3
Two-firm market structure outcomes for a sequential-move game

Market outcome	N	Conditions on profits
No firms	0	$\pi_1^M < 0 \quad \pi_2^M < 0$
Firm 1 monopoly	1	$\pi_1^M > 0 \quad \pi_2^D < 0$
Firm 2 monopoly	1	$\pi_2^M > 0 \quad \pi_1^M < 0$
	1	$\pi_2^D > 0 \quad \pi_1^D < 0 < \pi_1^M$
Duopoly	2	$\pi_2^D > 0 \quad \pi_1^D > 0$

firms' profits, it is therefore possible to write down a likelihood function for the number of firms.

While changing the focus from analyzing individual firm decisions to a single market outcome (N) can solve the multiplicity problem, it is not without its costs. One potential cost is the loss of information about firm heterogeneities. In particular, it may no longer be possible to identify all the parameters of individual firms' observed and unobserved profits from observations on the total number of firms than entered.[13]

3.2.2. *Timing: sequential entry with predetermined orders*

An alternative response to multiple equilibria in perfect-information, simultaneous-move entry games is to assume that firms instead make decisions sequentially. While this change is conceptually appealing because it guarantees a unique equilibrium, it may not be practically appealing because it requires additional information or assumptions. For instance, the researcher either must: know the order in which firms move; make assumptions that permit the order in which firms move to be recovered from the estimation; or otherwise place restrictions on firms profit functions or the markets firms can enter. We discuss each of these possibilities in turn.

When firms make their entry decisions in a predetermined order, it is well known that early movers can preempt subsequent potential entrants [e.g., Bresnaham and Reiss (1990, 1991a)]. To see this, recall the structure of the equilibrium payoff regions of Figure 29.1. There, the payoffs in the center rectangle would support either firm as a monopolist. Now suppose that we knew or were willing to assume that firm 1 (exogenously) moved first. Under this ordering, the equilibrium threshold conditions are as shown in Table 29.3.

The sole difference between Tables 29.3 and 29.2 is that the region where firm 2 can be a monopolist shrinks. Specifically, by moving first, firm 1 can preempt the entry of firm 2 in the center cross-hatched area in Figure 29.1.

[13] See, for example, Bresnahan and Reiss (1991a) and Andrews, Berry and Jia (2005).

This change eliminates the multiplicity problem and leads to a coherent econometric model. If, for example, the researcher assumes the joint distribution of unobserved profits is $\phi(\cdot, x, z, \theta)$, then the researcher can calculate the probability of observing any equilibrium D^* as

$$\Pr(D^*) = \int_{A(D^*,x,z,\theta)} \phi(\epsilon, x, z, \theta)\, \mathrm{d}\epsilon. \tag{25}$$

In this expression, $A(D^*, x, z, \theta)$ is the region of ϵ's that leads to the outcome D^*. For example, in Figure 29.1 $A(0, 1)$ would correspond to the northwest region of firm 2 monopolies. There are two main problems researchers face in calculating the probabilities (25) when there are more than a few firms: (1) how to find the region A; and (2) how to calculate the integral over that region.

The problem of finding and evaluating the region A can become complicated when there are more than a few firms. Berry (1992) solves this problem via the method of simulated moments, taking random draws on the profit shocks and then solving for the unique number and identity of firms. With a sufficient number of draws (or more complicated techniques of Monte Carlo integration) it is also possible to construct a simulated maximum likelihood estimator.

3.2.3. Efficient (profitable) entry models

One criticism that can be leveled against models that assume that firms move in a given order is that this can result in an inefficient first-mover preempting a much more efficient second-mover. While the preemption of more efficient rivals may be a realistic outcome, it may not be realistic for all markets.

An alternative modeling strategy would be assume that inefficient entry never occurs. That is, that the most profitable entrant always is able to move first. In our two-firm model, for example, we might think of there being two entrepreneurs that face the profit possibilities displayed in Figure 29.1. The entrepreneur who moves first is able to decide whether they will be firm 1 or firm 2, and then whether they will enter. In this case, the first entrepreneur will decide to be the entrant with the greatest profits. This means that the center region of multiple monopoly outcomes in Figure 29.1 will now be divided as in Figure 29.2. In Figure 29.2, the dark, upward-sloping 45° line now divides the monopoly outcomes. The area above the diagonal and to the northwest represents outcomes where firm 2 is more profitable than firm 1. In this region, the initial entrepreneur (the first-mover) chooses to be firm 2. Below the diagonal, the opposite occurs – the initial entrepreneur (the first-mover) chooses to be firm 1. The thresholds that would be used in estimation are thus as shown in Table 29.4.

This two-stage model of sequential has several advantages and disadvantages when compared to previous models. On the positive side it resolves the multiplicity problem and the need to observe which firm moved first. For example, if we observe a firm 2 monopoly we know that the first-mover chose to be firm 2 because this was the more profitable of the two monopolies. Yet another potential advantage of this model is that

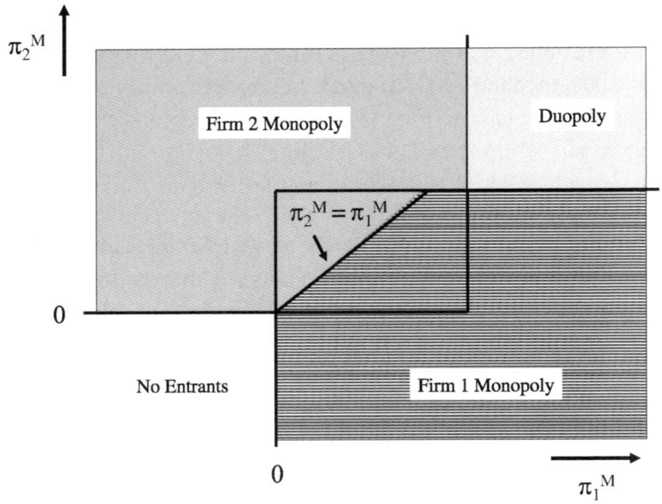

Figure 29.2. Multi-stage sequential monopoly model.

Table 29.4
Two-firm market structure outcomes for a two-stage sequential-move game

Market outcome	N	Conditions on profits		
No firms	0	$\pi_1^M < 0$		$\pi_2^M < 0$
Firm 1 monopoly	1	$\pi_1^M \geqslant 0,$	$\pi_1^M > \pi_2^M$	$\pi_2^D < 0$
Firm 2 monopoly	1	$\pi_2^M \geqslant 0,$	$\pi_2^M > \pi_1^M$	$\pi_1^D < 0$
Duopoly	2	$\pi_2^D \geqslant 0$		$\pi_1^D \geqslant 0$

in cases where the researcher observes which duopolist entered first, the researcher has additional information that potentially may result in more precise parameter estimates.

With these advantages come disadvantages however. Chief among them is a computational disadvantage. This disadvantage can be seen in the non-rectangular shape of the monopoly outcome regions. These non-rectangular shapes can considerably complicate estimation – particularly if the firms' unobserved profits are assumed to be correlated.

3.2.4. Estimating the probabilities of different equilibria

Another possible approach to multiplicity is to assume that the players move sequentially, but to treat the order as unknown to the econometrician. This approach is of limited use if the researcher does not have extra information that is correlated with who moves first. This is because a uniform likelihood model will mirror the multiplicity of the simultaneous-move model.

One response to this problem is to add a mechanism to the entry model that dictates the order in which the players move. Indeed, the assumption that the order is the same (or known) across all markets is a trivial example of a mechanism. One alternative mechanism is to assume that the order is randomly determined. Such a possibility was explored by Bjorn and Vuong (1984). One version of their approach would assign probabilities λ and $1 - \lambda$ to each of the two monopolies occurring. The researcher would then attempt to estimate this probability along with the other parameters.

Tamer (2003) extends this approach to let the probability of each equilibria depend on the exogenous x's observed in the data. In the two-firm case, he introduces an unknown function $H(x)$, which is the probability that firm 1 enters when the draws place us in the region of multiple equilibria. (More generally, one could let that probability depend on the unobservable as well, giving a new function $H(x, \epsilon)$.) Tamer estimates H as an unknown non-parametric function.

Tamer (2003) notes that, under suitable assumptions, the heterogeneous firm entry model is identified simply from information on the (uniquely determined) number of entering firms. However, adding an explicit probability for each equilibria can increase the efficiency of the maximum likelihood estimates.

There are several potential shortcomings of this approach. At a practical level, depending upon how this probability is specified and introduced into the estimation, the researcher may or may not be able to estimate these probabilities consistently. Additionally, once there are more than two potential entrants, the number of payoff regions that can support multiple outcomes can proliferate quickly, necessitating the introduction of many additional probability parameters to account for the frequency with which each outcome occurs. On a more general level, there is the conceptual issue of whether it makes sense to view firms as randomly participating when they know another firm could take their place.

3.2.5. A bounds approach

Manski (1995) has suggested using a "bounds" approach to estimation when the economic model is incomplete – that is, does not make complete predictions about observed outcomes.[14] Market structure models with multiple equilibria fit this case nicely.

The basic idea of Manski's approach is that while a model may not make exact predictions about outcomes, it still may restrict the range of possible outcomes. In some highly parameterized cases, these restrictions may still serve to point-identify the model. In other cases, the qualitative restrictions may identify a non-trivial set of parameters rather than a single point. One of Manski's contributions is to point out that "set identification" can be useful for testing particular hypotheses or illustrating the range of possible outcomes (of, say, a proposed policy). Ciliberto and Tamer (2003) and Andrews, Berry and

[14] See also Manski and Tamer (2002).

Jia (2005) use this general idea to formulate oligopoly entry models that place bounds on the demand and cost parameters of firms' profits. We can illustrate this general idea in a simple context.

Suppose that the profit for firm j of entering into market m is

$$\bar{\pi}(D_{-j}, x_j, \theta) + \epsilon_j, \tag{26}$$

D_{-j} is a vector of dummy variables indicating whether the firm's rivals have entered, x_j is a vector of profit shifters, θ is a vector of parameters to be estimated and ϵ_j is an unobserved profit shifter. If a firm enters, the best reply condition is satisfied

$$\bar{\pi}(D_{-j,m}, x_{jm}, \theta) + \epsilon_j \geqslant 0, \tag{27}$$

and if the firm does not enter, then

$$\bar{\pi}(D_{-j}, x_j, \theta) + \epsilon_j \leqslant 0. \tag{28}$$

In the case of multiple equilibria, these conditions are necessary but not sufficient, because the existence of multiple equilibria means that the same vectors of (x, ϵ) might also lead to another outcome, D'.

Using the distribution of ϵ, we can calculate the joint probability (across firms within a market) that the best reply conditions in (27) and (28) hold. This probability is *not* the probability of the observed entry choices, but it is an upper bound on that probability. This follows from the fact that necessary conditions are weaker than necessary-and-sufficient conditions. To be more formal, suppose that we observe the market structure outcome D_m in market m. For a given parameter vector θ, we can calculate $\Omega(D, x, \theta)$, the set of ϵ's that jointly satisfy the necessary conditions in (27) and (28) for a pure-strategy Nash equilibrium. By the definition of a necessary condition

$$\Pr\big(\epsilon \in \Omega(D, x, \theta_0)\big) \geqslant P_0(D \mid x). \tag{29}$$

That is the probability of the necessary condition holding must weakly exceed the probability of the equilibrium event.

The "identified set" of parameters is then the set of θ's that satisfy

$$\Pr\big(\epsilon \in \Omega(D, x, \theta)\big) \geqslant P_0(D \mid x). \tag{30}$$

A key question is whether this set is informative. For example, in practice the data and model may result in a set that is so large, it does not allow one to infer anything about demand and costs. On the other hand, it also is possible that the bounds are small enough so that the researcher can reject interesting hypotheses, such as the hypothesis that two firms do not compete with each other. Additionally, the identified set could place useful bounds on the outcomes of policy experiments, such as how market structure would change if the number of potential entrants changed.

These set identification arguments pose interesting econometric issues. These issues have recently attracted the interest of econometricians. For example, an important econometric issue is how one should go about forming a sample analog to (30). Others issues have to do with the rate of convergence and distribution of any estimator. Even more difficult is the question of how to place a confidence region on the set of parameters that satisfy the model. One of the first papers to address the inference problem in a general way is Chernozhukov, Hong and Tamer (2004). There also is on-going research by Andrews, Berry and Jia (2005), Ciliberto and Tamer (2003) and Shaikh (2006), among others.[15]

We now consider two empirical applications that rely on more traditional identification arguments and econometric methods.

3.3. Applications with multiple equilibria

3.3.1. Application: motel entry

Bresnahan and Reiss (1991a, 1991b) discuss a variety of approaches to modeling discrete games, including entry games. Several papers have adopted their structure to model firms' choices of discrete product types and entry decisions. Many of these papers also recognize the potential for multiple equilibria, and many adopt solutions that parallel those discussed above.

Mazzeo (2002), for example, models the entry decisions and quality choices of motels that locate near highway exits. Specifically, he has data on the number of high-quality and low-quality motels at geographically distinct highway exits. Thus, his discrete game is one where each potential entrant chooses a quality and whether to enter. It should be immediately clear that this is a setting where non-uniqueness and non-existence problems can easily arise. For example, consider the following table listing the (assumed symmetric) profit opportunities for high (H) and low (L) quality hotels as a function of the number of entrants of each type, N_L and N_H.

We note that the motels' profits decline as more motels of either type enter the local market. It is easy to verify that these profit outcomes support three simultaneous-move Nash equilibria: (2, 0), (1, 1) and (0, 2). Each of these outcomes results in two entrants.

Mazzeo recognizes the possibility of multiple outcomes and pursues two responses. The first is to assume that these firms move sequentially. This assumption guarantees a unique prediction for the game. Moreover, because here the firms are ex ante symmetric, it may also be possible to estimate parameters of the profit functions even when one does not know the exact order of entry. For example, in the above example, it is clear that (1, 1) is the unique sequential-move equilibrium provided we assume that the entry of a same-quality duopolist lowers profits more than a different-quality monopolist. With this assumption, it does not matter whether the first mover selected high or low quality, the second mover will always find it optimal to pick the other quality.

[15] Andrews, Berry and Jia (2005) consider a stylized empirical example of competition between WalMart and K-Mart, while Ciliberto and Tamer (2003) consider an airline-entry example in the spirit of Berry (1992).

Table 29.5
Entrant profits for qualities L and H entries are $(\pi_L(N_L, N_H), \pi_H(N_L, N_H))$

N_L	N_H 0	1	2	3
0	0, 0	0, 4	0, 1.5	0, −1
1	3, 0	2, 2	−1, −1	−2, −1
2	1, 0	−1, −1	−2, −2	−4, −3
3	−1, 0	−2, −3	−3, −4	−5, −5

As we have noted previously, in some cases the fact that firms move sequentially may advantage or disadvantage certain firms. Perhaps because a sequential-move equilibrium can result in inefficient outcomes, Mazzeo also considers two-stage equilibria where firms first make their entry decisions simultaneously and then make their quality decisions simultaneously. The equilibrium of this two-stage game in Table 29.5 is $(1, 1)$, as two firms initially commit to enter and then they split themselves among the qualities. This staging of the game here in effect selects the efficient entry outcome.

Because in general this second equilibrium concept need not result in unique entry and quality outcomes, Mazzeo must place additional structure on firms' observed and unobserved payoffs. In his empirical work, he assumes firm j of quality type k in market i has profits

$$\pi_{jki} = x_i\beta_k + g_k(N_{Li}, N_{Hi}, \theta) + \epsilon_{ki}, \tag{31}$$

where N_L and N_H are the numbers of high and low quality competitors. It is important to note that both the observable and unobservable portion of firm profits have no firm-level idiosyncrasies. In other words, profits are the same for all firms of a given quality in a given market. This assumption appears to be required because otherwise the specific order in which firms moved in could change the market structure outcome. This assumption also considerably simplifies estimation.

The function $g(\cdot)$ is introduced to allow the number of competitors of either quality to affect variable profits. Following Bresnahan and Reiss (1988), Mazzeo makes $g(\cdot)$ flexible by using dummy variables to shift $g(\cdot)$ with N_L and N_H. A key restriction, however, is that profits must decline faster with the entry of a firm of the same quality than the entry of a firm with a different quality. While this assumption seems reasonable in his application, it may not be applicable in others where the effect of entry depends more on factors idiosyncratic to the entrant.

In his empirical analysis, Mazzeo finds that the restrictions he uses result in non-rectangular boundaries for the market structure outcomes – the $A(D^*, x, z, \theta)$ in Equation (25). This leads him to employ frequency simulation when maximizing a likelihood function for the observed number of motels. His estimates suggest strong returns to differentiation. That is, that entry by the same quality rival causes profits to fall much more than if a different quality rival enters. Additionally, he finds that the choice of equilibrium concept appears to have little consequence for his estimates or predictions.

3.3.2. Application: airline city-pair entry

Several papers have developed econometric models of airlines' decisions to serve airline routes, including Reiss and Spiller (1989), Berry (1992) and Ciliberto and Tamer (2003). Unlike Mazzeo (2002), Berry (1992) develops a sequential-move entry model that allows for observed and unobserved firm heterogeneity.

For example, in several specifications Berry estimates a profit function with a homogeneous-product variable profit function for firm j in market m of

$$V(N_m, X_m) = X_m\beta - \delta\ln(N) + \epsilon_{m0}, \tag{32}$$

and a heterogeneous fixed cost term

$$F_{mj} = Z_{jm}\alpha + \epsilon_{mj}. \tag{33}$$

In these equations, X_m is a vector that includes distance between the endpoint cities and population, ϵ_{m0} is a normally distributed unobserved shock to all firms' variable profits, the Z are fixed cost variables that include a dummy if a firm serves both endpoints, and ϵ_{mj} is an independent error in each firm's profits.[16]

A key simplifying assumption in this specification is that only the total number of firms affects profits, meaning that firms are symmetric post-entry. This allows Berry to simplify the calculation of sequential-move equilibria. In his estimations, Berry uses the simulated method of moments approach of McFadden (1989) and Pakes and Pollard (1989). At candidate parameter values, he simulates and then orders the profits of the M potential entrants

$$\pi_1 > \pi_2 > \cdots > \pi_M. \tag{34}$$

He then uses the fact that the equilibrium number of firms, N^*, must satisfy

$$V(N^*, x, z, \theta) - F + \epsilon_N \geqslant 0, \tag{35}$$

and

$$V(N^* + 1, x, z, \theta) - F + \epsilon_{N^*+1} \leqslant 0. \tag{36}$$

Because of his symmetric competitor and variable profit assumptions, Berry can guarantee that there will be a unique N^* for any given set of profit parameters. An issue he does not address is what other types of profit specifications would guarantee a unique D^* equilibrium. Reiss (1996) considers a case where uniqueness of equilibrium is guaranteed by an assumption on the order of moves. In this case, full maximum likelihood estimation may be possible.

[16] Although Berry motivates the endpoint variable as affecting fixed costs, there are a number of reasons why the scale of operations could also affect variable profits. For example, airline hubs might allow airlines to pool passengers with different destinations, allowing the airlines to use larger, more efficient aircraft.

Table 29.6
Results from Berry (1992) on airline city-pair profits

Variable	Ordered probit	Firm probit	Full model
Constant	1.0	−3.4	−5.3
	(0.06)	(0.06)	(0.35)
Population	4.3	1.2	1.4
	(0.1)	(0.08)	(0.24)
Distance	−0.18	1.2	1.7
	(0.03)	(0.17)	(0.3)
Serving two endpoints	–	2.1	4.9
		(0.05)	(0.30)
Endpoint size	–	5.5	4.7
		(0.16)	(0.45)
ln(*N*)	1.8	–	0.53
	(0.05)		(0.12)

Besides modeling the equilibrium number of firms in the market, Berry's approach could be used to model the decisions of the individual potential entrants. To do this, one would simulate unobserved profit draws from $\phi(\epsilon, x, z, \theta)$ and then construct the probability of entry $\bar{D}_j$ for each potential entrant. In practice this would mean estimating via a frequency or smooth simulator

$$\bar{D}_j(x, z, \theta) = \int_{\bigcup A_j} \phi(\epsilon)\,\mathrm{d}\epsilon, \tag{37}$$

where $\bigcup A_j$ are all regions where firm j enters. The observed differences between the firms' decisions and the model's (simulated) predictions

$$\bar{D}_j - \bar{D}_j(x, z, \theta) = \nu_j \tag{38}$$

can then be used to form moment conditions.

Table 29.6 reports some of Berry's parameter estimates. The results and other estimates in Berry (1992) suggest that increases in the number of competitors reduces profits and that common heterogeneities in firms' fixed costs are important determinants of firm profit. Moreover, it appears that simple discrete choice models, like the bivariate probit (without competitive effects) and ordered probit (without firm heterogeneity), do not provide sensible models of entry.

These differences raise the question of what in the airline data allows Berry to separately estimate the effects of firm heterogeneity and competition. Berry suggests that variation in the number of potential entrants is key. His intuition appears to come from the order statistics literature. Berry and Tamer (2006) have attempted to formalize this intuition.

To conclude this subsection, we should emphasize that these examples illustrate only some of the compromises a researcher may have to make to rule out multiple equilibria. We should also emphasize that eliminating multiple equilibria in econometric models should not be an end in and of itself. For example, simply assuming firms move in a specific order may result in inconsistent parameter estimates if that order is incorrect. Moreover, it may well be that the multiplicity of pure-strategy equilibria is a fact of life and something that the econometric model should allow. In the next section we shall illustrate approaches that allow multiple outcomes.[17]

3.4. Imperfect information models

So far we have considered entry models in which potential entrants have perfect information about each other and the researcher has imperfect information about potential entrants' profits. In these models, the presence of multiple or no pure-strategy equilibria can pose non-trivial identification and estimation issues.

A natural extension of these models is to assume that, like the econometrician, potential entrants have imperfect information about each others' profits. In this case, potential entrants must base their entry decisions on expected profits, where their expectations are taken with respect to the imperfect information they have about competitors' profits. As we show below, the introduction of expectations about other players' profits may or may not ameliorate multiplicity and non-existence problems.

3.4.1. A two-potential entrant model

To appreciate some of the issues that arise in imperfect information models, it is useful to start with Bresnahan and Reiss' 2×2 perfect information entry game. Following Bresnahan and Reiss' notation, assume that the heterogeneity in potential entrants' profits comes in fixed costs. The two firms' ex post profits as function of their competitor's entry decision, D_j, can be represented as

$$\begin{aligned}\pi_1(D_1, D_2) &= D_1\big(\pi_1^M + D_2\Delta_1 - \epsilon_1\big),\\ \pi_2(D_1, D_2) &= D_2\big(\pi_2^M + D_1\Delta_2 - \epsilon_2\big),\end{aligned} \tag{39}$$

where the Δ_i represent the effect of competitor entry. To introduce private information in the model, imagine that firm i knows its own fixed cost unobservable ϵ_i, but it does not know its competitor's fixed cost unobservable ϵ_j. Assume also that firm i has a distribution $F_i(\epsilon_j)$ of beliefs about the other player's unobservable fixed costs ϵ_j.

Following the perfect information case, we must map the potential entrants' latent profit functions into equilibrium strategies for each potential entrant. Unlike the perfect information case, the potential entrants maximize expected profits, where they treat their competitor's action D_j as a function of the competitor's unknown fixed costs. Mathematically, firms 1 and 2 enter when their expected profits are positive, or

$$\begin{aligned}D_1 = 1 \quad &\Longleftrightarrow \quad D_1\big(\pi_1^M + p_2^1\Delta_1 - \epsilon_1\big) > 0,\\ D_2 = 1 \quad &\Longleftrightarrow \quad D_2\big(\pi_2^M + p_1^2\Delta_2 - \epsilon_2\big) > 0\end{aligned} \tag{40}$$

[17] See also Bresnahan and Reiss (1991a) for an analysis of a game with mixed strategies.

and $p_j^i = E_i(D_j)$ denotes firm i's expectation about the probability firm j will enter. In equilibrium, these probabilities must be consistent with behavior, requiring

$$p_2^1 = F_1(\pi_2^M + p_1^2 \Delta_2), \qquad p_1^2 = F_2(\pi_1^M + p_2^1 \Delta_1). \tag{41}$$

To complete the econometric model, the researcher must relate his or her information to the potential entrants' information. Absent application-specific details, there are many possible assumptions that can be entertained.

One leading case is to assume that the researcher's uncertainty corresponds to the firms' uncertainty. In this case, the econometric model will consist of the inequalities (40) and the probability equalities (41). Because the equations in (41) are non-linear, it is not immediately straightforward to show that the system has a solution or a unique solution. To illustrate the non-uniqueness problem, suppose the firms' private information has a $N(0, \sigma^2)$ distribution, $\pi_1^M = \pi_2^M = 1$ and $\Delta_1 = \Delta_2 = -4$. In the perfect information case where $\sigma^2 = 0$, this game has two pure strategy Nash equilibria ($\{D_1 = 1, D_2 = 0\}$ and $\{D_1 = 0, D_2 = 1\}$) and one mixed strategy equilibrium (both firms enter with probability 0.25). When σ^2 is greater than zero and small, there is a unique symmetric equilibrium where each firm enters with a probability slightly above 0.25. There also are two asymmetric equilibria, each with one firm entering with a probability close to one and the other with a probability close to zero. These equilibria parallel the three Nash equilibria in the perfect information case. As σ^2 increases above 1, the asymmetric equilibria eventually vanish and a unique symmetric equilibrium remains. This equilibrium has probabilities $p_2^1 = p_1^2$ approaching 0.5 from below as σ^2 tends to infinity.

Thus in this example there are multiple equilibria for small amounts of asymmetric information. The multiple equilibria appear because the model's parameters essentially locate us in the center rectangle of Figure 29.1, apart from the firm's private information. If, on the other hand, we had chosen $\pi_1^M = \pi_2^M = 1$ and $\Delta_1 = \Delta_2 = -0.5$, then we would obtain a single symmetric equilibrium with probability $p_2^1 = p_1^2$ approaching 0.5 from above as σ^2 tends to infinity and both players entering with probability 1 as σ^2 tends to zero. (The later result simply reflects that duopoly profits are positive for both firms.) These examples illustrate that introducing private information does not necessarily eliminate the problems found in complete information games. Moreover, in these games, there need be no partition of the error space that uniquely describes the number of firms.[18] Finally, any uncertainty the econometrician has about the potential entrants' profits above and beyond that of the firms will only tend to compound these problems.

[18] In the above example, uniqueness appears to be obtainable if the researcher focuses on symmetric equilibria or if restrictions are placed on Δ.

3.4.2. Quantal response equilibria

The above model extends the basic Bresnahan and Reiss duopoly econometric model to the case where potential entrants have private information about their payoffs and the econometrician is symmetrically uninformed about the potential entrants' payoffs. Independently, theorists and experimentalists have developed game-theoretic models to explain why players might not play Nash equilibrium strategies in normal form games. The quantal response model of McKelvey and Palfrey (1995) is one such model, and it closely parallels the above model. The motivation offered for the quantal response model is, however, different.

In McKelvey and Palfrey (1995), players' utilities have the form

$$u_{ij} = u_i(D_{ij}, p_{-i}) + \epsilon_{ij},$$

where D_{ij} is strategy j for player i and p_{-i} represents the probabilities that player i assigns to the other players playing each of their discrete strategies. The additive strategy-specific error term ϵ_{ij} is described as representing "mistakes" or "errors" the agent makes in evaluating the utility $u_i(\cdot,\cdot)$. The utility specification and its possibly non-linear dependence on the other players' strategies is taken as a primitive and is not derived from any underlying assumptions about preferences and player uncertainties.

A quantal response equilibrium (QRE) is defined as a rational expectations equilibrium in which the probabilities p each player assigns to the other players playing their strategies is consistent with the probability the players play those strategies. Thus, the probability $p_{ij} = \Pr(u_{ij} \geqslant \max_k u_{ik})$ for $k \neq j$ must match the probability that other players assign to player i playing strategy D_{ij}.

This quantal response model is similar to the private information entry model in the previous section. The two are essentially the same when the utility (profit) function $u_i(D_{ij}, p_{-i})$ can be interpreted as expected utility (profit). This places restrictions on the way the other players' strategies D_{-i} enter utility. In the duopoly entry model, the competitor's strategy entered linearly, so that $E_D u_1(D_1, D_2) = u_1(D_1, E_D D_2) = u_1(D_1, p_2^1)$. In a three-player model, profits (utility) of firm 1 might have the general form

$$\pi_1(D_1, D_2, D_3) = D_1\left(\pi_1^M + D_2\Delta_{12} + D_3\Delta_{13} + D_2 D_3\Delta_{123}\right).$$

In this case, independence of the players' uncertainties (which appears to be maintained in quantal response models) would deliver an expected profit function that depends on the player's own strategy and the p^i_j.

3.4.3. Asymmetric entry/location models

Quantal response models have been used to model data from a variety of experiments in which players have discrete strategies [see, for example, Goeree and Holt (2000)]. As in McKelvey and Palfrey (1995), interest often centers on estimating the variance of the errors in utility as opposed to parameters of the utility functions, $u_i(\cdot,\cdot)$. The estimated variance sometimes is used to describe how close the quantal response equilibrium is to a Nash equilibrium. A standard modeling assumption is that the utility errors have a Type 1 extreme value distribution and thus that the choice (strategy) probabilities can be calculated using a scaled logistic distribution. Most studies are able to identify the variance of ϵ_{ij} because they are modeling experimental choices in which the players' utilities are presumed to be the monetary incentives offered as part of a controlled experiment.

Seim (2000, 2006) introduces asymmetric information into an econometric models of potential entrants' location decisions.[19] Specifically, Seim models a set of N potential entrants deciding in which one, if any, of L locations the entrants will locate. In Seim's application, the potential entrants are video rental stores and the locations are Census tracts within a town.[20]

In Seim's model, if potential entrant i enters location l, it earns

$$\pi_{il}(\bar{n}^i, x_l) = x_l\beta + \theta_{ll}\sum_{j\neq i}^{N} D_{jl} + \sum_{h\neq l}\theta_{lh}\sum_{k\neq i} D_{kh} + \nu_{il}, \tag{42}$$

where D_{kh} denotes an indicator for whether store k has chosen to enter location h; $\bar{n}^i = n_0^i, \ldots, n_L^i$ denotes the number of competitors in each location (i.e., $n_h^i = \sum_{j\neq i} D_{jh}$); location 0 is treated as the "Do not enter any location"; x_l is a vector of profit shifters for location l; and β and θ are parameters. The own-location effect of competition on profits is measured by the parameter θ_{ll}, while cross-location effects are measured by θ_{lh}. The term ν_{il} is a store/location specific shock that is observed by the store but not by its rivals. Aside from ν, all of the stores' profits (in the same location) are identical.

Because a given store does not observe the other stores' ν's, the store treats the other stores' D_{jh} as random variables when computing the expected number of rival stores in each location h. By symmetry, each store's expectation that one of its rivals will enter location h is $p_h = E_D(D_{kh})$. Given $N-1$ rivals, the number of expected rivals in location h is then $(N-1)p_h$. We now see that the linearity of π in the D_{kh} is especially convenient, as

$$E_D\pi_{il}(\bar{n}^i, x_l) = x_l\beta + \theta_{ll}(N-1)p_l + \sum_{j\neq l}\theta_{lj}(N-1)p_j + \nu_{il} = \bar{\pi}_l + \nu_{il}. \tag{43}$$

For simplicity, one could assume that the ν's have the type 1 extreme value or "double-exponential" distribution that leads to multinomial logit choice probabilities.[21] In this case, Equation (43) defines a classic logit discrete choice problem. The $L+1$ entry probabilities, the p_l, then map into themselves in equilibrium. These entry probabilities then appear in the stores' profit and best response functions.

[19] The econometrics of such models are considered further in Aradillas-Lopez (2005).

[20] By way of comparison, the Bresnahan and Reiss model assumes there is only one location in town.

[21] In practice, Seim treats "no entry" as location 0 in the choice problem and uses a nested logit model of the unobservables, where the entry locations $l > 0$ are more "similar" than the no-entry location.

To calculate the Nash equilibrium entry probabilities $p_1, \ldots, p_L$ we must solve the non-linear system of equations[22]

$$
\begin{aligned}
p_0 &= \frac{1}{1 + \sum_{l=1}^{L} \exp(\bar{\pi}_l)}, \\
p_1 &= \frac{\exp(\bar{\pi}_1)}{1 + \sum_{l=1}^{L} \exp(\bar{\pi}_l)}, \\
&\vdots \\
p_L &= \frac{\exp(\bar{\pi}_L)}{1 + \sum_{l=1}^{L} \exp(\bar{\pi}_l)}.
\end{aligned} \tag{44}
$$

Seim argues that for fixed N, a solution to this equilibrium system exists and is typically unique, although as the relative variance of the ν's declines, the problem approaches the discrete problem and it seems that the non-uniqueness problem faced in perfect information simultaneous-move could reoccur. The single location model discussion above illustrates how and why this could happen.

Three other noteworthy issues arise when she estimates this model. The first is that in principle she would like to parameterize the scale of the logit error so that she could compare the model estimates to a case where the potential entrants had perfect information about each other's profits. Unfortunately, this cannot be done because the scale parameter is not separately identified from the profit parameters. The second issue is that the number of potential entrants in each market is unknown. Seim deals with this problem by making alternative assumptions about the number of potential entrants. The third is that some markets have small census tracts and others have large tracts. To be able to compare θ_{ij}'s across markets and to reduce the number she has to estimate, Seim associates the θ's with distance bands about any given location. Thus, two neighboring tracts, each ten miles away, would have their entrants weighted equally in a store's profit function. Naturally, competitors in nearer bands are thought to have greater (negative) effects on store profits than competitors in more distant bands, however, these effects are not directly linked to the geographic dispersion of consumers [as for example in the retail demand model of Davis (1997)].

Turning to estimation, the system (44) produces probabilities of entry for each firm for each location in a market. The joint distribution of the number of entrants in each location $\bar{n} = n_0, \ldots, n_L$ is given by the multinomial distribution

$$P(n_0, \ldots, n_L) = N! \prod_{j=0}^{L} \frac{p_j^{n_j}}{n_j!}.$$

Because the probabilities p_j depend on each other, some type of nested fixed-point algorithm will have to be used to evaluate the likelihood function for each new parameter vector. Similarly, generalized method of moment techniques that used the expected

[22] Seim's expressions differ somewhat because she uses a nested logit and includes market unobservables.

number of entrants in each location, combined with a nested fixed point algorithm, could be used to compute parameter estimates.

3.5. Entry in auctions

The IO literature has recently devoted considerable attention to estimating structural econometric models of auction participants' bids. Almost all of these empirical models presume that the number of participants is exogenously given. The number of bidders in an auction is then used as a source of variation to identify parameters of the auction model. Recently, there have been several attempts to develop and estimate structural models of auction participation decisions. These papers build on theoretical models that explore how participation and bids are related [e.g., McAfee and McMillan (1987), Levin and Smith (1994), and Pevnitskaya (2004)].

Auctions are a natural place in which to apply and extend private information models of entry. This is because the actual number of bidders is typically less than the total eligible to bid in any given auction. Additionally, in the standard auction set-up bidders are presumed to have private information about their valuations, which is analogous to potential entrants having private information about costs. As the theoretical literature has emphasized, auction models differ considerably depending upon the affiliation of participants' information, auction formats and auction rules. In addition, when considering entry, there is an issue of what players know when they bid versus what they know when they make their entry decisions.

To illustrate parallels and differences between auction participation and market entry models, consider a sealed-bid, private values auction with symmetric, risk-neutral bidders. In a first stage, assume that N potential bidders decide whether to pay a known entry cost K to enter, and in a second stage they bid after learning the number of "entering" bidders, n.

Conditional on entering and having $n-1$ rivals, bidder i with private value v_i maximizes expected profits of

$$\pi_i(v_i, b, n) = (v_i - b) \prod_{j \neq i}^{n} G(b, j) \tag{45}$$

by choosing b. In this expression, $G(b, j)$ is the probability that bidder j bids less than b. The first-order conditions for this maximization, along with any boundary conditions, determine the optimal bid functions as a function of the private information v_i and the number of bidders, n. Inserting these bid functions back into the profit function (45), delivers an expected equilibrium profit function $\pi(v_i, n)$ as a function of n.

To predict how many firms n will bid, we now need to know the timing of the private information. In Levin and Smith, for example, the N potential bidders do not know their valuations before they sink an entry cost K. In a symmetric equilibrium, the potential bidders randomize their entry decisions wherein they decide to pay the entry cost K

with probability p^*. In equilibrium then, expected profits

$$\sum_{n=1}^{N} \Pr(n-1, N-1) E_v \pi(v_i, n) - K$$

will equal zero. Here, E_v denotes the expectation with respect to the (symmetric) distribution of private values revealed post-entry. The term $\Pr(n-1, N-1)$ denotes the probability that $n-1$ of the $N-1$ rival firms choose to enter. In a symmetric equilibrium, this probability is the binomial probability

$$\Pr(n-1, N-1) = \binom{N-1}{n-1} p^{n-1} (1-p)^{N-n}.$$

This probability can serve as the basis for estimating p^* from the empirical distribution of n. In turn, estimates of p^* can be used to obtain an estimate of K.[23]

3.6. Other kinds of firm heterogeneity

The empirical applications we have discussed either model firm heterogeneities as part of fixed cost, or else model potential heterogeneity as a discrete set of firm types. There are a wide range of choices about endogenous market structure that we have not considered here but are obviously empirically important and would be useful extensions to the existing empirical literature on "structural" models of market structure. These extensions would include allowing for

- endogenous scale of operations;
- endogenous product characteristics in a continuous space;
- endogenous product quality.

Each of these topics is discussed at great length in the theoretical literature in IO and each of these topics has featured in descriptive empirical work on actual industries, but the tie between theory and empirical work is far from complete.

3.7. Dynamics

In a separate chapter in this volume, Ulrich Doraszelski and Ariel Pakes discuss a class of dynamic industry models that are intended to be applied. As in Ericson and Pakes (1995), these models incorporate firm heterogeneity, endogenous investment (with uncertain outcomes), imperfect competition and entry and exit. However, to date the empirical application of those models has been limited and the present empirical applications rely on calibration as much or more than on estimation. One reason for this is the "curse of dimensionality" that makes computation take a long time. There are

[23] Other estimation strategies are possible. Additionally, more heterogeneity can be introduced by making p and K depend on covariates.

two solutions to this curse. The first is the development of faster computational techniques and faster computers. The second is the development of econometric techniques to estimate some parameters without fully solving the dynamic model. In simpler entry models, this amounts to estimating some demand and marginal cost parameters without solving the entry game (but likely using instrumental variables to control for endogenous market structure).

There are a range of possible models that fall between the strictly static (or "cross-sectional") models of this chapter and the more complicated dynamic models exemplified by Ericson and Pakes (1995). A first set of steps in this direction is taken by Aguirregabiria and Mira (2007), Pakes, Ostrovsky and Berry (2004) and Pesendorfer and Schmidt-Dengler (2004). For example, one could consider a repeated entry game, where the variable profit function is symmetric (as in Bresnahan and Reiss) and heterogeneity only enters fixed cost [as in Berry (1992)]. One might assume that a fraction of the fixed costs are sunk and some fraction must be paid anew each period. To keep the model simple, one might follow Seim (2006) in assuming that each period's unobservable is i.i.d. and privately observed by the firm. In the dynamic context, the resulting ex post regret will affect future entry and exit decisions. One could track data on the number of firms in each market in each time period, learning about sunk costs via the degree to which history matters in predicting N as a function of current market conditions and past N. Such a model would be much easier to compute than models with richer notions of firm heterogeneity and investment, but of course this would come at the cost of considerable realism.

4. Conclusion

The models of this chapter use the logic of revealed preference to uncover parameters of profit functions from the cross-sectional distribution of market structure (i.e. "entry decisions") of oligopolist firms across markets of different sizes and types. We have highlighted the role that assumptions on functional form, distributions of unobservables and the nature of competition play in allowing us to estimate the parameters of underlying profits. Considerable progress has been made in applying these models to an increasingly rich set of data and questions. Considerable work remains in dealing with important limitations of the work, including difficult questions about dynamics and multiple equilibria.

References

Aguirregabiria, V., Mira, P. (2007). "Sequential estimation of dynamic discrete games". Econometrica 75 (1), 1–53.

Andrews, D., Berry, S., Jia, P. (2005). "Confidence regions for parameters in discrete games with multiple equilibria". Working Manuscript. Yale University.

Aradillas-Lopez, A. (2005). "Semiparametric estimation of a simultaneous game with incomplete information". Working Manuscript. Princeton University.
Bain, J.S. (1956). Barriers to New Competition, Their Character and Consequences in Manufacturing Industries. Harvard Univ. Press, Cambridge.
Berry, S.T. (1992). "Estimation of a model of entry in the airline industry". Econometrica 60 (4), 889–917.
Berry, S.T., Tamer, E. (2006). "Identification in models of oligopoly entry". Working Manuscript. Yale University.
Berry, S.T., Waldfogel, J. (1999). "Social inefficiency in radio broadcasting". RAND Journal of Economics 30 (3), 397–420.
Bjorn, P., Vuong, Q. (1984). "Simultaneous equations models for dummy endogenous variables: A game theoretic formulation with an application to labor force participation". Working Manuscript SSWP 537. California Institute of Technology.
Bourguignon, F., Chiappori, P. (1992). "Collective models of household behavior, an introduction". European Economic Review 36, 355–364.
Bresnahan, T.F. (1989). "Empirical methods for industries with market power". In: Schmalensee, R., Willig, R. (Eds.), Handbook of Industrial Organization, vol. 2. North-Holland, Amsterdam.
Bresnahan, T.F., Reiss, P.C. (1988). "Do entry conditions vary across markets?". Brookings Papers in Economic Activity: Microeconomic Annual 1, 833–882.
Bresnahan, T.F., Reiss, P.C. (1990). "Entry in monopoly markets". Review of Economic Studies 57, 57–81.
Bresnahan, T.F., Reiss, P.C. (1991a). "Empirical models of discrete games". Journal of Econometrics 48 (1–2), 57–81.
Bresnahan, T.F., Reiss, P.C. (1991b). "Entry and competition in concentrated markets". Journal of Political Economy 99 (5), 977–1009.
Caves, R. (1998). "Industrial organization and new findings on the mobility and turnover of firms". Journal of Economic Literature 36, 1947–1982.
Chernozhukov, V., Hong, H., Tamer, E. (2004). "Inference on parameter sets in econometric models". Working Manuscript. MIT Department of Economics.
Ciliberto, F., Tamer, E. (2003). "Market structure and multiple equilibria in the airline industry". Working Manuscript. Princeton University.
Davis, P. (1997). "Spatial competition in retail markets: Motion theaters". RAND Journal of Economics. In press.
Dunne, T., Roberts, M.J., Samuelson, L. (1988). "Patterns of firm entry and exit in U.S. manufacturing industries". RAND Journal of Economics 19 (4), 495–515.
Ericson, R., Pakes, A. (1995). "Markov perfect industry dynamics: A framework for empirical work". Review of Economic Studies 62, 53–82.
Geroski, P. (1995). "What do we know about entry?". International Journal of Industrial Organization 13, 421–440.
Goeree, J., Holt, C. (2000). "An explanation of anomalous behavior in binary-choice games: Entry, voting, public goods, and the volunteers dilemma". Working Manuscript. University of Virginia.
Heckman, J. (1978). "Dummy endogenous variables in a simultaneous equation system". Econometrica 46, 931–959.
Klein, R., Sherman, R. (2002). "Shift restrictions and semiparametric estimation in ordered response models". Econometrica 70, 663–692.
Kooreman, P. (1994). "Estimation of econometric models of some discrete games". Journal of Applied Econometrics 9, 255–268.
Levin, D., Smith, J. (1994). "Equilibrium in auctions with entry". American Economic Review 84, 585–599.
Lewbel, A. (2002). "Ordered response threshold estimation". Working Manuscript. Boston College.
Manski, C. (1995). Identification Problems in the Social Sciences. Harvard Univ. Press, Cambridge.
Manski, C., Tamer, E. (2002). "Inference on regressions with interval data on a regressor or outcome". Econometrica 70, 519–546.
Mazzeo, M. (2002). "Product choice and oligopoly market structure". RAND Journal of Economics 33 (2), 1–22.

McAfee, R.P., McMillan, J. (1987). "Auctions with entry". Economics Letters 23, 343–347.
McFadden, D. (1989). "Method of simulated moments for estimation of discrete response models without numerical integration". Econometrica 57, 995–1026.
McKelvey, R., Palfrey, T. (1995). "Quantal response equilibria for normal form games". Games and Economic Behavior 10, 6–38.
Pakes, A., Pollard, D. (1989). "Simulation and the asymptotics of optimization estimators". Econometrica 54, 1027–1057.
Pakes, A., Ostrovsky, M., Berry, S. (2004). "Simple estimators for the parameters of dynamic games, with entry/exit examples". Working Manuscript. Harvard University.
Pesendorfer, M., Schmidt-Dengler, P. (2004). "Identification and estimation of dynamic games". Working Manuscript. London School of Economics.
Pevnitskaya, S. (2004). "Endogenous entry in first-price private-value auctions: The selection effect". Working Manuscript. Ohio State University.
Reiss, P.C. (1996). "Empirical models of discrete strategic choices". American Economic Review 86, 421–426.
Reiss, P.C., Spiller, P.T. (1989). "Competition and entry in small airline markets". Journal of Law and Economics 32 (2), S179–S202.
Rysman, M. (2004). "Competition between networks: A study of the market for Yellow Pages". Review of Economic Studies 71, 483–512.
Seim, K. (2000). "Essays on spatial product differentiation". Ph.D. Dissertation. Yale University.
Seim, K. (2006). "An empirical model of firm entry and endogenous product-type choices". RAND Journal of Economics 37 (3).
Shaikh, A. (2006). "Inference for partially identified econometric models". Working Manuscript. Stanford University.
Sutton, J. (2007). "Market structure: Theory and evidence". In: Armstrong, M., Porter, R. (Eds.), Handbook of Industrial Organization, vol. 3. North-Holland, Amsterdam (this volume).
Sweeting, A. (2005). "Coordination games, multiple equilibria and the timing of radio commercials". Working Manuscript. Northwestern University.
Tamer, E. (2003). "Incomplete simultaneous discrete response model with multiple equilibria". Review of Economic Studies 70, 147–165.

Chapter 30

A FRAMEWORK FOR APPLIED DYNAMIC ANALYSIS IN IO

ULRICH DORASZELSKI

Harvard University

ARIEL PAKES

Harvard University

Contents

Handbook of Industrial Organization, Volume 3
Edited by M. Armstrong and R. Porter

DOI: 10.1016/S1573-448X(06)03030-5

Abstract

This paper reviews a framework for numerically analyzing dynamic interactions in imperfectly competitive industries. The framework dates back to Ericson and Pakes [1995. Review of Economic Studies 62, 53–82], but it is based on equilibrium notions that had been available for some time before, and it has been extended in many ways by different authors since. The framework requires as input a set of primitives which describe the institutional structure in the industry to be analyzed. The framework outputs profits and policies for every incumbent and potential entrant at each possible state of the industry. These policies can be used to simulate the distribution of sample paths for all firms from any initial industry structure. The sample paths generated by the model can be quite different depending on the primitives, and most of the extensions were designed to enable the framework to accommodate empirically relevant cases that required modification of the initial structure. The sample paths possess similar properties to those observed in (the recently available) panel data sets on industries. These sample paths can be used either for an analysis of the likely response to a policy or an environmental change, or as the model's implication in an estimation algorithm. We begin with a review of an elementary version of the framework and a report on what is known about its analytic properties. Much of the rest of the paper deals with computational issues. We start with an introduction to iterative techniques for computing equilibrium that are analogous to the techniques used to compute the solution to single agent dynamic programming problems. This includes discussions of the determinants of the computational burden of these techniques, and the mechanism implicitly used to select an equilibrium when multiple equilibria are possible. We then outline a number of techniques that might be used to reduce the computational burden of the iterative algorithm. This section includes discussions of both the implications of differences in modeling assumptions used in the alternative techniques, and a discussion of the likely relevance of the different techniques for different institutional structures. A separate section reports on a technique for computing multiple equilibria from the same set of primitives. The paper concludes with a review of applications of the framework and a brief discussion of areas where further development of the framework would seem warranted.

Keywords

Dynamic oligopoly, Markov perfect equilibrium, Computational techniques, Multiple equilibria, Applications

JEL classification: C73, C63, L13

1. Introduction

The applied analysis of dynamic interactions in imperfectly competitive industries is just beginning. This paper reviews a framework which has been developed to facilitate this analysis. The framework dates back to Ericson and Pakes (1995) (hereafter EP), and has been improved and generalized by a series of authors since that article. The EP framework worked to integrate a set of baseline facts from the empirical literature with notions of equilibrium from the theoretical literature.

The facts, drawn in part from the newly available panel data sets on the evolution of firms and industries, made it clear that for a framework to be rich enough to be taken to data it had to allow for heterogeneity among firms within a market (even for very narrowly defined markets), both firm and market (or sometimes industry) specific sources of uncertainty, and entry and exit [see, e.g., Dunne, Roberts and Samuelson (1988) and Davis and Haltiwanger (1992)]. The firm specific uncertainty is needed to account for the fact that we often see both simultaneous entry and exit and rank reversals in the fortunes of firms within a market (no matter how we define "fortunes"). The market (and/or) industry specific uncertainty is needed to rationalize the fact that often the firms competing in a given market (or industry) are subject to changes in costs or demand conditions which cause their profits to be positively correlated.

The EP framework is designed to track an oligopolistic industry over time. In each period, incumbent firms decide whether to remain in the industry and how much to invest, and potential entrants decide whether to enter the industry. Once the investment, entry, and exit decisions are made, firms compete in the product market. Firm heterogeneity is accounted for by encoding all payoff-relevant characteristics of a firm in its "state". Typically a firm's state describes its production capacity, cost structure, and/or the quality of its product. A firm is able to change its state over time through investment, and there is both firm and industry specific variability in the outcomes of the investment. This can generate both diversity of fortunes of seemingly similar firms and positive correlation in their profits.

Formally the EP framework is a dynamic stochastic game with a discrete state space. Dynamic stochastic games have a long tradition in economics. Dating back to Shapley (1953), these games have become central to the analysis of strategic interactions among forward-looking players in dynamic environments. See Filar and Vrieze (1997) and Basar and Olsder (1999) for textbook treatments.[1]

The equilibrium notion used in the EP framework is that of Markov perfect equilibrium. For applied work there were at least two virtues of the Markov perfect notion. First it involved familiar notions, as Markov processes are used intensively in applied work in

[1] This approach differs from continuous-time games with a continuum of states which date back to Isaacs (1954) (zero-sum games) and Starr and Ho (1969) (non-zero-sum games). See Basar and Olsder (1999) for a standard presentation of differential games and Dockner et al. (2000) for a survey of applications.

related fields. Perhaps more important, however, was the fact that Markov perfect equilibria deliver an empirically tractable way of analyzing outcomes. That is, they allow us to condition on a current state, hopefully a state that we might be able to read off the data, and generate a probability distribution of the subsequent state. That distribution can then be used for either estimation or for numerical analysis.[2]

The Markov perfect notion was used intensively in an influential set of theory papers examining dynamic issues in oligopolistic settings by Maskin and Tirole (1987, 1988a, 1988b). One lesson from these articles was just how rich a set of outcomes could be generated even from extremely stylized environments; far too stylized for anyone to think of using them to closely approximate behavior in any market. Partly this was the result of the possibility of multiple equilibria, a topic we examine in some detail below. However even more evident was the fact that very different types of behavior could be generated by changes in the primitives of the problem (the nature of the demand or cost functions, or the characteristics of investment processes allowed). Moreover the diverse patterns of outcomes illustrated by different industry studies reinforced the impression that, depending on the details of the institutional structure, different industries could have very different evolutionary patterns.

The EP framework copes with this result by providing a framework with an ability to "plug in" different primitives, and then numerically analyze their result. The framework delivers very little in the way of analytic results of applied interest; i.e. just about anything can happen. Indeed by adopting the framework the researcher essentially gives up on analytic elegance in favor of an ability to numerically analyze the more complex situations that might better approximate what we seem to observe in real data sets. Theoretical results from stylized environments are often used at a later stage as a guide to understanding the economics underlying the phenomena generated by the numerical results.

This paper provides an introduction to the EP framework and then considers issues that arise in using it to numerically analyze results from different specifications for its primitives. We begin by outlining the model in Section 2, and then, in Section 3, summarize what is known about questions of existence of equilibrium, the characteristics of the equilibrium when it does exist, and the potential for multiple equilibria. Section 4 provides an introduction to techniques for computing an equilibria, and then considers their computational burden. Section 5 considers techniques for alleviating this computational burden. In Section 6 we consider what is known about computing multiple equilibria (from the same set of primitives). Section 7 reviews applications and extensions of the framework. Section 8 points out some (of the many) topics that require further study, and Section 9 concludes.

[2] In fact there is some debate as to whether the concept of Markov perfect equilibrium restricts policies and outcomes in untestable ways, and hence weaker notions of equilibria, such as the notion of self-confirming equilibrium in Fudenberg and Levine (1993), are more appropriate for applied work. This is largely a topic beyond the scope of this paper, but we come back to a related issue in Section 5 below, where we provide a way of computing a weaker equilibrium notion.

2. Model

The EP framework is designed to capture the evolution of an industry with heterogeneous firms. The model is dynamic, time is discrete, and the horizon is infinite. There are two groups of firms, incumbent firms and potential entrants. An incumbent firm has to decide each period whether to remain in the industry and, if so, how much to invest. A potential entrant has to decide whether to enter the industry and, if so, how much to invest. We assume that entry, exit, and investment decisions are made simultaneously at the beginning of the period.

Once these decisions are made, product market competition takes place. For simplicity, we assume that the price or quantity that a firm sets in the product market has no effect on the dynamics of the industry. This reflects the traditional "static–dynamic" breakdown in teaching IO. Due to this "static–dynamic" breakdown, the profit function can be computed "off line" and fed into the algorithm for computing the equilibrium of the dynamic stochastic game. Hence, we essentially treat the per-period profit function as a primitive of the dynamic stochastic game.

For the reader who is familiar with this literature, we note that the model below differs from the model in EP in a few details. First, we treat setup costs and scrap values as privately known random variables in order to ensure the existence of an equilibrium.[3] Second, we assume that exit decisions are implemented after incumbent firms compete in the product market. That is, while entry, exit, and investment decisions are made at the beginning of the period, we assume that their realizations occur at the end of the period. Hence, a firm's current profit from product market competition is completely determined by the current state of the industry. Third, when we allow more than one potential entrant per period to come into the industry we assume that entry decisions, like exit decisions, are made simultaneously. Moreover, we allow a potential entrant to make an initial investment in order to improve the odds that it comes into industry in a more favorable state. Most of these changes make the model easier to compute.

Incumbent firms Incumbent firm i is described by its state $\omega_i \in \Omega$. EP assume that the state takes on integer values and provide conditions which insure that there are finite upper and lower bounds to the states that can occur in equilibrium (see Section 3.2 for details). Thus, without loss of generality, we take $\Omega = \{1, 2, \ldots, \bar{\omega}\}$. Typically the state of a firm encodes the characteristics of the products the firm sells or of the production process used to produce those products (e.g., the firm's capital stock or productivity), but it may also include variables that are not as directly "payoff relevant" (as, e.g., in models of collusion, see Section 7.5). A firm is able to change its state over time through its investment $x_i \geqslant 0$. While a higher investment today is no guarantee of a more

[3] Pakes and McGuire (1994) suggest treating a potential entrant's setup cost as a random variable to overcome convergence problems in their algorithm. Gowrisankaran (1995) is the first to make the connection between existence of equilibrium and randomization of both entry and exit decisions and Doraszelski and Satterthwaite (2003) provide a formal proof.

favorable state tomorrow, it does ensure a more favorable distribution over future states. Since a firm's transition from one state to another is subject to an idiosyncratic shock, there is variability in the fortunes of firms even if they carry out identical strategies. This variability in outcomes is necessary for the model to be able to rationalize the data on the evolution of firms.

Turning from investment to exit, we assume that at the beginning of each period each incumbent firm draws a random scrap value from a distribution $F(\cdot)$. Scrap values are independently and identically distributed across firms and periods.[4] Incumbent firm i learns its scrap value ϕ_i prior to making its exit and investment decisions, but the scrap values of its rivals remain unknown to it. If the incumbent decides to exit the industry, it collects its scrap value ϕ_i and perishes. Since this decision is conditioned on the privately known ϕ_i, it is a random variable from the perspective of other firms, and we use r_i to denote the probability that incumbent firm i *remains* in the industry.

Potential entrants In addition to incumbent firms, there are potential entrants. Entry has been treated differently in different papers. This proliferation of entry models is largely because there is no agreement, and very little in the way of empirical guidance, on the appropriate way to model entry; indeed this is one of our suggested directions for future research (see Section 8). For concreteness we assume here that there is a finite number $\mathcal{E}$ of potential entrants in each period and they make simultaneous entry decisions.

Potential entrants are short-lived and base their entry and investment decisions on the net present value of entering today; potential entrants do not take the option value of delaying entry into account. At the beginning of each period each potential entrant draws a random setup cost from a distribution $F^e(\cdot)$. Like scrap values, setup costs are privately known and independently and identically distributed across firms and periods. If potential entrant i enters the industry, it incurs its setup cost ϕ_i^e and chooses its initial investment $x_i^e \geqslant 0$. It takes the entrant a period to set up so it does not earn profits until the next period. In that period the entrant becomes an incumbent with an initial state whose distribution depends on x_i^e. We use r_i^e to denote the probability that potential entrant i *enters* the industry.

States At any point in time the industry is completely characterized by the list of states of the incumbent firms.[5] We refer to $\omega \equiv (\omega_1, \ldots, \omega_n)$ as the state of the industry or as

[4] In all the models that have been computed to date the random draws on scrap values are assumed to be independent over time. If this were not the case, then a firm's scrap value and its rivals' beliefs about it would become state variables of the model.

[5] To be precise, *after* incumbent firms and potential entrants have learned the realization of their scrap value and setup cost for the period, respectively, a complete description of the industry requires a list of scrap value and setup cost in addition to a list of states of the incumbent firms. Since these additional state variables would add to the computational burden, we integrate out over them. In effect, this means that we write down the equations that characterize the equilibrium *before* firms learn their realizations.

the "industry structure". The set of possible industry structures is

$$S = \{(\omega_1, \dots \omega_n): \omega_i \in \Omega,\ n \leqslant \bar{n}\},$$

where n is the number of currently active firms and $\bar{n}$ is the maximum number of firms that are ever active in the industry. We adopt the usual notation for partitioning vectors, e.g., if $\omega = (\omega_1, \dots, \omega_n)$, then $\omega_{-i} = (\omega_1, \dots, \omega_{i-1}, \omega_{i+1}, \dots, \omega_n)$.

In order to simplify the modeling of entry and exit, it is convenient to use a special state, say state $\varnothing$. This is the state from which an entrant enters or to which an exitor exits.

Symmetry and anonymity As does virtually all the applied literature, we restrict attention to models with symmetric and anonymous primitives and focus on equilibria in which values (i.e., payoffs) and policies (i.e., strategies) are also symmetric and anonymous.

We say that a set of functions $\{f_i(\cdot)\}_{i=1}^{n}$ is symmetric if

$$f_i(\omega_i, \omega_{-i}) = f_j(\omega_i, \omega_{-i})$$

for all indices i and j. Hence, there is no need to index the functions by i and j and we simply write $f(\cdot)$ from hereon. The function $f(\cdot)$ is anonymous (a.k.a., exchangeable) if

$$f(\omega_i, \omega_{-i}) = f(\omega_i, \omega_{\pi(-i)})$$

for all permutations $\pi(-i)$ of the indices in $-i$.

The importance of the symmetry and anonymity assumptions for applied work is that they insure that all relevant differences among firms are encoded in the firms' states (including possible differences in "types" of firms). This allows us to connect differences in equilibrium responses among firms to differences in the characteristics of those firms.[6]

Symmetry and anonymity reduce the size of the state space. Without symmetry and anonymity S grows as an exponential in $\bar{n}$, i.e., its cardinality ($\#S$) is greater than $\bar{\omega}^{\bar{n}}$. Once we restrict attention to symmetric and anonymous games the relevant state space grows as a polynomial in $\bar{n}$. That is, symmetry and exchangeability enables us to restrict the state space to

$$S^\circ \equiv \{(\omega_1, \omega_2, \dots, \omega_n): \omega_1 \in \Omega,\ \omega_2 \leqslant \omega_3 \leqslant \cdots \leqslant \omega_n,\ n \leqslant \bar{n}\} \subset S,$$

where $\subset$ is notation for a proper subset.

[6] In general one could be concerned with asymmetric and non-anonymous equilibria even in symmetric and anonymous games. The burden on applied work then becomes much greater. On the other hand, once we define the state variables of the problem the symmetry and anonymity assumptions should, at least in principle, be testable. Of course if the test rejects we are left with the problem of distinguishing whether the rejection is due to a misspecification of the state variables or the inappropriateness of the equilibrium assumptions.

Given symmetry and anonymity we can characterize industry structures more compactly as a set of "counting measures", i.e., as vectors of positive integers in which each integer represents the number of firms in state $\omega \in \Omega$. Formally, if $\mathcal{Z}^+$ is the set of non-negative integers then the state space can also be written as

$$S^\circ = \left\{ (\omega_i, s)\colon \omega_i \in \Omega,\ s = (s_1, \ldots, s_{\bar{\omega}}),\ s_\omega \in \mathcal{Z}^+,\ \sum_{\omega \in \Omega} s_\omega \leqslant \bar{n} \right\}.$$

Typically a program used to compute an equilibrium stores the detail it needs on the different industry structures in locations which are one-to-one with the elements of S°. However the program has to compute continuation values by integrating over possible future states from given initial states. Since the same future industry structure can arise from two different sets of firm-specific outcomes, it is convenient to compute continuation values by summing the probabilities of all possible firm-specific outcomes from that state.[7] As a result when we compute the state-to-state transitions we use the less concise representation of the state space, and for that reason we will use it here also.

Timing We assume that all decisions (pricing, investment, entry, and exit) are made as a function of the state of the industry at the beginning of the period. For simplicity we also assume that incumbents firms that decide to exit compete in the product market before they exit.[8] During the period the outcomes of the investment process are realized, potential entrants enter, and incumbent firms exit. At the end of the period the state of the industry is updated with the results of these processes.

Throughout we use ω to denote the state of the industry at the beginning of the period and ω' to denote its state at the end of the period (after the state-to-state transitions are realized). Firms observe the state at the beginning of the period as well as the outcomes of the entry, exit, and investment decisions during the period.

Product market competition Let $\pi(\omega_i, \omega_{-i})$ denote the current profit of incumbent firm i from product market competition when the industry is in state ω. Until we get to our discussion of extensions to the basic framework (our Section 7) we treat this per-period profit function as a primitive of the dynamic stochastic game. Up to "regularity conditions" (which we come back to when they are needed, in our Section 3) the EP

[7] The alternative here would be to explicitly formulate the multinomial formula for the probabilities of vectors of outcomes for a firm's competitors. This would undoubtedly be the efficient way of computing continuation values if the number of firms was large enough, but for the number of firms typical for current applications the savings in the number of elements in the summand does not compensate for the computational burden of setting up the multinomial probabilities.

[8] If exitors did not compete in the product market in the period they exit, then we would have to use expected profits as our profit measure where the expectation takes account of the exit decisions of a firm's competitors. Similarly, if we were to amend our earlier assumption and allow entrants to compete in the product market in the period they enter, then we would have to compute expected profits where the expectation takes account of entry decisions.

framework leaves the specification the profit function to the analyst. This typically requires the researcher to specify a demand system, a cost function, and an equilibrium assumption.

The existing literature has used a variety of different specifications including: price competition with differentiated products where a firm's state indexes the quality of its product [Pakes and McGuire (1994)]; price competition with differentiated products where a firm's state represents the share of consumers who are aware of the firm's product [Doraszelski and Markovich (2006)]; and quantity or price competition with homogeneous products where a firm's state determines its cost schedule through either its capacity or its capital stock [Berry and Pakes (1993), Gowrisankaran (1999), Besanko and Doraszelski (2004)]. It is important to keep in mind that the actual dynamics of the equilibria we compute (and no doubt of data on actual industries) depend on the properties of the per-period profit function in complex ways that we are only beginning to understand [see, e.g., Besanko and Doraszelski (2004) and Doraszelski and Markovich (2006)].

Below we use the Pakes and McGuire (1994) quality ladder model to illustrate the modeling of the product market. Incumbent firm i produces a product of quality ω_i. The consumers behave according to a standard discrete choice model (and so either purchase one product during the period or use all their money on the outside alternative). Consumer k's utility from choosing good i is given by $g(\omega_i) - p_i + \epsilon_{ik}$, where $g(\cdot)$ is an increasing bounded function of ω_i.[9] Here $g(\omega_i)$ provides the mean (across consumers) of the utility from choice i and ϵ_{ik} represents taste differences among consumers. The no-purchase alternative or outside good is denoted as product 0 and has utility ϵ_{0k}. The consumer specific terms $\epsilon_{0k}, \epsilon_{1k}, \ldots, \epsilon_{nk}$ are assumed to be independently and identically extreme value distributed across products and consumers. As is well known since the work of McFadden (1974) this results in the demands

$$q_i(p_1, \ldots, p_n; \omega) = M \frac{\exp(g(\omega_i) - p_i)}{1 + \sum_{j=1}^{n} \exp(g(\omega_j) - p_j)},$$

where $M > 0$ is the size of the market (the measure of consumers).

Assuming a constant marginal cost of $c \geqslant 0$, the price of firm i in state ω solves

$$\max_{p_i \geqslant 0} q_i(p_1, \ldots, p_n; \omega)(p_i - c).$$

The first-order conditions are given by

$$0 = \frac{\partial}{\partial p_i} q_i(p_1, \ldots, p_n; \omega)(p_i - c) + q_i(p_1, \ldots, p_n; \omega),$$

[9] Introducing the $g(\cdot)$ function is an easy way to insure profits are bounded. Specifically, Pakes and McGuire (1994) set

$$g(\omega_i) = \begin{cases} 3\omega_i - 4 & \text{if } \omega_i \leqslant 5, \\ 12 + \ln(2 - \exp(16 - 3\omega_i)) & \text{if } \omega_i > 5. \end{cases}$$

and have a unique solution [Caplin and Nalebuff (1991)]. The Nash equilibrium prices are found by numerically solving the system of first-order conditions. Profits are then computed as

$$\pi(\omega_i, \omega_{-i}) = q_i\big(p_1(\omega), \ldots, p_n(\omega); \omega\big)\big(p_i(\omega) - c\big).$$

State-to-state transitions The probability that the industry transits from today's state ω to tomorrow's state ω' is determined jointly by the investment decisions of the incumbent firms that remain in the industry, the decisions of potential entrants that enter the industry, and industry-wide shocks that represent movements in the demand or cost conditions facing the industry. Again, subject to mild regularity conditions, the primitives governing these transitions can vary with what seems appropriate for the study at hand, though as EP emphasize, to get their upper bound to Ω they use the assumption that a firm's state does not increase when it does not invest.

We come back to the relationship between the specification for the transition probabilities and computational and modeling issues below, but for now we suffice with the simple case where the transition probability for firm i's state depends only on its own investment and current state (and not on the investments or states of its competitors). Then what the analyst has to specify is a family of probability distributions for ω_i'; one for each possible ω_i, level of investment x_i, and industry-wide shock η (these represent factor prices or demand conditions that cause correlation between the outcomes of different firms in the same industry). Our notation for this family of distributions is

$$\mathcal{P}_{\omega'} \equiv \big\{p(\cdot \mid \omega_i, x_i, \eta)\colon\ \omega_i \in \Omega,\ x_i \in \mathcal{R}^+,\ \eta \in \Upsilon\big\},$$

where Υ is the set of values for η. We assume that $\mathcal{P}_{\omega'}$ is stochastically increasing (in the first-order stochastic dominance sense) in the natural order of both ω_i and x_i.

Industry-wide demand shocks Pakes and McGuire (1994), among others assume that incumbent firm i's state conditional on remaining in the industry evolves according to

$$\omega_i' = \omega_i + \nu_i - \eta,$$

where ν_i represents the outcome of the firm's investment process, and hence has a distribution which is stochastically increasing in x_i and independent across firms, and η represents the improvements in the outside alternative. These improvements in the mean utility from not purchasing any of the goods marketed occur with exogenously fixed probabilities and affect the desirability of all goods produced in the industry. We note that for any given application one might need to also allow for intertemporal changes in costs, or for a second industry wide random variable which moves all firms' marginal costs. Then the level of costs would also become a state variable in the problem.

In Pakes and McGuire (1994) $\mathcal{P}_{\omega'}$ is constructed from the family

$$\mathcal{P}_\nu \equiv \big\{p(\cdot \mid x_i)\colon\ x_i \in \mathcal{R}^+\big\}$$

and the probabilities $\{p(\eta)\}_{\eta\in\Upsilon}$. In the simplest case $\nu \in \{0, 1\}$ and $\mathcal{P}_\nu$ is

$$\Pr(\nu \mid x_i) = \begin{cases} \frac{\alpha x_i}{1+\alpha x_i} & \text{if } \nu = 1, \\ \frac{1}{1+\alpha x_i} & \text{if } \nu = 0, \end{cases} \tag{1}$$

where $\alpha > 0$ parameterizes the effectiveness of investment. This family is stochastically increasing in x_i as required. To complete the specification we need to specify the distribution of η and the simplest case here is to assume $\eta \in \{0, 1\}$, and $\eta = 1$ with probability δ. Note that this simplistic specification can be made somewhat more realistic by noting that the length of the decision making interval can be made small relative to, say, the interval at which data becomes available. For example if the data is annual and we assume the firm makes decisions monthly, the distribution for ω_i' given ω_i is a twelve fold convolution of the increments modeled above.

To complete the specification we note that a firm which exits does not invest and transits to the special state $\varnothing$ with probability one. A potential entrant who enters has the law of motion $\omega_i' = \omega^e + \nu_i - \eta$, where $\omega^e \in \Omega$ is an (exogenously given) initial state and ν_i is distributed with the same probabilities as are given above.

Firm-specific depreciation shocks Note that in the model above the firm specific outcome (the ν) can only increase the firm's state, as may be appropriate for a research and development or perhaps an advertising game. Besanko and Doraszelski (2004) among others assume that firm i's state evolves according to

$$\omega_i' = \omega_i + \nu_i - \eta_i,$$

where the realization of η_i is firm specific (in contrast to the industry-wide η in the previous specification). The probabilities for ν_i and η_i are derived just as in the model with industry shocks given above. That is the distribution of ν_i is given by a family of distributions which are increasing in x_i, and the distribution of η_i is determined by an exogenous "breakdown" probability.

Depending on what is encoded in a firm's state, more elaborate specifications of firm-specific depreciation shocks may be called for. In the context of physical capital, in particular, we often think of depreciation as being proportional to the stock. That is, absent investment, the capital stock tomorrow is with certainty a particular fraction of the capital stock today. Since fractional values of the capital stock are not allowed, we cannot reproduce deterministic proportional decay exactly, however there are a number of ways of modeling decay which are similar in certain respects. One is to assume that firm i owns ω_i machines and that each machine has a probability of δ per period of breaking down independent of other machines. Then firm i will own anywhere from 0 to ω_i machines next period, so that ω_i' is binomially distributed with support $\{0, 1, \ldots, \omega_i\}$ (before investment is taken into account). An alternative is to choose integer values that are on either side of the desired fraction and assign probabilities of transition to them which generate the right expected decay [see, e.g., Benkard (2004)].

Note that since a positive outcome from the research of one firm will take profits away from its competitors, if there were no source of correlation between the transitions of firms within an industry, as in the model with just firm-specific shocks, the model would predict a negative correlation between the profitability of different firms. In fact, the profits of firms within an industry are often (though not always) positively correlated, i.e., industry-wide shocks to demand or cost conditions often have larger impacts than the outcomes of rivalrous investment decisions. By allowing for both firm-specific and industry-wide shocks we let the specific application determine the profit correlations. For notational simplicity we focus on the industry-wide shock in what follows.

An incumbent's problem Suppose that the industry is in state ω. Incumbent firm i solves an intertemporal maximization problem to reach its exit and investment decisions. Let $V(\omega_i, \omega_{-i}, \phi)$ denote the expected net present value of all future cash flows to incumbent firm i, when the industry structure is given by ω and the firm has drawn a scrap value ϕ. $V(\omega_i, \omega_{-i}, \phi)$ is defined recursively by the solution to the following Bellman equation:

$$\begin{aligned} V(\omega_i, \omega_{-i}, \phi) &= \pi(\omega_i, \omega_{-i}) \\ &\quad + \max\Big\{\phi, \max_{x_i} -x_i + \beta E\big[V(\omega_i', \omega_{-i}', \phi') \mid \omega_i, \omega_{-i}, x_i\big]\Big\}, \end{aligned} \tag{2}$$

where β is the common discount factor, and where it is understood that E is the expectation operator which integrates out over the probability distribution of possible next period values for the firm's own state, its competitors' states, and its scrap value conditional on the current state and the firm's choice of investment. The firm's value consists of the current profit from product market competition ($\pi(\omega_i, \omega_{-i})$) plus the larger of the return to exiting the industry (ϕ) and the continuation value for remaining in the industry. The continuation value consists of the discounted (by β) expectation of next period's value minus the cost of the investment incurred in the interim.

To take the expectation required to determine its continuation value the firm must have a perception of the likely future states of its competitors conditional on the different possible outcomes of the industry-wide shock, η. We let the firm's perceived probability of the next period value of its competitors' state (ω_{-i}') conditional on η be $q(\omega_{-i}' \mid \omega_i, \omega_{-i}, \eta)$. In equilibrium these perceptions will have to satisfy certain conditions, and we will come back to these conditions below, but for now assume only that $q(\cdot)$ is the distribution used by the firm. Then we can write

$$E\big[V(\omega_i', \omega_{-i}', \phi') \mid \omega_i, \omega_{-i}, x\big] = \sum_{\nu} W(\nu \mid \omega_i, \omega_{-i}) p(\nu \mid x_i), \tag{3}$$

where

$$\begin{aligned} &W(\nu \mid \omega_i, \omega_{-i}) \\ &\quad \equiv \sum_{\omega_{-i}', \eta} \int_{\phi'} V(\omega_i + \nu - \eta, \omega_{-i}', \phi')\, \mathrm{d}F(\phi')\, q(\omega_{-i}' \mid \omega_i, \omega_{-i}, \eta) p(\eta). \end{aligned}$$

$W(\nu \mid \omega_i, \omega_{-i})$ is the expected discounted value of the firm conditional on the outcome of its investment being ν. To obtain it we had to integrate out over the distribution of possible outcomes for the firms' competitors, the firm's own future scrap value, and the outside alternative.

Note that neither $W(\cdot)$ nor $q(\cdot)$ are primitives of the problem. As a result different computational algorithms construct them in different ways, a point we will be much more explicit about in the computational section below.

The important point to note now is that if we (or the agent) were to know $\{W(\cdot)\}$, optimal behavior could be determined from a simple single agent optimizing problem. To do so substitute Equation (3) into (2) and obtain a Kuhn–Tucker condition

$$x_i\left(\beta\sum_{\nu} W(\nu \mid \omega_i, \omega_{-i})\frac{\partial p(\nu \mid x_i)}{\partial x_i} - 1\right) = 0 \quad \wedge \quad x_i \geqslant 0 \tag{4}$$

for the optimal x_i, say $x(\omega_i, \omega_{-i})$. Below we provide conditions where the solution to this equation is unique, as it will be, for example, if we use the $\mathcal{P}_\nu$ in Equation (1). In this case

$$x(\omega_i, \omega_{-i}) = \max\left\{0, \frac{-1 + \sqrt{\beta\alpha(W(1 \mid \omega_i, \omega_{-i}) - W(0 \mid \omega_i, \omega_{-i}))}}{\alpha}\right\} \tag{5}$$

if $W(1 \mid \omega_i, \omega_{-i}) \geqslant W(0 \mid \omega_i, \omega_{-i})$, and $x(\omega_i, \omega_{-i}) = 0$ otherwise.

Next we substitute $x(\omega_i, \omega_{-i})$ into Equation (2) and determine whether the firm continues. Letting $\chi(\omega_i, \omega_{-i}, \phi)$ be the indicator function which takes the value of one if the firm continues and zero otherwise we have

$$\begin{aligned}\chi(\omega_i, \omega_{-i}, \phi) = {} & \arg\max_{\chi \in \{0,1\}} (1-\chi)\phi \\ & + \chi\left(\beta\sum_{\nu} W(\nu \mid \omega_i, \omega_{-i}) p\big(\nu \mid x(\omega_i, \omega_{-i})\big) - x(\omega_i, \omega_{-i})\right).\end{aligned} \tag{6}$$

The probability of drawing a ϕ such that $\chi(\omega_i, \omega_{-i}, \phi) = 1$ determines the probability of the firm remaining active or

$$r(\omega_i, \omega_{-i}) = F\left(\beta\sum_{\nu} W(\nu \mid \omega_i, \omega_{-i}) p\big(\nu \mid x(\omega_i, \omega_{-i})\big) - x(\omega_i, \omega_{-i})\right). \tag{7}$$

An entrant's problem A potential entrant who chooses to enter must pay an entry fee and then becomes an incumbent firm in the next period. The entrant's decision on whether to enter is analogous to the incumbent's decision on whether to exit; i.e. it compares its continuation value to the cost of entry. Since the competitors of the potential entrant are given by the entire vector of active firms' states, or ω, the value of potential entrants i is given by

$$V^e(\omega, \phi^e) = \max\left\{0, \max_{x_i^e} -\phi^e - x_i^e + \beta \sum_\nu W^e(\nu \mid \omega) p(\nu \mid x_i^e)\right\}, \tag{8}$$

where $W^e(\cdot)$ is defined analogously to $W(\cdot)$ for an incumbent firm.

The potential entrant solves for its optimal investment $x^e(\omega)$ in a manner analogous to an incumbent firm, and then enters if and only if it is profitable to do so. Letting $\chi^e(\omega, \phi^e)$ be the indicator which takes the value of one if the potential entrant enters and zero otherwise

$$\chi^e(\omega, \phi^e) = \arg\max_{\chi \in \{0,1\}} \chi\left(-\phi^e - x^e(\omega) + \beta \sum_\nu W^e(\nu \mid \omega) p(\nu \mid x^e(\omega))\right). \tag{9}$$

So the probability that a potential entrant enters is

$$r^e(\omega) = F^e\left(-x^e(\omega) + \beta \sum_\nu W^e(\nu \mid \omega) p(\nu \mid x^e(\omega))\right). \tag{10}$$

3. Equilibrium

This section begins by providing a definition of equilibrium. We then provide sufficient conditions for the existence of an equilibrium that satisfy these definitions (Section 3.1). We do not know conditions which insure uniqueness of the equilibrium but we do have results which characterize any of the possible equilibria (Section 3.2), and we use those characteristics in our computational algorithms. To illustrate the issues underlying the multiplicity of equilibria, we consider a number of examples of multiple equilibria (Section 3.3). Our discussion is mostly based on EP, Doraszelski and Satterthwaite (2003), and Besanko et al. (2004).

We consider Markov perfect equilibria (MPE). A Markov prefect equilibrium insures that at each $\omega \in S^\circ$ each incumbent firm and each potential entrant:

- chooses optimal policies given its perceptions on likely future industry structures, and
- those perceptions are consistent with the behavior of each agent's competitors.

One way of checking that these conditions are satisfied is to show that the equilibrium generates a set of value functions and policies, one for each potential entrant and each incumbent at each $\omega \in S^\circ$, such that:

- given the policies, the value functions satisfies the Bellman equations in (2) and (8) for incumbents and potential entrants respectively, and
- given the value functions, the policies for investment and exit satisfy the optimality conditions in Equations (4) and (6) for incumbents (augmented to include a check of whether the extreme point for investment is a global maximum in cases where functional forms do not guarantee that), and the analogous equations for potential entrants.

Note that since the horizon is infinite and the influence of past play is captured in the current state, there is a one-to-one correspondence between subgames and states. Hence, any Markov perfect equilibrium is subgame perfect. Further since a best reply to Markovian strategies is a Markovian strategy, a Markov perfect equilibrium remains a subgame perfect equilibrium even if more general strategies are considered.

3.1. Existence

The extent to which the applied literature has faced the existence question is by testing whether the values and policies they computed in fact satisfy the equilibrium conditions up to some error. The fact that we allow for an error, makes this condition imperfect.[10] However since computers can only compute fixed points to machine precision, there is a sense in which we cannot determine whether numerical results satisfy any stronger notion of equilibrium than this. Indeed the reader that is only interested in computational issues should be able to skip this section and have no trouble with the rest of the paper.

This section asks a different question then that asked by the applied literature. In particular we ask for conditions that insure that there is an equilibrium in which the conditions given above hold exactly. The importance of an existence proof to applied work is that it provides conditions that ensure we are searching for an approximation to something that actually exists. The weakness is that the conditions we give for existence are sufficient but not necessary, so there may well be equilibria in situations which do not abide by the conditions in the proof.

We look for an equilibrium in pure strategies (computing mixed strategy equilibria increases the computational complexity of the algorithm markedly). The proof of existence requires a continuous mapping from policies into themselves. One reason for adding random scrap values/setup costs to the EP framework is that they allow us to treat the continuous exit and entry probabilities as the policies [in contrast to the discrete entry and exit decisions; see Doraszelski and Satterthwaite (2003)]. Continuity of this best-reply mapping can then be established under standard continuity assumptions on the transition functions.

Given continuity, one way to obtain a pure strategy equilibrium is to ensure that a firm's best reply is always unique.[11] As long as the densities of the scrap values and

[10] The theoretical literature on game theory does use the notion of ϵ-equilibrium, but it is not automatically satisfied by ensuring the equilibrium conditions up to a sufficiently small error; i.e. in an ϵ-equilibrium a player's strategy brings the player within ϵ of his best possible payoff, assuming that payoffs can be computed exactly. In the notion used in computation both payoffs and strategies are computed with error, and the connection between the computed strategies and an ϵ-equilibria has not been shown. In addition it is well known that an ϵ-equilibrium need not be close to an exact equilibrium.

[11] Escobar (2006) proposes a similar condition to ensure the existence of an equilibrium in pure strategies in the context of more general dynamic stochastic games with a countable state space and a continuum of actions. While Escobar's (2006) condition applies to games with continuous actions other than the investment decisions in the EP model, there is no systematic treatment of incomplete information as a means to purify the discrete entry/exit decisions.

setup costs are continuous the entry and exit best responses are unique [up to a set of measure zero which is sufficient for the argument in Doraszelski and Satterthwaite (2003)]. Turning to investment decisions, any family of distribution functions (our $\mathcal{P}_\nu$) which guarantee that, for any given distribution of the outcomes from the actions of the firm's competitors, the continuation value for the firm is concave in its investment choice will guarantee a unique best reply. This is true of the simple family used above (which is taken from EP). Doraszelski and Satterthwaite (2003) go further. They define a class of transition functions that are called unique investment choice (UIC) admissible and prove that if the transition function is UIC admissible, then a firm's investment decision is indeed uniquely determined. The UIC class generalizes the EP example by allowing transitions to more than immediately adjacent states, and also allows for the construction of median preserving spreads.

3.2. Characterization

EP provide conditions which insure that in equilibrium there is an $\bar{n}$ and a $\bar{\omega}$ such that if we start at an initial industry structure in which

- there are no more than $\bar{n}$ firms active, and
- each active firm has an $\omega_i \in \Omega$,

then, with probability one,

- there will never be more than $\bar{n}$ firms active, and
- we will never observe an active firm with an $\omega_i \notin \Omega$.

As a result $\#S^\circ$ is finite, and equilibrium values and policies are computable.[12]

They also show that any equilibrium defines a time homogeneous Markov process, for ω' given ω, defined by the family of distributions (or by the Markov transition kernel)

$$\mathcal{Q}_{\omega'} \equiv \{Q(\cdot \mid \omega):\ \omega \in S^\circ\}.$$

Moreover every process generated by the equilibrium conditions satisfies a fixed point to an operator which takes the set of time homogeneous Markov processes on S° into

[12] The proof restricts the profit function so that profits will be driven arbitrarily close to zero for n large enough regardless of the location of the incumbents, and that profits are bounded from above. It also assumes that the number of potential entrants in any given period is finite, that entry fees are bounded away from zero, and that if there is no investment, the firm's state cannot advance (i.e., $\Pr(\nu = 1 \mid x_i = 0) = 0$). The argument for the upper bound to ω is roughly as follows. The value function is bounded if profits are. The incentive to invest is the increment to the value function from increasing ω_i. Since the value function is bounded, for any given value of ω_{-i} that increment can be made arbitrarily close to zero. So eventually the increment has a value less than the cost of investment and investment shuts down. Once investment shuts down the firm's state cannot increase. The argument is completed by showing that their is only a finite number of possible ω_{-i}. The argument for the upper bound to n follows from the fact that profits can be driven arbitrarily small by increasing n, that there are finite number of potential entrants in each period, and that entry costs are bounded away from zero.

itself, and one can view the procedures for computing the equilibria that we discuss below as algorithms for finding such a fixed point.[13]

Since $\#S^\circ$ is finite, the process generating industry structures in the EP model is a finite state Markov chain. Consequently standard results in Markov chain theory [see, e.g., Freedman (1983)] insure that there is at least one recurrent class of states, say $R \subset S^\circ$, and with probability one each sample path (each sequence of $\{\omega_t\}_t$) will enter one of these recurrent classes in finite time. Once in the recurrent class the sample path will stay within it forever. Consequently the points in the recurrent class are visited infinitely often. EP go further and provide conditions which insure that there is only one such class, so the process is ergodic, though ergodicity is not necessary for the discussion that follows and it does require substantive conditions [for an example with more than one recurrent class see Besanko and Doraszelski (2004)].

In IO problems recurrent classes of points are typically much smaller then the state space or S°. Consider our quality competition example. As we increase market size (our M) we will typically generate equilibria with a higher $\bar{n}$, and $\#S^\circ$ will increase polynomially in $\bar{n}$. However as M increases the economics of the primitives will typically insure that, provided we start with a relatively large n at high enough states, we will never observe an industry structure with a small number of firms at low states, as entry will occur whenever the number and states of incumbents fall below certain thresholds. Thus $\#R$ can grow at a much slower rate that $\#S^\circ$. Indeed, at least in principle it need not grow in M at all [in our quality model it seems to grow less than linearly in M, see the example in Pakes and McGuire (2001)]. Similarly if we allow two characteristics of products, say mpg and engine size of vehicles, then in equilibrium we may never observe vehicles with either both mpg and engine size very large (as it would be too expensive to produce) or both engines and mpg very small (as no one would buy them).

Recall that all subgames initiated from the recurrent class will stay within that class forever. So if we were trying to analyze likely future outcomes in an industry and are willing to assume that (or could check whether) the current industry structure were in the recurrent class, then all we would require is information on policies on the recurrent class. Therefore a way to reduce the computational burden in applied problems is to design an algorithm which computes values and policies only on the recurrent class [see Pakes and McGuire (2001)].

Before leaving this section we want to emphasize that the nature of states in R, the transitions among those states, and the transitions into R all depend on the primitives of the problem and can vary greatly with different parameterizations for those primitives. As a result there is little in the way of characterizations of behavior that are directly

[13] To see this assume $\mathcal{Q}_{\omega'}$ is generated by our equilibrium conditions. Take any ω and use $Q(\cdot \mid \omega) \in \mathcal{Q}_{\omega'}$ to form the marginal distribution of the likely locations of each firm's competitors in the next period. Substitute this for $\{q(\cdot)\}$ in constructing the expected discounted value of future net cash flow conditional on investment outcomes, or the $\{W(\cdot)\}$, in Equation (3). Then form optimal policies for all agents just as described above. In equilibrium these policies will generate an objective distribution of outcomes which coincide with the $Q(\cdot \mid \omega) \in \mathcal{Q}_{\omega'}$ we started with.

relevant for policy or descriptive work that comes out of the general framework. Rather the goal is to have a framework which is flexible enough to generate a broad range of results and then let knowledge of the relevant institutions pick out the implications that seem relevant for the problems at hand.

3.3. Multiplicity

Doraszelski and Satterthwaite (2003) provide three examples that show that there need not be a unique equilibrium that is symmetric and anonymous. Multiplicity may arise from three sources:

- investment decisions,
- entry/exit decisions, and
- product market competition.

We now discuss each of these in turn, providing simple examples of the first two. Note that both the examples only consider equilibria that are symmetric and anonymous in the sense we defined earlier. Note also that the examples are all in the context of simple models where we can break out the static profit function and analyze it without considering investment, entry and exit decisions. Once this simplification is left behind, much richer examples of multiple equilibria can be generated, see Besanko et al. (2004).

Investment decisions Consider a model with $\bar{n} = 2$ firms and neither entry nor exit. Firm i's capacity in state $\omega_i \in \{1, 2, \ldots, 10\}$ is $5(\omega_i - 1)$. The state-to-state transitions are as in our example with a firm-specific depreciation shock with parameters $\alpha = 2.375$ and $\delta = 0.03$. The discount factor is $\beta = \frac{20}{21}$. Products are undifferentiated and firms compete in prices subject to capacity constraints. There are $M = 40$ identical consumers with unit demand and reservation price $v = 1$. The equilibrium of this Bertrand–Edgeworth product market game is unique and symmetric [see Chapter 2 of Ghemawat (1997)].

Figure 30.1 depicts two symmetric equilibria of the dynamic stochastic game. In both equilibria investment activity is greatest in states on or near the diagonal of the state space. That is, firms with equal or similar capacities are engaged in a "race" to become the industry leader. The difference in investment activity is greatest in state $(5, 5)$ where both firms invest 1.90 in the first equilibrium compared to 1.03 in the second one. Investment activity also differs considerably in states $(1, 6)$ and $(6, 1)$: in the first (second) equilibrium the smaller firm invests 2.24 (3.92) and the larger firm invests 1.57 (1.46). That is, in the second equilibrium, a firm that has fallen behind to state 1 strives to catch up and the industry leader (i.e., the firm in state 6) to some extent accommodates the laggard by reducing its investment.

Note that multiplicity rests on the dynamic nature of the game. Because product market competition takes place before investment decisions are carried out, a firm has no incentive to invest if $\beta = 0$. Hence, multiple equilibria cannot possibly arise in the static version of the game.

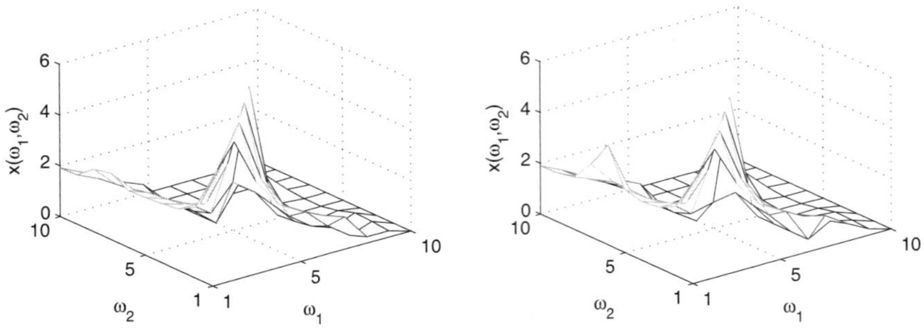

Figure 30.1. Two equilibria. *Source*: Doraszelski and Satterthwaite (2003).

Table 30.1
Two more equilibria

$r(\omega_1, \omega_2)$	$\omega_2 = 1$	$\omega_2 = 2$	$r(\omega_1, \omega_2)$	$\omega_2 = 1$	$\omega_2 = 2$
$\omega_1 = 1$	0.8549	0.8549	$\omega_1 = 1$	0.8549	0.1542
$\omega_1 = 2$	0.8549	0.8549	$\omega_1 = 2$	1	0.8549

Source: Doraszelski and Satterthwaite (2003).

Entry/exit decisions Consider a model with at most $\bar{n} = 2$ firms, $\bar{\omega} = 2$ active states plus one inactive state per firm, and the profits from product market competition given by

$$\pi(\omega_1) = 1, \qquad \pi(\omega_1, \omega_2) = 0.$$

That is, monopoly profits are one and duopoly profits are zero. While entry is prohibited, exit is permissible with a scrap value that is uniformly distributed on [14, 16]. The discount factor is again $\beta = \frac{20}{21}$. Finally, a firm cannot transit between its active states (in our example with a firm-specific depreciation shock this corresponds to $\alpha = 0$ and $\delta = 0$). Notice that the parameters are chosen such that each firm would want to exit if its rival stays, i.e., exiting is more attractive than being a duopolist, but each firm would want to stay if its rival exits, i.e., being a monopolist is more attractive than exiting. This gives rise to a "war of attrition".

One equilibrium has both firms play the same strategies in states $(1, 1)$, $(1, 2)$, $(2, 1)$, and $(2, 2)$. The left panel of Table 30.1 summarize this equilibrium. Another equilibrium is illustrated in the right panels of Table 30.1. In states $(1, 1)$ and $(2, 2)$ both firms make the same exit decisions as before. In state $(1, 2)$, however, firm 1 exits with high probability and firm 2 stays for sure whereas in state $(2, 1)$ firm 1 stays for sure and firm 2 exits with high probability. Note that the two equilibria differ starkly from each other: In the first equilibrium, a duopolistic industry may over time turn into either a monopolistic or an empty industry. In the second equilibrium, if the industry starts in states $(1, 2)$ or $(2, 1)$, then it always ends up as a monopoly.

Product market competition To determine the profit function we need to model competition in the product market. Depending on the nature of demand and cost primitives, and the assumptions on strategies, it is well known that we can generate multiple solutions to this static game. The different profit functions will generate different investment, entry, and exit incentives and hence different equilibria with different distributions of sample paths for industry structures. This is yet another source of multiplicity.

We conclude with some further details on how multiplicity arises. The value of continued play to firm i is determined by its value function in states ω' that may be reached from state ω. Holding the value of continued play fixed, the strategic situation in state ω is akin to a static game. If the reaction functions in this game intersect more than once, then multiple equilibria arise.

We say that the model satisfies stagewise uniqueness if the reactions functions intersect once irrespective of the value of continued play [Besanko et al. (2004)], i.e., there is only one set of Nash equilibrium policies conditional on the value of continued play. Note that stagewise uniqueness requires more than just UIC admissibility. In our investment example above, the transition function satisfies UIC admissibility, so that given a firm's beliefs about the value of continued play, its investment decision is uniquely determined. The mere fact that each firm has a well-defined reaction function (as opposed to a correspondence) does not guarantee that these functions intersect only once.

If the model satisfies stagewise uniqueness and there are multiple equilibria, the multiplicity must arise from firms' expectations regarding the value of continued play. That is rational expectations are consistent with more than one value of continued play at a least one node of the game tree.

As Besanko et al. (2004) point out, a sufficient condition for uniqueness of equilibrium in a dynamic stochastic game is that the model satisfies stagewise uniqueness and that movements through the state space are unidirectional, i.e., a firm's state can only move in one direction (either up or down). Stagewise uniqueness precludes players' decisions from giving rise to multiple equilibria, and unidirectional movements preclude their expectations from doing so. Though applied problems with this property are rare, it is instructive to consider the reasoning behind this argument.

To do so let there be $\bar{n} = 2$ firms and neither entry nor exit. Suppose that a firm can never move backward to a lower state (say because $\delta = 0$ rules out depreciation shocks). Hence, once the industry reaches state $(\bar{\omega}, \bar{\omega})$, it remains there forever, so that the value of future play in state $(\bar{\omega}, \bar{\omega})$ coincides with the value of being in this state. In conjunction with stagewise uniqueness, this uniquely determines the value of being in state $(\bar{\omega}, \bar{\omega})$. Next consider states $(\bar{\omega} - 1, \bar{\omega})$ and $(\bar{\omega}, \bar{\omega} - 1)$. The value of future play in states $(\bar{\omega} - 1, \bar{\omega})$ and $(\bar{\omega}, \bar{\omega} - 1)$ depends on the value of being in state $(\bar{\omega}, \bar{\omega})$. Stagewise uniqueness ensures that firms' decisions in states $(\bar{\omega} - 1, \bar{\omega})$ and $(\bar{\omega}, \bar{\omega} - 1)$ as well as the value of being in these states are uniquely determined. Further, since the value of future play in state $(\bar{\omega} - 1, \bar{\omega} - 1)$ depends on the value of being in states $(\bar{\omega} - 1, \bar{\omega})$ and $(\bar{\omega}, \bar{\omega} - 1)$, firms' decisions and the value of being in state $(\bar{\omega} - 1, \bar{\omega} - 1)$ are uniquely determined. Continuing to work backwards in this fashion establishes that the equilibrium is unique. Conversely, suppose a firm can never move forward to a higher state (say because $\alpha = 0$ renders investment completely ineffective). A similar argument establishes uniqueness of equilibrium except that the argument is anchored in state (1, 1) rather than state $(\bar{\omega}, \bar{\omega})$.[14]

4. Introduction to computation

There have been a number of different algorithms proposed for computing equilibria to these games. One possibility is to look at the problem of computing equilibria as the problem of solving the system of non-linear equations defined by our equilibrium conditions [see Chapter 5 of Judd (1998) for methods for solving non-linear equations systems]. However the applied problems we are interested in are typically too large to make direct application of Newton's method practical. Most applications therefore use some type of Gaussian method that break up the system of non-linear equations into smaller parts. The idea behind Gaussian methods is that it is harder to solve a large system of equations once than to solve smaller systems many times.

The Gaussian method we begin with is the backward solution method used in Pakes and McGuire (1994). This section begins by describing their algorithm, and concludes with a general discussion of two problems that can make it necessary to use more sophisticated algorithms in applied work. The first is the burden of computing equilibria, the second is the possibility of multiple equilibria. The later sections provide tools that ameliorate these two problems. First we discuss a number of computational methods that alleviate the computational burden. Among others we explain the continuous-time stochastic games due to Doraszelski and Judd (2004) and the stochastic approximation algorithm due to Pakes and McGuire (2001). Then we explain the homotopy methods used in Besanko et al. (2004) to address the multiplicity problem. We note however that neither problem is currently "solved", i.e., both computational burden and multiplicity can effectively limit the extent to which we can analyze particular applied problems.

4.1. *Gaussian methods*

Like all backward solution techniques the Pakes and McGuire (1994) algorithm is an iterative procedure which starts each iteration with a set of numbers in memory, provides a rule which updates those numbers in the course of the iteration, and checks to see if the updated numbers satisfy a convergence criterion at the end of the iteration. If not the algorithm begins a new iteration.

The algorithm holds in memory an expected value function and policy for each incumbent firm and each potential entrant in each state $\omega \in S^\circ$. The expected value function is defined as

$$V(\omega_i, \omega_{-i}) \equiv \int_\phi V(\omega_i, \omega_{-i}, \phi)\, \mathrm{d}F(\phi). \tag{11}$$

[14] As an aside we note unidirectional movements through the state space not only make a dynamic stochastic game much more tractable [see, e.g., Cabral and Riordan (1994)] but also greatly simplify computing an equilibrium [see, e.g., Judd, Schmedders and Yeltekin (2002)].

By keeping these expected values, instead of the values themselves in memory, we can ignore the continuous state variable ϕ in storing and recalling objects from memory.

From the definition of the Bellman equation in (2) and of the $W(\cdot)$ in Equation (3) we have

$$V(\omega_i, \omega_{-i}) = \pi(\omega_i, \omega_{-i}) + \big(1 - r(\omega_i, \omega_{-i})\big)\phi(\omega_i, \omega_{-i}) + r(\omega_i, \omega_{-i})\left\{ - x(\omega_i, \omega_{-i}) + \beta \sum_{\nu} W(\nu \mid \omega_i, \omega_{-i}) p(\nu \mid x_i)\right\}, \tag{12}$$

where

$$W(\nu \mid \omega_i, \omega_{-i}) \equiv \sum_{\omega'_{-i}, \eta} V(\omega_i + \nu - \eta, \omega'_{-i}) q(\omega'_{-i} \mid \omega_i, \omega_{-i}, \eta) p(\eta), \tag{13}$$

and $\phi(\omega_i, \omega_{-i})$ is the expectation of ϕ conditional on exiting in state (ω_i, ω_{-i}) (i.e. on $\chi(\omega_i, \omega_{-i}, \phi) = 0$).

An iteration circles through the states in some fixed order, updating *all* policies and expected values associated with each state every time it visits the state (any algorithm which updates all points at each iteration is a "synchronous" algorithm, we come back to this below).

Iterations Iterative techniques begin with an initial set of values and policies for all states in S°. There are a number of alternative ways to obtain the initial guesses. If no other information is available, reasonable initial guesses are often obtained by assuming the agent gets the profits from its state forever, and discounting that sum. That is, if we let the superscript 0 to denote guesses, then

$$V^0(\omega_i, \omega_{-i}) = \frac{\pi(\omega_i, \omega_{-i})}{1 - \beta}, \qquad r^0(\omega_i, \omega_{-i}) = 1, \qquad x^0(\omega_i, \omega_{-i}) = 0,$$
$$V^{e,0}(\omega) = r^{e,0}(\omega) = x^{e,0}(\omega) = 0.$$

Of course if there is some information available that allows one to form initial conditions which are likely to be closer to the true values than this, e.g., if one has available the equilibrium values from a set of parameters that are close to the set that underlies the current calculation, one would use them.

Iteration l determines $V^l(\cdot)$, $x^l(\cdot)$, $r^l(\cdot)$ $V^{e,l}(\cdot)$, $x^{e,l}(\cdot)$, $r^{e,l}(\cdot)$ from $V^{l-1}(\cdot)$, $x^{l-1}(\cdot)$, $r^{l-1}(\cdot)$, $V^{e,l-1}(\cdot)$, $x^{e,l-1}(\cdot)$, $r^{e,l-1}(\cdot)$. We now provide detail on how the values and policies are updated from one iteration to the next.

Updating policies and values Fix ω. For each incumbent and potential entrant we update the $W(\cdot)$'s by treating the continuation values in memory as the true expected values of being in a given state in the next period, and the policies in memory as the true policies of the firm's competitors. We then mimic the single agent problem discussed above for computing updated values and policies conditional on these $\{W(\cdot)\}$ (or $\{W^e(\cdot)\}$).

If we let l index iterations, the first step is constructing the $\{W^l(\cdot)\}$ from the policies and expected values in memory at iteration $l-1$. The calculation is simplified if we begin by constructing the probabilities of a firm's future state, counting exit as a possible outcome, conditional on the current states, the policies in memory and the outside shock. Recall that a firm either exits (to state $\varnothing$) or continues with state $(\omega+\nu-\eta)$, so if we use the probabilities for ν given x in Equation (1)

$$p^{l-1}(\omega_i' \mid \omega_i, \omega_{-i}, \eta) = \begin{cases} 1 - r^{l-1}(\omega_i, \omega_{-i}) & \text{if } \omega_i' = \varnothing, \\ r^{l-1}(\omega_i, \omega_{-i}) p(\nu_i \mid x^{l-1}(\omega_i, \omega_{-i})) & \\ \qquad\qquad\qquad\qquad \text{if } \omega_i' = \omega_i + 1 - \eta, & \\ r^{l-1}(\omega_i, \omega_{-i})(1 - p(\nu_i \mid x^{l-1}(\omega_i, \omega_{-i}))) & \\ \qquad\qquad\qquad\qquad \text{if } \omega_i' = \omega_i - \eta. & \end{cases}$$

Assuming that there is a fixed number, say $\mathcal{E}$, of potential entrants each period, we will also need the binomial probability that precisely $\mathcal{E}'$ of the $\mathcal{E}$ potential entrants enter conditional on iteration $l-1$'s policies which is constructed as

$$r^{e,l-1}(\mathcal{E}', \omega) \equiv \binom{\mathcal{E}}{\mathcal{E}'} r^{e,l-1}(\omega)^{\mathcal{E}'} \left[1 - r^{e,l-1}(\omega)\right]^{\mathcal{E}-\mathcal{E}'}.$$

Next take the $p^{l-1}(\cdot)$'s and the $r^{e,l-1}(\cdot)$'s and compute the firm's perceived probabilities of next periods values of its competitors state as

$$\begin{aligned} & q^l(\omega_{-i}' \mid \omega_i, \omega_{-i}, \eta) \\ & \quad = \prod_{j \neq i} p^{l-1}(\omega_j' \mid \omega_j, \omega_{-j}, \eta) \prod_{j=1}^{\mathcal{E}'} p\big(\nu_j' \mid x^{e,l-1}(\omega)\big) r^{e,l-1}(\mathcal{E}', \omega), \end{aligned}$$

where $p(\nu_j \mid \cdot)$ is as defined in Equation (1), and $x^{e,l-1}(\cdot)$ is the entry policy at iteration $l-1$.

Substituting $q^l(\cdot)$ into Equation (13) and calling up expected values from memory we compute

$$W^l(\nu \mid \omega_i, \omega_{-i}) \equiv \sum_{\omega_{-i}', \eta} V^{l-1}(\omega_i + \nu - \eta, \omega_{-i}') q^l(\omega_{-i}' \mid \omega_i, \omega_{-i}, \eta) p(\eta).$$

We now update continuation values and policies conditional on the $\{W^l(\cdot)\}$ for a given ω. For each incumbent i we solve the resultant single agent optimization problem for the optimal investment and exit decisions as follows

- Substitute $W^l(\cdot)$ for the generic $W(\cdot)$ in the Kuhn–Tucker condition (4) to obtain the optimal investment of the firm should it continue. In the simple case where ν only takes on the values $\{0, 1\}$, the optimal x satisfies

$$x\left(-1+\beta\left[W^l(1;\omega_i,\omega_{-i})-W^l(0;\omega_i,\omega_{-i})\right]\frac{\partial p(1\mid x)}{\partial x}\right)=0 \quad\wedge\quad x\geqslant 0.$$

Depending on the chosen functional forms for the transition probabilities, the solution to this problem, which we label $x^l(\omega_i,\omega_{-i})$, may or may not have a closed-form solution. Equation (5) exhibits the solution in case the success probability $p(1\mid x)=\frac{\alpha x}{1+\alpha x}$. The second-order condition is satisfied automatically here, but is has to be explicitly checked if more general functional forms are used.

- Substitute $x^l(\omega_i,\omega_{-i})$, $W^{l-1}(\nu;\omega_i,\omega_{-i})$ into Equation (6) to determine the exit policy, i.e. $\chi^l(\omega_i,\omega_{-i},\phi)$, and use that policy to determine the probability that incumbent firm i will draw a ϕ that induces it to remain in the industry as

$$r^l(\omega_i,\omega_{-i})=F\left(-x^l(\omega_i,\omega_{-i})+\beta\sum_\nu W^l(\nu;\omega_i,\omega_{-i})p\big(\nu\mid x^l(\omega_i,\omega_{-i})\big)\right).$$

- Substitute $W^l(\nu;\omega_i,\omega_{-i})$, $x^l(\omega_i,\omega_{-i})$, and $r^l(\omega_i,\omega_{-i})$ into (12) and take the value of the resultant expression as the continuation value $V^l(\omega_i,\omega_{-i})$. Place $V^l(\cdot)$, $x^l(\cdot)$, $r^l(\cdot)$ in memory. This completes the update for the incumbent firms at ω.

Updating values and policies for potential entrants, i.e., $V^{e,l}(\omega)$, $x^{e,l}(\omega)$, and $r^{e,l}(\omega)$, is analogous except that we use $W^{e,l-1}(\nu\mid\omega)$ to evaluate the expected discounted value of future net cash flows for the potential entrants, and the entrant bases its entry decision, and its investment should it enter, on the Bellman equation (8) instead of the incumbent's Bellman equation in (2). That completes our discussion of the updates that occur during an iteration.

Stopping rule The algorithm cycles through the state space until the changes in the values and policies from one iteration to the next are "small".[15] To quantify this, we require a measure of the distance between two sets of values and policies. Different distance measures or norms have been used in the literature, and as we shall see some of them make more sense for one algorithm than for another. For the Gaussian scheme described above, there is an argument for using the L_∞ or sup norm, as it is the strongest

[15] If one does not fix Ω and $\bar{n}$ at the outset, but rather allows the algorithm to solve for them [as did Pakes and McGuire (1994)], the sequence of iterations must typically be done more than once. For a fixed Ω we compute the fixed point with the constraint that there are never more that $\bar{n}$ firms active. Those values and policies are then used as initial conditions for a sequence of iterations that allows for a larger number of active firms. We repeat this procedure until $\bar{n}$ is so large that there are no states at which a potential entrant wants to enter. Ω is set as follows. First we compute values and policies for the monopoly problem. The value of ω at which a monopolist would exit and the value of ω at which the monopolist would stop investing become the lowest and highest values in Ω. Though a value of ω at which the monopolist would exit would induce exit no matter the market structure, it is possible for an oligopolist to still invest at an ω at which a monopolist would not. Thus once one computes the equilibrium values one must check to see that no firm wants to invest at $\bar{\omega}$. If this is not the case $\bar{\omega}$ is increased, and the computation is done again. For more detail see Pakes and McGuire (1994).

norm, and to use a norm which is close to "unit free", so we divide by $|V^l(\omega)|$. Therefore we take the relative difference in values at iteration l to be

$$\left\| \frac{V^l - V^{l-1}}{1 + |V^l|} \right\| = \max_{\omega \in S^\circ} \left| \frac{V^l(\omega) - V^{l-1}(\omega)}{1 + |V^l(\omega)|} \right|,$$

where the plus one is to avoid division by zero, and similarly for policies.[16]

There remains the issue of when to terminate the iterations. We would like a criterion that is based on the distance between the current iteration's policies and values and the true fixed point, and not just on the distance between subsequent iterates. Note that if the algorithm does converge (and there is no guarantee that it will), then convergence is linear as in all Gaussian schemes [Ortega and Rheinboldt (1970, p. 301)]. A sequence $\{z^l\}_{l=0}^{\infty}$ is said to converge linearly to the limit z^∞ if and only if

$$\lim_{l \to \infty} \frac{\|z^{l+1} - z^\infty\|}{\|z^l - z^\infty\|} \leqslant \theta < 1.$$

Assume temporarily that the first inequality can be strengthened to hold along the entire sequence of iterates, i.e.,

$$\left\|z^{l+1} - z^\infty\right\| \leqslant \theta \left\|z^l - z^\infty\right\| \tag{14}$$

for all l. This is similar to the contraction property of a single agent dynamic programming problem. Then the distance to the limit can be shown to be related to the distance between subsequent iterates by

$$\left\|z^l - z^\infty\right\| \leqslant \frac{\|z^{l+1} - z^l\|}{1 - \theta}.$$

Consequently to ensure that the current iterate is within a prespecified tolerance ϵ of the limit, we can stop once

$$\left\|z^{l+1} - z^l\right\| \leqslant \epsilon(1 - \theta). \tag{15}$$

Of course the algorithm described above is *not* a contraction mapping and the condition in Equation (14) does not, in general, hold along the entire sequence of iterates. On the other hand, if the algorithm converges, our experience is that it does hold after a "burn in" phase of several iterations. Figure 30.2 illustrates this point; it plots the relative difference in values and policies between iterations (on a log scale) versus the number of iterations. After iteration 50 or so, the distance decreases as a straight line until it hits machine precision around iteration 325. Unlike a single agent dynamic programming problem, however, we do not have an obvious guess for the convergence

[16] Note that in a single agent dynamic programming problem we would define a norm on absolute differences (instead of relative differences) and then derive error bounds from the contraction mapping theorem. Seeing that our problem is not a contraction we cannot derive error bounds in this way, and the argument for using relative differences is that at least it makes the distance measure, and the tolerance we will eventually use, scale invariant.

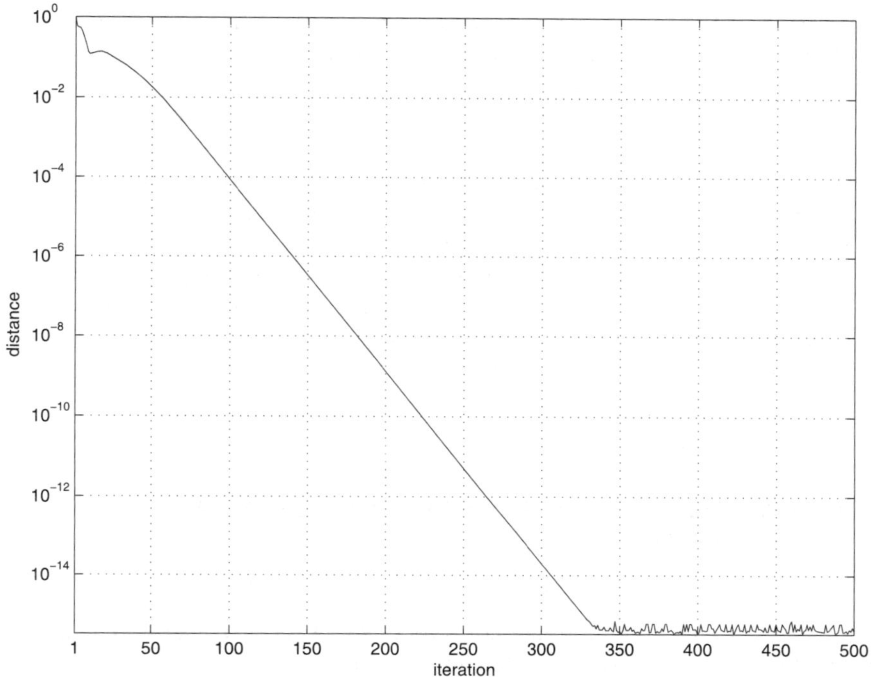

Figure 30.2. Relative difference in values and policies between iterations. *Source*: Doraszelski and Judd (2004) and own calculations.

factor. One way to resolve this problem is to estimate θ from the iteration history. There are many ways of doing this. For example, the slope of the straight line in Figure 30.2 is a direct estimate of $\log_{10}\theta$ because if the current and previous errors are related by $\|z^{l+1} - z^l\| = \theta\|z^l - z^{l-1}\|$, then the current and initial errors are related by $\|z^{l+1} - z^l\| = \theta^l\|z^1 - z^0\|$ and hence $\log_{10}\|z^{l+1} - z^l\| = l\log_{10}\theta + \log_{10}\|z^1 - z^0\|$. Alternatively, suppose we want to continue iterating until we are with ϵ of the limit. Then we could let k be the first iteration such that $\|z_k - z_{k-1}\| < 10\epsilon$ and l the first iteration such that $\|z_l - z_{l-1}\| < \epsilon$ to produce the estimate

$$\hat{\theta} = \left(\frac{\|z_l - z_{l-1}\|}{\|z_k - z_{k-1}\|}\right)^{\frac{1}{l-k}} \approx 10^{\frac{1}{k-l}}.$$

For further discussion see Judd (1998, pp. 42–44) and Doraszelski and Judd (2004).

Gauss–Jacobi vs. Gauss–Seidel Pakes and McGuire (1994) describe a Gauss–Jacobi scheme. That is when we compute the lth iteration values and policies we only use the information in memory from the $(l - 1)$st iteration. An alternative is to use a so-called Gauss–Seidel scheme [used, e.g., in Benkard (2004), Doraszelski and Judd

(2004)]. Consider the lth iteration. When we are at state ω we know the new guesses $V^l(\omega_i^\dagger, \omega_{-i}^\dagger)$, $r^l(\omega_i^\dagger, \omega_{-i}^\dagger)$, $x^l(\omega_i^\dagger, \omega_{-i}^\dagger)$, $V^{e,l}(\omega_i^\dagger, \omega_{-i}^\dagger)$, $r^{e,l}(\omega_i^\dagger, \omega_{-i}^\dagger)$, and $x^{e,l}(\omega_i^\dagger, \omega_{-i}^\dagger)$ in states $\omega^\dagger$ that are updated prior to state ω in each iteration. This information can be used when updating the values and policies at state ω requires values and policies from state $\omega^\dagger$.

In systems of linear equations it can be shown that if both Gauss–Jacobi and Gauss–Seidel schemes converge, then Gauss–Seidel schemes are faster [see, e.g., Section 2.6.2 in Bertsekas and Tsitsiklis (1997)]. There is some experience suggesting that this is also true in the systems of non-linear equations that characterize the equilibria of dynamic stochastic games.

Convergence We note that there is no proof that either of these algorithms converge. Moreover when a Gauss–Jacobi scheme converges, a Gauss–Seidel scheme may not, and vice versa. Again there is some experience that suggests that Gauss–Seidel schemes are more prone to convergence failures. Pakes and McGuire (1994) discuss a number of problems and fixes. In particular, it is frequently helpful to introduce dampening into the algorithm. In the lth iteration after computing $V^l(\cdot)$, $x^l(\cdot)$, $r^l(\cdot)$, $V^{e,l}(\cdot)$, $x^{e,l}(\cdot)$, $r^{e,l}(\cdot)$ dampening forms a convex combination of the new and the old guesses and uses these as input for the $(l+1)$th iteration. This may facilitate convergence by "smoothing out" the path that the algorithm takes; see Pakes and McGuire (1994, footnote 18) and Judd (1998, ch. 3) for details.

Software Pakes, Gowrisankaran and McGuire (1993) make Gauss and Matlab code publicly accessible. The code allows for three types of product market competition. One is a differentiated product model. Here equilibrium in the "spot" market is Nash in prices, and firms invest to improve the qualities of their products. The other two models are homogeneous product models; one has differences in marginal costs across firms and the other has differences in capacities. In these models equilibrium in the spot market is Nash in quantities and investment is directed at decreasing marginal cost (in the model with differences in marginal costs) or at increasing capacity (in the model with capacity constraints). For each model the user is allowed to specify values for parameters that set demand, production costs, sunk entry and exit fees, the efficacy of investments, and the discount rate. In addition the user specifies an initial market structure for the analysis. Finally there are additional modules which compute the solutions to a social planner's problem and to a "perfect cartel" problem based on the same parameters, and provide statistics which allow the user to compare these outcomes to those from equilibrium of the dynamic stochastic game. The publicly accessible code has been used extensively as a teaching tool, but it is not designed for computational efficiency and flexibility. For this reason researchers using variants of the EP framework have largely developed their own programs.

Doraszelski and Judd (2004) make a set of C codes with Matlab interface available upon request.

4.2. Computational burden

The computational burden of computing equilibria is large enough to often limit the type of applied problems that can be analyzed. There are two aspects of the computation that can limit the complexity of the models we analyze; the computer memory required to store the value and policies, and the CPU time required to compute the equilibrium. Here we assume that CPU time is the binding constraint, and analyze its properties.

The compute time is determined by three factors:

- the number of states per iteration,
- the time per state required to update values and policies, and
- the number of iterations.

Together the first two factors determine the time per iteration. The time to convergence is then given by the product of the time per iteration and the number of iterations. We examine the three factors in turn.

Number of states It is convenient to consider the number of states as a function of the maximum number of firms ever active, our $\bar{n}$, and of the number of possible values the firm-specific state variable can take on, say $\#\Omega$.[17] Recall that provided we restrict attention to symmetric and anonymous equilibria the number of states grows polynomially in both $\bar{n}$ and in $\#\Omega$. Even though there is no curse of dimensionality in the formal sense, the polynomial growth is often a challenge. Moreover, without special structure, $\#\Omega$ grows exponentially in the number of state variables that take on firm specific values. Suppose, for example, we want to model firms that differ in terms of both product quality and production capacity. If quality and capacity each take on one of $\bar{\omega}$ values, then $\#\Omega = \bar{\omega}^2$. Thus allowing for multiple sources of heterogeneity among firms can be especially costly. A similar problem arises if firms market more than one product, see Langohr (2003) and Song (2002).

Time per state This consists of computing the summation underlying the expected discounted value of future net cash flow given an investment outcome, or the relevant elements of $\{W(\cdot)\}$, and then solving for optimal policies and the probabilities of entry and exit given $\{W(\cdot)\}$. As noted for simple enough functional forms the optimal investment can be written down as an analytic function of the $\{W(\cdot)\}$, and provided the distributions of entry and exit fees can be evaluated analytically, so can the entry and exit probabilities.

However, as Pakes and McGuire (2001) point out, if we compute transition probabilities as we usually do using unordered states then the number of states that we need

[17] We note that in fact $\bar{n}$ and $\#\Omega$ are endogenous, but the map from primitives is too complex to be useful, and for many applied problems there is a priori information available on likely values for $\bar{n}$ and $\#\Omega$.

to sum over to compute continuation values grows exponentially in *both* the number of firms and the number of firm-specific state variables.[18] To see this, suppose that each firm can move to one of K states from one period to the next. For example if there were two firm-specific state variables and each could move up by one, down by one, or stay the same then $K = 3^2 = 9$. Then if there are n firms continuing from that state and $\mathcal{E}$ potential entrants, the total number of states that need to be summed over to obtain the continuation values for a given firm is $K^{n+\mathcal{E}-1}$.

Number of iterations There is little known about what determines the number of iterations and how it scales in the size of the problem. Somewhat surprisingly our experience has been that the number of iterations grows slowly if at all in $\#S^\circ$ but can vary greatly with the nature of the problem. Also the number of iterations does tend to increase with the discount factor β, and by quite a bit when β approaches one [Doraszelski and Judd (2004)].

Memory requirements Some of the more advanced algorithms to be discussed below have, at least in some applications, been able to decrease CPU time to such an extent that memory requirements typically become the binding constraint. This is a relatively recent phenomena and except for Pakes and McGuire (2001) very little attempt has been made to reduce memory requirements. This is an area which requires further attention.

Summary It should be clear from the discussion above that the burden of computing equilibria can often be a significant consideration in choosing the model we analyze. Indeed we typically can add enough sources of heterogeneity to any applied problem to make it impossible to compute the required equilibrium.[19] Moreover this same caveat will apply to the more sophisticated algorithms introduced below. On the other hand, all applied work can ever hope to accomplish is to form an approximation to the workings of real industries that is adequate for the problem being analyzed. What the more sophisticated algorithms allow us to do is weaken the dominance of computational considerations in considering the relevant tradeoffs.

4.3. Equilibrium selection

As we pointed out in Section 3.3, we generally have little reason to believe that there is a unique symmetric and anonymous equilibrium. This raises a number of issues for

[18] The alternative, that is distinguishing among the elements in the smaller set S° instead of S, which as we noted is not typically efficient for the kind of problems analyzed to date, would imply that the sum grows exponentially in the number of state variables per firm and geometrically in the number of firms.

[19] This also raises the question of what firms actually do and how close an approximation to actual behavior the Markov perfect framework provides. This is a topic which is largely beyond the scope of this paper, though it is touched on in Pakes and McGuire (2001). Our informal analysis indicates that perhaps the most frequent surprise in empirical work is just how good an approximation the Markov perfect framework gives [see, e.g., Benkard (2004)].

applied work. Some of them are not directly related to computation. Examples include the estimation of parameters in the presence of multiple equilibria, the ability of data to identify the equilibria (or the equilibrium selection rule) that is being played, and the issue of how to evaluate the possible outcomes of alternative policies in the presence of multiple equilibria [for more detail see, e.g., Pakes (2006) and the literature cited there].

Here we focus more narrowly on questions that involve the interaction between computation and multiple equilibria, starting with the fact that any algorithm which computes an equilibrium implicitly selects an equilibrium. Most applications have sufficed with the selected equilibrium, perhaps after performing some rudimentary search for alternatives.[20]

There is a sense in which any algorithm which converges is locally stable at least with respect to the path along which it converged. On the other hand, Besanko et al. (2004) prove, in the context of a dynamic model with learning-by-doing and organizational forgetting, that there is a set of equilibria that are unstable in the sense that they cannot be computed by the Pakes and McGuire (1994) algorithm. An interesting and unexplored question is whether there is something special about the equilibria an algorithm selects. For example, would a learning algorithm either converge to it or at least remain near it if started in an appropriate neighborhood? Perhaps even more important is whether decision making processes used by actual firms would converge to it. If we could characterize stability in these terms, then there would be grounds for excluding the equilibria which are unstable as unlikely to occur.

There remains the question of the rationale for the selected equilibrium. There is a sense in which the building blocks of the Pakes and McGuire (1994) algorithm are intuitively appealing. The algorithm combines value function iteration as familiar from dynamic programming with best reply dynamics (akin to Cournot adjustment) as familiar from static games. Since the ordering of the states does not affect iterates in a Gauss–Jacobi algorithm, the Pakes and McGuire (1994) algorithm is independent of the order in which states are visited. This means that different computers which use the same parameter values and the same (admittedly arbitrary) initial conditions to the Pakes and McGuire (1994) algorithm ought to obtain the same answer. Despite these features of the Pakes and McGuire (1994) algorithm, however, it is not clear that the equilibrium computed by it is the one we should focus on.

Undoubtedly the reasonableness of any selection depends on what the subsequent analysis is to be used for. If we were trying to demonstrate the feasibility of a theoretical proposition, or the feasibility of a particular change in outcomes as we vary some parameter, then probably any of the equilibria would be fine. On the other hand, if we

[20] Neither the Pakes and McGuire (1994) algorithm, nor the modifications that have been made to it to enable it to be used for a broader range of applied problems, offers a systematic approach to computing multiple equilibria. So to the extent that authors have searched for multiplicity, the search has been rather ad hoc, usually consisting of computing equilibria many times from different initial conditions, or different orders for cycling through the states in S°.

were trying to analyze how a particular industry is likely to respond to a proposed policy change, we need to be more careful. In this case, we would want to try to figure out which of the possible equilibria is more likely, or at least to bound the outcomes of interest that could arise. As noted above, the question of how to figure out which equilibria are more likely to arise is beyond the scope of this paper. However the possibility of bounding outcomes raises distinct computational questions. In particular can we compute all possible equilibria, or at least trace out a large subset of them? This is the multiplicity issue we come back to below.

5. Alleviating the computational burden

The computational burden of computing equilibria is oftentimes substantial, thus limiting the applications of the EP framework. In particular, there is a curse of dimensionality in (i) computing expectations over successor states, and in (ii) the size of the state space. This section outlines approaches to alleviating the computational burden. We begin with an overview of the ideas behind the techniques and the differences between them. We then proceed to a more detailed description of each of them, and we conclude with some thoughts for future research. The subsections of this section correspond to the different algorithms, and each should be readable independent of whether the others are read.

5.1. Overview

The first approach we describe, due to Doraszelski and Judd (2004), is designed to ease the burden of computing the expectation over successor states, and hence decreases the computation time needed to update values and policies at a particular state (it makes no attempt to alleviate the burden imposed by the number of states). Doraszelski and Judd (2004) set up a continuous-time model in which at any particular instant only one firm experiences a change in its state. As a result if each firm's transition can go to one of K states, and there are n firms, we only need to sum over $(K-1)\times n$ states to compute continuation values. This is in contrast to the K^n possible future states that we need to sum over in the computational algorithm described above.[21] This implies that the discrete- and continuous-time models discussed in this paper have different implications. As a result it may (but need not) be the case that one of the models provides a better approximation to behavior in a particular setting than the other. We come back

[21] Note that if we are willing to explicitly restrict players to move one at a time we could obtain similar gains from a discrete-time model in which decisions are made sequentially as a result of a random selection mechanism and outcomes are realized before the next decision is made. Discrete-time models with a deterministic order of moves have been investigated in classic articles by Maskin and Tirole (1988a, 1988b); see also Noel (2004) for a computable version of Maskin and Tirole (1988b) Edgeworth cycle model. From a computational point of view the deterministic order prevents us from using anonymity to reduce the size of the state space. It is the idea of using a random order of moves which preserves anonymity, see Doraszelski (2005).

to this point in our discussion of topics for further research as one of those topics is the role of timing assumptions in the models that have been used to date.

The second approach we describe for reducing the burden of computing equilibria is the stochastic algorithm of Pakes and McGuire (2001). This algorithm is designed to alleviate *both* the curse of dimensionality resulting from the need to calculate expectations over successor states at each point in the state space, and that arising from the growth in the number of points in that state space. It use simulations draws both to (i) approximate expectations, and to (ii) determine a recurrent class of points which eventually become the only points at which it computes equilibrium policies.

Using simulation instead of explicit integration to compute expectations makes the time per state linear in the number of firms (just as in the continuous-time model). The stochastic algorithm, however, also deals with the large size of the state space. It updates only one state at each iteration (the state visited at that iteration), and the same simulation draws used to compute the expectation are used to update the state visited. The algorithm eventually wanders into a recurrent class of points, and once in that class stays within it. That is, after an initial run in period the algorithm only computes expectations on this recurrent class of points, and, as noted, the cardinality of the recurrent class can be much smaller than that of the state space itself. The relationship of the cardinality of the recurrent class to that of the state space depends on the details of the model. However as discussed below for IO models with even a reasonably large number of state variables the cardinality of the recurrent class is often only a tiny fraction of that of the state space.

From a conceptual point of view the Pakes and McGuire (2001) algorithm is an adaptation of artificial intelligence algorithms which have been used extensively for both single agent problems and zero sum games [see Bertsekas and Tsitsiklis (1996)] to the problem of computing the equilibrium of dynamic games. It is therefore related to the recent theoretical literature on learning, both in macroeconomics [see, e.g., Sargent (1993) and Lettau and Uhlig (1999)] and in games [see, e.g., Fudenberg and Levine (1998)]. An additional rationale for the algorithm, then, is that the algorithm's path has an interpretation as an outcome of a learning process that might be a good approximation to behavior in certain situations.

We note that in both these subsections we provide numerical examples with computational time. The examples refer to models in which we increase the number of firms holding the states per firm constant. As we increase the realism of our models we will want to also consider how the computational complexity varies as we increase the number of state variables per firm. Unfortunately there has been very little experimentation with models with more than one state variable per firm.

Finally we also briefly consider parametric approximation methods similar to those discussed in Judd (1998), and approximations to the decision making process which might be relevant when there are a large number of firms as in Weintraub, Benkard and Van Roy (2005). The first set of methods are designed to reduce the number of points which we have to update at each iteration of the iterative process, the second changes the equilibrium concept in a way that simplifies computation.

Many of the ideas behind the algorithms we describe are complementary. This suggests building hybrids. For example one might want to combine the continuous-time approach of Doraszelski and Judd (2004) with the idea of focusing on the recurrent class due to Pakes and McGuire (2001). Alternatively the idea in Weintraub, Benkard and Van Roy (2005) of changing the equilibrium conditions may be further exploited by allowing for aggregate shocks and more detailed responses to a few "large" firms, still keeping the idea of a "fringe" of small firms whose every move need not be considered in computing future expectations.

5.2. Continuous-time models

Doraszelski and Judd (2004) develop continuous-time stochastic games with a finite number of states. We consider a variant of their game which mimics the assumptions of our discrete-time model as closely as possible.

The major difference is that in the discrete-time model the time path of the state is a sequence while in the continuous-time model that path is a piecewise-constant, right-continuous function of time. Jumps between states occur at random times according to a controlled non-homogeneous Poisson process. Thus we need to specify the hazard rates for each possible reason for a jump, and the probability of transitions conditional on the jump occurring. In a model with industry specific shocks there are four possible reasons for a jump; the investment of one of the incumbents produced a new outcome, the value of the outside alternative increased, an incumbent decided to exit, or a potential entrant decided to enter.

Setup The horizon is infinite and the state of the game at time t is $\omega_t = (\omega_{1t}, \ldots, \omega_{nt})$, where ω_{it} is the state of incumbent firm i at time t. Incumbent firm i has to sell its assets in order to exit the industry, and buyers for its assets arrive with hazard rate λ. Upon arrival the buyer makes a take-it-or-leave-it offer of a scrap value, ϕ_{it}, drawn randomly from a distribution $F(\cdot)$ with continuous and positive density. As in the discrete-time model, the offered scrap value is private information and hence is a random variable from the perspective of other firms. If it is above the incumbent firm's continuation value, the incumbent accepts it and leaves the industry. We let $\psi(\omega_{it}, \omega_{-it})$ (sometimes abbreviated to ψ_{it}) be the probability that incumbent firm i *exits*.

A continuing firm invests $x_{it} \geqslant 0$ per unit of time and the probability of its ω_{it} transiting to $\omega_{it} + 1$ in any time interval is increasing in this investment. If we use the familiar constant elasticity form that hazard becomes x_{it}^{γ}, where the parameter $\gamma > 0$ is the elasticity of the success hazard with respect to investment expenditures or, equivalently, (the negative of) the elasticity of the expected time to an investment success. As in the discrete-time model we allow for an industry wide shock which has a probability of occurring of δ per unit of time and decreases the state of all incumbents by one if it does occur.

We assume that there is always a finite number $\mathcal{E}$ of potential entrants. Potential entrant i has to acquire assets to enter the industry. Sellers of assets arrive with hazard rate

λ^e and make a take-it-or-leave-it offers of ϕ^e_{it}, which is assumed to be drawn randomly from a distribution $F^e(\cdot)$ with continuous and positive density. If the value of entering at state ω^e exceeds this entry cost the potential entrant i accepts the offer and immediately begins to invest. We let $r^e(\omega_t)$ denote the probability that potential entrant i accepts the offer and *enters* the industry.

At time t the hazard rate of a jump occurring depends on the firms' investment, entry, and exit policies at the given state; i.e. on $x_t = (x_{1t}, \ldots, x_{nt})$, $\psi_t = (\psi_{1t}, \ldots, \psi_{nt})$, and $r^e(\omega_t)$. If a jump occurs at time t then the change in the state of the industry depends on what generated the jump, and the transition rules given above. More specifically if we let $\mu(\omega' \mid \omega_t, x_t, \psi_t, r^e_t)$ be the hazard rate of a jump to ω' occurring conditional on current polices and ω we have

$$\mu\left(\omega' \mid \omega_t, x_t, \psi_t, r^e_t\right) = \begin{cases} \lambda\psi_{it} & \text{if } \omega' = (\varnothing, \omega_{-it}) \text{ for } i = 1, \ldots, n_t, \\ x^{\gamma}_{it} & \text{if } \omega' = (\omega_{it} + 1, \omega_{-it}) \\ & \quad \text{for } i = 1, \ldots, n_t, \\ \mathcal{E}\lambda^e r^e_t & \text{if } \omega' = \omega_t \cup \omega^e, \\ \delta & \text{if } \omega' = (\omega_{1t} - 1, \ldots, \omega_{nt} - 1), \end{cases} \tag{16}$$

where $\omega^e \cup \omega_t$ is shorthand for the vector obtained by adding an ω^e to the vector ω_t and reordering the result appropriately.[22]

The savings in the computation of the expectation over successor states results from the fact that to form that expectation we need only sum over the $2n + 2$ distinct ω' with positive hazards. This occurs because the model implies that in a short time interval there will be (with probability arbitrarily close to one) at most one jump. In the discrete-time model we must keep track of all possible combinations of firms' transitions between time t and time $t + 1$. Thus the computational burden of computing the expectation over successor states in the continuous-time model grows linearly in the number of firms, thereby avoiding the curse of dimensionality in that expectation.

Equilibrium At time t player i chooses an action x_{it} that depends solely on the current state ω_t. As in the discrete-time model, given that all his rivals adopt a Markovian strategy, a player faces a dynamic programming problem and Bellman's (1957) principle of optimality implies that he can do no better than to also adopt a Markovian strategy. For a statement of the principle of optimality in a continuous-time setting see, e.g., Intriligator (1971, p. 327). Furthermore, although the player gets to pick his action from scratch at each point in time, his optimal action changes only when the state of the game changes.

An incumbent's problem Suppose that the industry is in state ω. The Bellman equation for incumbent firm i is similar to the one in discrete time. To see this reinterpret $\pi(\cdot)$

[22] Were we to add the possibility of a firm specific depreciation component, we would add a hazard for $\omega' = (\omega_{it} - 1, \omega_{-it})$ for $i = 1, \ldots, n_t$ to the hazards defined above. Note that $\sum_{\omega'} \mu(\omega' \mid \omega_t, x_t, \psi_t, r^e_t)$ is the hazard rate of a change in the state of the game.

and x_i as flows per unit of time and note that over a short interval of length $\Delta > 0$ incumbent firm i solves the dynamic programming problem given by

$$V(\omega_i, \omega_{-i}) \approx \max_{x_i \geqslant 0} \big(\pi(\omega_i, \omega_{-i}) - x_i\big)\Delta + (1 - \rho\Delta)E\big\{\max\big\{\chi\phi', V(\omega_i', \omega_{-i}')\big\} \mid \omega_i, \omega_{-i}, x_i\big\},$$

where $(1 - \rho\Delta) \approx e^{-\rho\Delta}$ is the analog to the discrete-time discount factor β, χ is an indicator function which takes the value of one if a potential purchaser of the firm's assets arrives at the end of the interval of length Δ, and it is understood that the expectations presumes all other agents are making equilibrium choices. Evaluating the right-hand side of this equation we get

$$\begin{aligned} V(\omega_i, \omega_{-i}) \approx{}& \max_{x_i \geqslant 0} \big(\pi(\omega_i, \omega_{-i}) - x_i\big)\Delta \\ &+ (1 - \Delta\rho)\Bigg[\lambda\psi(\omega_i, \omega_{-i})\Delta E\big[\phi \mid \phi \geqslant V(\omega_i, \omega_{-i})\big] \\ &+ \sum_{\omega_i', \omega_{-i}'} q^c(\omega_i', \omega_{-i}' \mid \omega_i, \omega_{-i}, x_i)\Delta V(\omega_i', \omega_{-i}') \\ &+ \Bigg(1 - \lambda\psi(\omega_i, \omega_{-i})\Delta \\ &- \sum_{\omega_i', \omega_{-i}'} q^c(\omega_i', \omega_{-i}' \mid \omega_i, \omega_{-i}, x_i)\Delta\Bigg)V(\omega_i, \omega_{-i})\Bigg], \end{aligned}$$

where

$$\psi(\omega_i, \omega_{-i}) = 1 - F\big(V(\omega_i, \omega_{-i})\big)$$

is the probability of exit and

$$\begin{aligned} &q^c(\omega_i', \omega_{-i}' \mid \omega_i, \omega_{-i}, x_i) \\ &\quad = \mu\big(\omega_i', \omega_{-i}' \mid \omega_i, \omega_{-i}, x_i, x_{-i}(\omega_i, \omega_{-i}), 0, \psi_{-i}(\omega_i, \omega_{-i}), r^e(\omega_i, \omega_{-i})\big) \end{aligned} \tag{17}$$

are the equilibrium perceptions of incumbent firm i about state-to-state transitions. The value of zero for ψ_i reflects the fact that these perceptions are conditional on continuing on in the industry.

This last equation breaks up the hazard rate of a change in the state of the industry into a part that is due to exit, $\lambda\psi_i(\cdot)$, and a part that is due to all other possible change in the state, $\sum_{\omega_i', \omega_{-i}'} q^c(\omega_i', \omega_{-i}' \mid \omega_i, \omega_{-i}, x_i)$. The first term reflects the fact that the firm earns the flow profits minus investment over the Δ period. Exit occurs with probability $\lambda\psi_i(\cdot)\Delta$ and, similar to the discrete-time model, the expected scrap value conditional on exiting is $\mathrm{E}\{\phi \mid \phi \geqslant V(\omega_i, \omega_{-i})\}$ rather than its unconditional expectation $\mathrm{E}\{\phi\}$. The next term covers the possibility of some other change in the state, including an investment success and a depreciation shock. The final term covers the possibility that nothing changes between time t and time $t + \Delta$.

As $\Delta \to 0$, the above equation simplifies to the Bellman equation

$$\begin{aligned}\rho V(\omega_i, \omega_{-i}) = \max_{x_i \geqslant 0} \pi(\omega_i, \omega_{-i}) - x_i \\ + \lambda \psi(\omega_i, \omega_{-i})\big(E\big[\phi \mid \phi \geqslant V(\omega_i, \omega_{-i})\big] - V(\omega_i, \omega_{-i})\big) \\ + \sum_{\omega_i', \omega_{-i}'} q^c(\omega_i', \omega_{-i}' \mid \omega_i, \omega_{-i}, x_i)\big(V(\omega_i', \omega_{-i}') - V(\omega_i, \omega_{-i})\big).\end{aligned} \tag{18}$$

Hence, $V(\omega_i, \omega_{-i})$ can be interpreted as the asset value to incumbent firm i of participating in the game. This asset is priced by requiring that the opportunity cost of holding it, $\rho V(\omega_i, \omega_{-i})$, equals the current cash flow, $\pi(\omega_i, \omega_{-i}) - x_i$, plus the expected capital gain or loss due to exit or some other change in the state.

The strategy of incumbent firm i is found by carrying out the maximization problem on the RHS of the Bellman equation (18). In particular, the optimal investment decision is

$$\begin{aligned}x(\omega_i, \omega_{-i}) = \arg\max_{x_i} -x_i \\ + \sum_{\omega_i', \omega_{-i}'} q^c(\omega_i', \omega_{-i}' \mid \omega_i, \omega_{-i}, x_i)\big(V(\omega_i', \omega_{-i}') - V(\omega_i, \omega_{-i})\big).\end{aligned} \tag{19}$$

Given a success hazard of x_i^γ with $0 < \gamma < 1$, this simplifies to

$$x(\omega_i, \omega_{-i}) = \max\big\{0, \big(\gamma\big(V(\omega_i + 1, \omega_{-i}) - V(\omega_i, \omega_{-i})\big)\big)^{\frac{1}{1-\gamma}}\big\}.$$

More generally, the optimal investment decision satisfies a Kuhn–Tucker condition similar to the discrete-time model. An incumbent exits if the optimized continuation value is less than the offered scrap value. This gives an exit probability of

$$\psi(\omega_i, \omega_{-i}) = 1 - F\big(V(\omega_i, \omega_{-i})\big). \tag{20}$$

An entrant's problem Suppose that the industry is in state ω. If $V(\omega, \omega^e)$ is the value of entering the industry in state ω^e (holding fixed the other firms in state ω) and continuing on as an incumbent, then an entrant will enter if and only if $V(\omega, \omega^e) \geqslant \phi^e$. Consequently the probability of entry conditional on a seller of assets appearing at a particular instant is

$$r^e(\omega) = F^e\big(V(\omega, \omega^e)\big), \tag{21}$$

and the hazard rate of entry is $\mathcal{E}\lambda^e r^e(\omega)$.

Computation While Doraszelski and Judd (2004) use a Gauss–Seidel algorithm to compute the equilibrium to their continuous-time model, here we provide a Gauss–Jacobi algorithm that is analogous to Pakes and McGuire (1994) algorithm for the discrete-time model. As usual we begin with an initial set of values and policies for all states $\omega \in S^{\circ}$. Iteration l then maps old guesses into new guesses as it cycles over the state space S° in some predetermined order.

Specifically, to update the values and policies for an incumbent firm in state ω, we proceed as follows. First, we use the optimality condition in Equation (19) to update the investment decision as

$$x^l(\omega_i, \omega_{-i}) = \arg\max_{x_i} -x_i + \sum_{\omega_i', \omega_{-i}'} q^{c,l-1}(\omega_i', \omega_{-i}' \mid \omega_i, \omega_{-i}, x_i) \\ \times \big(V^{l-1}(\omega_i', \omega_{-i}') - V^{l-1}(\omega_i, \omega_{-i})\big),$$

where $q^{c,l-1}(\omega_i', \omega_{-i}' \mid \omega_i, \omega_{-i}, x_i)$ is constructed by substituting the policies of the other firms from the previous iteration into Equation (17). Second, we use Equation (20) to update the exit decision as

$$\psi^l(\omega_i, \omega_{-i}) = 1 - F\big(V^{l-1}(\omega_i, \omega_{-i})\big).$$

Third, we use $x^l(\omega_i, \omega_{-i})$ and $\psi^l(\omega_i, \omega_{-i})$ to update the value as

$$V^l(\omega_i, \omega_{-i}) \\ = \frac{1}{\rho + \lambda\psi^l(\omega_i, \omega_{-i}) + \sum_{\omega_i', \omega_{-i}'} q^{c,l-1}(\omega_i', \omega_{-i}' \mid \omega_i, \omega_{-i}, x^l(\omega_i, \omega_{-i}))} \\ \times \Big\{\pi(\omega_i, \omega_{-i}) - x^l(\omega_i, \omega_{-i}) + \lambda\psi^l(\omega_i, \omega_{-i})E\big[\phi \mid \phi \geqslant V^{l-1}(\omega_i, \omega_{-i})\big] \\ + \sum_{\omega_i', \omega_{-i}'} q^{c,l-1}\big(\omega_i', \omega_{-i}' \mid \omega_i, \omega_{-i}, x^l(\omega_i, \omega_{-i})\big) V^{l-1}(\omega_i', \omega_{-i}')\Big\}. \tag{22}$$

By rearranging Equation (18) and dividing through by the sum of the discount factor and the hazard rate of a change in the state of the industry, we ensure that Equation (22) would be a contraction were we to iterate on it holding the policies of the other firms fixed (just as it is in the equation which updates values in the discrete-time model). Fourth, we update the entry probability conditional on the appearance of a seller of assets by setting

$$r^{e,l}(\omega) = F^e\big(V^{l-1}(\omega, \omega^e)\big).$$

The smaller number in successor states in the continuous-time model may allow us to speed up the computations in one other way. Prior to adding each of the terms that enter in the expectation over successor states, both the continuous- and the discrete-time algorithms need to look them up in computer memory. This requires the algorithms

Table 30.2
Time to convergence and ratio of discrete to continuous time in terms of time per iteration, number of iterations, and time to convergence. Stopping rule is "distance to truth $< 10^{-4}$". Entries in italics are based on an estimated 119 iterations to convergence in discrete time

#Firms	Discrete time (min)	Continuous time (min)	Ratio time per iteration	Ratio number of iterations	Ratio time to convergence
2	1.80×10^{-4}	1.12×10^{-4}	1.73	0.93	1.61
3	1.42×10^{-3}	8.83×10^{-4}	2.88	0.56	1.60
4	1.13×10^{-2}	4.43×10^{-3}	6.10	0.42	2.54
5	8.78×10^{-2}	1.70×10^{-2}	14.57	0.36	5.18
6	6.42×10^{-1}	5.34×10^{-2}	37.12	0.32	12.03
7	4.44×10^{0}	1.47×10^{-1}	98.26	0.31	30.19
8	2.67×10^{1}	3.56×10^{-1}	249.38	0.30	74.94
9	1.66×10^{2}	7.95×10^{-1}	709.04	0.29	208.85
10	*9.28×10^{2}*	1.77×10^{0}	1800.00	*0.29*	*523.72*
11	*4.94×10^{3}*	3.30×10^{0}	5187.50	*0.29*	*1498.33*
12	*2.46×10^{4}*	6.18×10^{0}	13,770.00	*0.29*	*3977.26*
13	*1.27×10^{5}*	1.13×10^{1}	39,033.56	*0.29*	*11,246.96*
14	*6.00×10^{5}*	2.02×10^{1}	103,195.27	*0.29*	*29,734.23*

Source: Doraszelski and Judd (2004).

to compute the addresses of the successor states in computer memory and imposes a further cost. One way to speed up the computations is to compute these addresses once and then store them for future reference. Precomputed addresses decreases running times but increases memory requirements. When the number of successor states is small enough the savings from this prior computation outweigh the costs, so it is frequently useful in the continuous-time model, but not in the discrete-time model. We note also that the homotopy methods that we discuss in Section 6 can use the continuous-time models just as the Gaussian methods described here do, and that this would result in similar reductions of the computational burden.

Example Doraszelski and Judd (2004) use a modified version of the Pakes and McGuire (1994) quality ladder model to compare the continuous- and discrete-time approaches. In order to avoid the existence problems that may arise from the discrete nature of firms' entry and exit decision (see Section 3.1 for details), they abstract from entry and exit. Moreover, they differ from the original quality ladder model in that their shocks are independent across firms whereas Pakes and McGuire (1994) assume an industry-wide shock (see Section 2).

As Table 30.2 shows, each iteration of the continuous-time algorithm is far faster than its discrete-time equivalent. Partly offsetting this is the fact that for comparable games the continuous-time algorithm needs more iterations to converge to the equilibrium. The reason that the continuous-time algorithm suffers an iteration penalty is that the continuous-time "contraction factor", i.e.

$$\frac{\sum_{\omega_i',\omega_{-i}'} q^{c,l-1}(\omega_i',\omega_{-i}' \mid \omega_i,\omega_{-i},x^l(\omega_i,\omega_{-i}))}{\rho+\lambda\psi^l(\omega_i,\omega_{-i})+\sum_{\omega_i',\omega_{-i}'} q^{c,l-1}(\omega_i',\omega_{-i}' \mid \omega_i,\omega_{-i},x^l(\omega_i,\omega_{-i}))}$$

in Equation (22) varies with firms' policies and substantially exceeds the discrete-time discount factor β. Even though the continuous-time algorithm needs more iterations, the loss in the number of iterations is small when compared to the gain from avoiding the curse of dimensionality and the (much smaller) gain from precomputed addresses. Table 30.2 illustrates this comparison and the total gain from continuous time. Continuous time beats discrete time by 60% if $n = 3$, a factor of 12 if $n = 6$, a factor of 209 if $n = 9$, a factor of 3977 if $n = 12$, and a factor of 29,734 if $n = 14$.

Software Doraszelski and Judd (2004) make a set of C codes with Matlab interface available upon request.

5.3. *Stochastic approximation algorithm*

The stochastic algorithm breaks the curses of dimensionality in the number of elements of the summand in calculating the expectation over future states *and* in the number of states. It is able to do so because

- it never attempts to obtain accurate policies on the entire state space, just on a recurrent class of points, and the number of points in the recurrent class need not grow in any particular way with the dimension of the state space, and
- it never calculates integrals over possible future values, rather it approximates those integrals with an average of past outcomes.

To ease exposition of how this is done this section will modify the presentation in two ways. First we will initially assume that the exit and entry costs are fixed numbers, our (ϕ, ϕ^e), rather than draws from distributions, and that there is only one potential entrant in each period (who will either enter or not as a deterministic function of equilibrium values). Accordingly since all incumbents have the same ϕ we do not include ϕ as an argument of the value function. We include a paragraph indicating how to modify the algorithm to revert to the initial specification below.

Second we will rewrite the value function in a way that makes it explicit that the equilibrium conditions can be expressed as a fixed point in the $\{W(\cdot)\}$, i.e. in the expected discounted value of future net cash flows conditional on the different possible outcomes of the firm's investment expenditures, rather than as a fixed point in the values per se. That is we rewrite the fixed point conditions at every $\omega \in S^\circ$ so that incumbent values are given by

$$V(\omega_i,\omega_{-i} \mid W) = \pi(\omega_i,\omega_{-i}) + \max\left\{\phi, \max_{x_i}\left(-x_i + \beta\sum_{\nu} W(\nu \mid \omega_i,\omega_{-i})p(\nu \mid x_i)\right)\right\} \tag{23}$$

potential entrants values are given by

$$V\big(\omega^e, \omega \mid W\big) = \max\left\{0, -\phi^e + \max_{x^e}\left(-x^e + \beta \sum_{\nu} W\big(\nu \mid \omega^e, \omega\big)p\big(\nu \mid x^e\big)\right)\right\} \tag{24}$$

and

$$W(\nu \mid \omega_i, \omega_{-i}) = \sum_{\omega'_{-i}, \eta} V(\omega_i + \nu - \eta, \omega'_{-i} \mid W)q(\omega'_{-i}, \omega, \eta)p(\eta), \tag{25}$$

where $q(\omega'_{-i}, \omega, \eta)$ are derived from the policies generated by Equations (23) and (24) and the primitives of the problem. Note that here and below when $i = e$ it is understood that $\omega_{-i} = \omega$, the vector of all of the incumbents ω's.

Writing the value function in this way makes it clear that the $W(\cdot)$ are sufficient statistics for agents' behavior. That is if we knew the $W(\cdot)$'s we would know equilibrium policies and values. The stochastic algorithm recasts the search for equilibrium as a search for a set of numbers, the $\{W(\cdot)\}$, that satisfy the fixed point implicit in the definition of the value function in terms of $W(\cdot)$, our $V(\cdot \mid W)$ in Equations (23) and (24), and the definition of $W(\cdot)$ in terms of $V(\cdot \mid W)$ in Equation (25).

Iterative search procedure The stochastic algorithm is also iterative. However in contrast to the other algorithms discussed here it is *asynchronous*; it only calculates policies for a single state at each iteration. Consequently it must hold in memory both

- a location, and
- estimates of the expected discounted value of the future net cash flows that would result from each possible outcome of each firm's actions (i.e. of the $W(\cdot)$'s in Equations (23) and (24)).

Let $W(\omega)$ refer to the vector of values of $W(\nu; \omega_i, \omega_{-i})$ associated with the incumbents and potential entrant at ω, W refer to the entire collection of $W(\omega)$ (so $W = \{W(\omega){:}\ \omega \in S^\circ\}$), and l index iterations. Then an iteration must update both the location, say ω^l, and the estimates of equilibrium $W(\cdot)$, or W^l.

In the first step of the update incumbents and the potential entrant at the current location chose the policies that maximizes the current iteration's estimate of expected discounted values of net cash flows. That is the first step substitutes components of $W^l(\omega^l)$ for the equilibrium components of $W(\omega)$ appearing in Equations (23) and (24), and then determines the optimal policies implied by these estimates in a manner analogous to that described in Equations (4), (6), and (9) above.

These policies determine the distribution of the next location. To get the actual realization of that location we take computer generated pseudo-random draws from the distributions determined by these policies and the primitives of the model. Then a potential entrants whose policy was to enter does so at the state determined by the simulated draws, incumbents whose policy were to continue update their state with their simulated draws, and incumbents whose policy was to exit do so. More precisely the location of the firms active in $l+1$ are given by $\omega_i^l + \nu_i^{l+1} - \eta^{l+1}$ for continuing incumbents and $\omega^e + \nu_e^{l+1} - \eta^{l+1}$ for a new entrant that enters. Here the ν_i^{l+1} and ν_e^{l+1} are draws from the distributions $p(\nu \mid x_i^l)$ and $p(\nu \mid x_e^l)$, where the x's are the policies determined above, while η^{l+1} is a draw from $p(\eta)$ (the distribution of increments to the outside alternative). The vector of new states, re-ordered to be in their natural order, becomes ω^{l+1}, the new location.

To complete the iteration we need also to update the estimates of the W. We only update the estimates of $\{W(\omega^l)\}$ (the components of W associated with the location of the algorithm at iteration l). From Equation (25), each equilibrium $W(\nu; \omega_i, \omega_{-i})$ is an expectations of the discounted value of the firm's state in the next period conditional on a realization of its own investment outcome. The expectation is over the possible outcome of the competitors' states and of the outside alternative.

The update of the estimate of $W(\omega^l)$ acts as if the random draws on the outcomes of the competitors' states and of the outside alternative are random draws from the equilibrium distribution of outcomes for the competitors' states and from the outside alternative; i.e. as if they are random draws from the equilibrium $q(\omega'_{-i}, \omega, \eta)$ and $p(\eta)$. It then evaluates the integrand at the new state by acting as if the current iteration's estimate of $W(\omega^l)$, our $W^l(\omega^l)$, were the equilibrium values of $W(\omega^l)$. That is it acts as if $V(\omega_i^l + \nu - \eta^{l+1}, \omega_{-i}^{l+1} \mid W^l)$, formed from the random draws and $W^l(\omega^l)$ and computed as in Equation (23), is the equilibrium value associated with that point. $V(\omega_i^l + \nu - \eta^{l+1}, \omega_{-i}^{l+1} \mid W^l)$ is then treated as a random draw from the integral determining W and averaged with the current iterations estimate of W, or W^l, to obtain W^{l+1}. That is to form its $W^{l+1}(\cdot)$ the algorithm chooses an $\alpha(\omega, l) > 0$ and sets

$$W^{l+1}(\nu; \omega_i^l, \omega_{-i}^l) = \frac{1}{1+\alpha(\omega, l+1)} V(\omega_i^l + \nu - \eta^{l+1}, \omega_{-i}^{l+1} \mid W^l) + \frac{\alpha(\omega, l)}{1+\alpha(\omega, l+1)} W^l(\nu; \omega_i, \omega_{-i}). \tag{26}$$

So $W^{l+1}(\nu_i; \omega_i, \omega_{-i}) - W^l(\nu_i; \omega_i, \omega_{-i})$ is greater than, equal to, or less than zero according as $V(\omega_i^l + \nu - \eta^{l+1}, \omega_{-i}^{l+1} \mid W^l) - W^l(\nu_i; \omega_i, \omega_{-i})$ is greater than, equal to, or less than zero.

If $\alpha(\omega, l)$ equals the number of times the state $\omega = \omega^l$ had been visited prior to iteration l, then the formulae in (26) produces the simple of average of the values obtained from those visits. In general there are "better" ways of choosing the $\alpha(\cdot)$ then this. This because the earlier outcomes should be less precise estimates of the numbers we are after (and hence should receive less weight; we provide one example below). On the other hand, all proposed weighting schemes satisfy Robbins and Monro (1951) convergence conditions; i.e. the sum of the weight increase without bound as the number of visits increase, but the sum of the squared weights remains bounded (conditions which are satisfied by simple averages).

Two conceptual points about the updates. First if $W^l(\omega^l)$ equals the equilibrium $W(\omega^l)$ then the expectation of the $V(\omega_i^l + \nu - \eta^{l+1}, \omega_{-i}^{l+1} \mid W^l)$ is also the equilibrium $W(\omega^l)$. That is once we are at the equilibrium values of $W(\omega^l)$ we will tend to stay there. However as is explained below the algorithm only repeatedly visits points in a recurrent subset of the state space. As a result we should not expect the algorithm to generate precise estimates of the equilibrium $W(\omega)$'s associated with ω's that are outside the recurrent class. Consequently below we modify the conditions which define equilibrium policies and values so that they pertain only to a recurrent class of points, and show why they are relevant for subgames starting from an initial condition in the recurrent class. We then discuss tests of whether these equilibrium conditions are satisfied by the estimate of W outputted by the algorithm.

Second use of the Monte Carlo draw to both determine the evolution of the state, and to estimate the returns to alternative actions, mimics what would happen were agents actually implementing policies based on our procedure and then using the actual market outcomes to update their estimate of the implications of their actions. This provides both the link to the learning literature in economic theory, and the reason one might want to use the algorithm as a behavioral model in certain instances. That is if we knew the $W(\cdot)$'s that the agents' perceived at any point in time, and were willing to specify how those agents updated their perceptions of W as a result of information that accumulated over time, we could generate a probability distribution over sample paths for both the policies followed and the states achieved.

Computational burden We now review the reasons for the stochastic algorithm's computational savings. First the location of the stochastic algorithm will eventually wander into a recurrent class of points (our R), and once within that R will stay within it forever (with probability one). That is after an initial run in period the stochastic algorithm only updates the values and policies associated with points in this recurrent class (the other algorithms update on the entire state space). In the examples we have computed the recurrent class tends to grow linearly in the number of state variables, thus overcoming one of the two aspects of the curse of dimensionality noted in the last section.

Second the stochastic algorithm does not require a summation over possible future states to update the information in memory at each point visited. The computational burden at a point involves only; determining the optimal policies given $W^l(\omega^l)$, drawing the random variables whose distributions are determined by these policies, and updating the estimates of $W(\omega)$ with Equation (26). The computational burden of these tasks grows linearly in the number of firms active at the state, thus eliminating the second aspect of the curse of dimensionality noted in the last section.

However unlike the deterministic updates used in the other algorithms discussed here, the Monte Carlo estimate of $W(\omega)$ contains the variance induced by the simulated draws on outcomes. If the estimates of $W(\omega)$ settles down, the precision of the Monte Carlo estimate of the integral will become proportional to the number of times the state is visited. As a result the accuracy of the estimates at a point depend on the number of visits to the point, and sufficient accuracy can take a larger number of iterations per point than the other algorithms discussed here. On the other hand, the precision of the Monte Carlo estimate of the integral does not (necessarily) depend on the dimension of the integral being estimated, while the cost of doing the summation explicitly does. So the number of visits needed for given accuracy need not (and in our experience does not) depend on the number of state variables.

Equilibrium policies and stopping rules Let $\tilde{W}$ be a particular value of W. As noted once we substitute $\tilde{W}(\omega)$ into Equations (23) and (24) we determine policies for all agents active at that ω (though these policies will not, in general, be equilibrium policies). These policies determine the probabilities of transiting to any future state if the policies generated by $\tilde{W}(\omega)$ are followed. Let those probabilities be given by $q(\omega', \omega \mid \tilde{W}(\omega))$, $\forall \omega' \in S^\circ$. Now order the states and arrange these probabilities into a row vector in that order, say $q(\omega \mid \tilde{W}(\omega))$. Do this for each $\omega \in S^\circ$, and combine the resultant rows into a matrix whose rows are ordered by the same order used to order the elements in each row. The result is a Markov matrix (or transition kernel) for the industry structures, say $Q(\cdot,\cdot \mid \tilde{W})$. This matrix defines the Markov process for industry structures that would be generated if all agents acted as if $\tilde{W}$ were the true expected discounted values of alternative outcomes.

Any finite state Markov kernel generates a stochastic process with at least one recurrent class. Say $\tilde{R} \subset S^\circ$ is a recurrent class of the Markov process defined by $Q(\cdot,\cdot \mid \tilde{W})$, i.e. if we start the process at an $\omega^0 \in \tilde{R}$ and follow the policies generated by $\tilde{W}$ then each element of all possible sequences, $\{\omega^k\}_{k=0}^{\infty}$, will be in $\tilde{R}$ with probability one. Call the subvector of $\tilde{W}$ which contains the elements of $\tilde{W}$ associated with the points in $\tilde{R}$, $\tilde{W} \mid \tilde{R}$. Since $\tilde{R}$ is a recurrent class of $Q(\cdot,\cdot \mid \tilde{W})$, $\tilde{W} \mid \tilde{R}$ contains all information needed to analyze any game starting from any initial condition $\omega^0 \in \tilde{R}$. That is $\tilde{W} \mid \tilde{R}$ generates policies "for subgames from $\tilde{R}$".

Pakes and McGuire (2001) provide conditions which insure that $\tilde{W} \mid \tilde{R}$ generates *equilibrium* policies for subgames from $\tilde{R}$. They then propose a procedure which identifies a recurrent class of $Q(\cdot,\cdot \mid \tilde{W})$, our $\tilde{R}$, and tests whether $\tilde{W} \mid \tilde{R}$ satisfies the equilibrium conditions. We explain their procedure next. More details on the conceptual issues underlying these calculations are given below.

Say we want to test whether a subset of the $\tilde{W}$ outputted by the algorithm, and the associated values and policies, are equilibrium policies for a recurrent class of $Q(\cdot,\cdot \mid \tilde{W})$. First we need to obtain a candidate for a recurrent class of $Q(\cdot,\cdot \mid \tilde{W})$. To do so use the policies generated by $\tilde{W}$ to simulate $\{\omega^j\}_{j=1}^{J_1+J_2}$. Let $R(J_1, J_2)$ be the set of states visited at least once between $j = J_1$ and $j = J_2$. Then, as both J_1 and $J_2 - J_1 \to \infty$, $R(J_1, J_2)$ must converge to a recurrent class of the process $Q(\cdot,\cdot \mid \tilde{W})$. As we shall see it typically does not take long to generate a million iterations of the stochastic algorithm. As a result it is easy to simulate several million draws, throw out a few million, and then consider the locations visited by the remainder as the recurrent class.

Let $\tilde{W} \mid \tilde{R}(J_1, J_2)$ contain the components of the $\tilde{W}$ vector outputted from the algorithm that are needed to obtain the policies for all the $\omega \in R(J_1, J_2)$. Pakes and McGuire (2001) test of whether $W \mid \tilde{R}(J_1, J_2)$ generates equilibrium policies for subgames starting in $R(J_1, J_2)$ consists of checking if Equations (23) and (24) are satisfied to sufficient accuracy with W computed from (25) after substituting $V(\cdot \mid \tilde{W})$ for $V(\cdot \mid W)$ into that equation. Sufficient accuracy is defined in terms of a norm on the $\omega \in R(J_1, J_2)$ (and the comparison is made for each incumbent and potential entrant at those ω). Since the stochastic algorithm is designed to obtain more accurate estimates of policies and values for points that are visited more frequently, Pakes and McGuire (2001) suggest using a weighted sum of squares norm with weights proportional to the number of visits to the point. Note that this test is the same as the test used to stop the Gaussian algorithm in Section 4 except that now we confine the test to points in $R(J_1, J_2)$ and use a weighted norm.

If the researcher is particularly interested in policies and values from a given point, say a point which reflects the structure of a particular industry at a time of interest, the test can be altered to reflect that fact. More generally the algorithm, as programmed in Pakes and McGuire (2001), outputs a count of how many times each point has been visited. This provides a good indication of how precisely the values and policies at the given point have been estimated. Local restart procedures are advisable if, for some reason, the researcher is interested in a point rarely visited by the natural progression of the algorithm.

Note that the computational burden of the test in Pakes and McGuire (2001) goes up either geometrically or exponentially in the dimension of the state space (depending on the type of states). Moreover the test is the *only* aspect of the stochastic algorithm whose computational burden grows more than linearly in the dimension of the state space. So as we increase the number of state variables the computational burden of the test eventually outweighs the burden of the rest of the algorithm (see below). As a result Fershtman and Pakes (2005) developed an alternative test which both circumvents this curse, and is easy to apply. We come back to this alternative test below.

Equilibrium: conceptual issues We now provide more detail on the conceptual issues underlying the notion of equilibrium and the test (a reader not interested in these details should be able to skip this section and have no difficulty with the sections that follow).

Formally the conditions being tested above are not sufficient to guarantee that the policies and values outputted by the algorithm are Markov perfect equilibrium policies and values for states in the recurrent class. To see this note that though all points in the recurrent class only communicate with other points in the recurrent class if optimal policies are followed, there are points in the recurrent class that could communicate with points outside the recurrent class if feasible (though in-optimal) policies are followed. When this occurs the $V(\cdot,\cdot \mid \tilde{W})$ needed to check Equation (25) will contain values which the test does not insure are equilibrium values (since they are points which are not in the recurrent class we do not test the condition in Equation (23) for them). For an example of this recall that $\bar{n}$ is the maximum number of agents ever active, and consider a state in $R(J_1, J_2)$ with $\bar{n}$ firms active. To determine whether the policies at that state are optimal we need to know what values would be were the potential entrant to enter and no incumbent exit; i.e. what the values would be if there were $\bar{n}+1$ firms active. We do not check whether the values at such states satisfy our equilibrium conditions.[23]

Pakes and McGuire (2001) call points that are in $\tilde{R}$ but could communicate with points outside of $\tilde{R}$ if feasible (though in-optimal) policies were followed, boundary points of $\tilde{R}$. Points in $\tilde{R}$ that are not boundary points are called interior points of $\tilde{R}$. Interior points could not communicate with a point outside of $\tilde{R}$ under any feasible policy. They then show that when the test needs to use a $V(\cdot,\cdot \mid \tilde{W})$ associated with an $\omega \notin \tilde{R}$ to compute a W (using Equation (25)) to check Equation (23) or (24) at a point in $\tilde{R}$, then that $V(\cdot,\cdot \mid W)$ need not satisfy the equilibrium condition (Equation (23) or (24)) exactly; it only needs to be larger than the true equilibrium value. The reason is that if the firm chooses not to undertake a policy that would lead them to a point outside of $\tilde{R}$ when those points are evaluated too highly, we know they would not chose such an action if those points were evaluated at their true values. They then consider ways of bringing the weaker condition into the test for equilibrium at boundary points, and report that boundary points are visited so infrequently that bringing in different reasonable ways of checking these conditions had no effect on the estimates.[24] We note, however, that as in single agent applications of stochastic algorithms (see the references below), to minimize the probability that the algorithm ignores relevant actions they initialized the algorithm with an initial estimate of W (a W^0) thought to be much larger than the equilibrium W (two candidates are the value function from the one firm problem and $\pi(\omega_i, \omega_{-i})/(1-\beta)$). This tends to make the program stop at a set of W which are, if anything, too large, and this in turn insures that the conditions required for boundary points are satisfied (though we cannot prove this in the context of the dynamic games that we are considering here).

Fershtman and Pakes (2005) treat this issue differently. They consider a notion of equilibrium whose conditions can be consistently tested on actual data. They call their equilibrium notion applied Markov perfect equilibrium; it is closely related to the notion of self-confirming equilibrium in Fudenberg and Levine (1993). The conditions of applied Markov perfect equilibrium only place restrictions on policies and values on the recurrent class of points. Roughly those conditions are that (i) in equilibrium policies at those points must be optimal with respect to the equilibrium W, and (ii) for every (ω_i, ω_{-i}) associated with a point in the recurrent class and every ν, $W(\nu; \omega_i, \omega_{-i})$ must satisfy the fixed point condition in Equation (25) only if optimal policies indicate that the probability of that ν is greater than zero. One test of the sufficient conditions for applied Markov perfect equilibrium is the test introduced above, but they introduce a test that is less computationally burdensome (see below).

[23] Moreover since the algorithm does not visit points with $\bar{n}+1$ agents active repeatedly, it cannot be expected to produce an accurate estimates of the values at that point.

[24] Given this fact they found it computationally efficient to set the probability of events that would lead from an $\omega \in R(J_1, J_2)$ to a point outside of $R(J_1, J_2)$ to zero, and renormalize the remaining probabilities appropriately.

Experience with stochastic algorithms Most of the experience with stochastic algorithms is with single agent problems or zero sum games in which all points are recurrent [for an easy to read review see Barto, Bradtke and Singh (1995)]. In these problems one can generally prove convergence [in probability, or almost surely, see Bertsekas and Tsitsiklis (1996)]. These proofs require one to start with an *overestimate* of the estimated values (so all points are tried before they are discarded). The striking result from the numerical exercises is that the imprecision in their estimates at points with little weight in the ergodic distribution *does not* seem to impact adversely on the precision of the estimates of the values associated with points with heavy weight in the ergodic distribution (see also below).

Once we move to dynamic games we cannot guarantee convergence of the stochastic algorithm (just as we could not for the deterministic algorithms discussed above). On the other hand, the two applications of the stochastic algorithm we know of have never experienced a convergence problem. Interestingly those models worked with the version of the EP model which assumes a single known entry fee and exit value, just as we have done in this section. This is precisely the version of the EP model which Pakes and McGuire (1994) found often generate convergence problems when computed with their Gaussian algorithm. This makes the absence of convergence problems in the stochastic algorithm particularly notable.

To allow for random entry and exit fees we need only modify the algorithm slightly. Equation (23) must be modified to read

$$V(\omega_i, \omega_{-i} \mid W) = \pi(\omega_i, \omega_{-i}) + \left[1 - r(\omega_i, \omega_{-i} \mid W)\right]\phi(\omega_i, \omega_{-i} \mid W) + r(\omega_i, \omega_{-i} \mid W)\left\{ - x(\omega_i, \omega_{-i} \mid W) + \beta \sum_{\nu} W(\nu \mid \omega_i, \omega_{-i}) p\big(\nu \mid x(\omega_i, \omega_{-i} \mid W)\big)\right\},$$

where $r(\omega_i, \omega_{-i} \mid W)$ is the probability of drawing a random exit fee less than the continuation value, and $\phi(\omega_i, \omega_{-i} \mid W)$ is the expected value of the exit fee conditional on it being greater than the continuation value. These values are calculated from the exit policy at each (ω_i, ω_{-i}) and held in memory. Similarly the entry policy becomes a value for ϕ^e above which the potential entrant does not enter, and that value is also held in memory at (ω_i, ω_{-i}).

Example To illustrate Pakes and McGuire (2001) computed the same equilibrium computed pointwise in Pakes and McGuire (1994), and showed that the stochastic algorithm computed estimates whose implications are indistinguishable from those of the Gaussian algorithm.

The model in Pakes and McGuire (1994) has only one state per firm, so the only dimension in which we can trace out the relationship between the components of computational burden, and the size of the problem, is as we increase $\bar{n}$. $\bar{n}$ for Pakes and

McGuire (1994) problem is largely determined by their M (the number of consumers serviced by the market). So we will focus on how the components of the computational burden changes as we push M up from Pakes and McGuire (1994) initial $M = 5$ by units of 1 until $M = 10$. Recall that we know that the time per state in the stochastic algorithm scales linearly in the number of firms, but we do not know how the size of the recurrent class increases in the number of state variables, so this is the issue we are particularly interested in.

The version of the algorithm used in Pakes and McGuire (2001) downweighs the early estimates of continuation values (which, recall, are imprecisely estimated). It does so by restarting the algorithm after each of the first seven million iterations, using the terminal values from those iterations as starting values of the next million iterations. The algorithm then begins a long run which was interrupted every million iterations to run the test. The test compared the estimates of the values obtained from the current estimate of W and Equations (23) and (24) to the estimates obtained from Equations (23) and (24) when the W estimates were obtained from the calculation in Equation (25) (the weights were set proportional to the number of visits to the location in the last million draws). If the weighted correlation between the two estimates of the value function was over 0.995 and the difference between their weighted means were less than 1%, the algorithm stopped. The bottom panel of the table provides statistics which enable us to assess how the computational burden changed with market size. The top panel of Table 30.3 provides the distribution of the number of firm's active from a 100,000 period simulation and our estimated policies.

The number of points in the last row refers to the number of points visited at least once in the last million iterations. This will be our approximation to the size of the recurrent class (#R). There were 21,300 such points when $M = 5$. As expected $\bar{n}$ increases in M. However #R *does not* increase geometrically in $\bar{n}$. The top part of the panel makes it clear why; when we increase M the number of distinct points at which there are a large number of firms active does increase, but the larger market no longer supports configurations with a small number of firms. Indeed though the function relating #R to M seems initially convex, it then turns concave giving the impression that it may asymptote to a finite upper bound. The ratio of the number of states at which we compute policies and values in the stochastic algorithm to that in the Gaussian algorithms described above is $\#R/\#S$. $\#R/\#S \approx 3.3\%$ when $\bar{n} = 6$, about 0.4% when $\bar{n} = 10$ (then $\#S \approx 3.2 \times 10^7$), and would decline further for larger $\bar{n}$. We note here that we have gotten reductions at least as large as this when we computed equilibria to models that had more than one state per firm. In particular in models where products had more than one dimension which could vary with the firms' investments, there were typically many combinations of characteristics that were not profitable to produce, and the stochastic algorithm would simply never visit them.

The other two components of computational time are the time needed to update values and compute policies at each state, and the number of iterations. As noted we expected the time per state to be a function of the number of firms active at the state, and what the table shows is that the ratio of the average number of active firms to the time per

Table 30.3
Comparisons for increasing market size[a]

$M =$	5	6	7	8	9	10
Percentage of equilibria with n firms active						
$n =$						
3	58.3	00.8	00.0	00.0	00.0	00.0
4	33.7	77.5	48.9	04.4	00.7	00.1
5	06.3	16.8	41.4	62.3	33.0	07.2
6	01.5	04.2	07.3	25.0	44.3	41.8
7	00.2	00.6	02.2	06.5	15.3	34.3
8	00.0	00.1	00.2	01.7	05.9	13.1
9	00.0	00.0	00.0	00.0	00.8	03.5
10	00.0	00.0	00.0	00.0	00.0	00.0
Average n						
	3.43	4.26	4.64	5.39	5.95	6.64
Minutes per million iterations						
	5.5	6.5	7.5	8.6	10	11
Minutes per test						
	3.6	8.15	17.1	42.8	100	120
Number of iterations (millions)						
	$7+5$	$7+2$	$7+21$	$7+4$	$7+9$	$7+3$
Number of points (thousands)						
	21.3	30.5	44.2	68.1	98.0	117.5

Source: Pakes and McGuire (2001).
[a]All runs were on a Sun SPARCStation 2.

million iterations was essentially constant as we increased M (it varied between 1.53 and 1.65 min). The good news was that the number of iterations until our test criteria was satisfied did not tend to increase in M (though it did vary quite a bit between runs).

Thus *absent* test times, the average CPU time needed for our algorithm seems to grow *linearly* in the average number of firms active. Given the theoretical discussion this is as good as we could have expected. Comparing the level of our CPU times to those from backward solution algorithms we find that when $\bar{n} = 6$ the stochastic algorithm took about a third of the CPU time, when $\bar{n} = 10$ even the most optimistic projection for the backward techniques leads to a ratio of CPU times of 0.09%. If $\bar{n}$ grew much beyond that, or if there were more than one state variable per firm, the backward solution algorithm simply could not be used (even on the most powerful of modern computing equipment). In contrast, we have analyzed several such problems on our workstation.

As noted the *test* times do grow exponentially in the number of firms and in our runs they rose from about 3 min when $M = 5$ to over two hours when $M = 10$. By $M = 10$ the algorithm spends ten times as much time computing the test statistic after each million iterations as it spends on the iterations themselves. So we now outline a modification to the test due Fershtman and Pakes (2005) which circumvents this problem.

A more computationally efficient test Fershtman and Pakes (2005) provide a test of the equilibrium conditions on the recurrent class whose: (i) computational burden scales linearly in both the number of points in the recurrent class and the number of states at each point (and so is not subject to a curse of dimensionality), and (ii) has an interpretation as a norm in the percentage difference between the actual expected values generated by the estimate of W and the values implied by the Bellman equations (23) and (24).

Say we want to test whether a $\tilde{W}$ generates equilibrium policies and values on the recurrent class. One way to view what we want a test to do is to measure the difference between the estimate of $V(\omega_i, \omega_{-i} \mid \tilde{W})$ from Equations (23) and (24), and the expected discounted values of future net cash flows that each agent would obtain were all agents using the policies generated by $\tilde{W}$. Fershtman and Pakes (2005) suggest approximating the expected returns the agents would earn from following the policies generated by $\tilde{W}$ with averages of the discounted value of net cash flows earned from different sample paths that are simulated using the policies generated by $\tilde{W}$, and comparing that to the values, $V(\omega_i, \omega_{-i} \mid \tilde{W})$, from Equations (23) and (24). The squared differences between the $V(\omega_i, \omega_{-i} \mid \tilde{W})$ from these equations and the average of the discounted value over the simulated sample paths is a sum of (i) the sampling variance in the average of the discounted value of the simulated sample paths (we will refer to this as the sampling variance term), and (ii) the difference between the *expectation* of the discounted net cash flows from the simulated paths and the value functions estimates in Equations (23) and (24) (we will refer to this as the "bias" term). Fershtman and Pakes (2005) subtract a consistent estimate of the sampling variance term from this squared difference to obtain a test statistic which, at least in the limit, will depend only on the bias term.

More precisely for each state in the recurrent class use the policies generated by $\tilde{W}$ to simulate the algorithm T iterations into the future and keep track of the discounted value of net cash flows generated over those T iterations. Add this sum to the discounted value Equation (23) assigns to the terminal state; i.e. if the terminal state is $(\omega_i^T, \omega_{-i}^T)$ add $\beta^T V(\omega_i^T, \omega_{-i}^T \mid \tilde{W})$ as computed from Equation (23). Call this sum an estimated value of the simulated path. Compute several independent estimates of the value of the simulated path from each state, and compute the average and variance of those values.

If we let the average of the values of the simulated paths be $VS(\omega_i, \omega_{-i} \mid \tilde{W}, T)$, and E be the expectation operator over the simulated random draws then

$$\begin{aligned} E&\left(\frac{VS(\omega_i, \omega_{-i} \mid \tilde{W}, T)}{V(\omega_i, \omega_{-i} \mid \tilde{W})} - 1\right)^2 \\ &= E\left(\frac{VS(\omega_i, \omega_{-i} \mid \tilde{W}, T) - E[VS(\omega_i, \omega_{-i} \mid \tilde{W})]}{V(\omega_i, \omega_{-i} \mid \tilde{W})}\right)^2 \\ &\quad + \left(\frac{E[VS(\omega_i, \omega_{-i} \mid \tilde{W}, T)] - V(\omega_i, \omega_{-i} \mid \tilde{W})}{V(\omega_i, \omega_{-i} \mid \tilde{W})}\right)^2. \end{aligned} \tag{27}$$

The first term in this expression is the variance term, and the second term is the bias. Moreover the variance term can be unbiasedly estimated from the variance across the simulated sample paths; i.e. we can form $\widehat{\mathrm{Var}}(\frac{VS(\omega_i,\omega_{-i})}{V(\omega_i,\omega_{-i}|\tilde{W})})$ such that

$$E\left[\widehat{\mathrm{Var}}\left(\frac{VS(\omega_i,\omega_{-i})}{V(\omega_i,\omega_{-i}\mid\tilde{W})}\right)\right] = E\left(\frac{VS(\omega_i,\omega_{-i}\mid\tilde{W},T)-E[VS(\omega_i,\omega_{-i}\mid\tilde{W})]}{V(\omega_i,\omega_{-i}\mid\tilde{W})}\right)^2.$$

Consequently

$$E\left[\left(\frac{VS(\omega_i,\omega_{-i}\mid\tilde{W},T)}{V(\omega_i,\omega_{-i}\mid\tilde{W})}-1\right)^2-\widehat{\mathrm{Var}}\left(\frac{VS(\omega_i,\omega_{-i})}{V(\omega_i,\omega_{-i}\mid\tilde{W})}\right)\right] = \left(\frac{E[VS(\omega_i,\omega_{-i}\mid\tilde{W},T)]-V(\omega_i,\omega_{-i}\mid\tilde{W})}{V(\omega_i,\omega_{-i}\mid\tilde{W})}\right)^2.$$

This provides us with an unbiased estimate of the bias term. Since the variance (and higher-order moments) of this estimate of the bias is finite, any weighted average of independent estimates of the bias terms over the recurrent class of points will converge to the same weighted average of the true bias term across these points (a.s.). It is weighted averages of this form that Fershtman and Pakes (2005) use as a test statistic.

Potential usefulness The usefulness of the stochastic algorithm is likely to vary from problem to problem. There are some problems which it cannot be applied to without further adaptation; a good example being problems in which we want to constrain "off the equilibrium path" behavior in a more detailed way (as in many collusion models). Where we can use it, the tradeoff between using it and the other algorithms can be thought of as a tradeoff between number of iterations, number of states, and the time per state at each iteration. The stochastic algorithm can be expected to do particularly well when (i) the dimension of the recurrent class is small relative to the dimension of the state space, and (ii) the formulae for computing the probability distribution over future possible outcomes is complicated. This last point is particularly important in computing equilibria to models with asymmetric information, as the stochastic algorithm can compute those equilibria without ever actually computing posterior distributions at any given state [and the posteriors are often horribly complex; for more detail see Fershtman and Pakes (2005)].

5.4. Function approximation methods

Function approximation techniques attempt to approximate either the value or the policy function (or both) by a sufficiently rich set of basis functions (e.g. polynomials or splines). Judd (1998) discusses these methods in some detail in the context of dynamic programming models.

In the context of dynamic games function approximation methods have been used mostly for dynamic games with a continuum of states and without entry and exit. These games pose both theoretical [see, e.g., Whitt (1980)] and computational challenges. In particular, they require an entirely different set of techniques to compute an equilibrium since players' values and policies can no longer be represented as (finite-dimensional) vectors and instead have to be represented as (infinite-dimensional) functions. Judd (1998) gives an introduction to these so-called projection techniques and Rui and Miranda (1996, 2001), Doraszelski (2003), and Hall, Royer and Van Audenrode (2003) apply them to dynamic games with a continuum of states.

There has been some attempt to apply these techniques to games with discrete state spaces. Pakes and McGuire (1994) provide one example and some theoretical results on the dimensionality reductions available from these techniques. Briefly they consider a polynomial basis, and project an initial estimate of the value functions at a small number of points down onto this basis to obtain initial coefficients of the basis functions. These coefficients and the basis functions allow one to construct continuation values for each firm operating at the basis points. These continuation values, in turn, can be used to obtain policies and new estimates of the values for all firms active at those points. The new value functions are projected down against the basis functions to obtain new coefficients and the process is repeated.

Pakes and McGuire (1994) show that if one restricts the basis functions to functions which preserve symmetry and anonymity (what they call an "exchangeable" basis), the number of basis functions needed for any order of polynomial, and hence the number of points we need to keep track of, is bounded by a finite constant (i.e. does not grow in $\bar{n}$ at all). Moreover moment generating functions can be used to reduce the computational burden from computing continuation values at a given point. So the potential for decreasing the computational burden of computing equilibrium for large markets using this technique is dramatic. On the other hand, they also report that in their particular example with $\bar{n} = 6$ there were extensive convergence problems.

The convergence problems were likely to result from the fact that in their model the firm's value function can be a discontinuous function of its competitor's policies (entry and exit by competitors can cause jumps in the value function), and the polynomials they used have problems approximating discontinuities. So these problems may well disappear if either different forms of approximations were used (e.g. splines), or if the number of firms grew larger (in which case exit by any one firm should have a smaller effect on the value of its competitors). This suggests that function approximation might still be a useful technique for problems with a large number of firms (as is often the case in the dynamic models used in trade, development, and productivity), though such applications might require some further technical developments.

5.5. *Oblivious equilibrium*

Weintraub, Benkard and Van Roy (2005) propose an approximation method for analyzing EP-style dynamic models of imperfect competition. They derive an algorithm for computing an "oblivious" equilibrium in which each firm is assumed to make decisions based only on its own state, an aggregate shock, and knowledge of the long run average industry state. When firms chose their controls they ignore the influence of current and past values of the aggregate shock, and current information about rivals' states, on likely future states.

They prove that if the distribution of firms obeys a certain "light-tail" condition, then as the market size becomes large oblivious equilibrium closely approximates a Markov perfect equilibrium in a certain sense. The light tail condition is more likely to be satisfied in industries where there are no firms that are clearly dominant.

They also derive a performance bound that can be used to assess how well the approximation performs in any given applied problem. Finally, Weintraub, Benkard and Van Roy (2005) apply these methods to a dynamic investment game and find that the approximation typically works well for markets with hundreds of firms, and in some cases works well even for markets with only tens of firms.

6. Computing multiple equilibria

Below we review the homotopy method to computing multiple equilibria in the EP framework due to Besanko et al. (2004). At the end of this section, we briefly discuss how the problem of multiple equilibria has been handled in other settings.

A drawback of all the computational methods discussed above is that they offer no systematic approach to computing multiple equilibria. Homotopy or path-following methods partially resolve this issue.[25] Starting from a single equilibrium computed for a particular value of the parameter vector, the homotopy algorithm traces out an entire path of equilibria obtained by varying the parameter vector. Whenever we can find such a path and the path folds back on itself, then the homotopy algorithm will identify multiple equilibria. We note at the outset that there is no guarantee that any given path computes all possible equilibria at a given value of the parameter vector [unless the system of equations that defines the equilibrium happens to be polynomial; see Judd and Schmedders (2004)]. Moreover, homotopy methods are computationally demanding.

We begin with a simple example which explains how the homotopy algorithm works. Consider the single non-linear equation $H(x, \tau) = 0$, where

$$H(x, \tau) = -15.289 - \frac{\tau}{1 + \tau^4} + 67.500x - 96.923x^2 + 46.154x^3. \tag{28}$$

[25] Recall that two functions $f : X \to Y$ and $g : X \to Y$ from one topological space X to another Y are called homotopic if one can be continuously deformed into the other, i.e., if there exists a continuous function H: $X \times [0, 1]$ such that $H(x, 0) = g(x)$ and $H(x, 1) = f(x)$ for all $x \in X$. Such a deformation is called a homotopy. See Zangwill and Garcia (1981) for an introduction to homotopy methods, Schmedders (1998, 1999) for an application to general equilibrium models with incomplete asset markets, and Berry and Pakes (2006) for an application to estimating demand systems.

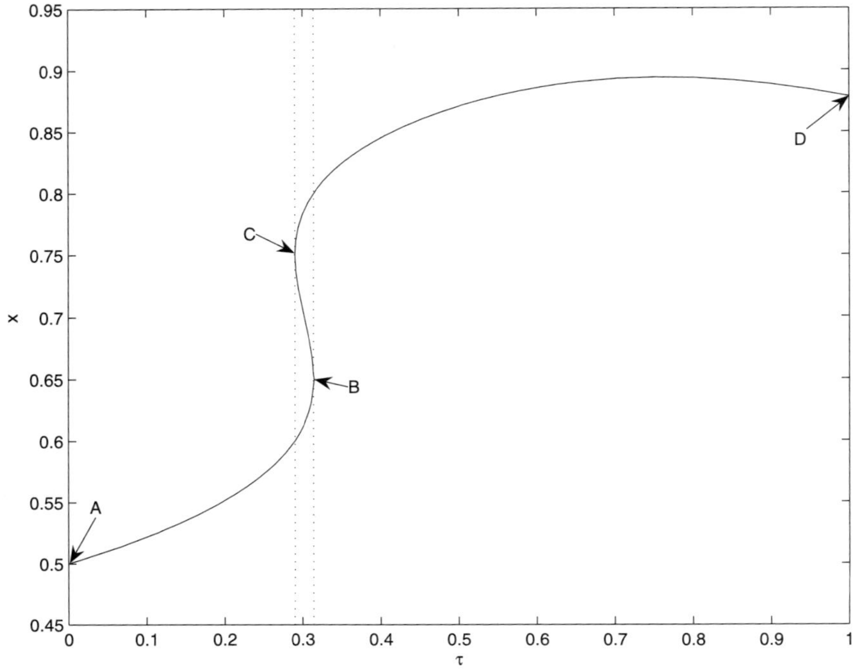

Figure 30.3. Homotopy example. *Source*: Besanko et al. (2004).

Equation (28) implicitly defines the relationship between an endogenous variable x and an exogenous parameter τ (in our case τ would be one of the parameters of the model). The object of interest is the set of solutions $H^{-1} = \{(x, \tau) \mid H(x, \tau) = 0\}$ as graphed in Figure 30.3. Inspection of Figure 30.3 shows that there are multiple solutions to Equation (28), e.g., at $\tau = 0.3$ there are three solutions: $x = 0.610$, $x = 0.707$, and $x = 0.783$. Finding these solutions is trivial once the graph is drawn, but producing the graph is less than straightforward even in this very simple case. Whether one solves $H(x, \tau) = 0$ for x taking τ as given or for τ taking x as given, the result is a multi-valued correspondence, not a single-valued function.

To apply the homotopy method, we introduce an auxiliary variable s that indexes each point on the graph starting at point A for $s = 0$ and ending at point D for $s = \bar{s}$. The graph is just the parametric path given by a function pair $(x(s), \tau(s))$ that satisfies $H(x(s), \tau(s)) = 0$ or, equivalently, $(x(s), \tau(s)) \in H^{-1}$. Since there are infinitely many such function pairs, we need a simple way to pick out a member of this family. To do this, we differentiate $H(x(s), \tau(s)) = 0$ with respect to s to obtain

$$\frac{\partial H(x(s), \tau(s))}{\partial x} x'(s) + \frac{\partial H(x(s), \tau(s))}{\partial \tau} \tau'(s) = 0. \tag{29}$$

This single differential equation in two unknowns, $x'(s)$ and $\tau'(s)$, captures the conditions that are required to remain "on path". One possible approach for tracing out a path in H^{-1} is thus to solve Equation (29) for the ratio $\frac{x'(s)}{\tau'(s)}$, i.e., the direction of the next step along the path from s to $s+\mathrm{d}s$. This approach, however, creates difficulties because the ratio may switch from $+\infty$ to $-\infty$, e.g., at point B in Figure 30.3. So instead of solving for the ratio, we solve for each term of the ratio. To do this, we use the system of differential equations given by

$$x'(s) = \frac{\partial H(x(s), \tau(s))}{\partial \tau}, \tag{30}$$

$$\tau'(s) = -\frac{\partial H(x(s), \tau(s))}{\partial x} \tag{31}$$

to determine the next step along the path. Now we have avoided the problem of dividing by zero when the path folds back on itself.

These are the so-called basic differential equations for our simple example. Their significance is that they reduce the task of tracing out the set of solutions to solving a system of differential equations. Given an initial condition this is can be done using a variety of methods [see, e.g., Judd (1998, ch. 10)]. In our example, note that if $\tau = 0$, then $H(x, \tau) = 0$ is easily solved for $x = 0.5$. This provides the initial condition (point A in Figure 30.3). From there the homotopy algorithm follows the path until it reaches $\tau = 1$ (point D). Whenever $\tau'(s)$ switches sign from positive to negative (point B), the path is bending backward and there are multiple solutions. Conversely, whenever the sign of $\tau'(s)$ switches back from negative to positive (point C), the path is bending forward.[26]

Besanko et al. (2004) apply the homotopy method to computing equilibria in their model of learning-by-doing and organizational forgetting. They write the system of nonlinear equations that defines an equilibrium as $H(x, \tau) = 0$. The system contains the Bellman equation and optimality conditions for each firm's policy at each state in S°. τ is a parameter of the model; in their case the rate of depreciation δ. The object of interest is the set of equilibria $H^{-1} = \{(x, \tau) \mid H(x, \tau) = 0\}$.

Proceeding as in our simple example, they define a parametric path to be a set of functions $y(s) = (x(s), \tau(s))$ such that $y(s) \in H^{-1}$. Here $x(s)$ is the vector of value functions, policies, and exit or entry probabilities associated with each firm at each state. As s varies $y(s)$ describes a path in H^{-1}, that satisfies

$$H\big(y(s)\big) = 0.$$

[26] In computing equilibria to their learning-by-doing model Besanko et al. (2004) prove that on the portion of the path that is backward bending (in Figure 30.3 this is the part of the path between points B and C) the mapping that provides the iterations for the Pakes and McGuire (1994) algorithm has an eigenvalue outside of the complex unit circle and is therefore unstable. It follows that, holding fixed the homotopy parameter, "inbetween" two equilibria with $\tau'(s) > 0$, there is one equilibrium with $\tau'(s) \leqslant 0$ that cannot be computed using the Pakes and McGuire (1994) algorithm.

Differentiating both sides with respect to s yields the conditions that are required to remain on path

$$\sum_i \frac{\partial H(y(s))}{\partial y_i} y_i'(s) = 0. \tag{32}$$

This is a system differential equations with the same number of unknowns as equations.

As before there is at least one solution and it obeys the basic differential equations

$$y_i'(s) = (-1)^{i+1} \det\left(\left(\frac{\partial H(y(s))}{\partial y}\right)_{-i}\right) \tag{33}$$

for all i, where the notation $(\cdot)_{-i}$ is used to indicate that the ith column is removed from the Jacobian $\frac{\partial H(y(s))}{\partial y}$ [see Zangwill and Garcia (1981, pp. 27–28) for the proof]. Note that Equation (33) reduces to Equations (30) and (31) if x is a scalar instead of a vector. Given an initial condition the basic differential equations (33) can be solved using numerical methods.

A few comments are in order. First, if the Jacobian has less than full rank, then the determinants of all its submatrices are zero. Thus, $y_i'(s) = 0$ for all i and the homotopy algorithm stalls. Indeed, a central condition in the mathematical literature on homotopy methods is that the Jacobian has full rank [see, e.g., Zangwill and Garcia (1981)]. If so, the homotopy is called regular and the algorithm is guaranteed to trace out a path.[27] Unfortunately, proving that the Jacobian has full rank is frequently difficult when the goal is to follow an economically meaningful parameter such as the rate of depreciation δ or the discount factor β.

Second, $H(\cdot)$ must be continuously differentiable. This means that we need the distribution of scrap values $F(\cdot)$ and setup costs $F^e(\cdot)$ to be differentiable. Also the investment decisions which, since zero investment is a possible outcome, are typically characterized by Kuhn–Tucker conditions should be reformulated as continuously differentiable equations [Judd, Kübler and Schmedders (2003) show how to do this].[28]

Finally we note that the homotopy algorithm is computationally demanding. Computing the Jacobian is a major burden. Numeric derivatives are slow to compute and though analytic derivatives speed up the computations, deriving and coding them by hand is time consuming and error prone. One alternative is to use automatic differentiation software that takes a procedure for computing a function as input and produces a procedure for computing its derivatives as output. However even with analytic derivatives the computational demands of homotopy algorithm that have been used to date are such they have been restricted to relatively small systems of non-linear equations. On

[27] The mathematical literature calls this the continuation problem and has developed methods for dealing with the bifurcations that may arise if the Jacobian has less than full rank [see, e.g., Kalaba and Tesfatsion (1991)].

[28] The mathematical literature has developed piecewise linear homotopy methods that can handle problems with discontinuous equations [see, e.g., Eaves (1972) and Judd (1998, ch. 5)].

the other hand, there has been very little exploration of methods which might reduce its computational burden. Some initial experience suggests that exploiting sparsity patterns in the Jacobian yields substantial gains.

Software A number of software packages implement homotopy methods. Besanko et al.'s (2004) programs are based on Hompack [Watson, Billups and Morgan (1987)], which is written in Fortran 77, and are available upon request. Hompack 90 is able to exploit sparsity patterns and is described in Watson et al. (1997). There are numerous software packages available for automatic differentiation, e.g., ADIFOR for Fortran 77 and ADIC for C.

Summary The problem of finding all solutions to a system of non-linear equations is largely unresolved in the mathematics literature. Indeed, as already noted, there is no guarantee that the homotopy algorithm finds all the equilibria of our dynamic stochastic game. In some cases it is possible to exploit the structure of the system of equations. For example, the system of equations that characterizes the set of Nash equilibria in static games is polynomial [see, e.g., McKelvey and McLennan (1996)]. For polynomial systems, in turn, there are methods that are guaranteed to find all solutions. These all-solutions homotopies have been implemented in the freely-available software package Gambit [McKelvey, McLennan and Turocy (2006)] and used by Bajari, Hong and Ryan (2004) in the context of static games and by Judd and Schmedders (2004) to construct a computational uniqueness proof for dynamic games in which movements through the state space are unidirectional. Jia (2006) imposes supermodularity conditions on a two-stage game and uses the fact that in supermodular games there is a best and a worst equilibrium to delineate the set of subgame perfect equilibria.

Finally, there are methods for computing the entire set of subgame perfect equilibria in repeated games [see, e.g., Judd, Yeltekin and Conklin (2003)]. Recently, these methods have been extended to game with state variables [Conklin and Judd (1996), Judd and Yeltekin (2001)]. Unfortunately, however, none of the available methods is anywhere near capable of handling the large games that are typical for applications of EP's framework.

7. Applications and extensions

There is a large and active literature using the EP framework in IO, and, most recently, it has also been used in other fields such as international trade [Erdem and Tybout (2003)] and finance [Goettler, Parlour and Rajan (2005), Kadyrzhanova (2006)]. As Table 30.4 shows, there are too many applications to discuss all of them in detail. Instead we focus on some of the larger themes in this literature. They allow us to both (i) illustrate how the framework has been extended by various authors to approximate alternative institutional structures, and (ii) point out some of the problems that need to be overcome before the framework can be applied to particular topics of obvious interest.

Table 30.4
Applications of EP's framework

Application	Paper(s)
Advertising	Doraszelski and Markovich (2006), Dube, Hitsch and Manchanda (2005)
Capacity accumulation	Besanko and Doraszelski (2004), Ryan (2005), Beresteanu and Ellickson (2005)
Collusion	Fershtman and Pakes (2000, 2005), de Roos (2004)
Competitive convergence	Langohr (2003)
Consumer learning	Ching (2003)
Firm size and growth	Laincz and Rodrigues (2004)
Learning-by-doing	Benkard (2004), Besanko et al. (2004)
Mergers	Berry and Pakes (1993), Gowrisankaran (1999), Chen (2004)
Network effects	Jenkins et al. (2004), Markovich (2004), Markovich and Moenius (2005), Chen, Doraszelski and Harrington (2004)
Productivity growth	Laincz (2005)
R&D	Gowrisankaran and Town (1997), Auerswald (2001), Song (2002), Judd, Schmedders and Yeltekin (2002), Fershtman and Markovich (2006)
Technology adoption	Schivardi and Schneider (2005)
International trade	Erdem and Tybout (2003)
Finance	Goettler, Parlour and Rajan (2005), Kadyrzhanova (2006)

We begin with a brief review of the empirical work using the EP framework. This includes a small literature on testing the EP model against known alternatives, and a small but growing literature on using the framework to analyze the impacts of different policy or environmental changes. Notably absent from this subsection is a review of the recent literature which uses the EP framework to structure estimation algorithms. The relevant literature here includes Aguirregabiria and Mira (2007), Bajari, Benkard and Levin (2006), Pakes, Ostrovsky and Berry (2006), Pesendorfer and Schmidt-Dengler (2003) and has been recently reviewed in Ackerberg et al. (2005).

We then turn to applied theory papers which use the framework. Our starting point are models of capacity and advertising dynamics. These models preserve the traditional "static–dynamic" breakdown we used to introduce the framework in prior sections. They illustrate nicely just how rich the industry dynamics generated by the framework can be even in this "textbook" setting. This fact is accentuated by comparing the results using the EP framework to other – typically analytically tractable – dynamic models. Next we discuss models of mergers. The EP framework in its basic form is well suited to analyze the effect of a "one-time" exogenously specified merger on the future evolution of an industry. The papers which do this analysis emphasize the importance of explicitly modeling how a merger affects firms' incentives for investment, entry, and exit. By taking into account how these incentives evolve after a merger has taken place, these papers often arrive at welfare implications that are quite different from those obtained in simpler models. There has also been some work on endogenizing merger activity. This requires a much richer stage game to be played in each period; firms not only choose quantities/prices but also whether and with whom to merge.

Next we turn to models of learning-by-doing, network effects, and collusion. These types of models depart from the traditional "static–dynamic" breakdown in teaching IO, i.e. in these models the price or quantity that a firm sets in the product market has a direct effect on the dynamics of the industry. Consequently, the profit function can no longer be computed "off line". After providing a brief review of how to modify the framework to allow for this possibility we review some of the results from this literature. Again the emphasis is on dynamic effects that have not been captured by simpler models. As we shall see they often shed new light on both policy issues and our understanding of the implications of different environments.

7.1. Empirics

First a brief note on testing. Pakes and Ericson (1998) show that the Markov nature of the equilibrium process distinguishes the EP model from industry equilibrium models based on learning about a time-invariant parameter such as the dynamic equilibrium model of Jovanovic (1982). They formalize this distinction by developing a non-parametric test, versions of which have been used to determine the appropriateness of the different types of models for different data sets [see, e.g., Bhattacharjee (2005), Klette and Raknerud (2002), and Abbring and Campbell (2003)].

The test assumes there is an observable variable which orders the ω_i of active firms (in their application the variable used was sales), and follows the values of this variable in cohorts of surviving firms over time. If the EP framework is appropriate, the dependence of the conditional distribution of current size, conditional on a few past sizes, on the initial size should disappear as we increase the age of the firm (formally a ϕ-mixing condition is satisfied). If the learning model is appropriate that dependence never disappears. Interestingly Pakes and Ericson (1998) find a sharp distinction between manufacturing and retail firms in their Wisconsin data set; it is clear that manufacturing firms satisfy the ϕ-mixing condition while retail firms do not. That is at least in their data the EP model seems more appropriate for manufacturing firms while a model based on learning about time-invariant parameters seems more appropriate for retail trade.

In addition, a number of papers apply variants of the EP framework to analyze policy or environmental changes in a variety of industries. In the first effort along these lines, Gowrisankaran and Town (1997) present a dynamic model of the hospital industry in which non-profit and for-profit hospitals coexist and compete. They are differentiated by their objective functions, investment technologies, and taxation rates. In their model patients, who differ by income and type of insurance coverage, chose admission to their preferred hospital. Hospitals choose investment, entry, exit, and pricing strategies. Gowrisankaran and Town (1997) first estimate the parameters of the model and then use it to examine the effects of changes in the Medicare reimbursement system, universal health-care coverage, and taxation of non-profits. The results were striking; the effect of the policy changes on entry, investment and exit policies often implied that the original goals of the policy changes would not only not be achieved, but in some cases the dynamic implications would quickly result in an environment that was worse than the original situation with respect to the stated policy goal.

Ryan (2005) evaluates the welfare costs of the 1990 Amendments to the Clean Air Act on the U.S. Portland cement industry. The typical cost analysis of an environmental regulation consists of an engineering estimate of the compliance costs. In industries where fixed costs are an important determinant of market structure this static analysis ignores the dynamic effects of the regulation on entry, investment, and market power. Ryan (2005) accounts for these effects through a dynamic model of oligopoly in the tradition of EP. He recovers the entire cost structure of the industry, including the distribution of sunk entry costs and adjustment costs of investment, and finds that the Amendments have significantly increased the sunk cost of entry. Simulating the welfare effects of the Amendments, he shows that a static analysis misses the welfare penalty on consumers, and obtains the wrong sign on the welfare effects on incumbent firms.

The EP framework has also been applied to particular industries in order to shed light on the institutional arrangements in those industries. Song (2002) analyzes a research joint venture (RJV) led by SEMATECH in the semiconductor industry using the dynamic model of oligopoly. The paper first estimates firms' states, using product level data, and solves for the equilibrium research expenditures. Results show that a firm's research expenditure in SEMATECH is one-fifth of what it would be in competitive research. Lower research expenditures result in higher net profits in RJVs, although variable profits are similar in both regimes. RJVs are also more likely to generate higher consumer surplus than competitive research. The paper also shows that firms react differently for the same changes in the product market, depending on whether they cooperate or compete in research.

Beresteanu and Ellickson (2005) examine competition between supermarket chains using a dynamic model of strategic investment. Employing an eight-year panel dataset of store level observations that includes every supermarket operating in the United States, they develop and estimate a fully dynamic model of chain level competition. The estimated parameters of the structural model are then used to evaluate the competitive impact from the introduction of superstores.

There are a number of other papers which use variants of the framework to analyze particular issues in different industries [Benkard (2004), Ching (2003), de Roos (2004), Dube, Hitsch and Manchanda (2005), Jenkins et al. (2004)], some of which we will return to after we introduce more complex variants of the EP framework. Overall these papers have shown both that (i) the framework is at least reasonably well suited for applied dynamic analysis in a variety of industries, and (ii) that the dynamic effects of policy changes should not be ignored and often outweigh (sometimes reversing) the static effects.

7.2. Capacity and advertising dynamics

Empirical evidence suggests that there are substantial and persistent differences in the sizes of firms in most industries. For example, Mueller (1986) found that in 44 percent of 350 U.S. manufacturing industries, the identity of the industry leader remained unchanged over a twenty-two year period, and that the correlation between market shares over this period was 0.66 [see also Gort (1963) among others].

Asymmetric industry structures can, of course, arise as the outcome of a game in which firms differ in their economic fundamentals (e.g., cost structures) or their strategic positions at the outset of the game (e.g., first versus later mover). However, this begs the question: How do such differences in initial conditions arise in the first place? A number of papers has shown that asymmetric industry structures can arise as the outcome of a capacity accumulation game played by ex ante identical firms [e.g., Saloner (1987), Maggi (1996), and Reynolds and Wilson (2000)]. Though valuable in highlighting that substantial differences in firm size can arise endogenously for strategic reasons, these models are less satisfactory in explaining the persistence of these differences over time which is highlighted by the evidence. This is because these papers consider an unchanging competitive environment. Once an equilibrium has been reached, nothing further happens to upset the positions of firms. That is, asymmetric industry structures persist in these models by default. Ideally, however, one would like to understand whether there are circumstances under which asymmetric industry structures persist in a competitive environment that changes over time, for example, because of firm-specific shocks. The competitive environment can also change due to feedback effects. For example, if large firms invest more aggressively than small firms, then a small initial asymmetry may become larger over time, but it may vanish otherwise. In general, one would expect feedback effects to play a role whenever the time horizon under consideration is long enough to allow firms to interact repeatedly.

For these reasons, an important question is when substantial and persistent size differences can arise endogenously in equilibrium in a market in which ex ante identical firms interact repeatedly and are subject to firm-specific shocks that continuously alter their positions. To address this question, Besanko and Doraszelski (2004) use the EP framework to track the evolution of an oligopolistic industry. Consistent with the empirical evidence, their dynamic model of capacity accumulation is able to explain the substantial and persistent differences in the sizes of firms.

Besanko and Doraszelski (2004) demonstrate that industry dynamics depend critically on the mode of product market competition and on the degree to which investment is reversible, as measured by the rate of depreciation. Under quantity competition, each firm accumulates enough capacity to supply the Cournot quantities, leading to an industry structure of equal-sized firms independent of whether investment is irreversible (zero depreciation) or reversible (positive depreciation). With positive depreciation, firms tend to hold idle capacity out of a precautionary motive. By contrast, under price competition, there are forces that propel the industry towards asymmetric structures. In particular, if investment is reversible, then the industry evolves towards an outcome with one dominant firm and one small firm. Industry dynamics in this latter case resemble a rather brutal preemption race. During this race, firms invest heavily as long as they are of equal size even though this leads to substantial industry-wide overcapacity. Once one of the firms manages to pull slightly ahead in this race, however, the smaller firm "gives up", thereby propelling the larger firm eventually into a position of dominance.

Their paper sheds new light on the relationship between preemption and reversibility. Besanko and Doraszelski (2004) show that, under price competition, the preemption race between contending firms becomes more brutal as investment becomes more reversible. This stands in marked contrast to the usual intuition that depreciation reduces the commitment power of capacity and that capacity accumulation can therefore only lead to a temporary advantage. The key insight underlying their result is that with reversible investment the consequences to a firm of falling behind its rival are not fatal: the firm can allow its capacity to depreciate and assume the more profitable posture of a "puppy dog". The higher is the rate of depreciation, the easier it is for a lagging firm to "disengage" from the preemption race and hence the more attractive it is for firms to enter in such a race in the first place.

Laincz and Rodrigues (2004) further pursue the idea of using the EP framework to explain stylized facts about industry structure and dynamics. To this end, they develop a dynamic model of the firm size distribution. Their model allows for continually falling marginal costs through process R&D [as in Laincz (2005)]. Empirical studies of the firm size distribution often compare the moments to a log-normal distribution as implied by Gibrat's Law and note important deviations. Thus, the first, and basic questions they ask are how well does the dynamic industry model reproduce Gibrat's Law and how well does it match the deviations uncovered in the literature. They show that the model reproduces these results when testing the simulated output using the techniques of the empirical literature. They then use the model to study how structural parameters affect the firm size distribution. They find that, among other things, fixed and sunk costs increase both the mean and variance of the firm size distribution while generally decreasing the skewness and kurtosis. The rate of growth in an industry also raises the mean and variance, but has non-monotonic effects on the higher moments.

Turning from capacity to advertising dynamics, it is worth noting that during 2003 close to 250 billion dollar was spent on advertising in the U.S., well above 2% of GDP. Practitioners know very well the value of advertising to achieving their long-term market share and profitability goals and presume that advertising is capable of giving them a sustainable competitive advantage over their rivals. The existing dynamic models of advertising competition, however, suggest quite the opposite. In these models there is a globally stable symmetric steady state [see, e.g., Friedman (1983), Fershtman (1984), Chintagunta (1993), Cellini and Lambertini (2003)]. Consequently, any differences among firms are bound to vanish over time, and there is no room for a sustainable competitive advantage, not even if firms enter the market one by one and thus differ in their strategic positions at the outset of the game [Fershtman, Mahajan and Muller (1990)].

Doraszelski and Markovich (2006) attempt to reconcile theory and observation by showing that advertising can indeed have a lasting effect on the structure of an industry. To this end, they propose a dynamic model of advertising competition based on the EP framework to track the evolution of an industry. Within this dynamic framework, they study two different models of advertising: In the first model, advertising influences the goodwill consumers extend towards a firm ("goodwill advertising"), whereas in the second model it influences the share of consumers who are aware of the firm ("awareness advertising"). They show that asymmetries may arise and persist under goodwill as well as awareness advertising. The basis for a strategic advantage, however, differs greatly in the two models of advertising.

Under goodwill advertising, the size of the market and the cost of advertising are key determinants of industry structure and dynamics. In particular, goodwill advertising leads to an extremely asymmetric industry structure with a large and a small firm if the market is small or if advertising is expensive. Because the marginal benefit of advertising is small relative to its cost, a small firm has only a weak incentive to advertise when competing against a large firm and, in fact, may choose not to advertise at all. If the market is large or if advertising is cheap, on the other hand, even a small firm has a fairly strong incentive to advertise. In this case we obtain a symmetric industry structure with two large firms.

In contrast to the cost/benefit considerations that give rise to a strategic advantage under goodwill advertising, whether or not asymmetries arise and persist under awareness advertising depends on the intensity of product market competition. If competition is soft, the industry evolves towards a symmetric structure, but it evolves towards an asymmetric structure if competition is fierce. Industry dynamics in this latter case resemble a preemption race. In this race, both firms start off advertising heavily and continue to do so as long as they are neck-and-neck. Once one firm gains a slight edge over its competitor, however, there is a marked change in advertising activity. While the smaller firm scales back the larger firm ratchets up its advertising, thus eventually securing itself a position of dominance. The ensuing asymmetric industry structure persists because it is in the self-interest of the smaller firm to stay behind. In fact, the nature of product market competition is such that once the smaller firm tries to grow, the larger firm responds aggressively by triggering a "price war", thereby pushing prices and hence profits down. This gives the smaller firm an overwhelming incentive to remain inconspicuous. In sum, the central idea of their model of awareness advertising is that "more is less". This is a rationale for persistent asymmetries that has mostly been ignored in the literature on dynamic games.

The benefits from improving upon earlier work are most obvious in comparison to linear–quadratic games [Friedman (1983), Cellini and Lambertini (2003)]. Since the law of motion in such a game is given by a system of linear difference (or differential) equation, the dynamics are generically either explosive and thus inconsistent with equilibrium or there is a globally stable symmetric steady state. Hence, the very nature of a linear–quadratic game goes against the notion of a sustainable competitive advantage. Taken together, Doraszelski and Markovich's (2006) departures from earlier work lead to a model of advertising competition that exhibits much richer dynamics. On the other hand, they force them to leave analytically tractable modeling frameworks such as linear–quadratic games behind.

Dube, Hitsch and Manchanda (2005) use the EP framework to study a higher-frequency feature of firms' advertising policies in more detail. More specifically, they develop a model of dynamic advertising competition in order to explain "pulsing", a widely observed phenomenon in many consumer-goods industries whereby firms systematically switch advertising on and off at a high-frequency. Hence, we observe periods of zero and non-zero advertising, as opposed to a steady level of positive advertising. Using an estimated demand system for the frozen entree product category, they verify whether the use of pulsing can be justified as an equilibrium advertising practice. They find evidence for a threshold effect, which is qualitatively similar to the S-shaped advertising response that the theoretical literature has put forth as an explanation for pulsing. Their estimates imply that firms should indeed pulse in equilibrium. Predicted advertising in equilibrium is higher, on average, than observed advertising. On average, the optimal advertising policies yield a moderate profit improvement over the profits under observed advertising.

7.3. Mergers

Almost all of the formal models of merger activity condition on the cost, qualities, and variety of products sold in the market. These models hold the distribution of characteristics of the products being marketed (as well as the nature of competition) fixed, and analyze the impact of the ownership change on producer and consumer surplus. The producer surplus analysis provides a vehicle for analyzing the incentives to merge, while either the consumer surplus or the sum of the two provides the vehicle for analyzing whether the merger might be socially beneficial.

As noted in Stigler's (1968) investigation of the U.S. Steel mergers, the results from such a "static" analysis of mergers can easily be overturned by simple dynamic considerations (his discussion allowed for adjustment costs in an analysis of mergers in a homogeneous homogeneous goods industry). The first attempts to build a model to analyze the dynamic effects of mergers are Berry and Pakes (1993) and Cheong and Judd (2006). Both papers analyze the impact of a "one-time" exogenously specified merger in a dynamic model which allows for investment but does not allow for any further mergers. These papers show that mergers can be beneficial to *both* the firms merging and to society, even if the profits of the merging firms *and* consumer surplus falls at the time of the merger. The predominant reason is that there is less of an incentive to invest in the merged industry, and the Markov perfect equilibrium generates more investment than a social planner would [see Mankiw and Whinston (1986) for the intuition underlying these arguments].

Chen (2004) extends the dynamic model of capacity accumulation due to Besanko and Doraszelski (2004) in which firms produce nearly homogeneous products and compete in prices to investigates the price and welfare effects of mergers. In contrast to the results stressed in the results cited in the last paragraph, Chen (2004) finds that mergers reduce welfare. This negative effect results from the fact that certain firms in the postmerger industry optimally choose to let their capacities shrink, resulting in higher prices and lower consumer surplus. This divergence in results emphasizes both just how rich a set of outcomes the framework can generate, and the importance of programming an appropriate institutional structure into the model before coming to any policy conclusions.

To be more realistic a model which investigated the dynamic impacts of mergers would want to allow mergers to arise endogenously, and not just investigate the impacts of a "one-time" exogenously specified merger. In particular one might think that a merger by one firm might lead to further mergers of competitors, as it has often been noted that there tend to be "merger waves". There are many unsolved problems here, not least among them being the diversity of views on the factors motivating merger activity in different industries. In addition to specifying the possible sources of gains from mergers, a merger model must also specify a market mechanism for determining which among the possible profitable mergers at any point of time are in fact consummated.

One such mechanism is provided in Gowrisankaran (1999). He takes the capacity-constrained quantity-setting game with homogeneous goods and adds to it a merger game. The merger game occurs at the beginning of each period and proceeds in the following sequential manner. The largest firm is allowed to choose a merger partner first. All other firms present the largest firm with a "take-it-or-leave-it" price at which they are willing to be bought. Information is symmetric except that the largest firm draws a "synergy" value for each merger which is known only to it; i.e. the synergy value for a given firm is not known to any of the firms that might be acquired. The largest firm chooses to merge with the firm which generates the highest net merger value provided that value is positive. The net merger value is the expected discounted value of future net cash flow if a merger would take place net of the price of the acquisition and what the value of the firm would be if the merger did not take place. If a merger takes place the process restarts (there are new take-it-or-leave-it offers, and new synergy values), and the (new) largest firm can choose another merger partner. When the largest firm chooses not to merge further, the second largest firm gets to choose a merger partner in the same way. This process continues until the smallest active firm chooses not to merge further. At that point production, investment, and then exit followed by entry and investment decisions are made. All offers and actions are made to maximize the expected discounted value of future net cash flows given the agents' information sets, and the equilibrium is Markov perfect.

Perhaps the most striking part of this analysis is that it can be done. Given the quantitative magnitude of the merger phenomena in recent years and the extent that it can be impacted by policy, any step in developing a usable models of mergers is welcome. Still, it is clear that we are only at the beginnings of developing realistic dynamic models that allow for mergers; a lot of work remains to be done.

7.4. Learning-by-doing and network effects

In the simple special case of the framework described above the distribution of the next period's state, conditional on today's states and firms' investment, entry, and exit decisions, is independent of the prices or quantities that the firms set in the product market. This is the assumption which allows us to compute the profit function "off line" and to study static equilibrium without considering the impact of pricing or quantity decisions on future profits. The assumption is, however, inappropriate whenever either (i) future cost, (ii) future demand, or (iii) the choice of equilibrium prices or quantities in future periods, depends on the prices or the quantities set in the current period. Relevant cases when this assumption is inappropriate include models with learning-by-doing, adjustment costs, durable goods, experience goods, collusion, and network effects.

In all these cases the profit function can no longer be computed "off line" and fed into the algorithm for computing the equilibrium of the dynamic stochastic game. The reason is that the choice rule for prices or quantities will now have to account for the impact of the choice on future cash flows as well as on current profits. As a result we cannot solve for prices or quantities without knowing the value function, and this makes for a more difficult computational problem. The collusion case has a slightly different structure then the others and we discuss it in a separate section below. Here we consider only the cases where the price or quantity set today have an independent effect on future demand or cost conditions.

The modification to the first-order condition needed to accommodate these cases differs depending on whether the firm's control is price or quantity. To see this consider a setting with learning-by-doing. Let ω_i be the stock of experience or know-how of firm i that determines its cost of production. The law of motion for firm i's state is

$$\omega_i' = \omega_i + \nu_i - \eta_i,$$

where the random variable ν_i indicates additions to the stock of experience and the random variable η_i represents firm-specific depreciation of experience (also called organizational forgetting in the literature). The distribution of ν_i is stochastically increasing in the sales q_i of firm i.

In games of quantity competition a firm can change its control without directly affecting the quantities, and therefore state-to-state transitions, of its competitors. Then the Nash first-order condition only involves the derivative of the firm's current profit and transition probabilities for its own state with respect to the control. In contrast, in games of price competition any change in the firm's control induces a change in the quantities, and therefore in the probabilities of the state-to-state transitions, of the firm's competitors. This adds further derivatives to the Nash first-order condition.[29] Benkard (2004) analyzes a learning-by-doing model with quantity competition and since his work has

[29] This also happens when the control is a bid in a repeated auction with capacity constraints, see Jofre-Bonet and Pesendorfer (2003).

the added realism of a model built up from estimated parameters, we begin with an outline of it. Later we discuss the model of learning-by-doing and organizational forgetting of Besanko et al. (2004) as an example of a price setting game.

Benkard's (2004) goal is to analyze competition in the market for wide bodied commercial aircraft. Benkard adds estimates of demand parameters to the cost functions he estimates in Benkard (2000), and then computes and analyzes a model of dynamic quantity competition among producers which is a reasonably realistic approximation to the competition that occurred in the commercial aircraft market at the time the Lockheed Tristar was being introduced. Benkard (2004) finds that the effect of current quantity on future costs, and through future costs on its future competitive status, will induce the firm to produce large quantities in the early production years (the experience curve is steep early on in the production process). In fact production in the early years is pushed so far that price falls well below marginal cost in those years. This implication is clearly borne out by the price and cost data, and is inconsistent with a static quantity setting model. Benkard (2004) then proceeds to an analysis of the producer and consumer surplus generated by the outcomes of the interactions in this market, and a series of counterfactuals allow him to analyze what would have been likely to happen if we had imposed other institutional constraints.

As pointed out by Benkard (2004), organizational forgetting, i.e., depreciation of experience, is needed to explain the dynamics in the market for wide-bodied airframes in the 1970s and 1980s. It is often said that learning-by-doing promotes market dominance because it gives a more experienced firm the ability to profitably underprice its less experienced rival. However if learning-by-doing can be "undone" by organizational forgetting, then there is a question of whether organizational forgetting can reverse the market dominance effects of learning-by-doing. Besanko et al. (2004) find that this is not necessarily the case; on the contrary, over a wide range of parameterizations, organizational forgetting tends to make firms more instead of less aggressive. This aggressive pricing behavior, in turn, puts the industry on a path towards market dominance. They extend Cabral and Riordan's (1994) model of learning-by-doing by allowing for organizational forgetting. In the absence of organizational forgetting, the price that a firm sets reflects two goals. First, by winning a sale, the firm moves down its learning curve. Second, the firm prevents its rival from moving down its learning curve. Organizational forgetting accentuates these possibilities; by winning a sale, a firm makes itself less vulnerable to future losses from organizational forgetting and, at the same time, it makes its rival more vulnerable. This creates strong incentives to cut prices.

Incorporating organizational forgetting in the model as suggested by the empirical studies of Argote, Beckman and Epple (1990), Darr, Argote and Epple (1995), Benkard (2000), and Thompson (2003) into the Cabral and Riordan (1994) model of learning-by-doing makes the model much less analytically tractable. As a result Besanko et al. (2004) move from the elegance of the analytic results in Cabral and Riordan (1994) to numerical analysis. On the other hand, adding organizational forgetting to a model of learning-by-doing leads to a rich array of pricing behaviors and industry dynamics that the existing literature never considered.

In particular, Besanko et al. (2004) show that the model with both learning-by-doing and organizational forgetting can give rise to multiple equilibria, whereas a model with learning-by-doing alone cannot. They show that with their parameterization these equilibria range from "peaceful coexistence" to "trench warfare". If the inflow of know-how into the industry due to learning-by-doing is substantially smaller than the outflow of know-how due to organizational forgetting, then it is virtually impossible that both firms reach the bottom of their learning curves. Conversely, if the inflow is substantially greater than the outflow, then it is virtually inevitable that they do. In both cases, the primitives of the model tie down the equilibrium. This is no longer the case if the inflow roughly balances the outflow, and the stage is set for multiple equilibria. If firms believe that they cannot profitably coexist at the bottom of their learning curves and that instead one firm comes to dominate the market, then both firms cut their prices in the hope of acquiring a competitive advantage early on and maintaining it throughout. This aggressive pricing behavior, in turn, leads to market dominance. However, if firms believe that they can profitably coexist, then neither firm cuts its price, thereby ensuring that the anticipated symmetric industry structure actually emerges. Consequently, in addition to the degree of organizational forgetting, the equilibrium by itself is an important determinant of pricing behavior and industry dynamics.

Just as learning-by-doing can lead to decreasing cost over time, network effects can lead to increasing utility over time. Markovich (2004) and Markovich and Moenius (2005) model the dynamics caused by the interactions between hardware and software choices; that is by "indirect" network effects. Consumers make a hardware choice that lasts two periods. Software is designed to run on one, and only one, of the two types of hardware. Software firms must commit to one of the two types of hardware when they enter, and then can invest to improve the quality of their product, or exit, just as in the core version of our model. The demand for a given software product depends not only on the qualities of software products available for each of the two hardware types, but also on the number of consumers who have purchased the different types of hardware in the past. Thus consumer demand for hardware products depends on beliefs about the likelihood of future software products available for each hardware type, while the entry exit and investment decisions of software firm's depends on their beliefs on the future hardware purchases of consumers.

Markovich (2004) shows that with her parameterization excess inertia does not occur. A platform would be the standard in the market only if it is better than the competing platforms. Furthermore, if the industry's competitors (the outside alternative) are not progressing too quickly the equilibrium is one where both types of hardware are produced (the "variety" equilibrium), while if the competitors to the industry are growing quickly we see an equilibrium with only a single type of hardware produced (the "standardization" equilibrium). Markovich and Moenius (2005) find that network effects tie together the performance of firms using the same platform. This is driven by two effects: a successful competitor increases its platform's market share, and that in turn increases the incentives to invest in quality for all firms on this platform. So a firm may even enjoy a windfall increase in its market value resulting when a competitor on the same platform has a success.

Jenkins et al. (2004) apply a dynamic model with network externalities to a stylized description of the browser war between Netscape and Microsoft [see also Hall, Royer and Van Audenrode (2003)]. They show that network effects may be a substantial barrier to entry, giving both entrants and incumbents powerful strategic incentives to tip the market. An incumbent that dominates a market through share and scope has an incentive to maintain share as a barrier that makes entry costly and risky. An entrant has an incentive to grab market share to overcome the incumbent's advantage. In the browser war between Netscape and Microsoft, network effects appear to have sharpened strategic incentives and driven a "no-holds-barred" battle for market share. Counterfactual experiments that compare "as is" market trajectories with "but for" trajectories suggest Microsoft's "bad acts" may have been decisive in tipping the market.

7.5. Collusion

Most of the theoretical work on collusion and price wars assumes a fixed or exogenously changing environment. Though these assumptions help clarify what determines when a collusive agreement can be enforced and hence when it breaks down [see, in particular, the classic work of Green and Porter (1984) and Abreu, Pearce and Stacchetti (1986)], they limit the investigation of the implications of collusion to its impact on prices ignoring the (possibly equally important) effects of collusion on the costs, qualities, and varieties of the products marketed.

If we are willing to give up on the elegance of analytic results and rely instead on numerical analysis, it is not difficult to analyze collusive models that allow for heterogeneity among firms who invest to develop their products, and can enter and exit. Fershtman and Pakes (2000) assume that firms either collude to set prices or set prices as in a static Nash pricing equilibrium. Collusive prices and profits are determined by the outcomes of a Nash bargaining game in which the threat value is the profits from the static, Nash in prices, equilibrium. The choice of which price vector to play depends on whether any incumbent has deviated from collusive prices in the past, and on whether the punishments currently available are sufficient to insure no firm has an incentive to deviate in the current period. If there is an incumbent who has deviated, the static Nash in price solution is played as long as that incumbent remains active. As in much of the repeated game literature no incumbent ever deviates.[30] However there are tuples of states for which the punishment of reverting to non-collusive prices is not sufficient to support collusion, and this generates "price wars" (reversions to a Nash pricing equilibrium).

Fershtman and Pakes (2000) find that collusion is hard to sustain when either one of the firms does not keep up with the advances of its competitors, or a "low quality"

[30] See Green and Porter (1984) and Abreu, Pearce and Stacchetti (1986) and Judd, Yeltekin and Conklin (2003) for a method to compute the set of subgame perfect equilibria in repeated games.

entrant enters. In either case there will be an active firm that is quite likely to exit in the near future. Not only is it hard to punish a firm who is likely to exit after it deviates, but if one of the competitors is near an exit state the other incumbent(s) has an incentive to price predatorily (that is to deviate themselves) in order to hasten that exit.

Formally the difference between the Fershtman and Pakes (2000) model and the original EP framework is that they introduce a second state variable for each firm and let price choices depend on it. The second state variable, borrowed from the repeated game literature, is an indicator function which is one if the given firm has ever deviated from the collusive agreement in the past.[31] The Bellman equation for an incumbent firm is then more complicated because now at each state vector for which no one has deviated in the past, we must check to see that no one has an incentive to deviate in the current period. If either someone has deviated in the past, or someone has an incentive to deviate in the current period, then static Nash pricing ensues. If neither of these conditions are satisfied, then the collusive prices are played. With this modification to the Bellman equation one can compute equilibrium values iteratively, using techniques analogous to those described in Section 4.1. Note that this implies that policies are computed for values of the state vector in which each incumbent firm has deviated in the past, as well as for cases when none have ever deviated. Since, in the equilibria that Fershtman and Pakes (2000) compute, no firm ever deviates, this implies that they need to compute values and policies which should never actually be observed (states that are "off the equilibrium path").

The results illustrate the potential importance of dynamic considerations in evaluating the benefits and costs of collusion. In particular for the parameter values they chose consumers prefer the collusive equilibria to the equilibria with no collusion; i.e. the greater quality and variety of goods that are marketed in the collusive equilibria more than compensates consumers for the higher prices they have to pay when there is collusion.

As Fershtman and Pakes (2000) note there are many ways to model collusion in a numerically tractable way and the choice among the possibilities should probably be made with a particular industry in mind. de Roos (2004) computes a model designed to match the available data on the lysine cartel that operated in the 1990s. In his model firms' profits in the collusive regime are based on their market shares at the time the collusion agreement is struck and there is a punishment regime in addition to a non-cooperative and a collusive regime.

[31] This had been used previously to allow for collusion in Markov perfect settings, see Haurie and Tolwinski (1986), Tolwinski, Haurie and Leitmann (1986), and Reynolds (1991). It is sometimes also possible to construct collusive equilibria without adding another state variable, see Fudenberg and Tirole (1983) and Nocke (in press).

8. Topics for further study

There are a number of topics of potential importance to the successful use of the EP framework which have not yet been studied. Some of them involve a more in depth examination of the basic behavioral assumptions used in that framework. Others involve extensions to the framework which would be required to apply it to settings of obvious empirical importance. We now briefly outline four among those topics that we think may well be particularly important.

Entry There has been a proliferation of entry models in which the potential entrants are short lived (i.e. entrants either enter this period or disappear, but cannot delay entry until the next period). EP assume that there is a finite number of potential entrants each period whose entry decisions are made sequentially. Letting n be the number of currently active firms, Doraszelski and Satterthwaite (2003) assume that every period there are $\bar{n} - n$ potential entrants that make simultaneous decisions on whether to enter. Pakes, Ostrovsky and Berry (2006) assume that the number of potential entrants is a random draw from a known distribution, and the potential entrants who do appear make their entry decisions simultaneously. As noted part of the reason for this proliferation is an absence of empirical facts on entry.

In any given applied setting it may be preferable to tie the number of potential entrants to particular exogenous state variables. As long as the exogenous state variable(s) evolve as a Markov process, this just requires us to add a state variable(s) to the model. It is also relatively easy to allow potential entrants to delay entry provided the number of active potential entrants in each period are observed by the other agents in the industry and the next period entry costs of the agents who do delay are independent of their current entry cost. This just requires us to add a state variable which specifies the number of potential entrants in each period.

It is more difficult to allow potential entrants in a given year to wait and enter in a future period when either (i) the number of available potential entrants is unknown to the other agents in the market, and/or (ii) when a potential entrant who delays in a given period has a setup cost in a following period which is correlated with their current setup cost. The difficulty does not lie in formulating the Bellman equation for the potential entrant; it is easy enough to add to that equation an option of remaining in the industry as a potential entrant in the next period. What is harder is to keep track of the number of potential entrants and the distribution of their setup costs when either the potential entrant's setup costs are correlated over periods, or when past potential entrants may (but need not) still be present (as they may have left to engage in some other activity). The reason is that then the number of potential entrants and the distribution of their setup costs depends on past states; i.e. then the incumbent firms would use the observation that there were potential entrants who had not entered in prior periods to infer the number and potential setup costs of the potential entrants in the current period.

There are a number of possible workable alternatives here. For example we might allow potential entrants to delay by a small number of periods and then keep track of their number and the distribution of their setup costs over those periods. Alternatively we could keep track of sufficient statistics for the distribution of the number of potential entrants and their setup costs (as is done in the asymmetric information model discussed below). Yet another alternative is to assume that the setup cost is composed of a deterministic part that is publicly known and a random part that is privately observed and then allow for a number of different types of entrants according to the deterministic part of setup costs (assuming the privately observed costs are independent over time). We do not know of anyone who has explored these (or any other) alternatives to date.

Timing There are at least two aspects of timing that we have not delved into. One is the timing of when decisions are made. The other is the timing of the realizations of random variables and any lags between their updated values and the values of the "payoff relevant" random variables that affect the profit function. We begin with the timing of decisions.

The continuous-time model assumes that controls can be changed continuously while the discrete time version assumes that they can only be changed at fixed intervals. Though it may be the case that one (or both) of these alternatives provide an adequate approximation to a given setting, there may well be other cases in which the timing of decisions is crucial to an understanding of outcomes, and the simple alternatives we have put forth are not rich enough to capture essential features of the environment. For example it is likely that firms have a planned schedule of meetings of the decision-making staff, but that extra meetings can be called when a change in the state of the industry warrants it. This makes the timing of decisions endogenous, a feature which is not allowed in (but could be added to) the framework. In cases where there are sharp changes in values resulting from being a first mover, a model with the endogenous timing of decisions may be necessary.

Relatedly we note that we are currently constraining decisions on our two instruments, price and investment, to occur at the same time. This may not lead to an adequate approximation for some industries; i.e. in some environments it may be more appropriate to have different (possibly endogenous) lengths of time for price commitment than for changes in investment policies. Moreover as we add further controls we should keep in mind that decisions on different controls need not be perfectly aligned.[32]

The continuous- and discrete-time models also treat realizations of the investment process differently. Starting at any initial state the continuous-time model will generate a change to one firm's state at some future time. The probability of the change occurring to any particular firm depends on the investments of all firms. After that change every agent will face the new industry state which consists of an updated state for the firm whose state experienced the change, and exactly the same state for the $n - 1$ firms that did not. As in all Markov perfect models the game then continues from this new state. As a result to compute the continuation value in the continuous-time model we need only

[32] We thank Joe Harrington for pointing this out to us.

compute probabilities for which agent's state is the next to change and an integral over where it is likely to change to should it change; a computation whose burden is linear in the number of firms. Note that this implies that the investments made by $n - 1$ firms in the interval of time between the initial state and the changed state vector will, with probability one, have no impact on the sample path of any of the agents. The discrete-time model assumes that realizations of all firms random outcomes occur between the instants when successive decisions are made. This forces the agent to take account of the possibility of simultaneous changes in all firms' states in the time interval between its current and future decisions, and hence in calculating continuation values. However even in the discrete-time model once a period has elapsed the investment made prior to that period is irrelevant for future sample paths.

Note that both specifications of investment assume that either the investment is successful, and leads to an immediate change in a "payoff relevant" random variable, or it is "lost". It may be that there are additional ordering, delivery and/or installation lags before the output of the investment activity can be embodied in marketable goods or services. Alternatively the whole idea that each new piece of information leads to an increment in profits may be too narrow a conceptualization to adequately characterize the investment process in some industries. Consider, for example, pharmaceutical research. Even if investments do not lead to the discovery of a new drug in the current period, they may still yield information which changes the firm's perceptions of its (or of other firms') likely state in the future. If the information produced but not embodied in current output is known to all we could accommodate it by adding additional state variables to the model.[33] Alternatively it may well be important to account for the possibility that not all the information the firm discovers is known to the firm's competitors. In that case we would have to move to a model with private information which is correlated over time, like the model of asymmetric information model discussed below. In fact there has been very little investigation of the relationship of these timing issues to either the implications of the model, to its computational burden, or to the ability of the model to adequately mimic real-world environments.

Asymmetric information In many situations it is natural to think that firms know more about their own state (their cost structure, the status of their research programs, etc.) then about their rivals' states. This leads us to the theoretical literature on asymmetric information [see Green and Porter (1984), Abreu, Pearce and Stacchetti (1986), Athey and Bagwell (2001), Athey, Bagwell and Sanchirico (2004)]. In these models firms observe the actions of (and/or signals sent by) their competitors and use them to formulate posterior distributions on their competitors' states. At least from a computational point of view constructing these posteriors is difficult. They depend on all the variables that

[33] If it is one-to-one with investment expenditures, then we would add a state that measures the dollar value of the relevant investments. Alternatively there may be intermediate stages a firm must pass before it can embody the output of the research in a marketable good or service and we would add the state achieved; see, e.g., Doraszelski (2003) discussion of this point in the context of R&D race models.

contain information on a firm's competitors, and on the equilibrium conditions which tell the firm how to extract information on the competitors' states from whatever they observe. As a result the integral over successor states needed to determine policies is typically quite complicated.

Fershtman and Pakes (2005) present a different approach to computing equilibria in dynamic games with asymmetric information which circumvents the problem of computing posteriors. The idea is to obtain estimates of the expected future discounted value of net cash flows conditional on everything the firm knows. To do this they enlarge the state space to allow for informationally relevant variables, that is variables that contain information on the states of its competitors, as well as payoff relevant random variables. The estimates of the expected discounted values conditional on all observables are obtained from a "learning process" similar to that used in stochastic algorithm (see Section 5.3). Therefore there is no curse of dimensionality in the computation of the integral determining the value of successor states, and the algorithm converges to a recurrent class of the game in these states (which again need not grow in any particular way as a function of the number of state variables). This is a literature which is still in its infancy. On the other hand, as noted above, there are a number of environments in which asymmetric information is likely to play a central role, so it is probably worth developing further.

Dynamic consumers There are many situations in which it seems appropriate to allow consumers as well as producers to be forward looking. Analyzing markets with either durable or experience goods are two examples which, in and of themselves, are important enough to warrant detailed consideration of the relevant issues. When consumers, as well as producers, are forward looking, the fixed point that defines equilibrium values and policies requires consumers to maximize expectations based on consistent perceptions of the likelihood of future producer states, and producers to maximize expectations based on consistent perceptions on the likelihood of future consumer states; i.e. the conditions we used to define equilibrium in Section 3 must be augmented to insure the optimality of consumer decisions. Though this is not conceptually difficult, it does imply that the state variables determining behavior include the distribution of consumer, as well as that of producer, characteristics; a fact which, without further developments, is likely to increase the burden of computing equilibria significantly.

There have been some attempts to allow for dynamic consumers. Markovich (2004) and Markovich and Moenius (2005) have consumers that look two periods into the future in an oligopoly model and Nair (2005) has two types of forward-looking consumers in a monopoly model. Ching (2003) incorporates consumers learning into a dynamic model of the market for clonidine, a prescription drug, using estimated parameters from Ching (2002). However, he assumes that consumers base their purchase decision solely on their utility in the current period. Since most of manufacturing produces durable goods, and markets with experience goods typically raise a number of important policy issues (think of the market for prescription pharmaceuticals), the fact that we know of so few applications of equilibrium modeling when both consumers and producers are forward looking testifies to the difficulty of computing the equilibria from such models. Advances in computing hardware will no doubt help here, but this is definitely an area where algorithmic advances would be most welcome.

9. Conclusions

Dynamic analysis of imperfectly competitive markets is still in its infancy. Indeed there remain open questions in just about every dimension of the analysis. We have pointed out a number of ways one could make our assumptions richer. However even if we accept the modeling assumptions there remains an open and important theoretical question about how to select among multiple equilibria and about the relationship of the output of the algorithm to that selection mechanism. On a more applied front the extensions of the framework needed to analyze topics of obvious importance to the economy, such as the analysis of markets for durable, experience, or (most types of) network goods, are not yet available. Moreover the burden of currently available techniques for computing the equilibria to the models we do know how to analyze is still large enough to be a limiting factor in the analysis of many empirical and theoretical issues of interest. Finally we have adhered throughout to the notion of Markov perfect equilibria. Weaker notions of equilibria may be all that one can justify when describing the evolution of the industries we want to study [see, e.g., Fudenber and Levine's (1993) notion of self-confirming equilibrium]. The weaker notions may also be easier to use in applied work [see Fershtman and Pakes (2005)], and have different implications then the stronger Markov perfect notion [see, e.g., Esponda (2005)].

On the other hand, we have to start somewhere. Moreover perhaps the most notable aspect of the applied results thus far is that even given all their assumptions and limitations they have reproduced phenomena that we observe in actual industries rather closely (see the discussion in Section 7 and the literature cited there). At the very least this has generated a deeper understanding of those phenomena. Of course we want to push the tools reviewed here further, possibly far enough to use to form predictions that would be accurate enough to use in policy analysis. The predictive accuracy of the current tools has not really been analyzed in any formal way, and is likely to vary with both the institutional setting and the issues of interest. Still one has to keep in mind that policy choices are often based on predictions of some form, and a computational tool would at least have the advantage of enabling an internally consistent quantitative assessment of alternatives.

Acknowledgements

We would like to thank numerous colleagues for helpful discussions. Joe Harrington, Ken Judd, Rob Porter, and Michael Riordan gave us useful feedback on an earlier draft of this chapter. Pakes would like to thank his NSF grant for financial support and acknowledge the important role of Richard Ericson and Paul McGuire in developing the techniques reported on here. This paper supercedes his NBER discussion paper with the same title [Pakes (2000)].

References

Abbring, J., Campbell, J. (2003). "The entry and survival thresholds of a dynamic oligopoly". Working paper. University of Amsterdam, Amsterdam.

Abreu, D., Pearce, D., Stacchetti, E. (1986). "Optimal cartel equilibria with imperfect monitoring". Journal of Economic Theory 39 (1), 251–269.

Ackerberg, D., Benkard, L., Berry, S., Pakes, A. (2005). "Econometric tools for analyzing market outcomes". In: J. Heckman (Ed.), Handbook of Econometrics, vol. 6. North-Holland, Amsterdam. In press.

Aguirregabiria, V., Mira, P. (2007). "Sequential estimation of dynamic discrete games". Econometrica 75 (1), 1–54.

Argote, L., Beckman, S., Epple, D. (1990). "The persistence and transfer of learning in an industrial setting". Management Science 36 (2), 140–154.

Athey, S., Bagwell, K. (2001). "Optimal collusion with private information". RAND Journal of Economics 32 (3), 428–465.

Athey, S., Bagwell, K., Sanchirico, C. (2004). "Collusion and price rigidity". Review of Economic Studies 72 (2), 317–349.

Auerswald, P. (2001). "The complexity of production, technological volatility and inter-industry differences in the persistence of profits above the norm". Working paper. Harvard University.

Bajari, P., Benkard, L., Levin, J. (2006). "Estimating dynamic models of imperfect competition". Econometrica. In press.

Bajari, P., Hong, H., Ryan, S. (2004). "Identification and estimation of discrete games of complete information". Working paper. Duke University, Durham.

Barto, A., Bradtke, S., Singh, S. (1995). "Learning to act using real-time dynamic programming". Artificial Intelligence 72 (1), 81–138.

Basar, T., Olsder, J. (1999). Dynamic Noncooperative Game Theory, second ed. Society for Industrial and Applied Mathematics, Philadelphia.

Bellman, R. (1957). Dynamic Programming. Princeton Univ. Press, Princeton.

Benkard, L. (2000). "Learning and forgetting: The dynamics of aircraft production". American Economic Review 90 (4), 1034–1054.

Benkard, L. (2004). "A dynamic analysis of the market for wide-bodied commercial aircraft". Review of Economic Studies 71 (3), 581–611.

Beresteanu, A., Ellickson, P. (2005). "The dynamics of retail oligopoly". Working paper. Duke University, Durham.

Berry, S., Pakes, A. (1993). "Some applications and limitations of recent advances in empirical industrial organization: Merger analysis". American Economic Review 83 (2), 247–252.

Berry, S., Pakes, A. (2006). "The pure characteristics demand model". International Economic Review. In press.

Bertsekas, D., Tsitsiklis, J. (1996). Neuro-Dynamic Programming. Athena Scientific, Belmont.

Bertsekas, D., Tsitsiklis, J. (1997). Parallel and Distributed Computation: Numerical Methods. Athena Scientific, Belmont.

Besanko, D., Doraszelski, U. (2004). "Capacity dynamics and endogenous asymmetries in firm size". RAND Journal of Economics 35 (1), 23–49.

Besanko, D., Doraszelski, U., Kryukov, Y., Satterthwaite, M. (2004). "Learning-by-doing, organizational forgetting, and industry dynamics". Working paper. Northwestern University, Evanston.

Bhattacharjee, A. (2005). "Models of firms dynamics and the hazard rate of exits: Reconciling theory and evidence using regression models". Working paper. University of St. Andrews, St. Andrews.

Cabral, L., Riordan, M. (1994). "The learning curve, market dominance, and predatory pricing". Econometrica 62 (5), 1115–1140.
Caplin, A., Nalebuff, B. (1991). "Aggregation and imperfect competition: On the existence of equilibrium". Econometrica 59 (1), 26–59.
Cellini, R., Lambertini, L. (2003). "Advertising with spillover effects in a differential oligopoly game with differentiated goods". Central European Journal of Operations Research 11, 409–423.
Chen, J. (2004). "Bias in merger evaluation due to cost misspecification". Working paper. UC Irvine, Irvine.
Chen, J., Doraszelski, U., Harrington, J. (2004). "Avoiding market dominance: Product compatibility in markets with network effects". Working paper. Harvard University, Cambridge.
Cheong, K., Judd, K. (2006). "Mergers and dynamic oligopoly". Journal of Economic Dynamics and Control. In press.
Ching, A. (2002). "Consumer learning and heterogeneity: Dynamics of demand for prescription drugs after patent expiration". Working paper. Ohio State University, Columbus.
Ching, A. (2003). "A dynamic oligopoly structural model for the prescription drug market after patent expiration". Working paper. University of Wisconsin, Madison.
Chintagunta, P. (1993). "Investigating the sensitivity of equilibrium profits to advertising dynamics and competitive effects". Management Science 39 (9), 1146–1162.
Conklin, J., Judd, K. (1996). "Computing value correspondences for repeated games with state variables". Working paper. Hoover Institution, Stanford.
Darr, E., Argote, L., Epple, D. (1995). "The acquisition, transfer, and depreciation of knowledge in service organizations: Productivity in franchises". Management Science 41 (11), 1750–1762.
Davis, S., Haltiwanger, J. (1992). "Gross job creation, gross job destruction, and employment reallocation". Quarterly Journal of Economics 107 (3), 819–863.
de Roos, N. (2004). "A model of collusion timing". International Journal of Industrial Organization 22, 351–387.
Dockner, E., Jorgensen, S., Van Long, N., Sorger, G. (2000). Differential Games in Economics and Management Science. Cambridge Univ. Press, Cambridge.
Doraszelski, U. (2003). "An R&D race with knowledge accumulation". RAND Journal of Economics 34 (1), 19–41.
Doraszelski, U. (2005). "A note on dynamic stochastic games with sequential moves". Working paper. Harvard University, Cambridge.
Doraszelski, U., Judd, K. (2004). "Avoiding the curse of dimensionality in dynamic stochastic games". Technical working paper No. 304. NBER, Cambridge.
Doraszelski, U., Markovich, S. (2006). "Advertising dynamics and competitive advantage". RAND Journal of Economics. In press.
Doraszelski, U., Satterthwaite, M. (2003). "Computable Markov-perfect industry dynamics: Existence, purification, and multiplicity". Working paper. Harvard University, Cambridge.
Dube, J., Hitsch, G., Manchanda, P. (2005). "An empirical model of advertising dynamics". Quantitative Marketing and Economics 3, 107–144.
Dunne, T., Roberts, M., Samuelson, L. (1988). "Patterns of firm entry and exit in U.S. manufacturing". RAND Journal of Economics 19 (4), 495–515.
Eaves, C. (1972). "Homotopies for computation of fixed points". Mathematical Programming 3 (1), 1–22.
Erdem, E., Tybout, J. (2003). "Trade policy and industrial sector responses: Using evolutionary models to interpret the evidence". Working paper No. 9947. NBER, Cambridge.
Ericson, R., Pakes, A. (1995). "Markov-perfect industry dynamics: A framework for empirical work". Review of Economic Studies 62, 53–82.
Escobar, J. (2006). "Time-homogenous Markov equilibrium in dynamic stochastic games". Working paper. Stanford University, Stanford.
Esponda, I. (2005). "Behavioral equilibrium in economies with adverse selection". Working paper. Stanford University, Stanford.
Fershtman, C. (1984). "Goodwill and market shares in oligopoly". Economica 51 (203), 271–281.

Fershtman, C., Markovich, S. (2006). "Patent regimes in an asymmetric dynamic R&D race". Working paper. Northwestern University, Evanston.

Fershtman, C., Pakes, A. (2000). "A dynamic oligopoly with collusion and price wars". RAND Journal of Economics 31, 294–326.

Fershtman, C., Pakes, A. (2005). "Finite state dynamic games with asymmetric information: A framework for applied work". Working paper. Harvard University, Cambridge.

Fershtman, C., Mahajan, V., Muller, E. (1990). "Market share pioneering advantage: A theoretical approach". Management Science 36 (8), 900–918.

Filar, J., Vrieze, K. (1997). Competitive Markov Decision Processes. Springer, New York.

Freedman, D. (1983). Markov Chains. Springer, Berlin.

Friedman, J. (1983). "Advertising and oligopolistic equilibrium". Bell Journal of Economics 14 (2), 464–473.

Fudenberg, D., Levine, D. (1993). "Self-confirming equilibrium". Econometrica 61 (3), 523–545.

Fudenberg, D., Levine, D. (1998). The Theory of Learning in Games. MIT Press, Cambridge.

Fudenberg, D., Tirole, J. (1983). "Capital as commitment: Strategic investment to deter mobility". Journal of Economic Theory 31 (2), 227–250.

Ghemawat, P. (1997). Games Businesses Play. MIT Press, Cambridge.

Goettler, R., Parlour, C., Rajan, U. (2005). "Equilibrium in a dynamic limit order market". Journal of Finance 60 (5), 2149–2192.

Gort, M. (1963). "Analysis of stability and changes in market shares". Journal of Political Economy 71, 51–63.

Gowrisankaran, G. (1995). "A dynamic analysis of mergers". Ph.D. thesis. Yale University, New Haven.

Gowrisankaran, G. (1999). "A dynamic model of endogenous horizontal mergers". RAND Journal of Economics 30 (1), 56–83.

Gowrisankaran, G., Town, R. (1997). "Dynamic equilibrium in the hospital industry". Journal of Economics and Management Strategy 6 (1), 45–74.

Green, E., Porter, R. (1984). "Noncooperative collusion under imperfect price information". Econometrica 52 (1), 87–100.

Hall, R., Royer, J., Van Audenrode, M. (2003). "Potential competition and the prices of network goods: Desktop software". Working paper. Hoover Institution, Stanford.

Haurie, A., Tolwinski, B. (1986). "Definition and properties of cooperative equilibria in a two-player game of infinite duration". Journal of Optimization Theory and Applications 46, 525–534.

Intriligator, M. (1971). Mathematical Optimization and Economic Theory. Prentice Hall, Englewood Cliffs.

Isaacs, R. (1954). Differential Games. John Wiley & Sons, New York.

Jenkins, M., Liu, P., Matzkin, R., McFadden, D. (2004). "The browser war: Econometric analysis of Markov perfect equilibrium in markets with network effects". Working paper. Stanford University, Stanford.

Jia, P. (2006). "What happens when Wal-Mart comes to town: An empirical analysis of the discount retailing industry". Working paper. Yale University, New Haven.

Jofre-Bonet, M., Pesendorfer, M. (2003). "Estimation of a dynamic auction game". Econometrica 71 (5), 1143–1489.

Jovanovic, B. (1982). "Selection and the evolution of industry". Econometrica 50 (3), 649–670.

Judd, K. (1998). Numerical Methods in Economics. MIT Press, Cambridge.

Judd, K., Schmedders, K. (2004). "A computational approach to proving uniqueness in dynamic games". Working paper. Hoover Institution, Stanford.

Judd, K., Yeltekin, S. (2001). "Computing supergame equilibria with state variables". Working paper. Hoover Institution, Stanford.

Judd, K., Kübler, F., Schmedders, K. (2003). "Computational methods for dynamic equilibria with heterogeneous agents". In: Dewatripont, M., Hansen, L., Turnovsky, S. (Eds.), Advances in Economics and Econometrics: Theory and Applications, Eighth World Congress, vol. 3. Cambridge Univ. Press, Cambridge.

Judd, K., Schmedders, K., Yeltekin, S. (2002). "Optimal rules for patent races". Working paper. Hoover Institution, Stanford.

Judd, K., Yeltekin, S., Conklin, J. (2003). "Computing supergame equilibria". Econometrica 71 (4), 1239–1254.

Kadyrzhanova, D. (2006). "The leader-bias hypothesis: Corporate control dynamics in industry equilibrium". Working paper. Columbia University, New York.

Kalaba, R., Tesfatsion, L. (1991). "Solving nonlinear equations by adaptive homotopy continuation". Applied Mathematics and Computation 41 (2), 99–115.

Klette, T., Raknerud, A. (2002). "How and why do firms differ?" Working paper. University of Oslo, Oslo.

Laincz, C. (2005). "Market structure and endogenous productivity growth: How do R&D subsidies affect market structure?". Journal of Economic Dynamics and Control 29, 187–223.

Laincz, C., Rodrigues, A. (2004). "A theoretical foundation for understanding firm size distributions and Gibrat's law". Working paper. Drexel University, Philadelphia.

Langohr, P. (2003). "Competitive convergence and divergence: Capability and position dynamics". Working paper. Northwestern University, Evanston.

Lettau, M., Uhlig, H. (1999). "Rules of thumb versus dynamic programming". American Economic Review 89 (1), 148–174.

Maggi, G. (1996). "Endogenous leadership in a new market". RAND Journal of Economics 27 (4), 641–659.

Mankiw, N.G., Whinston, M. (1986). "Free entry and social inefficiency". RAND Journal of Economics 17 (1), 48–58.

Markovich, S. (2004). "Snowball: A dynamic oligopoly model with network externalities". Working paper. Northwestern University, Evanston.

Markovich, S., Moenius, J. (2005). "Winning while losing: Competition dynamics in the presence of indirect network effects". Working paper. Northwestern University, Evanston.

Maskin, E., Tirole, J. (1987). "A theory of dynamic oligopoly. III. Cournot competition". European Economic Review 31 (4), 947–968.

Maskin, E., Tirole, J. (1988a). "A theory of dynamic oligopoly. I. Overview and quantity competition with large fixed costs". Econometrica 56 (3), 549–569.

Maskin, E., Tirole, J. (1988b). "A theory of dynamic oligopoly. II. Price competition, kinked demand curves, and Edgeworth cycles". Econometrica 56 (3), 571–599.

McFadden, D. (1974). "Conditional logit analysis of qualitative choice behavior". In: Zarembka, P. (Ed.), Frontiers of Econometrics. Academic Press, New York, pp. 105–142.

McKelvey, R., McLennan, A. (1996). "Computation of equilibria in finite games". In: Amman, H., Kendrick, D., Rust, J. (Eds.), Handbook of Computational Economics. North-Holland, Amsterdam, pp. 87–142.

McKelvey, R., McLennan, A., Turocy, T. (2006). "Gambit: Software tools for game theory". Technical report. California Institute of Technology, Pasadena. Available at: http://econweb.tamu.edu/gambit.

Mueller, D. (1986). Profits in the Long Run. Cambridge Univ. Press, Cambridge.

Nair, H. (2005). "Intertemporal price discrimination with forward-looking consumers: Application to the US market for console video-games". Quantitative Marketing and Economics. In press.

Nocke, V. (in press). "Collusion and dynamic (under-) investment in quality". RAND Journal of Economics.

Noel, M. (2004). "Edgeworth cycles and focal prices: Computational dynamic Markov equilibria". Working paper. UC San Diego, San Diego.

Ortega, J., Rheinboldt, W. (1970). Iterative Solution of Nonlinear Equations in Several Variables. Academic Press, New York.

Pakes, A. (2000). "A framework for applied dynamic analysis in IO". Working paper No. 8024. NBER, Cambridge.

Pakes, A. (2006). "Econometrics and theory in empirical IO". Fisher Schulz lecture. Harvard University, Cambridge.

Pakes, A., Ericson, R. (1998). "Empirical implications of alternative models of firm dynamics". Journal of Economic Theory 79, 1–45.

Pakes, A., McGuire, P. (1994). "Computing Markov-perfect Nash equilibria: Numerical implications of a dynamic differentiated product model". RAND Journal of Economics 25 (4), 555–589.

Pakes, A., McGuire, P. (2001). "Stochastic algorithms, symmetric Markov perfect equilibrium, and the "curse" of dimensionality". Econometrica 69 (5), 1261–1281.
Pakes, A., Gowrisankaran, G., McGuire, P. (1993). "Implementing the Pakes–McGuire algorithm for computing Markov perfect equilibria in Gauss". Working paper. Yale University, New Haven.
Pakes, A., Ostrovsky, M., Berry, S. (2006). "Simple estimators for the parameters of discrete dynamic games (with entry/exit examples)". RAND Journal of Economics. In press.
Pesendorfer, M., Schmidt-Dengler, P. (2003). "Identification and estimation of dynamic games". Working paper No. 9726. NBER, Cambridge.
Reynolds, S. (1991). "Dynamic oligopoly with capacity adjustment costs". Journal of Economic Dynamics and Control 15 (3), 491–514.
Reynolds, S., Wilson, B. (2000). "Bertrand–Edgeworth competition, demand uncertainty, and asymmetric outcomes". Journal of Economic Theory 92, 122–141.
Robbins, H., Monro, S. (1951). "A stochastic approximation technique". Annals of Mathematical Statistics 22, 400–407.
Rui, X., Miranda, M. (1996). "Solving nonlinear dynamic games via orthogonal collocation: An application to international commodity markets". Annals of Operations Research 68, 89–108.
Ryan, S. (2005). "The costs of environmental regulation in a concentrated industry". Working paper. Duke University, Durham.
Saloner, G. (1987). "Cournot duopoly with two production periods". Journal of Economic Theory 42 (1), 183–187.
Sargent, T. (1993). Bounded Rationality in Macroeconomics: The Arne Ryde Memorial Lectures. Clarendon Press, Cambridge.
Schivardi, F., Schneider, M. (2005). "Strategic experimentation and disruptive technological change". Working paper. New York University, New York.
Schmedders, K. (1998). "Computing equilibria in the general equilibrium model with incomplete asset markets". Journal of Economic Dynamics and Control 22, 1375–1401.
Schmedders, K. (1999). "A homotopy algorithm and an index theorem for the general equilibrium model with incomplete asset markets". Journal of Mathematical Economics 32 (2), 225–241.
Shapley, L. (1953). "Stochastic games". Proceedings of the National Academy of Sciences 39, 1095–1100.
Song, M. (2002). "Competition vs. cooperation: A dynamic model of investment in the semiconductor industry". Working paper. Harvard University, Cambridge.
Starr, A., Ho, Y. (1969). "Nonzero-sum differential games". Journal of Optimization Theory and Applications 3 (3), 184–206.
Stigler, G. (1968). The Organization of Industry. University of Chicago Press, Homewood.
Thompson, P. (2003). "How much did the Liberty shipbuilders forget?" Working paper. Florida International University, Miami.
Tolwinski, B., Haurie, A., Leitmann, G. (1986). "Cooperative equilibria in differential games". Journal of Mathematical Analysis and Applications 119, 182–202.
Vedenov, D., Miranda, M. (2001). "Numerical solution of dynamic oligopoly games with capital investment". Economic Theory 18, 237–261.
Watson, L., Billups, S., Morgan, A. (1987). "HOMPACK: A suite of codes for globally convergent homotopy algorithms". ACM Transactions on Mathematical Software 13 (3), 281–310.
Watson, L., Sosonkina, M., Melville, R., Morgan, A. (1997). "HOMPACK90: A suite of Fortran 90 codes for globally convergent homotopy algorithms". ACM Transactions on Mathematical Software 23 (4), 514–549.
Weintraub, G., Benkard, L., Van Roy, B. (2005). "Markov perfect industry dynamics with many firms". Working paper. Stanford University, Stanford.
Whitt, W. (1980). "Representation and approximation of noncooperative sequential games". SIAM Journal of Control and Optimization 18 (1), 33–48.
Zangwill, W., Garcia, C. (1981). Pathways to Solutions, Fixed Points, and Equilibria. Prentice Hall, Englewood Cliffs.

Chapter 31

COORDINATION AND LOCK-IN: COMPETITION WITH SWITCHING COSTS AND NETWORK EFFECTS

JOSEPH FARRELL

University of California
e-mail: farrell@econ.berkeley.edu

PAUL KLEMPERER

Nuffield College, Oxford University
e-mail: paul.klemperer@economics.ox.ac.uk

Contents

Handbook of Industrial Organization, Volume 3
Edited by M. Armstrong and R. Porter

DOI: 10.1016/S1573-448X(06)03031-7

Abstract

Switching costs and network effects bind customers to vendors if products are incompatible, locking customers or even markets in to early choices. Lock-in hinders customers from changing suppliers in response to (predictable or unpredictable) changes in efficiency, and gives vendors lucrative ex post market power – over the same buyer in the case of switching costs (or brand loyalty), or over others with network effects. Firms compete ex ante for this ex post power, using penetration pricing, introductory offers, and price wars. Such "competition for the market" or "life-cycle competition" can adequately replace ordinary compatible competition, and can even be fiercer than compatible competition by weakening differentiation. More often, however, incompatible competition not only involves direct efficiency losses but also softens competition and magnifies incumbency advantages. With network effects, established firms have little incentive to offer better deals when buyers' and complementors' expectations hinge on non-efficiency factors (especially history such as past market shares), and although competition between incompatible networks is initially unstable and sensitive to competitive offers and random events, it later "tips" to monopoly, after which entry is hard, often even too hard given incompatibility. And while switching costs can encourage small-scale entry, they discourage sellers from raiding one another's existing customers, and so also discourage more aggressive entry. Because of these competitive effects, even inefficient incompatible competition is often more profitable than compatible competition, especially for dominant firms with installed-base or expectational advantages. Thus firms probably seek incompatibility too often. We therefore favor thoughtfully pro-compatibility public policy.

Keywords

Switching costs, Network effects, Lock-in, Network externalities, Co-ordination, Indirect network effects

JEL classification: L130, L150, L120, L140, D430, D420

1. Introduction

The economics of switching costs and network effects have received a great deal of popular, as well as professional, attention in the last two decades.[1] They are central to the "new economy" information technology industries. But these new topics are closely linked to traditional concepts of contract incompleteness, complementarity, and economies of scale and scope.

Both switching costs and proprietary network effects arise when consumers value forms of *compatibility* that require otherwise separate purchases to be made from the same firm. Switching costs arise if a consumer wants a group, or especially a series, of his own purchases to be compatible with one another: this creates economies of scope among his purchases from a single firm. Network effects arise when a user wants compatibility with *other* users so that he can interact or trade with them, or use the same complements; this creates economies of scope between different users' purchases.

These economies of scope make a buyer's best action depend on other, complementary transactions. When those transactions are in the future, or made simultaneously by others, his *expectations* about them are crucial. When they are in the past, they are *history* that matters to him. History also matters to a firm because established market share is a valuable asset: in the case of switching costs, it represents a stock of individually locked-in buyers, while in the case of network effects an installed base directly lets the firm offer more network benefits and may also boost expectations about future sales.

Vying for valuable share, firms may compete hard for early adoptions, notably with penetration pricing but perhaps also in less efficient ways. Early sales induce lucrative follow-on sales, which we often call locked-in, although lock-in is seldom absolute. Both switching costs and proprietary network effects thus shift the locus of competition from smaller to larger units of sales, as economies of scope, tying, and bundling do.

When switching costs are high, buyers and sellers actually trade streams of products or services, but their contracts often cover only the present. Similarly, network effects push large groups of users toward doing the same thing as one another, but contracts usually cover only a bilateral transaction between a seller and one user. If users choose sequentially, early choices constrain later buyers and create "collective switching costs"; if users choose simultaneously, they face a coordination problem. Clever contracts can solve these problems, but ordinary contracts generally do not.

Because firms compete to capture buyers, those problems are more subtle than the mere fact that buyers are locked in ex post. For example, in the simplest switching-cost models, initial sales contracts do not specify future prices, yet competition for the stream of purchases is efficient. Similarly, in some simple network models, users efficiently coordinate and network effects cause no trouble. As such models illustrate, conventional competition "in the market" *can* be replaced by well-functioning competition "for the

[1] Recent short (less than 2000 words each) non-technical summaries of the economics of switching costs and network effects can be found in Klemperer (in press a) and Klemperer (in press b), respectively.

market" – for a buyer's lifecycle requirements in the case of switching costs, or for the business of many buyers when there are network effects. Early adoptions are often pivotal and competition focuses on them; later, locked-in buyers pay more and create ex post rents; but ex ante competition passes those rents through to the pivotal buyers. This can be efficient, though it raises distributional issues unless (as in simple switching cost markets) locked-in buyers were themselves previously pivotal.

But these simplest models are misleading: things do not usually work so well. Despite ex ante competition for the market, incompatibilities often reduce efficiency and harm consumers in a number of ways:

Direct costs are incurred if consumers actually switch or actually adopt incompatible products.[2] Consumers may avoid those costs by not switching, or by buying from the same firm, but that ties together transactions and thus often obstructs efficient buyer–seller matching. Variety may be more sustainable if niche products do not force users to sacrifice network effects or incur switching costs by being incompatible with mainstream products. Entrants lack installed bases and consumers' expectations may naturally focus on established firms, so entry with network effects, and large-scale entry with switching costs, are hard. These entry hurdles may be broadly efficient *given* incompatibility, but they nevertheless represent a social cost of incompatibility.

Ex ante competition often fails to compete away ex post rents: switching costs typically raise oligopoly profits and proprietary network effects often do, especially if expectations fail to track relative surplus. And even when ex ante competition dissipates ex post rents, it may do so in unproductive ways such as through socially inefficient marketing; at best it induces "bargain-then-ripoff" pricing (low to attract business, high to extract surplus) that normally distorts buyers' quantity choices, gives consumers wrong signals about whether to switch, and (in the case of network effects) provides artificial incentives to be or appear pivotal.

Thus while incompatibility does not necessarily damage competition, it often does.

1.1. Switching costs

A product has classic switching costs if a buyer will purchase it repeatedly and will find it costly to switch from one seller to another. Switching costs also arise if a buyer will purchase follow-on products such as service and repair, and will find it costly to switch from the supplier of the original product.

Large switching costs lock in a buyer once he makes an initial purchase, so he is effectively buying a series of goods, just as (more generally) with strong enough relationship-specific economies of scope, sellers compete on bundles of goods rather than single goods. Sometimes sellers offer complete ("life-cycle") contracts that specify all prices. But often contracts do not specify all the future prices, so that a long-term

[2] Firms may also dissipate resources creating and defending incompatibility.

relationship is governed by short-term contracts. This pattern creates ex post monopoly, for which firms compete ex ante.[3]

Some of the same issues arise if contracts are incomplete for other reasons. For instance, shops often advertise some, but not all, of their prices: the consumer learns others only once he is in the shop and will find it costly to go elsewhere. Just as with dynamic switching costs, this tends to produce ripoffs on un-advertised (small print) prices and corresponding bargains on advertised (loss leader) prices.

The same consumer-specific economies of scope are present in "shopping-cost" markets where consumers face costs of using different suppliers for different goods in a single period and with all prices advertised, but neither time nor commitment problems arise. Such shopping costs encourage firms to offer a full (perhaps too broad) product line – and so help explain multi-product firms – but can lead firms to offer similar products to each other so that there may be too little variety in the market as a whole. We argue below that the shopping-cost framework is the best way to understand the "mix and match" literature.

Switching costs shift competition away from what we normally think of as the default (a single consumer's needs in a single period) to something broader – a single consumer's needs over time. Even when that long-term relationship is governed by short-term contracts, this shift need not cause competitive problems: competing on first-period terms can be an adequate proxy for competition with complete contracts. Likewise, the theory of bilateral contracts with hold-up shows that when parties cannot readily contract on future variables and there are switching costs, it can be efficient to accept that hold-up will occur and to compensate the prospective victim up front. But this only works if the parties can efficiently transfer rents across periods; often, instead, "hold up" or "bargain-then-ripoff" pricing distorts quantity choices, incentives to switch suppliers, and entry incentives.

The bargain-then-ripoff structure is clearest when new and locked-in customers are clearly distinguished and can be charged separate bargain and ripoff prices, respectively. This will be the case when prices are individually negotiated (and existing customers are known); it will also be the case when locked-in buyers buy separate "follow-on" products such as parts and service, rather than repeatedly buying the same good.

If, however, each firm has to set a single price to old (locked-in) and new customers, then its trade with a locked-in customer affects its trade with a new customer and the problem is no longer bilateral. A form of bargain-then-ripoff pricing sometimes survives, with firms engaging in repeated "sales", but prices will often instead be a compromise between high prices to exploit locked-in buyers and lower prices to build a locked-in customer base.

[3] Williamson (1975) stressed the "fundamental transformation, in which the initial winner of a bidding competition thereafter enjoys an advantage over rival suppliers because of its ownership of or control over transaction specific assets".

Whether with bargain-then-ripoff dynamics or with a single compromise price, switching costs may either raise or lower average oligopoly prices. The outcome depends heavily on how consumers form expectations about future prices, but on balance switching costs seem more likely to increase prices. Furthermore, switching costs can segment an otherwise undifferentiated market as firms focus on their established customers and do not compete aggressively for their rivals' buyers, letting oligopolists extract positive profits.

Switching costs also affect entry conditions, in two opposing ways. They hamper forms of entry that must persuade customers to pay those costs. So in a classic switching-cost market they hamper large-scale entry that seeks to attract existing customers (for instance to achieve minimum viable scale, if the market is not growing quickly). Likewise, shopping costs make single-product entry hard.

On the other hand, if incumbents must set a single price to old and new buyers, a firm with a larger customer base puts relatively more weight on harvesting this base than on winning new customers. Thus switching costs create a fat-cat effect that actually encourages entry that focuses purely on new customers, and makes competition stable: large shares tend to shrink and small shares to grow. More generally, the tradeoff between harvesting and investing depends on interest rates, the state of the business cycle, expectations about exchange-rates, etc., with implications for macroeconomics and international trade.

1.2. Network effects

A good exhibits *direct* network effects if adoption by different users is complementary, so that each user's adoption payoff, and his incentive to adopt, increases as more others adopt. Thus users of a communications network or speakers of a language gain directly when others adopt it, because they have more opportunities for (beneficial) interactions with peers.

Indirect network effects arise through improved opportunities to trade with the other side of a market. Although buyers typically dislike being joined by other buyers because it raises price given the number of sellers, they also like it because it attracts more sellers. If thicker markets are more efficient, then buyers' indirect gain from the re-equilibrating entry by sellers can outweigh the terms-of-trade loss for buyers, and vice versa; if so, there is an indirect network effect.

From a cooperative game theory perspective, network effects are just economies of scale: the per-buyer surplus available to a coalition of buyers and a seller increases with the size of the coalition.[4] But the contracting and coordination issues seem much harder.

[4] The analogy becomes weaker if network effects are less anonymous. Likewise, switching costs correspond to economies of scope on the production side in a single-consumer context, but the analogy is imperfect with many consumers because individual customer–supplier matches matter in switching-cost markets.

Unless adoption prices fully internalize the network effect (which is difficult), there is a positive externality from adoption, and a single network product tends to be under-adopted at the margin. But when one network competes with another, adopting one network means not adopting another; this dilutes or overturns that externality.

More interestingly, network effects create incentives to "herd" with others. Self-fulfilling expectations create multiple equilibria and cause chicken-and-egg or critical-mass behavior with positive feedback or "tipping": a network that looks like succeeding will as a result do so.

How adopters form expectations and coordinate their choices dramatically affects the performance of competition among networks. If adopters smoothly coordinate on the best deal, vendors face strong pressure to offer such deals. Indeed, competition may be unusually fierce because all-or-nothing competition neutralizes horizontal differentiation – since adopters focus not on matching a product to their own tastes but on joining the expected winner.

Smooth coordination is hard, especially when different adopters would prefer different coordinated outcomes, as in the Battle of the Sexes, perhaps because each has a history with a different network and faces individual switching costs. However, some institutions can help. Consensus standard setting (informally or through standards organizations) can help avert "splintering"; contingent contracts seem theoretically promising but little used; and – most important – adoption is very often sequential. If one trusts long chains of backward induction, fully sequential adoption eliminates the starkest coordination traps, in which an alternative equilibrium would be strictly better for all.

However, sequential adoption may not help overall efficiency in the Battle-of-the-Sexes case. Sequential adoption translates multiple static (simultaneous-adoption) equilibria into the adoption dynamics characteristic of network markets: *early instability and later lock-in*. In particular, sequential adoption implements tradeoffs between early and late efficiencies that are not generally efficient. Because early adoptions affect later ones, long-term behavior is driven by early events, whether accidental or strategic. Thus early adopters' preferences count for more than later adopters': "excess early power".

These adoption dynamics are the essence of competition if each network is competitively supplied, and the playing field for competition if each network is proprietary to one "sponsor". Sponsors compete ex ante, in particular with penetration pricing, and perhaps also using other tactics such as pronouncements, to appeal to the pivotal early adopters, since the ex post lock-in creates ex post dominance and profits. This competition for the market can neutralize or overturn excess early power if sponsors' anticipated later relative efficiency feeds through into their early willingness to set low penetration prices. But where that feed-through is obstructed or asymmetric, networks that appeal to early pivotal customers thrive, while late developers have a hard time. Much has been written on whether incompatible transitions are even harder than they should be, given ex-post incompatibility, but whether there is such "excess inertia" or its opposite, "excess momentum", long-term choices still hinge mainly on early preferences and early information. In Section 3.2 below, we illustrate these themes in the famous case of the QWERTY keyboard.

If such incompatible competition does not tip all the way to one network, it sacrifices network benefits and may segment the market; if it does tip, it sacrifices matching of products to customers or to time periods and loses the option value from the possibility that a currently inferior technology might become superior. Moreover, if adopters do not coordinate well, or coordinate using cues – such as history – other than the surpluses firms offer, the direct loss in performance is exacerbated by vendors' weaker incentive to offer good deals. For example, if one firm clearly has the *ability* to offer the highest quality, so buyers know it could profitably recapture the market even after losing any one cohort's business, they may quite rationally all buy from it even if it never actually produces high quality or offers a low price. Finally, the excess power of early adopters biases outcomes towards networks that are more efficient early on, when unsponsored networks compete; biases outcomes in favor of sponsored over unsponsored alternatives; and often biases the outcome even when both alternatives are sponsored.

If firms choose to compete with compatible products, then consumers obtain full network benefits even when they do not all buy from the same firm. This raises consumers' willingness to pay, which can persuade firms to make their products compatible. But, as with switching costs, compatibility often sharpens competition and neutralizes the competitive advantage of a large installed base; furthermore, while switching costs tend to soften competition, hindering attempts to lure customers from rivals (though they may facilitate small-scale entry, they also encourage entry to stay small), proprietary network effects tend to make competition all-or-nothing, with risks of exclusion. Thus large firms and those who are good at steering adopters' expectations may prefer their products to be incompatible with rivals'. If others favor compatibility, this can lead to complex maneuvering, but intellectual property can help firms insist on incompatibility.

1.3. Strategy and policy

Switching costs and proprietary network effects imply complementarities that in turn make success selling in one period or to one customer an advantage in another. This central fact has important implications for competitive strategy and for public policy.

For a firm, it makes market share a valuable asset, and encourages a competitive focus on affecting expectations and on signing up pivotal (notably early) customers, which is reflected in strategies such as penetration pricing; competition is shifted from textbook competition in the market to a form of Schumpeterian competition for the market in which firms struggle for dominance.

For a consumer, it may make early choices tantamount to long-term commitments – necessitating great care and raising the value of accurate information at that stage; it may make those choices a coordination problem with other adopters, or it may mean that there is no real choice because of what others have done or are expected to do.

And for policy, these facts collectively have broad repercussions. Because early choices are crucial, consumer protection (against deception, etc.) and information can be key; because coordination is often important and difficult, institutions such as standards organizations matter. Finally, because competition for the market differs greatly from competition in the market, competition policy gets involved in issues of compatibility, as well as in the analysis of mergers, monopolization, intellectual property, and predation, all of which behave differently in the presence of switching costs and network effects.

2. Switching costs and competition

2.1. Introduction

A consumer faces a *switching cost* between sellers when an investment specific to his current seller must be duplicated for a new seller.[5] That investment might be in equipment, in setting up a relationship, in learning how to use a product, or in buying a high-priced first unit that then allows one to buy subsequent units more cheaply (when firms' prices are non-linear). Switching costs may be psychological.[6] Klemperer (1995) gives many examples of each of these kinds of switching costs, and Section 2.2 discusses empirical evidence for switching costs.

Switching costs may be *learning* costs, in which case a consumer who switches from firm A to firm B has no switching cost of later buying from either firm. Alternatively, switching costs may be *transactional*, in which case a consumer who switches from A to B would incur an additional switching cost if he reswitched back to A (an example is the cost of returning rented equipment and renting from a new supplier). Of course, many switching costs have both learning and transactional aspects.

We will generally assume that switching costs are real social costs, but there can also be *contractual* or pecuniary switching costs (that are not social costs). Examples include airlines' "frequent-flyer" programs, and "loyalty contracts" that rebate a fraction of past payments to consumers who continue to patronize the firm. These pecuniary switching costs are a form of quantity discount or bundling. Lars Stole (2007) discusses such price discrimination strategies elsewhere in this Volume, so we will focus mainly on " real" switching costs.[7]

[5] There can also be switching costs among different products of a single firm, as there were among IBM computers until the internally compatible System/360 family. But we (following the economics literature) focus on switching costs between firms.

[6] Social psychologists have shown that consumers change their own preferences in favor of products that they have previously chosen or been given, in order to reduce "cognitive dissonance" [Brehm (1956)].

[7] Typically, a consumer who has not previously bought from any firm incurs a start-up cost similar to (or greater than) the new investment (switching cost) that a brand switcher must make. We will use the term "switching cost" to include these start-up costs. So a consumer may have a "switching cost" of making a first purchase. In many models consumers have high enough willingnesses to pay that this cost has little consequence since it does not affect consumers' preferences between firms.
Sometimes costs of forming a new relationship fall upon the supplier, not (or as well as) on the customer, and firms' costs of serving new customers have parallels to consumers' switching costs [see Klemperer

We assume consumers have perfect information about the existence and qualities of all firms' products, even before purchasing any. So "new" consumers who have not yet developed an attachment to any particular product are especially important in markets with switching costs. In contrast, "search costs" directly affect even consumers' initial purchases. But search costs and switching costs have much in common, and models of the effects of switching costs can also apply to search costs. For example, either kind of friction makes a firm's market share important for its future profitability (see Section 2.6) and much empirical work does not distinguish between search and switching costs.[8] For a survey of search costs, see, for example, Stiglitz (1989) in Volume 1 of this Series.

"Experience-good" markets in which each consumer needs to purchase a product to determine its quality [see Nelson (1970)] and so prefers to repurchase a brand he tried and liked rather than try a new brand of unknown quality, also have much in common with switching-cost markets. But with experience goods, unlike with switching costs, complications can arise from the possibility of prices signaling qualities, and from the existence of consumers who disliked the product they last purchased.[9,10]

Switching costs not only apply to repeat-purchases of identical goods. An important class of examples involves "follow on" goods, such as spare parts and repair services, bought in "aftermarkets": buyers face additional "switching" costs if the follow-on goods are not compatible with the original purchase, as may be the case if they are not bought from the same firm.[11]

(1995)]. Firms' switching costs have been less studied, but in some contexts, such as the simple model of the next subsection, the total prices (including any switching costs) paid by consumers are unaffected by whether firms or consumers actually pay the switching costs. Thus the equilibrium incidence need not coincide with the apparent incidence of switching costs.

[8] For example, empirical findings about the credit card [Ausubel (1991), etc. – see footnote 66] and telecommunications [see, e.g., Knittel (1997)] markets, and about the effects of firms' discount rates on prices [Froot and Klemperer (1989), Chevalier and Scharfstein (1996), Fitoussi and Phelps (1988), etc.] could be the result of either switching or search costs. On the other hand, Moshkin and Shachar (2000) develop a discrete-choice empirical model to estimate how many consumers behave as if they have switching costs and search costs, respectively. Their test is based on the fact that whereas the switching probability of a consumer facing search costs depends on the match between his tastes and the attributes of the alternative he last chose, the switching probability of a consumer facing switching costs depends on the match between his tastes and the attributes of all available alternatives. Using panel data on television viewing choices, they suggest 72% of viewers act as if they have switching costs between TV channels, while 28% act as if they have search costs. See also Wilson (2006).

[9] Schmalensee (1982) and Villas Boas (2006) analyse models of experience goods that show similarities to switching costs models. Hakenes and Peitz (in press) and Doganoglu (2004) model experience goods when there are also learning or transactional switching costs; Doganoglu shows that adding small switching costs to Villas Boas' (2006) model can sometimes reduce price levels.

[10] For related models in which consumers differ in their "quality" from firms' point of view, and firms are uncertain about consumers they have not supplied and can exploit those they know to be of "high quality", see, for example, Nilssen (2000) and Cohen (2005) on insurance markets and Sharpe (1990) and Zephirin (1994) on bank loan markets.

[11] Aftermarkets have been much studied since a US Supreme Court decision (ITS v. Kodak) held that it was conceptually possible for ITS, an independent repair firm, to prove that Kodak had illegally monopolized the

Similar issues arise when retailers each advertise the prices of only some of their products (often the "loss leaders"), but expect consumers who enter their stores to buy other products also.[12] See, for example, Lal and Matutes (1994) and Lee and Png (2004). In these models, consumers decide whether or not to buy the advertised goods before entering a store, that is, consumers are making purchase decisions about the advertised goods and the unadvertised ("follow-on") products in different "periods".[13]

If all prices are advertised, consumers may incur switching costs, or "shopping costs", at a single date by choosing to buy related products from multiple suppliers rather than from a single supplier. In this case a static (single-period) model is appropriate. (These "shopping costs" can be real social costs or contractual costs created by quantity discounts and bundling.)

Either in a static context, or in a dynamic context when firms can commit to future prices and qualities, a market with switching costs is closely analogous to a market with economies of scope in production; with switching costs each individual consumer can be viewed as a market with economies of scope between "purchases now" and "purchases later". Just as a market with large production economies of scope is entirely captured by the firm with the lowest total costs in the simplest price-competition model, so in a simple model with complete contracts each individual buyer's lifetime requirements in a market with large switching costs are filled by the lowest-cost supplier of those requirements. That is, firms compete on "lifecycle" prices and the market lifecycle price is determined by lifecycle costs, with any subdivision of the lifecycle price being arbitrary and meaningless. In this case, the outcome is efficient and switching costs confer no market power on firms.

However, most of the literature focuses on dynamic problems and emphasizes the resulting commitment problems. The simple analogy in the paragraph above – including the efficiency of the outcome – *can* survive even if firms cannot credibly commit to future prices or qualities. But even small steps outside the simplest story suggest ways in which the analogy and the efficiency break down (Section 2.3). The analogy is still weaker if firms cannot discriminate between different customers (Section 2.4), or consumers use multiple suppliers (Section 2.5). After treating these cases (and having discussed empirical evidence in Section 2.2), we analyze the "market share" competition that switching costs generate (Section 2.6). All this discussion takes both the switching costs and the number of firms as exogenous, so we then consider entry (Section 2.7) and endogenous switching costs (Section 2.8), before addressing implications for competition policy (Section 2.9).

aftermarket for servicing Kodak photocopiers: see, e.g., Shapiro (1995), Shapiro and Teece (1994), MacKie-Mason and Metzler (1999), and Borenstein, MacKie-Mason and Netz (1995, 2000).

[12] If the unadvertised follow-on product is always purchased, it can be interpreted as the "quality" of the advertised product – see Ellison (2005) and Vickers (2004).

[13] Gabaix and Laibson (2006) analyse this case when only some consumers are rational.

2.2. Empirical evidence

The empirical literature on switching costs is much smaller and more recent than the theoretical literature.[14,15] Some studies test specific aspects of the theory (see later sections), but only a few studies directly attempt to measure switching costs.

Where micro data on individual consumers' purchases are available, a discrete choice approach can be used to explore the determinants of a consumer's probability of purchasing from a particular firm. Greenstein (1993) analyses federal procurement of commercial mainframe computer systems during the 1970s, and finds that an agency is likely to acquire a system from an incumbent vendor, even when controlling for factors other than the buyer's purchase history that may have influenced the vendor–buyer match; he suggests switching costs were an important source of incumbent advantage in this market.[16] Shum (2004) analyzes panel data on breakfast cereal purchases, and finds that households switching brands incur average implicit switching costs of \$3.43 – which exceeds every brand's price! (However he also finds advertising can be effective in attracting customers currently loyal to rival brands.)

Because switching costs are usually both consumer-specific and not directly observable, and micro data on individual consumers' purchase histories are seldom available, less direct methods of assessing the level of switching costs are often needed. Kim et al. (2003) estimate a first-order condition and demand and supply equations in a Bertrand oligopoly to extract information on the magnitude and significance of switching costs from highly aggregated panel data which do not contain customer-specific information. Their point estimate of switching costs in the market for Norwegian bank loans is 4.12% of the customer's loan, which seems substantial in this market, and their results also suggest that switching costs are even larger for smaller, retail customers.[17] Shy (2002) argues that data on prices and market shares reveal that the cost of switching between banks varies from 0 to 11% of the average balance in the Finnish market for bank accounts. He also uses similar kinds of evidence to argue that switching costs in the Israeli cellular phone market approximately equal the price of an average phone.

One defect of all these studies is that none of them models the dynamic effects of switching costs that (as we discuss below) are the main focus of the theoretical literature;

[14] Experimental studies are even fewer and more recent, but include Cason and Friedman (2002), and Cason, Friedman and Milam (2003). See footnote 36.

[15] The theoretical literature arguably began with Selten's (1965) model of "demand inertia" (which assumed a firm's current sales depended in part on history, even though it did not explicitly model consumers' behavior in the presence of switching costs), and then took off in the 1980s.

[16] Breuhan (1997) studies the switching costs associated with the Windows and DOS operating systems for personal computers. See Chen (2005) for a general survey of the literature on switching costs in information technology.

[17] Sharpe (1997) studies the bank retail deposit market and argues that the data support the model of Klemperer (1987b). See also Waterson (2003).

in effect, these empirical studies assume consumers myopically maximize current utility without considering the future effects of their choices.[18]

Other empirical studies, many of which we will discuss below in the context of specific theories, provide evidence for the importance of switching costs for credit cards [Ausubel (1991), Calem and Mester (1995), Stango (2002)]; cigarettes [Elzinga and Mills (1998, 1999)]; computer software [Larkin (2004)]; supermarkets [Chevalier and Scharfstein (1996)]; air travel, and alliances of airlines in different frequent-flyer programs [Fernandes (2001), Carlsson and Löfgren (2004)]; individual airlines for different flight-segments of a single trip [Carlton, Landes and Posner (1980)]; phone services [Knittel (1997), Gruber and Verboven (2001), Park (2005), Shi et al. (2006), Viard (in press)]; television viewing choices [Moshkin and Shachar (2000)]; online brokerage services [Chen and Hitt (2002)]; electricity suppliers [Waterson (2003)]; bookstores [Lee and Png (2004)]; and automobile insurance [Schlesinger and von der Schulenberg (1993), Israel (2005), Waterson (2003)].

There is also an extensive empirical marketing literature on brand loyalty (or "state dependence") which often reflects, or has equivalent effects to, switching costs. Seetharaman et al. (1999) summarize this literature; a widely cited paper is Guadagni and Little's (1983) analysis of the coffee market.[19] Finally, Klemperer (1995) gives many other examples of markets with switching costs, and UK Office of Fair Trading (2003) presents useful case studies.

2.3. *Firms who cannot commit to future prices*

2.3.1. *Bargains followed by ripoffs*

The core model of the switching costs literature posits that firms cannot commit to future prices.

The simplest model has two periods and two symmetric firms, with costs c_t in periods $t = 1, 2$.[20] A single consumer has a switching cost s and reservation price $r_t > c_t + s$ for one unit of the period-t good, firms set prices, and there is no discounting. Then in period 2 the firm that sold in period 1 will exercise its ex post market power by pricing (just below) $c_2 + s$ (the rival firm will offer price c_2 but make no sale). Foreseeing this, firms are willing to price below cost in period 1 to acquire the customer who will

[18] But Viard (in press) studies the impact of number portability on prices in the U.S. market for toll-free numbers using a dynamic model in which consumers consider the future effects of their choices.

[19] Jacoby and Chestnut (1978) survey earlier attempts in the marketing literature to measure brand loyalty. Theoretical marketing papers include Wernerfelt (1991) (see footnote 34), Villas Boas (2006) (see footnote 9), and Kim et al. (2001) who study incentives to offer reward programs that create pecuniary switching costs. Seetharaman and Che (in press) discusses adopting switching costs models to model "variety seeking" consumers with negative switching costs.

[20] $c_2 \neq c_1$ is especially natural if the second-period good is spare parts/repair services/consumables for a first-period capital good.
It makes no difference if there are $n > 2$ firms.

become a valuable follow-on purchaser in period 2; undifferentiated competition to win the customer drives period-1 prices down to $c_1 - s$.

Note that in this simple model the consumer's expectations do not matter. Competition among non-myopic firms makes buyer myopia irrelevant.[21]

Although first-period prices are below cost, there is nothing predatory about them, and this pattern of low "introductory offers" or "penetration pricing" (see Section 2.6), followed by higher prices to exploit locked-in customers is familiar in many markets. For example, banks offer gifts to induce customers to open new accounts, and Klemperer (1995) gives more examples.[22] This "bargains-then-ripoffs" pattern is a main theme of many two-period models in the switching-costs literature, including Klemperer (1987a, 1987b, 1995, Section 3.2), Basu and Bell (1991), Padilla (1992), Basu (1993), Ahtiala (1998), Lal and Matutes (1994), Pereira (2000), Gehrig and Stenbacka (2002), Ellison (2005), and Lee and Png (2004). Of these models, Klemperer (1995, Section 3.2) is particularly easy to work with and to extend for other purposes.[23]

Although the switching cost strikingly affects price in each period, it does not affect the life-cycle price $c_1 + c_2$ that the consumer pays in the simple model of this subsection. As in the case of full commitment noted in Section 2.1, we can here view the life-cycle (the bundle consisting of the period-1 good and the period-2 good) as the real locus of competition, and competition in *that* product has worked exactly as one would hope. In particular, the absence of price commitment did not lead to any inefficiency in this very simple model.

2.3.2. *Inefficiency of the price-path*

Although the outcome above is socially efficient, the inability to contract in period 1 on period-2 prices in general leads to inefficiencies, even if firms still earn zero profits over the two periods. Even slight generalizations of the simple model above show this.

[21] Because firms are symmetric and so charge the same price in period 2, the consumer is indifferent in period 1. If firms A, B had different costs c_{A2} and c_{B2} in period 2, then if A made the period-1 sale, its period-2 price would be $p_{A2} = c_{B2} + s$ (that is, constrained by B), while if B made the period-1 sale, its period-2 price would be $p_{B2} = c_{A2} + s$. In this case, the prices that firms charge in period 1 (and hence also firms' incentives to invest in cost reduction, etc.) depend on whether the consumer has rational expectations about the period-2 prices it will face or whether the consumer acts myopically. We discuss the role of expectations in Section 2.4.5. Other simple models such as that in Klemperer (1995, Section 3.2) sidestep the issue of consumers' expectations by assuming period-2 prices are constrained by consumers' reservation price r_2, hence independent of consumers' period-1 choice. The distinction between these modeling approaches is crucial in some analyses of network effects (see Section 3.7.3).
It is important for the modeling that the customer buys from just one firm in period 1. If a unit mass of consumers splits evenly between the firms in period 1, there may be no pure-strategy equilibrium in period 2. See footnote 31.

[22] Skott and Jepsen (2000) argue that a tough drug policy may encourage the aggressive marketing of illegal drugs to new users, by increasing the costs of switching between dealers.

[23] For example, the many-period extension of this model is Beggs and Klemperer (1992).

In particular, if the consumer has downward-sloping demand in each period and firms are restricted to linear pricing (i.e. no two-part pricing), or if firms face downward-sloping demands because there are many heterogeneous consumers with different reservation prices among whom they cannot distinguish, then there will be excessive sales in period 1 and too few sales in period 2 [Klemperer (1987a)].[24]

Our simple model also assumed that ex-post profits can feed through into better early deals for the consumers. In practice this may not be possible. For example, setting very low introductory prices may attract worthless customers who will not buy after the introductory period.[25] If for this or other reasons firms dissipate their future profits in unproductive activities (e.g., excessive advertising and marketing) rather than by offering first-period customers truly better deals, or if, for example, risk-aversion and liquidity concerns limit the extent to which firms charge low introductory-period prices to the consumers whom they will exploit later, then consumers are made worse off by switching costs, even if competition ensures that firms are no better off.

In our simple model firms make zero profits with or without switching costs. But switching costs and the higher ex-post prices and lower ex-ante prices that they create can either raise or lower oligopolists' profits. The reason is that, in cutting its first-period price, each firm sets its *marginal* first-period profit sacrifice equal to its marginal second-period gain, so the *total* first-period profit given up can be greater or less than the total second-period gain [see, especially, Klemperer (1987a, 1987b)]. However, the arguments we will review in Section 2.4 (which also apply to two-period models) suggest firms typically gain from switching costs.[26]

Finally note that while we (and the literature) primarily discuss firms exploiting locked-in consumers with high prices, consumers can equally be exploited with low qualities. And if it is hard to contract on future quality, contracting on price does not easily resolve the inefficiencies discussed above.[27]

2.4. *Firms who cannot discriminate between cohorts of consumers*

In our first bargains-then-ripoffs model, we assumed that there was just one customer. It is easy to see that the basic lessons extend to the case where there are many customers but firms can charge different prices to "old" and "new" consumers, perhaps because

[24] Thus discussions of aftermarket power point out the possibility of sub-optimal tradeoffs between aftermarket maintenance services, self-supplied repair, and replacement of machines. See Borenstein, MacKie-Mason and Netz (2000), for instance.

[25] This is a particular problem if the introductory price would have to be negative to fully dissipate the ex-post rents. There may also be limits on firms' ability to price discriminate in favor of new customers without, for example, antagonizing their "regular" customers. See Section 2.4 for the case in which price-discrimination is infeasible.

[26] See, especially, Klemperer (1987b). Ellison (2005) argues that firms gain from switching costs for a natural type of demand structure.

[27] Farrell and Shapiro (1989) show that price commitments may actually be worse than pointless. See footnote 78.

"old" consumers are buying "follow on" goods such as spare parts. But when old consumers buy the same good as new consumers, it can be difficult for firms to distinguish between them. We now consider this case when a new generation of consumers arrives in the market in each of many periods.

2.4.1. Free-entry model

Even if firms cannot distinguish between cohorts of consumers, we may get the same pricing pattern if firms specialize sufficiently. In particular, in a simple model with free entry of identical firms and constant returns to scale, in each period some firm(s) will specialize in selling to new consumers while any firm with any old locked-in customers will sell only to those old customers.

If consumers have constant probability ϕ of surviving into each subsequent period, new-entrant firms with constant marginal costs c and discount factor δ offer price $c-\phi\delta s$ and sell to any new consumers, while established firms charge s more, i.e., charge $c + (1 - \phi\delta)s$ in every period.[28] That is, established firms charge the highest price such that no "old" consumers want to switch, and new entrants' expected discounted profits are zero. Thus the price paths consumers face are exactly as if firms could perfectly discriminate between them. In either case one can think of every (new and old) consumer as getting a "discount" of $\phi\delta s$ in each period reflecting the present value of the extent to which he can be exploited in the future, given his option of paying s to switch to an entrant; simultaneously, every "old" consumer is indeed exploited by s in every period. The outcome is socially efficient.

2.4.2. Do oligopolists hold simultaneous sales?, or staggered sales?, or no sales?

Just as in the free-entry model, if there is a small number of firms who face no threat of entry and who cannot distinguish between cohorts of consumers, it is possible that in every period one firm might hold a "sale", setting a low price to attract new consumers, while the other(s) set a higher price to exploit their old consumers. Farrell and Shapiro (1988) explore such an equilibrium in a model that has just one new and one old consumer in each period. Since this assumption implies that in any period one firm has no customer base while the other already has half the market "locked-in", it is not surprising that this model predicts asynchronous sales. However, Padilla's (1995) many-customer model yields somewhat similar results: firms mix across prices but a firm with more locked-in customers has more incentive to charge a high price to exploit them,

[28] See Klemperer (1983). This assumes all consumers have reservation prices exceeding $c + (1 - \phi\delta)s$ for a single unit in each period, and that all consumers survive into the next period with the same probability, ϕ, so a consumer's value is independent of his age. If consumers live for exactly two periods the price paths in general depend on whether firms can directly distinguish between old and new consumers (as in the previous subsection) or cannot do this (as in this section).

and so sets high prices with greater probabilities than its rival.[29] These papers illustrate how switching costs can segment an otherwise undifferentiated products market as firms focus on their established customers and do not compete aggressively for their rivals' buyers, letting oligopolists extract positive profits.

More generally it is unclear whether oligopolists will hold sales simultaneously or will stagger them. On the one hand, it might make most sense to forgo short run profits to go after new customers when your rivals are not doing so. On the other hand, if switching costs are learning costs, then staggered sales cause switching and create a pool of highly mobile consumers who have no further switching costs, intensifying future competition (see Section 2.5). Klemperer (1983, 1989) and the extension of the latter model in Elzinga and Mills (1999) all have simultaneous sales.[30,31]

Another possibility is that rather than holding occasional sales, each oligopolist in every period sets a single intermediate price that trades off its incentive to attract new consumers and its incentive to exploit its old customers. In a steady state, each firm's price will be the same in every period. Such an equilibrium could break down in several ways: if the flow of new consumers is too large, a firm would deviate by cutting price significantly to specialize in new consumers. If some consumers' switching costs and reservation prices are too large, a firm would deviate by raising price significantly to exploit old customers while giving up on new ones. And if firms' products are undifferentiated except by switching costs, a firm might deviate to undercut the other slightly and win all the new consumers.[32] But when none of these breakdowns occurs, there

[29] Farrell and Shapiro assume firms set price sequentially in each period, but Padilla assumes firms set prices simultaneously. See also Anderson, Kumar and Rajiv (2004).

[30] Elzinga and Mills' model fits with observed behavior in the cigarette market. See also Elzinga and Mills (1998).

[31] In a single-period model in which all consumers have the same switching cost, s, and many customers are already attached to firms before competition starts, the incentive to either undercut a rival's price by s or to overcut the rival's price by just less than s generally eliminates the possibility of pure-strategy equilibria if s is not too large: numerous papers [Baye et al. (1992), Padilla (1992), Deneckere et al. (1992), Fisher and Wilson (1995), Green and Scotchmer (1986), Rosenthal (1980), Shilony (1977), Varian (1980)], analyse single-period models of switching costs (or models that can be interpreted in this way) that yield mixed strategy equilibria, and Padilla (1995) finds mixed-strategy equilibria in a multi-period model. However, adding more real-world features to some of these models yields either asymmetric pure-strategy equilibria or symmetric pure-strategy Bayesian–Nash equilibria (if information is incomplete) rather than mixed-strategy equilibria.

Asymmetric pure-strategy equilibrium can be interpreted as asynchronous sales. Like Farrell and Shapiro (1988), Deneckere et al. find that if firms can choose when to set their prices, the firm with fewer locked-in customers sets price second and holds a "sale".

Symmetric Bayesian equilibria correspond to "tradeoff pricing" of the kind discussed in the next paragraph of the text. Bulow and Klemperer (1998, Appendix B) give an example of this by incorporating incomplete information about firms' costs into a one-period model with switching costs that would otherwise yield mixed-strategy equilibria.

Gabrielsen and Vagstad (2003, 2004) analyse when a pure-strategy equilibrium that looks like monopoly pricing exists in a single-period duopoly with heterogeneous switching costs.

[32] However, if consumers have rational expectations about future prices, a small price cut may win only a fraction of new consumers; see Section 2.4.5 below.

may be a stationary "no-sales" equilibrium: much of the literature examines such equilibria.[33]

Beggs and Klemperer (1992) explore a no-sales equilibrium in which in period t, firm i sets price

$$p_t^i = c^i + \alpha + \beta\sigma_{t-1}^i + \gamma(c^j - c^i), \quad (1)$$

where c^i is i's cost, σ_{t-1}^i is i's previous-period market share (i.e., the fraction of consumers i sold to in the previous period) and α, β, and γ are positive constants. These constants depend on four parameters: the discount factor, the market growth rate, the rate at which individual consumers leave the market, and the extent to which the firms' products are functionally differentiated; when firms are symmetric, the steady-state equilibrium price increases in the last of these four variables and decreases in the other three.[34]

2.4.3. *Oligopoly dynamics*

We have seen that sometimes a lean and hungry firm with few locked-in customers holds a sale while its rivals with larger customer bases do not. Similarly, in no-sale models in which all firms sell to both old and new consumers, a firm with more old locked-in customers has a greater incentive to exploit them, so will usually price higher and win fewer new unattached consumers. In both cases, the result is stable industry dynamics as more aggressive smaller firms catch up with larger ones.

In the equilibrium of Beggs and Klemperer's (1992) no-sale duopoly model, described in (1) above, for example, $\beta > 0$, so larger firms charge higher prices, yielding stable dynamics. Indeed, it can be shown that $\sigma_t^i = \sigma^i + (\mu)^t(\sigma_0^i - \sigma^i)$ in which σ^i is firm i's steady-state market share and $0 < \mu << \frac{1}{2}$, so the duopoly converges rapidly and monotonically back to a stable steady state after any shock. Chen and Rosenthal (1996) likewise demonstrate a tendency for market shares to return to a given value, while in Taylor (2003) any initial asymmetries in market shares between otherwise symmetric firms may persist to some extent but are dampened over time.

However, the opposite is possible. If larger firms have lower marginal costs, and especially if economies of scale make it possible to drive smaller firms completely out of the market, then a larger firm may charge a lower price than its smaller rivals. In this case, any small advantage one firm obtains can be magnified and the positive-feedback dynamics can result in complete dominance by that firm. This is just as is typical with

[33] Even if there are occasional "sales", firms will balance exploiting the old with attracting the new in "ordinary" periods, and this literature is relevant to these ordinary periods.
In the case of monopoly, both stationary " no-sales" models [see Holmes (1990)] and models in which periodic sales arise in equilibrium [see Gallini and Karp (1989)] can be constructed.

[34] Klemperer (1995) discusses this model further: variants are in Chow (1995) and To (1995). Other important "no-sales" models are von Weizsäcker (1984) and Wernerfelt (1991); Phelps and Winter's (1970) and Sutton's (1980) models of search costs, and Radner's (2003) model of "viscous demand", are related.

network effects (see Section 3.5.3) – indeed, switching costs create positive network effects in this case, because it is more attractive to buy from a firm that other consumers buy from [Beggs (1989)].

So switching-costs markets *can* "tip" like network-effects markets. But the simple models suggest a presumption that markets with switching costs are stable, with larger firms acting as less-aggressive "fat cats".[35]

2.4.4. The level of profits

A central question in policy and in the literature is whether switching costs raise or lower oligopoly profits. In the simple two-period model of Section 2.3.1 they do neither, but many non-theorist commentators, notably Porter (1980, 1985), believe switching costs raise profits, and both a small body of empirical evidence including Stango (2002), Park (2005), Viard (in press) and Shi et al. (2006), and also the laboratory evidence of Cason and Friedman (2002) support this view.[36] As we discuss next, most models that are richer than the simple model tend to confirm this popular idea that switching costs raise profits.

If duopolists who cannot discriminate between old and new buyers hold asynchronous sales, they can earn positive profits in price competition even if their products are undifferentiated except by switching costs. The switching costs segment the market, and when one firm (generally the firm with the larger customer base) charges a high price to exploit its locked-in customers, the other firm then has market power even over new consumers because it can operate under the price umbrella of its fat-cat rival [see Farrell and Shapiro (1988) and Padilla (1995)]. So in these models, a duopolist earns positive profits even in a period in which it starts with no locked-in customers. (However, if there were two identical new firms entering in every period, they would not generally earn any profits.)

Furthermore, if switching costs are heterogeneous, a similar effect means even duopolists who can (and do) discriminate between old and new customers can earn positive profits in price competition with products that are undifferentiated except by switching costs – see our discussion of Chen (1997) and Taylor (2003) in Section 2.5.1, below.

In addition, the symmetric stationary price of a "no-sales" equilibrium of the kind described in Section 2.4.3 is also usually higher than if there were no switching costs. There are two reasons:

[35] In the terminology introduced by Fudenberg and Tirole (1984). In the terminology introduced by Bulow, Geanakoplos and Klemperer (1985a, 1985b), there is strategic complementarity between a firm's current price and its competitors' future prices. See also Farrell (1986).

[36] However, Dube et al. (2006) have very recently calibrated a model with data from the orange juice and margarine markets, where consumers exhibit inertia in their brand choices, and come to the opposite conclusion.

First, the "fat cat" effect applies here too, though in the indirect way discussed in Section 2.4.3; firms price less aggressively because they recognize that if they win fewer customers today, their rivals will be bigger and (in simple models with switching costs) less aggressive tomorrow.

Second, when consumers face switching costs, they care about expected future prices as well as current prices. Depending on how expectations of future prices react to current prices, this may make new customers (not yet locked into any firm), react either more or less elastically to price differences. However, as we now discuss, the presumption is that it makes their response less elastic than absent switching costs, thus raising firms' prices and profits.

2.4.5. *The effect of consumers' expectations on prices*

How consumers' expectations about future prices depend on current prices critically affects competition and the price level – just as in other parts of the lock-in literature.[37] Consumers' expectations about their own future tastes also matter in a market with real (functional) product differentiation; we assume consumers expect some positive correlation between their current and future tastes.

In a market without switching costs, a consumer compares differences between products' prices with differences between how well they match his current tastes. But with switching costs, he recognizes that whichever product he buys today he will, very likely buy again tomorrow. So switching costs make him more willing to change brands in response to a price cut if, roughly speaking, he expects that price cut to be more permanent than his tastes; they will lower his willingness to change in response to a price cut if he expects the price cut to be less permanent than his tastes.

(i) *Consumers who assume any price cut below their expected price will be maintained in the future*

If consumers expect a firm that cuts price today to maintain that price cut forever then, relative to the case of no switching costs, they are more influenced by such a price cut than by their current (impermanent) product preferences.[38] (In the limit with infinite switching costs, a consumer's product choice is forever, so unless his preferences are also permanent, products are in effect less differentiated.) So switching costs then *lower*

[37] Consumers' expectations about how future prices depend on costs are, of course, also important in determining whether firms have the correct incentives to invest in future cost reduction. This issue does not seem to have been directly addressed by the switching-costs literature, but we discuss in Section 3.7 how a network-effects model can be reinterpreted to address it. See also footnote 21.

[38] A related model with these expectations is Borenstein, MacKie-Mason and Netz (2000). In their model, consumers buy a differentiated durable good ("equipment") from one of two firms and must then buy an aftermarket product ("service") in the next period from the same firm. High service prices generate profits from locked-in customers, but deter new customers from buying equipment because they expect high service prices in the following period. So the stationary equilibrium service price lies between marginal cost and the monopoly price, even if firms' products are undifferentiated except by switching costs.

equilibrium prices; see von Weizsäcker's (1984) model in which each firm chooses a single once-and-for-all price (and quality) to which it is (by assumption) committed forever, but in which consumers are uncertain about their future tastes.[39]

We will see below (see Section 3.7) that a similar effect arises when there are strong proprietary network effects and differentiated products. Then, consumers' desire to be compatible with others overwhelms their differences in tastes and drives firms whose networks are incompatible towards undifferentiated Bertrand competition. Here, with switching costs, each consumer's desire to be compatible with his future self (who in expectation has tastes closer to the average) likewise reduces effective differentiation and drives the firms towards undifferentiated Bertrand competition.

(ii) *Consumers whose expectations about future prices are unaffected by current prices*
If consumers expect that a firm that unexpectedly cuts price this period will return to setting the expected price next period, then price changes are less permanent than, and so influence consumers less than, taste differences. So switching costs raise price levels. Each consumer is making a product choice that his future selves must live with, and his future selves' preferences (while possibly different from his own) are likely to be closer to his currently-preferred product than to other products. Consumers are therefore less attracted by a current price cut than absent switching costs.

(iii) *Consumers with rational expectations*
If consumers have fully rational expectations they will recognize that a lower price today generally presages a higher price tomorrow. As we discussed above, a firm that wins more new consumers today will be a "fatter cat" with relatively greater incentive to price high tomorrow; and we expect that this will typically be the main effect, although other effects are possible.[40] So consumers with rational expectations will be even less sensitive than in (ii) to price cutting, and switching costs thus raise prices.[41]

[39] The effect we discussed in the previous Section 2.4.4 – that firms moderate price competition in order to fatten and so soften their opponents – is also eliminated by von Weizsäcker's commitment assumption.

[40] See, e.g., Beggs and Klemperer (1992), Klemperer (1987a, 1987b, 1987c), Padilla (1992, 1995). As discussed above, the fat cat effect can be reversed if, e.g., economics of scale or network effects are strong enough. [Doganoglu and Grzybowski (2004) show how appending network benefits to Klemperer's (1987b) model lowers prices.] Another caveat is that with incomplete information about firms' costs a lower price might signal lower costs, so consumers might rationally expect a lower price today to presage a lower price tomorrow. But if there is incomplete information about costs, firms might price high in order to signal high costs and thus soften future competition. [A search-costs model that is suggestive about how firm-specific cost shocks might affect pricing in a switching-costs model is Fishman and Rob (1995).] Furthermore, if firms differ in the extent that they can or wish to exploit locked-in customers, consumers will expect that a lower price today means a higher price tomorrow, which will also be a force for higher prices.

[41] Holmes (1990) analyses price-setting by a monopolist facing overlapping generations of consumers who must sink set-up costs before using the monopolist's good. He finds that if consumers have rational expectations, then prices are higher than those that would prevail if the firm could commit to future prices. The reason is similar: rational consumers are insensitive to price cuts because they understand that a low price today will encourage other consumers to sink more costs which in turn results in higher future prices.

In summary, while there is no unambiguous conclusion, under either economists' standard rational-expectations assumption [(iii)], or a more myopic assumption [(ii)], switching costs raise prices overall. Only if consumers believe unanticipated price changes are more permanent than their product preferences do switching costs lower prices. For these reasons, Beggs and Klemperer (1992) argue that switching costs tend to raise prices when new and old customers are charged a common price. There is therefore also a more general presumption that switching costs usually raise oligopolists' total profits.

2.4.6. *Collusive behavior*

Like most of the literature, the discussion above assumes non-cooperative behavior by firms, without strategic threats of punishment if others compete too hard.[42]

One should also ask whether switching costs hinder or facilitate collusion, in which high prices are supported by firms punishing any other firm thought to have deviated. While many people's intuition is that switching costs support collusion, this remains unclear as a theoretical matter:

Switching costs make deviating from a collusive agreement less profitable in the short run, because it is harder to quickly "steal" another firm's customers. But, for the same reason, switching costs make it more costly to punish a deviating firm. So it is not obvious whether collusion is easier or harder on balance, and in Padilla's (1995) and Anderson et al.'s (2004) models, which incorporate both these effects, switching costs actually make collusion more difficult.

Switching costs may also make it easier for firms to monitor collusion, because the large price changes necessary to win away a rival's locked-in customers may be easy to observe. And switching costs may additionally facilitate tacit collusion by providing "focal points" for market division, breaking a market into well-defined submarkets of customers who have bought from different firms. However, while these arguments are discussed in Stigler (1964) and Klemperer (1987a), they have not yet been well explored in the literature, and do not seem easy to formalize satisfactorily. Furthermore, if collusion is only easier after most customers are already locked-in, this is likely to induce fiercer competition prior to lock-in, as in the simple bargain-then-ripoff model.

2.5. *Consumers who use multiple suppliers*

In the models above, as in most leading models of switching costs, switching costs affect prices but there is no switching in equilibrium. In reality a consumer may actually switch, and use different suppliers in different periods, either because firms' products

[42] For example, Beggs and Klemperer assume each firm's price depends only on its current market share and not otherwise on history, and rule out the kind of strategies described by, for example, Abreu (1988) or Green and Porter (1984) that support collusive outcomes in contexts without switching costs.

are differentiated and his tastes change, or because firms' relative prices to him change over time, as they will, in particular, when each firm charges new customers less than existing customers.

Furthermore, although we assumed above that each consumer buys one unit from one firm in each period, a consumer who values variety may buy multiple products even in a single period. Consumers may therefore use multiple suppliers in a period or, as we will discuss, each firm may produce a range of products.

2.5.1. Paying consumers to switch

Most of the switching costs literature assumes a firm offers the same price to all consumers in any given period. However, as the bargains-then-rip-offs theme stresses, firms would often like to price discriminate between their old locked-in customers, unattached (new) customers, and customers locked-in to a rival. And firms often do pay consumers to switch to them from rivals. For example, long-distance phone carriers make one-time payments to customers switching from a rival; credit card issuers offer lower interest rates for balance transfers from another provider; and economics departments pay higher salaries to faculty members moving from other departments. How does the possibility of such discrimination affect pricing?

Chen (1997) analyses a two-period, two-firm, model in which each firm can charge one price to its old customers and another to other consumers in the same period. In effect, second-priced consumers are in two separate markets according to which firm they bought from in the first period. Each of these "markets" is like the second period of our core (Section 2.3.1) two-period model. In that model all consumers had the same switching costs, s, so the period-2 incumbent charged a price just low enough to forestall actual switching.[43] But in Chen's model, old consumers have heterogeneous switching costs (and firms cannot discriminate between them, perhaps because they cannot observe individual consumers' switching costs), so firms charge higher prices than their rivals to their old consumers but consumers with low switching costs switch firms.

In Chen's model both firms' second-period profits and their total discounted profits are lower than if they could not discriminate between old and new customers. However, consumers might also be worse off overall, because of the costs of actually switching.

[43] Likewise, the simple model of Section 2.4.1 shows that if firms can price discriminate, the price will be $c + (1 - \phi\delta)s$ to all old consumers, and will be s lower to new consumers, but no consumers will ever actually switch. Similarly, Nilssen (1992) observes that if each firm can charge a different price to each consumer, there will be no actual switching. Nilssen showed that transactional switching costs give consumers less incentives to switch than do learning switching costs. Thus transactional costs lead to lower prices for new consumers, higher prices for loyal consumers, and so also a bigger within-period quantity distortion if there is downward-sloping demand in each period. [Gabrielsen and Vagstad (2003, 2004) note that two-part tariffs can in theory avoid this distortion.]

Firms' total discounted profits are nevertheless higher than absent switching costs because (as in Section 2.4.4) the switching costs segment the market, so firms have some market power even over customers who are new to them in the second period.[44,45]

In Chen's two-firm model, consumers who leave their current supplier have only one firm to switch to, so this other firm can make positive profits even on new customers, and the duopolists earn positive profits in equilibrium. But with three or more firms, there are always at least two firms vying for any consumer willing to leave his current supplier and, if products are undifferentiated, these firms will bid away their expected lifetime profits from serving those consumers in their competition to attract them. So, as Taylor (2003) shows, with three or more firms, firms earn positive rents only on their current customers, and these rents are competed away ex ante, as in our core model.

These models of "paying customers to switch" suggest repeat buyers pay higher rather than lower prices. While this is often observed, we also often observe the opposite pattern in which customers are rewarded for loyalty. Taylor's model provides one possible explanation. He shows that if switching costs are transactional, consumers may move between suppliers to signal that they have low switching costs and so improve their terms of trade. Because this switching is socially costly, equilibrium contracts may discourage it through "loyal customer" pricing policies that give better terms to loyal customers than to those who patronized other firms in the past. But Taylor nevertheless finds that firms charge the lowest prices to new customers.

Shaffer and Zhang (2000) study a single-period model that is similar to the second period of Chen's model but in which the distributions of switching costs from the two firms are different. If firm A's customers have lower and more uniform switching costs than firm B's, then A's loyal-customer demand is more elastic than its new-customer demand, so it may charge a lower price to its loyal customers than to customers switching from B. But this rationale is asymmetric, and this model never results in both firms charging lower prices to loyal customers than to switching customers.[46]

[44] Because in this model a firm's old and new customers are effectively in unconnected markets, both of the firm's prices are independent of its previous-period market share, by contrast with the no-price-discrimination models discussed above. This feature allows Taylor (2003) to extend Chen's model to many periods and many firms, but Arbatskaya (2000) shows that the "independence" result does not persist if there is functional product differentiation as well as switching costs.

[45] Gehrig and Stenbacka (2004a) develop a model in which the last two periods are similar to Chen's model, and in which profits are increasing in the size of switching costs; in Gehrig and Stenbacka's *three*-period model firms therefore (non-cooperatively) make product choices that maximize the switching costs between them. See also Gehrig and Stenbacka (2004b). In another related model, Gehrig and Stenbacka (2005) find that when goods are vertically differentiated and consumers have switching costs, two firms choose to produce the highest quality, by contrast with most models of vertical product differentiation in which just one firm produces the top quality.

[46] Lee (1997) also studies a one-period switching-cost model similar to the second period of Chen's model. Fudenberg and Tirole (2000) explore a two-period model with some similar features to Chen's, in which firms price discriminate between consumers based on their past demands, but with real functional product differentiation between firms and without real (socially costly) switching costs; they too find that loyal customers

There are also models of contractual switching costs that result in lower effective prices to repeat customers than to new customers, and contracts that favor repeat customers arise endogenously in some of these models (see Section 2.8.3). But the literature has found it hard to explain how real switching costs might generate discrimination in favor of old customers.

2.5.2. *Is there too much switching?*

Consumers decide whether or when to switch, and pay the switching costs. So there will generally be the wrong amount of switching if (i) firms' relative prices to a consumer fail to reflect their relative marginal costs,[47] or (ii) consumers switch (or not) in order to affect firms' future prices, or (iii) consumers' switching costs are not real social costs. Most simple models recognize no efficiency role for switching, so any switching in such models is inefficient.

(i) *Price differences do not reflect cost differences*
The bargains-then-ripoffs theme predicts that, when they can do so, firms charge lower prices to their new consumers. As a result, a given consumer will face different prices from different firms that do not reflect any cost differences between firms. This is true even when all firms symmetrically charge high prices to old customers and lower prices to new customers. Although some simple models such as our core (Section 2.3.1) model predict no switching, in general inefficient switching results.[48]

When firms do not price discriminate between new and old consumers, the same result applies for a slightly different reason. As we saw in Section 2.4, a firm with a larger customer base will then charge a larger markup over its marginal cost. So if consumers have differing switching costs, such a firm's price exploits its old high switching-cost customers and induces its low switching-cost consumers to switch to a smaller firm or entrant. Thus Gabszewicz, Pepall and Thisse (1992), Farrell and Shapiro (1988), and Wang and Wen (1998) also predict excessive switching to smaller firms and entrants.

are charged higher prices than switchers. However, they also show that firms may wish to offer long-term contracts that offer consumers a high period-one price in return for a guaranteed low period-two price (see Section 2.8.3). [Villas-Boas (1999) analyses a many-period model similar to Fudenberg and Tirole's but does not consider long-term contracts.] Acquisti and Varian (2005) present a related two-period monopoly model which can be interpreted as being of consumers with switching costs.

[47] Consumers must also have rational expectations about future price differences, etc.

[48] Even if all consumers have the same switching cost, if an entrant's production cost plus that switching cost exceeds the incumbent's production cost, then in a *quantity*-competition model the entrant will sell to some of them, thus inducing inefficient switching [Klemperer (1988)]. This result is just the standard oligopoly result that a higher-cost firm wins a socially excessive market share (though at a smaller markup).
A caveat is that these excessive-switching results take the number of firms as given. If the switching costs mean there is too little entry from the social viewpoint (see Section 2.7.2) then there may for this reason be too little switching.

(ii) *Consumers switch in order to affect prices*
If a consumer is a large fraction of the market, or if firms can discriminate between consumers (so each consumer is, in effect, a separate market), a consumer may switch to affect future prices.

If switching costs are learning costs, switching strengthens a consumer's outside option, so he may switch in order to strengthen his bargaining position – by switching he effectively creates a second source of supply and thereby increases the competition to supply him in the future [Lewis and Yildirim (2005)]. And even if switching costs are transactional (and firms are imperfectly informed about their magnitude), we saw in Section 2.5.1 that consumers may switch to signal that their switching costs are low and so improve their terms of trade.

Strategic consumers may also commit to ignore switching costs (or acting as if their switching costs were lower than they truly are) in their future purchase decisions, in order to force the incumbent supplier to price more competitively [Cabral and Greenstein (1990)][49]; this strategy will generally increase the amount of switching.

In all these cases, socially costly switching in order to affect prices is inefficient to the extent that it merely shifts rents from firms to the customer who switches. On the other hand, if firms cannot discriminate between consumers, such switching usually lowers prices and so improves the efficiency of other consumers' trades with sellers, so there may then be less switching than is socially desirable.

(iii) *Switching costs are not real social costs*
If switching costs are contractual, and not social costs, consumers will ceteris paribus switch less than is efficient. But if real (social) switching costs exist, then contractual switching costs may prevent socially inefficient switches of the types discussed above.[50]

2.5.3. *Multiproduct firms*

A consumer who buys several products in a single period may incur additional "shopping costs" for each additional supplier used. These shopping costs may be the same as the switching costs incurred by consumers who change suppliers between periods. However, the dynamic and commitment issues that switching-cost models usually emphasize no longer arise. In particular, firms and consumers can contract on all prices, so the analogy with economies of scope in production is particularly strong.[51] Thus

[49] The literature has largely assumed that consumers have no commitment power (see Section 2.8 for exceptions).

[50] In Fudenberg and Tirole (2000) firms endogenously offer long term contracts that create contractual switching costs that reduce inefficient switching to less preferred products and increase social welfare, conditional on firms being permitted to price discriminate between old and new customers.

[51] But some superficially single-period contexts are better understood as dynamic. For instance, supermarkets advertise just a few "loss leaders"; unadvertised prices are chosen to be attractive once the consumer is in the shop ("locked in") but might not have drawn him in. (See Section 2.1.)

shopping costs provide an efficiency reason for multiproduct firms just as economies of scope in production do.[52]

The analogy is not perfect, because switching costs and shopping costs are based on specific consumer–firm matches, whereas the production-side economies of scope emphasized by Panzar and Willig (1981) and others depend only on a firm's total sales of each product and not on whether the same consumers buy the firm's different products or whether some consumers use multiple suppliers.[53]

However, the analogy is particularly good if firms' product lines are sufficiently broad that most consumers use just one supplier. For example, Klemperer and Padilla (1997) demonstrate that selling an additional product can provide strategic benefits for a firm in the markets for its current products if consumers have shopping costs of using additional suppliers (because selling an extra variety can attract demand away from rival suppliers for this firm's existing varieties). This parallels Bulow et al.'s (1985a) demonstration of the same result if consumers' shopping costs are replaced by production-side economies of scope (because selling an additional variety lowers the firm's marginal costs of its existing products). In both cases each firm, and therefore the market, may therefore provide too many different products. More obviously, mergers can be explained either by consumer switching costs [Klemperer and Padilla (1997)] or by production economies of scope.

Some results about *single*-product competition over *many* periods with switching costs carry over to *multi*-product competition in a *single* period with shopping costs. For example, we suggested in Section 2.4.2 that when switching costs are learning costs, oligopolists might benefit by synchronizing their sales to minimize switching and so reduce the pool of highly price-sensitive (no-switching cost) customers. Likewise multiproduct firms competing in a single period may have a joint incentive to minimize the number of consumers who buy from more than one firm. Indeed Klemperer (1992, 1995, ex. 4) shows that firms may inefficiently offer similar products to each other, or similar product lines to each other, for this reason. Taken together with the previous paragraph's result, this suggests that each firm may produce too many products, but that there may nevertheless be too little variety produced by the industry as a whole.

An important set of shopping-cost models are the "mix-and-match" models pioneered by Matutes and Regibeau (1988), Economides (1989) and Einhorn (1992). Most of this literature takes each firm's product-line as given, and asks whether firms prefer to be compatible (no shopping costs) or incompatible (effectively infinite shopping costs); see Sections 2.7.3 and 2.8.

[52] Examples include supermarkets, shopping malls, hospitals and airlines: Dranove and White (1996) models hospitals as multi-product providers with switching costs between providers. Several studies document that travelers strongly prefer to use a single airline for a multi-segment trip, and the importance of these demand-side complementarities in air travel [e.g. Carlton, Landes and Posner (1980)].

[53] As we noted in Section 2.1, if firms can discriminate between consumers, then each consumer becomes an independent market which, in the presence of switching costs, is closely analogous to a market with production economies of scope.

Similarly, when firms "bundle" products [see, e.g., Whinston (1990), Matutes and Regibeau (1992), Nalebuff (2000, 2004)] they are creating contractual shopping costs between their products; we discuss bundling briefly in Sections 2.7.3 and 2.8.[54]

"Shopping costs" models are distinguished from other "switching costs" models in that consumers can observe and contract on all prices at the same time in the "shopping costs" models. We will henceforth use the term switching costs to cover all these costs, but continue to focus mainly on dynamic switching costs.

2.6. *Battles for market share*

2.6.1. *The value of market share*

We have seen that with switching costs (or indeed proprietary network effects – see Section 3.7), a firm's current customer base is an important determinant of its future profits.

We can therefore write a firm's current-period value function (i.e., total discounted future profits), V_t, as the sum of its current profits, π_t, and its discounted next-period value function $\delta V_{t+1}(\sigma_t)$, in which δ is the discount factor and the next-period value function, $V_{t+1}(\cdot)$, is a function of the size of its current-period customer base, σ_t.

$$V_t = \pi_t + \delta V_{t+1}(\sigma_t). \tag{2}$$

For example, in our core model with free entry, $V_{t+1} = s\sigma_t$, and Biglaiser, Crémer and Dobos (2003) have explored various cases in which this simple formula holds. More generally, however, (2) is a simplification. In general, the firm's future profits depend on its customers' types and their full histories, how market share is distributed among competing firms, how many consumers in the market make no purchase, etc. However, V_{t+1} depends only on current-period market share in models such as Klemperer (1987b, 1995), Farrell and Shapiro (1988), Beggs and Klemperer (1992), Padilla (1992, 1995), and Chen and Rosenthal (1996), which all model just two firms and a fixed set of consumers whose reservation prices are high enough that they always purchase. (For example, Equation (1) shows for Beggs and Klemperer's model how prices, and therefore also quantities, and hence value functions, in a period depend on the firm's previous-period market share.) So σ_t is often interpreted as "market share", and this explains firms' very strong concern with market shares in markets with switching costs and/or (we shall see) network effects.[55]

[54] Varian's (1989) and Stole's (2007) surveys describe models of quantity discounts and bundling in Volume 1 and the current volume of this Series, respectively.

[55] Because switching costs make current market share such an important determinant of a manufacturer's future profits, Valletti (2000) suggests they may provide a motive for vertical integration with retailers to ensure sufficient investment in a base of repeat subscribers.

2.6.2. Penetration pricing

From (2), the firm's first-order condition for the optimal choice of a period-t price is

$$0 = \frac{\partial V_t}{\partial p_t} = \frac{\partial \pi_t}{\partial p_t} + \delta \frac{\partial V_{t+1}}{\partial \sigma_t} \frac{\partial \sigma_t}{\partial p_t}. \tag{3}$$

Provided that the firm's value function is increasing in its market share,[56] therefore, the firm charges a lower price or sets a higher quantity[57] than would maximize short-run profits, in order to raise its customer base and hence its future profits. That is, $\partial \pi_t / \partial p_t > 0$ (since we assume $\partial \sigma_t / \partial p_t < 0$).

In the early stages of a market, therefore, when few consumers are locked in, so even short-run profit-maximizing prices are not high relative to costs, Equation (3) implies low penetration pricing, just as in the core two-period model.[58,59] Equation (3) also suggests that the larger the value of the future market, V_{t+1}, the deeper the penetration pricing will be. For example, a more rapidly growing market will have lower prices.[60]

2.6.3. Harvesting vs investing: macroeconomic and international trade applications

As Equations (2) and (3) illustrate, the firm must balance the incentive to charge high prices to "harvest" greater current profits ((3) showed π_t is increasing in p_t) against the incentive for low prices that "invest" in market share and hence increase future profits (V_{t+1} is increasing in σ_t, which is decreasing in p_t).

Anything that increases the marginal value of market share will make the firm lower price further to invest more in market share. Thus, for example, a lower δ, that is,

[56] This case, $\partial V_{t+1}/\partial \sigma_t > 0$, seems the usual one, although in principle, stealing customers from rival(s) may make the rival(s) so much more aggressive that the firm is worse off. See Banerjee and Summers (1987), Klemperer (1987c).
In Beggs and Klemperer (1992), V_{t+1} is quadratic in σ_t. [The fact that the sum of the duopolists' value functions is therefore maximized at the boundaries is consistent with stable dynamics because lowering current price is less costly in current profits for the firm with the smaller market share. See Budd et al. (1993).]

[57] We can perform a similar analysis with similar results for a quantity-setting firm. The analysis is also unaffected by whether each firm sets a single price to all consumers or whether, as in Section 2.5, each firm sets different prices to different groups of consumers in any period.

[58] It is unclear whether we should expect "penetration pricing" patterns from a monopolist, since $\partial V_{t+1}/\partial \sigma_t$ may be smaller in monopoly – where consumers have nowhere else to go – than in oligopoly, and (if goods are durable) durable-goods effects imply falling prices in monopoly absent switching-cost effects (Equation (3) only implies that early period prices are lower than in the absence of switching-costs, not that prices necessarily rise). Cabral et al. (1999) show it is hard to obtain penetration pricing in a network-effects monopoly model (see Section 3.6).

[59] Of course, as noted in Section 2.3.2, in a more general model the "penetration" might be through advertising or other marketing activities rather than just low prices.

[60] Strictly, (3) tells us prices are lower if $\partial V_{t+1}/\partial \sigma_t$ is larger, but this is often true for a more rapidly growing market. See, for example, Beggs and Klemperer (1992), Borenstein, MacKie-Mason and Netz (2000) and also Holmes' (1990) steady-state model of a monopolist selling a single product to overlapping generations of consumers who incur set-up costs before buying the product.

a higher real interest rate, reduces the present value of future market share (see (2)) so leads to higher current prices (see (3): lower δ implies lower $\partial \pi_t / \partial p_t$ implies higher p_t[61]).

Chevalier and Scharfstein (1996) develop this logic in a switching-cost model based on Klemperer (1995). They argue that liquidity-constrained firms perceive very high real interest rates and therefore set high prices, sacrificing future profits in order to raise cash in the short term. They provide evidence that during recessions (when financial constraints are most likely to matter) the most financially-constrained supermarket chains indeed raise their prices relative to other chains, and Campello and Fluck's (2004) subsequent empirical work shows that these effects are larger in industries where consumers face higher switching costs.[62]

Fitoussi and Phelps (1988) use a similar logic (emphasizing search costs rather than switching costs) to argue that high interest rates contributed to the high rates of inflation in Europe in the early 1980s.

Froot and Klemperer (1989) also apply the same logic to international trade in a model of competition for market share motivated by switching costs and network effects. A current appreciation of the domestic currency lowers a foreign firm's costs (expressed in domestic currency) and so tends to lower prices. However, if the appreciation is expected to be only temporary then the fact that the domestic currency will be worth less tomorrow is equivalent to an increase in the real interest rates which raises prices. So exchange-rate changes that are expected to be temporary may have very little impact on import prices. But if the currency is anticipated to appreciate in the future, both the "cost effect" and "interest-rate effect" are in the same direction – market share tomorrow is probably worth more if future costs are lower, and tomorrow's profits are worth more than today's profits, so for both reasons today is a good time to invest in market share rather than harvest current profits. So import prices may be very sensitive to anticipated exchange-rate changes. Froot and Klemperer (1989) and Sapir and Sekkat (1995) provide empirical support for these theories.[63]

2.7. Entry

Switching costs may have important effects on entry: with real, exogenous switching costs, small-scale entry to win new, unattached, consumers is often easy and indeed often too easy, but attracting even some of the old "locked-in" customers may not just be hard, but also be too hard from the social standpoint.

[61] See Klemperer (1995). We assume stable, symmetric, oligopoly and that the dominant effect of lowering δ is the direct effect.

[62] See also Campello (2003). Beggs and Klemperer (1989, Section 5.3) and Klemperer (1995) provide further discussion of how "booms" and "busts" affect the trade-offs embodied in Equation (3) and hence affect price–cost margins.

[63] For other applications of switching-costs theory to international trade, see Tivig (1996) who develops "J-curves" (since sales quantities respond only slowly to price changes if there are switching costs), Gottfries (2002), To (1994), and Hartigan (1995).

Furthermore, firms may also create unnecessary switching costs in order to discourage entry.

2.7.1. *Small-scale entry is (too) easy*

We saw in Section 2.4 that if firms cannot discriminate between old and new consumers, then the "fat cat" effect may make small scale entry very easy: incumbent firms' desire to extract profits from their old customers creates a price umbrella under which entrants can profitably win new unattached (or low switching cost) customers. And even after entry has occurred, the erstwhile incumbent(s) will continue to charge higher prices than the entrant, and lose market share to the entrant, so long as they remain "fatter" firms with more old consumers to exploit.

So if there are no economies of scale, even an entrant that is somewhat less efficient than the incumbent(s) can enter successfully at a small scale that attracts only unattached buyers.[64] [See Klemperer (1987c), Farrell and Shapiro (1988), Gabszewicz, Pepall and Thisse (1992), Wang and Wen (1998), etc.]

Of course, the flip-side of this is that the same switching costs that encourage new entry also encourage the new entrants to remain at a relatively small scale unless there are many unattached buyers.[65]

2.7.2. *Large scale entry is (too) hard*

While the fat-cat effect gives new entrants an advantage in competing for new customers, it is very hard for them to compete for customers who are already attached to an incumbent. There is also adverse selection: consumers who switch are likely to be less loyal, hence less valuable, ones.[66] So entry may be hard if small-scale entry is impractical, due perhaps to economies of scale, or to network effects. Furthermore, even

[64] This result depends on there being (sufficient) new customers in each period (which is a natural assumption). For an analogous result that entry was easy into just one product in a shopping-cost market, there would have to be sufficient buyers without shopping costs, or who wished to purchase just that product (this may be a less natural assumption). Failing that, "small scale" entry in a shopping cost market is not easy.
Our assumption of no discrimination between old and new consumers means the easy-entry result also does not apply to aftermarkets. Entry may be hard in this case if first-period prices cannot fall too low, and the incumbent has a reputational or similar advantage. For example, the UK Office of Fair Trading found in 2001 that new entry was very hard into the hospital segment of the market served by NAPP Pharmaceutical Holdings Ltd where prices were less than one-tenth of those in the "follow-on" community market.

[65] Good (2006) shows that, for this reason, switching costs may lead an incumbent firm to prefer to delay innovation and instead rely on new entrants to introduce new products which the incumbent can then imitate.

[66] Some work on the credit card market emphasizes this adverse-selection problem: creditworthy borrowers may have been granted high credit limits by their current card issuers so have higher switching costs. Furthermore, low-default risk customers may be less willing to switch (or even search) because they do not intend to borrow – but they often do borrow nevertheless [Ausubel (1991)]. Calem and Mester (1995) provide empirical evidence that this adverse selection is important, Ausubel provides evidence that the U.S. bank credit card issuing market earns positive economic profit and attributes this, at least in part, to switching costs or search costs, and Stango (2002) also argues that switching costs are an important influence on pricing.

new consumers may be wary of buying from a new supplier if they know that it can only survive at a large scale, since with switching costs consumers care about the future prospects of the firms they deal with.

Of course, this does not imply that there is *too* little large-scale entry. If switching costs are social costs, then large-scale entry may not be efficient even if the entrant's production costs are modestly lower than an incumbent's. That is, to some extent these obstacles to profitable large-scale entry reflect social costs of such entry.

However, this reflection is imperfect. If the entrant cannot discriminate between consumers, then large-scale entry requires charging all consumers a price equal to the incumbent's price less the marginal old buyer's switching cost. But socially the switching cost applies only to the old switching buyers, not to the new consumers, and only applies to switching buyers at the average level of their switching cost, not at the marginal switching cost. So efficient large-scale entry may be blocked.

Furthermore, entry can sometimes be strategically blockaded. In particular, an incumbent may "limit price", that is, cut price to lock in more customers and make entry unprofitable at the necessary scale, when entry at the same scale would have been profitable, and perhaps efficient, if the additional customers had not been "locked-up" prior to entry [see Klemperer (1987c)].[67]

Of course, entry can be too easy or too hard for more standard reasons. Entry can be too hard if it expands market output, and consumers rather than the entrant capture the surplus generated. And entry is too easy if its main effect is to shift profits from the incumbent to the entrant.[68] But these caveats apply whether or not there are switching costs; the arguments specific to switching costs suggest that entry that depends for its success on consumers switching is not just hard, but too hard.

2.7.3. *Single-product entry may be (too) hard*

If switching costs (or shopping costs) "tie" sales together so consumers prefer not to patronize more than one firm, and consumers wish to buy several products (see Section 2.5.3), then an entrant may be forced to offer a full range of products to attract new customers (let alone any old consumers). If offering a full range is impractical, entry can effectively be foreclosed. Thus in Whinston (1990), Nalebuff (2004), and Klemperer

[67] The incumbent's advantage is reduced if it does not know the entrant's costs, or quality, or even the probability or timing of entry, in advance of the entry. Gerlach (2004) explores the entrant's choice between pre-announcing its product (so that more consumers wait to buy its product) and maintaining secrecy so that the incumbent cannot limit price in response to the information.

[68] Klemperer (1988) illustrates the latter case, showing that new entry into a mature market with switching costs can sometimes be socially undesirable. The point is that just as entry of a firm whose costs exceed the incumbent's is often inefficient in a standard Cournot model without switching costs [Bulow et al., 1985a, Section VI E, Mankiw and Whinston (1986)] so entry of a firm whose production cost *plus* consumers' switching cost exceeds the incumbent's production cost is often inefficient in a quantity-setting model with switching costs (see footnote 48).

and Padilla (1997), tying can foreclose firms that can only sell single products. In Whinston and Nalebuff the "switching costs" are contractual, while in Klemperer and Padilla the products are "tied" by real shopping costs.[69] If the switching/shopping costs are real, entry need not be too hard *given* the switching costs, but the arguments of the previous subsection suggest it often may be.

2.7.4. Artificial switching costs make entry (too) hard

The previous discussion addressed whether entry is too easy or too hard, taking the switching costs as given: we observed that switching costs make certain kinds of entry hard, but that this is at least in part because they also make entry socially costly, so entry may not be very much *too* hard given the switching costs. A larger issue is whether the switching costs are inevitable real social costs. They may instead be contractual,[70] or may be real but caused by an unnecessary technological choice that an entrant cannot copy. In these cases, it is the incumbent's ability to choose incompatibility that is the crucial entry barrier.

2.8. Endogenous switching costs: choosing how to compete

Market participants may seek to either raise or to lower switching costs in order to reduce inefficiencies (including the switching cost itself), to enhance market power, to deter new entry, or to extract returns from a new entrant.

2.8.1. Reducing switching costs to enhance efficiency

As we have seen, a firm that cannot commit not to exploit its ex-post monopoly power must charge a lower introductory price. If the price-path (or quality-path) is very inefficient for the firm and consumers jointly, the firm's surplus as well as joint surplus may be increased by nullifying the switching costs. Thus, for example, a company may license a second source to create a future competitor to which consumers can costlessly switch [Farrell and Gallini (1988)].[71]

Likewise, firms producing differentiated products (or product lines) may deliberately make them compatible (i.e., choose zero switching costs). This increases the variety of options available to consumers who can then "mix-and-match" products from more

[69] Choi (1996a) shows that tying in markets where R&D is critical can allow a firm with an R&D lead in just one market to pre-empt both. The welfare effects are ambiguous.

[70] This includes those created by "loyalty contracts", "exclusive contracts" and " bundling" or "tying", etc.

[71] In Gilbert and Klemperer (2000) a firm commits to low prices that will result in rationing but will not fully exploit the consumers ex-post, to induce them to pay the start-up costs of switching to the firm.

than one firm without paying a switching cost. So eliminating switching costs can raise all firms' demands, and hence all firms' profits.[72]

Where suppliers are unwilling to reduce switching costs (see below), third parties may supply converters,[73] or regulators may intervene.

We have also already noted that customers may incur the switching (or start-up) cost of using more than one supplier, or may pre-commit to ignoring the switching costs in deciding whether to switch,[74] in order to force suppliers to behave more competitively.[75]

Finally, firms may be able to mitigate the inefficiencies of distorted prices and/or qualities by developing reputations for behaving as if there were no switching costs.[76]

2.8.2. Increasing switching costs to enhance efficiency

Firms may also mitigate the inefficiencies of distorted prices and qualities by contracting, or even vertically integrating, with their customers.[77,78] Likewise, Taylor (2003) finds firms might set lower prices to loyal consumers to reduce inefficient switching. Of course, a downside of these strategies of increasing switching costs is that they also limit the variety available to consumers unless they pay the switching costs.

2.8.3. Increasing switching costs to enhance oligopoly power

Although switching costs typically reduce social surplus, we saw in Sections 2.3–2.5 that they nevertheless often increase firms' profits. If so, firms jointly prefer to commit (before they compete) to real social switching costs than to no switching costs. Thus, firms may artificially create or increase switching costs.

[72] See Matutes and Regibeau (1988), Economides (1989), Garcia Mariñoso (2001), Stahl (1982), etc. But the mix-and-match models reveal other effects too; see Section 2.8.4. Note that many models ignore the demand-reducing effect of switching costs by considering a fixed number of consumers all of whom have reservation prices that are sufficiently high that total demand is fixed.

[73] See Section 3.8.3 for more on converters.

[74] See Cabral and Greenstein (1990).

[75] Greenstein (1993) discusses the procurement strategies used by U.S. federal agencies in the late 1970s to force suppliers of mainframe computers to make their systems compatible with those of their rivals.

[76] See Eber (1999). Perhaps more plausibly firms may develop reputations for, or otherwise commit to, treating old and new customers alike (since this behavior is easy for consumers to understand and monitor); this behavior may also mitigate the inefficiencies due to the distorted prices (though see footnote 78) – it is most likely to be profitable if bargain-then-ripoff pricing is particularly inefficient.

[77] See Williamson (1975) and Klein, Crawford and Alchian (1978).

[78] However *incomplete* contracts to protect against suppliers' opportunism may be less desirable than none at all. Farrell and Shapiro (1989) call this the Principle of Negative Protection. The point is that it is better (ex ante) for customers to be exploited efficiently than inefficiently ex-post. So if contracts cannot set all future variables (e.g. can set prices but not qualities), so customers anyway expect to be exploited ex-post, it may be better that there are no contracts.

Of course, a firm may prefer switching costs *from* but not *to* its product if it can achieve this, especially where the switching costs are real social costs. Adams (1978) describes how Gillette and its rivals tried to make their razor blades (the profitable follow-on product) fit one another's razors but their razors accept only their own blades. However, Koh (1993) analyses a model in which each duopolist chooses a real social cost of switching to it, and shows the possibility that each chooses a positive switching cost in order to relax competition.[79]

In Banerjee and Summers (1987) and Caminal and Matutes (1990) firms have the option to generate contractual switching costs by committing in period zero to offering repeat-purchase coupons in a two-period duopoly, and both firms (independently) take this option.[80] Similarly Fudenberg and Tirole (2000) explore a two-period model in which firms can price discriminate between consumers based on their past demands; if firms can also offer long term contracts – that is, generate contractual switching costs – then firms do offer such contracts in equilibrium, in addition to spot contracts.[81]

2.8.4. *Reducing switching costs to enhance oligopoly power*

An important class of models which suggests that firms may often be biased towards too much compatibility from the social viewpoint is the "mix-and-match" models (see Section 2.5) in which different firms have different abilities in producing the different components of a "system". Consumers' ability to mix-and-match the best product(s) offered by each firm is an efficiency gain from compatibility (that is, from zero rather than infinite shopping costs), but firms' private gains from compatibility may be even greater because – perhaps surprisingly – compatibility can increase prices.

In the simplest such model, Einhorn (1992) assumed that a single consumer wants one each of a list of components produced by firms A, B, with production costs a_i and b_i respectively for component i. In compatible competition the price for each component is $\max\{a_i, b_i\}$, so the consumer pays a total price $\sum_i \max\{a_i, b_i\}$ for the system. But if the firms are incompatible, the Bertrand price for a system is $\max\{\sum_i a_i, \sum_i b_i\}$ which is lower unless the same firm is best at everything: if different firms are best at providing different components, then the winning seller on each component appropriates its full efficiency margin in compatible competition, but in *in*compatible competition the winner's margin is its efficiency advantage where it is best, *minus* its rival's advantage where its rival is best. Firms thus (jointly) more than appropriate the efficiency gain from compatibility, and consumers actually prefer incompatibility.

This result depends on (among other assumptions) duopoly at each level. If more than two firms produce each component, the sum of the second-lowest cost of each

[79] Similarly Bouckaert and Degryse (2004) show in a two-period credit market model that each bank may reduce switching costs *from* itself, in order to relax competition.

[80] However, Kim and Koh (2002) find that a firm with a small market share may reduce contractual switching costs by choosing to honor repeat-purchase coupons that its rivals have offered to their old customers.

[81] These papers are discussed in more detail elsewhere in this Volume, in Stole (2007).

component (which the consumer pays under compatibility) may easily be lower than the second-lowest system cost when firms are incompatible, so consumers often prefer compatibility and firms' incentives may be biased either way [see Farrell, Monroe and Saloner (1998)].[82]

The "order-statistic" effect emphasized in these models is not the only force, however. Matutes and Regibeau (1988) stressed that under compatibility a price cut by one firm in one component increases demand for the *other* firms' complements, whereas under incompatibility all of this boost in complementary demand accrues to the firm, so compatibility reduces incentives to cut prices.[83] Economides (1989) argued that, unlike the Einhorn result, this logic does not depend on duopoly, so provides a clear argument why firms may try too hard to reduce switching costs and shopping costs.[84]

2.8.5. *Increasing switching costs to prevent or exploit entry*

The mix-and-match literature of the previous subsection ignores the fact that entry provides a much greater discipline on prices when compatibility means a new firm can enter offering just one component of a system than when any entrant needs to offer a whole system.

More generally, we have seen (Section 2.7) that an incumbent firm may protect a monopoly position against entry by writing exclusionary contracts, or by artificially creating real switching costs through technological incompatibility with potential entrants.[85] Imposing contractual switching costs (but not real social switching costs) can

[82] Einhorn's results, but not those of Farrell, Monroe and Saloner, are qualitatively unaffected by whether or not firms know their own efficiencies in each component. The analysis of these two papers is related to Palfrey (1983).

[83] Matutes and Regibeau (1992) allowed firms to set separate prices for bundles (not necessarily the sum of the component prices) and found that the force toward compatibility weakens. Furthermore, compatibility also changes the structure of demand, so even Matutes and Regibeau (1988) found that firms are sometimes biased towards incompatibility. And Klemperer (1992) also shows that firms may prefer incompatibility to compatibility when the latter is socially preferred, and that the firms may even distort their product choices to sustain incompatibility. Garcia Mariñoso (2001) examines a mix-and-match model in which purchase takes place over two periods, and finds that firms are biased towards compatibility because it reduces the intensity of competition in the first period – see also Haucap (2003) and Garcia Mariñoso (2003). (All these models, unlike Einhorn and Farrell, Monroe and Saloner, assume some product differentiation between firms' components even under compatibility.) See also Anderson and Leruth (1993).

[84] Most of the "mix-and-match" literature assumes that each firm offers a full line of products, but DeNicolo (2000) analyzes competition with one full-line and a pair of specialist firms. In our terminology, there are then no additional shopping costs of buying from an additional specialist firm after having bought from one of the specialist firms, but the specialist firms do not internalize the complementarities between them.

[85] Imposing switching costs would not be worthwhile for the incumbent if they reduced consumers' willingnesses to pay by more than the gains from excluding entry. In models such as Rasmusen, Ramseyer and Wiley (1991), and Segal and Whinston (2000), it is unprofitable to enter and serve only one customer, so no customer loses by signing an exclusive contract if other customers have already done so; in equilibrium this can mean that no customer needs to be compensated for signing an exclusive contract.
Deterring entry is also profitable if it can transfer rents from an entrant to the incumbent.

also enable an incumbent to extract rents from an entrant without preventing its entry – the entrant is forced to pay a fee (the "liquidated damages") to break the contracts.[86]

2.9. Switching costs and policy

As we have seen, with (large) switching costs firms compete over streams of goods and services rather than over single transactions. So one must not jump from the fact that buyers become locked in to the conclusion that there is an overall competitive problem. Nor should one draw naïve inferences from individual transaction prices, as if each transaction were the locus of ordinary competition. Some individual transactions may be priced well above cost even when no firm has (ex-ante) market power; others may be priced below cost without being in the least predatory.[87,88] Thus switching-cost markets can be more competitive than they look, and switching costs need not generate supernormal profits, even in a closed oligopoly. These points emerge clearly from the core two-period model with which we began.

But, as our further discussion shows, while switching costs need not cause competitive problems, they probably do make competition more fragile, especially when they coexist with ordinary scale economies (or, as we will see in Section 3, with network effects). Because large-scale entry into switching-cost markets is hard (whether or not inefficiently so), there may be much more incentive for monopolizing strategies such as predation or merger than there is in markets in which easy entry limits any market power. Thus switching costs, in combination with other factors, could justify heightened antitrust scrutiny.[89]

Furthermore, while sometimes (as in our core model) firms must give all their ex post rents to consumers in ex ante competition, that is not always true. The ex post rents may be less than fully competed away, as in most of the oligopoly models we discussed. Or,

[86] See Aghion and Bolton (1987) and Diamond and Maskin (1979).

[87] For instance, in an aftermarket context such as the Kodak case, the fact that repair services are priced well above cost does not by itself prove that there is a serious competitive problem.

[88] Another naïve argument is that if one observes little or no switching, then firms do not constrain one another's prices: firms that compete on a life-cycle basis (rather than on an individual transaction basis) constrain one another's life-cycle prices and, of course, firms may be constrained even ex post by the threat of customer switching even when that threat is not carried out in equilibrium.

[89] For example, the UK Competition Commission in July 2001 blocked the proposed merger of two banks, Lloyds TSB and Abbey National, even though Abbey National accounted for only 5 per cent of the market for personal banking. An important part of the Commission's reasoning was that consumer switching costs, combined with some scale economies, make new entry very hard, and that existing firms with low market shares tend to compete more aggressively than larger firms in markets with switching costs, so smaller firms are particularly valuable competitors to retain. (Klemperer is a UK Competition Commissioner, but was not involved in this decision.) See also Lofaro and Ridyard (2003).
Footnote 64 gives another example where policy makers were concerned that entry was very hard in a market with switching costs. In this case the UK regulator (the Director of the Office of Fair Trading) limited NAPP's aftermarket price to no more than five times the foremarket price in order to ameliorate the bargains-then-ripoffs price pattern. (He also limited the absolute level of the aftermarket price.)

if the ex post rents are dissipated in unproductive activities such as excessive marketing or advertising, then consumers are harmed by switching costs even if firms are no better off. So switching costs often do raise average prices. Moreover, as in our core model, switching costs often cause a bargain-then-ripoff pattern of prices, and (going beyond the core model) this can be inefficient even when the average level of prices remains competitive; they make matching less efficient by discouraging re-matching or the use of multiple suppliers; and, of course, they result in direct costs when consumers do switch.

For these reasons, despite the warnings in the first paragraph of this subsection, markets may indeed perform less well with switching costs than without, so policy intervention to reduce switching costs may be appropriate.[90] For example, policy might cautiously override intellectual property rights, especially of copyright-like intellectual property that may have little inherent novelty, if those rights are used only as a tool to enforce incompatibility and so create private rewards that bear no relationship to the innovation's incremental value.[91]

In general firms may be biased either towards or against compatibility relative to the social standpoint. But switching costs seem more likely to lower than to raise efficiency, so when firms favor switching costs the reason is often because they enhance monopoly or oligopoly power by directly raising prices or by inhibiting new entry.[92] This suggests that policy-makers should take a close look when firms with market power choose to have switching costs (through contract form or product design) when choosing compatibility would be no more costly.[93,94]

[90] Gans and King (2001) examine the regulatory trade-offs in intervening to reduce switching costs and show that who is required to bear the costs of ameliorating switching costs can importantly affect the efficiency of the outcome. See also Galbi (2001).
Viard (in press) found that the introduction of number portability for U.S. toll-free telephone services substantially reduced switching costs and led to the largest firm substantially reducing prices; the U.S. wireless industry strongly resisted the introduction of number portability in the wireless market. Aoki and Small (2000) and Gans, King and Woodbridge (2001) also analyse number portability in the telecoms market.
The UK government is currently considering recommendations to reduce switching costs in the mortgage market, see Miles (2004).

[91] Thus, for example, the European Commission in 2004 ruled that Microsoft had abused its market power by, inter alia, refusing to supply interface infrastructure to competitors, thus making entry hard by products that could form part of a "mix-and-match" system with Microsoft's dominant Windows PC operating system. Microsoft was ordered to provide this information even if it was protected by intellectual property.

[92] A caveat is that firms often do not make a coordinated joint choice of whether to compete with switching costs or without, and different firms may be able to control the costs of different switches. See Section 2.8.

[93] For example, the Swedish competition authority argued that Scandinavian Airlines' "frequent-flyer" program blocked new entry on just one or a few routes in the Swedish domestic air-travel market in which entry on the whole range of routes was impractical (see Section 2.7.3), and the airline was ordered to alter the program from October 2001. A similar decision was made by the Norwegian competition authority with effect from April 2002. Fernandes (2001) provides some support for these decisions by studying alliances formed by U.S. airlines, and showing that "frequent-flyer" programs that cover more routes are more attractive to consumers and confer greater market power on the airlines operating the programs. See also Klemperer and Png (1986).

[94] A caveat is that the policy debate is often held ex-post of some lock-in. At this point incumbents' preference to maintain high switching costs is unsurprising and does not prove that switching costs raise prices

3. Network effects and competition

3.1. Introduction

It can pay to coordinate and follow the crowd. For instance, it is useful to speak English because many others do. A telephone or a fax machine or an email account is more valuable if many others have them. Driving is easier if everyone keeps right – or if everyone keeps left. While following the crowd may involve a variety of choices, we follow the literature in using the metaphor of "adoption of a good", construed broadly. We say that there are *network effects* if one agent's adoption of a good (a) benefits other adopters of the good (a "total effect") and (b) increases others' incentives to adopt it (a "marginal effect").

Classic (or *peer-to-peer*) *network effects* arise when every adoption thus complements every other, although the effects may be "localized": for instance, an instant-messaging user gains more when her friends adopt than when strangers do. Indeed, adoption by spammers or telemarketers harms other adopters and makes them less keen to adopt, yet a few such nuisance adopters will not overturn the overall network effect: "generally" increased adoption makes the good more appealing.

An important kind of network effect arises when following the crowd enhances opportunities to trade. If thicker markets work better, then all traders want to join (adopt) a big market, and gain when the market grows. This fits the definition if each trader expects both to buy and to sell; but when traders can be divided into buyers and sellers, it is not true that each trader's arrival makes all others better off or encourages them to adopt. Each buyer gains when more sellers join, but typically loses when more other buyers join: he does not want to trade with them and may suffer an adverse terms-of-trade effect. Thus the effect of a buyer's adoption on sellers fits the definition above, as does the effect of a seller's adoption on buyers, but the buyer–buyer spillovers and the seller–seller spillovers often go the other way. *Indirect network effects* describe market-thickness effects from one side of the market, typically buyers, as the other side re-equilibrates. That is, when an additional buyer arrives, the "marginal effect" on sellers attracts additional sellers, and the total and marginal effects of additional sellers on buyers can then be attributed (indirectly, hence the name) to the additional buyer. If those effects outweigh any adverse terms-of-trade effect of the new buyer on other buyers, they induce network effects among buyers, treating sellers not as adopters subject to the definition but as a mere background mechanism.

This can all take place in terms of just one good. For instance, a firm's price policies create a network effect among buyers if price falls when demand rises. This can reflect production-side *economies of scale* if those are passed through to consumers.

overall (nor do the switching costs necessarily cause inefficiencies). Reducing switching costs ex-post also expropriates the incumbents' ex-ante investments, which may be thought objectionable, though the fear of expropriation of this kind of ex-ante investment seems unlikely to harm dynamic efficiency (and may in fact improve efficiency).

For example, if public transport is always priced at average cost, it gets cheaper the more it is used. Similarly, Bagwell and Ramey (1994) and Bagwell (2007) show how economies of scale in retailing can encourage consumers to coordinate (perhaps by responding to advertising) on large retailers. With or without scale economies, a firm's price policy can create an artificial network effect among buyers, as when a mobile-phone provider offers subscribers free calls to other subscribers. If a product will be abandoned without sufficient demand, one can view that as a price increase; thus buyers who will face switching costs want to buy a product that enough others will buy [Beggs (1989)]. At the industry rather than firm level, there may be price-mediated network effects in decreasing-cost competitive industries; or a larger market may support more sellers and thus be more competitive [Rasmusen, Ramseyer and Wiley, 1991; Segal and Whinston (2000)] or more productively efficient [Stigler (1951)].

But, usually, the concept gets an additional layer: the background mechanism is re-equilibration of sellers of *varied complements* to a "platform" that buyers adopt. For instance, when more buyers adopt a computer hardware platform, more vendors supply software that will run on it, making the computer (with the option to buy software for it) more valuable to users: the hardware–software paradigm.[95] Similarly, buyers may want to buy a popular car because a wider (geographic and other) variety of mechanics will be trained to repair it, or may hesitate to buy one that uses a less widely available fuel. We give more examples in Section 3.2 and discuss indirect network effects further in Section 3.3.2.[96]

While such indirect network effects are common – indeed, Rochet and Tirole (2003) argue that network effects predominantly arise in this way – it is worth warning against a tempting short-cut in the logic. Even in classic competitive markets, "sellers like there to be more buyers, and buyers like there to be more sellers", and this does not imply network effects if these effects are pecuniary and cancel one another. Indirect network effects driven by smooth free entry of sellers in response to additional buyers can only work when larger markets are more efficient, as we discuss further in Section 3.3.5.

Section 3.2 describes some case studies and empirical work. Section 3.3, like the early literature, explores whether network effects are externalities and cause network goods to be under-adopted at the margin, a question that draws primarily on the total effect. But the modern literature focuses on how the marginal effect can create multiple equilibria among adopters, making coordination challenging and giving expectations

[95] Somewhat confusingly, a leading example puts Microsoft's Windows in the role of "hardware" and applications software in the role of "software".

[96] For theories of indirect network effects through improved supply in a complement see Katz and Shapiro (1985), Church and Gandal (1992, 1993), Chou and Shy (1990), and Economides and Salop (1992); Gandal (1995a) and Katz and Shapiro (1994) review this literature. Liebowitz and Margolis (1994) argue that indirect network effects lack the welfare properties of direct effects; see also Clements (2004); but Church, Gandal and Krause (2002) argue otherwise.

Presumably we could have network effects with several classes of adopter, each class benefiting only from adoption by one other class, but in practice models tend to assume either classic (single-class) or indirect (two-class) cases, although multi-component systems are sometimes studied.

a key role in competition and efficiency. As a result, network markets often display unstable dynamics such as critical mass, tipping, and path dependence, including collective switching costs. Section 3.4 argues that coordination is central and can be hard even despite helpful institutions. Section 3.5 discusses how adoption in network markets favors the status quo; such "inertia" has important implications for competition. Sections 3.3–3.5 thus study adopters' collective behavior, given their payoff functions including prices. Those sections thus describe adoption dynamics when each network good is unsponsored (competitively supplied), and also describe the demand side generally, including when each network good is strategically supplied by a single residual claimant or sponsor.

Turning to the supply side of network-effect markets, Section 3.6 discusses how a sponsor might address coordination and externality problems; Section 3.7 considers competition between sponsors of incompatible network products. In light of this analysis of incompatible competition, Section 3.8 asks whether firms will choose to compete with compatible or incompatible products, and Section 3.9 discusses public policy.

3.2. Empirical evidence

3.2.1. Case studies

We discuss some of the most prominent cases in which it has been argued that network effects are important:

Telecommunications Much early literature on network effects was inspired by telecommunications. Since telecommunications at the time was treated as a natural monopoly, the focus was mainly on how second-best pricing might take account of network effects/externalities, and on how to organize "universal service" cross-subsidies to marginal (or favored) users.[97]

Modern telecommunications policy stresses facilitating efficient competition. Compatibility in the form of interconnection, so that a call originated on one network can be completed on another, is fundamental to this.[98] Unlike many compatibility decisions elsewhere, it is often paid for, and is widely regulated. Brock (1981) and Gabel (1991) describe how, in early unregulated U.S. telephone networks, the dominant Bell system refused to interconnect with nascent independent local phone companies. Some users then subscribed to both carriers, somewhat blunting the network effects, as do similar "multi-homing" practices such as merchants accepting several kinds of payment cards.

[97] See for instance (in chronological order) Squire (1973), Rohlfs (1974), Kahn and Shew (1987), Einhorn (1993), Panzar and Wildman (1995), Barnett and Kaserman (1998), Crémer (2000), Yannelis (2001), Mason and Valletti (2001), Gandal, Salant and Waverman (2003) and also Shy (2001).

[98] Besen and Saloner (1989, 1994) studied standards and network effects in telecommunications; the International Telecommunications Union (ITU) has an entire "standardization sector".

Standards issues also arise in mobile telephony, although users on incompatible standards can call one another. Most countries standardized first- and second-generation air interfaces, predominantly on GSM, but the U.S. did not set a compulsory standard for the second-generation air interface.

Radio and television Besen and Johnson (1986) discuss standards obstacles to the adoption of AM stereo in the U.S. after the government declined to mandate a standard; they argue that the competing standards were similar enough, and demand limited enough, for such a leadership vacuum to stall the technology. Greenstein and Rysman (2004) give a similar interpretation of the early history of 56kbps modem standards.

In television, governments have imposed standards, but they differ among countries; Crane (1979) interprets this as protectionist trade policy. Besen and Johnson describe how the U.S. initially adopted a color TV standard that was not backward compatible with its black-and-white standard, so that color broadcasts could not be viewed at all on the installed base of sets; after brief experience with this, the FCC adopted a different standard that was backward-compatible. Farrell and Shapiro (1992) discuss domestic and international processes of picking high-definition television standards.

Microsoft Powerful network effects arise in computer platforms including operating systems, and Bresnahan (2001b) argues that internal strategy documents confirm that Microsoft understands this very well. Because they have many users, Microsoft's operating system platforms attract a lot of applications programming. An indirect network effect arises because application software writers make it their first priority to work well with the dominant platform, although many applications are "ported" (a form of multi-homing), softening this effect. As we explore below, incompatible competition (and entry in particular) may well be weak *unless* applications programmers, consumers, and equipment manufacturers would rapidly coordinate and switch to any slightly better or cheaper operating system.[99]

The U.S. antitrust case against Microsoft relied on this network effect or "applications barrier to entry", but did not claim that Windows is "the wrong" platform. Rather, Microsoft was convicted of illegal acts meant to preserve the network barrier against potential weakening through the Netscape browser and independent "middleware" such as Java.[100]

[99] A barrier to incompatible entry matters most if there is also a barrier (here, intellectual property and secrecy) to compatible entry.

[100] Both the Department of Justice and Microsoft have made many documents available on their web sites, http://www.usdoj.gov/atr/ and http://www.microsoft.com/, respectively. A good introduction to the case is the 2001 decision of the DC Court of Appeals. A discussion by economists involved in the case is Evans et al. (2000); Fisher (2000) and Schmalensee (2000) give briefer discussions. See also Evans and Schmalensee (2001), Gilbert and Katz (2001), Whinston (2001) and Rubinfeld (2003). Werden (2001) discusses the applications barrier to entry. Lemley and McGowan (1998b) discuss Java, and Gandal (2001) discusses the Internet search market. (Farrell worked on this case for the Justice Department.)

Others complain that Microsoft vertically "leverages" control from the operating system to other areas, such as applications and servers. The European Commission's 2004 order against Microsoft addressed both leverage into media viewers and interface standards between PCs and servers.

In software more generally, Shurmer (1993) uses survey data and finds network effects in word processing and spreadsheet software; Liebowitz and Margolis (2001) however argue that product quality largely explains success. Gawer and Henderson (2005) discuss Intel's response to opportunities for leverage.

Computers Gabel (1991) contrasts case studies of standards in personal computers and in larger systems. In personal computers, initial fragmentation was followed by the rise of the IBM/Windows/Intel (or "Wintel") model, whose control passed from IBM to Intel and Microsoft. The standard, which lets many firms complement the microprocessor and operating system (and to a lesser extent lets others, such as AMD and Linux, compete with those), has thrived, in part due to the attraction of scale for applications software vendors and others, and relatedly due to the scope for specialization: see Gates, Myrhvold and Rinearson (1995), Grove (1996), and Langlois (1992). Outside this standard only Apple has thrived.

Credit cards From the cardholder side, a credit card system has indirect network effects if cardholders like having more merchants accept the card and do not mind having more other cardholders. The question is more subtle on the merchant side since (given the number of cardholders) each merchant loses when more other merchants accept a card. Since this negative "total effect" applies whether or not this merchant accepts the card, Katz (2001) and Rochet and Tirole (2002) show that the "marginal effect" (adoption encourages others to adopt) may apply but the total effect may fail even taking into account re-equilibration on the customer side, if card penetration is already high and total spending does not rise much with cardholding.

Network effects color inter-system competition, and dominant systems could remain dominant partly through self-fulfilling expectations, although both merchants and cardholders often "multi-home", accepting or carrying multiple cards, which weakens network effects [Rochet and Tirole (2003)]. The biggest card payment systems, Visa and Mastercard, have in the past been largely non-profit at the system level and feature intra-system competition: multiple banks "issue" cards to customers and "acquire" merchants to accept the cards. The systems' rules affect the balance between inter- and intra-system competition. Ramsey-style pricing to cardholders and merchants may require "interchange fees", typically paid by merchants' banks to cardholders' banks: see, e.g., Katz (2001), Schmalensee (2002) and Rochet and Tirole (2002). But such fees (especially together with rules against surcharges on card purchases) may raise prices to non-card customers [Schwartz and Vincent (2006), Farrell (2006)].

The QWERTY keyboard David (1985) argued that the QWERTY typewriter keyboard became dominant through "historical small events". He suggested that QWERTY remains dominant despite being inferior (at least on a clean-slate basis) to other keyboard designs, notably the "Dvorak Simplified Keyboard" (DSK). Switching costs arise because it is costly to re-learn how to type. Network effects may arise "directly" because typists like to be able to type on others' keyboards, and "indirectly" for various reasons, e.g. because typing schools tend to teach the dominant design.

Liebowitz and Margolis (1990, 2001) deny that QWERTY has been shown to be substantially inferior, claiming that the technical evidence is mixed, weak, or suggests a relatively small inferiority – perhaps a few percent. If the penalty is small, switching (retraining) could be privately inefficient for already-trained QWERTY typists *even without* network effects. And evidently few users find it worth switching given all the considerations *including* any network effects.

But new users (who would not have to re-train from QWERTY) would find it worth adopting DSK or another alternative, *if* network effects did not outweigh their clean-slate stand-alone advantages. Combined with the technical evidence, this gives a lower bound on the strength of these network effects. If most typists type for a fifth of their working time and QWERTY has a stand-alone disadvantage of 5 percent, for instance, revealed preference of new QWERTY students suggests that the network effect is worth at least one percent of earnings.[101] Yet many would doubt that network effects are terribly strong in keyboard design: most typists work mostly on their own keyboards or their employer's, and DSK training and keyboards are available (PC keyboards can be reprogrammed). We infer that even easily disparaged network effects can be powerful.[102]

But the efficiency of typing is mostly a parable; the deeper question is whether the market test is reliable. That question splits into two:

(a) *Ex ante: did QWERTY pass a good market test when the market tipped to it?* Can we infer that it was best when adopted, whether or not it remains ex post efficient now? A short-run form of this question is whether contemporary users liked QWERTY best among keyboards on offer; a long-run version is whether the market outcome appropriately took into account that not all keyboards had been tried and that taste and technology could (and later did) change.

On the short-run question, David suggests that "small" accidents of history had disproportionate effects; a prominent typing contest was won by an especially good typist who happened to use QWERTY. He suggests that the outcome was somewhat *random*

[101] Since widespread dissemination of the PC, many typists type less than this; but for most of the keyboard's history, most typing probably was done by typists or secretaries who probably typed more than this.

[102] If one were very sure that network effects are weak, one might instead infer that the clean-slate stand-alone penalty of QWERTY must be small indeed, even negative. Even aside from the ergonomic evidence, however, that view is hard to sustain. For instance, the keyboard design problem differs among languages and has changed over time, yet QWERTY and minor variations thereof have been persistently pervasive. Thus if network effects were unimportant, the evidence from new typists' choices would imply that QWERTY was remarkably optimal in a wide range of contexts. And even if QWERTY is actually the best of all designs, the many people who believe otherwise would adopt DSK if they did not perceive network effects to be bigger.

and thus may well have failed even the short-run test. Liebowitz and Margolis argue that because both typing-contest and market competition among keyboards was vigorous, one can presume that the outcome served short-run contemporary tastes.

A fortiori, David presumably doubts that the market's one-time choice of QWERTY properly took long-run factors into account. Liebowitz and Margolis do not directly address the long-run question, but suggest that it should not be viewed as a market failure if QWERTY won because technically superior alternatives were not yet on the market.[103] In Sections 3.5–3.7 below we discuss market forces toward contemporaneous efficiency.

(b) *Ex post: as of now, would a switch be socially efficient?* Many students of keyboard design believe DSK is better on a clean-slate basis. But the slate is not clean: there is a huge installed base of equipment and training. As things stand, no switch is taking place; should one? This question in turn can take two different forms.

In a *gradual switch*, new users would adopt DSK while trained QWERTY typists remained with QWERTY. This would sacrifice network benefits but not incur individual switching costs; it would presumably happen without intervention if switching costs were large but network effects were weak compared to DSK's stand-alone advantage. Private incentives for a gradual switch can be too weak ("excess inertia") because early switchers bear the brunt of the lost network benefits (see Section 3.5 below). But equally the private incentives can be too strong, because those who switch ignore lost network benefits to those who are stranded.

In a *coordinated switch*, everyone would adopt DSK at once (already-trained QWERTY typists would retrain). Thus society would incur switching costs but preserve full network effects. Because new users would unambiguously gain, already-trained QWERTY typists will be too reluctant to participate. Even if they were willing, coordination (to preserve full network benefits) could be a challenge; if they were opposed, compulsion or smooth side payments could be required for an efficient coordinated switch; of course, compulsion can easily lead to inefficient outcomes, and side payments seem unlikely to be smooth here.

Video recordings: Betamax versus VHS; DVD and DIVX Gabel (1991) and Rohlfs (2001) argue that the VCR product overcame the chicken-and-egg problem by offering substantial stand-alone value to consumers (for "time-shifting" or recording programs off the air) even with no pre-recorded programming for rent. By contrast, RCA and CBS introduced products to play pre-recorded programming (into which they were vertically integrated), but those failed partly because they did not offer time-shifting; laser disks suffered the same fate.

Later, the VCR market tipped, generally to VHS and away from Betamax – though Gabel reports that (as of 1991) Betamax had won in Mexico. The video rental market

103 Below, we discuss what institutions might have supported a long-run market test.

created network effects (users value variety and convenience of programming availability, rental outlets offer more variety in a popular format, and studios are most apt to release videos in such a format). The rise of these network effects hurt Sony, whose Betamax standard was more expensive (VHS was more widely licensed) and, according to some, superior at equal network size, although Liebowitz and Margolis (1994) argue not. Gabel (1991) suggests that the strength of network effects may have surprised Sony.

Cusumano, Mylonadis and Rosenbloom (1992) describe the VHS–Betamax battle. Park (2004b) and Ohashi (2003) develop dynamic model of consumer choice and producer pricing for the VCR market and assess the extent to which network effects contributed to the tipping.

In the next generation of video, Dranove and Gandal (2003) and Karaca-Mandic (2004) found substantial indirect network effects in DVD adoption. Dranove and Gandal found that a preannouncement of a competing format, DIVX, delayed DVD adoption. Both papers find cross-effects such that the content sector as a whole could profitably have subsidized hardware sales, which could motivate vertical integration.

DVD players (until recently) did not record, like the laser disk product, but many households are willing to own both a VCR and a DVD player, allowing DVD's other quality advantages to drive success in a way that the laser disk could not. Again, such multi-homing blunts the network effects and can help with the chicken-and-egg problem.

Sound recordings and compact disks Farrell and Shapiro (1992) argued that although prices of CDs and players fell during the period of rapid adoption, it would be hard to explain the adoption path without network effects; on the other hand, since CD players could be connected to existing amplifiers and loudspeakers, multi-homing was easy.

Gandal, Kende and Rob (2000) estimated a simultaneous-equations model of adoption in terms of price and software availability, stressing the cross-effects that would lead to indirect network effects.

Languages Human languages display classic network effects. Changes in patterns of who talks with whom presumably explain the evolution of language, both convergent (dialects merging into larger languages) and divergent (development of dialects). English is dominant, but there have been previous bandwagons such as French in diplomacy, or Latin as *lingua franca*.

Some Americans argue for "English only" laws based on a network externality; across the border, Canadians intervene to discourage *de facto* standardization on English [Church and King (1993)]. As we discuss in Section 3.3.5 below, the net externality involved in choosing between two network goods (such as languages) is ambiguous. Of course, many people learn more than one language, but native English speakers are less apt to do so. Shy (1996) stresses that who learns a second language can be indeterminate and/or inefficient, as Farrell and Saloner (1992) noted for converters or adapters generally.

Law Klausner (1995) and Kahan and Klausner (1996, 1997) argue that contracts and corporate form are subject to network effects (especially under common law), as it is valuable to use legal forms that have already been clarified through litigation by others, although Ribstein and Kobayashi (2001) question this empirically. Radin (2002) discusses standardization versus customization in the law generally.

Securities markets and exchanges Securities markets and exchanges benefit from liquidity or thickness: see Economides and Siow (1988), Domowitz and Steil (1999), Ahdieh (2003). When there is more trade in a particular security its price is less volatile and more informative, and investors can buy and sell promptly without moving the market. This helps explain why only a few of the imaginable financial securities are traded, and why each tends to be traded on one exchange unless institutions allow smooth cross-exchange trading.

Not only do buyers wish for more sellers and vice versa, but this positive cross-effect outweighs the negative own-effect (sellers wish there were fewer other sellers); the difference is the value of liquidity, an efficiency gain from a large (thick) market. This fuels a network effect.

If products are differentiated, a larger network offers more efficient matches. This is the network effect behind eBay, and could be important in competition among B2B (business-to-business) exchanges [FTC 2000; Bonaccorsi and Rossi (2002)]. This also captures part of the value of liquidity, in that a larger market is more likely to have "coincidence of wants".

3.2.2. Econometric approaches

Quantitative work on network effects has focused on two questions. First, it aims to estimate and quantify network effects. Second, some less formal work aims to test implications of the theory, notably the possibility of persistent inefficient outcomes.

The theory of network effects claims that widespread adoption causes high value. How can one test this? Clearly one cannot simply include demand for a good as an econometric predictor of demand for that good. At the level of individual adoptions, it may be hard to disentangle network effects from correlations in unobserved taste or quality variables [Manski (1993)]. Moreover, dynamic implications of network effects may be hard to distinguish econometrically from learning or herding.

Meanwhile, the theory predicts path dependence, which implies both large "errors" and a small number of observations (a network industry may display a lot of autocorrelation). Likewise it predicts that modest variations in parameters will have unpredictable effects, and focuses largely on claims about efficiency, all of which makes testing a challenge. Nevertheless, some work aims to quantify these effects.

A popular hedonic approach compares demand for two products that differ in the network effects expected; the approach aims to isolate this effect from that of other quality variables. A natural proxy for expected network effects is previous sales: lagged sales or the installed base, relying on some inertia in network size. Thus Brynjolfsson and Kemerer (1996) estimated that the value of an installed base of spreadsheet users represented up to 30% of the price of the market leader in the late 1980s; similarly Gandal (1994, 1995b) found a premium for Lotus-compatibility in PC spreadsheets. Hartman and Teece (1990) find network effects in minicomputers. This approach risks misinterpreting unobserved quality as network effects; but Goolsbee and Klenow (2002) find evidence of strictly local network effects in the adoption of PCs, using geographic variation to control for unobserved quality.

Another econometric approach rests on the fact that large adopters may better internalize network effects, and may care less than smaller adopters about compatibility with others. Saloner and Shepard (1995) found that banks with more branches tended to install cash machines (ATMs) sooner. Gowrisankaran and Stavins (2004) also use geographic variation to estimate network effects for automated transactions by banks. Gowrisankaran and Ackerberg (in press) aim to separate consumer-level from bank-level network effects.[104]

It is easier to identify cross-effects between complementary groups, estimating how more adoption by one affects demand by the other (but recall that complementarities need not imply network effects). Rosse (1967) documented that newspaper advertisers pay more to advertise in papers with more readers, although news readers may not value having more advertisements; by contrast, readers do value having more advertisements in the Yellow Pages [Rysman (2004)]. Dranove and Gandal (2003) and Karaca-Mandic (2004) also focus on the cross-effects.

Testing the central efficiency implications of the theory is hard, because (a) it is hard (and not standard economic methodology) to directly assess the efficiency of outcomes, and (b) the theory's prediction that outcomes depend sensitively on early events and are insensitive to later events, costs and tastes, is also hard to test. Liebowitz and Margolis (2001) argue that software products succeed when measured quality is higher, and that prices do not systematically rise after the market tips; they infer that network effects seem unimportant.[105] Bresnahan and Greenstein (1999) argues that effective competition for the market occurs only at rather rare "epochs" or windows of opportunity, so that high quality may be necessary but is not sufficient for success.

Fascinating though they are, these case studies and empirics do not satisfyingly resolve the theoretical questions raised below, in particular, those concerning the efficiency of equilibria.

3.3. Under-adoption and network externalities

In this sub-section we follow the early literature on network effects in focusing on the single-network case and on the total effect or (often) adoption externality.

[104] See also Guibourg (2001) and Kauffman and Wang (1999).

[105] Liebowitz and Margolis (1994) suggest that network effects may be essentially exhausted at relevant scales, so that the *u* function flattens out, as Asvanund et al. (2004) found in file sharing. However, Shapiro (1999) argues that network effects are less likely than classic scale economies to be exhausted.

3.3.1. Formalities

Each of K players, or adopters, chooses an action: to adopt a product or not, or to adopt one product (network) or another. We often interpret these players not as individuals but as "groups" of adopters, where group i is of size n_i and $\sum n_i = N$. Often (but see Section 3.3.2), we treat each group as making an all-or-nothing choice, to adopt or not, or to adopt one product or its rival.

Player i has payoff $u_a^i(x)$ from action a if a total of x adopters choose action a; for simplicity, assume there is only one alternative, a'.[106] Recalling our definition in Section 3.1, we say that there are *network effects* in a if, for each i, both the payoff $u_a^i(x)$ and the adoption incentive $u_a^i(x) - u_{a'}^i(N - x)$ are increasing in x.[107] At this point we are considering adoption incentives, so these payoffs include prices.

For simplicity, the literature often takes $K = 2$, though the problems might not be very interesting with literally only two adopters. Consider two groups choosing whether or not to adopt a single product. If a non-adopter's payoff is unaffected by how many others adopt, then we can normalize it as zero, and (dropping the subscript) write $u^i(x)$ for i's payoff from adoption, as in Figure 31.1.

	Group 2 adopts	Group 2 does not adopt
Group 1 adopts	$u^1(N), u^2(N)$	$u^1(n_1), 0$
Group 1 does not adopt	$0, u^2(n_2)$	$0, 0$

Figure 31.1. Adoption payoffs from single network good.

Network effects arise for this single product if $u^i(N) > u^i(n_i)$ for $i = 1, 2, \ldots, K$[108]; in Section 3.3.3, we show that this implies both parts of our definition. However, often the leading alternative to one network product is another, as in Figure 31.2.

	Group 2 adopts A	Group 2 adopts B
Group 1 adopts A	$u_A^1(N), u_A^2(N)$	$u_A^1(n_1), u_B^2(n_2)$
Group 1 adopts B	$u_B^1(n_1), u_A^2(n_2)$	$u_B^1(N), u_B^2(N)$

Figure 31.2. Adoption payoffs with rival network goods.

[106] It is not immediately clear how best to extend the definition to more than two alternatives: for which alternative(s) a' must the "adoption incentive" described in the text increase with adoption of a, and which alternatives does that adoption displace? The literature has not focused on these questions and we do not address them here.

[107] In reality network benefits are not homogeneous [Beige (2001) discusses local network effects, or communities of interest]. Also note that if $u_a^i(x)$ is linear in x and independent of i, then the total value of the network is quadratic in x: "Metcalfe's law". Swann (2002) and Rohlfs (2001) argue that this is very special and even extreme.

[108] We often assume for clarity that u is *strictly* increasing when there are network effects.

Network effects arise if $u_a^i(N) > u_a^i(n_i)$ for $i = 1, 2$ and $a = A, B$; again, this implies both parts of our definition.

Network effects are *strong* if they outweigh each adopter's preferences for A versus B, so that each prefers to do whatever others do. Then "all adopt A" and "all adopt B" are both Nash equilibria of the simultaneous-move non-cooperative game whose payoff matrix is Figure 31.2. Strong network effects thus create multiple equilibria if adoption is simultaneous (not literally, but in the game-theoretic sense that players cannot react to others' actual choices but must base their actions on expectations). For a single network product (Figure 31.1), network effects are strong if, for all i, $u^i(N) > 0$ (each would adopt if others do, or more precisely if he expects others to adopt) and $u^i(n_i) < 0$ (each will not if others do not). Thus "no adoption" can be an equilibrium even for valuable network goods: the chicken-and-egg problem [Leibenstein (1950)], especially in the "fragmented" case where groups are small in the sense that each $u^i(n_i)$ is small relative to $u^i(N)$.

3.3.2. *What are the groups?*

Calling each kind of adopter a group, even though it does not act as a single player, can help focus on the complementarity of adoption by different kinds of adopter. For instance, in camera formats, we might make photographers one group and film processors the other. Then each group's benefit from adoption increases when the other group adopts more strongly. Often this reformulation greatly reduces the number of groups: here, from millions of individuals to two groups.

This departs from our formal definition in two ways. First, each group does not coordinate internally and does not make an all-or-nothing adoption choice; rather, some but not all members of each group adopt. Second, there may be no intra-group network effects; there may even be intra-group congestion. Thus, given the number of photographers, a developer prefers fewer other developers for competitive reasons, just as with merchants accepting credit cards.

A different reformulation of the groups views only photographers as adopters, and diagnoses an "indirect network effect" among them, mediated through the equilibrium response of film processors. Doing so returns us to the strict framework above, but pushes the processors into the background.

Another way in which identifying groups is a non-trivial modeling choice is that adoption choices often are made at several different vertical levels (see Section 3.8.3ii). For instance, in the PC industry, memory technology is chosen by memory manufacturers, by producers of complements such as chipsets, by computer manufacturers (OEMs), and/or by end users or their employers. Even in a simple model, "adopters" may be vendors, or may be end users choosing between standards if vendors have chosen incompatible technologies.

3.3.3. Total and marginal effects

Our definition of network effects requires that (a) one agent's adoption of a good benefits other adopters, and that (b) his adoption increases others' incentive to adopt. We call these respectively the *total effect* and the *marginal effect*. We noted above that the marginal effect might apply to merchants' decisions to accept credit cards even if the total effect does not, if a merchant's adoption hurts his rivals who do not adopt more than it hurts those who do. On the other hand, the total effect can apply where the marginal effect does not: if one firm in a standard Cournot oligopoly chooses a lower output, it benefits other firms who have chosen a low output, but those other firms then typically have an incentive to *increase* their output.[109]

Although the two conditions are logically separate, definitions in the literature often mention only the total effect. The (seldom explicit) reason is that if the total effect holds *for both alternatives* A and B then the marginal effect follows. Group 2's incentive to adopt A rather than B is $u_A^2(N) - u_B^2(n_2)$ if group 1 has adopted A; it is $u_A^2(n_2) - u_B^2(N)$ if group 1 has adopted B. The marginal effect therefore holds if $u_A^2(N) - u_B^2(n_2) > u_A^2(n_2) - u_B^2(N)$, or $u_A^2(N) + u_B^2(N) > u_A^2(n_2) + u_B^2(n_2)$; but this follows from adding the two total-effect conditions $u_y^i(N) > u_y^i(n_i)$ for $i = 2$ and $y = A, B$.

The early literature focused on a single network with a scale-independent outside good. Thus (as in Figure 31.1) each group's payoff from B is independent of others' choices, so there are network effects in A if and only if the total effect holds for A. Accordingly, although the early literature generally stressed the total effect, the marginal effect follows. By contrast, recent work stresses competing networks, with much more stress on the marginal effect, which is essentially Segal's (1999) "increasing externalities" or Topkis' (1978, 1998) "supermodularity" [see also Milgrom and Roberts (1990)].

3.3.4. Under-adoption of a single network

Two forms of under-adoption threaten a network good. First, the marginal effect causes a chicken-and-egg coordination problem. Second, if the network effect is an externality (see below), there is too little incentive to adopt at the margin, because the total effect means that adoption benefits other adopters. We discuss this marginal externality here and the chicken-and-egg problem in Section 3.4.2 below.

In Figure 31.1, if $u^1(N) > 0 > u^2(N)$ then player 1 would like the "all adopt" outcome but, even if he adopts, player 2 will not. If $u^1(n_1) < 0$ then the unique equilibrium is no adoption; if instead $u^1(n_1) > 0$ then equilibrium is adoption by group 1 alone. In either case, if $u^1(N) + u^2(N) > \max[u^1(n_1), 0]$ then adoption by all would increase

[109] Other firms would have an incentive to reduce their outputs if firms' outputs are "strategic complements" [Bulow, Geanakoplos and Klemperer (1985a, 1985b)], and the marginal effect then does apply.

total surplus. Since each player likes the other to adopt, each one's adoption incentive is too weak from the viewpoint of adopters jointly.

The efficient outcome can still be an equilibrium if this bias is not too strong, and this generic observation takes an interesting form here. Say that preferences are *similar* if the players agree on the best outcome, so $u^i(N)$ has the same sign for all i. Then the efficient outcome, which is either "all adopt" or "no adoption", is an equilibrium of the simultaneous-adoption game suggested by Figure 31.1, as Liebowitz and Margolis (1994) noted. Moreover, while this equilibrium need not be unique, it is each player's best feasible outcome, and many institutions (including side payments, sequential moves and commitment, and communication) preserve and reinforce it.

But normally the bias will cause wrong choices. In a static framework, it makes the network too *small*.[110] If adoption is dynamic, for instance if costs fall over time, the same logic makes adoption too *slow*.[111] It is efficient to subsidize a marginal adopter for whom the cost of service exceeds his private willingness to pay, but exceeds it by less than the increase in other adopters' value. Such subsidies can be hard to target, as we discuss next, but there is a deeper problem too, even with perfectly discriminatory prices. With complete information and adopter-specific pricing, Segal (1999) finds that without externalities on non-traders, efficiency results if the sponsor simultaneously and publicly makes an offer to each adopter, but because there are positive externalities on efficient traders, there is too little adoption when offers are "private," or essentially bilateral. Efficiency requires multilateral bargaining, in which trade between the sponsor and one trader depends on trade with others.

3.3.5. *Are network effects externalities?*

Network effects often involve externalities, in the sense that prices do not fully incorporate the benefits of one person's adoption for others. Indeed, early literature often simply called network effects "network externalities". But network effects are not always externalities, as Liebowitz and Margolis (1994) stressed.

Liebowitz and Margolis argue that many indirect network effects are pecuniary. If adoption by buyers just lowers price, it might be that Figure 31.1 describes payoffs to buyers, but sellers bear an equal negative effect. Then, while *buyers jointly* could be made better off by a well-targeted small subsidy from inframarginal to marginal buyers, no such subsidy can make *everyone* (sellers included) better off. However, the microfoundations of such pecuniary network effects seem unclear. Decreasing costs in

110 Beige (2001) shows that equilibrium locally maximizes a "harmony" function that counts only half of the network effects in the sum of payoffs.

111 Dynamic adoption paths with falling prices or other "drivers" of increasing adoption have been studied by (e.g.) Rohlfs (1974), Farrell and Shapiro (1992, 1993), Economides and Himmelberg (1995), Choi and Thum (1998), and Vettas (2000). Prices may fall over time because of Coasian dynamics: see Section 3.6. Adoption paths can also be driven by the strengthening of network effects: human languages with more trade and travel; computer programming languages with more modularity and re-use; VCRs with more movie rental.

a competitive industry often reflect a real economy of scale (perhaps upstream), so there is an efficiency (not just pecuniary) benefit of coordination. With no real economy of agglomeration, it is unclear how a sheer price shift can both favor buyers and also induce additional entry by sellers, as we noted in Section 3.1. Church, Gandal and Krause (2002) stress that there can be a real efficiency gain when a larger "hardware" network attracts more varied "software", not just lower prices.

More compellingly, *any* economic effect is an externality only if not internalized. A network effect might be internalized through side payments among adopters, although this will be hard if there are many players or private information. Alternatively (see Sections 3.6 and 3.7) a seller who can capture the benefits of a larger network might internalize network effects and voluntarily subsidize marginal adopters, as in Segal's (1999) model of public offers. But unless a seller can accurately target those adopters, subsidy is costly, and while it may sometimes work well enough, it seems clear that it often will not. Indeed, first-best pricing would require the price to each adopter to be equal to incremental cost less his external contribution to others, and such pricing jeopardizes profits and budget balance. Suppose for instance that a good will be supplied if and only if all K groups agree. For first-best adoption incentives, the price facing group i should be equal to the cost C of supplying the good to all, less the additional surplus accruing to groups other than i as a result of group i's agreeing: $p_i = C - \sum_{j \neq i} u^j(N)$. Hence $\sum p_i - C = (K-1)[C - \sum u^i(N)]$, so costs are covered if and only if adoption is inefficient! (First-best incentives require that each adopter be a residual claimant, leaving the vendor a negative equity interest at the margin.) For these reasons, adoption prices will often not fully internalize network effects, and a profitably supplied single network good will be under-adopted.

Third, any externalities are smaller and ambiguous when networks compete. To illustrate, suppose that $K = 3$, and that groups 1 and 2 have adopted A and B, respectively; now group 3 is choosing. A-adopters (group 1) gain if group 3 adopts A, but B-adopters gain if it adopts B. When each choice means rejecting the other, the net effect on others is ambiguous.[112]

3.4. The coordination problem

When networks compete, we just noted that any conventional externality becomes weaker and ambiguous. The same logic, however, *strengthens* the marginal effect –

112 To quantify, treat K as large, and approximate the set of adopters with a continuum. A small shift of $\mathrm{d}x$ users from a network of size x_A to one of size x_B has a net effect on other adopters of $e = [x_B u'_B(x_B) - x_A u'_A(x_A)]\,\mathrm{d}x$: this has ambiguous sign and is smaller in magnitude than at least one of the $x_i u'_i(x_i)\,\mathrm{d}x$. The incentive to "splinter" from what most others are doing is too strong at the margin (defection imposes a negative net externality, or conformity confers a positive externality) if $e < 0$ whenever $x_B < x_A$. When the goods are homogeneous except for network size, that condition is that $xu'(x)$ is increasing: see Farrell and Saloner (1992). In the convenient (if unrealistic) Metcalfe's Law case $u(n) = vn$, there is thus too much incentive to defect from a network to which most players will adhere. Then there is not just a benefit but a positive externality from conformity.

the fact that adoption encourages others to adopt the same network. A user's adoption of A instead of B not only directly makes A more attractive to others but also makes the alternative, B, less so.[113] For instance, part of the positive feedback in the adoption of CDs was the declining availability of LP records as CDs became more popular.

Through the marginal effect, strong network effects create multiple adoption equilibria and hence coordination problems. Optimal coordination is hard, as everyday experience and laboratory experiments [Ochs (1995), Gneezy and Rottenstreich (2004)] confirm. Coordination problems include actual breakdowns of coordination (Section 3.4.1) and coordination on the wrong focal point (Section 3.4.2). Coordination is especially difficult – and the institutions to aid it work less well – when (as in the Battle of the Sexes) the incentive for coordination coexists with conflict over what to coordinate on.

3.4.1. Coordination breakdowns: mistakes, splintering, and wait-and-see

Coordination "breaks down" when adopters choose incompatible options but would all prefer to coordinate. This can happen in at least two ways, which we call confusion and splintering. Economic theorists' equilibrium perspective pushes them toward (probably over-) optimistic views on the risks of such failures, but case studies and policy discussion often implicate coordination failures.

Confusion Coordination can break down by mistake or confusion if adopters do not know what others are doing.[114] Common knowledge of plans averts such confusion, and the simplest models assume it away by focusing on pure-strategy equilibrium, in which by definition players know one another's strategies and do not make mistakes.[115] Other models use mixed-strategy equilibrium,[116] which may be too pessimistic about coordination: each player's attempt to coordinate with others is maximally difficult in mixed-strategy equilibrium.[117]

Splintering Second, coordination can break down even in pure-strategy equilibrium with strategic certainty. This happens if product differentiation discourages unilateral

[113] With a continuum of adopters, the gain in A's relative attractiveness from a small increase in its adoption at B's expense is proportional not just to $u'_A(x_A)$, as it would be if A were the only network good, but to $u'_A(x_A) + u'_B(x_B)$. Note that this strengthening of the marginal effect depends on the total effect in both A and B.

[114] In *The Gift of the Magi*, a famous short story by O. Henry, Jim sold his watch to buy his wife Della a comb; Della sold her hair to buy Jim a watch-chain. Their plans were secret because each was meant as a Christmas surprise for the other.

[115] Rationalizability, on the other hand, unhelpfully permits any outcome in a simultaneous-adoption game with strong network effects.

[116] See for instance Dixit and Shapiro (1986), Farrell (1987), Farrell and Saloner (1988), Bolton and Farrell (1990), Crawford (1995).

[117] But mixed-strategy equilibrium can be defended as a shorthand for a symmetric Bayesian–Nash equilibrium with incomplete information.

moves (e.g. to slightly larger networks) but is weak enough that a coordinated move of everyone on networks B, C and D to network A would benefit all.

When there are just two networks A and B splintering is impossible if the users of each network can optimally coordinate as a group, but can arise if, for example, a coordinated move of everyone on network B to network A would benefit all of them, but the users of B cannot coordinate.

The incompatible outcome is thus (in game-theory language) an equilibrium but not coalition-proof: if multiple decision makers could coordinate a move they would all do better. We call this *splintering*: a dysfunctional equilibrium with multiple small and consequently unsuccessful networks instead of one large and successful one. Common knowledge of plans does *not* avert these problems; their solution requires a leadership-like ability to focus on "let's all do X instead".

Evidence that splintering is important includes the demand for consensus compatibility standards, which provide just such leadership.[118] Such standards (see Section 3.4.3) go beyond mere communication of plans, since common knowledge need not cure the problem. For instance, following Thompson (1954), Hemenway (1975) and Gabel (1991) argue that early twentieth-century standardization of auto parts mainly reduced spurious variety. Even before the standardization meetings any manufacturer could have chosen to match another's (non-proprietary, non-secret) specifications; apparently such a unilateral move would not pay, but a coordinated voluntary move did.[119] But consensus standards generally are non-binding and do not involve side payments, so they would not affect a failure to standardize that was a coalition-proof equilibrium reflection of (say) differences in tastes.

There is little theoretical work on splintering, although Kretschmer (2001) explores how it can retard innovation when there are multiple alternatives to a single established standard.[120] But it features prominently in case studies. Postrel (1990) argued that quadraphonic sound in the 1970s failed because competing firms sponsored incompatible quad systems and because hardware producers did not adequately manage complements (recorded music). Rohlfs (2001) describes how competing incompatible fax systems (invented in 1843) stalled for over a century until consensus standardization in the late 1970s.[121] Augereau, Greenstein and Rysman (in press) claim that the adoption of 56kbps modem technology in aggregate was stalled by the coexistence of two equally good incompatible standards until the ITU issued a third that became focal.

[118] An optimistic view would be that consensus standards promptly solve the problem wherever it arises, so splintering never persists. But finding consensus standards seems slow and painful, which casts doubt on such optimism. If the pain and slowness arises from difficulty in finding Pareto-improving coordinated shifts, however, then the theory sketched in the text is incomplete.

[119] The point is not that there are increasing returns in compatibility benefits, but that a critical mass may be necessary to overcome differences in tastes, beliefs, etc.

[120] Goerke and Holler (1995) and Woeckener (1999) also stress inefficiencies of splintering.

[121] Economides and Himmelberg (1995) estimated a demand system for the adoption of fax under a single standard.

Saloner (1990) discusses splintering among Unix implementations (widely blamed for slow adoption of Unix until Linux became relatively focal). Besen and Johnson (1986) argued that AM stereo was adopted slowly because there were competing, broadly comparable, standards and no player could start a strong bandwagon: adopters (radio stations) avoided explicit coordination because of antitrust fears, and the FCC did not take a lead. Microsoft was accused of "polluting" or intentionally splintering the Java standard when it perceived the latter as a threat to its own non-Java standard. Rysman (2004) notes that competition in yellow pages may involve splintering, thus reducing network benefits (although he finds that this does not outweigh losses from monopoly). He does not assess whether advertisers and users might instead all coordinate on the directory that offers them jointly the best deal – a sunnier non-splintering view of incompatible competition that theory has tended to find focal.

Do similar splintering concerns arise with traditional economies of scale? In terms of cooperative game theory (how much surplus is generated by various groups of participants) network effects and economies of scale are isomorphic, so concerns about splintering parallel classic concerns about inefficiently small-scale production in monopolistic competition. Modern models of the latter, since Spence (1976) and Dixit and Stiglitz (1977), mostly attribute splintering among monopolistically competitive firms to horizontal product differentiation, and because variety is valuable, these models find that although each firm is too small to minimize average cost, it need not be too small for overall efficiency. But the classical suspicion that equilibrium involves too much fragmentation re-surfaces in that a popular claimed efficiency motive for horizontal mergers is achieving more efficient scale.[122]

Fear of breakdowns Even mere fear of coordination breakdowns may delay adoption as people wait to see what others will do.[123] This can inefficiently slow adoption through strategic uncertainty rather than because of the externality from adoption.

3.4.2. *Coordinating on the wrong equilibrium*

Because coordination is hard, clumsy cues such as tradition and authority are often used. Schelling (1960) suggested that two people wishing to meet in New York might well go, by tradition, to Grand Central Station at noon. Many species of animals meet at fixed times or places for mating. Human meetings, and work hours, are often arranged in advance, and thus do not respond sensitively to later-revealed information about what is convenient for participants. The persistence of such clumsy solutions testifies to the difficulty of flexible optimal coordination. It would therefore be surprising if multiple adopters of networks always coordinated on the choice that gives them the most surplus.

[122] For a skeptical view see Farrell and Shapiro (2001). A merger removes all competition between firms, whereas a common standard replaces incompatible competition with compatible competition; see Section 3.9.

[123] Kornish (2006) describes a "decision-theoretic" model of adoption timing under strategic uncertainty, but takes as given the behavior of all agents but one.

Other parts of economics have studied the possibility of (perhaps persistent) coordination on the wrong equilibrium. Rosenstein-Rodan (1943) and Murphy, Shleifer and Vishny (1989) suggested that industrialization requires a "Big Push" that coordinates many sectors of the economy and that may not happen under *laissez-faire*. That is, industrialization is a "good" equilibrium, but the economy may stay at the "bad" pre-industrial equilibrium without major intervention. Modern economic geography sees patterns of development as partly fortuitous [Saxenian (1994), Krugman (1991a), Davis and Weinstein (2002)]. Macroeconomists have studied how otherwise irrelevant "sunspot" signals can guide economies to good or bad equilibria[124]; game theory has studied how cheap talk can do so.

Starting from a bad equilibrium, there would (by definition) be joint rewards for getting to a better equilibrium, but no rewards to individually deviating. As Liebowitz and Margolis (1994, 1995) stressed, this can suggest a role for an entrepreneur: in Sections 3.6–3.8 below, we note some entrepreneurial tactics.

i. *Single network* With a single network (Figure 31.1), voluntary adoption is weakly Pareto-improving, so an equilibrium with more adoption Pareto-dominates one with less. Dybvig and Spatt (1983) show that there is a *maximal equilibrium*, in which all players who adopt in any equilibrium adopt. This maximal equilibrium is Pareto preferred to all other equilibria, which thus have too little adoption.[125]

As in any game with multiple equilibria, *expectations are key*. If players expect others to adopt, they too will adopt. Shifting from a simultaneous-move perspective to a more dynamic one (informally at this point), implications include positive feedback and critical mass: once enough adoption happens or is confidently foreseen, further self-reinforcing adoption follows. Similarly lack of adoption is self-reinforcing: a network product can enter a "death spiral" (a dynamic form of the chicken-and-egg problem) if low adoption persuades others not to adopt.[126]

While they both involve under-adoption, this chicken-and-egg problem is quite different from the marginal externality in Sections 3.3.4 and 3.3.5 above. The marginal problem arises only when preferences are not similar,[127] could typically be helped by small subsidies to marginal adopters, and cannot be solved by voluntary joint action without side payments; whereas the chicken-and-egg problem arises even with identical adopters, might be solvable by coordinating better without side payments, and often cannot be helped by small subsidies.

[124] See e.g. Cooper (1999), Cooper and John (1988), Diamond (1982), and Bryant (1994).

[125] This is characteristic of games with supermodularity [Topkis (1978, 1998) or Milgrom and Roberts (1990)] or "strategic complements" [Bulow, Geanakoplos and Klemperer (1985a, 1985b)].

[126] Schelling (1978) describes such dynamics in a wide range of applications. Of course, the dynamics can also work in the other direction, with critical mass and take-off. Jeitschko and Taylor (2001) study the stability of "faith-based coordination".

[127] This assumes, as does most of the literature, that each adopter's choice is zero-one. When each adopter makes a continuous quantity choice a marginal problem arises even if preferences are identical.

ii. *Competing networks* Similar coordination problems can cause the adoption of the wrong network good. In Figure 31.2, if players expect others to adopt *A*, they will do so, but expectations in favor of *B* are equally self-fulfilling. And if expectations clash, so too will choices. What, then, drives expectations? In general one must look to cues outside Figures 31.1 and 31.2, as we discuss in the rest of this subsection.

Clumsy coordination can also blunt competitive pressures among networks, since business does not reliably go to the best offer, as we discuss in Section 3.7.

3.4.3. Cheap talk and consensus standards

A natural response to a coordination problem is to talk. Credible talk can make plans common knowledge and thus avert confusion-based coordination failures, and may help adopters coordinate changes in plans and thus escape splintered equilibria or coordination on the wrong focal point. In fact, many voluntary "consensus standards" are reached through talk, sometimes mediated through standards organizations; David and Shurmer (1996) report that consensus standardization has grown dramatically.[128] Large official organizations often have formal procedures; smaller consortia may be more flexible.[129] The economics literature on consensus standards is less developed than that on de facto or bandwagon standards, perhaps because reaching consensus seems political rather than a narrowly economic process.

Game theory finds that cheap talk works less well the more conflict there is. At the vendor level, conflict can arise because not everyone wants to coordinate: see Section 3.8 below. Discussion of consensus standards has focused more on conflict that arises if all players want to coordinate but disagree over what to coordinate on, as in the Battle of the Sexes. For example, when a promising new technology arrives, conflict is likely between the "installed base" of those who are more locked in to an old technology and those who are less so. Gabel (1991) argues that conflict is likely between those who are and are not vertically integrated. Conflict may also arise because active participants in standards organizations tend to have vested interests (which indeed may motivate them to bear the costs of participating).[130] Vested interest may be especially strong when potential standards incorporate intellectual property.

[128] Some practitioners reserve the term "standard" for formal consensus coordination. Standards organizations include the International Telecommunications Union (ITU), and a wide variety of national standards bodies such as ANSI in the U.S.; ANSI is an umbrella organization for specialized industry standards development. There are also many informal standards fora.

[129] On the institutions, see e.g. Hemenway (1975), Kahin and Abbate (1995). On the economics of consensus standards development see also Besen and Saloner (1994). Cargill (1989) and Berg and Schumny (1990) describe the standards process in information technology.

Weiss and Sirbu (1990) econometrically study technology choices in voluntary consensus standards committees. Lehr (1995) describes consensus standardization in the Internet. See also OECD (1991), Grindley (1995), and Simcoe (2003).

[130] Weiss and Sirbu (1990), Farrell and Simcoe (2007) [see also Farrell (1993)].

As a result, attempts to coordinate through talk may induce bargaining delays that dissipate much of the gains from coordination. The economics literature stresses this observation, echoing concerns of many standards participants. Economists have modeled the process as a war of attrition: participants who favor standard A hope that those who favor B will give up rather than delay further. Farrell and Saloner (1988) introduced such a model with complete information and two participants, and compared "committee" versus "bandwagon" standardization, and against a hybrid mechanism.[131] Farrell and Simcoe (2007) and David and Monroe (1994) observe that when there is private information about the quality of proposed standards, the war of attrition may select for good proposals, although at a high cost [Simcoe (2003) shows how similar results can emerge from rational search by interested parties]. They then assess efficiency consequences of rules in the consensus standards process. For instance, many standards organizations limit the exploitation of intellectual property embodied in standards [Lemley (2002)], and this may reduce delays as well as limit patent-holders' ex post market power. Simcoe (2003) analyzes data from the Internet Engineering Task Force and finds evidence that more vested interest (measured as more patents, or more commercial participation) causes more delay. Another response is to seek rapid consensus before vested interest ripens.

With two players (as in those models), either can ensure immediate consensus by conceding. With more players, Bulow and Klemperer (1999) show that delays can be very long if conceding brings no reward until others also concede, as is the case if (as in many standards organizations) a standard requires near-unanimous consensus.[132]

3.4.4. Coordination through sequential choice

Game theory claims that with full information and strong network effects, fully sequential adoption ensures coordination on a Pareto-undominated standard. The argument [Farrell and Saloner (1985)] is fairly convincing with two groups. For simplicity, consider the single-network case. Suppose that $u^i(N) > 0 > u^i(n_i)$ for all i, so that adoption is an efficient equilibrium and non-adoption is an inefficient equilibrium of the simultaneous-adoption game. If group 1 first adopts, then group 2 will also adopt: knowing this, group 1 can (and therefore will) get $u^1(N)$ by adopting. By moving first,

131 In a hybrid mechanism, compatibility may result either by consensus or by one proponent driving a market bandwagon (but if both try simultaneously, the result is incompatibility). Thus the consensus standards process competes directly against the bandwagon process; Gabel (1991) stresses that network effects can be realized through consensus, bandwagons, or other means. Besen and Farrell (1991) note a different form of competition among processes: less-formal consensus processes may act faster than more formal ones such as the International Telecommunications Union (ITU); Lerner and Tirole (2006) study forum-shopping equilibria in consensus standards.

132 By contrast, they show that if a player can cease to bear delay costs by unilaterally conceding (as in oligopolists competing to win a natural monopoly), a multi-player war will quickly collapse to a two-player one. Political scientists analogously have Duverger's Law, a claim that most elections will have two serious candidates.

group 1 can start an irresistible bandwagon: it need not fear that adoption will give it only $u^1(n_1)$; thus only the efficient equilibrium is subgame-perfect when adoption is sequential.

The argument extends in theory to any finite number of players, and to the choice between two (or more) networks.[133] But it is much less compelling with many players: it assumes that each adopter sees all previous choices before making his own, and assumes strong common knowledge of preferences and of rationality to forge a chain of backward induction with (on the order of) K steps, an unreliable form of reasoning (empirically) when K is large. Thus the theoretical result is surely too strong: the first player should not count on it if $u^1(n)$ is very negative for small n; and if players will not rely on the result, it becomes false. But it does express one possible route out of inefficient coordination traps: an influential adopter could try to start a bandwagon. In this respect influence is related to size: when a big player moves, it shifts others' incentives by more than when a small player moves. Indeed, it may even become a dominant strategy for others to follow, surely a stronger bandwagon force than backward induction in the subgame among the remaining players. Thus size confers leadership ability, and markets with at least one highly concentrated layer are less apt (other things, notably conflict, equal) to be caught in pure coordination traps. Illustrating this idea, Holmes (1999) discusses the role of large players in the geographic shift of the U.S. textile industry; Bresnahan (2001a) discusses AOL's role (as a large and potentially pivotal user) in the Netscape–Microsoft battle for browser share.

This result is optimistic about the ability of adoption bandwagons to avert Pareto-inferior outcomes. As we see next, however, bandwagons may be less good at balancing early and late adopters' preferences.

3.5. *Inertia in adoption*

Individual switching costs can cause problems, as in Section 2 above, but at least each user makes his own choice. Network effects, by binding together different users' choices, might generate a stronger and more worrying form of inertia, locking society in to an inefficient product (or behavior) because it is hard to coordinate a switch to something better but incompatible – especially where network effects coexist with individual switching costs. In a range of cases, including QWERTY, English spelling, VHS, and many computer software products, some suggest that a poor standard *inefficiently* persists because network effects create excessive inertia. Liebowitz and Margolis (1990, 1995) are skeptical (notably in QWERTY) and argue (2001) that success in computer software has followed trade reviewers' assessments of product quality; but Bresnahan and Greenstein (1999) argues that this has been true only in wide-open periods and that high quality is necessary but not sufficient for success. It is hard to test ex

[133] Farrell and Saloner (1985) also show (with two groups) that cheap talk need not help when information on preferences is incomplete; Lee (2003) extends this to K groups.

post excess inertia in case studies by directly assessing the efficiency of outcomes; we focus instead on the economic logic. Here we ask how much inertia there is in adoption dynamics at given prices. In Sections 3.6 and 3.7, we ask how sponsors' price and other strategies affect it.

3.5.1. Ex post inertia

Inertia arises ex post if later adopters remain compatible with the installed base even though an alternative would be better if network effects were neutralized. Just as contestability theory observes that economies of scale alone do not create an advantage to incumbency, so too network effects alone need not generate inertia: in principle everyone could instantly shift to coordinate on the better alternative. But there are usually some sunk costs or switching costs; and if expectations center on the status quo then inertia results even if there are no tangible intertemporal links.

Inertia surely is often substantial: Rohlfs (2001) argues from the history of fax that a network product without stand-alone value must be "truly wonderful and low-priced" to succeed; he and others attribute the VCR's success to its offering stand-alone value; Shapiro and Varian (1998) quote Intel CEO Andy Grove's rule of thumb that an incompatible improvement must be "ten times better".

Inertia can be efficient: incompatibility with the installed base is a real social cost if the status quo has network effects. But inertia is ex post "excess" if it would be more efficient for later adopters to switch, *given* earlier adopters' choice. (As that phrasing suggests, we follow the literature in assuming here that the installed base will not switch; if it would, then later adopters would sacrifice no network benefits and would collectively have excessive incentives to switch.) For example, it would be ex post excess inertia if society should switch to the DSK typewriter keyboard, counting the full social costs, but network effects and switching costs *inefficiently* prevent this. This requires that pivotal movers inefficiently fail to move, because they expect others not to move (the "horses" problem), or because they bear a larger share of the costs than of the benefits of moving (the "penguins" problem).[134]

In a simple two-group case where group 1 is committed and group 2 optimally coordinates internally, neither of these can happen, so inertia cannot be ex post excessive. In Figure 31.2, suppose that group 1 has irreversibly adopted (say) A. To be adopted by group 2, B must be substantially better: $u_B^2(n_2) > u_A^2(N)$, or equivalently $u_B^2(n_2) - u_A^2(n_2) > u_A^2(N) - u_A^2(n_2)$. That is, B's quality or price advantage (assessed by group 2) must outweigh the additional network benefit of compatibility with group 1 (assessed by group 2 when it adopts A). Of course, there is inertia: if group 2 values compatibility with group 1, B will fail unless it is much better than A. But to maximize total

[134] Farrell and Saloner (1986a) analogize the first problem to horses tied to one another who will not wander far or fast, because none can move independently and staying still is more focal than moving in a particular direction at a particular speed. They [and, e.g., Choi (1997a)] analogize the second problem to penguins, wishing to dive for fish but concerned that the first one in is most vulnerable to predators.

surplus ex post, group 2 should adopt B only if $u_B^2(n_2) > u_A^2(N) + [u_A^1(N) - u_A^1(n_1)]$. Group 2 internalizes only part of the social benefit of inter-group compatibility, and is thus too ready to strand group 1. Far from excess inertia, this model displays ex post "excess momentum".[135]

This result instructively contradicts the popular intuition that inertia is obviously ex post excessive. But with more than two groups, ex post excess inertia may well occur, because optimal coordination among ex post adopters may well fail due to coordination problems and/or free-riding. To see this, return to the sequential adoption model of Farrell and Saloner (1985). Adopters $1, 2, \ldots, K$ arrive in sequence and, on arrival, irreversibly choose to adopt A or B. Because of idiosyncratic preferences or relative technological progress over time, adopters have different preferences between A and B. There are network effects: adopter i gets payoff $u_z^i(x_z)$, where x_z is the total number of adopters on his network $z = A, B$.

Arthur (1989) simplified this framework by assuming that an adopter gets network benefits only from previous adoptions, not future ones; thus adopters need not form expectations about the future. He showed that a technology favored by enough *early* adopters can become permanently locked in. If the relative network sizes ever become lopsided enough to outweigh the strongest idiosyncratic preferences, all subsequent adopters follow suit, because none wants to lead a new bandwagon, even if he knew that all future adopters would join it. There is a free-rider problem in overcoming an installed-base lead. Thus suppose that network effects make $x = 2$ much more valuable than $x = 1$, and that most adopters prefer B, but that by chance the first adopter prefers, and adopts, A. Adopter 2, then, who prefers B, must compare $u_B^2(1)$ against $u_A^2(2)$. He may adopt A only because $x = 1$ is so undesirable, in which case he and all subsequent adopters would pick A; while if he chose B, then other B-lovers would be happy choosing B thereafter.[136] This is extreme, but getting a new network up to critical mass can generally be costly for the pioneer, harmful to the installed base, but valuable to those who arrive later.

Arthur's assumption that adopters do not care about future adoptions seems to fit learning-by-doing with spillovers rather than most network effects, but we can usefully re-formulate it. Adopters more generally get the present value of a flow of network benefits, where the flow is increasing in adoptions to date. Then if adopter 2 adopts B and others follow, his sacrifice of network benefits is only temporary.

In this broader framework, Arthur's model assumes that adopters are infinitely impatient, thus both ignoring coordination problems and exaggerating the free-rider problem.

[135] Farrell and Saloner (1986b) phrased this result in terms of "unique equilibrium" because they did not assume that each group optimally coordinates. Ellison and Fudenberg (2000) use essentially this model with optimal coordination to argue that there may be excessive innovation. If early adopters (group 1 here) would switch ex post to retain compatibility with group 2, group 2 is clearly again too willing to choose B. See also Shy (1996) and Witt (1997).

[136] This is similar to the "informational herding" literature: see e.g. Banerjee (1992), Scharfstein and Stein (1990), Ellison and Fudenberg (1993, 1995), Bikhchandani, Hirshleifer and Welch (1992). Berndt, Pindyck and Azoulay (2003) argue that informational herding creates network effects in anti-ulcer drugs.

On the other hand, Farrell and Saloner (1986a) considered ex ante identical adopters with a finite discount rate. Adopters adopt immediately on arrival, and good B becomes available at date T. Specializing their model in the opposite direction from Arthur's, if identical adopters are infinitely patient *and* can optimally coordinate from any point on, the problem reduces to the two-group model outlined above in which ex post excess inertia cannot arise.

But the coordination problem re-emerges as soon as we depart from Arthur's infinite impatience. In particular, if previous history is the leading cue for coordination, then a patient small adopter 2 will compare $u_B^2(1)$ against $u_A^2(K)$,[137] so that an early lead would be even *more* powerful than Arthur's model suggests; it may be a self-fulfilling prophecy that a minority network will never grow. And if there are many contenders to displace the incumbent, adopters might expect splintering among those who abandon the incumbent [Kretschmer (2001)]. By the same logic, if everyone expects the new network to take over then it often will do so even if it is inefficient.

With identical adopters, the inductive logic of Farrell and Saloner (1985) suggests that the first adopter to arrive after T is pivotal. If he prefers that everyone forever stick to A, he can adopt A and thus make the next adopter feel all the more strongly the same way; similarly if he prefers that all from now on adopt B.[138] Because of the free-rider problem, the pivotal adopter may have too little incentive to adopt the new network, B; on the other hand, adopting B strands the installed base. As in Section 3.3.5 above, the net externality can run in either direction, so ex post excess inertia and excess momentum are both possible, even in unique equilibrium. If we eschew the long chain of backward induction and instead assume that the date-T adopter expects others' future choices to be unaffected by his own (he is small), then there are typically multiple equilibria and expectations determine the outcome, which can be biased in either direction. This would presumably also be the case if nobody knows which adopter is pivotal.

Farrell and Saloner (1986a) and Ostrovsky and Schwarz (2005) describe other models in which adopters are currently on A, and choose when, if at all, to switch to B. In these models, efficient coordination is hindered by delays before other adopters can follow an early mover's lead. Each is most easily described for two adopters. In Farrell and Saloner, each adopter has only occasional opportunities to adopt a new technology, so even if each adopts as soon as possible, adopting first entails a temporary loss of network benefits. If that is painful enough, no adopter is willing to lead; the private cost may be either greater or less than the social cost. In Ostrovsky and Schwarz, each adopter chooses a "target" time to adopt, and if there were no noise, immediate adoption by all would be a Pareto-dominant equilibrium. But when actual adoption time is affected by (continuous) noise, Pareto-dominance is not enough. Each adopter i can contemplate slightly delaying its adoption, by $\mathrm{d}t$. If p_i is the probability that it will be the first to

[137] This makes what may seem an unduly pessimistic assumption about later adopters' expectations if adopter 2 picks B. But that pessimistic assumption seems more natural if we are instead discussing adopter 3 after two A-adoptions.

[138] Thus his preference is evaluated assuming that all subsequent adopters follow his lead.

adopt, slight delay is privately desirable with probability p_i and then yields a gain of $[u^i_A(2) - u^i_B(1)]\,\mathrm{d}t$; it is privately undesirable with probability $1 - p_i$ and then yields a loss of $[u^i_B(2) - u^i_A(1)]\,\mathrm{d}t$. Hence if $(1 - p_i)[u^i_B(2) - u^i_A(1)] < p_i[u^i_A(2) - u^i_B(1)]$, or $p_i > r_i \equiv \frac{u^i_B(2) - u^i_A(1)}{u^i_B(2) - u^i_A(1) + u^i_A(2) - u^i_B(1)}$, it will prefer to delay slightly. Thus in any equilibrium with adoption by all, $p_i \leqslant r_i$ for all i. But $\sum p_i = 1$, so if $\sum r_i < 1$ then there is no equilibrium with adoption, even if all would gain ($u^i_B(2) > u^i_A(2)$ for all i) and there is only a little noise. However much each player expects others (collectively) to delay, he wants to delay slightly more.

Entry Our discussion of inertia also informs us about competitive entry of a product that is incompatible with an established network. Inertia implies that even if an entrant offers a better deal, network effects aside, to new adopters, they may (and perhaps should) stick to the installed base, assuming that the base itself will not move (perhaps because of individual switching costs). Incompatible entry is difficult, and Fudenberg and Tirole (2000) show that limit pricing can be powerful with network effects.

If new adopters optimally coordinate, this inertia is presumably because, for them, compatibility with the installed base outweighs the new product's advantages. As noted above, inertia can be ex post efficient given incompatibility,[139] although even ex post excess momentum (too-strong incentives for such entry) is possible. The point here is not whether incompatible entry is *too* hard ex post, given incompatibility and the installed base, but the fact that even efficient (indeed, even less-than-efficient) inertia can confer ex post market power on the established network.

Some incompatible innovation/entry succeeds in overcoming inertia. Of course, a product that is "ten times better" may simply outweigh inertia. But inertia can be lowered in other ways, as Bresnahan and Greenstein's (1999) discussion of competitive transitions in the computer industry stresses.

First, compatibility with the installed base eliminates the coordination and free-rider problems, and lowers individual switching costs; even partial compatibility through converters (see Section 3.8) can help. Similarly, multi-homing or double purchase [de Palma, Leruth and Regibeau (1999)] mitigates pivotal adopters' losses of network benefits if they switch; Shapiro (1999) thus argues that exclusive dealing[140] by incumbents in network markets is especially threatening. Complementors can also multi-home, as when applications software providers "port" their programs from one operating system to another.

[139] Moreover, we saw that ex post excess inertia, blocking ex post efficient incompatible entry, is plausible when there are free-rider or coordination problems among adopters, and perhaps especially if expectations track history; Krugman (1991b) discusses the relationship between expectations and history. Since those problems may become more severe as the installed base grows, incompatible entrants may face "narrow windows" of opportunity [David (1986)].

[140] Broadly speaking this means agreements that make it hard for an entrant to thrive with small scale or limited scope.

Rapid market growth makes the installed base less important relative to new adopters, and can thus mitigate pivotal adopters' transient losses of network benefits if they lead a switch [Farrell and Saloner (1986a)]; large players may both suffer less from such losses and be especially effective leaders of a bandwagon. When expectations otherwise focus on the incumbent, mechanisms such as consensus standards to help adopters coordinate on the best deal can also lower entry barriers. Finally, just as splintering among innovators tends to preserve the status quo [Kretschmer (2001)], disarray and incompatibility in the installed base may open up opportunities for a "strong leader" that can offer coordination as well as (or instead of) a better product.

As this last point suggests, successful static compatibility or standardization might retard (incompatible) innovation. Although the logic requires care – it is natural that the better the status quo, the less likely a good system is to engage in costly change – this might be an argument (in the spirit of maintaining biodiversity) against static standardization, as Cabral and Kretschmer (2007) explore. But while marketwide compatibility may retard incompatible replacement of the compatible outcome, mix-and-match compatibility encourages component innovation [Langlois (1992)].

3.5.2. Early power

When there will be inertia – even ex post efficient inertia – early movers' choices determine later adoptions. Thus early movers might strategically or inadvertently commit to a standard that is bad for later adopters but will not be abandoned. We say there is *excess early power* if early movers adopt and are followed but this is ex ante inefficient: efficiency might demand instead that they defer to later adopters' preferences, or that they wait. That is, early adopters have excess power if their preferences weigh too heavily (relative to later adopters') in the collective choice of what is adopted.

Such an ex ante problem is sometimes called excess inertia, but we prefer to distinguish it more sharply from the ex post problem discussed above. They differ not only in timing, but in that ex post excess inertia concerns *later* adopters' choices, while ex ante excess early power concerns *early* adopters' choices. Excess early power does not imply ex post excess inertia: for instance, with two groups we saw that if group 2 optimally coordinates then there cannot be ex post excess inertia, but if inter-group network effects are strong and group 1 optimally coordinates, it has all the power. But the two concepts reflect the same force: the stronger ex post inertia will be, the more power early adopters have.

Arthur's model predicts excess early power; foresight complicates but does not fundamentally change the picture. Moving first gives commitment: early adopters are pivotal (early power), and the more they recognize that later adoptions will have to follow, the less sensitive early adopters will be to later preferences. Like inertia, early power can be efficient but can readily go too far: with strong network effects, long-run network technology choice can be determined by first-mover advantage and by historical small events.[141] With positive (not necessarily small) probability, almost all adopters choose A but total surplus would have been greater had almost all chosen B.[142]

Lock-in could go the other way, in which case foresight weakens early power: if group 2 finds adopting B a dominant strategy, while group 1 wants to adopt whatever it expects group 2 to adopt, then group 2 is pivotal.[143] But that requires network effects to be strong for group 1 but weak for group 2, so reverse lock-in seems likely to be rarer and weaker than forward lock-in. Thus Farrell and Saloner (1985) found that, given preferences, each player is better off moving earlier: this "New Hampshire Theorem" says that earlier adopters' preferences get more weight than later adopters' in the collective outcome,[144] which strongly suggests excess early power.[145]

In summary, early adopters have the strategic advantage: there is a reasonable presumption of excess early power at the adopter level. As we see in Section 3.7.2 below, however, this need not imply that early advantages confer sustained success when sponsors of competing standards compete using penetration pricing.

3.5.3. Positive feedback and tipping

We have seen how early choices are powerful, able either to help coordination or to wield disproportionate influence. Thus any early lead in adoptions (whether strategic or accidental) will tend to expand rather than to dissipate. Network markets are "tippy": early instability and later lock-in.

To explore this, consider a continuum of identical adopters who only want to coordinate. There are three kinds of static pure-strategy Nash equilibria: all adopt A, all adopt B, and many splintered equilibria in which half adopt A and half adopt B (and all are indifferent). Now suppose market shares are randomly perturbed, and at each instant some adopters can change their move in response to current shares. Then as soon as the shares are unequal, those who can choose will adopt the majority product; this makes the half-and-half equilibrium unstable. The point carries over even with some horizontal product differentiation.[146]

141 Thus it can create a "butterfly effect": a butterfly flapping its wings might cause a hurricane years later and thousands of miles away.

142 In principle this might also arise if good A is worth more than B when each network is small but B is worth more than A when each network is large. As Liebowitz and Margolis (1994) observe, there is no obvious reason to expect that.

143 Holmes (1999) shows how adopters who care less than others about network effects (relative to their preferences between products, or in his case locations) can lead a transition. He uses this in explaining the migration of the U.S. cotton textile industry. Large groups that can successfully coordinate internally are thus prime candidates to be pivotal movers and get the best deals. Bresnahan (2001a) explored this in the context of AOL's adoption of Internet Explorer during the Netscape–Microsoft browser war.

144 Holding an early primary, as New Hampshire does, gives a state more influence when bandwagon effects are important in a national election.

145 Excess late power (sometimes called ex ante excess momentum) is also possible, because the outcome depends only on ordinal preferences and not on their intensity.

146 With a finite number of adopters rather than a continuum, the same force prevents equal shares being an equilibrium at all. See, e.g., Katz and Shapiro (1985, 1994). Echenique and Edlin (2004) show that strategic

Although sketchy, such dynamics suggest that re-equilibration by others (which is central to indirect network effects) strengthens instability.

Arthur (1989, 1990) and Arthur and Lane (1993) similarly find that if prices are fixed, and adoption decisions depend only on past adoptions (current shares of installed base), then one product or technology will come to dominate.[147,148]

3.5.4. Option value of waiting

We have seen that early adoption can freeze a technology choice and foreclose what would otherwise be later adopters' preferred choices. Above, we asked whether early adopters instead ought to defer to the known preferences of later adopters. When those preferences (and/or later costs) are not known early on, waiting can thus be efficient. Lock-in – even lock-in to a choice that's optimal given available information at the time – sacrifices social option value.

Just as future preferences are often under-weighted by market forces, option value will be. And institutions may be less apt to repair this: it is probably easier to acquire residual rights in one potential network with a clear future than to internalize the gains from waiting for something unpredictable. Whether or not the Dvorak keyboard is better than QWERTY, there clearly was a chance in 1888 that something better would later appear. How might incentives at that date incorporate this option value – what would persuade early generations of typists to wait, or to adopt diverse keyboards, *if* that was socially desirable in the long run? In principle the option value might be internalized by a century-long monopoly on typing so that the monopoly could price the loss of option value into early adoptions, or by a futuristic patent on a range of alternative keyboards so that Dr. Dvorak's grandparents could subsidize waiting or diversity. Even if there had been many individual long-lived patents on particular keyboards, their proprietors would have faced a public-good problem in encouraging waiting. These institutions seem far from reality. It might well *not* have been efficient for nineteenth-century typists to wait, or to use keyboards they did not like, in order to preserve a more realistic option for a different design in 1940. But it is hard to think that the market gave a very good *test of whether or not* that would have been desirable.

Sometimes option value could be preserved by making later products compatible with early adoption. Section 3.8 below discusses incentives to do this, but clearly early adopters, or a sponsor of a product that they favor, may not want to ensure compatibility if they expect ex post inertia (excess or not) under incompatibility, as they gain from

complementarities make mixed-strategy equilibria unstable, unless adopters have perverse beliefs about how shares will evolve.

[147] In these models, the probability of winning a consumer is a function of prices and shares of installed base; this assumption is rationalized by horizontal differentiation.

[148] In Ellison and Fudenberg (2003) and Ellison, Fudenberg and Möbius (2004), there may be a plateau of non-tipped outcomes from which no player unilaterally wants to move, if buyers dislike (slightly) outnumbering sellers more than they like being in a bigger market.

excess early power. Indeed, Choi (1994b) and Choi and Thum (1998) confirm that pre-emption competition for the New Hampshire first-mover advantage can make adoption inefficiently fast when moving quickly can drive a bandwagon. Recall however that adoption may be too slow because of the externality or because early adoption risks coordination failure.

3.6. Sponsored price and strategy for a single network

Having discussed the demand side of network markets – adopters' choices given the offers they face – we turn to the supply side. This section primarily discusses a network monopoly, but most of the insights apply equally to a firm trying to establish its standard against a rival standard, as Section 3.7 further explores.

A sponsor seeking to establish its network has two generic strategies. First, it may focus selling effort on pivotal adopters, whose choices strongly affect others'. In particular, when a network involves different *classes of adopters* (for instance a credit card network that must be adopted by consumers and merchants) a sponsor can choose where to focus its marketing or price-cutting; and when there are different *adoption dates* a sponsor can choose (subject to commitment issues) when to do so. Second, a sponsor might seek to visibly *commit* to ensuring widespread adoption, or otherwise work on *expectations*.

3.6.1. Pricing to different groups: penetration pricing

First consider separate prices to two classes or groups of adopters with inter-group network effects.[149] These groups might be peers at different dates (early and late adopters), or two sides of a market. As Rochet and Tirole (2002, 2006) and Armstrong (2006) observe, such two-sided markets include credit cards, brokers, auctions, matchmakers, conferences, journals, computer platforms, and newspapers.

Suppose first that the sponsor simultaneously commits to both prices. Increased sales to one group raise the other group's demand: the inter-group marginal network effect. So in broadly Ramsey fashion the optimal price to group 1 will be lower, the more strongly group 2's demand responds to adoption by group 1 and the more profitable (endogenously) are sales to group 2, as well as the higher group 1's own demand elasticity (as usual).[150] Thus a single seller's optimal prices to the two groups may well be asymmetric; indeed, one side often pays zero or below cost.[151]

[149] We consider only simple prices; Sundararajan (2003) discusses non-linear pricing with network effects.

[150] As we noted in Section 3.3.2, there may be intra-group network effects (or congestion effects if the groups are different sides of a market). These affect the welfare economics, but for profit-maximizing pricing we can treat each group as a demand curve.

[151] See for instance Parker and Van Alstyne (2005), Schmalensee (2002), Rochet and Tirole (2006). As we saw in Section 3.3.2 above, first-best prices would be below marginal cost for both groups. Ramsey pricing looks qualitatively similar to profit-maximizing pricing because the problems are closely related.

At an abstract level this is simply pricing with complementarities, as in Gillette's early strategy of giving away razors and making money on blades [Adams (1978)]; but here the complementarities are between different customers' adoption choices. If there is no single sponsor, implementing an optimal markup structure may require payments between sectors such as the credit card interchange fees discussed in Section 3.2; if that's hard to do well, it can encourage vertical integration.

With early and late groups the analysis is the same if the seller commits to a price path. For Ramsey-style reasons, low-then-high penetration pricing is privately (and can be socially) efficient in the usual case where early adopters are pivotal.

Finally, with early and late groups but no commitment, low–high pricing is even further encouraged. The seller will predictably set a second-period price higher than would be optimal ex ante, since ex post it will not take into account the effect on first-period adoption. Thus first-period adopters will expect a high future price, lowering first-period demand; and incompatible competition among sponsors will lower first-period prices in anticipation of the ex post rents. All these forces push towards bargain-then-ripoff penetration pricing, the reverse of Coasean dynamics.[152]

That commitment problem puts a sponsored network at a disadvantage against an open (competitively supplied) network product in the relatively rare case of reverse lock-in where second-period adopters are pivotal. A proprietary sponsor might then seek even costly forms of commitment such as (delayed) free licensing of a technology [Farrell and Gallini (1988), Economides (1996b)]. But sellers of an open product cannot recoup investment in below-cost early prices, so a sponsored product has an advantage when (as is probably typical) overall adoption responds more sensitively to early prices than to sophisticated predictions of later prices [Katz and Shapiro (1986a)].

3.6.2. Single monopoly price

Above, we separated the two roles of p: each adopter viewed the price facing him in the ordinary way, and based his relevant expectations on the price facing the complementary group. With switching costs, the ex ante and ex post prices are similarly separable when locked-in customers buy a distinct good such as service; otherwise they may have to be equal, as we discussed in Section 2.4. Similarly here prices to two sides of a market are presumably separable, but with two groups of peer adopters they may not be. In that case it is natural to suppress the two groups and simply study overall demand at the given price.

[152] Cabral, Salant and Woroch (1999) study monopoly penetration pricing of durable network goods when buyers have rational expectations. In certain classes of example, they find that Coase-conjecture price dynamics tend to predominate over penetration pricing: prices fall rather than rise over time, especially when there is complete information. Bensaid and Lesne (1996) find however that strong network effects remove the time-consistency Coase problem and cause optimal prices to increase over time. See also Mason (2000) and Choi (1994a). Radner and Sundararajan (2005) study a network monopolist's dynamic pricing problem when adopters expect each period's network size to be equal to last period's; they find extreme bargain-then-ripoff pricing (the monopolist prices at zero until the network reaches its desired size).

The "fulfilled-expectations demand curve" then matches each price p with those penetration levels x such that, when adopters expect penetration x, just x of them will adopt at price p: see e.g. Leibenstein (1950), Rohlfs (1974), Katz and Shapiro (1985), Economides (1996a). Such a demand curve is more elastic than each of the fixed-expectations curves of which it is built [Leibenstein (1950)]. Gabel (1991) suggests that Sony, Betamax's sponsor in VCRs, may have optimized against a less elastic (perhaps short-run) perceived demand curve because it did not anticipate video-rental network effects. Monopoly deadweight loss may be more severe with network effects: monopoly not only deters marginal adoption, but also lowers surplus of inframarginal adopters.[153]

Multiple equilibria in adoption at price p now show up as multiple intersections of the demand curve with a horizontal line at p. To pin down demand at p, one might rule out "unstable" equilibria (at which demand is upward-sloping); but if there is an unstable equilibrium, there are at least two stable equilibria. However one selects an adoption equilibrium for each p, there may well be discontinuous changes in behavior as a parameter such as cost varies continuously, as in catastrophe theory.[154] Even if a network product only gradually becomes cheaper or better over time, it may suddenly acquire critical mass and take off.[155]

A strategic monopoly seller might persuade adopters to coordinate on the largest equilibrium x given p. If so, we say that the seller can "affect expectations" and pick any (x^e, p) such that x^e is an adoption equilibrium at price p. The next subsection discusses some tactics for affecting expectations in this sense.

3.6.3. *Commitment strategies*

Since demand depends on expectations, a network sponsor can gain from commitment to size, to inspire confidence and optimism. Commitment can address both the marginal and multiple-equilibrium underadoption problems identified in Section 3.3 above.

One commitment is simply selling products early on. Sellers boast about (even exaggerate) sales. To be a useful commitment, sales must be visible and irreversible, so this strategy makes most sense for durables. Network effects typically arise from use, not from mere possession, so dumping (e.g., free) units on the market may be discounted. The most effective sales are to influential adopters whose adoption will boost others' by the most.

153 Farrell and Shapiro (1992) argue this in a linear example; but Lambertini and Orsini (2001), stressing network quality, reach different conclusions. One problem is that it is not clear what the demand curve "would be" without network effects. Rysman (2004) shows that, even if competition involves splintering, it is better than monopoly in his calibrated model of the market for Yellow Pages.

154 Indeed, if the rational-expectations demand curve has an upward-sloping portion, there is typically no everywhere-continuous selection of adoption equilibrium, even if there is everywhere a locally continuous selection.

155 Rohlfs (2001), Farrell and Shapiro (1992), and Economides and Himmelberg (1995) suggest examples of sudden success that might reflect such tipping. Liebowitz and Margolis (2001) question that interpretation and argue that price and share dynamics in computer software seem inconsistent with tipping.

A blunt early-sales strategy is of course *penetration pricing*, as discussed above. As we will see in Section 3.7 below, competition can induce penetration pricing as the form of competition for the market. When a monopoly engages in penetration pricing, however, it would seem to be leaving money on the table relative to convincing early buyers in some other fashion that the long-run network size will be large. Thus we focus here on means to commit to that.

To encourage early adoption, a seller would like to commit to selling more later than it will then wish to sell, a point made by Katz and Shapiro (1986a) and put in a broader framework by Segal (1999). This kind of commitment strategy can operate even when there is a single equilibrium; commitment shifts the equilibrium. We have already noted some tactics such as second-sourcing that might help such a commitment. One might model commitment in a reduced-form way through assumptions about a sponsor's strategic variable. Rather than just setting a price, a sponsor might seek to commit to quantities sold or to the utility it will give each (type of) adopter.

Reputation and general market credibility can help communicate commitment or boost expectations. Another commitment strategy is to open a standard to guarantee competitive future behavior, increasing early adopters' expectations of long-run network size. And integration with complementors might visibly improve incentives for supply of complements, as well as facilitate Ramsey-style cross-pricing.

When there are multiple equilibria, some of the same commitment tactics can help ensure a more favorable equilibrium. Rohlfs (2001) develops a model of irreversible adoption by many small buyers that involves dynamics at two levels. First, at any time buyers adopt if they want to do so given prices and given the current installed base, but they lack foresight and the adoption-equilibrium selection is thus pessimistic: there may be other equilibria with more adoption. In the second kind of dynamics, sponsors try to push the market past critical mass and generate positive feedback. For instance, a sponsor may dump enough units on the market to enter the basin of attraction of a preferred equilibrium.

In addition to the use of equilibrium-path price discrimination (penetration pricing), out-of-equilibrium (discriminatory) offers can eliminate an equilibrium that the seller dislikes, as we discuss next and as Segal and Whinston (2000) explored in the context of exclusive dealing. As that case illustrates, these equilibrium-selection tactics can work against buyers when networks compete, whereas in the case of a single network both seller and buyers prefer an equilibrium with more adoption.[156]

3.6.4. Contingent contracts

Commitment through contracts could in principle overcome the coordination problem, as Dybvig and Spatt (1983) noted. Suppose a seller offers buyers a contract: "The

[156] The reason is that one player's adoption of network A hurts – relative to the alternative – those who adopt B; thus in Segal's (1999) terms there is a negative externality on non-traders, leading to conflict at equilibrium when offers are public (full commitment by the seller). See also Segal (2003).

price is $p < u(N)$ if all other buyers also adopt (which I expect); if not, the price is $p' < u(n_i)$." Each buyer should accept this contract whatever he expects other buyers to do. Of course, p' may have to be (perhaps far) below cost, so the seller will make a loss if some buyers reject the offer. But in principle success depends only on buyers' individual rationality, not on their coordinating.

Likewise, the theory suggests, a contingent contract can profitably attract buyers away from coordination on the wrong network if a better alternative has a residual claimant (sponsor). Thus, suppose that buyers expect one another to adopt A, and that $u_B(n_i) - c_B < u_A(N) - p_A < u_B(N) - c_B$.[157] Seller B offers the contract: "If x of you buy B, the price will be $u_B(x) - u_A(N) + p_A - k$." For $k > 0$, it is a dominant strategy for each buyer to accept, and the contract is profitable if all buyers do so and k is small enough. Indeed, as we noted in the previous subsection, such a contract may inefficiently succeed: Segal (1999) and Jullien (2001) show that, because adoption of B imposes a negative externality on those who continue to buy A, there will be excessive adoption of B even if initial expectations favor A, when B (but not A) can offer public flexible pricing under complete information. But Park (2004a) applies mechanism-design methods and finds that such contingent inducement schemes (and a range of other schemes) will induce less than efficient adoption when the seller has incomplete information about adopters' tastes.

It is not surprising that some flexible contracting can in theory solve coordination problems.[158] At the level of cooperative game theory, network effects are like ordinary economies of scale: in each case a coalition consisting of a seller and x buyers achieves more surplus per buyer as x increases. Indeed, Sutton's (1998, chs. 14.2 and 15.2) models of network effects and learning effects are formally identical. Since simple contracts often enable efficient competition with economies of scale (even dynamically if contestability holds), *some* contracts would in principle do so with network effects.[159]

Contingent contracts might be differently implemented depending on whether adopters make a one-time purchase or continue to buy in order to use the network. When adopters will continue to trade with the seller over time, penetration pricing can become contingent pricing[160]; one version is usage-based pricing.[161] With one-time purchases, a seller might either charge low prices and later collect top-up fees if the network succeeds, or charge prices consonant with a successful network, promising refunds if the network falls short. Refund promises might not be believed, either because a

157 Recall here that c_A is the production cost of good A, etc.

158 Thum (1994) also considers how contract form affects efficiency.

159 One could also reach the same optimistic view via the Coase Theorem.

160 Another view of penetration pricing with one-time purchases is that it is an attempt at contingent pricing but sacrifices part of the surplus from early adopters: they "ought to" see that the network will succeed and hence be willing to pay a lot, but they do not.

161 Oren and Smith (1981) and Rohlfs (2001). That is, if each adopter's use of a telecommunications product, say, is proportional to the value he derives from it, then traffic-sensitive pricing may solve the chicken-and-egg problem even at the cost of inefficiently deterring usage given network size. See also Carter and Wright (1999).

nascent B-supplier would lack funds for such a large, non-diversifiable risk, or because buyers would suspect fine print in the contract.

Despite the advantages of contingent contracts, they do not seem the norm in network markets.[162] Very low, especially negative, prices may be problematic, as we discussed in Section 2, and the nuisance adopter issue is arguably worse here because network benefits normally hinge on use, not just possession, of the good. Especially if A is well established, this can make users' opportunity costs of adopting B large and hard to observe. Thus contingent contracts might work better against the single-network chicken-and-egg problem than to help an entrant displace an established network rival.

While cost-side economies of scale often do not raise the coordination issues that we argue are central in network effects, this is not a fact of technology and preferences: it hinges on the contracts used. Thus contract theory should play more role in the study of network effects than it has hitherto, and in particular understanding the use, or lack of use, of contingent contracts would be an important advance.

3.7. Sponsored pricing of competing networks

In incompatible competition firms vie to control expectations. Competition will focus on pivotal customers; these are often early adopters – as with switching costs, where competition is largely for early purchases. Central questions are whether more efficient firms reliably win and whether profits reflect only their efficiency advantage.

3.7.1. Competition with cost/quality differences

Consider incompatible competition with purely vertical differentiation: either a cost difference or a quality difference valued equally by all consumers. First we treat efficiency advantages as fixed over time; in Section 3.7.2 we allow them to vary. Expectations may respond in various ways to quality and price differences: for instance they may track surplus, track quality, track past success, or stubbornly favor one firm.[163]

We say expectations *track surplus* if each buyer expects all others to buy the product that, network effects held constant, offers the most surplus. For instance, suppose firms set prices just once and then there is a sequence of adoption choices by small cohorts. If adopters have similar preferences (agree on which product offers them more surplus if all adopt it), one might expect adoption of that product.[164] Price competition then works just as it would if the products were compatible. The efficient product wins, and (with non-drastic efficiency differences) consumers get the same surplus as they would if the second-best product were offered at average cost and adopted by all. Consumers capture

[162] Arguably this suggests either that there is no problem to be solved, or that (as we suspect) the contracts are problematic. See also Innes and Sexton (1994) and Haruvy and Prasad (2001).

[163] These terms are from Farrell and Katz (1998).

[164] As we saw in Section 3.4.4, this is the unique subgame-perfect equilibrium. As we argued there, this may not be conclusive; but it is one plausible expectation.

the network effect and any economies of scale. Quality competition also is therefore just as under compatibility.[165]

But this changes dramatically if instead expectations *track quality*. Although this is a static model, this assumption can be motivated because, as Katz and Shapiro (1992) showed, this is the equilibrium if sponsors can adjust prices in response to adoption dynamics: suppose for instance that A has higher quality (or lower costs), and that this outweighs the network gain from adoption by a single additional cohort. Then, A will not fail through a bandwagon effect that starts because a *few* buyers adopt B instead. Rather, such a loss will lead A's sponsor to cut its price to subsequent adopters: it can profitably do what it takes to win, even coming from a bit behind in installed base.[166] So each adopter will recognize that even if he and his cohort adopt product B, product A will still win the rest of the market. Since no buyer is pivotal, the price to any buyer (or cohort) should not affect expectations. So rational expectations will *track quality* – focus on the network with higher quality (or lower costs) – and ignore any period's prices.

In this case, if A has higher quality it wins current sales if[167]: $u_A(N) - p_A \geqslant u_B(1) - c_B$, or $p_A - c_A \leqslant [u_A(N) - u_B(N)] + [u_B(N) - u_B(1)] - [c_A - c_B]$. Its profit is equal to its actual (cost and/or quality) advantage plus the network effect. If A visibly *could* make consumers a significantly better offer than can B, it need not *actually* match B's offer! Consumers would get more surplus if they all adopted the losing network B priced at cost.[168]

Of course, when such lucrative expectations track quality, firms will compete intensely on quality. Consumers gain from additional quality created by the second highest-quality firm.[169] The network effect accrues to the winner, and/or is dissipated in quality competition, which can therefore be socially excessive.

Worse, other factors might make consumers expect a product to win the market even after (out of equilibrium) losing a round or two – making expectations stubbornly unresponsive to price or performance. For instance, this logic would focus expectations on a firm that plainly *could* dramatically improve its product if necessary – even if it never actually does so. Other forces might include deep pockets, history or reputation, a convincing road-map for future products, control of a key complement, control of formal

165 Baake and Boom (2001) and Bental and Spiegel (1995) discuss static competition with network effects and quality differentiation when consumers' willingness to pay for quality varies.

166 Therefore B will not attempt penetration pricing: there is no follow-on gain to winning a cohort or two. See Fudenberg et al. (1983) on races without leapfrogging.

167 We assume that each adopter is of size 1 and that a losing seller is willing to price down to cost.

168 This is an instance of the principle that pivotal adopters get the surplus: when there are no such buyers, firms can keep the surplus. [Raskovich (2003) argues, on the other hand, that pivotal buyers find themselves saddled with the responsibility of ensuring that a good is actually provided.] In predatory pricing policy, Edlin (2002) discusses how a firm's ability to make a better offer can forestall the need to do so (to consumers' detriment).

169 As always when competition gives no gross return to investment by a subsequent "loser", there can be equilibria in which only one firm invests. Thus details of the quality competition game may be important.

standards efforts, or marketing activity. As we saw, a seller thus favored by expectations can extract profits commensurate with the network effects, and may thus profitably control the market even with an inferior product or offering – provided, crucially, that its inferiority does not loosen its control of expectations. Such dysfunctional patterns of expectations may be most likely where adopters have dissimilar preferences, hindering attempts (e.g. through talk) to coordinate better.

When expectations thus *stubbornly* favor one firm, it has monopoly-like incentives for quality improvement. Its rivals cannot gain from ordinary innovation. But if B's quality improves so much that each user will adopt B no matter what he expects others to do, then adopters should now give B the benefit of expectations. Thus A's rivals have strong incentives for dramatic innovation (Grove's "ten times better").

Thus these models suggest that quality competition can produce stronger incentives for innovation than monopoly (even inefficiently strong incentives), while expectations-dominant firms have incentives for incremental innovation and other firms have little incentive for other than breakthrough innovation.

If expectations track past market success, they reinforce installed base in giving past winners an advantage in future competition. This increases collective switching costs and accentuates the bargain-then-ripoff pattern of dynamic competition.

3.7.2. Competition with cost/quality differences that vary over time

Now suppose that competing networks' efficiency advantages may shift over time. We revisit the inertia questions of Section 3.5 but now when competing networks are strategically priced. In doing so we address the scope for competitive entry (perhaps via penetration pricing) by a sponsored network product that must come from behind in network size and hence (often) in static efficiency, but that might become more efficient than an incumbent if widely adopted.

As we saw in Section 3.5, if early efficiency advantages determine offers to the pivotal early adopters, then a technology with an early lead will beat a technology that will (or may) be better later. This is the New Hampshire Theorem: early power for any given prices. In particular, if each network is competitively supplied, there is excess early power: a bias toward the one that early adopters prefer.

Now suppose instead that network sponsors compete for early adopters through penetration pricing. We describe how competitive penetration pricing can yield efficient adoption choices in favorable circumstances. More realistically, biases can arise in either direction, but we argue that excess early power remains more likely than its opposite.

Suppose that A has costs a_t in period t, while B has costs b_t, and that network effects are strong: second-period adopters would follow first-period adopters if both products were priced at cost, and will pay r for a product compatible with first-period adoption. Finally, suppose that if a firm fails to win first-period sales, it exits (it knows it will lose in the second period). Then A would price as low as $a_1 - (r - a_2)$ to win first-period sales, while B would go down to $b_1 - (r - b_2)$. Consequently, second-period efficiencies feed through efficiently into first-period penetration pricing, and the firm that can more efficiently provide the good in both periods wins sales in both periods, if each cohort optimally coordinates internally and first-period buyers correctly foresee second-period behavior. In this model, collective technology choice is efficient, and the pivotal (first-period) adopters get the benefit of competition.[170]

How robust is this optimistic result? Second-period efficiency can feed through *more* strongly than is efficient into first-period penetration pricing. In Katz and Shapiro (1986a), a first-period loser does not exit but continues to constrain pricing. Thus the second-period prize for which A is willing to price below its cost in the first period is $b_2 - a_2 + \beta$, where β represents a network-size advantage[171]; similarly B expects a second-period prize of $a_2 - b_2 + \beta$ for winning the first period. So firm A wins first-period (and hence all) sales if and only if $a_1 - [b_2 - a_2 + \beta] \leqslant b_1 - [a_2 - b_2 + \beta]$. Second-period efficiency is *double*-counted relative to first-period efficiency, leading to excess late power[172] despite the excess early power for any given prices: strategic pricing here *reverses* the adoption-level bias.

Or feed-through can be *weaker* than is efficient. There is *no* feed-through when both standards are unsponsored (firms cannot later capture gains from establishing a product). Uncertainty and capital market imperfections can weaken feed-through.[173] Feed-through is also inefficient if first-period competition is not entirely through better offers but consists of rent-seeking through unproductive marketing. Feed-through can work efficiently even if consumers do not know why they are getting good first-period offers, or do not know the extent of gouging, provided the latter is symmetric. But, as we saw in Section 2, bargain-then-ripoff competition can cause inefficiencies.

As Katz and Shapiro (1986a) also noted, when one product is sponsored but its rival is not, feed-through is *asymmetric*, biasing the outcome toward the sponsored product. And, as Farrell and Katz (2005) note, feed-through is also asymmetric if A would stay in the market for the second period after losing the first, but B would exit if it lost the first round.[174]

170 Welfare may still be lower than under compatibility if different products would then be adopted in different periods, although firms have an incentive to achieve compatibility in that case [Katz and Shapiro (1986b); see Section 3.8 below].

171 Specifically, β is the difference in value between a network of all consumers and one consisting only of second-generation consumers. With strong network effects, β exceeds second-period cost differences.

172 This is why Katz and Shapiro (1986a) find excess late power (or "new-firm bias") with sponsored products when network effects are strong. When network effects are weaker, they found a new-firm bias for a different reason. The ("new") firm with the second-period advantage certainly would win second-period sales if it won first-period sales; but the other firm with the second-period disadvantage might not. The "old" firm would like to commit to doing so, in order to offer first-period customers a full network, but cannot.

173 Feed-through will be weakened (as in switching-cost markets) if firms cannot lower first-period prices enough to pass through all prospective ex post profits to the pivotal early adopters (e.g. because of borrowing constraints, or because negative prices attract worthless demand).

174 Then, A's second-period prize for winning the first period is $r - a_2$, but B's is only $\min[r - b_2, a_2 - b_2 + \beta]$. Thus if $r > a_2 + \beta$, feedthrough is asymmetric and A wins both periods if and only if $a_1 - [r - a_2] \leqslant b_1 - [a_2 - b_2 + \beta]$, or $a_1 + a_2 \leqslant b_1 + b_2 + [r - a_2 - \beta]$. The last term in brackets is a bias toward the firm with a reputation for persistence.

To summarize, at given prices, network effects cause pivotal adopters' preferences to be over-weighted; since early adopters are often pivotal, products that appeal to them fare better than products that appeal comparably to later adopters. That is, there is typically excess early power for any given prices. But relative efficiencies in serving non-pivotal adopters may feed through into prices to pivotal adopters, and thus into the outcome. This feed-through can be zero (as with unsponsored products), weak, correct (as in the model above where first-round losers exit), or excessive [as in Katz and Shapiro (1986a) and Jullien (2001)]. Nevertheless, in general we think feed-through seems likely to be too weak, even if buyers optimally coordinate: the arguments for optimal or excessive feed-through put a lot of weight on firms' ability to predict future quasi-rents and incorporate them into today's pricing. Perhaps more importantly, however, feed-through can be asymmetric for reasons unrelated to the qualities of the competing products, and the asymmetry probably tends to favor established or sponsored products over nascent or unsponsored ones.

Thus entry by an incompatible product is often hard, and may well be *too* hard even *given* the incumbent's installed base and *given* incompatibility. Switching costs and network effects can work in tandem to discourage incompatible entry: switching costs discourage large-scale entry (which would require the installed base to switch) while network effects discourage gradual, small-scale entry (offering a small network at first).

A switching-cost analogy The models above have close switching-cost analogies, although the switching-cost literature has not stressed efficiency differences between firms. With costs as described above and no network effects or quality differences but a switching cost s, suppose first that each buyer expects to face a second-period price p_2 that is independent of which seller he is locked into. Then of course he will buy the lower-priced product in the first period. If he is correct about second-period pricing (for instance, if his reservation price r is low enough that switching can never pay, so $p_2 = r$), then seller A is willing to price down to $a_1 - [p_2 - a_2]$ in the first period, and similarly for B. Hence, the firm with lower life-cycle costs makes the sale, as efficiency requires. This is the switching-cost analogy to the model with exit above.[175]

But if second-period prices are instead constrained by the buyer's option to switch, then A will price at $b_2 + s$ in the second period if it wins the first, while B will price at $a_2 + s$ if it does. If myopic buyers do not foresee this difference then second-period costs are double-counted relative to first-period costs: this is an asymmetric version of the model in Section 2.3.1 above, and is the switching-cost analogy to Katz and Shapiro (1986a). Finally, if second-period prices are constrained by the option to switch and buyers have rational expectations and know firms' second-period costs, then the buyer chooses A only if its first-period price is at least $b_2 - a_2$ lower than B's, and again the firm with lower lifecycle costs wins.

[175] See also Section 3.2 of Klemperer (1995).

3.7.3. *Static competition when consumers' preferences differ*

Without network effects, or with compatibility, horizontal differentiation has several effects. First, tipping is unlikely: a variety of products make sales. Second, prices reflect each firm's marginal cost and its market power due to the horizontal differentiation (in a Hotelling model, for instance, the level of transport costs). Third, if a seller modestly improves its product, it gets modestly higher share and profits.

With strong network effects and incompatibility, all these lessons change. Buyers want to coordinate and all adopt a single network, though they disagree on which one. If they will succeed in doing so, and if their collective choice is responsive to changes in quality or price, then firms are competing for the market, which blunts horizontal differentiation. Thus, strong proprietary *network effects can sharpen price competition* when expectations are up for grabs and will track surplus[176]; Doganoglu and Grzybowski (2004) contrast this with competition-softening switching costs. Product improvement by the leader does not change market shares; nor does marginal product improvement by other firms. If price reflects cost, it will reflect the loser's average cost, because the loser is willing to price down that far in competition for the whole market.

When differentiation is stronger, or network effects weaker, niche minority products such as Apple can survive. Multiple products can also survive if network effects are primarily localized within subgroups of adopters, segmenting the market. But the strategy of selling only to closely-matching buyers is less appealing than under compatibility (or than without network effects), and if network effects strengthen or become less localized, or the dominant network grows, niches may become unsustainable, as speakers of "small" human languages are finding and as Gabel (1987) argues was the case for Betamax.

3.7.4. *Dynamic competition when consumers' preferences differ*

Just as excess early power at fixed prices need not imply excess early power when firms compete in penetration pricing, tipping at given prices might not imply tipping when sponsors price to build or exploit market share. If one network gets ahead, will its sponsor raise price to exploit that lead and thus dissipate it, as (recall Section 2.7.1) happens with switching costs, repeated sales of a single good, and no price discrimination; or will it keep price low and come to dominate the market? The literature suggests the answer is ambiguous. Arthur and Rusczczynski (1992) studied this question when firms set prices in a many-period dynamic game; Hanson (1983) considered a similar model. In stochastic duopoly they find that if firms have high discount rates, a large firm tends

[176] Large buyers in oligopoly markets often negotiate discounts in return for exclusivity. One possible explanation is that a "large buyer" is really a joint purchasing agent for many differentiated purchases; exclusivity commits the buyer to ignore product differentiation and thus sharpens price competition. See Dana (2006).

to lose share by pricing high for near-term profit. But if firms have lower discount rates, a large firm sets low prices to reinforce its dominant position.[177]

In summary, strong network effects tend to cause tipping or unstable (positive feedback) dynamics at given prices (including the case of unsponsored standards and constant costs); sometimes, they also do so where sponsors strategically set prices.

3.8. Endogenous network effects: choosing how to compete

Incompatibility of competing products can be inevitable, but is often chosen. Why would a firm prefer one form of competition over another?

When firms do not compete, or when competition is equally fierce either way, efficiency effects should normally govern: firms internalize efficiency advantages of compatibility choices. But competitive effects modify this, and can readily reverse it. Finally, when firms disagree on how to compete, who gets to choose?

3.8.1. Efficiency effects

Incompatibility has some obvious inefficiencies. Network benefits are lost if some adopters are unwilling to follow the crowd (network effects are weak) or the market splinters because adopters choose simultaneously or in ignorance. If, on the other hand, the market cleanly tips, it worsens matching of products to consumers when tastes differ or if the market tips the wrong way. When networks' future relative advantages are uncertain, compatibility makes switching easier (whether or not inertia is efficient given incompatibility) and thus preserves option value and reduces adopters' incentives either to wait and see which network wins or to adopt hastily and pre-empt.

Compatibility can also enable mix-and-match of complements. When the best hardware and the best software may not come from the same family, compatibility yields a direct mix-and-match efficiency gain.

But compatibility need not be efficient. Compatibility may require costly adapters or impose design constraints that may be severe if a standard requires a slow-moving consensus process. Proprietary control of a standard can encourage investment in development or in penetration pricing. It thus makes sense to supplement thinking directly about the pluses and minuses of compatibility with thinking about firms' competitive incentives.

3.8.2. Competitive effects

The first competitive effect is *leveling*: compatibility neutralizes the competitive advantage of one firm having a larger installed base or being better at attracting expectations.

[177] Dosi, Ermoliev and Kaniovski (1994) find that market sharing can occur if firms adjust prices in response to market shares according to an exogenous non-optimal rule.

When firm 1 is larger than firm 2, so $x_1 > x_2$, compatibility boosts the value of firm 1's product from $u(x_1)$ to $u(x_1 + x_2)$, and firm 2's product from $u(x_2)$ to $u(x_1 + x_2)$. Since a firm's profit is increasing in the value of its own product and decreasing in that of its rival, compatibility helps the large firm less and hurts it more than it helps or hurts the small firm *if* we can take the (expected) sizes x_1 and x_2 as broadly given. So a firm with a big locked-in installed base, or a firm that is exogenously expected to be big, is apt to resist compatibility with a smaller but fierce rival.[178]

Thus the dominant Bell system declined to interconnect with upstart independents in the early post-patent years of telephone competition in the U.S., and Faulhaber (2002, 2004) describes AOL's failure to interlink with rivals' instant messaging systems. Borenstein (2003) similarly argues that interline agreements between airlines, which let customers buy discount tickets with outbound and return on different airlines, help smaller airlines much more than larger ones; interlining has declined over time. Bresnahan and Greenstein (1999) describes how Word Perfect sought compatibility with the previously dominant WordStar, but then fought compatibility with its challengers.

Second is the *un-differentiating effect*. As in Section 3.7.3, when tipping is likely and size is (or expectations are) completely up for grabs, incompatibility can neutralize ordinary horizontal differentiation that would soften price competition in compatible competition. Even when it is less efficient, incompatible competition can then be sharper. But when tipping is unlikely, incompatibility can *create* horizontal differentiation (segment the market), as in switching-cost markets.[179] Thus firms' incentives will depend on the likelihood of tipping and on whether expectations are largely exogenous or are symmetrically competed for. Real-world frictions, including switching costs, limit short-run shifts of customers (or expectations), and simple network models that understate such frictions will thus overestimate the strength of incompatible competition.

Third, if each side has proprietary complements that remain fixed independent of scale, and compatibility enables mix-and-match, duopoly models suggest that firms' private gains from compatibility exceed the social gains, but this is less clear with more than two firms (see Section 2.8.4). We digress briefly here to discuss the relationship between these mix-and-match models and indirect network effects.

Indirect network effects and mix-and-match Both indirect network effects and the mix-and-match literature discussed in Section 2.8.4 above study modularity (mix-and-match) versus proprietary complements in a systems market, but the two literatures are

[178] See for instance Katz and Shapiro (1985), de Palma and Leruth (1996), Crémer, Rey and Tirole (2000), and Malueg and Schwartz (2006). Belleflamme (1998) explores how the leveling effect varies with the number of firms and with the form (e.g. Cournot vs Bertrand) of competition. It may be particularly unfortunate if large players resist compatibility, since they tend to be best at leading bandwagons.

[179] Augereau, Greenstein and Rysman (in press) find that when ISPs chose between incompatible 56kbps modems, there was less compatibility than random choice would imply in each local market. They attribute this to ISPs' desire for horizontal differentiation, though it may have been more a switching-cost effect (consumers invested in modems) than a network effect.

surprisingly hard to relate; we note some key differences, but future research should develop a more unified understanding.

When more customers buy "hardware" of type A, the demand for A-compatible "software" increases, so there is more profit to be made from providing such software if entry does not dissipate that profit. The mix-and-match literature, like the bundling literature [e.g. Nalebuff (2000)], allows for this profit increase to be captured by the A-hardware provider through vertical integration. It then studies pricing and profits when this fact *does not induce additional entry* into A-compatible software.

In contrast, as we discussed in Section 3.1, the indirect network effect literature assumes that when more A-hardware is sold, the boost in A-software demand *does induce additional (re-equilibrating) software entry*, making A's hardware more attractive to customers and thus indirectly increasing hardware profits. But a boost in software profits is not part of this calculation, both because entry dissipates software profits and because most models assume there is no integration.

We also note that with indirect network effects, tipping at the hardware level increases software variety while reducing hardware variety.[180]

3.8.3. *Institutions and rules: who chooses?*

If participants disagree on compatibility, who chooses? This question arises at several levels. We pose it primarily as a tussle among competing vendors with different preferences over how to compete. Another version of the question pits one vertical layer against another: often customers against vendors. A third version concerns the various means to achieve network benefits. Finally, there may be (as in television) compatibility domestically but not internationally.

i. *Horizontal competitors* Sometimes side payments can be made smoothly enough that the outcome is the one that maximizes *joint* profits. If side payments are fixed or one-shot, efficiency effects and the ferocity/softness of competition will drive the joint decision. And if firms can charge one another running royalties for compatibility, that may itself soften compatible competition. In telecommunications, interconnection (compatibility) is largely compulsory but charges for interconnection are common; Ennis (2002) shows that the curvature of the network-benefit function can determine equilibrium payments, while Hermalin and Katz (2005) show how efficient carrier-to-carrier pricing depends on demand elasticities. Brennan (1997) and Laffont, Rey and Tirole (1998a) ask whether competing firms can use such charges to support monopoly outcomes as non-cooperative equilibria. Similar concerns may arise if firms agree to include one another's intellectual property in a consensus standard or a patent pool, as

[180] When indirect network effects are proprietary (mixing and matching is impossible), tipping at the hardware level tends to *improve* the match between customers' software tastes and the software varieties endogenously provided, by increasing the size of the winning hardware platform's market (though tipping worsens hardware matches).

Gilbert (2004) stresses.[181] But these strategems might be hard to distinguish in practice from side payments to encourage efficient compatibility.

In other cases firms choose how to compete non-cooperatively without smooth side payments. As above, any firm wants to offer its customers bigger network benefits, and wants its rival's customers to get smaller network benefits. Thus each firm would like to *offer* a one-way converter that gives its customers the network benefits of compatibility with its rivals' customers; but would like to *block* converters in the other direction.[182] In a non-cooperative framework, then, if any firm can block such a one-way converter (e.g. through intellectual property or by secretly or frequently changing an interface), incompatibility results. But if any firm can unilaterally offer a one-way converter, compatibility results.

One can then study incentives for two-way compatibility by thinking of converters in the two directions as inseparably bundled. If both sides want compatibility, or if neither does, the question of who chooses is less prominent. If the firms disagree, incompatibility results if the firm who dislikes compatibility (typically the larger or expectations-dominant player) can prevent it, perhaps through intellectual property or through secrecy or frequent changes of interface.[183] MacKie-Mason and Netz (2007) explore micro-analytics and institutions of such strategies. On the other hand, compatibility results if it is easier to imitate than to exclude, as Gabel (1991) argues it was for auto parts.

With more than two firms, compatible coalitions may compete against incompatible rivals.[184] Extending Katz and Shapiro (1985), Crémer, Rey and Tirole (2000) describe a dominant firm's incentive for targeted (at one smaller rival) degradation of interconnection even if it has no incentive for uniform degradation. But Malueg and Schwartz (2006) observe that a commitment to compatible competition may attract users and deter degradation; Stahl (1982), Dudey (1990), and Schulz and Stahl (1996) similarly discuss incentives to locate near competitors. Cusumano et al. (1992) suggest that this was important in VHS's victory over Betamax.

ii. *Vertical locus of compatibility choice* Network benefits can result from choices at various vertical layers (see Section 3.3.2). The efficiency effects may broadly be the same, but competitive effects may differ according to the vertical layer at which compatibility happens. Many consensus standards organizations bring together participants

[181] Firms might also sustain price collusion by threatening to withdraw cooperation on compatibility.

[182] See Manenti and Somma (2002). Adams (1978) recounts how Gillette and others fought this battle of one-way converters in the razor/blade market.

[183] Besen and Farrell (1994) analyze compatibility choice in these terms. Farrell and Saloner (1992) analyzed effects of two-way converters, and also found that converters can reduce static efficiency; Choi (1996b, 1997b) finds that converters can block the transition to a new technology. See also David and Bunn (1987), Kristiansen (1998), and Baake and Boom (2001).

[184] Axelrod et al. (1995), Economides and Flyer (1998), and Farrell and Shapiro (1993) also study coalitions in network markets with more than two players.

from multiple layers, though few true end users attend. The literature's focus on competing interests is a simplification of the web of interests that results. In particular, end users often compete with one another less than do the vendors who sell to them, making it easier for end users than for vendors to agree on standards; but there are typically many end users, making it hard.

A value-chain layer with a single dominant provider may also be a relatively likely locus for standards. Thus for instance Intel has championed, even imposed, compatibility in some layers complementary to its dominant position. In favorable cases, a dominant firm has salutary incentives to influence complementary layers.

iii. *Means to network benefits* One way to achieve network benefits is that all the players at one vertical layer of a value chain – perhaps vendors, perhaps end users – decide to adopt the same design. That in turn can happen through various mechanisms of coordination, including consensus agreements and sequential bandwagons, but also including tradition, authority, or the use of sunspot-like focal points. Another path to network benefits is the use of converters or adapters,[185] or the related multi-homing strategies such as learning a second language.[186]

iv. *International trade* Just as firms might choose incompatibility for strategic advantage, so too may nations pursuing domestic (especially producers') benefits at the expense of foreigners'. As in strategic trade with economies of scale, one strategy conscripts domestic consumers as a protected base to strengthen domestic firms in international competition: incompatibility may be a tool to do so, and Crane (1979) argues that this was why governments imposed incompatible standards in color television.[187] As with competing firms, Jensen and Thursby (1996) note that a country may prefer compatibility when its standard is behind, but will shift to preferring incompatibility if it wins. Gandal and Shy (2001) argue that countries will not choose standards autarky but may inefficiently form standardization unions that exclude some countries (as indeed happened in color TV).[188]

[185] See David and Bunn (1987), Farrell and Saloner (1992), and Choi (1996b, 1997b). Because converters affect competition between otherwise incompatible networks, they may be subsidized or provided by sponsors of networks or may be independently supplied. Because network transitions are not first-best, strange effects can occur: for instance Choi shows that they can retard a transition.

[186] See de Palma et al. (1999) Multi-homing is also discussed in the context of two-sided markets by Rochet and Tirole (2003).

[187] Farrell and Shapiro (1992) and Rohlfs (2001) discuss this in terms of network effects. Note also that U.S. high-definition standards however contain many "options", which might threaten compatibility.

[188] Walz and Woeckener (2003) also find forces for inefficient incompatibility in trade policy. Kubota (1999) notes that transfer payments can make this less likely. Adams (1996), Choi, Lim and Yu (1999), Gandal (2002), Matutes and Regibeau (1996), and Klimenko (2002) also study trade policy with network effects.

3.9. Network effects and policy

Economists disagree on the strength and efficiency of incompatible competition. In our judgment, this largely reflects different views on how well adopters coordinate in the presence of network effects.[189]

Optimists expect that adopters can find ways to coordinate on shifting to any better offer that might be available: bandwagon leadership, communication (including through standards organizations), and penetration pricing all help. In a static framework, such good coordination makes the market behave as if there were a single adopter. Relative to compatible competition, incompatible competition then sacrifices variety but neutralizes horizontal differentiation, sharpening competition (possibly even making it fiercer than compatible competition). In a dynamic framework adopters often invest in the standard they adopt, creating individual switching costs. These can interact with network effects to create large collective switching costs, but (as we saw in the simplest models of Section 2) a switching-cost market may perform tolerably well, giving adopters up-front the quasi-rents that will later be gouged out of them.[190] Thus in the optimists' view, competition for the market works well, both in a static framework and dynamically.[191]

Pessimists see coordination as more likely to fail, or to succeed only by tracking cues other than adopter surplus, notably history. That implies several layers of pessimism about markets with proprietary network effects. First, both splintering and coordination on the "wrong" standard are possible, so that adopters collectively may fail to take the best deal offered. Second, because offering better deals is thus unreliable as a way to win the market, sponsors focus more on attracting expectations in other ways and on arranging to extract more rent if they do win – so sponsors offer less good deals. Third, if expectations track history rather than surplus, collective switching costs come to include the value of network effects, cementing us into what can be badly outdated (or just bad) standards.

Fourth, the strong competitive advantage conferred on a firm that attracts adopters' expectations opens up new avenues for mischief. Exclusive dealing may be especially problematic [see Shapiro (1999)], and product preannouncements by incumbents can block efficient entrants' "narrow windows" of opportunity. There is more than usual scope for predation if, as seems likely, expectations tend to center on the products of a

[189] Pessimists include David (1985) and Arthur (e.g., 1988, 1989) who contend long-run technology choice is inefficiently driven by accidental short-run small events. Liebowitz and Margolis (e.g., 1994, 1996, 1998a, 1998b) are famously optimistic. Between these extremes, Bresnahan and Greenstein (1999) suggests that in the computer industry long periods of lock-in are punctuated by occasional "epochs" of competition for the market when barriers due to network effects and switching costs are much lower than usual because of a shift of the incumbent's standard or a strong independent complement. See also Economides and White (1994).

[190] With individual switching costs, this broadly applies to each adopter. With network effects and collective switching costs, the up-front bargains are targeted on pivotal (typically early) adopters; other adopters may only experience the later rip-offs.

[191] Demsetz (1968) is often cited on competition for the market, although the idea goes back to Chadwick (1859). Contestability [Baumol, Panzar and Willig (1983)] is closely related.

powerful incumbent firm, because achieving the status of dominant incumbent will be especially profitable (making recoupment more likely, for instance) even after a more efficient rival attempts (re-)entry. And (whether or not incompatible entry would be efficient) the difficulty of entry, especially gradual or small-scale entry, sharpens other competitive concerns. For instance, a merger among incumbents who would jointly control an established standard may do more harm than a similar merger if entrants could be compatible.[192]

If proprietary network effects coupled with imperfect coordination creates competitive problems, might those problems be addressed directly? Of course, but doing so effectively is very hard because the dynamics of markets with proprietary network effects are complex. For example, recognizing that product preannouncements can be anticompetitive in such a market does not point to any reliably helpful policy interventions; banning or controlling product preannouncement is obviously problematic.[193] Likewise, conventional anti-predation policy starts from a suspicion of below-cost pricing; but in network industries below-cost pricing early on or to pivotal adopters is a big part of incompatible competition, just as with individual switching costs. Thus, addressing the problems directly is probably not enough.

Still taking as given that there will be incompatible competition, a more promising approach probably is to help adopters coordinate better. Information policy (helping adopters know what they are choosing), or contract policy (enforcing sponsors' promises) may help; because of the externalities among adopters, private incentives to research alternatives or to extract and enforce promises may well be too low.[194] Sensibly, policy generally seems recently to be moving to protect standard-setting organizations' ability to help focus adopters' expectations. In particular, these organizations have been lamentably spooked by fear of antitrust complaints (notably for taking account of the pricing of patent licenses), and we applaud policies to assuage that fear and to help them protect themselves against patent "trolls" whose patents have inadvertently been written into consensus standards.[195]

[192] Robinson (1999) describes concerns that the MCI-WorldCom combination would have so large a share in the Internet backbone market that it might profitably deny efficient interconnection. Crémer et al. (2000), Dewatripont and Legros (2000), Ennis (2002), and Malueg and Schwartz (2006) discuss the economics of this concern.

[193] Farrell and Saloner (1986b) and Haan (2003) explore the anticompetitive potential of preannouncements or vaporware; Dranove and Gandal (2003) found preannouncement had a significant effect in DVDs. Fisher (1991) and others have stressed the difficulty of crafting good policies to address this concern.

[194] Large, forward-looking buyers can also take into account the effects of their purchases on future market power. For example, government procurement might sensibly eschew offers by sponsors of proprietary networks (e.g. Microsoft) that are more attractive in the short run (e.g., cheaper, or come with free training) than competing open networks (e.g. based on Linux) if the latter would benefit future competition.

[195] Since much of the harm from hold-up is borne downstream, standards organizations have insufficiently strong incentives to avoid these problems (e.g. by requiring disclosure in advance and "reasonable and non-discriminatory" (RAND) licensing). For similar reasons there can be an incentive for firms to agree to charge one another running royalties for compatibility, perhaps by agreeing to incorporate one another's intellectual property in a standard: see Gilbert (2004) and Laffont, Rey and Tirole (1998a, 1998b).

But we think that even with such policies adopters will often not coordinate well enough to make incompatible competition work efficiently. So the best policy may be to encourage compatibility and compatible competition. This conclusion is reinforced by the fact that – in large part because of the problems above – the incentives of firms, especially dominant firms, are often biased towards incompatibility.[196] Denial of compatibility is profitable if this allows a firm to retain adopters' expectations and remove them from rivals.

Sometimes government should mandate a standard to ensure compatibility, just as other organizations often impose internal compatibility (indeed firms enforce internal compatibility by fiat more often than governments), and so avoid splintering or confusion or inefficient variety. Most nations do this in broadcasting, all insist that everyone drive on the same side of the road,[197] and many mandate mobile phone standards. But government should not always seek rapid standardization when the merits of competing standards are unclear. Considerations akin to biodiversity can suggest prolonging rather than cutting short market experimentation; the case for mandated standardization is strongest when technological progress is unlikely (as with weights and measures standards, which side of the road to drive on, or currency).[198] Moreover, government may be inexpert, and standards may need to evolve, and (partly as a result) compliance may not be clear. So governments wisely, we think, seldom intervene to displace an established standard because it was thought inefficient. (And when they do change a standard it is typically to replace a previously mandated standard – as with weights and measures, driving-sides, and currencies – rather than to second-guess a previous market choice.)

We are therefore most enthusiastic about facilitating, rather than directly requiring, compatibility. Standards organizations help when all want to coordinate, but when powerful players resist compatibility we are sympathetic to policies that give more power to complementors and competitors who want compatibility, in the analysis of Section 3.8. Thus telecommunications policy gives competitors the right of interconnection

[196] When network effects are indirect, compatibility is part of the broader question of vertical openness: if A wants to complement B, can B say no, or set terms such as exclusivity? The "one monopoly rent theorem" that suggests B will choose an efficient policy (because having better complements makes its product more appealing) can fail for a range of reasons [such as price discrimination, see, e.g., Farrell and Weiser (2003)], even absent network effects. But with indirect network effects, vertical integration creates particular concerns if independent complementors can be important potential entrants, as Bresnahan and Greenstein (2001) argue in the computer industry (the trial court in the U.S. Microsoft case echoed this logic with its proposed remedy of breaking up Microsoft into an operating system company and one that would initially sell applications, though the appeals court overturned this).

[197] Failure to say which side of the road people should drive would induce confusion (see Section 3.4 above), and saying "drive on the right" without enforcement leads to inefficient variety (those drivers that buck the norm may take account of their own sacrifice of compatibility benefits, but they also spoil those benefits for others).

Besen and Johnson (1986) argue that government failure to set a standard in AM stereo led to splintering.

[198] Cabral and Kretschmer (2007) find that in Arthur's (1989) model it is ambiguous whether policy should retard or accelerate lock-in.

on regulated terms, and the EU and increasingly the U.S. have done this for computer software.[199] Firms often enforce incompatibility through intellectual property that may have little or no inherent innovative value; in such cases, we favor a right to achieve compatibility despite the intellectual property.

How do these lessons and views relate to those we suggested for switching-cost markets in Section 2.9 above? In antitrust terms, incompatible competition with network effects tends to increase the risks of exclusion, whereas incompatible competition with switching costs is more apt to soften competition. But in both cases we emerge with a cautious preference for compatible competition, which often has direct efficiency benefits and is apt to be more competitive. Firms' own incentives somewhat align with direct efficiency effects but (especially for dominant firms) often include competitive effects with the "wrong sign". Thus one might especially suspect that firms have picked incompatibility inefficiently if compatibility would be low-cost or would even save costs directly, or if a firm imposes incompatibility while its rivals seek compatibility.

4. Conclusion

Switching costs and network effects create fascinating market dynamics and strategic opportunities. They link trades that are not readily controlled by the same contract: future trades in the case of switching costs, and trades between the seller and other buyers in the case of network effects. We have stressed that the result *can* be efficient competition for larger units of business – "competition for the market". Thus neither switching costs nor network effects are inherently and necessarily problematic. But they very often make competition, perhaps especially entry, less effective. So we favor cautiously pro-compatibility public policy. And policymakers should look particularly carefully at markets where incompatibility is strategically chosen rather than inevitable.

Acknowledgements

We are grateful to many friends and colleagues for numerous helpful suggestions and comments over several substantial rewrites of this paper since our first 1997 draft. Special thanks are due to Alan Beggs, Simon Board, Tim Bresnahan, Yongmin Chen, Matthew Clements, David Gill, Jonathan Good, Moshe Kim, Catherine McNeill, Markus Mobius, Meg Meyer, Tore Nilssen, Hiroshi Ohashi, Pierre Regibeau, Garth Saloner, Marius Schwartz, Oz Shy, Rebecca Stone, John Vickers, Matthew White, Miguel Villas-Boas, and the Editors of this volume. Joe Farrell was chief economist at the

[199] See Lemley and McGowan (1998a), Menell (2002), and Samuelson and Scotchmer (2002). But Llobet and Manove (2006) argue that because incumbents may build smaller networks if entrants can share them, R&D subsidies are better policy than compatibility rights. Kristiansen and Thum (1997) stress that network size is a public good in compatible competition.

Federal Communications Commission 1996–1997 and at the Antitrust Division of the Department of Justice 2000–2001, and Paul Klemperer served as a Member of the UK Competition Commission 2001–2005, but all the views expressed are personal ones.

References

Abreu, D. (1988). "On the theory of infinitely repeated games with discounting". Econometrica 56, 383–396.
Acquisti, A., Varian, H. (2005). "Conditioning prices on purchase history". Marketing Science 24, 367–381.
Adams, R.B. (1978). C.K. Gillette: The Man and His Wonderful Shaving Device. Little Brown & Co., Boston.
Adams, M. (1996). "Norms, standards, rights". European Journal of Political Economy 12, 363–375.
Aghion, P., Bolton, P. (1987). "Contracts as a barrier to entry". American Economic Review 77, 388–401.
Ahdieh, R.B. (2003). "Making markets: Network effects and the role of law in the creation and restructuring of securities markets". Southern California Law Review 76, 277–350.
Ahtiala, P. (1998). "The optimal pricing of computer software and other products with high switching costs". Working Paper. University of Tampere.
Anderson, S.P., Leruth, L. (1993). "Why firms may prefer not to price discriminate via mixed bundling". International Journal of Industrial Organization 11, 49–61.
Anderson, E.T., Kumar, N., Rajiv, S. (2004). "A comment on: Revisiting dynamic duopoly with consumer switching costs". Journal of Economic Theory 116, 177–186.
Aoki, R., Small J. (2000). "The economics of number portability: Switching costs and two part tariffs". In: Marching into the New Millenium: Economic Globalization Conference Proceedings, June 3–4. Tamkank University.
Arbatskaya, M. (2000). "Behaviour-based price discrimination and consumer switching". In: Baye, M.R. (Ed.), Industrial Organization. In: Advances in Applied Microeconomics, vol. 9. JAI Press, New York, pp. 149–171.
Armstrong, M. (2006). "Competition in two-sided markets". RAND Journal of Economics 37, 668–691.
Arthur, W.B. (1988). "Competing technologies". In: Dosi, G., Freeman, C., Silverberg, G. (Eds.), Technical Change and Economic Theory. Pinter, London, pp. 590–607.
Arthur, W.B. (1989). "Competing technologies, increasing returns, and lock-in by historical events". Economic Journal 99, 116–131.
Arthur, W.B. (1990). "Positive feedbacks in the economy". Scientific American (February), 92–99.
Arthur, W.B., Lane, D.A. (1993). "Information contagion". Economic and Dynamics and Structural Change 4, 81–104.
Arthur, W.B., Rusczcynski, A. (1992). "Dynamic equilibria in markets with a conformity effect". Archives of Control Sciences 37, 7–31.
Asvanund, A., Clay, K., Krishnan, R., Smith, M. (2004). "An empirical analysis of network externalities in peer-to-peer music sharing networks". Information Systems Research 15, 155–174.
Augereau, A., Greenstein, S., Rysman, M. (in press). "Coordination vs. differentiation in a standards war: 56K modems". RAND Journal of Economics. In press.
Ausubel, L. (1991). "The failure of competition in the credit card market". American Economic Review 81, 50–81.
Axelrod, R., Mitchell, W., Thomas, R., Bennett, S., Bruderer, E. (1995). "Coalition formation in standard-setting alliances". Management Science 41, 1493–1508.
Baake, P., Boom, A. (2001). "Vertical product differentiation, network externalities, and compatibility decisions". International Journal of Industrial Organization 19, 267–284.
Bagwell, K. (2007). "The economic analysis of advertising". In: Armstrong, M., Porter, R. (Eds.), Handbook of Industrial Organization, vol. III. North-Holand, Amsterdam (this volume).
Bagwell, K., Ramey, G. (1994). "Coordination economies, advertising and search behavior in retail markets". American Economic Review 84, 498–517.

Banerjee, A. (1992). "A simple model of herd behavior". Quarterly Journal of Economics 107, 797–817.

Banerjee, A., Summers, L.H. (1987). "On frequent-flyer programs and other loyalty-inducing economic arrangements". Working Paper. Harvard University.

Barnett, A.H., Kaserman, D.L. (1998). "The simple welfare economics of network externalities and the uneasy case for subscribership subsidies". Journal of Regulatory Economics 13, 245–254.

Basu, K. (1993). "Switching costs and rural credit". In: Lectures in Industrial Organization Theory. Blackwells, Oxford, pp. 202–204.

Basu, K., Bell, C. (1991). "Fragmented duopoly: Theory and applications to backward agriculture". Journal of Development Economics 36, 145–165.

Baumol, W., Panzar, J., Willig, R. (1983). "Contestable markets: An uprising in the theory of industry structure: Reply". American Economic Review 73, 492–496.

Baye, M.R., Kovenock, D., de Vries, C.G. (1992). "It takes two to tango: Equilibria in a model of sales". Games and Economic Behavior 4, 493–510.

Beggs, A. (1989). "A note on switching costs and technology choice". Journal of Industrial Economics 37, 437–440.

Beggs, A., Klemperer, P.D. (1989). "Multiperiod competition with switching costs". Discussion Paper 45. Nuffield College, Oxford University.

Beggs, A., Klemperer, P.D. (1992). "Multiperiod competition with switching costs". Econometrica 60, 651–666.

Beige, O. (2001). "The structure of coordination: Three essays on network externalities, expert influence and party-line voting". Ph.D. Dissertation. Haas School of Business, University of California, Berkeley.

Belleflamme, P. (1998). "Adoption of network technologies in oligopolies". International Journal of Industrial Organization 16, 415–444.

Bensaid, B., Lesne, J.P. (1996). "Dynamic monopoly pricing with network externalities". International Journal of Industrial Organization 14, 837–855.

Bental, B., Spiegel, M. (1995). "Network competition, product quality, and market coverage in the presence of network externalities". Journal of Industrial Economics 43, 197–208.

Berg, J.L., Schumny, H. (1990). An Analysis of the Information Technology Standardization Process: Proceedings. Elsevier, Amsterdam.

Berndt, E., Pindyck, R., Azoulay, P. (2003). "Consumption externalities and diffusion in pharmaceutical markets: Antiulcer drugs". Journal of Industrial Economics 51, 243–270.

Besen, S., Farrell, J. (1991). "The role of the ITU in standardization: Pre-eminence, impotence or rubber stamp?". Telecommunications Policy 15, 311–321.

Besen, S., Farrell, J. (1994). "Choosing how to compete: Strategies and tactics in standardization". Journal of Economic Perspectives 8, 117–131.

Besen, S., Johnson, L. (1986). "Compatibility standards, competition, and innovation in the broadcasting industry". Rand Report, #R-3453-NSF, November.

Besen, S., Saloner, G. (1989). "The economics of telecommunications standards". In: Crandall, R.W., Flamm, K. (Eds.), Changing the Rules: Technological Change, International Competition, and Regulations in Communications. Brookings Institution, Washington, DC, pp. 177–220.

Besen, S., Saloner, G. (1994). "Compatibility standards and the market for telecommunications services". In: Thomas, A., Morton, M. (Eds.), Research Studies. Information Technology and the Corporation of the 1930s. Oxford Univ. Press, Oxford, pp. 149–183.

Biglaiser, G., Crémer, J., Dobos, G. (2003). "You won't get rich on switching costs alone". Working Paper. Universities of North Carolina and Toulouse, November.

Bikhchandani, S., Hirshleifer, D., Welch, I. (1992). "A theory of fads, fashion, custom, and cultural change in informational cascades". Journal of Political Economy 100, 992–1026.

Bolton, P., Farrell, J. (1990). "Decentralization, duplication, and delay". Journal of Political Economy 98, 803–826.

Bonaccorsi, A., Rossi, C. (2002). "The adoption of business to business e-commerce: Heterogeneity and network externality effects". LEM Working Paper, May.

Borenstein, S. (2003). "Inter-lining and competition in the US airline industry". Working Paper. University of California, Berkeley.
Borenstein, S., MacKie-Mason, J.K., Netz, J.S. (1995). "Antitrust policy in aftermarkets". Antitrust Law Journal 63, 455–482.
Borenstein, S., MacKie-Mason, J.K., Netz, J.S. (2000). "Exercising market power in proprietary aftermarkets". Journal of Economics and Management Strategy 9, 157–188.
Bouckaert, J., Degryse, H. (2004). "Softening competition by inducing switching in credit markets". Journal of Industrial Economics 52, 27–52.
Brehm, J.W. (1956). "Post-decision changes in the desirability of alternatives". Journal of Abnormal and Social Psychology 52, 384–389.
Brennan, T. (1997). "Industry parallel interconnection agreements". Information Economics and Policy 9, 133–149.
Bresnahan, T. (2001a). "The economics of the Microsoft case". Working Paper. Stanford University, Department of Economics.
Bresnahan, T. (2001b). "Network effects and Microsoft". Working Paper. Stanford University, Department of Economics.
Bresnahan, T., Greenstein, S. (1999). "Technological competition and the structure of the computer industry". Journal of Industrial Economics 47, 1–40.
Bresnahan, T., Greenstein, S. (2001). "The economic contribution of information technology: Towards comparative end user studies". Journal of Evolutionary Economics 11, 95–118.
Breuhan, A. (1997). "Innovation and the persistence of technical lock-in". Ph.D. Dissertation. Stanford University.
Brock, G.W. (1981). The Telecommunications Industry: The Dynamics of Market Structure. Harvard Univ. Press, Cambridge.
Bryant, J. (1994). "Coordination Theory, the Stag Hunt, and Macroeconomics". In: Friedman, J.W. (Ed.), Problems of Coordination in Economic Activity. Kluwer Academic Publishers, Boston.
Brynjolfsson, E., Kemerer, C. (1996). "Network externalities in microcomputer software: An econometric analysis of the spreadsheet market". Management Science 42, 1627–1647.
Budd, C., Harris, C., Vickers, J. (1993). "A model of the evolution of duopoly: Does the asymmetry between firms tend to increase or decrease?" Review of Economic Studies 60, 543–753.
Bulow, J., Klemperer, P.D. (1998). "The tobacco deal". In: Brookings Papers on Economic Activity: Microeconomics, pp. 323–394.
Bulow, J., Klemperer, P.D. (1999). "The generalized war of attrition". American Economic Review 89, 175–189.
Bulow, J., Geanakoplos, J., Klemperer, P.D. (1985a). "Multimarket oligopoly: Strategic substitutes and complements". Journal of Political Economy 93, 488–511.
Bulow, J., Geanakoplos, J., Klemperer, P.D. (1985b). "Holding idle capacity to deter entry". Economic Journal 95, 178–182.
Cabral, L., Greenstein, S. (1990). "Switching costs and bidding parity in government procurement of computer systems". Journal of Law, Economics, and Organization 6, 463–469.
Cabral, L., Kretschmer, T. (2007). "Standards battles and public policy". In: Greenstein, S., Stango, V. (Eds.), Standards and Public Policy. Cambridge Univ. Press, pp. 329–344.
Cabral, L., Salant, D.J., Woroch, G.A. (1999). "Monopoly pricing with network externalities". International Journal of Industrial Organization 17, 199–214.
Calem, P., Mester, L. (1995). "Consumer behavior and the stickiness of credit-card interest ates". American Economic Review 85, 1327–1336.
Caminal, R., Matutes, C. (1990). "Endogenous switching costs in a duopoly model". International Journal of Industrial Organization 8, 353–374.
Campello, M. (2003). "Capital structure and product markets interactions: Evidence from business cycles". Journal of Financial Economics 68, 353–378.
Campello, M., Fluck Z. (2004). "Product market: Performance, switching costs, and liquidation values: The real effects of financial leverage". Working Paper. University of Illinois and Michigan State University.

Cargill, C.F. (1989). Information Technology Standardization. Digital Press, Bedford, MA.

Carlsson, F., Löfgren, A. (2004). "Airline choice, switching costs and frequent flyer programs". Working Paper. Gothenburg University, January.

Carlton, D.W., Landes, W.M., Posner, R.A. (1980). "Benefits and costs of airline mergers: A case study". Bell Journal of Economics 80, 65–83.

Carter, M., Wright, J. (1999). "Interconnection in network industries". Review of Industrial Organization 14, 1–25.

Cason, T.N., Friedman, D. (2002). "A laboratory study of customer markets". Advances in Economic Analysis and Policy 2. Article 1. http://www.bepress.com/bejeap/advances/vol2/iss1/art1.

Cason, T.N., Friedman, D., Milam, G.H. (2003). "Bargaining versus posted price competition in customer markets". International Journal of Industrial Organization 21, 223–251.

Chadwick, E. (1859). "Results of different principles of legislation and administration in Europe: Of competition for the field, as compared with competition within the field, of service". Journal of the Statistical Society of London 22, 381–420.

Chen, P.-Y. (2005). "Information technology and switching costs". In: Handbook on Economics and Information Systems. Elsevier, Amsterdam. Preliminary Draft.

Chen, P.-Y., Hitt, L. (2002). "Measuring switching costs and their determinants in Internet enabled businesses: A study of the on-line brokerage industry". Information Systems Research 13, 255–274.

Chen, Y. (1997). "Paying customers to switch". Journal of Economics and Management Strategy 6, 877–897.

Chen, Y., Rosenthal, R.W. (1996). "Dynamic duopoly with slowly changing customer loyalties". International Journal of Industrial Organization 14, 269–296.

Chevalier, J., Scharfstein, D. (1996). "Capital-market imperfections and countercyclical markups: Theory and evidence". American Economic Review 86, 703–725.

Choi, J.P. (1994a). "Network externality, compatibility choice, and planned obsolescence". Journal of Industrial Economics 42, 167–182.

Choi, J.P. (1994b). "Irreversible choice of uncertain technologies with network externalities". RAND Journal of Economics 25, 382–401.

Choi, J.P. (1996a). "Pre-emptive R&D, rent dissipation, and the leverage theory". Quarterly Journal of Economics 111, 1153–1181.

Choi, J.P. (1996b). "Do converters facilitate the transition to a new incompatible technology – A dynamic analysis of converters". International Journal of Industrial Organization 14, 825–835.

Choi, J.P. (1997a). "Herd behavior, the penguin effect, and the suppression of informal diffusion: An analysis of informational externalities and payoff interdependency". RAND Journal of Economics 28, 407–425.

Choi, J.P. (1997b). "The provision of (two-way) converters in the transition process to a new incompatible technology". Journal of Industrial Economics 45, 167–182.

Choi, J.P., Thum, M. (1998). "Market structure and the timing of technology adoption with network externalities". European Economic Review 42, 225–244.

Choi, S.C., Lim, K.S., Yu, P.I. (1999). "Strategic joint ventures with developing country in battles for technical standards". Japan and the World Economy 11, 135–149.

Chou, C.F., Shy, O. (1990). "Network effects without network externalities". International Journal of Industrial Organization 8, 259–270.

Chow, G.C. (1995). "Multiperiod competition with switching costs: Solution by Lagrange multipliers". Journal of Economic Dynamics and Control 19, 51–57.

Church, J., Gandal, N. (1992). "Network effects, software provision, and standardization". Journal of Industrial Economics 40, 85–103.

Church, J., Gandal, N. (1993). "Complementary network externalities and technological adoption". International Journal of Industrial Organization 11, 239–260.

Church, J., King, I. (1993). "Bilingualism and network externalities". Canadian Journal of Economics 26, 337–345.

Church, J., Gandal, N., Krause, D. (2002). "Indirect network effects and adoption externalities". Working Paper 02-30. Foerder Institute for Economic Research.

Clements, M. (2004). "Direct and indirect network effects are they equivalent?". International Journal of Industrial Organization 22, 633–645.
Cohen, A. (2005). "Asymmetric information and learning: Evidence from the automobile insurance market". Review of Economics and Statistics 87, 197–207.
Cooper, R. (1999). Coordination Games: Complementarities and Macroeconomics. Cambridge Univ. Press, Cambridge, MA.
Cooper, R., John, A. (1988). "Coordinating coordination failures in Keynesian models". Quarterly Journal of Economics 103, 441–463.
Crane, R.J. (1979). The Politics of International Standards: France and the Color T.V. War. Norwood, New Jersey.
Crawford, V.P. (1995). "Adaptive Dynamics in Coordination Games". Econometrica 63, 103–143.
Crémer, J. (2000). "Network externalities and universal service obligation in the Internet". European Economic Review 44, 1021–1031.
Crémer, J., Rey, P., Tirole, J. (2000). "Connectivity in the commercial Internet". Journal of Industrial Economics 48, 433–472.
Cusumano, M.A., Mylonadis, Y., Rosenbloom, R.S. (1992). "Strategic maneuvering and mass market dynamics: The triumph of VHS over Beta". Business History Review 66, 51–94.
Dana, J. (2006). "Buyer groups as strategic commitments". Working Paper. Northwestern University.
David, P. (1985). "Clio and the economics of QWERTY". American Economic Review 75, 332–337.
David, P. (1986). "Narrow windows, blind giants and angry orphans: The dynamics of systems rivalries and dilemmas of technology policy". CEPR Paper #10. Stanford University, March.
David, P., Bunn, J.A. (1987). "The economics of gateway technologies and network evolution: Lessons from electricity supply history". Information Economics and Policy 3, 165–202.
David, P., Monroe, H. (1994). "Standards development strategies under incomplete information". Mimeo.
David, P., Shurmer, M. (1996). "Formal standards-setting for global telecommunications and information services towards an institutional regime transformation?". Telecommunications Policy 20, 789–815.
Davis, D.R., Weinstein, D.E. (2002). "Bones, bombs and breakpoints: The geography of economic activity". American Economic Review 92, 1269–1289.
Demsetz, H. (1968). "Why regulate utilities?". Journal of Law and Economics 12, 229–239.
Deneckere, R., Kovenock, D., Lee, R. (1992). "Model of price leadership based on consumer loyalty". Journal of Industrial Economics 41, 147–156.
DeNicolo, V. (2000). "Compatibility and bundling with generalist and specialist firms". Journal of Industrial Economics 48, 177–188.
de Palma, A., Leruth, L. (1996). "Variable willingness to pay for network externalities with strategic standardization decisions". European Journal of Political Economy 12, 235–251.
de Palma, A., Leruth, L., Regibeau, P. (1999). "Partial compatibility with network externalities and double purchase". Information Economics and Policy 11, 209–227.
Dewatripont, M., Legros, P. (2000). "Mergers in emerging markets with network externalities: The case of telecoms". CIC Working Paper #FS IV 00-23. Wissenschaftszentrum, Berlin.
Diamond, P. (1982). "Aggregate demand management in search equilibrium". Journal of Political Economy 90, 881–894.
Diamond, P., Maskin, E. (1979). "An equilibrium analysis of search and breach of contract I: Steady states". Bell Journal of Economics 10, 282–316.
Dixit, A.K., Shapiro, C. (1986). "Entry dynamics with mixed strategies". In: Thomas, L.G. (Ed.), The Economics of Strategic Planning: Essays in Honor of Joel Dean. Lexington Books/Heath, Lexington, MA/Toronto, pp. 63–79.
Dixit, A.K., Stiglitz, J. (1977). "Monopolistic competition and optimum product diversity". American Economic Review 67, 297–308.
Domowitz, I., Steil, B. (1999). "Automation, trading costs, and the structure of the securities trading industry". Brookings–Wharton Papers on Financial Services 2, 33–92.
Doganoglu, T. (2004). "Switching costs, experience goods and dynamic price competition". Working Paper. University of Munich, April.

Doganoglu, T., Grzybowski, L. (2004). "Dynamic duopoly competition with switching costs and network externalities". Working Paper. University of Munich, January.

Dosi, G., Ermoliev, Y., Kaniovski, Y. (1994). "Generalized urn schemes and technological dynamics". Journal of Mathematical Economics 23, 1–19.

Dranove, D., Gandal, N. (2003). "The DVD vs. DIVX standard war: Network effects and empirical evidence of preannouncement effects". Journal of Economics and Management Strategy 12, 363–386.

Dranove, D., White, W.D. (1996). "Specialization, option demand, and the pricing of medical specialists". Journal of Economics and Management Strategy 5, 277–306.

Dube, J.-P., Hitsch, G.J., Rossi, P.E. (2006). "Do switching costs make markets less competitive?" Working Paper. Graduate School of Business, University of Chicago.

Dudey, M. (1990). "Competition by choice: The effect of consumer search on firm location decisions". American Economic Review 80, 1092–1104.

Dybvig, P.H., Spatt, C.S. (1983). "Adoption externalities as public goods". Journal of Public Economics 20, 231–247.

Eber, N. (1999). "Switching costs and implicit contracts". Journal of Economics (Zeitschrift-für-Nationalökonomie) 69, 159–171.

Echenique, F., Edlin, A. (2004). "Mixed equilibria in games of strategic complements are unstable". Journal of Economic Theory 118, 61–79.

Economides, N. (1989). "Desirability of compatibility in the absence of network externalities". American Economic Review 79, 1165–1181.

Economides, N. (1996a). "The economics of networks". International Journal of Industrial Organization 14, 673–699.

Economides, N. (1996b). "Network externalities, complementarities, and invitations to enter". European Journal of Political Economy 12, 211–233.

Economides, N., Flyer, F. (1998). "Equilibrium coalition structures in markets for network goods". Annales d'Economie et de Statistique 49/50, 361–380.

Economides, N., Himmelberg, C. (1995). "Critical mass and network evolution in telecommunications". In: Brock, G.W. (Ed.), Toward a Competitive Telecommunications Industry: Selected Papers from the 1994 Telecommunications Policy Research Conference. Lawrence Erlbaum Associates Manwah, New Jersey.

Economides, N., Salop, S. (1992). "Competition and integration among complements, and network market structure". Journal of Industrial Economics 40, 105–123.

Economides, N., Siow, A. (1988). "The division of markets is limited by the extent of liquidity (spatial competition with externalities)". American Economic Review 78, 108–121.

Economides, N., White, L.J. (1994). "Networks and compatibility: Implications for antitrust". European Economic Review 38, 651–662.

Edlin, A. (2002). "Stopping above-cost predatory pricing". Yale Law Journal 111, 941–991.

Einhorn, M.A. (1992). "Mix and match compatibility with vertical product dimensions". RAND Journal of Economics 23, 535–547.

Einhorn, M.A. (1993). "Biases in optimal pricing with network externalities". Review of Industrial Organization 8, 741–746.

Ellison, G. (2005). "A model of add-on pricing". Quarterly Journal of Economics 120, 585–637.

Ellison, G., Fudenberg, D. (1993). "Rules of thumb and social learning". Journal of Political Economy 101, 612–643.

Ellison, G., Fudenberg, D. (1995). "Word-of-mouth communication and social learning". Quarterly Journal of Economics 110, 93–125.

Ellison, G., Fudenberg, D. (2000). "The Neo-Luddite's lament: Excessive upgrades in the software industry". RAND Journal of Economics 31, 253–272.

Ellison, G., Fudenberg, D. (2003). "Knife-edge or plateau: When do market models tip?". Quarterly Journal of Economics 118, 1249–1278.

Ellison, G., Fudenberg, D., Möbius, M. (2004). "Competing auctions". Journal of the European Economic Association 2, 30–66.

Elzinga, G., Mills, D. (1998). "Switching costs in the wholesale distribution of cigarettes". Southern Economic Journal 65, 282–293.

Elzinga, G., Mills, D. (1999). "Price wars triggered by entry". International Journal of Industrial Organization 17, 179–198.

Ennis, S. (2002). "Network connection and disconnection". U.S. Department of Justice Working Paper #02-5.

Evans, D., Schmalensee, R. (2001). "Some economic aspects of antitrust analysis in dynamically competitive industries". NBER Working Paper #W8268.

Evans, D., Fisher, F.M., Rubinfeld, D.L., Schmalensee, R.L. (2000). "Did Microsoft harm consumers? – Two opposing views". AEI-Brookings Joint Center for Regulatory Studies.

Farrell, J. (1986). "A note on inertia in market share". Economics Letters 21, 73–75.

Farrell, J. (1987). "Cheap talk, coordination and entry". RAND Journal of Economics 18, 34–39.

Farrell, J. (1993). "Choosing the rules for formal standardization". Working Paper. University of California, Berkeley, Department of Economics.

Farrell, J. (2006). "Efficiency and competition between payment instruments". Review of Network Economics 5, 19–44.

Farrell, J., Gallini, N.T. (1988). "Second-sourcing as a commitment: Monopoly incentives to attract competition". Quarterly Journal of Economics 103, 673–694.

Farrell, J., Katz, M.L. (1998). "The effects of antitrust and intellectual property law on compatibility and innovation". Antitrust Bulletin 43, 609–650.

Farrell, J., Katz, M.L. (2005). "Competition or predation? Consumer coordination, strategic pricing, and price floors in network markets". Journal of Industrial Economics 53, 203–232.

Farrell, J., Saloner, G. (1985). "Standardization, compatibility and innovation". RAND Journal of Economics 16, 70–83.

Farrell, J., Saloner, G. (1986a). "Installed base and compatibility: Innovation, product preannouncements, and predation". American Economic Review 76, 940–955.

Farrell, J., Saloner, G. (1986b). "Standardization and variety". Economics Letters 20, 71–74.

Farrell, J., Saloner, G. (1988). "Coordination through committees and markets". RAND Journal of Economics 19, 235–252.

Farrell, J., Saloner, G. (1992). "Converters, compatibility, and the control of interfaces". Journal of Industrial Economics 40, 9–35.

Farrell, J., Shapiro, C. (1988). "Dynamic competition with switching costs". RAND Journal of Economics 19, 123–137.

Farrell, J., Shapiro, C. (1989). "Optimal contracts with lock-in". American Economic Review 79, 51–68.

Farrell, J., Shapiro, C. (1992). "Standard setting in high-definition television". In: Brookings Papers on Economic Activity, Microeconomics, pp. 1–77.

Farrell, J., Shapiro, C. (1993). "The dynamics of bandwagons". In: Friedman, J.W. (Ed.), Problems of Coordination in Economic Activity. Kluwer Academic Publishers, Boston, pp. 149–184.

Farrell, J., Shapiro, C. (2001). "Scale economies and synergies in horizontal merger analysis". Antitrust Law Journal 68, 685–710.

Farrell, J., Simcoe, T. (2007). "Choosing the rules for formal standardization". Working Paper. University of California, Berkeley.

Farrell, J., Weiser, P. (2003). "Modularity, vertical integration, and open access policies: Towards a convergence of antitrust and regulation in the Internet age". Harvard Journal of Law and Technology 17, 85–135.

Farrell, J., Monroe, H.K., Saloner, G. (1998). "The vertical organization of industry: System competition versus component competition". Journal of Economics and Management Strategy 7, 143–182.

Faulhaber, G. (2002). "Network effects and merger analysis: Instant messaging and the AOL-Time Warner case". Telecommunications Policy 26, 311–333.

Faulhaber, G. (2004). "Access and network effects in the new economy: AOL-Time Warner". In: Kwoka, J., White, L. (Eds.), The Anti-trust Revolution. Oxford University Press, pp. 453–475.

Federal Trade Commission (2000). "Entering the 21st century: Competition policy in the world of B2B electronic marketplaces: A report". The Commission, Washington, DC.

Fernandes, P. (2001). "Essays on customer loyalty and on the competitive effects of frequent-flyer programmes". Ph.D. Thesis. European University Institute.
Fisher, F.M. (1991). "Organizing industrial organization: Reflections on the handbook of industrial organization". In: Brookings Papers on Economic Activity, Microeconomics, pp. 201–225.
Fisher, F.M. (2000). "The IBM and Microsoft cases: What's the difference?". American Economic Review 90, 180–183.
Fisher, E.O'N., Wilson, C.A. (1995). "Price competition between two international firms facing tariffs". International Journal of Industrial Organization 13, 67–87.
Fishman, A., Rob, R. (1995). "The durability of information, market efficiency and the size of firms". International Economic Review 36, 19–36.
Fitoussi, J.-P., Phelps, E. (1988). The Slump in Europe: Reconstructing Open Economy Theory. Blackwells, Oxford.
Froot, K.A., Klemperer, P.D. (1989). "Exchange rate pass-through when market share matters". American Economic Review 79, 637–654.
Fudenberg, D., Tirole, J. (1984). "The fat-cat effect, the puppy-dog ploy and the lean and hungry look". American Economic Review 74, 361–366.
Fudenberg, D., Tirole, J. (2000). "Customer poaching and brand switching". RAND Journal of Economics 31, 634–657.
Fudenberg, D., Gilbert, R., Stiglitz, J., Tirole, J. (1983). "Preemption, leapfrogging and competition in patent races". European Economic Review 22, 3–31.
Gabaix, X., Laibson, D. (2006). "Shrouded attributes, consumer myopia and information suppression in competitive markets". Quarterly Journal of Economics 121, 505–540.
Gabel, H.L. (1987). Product Standardization and Competitive Strategy. North-Holland, Amsterdam.
Gabel, H.L. (1991). Competitive Strategies for Product Standards. McGraw-Hill, London.
Gabrielsen, T.S., Vagstad, S. (2003). "Consumer heterogeneity, incomplete information and pricing in a duopoly with switching costs". Information Economics and Policy 15, 384–401.
Gabrielsen, T.S., Vagstad, S. (2004). "On how size and composition of customer bases affect equilibrium in a duopoly with switching costs". Review of Economic Design 9, 59–71.
Gabszewicz, J., Pepall, L., Thisse, J. (1992). "Sequential entry, with brand loyalty caused by consumer learning-by-doing-using". Journal of Industrial Economics 40, 397–416.
Galbi, D.A. (2001). "Regulating prices for shifting between service providers". Information Economics and Policy 13, 191–198.
Gallini, N., Karp, L. (1989). "Sales and consumer lock-in". Economica 56, 279–294.
Gandal, N. (1994). "Hedonic price indexes for spreadsheets and an empirical test for network externalities". RAND Journal of Economics 25, 160–170.
Gandal, N. (1995a). "A selective survey of the indirect network externalities: A discussion". Research in Law and Economics 17, 23–31.
Gandal, N. (1995b). "Competing compatibility standards and network externalities in the PC software market". Review of Economics and Statistics 77, 599–603.
Gandal, N. (2001). "The dynamics of competition in the Internet search engine market". International Journal of Industrial Organization 19, 1103–1117.
Gandal, N. (2002). "Compatibility, standardization, and network effects: Some policy implications". Oxford Review of Economic Policy 18, 80–91.
Gandal, N., Shy, O. (2001). "Standardization policy and international trade". Journal of International Economics 53, 363–383.
Gandal, N., Kende, M., Rob, R. (2000). "The dynamics of technological adoption in hardware/software systems: The case of compact disc players". RAND Journal of Economics 31, 43–61.
Gandal, N., Salant, D., Waverman, L. (2003). "Standards in wireless telephone networks". Telecommunications Policy 27, 325–332.
Gans, J., King, S. (2001). "Regulating endogenous customer switching costs". Contributions to Theoretical Economics 1 (1). http://www.bepress.com/bejte/contributions/vol1/iss1/art1.

Gans, J., King, S., Woodbridge, G. (2001). "Numbers to the people: Regulation, ownership, and local number portability". Information Economics and Policy 13, 167–180.
Garcia Mariñoso, B. (2001). "Technological incompatibility, endogenous switching costs and lock-in". Journal of Industrial Economics 49, 281–298.
Garcia Mariñoso, B. (2003). "Endogenous switching costs and exclusive systems: A reply". Review of Network Economics 1, 36–40.
Gates, B., Myrhvold, N., Rinearson, P. (1995). The Road Ahead. Viking, New York.
Gawer, A., Henderson, R. (2005). "Platform owner entry and innovation in complementary markets: Evidence from Intel". NBER Working Paper 11852.
Gehrig, T., Stenbacka R. (2002). "Introductory offers in a model of strategic competition". Working Paper. University of Freiburg and Swedish School of Economics, Helsinki.
Gehrig, T., Stenbacka, R. (2004a). "Differentiation-induced switching costs and poaching". Journal of Economics and Management Strategy 13, 635–655.
Gehrig, T., Stenbacka, R. (2004b). "Information sharing and lending market competition with relationship benefits and poaching". Working Paper. University of Freiburg and Swedish School of Economics, Helsinki.
Gehrig, T., Stenbacka, R. (2005). "Two at the top: Quality differentiation in markets with switching costs". CEPR Discussion Paper #4996. Universität Freiburg and Swedish School of Economics.
Gerlach, H.A. (2004). "Announcement, entry, and preemption when consumers have switching costs". RAND Journal of Economics 35, 184–202.
Gilbert, R.J. (2004). "Antitrust for patent pools: A century of policy evolution". Stanford Technology Law Review.
Gilbert, R.J., Katz, M.L. (2001). "An economist's guide to U.S. v. Microsoft". Journal of Economic Perspectives 15, 25–44.
Gilbert, R.J., Klemperer, P.D. (2000). "An equilibrium theory of rationing". RAND Journal of Economics 31, 1–21.
Gneezy, U., Rottenstreich, Y. (2004). "The power of the focal point is limited: Even minor pay off asymmetry yields massive coordination failure". Working Paper. University of Chicago Business School.
Goerke, L., Holler, M.J. (1995). "Voting on standardisation". Public Choice 83, 337–351.
Good, J.B. (2006). "The incentive for a dominant firm to innovate". M. Phil. Thesis. Oxford University.
Goolsbee, A., Klenow, P.J. (2002). "Evidence on learning and network externalities in the diffusion of home computers". Journal of Law and Economics 45, 317–344.
Gottfries, N. (2002). "Market shares, financial constraints, and pricing behavior in the export market". Economica 276, 583–607.
Gowrisankaran, G., Ackerberg, D. (in press). "Quantifying equilibrium network externalities in the ACH banking industry". RAND Journal of Economics.
Gowrisankaran, G., Stavins, J. (2004). "Network externalities and technology adoption: Lessons from electronic payments". RAND Journal of Economics 35, 260–276.
Green, E.J., Porter, R.H. (1984). "Noncooperative collusion under imperfect price information". Econometrica 52, 87–100.
Green, J., Scotchmer, S.A. (1986). "Switching costs as an explanation for price dispersion". Working Paper. Graduate School of Public Policy, University of California, Berkeley.
Greenstein, S.M. (1993). "Did installed base give an incumbent any (measurable) advantage in federal computer procurement". RAND Journal of Economics 24, 19–39.
Greenstein, S.M., Rysman, M. (2004). "Testing for agglomeration and dispersion". Economics Letters 86, 405–411.
Grindley, P. (1995). Standards Strategy and Policy: Cases and Stories. Oxford Univ. Press, Oxford.
Grove, A. (1996). Only the Paranoid Survive. Doubleday Publishing.
Gruber, H., Verboven, F. (2001). "The evolution of markets under entry and standards regulation – The case of global mobile telecommunications". International Journal of Industrial Organization 19, 1189–1212.
Guadagni, P., Little, J. (1983). "A logit model of brand choice calibrated on scanner data". Marketing Science 1, 203–238.

Guibourg, G. (2001). "Interoperability and network externalities in electronic payments". Sveriges Riksbank Working Paper Series, September, #126.

Haan, M. (2003). "Vaporware as a means of entry deterrence". Journal of Industrial Economics 51, 345–358.

Hakenes, H., Peitz, M. (in press). "Observable reputation trading". International Economic Review.

Hanson, W.A. (1983). "Bandwagons and orphans: Dynamic pricing of competing technological systems subject to decreasing costs". Working Paper. Stanford University.

Hartigan, J.C. (1995). "Perverse consequences of the GATT: Export subsidies and switching costs". Economica 63, 153–161.

Hartman, R., Teece, D. (1990). "Product emulation strategies in the presence of reputation effects and network externalities: Some evidence from the minicomputer industry". Economics of Innovation and New Technology 1, 157–182.

Haruvy, E., Prasad, A. (2001). "Optimal freeware quality in the presence of network externalities: An evolutionary game theoretical approach". Journal of Evolutionary Economics 11, 231–248.

Haucap, J. (2003). "Endogenous switching costs and exclusive systems applications". Review of Network Economics 1, 29–35.

Hemenway, D. (1975). Industrywide Voluntary Product Standards. Ballinger Publishing Co., Cambridge.

Hermalin, B., Katz, M. (2005). "Customer or complementor? Intercarrier compensation with 2-sided benefits". Working Paper. University of California, Berkeley.

Holmes, T.J. (1990). "Consumer investment in product specific capital: The monopoly case". Quarterly Journal of Economics 105, 789–801.

Holmes, T.J. (1999). "How industries migrate when agglomeration economies are important". Journal of Urban Economics 45, 240–263.

Innes, R., Sexton, R. (1994). "Strategic buyers and exclusionary contracts". American Economic Review 84, 566–584.

Israel, M.A. (2005). "Tenure dependence in consumer–firm relationships: An empirical analysis of consumer departures from automobile insurance firms". RAND Journal of Economics 36, 165–192.

Jacoby, J., Chestnut, R.W. (1978). Brand Loyalty: Measurement and Management. John Wiley and Sons, New York.

Jeitschko, T.D., Taylor, C.R. (2001). "Local discouragement and global collapse: A theory of coordination avalanches". American Economic Review 9, 208–244.

Jensen, R., Thursby, M. (1996). "Patent races, product standards, and international competition". International Economic Review 37, 21–49.

Jullien, B. (2001). "Competing in network industries: Divide and conquer". Working Paper. IDEI and GREMAQ, University of Toulouse.

Kahan, M., Klausner, M. (1996). "Path dependence in corporate contracting: Increasing returns, herd behavior, and cognitive biases". Washington University Law Quarterly 74, 347.

Kahan, M., Klausner, M. (1997). "Standardization and innovation in corporate contracting (or "the economics of boilerplate")". Virginia Law Review 83, 713.

Kahin, B., Abbate, J. (1995). Standards Policy for Information Infrastructure. MIT Press, Cambridge.

Kahn, A.E., Shew, W.B. (1987). "Current issues in telecommunications regulation: Pricing". Yale Journal on Regulation 4, 191–256.

Karaca-Mandic, P. (2004). "Estimation and evaluation of externalities and complementarities". Ph.D. Dissertation. University of California, Berkeley.

Katz, M.L. (2001). "Network effects, interchange fees, and no-surcharge rules in the Australian credit and charge card industry". Commissioned report, Reserve Bank of Australia.

Katz, M.L., Shapiro, C. (1985). "Network externalities, competition and compatibility". American Economic Review 75, 424–440.

Katz, M.L., Shapiro, C. (1986a). "Product compatibility choice in a market with technological progress". Oxford Economic Papers 38, 146–165.

Katz, M.L., Shapiro, C. (1986b). "Technology adoption in the presence of network externalities". Journal of Political Economy 94, 822–841.

Katz, M.L., Shapiro, C. (1992). "Product introduction with network externalities". Journal of Industrial Economics 40, 55–83.

Katz, M.L., Shapiro, C. (1994). "System competition and network effects". Journal of Economic Perspectives 8, 93–115.

Kauffman, R., Wang, Y.M. (1999). "Network externalities and the determinants of network survival". MIS Research Center Working Paper 99-03.

Kim, B.-D., Shi, M., Srinivasan, K. (2001). "Reward programs and tacit collusion". Marketing Science 20, 99–120.

Kim, J.-Y., Koh, D.-H. (2002). "Attracting the rival's customers in a model with switching costs". Japanese Economic Review 53, 134–139.

Kim, M., Kliger, D., Vale, B. (2003). "Estimating switching costs: The case of banking". The Journal of Financial Intermediation 12, 25–56.

Klausner, M. (1995). "Corporations, corporate law, and networks of contracts". Virginia Law Review 81, 757–852.

Klein, B., Crawford, R.G., Alchian, A.A. (1978). "Vertical integration, appropriable rents, and the competitive contracting process". Journal of Law and Economics 21, 297–326.

Klemperer, P.D. (1983). "Consumer switching costs and price wars". Working Paper. Stanford Graduate School of Business.

Klemperer, P.D. (1987a). "Markets with consumer switching costs". Quarterly Journal of Economics 102, 375–394.

Klemperer, P.D. (1987b). "The competitiveness of markets with switching costs". RAND Journal of Economics 18, 138–150.

Klemperer, P.D. (1987c). "Entry deterrence in markets with consumer switching costs". Economic Journal (Supplement) 97, 99–117.

Klemperer, P.D. (1988). "Welfare effects of entry into markets with switching costs". Journal of Industrial Economics 37, 159–165.

Klemperer, P.D. (1989). "Price wars caused by switching costs". Review of Economic Studies 56, 405–420.

Klemperer, P.D. (1992). "Equilibrium product lines: Competing head-to-head may be less competitive". American Economic Review 82, 740–755.

Klemperer, P.D. (1995). "Competition when consumers have switching costs". Review of Economic Studies 62, 515–539.

Klemperer, P.D. (in press a). "Switching costs". In: Durlauf, S.N., Blume, L.E. (Eds.) The New Palgrave: A Dictionary of Economics, second ed., Palgrave-Macmillan, Basingstoke.

Klemperer, P.D. (in press b). "Network effects". In: Durlauf, S.N., Blume, L.E. (Eds.), The New Palgrave: A Dictionary of Economics, second ed., Palgrave-Macmillan, Basingstoke.

Klemperer, P.D., Padilla, A.J. (1997). "Do firms' product lines include too many varieties?". RAND Journal of Economics 28, 472–488.

Klemperer, P.D., Png, I. (1986). "Frequent-flyer plans: Marketing device with insidious effects". Los Angeles Times. Section IV, June 8, 3.

Klimenko, M. (2002). "Strategic interoperability standards and trade policy in industries with network externalities". IRPS Working Paper.

Knittel, C.R. (1997). "Interstate long distance rate: Search costs, switching costs and market power". Review of Industrial Organization 12, 519–536.

Koh, D.-H. (1993). "Competition by endogenous switching time". UCLA Graduate School of Management Working Paper.

Kornish, L. (2006). "Technology choice and timing with positive network effects". European Journal of Operational Research 173, 268–282.

Kretschmer, T. (2001). "Competition, inertia and network effects". INSEAD Working Paper.

Kristiansen, E.G. (1998). "R&D in the presence of network externalities: Timing and compatibility". RAND Journal of Economics 29, 531–547.

Kristiansen, E.G., Thum, M. (1997). "R&D incentives in compatible networks". Journal of Economics 65, 55–78.

Krugman, P. (1991a). Geography and Trade. Leuven University Press/MIT Press, Cambridge.
Krugman, P. (1991b). "History versus expectations". Quarterly Journal of Economics 106, 651–667.
Kubota, K. (1999). "Trade negotiations in the presence of network externalities". Mimeo. World Bank – Country Economics Department.
Laffont, J.J., Rey, P., Tirole, J. (1998a). "Network competition. I. Overview and nondiscriminatory pricing". RAND Journal of Economics 29, 1–37.
Laffont, J.J., Rey, P., Tirole, J. (1998b). "Network competition. II. Price discrimination". RAND Journal of Economics 29, 38–56.
Lal, R., Matutes, C. (1994). "Retail pricing and advertising strategies". Journal of Business 67, 345–370.
Lambertini, L., Orsini, R. (2001). "Network externalities and the overprovision of quality by a monopolist". Southern Economic Journal 67, 969–982.
Langlois, R.N. (1992). "External economies and economic progress: The case of the microcomputer industry". Business History Review 66, 1–50.
Larkin, I. (2004). "Switching costs and competition in enterprise software: Theory and evidence". Working Paper. UC Berkeley.
Lee, B. (1997). "Markets with consumer switching benefits". Working Paper. Management Research Lab, Korea Telecom.
Lee, R. (2003). "The adoption of standards with incomplete information". Harvard Undergraduate Thesis (Economics).
Lee, S-Y.T., Png, I.P.L. (2004). "Buyer shopping costs and retail pricing: An indirect empirical test". Review of Marketing Science 2. http://www.bepress.com/romsjournal/vol2/iss1/art6.
Lehr, W. (1995). "Compatability standards and interoperability: Lessons from the Internet". In: Kahin, B., Abbate, J. (Eds.), Standards Policy for Information Infrastructure. MIT Press, Cambridge, pp. 121–147.
Leibenstein, H. (1950). "Bandwagon, snob and Veblen effects in the theory of consumers' demand". Quarterly Journal of Economics 64, 183–207.
Lemley, M.A. (2002). "Intellectual property rights and standard setting organizations". California Law Review 90, 1889–1980.
Lemley, M.A., McGowan, D. (1998a). "Legal implications of network economic effects". California Law Review 86, 479–612.
Lemley, M.A., McGowan, D. (1998b). "Could Java change everything? The competitive propriety of a propriety standard". Antitrust Bulletin 43, 715–773.
Lerner, J., Tirole, J. (2006). "A model of forum shopping". American Economic Review 96, 1091–1113.
Lewis, T.R., Yildirim, H. (2005). "Managing switching costs in multiperiod procurements with strategic buyers". International Economic Review 46, 1233–1269.
Liebowitz, S.J., Margolis, S.E. (1990). "The fable of the keys". Journal of Law and Economics 33, 1–25.
Liebowitz, S.J., Margolis, S.E. (1994). "Network externality: An uncommon tragedy". Journal of Economic Perspectives 8, 133–150.
Liebowitz, S.J., Margolis, S.E. (1995). "Path dependence, lock-in and history". Journal of Law Economics and Organization 11, 205–226.
Liebowitz, S.J., Margolis, S.E. (1996). "Should technology choice be a concern of antitrust policy?". Harvard Journal of Law and Technology 9, 284–317.
Liebowitz, S.J., Margolis, S.E. (1998a). "Network effects and externalities". In: The New Palgrave Dictionary of Economics and the Law, vol. II. MacMillan, Basingstoke, pp. 671–674.
Liebowitz, S.J., Margolis, S.E. (1998b). "Path dependence". In: The New Palgrave Dictionary of Economics and the Law, vol. III. MacMillan, Basingstoke, pp. 17–23.
Liebowitz, S.J., Margolis, S.E. (2001). Winners, Losers and Microsoft: Competition and Antitrust in High Technology, second ed. The Independent Institute, Oakland, CA, USA.
Llobet, G., Manove, M. (2006). "Network size and network capture". Working Paper. CEMFI and Boston University.
Lofaro, A., Ridyard, D. (2003). "Switching costs and merger assessment – Don't move the goalposts". European Competition Law Review 6, 268–271.

MacKie-Mason, J.K., Metzler, J. (1999). "Links between vertically related markets: ITS vs. Kodak". In: Kwoka, J., White, L. (Eds.), The Antitrust Revolution. Oxford Univ. Press, Oxford.
MacKie-Mason, J., Netz, J. (2007). "Manipulating interface standards as an anti-competitive strategy". In: Greenstein, S., Stango, V. (Eds.), Standards and Public Policy. Cambridge Univ. Press, Cambridge, UK, pp. 231–259.
Malueg, D., Schwartz, M. (2006). "Compatability incentives of a large network facing multiple rivals". Journal of Industrial Economics 54, 527–567.
Manenti, F.M., Somma, E. (2002). "One-way compatibility, two-way compatibility and entry in network industries". Working Paper. Southern European Research in Economic Studies, Series #4.
Mankiw, N.G., Whinston, M.D. (1986). "Free entry and social inefficiency". RAND Journal of Economics 17, 48–58.
Manski, C. (1993). "Identification of endogenous social effects: The reflection problem". Review of Economic Studies 60, 531–542.
Mason, R. (2000). "Network externalities and the Coase conjecture". European Economic Review 44, 1981–1992.
Mason, R., Valletti, T. (2001). "Competition in communication networks: Pricing and regulation". Oxford Review of Economic Policy 17, 389–415.
Matutes, C., Regibeau, P. (1988). "Mix and match: Product compatibility without network externalities". RAND Journal of Economics 19, 221–234.
Matutes, C., Regibeau, P. (1992). "Compatibility and bundling of complementary goods in a duopoly". Journal of Industrial Economics 40, 37–54.
Matutes, C., Regibeau, P. (1996). "A selective review of the economics of standardization: Entry deterrence, technological progress and international competition". European Journal of Political Economy 12, 183–209.
Menell, P. (2002). "Envisioning copyright law's digital future". New York Law Review 62 (3).
Milgrom, P., Roberts, J. (1990). "Rationalizability, learning, and equilibrium in games with strategic complementarities". Econometrica 58, 1255–1277.
Miles D. (2004). "The UK mortgage market: Taking a longer-term view". Report for the UK Treasury. The Stationery Office, UK.
Moshkin, N., Shachar, R. (2000). "Switching cost or search cost?". Working Paper #3-2000. Foerder Institute for Economic Research.
Murphy, K., Shleifer, A., Vishny, R. (1989). "Industrialization and the big push". Journal of Political Economy 97, 1003–1026.
Nalebuff, B. (2000). "Competing against bundles". In: Hammond, P.J., Myles, G.D. (Eds.), Incentives, Organization, and Public Economics. Oxford Univ. Press, Oxford, pp. 323–335.
Nalebuff, B. (2004). "Bundling as an entry barrier". Quarterly Journal of Economics 119, 159–188.
Nelson, P. (1970). "Information and consumer behavior". Journal of Political Economy 78, 311–329.
Nilssen, T. (1992). "Two kinds of consumer switching costs". RAND Journal of Economics 23, 579–589.
Nilssen, T. (2000). "Consumer lock-in with asymmetric information". International Journal of Industrial Organization 18, 641–666.
Ochs, J. (1995). "Coordination problems". In: Kagel, J., Roth, A. (Eds.), The Handbook of Experimental Economics. Princeton Univ. Press, Princeton, pp. 195–251.
OECD (1991). Information Technology Standards: The Economic Dimension. Paris.
Office of Fair Trading (2003). "Switching costs: Annex C". Economic Discussion Paper #5. London, UK.
Ohashi, H. (2003). "The role of network externalities in the U.S. VCR market, 1978–1986". Journal of Economics and Management Strategy 12, 447–494.
Oren, S.S., Smith, S.A. (1981). "Critical mass and tariff structure in electronic communications markets". The Bell Journal of Economics 12, 467–487.
Ostrovsky, M., Schwarz, M. (2005). "The adoption of standards under uncertainty". RAND Journal of Economics 4, 816–832.
Padilla, A.J. (1992). "Mixed pricing in oligopoly with consumer switching costs". International Journal of Industrial Organization 10, 393–412.

Padilla, A.J. (1995). "Revisiting dynamic duopoly with consumer switching costs". Journal of Economic Theory 67, 520–530.
Palfrey, T. (1983). "Bundling decisions by a multiproduct monopolist with incomplete information". Econometrica 51, 463–483.
Panzar, J.C., Wildman, S.S. (1995). "Network competition and the provision of universal service". Industrial and Corporate Change 4, 711–719.
Panzar, J.C., Willig, R.C. (1981). "Economies of scope". American Economic Review 71, 268–272.
Park, I.-U. (2004a). "A simple inducement scheme to overcome adoption externalities". Contributions to Theoretical Economics 4: Article 3. http://www.bepress.com/bejte/contributions/vol4/iss1/art3.
Park, S. (2004b). "Quantitative analysis of network externalities in competing technologies: The VCR case". Review of Economics and Statistics 86, 937–945.
Park, M.J. (2005). "The economic impact of wireless number portability". Working Paper. SIEPR 04-017, Stanford University.
Parker, G., Van Alstyne, M. (2005). "Two-sided network effects: A theory of information product design". Management Science 51, 1494–1504.
Pereira, P. (2000). "Price dynamics with consumer search and cost volatility". Working Paper. University of Madrid.
Phelps, E., Winter, S. (1970). "Optimal price policy under atomistic competition". In: Phelps, E. (Ed.), Microeconomic Foundations of Employment and Inflation Theory. Norton, New York, pp. 309–337.
Porter, M.E. (1980). Competitive Strategy. Macmillan Publishing Co., New York.
Porter, M.E. (1985). Competitive Advantage. Macmillan Publishing Co., New York.
Postrel, S.R. (1990). "Competing networks and proprietary standards: The case of quadraphonic sound". Journal of Industrial Economics 39, 169–185.
Radin, M.J. (2002). "Online standardization and the integration of text and machine". Fordham Law Review 70, 1125.
Radner, R. (2003). "Viscous demand". Journal of Economic Theory 112, 189–231.
Radner, R., Sundararajan, A. (2005). "Dynamic pricing of network goods with boundedly rational consumers". Working Paper. Stern School of Business.
Raskovich, A. (2003). "Pivotal buyers and bargaining position". Journal of Industrial Economics 51, 405–426.
Rasmusen, E., Ramseyer, J.M., Wiley, J. (1991). "Naked exclusion". American Economic Review 81, 1137–1145.
Ribstein, L., Kobayashi, B. (2001). "Choice of form and network externalities". William & Mary Law Review 43, 79–140.
Robinson, C. (1999). "Network effects in telecommunications mergers: MCI WorldCom merger: Protecting the future of the Internet, before the Practicing Law Institute, San Francisco, CA, August". http://www.usdoj.gov/atr/public/speeches/3889.htm.
Rochet, J.C., Tirole, J. (2002). "Cooperation among competitors: The economics of credit card associations". RAND Journal of Economics 33, 1–22.
Rochet, J.C., Tirole, J. (2003). "Platform competition in two-sided markets". Journal of the European Economic Association 1, 990–1029.
Rochet, J.C., Tirole, J. (2006). "Two-sided markets: A progress report". RAND Journal of Economics 37, 645–667.
Rohlfs, J. (1974). "A theory of interdependent demand for a communications service". Bell Journal of Economics 5, 16–37.
Rohlfs, J. (2001). Bandwagon Effects in High Technology Industries. MIT Press, Cambridge.
Rosenstein-Rodan, P. (1943). "Problems of industrialization of Eastern and South-Eastern Europe". The Economic Journal 53, 202–211.
Rosenthal, R. (1980). "A model in which an increase in the number of sellers leads to a higher price". Econometrica 48, 1575–1580.
Rosse, J.N. (1967). "Daily newspapers, monopolistic competition, and economies of scale". American Economic Review, Papers and Proceedings 57, 522–533.

Rubinfeld, D. (2003). "Maintenance of Monopoly: US v. Microsoft (2001)". In: Kwoka, J.E., White, L.J. (Eds.), The Antitrust Revolution. Oxford Univ. Press, Oxford.
Rysman, M. (2004). "Competition between networks: A study of the market for yellow pages". The Review of Economic Studies 71, 483–512.
Saloner, G. (1990). "Economic issues in computer interface standardization". Economics of Innovation and New Technology 1, 135–156.
Saloner, G., Shepard, A. (1995). "Adoption of technologies with network effects: An empirical examination of the adoption of automated teller machines". RAND Journal of Economics 20, 479–501.
Samuelson, P., Scotchmer, S. (2002). "The law and economics of reverse engineering". Yale Law Journal 111, 1575–1664.
Sapir, A., Sekkat, K. (1995). "Exchange rate regimes and trade prices: Does the EMS matter?". Journal of International Economics 38, 75–94.
Saxenian, A. (1994). Regional Advantage. Harvard Univ. Press, Cambridge.
Scharfstein, D., Stein, J. (1990). "Herd behavior and investment". American Economic Review 80, 465–479.
Schelling, T.C. (1960). The Strategy of Conflict. Harvard Univ. Press, Cambridge.
Schelling, T.C. (1978). Micromotives and Macrobehavior. Norton, New York.
Schlesinger, H., von der Schulenburg, J.M.G. (1993). "Consumer information and decisions to switch insurers". The Journal of Risk and Insurance 60, 591–615.
Schmalensee, R. (1982). "Product differentiation advantages of pioneering brands". American Economic Review 72, 349–365.
Schmalensee, R. (2000). "Antitrust issues in Schumpeterian industries". American Economic Review 90, 192–196.
Schmalensee, R. (2002). "Payment systems and interchange fees". Journal of Industrial Economics 50, 103–122.
Schulz, N., Stahl, K. (1996). "Do consumers search for the highest price? Oligopoly equilibrium and monopoly optimum in differentiated product markets". RAND Journal of Economics 3, 542–562.
Schwartz, M., Vincent, D. (2006). "The no-surcharge rule and card user rebates: Vertical control by a payment network". Review of Network Economics 5, 72–102.
Seetharaman, P.B., Che, H. (in press). "Price competition in markets with consumer variety seeking". Marketing Science.
Seetharaman, P.B., Ainslie, A., Chintagunta, P.K. (1999). "Investigating household state dependence effects across categories". Journal of Marketing Research 36, 488–500.
Segal, I.R. (1999). "Contracting with externalities". Quarterly Journal of Economics 114, 337–388.
Segal, I.R. (2003). "Coordination and discrimination in contracting with externalities: Divide and conquer?". Journal of Economic Theory 113, 147–181.
Segal, I.R., Whinston, M.D. (2000). "Naked exclusion: Comment". American Economic Review 90, 296–311.
Selten, R. (1965). "Spieltheoretische behandlung eines Oligopolmodells mit nachfrägetragheit". Zeitschrift für die Gesamte Staatswissenschaft 121, 301–324 and 667–689.
Shaffer, G., Zhang, Z.J. (2000). "Pay to switch or pay to stay: Preference-based price discrimination in markets with switching costs". Journal of Economics and Management Strategy 9, 397–424.
Shapiro, C. (1995). "Aftermarkets and consumer welfare: Making sense of Kodak". Antitrust Law Journal 63, 483–512.
Shapiro, C. (1999). "Exclusivity in network industries". George Mason Law Review, Spring.
Shapiro, C., Teece, D.J. (1994). "Systems competition and aftermarkets: An economic analysis of Kodak". The Antitrust Bulletin 39, 135.
Shapiro, C., Varian, H.R. (1998). Information Rules – A Strategic Guide to the Network Economy. Harvard Business School Press, Boston.
Sharpe, S.A. (1990). "Asymmetric information, bank lending and implicit contracts: A stylized model of customer relationships". Journal of Finance 45, 1069–1087.
Sharpe, S.A. (1997). "The effect of consumer switching costs on prices: A theory and its application to the bank deposit market". Review of Industrial Organization 12, 79–94.

Shi, M., Chiang, J., Rhee, B. (2006). "Price competition with reduced consumer switching costs: The case of "wireless number portability" in the cellular phone industry". Management Science 52, 27–38.

Shilony, Y. (1977). "Mixed pricing in oligopoly". Journal of Economic Theory 14, 373–388.

Shum, M. (2004). "Does advertising overcome brand loyalty? Evidence from the breakfast-cereals market". Journal of Economics & Management Strategy 13, 241–272.

Shurmer, M. (1993). "An investigation into sources of network externalities in the packaged PC software market". Information Economics and Policy 5, 231–251.

Shy, O. (1996). "Technology revolutions in the presence of network externalities". International Journal of Industrial Organization 14, 785–800.

Shy, O. (2001). The Economics of Network Industries. Cambridge Univ. Press, Cambridge.

Shy, O. (2002). "A quick-and-easy method for estimating switching costs". International Journal of Industrial Organization 20, 71–87.

Simcoe, T. (2003). "Committees and the creation of technical standards". Working Paper. University of California, Berkeley, Haas School of Business.

Skott, P., Jepsen, G.T. (2000). "Paradoxical effects of drug policy in a model with imperfect competition and switching costs". Journal of Economic Behaviour and Organization 48, 335–354.

Spence, A.M. (1976). "Product selection, fixed costs, and monopolistic competition". Review of Economic Studies 43, 217–235.

Squire, L. (1973). "Some aspects of optimal pricing for telecommunications". Bell Journal of Economics 4, 515–525.

Stahl, K. (1982). "Differentiated products, consumer search, and locational oligopoly". Journal of Industrial Economics 37, 97–113.

Stango, V. (2002). "Pricing with consumer switching costs: Evidence from the credit card market". Journal of Industrial Economics 50, 475–492.

Stigler, G. (1951). "The division of labor is limited by the extent of the market". Journal of Political Economy 59, 185–193.

Stigler, G. (1964). "A theory of oligopoly". The Journal of Political Economy 72, 44–61.

Stiglitz, J.E. (1989). "Imperfect information in the product market". In: Schmalensee, R., Willig, R.D. (Eds.), Handbook of Industrial Organization, vol. 1. North-Holland, Amsterdam, pp. 769–847.

Sundararajan, A. (2003). "Network effects, nonlinear pricing and entry deterrence". Working Paper. Stern School of Business, New York University.

Stole, L.A. (2007). "Price discrimination in competitive environments". In: Armstrong, M., Porter, R. (Eds.), Handbook of Industrial Organization, vol. III. North-Holland, Amsterdam (this volume).

Sutton, J. (1980). "A model of stochastic equilibrium in a quasi-competitive industry". Review of Economic Studies 47, 705–722.

Sutton, J. (1998). Technology and Market Structure: Theory and History. MIT Press, Cambridge.

Swann, G.M.P. (2002). "The functional form of network effects". Information Economics and Policy 14, 417–429.

Taylor, C. (2003). "Supplier surfing: Competition and consumer behavior in subscription markets". RAND Journal of Economics 34, 223–246.

Thompson, G.V. (1954). "Intercompany technical standardization in the early American automobile industry". The Journal of Economic History 14, 1–20.

Thum, M. (1994). "Network externalities, technological progress, and the competition of market contracts". International Journal of Industrial Organization 12, 269–289.

Tivig, T. (1996). "Exchange rate pass-through in two-period duopoly". International Journal of Industrial Organization 14, 631–645.

To, T. (1994). "Export subsidies and oligopoly with switching costs". Journal of International Economics 37, 97–110.

To, T. (1995). "Multiperiod competition with switching costs: An overlapping generations formulation". Journal of Industrial Economics 44, 81–87.

Topkis, D.M. (1978). "Minimizing a submodular function on a lattice". Operations Research 26, 305–321.

Topkis, D.M. (1998). "Supermodularity and complementarity". In: Kreps, D.M., Sargent, T.J., Klemperer, P. (Eds.), Frontiers of Economic Research Series. Princeton Univ. Press, Princeton.
Valletti, T.M. (2000). "Switching costs in vertically related markets". Review of Industrial Organization 17, 395–409.
Varian, H. (1980). "A model of sales". American Economic Review 70, 651–659.
Varian, H. (1989). "Price discrimination". In: Schmalensee, R., Willig, R.D. (Eds.), Handbook of Industrial Organization, vol. 1. North-Holland, Amsterdam, pp. 597–654.
Vettas, N. (2000). "Investment dynamics in markets with endogenous demand". Journal of Industrial Economics 48, 189–203.
Viard, B.V. (in press). "Do switching costs make markets more or less competitive?: The case of 800-number portability". RAND Journal of Economics.
Vickers, J.S. (2004). "Economics for consumer policy". Proceedings of the British Academy 125, 285–310.
Villas-Boas, M. (1999). "Dynamic competition with customer recognition". RAND Journal of Economics 30, 604–631.
Villas-Boas, M. (2006). "Dynamic competition with experience goods". Journal of Economics and Management Strategy 15, 37–66.
von Weizsäcker, C.C. (1984). "The cost of substitution". Econometrica 52, 1085–1116.
Walz, U., Woeckener, B. (2003). "Compatibility standards and strategic trade policy". CEPR Discussion Paper #3815. Universities of Frankfurt and Stuttgart.
Wang, R., Wen, Q. (1998). "Strategic invasion in markets with switching costs". Journal of Economics and Management Strategy 7, 521–549.
Waterson, M. (2003). "The role of consumers in competition and competition policy". International Journal of Industrial Organization 21, 129–150.
Weiss, M., Sirbu, M. (1990). "Technological choice in voluntary standards committees: An empirical analysis". Economics of Innovation and New Technology 1, 111–133.
Werden, G.J. (2001). "Network effects and conditions of entry: Lessons from the Microsoft case". Antitrust Law Journal 69, 87–111.
Wernerfelt, B. (1991). "Brand loyalty and market equilibrium". Marketing Science 10, 229–245.
Whinston, M.D. (1990). "Tying, foreclosure and exclusion". American Economic Review 80, 837–859.
Whinston, M.D. (2001). "Exclusivity and tying in US v. Microsoft: What we know, and don't know". Journal of Economic Perspectives 15, 63–80.
Williamson, O.E. (1975). Markets and Hierarchies: Analysis and Anti-trust Implications. Free Press, New York.
Wilson, C.M. (2006). "Markets with search and switching costs". Centre for Competition Policy Working Paper 06-10. University of East Anglia.
Witt, U. (1997). "Lock-in vs. critical masses: Industrial change under network externalities". International Journal of Industrial Organization 15, 753–773.
Woeckener, B. (1999). "Network effects, compatibility decisions, and monopolization". Zeitschrift für Wirtschafts und Sozialwissenschaften 119, 23–44.
Yannelis, D. (2001). "On the simple welfare economics of network externalities". International Journal of Social Economics 28, 344–348.
Zephirin, M.G. (1994). "Switching costs in the bank deposit market". Economic Journal 104, 455–461.

Chapter 32

AN EMPIRICAL PERSPECTIVE ON AUCTIONS

KEN HENDRICKS
University of Texas

ROBERT H. PORTER
Northwestern University

Contents

Handbook of Industrial Organization, Volume 3
Edited by M. Armstrong and R. Porter

DOI: 10.1016/S1573-448X(06)03032-9

Abstract

We describe the economics literature on auction markets, with an emphasis on the connection between theory, empirical practice, and public policy, and a discussion of outstanding issues. We describe some basic concepts, to highlight some strengths and weaknesses of the literature, and so indicate where further research may be warranted. We discuss identification and estimation issues, with an emphasis on the connection between theory and empirical practice. We also discuss both structural and reduced form empirical approaches.

Keywords

Auctions, Bidding, Identification, Estimation, Collusion, Bid rigging

JEL classification: D44, D82, C1

1. Introduction

Auctions are an important market institution. Our purpose in this chapter is to review the theoretical and empirical literature on bidding in auction markets, although the discussion of the theory will be limited to instances where the models have a direct bearing on some empirical literature. The emphasis is instead on empirical work.

There are many auction markets in which excellent data are available. There are several different types of auction data sets that have been analyzed in the literature. These include government sales, such as sales of timber and mineral rights, oil and gas rights, treasury bills, and import quotas, privatization sales, spectrum auctions and auctions of SO_2 emission permits. Auctions are important in government procurement, including defense contracts, and contracts for highway construction and repair, and for school milk. In the private sector, auction houses such as Sotheby's and Christies sell art, wine and memorabilia. There are agricultural sales (e.g., eggplants in Marmande, France), estate sales, real estate auctions, and used durable goods sales, for used cars and farm machinery. Burlington Northern has employed auctions to allocate future railcar capacity. The recently created wholesale electricity markets in the United Kingdom, Australia, various regions in the United States, and elsewhere often employ auctions. There are also now many Internet auctions, with eBay the most prominent. [See, e.g., Bajari and Hortacsu (2004).] Finally, auctions are frequently the subject of experimental research, both in the laboratory and in field experiments.

Auction data sets are often better than the typical data set in industrial organization. The auction game is relatively simple, with well-specified rules. The actions of the participants are observed directly, and payoffs can sometimes be inferred.

Why use an auction as a trading mechanism, rather than posting prices, bargaining or contracting? There is usually some uncertainty about the buyers' willingness to pay, and heterogeneity among potential buyers. Also, some degree of product heterogeneity is often present, so that past transactions are not a reliable guide to current market prices. In these circumstances, auctions can be an effective price discovery process.

There are *many* possible auction mechanisms. They can be characterized in terms of (1) a message space (i.e., what information do the bidders send to the seller) and (2) the seller's allocation rule, specifying which, if any, bidders might receive the item, and the probability that they receive it, and payments from (or transfers to) the bidders, as a function of the messages received. For example, consider a seller who has one item to allocate, and where messages are bids. Then one can roughly categorize common auction mechanisms into one of four cells:

	Highest bid	Second highest
Open	Dutch	English
Closed	FPSB	Vickrey (SPSB)

In closed auctions, submitted bids are considered simultaneously by the seller. In a first price, sealed bid (FPSB) auction, the item is awarded to the highest bidder, who pays his bid. In a Vickrey or second price sealed bid (SPSB) auction, the highest bidder wins and pays the highest losing bid. In open auctions, bidders call out their bids sequentially. In a Dutch auction, the seller starts the auction at a high price, and lowers the price until a bidder says "stop". That bidder wins the item at the stop price. Thus, only the winning "bid" is submitted. In an English auction, the seller starts the auction at a low price, and the price increases until no bidder is willing to raise it further. As we will describe in more detail in Section 3, there are many ways to run an English auction. Under several variants, the winning bidder acquires the item at the drop out price of the last remaining losing bidder, so that the outcome is like a second price auction. Similarly, the Dutch auction is akin to a FPSB auction. Variations on these mechanisms include secret or publicly announced reserve prices or minimum bids, and entry fees or subsidies.

In this chapter we describe the economics literature on auction markets, with an emphasis on the connection between theory, empirical practice, and public policy, and a discussion of outstanding issues. Auction markets are the subject of a large and distinguished theoretical literature. Klemperer (2004), Krishna (2002) and Milgrom (2004) provide excellent summaries of the theory and applications to public policy issues. There are also older thorough surveys by McAfee and McMillan (1987) and by Wilson (1993). An extensive empirical literature using data from auction markets has emerged recently. Our goal in this chapter is to provide an introduction to the empirical literature. Our intention is to describe some basic concepts, and to highlight some strengths and weaknesses of the literature, and so indicate where further research may be warranted. There are two other contemporaneous reviews of note, which complement our chapter. Athey and Haile (2008) survey various approaches to the estimation of structural models of equilibrium bidding, with an emphasis on non-parametric identification issues. Paarsch and Hong (2006) also discuss structural modeling, with an emphasis on estimation issues, often in a parametric context. We will also discuss identification and estimation issues, but our emphasis will be on the connection between theory and empirical practice. We will also discuss both structural and reduced form empirical approaches. The surveys by Hendricks and Paarsch (1995) and by Laffont (1997) describe some of the early empirical analysis of auction data sets. Finally, Kagel (1995) surveys the considerable literature on laboratory experimental auction markets, and Harrison and List's (2004) survey of field experiments describes some auction market field experiments. We refer to the experimental literature only occasionally, and interested readers should consult the surveys for more detail.

Auctions offer the prospect of a close connection between theory and empirical work. Moreover, much of the theoretical work on auctions has specific positive or normative goals in mind, and so empiricists are not usually required to re-cast the theory before testing theoretical predictions. Given a specific auction mechanism, the positive role of theory is to describe how to bid rationally, which usually involves characterizing the Bayesian Nash equilibrium (BNE) of the bidding game. Given the number of bidders, the joint distribution of their valuations and signals, and some behavioral assumption, the normative role of theory is to characterize optimal or efficient selling mechanisms. These two roles are reflected in the way theoretical work has been employed to guide empirical work and policy advice. Theory helps to shed light on how to interpret patterns in the data, suggests comparative static results that can be tested, and guides optimal mechanism design.

Empirical work also has positive and normative goals. The positive goal is to answer questions such as how agents behave, and whether their valuations are correlated and, if so, the sources of the correlation. Given the auction environment, a bidder's strategy is a mapping from his private information to a bid. Hence, a realization of bidder signals induces a distribution of bids. One can then ask whether an observed bid distribution is consistent with BNE, and test for such properties as independence. With experimental data, the researcher knows what signals were received, but not the preferences of the bidders, and one can compare predicted to actual bids under different assumptions concerning preferences. Thus, the consistency question is well defined. However, with field data, the researcher does not know what signals were received, and real modeling issues arise in examining the consistency question. The positive analysis can be of more than academic interest, since bid rigging or collusion may be distinguishable from non-cooperative behavior, if the two have different positive implications. One can also ask whether risk aversion is an important feature.

The normative goal of empirical work is to answer questions such as what the revenue maximizing or efficient auction might be. If one knows or one can estimate the relevant features of the auction environment, especially the joint distribution of valuations and signals for potential bidders, and one knows which behavioral model is appropriate, then optimal auction design is feasible. Alternatively, one can test whether the auction design is optimal. For example, McAfee and Vincent (1992) ask whether the reserve price is chosen optimally in the first-price, sealed bid (FPSB) auctions they study.

For want of a better description, there have been two kinds of approaches adopted in the empirical literature, which we term *reduced form* and *structural*. Reduced form analysis tests predictions of the theory to draw inferences about behavior and the bidding environment. The goal of the structural approach is to estimate the data generating process directly, in particular the joint distribution of valuations and signals, usually under the assumption of risk neutrality and BNE. The strategy is to characterize the Bayesian Nash equilibrium of the auction to obtain a functional relationship between signals and bids, and therefore between the distributions of signals and bids. Assuming a BNE equilibrium exists, one can use the relationship between signal and bid distributions to construct a likelihood function for the data. The difficulty, or constraint on applicability, is that equilibrium strategies can be complex, they are often highly nonlinear, and there may not be a closed-form representation for the bid strategy, or more precisely, for the inverse bid function. In addition, there are the usual existence and uniqueness issues to worry about. We will survey papers according to this perspective, to give a flavor of what's being done, where progress has been made, and what the outstanding issues are.

This survey is concerned primarily with single object auctions. The data, of course, often consists of many auctions, conducted either sequentially over time or simultaneously. For much of this survey, we follow the literature and treat each auction as an independent event, ignoring any factors, strategic or structural, that link participation and bidding decisions across auctions. Section 2 describes a model of bidding and introduces the notation we employ throughout. Section 3 focuses on structural estimation of second-price auctions. Section 4 discusses structural estimation of first-price auctions. Section 5 looks at tests that distinguish between information environments, and Section 6 describes tests of the theoretical implications of equilibrium bidding. Section 7 reviews empirical work that compares revenues across auction formats, in both single- and multi-unit settings. Section 8 examines work on collusion or bid rigging schemes. We close with a brief discussion of some outstanding empirical issues.

2. Model and notation

In this section we describe a model of bidding based upon the general symmetric information model introduced by Milgrom and Weber (1982). This model will serve to establish the notation that will be used throughout this chapter. Random variables will be denoted by upper case and realizations by lower case.

Consider a bidding environment in which n potential risk neutral buyers bid to purchase a single item. The buyers are indexed by i. Each bidder i observes a real-valued signal x_i. Here X_i is private information, observed only by bidder i. In addition, there is some random variable V, which may be multidimensional, and which influences the value of the object to the bidders. The values of $(V, X_1, \ldots, X_n)$ are governed by some joint distribution denoted by F. The joint distribution is assumed to be symmetric in the signals and to have a density function f. Let $x_{-i} = (x_1, \ldots, x_{i-1}, x_{i+1}, \ldots, x_n)$. A generic signal is denoted by X with realization x. Bidder i's payoff or valuation is given by $U_i = u_i(V, X_i, X_{-i})$ in the event that bidder i obtains the object being sold. The seller announces a minimum bid, or reserve price, r.

The primitives of the model are the number of bidders n, the distribution function F, and the utility functions $\{u_i\}_{i=1}^n$. These are assumed to be common knowledge among the buyers. The main assumptions of the model are (i) u_i is non-negative, continuous, increasing in each argument and symmetric in the components of X_{-i} and (ii) $(V, X_1, \ldots, X_n)$ are affiliated.[1] These two assumptions imply that the valuations $U_1, \ldots, U_n$ are affiliated random variables. Let $Y_1, \ldots, Y_{n-1}$ denote the ordering of the largest through the smallest signals from $(X_2, \ldots, X_n)$, the signals of bidder 1's rivals. By Theorem 2 of Milgrom and Weber (1982), $(V, X_1, Y_1, \ldots, Y_{n-1})$ are affiliated random variables.

There are several restrictive aspects of the model worth noting. First, the assumption that private information is single-dimensional rules out situations in which bidders have

[1] The n random variables $X = (X_1, \ldots, X_n)$, with joint density $f(x)$, are affiliated if, for all x and y, $f(x \wedge y) f(x \vee y) \geqslant f(x) f(y)$, where $\wedge$ denotes the component-wise minimum, and $\vee$ the component-wise maximum. If random variables are affiliated, then they are non-negatively correlated. See Milgrom and Weber (1982).

private information about the different components of their payoffs. The only empirical work in auctions that we know of that allows for multi-dimensional signals is Cantillon and Pesendorfer (2004). Second, symmetry of F in the signals rules out the possibility that some bidders have more precise signals of common unknown components of the payoffs. We relax this assumption when we discuss auctions with asymmetrically informed bidders. Third, there is an implicit assumption that, in the event that someone else obtains the object, bidder i's valuation is independent of the identity of that agent. Jehiel and Moldovanu (2003) consider the strategic implications of the alternative assumption that the winner's identity matters, as in an auction of an input prior to downstream oligopoly competition, for example. Fourth, the assumption that the number of potential bidders is common knowledge can be relaxed to account for uncertainties about whether rivals are serious bidders. For example, a costly decision to acquire a signal might be private. See Hendricks, Pinkse and Porter (2003), for an example of this sort of model.

A bidding (pure) strategy for bidder i is a correspondence $\beta_i : X_i \rightarrow \Re_+$. It maps the private signal into a non-negative real number. As we shall see, empirical work in auctions relies heavily upon the assumption that β_i is a strictly increasing function and hence invertible. Theoretical work in auctions informs us that the conditions under which a Bayesian Nash equilibrium in non-decreasing bid functions exists are affiliation of $(V, X_1, \dots, X_n)$ and symmetric payoff functions u_i. If either of these conditions are not satisfied, an equilibrium in increasing bid functions may not exist, although we will consider special cases in which such an equilibrium exists. For a discussion, see Athey (2001) or Krishna (2002, Appendix G).

Two special cases of the above model are frequently discussed in the theoretical literature:

1. Private values: $u_i(v, x_i, x_{-i}) = x_i$. Bidder i knows his own valuation and is only uncertain about how much others value the item.
2. Pure common values: $u_i(v, x_i, x_{-i}) = v$ (or one component of v when it is multi-dimensional). All buyers have the same valuation, which is unknown to them when they bid. If so, then each buyer's signal may be informative. However, each bidder i knows only its own signal and does not observe the other bidders' signals, x_{-i}.

The presence of common components in bidders' payoffs does not imply that valuations are not private. When the common components are known to the bidders, then bidders may be uncertain about their rivals' valuations but they know their own private valuations. When the common components are uncertain then, in terms of our notation, the important strategic issue is whether rival signals are informative about the realization of the common component V, given the realization of their own private signal, x_i. If the distribution of V conditional on x_i is independent of X_{-i}, then the bidding environment is one with private values. In practice, the private valuation can then be defined as the expected value of $u_i(V, X_i, X_{-i})$ given the signal x_i received by bidder i, which in a private values environment is independent of X_{-i}. The location of the signal distribution is arbitrary, and if $E[U_i \mid X_i = x_i,\ X_{-i} = x_{-i}] = f(x_i)$ for some monotone increasing function f, signals can be re-normalized to equal $f(x_i)$. In a common values environment, the distribution of V conditional on x_i is not independent of X_{-i} and the realization x_{-i} matters, i.e., $E[U_i \mid X_i = x_i,\ X_{-i} = x_{-i}]$ depends on x_{-i}. In summary, if valuations depend on known common components, or on unknown common components about which bidders have no private information, then the bidding environment can be characterized as one of private values (PV). If valuations depend on unknown common components about which bidders have private information, then we will characterize the bidding environment as one of common values (CV), and distinguish the special case in which valuations depend solely on the unknown common component as pure common values (PCV). Within the private and common values bidding environments, we will sometimes distinguish between independent signals (IPV and ICV, respectively) and affiliated signals (APV and ACV, respectively).[2]

Consider, for example, the bidding environment for offshore oil and gas leases. The argument for the common value case is that the firms are uncertain about common components of the value of the lease being sold, such as the size of any oil or gas deposits under the tract, the prices of oil and gas over the likely production horizon if the lease is productive, and the common costs of exploration and development. The first component is likely to lead to common values, to the extent that firms have private information about the size of the deposits based on the seismic data they obtain, and especially their interpretation of that data. In contrast, firms may not have private information about future prices, and uncertain prices are then not inconsistent with private values.

Alternatively, one might argue that there is little discrepancy in private assessments of these common components, and instead that valuations differ because of differences in bidder specific components of valuations. The most likely sources of bidder payoff heterogeneity are the private components of exploration and drilling costs. Bidders are not likely to differ in their valuation of recovered deposits, to the extent that there is a well-developed market for oil and gas. Under this alternative view, valuations are best modeled as private, although they may be affiliated because of the common unknown components of payoffs that may be correlated with publicly available information.

An intermediate case, introduced by Wilson (1977), that nests the private and pure common value cases assumes that $u_i(v, x_i, x_{-i}) = u(v, x_i)$. Here bidder i's valuation has a common component and an idiosyncratic component, and the former affects every bidder's payoff in the same way. In terms of oil and gas auctions, the Wilson model allows the bidders' payoffs to depend upon the common, unknown size of the deposit and upon their private drilling costs. Private information, however, must still be real-valued. Consequently, the private signal plays two roles: it is informative of the size

[2] The theoretical literature classifies auctions in terms of the "reduced form" valuation

$$w(x_i, x_{-i}) = E[U_i \mid X_i = x_i,\ X_{-i} = x_{-i}]$$

rather than the primitives. Values are private if $w(x_i, x_{-i}) = x_i$ and interdependent otherwise. Common values is a special case of interdependent values.

of the deposit and of drilling costs. The Wilson model is a restricted class of common values models, but we shall adopt it as the base model since almost all empirical work on auctions can be discussed in the context of this model. Throughout the remainder of this chapter, we will often use common values to refer to the Wilson model when discussing empirical work.

As we shall see, one of the important roles of empirical work on auctions is to determine whether values are private or common. The distinction is fundamental to both the positive goal of characterizing bidding behavior and the normative goal of auction design. In an independent private values environment, the standard logic of competitive markets prevails and more competition raises bids and increases revenues. [Note, however, that this result need not obtain in an APV environment, as shown by Pinkse and Tan (2005).] On the other hand, if the common component is the main determinant of bidder valuations, then more competition does not necessarily lead to higher bids and more revenue. Winning the auction is an informative event, with respect to the value of the item. The information is "bad news", and it has sometimes been called the "winner's curse". A bidder is more likely to bid high and win the item when he overestimates the item's value. In particular, bidding one's ex ante expectation (i.e., not conditioning on the event of winning) is an inferior strategy; one needs to bid more conservatively. As a result, restricting the number of bidders can be a revenue enhancing policy for the seller.

More formally, suppose the common value of the item, v, is unknown to the bidders and independent of the identity of the winner. Given a signal x, bidder *1*'s ex ante estimate of the item is

$$v_1(x) = E[V \mid X_1 = x] = \int v f_{V|X_1}(v \mid x)\,\mathrm{d}v,$$

where $f_{V|X_1}$ is the posterior conditional density function, derived by Bayes rule. By construction, $E[V_1 \mid v] = v$, where $V_1 = v_1(X_1)$, so that ex ante estimates are conditionally unbiased. Suppose the bidding strategy for each bidder i is monotone increasing in its signal. Then, in a symmetric equilibrium, the winner is the bidder with the highest signal, and hence the highest estimate. But

$$E\Big[\max_i\{V_i\} \mid v\Big] \geqslant \max_i\big\{E[V_i \mid v]\big\} = v$$

by Jensen's inequality, since max is a convex function. This is in essence the winner's curse. Winning is bad news [in the sense of Milgrom (1981a)] for bidder *1*, since

$$E[V \mid X_1 = x,\ Y_1 < x] < E[V \mid X_1 = x].$$

Recall that Y_1 is defined to be the maximum signal among bidder *1*'s rivals, and if bidders employ symmetric strategies bidder *1* wins only when his signal is highest, and therefore exceeds Y_1. Thus, independent of strategic considerations, bidder *1* should bid less than his ex ante estimate V_1 to account for the information contained in the event that he has the highest bid.

3. Structural analysis of second-price auctions

In structural estimation, the empirical researcher posits a theory of equilibrium bidding and estimates the unobserved bidders' utilities and the joint distribution of their signals from bid data. Interest in this exercise is based on the normative objective of finding the optimal selling mechanism, or the positive objective of describing behavior, or distinguishing between alternative behavioral models, such as competition vs collusion, or risk neutrality vs risk aversion. This section reviews the work that has been done on English and second-price, sealed bid auctions.

3.1. Theory

It will be useful to first characterize bidder's payoffs and the symmetric Bayesian Nash equilibrium for an English auction. In deriving the equilibrium, we take the perspective of bidder *1*. Define

$$w(x, y) = E\big[u(V, x) \mid X_1 = x,\ Y_1 = y\big]$$

and let $\underline{x}$ denote the lower bound of the support of X_i. The function $w(x, y)$ denotes the expected payoff of the bidder, given a signal x, in the event that the highest rival signal is y.

There are many ways to run an English auction. In one variant, bidders call out their bids, while in another the auctioneer calls out the bids. Bids may rise continuously or in increments. A bidder's willingness to pay the bid called may be privately communicated to the auctioneer or it may be observed by rival bidders. These institutional details matter since they affect equilibrium behavior. As a result, the different variants of English auctions constitute different data generating mechanisms, and the analyst needs to bear this in mind in interpreting bids and deriving the likelihood function for the data.

Most empirical work is based on a version of the English auction known as a button auction. In this auction, the price rises continuously and bidders stay active as long as they keep their fingers on the button. A bidder wins once all other bidders take their fingers off their buttons, and the price paid is the exit point of the penultimate active bidder. In this context, a strategy for bidder i specifies, at any bid level, whether to stay active or drop out of the bidding. The symmetric equilibrium is characterized by a "no regret" property: a bidder remains active as long as his expected value of the object conditional on winning at the current price exceeds that price, and he drops out otherwise. The critical issue in characterizing the bidder's drop out point is what he observes about rivals' bidding decisions.

One possibility is to assume that each bidder does not observe the prices at which rival bidders drop out. The only inference an active bidder can draw from the fact that the bidding has not ended is that at least one rival is still active. In this case, the equilibrium strategy for bidder *1* is to drop out at

$$\beta(x) = E\big[u(V, x) \mid X_1 = x,\ Y_1 = x\big] = w(x, x). \tag{1}$$

The reasoning is as follows. Suppose bidder *1*'s rivals bid according to the above strategy and bidding has reached $b = \beta(y)$. Bidder *1*'s payoff conditional upon winning is $w(x, y) - b$, because to win means that everyone else has dropped out and at least one rival has signal y. Affiliation implies that bidder *1*'s payoff is positive if $x > y$ and negative if $x < y$. Hence, he should stay active until the bidding reaches $\beta(x)$ and then drop out. The English auction with unobserved exits is strategically equivalent to a second-price, sealed bid auction. In that case, Equation (1) represents bidder *1*'s bid strategy.

Another formulation assumes that active bidders observe the prices at which rivals drop out of the bidding. Furthermore, no bidder who drops out can become active again. In this case, bidder *1*'s strategy at any bid will depend upon how many rivals have previously dropped out and the prices at which they dropped out. Let β_k specify the price at which bidder *1* drops out of the bidding if k rivals have dropped out previously, at the prices $b_1, \ldots, b_k$. The no regret property implies that

$$\beta_k(x) = E\big[u(V, x) \mid X_1 = x,\ Y_1 = \cdots = Y_{n-k-1} = x,\\ Y_{n-k} = \eta_{k-1}(b_k), \ldots, Y_{n-1} = \eta_0(b_1)\big]. \tag{2}$$

Here $\eta_k()$ denotes the inverse of the function $\beta_k()$. (To economize on notation, we suppress the dependence of the bid on $b_1, \ldots, b_k$.) The reasoning is similar to the case considered before. At any bid $b = \beta_k(y)$, bidder *1* calculates the expected value of the object conditional on winning and the prices at which k rivals have dropped out in prior rounds. Given those prices, and the inverse bidding rule with $n - k$ remaining rivals, the signals of the bidders who dropped out can be inferred. For example, the first bidder to drop at price b_1 must have had the signal $\eta_0(b_1)$. In this case, however, winning at b means that the $n - k - 1$ rivals who were active in the previous round of bidding must all drop out at b. For this to happen, they must all have the same signal, y. Affiliation implies that bidder *1*'s payoff from staying active is positive if $x > y$ and negative if $x < y$.

In most auctions, sellers set a reserve price, r. If $r > w(\underline{x}, \underline{x})$, the expected value if all bidders have the lowest possible signal, then bidders with low signals may not participate. Let x^* denote the participation threshold. In the symmetric equilibrium of the button auction described above, Milgrom and Weber (1982) show that the participation threshold for each bidder is given by

$$x^*(r) = \inf\big\{x \mid E\big[w(x, Y_1) \mid X_1 = x,\ Y_1 < x\big] \geqslant r\big\}.$$

Since affiliation implies that expectations are increasing in x and y, x^* is unique. Bidders with signals less than x^* do not bid, and bidders with signals larger than x^* participate. Therefore, the marginal participant is someone who is just willing to pay r even if he finds out that no one else is willing to pay r. It is straightforward to show that the screening level is increasing in r and, in a common values model, increasing in n, the number of bidders. In the latter case, the participation threshold x^* increases in n to compensate for more rivals having pessimistic signals.

When values are private, the information conveyed by bidders who drop out is irrelevant to each bidder's participation and bidding decisions. Each bidder bids if and only if his value exceeds r, that is $x^*(r) = r$. The equilibrium strategy given in Equations (1) and (2) reduces to $\beta(x) = \beta_k(x) = x$. Each bidder stays active until bidding reaches his private value and then drops out. The private values equilibrium is compelling because it is unique if one restricts attention to weakly dominant strategies. It is also an equilibrium in private values auctions with asymmetric bidders.

When values are common, the equilibrium is not unique. Bikhchandani, Haile and Riley (2002) characterizes the set of symmetric separating equilibria in English auctions with common values. They show that there are many ways for the $n - 2$ bidders with the lowest valuations to exit the auction. The restriction to symmetric equilibria does pin down the transaction price since the equilibrium to the subgame that begins after the $n - 2$ bidders with the lowest valuations drop out is unique. Unfortunately, this subgame has a continuum of asymmetric equilibria.

Consider the following simple example, which Klemperer (1998) calls the wallet game. There are two players, denoted by *1* and *2*. Each player's wallet contains money. Let X_i denote the money in player i's wallet, and assume that X_1 and X_2 are independent random variables uniformly distributed on $[0, \bar{x}]$. Each player knows how much is in his own wallet but does not know the amount in his rival's wallet. They are asked to bid for the sum of the contents of the two wallets in a second-price, sealed bid auction. Klemperer shows that the auction has a continuum of equilibria indexed by $\alpha > 0$ in which

$$\beta_1(x_1) = (1 + \alpha)x_1, \qquad \beta_2(x_2) = \left(1 + \frac{1}{\alpha}\right)x_2.$$

Here α can be interpreted as a measure of how aggressively player *1* bids. The symmetric equilibrium, where $\alpha = 1$, is for each player to bid twice the amount in his wallet, as $w(x, x) = 2x$. But, if player *1* bids more aggressively, player *2* will bid less aggressively since he knows that if he wins, the amount in player *1*'s wallet is less than half of the price that he has to pay. Conversely, if player *1* bids less aggressively, then player *2* can afford to bid more aggressively.

The wallet game illustrates the effects of common values. The symmetric equilibrium is no longer in dominant strategies, and it is no longer unique. In fact, there are typically many asymmetric equilibria. The wallet game result is a special case of a more general result established by Milgrom (1981b). He proves that for every continuous, increasing function g, the two player, second-price, common values auction has an equilibrium in which

$$\beta_1(x_1) = w\big(x_1, g(x_1)\big), \qquad \beta_2(x_2) = w\big(g^{-1}(x_2), x_2\big).$$

Bikhchandani and Riley (1991) establish similar results for common value English auctions in which bidder exit times are observable.

The symmetric equilibria may not be robust to slight asymmetries in the payoffs. In the wallet game, suppose player *1* values the contents of the wallets by a small amount θ

in addition to the total amount of money, whereas player *2* only cares about the money. In that case, Klemperer (1998) shows that the equilibrium consists of player *2* always bidding x_2 and bidder *1* bidding $x_1 + \bar{x}$. Thus, bidder *1* always wins and pays x_2. The intuition is that it is common knowledge that bidder *1* values the object more than bidder *2*, and bidder *1* can use this fact to threaten credibly to always bid more than bidder *2*.

Many oral, ascending price auctions are open outcry auctions in which bidders call out their bids. These are continuous time, dynamic games that are difficult to formalize since bidders can announce a "jump" bid at any time. Bidders can use jump bids to signal information about their valuations [as in Avery (1998)]. The idea behind a jump bid is to convince rival bidders to concede the auction before the bidding reaches their values. The strategy can be effective because, if a bidder is certain that his value is less than the value of the jump bidder, then dropping out of the auction is a weakly dominant strategy. As a result, the jump bidder may win the auction at a lower price than he would have had to pay in the equilibrium in which bids increase incrementally. The jump bidder does run the risk of paying more than might have been necessary to win. A jump bid could also be effective if it is costly to continue submitting bids. Then a player might drop out early, if he views his chances of winning as low.

More generally, it is inherently difficult to model continuous time, dynamic games with few limitations on the strategy space. Absent any such limitations, such as those of the button auction, the theoretical literature does not suggest a suitable behavioral model for open outcry auctions.

3.2. Estimation

We now turn to a discussion of estimation issues. The structural econometric exercise we consider consists of finding F, the joint distribution of private signals and the payoff relevant random variable, V, that best rationalizes the bidding data.

Consider first the case of a button auction with symmetric independent private values. The mechanism generating the data consists of the identity function, $\beta(x) = x$, for signals above the reserve price r. Denote the common distribution of bidder values by F_X, which we wish to estimate. As discussed above, the bid levels at which bidders drop out of the auction are often not observed with the exception of course of the bidder with the second-highest valuation. Suppose therefore that the only data available are

$$\{w_t, n_t, r_t\}_{t=1}^{T} \quad \text{if } m_t \geqslant 1,$$

where w_t denotes the winning bid, n_t the number of potential bidders, and r_t the reserve price in auction $t = 1, \dots, T$. Here m_t denotes a latent (unobserved) variable, the number of bidders who are active, by which we mean those whose values exceed the reserve price, and therefore submit bids. We assume that we observe data only from auctions in which at least one bid is submitted. The winning bid $w_t = \max\{x_{2:n_t}, r_t\}$, the maximum of the second highest order statistic from a sample of n_t valuations and the reserve price.

Donald and Paarsch (1996) describe how to construct the likelihood function. The researcher needs to take into account three possible outcomes:

1. If $m_t = 0$, $\Pr\{m_t = 0\} = F_X(r_t)^{n_t}$.
2. If $m_t = 1$, then $w_t = r_t$ and $\Pr\{m_t = 1\} = n_t F_X(r_t)^{n_t-1}[1 - F_X(r_t)]$.
3. If $m_t > 1$, then $w_t \sim h_t(w) = n_t(n_t - 1)F_X(w)^{n_t-2}[1 - F_X(w)]f_X(w)$.

The first outcome occurs when no bids are submitted at an auction. We interpret this event as evidence that all of the bidders' valuations are below the reserve price. The second outcome occurs when the winning bid in the auction is the reserve price. We interpret this event as the case where only one bidder values the item more than the reserve price. The third, and final, outcome arises when the winning bid exceeds the reserve price. In this case, $n_t - 2$ bidders have valuations below w_t, the winning bidder's valuation exceeds w_t, and the second highest valuation is equal to w_t. Let

$$D_t = \begin{cases} 1 & \text{if } m_t = 1, \\ 0 & \text{if } m_t > 1. \end{cases}$$

Then the likelihood function for the data set, which includes only auctions in which bids are submitted, is

$$L = \prod_t \left[\frac{h_t(w_t)^{1-D_t} \Pr\{m_t = 1\}^{D_t}}{(1 - \Pr\{m_t = 0\})} \right].$$

Estimation then might proceed by choosing a family for $F_X(\cdot \mid \theta)$, parameterized by θ, and recovering the distribution function F_X above r using maximum likelihood methods. Note that this method remains valid when the assumptions of risk neutrality and/or symmetry are relaxed since $b_{it} = x_{it}$ remains a dominant strategy. In the asymmetric case, one recovers F_{X_i} above r for each bidder i.

Interest in this exercise is based on the normative objective of selecting the optimal auction design, such as finding the revenue maximizing reserve price. Note that in IPV auctions, the optimal reserve price is independent of n and depends only upon F_X. For example, in the English button auction, expected revenue to the seller who values the item at x_0 is

$$R = x_0 F_X(r)^n + rnF_X(r)^{n-1}\big[1 - F_X(r)\big] + \int_r^{\bar{x}} wn(n-1)F_X(w)^{n-2}\big[1 - F_X(w)\big]f_X(w)\,\mathrm{d}w.$$

The first term corresponds to events when the item is not sold, the second when the item is sold at the reserve price, and the third when the winning bid exceeds r. Differentiating with respect to r yields the optimal reserve price as the solution to

$$r = x_0 + \big[1 - F_X(r)\big]/f_X(r).$$

Thus the optimal reserve price in an IPV auction depends only on x_0 and F_X, and not the number of bidders. [See, for example, Riley and Samuelson (1981).]

If the bid levels at which losing bidders drop out of the auction are observed, then the likelihood function becomes

$$L = \prod_{t=1}^{T} \left\{ [1 - F_X(w_t)] \left(\prod_{i=2}^{m_t} f_X(b_{it}) \right) F_X^{n_t - m_t}(r_t) \right\},$$

where b_{it} denotes the drop out point of bidder i for object t, $i = 1, \ldots, n_t$, and bids are ordered so that $b_{1t} \geqslant b_{2t} \geqslant \cdots \geqslant b_{m_t} \geqslant r_t$. The highest bid is not observed, in the sense that the winning bidder may have been willing to stay active at a higher price than w_t. If i did not submit a bid, we define $b_{it} \equiv 0$. If more than one bidder is active, then the winning bid is b_{2t}. If only one bidder is active, then the winning bid, and the lower bound on x_{1t}, is the reserve price r_t. If the reserve price is binding, then the likelihood function should be modified as above to account for the sample selection associated with observing auction outcomes only if $m_t \geqslant 1$.

If the number of potential bidders n_t is not observed, the researcher could assume $n_t = n$ for all t and estimate n as a parameter. Alternatively, one could assume $n = \max_t\{m_t\}$, i.e., the maximum number of active bidders observed in any auction, or a count of all bidders who are ever active. A third approach is to assume that n_t is the realization of a random variable N which has some distribution (e.g., Poisson) and estimate the distributional parameters (here of a truncated Poisson, since $n_t \geqslant m_t$). Note that in this case, where values are private, bidding behavior is independent of the number of bidders n_t. Hence, one could instead specify the likelihood function as

$$L = \prod_{t=1}^{T} \left\{ \prod_{i=1}^{m_t} \left[f_X(b_{it}) / \left(1 - F_X(r_t)\right) \right] \right\}.$$

That is, observed bids are draws from the truncated distribution $f_X/(1 - F_X)$ above the reserve price r_t.

Observable heterogeneity in the items being auctioned can be accommodated by conditioning the distribution of values on a vector of covariates, Z_t. In this case, one recovers the family of conditional distributions, $F_X(\cdot \mid Z_t = z_t)$. For example, one could express

$$x_{it} = \alpha + z_{it}\beta + u_{it}.$$

Then

$$x_{it} \geqslant b_{it} \quad \Longleftrightarrow \quad u_{it} \geqslant b_{it} - \alpha - z_{it}\beta.$$

Heterogeneity in the items that is observed by the bidders but not by the researcher is a much bigger problem. The presence of unobserved heterogeneity implies that the signals x_{it} (and therefore the bids) are not independent given t nor is their distribution identical across t. Furthermore, if n_t is not observed and unobserved heterogeneity is present, the researcher has an identification problem: are a few, low bids observed because n_t is low, or because $F_X(\cdot \mid Z_t = z_t)$ is unfavorable?

When values are private but affiliated, it is still a dominant strategy for bidder i to bid his signal and to participate if x_i exceeds r. From an empirical viewpoint, the researcher needs to treat the auction rather than the individual bid as the unit of observation, and the joint distribution of signals, $F_{\langle X\rangle}$, rather than F_X as the object of interest. Sample size may become a problem. If all bids are observed, then it is straightforward to specify and maximize a likelihood function to obtain an estimate of $F_{\langle X\rangle}$. If some of the bids are not observed due to censoring, the specification of the likelihood function is complicated by the need to integrate over some of the components of $F_{\langle X\rangle}$. With more than two bidders, these integrations are likely to render the maximum likelihood approach infeasible. An alternative approach is simulation methods [McFadden (1989) and Pakes and Pollard (1989)]. Note that, because these auctions are dominance solvable, signals do not have to be affiliated.

In many instances, researchers observe submitted bids in an open outcry English auction. Any given bidder may submit many bids, or none. Let b_{it} now denote the highest bid submitted by bidder i for object t, $i = 1, \ldots, n_t$. If bidder i did not submit a bid, let $b_{it} = 0$. But note that bidder i might be active yet not submit a bid. Order the bidders so that $b_{1t} \geqslant b_{2t} \geqslant \cdots \geqslant b_{m_t} \geqslant r_t$, where now m_t denotes the number of bidders who submit a bid, as opposed to the number of active bidders. Here the winning bid is submitted by the bidder with the highest valuation, and so $w_t = b_{1t}$. If agents play according to their dominant strategy (i.e., stay active until the high bid surpasses their valuation), then we know that $x_{1t} \geqslant b_{1t}$, $x_{it} \in [b_{it}, w_t]$ for $i = 2, \ldots, m_t$, and $w_t \geqslant x_{it}$for $i = m_t + 1, \ldots, n_t$. Both the winning bidder and the losing bidders are willing to pay at least their final bid, whereas the willingness to pay of losing bidders is less than the winning bid. The absence of a bid by bidder i implies that x_{it} is less w_t, but not necessarily less than the reserve price r_t. If we observe n_t, and if we assume that the second highest bidder drops out at the winning bid, or just below, then the likelihood function is as described above for the button version of an English auction. The winning bid is then distributed according to the density function $h_t(w_t)$, as defined at the beginning of this section, when there is more than one active bidder. Maximum likelihood estimation is possible even without observing the losing bids. Losing bid information might be used to obtain a more efficient estimator of F_X, although it is not clear how to do so, as there is not a one-to-one mapping from valuations to bids.

The problem with the likelihood approach in this context is the assumption that the winning bid equals the second highest valuation. If bids rise in discrete steps, or especially if there is jump bidding, with bids increasing faster than the required minimum increment, then the assumption is unlikely to be valid.

The likelihood approach as described here is parametric. Haile and Tamer (2003) propose a non-parametric approach to address the problem of inference when bidders do not indicate whether they are "in" as the ascending auction proceeds, which we describe in the next section. Their approach exploits the information embodied in the losing bids, and they do not require that the winning bid equal the second highest valuation.

We now discuss two empirical studies of bidding in ascending auctions.

Bajari and Hortacsu (2003) study bidding and auction design issues in eBay coin auctions. They treat this environment as a second-price, sealed bid auction. They note that eBay auctions have hard closing times, in that bids are not accepted after a pre-specified time. Moreover, a disproportionate fraction of bids are submitted close to the ending time, a practice known as sniping. Some preliminary empirical analysis indicates that, in their sample, winning bid levels are not correlated with early bidding activity, as measured by a dummy variable indicating whether the losing bids were submitted more than 10 minutes before the closing time (in which case the winning bidder would have had time to respond). They argue that the auctions they study are therefore strategically equivalent to a second price sealed bid auction.

A second potentially controversial assumption is that the coin auctions they study are a pure common value environment. They point to an active resale market, and to some evidence that bids are negatively correlated with the number of people who bid. The latter is likely endogenous, but the correlation persists if they use minimum bids as an instrument. Negative correlation between bids and the number of bidders is not consistent with private values in a second price sealed bid auction, as bidding one's value is a dominant strategy. As Bajari and Hortacsu note, the eBay coin market should probably instead be modeled as a more general common values setting, but to do so would be technically challenging.

Bajari and Hortacsu restrict attention to symmetric equilibria, so that bids are generated according to the strategy described above, whereby $\beta(x) = w(x, x)$, if x is greater than or equal to the screening level $x^*(n, r)$. In a common values environment, the screening level depends on the number of bidders, which we make explicit here. Although this is the unique symmetric equilibrium, as noted above there are a continuum of asymmetric equilibria in second price sealed bid auctions with common values. They also assume that the common value is normally distributed, with mean and variance linear functions of observable covariates, and that signals conditional on the common value are unbiased and normally distributed, with variance proportional to the variance of the common value, v. Given these assumptions, the likelihood function for the bid data is well defined but difficult to estimate. One complication is that the inverse mapping from bids to signals is no longer the identity function. The likelihood that bidder i submits a bid b_{it} in auction t, conditional on the common value, is given by

$$f_{B|V}(b_{it} \mid v_t) = f_{X|V}\big(\eta(b_{it}) \mid v_t\big)\eta'(b_{it}),$$

where η denotes the inverse bid function, and $f_{X|V}$ is the density of the signals conditional on the common value.[3] Since neither η nor its derivative η' are available in closed form, they must be estimated numerically. A second complication is that, in auctions with binding reserve prices, each bidder's participation decision depends upon the level of competition. As noted above, the screening level is a decreasing function of the number of bidders; the winner's curse causes expected profits to fall. This is not true

[3] Affiliation implies that $\beta(x)$ is strictly increasing in x, so the inverse function exists.

in private value auctions, where each bidder participates as long as his value exceeds r. The likelihood function for the data is

$$L = \prod_{t=1}^{T} \left\{ \int F_{X|V}\big(x^*(n_t, r_t) \mid v\big)^{n_t - m_t} \left[\prod_{i=2}^{m_t} f_{B|V}(b_{it} \mid v) \right] \right.$$
$$\left. \times \big(1 - F_{X|V}\big(\eta(w_t) \mid v\big)\big)^{1\{m_t \geqslant 1\}} f_V(v)\, \mathrm{d}v \right\},$$

where $1\{m_t \geqslant 1\}$ is an indicator variable for at least one active bidder in the auction, and $x^*(n_t, r_t)$ is the screening level, below which the signals of inactive bidders fall. Although eBay observes all bids, the data records only the losing bids and not b_{1t}, the winning bid. As above, if the auction receives only one bid, then b_{1t} is bounded below by the announced reserve price r_t. The likelihood contains no correction for sample selection since auctions that attract no bidders are observed and are assigned a positive probability. Finally, Bajari and Hortacsu argue that in eBay auctions, the number of rival bidders is not known to the bidders. They assume that n_t follows a Poisson distribution, with mean determined endogenously by a zero ex ante expected profit condition. Bidders are assumed to incur an entry cost before learning their signal. The function $w(x, x)$ must be modified to be the expectation of the common value, conditional on the bidder's signal x, where the expectation is now over both the realizations of the rival bidders' signals and the number of rival bidders. The screening level must also be modified to account for this uncertainty.

Bajari and Hortacsu's analysis of reserve price policy demonstrates the value of structural estimation. One caveat, which is more a complaint about the empirical eBay literature, is that the auctions are treated in isolation, when similar items are often sold at the same time. Thus the optimal reserve price calculation is treated like a monopoly pricing problem, and the bidder participation decision does not account for the outside option of bidding for comparable items.

Hong and Shum (2003) estimate a structural model of an asymmetric, ascending auction in a common value environment, where bidder's preferences depend on an idiosyncratic component and an unknown common component. The basic idea of their paper is to infer bidders' real-valued private signals from the bids at which they drop out, and to build a likelihood function for the observed drop out sequence. One can thus obtain estimates of the parameters of the distribution of bidder valuations. Since the likelihood function involves high-dimensional integrals, Hong and Shum adapt the simulated non-linear least-squares method developed by Laffont, Ossard and Vuong (1995) for first-price auctions, which is described in more detail below, to estimate their model.

Hong and Shum tackle a difficult problem using state-of-the-art econometrics. The main weakness is the restricted domain of application. The key step in the analysis infers the bidders' private signals from the bids at which they drop out. From a computational viewpoint, this works only for the class of preferences which admits closed-form solutions for the conditional expectations, since these can be inverted. Hong and Shum use Wilson's (1998) log-additive specification with the common and idiosyncratic components distributed lognormal. From a practical viewpoint, drop out bids are typically not observed, for example because bidders do not have to bid to be active. This is a problem with the data from the FCC auctions that Hong and Shum examine. Hong and Shum assign a dropout price to a given bidder equal to the last submitted bid of the next bidder to drop out on a given local spectrum license.

In a simultaneous English auction, such as the PCS spectrum auction, there may be payoff complementarities across objects, binding budget constraints, or activity rules based on overall participation. There will then be strategic interdependence across objects, and inferring valuations from bids may be difficult. For example, with the FCC activity rules, bidder i may bid more than x_{it} for t in order to retain eligibility to bid on other licenses (a practice known as "parking"). An extreme example of such bidding behavior occurred when Sprint bid on both Oklahoma City C block licenses at once, even though the rules stipulated that they could win at most one of the two licenses.

3.3. Identification

Identification is central to structural estimation, and it informs the interpretation of reduced form estimates of comparative static properties. The models presented in the previous section are identified by functional form assumptions but may not be non-parametrically identified. Non-parametric identification reduces to the following question: given an equilibrium, is there a one-to-one relationship between the joint distribution of bidder values and the joint distribution of bids? One could argue that this standard of identification is too much to ask. After all, economists often make parametric assumptions in estimating demand and supply functions. One difference between these studies and empirical studies of bidding is that the main object of interest in structural models of auctions is often the distribution of the idiosyncratic private component of bidder valuations, and not the deterministic component of bidder valuations. Theory provides some insight on how bidder and auction characteristics should affect bidder valuations, but it offers little guidance on the functional form of the distribution of the idiosyncratic component. Yet the latter is often the primary source of bidder rents and the focus of mechanism design. Consequently, we believe that it is desirable for auction models to be identified non-parametrically. If identification is only by functional form, then a given parametric family of distributions for valuations may not approximate the true unknown distribution, and so specification can play a pivotal role in the analysis.

Athey and Haile (2002) synthesize and extend a fragmented literature on identification of the distribution of bidder values (or information) in a variety of auction settings, including English and second-price auctions. They show when non-parametric identification of valuations is possible, and, if so, what kinds of data are needed. The necessary data depends on whether the value distribution is symmetric or asymmetric, whether values are correlated, and whether the correlating factors are observed. In button auctions with private values, the bid function is the identity function, so bids have a clear interpretation, as losing bids correspond to valuations, and the winning bidder's valuation must not be less than the winning bid. Athey and Haile show, however, that the general private value model is not identified unless *all* bids are observed. This is a problem in English auctions, since the highest valuation is not observed, but known only to be bounded below by the winning bid. However, if bidder valuations are independent and symmetric, and if the winning bid equals the second highest valuation, then only the winning bid and the number of bidders needs to be observed. The winning bid is then the second highest order statistic from a sample of size n whose distribution is uniquely determined by the marginal distribution, F_X. The asymmetric IPV model is also identified if, in addition to the winning bid, the identity of the winner is known. Li, Perrigne and Vuong (2000) show that a restricted class of pure common values auctions is identified if all bids are observed. For example, suppose that signals are independent conditional on the common value, and that signals are additively separable in the common value and the idiosyncratic information. But non-parametric identification fails when there are idiosyncratic value components, i.e., for more general common values settings, or if some bids are not observed.

A second challenge to the structural approach is multiplicity of equilibria. The equilibrium of the second-price, sealed bid auction, and that of the English button auction, is unique if values are private. But, as noted above, in the English button auction with common values, Bikhchandani, Haile and Riley (2002) have shown that there are many ways in which the bidders who do not have one of the two highest values might exit the auction. This multiplicity calls into question the interpretation of the losing bids as the valuations of the losing bidders. Hence, one should not draw strong inferences from the last bid of losing bidders, apart from the highest losing bid. The winning bid is unique in the symmetric equilibrium. But there is a continuum of asymmetric equilibria in which auction outcomes have quite different implications for the distribution of valuations. The latter point also applies to second-price, sealed bid auctions with common values. Thus, in our view, the structural modeling program that identifies the distribution of valuations by inverting the mapping from values or their order statistics to bids is on solid ground when values are private, but it is on shaky ground when values are common. In the latter case, the model has many equilibria, and even after selecting an equilibrium and assuming that bidders play according to this equilibrium in all of the auctions, the model can only be identified by functional form.

Most second-price auctions are open outcry auctions, and not sealed bid or English button auctions. The free form bidding can generate many possible bid histories for any profile of private signals. The observed bids in these histories are not very informative, even when values are private. Bidders often do not have to indicate whether they are "in" or "out" at every high bid, and even if they do, the bid increments associated with jump bids can be large. Thus, final recorded bids of bidders may be a poor approximation of their values, and even the winning bid may not be a good approximation of the second-highest valuation. As a result, the likelihood function is not well defined, since the distribution of final bids is not unique given the distribution of values, nor is the distribution of values uniquely defined given the observed distribution of final bids. This is one reason why there have been almost no structural econometric studies of English auctions.

Haile and Tamer (2003) provide a novel solution to the non-uniqueness problem in the IPV model. They exploit two plausible components of equilibrium play. First, the winning bidder may have been willing to bid more than the final bid, as noted above. In addition, none of the other bidders submit a bid more than they were willing to pay. Second, losing bidders were not willing to raise the winning bid by the minimum bid increment. This assumes that there are no costs associated with submitting bids, or with keeping bidding open. The latter feature would not necessarily be satisfied in an equilibrium with jump bidding. The upper bound on the valuations of bidders may also be violated if bidders collude. These two suppositions can be shown to provide bounds on the distribution of valuations, which are assumed to be private.

Let x_i denote the private value of bidder i, and b_i the highest bid submitted by that bidder. If a bidder does not submit a bid, then let b_i be zero. The two behavioral assumptions are then: (A1) $x_i \geqslant b_i$ for all i and (A2) $x_i \leqslant w + \Delta$ for all i except the winning bidder, where Δ denotes the minimum bid increment. These two assumptions are not sufficient to identify F_X, the distribution of private values, which for convenience are here assumed to be independent and identically distributed. But the two assumptions do put bounds on F_X. The first assumption bounds values below by observed bids, and hence the observed distribution of bids bounds F_X from above. Similarly, the second assumption bounds F_X from below.

The bounds can be derived as follows. Suppose that there are n bidders (as opposed to the number of players who submit bids). Denote the distribution function of the ith highest order statistic from the distribution F_X by $F_{i:n}$. Let $G_{i:n}$ denote the empirical distribution the ith highest bid. Then assumption (A1) implies that $F_{i:n}(x) \leqslant G_{i:n}(x)$ for all i, n, and x. Similarly, (A2) implies that $F_{2:n}(x) \geqslant G_{1:n}(x + \Delta)$ for all n and x. If all losing bidders were not willing to raise the winning bid by the minimum bid increment, it suffices to characterize the highest losing bidder.

These bounds are not the end of the story, since the ordering of bids does not necessarily correspond to the order of valuations. For example, a bidder with an intermediate value might not bid at all, and so register a zero bid, while a lower value bidder might submit a bid early in the auction. Nevertheless, Haile and Tamer show how to pool the bounds across n and i in the case of the upper bound, and across n for the lower bound, in order to derive upper and lower bounds on F_X for all values of x.

If bidders employ the dominant strategy of the button auction, and so the losing bidders' final bids equal their valuation, then it can be shown that the upper and lower bounds coincide, and F_X is uniquely determined. Otherwise, there will be a gap between the bounds on F_X.

An important identifying assumption is that the number of bidders is known. In the Forest Service auctions considered by Haile and Tamer, bidders pre-qualify by submitting a sealed bid, usually at the reserve price, that serves as a binding lower bound on the bid in the subsequent English auction. Given the number of pre-qualified bidders, Haile and Tamer exploit properties of order statistics to derive bounds on the distribution of valuations. These bounds are surprisingly tight, and they show that they also imply a relatively tight bound on the implied optimal reserve price, i.e., the reserve price that would maximize the seller's revenues. They also provide some Monte Carlo evidence that indicates that their bounds approach can provide much better estimates than a structural model that assumes exit prices reflect valuations, especially when there is jump bidding, or when some bidders are silent (i.e., they never submit a bid, although their valuation exceeds the outstanding high bid at some point before the end of the auction).

In conclusion, the structural maximum likelihood methods that exploit the information embodied in the winning bid, described in the previous subsection, are valid only if the winning bid can be interpreted as the second highest valuation. The interpretation of losing bids is problematic in many instances. The non-parametric bounds approach of Haile and Tamer indicates how to circumvent both of these potential difficulties in private values environments.

4. Structural analysis of first price auctions

In this section we discuss structural estimation of first price, sealed bid auctions. There are few empirical studies of field data from Dutch auctions. A notable exception is Laffont, Ossard and Vuong (1995), which we discuss below. [See also van den Berg and van der Klaauw (2000).] We first review the theory of equilibrium bidding, then describe the main estimation approaches, and end with a discussion of identification issues.

4.1. Theory

In a first-price sealed bid auction, each bidder must independently submit a bid to the auctioneer. The high bidder wins and pays his bid, if it exceeds the reserve price. For example, in federal offshore oil and gas auctions, the Department of Interior announces several months in advance that it intends to sell production rights to a set of tracts in a specific geographical area. The announced reserve price for wildcat tracts was \$15 per acre in the 1960s, for example. Firms are invited to submit bids in sealed envelopes at any time prior to the sale date. On the day of the sale, the envelopes are opened, and the values of the bids and the identities of the bidders are announced. The firm or consortium that submits the highest bid on a tract is usually awarded the tract at a price equal to its bid, although the government rejected as inadequate many high bids above the announced reserve price.

Assume that bidder *1*'s rivals in a first-price sealed bid auction are using a common increasing bid function β that has an inverse function η at bids above the reserve price. Then bidder *1*'s profits from bidding b given a signal x are

$$\pi(b, x) = \int_{\underline{x}}^{\eta(b)} \big[w(x, y) - b\big]\,\mathrm{d}F_{Y_1|X_1}(y \mid x).$$

The bidder wins in the event that the highest rival bid is less than b or, equivalently, that the highest rival signal is less than $\eta(b)$. Differentiating with respect to b and imposing the symmetry restriction that bidder *1*'s best reply is $b = \beta(x)$ yields the differential equation

$$\big[w(x,x) - \beta(x)\big] f_{Y_1|X_1}(x \mid x) - \beta'(x) F_{Y_1|X_1}(x \mid x) = 0. \tag{3}$$

If the auction has a binding reserve price, then bidders who obtain very low signals may not bid. The participation decision in the symmetric equilibrium of the first-price sealed bid auction is the same as in the second-price sealed bid auction. The screening level $x^*(r)$ is the lowest signal at which the expected value of the object conditional on winning is at least the reserve price. We assume that the reserve price is binding so that $x^*(r)$ exists and exceeds $\underline{x}$, the lowest possible signal.

The equilibrium bid function for $x \geqslant x^*$ is obtained by solving Equation (3) subject to the boundary condition $\beta(x^*) = r$. It is given by

$$\beta(x) = rL(x^* \mid x) + \int_{x^*}^{x} w(s,s)\,\mathrm{d}L(s \mid x),$$

where

$$L(s \mid x) = \exp\left\{-\int_{s}^{x} \frac{f_{Y_1|X_1}(t \mid t)}{F_{Y_1|X_1}(t \mid t)}\,\mathrm{d}t\right\}.$$

We define $\beta(x) = 0$ for $x < x^*$. The symmetric equilibrium exists under fairly weak regularity conditions on F. The assumption of a binding reserve price ensures that there is a unique symmetric equilibrium. See the account in Athey and Haile (2008), for example.

In the special case of affiliated private values, the equilibrium bid function reduces to

$$\beta(x) = x - \frac{\int_r^x F_{Y_1|X_1}(s \mid x)\,\mathrm{d}s}{F_{Y_1|X_1}(x \mid x)}$$

which further reduces to

$$\beta(x) = x - \frac{\int_r^x F_X(s)^{n-1}\,\mathrm{d}s}{F_X(x)^{n-1}}$$

in the case of independent private values. The bid falls below the valuation by a mark-down factor. In the case of private values, the mark-down factor, $x - \beta(x)$, is decreasing in the number of bidders, n, and increasing in the dispersion of the value distribution. If there was no dispersion in values, then the equilibrium strategy is to bid one's own value. The equilibrium bid strategy for bidder *1*, in the case of private values, can also be expressed as

$$\beta(x) = E\big[\max\{r, Y_1\} \mid X_1 = x,\ Y_1 \leqslant x\big].$$

The bid equals the expectation of the highest rival signal, where the seller's reserve price is treated like another rival signal, conditional on having the highest signal and therefore being the winning bidder in a symmetric equilibrium. This amount corresponds to the expected payment in a second price private values auction, conditional on being the winning bidder.

In the case of independent private values, Lebrun (1996, 1999) and Maskin and Riley (2000a, 2000b) have extended the existence and uniqueness results to auctions with asymmetric bidders under the assumption that the supports of the bidder distributions are identical and F_{X_i} satisfies certain mild regularity conditions.

4.2. Estimation

The IPV model can be estimated in a variety of ways. Paarsch (1992) derives a maximum likelihood estimator and applies it to procurement auctions for treeplanting contracts in British Columbia. Donald and Paarsch (1993) discuss related econometric issues in more detail. Suppose the data consists of $\{w_t, r_t, n_t\}_{t=1}^T$ for the sample where the number of submitted bids $m_t \geqslant 1$. Their approach relies on functional form assumptions, as the class of distributions considered guarantee that (β, η) have closed form representations. The winning bid w_t is observed if and only if the highest signal $x_{(1:n_t)} \geqslant r_t$, otherwise no bids are observed. The probability of the latter event is $F_X(r_t)^{n_t}$. The probability distribution function of w is

$$h_t(w) = n_t F_X\big(\eta_t(w)\big)^{n_t-1} f_X\big(\eta_t(w)\big)\eta_t'(w) = \frac{n_t F_X\big(\eta_t(w)\big)^{n_t}}{(n_t-1)(\eta_t(w)-w)}.$$

Note that the bid and inverse bid functions depend on t since the number of bidders n_t and the reserve price r_t vary across auctions. Note also that the valuation distribution F_X is assumed to be independent of n_t. The bid and inverse bid functions also both depend on the parameters of F_X, which we suppress for notational convenience. Therefore the likelihood function is

$$L = \prod_t \big\{h_t(w_t)/\big[1 - F_X(r_t)^{n_t}\big]\big\}.$$

The parameters of F_X are chosen to maximize L subject to $w_t \leqslant \beta_t(\bar{x})$ for all t, where $\bar{x}$ is the highest possible signal, and subject to the requirement that β, η, and F_X be conformable. Clearly, the main difficulty with this estimation approach lies in computing the inverse η_t, which is typically non-linear and often does not have a closed form solution. Another technical issue associated with the maximum likelihood method is that the asymptotic distribution of the estimator is non-standard, since the upper bound of the support of the bid distribution depends upon the parameters of interest. Moreover, the likelihood function may be discontinuous at the associated boundary of the parameter space. See Donald and Paarsch (1993, 1996, 2002) for more detail, as well as Chernozhukov and Hong (2004) and Hirano and Porter (2003), who advocate Bayesian estimators.

In his thesis, Bajari (1997) extends the likelihood approach to auctions with asymmetric bidders. His application is to procurement auctions of highway repair contracts in Minnesota. The lowest bid wins, and there is no reserve price, so the data consists of $\{\{b_{it}, z_{it}\}_{i=1}^{n_t}, n_t, z_t\}_{t=1}^{T}$, where z_{it} is the vector of firm i characteristics in auction t and z_t is the vector of contract t characteristics. The firm specific characteristics are the distances between the locations of firms and contract t, and measures of the firms' committed capacities at the time of auction t. The likelihood of firm i submitting bid b_{it} in auction t is given by

$$f_{B_i}(b_{it} \mid z_{it}, z_t) = f_{X_i}\big(\eta_{it}(b_{it}) \mid z_{it}, z_t\big)\eta_{it}'(b_{it}).$$

In this case, the inverse bid functions and their derivatives are obtained by numerically solving the system of n_t differential equations derived from the firms' first-order conditions. Bajari takes a Bayesian approach to estimation, simulating the posterior distribution of the parameters by taking random draws from a prior and evaluating the likelihood function for each draw. The Bayesian approach finesses some of the technical difficulties that arise with maximum likelihood estimators. It is also computationally easier to implement than maximum likelihood and allows the researcher to compare non-nested models such as collusion versus competition in a relatively straightforward way. The prior distribution must be chosen with care, however.

The main drawbacks of the likelihood approach are discussed in Bajari (1998). One difficulty is that the approach is computationally intensive. The need for flexible functional forms means that the inverse bid functions have to be computed numerically. A second difficulty is that the likelihood function typically does not have full support, which means that zero likelihoods often arise in practice. Outliers may be difficult to rationalize, and they can have a disproportionate effect on estimated parameter values.

Laffont, Ossard and Vuong (1995) develop a simulated non-linear least-squares estimator. They exploit the fact that the bid function in the FPSB auction in an IPV environment can be expressed as

$$\beta(x) = E\big[\max\{r_t, X_{2:n_t}\} \mid X_{1:n_t} = x\big],$$

where $X_{k:n_t}$ denotes the kth highest order statistic from a sample of size n_t. The winning bid therefore satisfies

$$w_t = \beta(x_{1:n_t}) = E\big[\max\{r_t, X_{2:n_t}\} \mid X_{1:n_t} = x_{1:n_t}\big].$$

Hence, the expectation of the winning bid, conditional on at least one bid being submitted, is

$$E[W_t \mid X_{1:n_t} \geqslant r_t] = E\big[\max\{r_t, X_{2:n_t}\} \mid X_{1:n_t} \geqslant r_t\big].$$

The expectation involves high-dimensional integrals. Instead of computing it, Laffont, Ossard and Vuong use simulation to approximate the expectation. They choose an "importance function" to weight the simulated samples. They then choose the parameters of F_X to minimize the average squared distance between the observed sample of winning bids, $\{w_t\}$, and the simulated sample mean of $\max\{r_t, x_{2:n_t}\}$, conditional on $x_{1:n_t}$ exceeding the reserve price, after correcting for the estimation error of the simulated sample. Laffont, Ossard and Vuong apply this method to eggplant sales in Marmande, France. Their method circumvents the need to compute the inverse bid function at each parameter value. As a result, their method allows for a much larger set of distributions than do maximum likelihood methods, although they just consider the lognormal distribution in their application. In their data, as in many applications, the number of bidders n_t is not observed. The authors assume the number is constant, n, treat n as a parameter, and estimate it.

The main restriction in applying their method is that it relies heavily upon the assumptions of the symmetric IPV model. If bidder valuations are not independent draws, or the distributions from which they are drawn are not symmetric, the bid function cannot be expressed as a conditional expectation of a second-order statistic. Independence may be a problem in theory, but it may be more of a problem in practice because of unobserved heterogeneity. For example, the bidders may all observe some factor that shifts the location of the distribution of values, where that factor is not observed in the data. In the application, unobserved heterogeneity that is also observed by the seller might result in correlation between the reserve price and the distribution of bidder valuations, in which case the reserve price is not exogenous. Symmetry is also frequently a problem. For example, in the Marmande eggplant market, one buyer was much larger. Laffont, Ossard and Vuong show how to adapt their method to account for this latter issue, under the assumption that the large buyer's valuation can be represented as a draw from F_X^k, where k can be thought of as the number of agents the large buyer represents as an intermediary at the auction. Then the large buyer's valuation is the highest of the k agents he represents, where the agents' valuations are drawn from the same distribution as the other bidders.

A third estimation procedure for private value models has been developed by Elyakime et al. (1994) and by Guerre, Perrigne and Vuong (2000). Their method can be non-parametric, and so not rely upon functional form assumptions. It is computationally easy to implement, nor does it require bidders' values to be independently or identically distributed. Suppose the researcher has data available on all bids submitted,

$$\left\{\{b_{it}\}_{i=1}^{m_t},\ n_t, r_t\right\}_{t=1}^{T}$$

plus perhaps covariates Z_t for auction t where $m_t \geqslant 1$. Here n_t again denotes the number of potential bidders, and m_t the number who submit bids. Now assume that $n_t = n$ for all t. In practice, applications of this method often estimate the value distribution separately for each value of n_t. In a symmetric equilibrium, the optimal bid for bidder *1* with signal $x_1 = \eta(b)$ solves

$$\big(\eta(b) - b\big) f_{Y_1|X_1}\big(\eta(b) \mid \eta(b)\big)\eta'(b) - F_{Y_1|X_1}\big(\eta(b) \mid \eta(b)\big) = 0.$$

Define $M_1 = \beta(Y_1)$ as the maximum bid of bidder *1*'s rivals, and let the conditional distribution of M_1 given bidder *1*'s bid B_1 be denoted by $G_{M_1|B_1}(\cdot \mid \cdot)$ and its density by $g_{M_1|B_1}(\cdot \mid \cdot)$. Monotonicity of β and η implies that for any $b \in (r, \beta(\overline{x}))$

$$G_{M_1|B_1}(m \mid b) = F_{Y_1|X_1}\big(\eta(m) \mid \eta(b)\big).$$

Here $G_{M_1|B_1}(m \mid b)$ is the probability that the highest bid among bidder *1*'s rivals is less than m conditional upon bidder *1*'s bid of b. The associated density function is given by

$$g_{M_1|B_1}(m \mid b) = f_{Y_1|X_1}\big(\eta(m) \mid \eta(b)\big)\eta'(m).$$

Substituting the above relations into the first-order condition for bidder *1* yields

$$\eta(b) = b + \frac{G_{M_1|B_1}(b \mid b)}{g_{M_1|B_1}(b \mid b)}.$$

In the special case of IPV, $G_{M_1|B_1} = G^{n-1}$, where G is the marginal bid distribution of individual bidders, $g_{M_1|B_1} = (n-1)gG^{n-2}$, and the inverse bid function for bidder *1* is given by

$$\eta(b) = b + \frac{G(b)}{(n-1)g(b)}.$$

The estimation procedure consists of two steps.

Step 1. Estimate $\hat{g}_{M_i|B_i}(m \mid b)$, $\hat{G}_{M_i|B_i}(m \mid b)$, either parametrically or non-parametrically, from the observed bids of all bidders. Here bidders are treated symmetrically, and auctions as independent and identical implicitly, except to the extent that one conditions on observable auction characteristics. Form "data",

$$\hat{x}_{it} = b_{it} + \frac{\hat{G}_{M_i|B_i}(b_{it} \mid b_{it})}{\hat{g}_{M_i|B_i}(b_{it} \mid b_{it})}.$$

This yields a sample of pseudo-values $\{\hat{x}_{it}\}_{i=1}^{n}$, $t = 1, \ldots, T$.

Step 2. Given $\{\{b_{it}, \hat{x}_{it}\}_{i=1}^{n}\}_{t=1}^{T}$, for the subsample with $n_t = n$, estimate $f_X(\hat{x}_{it})$ and $F_X(\hat{x}_{it})$. One can also estimate β, parametrically or non-parametrically, as $b_{it} = \beta(\hat{x}_{it})$. If the value distribution F_X is assumed to be identical across subsamples with different numbers of bidders, the data from these subsamples can be pooled at this stage. In principle, the symmetry assumption (of F_X across n_t) can be tested. (This assumption might equivalently be viewed as an assumption that the variation in the number of bidders is exogenous.) Note that one could not similarly pool estimation of the bid function across subsamples, as the bid function should depend on the number of bidders.

In their application to French timber auctions, Elyakime, Laffont, Loisel and Vuong modified the method to account for the fact that r_t is not announced to the bidders, so that there is a secret reserve price. The seller is treated as another potential bidder, but with an objective function that differs from that of the buyers. This can confound the estimation of F_X, since the bidding behavior of the buyers depends upon the distribution of seller valuations. Also, the researcher must recover two distributions instead of one. The authors simplify matters by assuming that seller always sets the reserve price equal to her valuation, which is optimal in their framework. They also assume that the seller valuation, and hence her behavior, is independent of the buyers' valuations. Their method relies heavily upon the independence assumption.

Since the two-step approach is based on first-order conditions, it is easily modified in an IPV model to deal with asymmetric bidders. Bidder *1* with signal x_1 chooses his bid, given that there are n potential bidders, to maximize

$$\pi_1(b, x_1) = (x_1 - b) \prod_{j=2}^{n} F_j\big(\eta_j(b)\big).$$

His optimal bid solves

$$\big(\eta_1(b) - b\big) \sum_{j=2}^{n} \frac{f_{X_j}(\eta_j(b))\eta_j'(b)}{[1 - F_{X_j}(\eta_j(b))]} = 1.$$

Using the same change of variables as above, each bidder's inverse bid function can be expressed as a function of his rivals' bid distributions,

$$\eta_i(b) = b + \frac{1}{\sum_{j \neq i} \frac{g_{B_j}(b)}{[1 - G_{B_j}(b)]}}.$$

In this case, the sample of pseudo-values has to be generated separately for each bidder. The samples can then be used to estimate the bidders' valuation distributions. Applications of this approach include Bajari and Ye (2003), who study collusive bidding in auctions of highway repair contracts in Minnesota, and Bajari, Houghton and Tadelis (2006), who study auctions of highway repair contracts in California. The latter paper argues that researchers need to be careful in defining contract revenues since, in many cases, subsequent contract changes or renegotiations lead to payment adjustments. The authors assume that ex post adjustments, and ex ante beliefs about these adjustments, are the same for all bidders, and do not depend upon their costs or bids, and hence upon their private information. Given this assumption, contract revenues can be defined as the amount bid plus ex post adjustments, where the latter serves as a proxy for the bidders' expectations, and bidder markups can be estimated accordingly. The authors find that only a fraction of the ex post adjustments are passed through to bids, and attribute the difference from full pass-through to transaction costs.

Krasnokutskaya (2004) and Athey, Levin and Seira (2004) extend the two-stage approach to allow for auction characteristics that are observed by the bidders but not by the econometrician. The unobserved heterogeneity accounts for the positive correlation in bids within an auction. This is important because failure to account for this correlation leads to an upward bias in bidder markups. Krasnokutskaya takes a semi-parametric approach. In her application to Michigan highway procurement contracts, she assumes that bidder i's costs take the form

$$c_i = x_i v.$$

Here the private signal X_i is independent of X_j, but not necessarily identically distributed, and also independent of the common, and commonly known, component V. The multiplicative structure implies that bidder i's equilibrium bid strategy can be decomposed into a component that is common to all bidders and an idiosyncratic component that is a function of his private signal

$$\beta(c_i) = v\alpha_i(x_i).$$

Let A_i denote the idiosyncratic component. Krasnokutskaya shows that, under mild regularity conditions, the distribution functions of V and the A_i's are uniquely determined from the joint distribution of two bids. Thus, the probability distribution functions of V and the A_i's can be obtained non-parametrically, based on bid data from auctions with at least two bidders. To generate a sample of pseudo-values for bidder i, first draw a random sample of L pseudo-bids $\{a_i\}_{i=1}^{L}$ from the estimated distribution of A_i and then use the inverse bid function under the assumption that $v = 1$ to infer the pseudo-value $\hat{x}_i$ associated with each a_i. The sample of pseudo-values can then be used to non-parametrically estimate F_{X_i}. Note that, while the distributions of V and the A_i's are identified, one cannot uniquely decompose any individual bid into its two components.

Athey, Levin and Seira (2004) study timber auctions. They distinguish between two types of bidders, mills and loggers. Mills are thought to have stochastically higher willingness to pay for cutting rights than loggers. Athey, Levin and Seira adopt a parametric approach. They assume that the distribution of bids for each bidder type conditional on V, the unobserved auction characteristic, is Weibull, and that V has a Gamma distribution. Here V is assumed to be independent of the observable auction characteristics, including the number of bidders. After integrating V out of the likelihood function, the parameters of the distributions of B_i and V are estimated by maximum likelihood. The procedure yields estimates of the conditional distributions of bids and inverse bid functions for loggers and mills. Since v is not observed, it is not possible to use the inverse bid function to infer a bidder's values from his bids. However, one can still recover the conditional distribution function of values for loggers, $F_{X_L|V}$, and for mills, $F_{X_M|V}$, from the identities

$$F_{X_k|V}(x \mid v) = G_k\big(\eta_k(b, v) \mid v\big), \quad \text{for } k = L, M.$$

The average bid functions and the unconditional distributions of bidder values are obtained by integrating $\beta(x, v)$ and $F_{X_k|V}$ over v, for $k = L, M$.

4.3. Identification

Laffont and Vuong (1996) discuss identification in first-price sealed bid auctions. In the symmetric common values model, the optimal bid by bidder *1* with signal $x_1 = \eta(b)$ satisfies

$$w\big(\eta(b), \eta(b)\big) = b + \frac{G_{M_1|B_1}(b \mid b)}{g_{M_1|B_1}(b \mid b)} \equiv \xi(b, G).$$

Recall that in the case of independent private values, this equation reduces to

$$\eta(b) = b + \frac{G(b)}{(n-1)g(b)}.$$

It then follows in the IPV case that F_X is identified from G if η is strictly increasing and $\lim_{b\downarrow r} \eta(b) = r$, i.e., there is not a mass point in the bid distribution at r. The identification condition requires G/g to be well-behaved, which is an equilibrium requirement of the data. Furthermore, a distribution G can be rationalized by F if and only if η satisfies the above properties. A similar argument establishes that affiliated private value models are also identified.

In the common values model,

$$w\big(\eta(b), \eta(b)\big) = E\big[u(x, V) \mid X = \eta(b),\ Y = \eta(b)\big].$$

Thus, $\xi(b, G)$ identifies bidder 1's expected utility conditional on the event that his signal is $\eta(b)$ and the maximum signal of his rivals is also $\eta(b)$. This conditional expectation is invariant to any increasing transformation of the signal. Even in a pure common values model, if X is normalized so that $E[X \mid V = v] = v$, mean-preserving transformations of $F_{X|V}$ cannot be distinguished in the data. Hence, knowing the value of $w(\eta(b), \eta(b))$ is not sufficient to identify the value of the signal $x = \eta(b)$, and G does not identify F. In fact, as Laffont and Vuong note, by defining a new signal

$$\tilde{x} = w(x, x)$$

and utility $u(\tilde{x}) = \tilde{x}$, one can transform the affiliated common values (ACV) model into an affiliated private value (APV) model. If the reserve price is not binding, then any symmetric ACV model is observationally equivalent to some symmetric APV model. Laffont and Vuong extend this result to asymmetric models.

In summary, Laffont and Vuong (1996) and Athey and Haile (2002) have shown that, while private value models are often identified, common value models are typically not identified, at least not without imposing strong restrictions on the primitives or on the type of data that are available. The lack of identification challenges the usefulness of the structural program for the class of common values models. One alternative, discussed by Hendricks, Pinkse and Porter (2003) in their study of auctions of offshore oil and gas leases, is to assume a pure common value model and augment bid data with ex post data on lease values. In this case, one can resolve the identification problem by imposing a moment restriction on the joint distribution of (X_{it}, V_t). For example, Wilson (1977) adopts the normalization $E[X_{it} \mid V_t = v] = v$, where signals are measured so that the mean signal on a tract is equal to the tract's value. Hendricks, Pinkse and Porter instead assume that

$$E[V_t \mid X_{it} = x,\ Z_t = z] = x.$$

The condition states that if a firm obtains a signal x on a tract with observable characteristics z, then the expected value of that tract is equal to the value of the signal. Signals are normalized in terms of ex post value and the bidders' posterior estimates are assumed to be correct on average. Identification of the bid function follows immediately from the above condition and monotonicity of the bid function, since

$$x = E[V_t \mid X_{it} = x,\ Z_t = z] = E\big[V_t \mid B_{it} = \beta(x, z),\ Z_t = z\big]$$
$$\Longrightarrow \quad \eta(b, z) = E[V_t \mid B_{it} = b,\ Z_t = z]. \tag{4}$$

The inverse bid function can be estimated as follows. For every bid level b on a tract with characteristics z, define a neighborhood $B(z)$ of b, and compute the average ex post value of all leases with characteristics z that received a bid in $B(z)$. To implement this idea, the authors employ a kernel estimator of the mean ex post value in the neighborhood of any bid b for tracts with similar characteristics. The inverse bid function can be used to generate the sample of signals $\{\{\hat{x}_{it}\}_{i=1}^{n_t}\}_{t=1}^{T}$ which, together with the sample of ex post values $\{v_t\}_{t=1}^{T}$, can be used to identify F.

Within the class of private value models, there is a second identification problem that remains an open issue. Can the APV model be distinguished from an IPV model with unobserved heterogeneity? In the former model, the correlation in bids is generated by a common factor that is not observed by the bidders; in the latter model, the correlation is generated by a common factor that is observed by the bidders but not by the econometrician. Krasnokutskaya (2004) conjectures that the two models are observationally equivalent.

5. Tests of private versus common values

The identification results make it important to develop ways of distinguishing between private and common value environments. Another reason is auction design. If the idiosyncratic component of valuations is the main determinant of bids, and values are independent, then under the standard logic of competitive markets more competition implies lower procurement costs. On the other hand, if the common component is the main determinant, more competition does not necessarily lead to lower procurements costs because bidders have to worry about the winner's curse. Restricting the number of bidders can then be a revenue enhancing policy.

Paarsch (1992) attempts to distinguish between a PCV model and an IPV model by estimating the structural parameters of each model and comparing the models using a non-nested hypothesis test. However, he has to adopt restrictive parametric assumptions on the distribution of bidder valuations in order to estimate the structural parameters of the IPV and PCV models. More recently, non-parametric tests have been developed that exploit the fact that the APV and ACV models are not observationally equivalent if reserve prices are binding or if the number of bidders varies across auctions.

In a sealed bid, second-price auction with a binding reserve price, the marginal participant's valuation conditional on winning is

$$r = E\big[u(V, x) \mid X_1 = x^*,\ Y_1 < x^*\big]$$

but he bids

$$\beta(x^*) = E\big[u(V, x) \mid X_1 = x^*,\ Y_1 = x^*\big].$$

These two equations yield an interesting, and testable, prediction, first noted by Milgrom and Weber (1982). The bid submitted by a bidder with signal equal to the screening level x^* is equal to the reserve price r if values are private, but $\beta(x^*)$ is strictly larger than r if values are affiliated. In the latter case, the lower bound of the support of the distribution of submitted bids in the second-price auction exceeds r. Moreover, the lower bound is increasing in the number of bidders and in any variable that is affiliated with V. Similarly, in an English auction with common values, the support of the distribution of prices should exhibit a gap above the reserve price r. When only one bidder is active, the price is r. When two or more bidders are willing to bid, the price is strictly above r.

Hendricks, Pinkse and Porter (2003) show that an analogous result holds in first-price auctions. In a private values model, the function ξ defined in Section 4.3 must satisfy the boundary condition, $\lim_{b\downarrow r} \xi(b, G(b)) = r$, which implies

$$\lim_{b\downarrow r} \frac{G_{M_{it}|B_{it}}(b \mid b)}{g_{M_{it}|B_{it}}(b \mid b)} \to 0.$$

By contrast, in a common values environment, ξ is discontinuous at r, which implies that

$$\lim_{b\downarrow r} \frac{G_{M_{it}|B_{it}}(b \mid b)}{g_{M_{it}|B_{it}}(b \mid b)} \to c > 0$$

for some constant c. Therefore, it is possible in principle to distinguish between the two models by examining the behavior of $G_{M_{it}|B_{it}}$ near the reserve price. In practice, reserve prices are often set so that the number of bids near the reserve are too few to implement the test with confidence.

Haile, Hong and Shum (2004) develop a test that exploits exogenous variation in the number of bidders. Let $\hat{G}_n$ denote an estimate of $G_{M_i|B_i}$ for auctions with n bidders and define

$$\hat{x}_{it} = \xi\big(b_{it}, \hat{G}_n(b_{it})\big)$$

as the pseudo-value corresponding to bidder i's bid in auction t. Under the hypothesis of private values, this is an estimate of bidder i's valuation of item t but, under the hypothesis of common values, it is an estimate of the latent conditional expectation $w(\eta(b_{it}), \eta(b_{it}))$. This expectation is decreasing in n if the common component is important, since winning against more bidders is worse news. Let $\hat{F}_n$ denote the estimate of the empirical distribution of pseudo-values in auctions with n bidders. Haile, Hong and Shum propose testing whether $\hat{F}_n$ is invariant to n, as implied by the private value hypothesis, against the alternative that $\hat{F}_n$ is strictly increasing in n, as implied by the common values hypothesis. A similar test can be applied to bids in SPSB auctions and to losing bids in English button auctions. Note that a maintained hypothesis is that the variation in the number of bidders is exogenous, and hence independent of the distribution of values. Haile, Hong and Shum propose an instrumental variables procedure for cases where the number of bidders is endogenous.

Some early studies test private versus common values in a FPSB format by testing for monotonicity of the bidding strategy β in the number of bidders n. In an independent private values environment, β is strictly increasing in n, as competition causes bidders to bid more aggressively. Recall that the optimal strategy in a FPSB auction with IPV and a minimum bid r can be expressed as

$$\beta(x) = E\big[\max\{r, X_{2:n}\} \mid X_{1:n} = x\big].$$

This expectation is increasing in n, as it is the expectation of a monotone function of the highest order statistic from a sample of size $n - 1$. But what does theory predict about the behavior of β with respect to n in a common value environment?

Wilson (1993) discusses several examples in which equilibrium bid strategies may be decreasing or non-monotone in the number of potential bidders. Consider the pure common value example in which F_V and $F_{X|V}$ are lognormal distributions and the reserve price is not binding. Wilson (1993) then shows that if F_V, the prior distribution of the common value, is diffuse,

$$\beta(x_i) = k(n)x_i,$$

so that the equilibrium bid is proportional to the signal, where the factor of proportionality depends on the number of bidders and the informativeness of their signals. Signals are more informative the lower the variance of $F_{X|V}$, and bidding is more aggressive the lower this variance. Wilson provides some examples in which $k(n)$ is increasing for small n, and then decreasing after $n = 2$ or 4. When the number of bidders is small, increasing competition leads to more aggressive bids. But this effect diminishes as the number of bidders increases, and eventually winner's curse considerations dominate the competitive effect. There are no general results, however.

It is important not to focus on the winning bid in the above exercises, since the expected winning bid in a CV environment, $E[\beta(X_{1:n})]$, is monotone increasing in n for many examples. [There are exceptions, however. Bulow and Klemperer (2002) provide one counter-example.] One should use the vector of all bids or a summary statistic, such as the average bid. Several studies have examined the sale of oil and gas leases. The basic idea of the test is to regress bids or average bid on the number of bids submitted n, and n^2, or some other function of n, and Z, a vector of observable characteristics (e.g., area and date of sale, tract acreage, water depth, etc.). An IPV model often matches the data better than CV, in the sense that β is increasing in n over the observed range of n (typically, from 1 to 18 bids).

Hong and Shum (2002) study the effects of winner's curse considerations on bidding in procurement auctions for highway repair contracts and quantify its importance. They use the Wilson (1998) log-additive model of preferences, which has the PV and PCV models as special cases. Identification is achieved by adopting parametric distributional assumptions. Given the functional form assumptions, they follow Laffont, Ossard and

Vuong (1995) and use simulation methods to generate a bid distribution from the equilibrium relationship between bids and signals. But, instead of trying to match the mean of the bid distribution, Hong and Shum exploit the monotonicity of the bid function and focus on matching the quantiles of the equilibrium bid distribution and the actual bid distribution. Simulating the quantiles of the equilibrium bid distribution is substantially easier than simulating its moments. They then show that procurement costs rise as competition intensifies, consistent with a CV model but not with private values.

The main limitation of tests that exploit the variation in the number of bidders is that, in most data sets, the number of bidders is endogenous. The problem is that the number of bidders is often correlated with unobserved characteristics of the item. For example, in the Hong and Shum study on highway contracts, the basic empirical regularity observed in the data is that bids are higher on contracts with more bidders. If the contracts are identical, then this fact can be attributed to the winner's curse, which counsels less aggressive bidding as the number of competitors increase. However, contracts are not identical, and the larger, more valuable contracts are likely to attract more bidders. The absence of good covariates like engineering estimates to control for contract heterogeneity means that their results may be due to the fact that the number of bidders is an imperfect proxy for the contract size. A similar problem arises with bidding for oil and gas auctions. Even if tract characteristics include an ex post proxy for V, ex ante bidder errors in expectation will be positively correlated with the number of bids submitted. If bidders are optimistic, more bid, and they bid aggressively. One solution is to employ a proxy or instrument for the number of potential bidders, but an instrumental variable may not be available. Many factors that are correlated with the participation decisions of firms will also be correlated with their valuations, and hence their bid levels. In their study of timber auctions, Haile, Hong and Shum adopt an instrumental variable strategy, exploiting variation in the number of nearby mills.

A second problem is that the comparative statics is with respect to a known number of *potential* bidders, not the number of submitted bids. If there is a binding reserve price, or if the support of V falls below zero, not all of the potential bidders will necessarily bid, and then there is a endogeneity problem. In the studies that test the monotonicity of the bid function in the number of bidders, the bias is towards the private values model, to the extent that the number of bids is positively correlated with bid levels. For example, in the oil and gas auctions, a potential bidder is more likely to submit a bid if tract is more likely to contain oil. Haile, Hong and Shum propose a clever test that exploits the fact that bidder's probability of participation does not depend upon the number of bidders in a private value environment but decreases with the number of rivals in a common value environment.

There is also a serious issue in many applications about whether the number of potential rivals is known by the bidders. In the OCS auctions, a bidder is classified as a potential bidder on a tract if it conducts detailed seismic studies. But bidders do not necessarily conduct such studies on every available tract. Furthermore, the decision to conduct a detailed analysis is essentially private. Thus, a firm may not know which tracts have been searched by its rivals. In this case, if the probability of search is higher on tracts that are perceived to be more likely to contain oil, the number of bids is likely to be positively correlated with bid levels even after controlling for tract values. The reason is the same as that given above.

Finally, the result that in a private values setting bids are increasing in the number of bidders relies on the assumption that private values are independently distributed. Pinkse and Tan (2005) show that if private valuations are instead affiliated, then equilibrium bids in a first price sealed bid auction can be decreasing in the number of bidders. Hence, bidding strategies that are decreasing in the number of bidders are not necessarily inconsistent with private values.

6. Tests of the theory

Structural models force a commitment to the theoretical model. Parametric methods entail joint hypotheses regarding preferences, behavioral assumptions, and the functional form of the value distribution. Non-parametric methods relax the last assumption, but retain the preference and behavioral assumptions. The behavioral assumption of non-cooperative bidding is crucial. If some bidders are colluding, some bids may be phony. Also, the effective number of bidders may be more than actual number submitting bids, due to coalitions. The existence of bidding coalitions may violate the symmetry assumption, since coalitions may have different objectives induced by their formation (when individual rationality or incentive compatibility constraints bind), or by the aggregation of their preferences or their information.

The theory of equilibrium bidding under the assumption of affiliated signals does deliver two tests that do not depend upon whether values are private or common. In first-price auctions, monotonicity of the equilibrium bid function implies that

$$\xi(b, \hat{G}) = b + \frac{\hat{G}_{M_i|B_i}(b \mid b)}{\hat{g}_{M_i|B_i}(b \mid b)}$$

is increasing in b, and the boundary condition on the equilibrium bid function implies that

$$\lim_{b \downarrow r} \xi(b, \hat{G}) \geqslant r.$$

These are consistency checks, akin to overidentifying restrictions. The monotonicity test has low power, however, as it can be satisfied by non-equilibrium strategies. For example, in a private values model, consider the strategy of bidding one's value, $\beta(x) = x$ if $x \geqslant r$. This strategy is monotone, and it satisfies the boundary condition $\eta(r) = r$. No such test is available in second-price auctions, where bids are simply interpreted as conditional expectations.

The second test is a variant of the test proposed by Haile, Hong and Shum for distinguishing between private and common value models. In first price auctions, equilibrium bidding implies that the empirical distribution of pseudo-values, $\hat{F}_n$, is non-decreasing in n. If this is not the case, then either the data are not consistent with equilibrium bidding or valuations are not common. A similar test applies to bids in second-price auctions and to losing bids in English auctions. Note that this test requires the number of bidders to be exogenous.

The lack of ex post data on bidder values makes it difficult to test the theory in private value auctions using field data, absent some alternative hypothesis. Bajari and Hortacsu (2005) use bid data from private value auction experiments to test the theory. Experimental data has two advantages over field data. First, the variation in the number of bidders is exogenous. Second, the realizations of the private values of the bidders, and the value distribution itself, are known. The main disadvantages are that bidders may not have sufficient experience, and the stakes are low. The authors evaluate the performance of several models of bidding by comparing the estimated valuations under the various models to the actual values. For example, in the case of risk neutral bidders with IPV, the estimated values are generated according to $\hat{x} = \xi(b, \hat{G})$. They find that the model that performs best is Bayesian Nash equilibrium with risk averse bidders.

6.1. Pure common value auctions

The theory of bidding in pure common value auctions can be tested when data on ex post values are available. Much of the early empirical interest in auctions with common values focused on the possibility that bidders may bid naively and be afflicted by the winner's curse. A (rather trivial) test of rationality, under which bidders anticipate the information revealed by winning, looks at individual rationality constraints. In private value first price sealed bid laboratory experiments, where valuations are observed by the researcher, individual rationality simply means not bidding more than the value. (Violations of this form of rationality are especially distressing. If the stakes are low, subjects may place too much value on winning for its own sake.) In field studies of common value auctions, the test often reduces to checking whether realized profits are positive.

Capen, Clapp and Campbell (1971) is perhaps most influential empirical auction paper addressing this issue. The authors compute ex post returns on offshore oil and gas auctions in the early years of these sales. They claim that bidders suffered from the winner's curse since, by their calculations, ex post returns were negative, i.e., the internal rate of return was less than that of Treasury bills. Their finding suggests that bidders violated the basic tenets of rational bidding. However, there are several reasons to doubt this conclusion. First, their measure of ex post returns is based on incomplete production histories. The wells they study were productive for many more years. Meade et al. (1980) compute, based on longer well histories, real internal rates of return of approximately 7 percent. Hendricks, Porter and Boudreau (1987) also find positive returns for most firms on wildcat tracts. In addition, negative ex post returns in small samples are not necessarily indicative of irrationality, if some unpredictable adverse common payoff shock occurred.

In a series of papers, we (with a number of different coauthors) have used data on bids, drilling costs, and oil production from federal sales of oil and gas leases on the Outer Continental Shelf (OCS) to study the impact of the winner's curse on bidding behavior and to re-examine the rationality issue. Oil and gas leases are classified into two categories. Wildcat tracts are located in previously unexplored areas. Prior to a wildcat auction, firms are allowed to conduct seismic studies, but they are not permitted to drill any exploratory wells. The seismic studies provide noisy, but roughly equally informative signals about the amount of oil and gas on a lease. We argue that wildcat auctions are likely to satisfy the symmetry assumption on the signal distribution. Drainage leases are adjacent to wildcat tracts where oil and gas deposits have been discovered previously. Firms that own adjacent tracts possess drilling information that makes them better informed about the value of the drainage tract than other firms, who are likely to have access only to seismic information. We argue that these auctions can be modeled by assuming one bidder has a private, informative signal and all other bidders have no private information.

For auctions of both types of leases, we ask the following question: do bidders behave as predicted by game theoretic models? In the case of drainage auctions, we study this question by examining whether the predictions of the theory are consistent with the data. In auctions with asymmetric information, knowing which bidders have better information allows us to generate testable predictions of equilibrium bidding based on bidders' identities. In the case of wildcat auctions, we address this question by testing whether the first-order conditions for optimality hold.

6.1.1. The asymmetric case

In the data set on drainage lease bidding, we can distinguish between firms owning adjacent wildcat leases (neighbors) and others (non-neighbors). This observable asymmetry between potential bidders appears to matter. Compared to wildcat auctions, drainage auctions have less entry (i.e., fewer bids submitted per tract), yet higher ex post returns. Drainage leases are more likely to be explored, and much more likely to be productive if explored. Although drainage tracts receive higher bids, their higher productivity translates into higher profits. Some numbers for the sample period 1954–1979 are as follows [Porter (1995)]:

	Wildcat	Drainage
Number of tracts	2510 (2255 sold)	295 (237 sold)
Number of bids	3.52	2.45
Mean high bid	\$5.5 million	\$7.4 million
Number of tracts drilled	1757 (78%)	211 (89%)
Number of productive tracts	881 (50%)	147 (70%)
Discounted revenues if productive	\$19.5 million	\$17.3 million

What is the explanation for lower entry and higher average returns on drainage leases? Two alternatives come to mind. One is asymmetries in information: neighbor firms are better informed about the value of the drainage tracts than non-neighbors. An alternative explanation is asymmetries in payoffs: neighbors have lower costs due to economies of scope. Either alternative can explain why entry does not drive ex post returns down to wildcat levels. Entry of non-neighbors might drive their own returns down to zero, but asymmetries protect the rents of neighbors, especially if they coordinate their bids.

Consider an environment in which one bidder, which we will refer to as I for informed, has a private, informative signal, X, concerning the unknown common value, V, and another bidder, called U for uninformed, has access only to public information. We will refer to I as the neighbor firm (if there is more than one, we assume that they collude) and U as a non-neighbor firm. In the OCS drainage auctions, more than one non-neighbor firm might potentially bid, but an important implication of equilibrium bidding is that the distributions of the neighbor bid and the maximum of the non-neighbor bids do not depend upon the number of uninformed bidders. (This result follows from the assumption that non-neighbor firms do not have any private information.) Hence we can assume without loss of generality that there is only one non-neighbor firm. Assume that r is the announced minimum bid, or reserve price, and that $E[V] > r$. If $E[V] < r$, then non-neighbor firms would never submit a bid.

The non-neighbor firm faces an acute case of the winner's curse in trying to win the tract from the better informed neighbor firm at a profitable price. Should it bid and, if so, how should it bid? Engelbrecht-Wiggans, Milgrom and Weber (1983) address this question. They show that U has to participate in equilibrium. If U does not participate, then I would bid the reserve price whenever $E[V \mid X = x]$ exceeds r. But, in that case, U could bid slightly more than r, win the auction for certain, and obtain a positive payoff of $E[V] - r$. Second, U has to bid randomly. If U used a pure strategy and bid $b > r$, then I's best reply is to bid slightly more than b if $E[V \mid X = x]$ exceeds b. But then U would suffer an extreme form of the winner's curse, as it would win only if $E[V \mid X = x]$ is less than b, i.e., the more informed bidder expects V to be less than U's bid b. Finally, U earns zero expected profit from its mixed strategy. In other words, there is a positive probability that U does not bid.

Consider next I's behavior and let G_U denote U's mixed strategy. The payoff to I from a bid of $b \geqslant r$ is given by

$$\pi_I(b, x) = \big(E[V \mid X = x] - b\big)G_U(b).$$

This payoff depends on the private signal X only through the expectation of the value of the tract. Define $H = E[V \mid X]$ as the sufficient statistic for I's information and let F_H denote its distribution. (Note that $E[H] = E[V]$, by the law of iterated expectations.) Then I's payoff can be written as

$$\pi_I(b, h) = (h - b)G_U(b),$$

and a pure bid strategy is a function $\beta_I(h)$. Let η_I denote its inverse.

As far as U is concerned, $\beta_I(H)$ is a random variable, which depends on the realization of the H, with distribution function $G_I(b) = F_H(\eta_I(b))$. Consequently, U's payoff from bidding $b \geqslant r$ is

$$\pi_U(b) = E\big[H - b \mid H < \eta_I(b)\big]F_H\big(\eta_I(b)\big).$$

Since I has to bid in such a way that U earns zero profits at any bid above r, its equilibrium bid strategy is given by

$$\beta_I(h) = \begin{cases} 0 & \text{if } h < r, \\ r & \text{if } h \in (r, \hat{h}), \\ E[H \mid H < h] = h - \frac{\int^h F_H(s)\,\mathrm{d}s}{F_H(h)} & \text{if } h > \hat{h} \end{cases}$$

where $\hat{h}$ satisfies $E[H \mid H < h] = r$. Clearly β is monotone increasing in h for $h \geqslant \hat{h}$. Therefore, $G_I(b) = F_H(\eta_I(b))$ for bids above the reserve price. Furthermore, as $h \to \infty$, $\beta(h) \to E[V]$. Therefore, the positive support of G_I is $(r, E[V])$. The remaining probability is concentrated at 0 (no bid) and at the reserve price r. The probability mass at these two bids are $F_H(r)$ and $F_H(\hat{h}) - F_H(r)$, respectively.

We turn next to characterizing U's mixed strategy. It has to bid so that I wants to bid according to β. Since $\beta(h)$ maximizes

$$\pi_I(b, h) = (h - b)G_U(b) \quad \text{s.t. } b \geqslant r,$$

$\beta(h)$ must solve

$$(h - b)g_U(b) - G_U(b) = 0 \quad \text{for all } b > r.$$

Substituting $\beta_I(h)$ for b, this first-order condition can be expressed as

$$\frac{g_U(\beta_I(h))\beta_I'(h)\,\mathrm{d}h}{G_U(\beta_I(h))} = \frac{f_H(h)\,\mathrm{d}h}{F_H(h)}.$$

Note that this equation holds for $h \geqslant \hat{h}$. Integrating both sides of this equation from $\hat{h}$ to h and applying the boundary condition $\beta_I(\hat{h}) = r$, yields

$$\frac{G_U(\beta_I(h))}{G_U(r)} = \frac{F_H(h)}{F_H(\hat{h})} \quad \text{for any } h \geqslant \hat{h}.$$

Since $\lim_{h\to\infty} G_U(\beta(h)) = 1$, it follows that $G_U(r) = F_H(\hat{h})$ and hence $G_U(\beta_I(h)) = F_H(h)$. Equivalently, $G_U(b) = F_H(\eta_I(b))$ for $b > r$. Continuity of expected profits implies that both bidders cannot have a mass point at r. Hence, the remaining probability of G_U is concentrated at 0. If there are n uninformed bidders, then G_U is the distribution of the maximum uninformed bid.

The equilibrium generates a number of testable predictions for drainage auctions. First, non-neighbor firms should have a lower aggregate participation rate than the neighbor firms. In the data, the participation rates for these two types of firms are 57%

and 87%, respectively. Second, neighbor firms should have a higher win rate than non-neighbor firms. In the data, neighbor firms account for 57% of the high bids. Third, non-neighbor firms should earn zero profits on average. The data are consistent with this prediction, at least prior to 1973, assuming a 5% real discount rate. Fourth, non-neighbor firms should earn negative expected profits on leases where neighbor firm(s) did not bid, since no neighbor bid is bad news. This pattern is found in the data, as the non-neighbor firms incurred significant (both statistically and economically) losses when no neighbor firm bid. Finally, the distribution of neighbor bids should have a mass point at r and should coincide with the distribution of the maximum non-neighbor bid above r. This last prediction is not consistent with the data. The two distributions coincide at higher bid levels but non-neighbor firms submitted relatively few low bids. (There were few low non-neighbor bids of any sort, and not just few low maximum non-neighbor bids.) Hendricks and Porter (1988) provide more detail.

We conclude that the simple theory of asymmetric information and common values can account for several features of the data, but not all. The simple theory ignores one important institutional feature, namely, that the government reserves the right to reject the high bid. In 1959–1979, the government rejected 58 of 295 high bids on drainage leases, approximately 20%. Rejection usually occurred when only one bid was submitted and the value of the bid was low.

We model the rejection policy as an unknown reserve price R with lower bound r, the announced reserve price, and upper bound $\bar{r}$. The high bid is rejected if $b < R$. The secret reserve price complicates the analysis considerably. The payoff of I is

$$\pi_I(b, x) = \big(E[V \mid X = x,\ b \geqslant R] - b\big) \Pr\{b \geqslant R \mid X = x\} G_U(b).$$

In this case, H is no longer a sufficient statistic for optimal bidding behavior. The private signal X may contain information that is relevant to the distributions of both V and R. Hendricks, Porter and Wilson (1994) assume that (V, X, R) are affiliated. This assumption implies that (i) $E[V \mid X, R]$ is non-decreasing in X and R, and (ii) the distribution $F_{R|X}$ satisfies the monotone likelihood ratio property with respect to realizations of X. These two properties are used to establish that $\beta_I(X)$ is non-decreasing. This in turn implies that (V, R, β_I) are affiliated and permits a characterization of the equilibrium bid distributions.

The main effects of the secret reserve price are captured in the special case where R is independent of (V, X), in which case H is a sufficient statistic for X. Let G_R denote the distribution of R. Then I's payoff from a bid of b is now

$$\pi_I(b, h) = (h - b) G_U(b) G_R(b).$$

Define

$$\beta_0(h) = \arg\max (h - b) G_R(b)$$

as the optimal strategy of I absent competition from uninformed bidders. The optimal bid function with U present is $\max\{\beta_0(h), \beta_I(h)\}$. In some cases, $\beta_0(h) > \beta_I(h)$ when

$h < \tilde{h}$ for some $\tilde{h} > r$. Then more aggressive bidding by I on the interval $[r, \tilde{h})$ means that $\pi_U(b) < 0$ for $b \in (r, \tilde{b})$, where $\tilde{b} = \beta(\tilde{h})$.

The predictions for the bid distributions have to be modified as follows: (i) G_I does not have a mass point if $G_R(r)$ is sufficiently close to 0; (ii) $G_U(b) \leqslant G_I(b)$ with strict inequality for $b \in (r, \bar{r})$ (stochastic dominance); and (iii) $G_U = G_I$ for $b > \bar{r}$. In the data, the bid distributions essentially coincide above $4 million. The probability of rejection at this bid level is very low. Stochastic dominance is evident, as depicted in Figure 1 of Hendricks, Porter and Wilson (1994), and significant. We conclude that the asymmetric information common value model with a secret reserve price can account for the main features of the data.

What about the assumption that there is only one neighbor? In the sample, the average number of neighboring wildcat tracts is 3.78. Yet non-neighbor bidding is independent of the number of neighbor firms. If neighbor firms are symmetrically informed, and if they bid competitively, then non-neighbor firms with no private information should not bid. At a minimum, one would expect less aggressive non-neighbor bidding as the number of neighbors increases, as the winner's curse is more severe. One could view participation by non-neighbor firms as evidence of coordination on the part of neighbor firms. Further, the high neighbor bid is independent of number of neighbors, and on tracts where more than one neighbor bids, neighbor profits are much higher. This evidence suggests coordination by the neighbor firms, with occasional phony bids to guard against rejection. Alternatively, the neighbor firms may themselves be asymmetric in some way. Note that it is relatively easy for neighbor firms to coordinate, as they could allocate production as a means of making side payments.

What about the alternative model in which there are cost asymmetries rather than information asymmetries? Several facts argue against this model. First, to avoid common pool problems, production on adjacent tracts is often unitized, with revenues allocated in proportion to area owned above the common pool. Second, non-neighbor firm profits are approximately zero. On tracts won by non-neighbors when neighbors do not bid, profits are negative because tracts are less likely to contain oil or gas deposits. This is inconsistent with unobserved cost differences being the predominant source of asymmetry.

The tests described above are reduced form. There is a role for structural estimation in this environment, in designing the optimal selling mechanism. But knowing only that information is asymmetric, and who has superior information, can be sufficient for optimal mechanism design. Hendricks, Porter and Tan (1993) discuss this issue.

6.1.2. The symmetric case

For wildcat tracts, Hendricks, Pinkse and Porter (2003) implement several tests of bidder rationality by comparing bids with ex post outcomes. One basic test is that actual rents, $v_t - w_t$, measured as the difference between discounted net revenues and the winning bid, should on average be positive. A second related test is that firms should expect to earn positive rents conditional on submitting the winning bid. To compute this expectation, we estimate the function

$$\phi(b) = E[V_t \mid B_{it} = b,\ M_{it} < b],$$

and evaluate it at b_{it}. The profit margin that firm i expects to earn upon winning tract t is $\phi(b_{it}) - b_{it}$. Averaging across firms and tracts, this profit margin should be positive. We find that actual rents and expected rents conditional on winning are significantly positive, and there is no evidence of adverse selection associated with winning. The magnitude of the actual rents are approximately equal to total entry costs, so it appears that on average firms earn zero profits.

Did bidders bid less than their expected tract value? To address this question, we estimate the function

$$\varsigma(b) = E[V_t \mid B_{it} = b]$$

and test the restriction that $\varsigma(b) > b$ at all bid levels. We also test the stronger restriction that firms should always bid less than the expected value of the tract conditional on winning, $\phi(b) > b$. We find that both $\varsigma(b) - b$ and $\phi(b) - b$ are significantly positive throughout the relevant range of bids, and furthermore that $\varsigma(b)$ is significantly larger than $\phi(b)$ at every bid level. The difference between these two functions is a measure of the informativeness of winning. This difference is greater on tracts with more potential bidders.

Our final test is a test of equilibrium bidding. Recall that, in a symmetric equilibrium, bids satisfy the first-order condition

$$E\big[V \mid X_i = \eta(b),\ Y_i = \eta(b)\big] = \xi(b, G).$$

We estimate the conditional expectation function,

$$\zeta(b) = E[V \mid B_i = b, M_i = b].$$

Since β is monotone, η is monotone as well, and hence these two equations imply that

$$\zeta(b) = \xi(b, G)$$

at any $b > r$. Equality of these two functions is an empirically testable implication of equilibrium bidding in wildcat auctions. We find that Bayesian Nash equilibrium cannot be rejected when competition is high (i.e., more than six potential bidders, by our measure), but equilibrium behavior is rejected when competition is low (six bidders or less). In the latter case, the data suggest that firms may have overbid.

In summary, we conclude that the winner's curse is evident in the data, but also that bidders are aware of its presence and bid accordingly, for the most part.

7. Revenues and auction design

The early theoretical work on auctions by Vickrey (1961, 1962) and Ortega Reichert (1968) studies the four standard single object auction formats, namely, Dutch, English,

FPSB, and SPSB, under the assumption that bidders are risk neutral, their valuations are private, and their signals are independent and identically distributed. The authors obtain a striking and surprising result: the expected revenues from all four formats are identical. In each case, the expected revenue to the seller in equilibrium is simply the expected value of $\max\{r, X_{2:n}\}$, where $X_{k:n}$ denotes the kth highest order statistic among the random variables $\{X_1, \ldots, X_n\}$. (The reserve price r can be interpreted as the bid of the seller, and as the second highest estimate in the event that no rival submits a bid. The revenue comparison assumes that r is constant across auction formats.) Myerson (1981) and Riley and Samuelson (1981) subsequently demonstrated that the revenue equivalence result holds under bidder risk neutrality in any auction format in which the bidder with the highest valuation wins and the bidder with the lowest possible valuation, $\underline{x}$, has zero expected payoff.

A number of empirical studies have examined the prediction of revenue equivalence. The prediction has also received the attention of the experimental literature. One strand of the empirical literature compares bid data from different auction formats. Although there are not many instances where different auction formats are run in parallel for similar auction environments, one example is U.S. Forest Service timber auctions [Hansen (1986)]. Hansen's econometric approach to test revenue equivalence is to regress winning bid on sales characteristics, Z_t, and an indicator variable

$$D_t = \begin{cases} 1 & \text{if auction } t \text{ is FPSB,} \\ 0 & \text{if auction } t \text{ is English.} \end{cases}$$

Hansen finds that the coefficient on D_t is significantly positive. Revenues in the FPSB auctions are about 10% higher than in English auctions. But, as Hansen argues, the Forest Service does not select auction type randomly. If one corrects for sample selection, where the Forest Service region is employed as an instrument for auction format, the coefficient on D_t is approximately zero. Hansen concludes that one cannot reject revenue equivalence. Athey, Levin and Seira (2004) find that, in more recent periods, revenues are higher in the FPSB auctions, even correcting for sample selection.

There are other implications of equilibrium bidding that could be tested. Higher moments of the distribution of seller revenues are not the same across auction formats. In particular, Matthews (1980) shows the FPSB winning bid distribution has lower variance than revenue in the SPSB and English auctions. Therefore, one might examine higher order moments of the distribution of prices, or properties of the entire distribution of prices. For example, Haile's (2001) method of moments estimator for the distribution of valuations in an English auction (with an active resale market) employs information on both the first and second moments of the bid distribution. But we know of no instance in which comparative statics properties across auction formats concerning higher order moments have been examined.

Rejection of revenue equivalence then leads one to ask why it occurs. What feature of equilibrium bidding in the symmetric, risk neutral IPV model is being rejected? One possibility is risk aversion [Holt (1980)]. Bidding one's valuation remains a dominant strategy in an English auction, but expected prices are higher in a FPSB, as risk averse bidders increase their bids to increase the probability of winning the auction. In a private values environment, bidders know their valuation net of their bid in the event they win, but are uncertain whether they will win the auction given their bid. Risk aversion therefore leads to more aggressive bidding. (In contrast, risk aversion may lead to less aggressive bidding in common value auctions, due to the winner's curse.) Haile (2001) argues that the presence of a resale market, and the consequent incentives to signal via bids in the original auction to affect subsequent resale negotiations, can account for FPSB revenue superiority.

Athey, Levin and Seira relax the assumption of symmetric bidders. They assume that a mill's willingness to pay for cutting rights is stochastically greater than a logger's willingness to pay since the latter has to sell its logs to a mill. Under this assumption, revenue equivalence does not hold and the auction format matters. In open, ascending price auctions, the bidder with the highest valuation wins but, in first-price, sealed bid auctions, this need not be the outcome. Mills shade their bids further below their valuations than do loggers in a FPSB auction, because of their favorable distribution of values. As a result, loggers are more likely to participate, and win, in a sealed bid auction than in an open auction, and sealed bid auctions may yield greater revenue. The main difficulty the authors face in testing these theoretical predictions is, again, that the choice of auction format is not random. The authors deal with this problem by using a non-parametric matching estimator, and assuming that the choice of auction format is a function of observable sale characteristics. The latter assumption is plausible since the data provide a rich set of sale characteristics. After controlling for sale characteristics, they find that the participation and win rates of loggers are higher in sealed bid auctions than in open auctions. In addition, winning bids in sealed bid auctions are significantly higher in Montana and Idaho, but similar to winning bids in open auctions in California.

Athey, Levin and Seira also explore the possibility that the FPSB revenue superiority in the Northern states may have been due to mills bidding less competitively in the open auctions. As we argue below, collusion can be easier to maintain in an English auction. To test this hypothesis, the authors use structural estimates of entry costs and the value distributions of loggers and mills from sealed bid auctions to predict average sale prices in the oral auctions under the assumption that mills behave competitively, and under the assumption that they bid collusively. For each tract, the mean parameter of the Poisson distribution determining the number of loggers is calibrated so that loggers are indifferent between entering and staying out. Thus, in contrast to other analyses of collusion in auctions which treat the number of bidders as fixed, collusion by mills affects the entry behavior of loggers. As a result, the impact of collusion on sale prices is not as large as it might have been had mills colluded in secret. Collusion is nevertheless profitable because loggers' valuations are stochastically lower than the mills' valuations. The main finding is that the average price in the Northern oral auctions lies below the average predicted price obtained under competition, and above that obtained under collusion. In California, average prices are not significantly different from the average predicted price obtained under competition.

The Athey, Levin and Seira paper illustrates the usefulness of structural estimation for building counterfactuals. Shneyerov (2005) pursues a similar strategy in studying the effects of auction format on revenues in municipal bond auctions. The auctions are first-price sealed bid, and Shneyerov wants to predict the revenue changes from switching from the FPSB format to either second-price sealed bid or an English button auction. Milgrom and Weber (1982) show that, in affiliated common value environments, the expected revenues of first-price auctions are lower than the expected revenues of sealed bid, second-price auctions, which in turn are lower than the expected revenues of English button auctions. The idea is that the SPSB format reveals rival information by making the winner's payment equal the highest rival bid. In an English button auction, rival signals are revealed by their exit decisions, further allaying the winner's curse. Before constructing the counterfactual, Shneyerov estimates the empirical distributions of the random variables, $\xi(B, \hat{G}_n)$, and tests the null hypothesis of private values against the alternative of affiliated values using one of the tests proposed by Haile, Hong and Shum (2004). He rejects the null, so that revenue gains are possible. The difficulty that he faces in constructing the counterfactual is that, in auctions with common values, the distribution of latent bidder valuations is not identified. Shneyerov observes, however, that $\xi(b, \hat{G}_n)$ is an estimate of the latent conditional expectation, $w(\eta(b), \eta(b))$, which is the amount that a bidder with signal $x = \eta(b)$ would bid in a second-price auction with n bidders. Hence, the pseudo-values generated by the two-step approach of Elyakime et al. (1994) and Guerre, Perrigne and Vuong (2000) can be interpreted as counterfactual bids in a second-price auction, and used to identify expected revenue from this auction format. Shneyerov finds that expected revenues from the second-price auction are approximately 20 percent higher than in the first-price auctions.

The second main result of Myerson (1981) and Riley and Samuelson (1981) is that the revenue maximizing mechanism in an IPV environment can be implemented by any of the standard auction formats with an appropriately specified reserve price. As we discussed in Section 3.1, the optimal reserve price for a seller who values the item at x_0 is the solution to

$$r = x_0 + \left[1 - F_X(r)\right] / f_X(r).$$

The optimal reserve price in an IPV auction depends only on x_0 and F_X, and not the number of bidders. Given an estimate of F_X, the seller can choose r to satisfy the above equation. Paarsch (1997) and Haile and Tamer (2003) estimate the optimal reserve price in an IPV environment.

McAfee and Vincent (1992) and McAfee, Quan and Vincent (2002) study the problem of setting optimal reserve prices in common value auctions when the seller does not have an estimate of F. This case is certainly relevant since, as noted earlier, F cannot be identified in these environments from bid data alone. McAfee and Vincent (1992) consider pure common value, first-price auctions and develop a distribution-free test statistic that the seller can compute from data on bids and ex post values to determine whether the reserve price is too low or too high. The test statistic allows for endogenous entry and stochastic participation. They apply the test to the data on federal offshore oil and gas auctions. They find that the federal government's revenue-maximizing reserve price was too low. In their 2002 paper, the authors extend the test to common value environments and to a broader class of auctions, including first price, second price and oral auctions. The extension does not require data on ex post values. They apply the test to real estate auctions.

7.1. Multi-unit auctions

The revenue equivalence theorem has been tested in sequential auctions under the assumption of unit demands. That is, each bidder's valuation refers to their valuation of the first unit they acquire, and the marginal value of any additional unit is assumed to be zero. Suppose that only the winning bid is revealed after each round. Let w_l denote the winning bid in the lth auction. It can be shown that in an IPV environment with risk neutral and symmetric bidders who have unit demands, the prices in a k-item, sequential first price auction should form a martingale, that is $E[w_l \mid w_{l-1}] = w_{l-1}$ for $l = 2, \ldots, k$, and furthermore, that $E[w_l] = E[X_{k+1:n}]$ for all l. This claim is also true of a SPSB sequence. In an English auction, the price sequence depends on what information is revealed to the bidders.

Ashenfelter (1989) tests this arbitrage condition for wine auctions. Identical cases of wine were sold sequentially via English auctions by an auction house. He finds evidence of a "declining price anomaly". Prices systematically and significantly decline over the sale sequence, although the magnitude of the decline is not large, a few percent. This pattern appears to violate the martingale prediction, as well as a more general notion of the implications of no arbitrage opportunities. Other studies that have examined this prediction include Ashenfelter and Genesove (1992) and Beggs and Graddy (1997), who respectively find that condominium and art prices also decline. In contrast, Donald, Paarsch and Robert (2006) find evidence of rising prices in auctions of Siberian timber export permits. Ashenfelter and Graddy (2003) provide a recent survey.

Is there a resolution to the anomaly? The martingale result relies on risk neutrality, the IPV assumption and the assumption of unit demands. A number of papers have shown that the conclusions are not robust. McAfee and Vincent (1993) study the effects of risk aversion. They show that in order to obtain declining prices, preferences must exhibit non-decreasing absolute risk aversion, which is not thought to be plausible. Milgrom and Weber (2000) show that affiliation implies that prices should (weakly) increase, as winner's curse concerns are mitigated as information is revealed. Finally, one might also question whether buyers only want one unit, and if not whether their valuations are independent across units. In some auctions with declining prices, initial winners have the option to buy more than one unit at their bid price, and the price decline may reflect the value of this option, as noted by Black and de Meza (1992).

The literature on the declining price anomaly illustrates the interaction between theory and empirical work in auctions. Here the theory generates a simple prediction, which is rejected by the data, inducing further theoretical work on the robustness of the predictions. It also illustrates an important theme of empirical work on auctions: tests of reduced form predictions are most compelling when the predictions are robust to the various maintained hypotheses.

Beggs and Graddy (1997) examine sequential sales of paintings, in part to see whether the order within the sequence matters. They find that sale rates and sale prices relative to pre-sale catalog estimates rise with bid order for the objects sold at the beginning of the day. Thereafter, sale rates and prices relative to estimates fall, similar to the declining price anomaly. Perhaps not surprisingly, there is a tendency to place higher value objects earlier in the sale, although not right at the beginning. Note that there is an implicit assumption in the econometric model that looking at prices relative to pre-sale estimates is sufficient to control for heterogeneity across dissimilar paintings. In sequential sales of identical objects, the variance of prices will evolve over time. An open issue is whether higher-order moments also vary with the pre-sale estimate, i.e. whether there is heteroskedasticity, as might result if the dispersion of valuations relative to the pre-sale estimate varies with the value of the object.

The revenue equivalence result also extends to simultaneous auctions of multiple identical objects when bidders have unit demands. Milgrom and Weber (2000) prove the following result in auctions where k units are auctioned simultaneously in an IPV environment with risk neutral bidders. Suppose the auction rules and equilibrium are such that the k highest types always win and that the lowest type has zero expected payoff. Then the expected payment of type x of bidder i at the Bayesian Nash equilibrium of the discriminatory auction (where the winning bidders pay their bid) is the same as in Vickrey's auction, where the winning bidders pay the highest rejected bid. The expected payment of that bidder is the expected valuation of the marginal losing bidder (including the seller, as represented by the reserve price), conditional on being among the set of winning bidders

$$E\big[\max\{X_{k+1:n}, r\} \mid x \geqslant \max\{X_{k+1:n}, r\}\big].$$

The Vickrey auction is also known as a uniform price auction. Another uniform price auction stipulates that the k highest bidders win and pay the lowest accepted bid, that is the lowest bid submitted by one of the k winning bidders. Note that, in the symmetric equilibria, the outcomes are the same and they are always efficient, because the items are allocated to the bidders who value them the most.

Treasury bills are an important example of a simultaneous item auction that has been run under both discriminatory and uniform pricing rules in a number of countries, such as the United States, Sweden, Switzerland, Mexico, Turkey and Korea. However, the unit demand assumption in these auctions typically fails. Bidders submit bid schedules, listing their willingness to pay for a varying number of items. Ausubel and Cramton (2002) provide examples under which either the uniform or the discriminatory format may yield higher revenues. Thus, the question as to which format yields more revenue is an empirical issue. Bikhchandani and Huang (1993) survey empirical studies that have addressed this issue using reduced form methods.

Several authors have recently employed structural estimation methods to recover the bidders' willingness to pay schedules. Hortacsu (2002) examines bidding in Turkish treasury auctions when a discriminatory format was employed. He assumes that values are private, and that buyers' private information is a real number (i.e., not multi-dimensional). An increase in the private signal leads to a monotonic increase in the bidder's marginal valuation schedule. Bidder's demand functions are assumed to be monotonic functions of their private signals. Thus, if a bidder's rivals adopt a given bid schedule, the bidder's best response can be computed for a given realization of his private information. As in the single unit case, one can define an inverse bid function, where now

$$v_i\big(\varphi_i(b,x),x\big) = b + \frac{G_i(b,\varphi_i(b,x))}{\partial G_i(b,\varphi_i(b,x))/\partial b}.$$

Here $\varphi_i(b,x)$ denotes the bid function specifying a quantity demanded by bidder i at price b, given a private signal x, and $v_i(q,x)$ is the marginal valuation of acquiring q units given the private signal. $G_i(b,\varphi_i(b,x))$ denotes the probability that the lowest winning bid is less than or equal to b, given that bidder i adopts the strategy $\varphi_i(b,x)$. This equation generalizes the expression for the inverse bid function in a single unit private value auction. Hortacsu proposes a method based on resampling to estimate $G_i(b,\varphi_i(b,x))$ and its derivative for each bidder, and thus recover a pseudo-sample of marginal valuations. Hortacsu shows that his method yields consistent estimates. After recovering the distribution of bidder valuations, he computes an upper bound on the counterfactual seller revenues that would be obtained in a uniform price auction, under the assumption that bidders would not bid more than their marginal values. This bound is less than the observed revenue in the discriminatory auction, suggesting that a uniform price format would not result in higher revenues. Such counterfactual comparisons are feasible only with structural estimates. Other structural estimation papers include Castellanos and Oviedo (2004), who study Mexican treasury auctions, and Fevrier, Preget and Visser (2004), who study French treasury auctions.

Several empirical studies of treasury bill and electricity markets, in which bidders submit bid schedules rather than bid prices, assume that the schedules are continuous functions. In practice, bidders often submit step functions with only a few steps, in some instances with many fewer steps than they would be permitted to use. Kastl (2005) argues that in some contexts the restriction to continuous bid schedules can mask important strategic issues, and that revenue comparisons based on continuous schedules may not be valid. In particular, revenues in uniform price auctions can exceed the bound derived by Hortacsu. His study of uniform price Czech treasury auctions indicates that the distinction between continuous and discrete schedules can matter empirically.

Kastl's empirical work exploits the fact that, although bid functions are not continuous, the price and quantity associated with any bid point are continuous variables. He characterizes the necessary conditions the price and quantity choices must satisfy, and his empirical work exploits the first-order condition for quantities. Wolak (2003, 2005) proposes an empirical method that accounts for both the price and quantity first-order conditions associated with each bid point, and he applies the method to determine the value of forward contracts in the Australian national electricity market.

8. Collusion

There is evidence of collusion in many auction markets. Examples include highway construction contracts, school milk delivery, timber sales, and spectrum auctions. Auction markets may be especially vulnerable to collusion. An auction is an effective price discovery mechanism under competition, and so can be attractive to sellers who are uncertain about the price they should receive. But the sellers may then be unable to determine when they are the victim of a bid rigging scheme. Collusion among bidders, if successful, can benefit the participants at the expense of their suppliers. The social losses usually outweigh the benefits. For example, if a bidding ring lowers the prices they offer to pay for products or services, relative to competitive levels, then sellers suffer a loss, and trade will be less likely to occur. The outcome may also be inefficient, if bidders outside the ring are more likely to win. Further, potential sellers will be less inclined to offer their products or services in the future. There will be social welfare losses to the extent that current and potential future gains from trade are foregone.

In this section, we describe various collusive schemes, the factors that facilitate or inhibit collusion among bidders in auction markets, as well as circumstances where detection is possible. Collusion in this instance means explicit, as opposed to tacit, cooperation, involving direct communication and perhaps side payments. These actions are usually surreptitious, either because they are illegal under antitrust laws, or because they are most effective if they are kept secret from the intended victims. We describe some results from the theoretical literature, and discuss a number of recent empirical studies. Two surveys that touch on some of the same issues, although not just for auction markets, are by Harrington (2005) and Porter (2005).

8.1. Collusive mechanisms

Collusion can take many different forms in auctions. The form often depends on the auction rules and characteristics of the environment [Hendricks and Porter (1989)]. But all bidding rings face a set of typical cartel problems: private information about the gains from trade, conflicting objectives, internal enforcement, detection by authorities or seller, and entry. An important feature of many collusive agreements, and a determinant of their success, is the need to reconcile disparate interests. Interests may differ for a number of reasons. For example, firms may have adopted technologies of differing vintages for historical reasons, they may serve non-overlapping and heterogeneous customer bases, or their payoffs may be subject to imperfectly correlated shocks. Side payments can solve some internal problems, but they may not be legal. Also, the contractual terms associated with side payments may not be enforceable. An unhappy conspirator whose loyalty cannot be purchased is more likely to report the collusion to antitrust authorities.

Theoretical studies have focused primarily on private information as a source of difficulties for a ring. In this literature, the ring's objective in an auction is viewed as a problem of mechanism design. The mechanism design approach is natural for legal cartels, which can write binding contracts to enforce side payments or allocative agreements, and to a lesser extent for illegal conspiracies where members communicate and may make side payments. Since most illegal rings operate in many auctions over time, they may be able to use repeated game strategies to enforce the mechanism played in an individual auction [Athey and Bagwell (2001), Athey, Bagwell and Sanchirico (2004)]. In a mechanism design framework, allocations and transfers are determined by internal messages. The collective goal is to win the auction when it is optimal to do so, and in those cases to allocate the good and divide the spoils among the participants. The ring mechanism must be incentive compatible and individually rational. That is, ring members must have an incentive to reveal their private information, and they must also participate voluntarily, so that there is no incentive to defect. The specification of these constraints, and the extent to which they are binding, will depend upon the auction rules and on the characteristics of the environment.

8.1.1. Private values

In a private values environment, the cartel has to overcome an adverse selection problem: the participants do not know how much fellow ring members are willing to pay for the item being auctioned, and each member wants to exploit this private information to argue for a bigger share of the spoils. Graham and Marshall (1987) and Mailath and Zemsky (1991) study collusion in second-price, IPV auctions. They show that ex post efficient collusion by any subset of bidders is possible. In a symmetric environment, the ring can easily implement the incentive compatible, ex post efficient cartel mechanism with a pre-sale knockout auction. In the knockout auction, the ring members bid for the right to be the ring's representative bidder in the seller's auction. The conspirator who bids the highest amount wins this right, and the winner pays an amount to the other ring members based on the bids submitted. Since the knockout auction has a symmetric equilibrium with monotone strategies, the winner is the member who has the highest valuation. The participation constraints are evaluated at the interim stage, after the members have obtained their values but before they have decided to participate in the ring. The payoff to a bidder who decides not to participate in a ring of size m is given by her equilibrium payoff in the seller's auction when she bids against a ring of size $m-1$ and $n-m$ non-ring bidders. This payoff is easily computed in a second-price, private value auction because participants have a dominant strategy to bid their value. Hence, a non-colluding bidder faces the same high bid whether her rivals form a ring (of any size) or not, assuming the ring selects the member with the highest valuation. The knockout auction satisfies the interim participation constraints, so bidders prefer the cartel mechanism to bidding non-cooperatively in the seller's auction.

McAfee and McMillan (1992) study collusion in first-price IPV auctions. They show that ex post efficient collusion is possible in these auctions if the ring includes all bidders. The all-inclusive ring can implement the incentive compatible, ex post efficient cartel mechanism using a first-price knockout auction in which the winning bidder pays his bid to the losing bidders, who share equally in this bid. Hendricks, Porter and Tan

(2006) extend this result to affiliated private value environments. McAfee and McMillan assume that the bidders have to make their participation decisions before they obtain their private information so that the relevant participation constraints are ex ante. They show that the bidders' expected cartel payoffs exceed the equilibrium payoff they would receive if everyone bid individually and non-cooperatively in the first price auction, and so everyone will want to join the ring. An alternative specification of the participation constraint is the equilibrium payoff in a first-price sealed bid auction in which one bidder bids against a ring of size $n - 1$. These payoffs are difficult to compute since the auction involves asymmetric bidders. McAfee and McMillan study a simple model in which each buyer's private value is an independent Bernoulli random variable. They show that the non-colluding bidder is better off ex ante than ring members. Thus, the all-inclusive ring is not stable, which may explain why most rings in first-price auctions are partial.

An alternative to a pre-sale knockout auction is a post-sale knockout, such as the one used by a bidding ring involving rare book dealers in England in 1919. After one large estate sale, the ring held a series of knockout auctions. Successively smaller subsets of the dealers conspired to deprive the seller, and then their fellow conspirators, of some of the gains. The book dealers differed according to expertise and scale of operation, and the larger and more experienced dealers stayed longer in the knockout process. The participants in the various knockout auctions shared the increases in bids over prices in the previous round. The original seller received less than 20 percent of the final settlement prices. (Note that this figure probably overstates the damage to the seller, as the ring settlement mechanism could induce conspirators to bid more than their valuations in the knockout auction.) Why did the larger ring members conspire with the smaller members? If they had not, the larger dealers would have had to outbid the smaller dealers at the original auction, and it would have been cheaper to share some of the collusive gains with them. But it is also in their interest to share only enough to buy the loyalty of the smaller dealers, and not the full difference between the original purchase price and what the larger dealers were willing to pay. A sequence of knockouts would limit the amount shared, assuming that smaller dealers were not aware that they would be excluded from later knockouts. [Porter (1992) provides a brief account.]

An imperfect solution that involves no side payments is the territorial division of bidding privileges, by region, by point in time, by incumbency, or even by pure randomization (via the submission of many identical bids). A scheme that assigns customers or territories to the participants would grant individual firms wide latitude within their own territories. Comanor and Schankerman (1976) provide evidence that rotating bid arrangements can be stable. Here firms take turns submitting serious bids for the ring. The serious bid may be optimized against the seller's acceptance rule, or against other bidders who are not co-conspirators. Other ring members may submit complementary bids to create the appearance of competition. McAfee and McMillan (1992) show that it may be optimal for a weak all-inclusive cartel (that is, one that cannot make side payments) to submit many identical bids at the reserve price, and so rely on the auctioneer to randomly select among them. In the 1950s, General Electric and Westinghouse assigned low bid privileges for electrical equipment contracts based on a phases-of-the-moon system [Smith (1961)], a practice that is unlikely to reflect differences in values.

Pesendorfer (2000) argues that a weak conspiracy that cannot make side payments may be forced to maintain relatively constant market shares, despite some losses from not allocating bidding rights to the low cost firm, in order to maintain internal discipline. He shows that, if there are many items being sold, the ring can achieve approximate internal efficiency via a ranking mechanism. That is, members rank items, and bidding privileges for individual items are assigned based on the submitted rankings. The ring does not achieve full internal efficiency, as minimal market shares must be guaranteed to ensure that participation constraints are satisfied. He compares Florida and Texas bid rigging schemes for providing school milk, and shows that market shares were less stable in Florida, where dairies used side payments.

8.1.2. Common values

In a pure common value auction environment, a ring's internal allocation problem is simpler, because all members value the item identically. As a result, cartels in these auctions can adopt equal division rules, in which all members share equally in the spoils. Given this sharing rule, cartel members have no incentive to misrepresent their information. They share a common goal, which is to bid only when the expected value of the item conditional on their pooled information exceeds the reserve price. The equal division sharing rule can be implemented without transfer payments by having every member submit the same bid (e.g., the reserve price) and letting the seller randomly select the winner, or by rotating bidding privileges over several auctions. However, participation constraints can be a problem.

Hendricks, Porter and Tan (2006) study all-inclusive cartel formation in a first-price auction with common values. The ring is assumed to form after the bidders have obtained their private information so the relevant participation constraints are interim. In the standard mechanism, bidders compare the equilibrium payoff (conditional on their private information) they would receive if everyone bid individually and non-cooperatively in the first price auction to their expected cartel payoff. We show that the equal division sharing rule does not generally satisfy these participation constraints, nor does the knockout tournament. Indeed, no incentive compatible, ex post efficient cartel mechanism may satisfy the participation constraints. The reason is that bidders have to bid cautiously in the first-price auction due to the winner's curse. As a result, a bidder with favorable information when commonly available signals are pessimistic is often able to earn a higher expected payoff from competitive bidding in the seller's auction. He will have to pay a somewhat higher price to the seller, but the surplus is not shared with other ring members, who are not likely to pose a competitive threat.

We also consider a second model of the participation constraint. Cramton and Palfrey (1995) have argued that the participation choices of bidders are informative about their types. If one or more bidders chooses not to participate, bidders should revise their beliefs accordingly before bidding in the first-price auction. The revision in beliefs will affect bidding behavior and hence payoffs, and should be anticipated by the bidders when they make their participation decisions. Cramton and Palfrey refer to this issue as the information leakage problem. They formalize the problem by assuming that bidders first play a veto game in which they simultaneously vote for or against the proposed cartel mechanism. If the mechanism is unanimously ratified, then the all-inclusive ring forms and the mechanism is implemented. If at least one bidder votes against the mechanism, then the all-inclusive ring does not form, bidders revise their beliefs, and they bid individually and non-cooperatively in the first-price auction. The cartel mechanism is ratifiable if it is not possible to construct a veto set such that the cartel payoff of every type in the set is less than their equilibrium payoff in the first-price sealed bid auction. The main difficulty with applying this solution concept in our context is computing the equilibrium payoffs to the veto set. If some bidders vote for and others vote against the cartel, then the seller's auction will involve asymmetric bidders. We show, however, that in the case of pure common values, one does not need to compute the equilibrium to prove that the cartel mechanism is ratifiable. The intuition behind this result is that the lowest type in the veto set makes zero profits in the auction. Since this type makes positive profits in the cartel mechanism, it is not possible to construct a veto set that makes everyone in the set better off. Hence, the all-inclusive cartel should always form. This conclusion generalizes to other voting models of joint venture formation.

The motivating example for our study is joint bidding in U.S. federal auctions of wildcat oil and gas leases in the Outer Continental Shelf off the coasts of Louisiana and Texas during the period 1954 to 1970. Joint bidding ventures for all firms were legal during this period. The potential gains from joint bidding appear to be substantial. The stakes are large, and the risks significant. By pooling geological data and expertise in interpreting the data, firms could reduce the risk of buying dry leases and, by pooling financial resources, they can bid for more leases and diversify away more of the tract-specific uncertainties. Despite these gains, solo bidding was the dominant form of bidding for the most active participants. Joint bids involving pairs of the most active firms represented less than 15% of all their bids, even though joint bidding agreements were legal. Furthermore, if these firms bid jointly, they almost always did so in pairs, and not in all-inclusive partnerships.

The standard model of participation constraints (i.e., passive beliefs) seems to be a better approximation to the firms' joint venture decisions in OCS auctions than the learning model. The reason is that the joint venture cover blocks of tracts, typically 25 to 50 tracts, and not individual tracts. If a bidder refuses to join the ring, then the other bidders may infer that the non-participating bidder has obtained favorable information about one or more tracts in the area, but they do not know which tracts and, since most are not worth bidding for, the inference is likely to have little impact on beliefs about individual tracts. The learning model of participation constraints suggests that the situation would have been quite different if the joint bidding decisions were taken on a tract by tract basis. In that case, refusal to bid jointly on a tract would cause beliefs about that tract, and therefore bidding behavior, to change. Information leakage would have forced the firms to participate. But, given passive beliefs, our results provide an explanation for the surprising low incidence of joint bidding, particularly on marginal tracts. Consistent with this explanation, we document a positive correlation between the incidence of joint bidding and the value of tracts. This correlation probably reflects the incentive for firms to find financial partners on tracts where the high bid is likely to be large. However, it may also reflect the fact that potential bidders are more likely to know their competition (i.e., who intends to bid) on high value tracts.

Solo bidding does not imply the absence of collusion. In testimony before Congress in the mid-1970s, Darius Gaskins of the Department of Interior argued that the collusive effects of joint ventures should not be measured solely in terms of tracts receiving joint bids. Joint bidding negotiations could allow partners to coordinate their solo bids. We find evidence of bid coordination by bidders who bid jointly in a sale. In particular, bidders are unlikely to submit competing solo bids if they have submitted a joint bid in another region in the same sale.

Finally, rings in common value environments may have to worry about a moral hazard problem, since each member has an incentive to free ride on the costly information gathering activities of other members. These difficulties may also explain the low incidence of joint bidding in the OCS auctions.

8.2. Enforcement

To succeed, a ring has to keep its members from deviating, by ensuring that it is in each of the conspirator's self-interest to adhere to the agreement. Robinson (1985) points out that enforcement is easier in SPSB or English private values (PV) auctions. [See also Milgrom (1987).] Suppose that the ring is ex post efficient, and therefore designates the member with the highest valuation to be its representative in the seller's auction. This agent's dominant strategy is to bid his valuation, independent of the competition he faces. Then the other ring members cannot gain from deviating and outbidding the designated bidder. The success of the ring depends only on how many potential bidders refrain from bidding, thereby lowering the expected price paid by the serious bidder when he wins. Similarly, in an English auction, the serious bidder only needs to outbid other submitted bids. There is an internal enforcement problem only if the serious bidder does not have the highest valuation among the ring members.

In FPSB PV auctions, the ring bidder optimally bids below his valuation. His bid is decreasing in the size of the ring, as more potential competition is eliminated. If the serious bid is low enough, another ring member might profitably deviate because the serious bid is below his valuation. A ring may then form only when the participants know that they will be competing against each other in subsequent auctions. In that case, the ring can credibly threaten to punish non-compliance in current play by expelling the deviator from the ring, or by dissolving the ring.

Marshall and Marx (2004) argue that collusion might even be possible in a one-shot FPSB auction, if side payments are feasible and if shill bids are employed to create the proper incentives within the FPSB auction. Shill bids, which are also known as complementary or phony bids, are submitted by ring members other than the designated bidder.

By design, a shill bid is less than the serious ring bid. The idea is that the designated ring representative bids more than would be optimal against outsiders, to ensure that other ring members do not defect. The purpose of a shill bid, just below the high ring bid, is to dissuade the designated bidder from bidding lower. Thus complementary bids may be employed by a ring to enforce internal discipline, and not just to create the appearance of competition.

In a multiple-unit simultaneous ascending bid format, such as the mechanism employed by the US Federal Communications Commission (FCC) to sell spectrum for PCS (personal communications services), punishments can be wide-ranging. Defections in the bidding for one object can induce responses elsewhere. In the FCC DEF block spectrum auction, a territorial division was achieved within the bidding process itself [Cramton and Schwartz (2000)]. The FCC employed a simultaneous ascending bid procedure, in which bidding was kept open on all licenses throughout the auction, and firms with enough eligibility could switch between licenses. Some bidders used trailing digits on their bids to communicate their future intentions. For example, one response to a new bidder in one's territory was to outbid that bidder on at least one other license where it held the standing high bid. The response bid's last three digits would be the identifying code of the original market, and the intended message was the offer to not compete on this license if the rival stays out of your territory. No overt communication is involved, unless the parties need to resolve how to interpret bid signals, and a territorial allocation can be achieved at relatively low bid prices. Gertner (1995) describes how these bidding strategies can be self-enforcing, and result in low prices. The auction rules could be amended to prevent this sort of signaling, for example by requiring new bids to be a fixed amount or fraction higher than the current high bid. There could also be a fixed ending time to the auction, in which case it would not be possible to retaliate after that time.

In a multi-unit uniform price auction, price is determined by a market clearing condition, where available supply equals demand. A version of this mechanism was employed by the England and Wales electricity auction market. [Wolfram (1998, 1999) provides an account.] Bidders can implicitly make it costly for rivals to steal market share by bidding low prices for infra-marginal supplies. A generating unit is infra-marginal if it is likely to be called on to supply power, but unlikely to be decisive in determining the market price. In multi-unit uniform price auctions, the gains from deviation can be limited by pricing infra-marginal units low, via "hockey stick" bidding, with low infra-marginal bids and high marginal bids.

An auction designer can combat this sort of bidding coordination by employing a different rationing rule [Kremer and Nyborg (2004)] or a downward sloping demand curve [LiCalzi and Pavan (2005), McAdams (2007)]. In this instance, a discriminatory auction, in which each supplying unit is paid the amount of its bid, might also induce more competitive bidding.

The ring also has to be able to control entry to prevent outsiders from capturing the benefits of collusion. Asymmetries in information or payoffs can act as a barrier to entry. For example, in auctions of drainage leases, neighbors with informational advantages over non-neighbors have obvious gains from coordination, and they would not have to worry that entry of non-neighbors would dissipate all of the gains. In general, firms with a favorable distribution of values, or those with better information, have an incentive to collude, and they will not want to share the gains with disadvantaged firms that do not pose a significant competitive threat.

8.3. Detection

Collusive schemes are often illegal, and a problem faced by antitrust authorities (such as the U.S. Department of Justice) is to detect their presence. Most cartels encounter operational problems. It is the manner in which a conspiracy deals with these problems that often facilitates the detection of the scheme. In some instances, one can do more than just look for direct evidence of the exertion of market power, such as high and persistent profits. In this subsection, we describe several papers that propose a variety of methods that are designed to distinguish between collusive and competitive bidding.

While statistical evidence that bidders seem to be colluding is not sufficient to establish guilt in a criminal price fixing case, such evidence can be used to guide an investigation. For example, suppose that examination of the data suggests the presence of a bid rigging scheme. The firms might be alerted that they are suspected of colluding, and informed that corporate leniency programs offer much reduced sentences and fines to those who confess first, thereby creating incentives for a "race to the courthouse". Econometric evidence may also be decisive in civil cases, where the burden of proof is less onerous.

Alternatively, antitrust authorities may pursue policies that inhibit successful collusion, by altering characteristics of the economic environment, such as pursuing an active merger policy. Further, the potential suppliers of the ring can alter the rules of the auctions they employ in response to the presence of collusion. For example, the seller can raise the minimum bid, adopt a secret reserve price, or not publicize bids to make it harder for the ring to detect cheating and maintain discipline.

Absent the direct evidence of a conspirator, a conspiracy may be difficult to detect. The constancy of market shares or geographical specialization, while consistent with a collusive assignment, are not in and of themselves evidence of collusion. There is a tendency to view bid rotation or incumbency bidding advantages as evidence of presence of collusion. However, these bidding patterns can be consistent with non-cooperative bidding. For example, bid rotation can be a competitive outcome in auctions of highway construction contracts where bidders' cost functions exhibit decreasing returns to scale. Firms with idle capacity are more likely to win the contract, but having won the contract, are less likely to bid or less likely to win another until some existing contracts are completed [Porter and Zona (1993)].

Similarly, incumbency patterns can reflect unobserved asymmetries among bidders. Those who won in the past may have done so because of location or other advantages that persist through time. Incumbents may have lower costs due to experience, or they may have an advantage with buyers who are reluctant to switch suppliers [Porter and

Zona (1999)]. An empirical challenge is to develop tests that can discriminate between collusive and non-cooperative explanations for rotation or incumbency patterns.

Most early empirical studies identified behavior that is difficult to reconcile with a non-cooperative bidding. An extreme example involves the submission of several identical bids. Mund (1960) and Comanor and Schankerman (1976) describe several instances of identical bids "independently" submitted in government procurement auctions. In 1955, five companies submitted identical sealed bids of \$108,222.58 for an order of 5640 one hundred capsule bottles of antibiotic tetracycline [Scherer and Ross (1990, p. 267)]. The submission of identical bids is virtually a zero probability event in a Bayesian Nash equilibrium if there is any dispersion in information or valuations across bidders.

Baldwin, Marshall and Richard (1997) study U.S. timber English auctions to see whether bidding was competitive or collusive, using structural methods. In an English auction, collusion can reduce the bid necessary to win. Under competition, the winning bid in a button IPV auction equals the second highest valuation. If the ring members are a subset of the potential bidders, the winning bid is affected only if the two highest valuation bidders are conspirators. Then the winning bid is no longer the second-order statistic of the valuations. If the highest non-ring valuation is the kth highest valuation overall, the winning bid will be the kth highest order statistic for $k > 1$, as the serious ring bidder outbids the highest non-conspirator. If the highest valuation bidder is not a ring member, $k = 1$, and the winning bid is the second highest valuation. Note that there is an implicit assumption of efficient collusion, where the cartel designates the member with highest value.

Baldwin, Marshall and Richard do not have firm specific information, and they assume that the valuation distribution is symmetric. Functional form then plays an important role in distinguishing between competition and collusion. In the former case, the winning bid is the second-order statistic from the valuation distribution, whereas in the latter case it is a mixture of the second- and higher-order statistics. One cannot distinguish between competition and collusion without some assumption concerning the functional form of the distribution of values. However, their method could be useful when there are observable bidder asymmetries.

The extension of the method to first price sealed bid auctions would be complicated, as bidding value is no longer a dominant strategy.

If the seller knows that a knockout auction has preceded the sale, it should set a higher reserve price. If the ring is not all-inclusive, it may also want to keep its presence unknown to other bidders, say because new potential bidders may enter the market in response to profitable opportunities. Therefore, it is in the interest of the ring to keep its meeting secret. Ring members may create the appearance of competition in order to avoid detection. Bidding rings may submit phony, or complementary, bids that are designed merely to be lower than the serious bid submitted by the ring. Then only the highest bid from the ring is serious. According to Preston McAfee, one conspiracy was investigated by the U.S. Department of Justice after a bidder submitted an envelope containing his own bid plus his notes from a pre-auction meeting. But phony bids, unlike serious bids, may not be related to the likely profits of the bidder in the event that it wins. Porter and Zona (1993) describe a bidding ring involving highway-paving jobs on Long Island in New York. A subset of the firms participated in pre-auction meetings in order to assign low bidding privileges for specific procurement contracts. The conspirators often submitted complementary bids above the low bid. How does this behavior manifest itself? The fact that the ring was not all-inclusive, plus the presence of phony bids, aids detection.

Porter and Zona split the data in two dimensions, distinguishing cartel from non-cartel bidders (those absent from meetings), and the low bid from a given set of bidders from higher bids from that set. Serious bids should depend on the costs of doing the job. Porter and Zona do not have good contract-specific information, and so they look at the rank distribution of bids within the two groups of firms, as opposed to bid levels. They test whether the identity of the low bidder is determined by same process as the ranking of higher bids. Bids by non-cartel members pass this test, whereas those from the ring do not.

The order of the bids submitted by non-conspirators was related to observable cost measures, such as firm capacity and the utilization rate of that capacity. The lowest non-conspirator bid was most likely to be submitted by the firm with the lowest cost. The lowest conspirator bid was determined by a similar process. In contrast, the order of the higher bids submitted by ring members was not correlated with the same cost measures.

Note that a ring could pass this test, were members aware that the ranking of bids might be examined. For example, suppose the ring is efficient and assigns low bidding rights to the low cost firm in the pre-auction meeting. If the serious bidder intends to bid some multiple of its costs in the auction, then the other conspirators could submit phony bids that were the same multiple of their costs.

Note also that the bid rank test exploits information concerning firms' participation in pre-auction meetings. However, it is not necessary to have this information. The rank test could be performed for any partition of the firms. Bajari and Ye (2003) conduct a similar exercise for several combinations of the larger bidders in Minnesota highway construction auctions, in order to determine who might be colluding.

In addition to creating the appearance of competition, complementary bids may also be intended to manipulate the expectations of the buyer. Feinstein, Block and Nold (1985) note that many agencies estimate the cost of projects on the basis of bidding on similar past projects. Multiple phony bids close to a relatively high bid may lead an unaware buyer to think that costs are higher than they are, and therefore not suspect collusion. Their analysis of data from North Carolina highway construction auctions suggests that contractors were indeed manipulating the information received by the buying agency.

If there is entry, and the entrants are not party to the collusive agreement, then the non-inclusive nature of the cartel may lead to evidence of its existence. As noted above, Porter and Zona distinguish complementary bids by a ring from non-winning bids submitted by a competitive fringe. Hendricks and Porter (1988) describe another example in our study of drainage auctions. Recall that an oil or gas lease is said to be a drainage lease if there has been prior exploration in the area. In that instance, the firms with prior drilling experience will have an informational advantage over firms that have access only to seismic data. In the offshore oil and gas drainage auctions, the identities of the firms owning the mineral rights on neighboring tracts ("neighbors") are known, and their numbers limited by the number of tracts previously sold and explored. Neighbors can gain from coordination, and they do not have to worry that the entry of non-neighbors will dissipate all of the gains. We find that neighbors earn high profits, whereas non-neighbors approximately break even. Despite relatively high overall returns, there is less entry (i.e., fewer bids are submitted per tract) than on wildcat leases, where bidders share similar information sources. The lower entry rates on drainage leases are consistent with asymmetries of information acting as an entry barrier.

If neighbors bid non-cooperatively in the drainage auctions, then there should not be entry by non-neighboring firms, if the latter do not have access to private drilling information. Yet there is entry by non-neighbors. Further, non-neighbors' bids are independent of the number of neighboring firms, rather than a decreasing function as winner's curse considerations would dictate. In addition, there are often multiple bids from the neighbors on a single drainage tract, yet their returns are an increasing function of the number of their bids submitted. Finally, the highest neighbor bid is independent of the number of neighbors, and their average bid level is a decreasing function of this number. This latter fact is consistent with the neighbors submitting only one serious bid, and the probability of submitting complementary bids being an increasing function of the number of neighboring leases in order to create the appearance of competition.

Porter and Zona (1999) provide evidence that the bidding behavior of some Ohio dairies for school milk contracts in the 1980s was more consistent with collusion than with competition. Bidder payoff asymmetries, based on plant locations, matter, as processed milk is costly to ship. Milk's value is low relative to its weight, and therefore competition is localized. Many dairies nevertheless bid for both local school district contracts and more distant school districts. That is, they submit bids relatively near their plants and they also submit bids well beyond their local territories. Porter and Zona's analysis of bidding levels shows that the more distant bids of the three Cincinnati dairies tended to be lower than their local bids, even after controlling for various covariates. In contrast, other dairies' bids are an increasing function of the distance from the school district to the firm's nearest plant. These features of bidding are consistent with a territorial allocation of nearby school districts by dairies with plants in the Cincinnati area to restrict competition, and relatively competitive bidding at more distant locations, which were perhaps outside the area of territorial allocation. If bidding for local districts had been competitive, local bids should have been lower than distant bids, because shipping costs were lower and because the Cincinnati area has many potential local suppliers. The effect of collusion is to relax the constraint on bids by removing marginal rivals. The effect is an "inverted price umbrella", consistent with a local monopoly constrained only by more distant rivals.

8.4. Collusion by sellers

We have discussed collusion among bidders in auctions. There are three other forms of auction market manipulation that may also blunt the incentives to engage in trade, and hence compromise the social value of auctions as a market institution. First, the recent investigation of Sotheby's and Christie's indicates that collusion among bidders is not the only potential antitrust concern in auction markets [e.g., Ashenfelter and Graddy (2004)]. To the extent that the market for providing auction services is concentrated, there may be collusion among auctioneers to raise service fees to potential sellers or buyers.

Second, recent events indicate that eBay auction rules can be manipulated by sellers who unilaterally submit phony or shill bids on their own items, in an attempt to obtain higher prices. Also, groups of sellers can inflate their eBay seller rankings by giving each other glowing reviews for service and product quality. These activities might best be characterized as fraudulent, rather than raising antitrust concerns. But they also reduce faith in the institution.

A third form of manipulation is the corruption of the seller by one or more bidders, or corruption of the auctioneer if he is an agent for the seller. For example, in a sealed bid auction a bidder could bribe the auctioneer to reveal the other bids. Armed with this knowledge, the bidder would not have to bid more than necessary to win. Burguet and Perry (2002) provide an analysis of this situation. Concerns about potential corruption of the bidding process are an important component of auction design, such as public procurement rules that limit the discretion of the auctioneer.

9. Further research issues

In this section, we conclude with a brief discussion of some outstanding issues.

9.1. Scoring rules

One extension of the standard static model of single-unit auctions considers auctions with scoring rules. In some cases, the seller (or the buyer in procurement auctions) is interested in soliciting and evaluating bids on more than one dimension. For example, the state of Louisiana sells its onshore oil and gas leases using an auction in which bidders submit a pair of numbers, a bonus and a royalty rate. The state's scoring rule is secret, but presumably it will select a bid with a high bonus bid if it believes that the likelihood of finding oil is low, and a bid with a high royalty rate if it believes that the likelihood of finding oil is high. In motivating their theoretical study of scoring auctions, Asker and Cantillon (2004) observe that 38 states in the United States evaluate bids for highway construction contracts on the basis of their costs as well as time to completion, weighted by a road user cost. In this case, the procurement authorities announce and commit to a specific scoring rule. The multi-dimensionality of the bid space is often associated with multi-dimensionality of the bidder type space, which greatly complicates the theoretical and empirical analysis.

Athey and Levin (2001) study scale auctions of timber, which employ scoring rules. In these auctions, a bidder submits a price for each species of tree, and her total bid is computed by multiplying these unit prices by the quantities announced by the Forest Service (FS). The tract is awarded to the bidder who is willing to pay the highest total bid, but her payment is based on the realized volumes of each species. Therefore, if she believes that actual relative volumes will differ from those announced by the FS, she has an incentive to skew her bid, allocating more of her total bid to species that she thinks the FS has overestimated. A risk neutral bidder would allocate all of her total bid to overestimated species, unless severely skewed bids are likely to be rejected. The decision is non-trivial if the bidder is risk averse, which seems relevant since the motivation for using scale auctions is to reduce the risk borne by the winners. Athey and Levin characterize equilibrium bidding when a tract has two species. The restriction to two species implies that a bidder's information can be summarized by her estimate of the proportion of one of the two species (ignoring uncertainty about the total volume of wood), so bidder types are one-dimensional. Given certain regularity conditions, the authors show that the skew (i.e., the difference in unit prices of the two species) and the total bid are increasing functions of the bidder's estimate. This theoretical result forms the basis of several predictions that are testable given the availability of the actual species volumes cut. The empirical results confirm the importance of equilibrium analysis.

9.2. Entry and dynamics

To date, researchers have used auctions to study the strategic effects of private information and the relevance of Bayesian Nash equilibrium. We believe that auctions can provide an important testing ground for studying two other important issues in industrial organization: entry and dynamics. Auctions are held repeatedly, and firms have to make frequent entry decisions. Auctions also provide a rich variety of settings (e.g., sealed bid versus oral, private versus common values) for studying entry decisions and outcomes. Recently, Bajari, Benkard and Levin (2005), Pakes, Ostrovsky and Berry (2005), Pesendorfer and Schmidt-Dengler (2004), and Aguirregabiria and Mira (2007) have developed estimators for dynamic games based on the approach taken by Hotz and Miller (1993). These papers make estimation of dynamic oligopoly models much more feasible, although the assumptions under which the estimators are valid can be quite restrictive. In particular, the dynamic game should consist of repeated stage games played in a stationary environment in which the unobservable shocks are independent across players and time. Private value auctions such as highway procurement auctions can come close to satisfying these assumptions.

Most of the empirical literature on auctions assumes that bidders treat auctions as static games, choosing their bids in each auction to maximize profits in that auction. This assumption is plausible in environments where there is no learning, and the time interval between auctions is sufficiently long that the outcome in the current auction is unlikely to influence the state of play in subsequent auctions. The state of play in an auction consists of the set of bidders and their value distributions. However, in some auctions, such as highway procurement contracts, the time between auctions can be quite short, often measured in weeks or even days. In these cases, the presence of capacity constraints or decreasing returns to scale introduces a dynamic element to the game. The bidder who wins the current auction may not have sufficient capacity to bid in the next auction, or it will have costs that are stochastically higher. As a result, the losers in the current auction are more likely to win the next auction. Bidders should anticipate the impact of the current auction outcome on the state of competition in future auctions and bid accordingly. The equilibrium mapping of valuations into bids in the dynamic game is not the same as in the static game, and estimating the distribution of costs under the assumption that bidders behave myopically may yield incorrect results. In particular, bidders may bid less aggressively if they anticipate that winning the current auction will put them at a competitive disadvantage in future auctions.

Jofre-Bonet and Pesendorfer (2003) estimate such a dynamic model using data from highway procurement auctions in California. The average duration between auctions was about 3 days. The state variables for each bidder are its backlog, measured as the dollar amount of work remaining from previous contract awards, the firm's size, measured by the number of plants in the region, and distance from the nearest plant to the project. Bidders' costs and contract characteristics are assumed to be independently distributed conditional on the state variables. In any given auction, bidders who are larger, those with closer plants, and those with less backlog have stochastically lower costs. The state of play changes with bidding outcomes and the location of contracts. Bidders who have an advantage in one auction may be at a disadvantage in another auction. The bidders are restricted to play symmetric Markovian strategies. Symmetry implies that the equilibrium is invariant to permutations of the bidder identities across states of play. The primitives of the model are the conditional cost distributions and the discount rate. Extending the first-order approach of Laffont and Vuong, the authors show that the inverse bid function in the dynamic game is equal to the bid plus a markdown factor that consists of two terms. The first is the usual term that accounts for the level of competition in the current auction. The second term accounts for the incremental impact of the outcome of the current auction on future payoffs. The latter term is weighted by the discount rate. Hence, forward looking bidders in the dynamic game bid less aggressively than myopic bidders.

One problem associated with estimating the dynamic auction model is that the primitives of model are not non-parametrically identified. Jofre-Bonet and Pesendorfer fix the discount rate in order to identify the conditional distribution of costs. This is an important issue, since rational behavior has to be assumed and cannot be tested. In particular, the data cannot distinguish between myopic bidders and forward-looking bidders, although the inferred costs and conditional distribution of costs will depend upon the assumed value of the discount rate. A potential source of identification is variation in the time between auctions. For example, in some inclement regions, highway procurement contracts are auctioned prior to the construction season, and have to be completed before the onset of winter. Hence, bidders in the last auction of the bidding season effectively can bid myopically, and ignore the impact of that auction outcome on future play.

Much of the empirical literature studies auctions under the assumption that the number of bidders is fixed. However, the number of bidders may be determined as part of the equilibrium to the auction game. In practice, participating in an auction can be costly. For example, bidders in timber auctions may have to cruise the stand to determine the type and volumes of available timber; bidders in oil and gas auctions have to conduct and analyze geological surveys, and bidders in highway procurement auctions have to develop cost estimates. When these costs are non-trivial and sunk at the bidding stage, the auction has to provide bidders with the prospect of sufficient rents that they will be able cover their entry costs, at least in expectation. The question then arises: does the auction attract too many or too few bidders? This issue is especially important when bidders are asymmetric since, in this case, the Revenue Equivalence Theorem does not hold and auction design matters. For example, the Athey, Levin and Seira (2004) study of oral and sealed bid timber auctions distinguishes between two kinds of bidders, loggers and mills. They argue that a mill's willingness to pay for cutting rights is stochastically greater than that of loggers, since the latter has to sell its logs to a mill. In open, ascending price auctions, the bidder with the highest valuation wins but, in first-price, sealed bid auctions, this need not be the outcome. As a result, loggers are more likely to participate, and win, in a sealed bid auction than in an open auction.

Standard market models use entry decisions by firms to draw inferences about post-entry behavior. In auctions, post-entry behavior is observable and can help identify entry costs and behavior. For example, Athey, Levin and Seira examine the effect of potential collusion by mills on entry rates of loggers; Athey and Levin (2005) and Krasnokutskaya and Seim (2005) examine the effects on entry of policies that exclude or subsidize certain classes of bidders. A fundamental problem that arises in estimating entry models is the multiplicity of equilibria. If entry is modeled as a simultaneous move, complete information game, then the entry game typically has many asymmetric pure strategy equilibria in which some firms are certain to enter and others stay out. There are also mixed strategy equilibria in which participation is random. The multiplicity of equilibria implies that the mapping from the unobservables to outcomes is not unique, and so the likelihood function is not well defined. The literature offers a number of ways of modifying the model to generates a well-defined likelihood function for the data: Bresnahan and Reiss (1990, 1991) and Berry (1992) restrict the payoffs of the players so that the number of entrants in the set of pure strategy equilibria is unique, and define the likelihood function in terms of this event; Seim (2005) "purifies" the mixed strategy equilibrium as an (often unique) Bayesian Nash equilibrium by assuming that players have different and private entry costs; Bajari, Hong and Ryan (2004) append a set of equilibrium selection rules to the model and estimate the joint probability distribution over outcomes and selection rules.[4] But, in auctions,

[4] Ciliberto and Tamer (2004) develop an estimation approach that allows for multiple equilibria but may sacrifice point identification. They use the theoretical entry model to define upper and lower bounds on the probabilities of the outcomes, and then estimate the parameters of the model by minimizing the distance between the empirical frequencies and these bounds.

the specific rules governing entry and bidding decisions in auctions may operate as a selection rule. Bidders may find it easier to coordinate on an asymmetric equilibrium in oral auctions where the bidders have to register and show up to bid than in sealed bid auctions, where the bidders mail or phone in their bids. In the latter case, the mixed strategy equilibrium may be a better description of entry behavior. For example, Athey, Levin and Seira assume that loggers play a mixed entry strategy, since the data are more consistent with an equilibrium in which too many or too few bidders enter ex post. Similarly, Li (2005) considers structural estimation of an IPV model with a binding reserve price, and entry determined by a symmetric mixed strategy equilibrium.

The structure of eBay auctions, and the availability of data from these auctions, gives researchers an opportunity to study participation and bidding decisions in a dynamic context. Sellers in an eBay auction choose the duration of the auction, but their choices are restricted to 1, 3, 5, 7 or 10 days. The discreteness of the duration menu, combined with the random arrival of sellers, means that the auctions for a product like TI-83 calculators or the Compaq Ipaq H3850 personal digital assistant can be ordered sequentially by their closing times. In fact, eBay often uses this ordering in presenting the choice set of auctions to potential bidders. A number of studies [e.g., Roth and Ockenfels (2002), Bajari and Hortacsu (2003)] have shown that most bidders "snipe", that is, they wait until the closing time of an auction to bid. The winning bidders usually then exit, since most bidders have unit demands. Losing bidders either exit (e.g., buy the item at the posted price in a buy-it-now auction or at a retail store) or bid again in a subsequent auction. If they bid again, and depending to some extent on the length of the time interval between closing times, losing bidders sometimes choose to participate in the same auction but more frequently participate in different auctions. In other words, most losing bidders do not participate in the next-to-close auction. The randomness in the participation decisions may be due in part to unobserved product heterogeneity, but more likely it reflects randomness in participation costs. A losing bidder has to wait until the next closing time to submit a bid, and the opportunity cost of participating in an auction will vary over time. The bidder may decide that he is better off coming back later in the day to submit a bid. Thus, to a first approximation, eBay auctions for a given product are a sequence of second-price, sealed bid auctions in which bidders arrive randomly and participate randomly.

As in the case of the static models, the first step of the research program consists of characterizing the Markov perfect equilibrium (or equilibria) to the dynamic game. This task is difficult since, in contrast to the highway auctions, the items in eBay auctions are close substitutes. If the intervals between auction closing times is short, losing bidders can learn about their rivals' valuations from their bids. The possibility for learning gives bidders a strategic incentive to bid in ways that make it difficult for rivals to draw inferences. The second step is to estimate the primitives of the model (the bidders' arrival and exit rates, the distribution of valuations, and the distribution of participation costs) treating the participation and bid data as the outcome of equilibrium play. The problems inherent in extending the structural program to dynamic auctions like eBay may prove intractable. However, the normative and positive goals of the research program are worthy of the effort.

We end this survey by noting that the theoretical and empirical literature surveyed in this chapter has emphasized the role of private information as the main source of rents in auctions, and the key determinant of strategic play. However, in many auctions, bidder asymmetries may be a more important source of market power. For example, Moshkin, Porter and Zona (2005) argue that dairies' bids to supply milk products to school districts in the Cincinnati area are largely determined by the distances between the diaries' plants and the schools, as well as other factors that are known by their rivals. They model the auction as a Bertrand pricing game in which costs are common knowledge and, in equilibrium, the lowest cost supplier wins the market by bidding the cost of the marginal rival. Collusion among bidders will affect the identity of the marginal rival. (They also consider a more general setting where fixed entry costs are private information, and where there may be some uncertainty about who will be awarded the contract.) Cost differences among suppliers is the traditional explanation for market power. Since bidder asymmetries in private value auctions can be accommodated using the first-order approach developed by Laffont and Vuong, it is possible to examine the relative importance of private information and bidder asymmetries as sources of rent.

Acknowledgements

We are grateful to Mark Armstrong, Phil Haile, Jakub Kastl, Paul Klemperer and Harry Paarsch for helpful comments.

References

Aguirregabiria, V., Mira, P. (2007). "Sequential estimation of dynamic discrete games". Econometrica 75, 1–54.

Ashenfelter, O. (1989). "How auctions work for wine and art". Journal of Economic Perspectives 3, 23–36.

Ashenfelter, O., Genesove, D. (1992). "Testing for price anomalies in real estate auctions". American Economic Review Papers and Proceedings 82, 501–505.

Ashenfelter, O., Graddy, K. (2003). "Auctions and the price of art". Journal of Economic Literature 41, 763–787.

Ashenfelter, O., Graddy, K. (2004). "Anatomy of the rise and fall of a price-fixing conspiracy, auctions at Sotheby's and Christie's". Mimeo. Princeton University.

Asker, J., Cantillon, E. (2004). "Properties of scoring auctions". Mimeo. Harvard University.

Athey, S. (2001). "Single crossing properties and the existence of pure strategy equilibria in games of incomplete information". Econometrica 69, 861–889.

Athey, S., Bagwell, K. (2001). "Optimal collusion with private information". RAND Journal of Economics 32, 428–465.

Athey, S., Haile, P. (2002). "Identification of standard auction models". Econometrica 70, 2107–2140.

Athey, S., Haile, P. (2008). "Nonparametric approaches to auctions". In: Heckman, J., Leamer, E. (Eds.). Handbook of Econometrics, vol. 6. Elsevier, Amsterdam. In press.

Athey, S., Levin, J. (2001). "Information and competition in U.S. Forest Service timber auctions". Journal of Political Economy 109, 375–417.
Athey, S., Levin, J. (2005). "Set-asides and subsidies in auctions". Mimeo. Stanford University.
Athey, S., Bagwell, K., Sanchirico, C. (2004). "Collusion and price rigidity". Review of Economic Studies 71, 317–349.
Athey, S., Levin, J., Seira, E. (2004). "Comparing open and sealed bid auctions: Theory and evidence from timber auctions". Mimeo. Stanford University.
Ausubel, L., Cramton, P. (2002). "Demand reduction and inefficiency in multi-unit auction". Mimeo. University of Maryland.
Avery, C. (1998). "Strategic jump bidding in English auctions". Review of Economic Studies 65, 185–210.
Bajari, P. (1997). "The first price auction with asymmetric bidders: Theory and applications". Unpublished Ph.D. Thesis. University of Minnesota.
Bajari, P. (1998). "Econometrics of sealed-bid auctions". Proceedings of the Business and Economic Statistics Section of the American Statistical Association, 41–49.
Bajari, P., Hortacsu, A. (2003). "The winner's curse, reserve prices, and endogenous entry: Empirical insights from eBay auctions". RAND Journal of Economics 34, 329–355.
Bajari, P., Hortacsu, A. (2004). "Economic insights from Internet auctions". Journal of Economic Literature 42, 457–486.
Bajari, P., Hortacsu, A. (2005). "Are structural estimates of auction models reasonable? Evidence from experimental data". Journal of Political Economy 113, 703–741.
Bajari, P., Ye, L. (2003). "Deciding between competition and collusion". Review of Economics and Statistics 85, 971–989.
Bajari, P., Benkard, L., Levin, J. (2005). "Estimating dynamic models of imperfect competition". Mimeo. Stanford University.
Bajari, P., Hong, H., Ryan, S. (2004). "Identification and estimation of discrete games of complete information". Mimeo. Duke University.
Bajari, P., Houghton, S., Tadelis, S. (2006). "Bidding for incomplete contracts: An empirical analysis". Mimeo. University of Michigan.
Baldwin, L., Marshall, R., Richard, J.F. (1997). "Bidder collusion at forest service timber sales". Journal of Political Economy 105, 657–699.
Beggs, A., Graddy, K. (1997). "Declining values and the afternoon effect: Evidence from art auctions". RAND Journal of Economics 28, 544–565.
Berry, S. (1992). "Estimation of a model of entry in the airline industry". Econometrica 60, 889–917.
Bikhchandani, S., Huang, C. (1993). "The economics of treasury securities markets". Journal of Economic Perspectives 7, 117–134.
Bikhchandani, S., Riley, J. (1991). "Equilibria in open common value auctions". Journal of Economic Theory 53, 101–130.
Bikhchandani, S., Haile, P., Riley, J. (2002). "Symmetric separating equilibria in English auctions". Games and Economic Behavior 38, 19–27.
Black, J., de Meza, D. (1992). "Systematic price differences between successive auctions are no anomaly". Journal of Economics & Management Strategy 1, 607–628.
Bresnahan, T., Reiss, P. (1990). "Entry in monopoly markets". Review of Economic Studies 57, 531–553.
Bresnahan, T., Reiss, P. (1991). "Empirical models of discrete games". Journal of Econometrics 48, 57–81.
Bulow, J., Klemperer, P. (2002). "Prices and the winner's curse". RAND Journal of Economics 33, 1–21.
Burguet, R., Perry, M. (2002). "Bribery and favoritism by auctioneers in sealed bid auctions". Mimeo. Rutgers University.
Cantillon, E., Pesendorfer, M. (2004). "Combination bidding in multi-unit auctions". Mimeo. London School of Economics.
Capen, E., Clapp, R., Campbell, W. (1971). "Competitive bidding in high-risk situations". Journal of Petroleum Technology 23, 641–653.
Castellanos, S., Oviedo, M. (2004). "Optimal bidding in the Mexican treasury securities primary auctions: Results from a structural econometric approach". Mimeo. Yale University.

Chernozhukov, V., Hong, H. (2004). "Likelihood estimation and inference in a class of nonregular econometric models". Econometrica 72, 1445–1480.
Ciliberto, F., Tamer, E. (2004). "Market structure and multiple equilibria in airline markets". Mimeo. Northwestern University.
Comanor, W., Schankerman, M. (1976). "Identical bids and cartel behavior". Bell Journal of Economics 7, 281–286.
Cramton, P., Palfrey, T. (1995). "Ratifiable mechanisms: Learning from disagreement". Games and Economic Behavior 10, 255–283.
Cramton, P., Schwartz, J. (2000). "Collusive bidding: Lessons from the FCC spectrum auctions". Journal of Regulatory Economics 17, 229–252.
Donald, S., Paarsch, H. (1993). "Piecewise pseudo-maximum likelihood estimation in empirical models of auctions". International Economic Review 34, 121–148.
Donald, S., Paarsch, H. (1996). "Identification, estimation, and testing in parametric empirical models of auctions within the independent private values paradigm". Econometric Theory 12, 517–567.
Donald, S., Paarsch, H. (2002). "Superconsistent estimation and inference in structural econometric models using extreme order statistics". Journal of Econometrics 109, 305–340.
Donald, S., Paarsch, H., Robert, J. (2006). "An empirical model of the multi-unit, sequential clock auction". Journal of Applied Econometrics 21, 1221–1247.
Elyakime, B., Laffont, J.J., Loisel, P., Vuong, Q. (1994). "First-price, sealed-bid auctions with secret reservation prices". Annales d'Economie et de Statistique 34, 115–141.
Engelbrecht-Wiggans, R., Milgrom, P., Weber, R. (1983). "Competitive bidding and proprietary information". Journal of Mathematical Economics 11, 161–169.
Feinstein, J., Block, M., Nold, F. (1985). "Asymmetric information and collusive behavior in auction markets". American Economic Review 75, 441–460.
Fevrier, P., Preget, R., Visser, M. (2004). "Econometrics of share auctions". Mimeo. University of Chicago.
Gertner, R. (1995). "Revenue and efficiency differences between sequential and simultaneous multiple-unit auctions with limited competition". Mimeo. University of Chicago.
Graham, D., Marshall, R. (1987). "Collusive bidder behavior at single-object second-price and English auctions". Journal of Political Economy 95, 1217–1239.
Guerre, E., Perrigne, I., Vuong, Q. (2000). "Optimal nonparametric estimation of first-price auctions". Econometrica 68, 525–574.
Haile, P. (2001). "Auctions with resale markets: An application to U.S. Forest Service timber sales". American Economic Review 91, 399–427.
Haile, P., Tamer, E. (2003). "Inference in an incomplete model of English auctions". Journal of Political Economy 111, 1–51.
Haile, P., Hong, H., Shum, M. (2004). "Nonparametric tests for common values in first-price sealed bid auctions". Mimeo. Yale University.
Hansen, R. (1986). "Sealed-bid versus open auctions: The evidence". Economic Inquiry 24, 125–142.
Harrington, J. (2005). "Detecting cartels". Mimeo. Johns Hopkins University.
Harrison, G., List, J. (2004). "Field experiments". Journal of Economic Literature 62, 1009–1055.
Hendricks, K., Paarsch, H. (1995). "A survey of recent empirical work concerning auctions". Canadian Journal of Economics 28, 315–338.
Hendricks, K., Porter, R. (1988). "An empirical study of an auction with asymmetric information". American Economic Review 78, 865–883.
Hendricks, K., Porter, R. (1989). "Collusion in auctions". Annales d'Economie et de Statistique 16–17, 217–230.
Hendricks, K., Pinkse, J., Porter, R. (2003). "Empirical implications of equilibrium bidding in first-price, symmetric, common value auctions". Review of Economic Studies 70, 115–145.
Hendricks, K., Porter, R., Boudreau, B. (1987). "Information, returns and bidding behavior in OCS auctions: 1954–1969". Journal of Industrial Economics 35, 517–542.
Hendricks, K., Porter, R., Tan, G. (1993). "Optimal selling strategies for oil and gas leases with an informed buyer". American Economic Review Papers and Proceedings 83, 234–239.

Hendricks, K., Porter, R., Tan, G. (2006). "Bidding rings and the winners curse". Mimeo. Northwestern University.

Hendricks, K., Porter, R., Wilson, C. (1994). "Auctions for oil and gas leases with an informed bidder and a random reservation price". Econometrica 62, 1415–1444.

Hirano, K., Porter, J. (2003). "Asymptotic efficiency in parametric structural models with parameter-dependent support". Econometrica 71, 1307–1338.

Holt, C. (1980). "Competitive bidding for contracts under alternative auction procedures". Journal of Political Economy 88, 433–445.

Hong, H., Shum, M. (2002). "Increasing competition and the winner's curse: Evidence from procurement". Review of Economic Studies 69, 871–898.

Hong, H., Shum, M. (2003). "Econometric models of ascending auctions". Journal of Econometrics 112, 327–358.

Hortacsu, A. (2002). "Mechanism choice and strategic bidding in divisible good auctions: An empirical analysis of the Turkish treasury auction market". Mimeo. University of Chicago.

Hotz, J., Miller, R. (1993). "Conditional choice probabilities and the estimation of dynamic models". Review of Economic Studies 60, 497–531.

Jehiel, P., Moldovanu, B. (2003). "Auctions with downstream interaction among buyers". RAND Journal of Economics 31, 768–791.

Jofre-Bonet, M., Pesendorfer, M. (2003). "Estimation of a dynamic auction game". Econometrica 71, 1443–1489.

Kagel, J. (1995). "Auctions: A survey of experimental research". In: Kagel, J., Roth, A. (Eds.), Handbook of Experimental Economics. Princeton Univ. Press, Princeton, NJ, pp. 501–585.

Kastl, J. (2005). "Discrete bids and empirical inference in divisible goods auctions". Mimeo. Northwestern University.

Klemperer, P. (1998). "Auctions with almost common values: The "wallet game" and its applications". European Economic Review 42, 757–769.

Klemperer, P. (2004). Auctions: Theory and Practice. Princeton Univ. Press, Princeton, NJ.

Krasnokutskaya, E. (2004). "Identification and estimation in highway procurement auctions under unobserved auction heterogeneity". Mimeo. University of Pennsylvania.

Krasnokutskaya, E., Seim, K. (2005). "Bid preference programs and participation in highway procurement programs". Mimeo. University of Pennsylvania.

Kremer, I., Nyborg, K. (2004). "Divisible-good auctions: The role of allocation rules". RAND Journal of Economics 35, 147–159.

Krishna, V. (2002). Auction Theory. Academic Press, San Diego.

Laffont, J.J. (1997). "Game theory and empirical economics: The case of auction data". European Economic Review 4, 1–35.

Laffont, J.J., Vuong, Q. (1996). "Structural analysis of auction data". American Economic Review Papers and Proceedings 86, 414–420.

Laffont, J.J., Ossard, H., Vuong, Q. (1995). "Econometrics of first-price auctions". Econometrica 63, 953–980.

Lebrun, B. (1996). "Existence of an equilibrium in first price auctions". Economic Theory 7, 421–443.

Lebrun, B. (1999). "First price auctions in the asymmetric N bidder case". International Economic Review 40, 125–142.

Li, T. (2005). "Econometrics of first-price auctions with entry and binding reservation prices". Journal of Econometrics 126, 173–200.

Li, T., Perrigne, I., Vuong, Q. (2000). "Conditionally independent private information in OCS wildcat auctions". Journal of Econometrics 98, 129–161.

LiCalzi, M., Pavan, A. (2005). "Tilting the supply schedule to enhance competition in uniform price auctions". European Economic Review 49, 227–250.

Mailath, G., Zemsky, P. (1991). "Collusion in second price auctions with heterogeneous bidders". Games and Economic Behavior 4, 467–486.

Marshall, R., Marx, L. (2004). "Bidder collusion". Mimeo. Duke University.
Maskin, E., Riley, J. (2000a). "Asymmetric auctions". Review of Economic Studies 67, 413–438.
Maskin, E., Riley, J. (2000b). "Equilibrium in sealed high bid auctions". Review of Economic Studies 67, 439–454.
Matthews, S. (1980). "Risk aversion and the efficiency of first and second price auctions". Mimeo. Northwestern University.
McAdams, D. (2007). "Adjustable supply in uniform-price auctions: Non-commitment as a strategic tool". Economics Letters 95, 48–53.
McAfee, P., McMillan, J. (1987). "Auctions and bidding". Journal of Economic Literature 25, 699–738.
McAfee, P., McMillan, J. (1992). "Bidding rings". American Economic Review 82, 579–599.
McAfee, P., Vincent, D. (1992). "Updating the reserve price in common-value auctions". American Economic Review Papers and Proceedings 82, 512–518.
McAfee, P., Vincent, D. (1993). "The declining price anomaly". Journal of Economic Theory 60, 191–212.
McAfee, P., Quan, D., Vincent, D. (2002). "How to set minimum acceptable bids, with an application to real estate auctions". Journal of Industrial Economics 50, 391–416.
McFadden, D. (1989). "A method of simulated moments for estimation of multinomial discrete response models without numerical integration". Econometrica 57, 995–1026.
Meade, W., Sorenson, P., Jones, R., Moseidjord, A. (1980). "Competition and performance in OCS oil and gas lease sales and development 1954–1969". Final Report to U.S. Geological Survey, Reston, VA.
Milgrom, P. (1981a). "Good news and bad news: Representation theorems and applications". Bell Journal of Economics 12, 380–391.
Milgrom, P. (1981b). "Rational expectations, information acquisition, and competitive bidding". Econometrica 49, 921–943.
Milgrom, P. (1987). "Auction theory". In: Bewley, T. (Ed.), Advances in Economic Theory: Fifth World Congress. Cambridge Univ. Press, Cambridge.
Milgrom, P. (2004). Putting Auction Theory to Work. Cambridge Univ. Press, Cambridge.
Milgrom, P., Weber, R. (1982). "A theory of auctions and competitive bidding". Econometrica 50, 1089–1122.
Milgrom, P., Weber, R. (2000). "A theory of auctions and competitive bidding, II". In: Klemperer, P. (Ed.), The Economic Theory of Auctions. Edward Elgar, Cheltenham, UK.
Moshkin, N., Porter, R., Zona, D. (2005). "Bid rigging in school milk auctions: Evidence from Ohio". Mimeo. Northwestern University.
Mund, V. (1960). "Identical bid prices". Journal of Political Economy 68, 150–169.
Myerson, R. (1981). "Optimal auction design". Mathematics of Operations Research 6, 58–73.
Ortega Reichert, A. (1968). "Models for competitive bidding under uncertainty". Ph.D. Dissertation. Stanford University.
Paarsch, H. (1992). "Deciding between the common and private value paradigms in empirical models of auctions". Journal of Econometrics 51, 191–215.
Paarsch, H. (1997). "Deriving an estimate of the optimal reserve price: An application to British Columbia timber sales". Journal of Econometrics 78, 333–357.
Paarsch, H., Hong, H. (2006). An Introduction to the Structural Econometrics of Auction Data. MIT Press, Cambridge, MA.
Pakes, A., Pollard, D. (1989). "Simulation and the asymptotics of optimization estimators". Econometrica 57, 1027–1057.
Pakes, A., Ostrovsky, M., Berry, S. (2005). "Simple estimators for the parameters of discrete dynamic games, (with entry/exit examples)". Mimeo. Harvard University.
Pesendorfer, M. (2000). "A study of collusion in first-price auctions". Review of Economic Studies 67, 381–411.
Pesendorfer, M., Schmidt-Dengler, P. (2004). "Least squares estimators for dynamic games". Mimeo. London School of Economics.
Pinkse, J., Tan, G. (2005). "The affiliation effect in first-price auctions". Econometrica 73, 263–277.
Porter, R. (1992). "Review of anatomy of an auction: Rare books at Ruxley lodge 1919 by Arthur Freeman and Janet Ing Freeman". Journal of Political Economy 100, 433–436.

Porter, R. (1995). "The role of information in U.S. offshore oil and gas lease auctions". Econometrica 63, 1–27.

Porter, R. (2005). "Detecting collusion". Review of Industrial Organization 26, 147–167.

Porter, R., Zona, D. (1993). "Detection of bid rigging in procurement auctions". Journal of Political Economy 101, 518–538.

Porter, R., Zona, D. (1999). "Ohio school milk markets: An analysis of bidding". RAND Journal of Economics 30, 263–288.

Riley, J., Samuelson, W. (1981). "Optimal auctions". American Economic Review 71, 381–392.

Robinson, M. (1985). "Collusion and the choice of auction". RAND Journal of Economics 16, 141–145.

Roth, A., Ockenfels, A. (2002). "Last minute bidding and the rules for ending second-price auctions: Evidence from eBay and Amazon auctions on the Internet". American Economic Review 92, 1093–1103.

Scherer, F.M., Ross, D. (1990). Industrial Market Structure and Economic Performance, third ed. Houghton Miflin, Boston, MA.

Seim, K. (2005). "An empirical model of firm entry with endogenous product-type choices". Mimeo. Stanford University.

Shneyerov, A. (2005). "An empirical study of auction revenue rankings: The case of municipal bonds". Mimeo. University of British Columbia.

Smith, R. (1961). "The incredible electrical conspiracy". Fortune 63, 132–180;
Smith, R., "The incredible electrical conspiracy". Fortune 63 (1961) 161–224.

Van den Berg, G., van der Klaauw, B. (2000). "Structural analysis of Dutch flower auctions". Mimeo. Free University Amsterdam.

Vickrey, W. (1961). "Counterspeculation, auctions and competitive sealed tenders". Journal of Finance 16, 8–37.

Vickrey, W. (1962). "Auctions and bidding games". In: Recent Advances in Game Theory. In: Princeton Conference Series, vol. 29. Princeton Univ. Press, Princeton, NJ, pp. 15–27.

Wilson, R. (1977). "A bidding model of perfect competition". Review of Economic Studies 44, 511–518.

Wilson, R. (1993). "Strategic analysis of auctions". In: Aumann, R., Hart, S. (Eds.), Handbook of Game Theory. North-Holland, Amsterdam.

Wilson, R. (1998). "Sequential equilibria of asymmetric ascending auctions". Economic Theory 12, 433–440.

Wolak, F. (2003). "Identification and estimation of cost functions using observed bid data: An application to electricity". In: Dewatripont, M., Hansen, L., Turnovsky, S. (Eds.), Advances in Econometrics: Theory and Applications. In: Eighth World Congress, vol. 2. Cambridge Univ. Press, Cambridge.

Wolak, F. (2005). "Quantifying the supply side benefits from forward contracting in wholesale electricity markets". Mimeo. Stanford University.

Wolfram, C. (1998). "Strategic bidding in a multi-unit auction: An empirical analysis of bids to supply electricity in England and Wales". RAND Journal of Economics 29, 703–725.

Wolfram, C. (1999). "Measuring duopoly power in the British electricity spot market". American Economic Review 89, 805–826.

Chapter 33

A PRIMER ON FORECLOSURE[1]

PATRICK REY

University of Toulouse (IDEI and GREMAQ)

JEAN TIROLE

University of Toulouse (IDEI and GREMAQ) and MIT

Contents

[1] Financial support for the initial research that eventually led to this chapter was provided by a grant from BellSouth New Zealand. The authors are grateful to Mark Armstrong, Paul Seabright, Chris Snyder, John Vickers and Lucy White for helpful comments on a previous draft.

Handbook of Industrial Organization, Volume 3
Edited by M. Armstrong and R. Porter

DOI: 10.1016/S1573-448X(06)03033-0

Abstract

This chapter analyzes the private rationale and the social costs and benefits of market foreclosure, here defined as a firm's restriction of output in one market through the use of market power in another market. The chapter first focuses on *vertical foreclosure* (in which full access to a bottleneck input is denied to competitors) and provides an overview of the theory of access to an essential facility in an unregulated environment. It considers a wide array of contexts: possibility of bypass of the bottleneck facility, upstream vs downstream location of this facility, and various exclusionary activities such as vertical integration and exclusive dealing. It identifies a number of robust conclusions as to the social and private costs and benefits of foreclosure. The chapter then turns to *horizontal foreclosure*, where the monopoly good is sold directly to the end-users, and analyzes recent theories of anti-competitive bundling aimed at reducing competition in the adjacent markets or at protecting the monopoly market. Finally, the chapter tackles exclusive customer contracts and discusses potential efficiency defenses for exclusionary behavior.

Keywords

Essential facility, Foreclosure, Vertical integration, Tie-ins, Antitrust

JEL classification: D4, K21, L42

1. Introduction

1.1. What is foreclosure?

This chapter provides a framework for the analysis of the private rationale as well as the social costs and benefits of market foreclosure. According to the received definition, foreclosure refers to a dominant firm's denial of proper access to an essential good it produces, with the intent of extending monopoly power from that segment of the market (the bottleneck segment) to an adjacent segment (the potentially competitive segment). Foreclosure can arise when the bottleneck good is used as an input (e.g., an infrastructure) by a potentially competitive downstream industry, or when it is sold directly to customers, who use the good in conjunction with other, perhaps complementary goods (e.g., system goods or aftersale services). In the former case, the firms in the competitive segment that are denied access to the essential input are said to be "squeezed" or to be suffering a secondary line injury. In the latter case, a tie may similarly distort or even eliminate effective competition from the rivals in the complementary segment.

An input produced by a dominant firm is essential if it cannot be cheaply duplicated by users who are denied access to it. Examples of inputs that have been deemed essential by antitrust authorities include a stadium, a railroad bridge or station, a harbor, a power transmission or a local telecommunications network, an operating system software and a computer reservation system.[2] The foreclosure or essential facility doctrine states that the owner of such an essential facility has an incentive to monopolize complementary or downstream segments as well. This doctrine was first elaborated in the U.S. in *Terminal Railroad Association v. U.S.* (1912), in which a coalition of railroad operators formed a joint venture owning a key bridge across the Mississippi River and the approaches and terminal in Saint Louis and excluded non-member competitors. The Supreme Court ruled that this practice was a violation of the Sherman Act. A version of the doctrine was invoked by the European Court of Justice in the celebrated *United Brands* (1978) decision, in which it held that United Brands Corporation enjoyed substantial market power in the banana market in Europe and engaged in exclusionary practices in related markets (distribution, ripening).[3]

Foreclosure varies in extent. It can be complete, as in the case of a refusal to deal (equivalently, an extravagant price can serve as "constructive refusal") or in the case of technical integration between complementary goods, or partial, as when the bottleneck owner favors some firms or products in the adjacent market to the detriment of other competitors. It can also be performed in various ways:

– The bottleneck owner can *integrate* with one or several firms in the complementary segment. For example, computer reservations systems were developed by major

[2] Extensive legal discussions of foreclosure can be found in Areeda (1981) and, especially, Hancher (1995).

[3] More recently still, the *Queensland Wire* case (which involved vertical integration and a vertical price squeeze) is perhaps the first such Australian case in 1989. The *Clear* case provides an example of application of the doctrine in New Zealand, in which the incumbent's local network is the essential facility.

airlines. Before the Civil Aeronautics Board (CAB)'s 1984 famous decision, it was perceived that smaller airlines, especially those competing head-to-head with the integrated firms, had to pay a high price for access to the reservation systems and received poor display of their flights on the travel agents' screens (a key competitive disadvantage given that most travel agents do not browse much through screen displays). The CAB attempted to impose equal access in price and quality to what were perceived to be essential facilities, namely computer reservation systems,[4] but did not demand the major airlines' divestiture of their computer reservation systems. In contrast, in the same year, U.S. courts forced AT&T to divest its regional operating companies (known as the RBOCs). Other examples of forced vertical separation include the UK brewing industry, in which, following an investigation by the Monopoly and Mergers Commission in 1989, the "majors" were instructed to divest pubs,[5] and the high voltage electricity transmission systems, that have been separated from generation in most countries.

The integrated firm can *refuse to deal* with potential competitors. Relatedly, it may make the bottleneck good incompatible with competitors' products or technologies, or engage in *tie-in* and refuse to unbundle, thereby denying access to the essential facility. For example, in *Port of Genoa* (1991), the European Court of Justice held that the harbor was an essential facility and that its use should not be reserved to the undertaking managing it[6]; in the U.S., *Otter Tail Power Co v. United States* (1973) established a duty for a vertically integrated power company to supply other companies. Famous tie-in cases in the U.S. include *International Salt* (1947), in which the producer of salt dispenser equipment bundled salt with the equipment, and *Chicken Delight* (1971), in which the franchiser tied various inputs (ingredients, cooking equipment) with the franchising contract. In Europe, the Commission charged IBM in 1980 for abusing its dominant position in CPUs for large mainframe computers, by tying other elements such as main memory or basic software. In *Tetra Pak* (1994), cartons were tied to the filling machines. On both sides of the Atlantic, a number of cases have also surfaced in the context of "after-markets", when a durable good manufacturer with market power excludes competitors from providing repairs, maintenance or spare parts.[7]

– In the presence of economies of scope or scale calling for cooperation among firms in the same market, a dominant group of firms may put its competitors at a disadvantage

[4] Similarly in 1988, the European Commission imposed a fine on Sabena for denying access to its computer reservation system to the price-cutting airline London European.

[5] Snyder (1994) performs an event study analysis of this industry and provides some evidence of non-competitive behavior. Slade (1998) however stresses that the vertical separation led to softer competition. These "beer orders" have been repealed in 2002.

[6] A related case is the *Sealink* decision (1992), where the same company operated ferry services and controlled the harbor.

[7] See, e.g., in Europe, *Hugin v. Commission* (1979), in which a manufacturer refused to supply spare parts for its cash machines and the Commission held that the manufacturer had a dominant position on its own spare parts. A hotly debated case in the U.S. is *Kodak*, who refused to sell replacement parts for photocopiers to owners unless the latter agreed not to use independent service organizations [see Borenstein, MacKie-Mason and Netz (1995) and Shapiro (1995) for a discussion of this case].

by *refusing to cooperate*. Famous cases include *Aspen Skying Co v. Aspen Highlands Skying Co* (1985),[8] in which the common owners of three mountains on the site discontinued the All-Aspen ski passes which enabled skiers to use these mountains as well a fourth, independently owned, one; and *Associated Press v. United States* (1945), in which members of the newspapers' cooperative could block membership by competing newspapers. Such cases have obvious implications for network industries.[9]

– Short of integration, the bottleneck owner can grant *exclusivity* to a subset of firms or *tie* its essential product with selected products on the complementary segment, and thus de facto exclude their rivals. For example, the Court held that the granting of exclusive rights by *Auckland Regional Authority* to Avis and Hertz for operating in the Auckland airport terminal violated sections 27 and 36 of the New Zealand Commerce Act. Similarly, the European Commission has investigated the 65 year contract between Eurotunnel and the incumbent operators, British Rail and SNCF, allocating the entire capacity available for passenger and freight rail transport to the two companies.

– Another instrument in the "forecloser's" toolbox is *second- and third-degree price discrimination*. Third-degree discrimination consists in charging different (cost-adjusted) prices to different customers. It generalizes exclusivity or tying arrangements by favoring some customers over the others, but gives the bottleneck owner some flexibility in serving discriminated-against customers. Even if outright third-degree price discrimination is prohibited, the bottleneck owner may be able to duplicate it in an apparently anonymous way, that is through second-degree price discrimination. For example, a loyalty program offered to all or rebates based on the rate of growth of purchases may target specific customers even though they formally are available to all customers. Similarly, substantial price discounts may allow the survival of only a few customers; for instance, a large enough fixed (that is, consumption independent) fee transforms a potentially competitive downstream industry into a natural monopoly industry. And in the case of complementary goods, conditional discounts (also known as "mixed bundling") can allow the firm to discriminate de facto among consumers according to their preferences for the different varieties of products. Such considerations (besides many others) played a role in the process of enacting the Robinson–Patman Act in the U.S. in 1936.[10] There was in particular a concern that independent wholesalers or retailers might not be able to compete with powerful chains buying their supplies at favorable prices.

[8] See, e.g., Ahern (1994).

[9] In *Aer Lingus* (1992), the European Commission condemned Aer Lingus for refusing to interline (a technique enabling the marketing of single tickets for combined flights) with British Midland.

[10] Interestingly, in *Hoffman La Roche*, the European Court of Justice upheld the Commission's condemnation of purchasing agreements or loyalty rebates while asserting the company's right to offer volume discounts as long as they are extended to all customers.

1.2. Remedies

Assuming that the intellectual argument underlying the rationale for and the detrimental impact of foreclosure is compelling, one must still design an informationally feasible policy that either reduces the incentive to exclude or impedes the impact of foreclosure, and verify that the cure has no strong side-effect.

A number of remedies have been considered by competition law practitioners. While we clearly should not restrict ourselves to the existing set of policies and should attempt to design better ones, it is useful to review the most prominent ones. It is convenient to group existing policies into five categories:

– *Structural policies.* Structural policies such as divestitures and line of business restrictions are often considered as a last resort, as they may involve substantial transaction costs of disentangling activities and may jeopardize the benefits of integration. Yet, in specific instances (as for the AT&T 1984 divestiture) policy makers may come to the conclusion that it is hard to design proper rules for access to the integrated bottleneck, and that alternative methods of foreclosure can be prevented under vertical separation.

Milder forms of vertical separation are sometimes considered; for instance, antitrust authorities may demand that the essential facility be commonly owned by all users, with the provision that new entrants be able to purchase shares and membership into the network "at a reasonable price" (as in the *Associated Press* case mentioned above). The joint ownership of an essential facility by competitors must then be granted an exemption from certain antitrust provisions (as is done for example for certain types of R&D joint ventures, of cooperatives and of patent pools).

– *Access price control.* In the tradition of fully distributed cost regulation of access in regulated industries, antitrust authorities sometimes compare the price of access with some measure of its cost. The principle of such a comparison was for example accepted by the European Court of Justice in *United Brands* (1978), although it did not apply it in the specific instance. As is well known, the measurement of marginal cost is a difficult empirical matter, while the allocation of common costs among product lines has weak theoretical underpinnings. Clearly, antitrust authorities lack the expertise and staff that is needed for conducting extensive cost studies; at best can one put the onus of proving overpricing on the excluded competitors, who may well have better cost information than the authorities.

– *Access quantity control.* Instead of trying to define the "right" access price, the authorities sometimes focus on the quantity of access. For example, following an investigation of the *Eurotunnel* exclusivity contract mentioned above, the European Commission asked that 25% of each operator (British Rail, SNCF)'s capacity be allocated to new entrants for passenger and freight services.

– *Price linkages.* Antitrust authorities often try to use other prices – for access or retail goods – as benchmarks for the access price.

A famous rule, variously called the *Efficient Component Pricing Rule* (ECPR), the Baumol–Willig rule, the imputation rule, the parity principle, and the non-discrimination rule, links the integrated monopolist's access and retail prices. The idea is to avoid "margin squeezes", so that an equally efficient competitor should be able to enter the downstream market: the access price charged to competitors should therefore not exceed the price charged by the integrated firm on the competitive segment, minus the incremental cost of that firm on the competitive segment. For example, in the U.S. the Interstate Commerce Commission expressed a preference for the use of ECPR in railroad disputes.

There are also various forms of mandated linkages between access charges. The bottleneck firm may be forced to offer the same tariffs to all users (nondiscrimination rules, ban on tying), or even to charge a single per-unit price. Or, it may be required to charge a price of access not exceeding its price for the final use of the bottleneck segment (for example, the access charge for the local telephone network may not be allowed to exceed the price of local calls for residential or business consumers).

Last, there may be mandated linkages between several firms' access prices, as in the case of reciprocity in access charges for two competing telecommunications networks (to the extent that each network, regardless of its size, enjoys monopoly power on the termination of calls to its subscribers, each network is an essential facility for the other).

– *"Common Carrier" policies*. By this expression, we mean the policy of turning the vertical structure of the industry upside down. It might appear that in a complementary goods industry, labeling one segment the "upstream segment" and the other the "downstream segment" is purely semantic. The analysis of Section 2 shows that it is not, because the downstream firms not only purchase goods (inputs) from the complementary segment but also are the ones who interact with the final consumers. Later, we will ask whether, in presence of differential competitiveness of the two segments, it is desirable to locate the more competitive segment upstream or downstream. The relevance of this question is illustrated (in a regulatory context) by Order 436 which created a structure that allows U.S. gas producers to directly sign contracts with the gas customers (and purchase access from the pipeline bottleneck) rather than staying mere suppliers of inputs to pipelines packaging a bundle of production and transport to final customers.

– *Disclosure requirements*. Another tool in the policymaker's box is the requirement that contracts for intermediate goods be made public, with the hope that more "transparency" in supply contracts will promote downstream competition. Note that transparency is not equivalent to the prohibition of access price discrimination among buyers. A disclosure requirement does not preclude different tariffs for different buyers.

1.3. Roadmap

Foreclosure can be defined in different ways. For the purpose of this survey, we will define foreclosure as a situation in which: (i) a firm dominates one market (bottleneck good); and (ii) it uses its market power in the bottleneck good market to restrict output in another market, perhaps but not necessarily by discouraging the entry or encouraging the exit of rivals. As discussed earlier, we analyze two types of situation:

- *Vertical foreclosure* may arise when a firm controls an input that is essential for a potentially competitive industry. The bottleneck owner can then alter competition by denying or limiting access to its input.[11]
- When instead the bottleneck good is not an input but is sold directly to final users, *horizontal foreclosure* may arise when the firm somehow bundles the potentially competitive good and the bottleneck good.

With this distinction between vertical and horizontal foreclosure come two distinct views on exclusionary behavior. Vertical foreclosure is motivated by the desire to restore a market power that is eroded by a commitment problem; that is, the exclusionary practice aims at increasing the perpetrator's profit. By contrast, horizontal foreclosure is an act of predation; as other predatory behaviors, it reduces the predator's current profit and is meant to lower the competitors' profitability, with the ultimate goal of inducing their exit and ultimately recouping the lost profit.[12]

We will focus on theories based on the exploitation or protection of *market power*. We will not discuss alternative theories of foreclosure which are based for example on bargaining power,[13] price discrimination [where, say, the complementary and potentially competitive product is used as a counting device; see, e.g., Bowman (1957)], the avoidance of "multiprincipal externalities" [Bernheim and Whinston (1986), Martimort (1996), Segal (1999)], the preservation of industry rents [Comanor and Rey (2000)],[14] or "information-based favoritism" (in which the bottleneck segment favors a subsidiary in the procurement of the complementary good, because it has superior information about the subsidiary or because it internalizes part of its rent).[15]

[11] Vertical relations involve many other facets than foreclosure. In the first volume of the *Handbook*, Katz (1989) offers for example an overview of the use of vertical restraints to improve vertical coordination and to soften interbrand competition between rival vertical structures, as well as of the early literature on foreclosure; and Perry (1989) discusses other motivations for vertical integration, such as price discrimination, rent extraction or the avoidance of double marginalization.

[12] In Europe, a refusal to deal was assessed in *Commercial Solvents* (1974) from the point of view of the elimination of competitors; however, starting with *United Brands* (1978), the European Court of Justice no longer requires that the refusal to deal may lead to the competitors' exit.
The link between tie-ins and predation is discussed in more detail in Tirole (2005).

[13] On this, see Hart and Tirole (1990) and especially, Bolton and Whinston (1993); de Fontenay and Gans (2005) revisit the issue using the more flexible multilateral bargaining developed by Stole and Zwiebel (1996).

[14] While we will focus on the consequences of the existence of a bottleneck in one market, Comanor and Rey study some of the implications of multi-stage incumbency.

[15] There is also an abundant literature on the strategic commitment effect of vertical arrangements; see, e.g., Caillaud and Rey (1995) for a review.

We will also abstract from the closely related access issues in regulated industries.[16] In such industries, price controls (and/or explicit or implicit earnings-sharing schemes)[17] often prevent regulated firms from making money in the bottleneck segment and create incentives for them to reap supra-normal returns in the competitive segment, which can only be achieved by foreclosing access to the bottleneck. For example, the regulation of access prices may induce the bottleneck owner to delay interconnection or degrade interconnection quality. Of course, to the extent that competition policy looks into the regulatory toolbox for possible remedies, some of the most salient public policies in the regulatory context are also prominent in the antitrust environment.

Finally, our definition of foreclosure, which involves two distinct markets, also rules out some exclusionary practices which may prevail within a single market, such as the use of long-term exclusive dealing arrangements as entry barriers [see Aghion and Bolton (1987) and Rasmusen, Ramseyer and Wiley (1991)]. We will nevertheless discuss the relationship between the long-term contracting literature and our notion of foreclosure in Section 4.

The objective of this chapter is twofold. First, it summarizes recent developments in the analysis of foreclosure, and sometimes extends the existing literature, by considering new modes of competition or by studying the impact of various forms of competition policy. In so doing, it develops a critical view of what, we feel, are misguided or insufficient policy interventions. Second, it builds a preliminary checklist of exclusionary complaints and bottleneck defenses, which may be useful for thinking about foreclosure.

The chapter is organized as follows. Section 2 focuses on vertical foreclosure. It first provides an informal overview of the argument, before developing the conceptual framework and identifying the private rationale for foreclosure. It also examines the impact of policies such as nondiscrimination laws and "common carrier" type policies, and applies the foreclosure argument to an analysis of vertical mergers and exclusive contracts. Section 3 turns to horizontal foreclosure through tie-ins. After an informal overview of the main arguments, it first focuses on Whinston's (1990) theory of entry deterrence, and then turns to recent developments relative to the impact of tie-ins on innovation and entry. Section 4 reviews theoretical contributions on exclusionary contracts, while Section 5 studies possible defenses for exclusionary behaviors. Section 6 concludes.[18]

[16] We refer the reader to existing surveys of the access pricing question: Laffont and Tirole (1999), Armstrong (2002).

[17] For example, the firm that is subject to cost-plus regulation in one market and is unregulated in another, potentially competitive market, has an incentive to allocate as much as possible of the common and fixed costs to the regulated market, with the result that entry will be more difficult in the competitive market. More generally, what matters is the sensitivity of the firm's profit to cost reductions in the various markets in which it is active: the firm will wish to "inflate" its costs in the markets that are subject to cost-based regulation and thus "subsidize" the goods that are either not regulated or subject to a more "price-cap" oriented regulation; see the discussion in Section 3.5.2 of Armstrong and Sappington (2007).

[18] Some of the themes covered in Sections 2 and 4 are covered in a more informal way by Vickers (1996).

2. Vertical foreclosure

For all its prominence in competition law, the notion of foreclosure until recently had poor intellectual foundations. Indeed, the intellectual impetus in the late seventies (reflected in the American antitrust practice of the eighties) cast serious doubt about its validity. In particular, the Chicago School, led, in this instance, by Bork (1978) and Posner (1976), thought that the "leverage" concept resulted from a confusion about the exercise of monopoly power. It argued that there is a single source of monopoly profit, and that a bottleneck monopolist can already earn the entire monopoly profit without extending its market power to related segments; and so in the absence of efficiency gains, vertical integration cannot increase the profitability of the merging firms. Relatedly, it questioned the rationale for excluding downstream competitors, who by offering product diversity, cost efficiency or simply benchmarking of the internal downstream producer, can be the source of extra monopoly profits.

Consider the following quintessential bottleneck situation: An upstream monopolist, U, produces a key input for downstream use. There is potential competition in the downstream segment, but it can emerge only if competitors have proper access to U's essential input. The bottleneck owner can therefore alter and even eliminate downstream competition by favoring one downstream firm – e.g., a downstream affiliate – and excluding others. According to the foreclosure doctrine, U has indeed an incentive to do so, in order to extend its monopoly power to the downstream segment. However, as pointed out by the Chicago School critique, in such a situation there is a single final market and therefore only one profit to be reaped, which U can get by exerting its market power in the upstream segment; U thus has no incentive to distort downstream competition – imperfect competition in the downstream market may actually adversely affect U's bargaining power and/or create distortions that reduce the profitability of the upstream market.

The Chicago School view has had the beneficial effect of forcing industrial economists to reconsider the foreclosure argument and to put it on firmer ground. The reconciliation of the foreclosure doctrine and the Chicago School critique is based on the observation that an upstream monopolist in general cannot fully exert its monopoly power without engaging in exclusionary practices. This fact is little acknowledged except in the specific contexts of patent licensing and of franchising. Consider for example a patent that covers the unique technology that can be used in a given productive process. The patentholder is then the owner of an essential facility (in the economic sense; on the legal front, courts are unlikely to mandate access, the traditional corollary of the "essential facility" labeling). Yet the patentholder is unlikely to make much money if it cannot commit not to flood the market with licenses; for, if everyone holds a license, intense downstream competition destroys the profit created by the use of the patent. Therefore, a patentholder would like to promise to limit the number of licenses. There is however a commitment problem: Once the patentholder has granted n licenses, it is then tempted to sell further licenses. Such expropriation is ex post profitable for the licensor, but depreciates the value of the first n licenses and, if anticipated, reduces the patentholder's ex ante profit. Intellectual Property (IP) law explicitly acknowledges this fact by conferring entire freedom to contract on the patentholder (except in a set of specified cases, in which compulsory licensing may be applied by competition authorities and/or governments to force access to the bottleneck piece of IP against "proper compensation"). A similar point can be made for franchising. Franchisees are unlikely to pay much to franchisors if they do not have the guarantee that competitors will not set up shop at their doorsteps.

A bottleneck owner faces a commitment problem similar to that of a durable-good monopolist: Once it has contracted with a downstream firm for access to its essential facility, it has an incentive to provide access to other firms as well, even though those firms will compete with the first one and reduce its profits. This opportunistic behavior ex ante reduces the bottleneck owner's profit (in the example just given, the first firm is willing to pay and buy less). There is thus a strong analogy with Coase's durable good analysis.[19] As is well known, a durable-good monopolist in general does not make the full monopoly profit because it "creates its own competition": By selling more of the durable good at some date, it depreciates the value of units sold at earlier dates; the prospect of further sales in turn makes early buyers wary of expropriation and makes them reluctant to purchase. As we will see, the analogy with the durable-good model also extends to the means of restoring monopoly power: the upstream monopolist's keeping ownership of supplies, exclusive dealing, retail price floor, reputation of the monopolist not to expropriate, and so forth.

The licensing and franchising examples mostly involve binary decisions for input transfer (grant or not a license or franchising agreement). But the commitment problem is very general and extends to situations in which downstream firms purchase variable amounts of the essential input. It is then not surprising that the loss of monopoly power associated with the commitment problem is more severe, the more competitive the downstream segment.[20] This proposition has two facets. First, the upstream bottleneck's profit is smaller, the larger the number of downstream firms. Second, for a given number of downstream firms, the upstream profit is smaller, the more substitutable the downstream units.

Bottlenecks are rarely pure bottlenecks. They most often compete with inferior goods or services. In the presence of such "bypass opportunities", an upstream bottleneck owner must face both the commitment problem and the threat of second sourcing by the downstream firms. A couple of interesting insights result from this extension of the basic framework. First, a vertically integrated firm controlling the bottleneck in general may want to supply a limited but positive amount of the essential input to the downstream affiliate's competitors, who would otherwise purchase the inferior good. The prospect

[19] See Coase (1972), as well as Tirole (1988, ch. 1) for an overview.

[20] In a recent debate in France on manufacturer–retailer relationships, some have advocated that the tough competition observed in the French retail market (which appears to be tougher than in neighboring countries, and in part due to the presence of large chains of independent retailers) generates "too much" destructive competition among their suppliers.

of productive inefficiency creates scope for profitable external sales by the bottleneck owner. Second, and relatedly, bypass possibilities create a distinction between two ways of restoring monopoly power, vertical integration and exclusive dealing. While exclusive dealing does not enable the bottleneck owner to supply several downstream firms, vertical integration in contrast provides enough flexibility to supply non-affiliates and yet favor the affiliate.

Our analysis has three broad policy implications. First, it does matter whether the more competitive of two complementary segments lies upstream or downstream. We show that prices are lower when the bottleneck owner lies upstream. This result is robust to the existence of bypass opportunities, and to the vertical structure of the industry (independent or vertically integrated bottleneck). Intuitively, an upstream bottleneck location has two benefits from a social welfare point of view. First, it creates a commitment problem not encountered by a downstream monopolist and thus reduces monopoly power. Second, in the presence of bypass opportunities, an upstream location of the bottleneck prevents productive inefficiency by creating a stage of competition that eliminates inferior substitutes. Our analysis thus shows that common carrier policies lower prices and raise production efficiency.

The second policy implication is that non-discrimination laws may have the perverse effect of restoring the monopoly power that they are supposed to fight. When an upstream bottleneck practices foreclosure by discriminating among competitors, it is tempting to impose a requirement that all competitors be offered the same commercial conditions. Non-discrimination rules however benefit the upstream bottleneck because, by forcing it to sell further units at the same high price as the initial ones, they help the bottleneck commit not to flood the market. A non-discrimination law is thus a misguided policy in this situation.[21]

The third policy implication is that ECPR (which was designed for a regulated environment, but is also used in antitrust contexts) often has little bite in unregulated environments. As pointed out by William Baumol in testimonies, ECPR only provides a link between access and final prices and is therefore only a partial rule. Moreover, the higher the final price, the higher the access price can be. In an unregulated environment, an integrated firm with upstream market power can thus exercise its market power by setting a high price for the final good and, at the same time, set a high access charge to prevent other firms in the competitive segment from becoming effective competitors.

Our analysis has also implications for business strategy. Interestingly, while the desire to foreclose often motivates vertical integration, it may alternatively call for divestiture. For example, we develop a rationale for the 1995 divestiture of AT&T manufacturing arm that is related to the official justification of this divestiture. With the impending competition in telecommunications between AT&T and the RBOCs, the latter, who were major buyers of AT&T equipment, would have been concerned that the AT&T

[21] To better focus on the impact of discrimination on the (in)ability to commit, this analysis does not account for potentially beneficial effects of bans on discrimination.

manufacturing arm would exclude them in order to favor its telecommunication affiliate.[22] The RBOCs might therefore have turned to alternative manufacturers. We provide necessary and sufficient conditions under which this smaller-customer-base effect dominates the foreclosure effect, and thus divestiture is preferred by the bottleneck owner to vertical integration.

2.1. *A simple framework*

As indicated above, when the monopolized market supplies an input used by a downstream industry, the motivation for foreclosure cannot be the desire to extend market power, since there is a single final product and thus a single monopoly profit. Foreclosure can however serve to protect rather than extend monopoly power. We analyze this rationale using the simplest framework.

An upstream firm, U, is a monopoly producer of an intermediate product with marginal cost c. It supplies two undifferentiated downstream firms, D_1 and D_2 (see Figure 33.1). We will refer to the upstream segment as the "bottleneck" or "essential facility" segment and to the downstream segment as the "competitive" segment (although it need not be perfectly competitive[23]). The downstream firms transform the intermediate product into an homogeneous final one, on a one-for-one basis and at zero marginal cost. They compete in the final goods market characterized by an inverse demand function $p = P(q)$. We will assume that the demand function is "well-behaved", in that the profit functions are (strictly) quasi-concave and that the Cournot game exhibit strategic substitutability.[24] Let Q^m, p^m, and π^m denote the whole vertical structure's or industry's monopoly output, price, and profit:

$$\begin{aligned} Q^m &= \arg\max_q \{(P(q) - c)q\}, \\ p^m &= P(Q^m), \\ \pi^m &= (p^m - c)Q^m. \end{aligned}$$

The interaction between the firms is modeled according to the following timing:

- Stage 1: U offers each D_i a tariff $T_i(\cdot)$; D_i then orders a quantity of the intermediate product, q_i, and pays $T_i(q_i)$ accordingly.
- Stage 2: D_1 and D_2 transform the intermediate product into the final good, observe each other's output and set their prices for the final good.

[22] In the absence of vertical separation, the integrated firm may attempt to create a level-playing field downstream through other means. A case in point is Nokia's creation of Nokia Mobile Software, an independent division separated from the rest of Nokia by a "Chinese Wall". This division writes the Nokia Series 60 middleware platform (running on top of the Symbian operating system) that is used not only by Nokia's phone division, but also by a number of its rival mobile makers. See Evans, Hagiu and Schmalensee (2006) for more detail.

[23] Despite perfect substitutability. The downstream firms may for example compete à la Cournot (see below); they could alternatively engage in some tacit collusion.

[24] A sufficient condition for that is $P'(q) + P''(q)q < 0$ for all q.

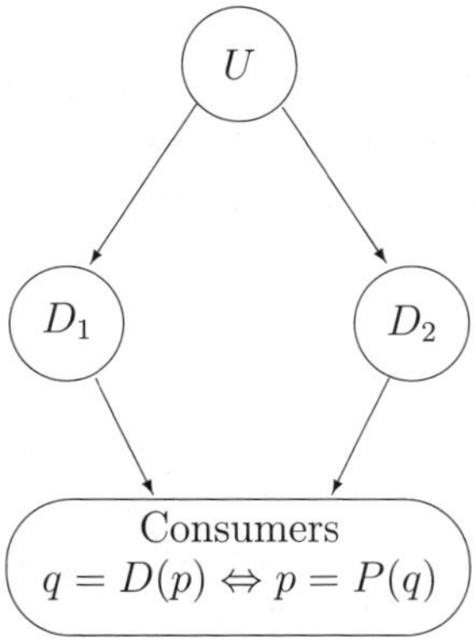

Figure 33.1. Basic framework.

This timing depicts a situation in which the supplier produces to order before the final consumers formulate their demand. The downstream firms are capacity constrained by their previous orders when they market the final product. Alternatively, the transformation activity is sufficiently time consuming that a downstream firm cannot quickly reorder more intermediate good and transform it if its final demand is unexpectedly high, or reduce its order if its final demand is disappointingly low. In Appendix C, we discuss the case in which final consumers are patient enough and the production cycle is fast enough that the downstream firms produce to order. Technically, the difference between these two modes of production resembles the distinction between Cournot and Bertrand competition.

We focus on perfect Bayesian equilibria. Given the quantities purchased in the first stage, the downstream firms play in the second stage a standard Bertrand–Edgeworth game of price competition with capacity constraints. For simplicity, we assume that the marginal cost c is sufficiently large relative to the downstream marginal cost (zero) that if the downstream firms have purchased quantities q_1 and q_2 in the viable range, they find it optimal to transform all units of intermediate product into final good and to set their price at $P(q_1 + q_2)$.[25] The second stage can then be summarized by Cournot revenue functions $P(q_1 + q_2)q_i$. As for the first stage, two cases can be distinguished, according to whether the tariff offered to one downstream firm is observed by the other or not.

2.1.1. *Commitment, observability and credibility*

Let us first consider, as a benchmark, the case where both tariffs offered by U are observed by both D_1 and D_2. In that case, U can fully exert its market power

[25] See Tirole (1988, ch. 5) for more detail.

and get the entire monopoly profit [see for example Mathewson and Winter (1984) and Perry and Porter (1989)]. For example, U can achieve this result by offering $(q_i, T_i) = (Q^m/2, p^m Q^m/2)$[26]: both D_1 and D_2 accept this contract and together sell the monopoly quantity, Q^m, at the monopoly price p^m.[27] In this world, there is no rationale for foreclosure. The upstream monopolist can preserve its monopoly power without excluding one of the competitors.

Sticking to those contracts, however, is not credible if the contracts are secret or can be privately renegotiated. Suppose for example that U and D_2 have agreed to $q_2 = Q^m/2$ (and $T_2 = p^m Q^m/2$); U and D_1 would then have an incentive to agree to the quantity, q_1, that maximizes their joint profit, i.e.:

$$q_1 = \arg\max_q \{[P(Q^m/2 + q) - c]q\} = R^C(Q^m/2) > Q^m/2,$$

where R^C denotes the standard Cournot reaction function, and the last inequality derives from a standard revealed preference argument.[28] Hence, U has an incentive to secretly convince D_1 to buy more than $Q^m/2$. Anticipating this, firm D_2 would turn down the monopolist's offer.

2.1.2. Secret contracts

From now on, we consider the game in which in the first stage, U offers *secret* contracts (that is, D_i observes the contract it is offered, but not the contract offered to D_j). In this game, U is subject to the temptation just described and thus faces a credibility problem. The contracts offered by U in equilibrium, as well as the responses from D_1 and D_2, depend on the nature of each downstream firm's conjectures about the contract offered to its rival. Since there is considerable leeway in specifying those beliefs, there are many perfect Bayesian equilibria: but, as we will see, one equilibrium stands out as the only plausible one in this context and we will therefore focus on this equilibrium.

[26] Since U has perfect information on D_1 and D_2 it can actually dictate their quantity choices – subject to their participation constraint – via adequately designed tariffs of the form "(q_i, T_i)": $T(q) = T_i$ if $q = q_i$ and $+\infty$ otherwise. Since U moreover makes take-it-or-leave-it offers, it can set T_i so as to extract D_i's entire profit.

[27] Although downstream firms are symmetric, an asymmetric allocation of the monopoly output between them would do as well. The symmetric allocation is however strictly optimal when downstream cost functions are (symmetric and) strictly convex.

[28] The first-order conditions for $q \equiv Q^m/2$ and $\hat{q} \equiv R^C(Q^m/2)$ are respectively $P(2q) - c + 2qP'(2q) = 0$ and $P(q + \hat{q}) - c + \hat{q}P'(q + \hat{q}) = 0$; since $P' < 0$, they cannot coincide for $\hat{q} = q$, and thus $\hat{q} \neq q$. From a revealed preference argument,

$$[P(q+q) - c](q+q) \geqslant [P(q+\hat{q}) - c](q+\hat{q}),$$
$$[P(q+\hat{q}) - c]\hat{q} \geqslant [P(q+q) - c]q,$$

implying $P(q+q) \geqslant P(q+\hat{q})$, and thus (since $\hat{q} \neq q$), $\hat{q} > q$.

To illustrate the role of conjectures, suppose that D_1 and D_2 assume that U makes the same offer (even unexpected ones) to both of them. Then it is credible for U to offer $(q_1, T_1) = (q_2, T_2) = (Q^m/2, p^m Q^m/2)$: Expecting that any offer it receives is also made to its rival, D_i refuses to pay more than $P(2q)q$ for any quantity q; U thus maximizes $(P(2q) - c)2q$ and chooses $q = Q^m/2$. Hence, under such a *symmetry* assumption on the downstream firms' conjectures, U does not suffer from any lack of credibility.

This symmetry assumption, which concerns unexpected offers (i.e., out-of-equilibrium ones) as well as expected ones, is however not very appealing. When the supplier supplies to order, it is more plausible to assume that, when a firm receives an unexpected offer it does not revise its beliefs about the offer made to its rival. Secrecy together with upstream production on order implies that, *from the point of view of the upstream monopolist*, D_1 and D_2 form two completely separate markets (of course, D_1 and D_2 themselves perceive a strong interdependency). Thus the monopolist has no incentive to change its offer to D_j when it alters D_i's contract. Such conjectures are called *passive* or *market-by-market-bargaining* conjectures.[29]

Under passive conjectures, D_i, regardless of the contract offer it receives from U, expects D_j to produce the candidate equilibrium quantity, q_j, and is thus willing to pay up to $P(q+q_j)q$ for any given quantity q. U, who extracts all of D_i's expected profit by making a take-it-or-leave-it offer, offers to supply q_i so as to maximize the joint profit in their *bilateral* relationship, namely:

$$q_i = \arg\max_q \{(P(q + q_j) - c)q\} \equiv R^C(q_j).$$

Hence, under passive conjectures the equilibrium is unique and characterized by the Cournot quantities, price and profits:

$$\begin{aligned}
&q_1 = q_2 = q^C, \quad \text{where } q^C = R^C(q^C) > Q^m/2,\\
&p_1 = p_2 = p^C = P(2q^C) < p^m,\\
&\pi_U = (p^C - c)2q^C = 2\pi^C < \pi^m,\\
&\pi_{D_1} = \pi_{D_2} = 0.
\end{aligned}$$

[29] Conjectures can be passive only if the downstream units have perfect information about the bottleneck's marginal cost; for example, assume that the bottleneck has private information about this marginal cost. The tariff offered to D_1, say, then signals information about the marginal cost; for example, a two-part tariff with a low marginal price may reveal a low marginal cost and therefore signal that D_2 is also offered a tariff with a low marginal cost and will produce a high quantity.
Thus, when the bottleneck has private information about its marginal cost, the downstream firms' conjectures can no longer be "passive". But they may still reflect the fact that the bottleneck bargains "market-by-market", that is attempts to maximize its profit in any given intermediate market (where an "intermediate market" corresponds to a D_i) without internalizing the impact of the contract on the other market, since its profits in the two markets are unrelated. A lack of transparency of the bottleneck's cost may nevertheless improve the bottleneck's commitment ability. The Coase problem with incomplete information about the bottleneck's cost function is developed in White (2000).

This result, due to Hart and Tirole (1990), and further analyzed by O'Brien and Shaffer (1992) and McAfee and Schwartz (1994), highlights the commitment problem faced by the supplier. Even though it is in a monopoly position, its inability to credibly commit itself gives room for opportunistic behavior and prevents it from achieving the monopoly outcome.

As already mentioned, this outcome is closely related to the phenomenon underlying the Coasian conjecture on the pricing policy of a durable good monopolist. If the monopolist can commit to future prices, it can obtain the monopoly profit by committing itself to never set its price below the monopoly level. However, once all monopoly sales have taken place (in the first period), it has an incentive to lower its price and exploit the residual demand. If the monopolist cannot commit itself on its future pricing policy, the buyers then delay their purchase in order to benefit from lower future prices, and the profit is reduced.

Suppose more generally that there are n identical downstream competitors. Then, by the same argument, the passive conjectures equilibrium is symmetric and satisfies

$$q = R^C\big((n-1)q\big),$$

where q is the output per downstream firm. Thus, the commitment problem becomes more severe, the larger the number of downstream firms. Indeed, the retail price on the competitive segment tends to marginal cost c and the industry profit tends to zero as the number of firms tends to infinity. Thus, we would expect bottleneck owners to be keener to foreclose access to the essential facility, the more competitive the downstream industry. The analogy with the durable good model again is obvious. There, the monopolist's commitment problem increases with the number of periods of sales. Indeed, and this is Coase's famous conjecture, the monopolist's profit vanishes as opportunities to revise prices become more and more frequent.[30]

Adding downstream firms is one way of increasing the intensity of downstream competition. Another relevant impact of competition on the extent of the commitment problem is obtained by varying the degree of downstream product differentiation. Let us, for the sake of this exercise only, depart from the perfect substitutes assumption and allow the two downstream firms to produce differentiated products. Under our assumptions, Bertrand–Edgeworth competition with capacities q_1 and q_2 yields retail prices $p_1 = P_1(q_1, q_2)$ and $p_2 = P_2(q_2, q_1)$. The equilibrium of the overall game is *still the Cournot equilibrium* of the simpler game in which the downstream firms face marginal cost c. If, as we would normally expect, the ratio of Cournot industry profit over monopoly profit increases with the degree of differentiation, the incentive to restore monopoly power is stronger, the more substitutable the downstream products.

[30] Caprice (2005a) shows that this effect is mitigated when the upstream dominant firm competes with an alternative supplier. In that case, while an increase in the number of downstream firms still decreases industry profits, it also allows the dominant supplier to get a bigger share of this smaller pie.

• *Restoring monopoly power*. In contrast with conventional wisdom, foreclosure here aims at *reestablishing rather than extending* market power: In order to exert its market power the upstream monopolist has an incentive to alter the structure of the downstream market. For example, excluding all downstream firms but one eliminates the "Coasian pricing" problem and restores U's ability to sustain the monopoly price; *exclusive dealing*, which de facto monopolizes the downstream market, thus allows U to exert more fully its upstream market power. [We define here exclusive dealing as an upstream firm's commitment not to deal with alternative downstream firms. Examples include exclusive license or franchise contracts.]

Alternatively, U may want to *integrate downwards* with one of the downstream firms, in order to eliminate the temptation of opportunism and credibly commit itself to reduce supplies to downstream firms.[31] For, suppose that the upstream firm internalizes the profit of its downstream affiliate, and that it supplies the monopoly quantity Q^m to this affiliate and denies access to the bottleneck good to non-integrated downstream firms. The integrated firm then receives the monopoly profit π^m. Any deviation to supply non-integrated producers can only result in a lower industry profit, and therefore in a lower profit for the integrated firm.

The bottleneck monopolist may conceive still other ways of preserving the monopoly profit. For instance, as noted by O'Brien and Shaffer (1992), a *market-wide resale price maintenance* (RPM), in the form of a price floor, together with a return option[32] would obviously solve the commitment problem; O'Brien and Shaffer further show that squeezing downstream margins through individual price ceilings can also help eliminate the scope for opportunism. Alternatively, allowing *tariffs* to be *contingent on both firms' outputs* is another such instrument: A contract of the form "$q_i = Q^m/2, T_i = p^m Q^m/2$,

[31] Again, there is an analogy with Coase's durable good model. A standard way for a durable-good monopolist of restoring commitment power is to refrain from selling. A durable-good monopolist who leases the good assumes ownership of existing units and thus is not tempted to expropriate the owners of previous production by flooding the market (it would expropriate itself), in the same way the integrated bottleneck owner is not tempted to expropriate its affiliate by supplying other downstream firms.

[32] The possibility for downstream units to return the wares at the marginal wholesale price is in general needed for obtaining the monopoly solution. Suppose that $c = 0$, and that when both sellers charge the same price but supply more than the demand at this price, the rationing follows a proportional rule (so, sellers sell an amount proportional to what they bring to the market). Let the upstream firm supply $q^m/2$ to each downstream firm and impose price floor p^m. Then the upstream firm can supply some more units at a low incremental price to one of the sellers, thus expropriating the other seller.

Relatedly, McAfee and Schwartz (1994) consider *most-favored-customer* (MFC) clauses. They allow downstream firms who have accepted a "first-stage" individualized contract offer to replace it in a "second stage" (that is, before downstream product market competition) by any offer made to any other downstream firm. They show that such MFC clauses do not quite solve the monopolist's commitment problem. By contrast, De Graba (1996) shows that, by offering two-part tariffs and by allowing downstream firms to apply the MFC term-by-term (that is, to choose the contract $(\min\{F_i\}, \min\{w_i\})$, where $\min\{F_i\}$ is the minimum of the fixed fees and $\min\{w_i\}$ is the minimum of the wholesale unit prices offered in the first stage), the monopolist restores its commitment power and is able to achieve the monopoly profit.

Table 33.1
Solving the commitment problem

Exclusionary behavior	Analogue for the durable-good monopolist
Exclusive dealing	Destruction of production unit
Profit sharing/vertical integration	Leasing
Retail price floor	Most favored nation clause
Reputation for implicit exclusive dealing	Reputation for not flooding the market
Limitation of productive capacity	Limitation of productive capacity

together with a hefty penalty paid by the supplier to the buyer if the buyer's competitor is delivered a higher quantity of the intermediate good, and thus produces a higher quantity of the final good" solves the opportunism problem.[33]

Recalling the various ways in which a durable-good monopolist can restore its commitment power[34] suggests several other commitment policies for the bottleneck owner. In an oft repeated relationship, the bottleneck owner may build a reputation with D_1, say, for practicing "implicit exclusive dealing". That is, the bottleneck owner may sacrifice short-term profit by not supplying D_2 in order to build a reputation and extract high payments from D_1 in the future, in the same way a durable-good monopolist may gain by refraining from flooding the market. In another analogy with the durable-good model, the bottleneck owner gains from facing a (publicly observed) tight capacity constraint (or more generally from producing under decreasing returns to scale). The downstream firms are then somewhat protected against expropriation by the capacity constraint.[35] Some of these analogies with the durable-good model are listed in Table 33.1.

2.1.3. *Empirical evidence*

2.1.3.1. Experimental evidence Martin, Normann and Snyder (2001) test this theory of foreclosure (with an upstream monopolist and a downstream duopoly) using experimental techniques. They compare three possible games: non-integration with public or secret offers and vertical integration. The first and the third, according to the theory, should yield the monopoly outcome, while the second should result in the Cournot outcome.

Martin et al. find only partial support for the theory. The monopolist's commitment problem is apparent in the data: total output and profit are similar and close to the

[33] In a smoother vein, the upstream monopolist could mimic vertical integration with contracts that capture all realized downstream profits, e.g., tariffs $T_i(q_i, q_j) = P(q_i + q_j)q_i$ that charge D_i according to the level of input delivered to D_i and D_j – a small discount for the particular choice $q_i = Q^m/2$ might help downstream firms to coordinate on the desired outcome – or contracts based on downstream revenues, if observable, rather than input – a contract of the form "give back (almost) all of your revenue" also eliminates the risk of opportunistic behavior.

[34] On this, see Tirole (1988, pp. 84–86).

[35] Alternatively, the upstream firm benefits if the downstream firms face capacity constraints.

monopoly level in the first and third games; by contrast, output is often, although not always, significantly higher and profit lower in the second game. But in addition, integration allows more surplus to be extracted from the unintegrated downstream firm, suggesting that bargaining effects play also a role. Under vertical integration, in the majority of cases the integrated player gets all the profit, as the theory predicts; downstream firms thus accept to get only a small profit, contrasting with other experiments in which players tend to reciprocate (retaliate) by wasting value when they are offered a small share of the pie.[36] In the non-integrated treatments, the industry profits are instead more evenly shared between the upstream monopolist and downstream firms.

Relatedly, Martin et al. indirectly investigate the nature of out-of-equilibrium beliefs under secret offers, by looking at downstream acceptance decisions as functions of the contract offer. They find that these beliefs are highly heterogeneous, and on the whole somewhere in between passive and symmetric beliefs. (Note, incidentally, that, as in other experiments, the rational behavior of a "rational player" does not coincide with the rational behavior under common knowledge of rationality. In particular, deviations by the upstream monopolist may signal some irrationality and it is not longer clear that passive conjectures are as rational as they are under common knowledge of rationality.)

2.1.3.2. Field studies Alternatively, one can look at the impact of vertical mergers on downstream rivals and end users. According to the foreclosure theory reviewed above, vertical integration may help upstream bottlenecks solve their commitment problem.[37] (At least) three implications may be tested:

(a) downstream rivals (D_2) receive less input from or pay a higher price to the upstream firm with market power (U), or more generally discrimination between D_1 and D_2 tilts market shares in the favor of D_1;
(b) if D_2 is publicly traded, then D_2's stock price goes down when the merger is announced;[38]
(c) the final customers suffer from the merger. Their decrease in welfare can be measured in (at least) two ways:
   - a decrease of their stock price if they are publicly listed,
   - an increase in the futures price if there is a future market for the final good.

As usual, the potential anti-competitive effects need to be traded off against potential benefits of vertical integration (such as the encouragement of investment in specific

[36] See, however, Roth et al. (1991) on the lack of fairness concerns in competitive environments.

[37] We are not aware of any empirical study testing another implication of foreclosure theory, namely that "turning an industry upside down" by mandating access to bottlenecks may make it more competitive (see below the discussion of the U.S. gas industry). This implication might be tested for example in the railroad or airline industries.

[38] This is not strictly the case in the model above, because U is assumed to extract the entire rents of the downstream units, and thus D_2's stock price does not react to the merger $U - D_1$. Relaxing this extreme assumption, e.g., by conferring some bargaining power on the downstream firms or by introducting private information about the latter's costs (so as to generate downstream rents), yields implication (b).

aspects), and more generally the various social benefits that are invoked in favor of a more lenient attitude of antitrust authorities toward market foreclosure (see Section 5).

Nor are individual tests perfect evidence of foreclosure effects. Test (a) (the destruction of the level-playing field between D_1 and D_2), if positive, may be alternatively interpreted through a standard monopoly pricing story, and might be positive even if D_1 and D_2 did not compete in the same product market (in which case foreclosure could not be a motive for vertical integration): When U has asymmetric information about D_1 and D_2's technology and profit, U may charge wholesale prices largely above its marginal cost because a fixed fee then does not suffice to handle the allocation of the downstream firm's rent. By contrast, if D_1's profit accrues to U, then U has an incentive to charge an internal marginal transfer price to D_1, regardless of whether D_1 and D_2 compete in the product market.[39]

Test (b) is subject to the potential criticism that specific increases in the merged entity's efficiency may hurt downstream rivals even in the absence of foreclosure intent. Namely, a merger that, say, encourages specific investments and reduces D_1's marginal cost makes D_1 a fiercer rival in the downstream product market. By contrast, mergers whose efficiency gains result from a reduction in fixed costs would have no such effect.

Test (c) is subject to the caveat that pre-merger stock or futures prices reflect market anticipations. Therefore, the evolution of such a price at the time of the merger depends on the impact of that particular merger, but also on what alternative scenario was anticipated as well. For example, if U was a potential entrant in the downstream market and decides instead to acquire one of the existing competitors, then market indicators may react negatively to the merger even in the absence of any foreclosure concern.[40]

We are aware of few empirical studies of modern foreclosure theory. Needless to say, this is an area that would deserve further investigations. Chipty (2001) considers implication (a) in the cable industry, and shows that integrated cable operators exclude rival channels. Snyder (1994, 1995a, 1995b) takes route (b), and conducts event studies looking at downstream rivals' stock market price reaction to various public announcements of a merger or of antitrust authorities's steps to undo existing mergers. His study of the vertical integration of beer manufacturers and pubs in the UK (Snyder, 1994, 1995a) looks at the reaction of the stock price of Guinness (then the only publicly listed non-integrated major beer producer) to the Monopolies and Mergers Commission's successive moves during its investigation of foreclosure in the brewing industry. He documents a positive reaction of Guinness's stock price to the MMC's and the government's anti-integration moves. His study of vertical integration of upstream crude

[39] While a vertical merger would thus generate discrimination between the integrated and non-integrated downstream firms, this would occur through a modification of the contract with the integrated subsidiary, while foreclosure motives would also involve a modification of the terms offered to the non-integrated firms. Thus, in principle, one might be able to distinguish the two types of motivations.

[40] Fridolfsson and Stennek (2003) stress a similar point in the context of horizontal mergers. When a merger is announced, the share prices of formerly potential targets and acquirers are reduced, since they are now out of play. Anti-competitive mergers may thus reduce competitors' share prices, despite increasing their profits; as a result event studies may not detect the competitive effects of mergers.

oil production and downstream refining in the U.S. oil industry (Snyder, 1995a, 1995b) delivers a small effect (negative impact of integration decision on rivals' stock price in event studies). Mullin and Mullin's (1997) study U.S. Steel's 1905–1906 "acquisition"[41] of a huge amount of low-extraction-cost iron ore properties on the Western Mesabi Range. Mullin and Mullin follow, inter alia, route (c), by measuring the event-study impact of the merger on the largest net consumers of iron and steel (railroads); they argue that the merger turned out to benefit these final consumers, suggesting that vertical integration was motivated by efficiency considerations (on which they bring another form of evidence).[42]

2.1.4. *Policy implications*

The previous subsection has presented the basic motivation for foreclosure and stressed the strong analogy with the Coasian pricing problem. We now derive some policy implications.

Upstream versus downstream bottlenecks The "Coasian pricing problem" is more likely to arise when bottlenecks are at more upstream levels, that is, when they have to supply (competing) intermediaries to reach final consumers. To see this, consider the more general framework, where two complementary goods, A and B, must be combined together to form the final good (on a one-to-one basis: one unit of good A plus one unit of good B produces one unit of the final good), good A being produced by a monopolist M (at constant marginal cost (c) whereas good B is produced by two competing firms C_1 and C_2 (at no cost).[43] In the case of telecommunications, for example, good A may correspond to the local fixed link segment and good B to the long distance segment. To stick to the previous framework, we denote by $p = P(q)$ the inverse demand for the final good.

The case where M is "upstream" (Figure 33.2a) is formally equivalent to the one analyzed above: M sells good A to C_1 and C_2, who combine it with good B to provide consumers with the final good. If M can make secret offers to both C_1 and C_2, then opportunism prevents M from fully exerting its monopoly power. The upstream monopolist obtains the Cournot profit.

If instead M is "downstream" (that is, C_1 and C_2 supply M, who then deals directly with consumers, as in Figure 33.2b), the situation is different: Being at the interface with consumers, M is naturally inclined to "internalize" any negative externality between C_1 and C_2, and is thus induced to maintain monopoly prices. Assuming M can still make

[41] More properly, the signing of a long-term lease giving U.S. Steel the exclusive right to mine.

[42] Riordan (1998) however questions their conclusions. In particular, he argues that incumbent railroads might well have benefited from *rising* steel prices, which would have limited entry and expansion plans.

[43] We use the generic notation $\{M, C_1, C_2\}$ when the location is endogenous – as here – or irrelevant – as in the horizontal foreclosure case studied in Section 3 – and the specific one $\{U, D_1, D_2\}$ for fixed vertical structures – such as studied previously.

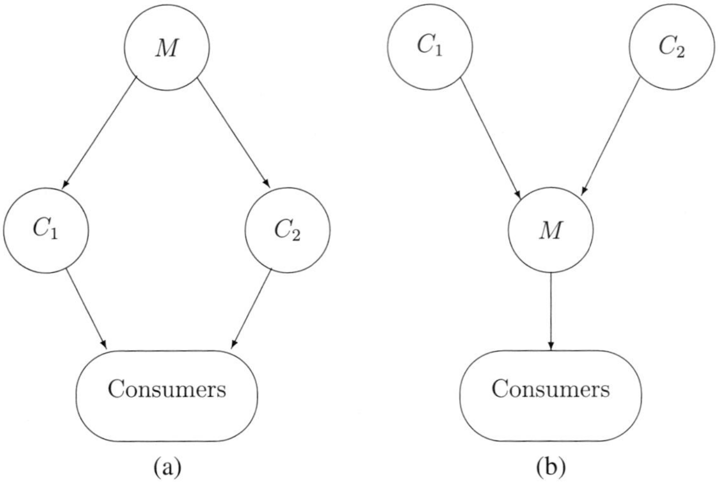

Figure 33.2. Upstream (a) versus downstream (b) bottlenecks.

take-it-or-leave-it offers to both C_1 and C_2, M can now at the same time extract all profits from them and charge the monopoly price to final consumers.[44] Hence, from either the consumers' or total welfare perspective, it is preferable to put the more competitive segment downstream. For example, in the above mentioned telecommunications example, it is preferable to let consumers deal directly with the competing long distance operators who then buy access from the fixed link operator. This idea may provide a rationale for the U.S. gas reform (FERC order 436, 1985)[45] and the "common carrier" concept, although some caution must be exerted in view of the regulatory constraints in those industries.

Non-discrimination laws Non-discrimination laws are often motivated by the protection of final consumers against abuses of a dominant position. It is well known that in

[44] Does this result depend on the assumption that the monopolist has all the bargaining power? Consider for example the opposite extreme: The upstream competitors make take-it-or-leave-it contract offers $T_i(q_i)$ to the downstream monopolist. This situation has been analyzed in depth by the literature on "supply functions equilibria" [e.g., Back and Zender (1993), Bernheim and Whinston (1986, 1998), Green and Newbery (1992), and Klemperer and Meyer (1989)]. As is well known, supply function games have multiple equilibria [see, e.g., Back and Zender (1993) and Bernheim and Whinston (1998)]. On the other hand, it is possible to select among differentiable equilibria by introducing enough uncertainty [Klemperer and Meyer (1989)]. This selection yields the same Bertrand competition outcome ($T_i(q_i) = 0$ for all q_i) as for the polar distribution of bargaining powers.

[45] Before the reform, pipelines (the bottleneck) sold gas to customers (distribution companies, large industrial customers) and purchased their gas internally or from independent producers who had no direct access to customers. Since the reform, producers can purchase access from pipelines and intereact directly with customers.

other contexts non-discrimination laws may have ambiguous effects, since they may favor some consumers to the detriment of others. But in the context described above, these laws adversely affect all consumers and total welfare: they eliminate opportunistic behavior and allow the bottleneck owner to fully exercise its monopoly power.[46]

To see this, return to the basic (Cournot) framework in which the monopolist is located upstream, and assume that U is restricted to offer the same tariff to both D_1 and D_2[47]:

- Stage 1: U offers the same tariff $T(\cdot)$ to both D_1 and D_2; D_i then orders a quantity of intermediate product, q_i and pays $T(q_i)$ accordingly.
- Stage 2: D_1 and D_2 transform the intermediate product into final good, observe each other's output and set their prices for the final good.

This game is played under complete information at each point of time. Thus there is no scope for opportunistic behavior from U. Formally, the situation is the same as with secret offers but "symmetric" beliefs, and in equilibrium U gets the entire monopoly profit. An *example* of an optimal tariff is $T(q) = F + wq$, where the fixed fee F and the wholesale price w satisfy:

$$q^C(w) = Q^m/2,$$
$$F = (p^m - w)Q^m/2,$$

where $q^C(w)$ denotes the Cournot equilibrium quantity (per firm) when firms' unit cost is w:

$$q^C(w) = \hat{q} \quad \text{such that} \quad \hat{q} = \arg\max_q \{(P(q+\hat{q}) - w)q\}.$$

In other words, the marginal transfer price w is set so as to lead to the desired monopoly price and quantities, and F is used to extract D_i's profit. Hence, if the upstream firm cannot discriminate between the two downstream firms (but can still offer a non-linear tariff, or at least require a – uniform – franchise fee), it can fully exert its market power and maintain the monopoly price: Non-discrimination laws here reduce consumer surplus and total welfare by enabling the monopolist to commit.

To obtain the monopoly profit, the upstream monopoly can alternatively offer the following non-discriminatory two-part tariff:

$$T(q_i) = \pi^m + cq_i.$$

[46] O'Brien and Shaffer (1992) already made this point in the context of Bertrand downstream competition. Caprice (2005b) notes that restoring commitment by banning price discrimination is not necessarily undesirable when there is an alternative supplier, since the dominant supplier may then want to commit to lower wholesale prices – see the discussion in footnote 52.

[47] This supposes some degree of ex post transparency; yet, in the absence of a ban on discrimination, there would still scope for opportunism if the downstream firms must sign their own contracts before observing the terms offered to the rivals.

That is, the wholesale price is equal to marginal cost and the fixed fee equal to the monopoly profit. It is then an equilibrium for D_1 to sign an agreement and for D_2 to turn it down.[48] The competitive sector then makes no profit, and the upstream monopolist obtains the full monopoly profit by monopolizing the downstream sector. Note that *the fixed fee de facto transforms a potentially competitive downstream industry into a natural monopoly (increasing returns to scale) industry*. Price discounts, an instance of second-degree price discrimination, are here a perfect substitute for the prohibited third-degree price discrimination. It is also interesting to note that such foreclosure ideas partly underlied the rationale for the 1936 Robinson–Patman Act in the U.S., although considerations such as differential access to backward integration (not to mention intense lobbying) were relevant as well.[49]

2.2. Restoring monopoly power: vertical integration

As we observed, vertical integration helps the upstream monopolist U to circumvent its commitment problem and to (credibly) maintain monopoly prices. Suppose that U integrates with D_1 as in Figure 33.3b. The upstream monopolist, if it receives D_1's profit, internalizes the impact of sales to D_2 on the profitability of units supplied to its subsidiary. Consequently, the "expropriation" problem disappears and U restricts supplies to D_2 as is consistent with the exercise of market power. We first analyze in detail the foreclosure effect of vertical integration under the possibility of bypass and then derive some policy implications.

2.2.1. Vertical integration and bypass of the bottleneck segment

In the simple framework above, vertical integration leads to the complete exclusion of the non-integrated downstream firm. This is clearly an extreme consequence, driven in particular by the absence of alternative potential supplier for D_2. We show however that the same logic holds, even when there exists a competing but less efficient second source for D_2.[50] The new feature is then that the vertically integrated firm may supply its competitor on the downstream segment, a sometimes realistic outcome.

[48] To be certain, there is a coordination problem here. But this problem is readily solved if U contacts one of the downstream firms first.

[49] If U is restricted to use *linear* prices, then the outcome is even worse for consumers and economic welfare, as well as for the monopolist, who still can commit but cannot prevent double marginalization.
Formally, when the above game is modified by restricting the tariff $T(\cdot)$ to be of the form $T(q) = wq$, U sets w so as to maximize $\Pi_U \equiv (w(Q) - c)Q$, where $w(Q) \equiv (q^C)^{-1}(Q/2)$ satisfies, from the downstream first-order conditions: $w(Q) = P(Q) + P'(Q)Q/2$. Hence, $\Pi'_U = P - c + P'Q + (2P' + P''Q)Q/2$ is negative for $Q = Q^m$, since the sum of the first three terms is then equal to zero and the term in bracket is then negative. Therefore, U "picks" a total quantity $Q < Q^m$ whenever its objective function is quasi-concave. This reflects the fact that U does not take into account the impact of a decrease of output on the downstream firms' profits.

[50] Here the other upstream firm produces a substitute. An interesting topic for future research would look at a bottleneck consisting of *complementary* goods produced by different upstream suppliers. Amelia Fletcher

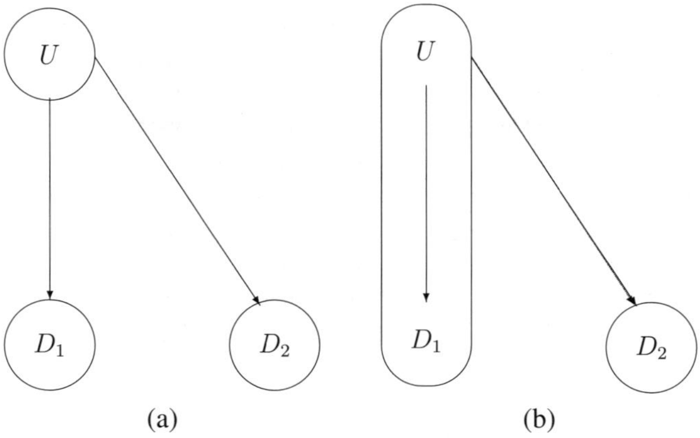

Figure 33.3. Vertical integration.

We generalize the model by introducing a second supplier, $\hat{U}$, with higher unit cost[51] $\hat{c} > c$. The timing is now as follows:

- Stage 1: U and $\hat{U}$ both secretly offer each D_i a tariff, $T_i(\cdot)$ and $\hat{T}_i(\cdot)$; each D_i then orders a quantity of intermediate product to each supplier, q_i and $\hat{q}_i$, and pays $T_i(q_i)$, $\hat{T}_i(\hat{q}_i)$, accordingly.
- Stage 2: D_1 and D_2 transform the intermediate product into final good, observe each other's output and set their prices for the final good.

In the absence of integration (Figure 33.4a), U, being more efficient, ends up supplying both D_1 and D_2, although under conditions that are more favorable to downstream units (lower fixed fees) than before, due to the potential competition from $\hat{U}$. More precisely [see Hart and Tirole (1990) for a formal proof], U supplies, as before, q^C to both downstream firms, but for a payment equal to $\pi^C - \max_q\{(P(q + q^C) - \hat{c})q\}$, since each downstream firm can alternatively buy from $\hat{U}$, who is willing to supply them at any price $\hat{p} \geqslant \hat{c}$. That is, the introduction of the alternative supplier does not affect final prices and quantities or the organization of production, but it alters the split of the profit between U and the downstream firms.[52]

suggested to us that a joint-marketing agreement (for example through the formation of a patent pool without independent licensing) might reduce welfare, despite the fact that the goods are complements, if it inhibits secret price discounts by creating protracted negotiations between upstream firms.

[51] We assume that the suppliers' costs are known. Hart and Tirole (1990) allow more generally the costs to be drawn from (possibly asymmetric) distributions. They show that U has more incentive to integrate vertically than $\hat{U}$ if realizations of c are statistically lower than those of $\hat{c}$, in the sense of first-order stochastic dominance.

[52] Interestingly, this may not be true in the case of public contracts. In the absence of $\hat{U}$, U could for example maintain the monopoly outcome by offering both firms ($q_i = Q^m/2$, $T_i = \pi^m/2$). When $\hat{U}$ is present, U could try to maintain the monopoly outcome ($q_i = Q^m/2$) and simply reduce the price to $\pi^m/2 - \hat{\pi}$, where $\hat{\pi} = \max\{[P(Q^m/2 + q) - \hat{c}]q\}$. However, if $\hat{U}$ is not too inefficient, namely, if $\hat{Q}^m = \max\{[P(q) - \hat{c}]q\} >$

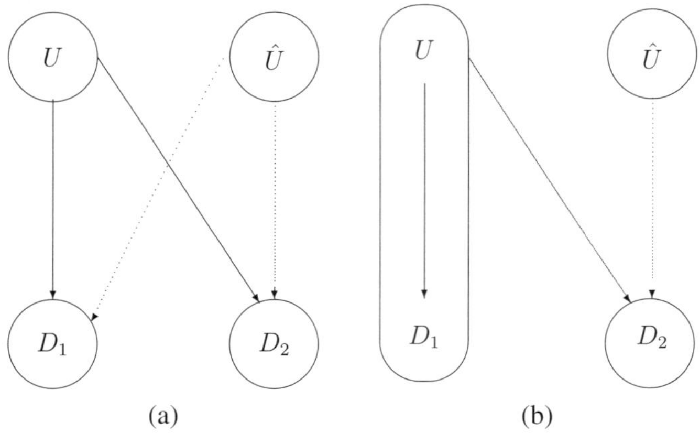

Figure 33.4. Vertical integration and bypass.

If U and D_1 integrate (Figure 33.4b), however, they again have an incentive to restrict supplies to D_2 as much as possible; however, D_2 can turn to $\hat{U}$ and buy $\hat{R}^C(q_1) \equiv \arg\max_q\{[P(q+q_1) - \hat{c}]q\}$. Consequently, in equilibrium U still supplies both downstream firms (and $\hat{U}$ does not sell), but the equilibrium quantities $\{q_1^C, q_2^C\}$ correspond to the "asymmetric" Cournot duopoly with costs c and $\hat{c}$, characterized by

$$q_1^C = R^C\left(q_2^C\right) \quad \text{and} \quad q_2^C = \hat{R}^C\left(q_1^C\right),$$

where $\hat{R}^C(q_1) \equiv \arg\max_q\{[(P(q+q_1)) - \hat{c}]q\}$.

Hence, vertical integration between U and D_1 still leads to a reduction in the supply to D_2, who now faces a higher opportunity cost ($\hat{c}$ instead of c). This new configuration entails a reduction of aggregate production as $-1 < R^{C\prime}(q) < 0$ and $\hat{R}^C(q) < R^C(q)$ imply $2q^C < q_1^C + q_2^C$ (see Figure 33.5); although q_1 increases, it increases less than q_2 decreases. Note however that production efficiency is maintained: Although U wants to reduce q_2 as much as possible, it still prefers to supply q_2^C rather than letting $\hat{U}$ supply it. Denoting by π_1^C and π_2^C the corresponding Cournot profits, the equilibrium profits are given by

$Q^m/2$, $\hat{U}$ would destroy this candidate equilibrium by offering $\hat{Q}^m$ to one downstream firm, at a lump-sum price between $\hat{\pi}$ and $\hat{\pi}^m$: that downstream firm would accept this contract, thereby discouraging the other firm from accepting U's offer. The analysis of competition in public contracts can actually be surprisingly complex – see Rey and Vergé (2002). Even when the alternative supply comes from a competitive fringe that does not behave strategically, the dominant manufacturer may deviate from joint profit maximization, e.g., by offering lower input prices, in order to reduce the rents obtained by the downstream firms – see Caprice (2005b), who notes that banning price discrimination may be a good idea in that case, since doing so may allow the dominant manufacturer to commit itself to low prices; this effect disappears, however, when contracts can be contingent on who supplies who: the dominant supplier can then reduce downstream rents by offering lower prices only "off the equilibrium", if one firm were to go to the alternative supplier.

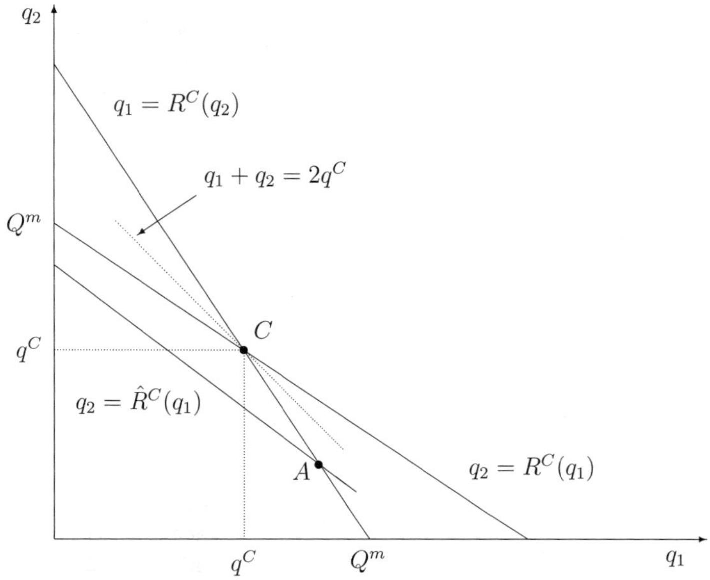

Figure 33.5. C: Cournot equilibrium ($c_1 = c_2 = c$). A: Asymmetric Cournot equilibrium ($c_1 = c < c_2 = \hat{c}$).

$$\pi_{U+D_1} = \pi_1^C + (\hat{c} - c)q_2^C, \qquad \pi_{D_2} = \pi_2^C.$$

Hence, D_2 is hurt by vertical integration, while $U - D_1$'s aggregate profit is higher, since industry profit is higher.[53] Vertical integration thus benefits the integrated firms and hurts the non-integrated one. Although it maintains production efficiency, it lowers consumer surplus and total welfare. Furthermore, the higher the cost of bypassing the bottleneck producer, the larger the negative impacts on consumers and welfare.[54] Last, it is interesting to note that vertical integration is more profitable, the less competitive the bypass opportunity (the higher $\hat{c}$ is).

The motivation for foreclosure is again here the preservation of an *existing* market power in a segment. By contrast, in Ordover, Saloner and Salop (1990), an upstream firm has no such market power and faces instead an equally efficient supplier. Yet, it is shown that such a firm may have an incentive to integrate vertically if (i) it can commit to limit its supplies to the downstream rivals and hence to expose them to the upstream competitor's market power thus created, and (ii) the upstream competitor can charge only linear prices so that its exercise of market power on the non-integrated down-

[53] The aggregate quantity is now lower, and lies between Q^m and $Q^C = 2q^C$ (and $q_1^C + q_2^C = Q^m$ for $\hat{c}$ sufficiently large), and production efficiency is maintained.

[54] Note that $\hat{U}$ or D_2 cannot gain by "fighting back" and integrating themselves. In equilibrium, D_2 gets actually exactly as much as it would being integrated with $\hat{U}$. For more general situations, in which "band-waggoning" may occur, see Hart and Tirole (1990).

stream firm operates through a high wholesale price rather than a high fixed fee. Several authors have built on Ordover et al. and relaxed some of their assumptions. In particular, Choi and Yi (2000) and Ma (1997) dispense in different settings with the commitment assumption, although not with the linear pricing one.[55]

2.2.2. *Policy implications*

Since vertical integration can lead to foreclosure and have a negative impact on consumers and total welfare, it is natural to ask which type of policy, short of structural separation, might nullify or at least limit this negative impact.

Upstream versus downstream bottleneck We noted that, in the absence of vertical integration, it is socially desirable to ensure if feasible that the most competitive segment of the market has access to final consumers. This is still the case under vertical integration as we now show.

Let us first consider the *no bypass* case, with a monopolist M in one segment (good A) and a competitive duopoly (C_1 and C_2) in the other segment (good B). Integration between M and, say, C_1, then leads to the perfect monopoly outcome even if the competitive segment is downstream (see the above analysis). In that case, whether the competitive segment (good B) or the monopolistic one (good A) is downstream does not matter (that is, given vertical integration between M and C_1, which segment is at the interface with consumers is irrelevant; however, M and C_1 only have an incentive to integrate if the bottleneck is upstream because a downstream bottleneck does not face the commitment problem).

In the richer framework with *possible bypass of the bottleneck segment*, however, whether this bottleneck is upstream or downstream again matters. The idea is that, when the bottleneck is downstream, then the less efficient alternative supplier cannot be shut down, which results in productive inefficiency. To see this, assume that there is now an alternative, but inferior supplier, $\hat{M}$, for good A. If the segment for good A is upstream, then formally the situation is the same as the one described in the previous subsection: The outcome is the asymmetric Cournot outcome $\{q_1 = R^C(q_2),\ q_2 = \hat{R}^C(q_1)\}$, but production is efficient (M supplies both C_1 and C_2). If instead good A is downstream (that is, M and $\hat{M}$ deal directly with final consumers), then, whether M is integrated with D_1 or not, both M and $\hat{M}$ have access to good B at marginal cost (zero), and M chooses to offer $q_1 = R^C(q_2)$, whereas $\hat{M}$ offers $q_2 = \hat{R}^C(q_1)$. As a result, the equilibrium quantities and prices are the same in both cases and correspond to the asymmetric Cournot duopoly, but production is organized inefficiently (q_2^C is produced by the inefficient alternative supplier $\hat{M}$, entailing a social loss $(\hat{c} - c)q_2^C$). [Note that M, if located downstream, is indifferent between integrating upstream with C_1 and remaining

[55] See also Salinger (1988) and Gaudet and Long (1996).

Table 33.2
Equilibrium allocation

	VI	NI		VI	NI
BU	M	C	BU	AC	C
BD	M	M	BD	AC	AC
				IP	IP
	No bypass (without $\hat{M}$)			Bypass (with $\hat{M}$)	

Notes. Vertical Integration (VI) or No Integration (NI); Bottleneck Upstream (BU) or Downstream (BD); M: pure Monopoly outcome; C: Cournot equilibrium ($c_1 = c_2 = c$); AC: Asymmetric Cournot equilibrium ($c_1 = c,\ c_2 = \hat{c}$); IP: Inefficient Production (loss $(\hat{c} - c)q_2^C$).

unintegrated.] Furthermore, whether the bottleneck is integrated or not, *it is again socially desirable to have the most competitive segment (good B) downstream, i.e. at the interface with final consumers.* Table 33.2 summarizes the equilibrium allocation.

ECPR[56] We now show that ECPR may not preclude or impose any constraint on foreclosure in our framework. That is, assuming that vertical integration between the upstream bottleneck and a downstream firm has taken place, the equilibrium outcome in the absence of ECPR satisfies ECPR.

Let us assume as a first step that bypass of the bottleneck is infeasible. As seen above, in the absence of any constraint the integrated firm $U - D_1$ *de facto* excludes D_2 and charges the monopoly price, p^m, in the final good market. We can check that the integrated bottleneck's optimal policy can be made consistent with ECPR by offering a linear access price w_2 to D_2 that (a) satisfies ECPR and (b) excludes D_2. Assuming as above that downstream unit costs are zero, to meet ECPR the access price must satisfy $w_2 \leqslant p^m - 0 = p^m$. But this cap on the access price does not really help D_2 to enter the market effectively. Indeed, suppose that the integrated firm sets a linear access charge $w_2 = p^m$, and that it produces $q_1 = Q^m$ in equilibrium. Buying q_2 units of intermediate good at that price p^m and transforming (at no cost) this intermediate good into final good yields:

$$\left[P\left(Q^m + q_2\right) - w_2\right]q_2 < \left[P\left(Q^m\right) - w_2\right]q_2 = 0.$$

D_2 has thus no viable activity under ECPR.

Second, consider the case where there is an alternative, less efficient supplier for the intermediate good ($\hat{U}$, with unit cost $\hat{c} > c$). In that case, the integrated firm $U - D_1$ produces $q_1^C > q^C$ whereas the non-integrated one, D_2, buys the intermediate good at $w_2 = \hat{c}$ and produces $q_2^C < q^C$; note that the equilibrium price for the final good,

[56] A much broader analysis of the impact of ECPR (in regulated and unregulated markets) can be found in Armstrong (2002).

$\hat{p}^C \equiv P(q_1^C + q_2^C)$, is necessarily higher than D_2's marginal cost, $\hat{c}$. Since $\hat{p}^C > \hat{c}$ and $w_2 = \hat{c}$ in the range where the threat of bypass is a constraint for the upstream monopolist, ECPR is again satisfied by the foreclosure outcome.

We conclude that, with or without the possibility of bypass, ECPR has no bite. The problem of course is not that ECPR is "wrong" per se, but rather that it is expected to perform a function it was not designed for.[57]

2.3. *Restoring monopoly power: exclusive dealing*

The previous section reviewed the dominant firm's incentives to vertically integrate in order to extend its market power. When used for that purpose, vertical integration gives rise to foreclosure and thus generates a social cost (vertical integration may also yield social benefits, which we discuss in the next section). To evaluate the social costs and benefits of preventing vertical integration, however, it may be necessary to investigate the alternative strategies available to dominant firms for implementing foreclosure and the relative costs of these strategies. One such strategy is "exclusive dealing" or "exclusive supply" agreements.[58]

2.3.1. *Basic framework: exclusive dealing as a substitute for vertical integration*

Consider, first, the basic framework, in which an upstream monopolist, U, sells to two downstream firms, D_1 and D_2. Vertical integration with, say, D_1, then allows U to monopolize the entire industry in the Cournot case. Consequently, D_2 is excluded from the market. Assuming now that vertical integration is prohibited, the upstream monopolist U can nevertheless achieve the same outcome by signing an exclusive agreement with D_1: By entering into such an agreement, U de facto commits itself not to sell to D_2 and thus eliminates the risk of opportunism. In this simple framework, an exclusive dealing arrangement is thus a perfect substitute for – and arguably a more straightforward solution to the commitment problem than – vertical integration. In particular, a policy that would prevent vertical mergers would have no effect if exclusive dealing were allowed.

Because it introduces a rigid constraint, exclusive dealing may actually be privately and socially less desirable than vertical integration. This is for example the case if there is some room for other upstream or downstream firms under vertical integration, as we now demonstrate.[59]

[57] See, e.g., Baumol, Ordover and Willig (1995) and Laffont and Tirole (1999) for a discussion of the facts that ECPR is only a partial rule, and that ECPR, even when it is optimal in the presence of other well-calibrated instruments, cannot achieve the optimum in the absence of these other instruments.

[58] Depending on the context, exclusive dealing agreements can take various forms: exclusive territories for retailers, exclusive license, and so form. These exclusive dealing agreements involve a commitment not to deal with other downstream firms, which may be easier to monitor and to enforce, and thus more credible than a commitment to deal with them "up to some level" (e.g., half of the monopoly quantity).

[59] Conversely, there may be circumstances where vertical integration might be an inferior substitute to exclusive dealing (e.g., because of internal organizational costs); a policy that would be more restrictive against exclusive deals than against vertical integration might then lead again to an alternative, less desirable solution.

2.3.2. Exclusive dealing generates production inefficiency in the presence of bypass

Consider next the case where there is an alternative, less efficient supplier, $\hat{U}$, with higher cost than U: $\hat{c} > c$. Although vertical integration with D_1 does not allow U to maintain the monopoly outcome, it nevertheless entails some foreclosure of D_2 and leads to a reduction of total output. However, in this context, the most efficient supplier, U, still supplies both downstream firms D_1 and D_2: U indeed does not want D_2 to buy from its rival (and in equilibrium, U supplies D_2 exactly the amount that D_2 would have bought from $\hat{U}$). In contrast, an exclusive agreement with D_1 would lead to the same reduction in output, but would moreover introduce an additional efficiency loss, since in that case D_2 would have to buy from $\hat{U}$ (compared with vertical integration, the additional welfare loss is equal to the loss in profit, namely $(\hat{c} - c)q_2^C$).[60]

Exclusive dealing is clearly profitable when the alternative supplier is quite inefficient, since in the limit case where $\hat{U}$ does not impose any competitive constraint, U gets the full monopoly profit with exclusive dealing and only the Cournot profit otherwise. When $\hat{U}$ is quite efficient (that is, $\hat{c}$ close to c), however, U may prefer serving both downstream firms. To see this, suppose that, before negotiating with D_1 and D_2, U can choose to auction off an exclusive dealing contract. If U does not offer exclusivity, the Cournot outcome (q^C, q^C) is achieved but each D_i gets a rent, equal to $r^N = \max_q\{(P(q^C + q) - \hat{c})q\}$; U thus obtains $\pi_U^N(\hat{c}) = 2(\pi^C - r^N)$, which is positive as long as $\hat{c} > c$. If instead U auctions the right to be supplied exclusively, the asymmetric Cournot outcome $(q_1^C(\hat{c}), q_2^C(\hat{c}))$ is achieved (where q_1^C and q_2^C, which coincide with q^C when $\hat{c} = c$, are respectively increasing and decreasing in $\hat{c}$) and each downstream firm bids up to what it would earn if it were to lose the auction, which is equal to $r^E = \max_q\{(P(q_1^C(\hat{c}) + q) - \hat{c})q\}$. Thus, by auctioning an exclusive deal, U can earn $\pi_U^E(\hat{c}) = \pi_1^C - r^E$. Both options (offering exclusivity or not) yield zero profit when the second supplier is equally efficient ($\pi_U^N = \pi_U^E = 0$ when $\hat{c} = c$) and become more profitable as $\hat{U}$ becomes less efficient; as already noted, the second option clearly dominates when $\hat{U}$ is sufficiently inefficient (π_U^1 is capped by the Cournot profit, while π_U^2 increases up to the full monopoly profit), but the first option might dominate when $\hat{U}$ is quite efficient ($\hat{c}$ close to c) and Cournot quantities do not react too much to cost asymmetry.[61]

[60] Chen and Riordan (in press) point out that a vertically integrated firm might still be able to monopolize the industry by entering into an exclusive deal with D_2, thereby committing itself not to compete in the downstream market; thus, vertical integration and exclusivity may together succeed in monopolizing the industry, even when vertical integration or exclusivity alone would not achieve that result.

[61] If a small asymmetry had no impact on quantities (i.e., $q_1 = q_2 = \hat{q}$ in the various configurations for $\hat{c}$ close to c), then clearly $\pi_U^N(\hat{c}) = 2(\hat{c} - c)\hat{q} > \pi_U^E(\hat{c}) = (\hat{c} - c)\hat{q}$. When both demand and costs are linear, however, quantities respond "enough" to cost asymmetry to make exclusive dealing always profitable; one can check that, for $P(q) = 1 - q$ and $c = 0$, U's profits are respectively $\pi_U^N(\hat{c}) = \frac{2}{9}(1 - (1 - \frac{3}{2}\hat{c})^2)$ and

2.3.3. Exclusive dealing and downstream product differentiation

Consider now the case where there is no alternative supplier, but there are two downstream firms producing differentiated products, which are sufficiently valuable that an integrated monopoly would choose to produce both. As in Section 2.3.2, vertical integration of the bottleneck with D_1 may again not lead to the full monopolization of the industry, but in general maintains D_2 alive. That is, the integrated firm $U - D_1$ may want to supply D_2, although in a discriminatory way, rather than forcing D_2 completely out of the market. In contrast, an exclusive agreement with D_1 would lead *de facto* to the exclusion of D_2, and might thus result in yet another inefficiency and reduction in welfare.[62]

2.3.4. Discussion

In the two situations just analyzed, exclusive dealing yields less profit to U than vertical integration, and ruling out vertical mergers but not exclusive dealing arrangements thus forces U to choose a socially less desirable outcome. In the first case, an exclusive dealing arrangement between the efficient upstream supplier and one of the downstream firms forces the other downstream firm(s) to switch to an alternative, less efficient supplier. In the second case, the exclusive dealing arrangement *de facto* excludes rival downstream firms and thus reduces the choice offered to final consumers, in contrast to what happens under vertical integration.

This raises an important issue for policy design: There is no point forbidding one practice (here, vertical integration) if it leads the firms to adopt practices (here, exclusive agreements) that are even less desirable from all (firms' and consumers') perspectives.

2.4. Further issues

Needless to say, our treatment is far from exhaustive. Let us mention a number of important topics or further developments.

– *Private incentives not to exclude.* We have emphasized the bottleneck's incentive to exclude in order to restore market power. To be certain, exclusion need not be complete, as when the bottleneck producer faces competition from a less efficient rival; but still

$\pi_U^E(\hat{c}) = \frac{1}{9}((1+\hat{c})^2 - (1-2\hat{c})^2)$, and thus

$$\mathrm{d}\pi_U^E(\hat{c})/\mathrm{d}\hat{c} = \frac{2}{3}(1-\hat{c}) > \mathrm{d}\pi_U^N(\hat{c})/\mathrm{d}\hat{c} = \frac{2}{3} - \hat{c}.$$

[62] There again, exclusive dealing is profitable as long as downstream differentiation remains limited, but may otherwise become unprofitable (in particular, U prefers serving both D_1 and D_2 when they do not really compete against each other).

then, the bottleneck owner does everything it can to restrict downstream output and just prefers to substitute its own production for that of the upstream rival. There are at least two situations, though, in which the bottleneck producer is less eager to exclude (we only sketch the reasoning; details and further discussion is provided in Appendix A).

First, independent users of the intermediate good may sink investments that orient their technology toward that of the upstream bottleneck or toward an alternative technology, for which there are competitive suppliers. They will choose the latter if they anticipate that the upstream bottleneck will practice foreclosure, for example if it has integrated downstream. The problem is one of commitment: to prevent inefficient choices of bypass technologies, the bottleneck owner would like to commit not to foreclose, which may require divesting downstream units, committing not to choose an exclusive customer, and so forth. Appendix A discusses in this light the voluntary divestiture of AT&T's equipment division (Lucent Technologies).

Second, and reversing the protection-of-specific-investments argument, an upstream bottleneck owner who has to sink specific investment does not want to face the prospect of hold-up in a bilateral monopoly situation with a favored downstream user [Chemla (2003)]. It is well known that competition protects investments in environments in which efficient long-term contracts are difficult to write. Certain forms of foreclosure may have the undesirable side-effect of leading to the expropriation of the upstream monopolist's investment through ex post bargaining.

– *The "Coasian logic" applies beyond industrial markets.* For example, in Cestone and White (2003), a financial intermediary (bank, venture capitalist, etc.) must develop some expertise in order to assess whether a line of business is promising, how to tailor the contract to the technology, or how to monitor the borrower. But once the intermediary has sunk the corresponding investment, nothing prevents it from funding another venture in the same line of business. That is, the financial intermediary becomes an upstream bottleneck who may be (sequentially) tempted to finance many competing ventures and may therefore not be able to extract rents (and possibly recoup the initial investment). The response to Coase's problem emphasized in Cestone–White is the ownership of equity stakes by the intermediary, which, at the cost of diluting the borrower's incentives, at least force the intermediary to internalize some of the loss of profit associated with the funding of competing ventures, while a debt contract would be more efficient in the absence of a commitment problem.

– *General results on contracting with externalities.* In an important, more abstract paper on contracting with externalities, Segal (1999) looks at more general situations in which a principal contracts with multiple agents and the contract with a particular agent exerts externalities on other agents (product-market-competition externalities in our framework). He obtain general results on the extent of trade between the principal and the agents when contracts are secret, as a function of the nature of the externalities, and then studies the case in which the principal is able to make public commitments.

– *Alternative conjectures.* As we have seen, the passive-conjecture assumption is a reasonable one in the Cournot situation in which the upstream monopolist produces to order. It is much less appealing in the case of Bertrand competition, and indeed in many games of contracting with externalities, where the contract signed with one downstream competitor affects the contracting terms that the upstream monopolist would like to offer to the competitor's rivals.

This strategic interdependence among the contracts signed with the different competitors has two implications. First, at the technical level, it creates non-concavities and, as a result, pure-strategy equilibria with passive beliefs may not exist anymore. This is because the gain from a multilateral deviation, i.e. a simultaneous change in the contracts offered to D_1 and D_2, may then exceed the total gains of the unilateral deviations, i.e. stand-alone modifications of the contract offered to one of the downstream firms. Rey and Vergé (2004) show that the unique "contract equilibrium", characterized by O'Brien and Shaffer (1992) using bilateral deviations, does not survive multilateral deviations when the cross elasticity is at least half of the direct demand elasticity.[63] Second, a downstream firm should anticipate that, if the supplier offers it an out-of-equilibrium contract, the latter has an incentive to change the contracts offered to the others. Passive beliefs thus appear less plausible. McAfee and Schwartz (1994) propose to consider instead *wary beliefs* where, when it receives an unexpected offer, a downstream firm anticipates that the supplier acts optimally with its rivals, given the offer just received. Rey and Vergé (2004) show that, when demand is linear, wary beliefs equilibria exist even when passive beliefs equilibria fail to exist, and these equilibria exhibit some degree of opportunism: the upstream firm does not fully exploit its market power, although it performs better than when downstream firms hold passive beliefs; in addition, prices are lower with Cournot than with Bertrand downstream competition.[64]

Segal and Whinston (2003) take another route and investigate in more general settings the set of conclusions that are robust to the choice of conjectures. They fully characterize equilibrium profits in offer games.

– *Bidding games.* We have mostly supposed so far that the upstream firm has the initiative and makes a take-it-or-leave-it offer to each downstream firm. Another stream of the literature studies situations where instead downstream rivals bid for the input supplied by an upstream monopolist. In the bidding games considered by Segal and Whinston (2003) and Martimort and Stole (2003), where the downstream rivals make

[63] Segal and Whinston (2003) note a similar existence problem when the manufacturer faces non-constant returns to scale. McAfee and Schwartz (1995) also point out that, when contracts are observed before the actual stage of downstream competition, the unique candidate equilibrium for passive beliefs may generate negative profits.

[64] Rey and Vergé also confirm the insight of O'Brien and Shaffer (1992), who pointed out that RPM can help an upstream manufacturer to exploit its market power. The idea is that RPM allows the upstream monopolist to squeeze its retailers' margins, thereby eliminating any scope for opportunism.

the offers but the upstream monopolist eventually chooses how much to supply, the equilibrium outcome is again competitive; in essence, each bidder then exerts an externality on the other, which the contracts cannot internalize despite using a common supplier.

In contrast, when the downstream firms eventually determine quantities and the offers are public, they can protect themselves again opportunistic behavior by the rivals, by offering a flexible contract that allows them to adapt their actual purchases to the terms offered by the rivals' contracts. Marx and Shaffer (2004) stress however that, even when contracts are public, coordination among the downstream firms may still fail and exclusive dealing may arise instead. The intuition is as follows: in any equilibrium where both downstream firms are active, the supplier must be indifferent between supplying both or only one firm, but each firm benefits from being an exclusive agent. This can be achieved through an exclusive dealing contract or, as noted by Marx and Shaffer, by making the fixed fee partly conditional on the downstream firm's eventually purchasing a positive quantity; in effect, a high enough conditional fixed fee deters the upstream monopolist from supplying its input to the rival, as the downstream firm would not purchase – and thus not pay the fee – in that case.[65] Rey, Thal and Vergé (2005) however show that allowing for contingent offers, where the terms of the contract depend on exclusivity, leads to the industry integrated outcome, with both retailers active and each receiving its contribution to total profits.

Another strand of literature looks at how downstream rivals may want to lock in the supplies of a competitively supplied input in order to monopolize the downstream market. In Stahl (1988) and Yanelle (1997), competing downstream firms bid up to corner supplies so as to become a downstream monopoly. In equilibrium, a single firm acquires all supplies and charges the monopoly price in the downstream price in the downstream market. This firm however makes no profit because it spends this monopoly profit to bid up supplies.

In Riordan (1998), the upstream market is served by a competitive industry, with an upward sloping supply curve. The downstream market is populated by a dominant firm and a competitive fringe. The dominant firm enjoys a first mover advantage in contracting for its input requirements. The upstream industry then supplies the downstream competitive fringe. An increase in the dominant firm's purchase of the input raises the fringe's marginal cost of production through a higher wholesale price (since the upstream supply curve is upward sloping) – a foreclosure effect; at the same time, the downstream dominant firm is not eager to produce much downstream and therefore to buy much upstream.

In this context, Riordan analyzes the impact of a prior and exogenous ownership stake in the upstream industry ("vertical integration"); that is, the dominant firm starts with input supplies $k_0 \geqslant 0$ and may want to increase its supplies beyond k_0. Riordan shows that an increase in k_0 raises both the wholesale and the final prices. Intuitively,

65 The conditional fixed fee can for example be set equal to the profit that the downstream firm can expect to achieve under exclusivity; the non-conditional part of the fee can then take the form of an upfront payment from the supplier to the downstream firm (as in the case of listing fees paid by manufacturers to large retailers).

the initial ownership stake makes it cheaper for the dominant firm to raise the fringe's marginal cost though an increase in the wholesale prices (the dominant firm is protected by ownership against the price increase for the first k_0 units). This increased foreclosure raises the downstream price as well. It would be interesting to investigate[66] whether the dominant firm has an incentive to buy the ownership stake k_0, though. In fact, the expectation of higher wholesale price raises the cost of acquiring a unit ownership stake, as k_0 grows. So the dominant firm ends up paying for the wholesale price increase, which may well dissuade it from acquiring the stake in the first place.

3. Horizontal foreclosure

We now turn to horizontal foreclosure, referring to situations in which: (i) a firm M is present in two final markets, A and B; and (ii) this firm M has substantial market power in market A, called for simplicity the "monopoly segment" and faces actual or potential competition in market B, labeled the "competitive segment". In such a situation, the traditional "leverage" concern is that M could foreclosure competitors in market B by tying the bottleneck good A to its own offering in B. This leverage theory has been used in many high-profile cases involving complements – particularly when product B has low value, or is even useless, unless combined with product A (memory or software and CPUs for mainframe computers, parts or maintenance services and original equipment, and so forth).

However, as the Chicago School pointed out, tying need not be a rational anticompetitive strategy for M. The key point is that, even though good A is sold separately, so there are indeed two markets and two profits to be made, M can extract its profit through its pricing in the monopoly market A rather than through seeking to exercise monopoly power in the adjacent market B. Furthermore, when the second product is a complement to the first, a monopolist that can exploit its market power for its own monopolized product has no interest in excluding low-cost and high-quality varieties from the market since their presence makes its own product more attractive to consumers: reducing competition in market B makes good A less desirable to the consumers.

To illustrate this, suppose that good B is useless unless combined with good A.[67] To simplify, suppose that consumers want one unit of each good. With a slight abuse of notation, consumers derive surplus A from good A alone, and an additional surplus B from M's version of good B, while several independent producers can produce a better version of good B, yielding a higher surplus $\hat{B} \geqslant B$ (provided, of course, that they also consume good A). M has constant unit costs a and b, respectively, in the two markets, while B-rivals produce at a lower cost $\hat{b} \leqslant b$.

[66] Along the lines of Burkart, Denis and Panunzi (1998), Joskow and Tirole (2000) and Gilbert, Neuhoff and Newbery (2004).

[67] A situation that would look very similar to that considered for vertical foreclosure. The crucial difference, though, is that good B (the counterpart of the "downstream" good) and good A are here sold separately.

– *Bundling*. By tying the bottleneck good A to its own version of B, M can foreclose rivals in market B and thus become a monopolist in both markets; it can then either sell the bottleneck good at price A and the other good at price B or the combination of the two goods at price $P^M = A + B$; both options result in a per-customer profit of

$$\pi^M = A - a + B - b.$$

– *Unbundling*. By contrast, in the absence of foreclosure, competition among the independent B producers leads them to offer the better version of B at their low marginal cost; consumers thus derive on market B a surplus equal to $\hat{B} - \hat{b}$; but then, M can increase the price it charges for good A from A to up to $A + \hat{B} - \hat{b}$ and realize a per-customer profit of

$$\pi^M + \Delta,$$

where

$$\Delta \equiv (\hat{B} - B) + (b - \hat{b})$$

denotes the technological advantage of the rivals. In other words, M loses from foreclosing access and becoming a B-monopolist. The point is that any additional surplus provided by B-competitors increases consumers' valuation of the bottleneck good, which M can then extract (at least partially) by exerting its market power on that segment.

Here again, the Chicago School view has led industrial economists to reconsider the leverage argument. Three lines of argument have been developed.[68]

First, when the products are relatively independent, the above observation does not apply: a second source of monopoly power does not devalue M's original monopolized product. If in addition the monopolist has a realistic chance of driving competitors out of – or of discouraging entry in – the adjacent market, then committing to sell the two goods as a bundle, and only as a bundle, can serve as a strategic commitment to be a tough competitor in market B – since then, any lost sale in B implies a lost sale as well in the core market A – and can thus deter potential competitors in market B.

Second, even when the two goods are complements, entry in the adjacent market B may facilitate entry in the monopolized market A. Then, the incumbent monopolist M may be tempted to deter entry in the adjacent market in order to help prevent entry in its core market.

Last, the mere fact that the integrated firm M is present in two complementary markets A and B affects that firm's incentives to invest in B, since any increase in competition in B enhances consumers' willingness to pay for the monopolized product in A. This, in turn, alters rivals' incentives to invest and innovate in the adjacent market.

These arguments are discussed in turn in the next three sections.

[68] See Whinston (2001) for an informal survey of this literature.

3.1. Entry deterrence in the tied market

The first response to the Chicago critique in the case of adjacent markets is Whinston's (1990) classic paper. His idea is best illustrated in the case in which goods A and B are *independent*. Suppose that M, the monopolist in market A, faces potential competition in market B from an entrant E, who has not yet incurred a fixed cost of entry. Whinston's key insight is that tying the two goods makes M de facto more aggressive in market B, and thus may discourage the rival from entering that market. A tie-in may thereby increase M's overall profit.

For example, consider the same example as above, except that:

- the demands for the two goods A and B are independent; that is, consumers as before have unit demands for each good, but now derive utility from good B whether or not they buy good A;
- in the B market, one potential entrant, E, must incur a sunk cost of entry in order to be active in the market;
- before the entry decision, M decides whether to sell the two goods as a bundle – and only as a bundle. Bundling then cannot be undone and therefore has commitment value.

So the timing goes as follows: (i) M chooses whether to bundle; (ii) E decides whether to enter, in which case it incurs a fixed cost f (in per-customer terms); (iii) M and E choose their prices (that is, depending on the bundling decision, M sets either a price P for the bundle or two distinct prices for A and B, while E sets a price for its B version if it entered the market).

– *Unbundling*. If goods A and B are sold separately, M sells the former at price A, so as to extract all consumer surplus, and thus makes a per-customer profit or margin $m_A = A - a$ on the A segment; in market B, E enters and drives M out of the market, yielding a profit Δ for E and a surplus $B - b$ for the consumers.

– *Bundling*. Suppose instead that M decides to sell the two goods as a bundle. For consumers, buying this bundle amounts to buying M's version of good B at an effective price of $P - A$. For M, the opportunity cost of a sale of good B is no longer b, but

$$b' = b - m_A;$$

that is, M's fictitious margin on good B should not be computed simply using B's marginal cost of production, b, but should also reflect the fact that M loses a sale on A (with value m_A) every time it loses a sale of B. This generates a more aggressive behavior by M in case of entry, since M would be willing to charge an effective price as low as b'; in other words, in order to maintain its sales M would be willing to charge for the bundle a price P as low as its marginal cost of production: $P = a + b$. This, of course, reduces E's profit, since E is now facing a more aggressive behavior from M in market B.

Tying can then successfully deter entry if E's competitive advantage, Δ, is small compared to the surplus generated by the bottleneck good, $m_A = A - a$; more precisely:

- if $\Delta < m_A$, M wins the competition since consumers prefer buying the bundle at marginal cost $a+b$ rather than buying the entrant's product at marginal cost $\hat{b}$:

$$(A+B)-(a+b) > \hat{B}-\hat{b} = B-b+\Delta \quad \Leftrightarrow \quad \Delta < m_A;$$

in that case, E cannot win the B market since M is willing to charge an "effective" price below the entrant's quality-adjusted cost;
- if $\Delta > m_A > \Delta - f$, if it enters E wins the competition but at a price which is too low to cover the cost of entry; E's margin m_E must be such that

$$\hat{B}-\hat{b}-m_E = B-b+\Delta-m_E \geqslant (A+B)-(a+b)$$

or

$$m_E \leqslant \Delta - m_A,$$

and thus does not allow E to recoup the per-customer entry cost f.

In both cases, bundling allows M to discourage E from entering the market. In the end, M charges $P = A+B$ for the bundle, and enjoys de facto per-customer profit $B-b$ in market B.[69]

This simple example identifies several conditions for a tie-in to be profitable[70]:

(a) *M must commit itself to a tie-in.* Otherwise, once entry occurs, M no longer has an incentive to bundle A and B. Suppose indeed that the potential competitor has already sunk the entry cost and is thus present in market B. In the absence of bundling M loses market B but makes a per-customer profit m_A in market A. In contrast, bundling reduces M's profit by Δ even if M wins the competition with the entrant: in order to maintain its position, M charges a maximal price of

$$P = A+b-\Delta$$

and makes a per-customer profit of only $m_A - \Delta$.

Therefore, the use of tying as an entry barrier relies on a strong commitment. Such commitment is more likely to obtain through technological choices (for example, making A irreversibly incompatible with competitive B versions, or by designing the two goods as a single integrated system) than through purely commercial bundling, where prices or conditional rebates can be subject to renegotiation, particularly in response to entry.

(b) *The strategy must deter entry (or induce exit) of competitors in market B.* As just observed, a tie-in is self-defeating if competitors stay in the market, because it increases the intensity of price competition: firms are more eager to make such price concessions, since a concession for one component then generates sales for all the components of the bundle.

[69] With variable demands (e.g., heterogeneous preferences) for the two goods, bundling per se can reduce M's profitability; even in that case, however, bundling may be a profitable strategy when it deters entry – see the discussion in Whinston (1990).

[70] Nalebuff (2003a) provides a full discussion of tying issues in the light of recent cases.

(c) *Goods A and B must be rather independent.* As pointed out by Whinston, when goods A and B are complementary the Chicago critique applies: the exit of competitors from market B mutilates good A (which it did not do under independent demands) and thus anticompetitive tie-ins are less likely for very complementary segments; if for example good B were useless unless combined with good A, then M would have no incentive to deter entry, since the entrant's competitive edge on B would reinforce consumer demand for the monopolized good A.

Suppose for instance that M is a price leader and modify the above-described stage (iii) as follows: M first choose its price(s) – for the bundle or for its components – and then E, if it entered, sets its price for B. Then, absent bundling and following E's entry, M would charge a low price (slightly above) $\hat{b} - (\hat{B} - B) = b - \Delta$ (thus below its own cost) for its B component, forcing E to sell at cost, and would recover (almost) all of E's added value through a high price $(A + B + \Delta)$ on the bottleneck component A. Of course, in practice M may not be able to extract all of E's added value: in the absence of price leadership, competition may allow E to keep part or even all of its technological advantage (Δ).[71] Still, M would have no incentive to bundle and deter entry, and as long as it extracts *some* of E's efficiency gain, it would actually have an incentive *to unbundle* and to encourage entry in the B-market.[72]

REMARK (*bundling and competition*). The fact that bundling intensifies competition has been further emphasized by Matutes and Regibeau (1988) and Economides (1989), who focus on the compatibility choices of competing firms that each offer all components of a system.[73] When firms opt for compatibility, "market-by-market" competition prevails, where firms compete separately for each component; in contrast, under incompatibility, consumers cannot "mix-and-match" rival firms' components: competition in bundles thus prevails and competition is again more intense.[74] The argument applies as

[71] When M and E set their prices simultaneously, there are many equilibria, generating any sharing of the gain Δ – see, e.g., Ordover, Sykes and Willig (1985). In particular, the prices that emerge when M acts as a price leader still constitute an equilibrium outcome when M and E set their prices simultaneously; the equilibrium that would obtain under the price leadership of E is also an equilibrium, in which E keeps all of its technological advantage Δ. Eliminating weakly dominated strategies however excludes any below cost pricing strategy for M and would thus single out the equilibrium where the entrant obtains all the benefits of its competitive advantage Δ.

[72] See Whinston (1990) for a fuller discussion of situations where tying can be a profitable entry deterrence device.

[73] Bundling, like (in-)compatibility choices, are examples of endogenous switching costs. Therefore, many insights from the analysis of switching costs [see Farrell and Klemperer (2007) for a detailed survey] apply here as well.

[74] These papers thus focus on the case of perfect complements, whereas Whinston (1990) studies mainly the case of independent goods. The distinction between independent goods and complements tends however to be blurred when total demand is fixed (the "whole market" is served, say). In the absence of bundling, or with compatible technologies in the case of complements, the same market-by-market competition then obtains whether the goods are complements or independent, while bundling or incompatible technologies

well to the case of mixed bundling, where firms set different prices for stand-alone components and bundles (in practice, this can take the form of conditional discounts, where consumers receive a discount on one component if they buy another component from the same firm).[75] Nalebuff (2000) extends the analysis to the case of an integrated firm competing against non-integrated rivals for a system with many components (that is, one firm offers a version of all components, and competes with a different firm for each component). Nalebuff points out that, while bundling intensifies price competition, it also gives a larger market share to the integrated firm than the latter would have without bundling; this is because the unintegrated firms face double – or multiple – marginalization problems.[76] Nalebuff further shows that, as the number of components becomes large (and double marginalization problems thus pile up), the gain in market share may become so important as to offset the price reduction that stems from the more intense competition. In that case, bundling may actually *benefit* the integrated firm.

In many markets, the complementary goods are or may be purchased sequentially (examples include razors and blades, mobile telephones and accessories such as car chargers, new cars and spare parts, and computers and component upgrades). In such markets, it is sometimes feared that manufacturers may tie the additional equipment to the original one, or else make their original equipment incompatible with the additional equipment of rival manufacturers, in order to "lock in" consumers and weaken price competition in the subsequent market. In that case, however, anticipating this risk of opportunism consumers are willing to pay less for their initial purchases.[77] That is, such as strategy would backfire, since the weakened ex post competition in the additional equipment market triggers stronger competition for the original sales.[78,79]

lead in both cases to the same system competition (a possible caveat concerns the possibility of buying two bundles in order to "mix and match", which may be relevant when unit costs are low and in the absence of technical integration). The distinction between independent and complementary goods plays a more important role when total demand is elastic; with complements, there is then an interaction across markets even in the absence of bundling.

[75] Choi submitted to the European Commission, in the context of the GE/Honeywell merger, a model in which a firm produces two complementary goods (e.g., aircraft engines and avionics) and competes with unintegrated firms in each market. Assuming linear demand and cost, Choi showed that rivals face tougher competition and can lose market share, in spite of lower prices, when the integrated firm is allowed to set a price for the bundle, in addition to component prices – see Choi (2001) and Nalebuff (2003b) for a fuller discussion of this case.

[76] The integrated firm recognizes that cutting the price of one component boosts the demand for complementary components. In the absence of bundling, however, this benefits all components – its own and the rivals' ones; in contrast, with bundling the integrated firm knows that any sacrifice in the price of one component benefits its own complementary components – and only its own – while unitegrated firms still fail to take into account such positive feedback.

[77] Even if consumers rationally anticipate this opportunism, the incentive still exists ex post as long as the supplier is unable to commit to future prices.

[78] See Klemperer (1995) for a comprehensive survey of oligopolistic competition with switching costs.

[79] Manufacturers will thus have an incentive to limit their ability to hold up the consumers. This can be done by developing a reputation; however, reputation building may prove difficult when the prices of the

3.2. Protecting the monopolized market

While a monopolistic supplier would suffer from the exit of efficient producers of complementary goods, this exit may make it easier to protect the position of the bottleneck supplier in its core market. This is for example the case when entry in one segment facilitates or encourages entry in the other segment. Two variants of this idea have been explored. Choi and Stefanadis (2001) emphasize that, when entry is risky (e.g., when it involves R&D projects that may or may not succeed), tying the two goods A and B reduces the expected return of entry in *each* market, since entry in one market is then profitable only when entry is successful in the other market as well; tying may in that case deter entry in *both* markets. Carlton and Waldman (2002) focus instead on the presence of economies of scope between entry decisions in the two markets. We explore these two ideas in turn.

We use a framework similar to the one above, except that M initially benefits from a monopoly position in both markets A and B, and that the two goods are valuable only when used together (perfect complementarity). In addition, we suppose now that an entrant E can potentially enter both markets.[80]

– *Risky entry*. Following Choi and Stefanadis (2001), suppose that in each market E can invest in R&D in order to enter that market. More precisely, by investing f in R&D in any of the two markets, E succeeds with probability ρ in developing a better variety of the good in question, which it can then produce at a lower cost; as before, we will denote by Δ the total gain in quality and cost. For simplicity, we assume symmetry between the two goods, and in particular Δ is the same for both. The R&D projects in the two markets are stochastically independent and the timing is as follows:

- M decides whether to bundle the two goods; tying is then irreversible and, in addition, customers cannot undo the tie, nor do they want to add a second version of a good they already have (either the technologies are incompatible or the marginal cost, and therefore the price of a component is high)[81];

subsequent purchases are not readily observable or when there is uncertainty about the exact need for additional equipment or services. Another possibility is to reduce endogenous switching costs and opt for "open standards" [Garcia Mariñoso (2001)], grant licenses, and so forth, so as to commit to strong competition in the additional equipment and services, as stressed in the second-sourcing literature – see Farrell and Gallini (1988) and Shepard (1987), and Kende (1998) for a recent application.

80 The analysis would apply as well to the case of independent entrants in the two markets. Potential coordination problems might then reinforce M's incentive to bundle and deter entry; see Choi and Stefanadis (2001) for an example of such a coordination problem with variable levels of investment.

81 This latter possibility is less relevant in the case of information goods since the marginal cost is very small (indeed, many Windows equipped computers now have at least three media players besides Microsoft's own version).
In the absence of a technological constraint, customers would be willing to pay up to Δ to use the entrant's component on top of the bundle and the impact of tying then largely depends on the production cost of the component. If the entrant produces one component at a marginal cost $\hat{a}$, it cannot sell that single component

- in each market, E decides whether to invest in R&D;
- M and E (in case of successful entry) set their price(s).

If E succeeds in entering both markets, it replaces M and gets 2Δ. If instead E succeeds in one market only, its profits depend on whether M tied the two goods. If M bundled the two goods, E gains nothing if it enters only one market, since one good is useless without the other. Since there is no point investing in only one market, E does not invest at all whenever

$$2f > 2\rho^2\Delta.$$

In the absence of bundling, and when E enters in one market only, competition takes place between M and E. As already noted, many equilibria then exist, in which M and E share the efficiency gain Δ in different ways.

If E fully appropriates Δ whenever a R&D project is successful, whatever the outcome of the other R&D project. E therefore chooses to invest – and then invests in both markets – if and only if

$$f < \rho\Delta.$$

Therefore, tying deters R&D and thus entry in both markets whenever

$$\rho^2 < \frac{f}{\Delta} < \rho.$$

Tying is then a profitable strategy for M since with probability ρ^2 it prevents E from replacing M in both markets, and M gains nothing when E enters a single market.[82]

As the analysis makes clear, the riskiness of entry projects plays a key role here. If both R&D projects were certain, entry would occur whenever $f < \Delta$, with or without bundling.[83]

at a profitable price if $\hat{a} > \Delta$, but can still get $\Delta - \hat{a}$ otherwise. Thus, when marginal costs are very small, in the absence of some form of technical integration tying would not prevent the entrant from retrieving most of its added value.

[82] If M can appropriate a share λ of E's technological gain when E enters in only one market (e.g., if M has a chance to act as a price leader), tying deters investment and entry occurs "less often", namely if and only if (R&D investments are strategic complements, so that E undertakes either both projects or none):

$$\rho[1 - \lambda(1 - \rho)] < \frac{f}{\Delta} < \rho;$$

furthermore, if it does deter investment, tying is profitable only when avoiding eviction by the entrant (with would otherwise happen with probability ρ^2) matters more to the monopolist than getting a share λ of the technological gain when only one project succeeds (which would happen with probability $2\rho(1 - \rho)$).

[83] It suffices that entry be risky in at least one market; tying may then deter investment and entry in the other market – which in turn may deter entry in the first one. For example, suppose that investing f brings the technological gain Δ with certainty in market A, whereas investing $\hat{f} = \rho f$ brings the innovation with probability ρ in market B. Then, in the absence of tying, entry would occur in both markets whenever $\Delta > f$, whereas with tying, entry (in both markets) only occurs when $\rho(2\Delta) > (1 + \rho)f$, that is, when $\Delta > (1 + \rho)f/(2\rho)(> f)$.

– *Economies of scale and scope*. Suppose now, following Carlton and Waldman (2002), that entry takes more time in one market than in the other. By reducing the profitability of being in one market only, tying may then again deter E from entering either or even both markets.[84] More precisely, suppose that:

- there are two periods, 1 and 2, and two perfect complements A and B; in each period, consumers have unit demands as before; to simplify notation we suppose that the interest rate is zero (firms maximize the sum of the profits obtained in the two periods);
- at the beginning of period 1, M decides whether to bundle the two goods; as before, tying is then irreversible and cannot be undone by customers;
- it is initially easier to enter the "adjacent market" (B) than the "core market" (A): E can enter market B in either period, while it can enter market A only in period 2; to market $i = A, B$, E must incur a fixed cost f_i (once for all);
- for simplicity, entry is not risky[85];
- in the absence of tying, when E enters in one market only, it fully appropriates its efficiency gain in that market;
- absent tying, entry in market A is profitable (we relax this assumption below), whereas entry in market B is profitable only when it generates profits in both periods: letting f_i and Δ_i denote, respectively, the cost of entry and E's technological edge in market i, we have:

  $$f_A < \Delta_A, \qquad \Delta_B < f_B < 2\Delta_B;$$

  in addition, entry in both markets is profitable only if E enters market B in period 1:

  $$\Delta_A + \Delta_B < f_A + f_B < \Delta_A + 2\Delta_B.$$

In the absence of tying, E enters market B in period 1 and market A in period 2, and then drives M out of the market. By tying the two goods together, M reduces the profitability of E's entering market B, from $2\Delta_B - f_B > 0$ to $\Delta_B - f_B < 0$. Tying thus deters E from entering market B, which allows M to protect its position and maintain its monopoly profit over the two periods.

Carlton and Waldman also point out that E may want to enter the core market in order to get a larger share of its efficiency gain in the adjacent market, rather than to exploit any efficiency gain in the core market itself. In that case again, tying may block entry in both markets. To see this, suppose now that: (i) when E enters market B only, in the absence of tying M appropriates a share λ of E's efficiency gain; and (ii) the following conditions hold:

$$\Delta_A < f_A < \Delta_A + \lambda\Delta_B,$$

[84] The analysis would formally be the same if, instead of two periods, there were two independent demands for good B: a stand-alone demand for B and a demand for the system $\{A, B\}$. In that case again, tying would reduce E's profitability, by restricting its customer base to those consumers that are interested in B on a stand-alone basis.

[85] That is, $\rho = 1$ in the previous notation.

$$\Delta_A + \Delta_B < f_A + f_B < (1 - \lambda)\Delta_B + \Delta_A + \Delta_B.$$

The first set of conditions asserts that, while entry in A is not per se profitable, it becomes profitable when it allows E to fully appropriate the share of the technological gain Δ_B that M would otherwise appropriate; thus, absent bundling, E enters both markets rather than market B only. The second set of conditions asserts that, as before, entering both markets in period 2 is not profitable whereas, absent bundling, entering market B in period 1 and market A in period 2 is profitable. In such a situation, tying the two goods blocks entry in both markets, since entry then generates profits in the second period only.

The analyses of Choi and Stefanadis and of Carlton and Waldman apply to industries where innovating in adjacent segments is sufficiently costly: if E were to enter the B-market anyway, there would be no point tying the two goods. For the sequential entry scenario, entry in the core segment must moreover be sufficiently delayed that the entrant does not want to incur the cost of entering the adjacent markets only; as pointed out by Carlton and Waldman, the argument is therefore more relevant when the core product A has both a long imitation lag (so that tying reduces the profitability of entering the B-segment during a significant amount of time) and a short lifetime (so that the profitability of eventually entering both segments is limited).

Finally, it would be interesting to explore further the dynamics of these models. If dominance and the strategic use of the multi-entry problem lead to high incumbency profits, then there is a high incentive to become the new incumbent.[86] E may therefore decide to enter, even if entry is unprofitable in the "short run" (period 2). It would therefore be important to add periods 3, 4, ..., to see if tying can still play a significant role.

3.3. Innovation by the monopoly firm in the competitive segment

It is sometimes argued that incumbent firms have an incentive to strategically invest in R&D in adjacent markets, in order to discourage competitive efforts (including innovation) by rival producers. On the face of it, this concern seems at odds with the standard intuition that innovation is desirable, that competition should apply to the innovation process as well as to manufacturing processes, and that intellectual property should be protected. Forcing M to share its innovation with its B-competitors might for example create an undesirable asymmetry in the competitive process. First, sharing induces the independent B-suppliers to free ride, reducing their R&D effort and probably product diversity. Second, access policies of this type could imply a de facto line-of business restriction, as M might stop engaging in innovations that would be competed away (note, though, that from the Chicago School argument, M still has *some* incentive to innovate even if it is forced to share the resulting intellectual property, as improvements in the

[86] For analyses of dynamic contestability in different environments, see Fudenberg and Tirole (2000), Maskin and Tirole (1987, 1988) and Segal and Whinston (2007).

adjacent market benefits M's core activity). Both arguments advocate protecting M's rights over its innovation.

While this simple analysis is broadly correct, there is a twist, though, that has been analyzed by Farrell and Katz (2000)[87]: R&D competition in market B is affected by the presence of one of the competitors, M, in the adjacent market A. Suppose for the sake of argument that A is sold on a stand-alone basis (a similar analysis applies to the case in which M produces an input that is then used internally by its B-division or sold to independent producers of good B). Then the value of A is higher, the lower the quality-adjusted price of the product offered (by M or its competitors) in segment B. This implies that M benefits from innovation in market B in two ways: directly through sales of component B if M's innovation in the B market is superior to those of its rivals; and indirectly through the increase in demand for good A – and this even if M's B-component remains inferior to its rivals'. The direct effect involves no asymmetry with B-market competitors, but the indirect effect exists only for the multi-product firm.

To fix ideas, suppose for example that all B-competitors produce the same good (no differentiation) and that innovations reduce production costs in that market. The indirect or spillover effect is then clearly identified when M's innovation in market B is dominated by a rival's innovation, in which case M makes no profit in the B-segment. In that case, a small increase in the quality of M's innovation in market B still leaves it dominated and thus does not generate any profit to M's B-division. Yet it increases M's profit if it forces the efficient B-rival to lower its price (squeezing quasi-rents from the independent B-producer), and thereby boosts the demand for complementary good A. This indirect effect takes another form when M's innovation in the B-segment dominates its rivals'. Then, beyond the direct impact on market B, a marginal increase in the quality of M's innovation increases the demand for M's integrated solution (this is an example of the vertical externality effect identified in Section 2).

The spillover effect implies that M's R&D efforts in segment B are higher than they would be if M's R&D division did not internalize the profit in the A segment. In turn, M's enhanced R&D effort reduces that of its rivals. As Farrell and Katz (2000) show, the overall welfare impact of M's B-division internalizing M's A-division's interests is ambiguous.

As usual, we should clarify the nature of the policy intervention that is being contemplated. Short of imposing structural remedies, no antitrust decision will prevent M's B-division from internalizing the A-division's interests; hence, the above analysis may seem irrelevant as it stands. One remedy that antitrust authorities may be tempted to adopt consists in mandating M to share its innovation in market B for some reasonably low licensing fee. This would not impact M's indirect benefit of innovation, which would still exert pressure on B-competitors and contribute to enhance demand for systems; however, this duty to share would reduce the direct benefit of innovation on market B; innovation sharing thus reduces investments by M (and may eliminate

[87] See also Choi et al. (2003).

them if there are fixed costs of R&D), and raises investments by rivals, with potentially detrimental welfare consequences, especially if M has substantial R&D expertise and is likely to produce a superior innovation.

The ambiguity of the welfare analysis suggests that such antitrust involvement is overall unlikely to foster innovation unless one demonstrates that (a) the reduction in independent B-producers' R&D effort due to M being vertically integrated more than offsets the increase in that of M, and (b) M's B-division can be effectively duplicated by entry in the B-market (e.g., through an effective divestiture and in the absence of economies of scope). It is therefore not surprising that antitrust authorities have traditionally shunned direct intervention in the competitive market.

Even if an analysis of this kind were used in a particular case as the basis for anti-trust intervention, the resulting intervention would run counter to the tradition of intellectual property law. That tradition seeks to resolve the tension between the benefits of competition and the protection of innovation by protecting the innovation from direct imitation, while encouraging rival innovations. Indeed (as the analysis above makes clear), while the quality of the best innovation determines the gross benefits to consumers who purchase it, the price at which they buy (and therefore the net benefits of the purchase) is determined by the quality of the second-best innovation (this is the same phenomenon as the fact that the price paid by the winner in an auction is determined by the valuation of the second-highest bidder). Consequently an innovation by rivals plays an important role in the process of keeping prices low, a role that IP law has consistently sought to protect. By contrast, intervention to restrict innovation by M in the B-segment would essentially consist in removing one firm's IP protection in order to protect the innovation of another firm from post-innovation rivalry.

Choi (2004) analyzes the impact of tying, rather than integration as such, on R&D incentives in the tied market. He considers a situation where M has a monopoly position in market A and faces competition in adjacent market B (goods A and B may, but need not be complements).[88] Choi starts from the observation that, in such a situation, tying generally increases competition and lowers prices, but also allows M to capture a larger share in the tied good market (as discussed in Section 3.1); as a result, tying tilts the R&D incentives in favor of M; tying can thus be interpreted as a credible commitment device to more aggressive R&D investment by M, and can discourage rivals' R&D investments. The change in R&D incentives allows M to increase its profits in the future, and can thus make tying a profitable strategy even if it intensifies competition in the short-term. The welfare implications are again ambiguous, since in the short-run tying reduces prices but restricts customer choice, and in the longer run it increases one firm's R&D incentives but reduces it rivals'.

[88] Relatedly, Choi (1996) considers the case where firms engage in a pre-emptive patent race for systems (that is, firms compete for both components); he shows that tying can mitigate the rent dissipation that can arise in such situations.

3.4. Summary

Competition in the adjacent market brings product variety, lower costs and lower prices. The Chicago School pointed out that competition in that market thereby enhances the value of the bottleneck good and boosts its owner's profit when the bottleneck good is marketed on a stand-alone basis and the two goods are complements. Bundling and foreclosure therefore must be either efficiency-driven or motivated by predatory intents. We reviewed two predation stories and hinted at their strengths and limits. First, bundling may be a way of deterring entry in (or inducing exit from) the adjacent market when goods are not complements (at least for a substantial fraction of the users). Second, bundling may allow a dominant firm to maintain its dominant position in its bottleneck market.

Given that the motivations for bundling may be rather unrelated to anti-competitive motives,[89] and that most firms, dominant or not, bundle goods and services on a routine basis, a rule of reason seems appropriate. The issue for economists is then to guide competition authorities in their handling of antitrust cases. To the extent that the anti-competitive foreclosure theories reviewed in this section are in fine predation stories (foreclosure in general leading, from the Chicago School argument, to a short-term profit sacrifice by the tying firm, with the prospect of a later recoupment), one possible approach is to treat tying cases through the lens of predatory behavior.[90] Whether one agrees with this viewpoint or not, there is clearly a need for economists to come up with clearer guidelines for the antitrust treatment of tying behaviors by dominant firms.

4. Exclusive customer contracts

Following our definition of foreclosure, we have so far discussed alternative ways in which an incumbent firm may strategically use its market power in one market in order to restrict competition in a related market. In some situations, the incumbent may use this market power to protect its position in the *same* market, even in the absence of interaction with related markets. For example, a supplier that currently benefits from a monopoly position may deter entry by locking customers into long-term exclusive arrangements. However, a Chicago critique again applies: customers should be reluctant to agree to such exclusive arrangements and should demand an appropriate compensation, that would dissipate the profitability of these arrangements.

To see this more precisely, suppose that an incumbent monopolist, M, faces a customer, C. This user is willing to buy one unit, which costs c and brings a gross surplus

[89] Among them: distribution cost savings, compatibility cost savings, accountability (liability, reputation) benefits, protection of intellectual property, market segmentation and metering; we discuss these efficiency motives in Section 5.

[90] For a discussion of the costs and benefits of this approach, see Tirole (2005) and the comments thereupon by Carlton and Waldman and by Nalebuff.

of S; and assume that a potential entrant E can enter with a lower cost $\hat{c} \leqslant c$ and generate a higher surplus $\hat{S} \geqslant S$. In the absence of entry, M could exploit its monopoly position, charge a price of S and thus get $S - c$ in profit. If instead entry occurs, competition drives the price down to $c + (\hat{S} - S)$; consumers then get a net surplus $S - c$, while E earns $\Delta = \hat{S} - S + c - \hat{c}$ and M is out of the market.

To prevent entry, M could try to lock-in the user through an exclusive contract. To capture this possibility, consider for example the following two-stage game:

- in the first stage, the incumbent offers C an exclusive contract at a given price p;
- in the second stage, if the exclusive contract has been accepted, C buys from M at price p; otherwise, E chooses whether to enter and then compete with M as above.

In the first stage, C anticipates that it will no longer benefit from competition if it signs an exclusive contract; thus, C does not accept an exclusive contract at a price p higher than c (which gives him the "competitive" surplus of $S - c$), so that such an exclusive contract cannot be profitable for M.

4.1. *Exclusionary clauses as a rent-extraction device*

Recognizing this issue, Aghion and Bolton (1987) pointed out that M could still use exclusive contracts in order to extract some of the entrant's technological advantage, Δ. For example, consider the following penalty contract: C buys from M at price p, or else must pay a penalty for breach d to M.[91] Then, in order to attract C, E must offer a price $\hat{p}$ such that $\hat{p} + d \leqslant p + \hat{S} - S$, or

$$\hat{p} \leqslant (p + \hat{S} - S) - d.$$

That is, the penalty for breach d is actually paid by E, and thus plays the role of an entry fee. It is then optimal for M to set d so as to reap the entrant's technological advantage. For example, the contract $(p = c, d = \Delta)$ forces the entrant to offer a price $\hat{p} = \hat{c}$, thus allowing M to appropriate Δ.

In this simple example, M can fine-tune the penalty for breach so as to extract the entire efficiency gain of the entrant, and thus entry occurs whenever it is efficient. The penalty for breach may discourage the entrant from investing in the new technology, though. Furthermore, Aghion and Bolton point out that, in practice, there may be some uncertainty about the entrant's technological superiority; in that case, maximizing its expected profit, the incumbent takes the risk of foreclosing entry if E is not much more efficient than M, so as to extract more of the efficiency gains when E has a large technological advantage.

EXAMPLE. Suppose that (i) E faces initially an uncertain cost (the same logic would apply to uncertainty about the quality advantage); and (ii) M and C sign a contract before this uncertainty is resolved. Once the cost $\hat{c}$ is realized, E decides whether to

[91] An alternative interpretation of this contract is that C pays d for the option of buying a unit at a price $p - d$.

enter the market, in which case it incurs an infinitesimal fixed cost of entry.[92] If for example $\hat{S} = S = 1$, $c = 1/2$ and $\hat{c}$ is uniformly distributed over $[0, 1]$, in the absence of any exclusivity entry occurs whenever $\hat{c} < 1/2$: if $\hat{c} \geqslant 1/2$, E does not enter and M earns $S - c = 1/2$ while if $\hat{c} < 1/2$, E enters and earns $\hat{c} - c$; since entry occurs with probability $1/2$, and E's expected cost is $1/4$ in case of entry, M's and E's expected profits are respectively $1/4$ and $1/8$. Now, suppose that M and C could levy a (non-contingent) *entry fee* f from E, and share the proceeds as desired; entry would then only occur when $\hat{c} + f \leqslant c$, thus with probability $(1/2 - f)$. Since entry per se does not affect M and C's total surplus (since E appropriates all the gain from its cost advantage when it enters), M and C would maximize the expected revenue from the fee, $(1/2 - f)f$ and thus choose $f = 1/4$, generating in this way an extra expected gain of $1/16$; entry would thus be restricted, and would only occur when $\hat{c} \leqslant 1/4$. But M and C can precisely achieve this outcome be signing a penalty contract of the form ($p = 3/4$, $d = 1/2$). Indeed, with this contract C is assured to pay no more than $3/4$ and thus earns the same expected profit as in the absence of exclusivity ($1/4$), while E only enters when $\hat{c} \leqslant p - d = 1/4$ and M earns either $p - c = 1/4$ in the absence of entry or $d = 1/2$ in case of entry. This contract thus replicates the optimal entry fee; entry is again restricted, while M's expected profit is increased by $1/16$.[93]

RENEGOTIATION. That exclusive contracts (in the form of a penalty for breach) have an exclusionary impact relies on the assumption that M and C cannot renegotiate their contract (say, M would forgive some of the penalty for breach) once E has made an offer. Otherwise, whenever this offer generates a surplus higher than $S - c$, M and C would indeed renegotiate the terms of their contract (say, M would forgive some of the penalty for breach) so as to benefit from E's offer. Given this, E would and could enter whenever entry is efficient. This point is recognized by Spier and Whinston (1995), who however emphasize that M may still have an incentive to block entry by over-investing in improving its own technology: by doing so, M forces E to concede a better deal; this strategic benefit can then be shared by M and C, e.g., through a lump-sum transfer in their initial contract.[94]

To see this more precisely, suppose for simplicity that M and E only differ in their costs of production ($\hat{S} = S$) and consider the following timing:

[92] This assumption ensures that E enters only if it can earn a positive profit. In the absence of any fixed cost, E would always "enter" the market and exert pressure on M; the analysis would be similar, in the sense that M's exclusionary behavior would lead to production inefficiency (that is, E may not supply C although it is more efficient than M).

[93] While M gets here the entire revenue from the fee, this revenue could be redisbuted to C through a simultaneous reduction in p and d.

[94] The general issue here is the commitment value of a contract that can be renegotiated later on. Katz (1991) and Caillaud, Jullien and Picard (1995) point out that such a contract may still involve some commitment when the relationship is subject to agency problems; e.g., in the form of moral hazard or adverse selection. See Caillaud and Rey (1995) for an introduction to this literature. In Spier and Whinston's model, there is indeed "moral hazard" since signing an exclusive agreement affects M's incentives to invest in its own technology.

(i) M offers an exclusive contract at a stipulated price of p, which C accepts or refuses.
(ii) M decides whether to invest in its technology: investing I reduces M's cost from $c = \bar{c}$ to $c = \underline{c}$; M's investment decision and/or actual cost is publicly observed.
(iii) E's cost $\hat{c}$ is drawn from a distribution over $[0, S]$ and publicly observed; E then sets its price, $\hat{p}$.
(iv) M and C can renegotiate their initial agreement (or sign one if M's first offer had been rejected); we assume that M and C bargain efficiently – as we will see, the division of the gains from trade is however irrelevant.
(v) C chooses its supplier.

Suppose that C accepts an exclusive contract with a stipulated price $p \leqslant S$. At stages (iv) and (v), either there is no renegotiation and C buys from M at p (this occurs if $\hat{p} > c$, since there is then no gain from renegotiation) or renegotiates the exclusivity agreement (if $\hat{p} \leqslant c$).[95] Anticipating this, at stage (iii) E does not enter if $\hat{c} > c$, otherwise it enters and quotes a price equal to c, leading M and C to renegotiate their initial agreement while minimizing their gains from renegotiation.[96] Therefore, entry occurs whenever it is efficient, *given* M's cost level, c. However, under an exclusive contract, M's ex post payoff is $p - c$, with or without renegotiation: C must buy at price p absent any renegotiation, and when renegotiation takes place, E leaves (almost) no gain from it, implying that M gets again $p - c$. This, in turn, implies that M chooses to invest whenever

$$\bar{c} - \underline{c} > I.$$

By contrast, M's investment is socially desirable only if

$$\big[1 - \hat{F}(\bar{c})\big](\bar{c} - \underline{c}) + \int_{\underline{c}}^{\bar{c}} (\hat{c} - \underline{c})\,\mathrm{d}\hat{F}(\hat{c}) > I,$$

where $\hat{F}$ denotes the cumulative distribution of E's cost. Note that the social benefit, which appears on the left-hand side of the above inequality, is lower than $\bar{c} - \underline{c}$; therefore, exclusivity leads to over-investment relative to what would be socially desirable, whenever

$$\big[1 - \hat{F}(\bar{c})\big](\bar{c} - \underline{c}) + \int_{\underline{c}}^{\bar{c}} (\hat{c} - \underline{c})\,\mathrm{d}\hat{F}(\hat{c}) < I < \bar{c} - \underline{c}.$$

In that case, after signing up a customer into a (renegotiable) exclusivity contract, M invests in its technology in order not only to reduce its cost when E is inefficient, but also

[95] Technically, there is no need for renegotiation when $\hat{p} = c$. To avoid an "openess" problem, however, we assume that M and C then take E's offer.

[96] This is why the relative bargaining power of M and C is irrelevant, as long as they bargain efficiently. Since it is strictly desirable for the two parties to renegotiate as long as $\hat{p} < c$, by setting a price (close to) $\hat{p} = c$, E induces renegotiation but actually appropriates (almost) all of the gains from it.

to force E to offer a better price ($\underline{c}$ instead of $\bar{c}$) when it efficient; this, however, implies that E enters less often than it would if M did not invest in its technology (E no longer enters when $\underline{c} < \hat{c} < \bar{c}$).[97]

More generally, exclusivity contracts in which downstream customers commit to purchase from an upstream supplier have the potential to deter investments by competing upstream suppliers. In Aghion and Bolton (1987), these investments take the form of an all-or-nothing entry decision. But the investment choice may more generally refer to an investment scale. In Stefanadis (1997), two upstream firms compete in the R&D market to obtain a patent on a process innovation that reduces the marginal cost of supplying the input. An exclusive contract with a downstream customer reduces the profitability of R&D for the upstream rival, and therefore the rival's R&D effort. In equilibrium, upstream firms lock in customers through exclusive contracts in order to reduce their rival's R&D expenditures in the subsequent innovation markets.

4.2. Scale economies and users' coordination failure

In a second contribution in the same paper, Aghion and Bolton (1987) also point out that the incumbent supplier, M, can play customers against each other in other to deter the entry of a more efficient competitor. While Aghion and Bolton's original analysis relies on commitment to conditional contracts[98] that may be difficult to implement (e.g., because of legal restrictions), Rasmusen, Ramseyer and Wiley (1991) and Segal and Whinston (2000) have shown that their insight is robust in the presence of scale economies.[99] To see this, suppose for example that there are n customers and that entry is viable only if E can sign up at least $m + 1 < n$ customers. M can therefore block entry by "bribing" a targeted group of $n - m$ customers into exclusive arrangements, by sharing the rents it gets from exploiting its monopoly power vis-à-vis the remaining m customers. This strategy is clearly successful when the monopoly rents exceed the benefits that the targeted customers can hope to derive together from free entry.

Even if this condition does not hold, however, M can still successfully deter entry by "playing customers against each other", that is, by relying on poor coordination among the customers: while customers may be better off if all reject exclusivity, they may fail to coordinate and accept exclusivity if they anticipate that the others will do – M may then not even need to bribe any customer.

Segal and Whinston (2000) stress that M's ability to discriminate among customers enhances the scope for successful exclusion. Without discrimination, M would fail to

[97] Whether M would invest in the absence of any initial agreement depends, among other things, on the price that E charges when it is less efficient than M and on C's ex post bargaining power. Spier and Whinston (1995) however confirm that M's incentive to invest (and thus limit entry) is maximal under exclusivity.

[98] Aghion and Bolton assumed that M could commit itself to charge prices that are conditional on how many customers accept exclusivity.

[99] Rasmusen, Ramseyer and Wiley (1991) meant to focus on non-discriminatory contracts but actually assume some form of discrimination. Segal and Whinston (2000) clarify this issue as well as the respective role of discriminatory offers and of customers' coordination problems.

deter the entry of an equally efficient competitor if customers coordinate – even only tacitly – on their favored equilibrium. By contrast, with discriminatory offers the above-mentioned scheme may succeed even if customers can explicitly coordinate their buying decisions.[100]

A related insight is obtained by Bernheim and Whinston (1998), who study a situation in which two suppliers compete sequentially for two customers. Bernheim and Whinston in particular show that the first customer may strategically choose to "exclude" one supplier so as to share with the other supplier the additional profits from its enhanced bargaining position vis-à-vis the second customer. To see this more precisely, consider the following framework:

- M and E simultaneously offer a contract to a first customer, C_1; each contract can be conditional on exclusivity (that is, it can stipulate different terms, depending on whether C_1 contracts with the other supplier as well). C_1 then accepts or rejects each offer; if C_1 buys a positive quantity from E (exclusively or not), E enters and incurs a fixed cost f;
- Then, M and E offer conditional contracts to a second customer, C_2; there again, contracts can be conditional on exclusivity and C_2 then chooses its supplier(s).

The payoffs are as follows. Let S_i denote the surplus that C_i can generate from dealing with both M and E (assuming that E enters) and S_i^M and S_i^E the surplus that C_i generates when dealing with M or E only. We assume that M and E offer partial substitutes:

$$S_i^M + S_i^E > S_i \left(> S_i^M, S_i^E > 0\right).$$

We will moreover assume that E's entry is socially efficient; that is,

$$S > S^M,$$

where

$$S \equiv S_1 + S_2 - f$$

denotes the total net surplus generated by the two suppliers and

$$S^M \equiv S_1^M + S_2^M$$

denotes the total surplus generated by M only.

Consider now the last stage of the game. Bernheim and Whinston show that, while this "common agency subgame" may involve both exclusive and non-exclusive equilibria, there is a Pareto-dominant equilibrium (for the suppliers); this equilibrium maximizes the joint surplus of the suppliers and the customer. If E entered the market, the

[100] This scheme is an example of "divide-and-conquer" strategies that were initially explored by Innes and Sexton (1994). Fumagalli and Motta (2006) stress however that such strategies are more difficult to implement when buyers are competing against each other, since then it is more difficult to compensate a deviant buyer who wants to buy from the more efficient entrant.

equilibrium involves no exclusivity and each supplier gets its "contribution" to the total surplus; that is, M gets $S_2 - S_2^E$, while E gets $S_2 - S_2^M$.[101] If instead E did not enter, then M enjoys a monopoly position and gets S_2^M.

Consider now the first stage. The same logic prevails, except that the relevant surpluses account for the suppliers' payoffs in the subsequent contracting stage. Thus, if C_1 chooses to deal with E (exclusively or not), E enters and the joint surplus of M, E and C_1 is given by

$$\hat{S} \equiv S_1 + \left(S_2 - S_2^E\right) + \left(S_2 - S_2^M - f\right);$$

the substitutability between the two suppliers implies that $\hat{S}$ is smaller than the total surplus S. If this substitutability is large enough, $\hat{S}$ may be even smaller than S^M, the surplus generated by M. In this case, while entry would be efficient (since $S > S^M$), the outcome of the first stage is that C_1 deals exclusively with M, so as to make M the monopoly supplier of C_2. That is, taking into account M's monopoly profit on C_2, M and C_1 can together generate more profits by excluding E, even if they could extract all of E's contribution to their joint surplus. Exclusive dealing then emerges as an anti-competitive device against (E and) C_2. The argument relies again on some form of coordination failure between the customers: if the two customers could side-contract, C_2 would be willing to compensate C_1 for opting for a non-exclusive relationship with M.

4.3. Summary

The Coasian or commitment theory of foreclosure reviewed in Section 2 insisted on the detrimental impact of downstream competition on upstream profit. To avoid the erosion of profit, downstream access to the upstream bottleneck was reduced relative to what would be socially optimal (assuming the very existence of this upstream bottleneck). By contrast, in the theories reviewed in this section, downstream users (who do not compete against each other) in a sense receive "too much" access to the bottleneck. In the rent-extraction theory, penalties for breach are used to force a more efficient upstream entrant to reduce its price; in the entry-deterrence theory, penalties for breach expose customers to a free-riding problem when the entrant faces a large fixed cost of entry and therefore needs a broad and profitable enough market in order to become a competitive threat. Either way, long-term contracts may create inefficiencies.

We have only touched on the issues associated with penalties for breach and dynamic price discrimination. More general approaches are surveyed by Armstrong (2006), Fudenberg and Villas-Boas (2005) and Stole (2007). Also, to draw tentative guidelines such as the ones that are currently debated for the application of European Article 82 on abuses of dominance, one needs to discuss possible efficiency defenses; we review some of them in the next section.

[101] The condition $S_2 - S_2^M < f$ would thus ensure that E does not want to enter when it fails to deal with C_1.

5. Potential defenses for exclusionary behaviors

Vertical or horizontal foreclosure may be socially beneficial in certain circumstances. First, it may enhance innovators' benefit from R&D efforts and thus foster their incentives to innovate or develop new products. Second, in situations where unrestrained competition in downstream or adjacent markets leads to excessive entry and duplication of fixed costs, foreclosure may help reducing excessive entry. Finally, integration may improve coordination between firms, for example by providing better incentives to monitor their efforts; foreclosure then is an undesired by-product of a useful institution. We briefly examine these defenses in turn. For expositional purposes we first focus on defenses that are relevant for vertical foreclosure, although some of them apply as well to horizontal foreclosure; we then turn to defenses that are specific to tying.

5.1. *Efficiency arguments for (vertical) foreclosure*

– *Forbearance as a reward to investment or innovation.* The antitrust authorities may refrain from prosecuting foreclosure activities because the monopoly position thus obtained compensates the bottleneck for its investment or innovative activity. This efficiency defense is similar to the logic underlying the patent system – as already noted, a prospective licensee would not pay much for using a new technology if it anticipates the licensor to "flood the market" with licensees. In both cases society is willing to tolerate static inefficiency, such as monopoly pricing, in order to promote dynamic efficiency. The same issue as for patents then arises: To what extent is forbearance an optimal mechanism for providing innovators with a rent? As recognized in *Aspen*, one cannot impose a general duty to deal with competitors. And even when such a duty is warranted, it would be unreasonable to mandate competitors' access to each and every aspect of a firm's activity on an unbundled basis.

Our discussion suggests one plausible dividing line to answer the question of when it is most desirable to force access: Is the origin of the bottleneck increasing returns to scale or scope (as may be the case of a bridge, a stadium, or a news agency) or an historical accident? Or does the bottleneck result from an innovative strategy? Intervention to avoid foreclosure and consequently to reduce the bottleneck profit seems more warranted in the former than in the latter case.

– *Free-riding by the downstream units on the marketing expenses of the upstream firm.* This argument states that the upstream firm must be able to recoup marketing expenses that will benefit downstream units. This argument is related to the above argument of forbearance as a reward to investment (see the discussion of Chemla's work in Appendix A.2).

– *Excessive entry.* Entry typically involves significant fixed costs, and excessive entry can therefore result in an inefficient duplication of these costs. In the absence of foreclosure, excessive entry can indeed occur due to the so-called "business-stealing" effect: when contemplating entering the market, a firm does not take into account that its prospective customers will in part simply switch away from existing products; the revenue generated by its product may thus exceed its social value.[102] In this context, foreclosure may be socially desirable when the duplication of the fixed cost is particularly harmful, and vertical or horizontal integration may yield a socially better outcome than no integration. We provide in Appendix B a short analysis of this issue using our vertical foreclosure framework.[103] The validity of this argument may however be difficult to assess in practice, since the characterization of the socially optimal number of firms is generally a complex matter.

– *Monitoring benefits of vertical integration.* Benefits of vertical integration are often mentioned as efficiency defenses. For example, control of a supplier by one of the buyers may put someone in charge of making sure that the technological choices of the supplier are in the best interest of the buyers. To be certain, the integrated buyer may then use its control right over the supplier to engage in non-price foreclosure, for instance by insisting on technological specifications that are biased in its favor. And, as in this paper, it may overcharge the buyers while keeping an internal transfer price equal to marginal cost and thus practice price foreclosure. These foreclosure practices are then arguably an undesirable by-product of an otherwise desirable activity, namely monitoring.

– *Costly divestitures.* Antitrust enforcers and regulators are often reluctant to force vertical separation because of the disruptive cost of disentangling deeply intertwined activities. That is, even if they would have prohibited the merger of two vertically-related firms, they do not order a divestiture when faced with the fait accompli of vertical integration.

– *Costly expansion of capacity or the costs incurred in order to provide access.* We have assumed that the cost of supplying competitors of a vertically integrated firm is the same as the cost of internal purchases. In practice, the former may exceed the latter, either because upstream decreasing returns to scale make marginal units more costly to supply than inframarginal ones, or because there is a genuine asymmetry between the costs of supplying the downstream affiliate and its competitors, due for example to compatibility costs. In essence, this efficiency defense amounts to saying that there is no foreclosure because discrimination among competitors is cost-based.

[102] See Salop (1979) and Mankiw and Whinston (1986) for detailed analyses of this issue.

[103] See Vickers (1995) for a related analysis of the relative cost and benefits of vertical integration in the context of a *regulated* upstream monopolist in which the regulator (i) controls the upstream firm's price but not its profit, (ii) operates direct transfers to the firm, and (iii) has no statutory power to regulate downstream entry. In this context, vertical integration leads to a higher (regulated) access price (since it is more difficult to extract the information from the integrated firm, the incentive scheme must be more high-powered, resulting in a higher access charge) but less duplication of fixed cost (because of foreclosure).

– *Fear of being associated with inferior downstream partners who might hurt the firm's reputation.* We have assumed that the only negative externality of supply by a downstream firm on the other downstream firms and thus indirectly on the upstream bottleneck is price mediated. That is, downstream entry depresses the final price and thus the industry profit; but it increases social welfare. There may be some other negative externalities on the upstream firm that are less socially desirable. In particular, misbehavior by a downstream firm may spoil the reputation of other downstream firms and of the upstream bottleneck. This argument, which relies on the existence of monitoring of the downstream firms, is often invoked for example in a franchising context, and used to justify strict quality controls.

– *Universal service.* It is sometimes argued that universal service obligations imposed by the regulator or the law should be compensated by a greater leniency vis-à-vis foreclosing behaviors; see, e.g., the 1993 decision of the European Commission in *Corbeau* (Decision *C 320/91*). This argument is simply a variant of the general argument that fixed costs must be recouped by market power in some market. And again one must wonder whether foreclosure is the most efficient means of creating market power.[104]

5.2. *Efficiency arguments for tying*

As we said earlier, some of the defenses listed above apply also in the horizontal context. Others are specific to that context. The most obvious such defense is the distribution cost savings associated with marketing two products together instead of separately. Other standard defenses of tying include:

– *Preventing inefficient substitution.* When two separately marketed goods are combined in variable proportions, market power over one good distorts customers' choices over the relative use of the two goods.[105] Consider for example a monopolist that produces a durable good, for which maintenance and repair services can be supplied by independent providers. If the monopolist prices its original equipment above (marginal) cost while maintenance is priced at cost, customers rely excessively on maintenance and replace their equipment insufficiently often. By tying the aftermarket services to the original purchase of the equipment, the monopolist generates more efficient replacement decisions, which improves social welfare. A similar argument applies when there is competition among original equipment manufacturers and customers face switching costs – in that case, tying can also improve both social and consumer welfare.[106]

[104] There is a further debate as to whether universal service should be financed through mark-ups on specific segments, as opposed to the policy of creating a competitively neutral universal service fund financing universal service through industry-wide taxes.

[105] See Vernon and Graham (1971), Schmalensee (1973), Su (1975), Warren-Boulton (1974) and Rust (1986).

[106] See Carlton and Waldman (2001), who further stress that monopolizing the used parts markets can be efficient when the supplier of the original equipment is also in the best position for re-manufacturing used parts into replacement parts.

– *Metering*. Relatedly, tying consumables may allow a supplier to meter usage and thus discriminate between high- and low-intensity users.[107] While such third-degree price discrimination has in general ambiguous welfare implications,[108] it can allow the supplier to recoup large investments and foster incentives to develop new products.

– *Signaling quality*. Tying consumables to the sale of the original equipment can give a high-quality seller an effective tool for signaling the quality of its product, when quality is not readily observable to buyers.[109] Indeed, if the manufacturer charges usage (through the tied consumables) rather than the initial purchase of the equipment, consumers then "pay" for the equipment only if they really use it, once they have found out its true quality.

6. Concluding remarks

Despite recent advances, some progress must still be made in order to better anchor the concept of foreclosure within the broader antitrust doctrine. First, a better integration between theory and applications should be achieved. This chapter has offered some guiding principles for thinking about the incentives for, and the feasibility and welfare implications of foreclosure. The link could be further strengthened. Relatedly, further empirical investigations will allow us to get a better feel for the magnitude of the effects involved and to assess the relevance of not only the scope for foreclosure, but also the theoretical factors affecting this scope (such as the competitiveness of upstream segments, the availability of alternative foreclosure strategies, or the location of the bottleneck).

In our discussion of efficiency defenses we hinted at some considerations calling for a milder antitrust treatment of exclusionary behavior, as when the bottleneck results from innovation or investment rather than returns to scale or scope, legal and regulatory interventions, or historical accident. Still, this discussion of efficiency defenses was somewhat of an addendum to the treatment of the anticompetitive effect, and the two should be better integrated.

This call for a unified treatment actually does not solely apply to theory. Indeed, the legal and regulatory framework exhibits, as we noted, a remarkable dichotomy between the treatment of intellectual property in which the practice of foreclosure is widely viewed as acceptable (except for some recent pushes for compulsory licensing and open access in certain contexts) and other areas in which foreclosure is systematically

[107] In *Chicken Delight* (1971), for example, the franchiser used packing items to measure the volume of activity of its franchisees; the franchiser's mark-up over the packing items then implemented a reliable revenue-sharing scheme. See Chen and Ross (1993, 1999) for applications to aftermarket services with, respectively, monopolistic and competitive manufacturers.

[108] See Katz (1987) and Tirole (1988).

[109] See Schwartz and Werden (1996).

viewed as socially detrimental. We have shown that the broad conceptual framework is the same, and offered guiding principles as to when foreclosure should be opposed or tolerated.

While we have tried to provide a comprehensive theoretical treatment within the confines of the topic of this paper, it would be desirable to broaden the scope of analysis in several directions. More complex forms of essential facilities have emerged, and corresponding theoretical frameworks should be developed. First, in markets such as telecommunications or the Internet, in which final consumers interact with each other through the mediation of the platforms' operator they are connected to, bottlenecks are endogenous in that they depend on the outcome of the "downstream" competition for consumers (by contrast, in our analysis, the bottleneck pre-exists downstream competition). Namely, each operator must rely on its competitors to terminate the connections initiated by their own consumers.[110] This competitive bottleneck problem, in which each operator needs access to its rivals' customers, exhibits many new and interesting features.[111] For example, an operator can reduce its need for access to a bottleneck it does not control by gaining market share and "internalizing" the interactions demanded by its customers. Furthermore, small players have more, rather than less, market power than big players in the wholesale market, provided that the latter are forced to interoperate; for, all players have the same – full monopoly – power on terminations toward their customers, and small players can demand very high termination prices without moving final prices much.

Bottlenecks that are governed by a cooperative arrangement rather than owned by a single entity would also deserve a full treatment on their own. Such bottlenecks can result from a desire to reap economies of scale, as in the case of a credit card or agricultural cooperative, or to eliminate multiple marginalization and offer a one-stop-shopping facility, as in the case of patent pools and joint marketing agreements. They can be run as for-profit entities or as not-for-profit associations. They raise interesting questions about the extent of access that should be granted to customers and for potential members. The previous considerations as to where the bottleneck nature comes from are relevant here as well. So, for example, a bottleneck created by economies of scale should in principle grant broad access, as long as this access does not amount to pure free riding on investments (financial and informational-learning) made by previous members. But the joint provision of the bottleneck gives rise to new questions such as the impact of new members on the governance of the bottleneck (with the possibility that dissonant objectives may hamper the functioning and reduce the efficiency of the bottleneck). We leave these and other fascinating issues for further research.

[110] Unless consumers "multi-home" on several platforms, a topic that has been studied only recently; see, e.g., Rochet and Tirole (2003).

[111] See, e.g., Armstrong (1998) and Laffont, Rey and Tirole (1998a, 1998b) for early analyses of telecommunications networks competition in a deregulated environment. More recent developments and further references to the subsequent literature can be found in Armstrong (2002), Laffont et al. (2003) and Jeon, Laffont and Tirole (2004).

Appendix A. Private incentives not to exclude

Section 2 emphasized the bottleneck owner's incentive to use various foreclosure strategies to preserve its market power. This section investigates whether the foreclosure activity can backfire on the bottleneck owner.

A.1. The protection of downstream specific investment: the 1995 AT&T divestiture

Interestingly, the foreclosure logic implies that a bottleneck owner may in some circumstances want to refrain from integrating vertically. To understand this, recall that under vertical integration, the excluded rivals on the competitive segment suffer a secondary line injury. Anticipating this, they may refrain from investing in assets that are specific to their relationship with the bottleneck owner, as these have low value if their firms have limited access to the essential input. This in turn may hurt the upstream bottleneck, which has a smaller industrial base downstream. And the independent downstream firms may start investing in assets that are specific to other upstream firms ($\hat{U}$) rather than to the bottleneck (U).

These ideas shed light on AT&T's 1995 voluntary divestiture of its manufacturing arm, AT&T Technology (now Lucent). One must recall that until then, AT&T and the RBOCs, who are major purchasers of AT&T made equipment, hardly competed in the final good markets. With AT&T's slow entry into the Intralata and the local telecommunications markets and with the 1996 Telecommunication Act allowing the RBOCs to enter the long distance market (provided that local loop competition developed sufficiently), competition between AT&T and the RBOCs on the final good markets was likely to become substantial. Consequently, the RBOCs may have been concerned about a possible foreclosure by AT&T Technology whenever such exclusion would favor the telecommunication branch of AT&T. There was thus a possibility that in a situation of vertical integration and increased product competition, the RBOCs would have turned more and more to alternative and non-vertically integrated manufacturers such as Northern Telecom, Alcatel, Siemens, or the Japanese manufacturers. The very threat of foreclosure could have substantially hurt AT&T's manufacturing arm, with the short-term gain from foreclosure more than offset by a long-term loss of manufacturing market share.

Let us formalize this argument in an extended version of the foreclosure model of Section 2. There are two upstream firms (manufacturers): U with unit cost c, and $\hat{U}$ with unit cost $\hat{c} > c$; U can be thought of as being AT&T Technology and $\hat{U}$ as being a rival manufacturer, since we will be primarily interested in those segments in which AT&T Technology had some competitive advantage and therefore foreclosure may occur. There are two downstream firms D_1 and D_2, both with unit cost 0; we will think of D_1 as being the telecommunications services branch of AT&T and D_2 as being the RBOCs. Last, there are two markets: market A (long distance) and market B (local).

Recall our basic argument: The integrated firm $U - D_1$ may want to divest when the competition between D_1 and D_2 gets more intense because D_2 then becomes more concerned about foreclosure and wants to sever or at least limit its relationship with U. We model this idea in a very simple albeit extreme way: We start from a situation of line-of-business restrictions in which D_1 is in market A only and D_2 is in market B only. Then line-of-business restrictions are lifted and D_1 and D_2 compete head-to-head in both markets. To formalize the idea that D_2 makes technological decisions (choice of standard, learning by using, etc.) that will in the future make purchases from U or $\hat{U}$ more desirable, we assume that ex ante D_2 makes a costless, but irreversible choice between U and $\hat{U}$. That is, ex post D_2 can purchase from a single supplier. This assumption is much stronger than needed, but models the basic idea in a very straightforward way. We also assume, without loss of generality, that D_1 picks U as its supplier.

The timing is as follows:

- Stage 1: U and D_1 decide whether they stay integrated or split.
- Stage 2: D_2 makes a technological choice that determines its supplier (U or $\hat{U}$).
- Stage 3: U and D_1 secretly agree on a tariff $T_1(\cdot)$. Simultaneously and also secretly, with probability α, the supplier chosen by D_2 at stage 2 makes a take-it-or-leave-it offer $T_2(\cdot)$ to D_2; with probability $1-\alpha$, D_2 makes a take-it-or-leave-it offer $T_2(\cdot)$ to this supplier. Then, the downstream firms order quantities from their suppliers and pay according to the agreed upon tariffs.
- Stage 4: D_1 and D_2 transform the intermediate product into the final goods. In case of line-of-business restrictions, each downstream firm sells the output in its own turf (markets A and B, respectively). In case of head-to-head competition, D_1 and D_2 observe each other's output in each market and set their prices for the final good in each market.

This timing calls for some comments. The last two stages are standard, except that we here have two final markets. Also, we introduce a more evenly distributed bargaining power: D_2 obtains on average a fraction $1-\alpha$ of the profit made in its relationship with the selected supplier (the same can be assumed for D_1, but this is irrelevant). We had earlier assumed that $\alpha = 1$, so D_2 never made any profit when facing a single supplier; we could maintain this assumption but find it more elegant to introduce some sharing of profit so that D_2 not be indifferent as to its choice of technology at stage 2.

We now analyze this game.

A.1.1. Line-of-business restrictions

Under line-of-business restrictions, D_1 and D_2 are monopolists in their respective markets. At stage 2, D_2 selects U as its supplier, as

$$(1-\alpha)\pi_B^m(c) > (1-\alpha)\pi_B^m(\hat{c}),$$

where $\pi_B^m(\tilde{c})$ is the monopoly profit in market B for unit cost $\tilde{c}$. Thus, the RBOCs turn to AT&T Technology if the latter has a competitive advantage.

Note also that, under line-of-business restrictions, vertical integration between U and D_1 has no impact on markets as foreclosure is not an issue.[112]

[112] A $U - D_1$ merger could however be motivated by (unmodeled) efficiency considerations.

A.1.2. Head-to-head competition

Let us now assume that D_1 and D_2 are in both markets. If U and D_1 are *vertically integrated*, then from Section 2.2, we know that if D_2 selects U at stage 2, D_2 is completely foreclosed from both downstream markets at stage 3. It then makes zero profit. By contrast, when selecting the inefficient supplier $\hat{U}$, D_2 makes a strictly positive profit as long as $\hat{U}$ is not too inefficient, that is as long as $\hat{c}$ is below the monopoly price for cost c in at least one of the markets. This formalizes the notion that the non-integrated downstream firm is likely to switch supplier when competition is introduced and the former supplier remains vertically integrated. Note that such switching generates production inefficiency.

Let $\pi_i^C(c, \hat{c})$ denote the Cournot profit in market $i = A, B$ of a firm with marginal cost c facing a firm with marginal cost $\hat{c}$; and let

$$\pi^C(c, \hat{c}) \equiv \pi_A^C(c, \hat{c}) + \pi_B^C(c, \hat{c})$$

be the overall profit.[113] This is the profit made by the integrated firm $U - D_1$ under head-to-head competition.

Let us now assume *vertical separation* of U and D_1. Then, for the same reason as under line-of-business restrictions, D_2 selects U at stage 2 as

$$(1 - \alpha)\pi^C(c, c) > (1 - \alpha)\pi^C(\hat{c}, c).$$

The aggregate profit of U and D_1 is then $(1 + \alpha)\pi^C(c, c)$. We thus conclude that it is in the interest of U and D_1 to split if and only if:

$$(1 + \alpha)\pi^C(c, c) > \pi^C(c, \hat{c}).$$

This condition admits a simple interpretation: Vertical integration results in foreclosure and in a flight of the non-integrated firm to the rival manufacturer. Foreclosure has a beneficial impact on the merging firms' profit but the loss of a downstream consumer is costly if U has some bargaining power in negotiations, that is if $\alpha > 0$. For $\hat{c}$ large, the *foreclosure effect* dominates[114]; conversely, the *smaller-customer-base effect* dominates for $\hat{c}$ close to c. More generally, strong downstream competition (e.g., from the removal of line-of-business restrictions) and/or weak upstream competition make foreclosure, and thus vertical integration, more attractive.[115]

[113] $\pi_i^C(c, \hat{c})$ should be replaced with $\pi_i^m(c)$ if $\hat{c} \geqslant p_i^m(c)$.

[114] For example, if $\hat{c} \geqslant \max(p_A^m(c), p_B^m(c))$, then $\pi^C(c, \hat{c}) = \pi^m(c) = \pi_A^m(c) + \pi_B^m(c) > 2\pi^C(c, c)$.

[115] We have assumed that D_2 has the same bargaining power $(1-\alpha)$ vis-à-vis U and $\hat{U}$. A new effect appears if D_2 has more bargaining power with $\hat{U}$, say because $\hat{U}$ is competitive, than with U. Then, due to differential bargaining positions, under head-to-head competition a divestiture may not suffice for U to keep D_2 as a customer. For example, if $\hat{U}$ is a competitive fringe producing at cost $\hat{c}$, D_2 buys from an unintegrated U if and only if $(1 - \alpha)\pi^C(c, c) > \pi^C(\hat{c}, c)$. It is easy to show that there exists α such that it is optimal for

A.2. Protecting upstream investment through downstream competition

Chemla (2003) develops the (Williamsonian) argument that downstream competition protects the bottleneck's investment against expropriation in a situation in which the downstream firms have non-negligible bargaining power. There is then a general trade-off between foreclosing competition downstream so as to exploit monopoly power and preserving competition there in order to protect upstream rents.

The thrust of his analysis is as follows: A bottleneck owner U faces n identical downstream firms $D_1, \ldots, D_n$. Consider the Cournot set up of Section 2, except that the bargaining power is split more evenly:

- Stage 1: U picks the number of downstream firms $m \leqslant n$ that are potentially active later on. For example, it communicates its technical specifications to m firms and these specifications are indispensable due to compatibility requirements. Without these specifications a downstream firm starts development "too late" and cannot compete at stages 2 and 3.
- Stage 2: With probability α, U makes secret take-it-or-leave-it offers $T_i(\cdot)$ to each D_i (in the subgroup selected at stage 1). With probability $1-\alpha$, all D_i's make (separate) take-it-or-leave-it offers $T_i(\cdot)$ to U. D_i then orders a quantity of intermediate product q_i and pays $T_i(q_i)$ accordingly.
- Stage 3: The D_i's that were selected at stage 1 transform the intermediate product into the final good, observe each other's output and set their prices for the final good.

Chemla further assumes that the bottleneck's cost $C(Q)$ is strictly convex rather than linear. The role of this assumption will become apparent shortly. The intuition for his results can be grasped from looking at the two polar cases of bargaining power. When $\alpha = 1$, the bottleneck has the entire bargaining power, and is only limited by the Coasian commitment problem. To commit not to supply beyond the monopoly output at stage 2, U optimally selects $m = 1$, that is forecloses the market. When $\alpha = 0$, the downstream firms have all the bargaining power. Under linear costs, they would entirely extract the bottleneck's rent at stage 2. This is not so under decreasing returns to scale in the provision of the essential input, as long as $m \geqslant 2$. In order for an offer by D_i to be accepted by U, D_i's payment must be at least equal to the incremental cost of q_i, and therefore each downstream firm must pay its incremental cost (close to the marginal cost for m large), leaving a rent to the bottleneck owner (as inframarginal costs are lower than incremental costs under decreasing returns to scale). Thus a bottleneck owner

$U - D_1$ to divest (for that α) if and only if

$$2\pi^C(c, c) > \pi^C(c, \hat{c}) + \pi^C(\hat{c}, c).$$

This condition is the necessary and sufficient condition for the existence of franchise-fee (or royalty-free) licensing in a Cournot duopoly (the firm with cost c licenses its technology to its rival with initial cost $\hat{c}$ for a franchise fee). It holds if $\hat{c}$ is close to c and does not hold for large $\hat{c}$'s [Katz and Shapiro (1985)], a conclusion in line with that obtained in the text.

may not want to engage in exclusionary practices when contracts are incomplete, in the sense that the bottleneck owner cannot contract on price when selecting the number m of buyers, and when the bottleneck owner has limited bargaining power against the remaining buyers of the essential input.

In this bargaining power story the upstream bottleneck has a motivation not to foreclose, namely the transfer of bargaining power. But this motivation is unrelated to social concerns, and it has actually too little incentive from a social viewpoint not to foreclose. Chemla also considers a second variation of the basic framework, in which U chooses some non-contractible investment e in marketing or design, that shifts the demand curve $p = P(Q, e)$ upwards: $\partial P/\partial e > 0$. This industry specific investment is chosen between stage 1 and stage 2 in the timing above and is observed by the downstream firms. Picking $m > 1$ protects somewhat the upstream firm against expropriation of the benefits of its investment when bargaining power lies downstream. That is, downstream competition at stage 2 gives the bottleneck owner an incentive to invest that would not exist if there were a single downstream firm ($m = 1$) that would impose a payment exactly equal to the bottleneck cost. Chemla shows that the bottleneck investment increases with the number of competing downstream firms m. This gives the upstream bottleneck a second incentive not to foreclose, which fits with the social concern of protecting investments.

Appendix B. Excessive entry and vertical foreclosure

As mentioned in Section 5, foreclosure may have the merit of limiting entry in situations where entry would otherwise be excessive. We briefly analyze this potential benefit in the context of vertical foreclosure. Consider our basic framework, except that there is now a large number of potential competitors, $D_1, D_2, \ldots,$ for the production of the downstream good, and that in the first stage, after U's contract offer, each downstream firm D_i chooses whether to enter (and accept the contract), in which case it has to pay a fixed cost f. [This fixed cost is a technological production cost and does not include the fixed fee associated with a two-part tariff for the intermediate good.]

All downstream firms produce the same homogeneous good, so that efficiency would dictate only one downstream entrant. To capture the risk of excessive entry, we further suppose that each D_i does not observe its competitors' entry decisions.[116] Under passive conjectures, U then offers each D_i an efficient bilateral contract, which can be thought of as a two-part tariff with a marginal access price equal to marginal cost c.

Let us denote by $\pi^C(n)$ and $Q^C(n) = nq^C(n)$ the per firm gross profit and the total output in the standard (Cournot) oligopolistic equilibrium with n active firms:

$$\pi^c(n) = \max_q \{[P((n-1)q^C(n) + q) - c]q\}.$$

[116] If entry were observable and contracts made contingent on the number of active firms, then U could perfectly monitor the number of active firms and achieve the entire monopolization of the industry by allowing only one active firm downstream.

And let us define:

$$\hat{\pi}(n) = \max_q \{ [P(Q^C(n) + q) - c] q \}.$$

In words, $\hat{\pi}(n)$ is the maximum profit gross of the fixed cost that a non-entering downstream could obtain if it entered, assuming that there are already n active firms, offering the output corresponding to the standard n-firm oligopolistic equilibrium. The functions $\pi^C(\cdot)$ and $\hat{\pi}^C(\cdot)$ are decreasing.

In the absence of vertical integration, a necessary and sufficient condition for an equilibrium with n active downstream firms is

$$\pi^C(n) \geqslant f \geqslant \hat{\pi}(n).$$

There may be several such equilibria. The optimal number of entrants for the industry, i.e. for U who in equilibrium recovers all profits through the fixed fee, maximizes total Cournot net profit $n[\pi^C(n) - f]$ in the relevant range defined above. Since total Cournot gross profit, $n\pi^C(n)$, is decreasing in n, so is total Cournot net profit. So the industry optimum has n_b entrants such that $\hat{\pi}(n_b) = f$, and the lowest industry profit is reached for n_w entrants such that $\pi^C(n_w) = f$; this latter equilibrium corresponds to the standard free entry equilibrium and yields zero profit to all firms.

Under vertical integration, U forecloses the downstream market. As a result the number of active downstream firms is equal to the one that is desirable from the point of view of productive efficiency ($n_i = 1$), but the price is the monopoly one. For example, in the linear demand case ($P(Q) = d - Q$), $n_w = (d - c)/\sqrt{f} - 1$, $n_b = (d - c)/2\sqrt{f} - 1$, and $Q^C(n) = (n/(n + 1))(d - c)$. If in the absence of foreclosure the firms end up in the "worst" equilibrium (from their point of view, but also from the point of view of the duplication of fixed costs), then foreclosure is socially desirable when the parameter $(d - c)/\sqrt{f}$ lies between 2 and 6.

Appendix C. Vertical foreclosure with Bertrand downstream competition

In the vertical foreclosure framework of Section 2, downstream competition was modeled in a Cournot, or more precisely in a Bertrand–Edgeworth way. It should however be clear that the commitment problem described above is robust to the nature of downstream competition. This Appendix notes however that a formalization "à la Bertrand" rather than "à la Bertrand–Edgeworth" is by no means straightforward and has not been properly addressed in the literature. With Bertrand competition, the marginal price charged to one downstream firm directly affects the profitability of the contracts signed with its competitors. Passive beliefs (which, recall, are the natural conjectures in the Bertrand–Edgeworth timing) thus appear less plausible, since downstream firms should anticipate that, if the supplier deviates with one of them, it has an incentive to change the contracts offered to the others. In addition, there may exist no equilibrium with passive beliefs, because the gain from a multilateral deviation may now exceed the total gains of the unilateral deviations.

To study this existence problem, let us assume that downstream firms produce differentiated goods, with symmetric final demands $D^i(p_1, p_2) = D(p_i, p_j)$, and change the timing as follows:

- Stage 1: U secretly offers each D_i a tariff $T_i(q_i)$.
- Stage 2: D_1 and D_2 simultaneously set their prices, p_1 and p_2, and then order q_1 and q_2 so as to satisfy demand (consumers observe both prices and choose freely between D_1 and D_2).

Assuming passive conjectures, D_i expects D_j to set the same equilibrium price p_j, regardless of the contract D_i is offered by U. Hence, given this expected price p_j, when facing a tariff $T_i(q_i)$, D_i chooses p_i so as to maximize $p_i D(p_i, p_j) - T_i(D(p_i, p_j))$. Assume that U can only charge two-part tariffs:

$$T_i(q_i) = F_i + w_i q_i.$$

D_i's first-order condition is

$$(p_i - w_i)\partial_1 D(p_i, p_j) + D(p_i, p_j) = 0, \tag{C.1}$$

which defines a reaction function $\tilde{R}^B(p_j; w_i)$ that is increasing in w_i ("B" stands for "Bertrand competition"). Given the candidate equilibrium price p_j, U will then "choose" D_i's price so as to maximize their aggregate profit:

$$(p_i - c)D(p_i, p_j) + (w_j - c)D(p_j, p_i).$$

This price p_i is characterized by

$$(p_i - c)\partial_1 D(p_i, p_j) + D(p_i, p_j) + (w_j - c)\partial_2 D(p_j, p_i) = 0. \tag{C.2}$$

Combining (C.1) and (C.2) yields:

$$(w_i - c)\partial_1 D(\cdot) + (w_j - c)\partial_2 D(\cdot) = 0. \tag{C.3}$$

Conditions (C.3), where $\partial_i D(\cdot)$ is evaluated at the Nash equilibrium retail prices, provide a system of two equations with two unknowns, the wholesale prices. A full rank argument then implies $w_1 = w_2 = c$: The equilibrium marginal transfer price equals the marginal cost. This in turn implies that a *candidate* equilibrium (for passive conjectures) must yield the Bertrand price and profit (with $R^B(p) \equiv \tilde{R}^B(p; c)$):

$$p_1 = p_2 = p^B < p^m \quad \text{such that} \quad p^B \equiv R^B(p^B)$$
$$\pi_U = 2\pi^B < \pi^m.$$

The reader may find this result, due to O'Brien and Shaffer (1992),[117] surprising for the following reason. The presumption under passive conjectures is that the downstream competitors wage whatever form of competition is relevant, internalizing exactly the

[117] They moreover show that the Bertrand equilibrium is still the unique candidate equilibrium, even when U can offer general non-linear tariffs.

marginal cost of upstream production. There is an extra twist under Bertrand competition, though: Because orders lag price setting, a change in the wholesale price w_i charged to a downstream competitor i affects its final price p_i and thus the profit $(w_j - c)D(p_j, p_i)$ made on downstream competitor j. But this indirect effect (which does not exist when orders are placed before demand is realized) vanishes exactly when $w_i = c$, that is when the wholesale price is equal to marginal cost.

Let us now show that, if demands are symmetric and the cross-price elasticity is at least one-half of the own-price elasticity, there exists no passive conjectures equilibrium. [Note that in the Hotelling case, the cross-price elasticity is equal to the own-price elasticity at a symmetric equilibrium. More generally what is needed for the reasoning below is that there is enough substitutability between the two products.]

With passive conjectures, the upstream firm's profit can be written as $\pi_i(w_i, w_j) + \pi_j(w_j, w_i)$, where

$$\pi_i(w_i, w_j) = \big(p_i^r(w_i) - w_i\big)D\big(p_i^r(w_i), p_j\big) + (w_i - c)D\big(p_i^r(w_i), p_j^r(w_j)\big),$$

and π_j is defined analogously. Fixing anticipated equilibrium prices (this is the passive conjectures assumption), $p_i^r(w_i)$ is defined by

$$p_i^r(w_i) = \arg\max(p_i - w_i)D\big(p_i, p_j^e\big).$$

Using the first-order condition for $p_i^r(\cdot)$, it is easy to show that at the candidate equilibrium ($w_i = c$),

$$\frac{\partial^2 \pi_i}{\partial w_i^2} = \frac{\partial D^i}{\partial p_i}\frac{\mathrm{d}p_i^r}{\mathrm{d}w_i}, \qquad \frac{\partial^2 \pi_i}{\partial w_i \partial w_j} = \frac{\partial D^i}{\partial p_j}\frac{\mathrm{d}p_j^r}{\mathrm{d}w_j}, \qquad \frac{\partial^2 \pi_i}{\partial w_j^2} = 0.$$

And so, the Hessian of $\pi_i + \pi_j$ is semi-definite negative only if

$$-\frac{\partial D^i}{\partial p_i} > 2\frac{\partial D^i}{\partial p_j}$$

(using the symmetry of the candidate equilibrium). Thus, if the cross-price elasticity is at least half of the own-price elasticity, U's above profit is not locally concave, implying that there exists a profitable multilateral deviation; therefore, there exists no passive conjectures equilibrium.

To circumvent this existence problem, Rey and Vergé (2004) consider the notion of *wary beliefs* introduced by McAfee–Schwartz, where a downstream firm that receives an unexpected offer then anticipates that the supplier acts optimally with its rivals, given the offer just received. In the context of linear model, Rey and Vergé show that wary beliefs equilibria exist even when passive beliefs equilibria fail to exist, and these equilibria exhibit some degree of opportunism: the upstream firm does not fully exploit its market power, although it performs better than when downstream firms have passive beliefs.

Vertical integration

Let us now assume that U and D_1 merge. The thorny issue of conjectures no longer arises since the non-integrated unit then knows that the integrated one purchases at marginal cost, and by construction the integrated downstream firm knows the tariff offered to the other one.

Through the choice of the marginal transfer price to D_2, w_2, U generates for D_2 a response to its expected price p_1^e given by

$$p_2^r(w_2; p_1^e) = \arg\max_{p_2}(p_2 - w_2)D(p_2, p_1^e).$$

[This is the same reaction curve as previously, but we now explicit the rival's expected price.]

Conversely, given a transfer price w_2 and an expected retail price p_2^e, $U - D_1$'s optimal response is given by

$$p_1^r(w_2; p_2^e) = \arg\max_{p_1}\{(p_1 - c)D(p_1, p_2^e) + (w_2 - c)D(p_2^e, p_1)\}.$$

Hence, a marginal transfer price w_2 generates a conditional equilibrium $(\hat{p}_1(w_2), \hat{p}_2(w_2))$ given by $p_1 = p_1^r(w_2; p_2)$ and $p_2 = p_2^r(w_2; p_1)$. The optimal transfer price then maximizes

$$(\hat{p}_1(w_2) - c)D(\hat{p}_1(w_2), \hat{p}_2(w_2)) + (\hat{p}_2(w_2) - c)D(\hat{p}_2(w_2), \hat{p}_1(w_2)).$$

Assuming the retail prices are strategic complements, both $\hat{p}_1$ and $\hat{p}_2$ increase with w_2. Moreover, the curve $\mathcal{F} \equiv (\hat{p}_1(w_2), \hat{p}_2(w_2))_{w_2}$ of feasible price pairs goes through the Bertrand equilibrium point (for $w_2 = c$), and never crosses the curve $p_1 = R^m(p_2)$.[118] Moreover, as w_2 goes to $+\infty$ (which amounts to exclusive dealing with D_1), $p_2(w_2)$ goes to $+\infty$ too (since $p_2(w_2) > w_2$). Hence the curve $\mathcal{F}$ crosses the curve $p_2 = R_2^m(p_1)$ to the left of the monopoly point M (see Figure 33.6).

It is clear that, starting from B ($w_2 = c$), a small increase in w_2, which increases both prices $\hat{p}_1$ and $\hat{p}_2$, strictly increases $U - D_1$'s aggregate profit. Hence vertical integration yields $w_2 > c$. The point I which represents the optimal pair of prices (p_1^*, p_2^*) actually lies above the curve $p_2 = R^m(p_1)$. To see this, evaluate the impact of a slight increase in w_2, starting from the value w_2 such that $\hat{p}_2 = R^m(\hat{p}_1(w_2))$:

$$\begin{aligned}
&\frac{\mathrm{d}}{\mathrm{d}w_2}\big((\hat{p}_1(w_2) - c)D(\hat{p}_1(w_2), \hat{p}_2(w_2)) + (\hat{p}_2(w_2) - c)D(\hat{p}_2(w_2), \hat{p}_1(w_2))\big)\\
&\quad = \frac{\mathrm{d}}{\mathrm{d}w_2}\big((\hat{p}_1(w_2) - c)D(\hat{p}_1(w_2), p_2) + (p_2 - c)D(p_2, \hat{p}_1(w_2))\big)\Big|_{p_2=\hat{p}_2(w_2)}\\
&\quad = (\hat{p}_2(w_2) - w_2)D_2(\hat{p}_2(w_2), \hat{p}_1(w_2))\frac{\mathrm{d}\hat{p}_1}{\mathrm{d}w_2} > 0,
\end{aligned}$$

[118] $p_1(w_2) = R^m(p_2(w_2)) \equiv \arg\max_{p_1}(p_1 - c)D(p_1, p_2(w_2)) + (p_2(w_2) - c)D(p_2(w_2), p_1)$ would require $p_2(w_2) = w_2$, which is impossible.

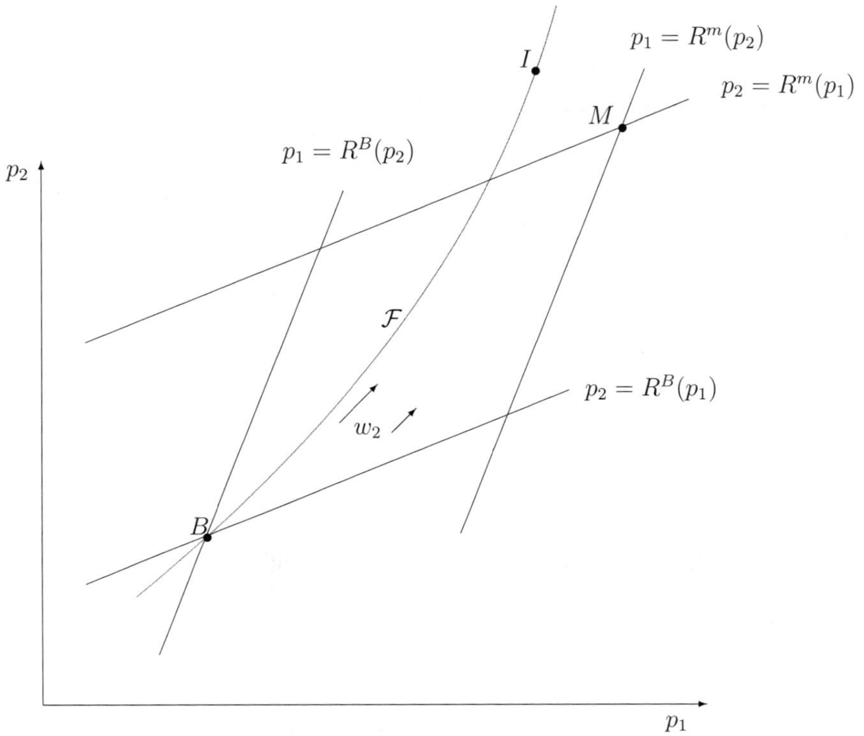

Figure 33.6. Bertrand competition and vertical integration.

where the first equality stems from $\hat{p}_2 = R^m(\hat{p}_1)$. Note finally that the equilibrium prices satisfy $w_2 > c$ and $p_2^* > p_1^*$ (since I lies to the right of $p_1 = R^m(p_2)$ and above $p_2 = R^m(p_1)$). In that sense, vertical integration does lead to foreclosure: The unintegrated firm D_2 faces a higher marginal transfer price and sets a higher price than its rival. Foreclosure in general is incomplete, however, when the two downstream firms are differentiated: In that case, vertical integration yields more profit than exclusive dealing (which would correspond here to $w_2 = \infty$).

References

Aghion, P., Bolton, P. (1987). "Contracts as a barrier to entry". American Economic Review 77, 388–401.

Ahern, P.J. (1994). "Refusal to deal after aspen". Antitrust Law Journal 63, 153–184.

Areeda, P. (1981). Antitrust Analysis, third ed. Little, Brown and Company, Boston.

Armstrong, M. (1998). "Network interconnection in telecommunications". Economic Journal 108, 545–564.

Armstrong, M. (2002). "The theory of access pricing and interconnection". In: Cave, M., Majumdar, S., Vogelsang, I. (Eds.), Handbook of Telecommunication Economics, vol. I. North-Holland, Amsterdam.

Armstrong, M. (2006). "Recent developments in the economics of price discrimination". In: Blundell, R., Newey, W., Persson, T. (Eds.), Advances in Economics and Econometrics: Theory and Applications, Ninth World Congress, vol. 2. Cambridge Univ. Press, Cambridge.

Armstrong, M., Sappington, D. (2007). "Recent developments in the theory of regulation". In: Armstrong, M., Porter, R. (Eds.), Handbook of Industrial Organization, vol. III. North-Holland, Amsterdam (this volume).
Back, K., Zender, J. (1993). "Auctions of divisible goods: On the rationale for the treasury experiment". Review of Financial Studies 6, 733–764.
Baumol, W., Ordover, J., Willig, R. (1995). "Notes on the efficient component pricing rule". Paper given at the Montreal Conference on Regulated Industries.
Bernheim, B.D., Whinston, M.D. (1986). "Common agency". Econometrica 54, 923–942.
Bernheim, B.D., Whinston, M.D. (1998). "Exclusive dealing". Journal of Political Economy 106, 64–103.
Bolton, P., Whinston, M. (1993). "Incomplete contracts, vertical integration, and supply assurance". Review of Economic Studies 60, 121–148.
Borenstein, S., MacKie-Mason, J.K., Netz, J.S. (1995). "Antitrust policy in aftermarkets". Antitrust Law Journal 63, 455–482.
Bork, R. (1978). Antitrust Paradox. Basic Books, New York.
Bowman Jr., W.S. (1957). "Tying arrangements and the leverage problem". Yale Law Journal 67, 19–36.
Burkart, M., Denis, G., Panunzi, F. (1998). "Why higher takeover premia protect minority shareholders". Journal of Political Economy 106, 172–204.
Caillaud, B., Rey, P. (1995). "Strategic aspects of delegation". European Economic Review 39, 421–431.
Caillaud, B., Jullien, B., Picard, P. (1995). "Competing vertical structures: Precommitment and renegotiation". Econometrica 63 (3), 621–646.
Caprice, S. (2005a). "Incentive to encourage downstream competition under bilateral oligopoly". Economics Bulletin 12 (9), 1–5.
Caprice, S. (2005b). "Multilateral vertical contracting with an alternative supplier: Discrimination and nondiscrimination". INRA-ESR Working Paper 2005-03.
Carlton, D.W., Waldman, M. (2001). "Competition, monopoly, and aftermarkets". NBER Working Paper 8086.
Carlton, D.W., Waldman, M. (2002). "The strategic use of tying to preserve and create market power in evolving industries". RAND Journal of Economics 33, 194–220.
Cestone, G., White, L. (2003). "Anti-competitive financial contracting: The design of financial claims". Journal of Finance 58 (5), 2109–2141.
Chemla, G. (2003). "Downstream competition, foreclosure and vertical integration". Journal of Economics, Management and Strategy 12, 261–289.
Chen, Y., Riordan, M.H. (in press). "Vertical integration, exclusive dealing, and ex post cartelization". RAND Journal of Economics.
Chen, Z., Ross, T. (1993). "Refusal to deal, price discrimination and independent service organizations". Journal of Economics and Management Strategy 2 (4), 593–614.
Chen, Z., Ross, T. (1999). "Refusal to deal and orders to supply in competitive markets". International Journal of Industrial Organization 17, 399–417.
Chipty, T. (2001). "Vertical integration, market foreclosure, and consumer welfare in the cable television industry". American Economic Review 91 (3), 428–453.
Choi, J.P. (1996). "Preemptive R&D, rent dissipation, and "leverage theory" ". The Quarterly Journal of Economics 110, 1153–1181.
Choi, J.P. (2001). "A theory of mixed bundling applied to the GE-Honeywell merger". Antitrust (Fall), 32–33.
Choi, J.P. (2004). "Tying and innovation: A dynamic analysis of tying arrangements". Economic Journal 114, 83–101.
Choi, J.P., Stefanadis, C. (2001). "Tying, investment, and the dynamic leverage theory". RAND Journal of Economics 32 (1), 52–71.
Choi, J.P., Yi, S.-S. (2000). "Vertical foreclosure with the choice of input specifications". RAND Journal of Economics 30, 717–743.
Choi, J.P., Lee, G., Stefanadis, C. (2003). "The effects of integration on R&D incentives in systems markets". Netnomics 5 (1), 21–32.
Coase, R. (1972). "Durability and monopoly". Journal of Law and Economics 15, 143.

Comanor, W.S., Rey, P. (2000). "Vertical restraints and the market power of large distributors". Review of Industrial Organization 17 (2), 135–153.
de Fontenay, C.C., Gans, J.S. (2005). "Vertical integration in the presence of upstream competition". RAND Journal of Economics 36 (3), 544–572.
DeGraba, P. (1996). "Most-favored-customer clauses and multilateral contracting: When nondiscrimination implies uniformity". Journal of Economics and Management Strategy 5, 565–579.
Economides, N. (1989). "The desirability of compatibility in the absence of network externalities". American Economic Review 71 (5), 1165–1181.
Evans , D., Hagiu , A., Schmalensee , R. (2006). "Invisible Engines: How Software Platforms Drive Innovation and Transform Industry". MIT Press, Cambridge.
Farrell, J., Gallini, N.T. (1988). "Second-sourcing as a commitment: Monopoly incentives to attract competition". The Quarterly Journal of Economics 103, 673–694.
Farrell, J., Katz, M. (2000). "Innovation, rent extraction and integration in systems markets". Journal of Industrial Economics 48 (4), 413–432.
Farrell, J., Klemperer, P. (2007). "Co-ordination and lock-in: Competition with switching costs and network effects". In: Armstrong, M., Porter, R. (Eds.), Handbook of Industrial Organization, vol. III. North-Holland, Amsterdam (this volume).
Fridolfsson, S.-O., Stenneck, J. (2003). "Why event studies do not detect the competitive effects of mergers – The out of play effect". Mimeo. Research Institute of Industrial Economics (IUI), Stockholm.
Fudenberg, D., Tirole, J. (2000). "Pricing under the threat of entry by a sole supplier of a network good". Journal of Industrial Economics 48 (4), 373–390.
Fudenberg, D., Villas-Boas, M. (2005). "Behavior-based price discrimination and customer recognition". Mimeo. Harvard University and UC Berkeley.
Fumagalli, C., Motta, M. (2006). "Exclusive dealing and entry: When buyers compete". American Economic Review 96 (3), 785–795.
Garcia Mariñoso, B. (2001). "Technological incompatibility, endogenous switching costs and lock-in". Journal of Industrial Economics 49 (3), 281–298.
Gaudet, G., Long, N.V. (1996). "Vertical integration, foreclosure and profits in the presence of double marginalisation". Journal of Economics and Management Strategy 5, 409–432.
Gilbert, R., Neuhoff, K., Newbery, D. (2004). "Allocating transmission to mitigate market power in electricity markets". RAND Journal of Economics 35 (4), 691–709.
Green, R., Newbery, D. (1992). "Competition in the British electricity spot market". Journal of Political Economy 100, 929–953.
Hancher, L. (1995). "European competition law implications for access pricing. Report for European Commission DGIV". Mimeo. Erasmus University, Rotterdam.
Hart, O., Tirole, J. (1990). "Vertical integration and market foreclosure". Brookings Papers on Economic Activity (Microeconomics) 1990, 205–285.
Innes, R., Sexton, R.J. (1994). "Strategic buyers and exclusionary contracts". American Economic Review 84 (3), 566–584.
Jeon, D.-S., Laffont, J.-J., Tirole, J. (2004). "On the receiver pays principle". RAND Journal of Economics 35, 85–110.
Joskow, P., Tirole, J. (2000). "Transmission rights and market power on electric power networks". RAND Journal of Economics 31, 450–487.
Katz, M. (1987). "The welfare effects of third-degree price discrimination in intermediate goods market". American Economic Review 77, 154–167.
Katz, M. (1989). "Vertical contractual relations". In: Schmalensee, R., Willig, R. (Eds.), Handbook of Industrial Organization, vol. I. North-Holland, Amsterdam.
Katz, M. (1991). "Game-playing agents: Unobservable contracts as precommitments". RAND Journal of Economics 22–23, 307–328.
Katz, M., Shapiro, C. (1985). "On the licensing of innovations". RAND Journal of Economics 16, 504–520.
Kende, M. (1998). "Profitability under an open versus a closed system". Journal of Economics and Management Strategy 7 (2), 307–326.

Klemperer, P. (1995). "Competition when consumers have switching costs". Review of Economic Studies 62 (4), 515–539.
Klemperer, P., Meyer, M. (1989). "Supply function equilibria in oligopoly under uncertainty". Econometrica 57, 1243–1277.
Laffont, J.-J., Tirole, J. (1999). Competition in Telecommunications. MIT Press, Cambridge.
Laffont, J.-J., Rey, P., Tirole, J. (1998a). "Network competition. I. Overview and nondiscriminatory pricing". RAND Journal of Economics 29 (1), 1–37.
Laffont, J.-J., Rey, P., Tirole, J. (1998b). "Network competition. II. Price discrimination". RAND Journal of Economics 29 (1), 38–56.
Laffont, J.-J., Marcus, S., Rey, P., Tirole, J. (2003). "Internet interconnection and the off-net-cost pricing principle". RAND Journal of Economics 34 (2), 370–390.
Ma, C.-T.A. (1997). "Option contracts and vertical foreclosure". Journal of Economics and Management Strategy 6, 725–753.
Mankiw, N.G., Whinston, M.D. (1986). "Free entry and social inefficiency". RAND Journal of Economics 17 (1), 48–58.
Martimort, D. (1996). "Exclusive dealing, common agency and multiprincipal incentive theory". RAND Journal of Economics 27 (1), 1–31.
Martimort, D., Stole, L.A. (2003). "Contractual externalities and common agency equilibria". Advances in Theoretical Economics 3 (1). Article 4.
Martin, S., Normann, H.-T., Snyder, C. (2001). "Vertical foreclosure in experimental markets". RAND Journal of Economics 32, 466–496.
Marx, L., Shaffer, G. (2004). "Upfront payments and exclusion in downstream markets". Mimeo.
Maskin, E., Tirole, J. (1987). "A theory of dynamic oligopoly. III. Cournot competition". European Economic Review 31, 947–968.
Maskin, E., Tirole, J. (1988). "A theory of dynamic oligopoly, I and II". Econometrica 56 (3), 549–599.
Mathewson, G.F., Winter, R. (1984). "An economic theory of vertical restraints". RAND Journal of Economics 15 (4), 27–38.
Matutes, C., Regibeau, P. (1988). "Mix and match: Product compatibility without network externalities". RAND Journal of Economics 19 (2), 219–234.
McAfee, R.P., Schwartz, M. (1994). "Opportunism in multilateral vertical contracting: Nondiscrimination, exclusivity, and uniformity". American Economic Review 84 (1), 210–230.
McAfee, R.P., Schwartz, M. (1995). "The non-existence of pairwise-proof equilibrium". Economics Letters 49, 251–259.
Mullin, J., Mullin, W. (1997). "United States Steel's acquisition of the Great Northern Ore properties: Vertical foreclosure or efficient contractual governance". Journal of Law, Economics and Organization 13, 74–100.
Nalebuff, B. (2000). "Competing against bundles". In: Hammond, P., Myles, G. (Eds.), Incentives, Organization, and Public Economics. Oxford Univ. Press, Oxford.
Nalebuff, B. (2003a). "Bundling, tying, and portfolio effects". DTI Economics Paper No. 1. Available at: http://www.dti.gov.uk/economics/papers.html.
Nalebuff, B. (2003b). "Bundling and the GE-Honeywell merger". In: Kwoka, J., White, L. (Eds.), The Antitrust Revolution, fourth ed. Oxford Univ. Press, Oxford.
O'Brien, D.P., Shaffer, G. (1992). "Vertical control with bilateral contracts". RAND Journal of Economics 23 (3), 299–308.
Ordover, J., Saloner, G., Salop, S.C. (1990). "Equilibrium market foreclosure". American Economic Review 80, 127–142.
Ordover, J.A., Sykes, A.O., Willig, R.D. (1985). "Nonprice anticompetitive behavior by dominant firms toward the producers of complementary products". In: Fisher, F.M. (Ed.), Antitrust and Regulation: Essays in Memory of John J. McGowan. MIT Press, Cambridge.
Perry, M.K. (1989). "Vertical integration: Determinants and effects". In: Schmalensee, R., Willig, R. (Eds.), Handbook of Industrial Organization, vol. I. North-Holland, Amsterdam.
Perry, M.K., Porter, R.H. (1989). "Can resale price maintenance and franchise fees correct sub-optimal levels of retail service?". International Journal of Industrial Organization 8 (1), 115–141.

Posner, R. (1976). Antitrust Law. University of Chicago Press, Chicago.
Rasmusen, E.B., Ramseyer, J.M., Wiley, J.S. (1991). "Naked exclusion". American Economic Review 81, 1137–1145.
Rey, P., Vergé, T. (2002). "RPM and horizontal cartels". CMPO Working Papers Series No. 02/047. Available at: http://www.bris.ac.uk/Depts/CMPO/workingpapers/wp47.pdf.
Rey, P., Vergé, T. (2004). "Bilateral control with vertical contracts". RAND Journal of Economics 35 (4), 728–746.
Rey, P., Thal, J., Vergé, T. (2005). "Slotting allowances and conditional payments". Mimeo. Université de Toulouse.
Riordan, M.H. (1998). "Anticompetitive vertical integration by a dominant firm". American Economic Review 88 (5), 1232–1248.
Rochet, J.-C., Tirole, J. (2003). "Platform competition in two-sided markets". Journal of the European Economic Association 1, 990–1029.
Roth, A.E., Prasnikar, V., Okuno-Fujiwara, M., Zamir, S. (1991). "Bargaining and market behavior in Jerusalem, Ljubljana, Pittsburgh, and Tokyo: An experimental study". American Economic Review 81, 1068–1095.
Rust, J. (1986). "When is it optimal to kill off the market for used durable goods". Econometrica 54, 65–86.
Salinger, M.A. (1988). "Vertical mergers and market foreclosure". The Quarterly Journal of Economics 77, 345–356.
Salop, S.C. (1979). "Monopolistic competition with outside goods". Bell Journal of Economics 10, 141–156.
Schmalensee, R. (1973). "A note on the theory of vertical integration". Journal of Political Economy 81, 442–449.
Schwartz, M., Werden, G. (1996). "A quality-signaling rationale for aftermarket tying". Antitrust Law Journal 64, 387–404.
Segal, I. (1999). "Contracting with externalities". The Quarterly Journal of Economics 114 (2), 337–388.
Segal, I., Whinston, M.D. (2000). "Naked exclusion: Comment". American Economic Review 90 (1), 296–309.
Segal, I., Whinston, M.D. (2003). "Robust predictions for bilateral contracting with externalities". Econometrica 71 (3), 757–791.
Segal, I., Whinston, M.D. (2007). "Antitrust in innovative industies". American Economic Review. In press.
Shapiro, C. (1995). "Aftermarkets and consumer welfare: Making sense of Kodak". Antitrust Law Journal 63, 483–511.
Shepard, A. (1987). "Licensing to enhance demand for new technologies". RAND Journal of Economics 18 (3), 360–368.
Slade, M.E. (1998). "Beer and the tie: Did divestiture of brewer-owned public houses lead to higher prices?". The Economic Journal 108, 565–602.
Snyder, C.M. (1994). "Vertical foreclosure in the British beer industry". In: Buyers, Suppliers, Competitors: The Interaction between a Firm's Horizontal and Vertical Relationship. PhD thesis. Department of Economics, MIT.
Snyder, C.M. (1995a). "Empirical studies of vertical foreclosure". In: Industry Economics Conference Papers and Proceedings, vol. 23. University of Melbourne and Bureau of Industry Economics, AGPS, Canberra, pp. 98–127.
Snyder, C.M. (1995b). "Interfirm effects of vertical integration: Event studies of the U.S. oil industry". Mimeo. George Washington University.
Spier, K.E., Whinston, M.D. (1995). "On the efficiency of privately stipulated damages for breach of contract: Entry barriers, reliance, and renegotiation". RAND Journal of Economics 26, 180–202.
Stahl, D.O. (1988). "Bertrand competition for inputs and walrasian outcomes". American Economic Review 78, 189–201.
Stefanadis, C. (1997). "Downstream vertical foreclosure and upstream innovation". Journal of Industrial Economics 65, 445–456.
Stole, L.A. (2007). "Price discrimination in competitive environments". In: Armstrong, M., Porter, R. (Eds.), Handbook of Industrial Organization, vol. III. North-Holland, Amsterdam (this volume).

Stole, L.A., Zwiebel, J. (1996). "Intra-firm bargaining under non-binding contracts". Review of Economic Studies 63, 375–410.

Su, T.T. (1975). "Durability of consumption goods reconsidered". American Economic Review 65, 148–157.

Tirole, J. (1988). The Theory of Industrial Organization. MIT Press, Cambridge.

Tirole, J. (2005). "The analysis of tying cases: A primer". Competition Policy International 1, 1–25.

Vernon, J.M., Graham, D.A. (1971). "Profitability of monopolization by vertical integration". Journal of Political Economy 79, 924–925.

Vickers, J. (1995). "Competition and regulation in vertically related markets". Review of Economic Studies 62, 1–18.

Vickers, J. (1996). "Market power and inefficiency: A contracts perspective". Oxford Review of Economic Policy 12, 11–26.

Warren-Boulton, F.R. (1974). "Vertical control with variable proportions". Journal of Political Economy 82, 783–802.

Whinston, M.D. (1990). "Tying, foreclosure, and exclusion". American Economic Review 80, 837–860.

Whinston, M.D. (2001). "Exclusivity and tying in U.S. v. Microsoft: What we know, and don't know". Journal of Economic Perspectives 15, 63–80.

White, L. (2000). "Foreclosure with incomplete information". Mimeo. Oxford University and University of Toulouse.

Yanelle, M.-O. (1997). "Banking competition and market efficiency". Review of Economic Studies 64, 215–239.

Chapter 34

PRICE DISCRIMINATION AND COMPETITION

LARS A. STOLE

University of Chicago, GSB

Contents

Handbook of Industrial Organization, Volume 3
Edited by M. Armstrong and R. Porter

DOI: 10.1016/S1573-448X(06)03034-2

Abstract

This chapter surveys the developments in price discrimination theory as it applies to imperfectly competitive markets. Broad themes and conclusions are discussed in the areas of first-, second- and third-degree price discrimination, pricing under demand uncertainty, bundling and behavior-based discrimination.

Keywords

Price discrimination, Oligopoly, Imperfect competition, Market segmentation, Demand uncertainty, Bundling

JEL classification: D400, L100, L400, L500

1. Introduction

Firms often find it profitable to segment customers according to their demand sensitivity and to price discriminate accordingly. In some settings, consumer heterogeneity can be directly observed, and a firm can base its pricing upon contractible consumer characteristics. In other settings, heterogeneity is not directly observable but can be indirectly elicited by offering menus of products and prices and allowing consumers to self-select. In both cases, the firm seeks to price its wares as a function of each consumer's underlying demand elasticity, extracting more surplus and increasing sales to more elastic customers in the process.

When the firm is a monopolist with market power, the underlying theory of price discrimination is now well understood, as explained, for example, by Varian (1989) in an earlier volume in this series.[1] On the other extreme, when markets are perfectly competitive and firms have neither short-run nor long-run market power, the law of one price prevails and price discrimination cannot exist.[2] Economic reality, of course, largely lies somewhere in between the textbook extremes, and most economists agree that price discrimination arises in oligopoly settings.[3] This chapter explores price discrimination in these imperfectly competitive markets, surveying the theoretical literature.[4]

Price discrimination exists when prices vary across customer segments in a manner that cannot be entirely explained by variations in marginal cost. Stigler's (1987) definition makes this precise: a firm price discriminates when the ratio of prices is different

[1] In addition to Varian (1989), this survey benefited greatly from several other excellent surveys of price discrimination, including Phlips (1983), Tirole (1988, ch. 3), Wilson (1993) and Armstrong (2006).

[2] It is straightforward to construct models of price discrimination in competitive markets without entry barriers in which firms lack long-run market power (and earn zero long-run economic profits), providing that there is some source of short-run market power that allows prices to remain above marginal cost, such as a fixed cost of production. For example, a simple free-entry Cournot model as discussed in Section 3.2 with fixed costs of production will exhibit zero long-run profits, prices above marginal cost, and equilibrium price discrimination. The fact that price discrimination can arise in markets with zero long-run economic profits suggests that the presence of price discrimination is a misleading proxy for long-run market power. This possibility is the subject of a recent symposium published in the *Antitrust Law Journal* (2003, vol. 70, No. 3); see the papers by Baker (2003), Baumol and Swanson (2003), Hurdle and McFarland (2003), Klein and Wiley (2003a, 2003b), and Ward (2003) for the full debate. Cooper et al. (2005) directly confront the issue of using price discrimination as proxy for market power by using a model in the spirit of Thisse and Vives (1988), which is discussed below in Section 3.4.

[3] Much empirical work tests for the presence of price discrimination in imperfectly competitive environments. An incomplete sample of papers and markets includes: Shepard (1991) – gasoline service stations, Graddy (1995) – fish market, Goldberg (1995), Verboven (1996), Goldberg and Verboven (2005) – European automobiles, Leslie (2004) – Broadway theater, Busse and Rysman (2005) – yellow pages advertising, Clerides (2004), Cabolis et al. (2005) – books, Cohen (2001) – paper towels, Crawford and Shum (2001) – cable television, McManus (2004) – specialty coffee, Nevo and Wolfram (2002) – breakfast cereal, Besanko, Dube and Gupta (2003) – ketchup, Miravete and Röller (2003) – cellular communications. For the minority viewpoint that price discrimination is less common in markets than typically thought, see Lott and Roberts (1991).

[4] Armstrong (2006) presents an excellent survey on these issues as well.

from the ratio of marginal costs for two goods offered by a firm.[5] Such a definition, of course, requires that one is careful in calculating marginal costs to include all relevant shadow costs. This is particularly true where costly capacity and aggregate demand uncertainty play critical roles, as discussed in Section 8. Similarly, where discrimination occurs over the provision of quality, as reviewed in Section 6, operationalizing this definition requires using the marginal prices of qualities and the associated marginal costs.

Even with this moderately narrow definition of price discrimination, there remains a considerable variety of theoretical models that address issues of price discrimination and imperfect competition. These include classic third-degree price discrimination (Section 3), purchase-history price discrimination (Section 4), intrapersonal price discrimination (Section 5), second-degree price discrimination and non-linear pricing (Section 6), product bundling (Section 7), and demand uncertainty and price rigidities (Section 8). Unfortunately, we must prune a few additional areas of inquiry, leaving some models of imperfect competition and price discrimination unexamined in this chapter. Among the more notable omissions are price discrimination in vertical structures,[6] imperfect information and costly search,[7] the commitment effect of price discrimina-

[5] Clerides (2002) contrasts Stigler's ratio definition with a price-levels definition (which focuses on the difference between price and marginal cost), and discusses the relevance of this distinction to a host of empirical studies.

[6] For example, in a vertical market where a single manufacturer can price discriminate across downstream retailers, there are a host of issues regarding resale-price maintenance, vertical foreclosure, etc. As a simple example, a rule requiring that the wholesaler offer a single price to all retailers may help the upstream firm to commit not to flood the retail market, thereby raising profits and retail prices. While these issues of vertical markets are significant, we leave them largely unexplored in the present paper. Some of these issues are considered elsewhere in this volume; see, for example, the chapter by Rey and Tirole (2007).

[7] The role of imperfect information and costly search in imperfectly competitive environments has previously received attention in the first volume of this series [Varian (1989, ch. 10, Section 3.4) and Stiglitz (1989, ch. 13)]. To summarize, when customers differ according to their information about market prices (or their costs of acquiring information), a monopolist may be able to segment the market by offering a distribution of prices, as in the model by Salop (1977), where each price observation requires a costly search by the consumer. A related set of competitive models with equilibrium price distributions has been explored by numerous authors including Varian (1980), Salop and Stiglitz (1977, 1982), Rosenthal (1980) and Stahl (1989). Unlike Salop (1977), in these papers each firm offers a single price in equilibrium. In some variations, firms choose from a continuous equilibrium distribution of prices; in others, there are only two prices in equilibrium, one for the informed and one for the uninformed. In most of these papers, average prices increase with the proportion of uninformed consumers and, more subtly, as the number of firms increases, the average price level can increase toward the monopoly level. These points are integrated in the model of Stahl (1989). Nonetheless, in these papers price discrimination does not occur at the firm level, but across firms. That is, each firm offers a single price in equilibrium, while the market distribution of prices effectively segments the consumer population into informed and uninformed buyers. Katz's (1984) model is an exception to these papers by introducing the ability of firms to set multiple prices to sort between informed and uninformed consumers; this contribution is reviewed in Section 3.5. At present, competitive analogs of Salop's (1977) monopoly price discrimination model, in which each firm offers multiple prices in equilibrium, have not been well explored.

tion policies,[8] collusion and intertemporal price discrimination,[9] price discrimination in aftermarkets[10], advance-purchase discounts,[11] price discrimination in telecommunications,[12] and the strategic effect of product lines in imperfectly competitive settings.[13]

It is well known that price discrimination is only feasible under certain conditions: (i) firms have short-run market power, (ii) consumers can be segmented either directly or indirectly, and (iii) arbitrage across differently priced goods is infeasible. Given that these conditions are satisfied, an individual firm will typically have an incentive to price discriminate, holding the behavior of other firms constant. The form of price discrimination will depend importantly on the nature of market power, the form of consumer heterogeneity, and the availability of various segmenting mechanisms.

When a firm is a monopolist, it is simple to catalog the various forms of price discrimination according to the form of consumer segmentation. To this end, suppose that a consumer's preferences for a monopolist's product are given by

$$U = v(q, \theta) - y,$$

where q is the amount (quantity or quality) consumed of the monopolist's product, y is numeraire, and consumer heterogeneity is captured in $\theta = (\theta_o, \theta_u)$. The vector θ has two components. The first component, θ_o, is observable and prices may be conditioned upon it; the second component, θ_u, is unobservable and is known only to the consumer. We say that the monopolist is practicing *direct* price discrimination to the extent that its prices depend upon observable heterogeneity. Generally, this implies that the price of purchasing q units of output will be a function that depends upon θ_o: $P(q, \theta_o)$. When the firm further chooses to offer linear price schedules, $P(q, \theta_o) = p(\theta_o)q$, we say the firm is practicing *third-degree* price discrimination over the characteristic θ_o. If

[8] While the chapter gives a flavor of a few of the influential papers on this topic, the treatment is left largely incomplete.

[9] For instance, Gul (1987) shows that when durable-goods oligopolists can make frequent offers, unlike the monopolist, they improve their ability to commit to high prices and obtain close to full-commitment monopoly profits.

[10] Tirole (1988, Section 3.3.1.5) provides a summary of the value of metering devices (such as two-part tariffs) as a form of price discrimination. Klein and Wiley (2003a) argue that such a form of price discrimination is common in competitive environments. In many regards, the economic intuition of two-part tariffs as a metering device is the same as the general intuition behind non-linear pricing which is surveyed in Section 6.

[11] Miravete (1996) and Courty and Li (2000) establish the economics behind sequential screening mechanisms such as advance-purchase discounts. Dana (1998) considers advance-purchase discounts in a variation of Prescott's (1975) model of perfect competition with aggregate demand uncertainty. Gale and Holmes (1992, 1993) provide a model of advance-purchase discounts in a duopoly setting.

[12] For example, see Laffont, Rey and Tirole (1998) and Dessein (2003).

[13] A considerable amount of study has also focused on how product lines should be chosen to soften second-stage price competition. While the present survey considers the effect of product line choice in segmenting the marketplace (e.g., second-degree price discrimination), it is silent about the strategic effects of locking into a particular product line (i.e., a specific set of locations in a preference space). A now large set of research has been devoted to this important topic, including significant papers by Brander and Eaton (1984), Klemperer (1992) and Gilbert and Matutes (1993), to list a few.

there is no unobservable heterogeneity and consumers have rectangular demand curves, then all consumer surplus is extracted and third-degree price discrimination is *perfect* price discrimination. More generally, if there is additional heterogeneity over θ_u or downward-sloping individual demand curves, third-degree price discrimination will leave some consumer surplus.

When the firm does not condition its price schedule on observable consumer characteristics, every consumer is offered the same price schedule, $P(q)$. Assuming that the unit cost is constant, we can say that a firm *indirectly* price discriminates if the marginal price varies across consumer types at their chosen consumption levels. A firm can typically extract greater consumer surplus by varying this price and screening consumers according to their revealed consumptions. This use of non-linear pricing as a sorting mechanism is typically referred to as *second-degree* price discrimination.[14] More generally, in a richer setting with heterogeneity over both observable and unobservable characteristics, we expect that the monopolist will practice some combination of direct and indirect price discrimination – offering $P(q, \theta_o)$, while using the non-linearity of the price schedule to sort over unobservable characteristics.

While one can categorize price discrimination strategies as either direct or indirect, it is also useful to catalog strategies according to whether they discriminate across consumers (*inter*personal price discrimination) or across units for the same consumer (*intra*personal price discrimination). For example, suppose that there is no interconsumer heterogeneity so that θ is fixed. There will generally remain some intraconsumer heterogeneity over the marginal value of each unit of consumption so that a firm cannot extract all consumer surplus using a linear price. Here, however, a firm can capture the consumer surplus associated with intraconsumer heterogeneity, either by offering a non-linear price schedule equal to the individual consumer's compensated demand curve or by offering a simpler two-part tariff. We will address these issues more in Section 5. Elsewhere in this chapter, we will focus on interpersonal price discrimination, with the implicit recognition that intrapersonal price discrimination often occurs in tandem.

The methodology of monopoly price discrimination can be both useful and misleading when applied to competitive settings. It is useful because the monopoly methods are valuable in calculating each firm's best response to its competitors' policies. Just as one can solve for the best-response function in a Cournot quantity game by deriving

[14] Pigou (1920) introduced the terminology of first-, second- and third-degree price discrimination. There is some confusion, however, regarding Pigou's original definition of second-degree price discrimination and that of many recent writers [e.g., see Tirole (1988)], who include self-selection via non-linear pricing as a form of second-degree discrimination. Pigou (1920) did not consider second-degree price discrimination as a selection mechanism, but rather thought of it as an approximation of first-degree using a step function below the consumer's demand curve and, as such, regarded both first and second-degrees of price discrimination as "scarcely ever practicable" and "of academic interest only". Dupuit (1849) gives a much clearer acknowledgment of the importance of self-selection constraints in segmenting markets, although without a taxonomy of price discrimination. We follow the modern use of the phrase "second-degree price discrimination" to include indirect segmentation via non-linear pricing.

a residual demand curve and proceeding as if the firm was a monopolist on this residual market, we can also solve for best responses in more complex price discrimination games by deriving residual market demand curves. Unfortunately, our intuitions from the monopoly models can be misleading because we are ultimately interested in the equilibrium of the firms' best-response functions rather than a single optimal pricing strategy. For example, while it is certainly the case that, *ceteris paribus*, a single firm will weakly benefit by price discriminating, if every firm were to switch from uniform pricing to price discrimination, profits for the entire industry may fall.[15] Industry profits fall depending on whether the additional surplus extraction allowed by price discrimination (the standard effect in the monopoly setting) exceeds any losses from a possibly increased intensity of price competition. This comparison, in turn, depends upon market details and the form of price discrimination, as will be explained. The pages that follow evaluate these interactions between price discrimination and imperfect competition.

When evaluating the impact of price discrimination in imperfectly competitive environments, two related comparisons are relevant for public policy. First, starting from a setting of imperfect competition and uniform pricing, what are the welfare changes from allowing firms to price discriminate? Second, starting from a setting of monopoly and price discrimination, what are the welfare effects of increasing competition? Because the theoretical predictions of the models often depend upon the nature of competition, consumer preferences and consumer heterogeneity, we shall examine a collection of specialized models to illuminate the broad themes of this literature and illustrate how the implications of competitive price discrimination compare to those of uniform pricing and monopoly.

In Sections 2–7, we explore variations on these themes by varying the forms of competition, preference heterogeneity, and segmenting devices. Initially in Section 2, we begin with the benchmark of first-degree, perfect price discrimination. In Section 3, we turn to the classic setting of third-degree price discrimination, applied to the case of imperfectly competitive firms. In Section 4, we examine an important class of models that extends third-degree price discrimination to dynamic settings, where price offers may be conditioned on a consumer's purchase history from rivals – a form of price discrimination that can only exist under competition. In Section 5, we study intrapersonal price discrimination. Section 6 brings together several diverse theoretical approaches to modeling imperfectly competitive second-degree price discrimination, comparing and contrasting the results to those under monopoly. Product bundling (as a form of price discrimination) in imperfectly competitive markets is reviewed in Section 7. Models of demand uncertainty and price rigidities are introduced in Section 8.

[15] Even a monopolist may be worse off with the ability to price discriminate when commitment problems are present. For example, the Coase conjecture argues a monopolist is worse off with the ability to charge different prices over time. As another example, when a monopolist can offer secret price discounts to its retailers, the monopolist may end up effectively competing against itself in the retail market.

2. First-degree price discrimination

First-degree (or perfect) price discrimination – which arises when the seller can capture all consumer surplus by pricing each unit at precisely the consumer's marginal willingness to pay – serves as an important benchmark and starting point for exploring more subtle forms of pricing. When the seller controls a monopoly, the monopolist obtains the entire social surplus, and so profit maximization is synonymous with maximizing social welfare. How does the economic intuition of this simple model translate to oligopoly?

The oligopoly game of perfect price discrimination is quite simple to analyze, even in its most general form. Following Spulber (1979), suppose that there are n firms, each selling a differentiated substitute product, but that each firm has the ability to price discriminate in the first degree and extract all of the consumer surplus under its residual demand curve. Specifically, suppose the residual demand curve for firm i is given by $p_i = D_i(q_i, q_{-i})$, when its rivals perfectly price discriminate and sell the vector $q_{-i} = (q_1, \ldots, q_{i-1}, q_{i+1}, \ldots, q_n)$. In addition, let $C_i(q_i)$ be firm i's cost of producing q_i units of output; the cost function is increasing and convex. As Spulber (1979) notes, the ability to then perfectly price discriminate when selling q_i units of output implies that firm i's profit function is

$$\pi_i(q_i, q_{-i}) = \int_0^{q_i} D_i(y, q_{-i})\,\mathrm{d}y - C_i(q_i).$$

A Nash equilibrium is a vector of outputs, $(q_1^*, \ldots, q_n^*)$, such that each firm's output, q_i^*, is a best-response to the output vector of its rivals, q_{-i}^*: formally, for all i and q_i, $\pi_i(q_i^*, q_{-i}^*) \geqslant \pi_i(q_i, q_{-i}^*)$. As Spulber (1979) notes, the assumption of perfect price discrimination – in tandem with the assumption that residual demand curves are downward sloping – implies that each firm i's profit function is strictly concave in its own output for any output vector of its rivals. Hence, the existence of a pure-strategy Nash equilibrium in quantities follows immediately. The equilibrium allocations are entirely determined by marginal-cost pricing based on each firm's residual demand curve: $D_i(q_i^*, q_{-i}^*) = C_i'(q_i)$.[16]

In this equilibrium of perfect price discrimination, each consumer's marginal purchase is priced at marginal cost, so, under mild technical assumptions, social surplus is maximized for a fixed number of firms.[17] In this setting, unlike the imperfect price discrimination settings which follow, the welfare effect of price discrimination is immediate, just as with perfect price discrimination under monopoly. Note, however, that

[16] This general existence result contrasts with the more restrictive assumptions required for pure-strategy Nash equilibria in which firms' strategies are limited to choosing a fixed unit price for each good. Spulber (1979) also demonstrates that if an additional stability restriction on the derivatives of the residual demand curves is satisfied, this equilibrium is unique.

[17] When firms can choose their product characteristics, as Spence (1976a) noted, if sellers can appropriately price discriminate, the social distortions are eliminated. Lederer and Hurter (1986) and MacLeod, Norman and Thisse (1988) more generally show that *for a fixed number of firms*, an equilibrium exists with efficient product choices. These papers assume that the industry configuration of firms is fixed.

while consumers obtain none of the surplus under the residual demand curves, it does not follow that consumers obtain no surplus at all; rather, for each firm i, they obtain no surplus from the addition of the ith firm's product to the current availability of $n - 1$ other goods. If the goods are close substitutes and marginal costs are constant, the residual demand curves are highly elastic and consumers may nonetheless obtain considerable surplus from the presence of competition. The net effect of price discrimination on total consumer surplus requires an explicit treatment of consumer demand. It may also be the case that each firm's residual demand curve is more elastic when its rivals can perfectly price discriminate than when they are forced to price uniformly. Thus, while each firm prefers the ability to perfectly price discriminate itself, the total industry profit may fall when price discrimination is allowed, depending on the form of competition and consumer preferences. We will see a clear example of this in the Hotelling-demand model of Thisse and Vives (1988) which examines discriminatory pricing based on observable location. In this simple setting, third-degree price discrimination is perfect, but firms are worse off and would prefer to commit collectively to uniform-pricing strategies.

The above conclusions take the number of firms, n, and their product characteristics as fixed. If the industry configuration is endogenous, additional welfare costs can arise. For example, if entry with fixed costs occurs until long-run profits are driven to zero, *and* if consumer surplus is entirely captured by price discrimination, then price discrimination lowers social welfare compared to uniform pricing. This conclusion follows immediately from the fact that when consumer surplus is zero and entry dissipates profits, there is zero social surplus generated by the market. Uniform pricing typically leaves some consumer surplus (and hence positive social welfare). In a general setting of spatial competition in which firms choose to enter and their product characteristics, Bhaskar and To (2004) demonstrate that perfect price discrimination always causes too much entry from a social welfare perspective. This is because the marginal firm captures its marginal social contribution relative to an inefficient allocation (rather than an efficient allocation of $n - 1$ firms), which over compensates entry. The intuition in Bhaskar and To (2004) is simply put: Suppose that the vector of product characteristics for the market is given by x, and let x_{-i} be the vector without the ith firm. Let $x^*(n)$ maximizes social welfare when there are n firms supplying output, and let $W(x^*(n))$ be the associated social surplus. With $n - 1$ firms in the market, the analogous characteristics vector and welfare level are $x^*(n - 1)$ and $W(x^*(n - 1))$, respectively. Now suppose that firm i is the marginal firm. Then its profits under perfect price discrimination are equal to $W(x^*(n)) - W^*(x^*_{-i}(n))$. Note that the firm's social contribution is $W(x^*(n)) - W^*(x^*(n-1))$. Because $W(x^*(n-1)) > W(x^*_{-i}(n))$, incentives for entry are excessive.

Rather than further explore the stylized setting of first-degree price discrimination, the ensuing sections turn to explicit analyses undertaken for a variety of imperfect price discrimination strategies.

3. Third-degree price discrimination

The classic theory of third-degree price discrimination by a monopolist is straightforward: the optimal price-discriminating prices are found by applying the familiar inverse-elasticity rule to each market separately. If, however, oligopolists compete in each market, then each firm applies the inverse-elasticity rule using its own residual demand curve – an equilibrium construction. Here, the cross-price elasticities of demand play a central role in determining equilibrium prices and outputs. These cross-price elasticities, in turn, depend critically upon consumer preferences and the form of consumer heterogeneity.

3.1. Welfare analysis

In the static setting of third-degree price discrimination, there are three potential sources of social inefficiency. First, aggregate output over all market segments may be too low if prices exceed marginal cost. To this end, we seek to understand the conditions for which price discrimination leads to an increase or decrease in aggregate output relative to uniform pricing. Second, for a given level of aggregate consumption, price discrimination will typically generate interconsumer misallocations relative to uniform pricing; hence, aggregate output will not be efficiently distributed to the highest-value ends. Third, there may be cross-segment inefficiencies as a given consumer may be served by an inefficient firm, perhaps purchasing from a more distant or higher-cost firm to obtain a price discount. A fourth set of distortions related to the dynamics of entry is taken up in Section 3.5.

In the following, much is made of the relationship between aggregate output and welfare. If the same aggregate output is generated under uniform pricing as under price discrimination, then price discrimination must necessarily lower social welfare because output is allocated with multiple prices. With a uniform price, interconsumer misallocations are not possible. Therefore, placing production inefficiencies aside, an increase in aggregate output is a necessary condition for price discrimination to increase welfare.[18] Robinson (1933) makes this point in the context of monopoly, but the economic logic applies more generally to imperfect competition, providing that the firms are equally efficient at production and the number of firms is fixed.[19] Because we can easily make

[18] Yoshida (2000), building on the papers of Katz (1987) and DeGraba (1990), considers third-degree price discrimination by an intermediate goods monopolist with Cournot competition in the downstream market, and finds a more subtle relationship between output and welfare. When demands and marginal costs are linear, price discrimination has no effect on the aggregate amount of intermediate good sold, but it may lead to an inefficient allocation of output among the downstream firms. Indeed, in Yoshida's (2000) model, if final output *rises*, social welfare must *fall*.

[19] Schmalensee (1981) extends Robinson's (1933) analysis to more than two segments and provides a necessary condition for aggregate quantity to rise in this general setting. Varian (1985) generalizes Schmalensee's (1981) necessary condition by considering more general demand and cost settings, and also by establishing

statements only about aggregate output for many models of third-degree price discrimination, this result proves useful in giving limited power to draw welfare conclusions.

To this end, it is first helpful to review the setting of monopoly in Robinson (1933). That work concludes that when a monopolist price discriminates, whether aggregate output increases depends upon the relative curvature of the segmented demand curves.[20] Particularly in the case of two segments, if the "adjusted concavity" (an idea we will make precise below) of the more elastic market is greater than the adjusted concavity of the less elastic market at a uniform price, then output increases with price discrimination; when the reverse is true, aggregate output decreases. When a market segment has linear demand, the adjusted concavity is zero. It follows that when demand curves are linear – providing all markets are served – price discrimination has no effect on aggregate output.[21] In sum, to make a determination about the effects of price discrimination on aggregate output under monopoly, one needs only to compare the adjusted concavities of each market segment. Below we will see that under competition, one will also need to consider the relationship between a firm's elasticity and the market elasticity for each market segment.

There are two common approaches to modeling imperfect competition: quantity competition with homogeneous goods and price competition with product differentiation. The simple, quantity-competition model of oligopoly price discrimination is presented in Section 3.2. Quantity competition, however, is not a natural framework in which to discuss price discrimination, so we turn our focus to price-setting models of competition. Within price-setting games, we further distinguish two sets of models based upon consumer demands. In the first setting (Section 3.3), all firms agree in their ranking of high-price (or "strong") markets and low-price (or "weak") markets. Here, whether the strong market is more competitive than the weak market is critical for many economic conclusions. In the second setting (Section 3.4), firms are asymmetric in their ranking of strong and weak markets; e.g., firm a's strong market is firm b's weak market and conversely. With such asymmetry, equilibrium prices can move in patterns that are not possible under symmetric rankings and different economic insights present themselves. Following the treatment of price-setting games, we take up the topics of third-degree price discrimination with endogenous entry (Section 3.5) and private restrictions on price discrimination (Section 3.6).

a lower (sufficient condition) bound on welfare changes. Schwartz (1990) considers cases in which marginal costs are decreasing. Additional effects arising from heterogeneous firms alter the application of these welfare results to oligopoly, as noted by Galera (2003). It is possible, for example, that price discrimination may lead to more efficient production across firms with differing costs, offsetting the welfare loss from consumer misallocations, and thus leading to a net welfare gain without an increase in aggregate output. In this paper, we largely examine models of equally efficient firms.

20 More precisely, Robinson defines the *adjusted concavity* of a segment demand curve to capture the precise notion of curvature necessary for the result. Schmalensee (1981) provides a deeper treatment which builds upon Robinson's work.

21 This finding was first noted by Pigou (1920), and so Robinson's analysis can be seen as a generalization to non-linear demand.

3.2. Cournot models of third-degree price discrimination

Perhaps the simplest model of imperfect competition and price discrimination is the immediate extension of Cournot's quantity-setting, homogeneous-good game to firms competing in distinct market segments. Suppose that there are m markets, $i = 1, \ldots, m$, and n firms, $j = 1, \ldots, n$, each of which produces at a constant marginal cost per unit. The timing of the output game is standard: each firm j simultaneously chooses its output levels for each of the i markets: $\{q_1^j, \ldots, q_m^j\}$. Let the demand curve for each market i be given by $p_i = D_i(Q_i)$, where $Q_i = \sum_j q_i^j$, and suppose that in equilibrium all markets are active. Setting aside issues of equilibrium existence, it follows that the symmetric equilibrium outputs, $\{q_1^*, \ldots, q_m^*\}$, satisfy, for every market i,

$$MC = D_i(nq_i^*) + D_i'(nq_i^*)q_i^* = p_i^*\left(1 - \frac{1}{n\varepsilon_i^m}\right),$$

where ε_i^m is the market elasticity for segment i.

Several observations regarding the effects of competition follow immediately from this framework. First, marginal revenues are equal across market segments, just as in monopoly. Second, under mild assumptions related to the change in elasticities and marginal costs, as the number of firms increases, the markup over marginal cost decreases in each market segment. It follows that each firm's profit also decreases and consumer surplus increases as n increases. Third, if each market segment has a constant elasticity of demand, relative prices across segments are constant in n and, therefore, an increase in firms necessarily decreases absolute price dispersion. Finally, in the spirit of monopolistic competition, one can introduce a fixed cost of production and allow entry to drive long-run profits to zero, thereby making the size of the market endogenous. In such a setting, both long-term market power and economic profit are zero, but fixed costs of entry generate short-run market power, short-run economic rents, and prices above marginal cost.

Aside from the effects of competition, one can also inquire about the welfare effects of price discrimination relative to uniform pricing. For Cournot oligopoly, the adjusted concavities are key to determining the effect of price discrimination on aggregate output. When demand curves are linear, these concavities are zero, and – providing all market segments are served – price discrimination has no effect on total sales. To see this clearly, let $Q_i = \alpha_i - \beta_i p_i$ be the demand function for segment i (or alternatively, $p_i = D_i(Q_i) = \alpha_i/\beta_i - Q_i/\beta_i$), and therefore $Q = \alpha - \beta p$ is the aggregate output across all segments at a uniform price of p, where $\alpha \equiv \sum_i \alpha_i$ and $\beta \equiv \sum_i \beta_i$. With constant marginal cost of production, c, the Cournot–Nash equilibrium under uniform pricing (i.e., with one aggregated market) is simply $Q^u = (\alpha - \beta c)(\frac{n}{n+1})$. Under price discrimination, the equilibrium total output in each segment is similarly given by $Q_i^{\text{pd}} = (\alpha_i - \beta_i c)(\frac{n}{n+1})$. Summing across segments, aggregate output under price discrimination is equal to that under uniform pricing: $Q^{\text{pd}} = \sum_i Q_i^{\text{pd}} = Q^u$. Given that firms are equally efficient at production and aggregate output is unchanged, price discrimination reduces welfare because it generates interconsumer misallocations. More generally, when demand curves are non-linear or some markets would not be served under uniform pricing, price discrimination may increase welfare. The ultimate conclusion is an empirical matter.

3.3. A tale of two elasticities: best-response symmetry in price games

In her study of third-degree price discrimination under monopoly, Robinson (1933) characterizes a monopolist's two markets as "strong" and "weak". By definition, a price discriminating monopolist sets the higher price in the strong market, and the lower price in the weak market. It is useful to extend this ranking to imperfectly competitive markets. Suppose that there are two markets, $i = 1, 2$. We say that market i is "weak" (and the other is "strong") for firm j if, for any uniform price(s) set by the other firm(s), the optimal price in market i is lower than the optimal price in the other market. Formally, if $BR_i^j(p)$ is the best-response function of firm j in market i, given that its rival sets the price p, then market 1 is weak (and 2 is strong) if and only if $BR_1^j(p) < BR_2^j(p)$ for all p. We say that the market environment satisfies *best-response symmetry* [using a phrase introduced by Corts (1998)] if the weak and strong markets of each firm coincide; alternatively, if the weak and strong markets of each firm differ, then the environment exhibits *best-response asymmetry*.[22]

When firms agree on their rankings of markets from strong to weak, the introduction of price discrimination causes the price in the strong market to rise (and the price in the weak market to fall) relative to the uniform price. Whether aggregate output rises or falls depends upon the magnitude of these movements. In particular, there exists a useful result from Holmes (1989) which predicts when aggregate output will rise or fall with price discrimination, and therefore provides some indication about its ultimate welfare effects. This result is not available when best responses are asymmetric, which creates a crucial distinction in what follows. In this section, we assume that there exists best-response symmetry; in the following section, we study best-response asymmetry along the lines of Corts (1998).

Borenstein (1985) and Holmes (1989) extend the analysis of third-degree price discrimination to settings of imperfect competition with product differentiation, underscoring the significance of cross-price elasticities in predicting changes in profits and surplus. In particular, Holmes (1989) builds upon the monopoly model of Robinson (1933) and demonstrates that under symmetric duopoly, it is crucial to know the ratio of market to cross-price elasticities, aside from the adjusted concavities of demand. The curvatures of the market demand curves are insufficient, by themselves, to predict changes in aggregate output when markets are imperfectly competitive.

[22] Note that a market might be "strong" for a monopoly but a "weak" market under duopoly if competition is more intense in the monopolist's "strong" market.

To understand the relevance of the ratio of market elasticity to cross-price elasticity, consider two markets, $i = 1, 2$, and duopolists, $j = a, b$, each offering products in both segments and producing with constant marginal cost of c per unit. We take market 2 to be the strong market and market 1 to be weak. Demand for firm j's output in market i depends upon the prices offered by each firm in market i: $q_i^j(p_i^a, p_i^b)$. These demand functions are assumed to be symmetric across firms (i.e., symmetric to permuting indices a and b), so we can write $q_i(p) \equiv q_i^a(p, p) \equiv q_i^b(p, p)$. The *market elasticity* of demand in market i (as a function of symmetric price $p = p_i^a = p_i^b$) is therefore

$$\varepsilon_i^m(p) = -\frac{p}{q_i(p)} q_i'(p).$$

Furthermore, j's own-price *firm elasticity* of demand in market i is

$$\varepsilon_{i,j}^f(p^a, p^b) = -\frac{p^j}{q_i^j(p^a, p^b)} \frac{\partial q_i^j(p^a, p^b)}{\partial p^j},$$

which at symmetric prices, $p = p_i^a = p_i^b$, is more simply

$$\varepsilon_i^f(p) = -\frac{p}{q_i(p)} q_i'(p) + \frac{p}{q_i(p)} \frac{\partial q_i^a(p, p)}{\partial p_i^b} = \varepsilon_i^m(p) + \varepsilon_i^c(p),$$

where $\varepsilon_i^c(p) > 0$ is the cross-price elasticity of demand at symmetric prices, p. Thus, the firm elasticity in a duopoly market is composed of two components: the market (or industry) elasticity and the cross-price elasticity. The former is related to the ability of a monopolist (or collusive duopoly) to extract consumer surplus; it measures the sensitivity of the consumer to taking the outside option of not consuming either good. The latter is related to the ability of a rival to steal business; it measures the consumer's sensitivity to purchasing the rival's product. While a monopolist will choose prices across markets such that

$$\frac{p_i - c}{p_i} = \frac{1}{\varepsilon_i^m(p_i)},$$

non-cooperative duopolists (in a symmetric price equilibrium) will set prices across markets such that

$$\frac{p_i - c}{p_i} = \frac{1}{\varepsilon_i^m(p_i) + \varepsilon_i^c(p_i)}.$$

Several results follow from this comparison.

• *Price effects of competition* From the above formulation of the inverse-elasticity rules, competition lowers prices in both markets compared to a price-discriminating monopolist, ceteris paribus, and therefore we expect competition to increase welfare in this simple third-degree price discrimination setting. The effect of competition on price dispersion across markets, however, is ambiguous and depends upon the cross-price elasticities. If the goods are close substitutes and market competition is fierce (i.e.,

$\varepsilon_1^c(p_1) \approx \infty$, $\varepsilon_2^c(p_2) \approx \infty$), prices will be close to marginal cost in each market and the price differential across markets will be negligible. Alternatively, if consumers in the weak market find the goods to be close substitutes (i.e., $\varepsilon_1^c(p_1) \approx \infty$) while consumers in the strong market exhibit powerful brand loyalties (i.e., $\varepsilon_2^c(p_2) \approx 0$), then the firms choose highly competitive prices in the weak market and close-to-monopoly prices in the strong market. Competition, in this setting, leads to greater price differentials across markets, relative to that of a price-discriminating monopolist. Testable implications for price dispersion are directly tied to estimates of the cross-price elasticities in each market.[23]

• *Output (and welfare) effects of price discrimination* A recurring policy question in the price discrimination literature is whether to allow third-degree price discrimination or to enforce uniform pricing. A key ingredient to understanding this question in the context of imperfectly competitive markets is the impact of price discrimination on output.

Consider the marginal profit to firm j from a change in price in market i (starting from a point of price symmetry):

$$D\pi_i(p) \equiv q_i^a(p) + (p - c)\frac{\partial q_i^a(p, p)}{\partial p_i^a}.$$

We further assume that these marginal profit functions decrease in price for each market segment. The third-degree discriminatory prices are determined by the system of equations, $D\pi_i(p_i^*) = 0$, $i = 1, 2$, while the uniform-price equilibrium is determined by $D\pi_1(p_u^*) + D\pi_2(p_u^*) = 0$.[24] Given our assumption of decreasing marginal profit functions, it is necessarily the case that $p_u^* \in (p_1^*, p_2^*)$.[25] This in turn implies that the output in market 2 decreases under price discrimination while the output in market 1 increases. The impact of price discrimination on aggregate output, therefore, is not immediately clear.

To determine the effect on aggregate output, suppose that due to arbitrage difficulties, a discriminating firm cannot drive a wedge greater than r between its two prices[26]; hence, $p_2 = p_1 + r$. It follows that, for a given binding constraint r, each firm will choose p_1 to satisfy $D\pi_1(p_1) + D\pi_2(p_1 + r) = 0$, the solution of which we denote

[23] Borenstein (1985) and Borenstein and Rose (1994) develop related theories indicating how competition may increase price dispersion. Borenstein and Rose (1994) find empirical evidence of various measures of increased price dispersion as a function of increased competition in airline ticket pricing.

[24] We assume that portions of each market are served under both forms of pricing.

[25] In the context of monopoly, the direction of price changes in third-degree price discrimination follows this pattern if the monopolist's profit function is strictly concave in price within each segment. When this is not the case (e.g., profit is bimodal in price), the direction of price changes is ambiguous, as shown by Nahata, Ostaszewski and Sahoo (1990).

[26] Leontief (1940) analyzes the effect of such a constraint on monopoly pricing. Schmalensee (1981) uses the technique to analyze aggregate output, as we do here.

parametrically as $p_1^*(r)$. By construction, $p_2^*(r) \equiv p_1^*(r) + r$. Hence, the effect on aggregate output from a fixed price differential of r can be characterized by

$$Q(r) = q_1\big(p_1^*(r)\big) + q_2\big(p_1^*(r) + r\big).$$

Because $r = 0$ corresponds to uniform pricing, it follows that if $Q(r)$ is everywhere increasing in r, then aggregate output increases from price discrimination. Alternatively, if $Q(r)$ is everywhere decreasing in r, aggregate output (and welfare) necessarily decreases. After some simplification, the condition that $Q'(r) > 0$ can be shown to be equivalent to the condition

$$\left[\frac{(p_2 - c)}{2q_2'(p_2)}\frac{d}{dp_2}\left(\frac{\partial q_2^a(p_2, p_2)}{\partial p_2^a}\right) - \frac{(p_1 - c)}{2q_1'(p_1)}\frac{d}{dp_1}\left(\frac{\partial q_1^a(p_1, p_1)}{\partial p_1^a}\right)\right]$$
$$+ \left[\frac{\varepsilon_2^c(p_2)}{\varepsilon_2^m(p_2)} - \frac{\varepsilon_1^c(p_1)}{\varepsilon_1^m(p_1)}\right] > 0.$$

The first bracketed expression is a straightforward variation of Robinson's adjusted-concavity condition found in the case of monopoly. When demands are linear (and adjusted concavities are zero), the elasticity-ratio test gives a sufficient condition for increased output:

$$\frac{\varepsilon_1^m(p_1)}{\varepsilon_2^m(p_2)} > \frac{\varepsilon_1^c(p_1)}{\varepsilon_2^c(p_2)}.$$

If the strong market (market 2) is more sensitive to competition in the sense that $\varepsilon_i^c/\varepsilon_i^m$ is larger, then price discrimination causes the strong market's output reduction to be less than the weak market's output increase. Accordingly, aggregate output rises. If the reduction in the strong market is sufficiently small relative to the weak market, then welfare will also rise. As an extreme example, when marginal cost is zero, optimal pricing requires that $\varepsilon_i^f(p_i) = 1$, and so $\varepsilon_i^m(p_i) = 1 - \varepsilon_i^c(p_i)$. The elasticity-ratio condition simplifies to the requirement that the strong market has a higher cross-price elasticity of demand: $\varepsilon_2^c(p_2) > \varepsilon_1^c(p_1)$.

From a social welfare point of view, the higher price should occur in the market with the lower market elasticity. This is also the pattern of monopoly pricing. Because each duopolist cares about its individual firm elasticity (which is the sum of the market and cross-price elasticities), this ordering may fail under competition and the higher price may arise in the more elastic market. While the average monopoly price exceeds the average duopoly price, the pattern of relative prices may be more inefficient under duopoly than under monopoly when firms are allowed to price discriminate. While competition is effective at controlling average prices, it is not effective at generating the correct pattern of relative prices. This is a key source of ambiguity in the welfare analysis.[27]

[27] I am grateful to Mark Armstrong for providing this insight, which provides further intuition regarding the desirability of intrapersonal price discrimination in competitive markets (Section 5).

• *Profit effects* The profit effects of price discrimination are more difficult to predict. While any individual firm's profit rises when allowed to price discriminate, the entire industry profit may rise or fall when all firms add price discrimination to their strategic arsenals. Two papers have made significant findings in this direction. Holmes (1989) analyzes the case of linear demand functions and finds that when the elasticity-ratio condition above is satisfied, profit (as well as output) increases. When the condition is violated, however, the effect on profits is ambiguous (though welfare necessarily falls). What is particularly interesting is that price discrimination decreases profits when the weak market has a higher cross-price elasticity but a lower market elasticity compared to the strong market. Because the market elasticity is lower in the weak market, a given increase in price would be more profitable (and more socially efficient) in the weak market than in the strong market. When profits fall due to price discrimination, it is because the weak market's significantly higher cross-price elasticity outweighs its lower market elasticity, and therefore price discrimination reduces the weak-market price. From a profit perspective (and a social welfare perspective), this lower price is in the wrong market, and thus profits decline relative to uniform pricing.

Related to this finding, Armstrong and Vickers (2001) consider a model of third-degree price discrimination in which each segment is a Hotelling market with uniformly distributed consumers, each of whom has identical downward-sloping demand. The market segments differ only by the consumers' transportation costs. They demonstrate that when competition is sufficiently intense (specifically, each segment's transportation cost goes to zero while maintaining a constant cost ratio), industry profits increase under price discrimination and consumer surplus falls. This outcome suggests that Holmes's (1989) numerical examples of decreased profits (reductions which Holmes notes are never more than a few percentage points) may not be robust to closely-related settings with intense competition. This finding, together with the other results of Holmes (1989), strengthens the sense that price discrimination typically increases profits in settings of best-response symmetry with sufficient competition.[28]

• *Inter-firm misallocations* The model examined in Holmes (1989) is symmetric across firms – no firm has a cost or product advantage over the other. This simplification obscures possibly significant, inter-firm misallocations that would arise in a model in which one firm has a comparative advantage in delivering value to consumers. The change from uniform pricing to price discrimination may either mitigate or amplify these distortions.

As an immediate illustration of this ambiguity, consider a duopoly setting in which both firms are local monopolists in their own strong markets and participate in a third, weak market. The strong-market demands are rectangular (although possibly different

[28] Armstrong and Vickers (2001) find that when the segment with the lower market elasticity also has a sufficiently higher cross-price elasticity (i.e., low transportation costs), welfare falls under price discrimination. The economics underlying this result are similar to Holmes's (1989) linear model of decreased profits – price discrimination causes the prices to fall and rise in the wrong markets.

between the firms). In the weak market, suppose that the firms are Hotelling (1929) duopolists in a market which is covered in equilibrium. Given these assumptions, the only social inefficiency is that some consumers in the weak market purchase from the "wrong" firm; this situation arises when the price differential across firms in the weak market is not equal to the difference in marginal costs. Under price discrimination, our assumption of rectangular demand curves implies that the strong-market, cross-firm price differential depends entirely on the consumer's valuations for each product. In the weak market, however, it is easy to see that the resulting price differential between the firms is smaller than the difference in marginal costs; the price discrimination equilibrium results in the high-cost firm serving too much of the market. Compare this outcome to the uniform-price setting: If the strong market is sufficiently important relative to the weak market, then the uniform-price differential will be close to the price-discriminating, inter-firm differential in the strong market. If the strong-market differential is close to the difference in marginal costs, then uniform pricing mitigates inefficiencies; if the differential in the strong market is smaller than the price-discriminating differential in the weak market, then uniform pricing amplifies the social distortions. In short, there are no robust conclusions regarding the effect of price discrimination on misallocated production.

3.4. When one firm's strength is a rival's weakness: best-response asymmetry in price games

The assumption that firms rank strong and weak markets symmetrically is restrictive, as it rules out most models with spatial demand systems in which price discrimination occurs over observable location; e.g., a weak (distant) market for firm a is a strong (close) market for firm b. The assumption of best-response symmetry in the previous analysis allowed us to conclude that the uniform price always lies between the strong and weak market prices under discrimination. Without such symmetry, this conclusion does not generally hold. Indeed, it is possible that all prices rise or fall following the introduction of price discrimination.

• *A simple model to illustrate recurring themes* We begin with a simple example of differentiated duopoly drawn from Thisse and Vives (1988) to illustrate some of the consequences of price discrimination when firms have dissimilar strengths and weaknesses across markets.[29] Consider a standard Hotelling (1929) model of duopoly in which two firms are located on the endpoints of a linear market. Each consumer has an observable location parameter, $\theta \in (0, 1)$, which is drawn from a uniform distribution across the market; each consumer demands at most one unit of output. A consumer at location θ who consumes from the left firm at price p_l obtains utility $z - \tau\theta - p_l$, while

[29] See related papers by Shaffer and Zhang (1995, 2000), Bester and Petrakis (1996), Liu and Serfes (2004) and Armstrong (2006, Section 3.4).

the same consumer purchasing from the right firm at price p_r obtains $z-\tau(1-\theta)-p_r$. In this sense, z represents the base value of the product, while τ is a measure of product differentiation and the intensity of competition. Each firm produces output at constant marginal (and average) cost equal to c.

In the analysis that immediately follows, we assume that z is sufficiently large so that the duopoly equilibrium exhibits competition (rather than local monopoly or kinked demand) and that the multi-plant monopolist covers the market. Critically, this assumption guarantees that industry demand is inelastic while the cross-price elasticity between products depends on $1/\tau$, which can be quite large. Among other things, the resulting relationship between the industry and cross-price elasticities induces intense competition in the duopoly setting.

As a benchmark, consider the case of uniform pricing. In the duopoly setting, it is straightforward to compute that in the Nash equilibrium, price is $p = c + \tau$ and each firm earns $\pi = \frac{1}{2}\tau$ in profits. Intuitively, a higher transportation cost translates into higher product differentiation, prices, and profits; indeed, τ is the unique source of profit in the Hotelling framework.

Now, suppose that firms are able to price discriminate *directly* on the consumer's location, θ, as in Thisse and Vives (1988). It follows in equilibrium that the more distant firm offers a price to the consumer of $p = c$ and the closer firm generates the same level of utility to make the sale.[30] Thus, the left firm offers a price of $p_l(\theta) = c + \tau(1 - 2\theta)$ for all $\theta \leqslant \frac{1}{2}$, and $p_l(\theta) = c$ for $\theta > \frac{1}{2}$; analogously, the right firm offers $p_r(\theta) = c + \tau(2\theta - 1)$ for $\theta \geqslant \frac{1}{2}$ and $p_r(\theta) = c$ for $\theta < \frac{1}{2}$. It immediately follows that price discrimination leads to a fall in equilibrium prices for *every* market segment: $p^d(\theta) \equiv \max\{p_l(\theta), p_r(\theta)\} < c + \tau$ for all $\theta \in (0, 1)$. Consequently, price discrimination also lowers profits which are now $\pi^d = \int_0^{\frac{1}{2}} \tau(1 - 2s)\,\mathrm{d}s = \frac{1}{4}\tau$, – exactly half of the profits that arise under uniform pricing.

Compare these duopoly outcomes to those which emerge when the two products are sold by a multi-plant monopolist. When the monopolist is restricted to offering the output of each plant at a uniform mill price, the price will be set so as to leave the consumer at $\theta = \frac{1}{2}$ with no surplus (providing z is sufficiently large); hence, $p = z - \frac{1}{2}\tau$ and per-plant profits under uniform pricing are $\pi = \frac{1}{2}(z - c - \frac{1}{2}\tau)$. If the multi-plant monopolist is able to price discriminate over consumer location, however, it can do much better. The firm would offer a price to extract all consumer surplus, $p^m(\theta) = z - \tau \min\{\theta, 1 - \theta\}$, and per-plant profits would increase to $\pi^m = \frac{1}{2}(z - c - \frac{1}{4}\tau)$. Unlike imperfect competition, price discrimination increases the prices and profits of the monopolist.

Several noteworthy comparisons can be made. First, consider the effect of price discrimination on profits and price levels. Profits for a monopolist increase with the ability to price discriminate by $\tau/4$, while industry profits for competing duopolists decrease by

30 Lederer and Hurter (1986) show that such marginal-cost pricing by the closest unsuccessful competitor is a common feature in pricing equilibria of location models.

$\tau/2$ when firms use discriminatory prices. Under duopoly, introducing price discrimination creates aggressive competition at every location and uniformly lowers every price: prices decrease from $p = c + \tau$ to $p^d(\theta) = c + \tau - 2\tau \min\{\theta, 1 - \theta\}$. Here, the business-stealing effect of price discrimination dominates the rent-extraction effect, so that duopolists are worse off with the ability to price discriminate. This result contrasts with that under best-response symmetry (Section 3.3) where price discrimination typically increases industry profits. Because welfare is constant in this simple setting, these profit conclusions imply that consumers are better off with price discrimination under competition and better off with uniform pricing under monopoly.[31]

Second, note that price discrimination generates a range of prices. Because perfect competition implies that all firms choose marginal cost pricing (even when allowed to price discriminate), a reasonable conjecture may be that an increase in competition reduces price dispersion relative to monopoly. In the present model, however, the reverse is true – competition increases dispersion.[32] The range of prices with price discriminating duopolists is $p^d(\theta) \in [c, c + \tau]$, twice as large as the range for the multiplant monopolist, $p^m(\theta) \in [z - \frac{1}{2}\tau, z]$. Intuitively, when price discrimination is allowed, duopoly prices are more sensitive to transportation costs because the consumer's distance to the competitor's plant is critical. A multiplant monopolist, however, is only concerned with the consumer choosing the outside option of purchasing nothing, so the relevant distance for a consumer is that to the nearest plant – a shorter distance. More generally, monopoly prices are driven by market elasticities, while duopoly prices are determined in tandem with the cross-price elasticity with respect to a rival's price. This suggests that whether dispersion increases from competition depends upon the specifics of consumer preferences.[33]

Third, if we generalize the model slightly so that firm a has higher unit costs than firm b, $c_a > c_b$, we can consider the impact of price discrimination on inter-firm mislocations. With uniform pricing, each firm chooses $p_j = \frac{2}{3}c_j + \frac{1}{3}c_{-j} + \tau$ and the price

[31] When drawing welfare conclusions, one must be especially careful given this model's limitations. Because the market is covered in equilibrium and inelastic consumers purchase from the closest plant, it follows that all regimes (price discrimination or uniform pricing, monopoly or duopoly) generate the same total social surplus. Hence, a richer model will be required to generate plausible welfare conclusions; we will consider such models later. That said, this simple model is useful for generating immediate intuitions about the effects of competition and price discrimination on profit, consumer surplus, price levels and price dispersion. Most importantly, the model illustrates the significance of relaxing best-response symmetry over strong and weak markets.

[32] Note that the range of duopoly prices contracts as τ becomes small. Because τ is a natural measure of the intensity of competition, we have the result that holding the number of firms fixed, increasing competitive pressures leads to less price dispersion.

[33] For example, if the base value also depends continuously upon location, $z(\theta)$, with $z'(\theta) < -\tau$ (respectively, $z'(\theta) > \tau$) for $\theta < \frac{1}{2}$ (respectively, $\theta > \frac{1}{2}$), then a multi-plant monopolist who sells to the entire market may offer a range of prices larger than would the duopolists. Whether competition increases or decreases price dispersion is unclear without more knowledge about market and cross-price elasticities. This ambiguity is no different from the setting of best-response symmetry; see Section 3.3.

differential is $(c_a - c_b)/3$. Because this price differential is smaller than the difference in firm costs, too many consumers purchase from the less efficient firm a. Under uniform pricing by a multi-plant monopolist, the differential is larger, $(c_a - c_b)/2$, but some misallocation remains. When price discrimination by location is allowed, however, efficiency in inter-firm allocations is restored for both duopoly and multi-plant monopoly settings. In the case of duopoly, efficiency arises because the marginal consumer, who is located at a point of indifference between the two endpoints, is always offered marginal cost pricing from both firms. In a monopoly, the monopolist extracts all consumer surplus using price discrimination and so eliminates any inter-plant misallocations. Although this setting is simplified, the intuition for why price discrimination decreases inter-firm misallocations can be generalized to a discrete-choice model in which the marginal consumer in equilibrium is offered marginal-cost prices under discrimination.

Fourth, consider the possibility of commitment. Given that profits are lower with price discrimination in the presence of competing firms, it is natural to wonder whether firms may find it individually optimal to commit publicly to uniform pricing in the hopes that this commitment will engender softer pricing responses from rivals. This question was first addressed in Thisse and Vives (1988), who add an initial commitment stage to the pricing game. In the first stage, each firm simultaneously decides whether to commit to uniform prices (or not); in the second stage, both firms observe any first stage commitments, and then each sets its price(s) accordingly.[34] One might conjecture that committing to uniform pricing may be a successful strategy if the second-stage pricing game exhibits strategic complementarities. It is straightforward to show in the present example, however, that the gain which a uniform-price firm would achieve by inducing a soft response from a rival is smaller than the loss the firm would suffer from the inability to price discriminate in the second stage. Formally, when one firm commits to uniform pricing and the other does not, the equilibrium uniform price is $p = c + \frac{1}{2}\tau$ and the optimal price-discriminatory response is $p(\theta) = c + \tau(\frac{3}{2} - 2\theta)$; these prices result in a market share of $\frac{1}{4}$ and a profit of $\pi = \frac{1}{8}\tau$ for the uniform pricing duopolist, and yield a market share of $\frac{3}{4}$ and a profit of $\pi = \frac{9}{16}\tau$ for the discriminator. Combined with the previous results on profits, it follows that choosing price discrimination in the first stage dominates uniform pricing: a Prisoners' Dilemma emerges.

• *General price effects from discrimination and competition* In the simple Hotelling model, prices decrease across all market segments when price discrimination is introduced. Because firms differ in their ranking of strong and weak markets in this example, one might wonder how closely this result depends upon best-response asymmetry. The answer, as Corts (1998) has shown, is that best-response asymmetry is a necessary condition for *all-out price competition* (defined as the case where prices drop in all markets

[34] When one firm commits to uniform pricing and the other does not, Thisse and Vives (1988) assume that the uniform-pricing firm moves first in the second-stage pricing game.

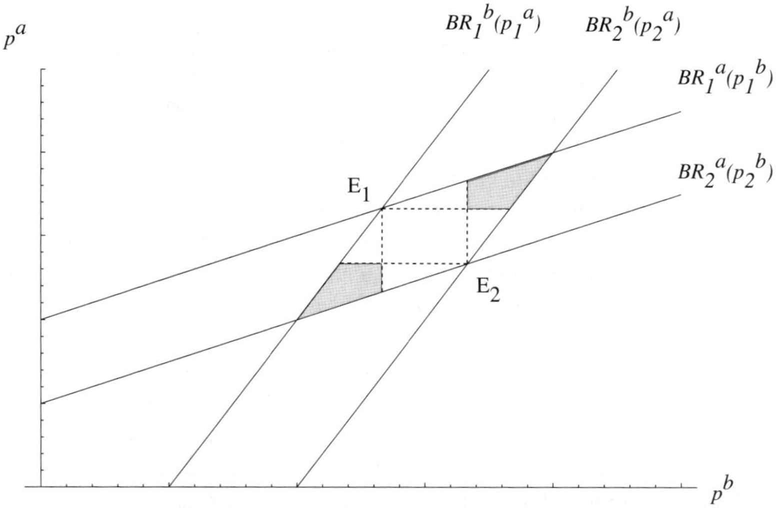

Figure 34.1. The possibility of all-out competition and all-out price gouging.

form competition) or all-out price increases (analogously, where prices increase in all markets).[35]

Recall that if firms have identical rankings over the strength and weakness of markets (and if profit functions are appropriately concave and symmetric across firms), it follows that the uniform price lies between the weak and strong market prices. When firms do not rank markets symmetrically in this sense, it is no longer necessary that the uniform price lies between the price discriminating prices. Indeed, Corts (1998) demonstrates that for any profit functions consistent with best-response asymmetry, either all-out competition or all-out price increases may emerge from price discrimination, depending on the relative importance of the two markets.

Suppose there are two markets, $i = 1, 2$ and two firms, $j = a, b$, and that market 1 is firm a's strong market but firm b's weak market. Mathematically, this implies that the best-response functions satisfy the following inequalities: $BR_1^a(p) > BR_2^a(p)$ and $BR_1^b(p) < BR_2^b(p)$. Graphically, the price-discrimination equilibrium for each market is indicated by the intersections of the relevant best-response functions; these equilibria are labeled E_1 and E_2 in Figure 34.1.

Depending on the relative importance of market 1 and market 2, firm j's uniform-price best-response function can be anywhere between its strong and weak best-response functions. With this insight, Corts (1998) shows that for any pair of prices

[35] Nevo and Wolfram (2002) and Besanko, Dube and Gupta (2003) empirically assess the possibility of all-out competition in breakfast cereals and ketchup, respectively. The former finds evidence consistent with best-response asymmetry and a general fall in prices in the breakfast cereal market; the latter, through empirical estimation of elasticities and simulations, finds no evidence of all-out competition in the branded ketchup market.

bounded by the four best-response functions, there exists a set of relative market weights (possibly different for each firm) that support these prices as an equilibrium. For example, if firm a finds market 1 to be sufficiently more important relative to market 2 and firm b has reverse views, then the uniform-price best-response functions intersect in the upper-right, shaded region, all-out competition emerges under price discrimination, and prices fall relative to the uniform-pricing regime. This is the intuition behind the simple Hotelling game above. There, each firm cares substantially more about its closer markets than its distant markets. On the other hand, if the uniform-price equilibrium is a pair of prices in the shaded region in the lower left, then price discrimination causes all segment prices to increase.

When the underlying demand functions induce either all-out competition or all-out price increases, the theoretical predictions are crisp. With all-out competition, price discrimination lowers all segment prices, raises all segment outputs, raises consumer utility and lowers firm profits. With all-out price increases, price discrimination has the opposite effects: all segment prices increase, all segment outputs decline, welfare and consumer surplus both decrease. When the underlying preferences do not generate all-out competition or price gouging (i.e., the uniform prices are not part of the shaded interiors of Figure 34.1) the impact of price discrimination is more difficult to assess. A more general treatment for settings of best-response asymmetry in which prices do not uniformly rise or fall would be useful to this end – perhaps focusing on market and cross-price elasticities in the manner of Holmes (1989).

3.5. Price discrimination and entry

The preceding analysis has largely taken the number of firms as exogenous. Given the possibility of entry with fixed costs, a new class of distortions arises: price discrimination may induce too much or too little entry relative to uniform pricing.

• *Monopolistic competition* If entry is unfettered and numerous potential entrants exist, entry occurs to the point where long-run profits are driven to zero. Under such models of monopolistic competition, social surplus is equated to consumer surplus. The question arises under free entry whether a change from uniform pricing to discrimination leads to higher or lower aggregate consumer surplus?

To answer this question, two effects must be resolved. First, by fixing the number of firms, does a change from uniform pricing to price discrimination lead to higher industry profits? We have already observed that price discrimination can either raise or lower industry profits, depending on the underlying system of demands. If price discrimination raises industry profits, then greater entry occurs; if price discrimination lowers profits, then fewer firms will operate in the market. Second, given that a move to price discrimination changes the size of the industry, will consumer surplus increase or decrease? Under uniform pricing, it is well known that the social and private values of entry may differ due to the effects of business stealing and product diversity; see, for example, Spence (1976b) and Mankiw and Whinston (1986). Generally, when comparing price discrimination to uniform pricing, no clear welfare result about the social efficiency of free entry exists, although a few theoretical contributions are suggestive of the relative importance of various effects.

Katz (1984), in a model of monopolistic competition with price discrimination, was one of the first to study how production inefficiencies from excessive entry may arise. He found the impact of price discrimination on social welfare is ambiguous and depends upon various demand parameters.[36] Rather than developing Katz's (1984) model, this ambiguity can be illustrated with a few simple examples.

As a first example, consider varying the linear market in Thisse and Vives (1988) to a circular setting, as in Salop (1979), where inelastic unit-demand consumers are uniformly distributed around a circular market; as entry occurs, firms relocate equidistant from one another. When the market is covered, all potential consumers purchase a good from the nearest firm, so the optimal number of firms is that which minimizes the sum of transportation costs and the fixed costs of entry, K. The sum of costs is $nK + \tau/4n$ and the socially efficient level of entry is $n^{\text{eff}} = \frac{1}{2}\sqrt{\frac{\tau}{K}}$. Under uniform pricing, each firm chooses an equilibrium price of $p = c+\tau/n$, leading to per-firm profits of $\pi^u = \tau/n^2 - K$. Free entry implies that entry occurs until $\pi^u = 0$, so $n^u = \sqrt{\frac{\tau}{K}} > n^{\text{eff}}$. Twice the efficient level of entry occurs with uniform pricing; the marginal social cost of additional entry, K, exceeds the benefit of lower transportation costs that competition generates. In contrast, under price discrimination, rivals offer $\hat{p}(\theta) = c$ to consumers located more distant than $1/2n$; consumers purchase from the closest firm at a price of $p(\theta) = c + \tau(\frac{1}{n} - 2\theta)$. Equilibrium profits are lower under price discrimination for a given n, $\pi^{\text{pd}} = \frac{\tau}{2n^2} - K$, so entry occurs up to the point where $n^{\text{pd}} = \sqrt{\frac{\tau}{2K}}$. It follows that $n^u > n^{\text{pd}} > n^{\text{eff}}$, so price discrimination increases social welfare relative to uniform pricing by reducing the value of entry. This conclusion, of course, is limited to the model at hand.[37]

It is also possible the price discrimination generates excessive entry relative to uniform pricing. To illustrate, suppose that consumer preferences are entirely observable so that a price-discriminating monopolist would capture all of the consumer surplus, unlike a uniform-pricing monopolist. To model imperfect competition, assume along the lines of Diamond (1971) that goods are homogeneous, but consumers must bear a small search cost for each visit to a non-local store to obtain a price quote. Each consumer obtains the price of the nearest (local) store at no cost. Then it is an equilibrium for all firms to offer the monopoly price schedule and for all consumers to purchase from their local store and not search. Firms follow identical pricing strategies, so there is no value to search, and each sells to its local consumers. Because of ex ante competition, firms enter this market until long-run profits are dissipated. Because more consumer surplus

[36] In particular, the proportion of informed to uninformed consumers is key.

[37] A similar result is found in Armstrong and Vickers (2001) but in the context of a different type of price discrimination.

remains under uniform pricing than under price discrimination, welfare is higher under uniform pricing while too much entry occurs under price discrimination.

• *Entry deterrence* Because it is natural to think that price discrimination may affect the ability of an incumbent firms to respond to local entry, entry deterrence and accommodation must also be considered in the welfare calculus.

One might imagine that firms are situated asymmetrically, as in Armstrong and Vickers (1993), where an incumbent firm serves two market segments, and potential entry can occur only in one of the segments. Here, price discrimination has no strategic value to the entrant given its limited access to a single market, but it does allow the incumbent to price lower in the newly entered market, while still maintaining monopoly profits from its captive segment. Hence, the incumbent's best-response discriminating prices following entry will generally result in a lower price in the attacked market than if uniform pricing across segments prevailed. It follows that the entrant's profits are higher following entry when price discrimination is banned. For sufficiently high entry costs, entry is blockaded whether or not the incumbent can price discriminate. For sufficiently low costs of entry, entry occurs regardless of whether the incumbent can price discriminate. For intermediate entry costs, the availability of price discrimination blockades entry, whereas uniform price restrictions accommodate the entrant and mitigate post-entry price reductions. Under uniform pricing, in Armstrong and Vickers's (1993) model, the prices in *both* markets are lower with entry than they would be with price discrimination and deterrence. Entrant profits and consumer surplus are also higher, while incumbent profits fall. This result is robust, providing that the monopoly price in the captive market exceeds the optimal discriminatory price in the competitive market. Armstrong and Vickers (1993) further demonstrate that the net welfare effects of uniform price restrictions are generally ambiguous, as the efficiencies from reduced prices must be offset against the inefficiencies from additional entry costs.[38]

The model in Armstrong and Vickers (1993) illustrates the possibility that uniform pricing reduces all prices relative to price discrimination, due entirely to entry effects. A restriction to uniform prices promotes entry, which in turn generates the price reductions. A similar theme emerges in Section 7 but for different economic reasons when we consider entry deterrence from bundling goods.

3.6. Collective agreements to limit price discrimination

There are two scenarios where we can make crisp comparisons of the social and collective incentives to price discriminate: (i) best-response asymmetry with all-out competition, and (ii) best-response symmetry with linear demands.

[38] See Aguirre, Espinosa and Macho-Stadler (1998) for extensions to this model which focus on the impact of other pricing policies, including FOB pricing, in this context. Cheung and Wang (1999) note that banning price discrimination may reduce entry when the monopoly price in the captive market is lower than the post-entry price of the competitive market.

When all-out competition is present, price discrimination lowers prices and profits. Hence, a collective agreement by firms to restrict price discrimination has the effect of raising prices for all consumers, lowering aggregate output, and lowering consumer surplus and total welfare. Collective incentives for discrimination are at odds with social welfare.

In the second setting of best-response symmetry with linear demands, Holmes (1989) demonstrates that if the elasticity-ratio condition is satisfied, then price discrimination increases industry profits. It follows that with linear demands, firms have a collective incentive to prohibit price discrimination only if the elasticity-ratio condition fails. Given that demands are linear, violation of the elasticity-ratio condition also implies that price discrimination lowers aggregate output and hence welfare. In this case, it follows that society benefits by allowing firms to agree collectively to limit price discrimination. There is also the possibility that the elasticity-ratio condition fails and price discrimination is welfare-reducing, but industry profits nonetheless increase under price discrimination. Here, restrictions on welfare-reducing price discrimination must come from outside the industry. No collective agreement restricting price discrimination would arise even though it is socially optimal. In short, with linear demands, a collective of firms would inadequately restrict price discrimination from a social vantage point.

Winter (1997) considers a variation of Holmes's (1989) analysis in the context of collective agreements to limit (but not prohibit) price discrimination by restricting the difference between the high and low prices. His conclusion for linear demands is similar: when firms have a collective desire to restrict price discrimination, it is socially efficient for them to be allowed to do so. As an illustration, suppose an extreme case in which each half of the strong market is captive to one of the firms (therefore, $\varepsilon_2^c = 0$), while the weak market has a positive cross-price elasticity of demand. In such a case, the elasticity-ratio test fails. At the equilibrium prices, a slight restriction on price discrimination causes the weak-market price to rise slightly and the strong-market price to fall by a similar margin. Because the weak market price is below the collusive profit-maximizing price, this price increase generates greater profits. Because the strong market's price is at the optimal monopoly price under discrimination (due to captive customers), a slight decrease causes only a negligible (second-order) reduction in profits. Hence, a slight restriction on price discrimination is jointly optimal for duopolists. Moreover, as a consequence of Holmes (1989), a restriction on the price differential (a lowering of r) raises aggregate output. Since aggregate output increases and the price differential decreases, welfare necessarily increases. It follows that industry agreements to limit price discrimination arise only if price discrimination reduces welfare, providing that adjusted demand concavities are insignificant. The results are less clear when demands are not linear and the adjusted concavity condition plays an important role.

In short, when profits are lower under price discrimination, firms in the industry would prefer to collude and commit to uniform pricing. Such collusion would decrease welfare if all-out competition would otherwise occur, and increase welfare when demand is linear and price discrimination would have reduced aggregate output.

• *Vertical restraints and downstream price discrimination* Although this survey largely ignores the impact of price discrimination on competing vertical structures, it is worth mentioning a sample of work in this area. We have already mentioned one strategic effect of price discrimination via secret price discounts by wholesalers to downstream firms: price discrimination may induce the upstream firm to flood the downstream market. A legal requirement that the wholesaler offer a single price to all retailers may instead induce the upstream firm to not over supply the retail market, thereby raising profits and retail prices.[39]

In other settings of wholesale price discrimination, if downstream market segments have different elasticities of demand but third-degree price discrimination is illegal or otherwise impractical because of arbitrage, vertical integration can be used as a substitute for price discrimination. Tirole (1988, Section 4.6.2) gives a simple model of such a vertical price squeeze. A monopoly wholesaler, selling to a strong market at price p_2 and to a weak market at price $p_1 < p_2$, may suffer arbitrage as the firms in the weak downstream market resell output to the strong segment. By vertically integrating into one of the weak-segment downstream firms, the wholesaler can now supply all output at the strong-segment price of p_2 while producing in the weak segment and using an internal transfer price no greater than p_1. Other firms in the weak market will be squeezed by the vertically integrated rival due to higher wholesale prices. The wholesaler effectively reduces competition in the weak segment to prevent arbitrage and to implement a uniform wholesale price.

Consider instead the case where it is the downstream retail firms that are the source of price discrimination. How do the various tools of resale price maintenance (RPM) by the upstream manufacturer impact profits and welfare when retailers engage in third-degree price discrimination? As the previous discussions suggested, a manufacturer who sells to imperfectly competitive, price-discriminating retailers would prefer to constrain retailers from discounting their prices to consumers who are highly cross-elastic, as this generates an unprofitable business-stealing externality. On the other hand, the manufacturer would like to encourage price discrimination across the full range of cross-price inelastic consumers as this action raises profits to the industry. Hence, the combination of competition and price discrimination generates a conflict in the vertical chain.

A simple duopoly example from Chen (1999) illustrates this conflict. Suppose that type-1 consumers are captive and buy only from the local retailer (if at all), while type-2 consumers comparison-shop for the lowest price. Both types have unit demands with reservation prices drawn from a uniform distribution on [0, 1]. Here, price discrimination arises simply because a consumer's outside option may depend upon his type (and the competing offer of a rival). It is assumed that competing retailers can identify consumer types costlessly, perhaps because only comparison-shopping consumers find coupons with targeted price reductions. Market 1 (comprised of type-1 consumers) has a measure of α; market 2 has a measure of $(1 - \alpha)$. Marginal costs

[39] For more on this and related points, see Rey and Tirole (2007), elsewhere in this volume.

are 0. The optimal prices which maximize the sum of retailers' and manufacturer's profits are $p_1 = p_2 = \frac{1}{2}$; total profit is $\frac{1}{4}$. When $\alpha \in (0, 1)$, this collective maximum cannot be achieved with two-part tariffs by themselves. A two-part tariff of the form $T(q) = F + wq$ will generate equilibrium prices by the retailers of $p_1 = \frac{1+w}{2}$ and $p_2 = w$; the conditionally optimal fixed fee will extract retailer profits, $F = \frac{1}{4}\alpha(1-w)^2$. The optimal wholesale price in this setting is

$$w^* = \frac{2(1-\alpha)}{4-3\alpha},$$

which implies retail prices will exceed the profit-maximizing prices of $\frac{1}{2}$. In effect, a classic double marginalization arises on each market segment. With the addition of either price ceilings or price floors, the two-part tariff again becomes sufficient to maximize the vertical chain's profit. For example, either $w = \frac{1}{2}$ and $F = 0$ in tandem with a price ceiling of $\frac{1}{2}$, or $w = 0$ and $F = \frac{1}{4}$ in tandem with a price floor of $\frac{1}{2}$, will achieve the desired retail prices. Moreover, RPM here has the desirable effect of lowering prices, raising output and making prices less dispersed across markets. With more general demand settings (specifically, type-1 consumers' valuations distributed differently than type-2 consumers), RPM can again implement the vertical chain's optimal retail prices, but its welfare effects are ambiguous. Chen (1999) places bounds on welfare changes which provide, among other things, that if output increases due to RPM, then welfare is necessarily higher, but, if output decreases, the change in welfare is ambiguous.

4. Price discrimination by purchase history

Consumer price sensitivities are often revealed by past purchase decisions. There are two related cases to consider. First, consumers may suffer costs if they switch to new products, so past customers may have more inelastic demands for their chosen brand than new customers. For example, a buyer of a particular word processing package may have to expend considerable cost to learn how to use the product effectively. Having expended this cost, choosing a competing software program is less attractive than it would have been initially. Here, purchase history is useful because an otherwise homogeneous good becomes differentiated ex post due to exogenous switching costs. It follows that competing firms may have an incentive to pay consumers to switch. Second, it may be that no exogenous switching cost exists but that the products are inherently differentiated, with consumers having strong preferences for one product or another. It follows that a customer who reveals a preference for firm a's product at current prices is precisely the person to whom firm b would like to offer a price reduction. In this case, purchase history operates through a different conduit of differentiation because it informs about a consumer's exogenous brand preference. Competing firms may have an incentive to lower prices selectively to poach consumers who purchased from a rival in the past. For example, consider a consumer who prefers a particular brand of frozen food. Rival brands may wish to target price reductions to these consumers by contracting with grocery stores to selectively print coupons on the reverse side of their sales receipts.

Regardless, the strategies of "paying customers to switch" [as in Chen (1997b)] or "consumer poaching" [as in Fudenberg and Tirole (2000)] can be profitable because purchase history provides a valuable instrument for the basis of dynamic third-degree price discrimination. It is not surprising, therefore, that such behavior-based price discrimination is a well-known strategy in marketing science.[40]

As the examples suggest, the literature takes two approaches to modeling imperfect competition and purchase-history price discrimination. The first set of models, e.g., Nilssen (1992), Chen (1997b), Taylor (2003), and others, assumes that the goods are initially homogeneous in period 1, but after purchase the consumers are partially locked in with their sellers; exogenous costs must be incurred to switch to different firms in future periods. The immediate result is that although prices rise over time as firms exploit the lock-in effects of switching costs, in period 1 firms compete over the future lock-in rents.

The second set of models assumes that products are horizontally differentiated in the initial period [e.g., Caminal and Matutes (1990), Villas-Boas (1999), Fudenberg and Tirole (2000), and others]. In the simplest variant, brand preferences are constant over time. It follows that a consumer who prefers firm a's product and reveals this preference through his purchase in period 1 will become identified as part of a's "strong" market segment (and firm b's "weak" market segment) in period 2. As we will see, when firms cannot commit to long-term prices, this form of unchanging brand preference will generate prices that *decrease* over time, and competition intensifies in each market.

The resulting price paths in the above settings rest on the assumption that firms cannot commit to future prices. This assumption may be inappropriate. One could easily imagine that firms commit in advance to reward loyal customers in the future with price reductions or other benefits (such as with frequent flyer programs). Such long-term commitments can be thought of as endogenous switching costs and have been studied in the context of horizontal differentiation by Banerjee and Summers (1987), Caminal and Matutes (1990), Villas-Boas (1999) and Fudenberg and Tirole (2000). Two cases have been studied: preferences that change over time and preferences that are static. In the first case, most papers assume that consumer valuations are independently distributed across the periods. If preferences change from period to period and firms cannot commit to future prices, there is no value to using purchase history as it is uninformative

[40] Kotler (1994, ch. 11) refers to segmenting markets based upon purchasing history as "behavioral segmentation" (e.g., user status, loyalty status, etc.), as opposed to geographic, demographic or psychographic segmentation. Rossi and Allenby (1993) argue that firms should offer price reductions to households "that show loyalty toward other brands and yet are price sensitive" (p. 178). Rossi, McCulloch and Allenby (1996) review some of the available purchase-history data. Acquisti and Varian (2005) study a general model of pricing conditional on purchase history and its application in marketing. See Shaffer and Zhang (2000) for additional references to the marketing literature. See also the forthcoming survey by Fudenberg and Villas-Boas (2005) for a review of the issues presented in this section.

about current elasticities. Public, long-term contracts between, say, firm a and a consumer, however, can raise the joint surplus of the pair by making firm b price lower in the second period to induce switching, as in the models of Caminal and Matutes (1990) and Fudenberg and Tirole (2000). In equilibrium, social welfare may decrease as long-term contracts induce too little switching. In the second category of price-commitment models, preferences are assumed to be fixed across periods. When preferences are unchanging across time, Fudenberg and Tirole (2000) demonstrate a similar effect from long-term contracts: firm a locks in some of its customer base to generate lower second-period pricing for switching, and thereby encourages consumers to buy from firm a in the initial period. With long-term contracts, some inefficient switching still occurs but less than when firms cannot commit to long-term prices; hence welfare increases by allowing such contracts.

We consider both switching-cost and horizontal-differentiation models of pricing without commitment in the following two subsections. We then turn to the effects of long-term price commitments when discrimination on purchase history is allowed.

4.1. Exogenous switching costs and homogeneous goods

Farrell and Klemperer (2007), in this volume, provide a thorough treatment of switching costs, so we limit our present attention to the specific issues of price discrimination over purchase history under imperfect competition.

One of the first discussions of purchase-history discrimination in a model of switching costs appears in Nilssen (1992).[41] Chen (1997b), builds on this approach by distributing switching costs in a two-period model, which results in some equilibrium switching. We present a variant of Chen's (1997b) model here.

Consider duopolists, $j = a, b$, selling identical homogeneous goods to a unit measure of potential consumers. In period 1, both firms offer first-period prices, p_1^j. Each consumer chooses a single firm from which to purchase one unit and obtains first-period utility of $v - p_1^j$. Consumers who are indifferent randomize between firms. Following the first-period purchase, each consumer randomly draws an unobservable switching cost, θ, that is distributed uniformly on $[0, \bar{\theta}]$. When price discrimination is allowed, firms simultaneously offer pairs of second-period prices, $\{p_{2a}^j, p_{2b}^j\}$, where p_{2k}^j is the second-period price offered by firm j to a consumer who purchased from firm k in period 1. A consumer who purchases from firm j in both periods obtains a present-value utility of

$$v - p_1^j + \delta(v - p_{2j}^j),$$

[41] In this model, however, there is no uncertainty over the size of the switching cost, and no consumer actually switches in equilibrium. The focus in Nilssen (1992) is primarily on how market outcomes are affected by the form of switching costs. Transaction costs are paid every time the consumer switches in contrast to learning costs which are only paid the first time the consumer uses a firm's product. These costs are indistinguishable in the two-period models considered in this survey.

and, if the consumer switches from firm j to firm k with switching cost θ, obtains

$$v - p_1^j + \delta\big(v - p_{2j}^k - \theta\big).$$

Beginning with the second period, suppose that firm a acquired a fraction ϕ^a of consumers in the first period. It follows that a consumer who purchased from firm a is indifferent to switching to firm b if, and only if,

$$v - p_{2a}^a = v - p_{2a}^b - \theta.$$

Consequently, firm a's retained demand is

$$\phi^a \int_{p_{2a}^a - p_{2a}^b}^{\bar{\theta}} \frac{1}{\bar{\theta}}\, \mathrm{d}\theta = \phi^a\left(1 - \frac{p_{2a}^a - p_{2a}^b}{\bar{\theta}}\right),$$

and firm b's switching demand is $\phi^a(p_{2a}^a - p_{2a}^b)/\bar{\theta}$, provided that the market is covered in equilibrium. It is straightforward to calculate the other second-period demand functions and profits as a function of second-period prices. Solving for the equilibrium, second-period, price-discriminating prices, we obtain $p_{2j}^j = c + \frac{2}{3}\bar{\theta}$ and $p_{2k}^j = c + \frac{1}{3}\bar{\theta}$ for $k \neq j$.[42] Using these prices, the associated equilibrium second-period profits are

$$\pi^j = \frac{\bar{\theta}}{3}\left(\frac{1}{3} + \phi^j\right),$$

a function solely of first-period market share.

First-period competition is perfect as the firm's goods are homogeneous. Chen (1997b) demonstrates that the unique subgame perfect equilibrium is for each firm to charge $p_1^j = c - \frac{\delta}{3}\bar{\theta}$, generating a present value of profits, $\frac{\delta}{9}\bar{\theta}$. In equilibrium, each firm sets its price so that the additional market share generated by a price decrease exactly equals the discounted marginal profit, $\delta\bar{\theta}/3$, derived from above. No additional profit is made from acquired first-period market share, but the firms continue to earn positive long-term profits because of the ability to induce switching in the second period and the underlying heterogeneity in preferences. Indeed, a firm who acquires zero first-period market share still earns profits of $\frac{\delta}{9}\bar{\theta}$. Prices increase over time, but more so for those consumers who are locked in. In equilibrium, all consumer types with switching costs below $\frac{\bar{\theta}}{3}$ inefficiently switch firms (i.e., one-third of the consumers switch), thereby revealing their price sensitivity and obtaining the discounted price.

Compare the price-discrimination outcome with what would emerge under uniform-pricing restrictions. In the second period, equilibrium prices will generally depend upon first-period market shares (particularly, prices depend upon whether the market share is above, below, or equal to $\frac{1}{2}$). A firm with a higher market share will charge a higher

[42] Remarkably, the second-period prices are independent of first-period market share, a result that Chen (1997b) generalizes to a richer model than presented here.

second-period price. When market shares are equal, computations reveal that second-period equilibrium prices are $p_2^j = c + \bar{\theta}$, $j = a, b$.[43] Hence, we are in the setting of all-out-competition as prices for both segments are lower under price discrimination relative to uniform pricing, consumer surpluses are higher, and firm profits are lower.

In the first period, unfortunately, the analysis is more complex because the second-period profit functions are kinked at the point where market shares are equal. This gives rise to multiple equilibria in which consumers realize that firms with larger market shares will have higher prices in the second period, and they take this into account when purchasing in period 1, leading to less elastic first-period demand. One appealing equilibrium to consider is a symmetric equilibrium in which the first-period prices constitute an equilibrium in a one-shot game.[44] Here, the equilibrium outcome is $p_1^j = c + \frac{2}{3}\bar{\theta}$, which is higher than the first-period price-discriminating price. Furthermore, the discounted sum of equilibrium profits is $\frac{5\delta}{6}\bar{\theta}$, which is higher than the price-discriminating level of $\frac{\delta}{9}\bar{\theta}$. Generally, Chen (1997b) demonstrates that regardless of the selected uniform-pricing equilibrium, the discounted sum of profits under uniform pricing is always weakly greater than the profits under price discrimination. Thus, price discrimination unambiguously makes firms worse off in the switching-cost model.

Consumers, on the other hand, may or may not be better off under uniform pricing, depending on the equilibrium chosen. In the selected "one-shot" equilibrium above, consumers are unambiguously better off under price discrimination. In other equilibria derived in Chen (1997b), both firms and consumers may be worse off under price discrimination. Regardless, price discrimination always reduces welfare because it induces inefficient switching, unlike uniform pricing. Of course, one must be careful when interpreting the welfare results in such models of inelastic demand as price discrimination has no role to increase aggregate output.

It might seem odd that firms earn positive profits in Chen (1997b) given that, ex ante, the duopolists' goods are homogeneous and competition is perfect in the first period. Profits are earned because only one firm (a monopoly) induces switching in the second period. Taylor (2003) makes this point (among others) by noting that in a model with three firms over two periods, both outside firms perfectly compete over prices in the second period, leading to zero profits from switching consumers, $p_{2k}^j = c$ for $k \neq j$.[45]

[43] Note that the computations for the uniform-price equilibrium are not straightforward because there is a kink at $\phi^a = \frac{1}{2}$ and profit functions are not differentiable at equilibrium prices. See Chen (1997b) for details.

[44] See Chen (1997b) for details.

[45] Taylor (2003) considers a more general T-period model; we simplify the present discussion by focusing on the 2-period variation. Taylor also studies a more complex setting of screening on unobservable characteristics. Specifically, Taylor assumes that there are two first-order, stochastically ranked distributions of switching costs. Consumers who draw from the low-cost distribution signal their type in equilibrium by switching, and hence generate lower prices in the future. This idea is closely related to the topic of second-degree price discrimination studied in Section 6 below.

At such prices, the inside firm will retain its consumer if and only if $\theta \geqslant p^j_{2j} - c$, so it chooses its retention price to maximize $(\bar{\theta} - (p^j_{2j} - c))(p^j_{2j} - c)$, or $p^j_{2j} = c + \frac{1}{2}\bar{\theta}$. Comparing this second-period price spread of $\frac{1}{2}\bar{\theta}$ to the previous duopoly spread of $\frac{1}{3}\bar{\theta}$, increased competition (going from duopoly to oligopoly, $n > 3$) leads to more inefficient switching and greater price dispersion. In a sense, this increased price dispersion is similar to the effect present in Thisse and Vives (1988) when one goes from monopoly to duopoly: increases in competition can differentially affect some market segments more than others, leading to a larger range of equilibrium prices. Here, going from two to three firms leads to increased competition among firms that induce switching, but does not influence the loyal customer price to the same degree.

Shaffer and Zhang (2000) consider a model similar to Chen (1997b), studying the case in which firms' demands are asymmetric and the effect these asymmetries may have on whether a firm "pays customers to switch" or instead "pays consumers to stay". It is, of course, always optimal for price-discriminating firms to offer a lower price to its more elastic segment of consumers. Focusing on the second period of a duopoly model, Shaffer and Zhang (2000) demonstrate that although charging a lower price to a competitor's customers is always optimal when demand is symmetric, with asymmetries it may be that one firm's more elastic consumer segment is its own customers. This latter situation arises, for example, when firm a's existing customer base has lower average switching costs, compared to firm b's loyal consumers. In such a setting, firm a finds its loyal consumer segment has a higher elasticity of demand than the potential switchers from firm b; firm a will charge a lower price to its loyal segment as a result. Hence, defending one's consumer base with "pay-to-stay" strategies can be optimal in a more general model.

4.2. Discrimination based on revealed first-period preferences

Instead of assuming exogenous switching costs arise after an initial purchase from either firm, one may suppose that consumers have exogenous preferences for brands that are present from the start, as in Fudenberg and Tirole (2000). To simplify the analysis, they model such horizontal differentiation by imagining a Hotelling-style linear market of unit length with firms positioned at the endpoints, and by assuming that each consumer's uniformly distributed brand preference, θ, remains fixed for both periods of consumption. Consumers have transportation costs of τ per unit distance, and firms produce with constant marginal and average costs of c per unit. In such a setting, consumers reveal information about their brand preference by their first-period choice, and firms set second-period prices accordingly.

Solving backwards from the second period, suppose that firm a captures the market share $[0, \hat{\theta}_1)$ and firm b captures the complement, $(\hat{\theta}_1, 1]$ in the first period. The second-period demand function derivations are straightforward. In the left segment (i.e., firm a's strong market and firm b's weak market), the marginal consumer, $\hat{\theta}^a_2$, who is indifferent between continuing to purchase from firm a at price p^a_{2a} and switching to firm b at price of p^b_{2a}, is given by

$$p^a_{2a} + \tau\theta^a_2 = p^b_{2a} + \tau\big(1 - \theta^a_2\big).$$

It follows that firm a's demand from retained consumers is

$$\hat{\theta}^a_2 = \frac{1}{2} + \left(\frac{p^b_{2a} - p^a_{2a}}{2\tau}\right),$$

and firm b's demand from switching consumers is

$$\hat{\theta}^b_2 = \hat{\theta}_1 - \hat{\theta}^a_2 = \hat{\theta}_1 - q^a_{2a} = \hat{\theta}_1 - \frac{1}{2} + \left(\frac{p^a_{2a} - p^b_{2a}}{2\tau}\right).$$

Similar derivations provide the retained demand for firm b and the switching demand for firm a. Using these demand functions, simple computations reveal that equilibrium second-period prices are $p^a_{2a}(\hat{\theta}_1) = p^b_{2b}(\hat{\theta}_1) = c + \frac{\tau}{3}(1 + 2\hat{\theta}_1)$ and $p^b_{2a}(\hat{\theta}_1) = p^a_{2b}(\hat{\theta}_1) = c + \frac{\tau}{3}(4\hat{\theta}_1 - 1)$. When the first-period market is equally split, we have $p^a_{2a} = p^b_{2b} = c + \frac{2}{3}\tau$ and $p^b_{2a} = p^a_{2b} = c + \frac{1}{3}\tau$.

The marginal consumer in the first period will ultimately switch in the second period, so the location $\hat{\theta}_1$ is determined by the relationship

$$p^a_1 + \tau\hat{\theta}_1 + \delta\big(p^b_{2a}(\hat{\theta}_1) + \tau(1 - \hat{\theta}_1)\big) = p^b_1 + \tau(1 - \hat{\theta}_1) + \delta\big(p^a_{2b}(\hat{\theta}_1) + \tau\hat{\theta}_1\big).$$

Simplifying, first-period demand is

$$\hat{\theta}_1\big(p^a_1, p^b_1\big) = \frac{1}{2} + \frac{3}{2\tau(3 + \delta)}\big(p^b_1 - p^a_1\big).$$

Providing $\delta > 0$, first-period demands are *less* sensitive to prices relative to the static one-shot game because an increase in first-period market share implies higher second-period prices. Using the equilibrium prices from the second period as a function of $\hat{\theta}_1$, one can compute second-period market shares as a function of $\hat{\theta}_1$. Because $\hat{\theta}_1$ is a function of first-period prices, second-period market shares and prices are entirely determined by first-period prices: $\hat{\theta}^a_2(\hat{\theta}_1(p^a_1, p^b_1))$ and $\hat{\theta}^b_2(\hat{\theta}_1(p^a_1, p^b_1))$. With these expressions, the present value of profit for firm a can now be written as a function of first-period prices. Computing the equilibrium is algebraically tedious but straightforward, leading one to conclude that first-period prices are $p^a_1 = p^b_1 = c + \tau + \frac{\delta}{3}\tau$, second-period prices are $p^a_{2a} = p^b_{2b} = c + \frac{2}{3}\tau$ for loyal customers, and $p^a_{2b} = p^b_{2a} = c + \frac{1}{3}\tau$ for switchers. The first-period market is split symmetrically with $\hat{\theta}_1 = \frac{1}{2}$, and the second-period segments are split at $\hat{\theta}^a_2 = \frac{1}{3}$ and $\hat{\theta}^b_2 = \frac{2}{3}$.

Compare this dynamic price discrimination game with the outcome under uniform pricing. Without the ability to condition second-period prices on first-period behavior, firms would offer the static prices in each period, $p^a_1 = p^a_2 = p^b_1 = p^b_2 = c + \tau$; consumers would pay a total of $(1 + \delta)(c + \tau)$ for the consumption stream, and no switching would arise. The absence of equilibrium switching under uniform pricing immediately implies that price discrimination lowers social welfare, although the modeling assumption of inelastic demand again limits the generality of this conclusion.

Several additional results emerge from a simple comparison of uniform pricing and price discrimination. First, in the price discrimination game, the "loyal" consumers in the intervals $[0, \frac{1}{3}]$ and $[\frac{2}{3}, 1]$ do not switch and their present-value payment is the same as in the uniform setting: $p_1^j + \delta p_{2j}^j = c + \tau + \frac{\delta}{3}\tau + \delta(c + \frac{2}{3}\tau) = (1+\delta)(c+\tau)$. Consumer surplus and profit for these intervals is unaffected by price discrimination. Second, the "poached" consumers in the interval $(\frac{1}{3}, \frac{2}{3})$ switch from one firm to the other. By revealed preference they could choose to be loyal but strictly prefer to switch firms; hence, consumer surplus increases for consumers with only moderate brand loyalties. Because such switching decreases social welfare, it follows that profits must decrease for these segments. The present-value price paid by these consumers for two periods of consumption is only $(1 + \delta)(c + \tau) - \frac{\delta}{3}\tau$, and hence lower than the price paid by loyal consumers. Price discrimination does not increase the present-value payment from any consumer segment and strictly reduces it to the middle segment, just as in models of all-out-competition.

The price path in the Fudenberg and Tirole (2000) model of product differentiation differs from the exogenous switching-cost model in Chen (1997b). In Fudenberg and Tirole (2000), prices *fall* over time as competition intensifies for the price-sensitive markets, while in Chen (1997b) prices *rise* over time as firms take advantage of buyer lock-in. One can understand the different dynamics by noting the different "network" effects present in each model.[46] In Chen (1997b), there is no network effect under price discrimination; second-period prices are independent of first-period market share. There is a network effect under uniform pricing, however, as a higher first-period market share generates a higher uniform price in the second-period. The reverse is the case in Fudenberg and Tirole (2000). Under price discrimination, there is a network effect as a larger first-period market share increases second-period prices. Under uniform pricing, there is no network effect as the second-period price is independent of first-period market share.

Villas-Boas (1999) studies a related but infinite-period, overlapping-generations model in which firms can only discriminate between returning customers and non-returning customers. Among these non-returning customers, a firm cannot distinguish between new consumers and customers who purchased from the rival firm in the first half of their economic lives. Whether this is a reasonable assumption depends upon the setting. If a firm wants to offer a lower price to new customers than to rival customers, this assumption may be plausible if masquerading as a new customer is possible. Of course, if a firm prefers to offer its rival customers the lower price, one might imagine a setting in which a consumer provides proof of purchase of a competing product; in that instance the assumption is less realistic and the model of Fudenberg and Tirole (2000) more appropriate. The steady-state results of Villas-Boas (1999) indicate

[46] See Farrell and Klemperer (2007) in this volume for a related discussion of networks.

that equilibrium prices are lower because each firm wants to attract the competitor's previous customers. Moreover, equilibrium prices decrease as consumers become more patient, due to increased indifference among marginal consumers over which product to buy initially. This movement toward indifference renders consumers more price sensitive, which in turn intensifies competition and makes customer retention more difficult. Finally, Villas-Boas (1999) demonstrates that, close to steady state, a greater previous-period market share results in a lower price to new customers and a higher price to existing customers. Thus, customer-recognition effects appear to make demand more inelastic in the previous period for reasons familiar to the other models of this section.

4.3. Purchase-history pricing with long-term commitment

Unlike the previous analyses which relied on short-term price agreements, we now ask what happens if a firm can write a long-term contract. The contract commits the firm to a second-period price to guarantee returning customers different terms than those offered to other customers. Banerjee and Summers (1987) and Caminal and Matutes (1990) were among the first to explore the use of long-term contracts to induce loyalty and generate endogenous switching costs.

Consider the setting of Caminal and Matutes (1990). As before, there are two firms and two periods of competition. The market in each period consists of a linear city of unit length, with firm a located at 0 and firm b located at 1, and consumers uniformly distributed across the interval. The difference with the previous models is that the location of each consumer is *independently distributed across periods*. Thus, a consumer's location in period 1, θ_1, is statistically independent of the consumer's location in period 2, θ_2. This independence assumption implies that there is no relevant second-period information contained in a consumer's first-period choice. It follows that if firms cannot commit to long-term prices, there is no value from price discrimination based upon purchase history.

Suppose, however, that price commitments are possible. The timing of the market game is as follows: First, firms simultaneously choose their first-period prices, p_1^j, and pre-commit (if they wish) to offer a second period price, p_{2j}^j, to customers purchasing in period 1 (i.e., period 1 customers are given an option contract for period 2). Consumers then decide from whom to purchase in period 1. At the start of the second period, each firm simultaneously chooses p_{2k}^j, $k \neq j$, which applies to non-returning consumers and returning customers if either $p_{2k}^j \leqslant p_{2j}^j$ or if firm j did not offer a price commitment. Caminal and Matutes (1990) demonstrate that subgame perfection requires that both firms commit to lower long-term prices for returning consumers. Calculating the subgame perfect equilibrium is straightforward, with the second-period poaching prices determined as functions of the second-period committed prices. These prices may be used to compute second-period profits and first-period market and derive equilibrium prices. Absent discounting, the equilibrium prices are $p_1^j = c + \frac{4\tau}{3}$, $p_{2j}^j = c - \frac{\tau}{3}$ and $p_{2k}^j = c + \frac{\tau}{3}$, $k \neq j$.

Caminal and Matutes (1990) find a few noteworthy results. First, equilibrium prices decline over time. Remarkably, the second-period commitment price is below even marginal cost. The reasoning of this is subtle. Suppose, for example, that firm b's poaching price in the second period was independent of firm a's second-period loyalty price. Because the consumer's second-period location is unknown at the time they enter into a long-term contract, firm a maximizes the joint surplus of a consumer and itself by setting $p_{2j}^{j} = c$ and pricing efficiently in the second period. Given that firm b's poaching price in reality *does* depend positively on firm a's second-period loyalty price, firm a can obtain a first-order gain in joint surplus by reducing its price slightly below cost and thereby reducing firm b's second-period price. This slight price reduction incurs only a corresponding second-order loss in surplus since pricing was originally at the efficient level. Hence, a firm can commit to a follow-on price below marginal cost in the second-period as a way to increase the expected surplus going to the consumer, and thereby raise the attractiveness of purchasing from the firm initially. Price commitment in this sense has a similar flavor to the models of Diamond and Maskin (1979) and Aghion and Bolton (1987), in which contractual commitments are used to extract a better price from a third party. Of course, as Caminal and Matures (1990) confirm, when both firms undertake this strategy simultaneously, profits fall relative to the no-commitment case and firms are worse off. Welfare is also lower as too little switching takes place from a social viewpoint because lock-in is always socially inefficient.

What are the effects of the presence of this commitment strategy? As is by now a familiar theme, although an individual firm will benefit from committing to a declining price path for returning customers, the firms are collectively worse off with the ability to write long-term price contracts. With commitment, there is also too much lock-in or inertia in the second-period allocations. Without commitment, social welfare would therefore be higher, as consumers would allocate themselves to firms over time to minimize transportation costs. The endogenous switching costs (created by the declining price path for returning consumers) decrease social welfare. As before, because market demand is inelastic in this model, there is an inherent bias against price discrimination, so we must carefully interpret the welfare conclusions.[47]

[47] Caminal and Matutes (1990) also consider a distinct game in which firms' strategies allow only for commitments to discounts (or coupons) rather than to particular prices. In this setting, a similar decreasing price path emerges for continuing consumers, and profits for firms are higher than with commitment to prices. Indeed, the profits are higher than if no commitments are allowed. The difference arises because committed prices do not have an impact on second-period profits from non-returning customers; this is not the case with committed discounts. With committed discounts, firms are reluctant to cut prices to non-returning customers, so second-period competition is less intense. This finding relates to that of Banerjee and Summers (1987), who show in a homogeneous product market that commitments to discounts for returning customers can be a collusive device which raises second-period prices to the monopoly level. Because profits are higher in the discount game, we might expect firms to choose such strategies in a meta-game that offers a choice between committed discounts and committed prices. Caminal and Matutes (1990) analyze this meta-game and conclude that, unfortunately for the firms, the price-commitment game is the equilibrium outcome. The analysis of Caminal and Matutes (1990) demonstrates that price discrimination over purchase history can generate

Closely related to Caminal and Matutes (1990), Fudenberg and Tirole (2000) also consider an environment in which price commitments can be made through long-term contracts, using an interesting variation in which consumer preferences are *fixed* across periods (i.e., location θ between firms a and b does not change). In this setting, there are no exogenous switching costs, but long-term contracts with breach penalties are offered which introduce endogenous switching costs in the sense of Caminal and Matutes (1990). While such contracts could effectively lock consumers into a firm and prevent poaching, the firms choose to offer both long-term and spot contracts in equilibrium so as to segment the marketplace. In equilibrium, consumers with strong preferences for one firm purchase long-term contracts, while those with weaker preferences select short-term contracts and switch suppliers in the second period. The firm utilizes long-term contracts to generate lower poaching prices, which benefit consumers located near the center of the market. The firm can extract concessions in the first period by locking in some customers with long-term contracts and thereby generate more aggressive second-period pricing [similar in spirit to Caminal and Matutes (1990)]. The long-term contracts generate a single-crossing property that segments first-period consumers: in equilibrium, consumers located near the middle of the market are more willing to purchase short-term contracts and switch in the second period to a lower-priced rival than consumers located at the extreme.

It is worth noting that a multi-plant monopolist would accomplish a similar sorting by selling long-term contracts for aa, bb and the switching bundles ab and ba. The monopolist can therefore segment the market, charging higher prices to the non-switchers and lower prices to the consumers who are willing to switch. The optimal amount of monopoly switching in the second period (given a uniform distribution) can be shown to be one-half of the consumers. Here, long-term contracts serve a similar segmentation function. Interestingly, Fudenberg and Tirole (2000) show that if consumers are uniformly distributed, one-fourth of the consumers will switch in the long-term contracting equilibrium with duopoly – less switching than in the case of short-term contracts alone, and still less switching than under monopoly. Hence, given price discrimination is allowed, allowing firms to use long-term contracts improves social welfare. This finding emerges because demand does not change across periods, in contrast to Caminal and Matutes (1990), who find that when preferences vary over time, long-term price commitments lead to too much lock-in and hence reduce social welfare.

5. Intrapersonal price discrimination

Intrapersonal price discrimination has received very little attention, partly because in the context of monopoly, the models and results are economically immediate. For example,

endogenous switching costs with declining price paths (loyalty rewards) and too much lock-in, assuming that demand information in the first period is independent of the second period.

consider a consumer with a known demand curve, $p = D(q)$, and a monopolist with constant marginal (and average) cost of production equal to c. Let q^* be the unique solution to $c = D(q^*)$. The monopolist increases profits by offering any of a host of equally optimal but distinct mechanisms that encourage efficient consumption on the margin: a fixed bundle of q^* units at a bundle price of $\int_0^{q^*} D(z)\,\mathrm{d}z$; a fully non-linear tariff of $P(q) = D(q)$; or a two-part tariff equal to $P(q) = v(c) + cq$, where $v(p) \equiv \max_q u(q) - pq$ is the consumer's indirect utility of consuming at the linear price p. In all examples, the monopolist effectively price discriminates in an intrapersonal manner: Different prices are charged to the same consumer for different units because the consumer's marginal values for those units vary according to consumption. These outcomes closely relate to third-degree price discrimination because the different units of consumption can be thought of as distinguishable market segments. Because consumers are homogeneous within each market – the reservation value is $D(q)$ in the qth unit market – price discrimination is perfect and social welfare is maximized. Note that if our downward sloping demand curve were instead generated by a continuous distribution of heterogeneous consumers with unit demands, then perfect price discrimination is no longer possible. There is no effective way to capture the infra-marginal surplus in this interpersonal analogue.

When markets are imperfectly competitive, intrapersonal price discrimination using non-linear prices allows firms to provide more efficiently a given level of consumer surplus while covering any fixed, per-consumer, production costs. This efficiency suggests that intrapersonal price discrimination may raise social welfare when firms compete. Following Armstrong and Vickers (2001), we address this possibility and related issues of consumer surplus and industry profit in the simplest discrete-choice setting in which there is a single market segment with homogeneous consumers.[48]

Suppose that there are two firms, $j = a, b$, and each is allowed to offer price schedules, $P_j(q_j)$, chosen from the set $\mathcal{P}$. Any restrictions on pricing, such as a requirement of uniform, per-unit prices, are embedded in $\mathcal{P}$. We assume that consumers make all of their purchases from a single firm. This one-stop-shopping assumption implies that a consumer evaluates his utility from each firm and chooses either the firm which generates the greatest utility or not to purchase at all.[49] A consumer who buys from firm j obtains indirect utility of

$$v_j \equiv \max_q u(q) - P_j(q).$$

Define $\pi(v)$ to be the maximal expected per-consumer profit that firm j can make, while choosing $P_j \in \mathcal{P}$ and generating an indirect utility of v for each participating

[48] Armstrong and Vickers (2001) also study the important settings of interpersonal third-degree price discrimination (discussed in Section 3.3) and the case of unobservable heterogeneity considered in Section 6.

[49] Holton (1957) provides an early discussion of one-stop shopping between supermarkets practicing price discrimination See also Bliss (1988) for a model of one-stop shopping.

consumer:

$$\pi(v) \equiv \max_{P_j \in \mathcal{P}} P_j(q) - C(q), \quad \text{such that } \max_q u(q) - P_j(q) = v.$$

Note that as fewer restrictions are placed on $\mathcal{P}$ and the set increases in size, $\pi(v)$ weakly increases. Thus, the per-consumer profit with unfettered price discrimination, $\pi^{\mathrm{pd}}(v)$, will typically exceed the per-consumer profit when prices are restricted to be uniform across units, $\pi^u(v)$.

Following the discrete-choice literature,[50] we can model duopoly product differentiation by assuming that each consumer's net utility from choosing firm j is the consumer's indirect utility plus an additive, firm-specific, fixed effect, $v_j + \varepsilon_j$; the outside option of no purchase is normalized to 0. For any joint distribution of the additive disturbance terms across firms, there exists a market share function, $\phi^a(v_a, v_b)$, which gives the probability that a given consumer purchases from firm a as a function of the indirect utilities offered by the two firms. Let $\phi^b(v_a, v_b) \equiv \phi^a(v_b, v_a)$ give the corresponding symmetric probability of purchase from firm b, where $\phi^a(v_a, v_b) + \phi^b(v_a, v_b) \leqslant 1$. With this notation in hand, we can model firms competing in utility space rather than prices. Firm a maximizes $\phi^a(v_a, v_b)\pi(v_a)$, taking v_b as given, and similarly for firm b. Armstrong and Vickers (2001) show with a few regularity assumptions that a symmetric equilibrium is given by each firm choosing a v to maximize $\sigma(v) + \log \pi(v)$, where $\sigma(v)$ is entirely determined by the structure of the market share functions.

Remarkably, one can separate the marginal effects of v on market share from its effect on per-consumer profit, which provides a powerful tool to understand the impact of intrapersonal price discrimination in competitive settings. For example, to model the competition for market share, $\phi(v_a, v_b)$, assume that the duopolists are situated at either end of a linear Hotelling-style market with transportation costs, τ, and uniformly distributed consumers.[51] Take the simplest case where per-consumer costs are $C(q) = cq + k$. We then consider two cases: when $k > 0$, there is a per-consumer cost of service; and when $k = 0$, there are constant returns to scale in serving a consumer. We define $\bar{v}$ to be the highest level of indirect utility that can be given to a consumer while earning nonnegative profits; formally,

$$\pi(\bar{v}) = 0 \quad \text{and} \quad \pi(v) < 0 \quad \text{for all } v > \bar{v}.$$

When there is a fixed-cost per consumer, $k > 0$, then $\bar{v} = v(c) - k$ when two-part tariffs are allowed, but $\bar{v} < v(c) - k$ when prices must be uniform. Thus, when $k > 0$ and per-consumer fixed costs exist, it follows that price discrimination generates greater

[50] Anderson, de Palma and Thisse (1992) provide a thorough survey of the discrete-choice literature.

[51] Formally, this framework violates a technical assumption used in Armstrong and Vickers's (2001) separation theorem, due to the kinked demand curve inherent in the Hotelling model. It is still true, however, that the equilibrium utility maximizes $\sigma(v) + \log \pi(v)$ if the market is covered. Here, $\sigma(v) = v/\tau$. Armstrong and Vickers (2001) also demonstrate that the Hotelling framework approximates the discrete-choice Logit framework when competition is strong.

utility than does uniform pricing: $\bar{v}^{\mathrm{pd}} > \bar{v}^{u}$. In such a setting, Armstrong and Vickers (2001) prove that allowing price discrimination increases consumer surplus and welfare relative to uniform pricing. As competition intensifies (i.e., $\tau \to 0$), firms attract consumers only by offering them utility close to the maximal zero-profit level. Because the relative loss in profits from a gain in indirect utility is never more than one-to-one, social surplus also increases. In a related model with free entry and firms competing equidistant on a Salop-style circular market, Armstrong and Vickers (2001) similarly demonstrate that price discrimination increases consumer surplus (which equals welfare) relative to uniform pricing. Because welfare increases under price discrimination, it follows that output must increase.

In the case when $k = 0$ and there is no per-consumer fixed cost, it follows that $\bar{v}^{\mathrm{pd}} = \bar{v}^{u} = v(c)$. Using a more subtle economic argument that requires Taylor expansions around $\tau = 0$, Armstrong and Vickers (2001) find that as competition intensifies (i.e., $\tau \to 0$), price discrimination increases welfare and profits, but this time at the expense of consumer surplus. In the free-entry analog on a circular market, they demonstrate that price discrimination again increases welfare and consumer surplus (profits are zero), relative to uniform pricing. It is more difficult to capture the economic intuition for these results, given that the analysis relies on second-order terms and $\tau \approx 0$. Because $\pi^{\mathrm{pd}}(\bar{v}) = \pi^{u}(\bar{v})$ and $\pi^{pd\prime}(\bar{v}) = \pi^{u\prime}(\bar{v})$, it can be shown that the second-order terms $\pi^{pd\prime\prime}(\bar{v}) > \pi^{u\prime\prime}(\bar{v})$ in the Taylor expansions drive the result. Taken together with the case for $k > 0$, the findings suggest that intrapersonal price discrimination is welfare-enhancing when competition is strong.

6. Non-linear pricing (second-degree price discrimination)

Unlike the setting of third-degree price discrimination, indirect (second-degree) discrimination relies on self-selection constraints, thus introducing an entirely new set of competitive issues.

In what follows, firms compete via price schedules of the form $P_j(q_j)$, and consumers choose which (if any) firms to patronize and which product(s) from the offered lines they will purchase. To model imperfect competition, we assume the product lines are differentiated.[52] The theoretical literature on second-degree price discrimination under imperfect competition has largely focused on characterizing equilibrium schedules and

[52] Other papers have modeled imperfect competition and non-linear pricing for homogeneous products by restricting firms to the choice of quantities (or market shares) as strategic variables, but we do not consider these approaches in this survey. Gal-Or (1983), De Fraja (1996), and Johnson and Myatt (2003) all consider the setting in which firms choose quantities of each quality level, and the market price schedule is set by a Walrasian auctioneer so as to sell the entire quantity of each quality. In a related spirit, Oren, Smith and Wilson (1983) consider two distinct models of imperfect competition with homogeneous goods. In the first, each firm commits to the market share it serves for each quality level; in the second model, each firm commits to the market share it serves for each consumer type.

the consequences of competition on efficiency; less attention has been spent on the desirability of enforcing uniform pricing in these environments. This is due in part to the extra technical complexity of second-degree price discrimination, and, to a lesser degree, to the impracticality of requiring uniform pricing when q refers to quality rather than quantity.

The variety of consumer preferences and competitive environments make it useful to distinguish a few cases. Two possible equilibrium configurations can arise: a consumer may purchase exclusively from one firm (referred to in the contract theory literature as *exclusive agency*) or may purchase different products from multiple firms (referred to as *common agency*). Second, within each agency setting, there are several possibilities regarding the unobservable heterogeneity of consumers. The two most common forms are what we will call *vertical* and *horizontal* heterogeneity. In the former, the consumer's marginal preferences for q (and absolute preferences for participating) are increasing in θ for each firm; in the latter, the consumer's marginal preferences for q and absolute preferences for participating are monotonic in θ, but the direction varies across firms with the result that a high-demand type for firm j is a low-demand type for firm k and conversely.[53] Under these definitions, vertical heterogeneity implies that firms agree in their ranking of type from high demand to low demand; under horizontal heterogeneity, two firms have reversed ranking for consumer types. In this sense, the taxonomy is similar in spirit to best-response symmetry and asymmetry under third-degree price discrimination.

Ideally, a model of competition among second-degree price-discriminating firms should incorporate both vertical and horizontal dimensions of heterogeneity to capture both a common ranking of marginal valuations for quality among consumers (holding brand preferences fixed) and a variety of brand preferences (holding quality valuations fixed). Unfortunately, multidimensional self-selection models are considerably more difficult to study, as they introduce additional economic and technical subtleties.[54] As a result, the literature has either relied upon one-dimensional models (either vertical or horizontal) for precise analytic results [e.g., Spulber (1989), Martimort (1992, 1996), Stole (1991), Stole (1995), Martimort and Stole (2005)], numerical simulations of multidimensional models [e.g., Borenstein (1985)], or further restrictions on preferences to simplify multidimensional settings to the point of analytical tractability [e.g., Armstrong and Vickers (2001), Rochet and Stole (2002), Ivaldi and Martimort (1994)]. While there are few general results across these different models, the range of approaches

[53] Formally, if preferences for firm j's goods are represented by $u^j(q_j, \theta)$, then vertical heterogeneity exists when $u^j_\theta > 0$ and $u^j_{q\theta} > 0$ for each j. Horizontal heterogeneity is said to exist between firms j and k if $u^j_{q\theta} > 0 > u^k_{q\theta}$ and $u^j_\theta > 0 > u^k_\theta$. Note that this notion of vertical heterogeneity should not be confused with the pure vertical differentiation preferences described in Gabszewicz and Thisse (1979, 1980) and Shaked and Sutton (1982, 1983), which require that all potential qualities are ranked in the same way by every consumer type when products are priced at cost.

[54] See Armstrong and Rochet (1999) and Rochet and Stole (2003) for surveys of multidimensional screening models.

successfully underscores a few recurring economic themes which we will illustrate in this section.

Before we survey the various approaches taken in the literature, we first review monopoly second-degree price discrimination to provide a benchmark and to introduce notation.

6.1. Benchmark: monopoly second-degree price discrimination

In the simplest monopoly model, the consumer has preferences $u(q,\theta) - P(q)$ over combinations of q and price, $P(q)$, where the consumer's one-dimensional type, θ, is distributed on some interval $\Theta = [\theta_0, \theta_1]$ according to the distribution and density functions, $F(\theta)$ and $f(\theta)$, respectively. Assume that the outside option of not consuming is zero and that the firm faces a per-consumer, convex cost of quality equal to $C(q)$. As in Mussa and Rosen (1978), we take q to represent quality, but it could equally well represent quantities.[55] We also assume that the consumer's preferences satisfy the standard single-crossing property that $u_{q\theta}(q,\theta) > 0$ and utility is increasing in type, $u_\theta(q,\theta) > 0$. In terms of consumer demand curves for q indexed by type, $p = D(q,\theta)$, single-crossing is equivalent to assuming the demand curves are nested in θ, with higher types exhibiting a greater willingness to pay for every increment of q.

The firm chooses the price schedule, $P(q)$, to maximize expected profits, given that consumers will select from the schedule to maximize individual utilities. Solving for the optimal price schedule is straightforward. For any $P(q)$, the firm can characterize the associated optimal purchase and surplus for a consumer of type θ as

$$q(\theta) \equiv \arg\max_q u(q,\theta) - P(q),$$
$$v(\theta) \equiv \max_q u(q,\theta) - P(q).$$

Expected profits can be written in terms of expected revenue less cost, or in terms of expected total surplus less consumer surplus:

$$\int_{\theta_0}^{\theta_1} \big(P\big(q(\theta)\big) - C\big(q(\theta)\big)\big)\,\mathrm{d}F(\theta) = \int_{\theta_0}^{\theta_1} \big(u\big(q(\theta),\theta\big) - C\big(q(\theta)\big) - v(\theta)\big)\,\mathrm{d}F(\theta).$$

The monopolist cannot arbitrarily choose $q(\theta)$ and $v(\theta)$, however, as the consumer's ability to choose q must be respected. Following standard arguments in the self-selection literature, we know that such incentive compatibility requires that $q(\theta)$ weakly increases in θ and that the consumer's marginal surplus is $v'(\theta) = u_\theta(q(\theta),\theta) > 0$. The requirement that the consumer wishes to participate, $v(\theta) \geqslant 0$, will be satisfied if and only if $v(\theta_0) \geqslant 0$, given that $v'(\theta) > 0$. Fortunately, for any surplus and quality functions that satisfy the incentive-compatibility and participation conditions, a unique price schedule (up to a constant) exists that implements $q(\theta)$.

[55] Maskin and Riley (1984) consider a more general model with non-linear pricing over quantities to explore, among other things, whether quantity discounts are optimal.

Integrating by parts and substituting for $v'(\theta)$ converts the firm's constrained-maximization program over $\{q(\theta), v(\theta)\}$ to a simpler program over $q(\theta)$ and $v(\theta_0)$. In short, the firm chooses $q(\theta)$ to maximize

$$\int_{\theta_0}^{\theta_1} \left(u\big(q(\theta), \theta\big) - C\big(q(\theta)\big) - \frac{1 - F(\theta)}{f(\theta)} u_\theta\big(q(\theta), \theta\big) - v(\theta_0) \right) \mathrm{d}F(\theta),$$

subject to $q(\theta)$ nondecreasing and $v(\theta_0) \geqslant 0$.

Assuming that the firm finds it profitable to serve the entire distribution of consumers, it will choose $v(\theta_0) = 0$ – a corner solution to the optimization program.[56] The integrand of firm's objective function is defined by

$$\Lambda(q, \theta) \equiv u(q, \theta) - C(q) - \frac{1 - F(\theta)}{f(\theta)} u_\theta(q, \theta).$$

This "virtual" profit function gives the total surplus less the consumer's information rents for a fixed type, θ. Choosing $q(\theta)$ to maximize $\Lambda(q, \theta)$ pointwise over θ will simultaneously maximize its expected value over θ. If this function is strictly quasi-concave (a reasonable assumption in most contexts), then the optimal $q(\theta)$ is determined by $\Lambda_q(q(\theta), \theta) = 0$ for every θ. If $\Lambda(q, \theta)$ is also supermodular (i.e., $\Lambda_{q\theta}(q, \theta) \geqslant 0$) – an assumption that is satisfied for a wide variety of distributions and preferences – then the resulting function $q(\theta)$ is weakly increasing in θ.[57] Hence, with a few regularity conditions, we have the firm's optimal choice. After setting $v(\theta_0) = 0$ and determining $q(\theta)$, constructing the unique price schedule is straightforward: one recovers $v(\theta) = v(\theta_0) + \int_{\theta_0}^{\theta_1} u_\theta(q(\theta), \theta)\, \mathrm{d}\theta$ and then constructs $P(q)$ from the equation $u(q(\theta), \theta) - P(q(\theta)) = v(\theta)$.

Because we are primarily interested in the consumption distortions introduced by the monopolist, we are more interested in $q(\theta)$ than $P(q)$. To understand the distortion, consider the first-order condition, $\Lambda_q(q(\theta), \theta) = 0$:

$$u_q\big(q(\theta), \theta\big) - C_q\big(q(\theta)\big) = \frac{1 - F(\theta)}{f(\theta)} u_{q\theta}\big(q(\theta), \theta\big) \geqslant 0. \tag{1}$$

In words, the marginal social benefit of increasing q (the marginal increase in the size of the pie) is set equal to the marginal loss from increased consumer surplus and reduced infra-marginal profits (a smaller slice of the pie). Alternatively, in the form $f(\theta)(u_q - C_q) = (1 - F(\theta))u_{q\theta}$, we see that the gain from increasing quality for some type θ is the probability, $f(\theta)$, of that type arising, multiplied by the increase in surplus which the

[56] For sufficiently large heterogeneity, it is possible that the firm will wish to serve a proper subset of types. Here, the lowest type served, θ_0^*, is determined by the point where the virtual profit (defined below) of the monopolist goes from positive to negative: $\Lambda(q(\theta_0^*), \theta_0^*) = 0$.

[57] For example, if preferences are quadratic and $(1 - F(\theta))/f(\theta)$ is non-increasing in θ, then $\Lambda(q, \theta)$ is supermodular. When $\Lambda(q, \theta)$ is not supermodular, one must employ control-theoretic techniques to maximize, subject to the monotonicity constraint. This "ironing" procedure is explained in Fudenberg and Tirole (1991, ch. 7).

marginal quality generates, $(u_q - C_q)$. The loss arises from all higher type consumers, $1 - F(\theta)$, who obtain more surplus by the amount $u_{q\theta}$. Thus, we have the marginal-versus-inframarginal tradeoff that is familiar to the classic monopolist: the marginal profit from selling to one more consumer must be set against the lowered price given to the higher-demand, inframarginal customers.

In standard models of price- or quantity-setting oligopolists, competition reduces the significance of the inframarginal term and fewer distortions arise. One might conjecture that the presence of competition should have the same general effect in markets with non-linear pricing – reducing the impact of the infra-marginal effect (and thereby reducing the distortions from market power). As we will see below, this is the case for a large class of models.

Two final remarks on monopoly price discrimination are helpful. First, the above model was one of vertical differentiation; consumers' willingness to pay increases in their marginal valuation of quality, θ, and the firm makes more profit per customer on the high types than on the low types. One could instead consider a model of horizontal differentiation with little difference in the character of the distortions. For example, suppose that consumer types are distributed over the positive real numbers, and a type represents the distance of the consumer to the monopolist firm. Here, closer consumers (low θ's) take on the role of valued, high-demand customers, so $u_\theta < 0$ and $u_{q\theta} < 0$. The analysis above executes with very minor modifications. Now, all consumers but the closest to the firm will have downward distortions in their quality allocation, and the first-order condition will be given by an analogue of the vertical uncertainty program:

$$u_q\big(q(\theta),\theta\big) - C_q\big(q(\theta)\big) = -\frac{F(\theta)}{f(\theta)} u_{q\theta}\big(q(\theta),\theta\big) \geqslant 0.$$

Hence, there is nothing conceptually distinct about horizontal or vertical preference heterogeneity in the context of monopoly, providing the relevant single-crossing property is satisfied.

Second, it is worth noting that a consumer's relevant "type" is completely summarized by the consumer's demand curve; therefore, we should be able to find similar conclusions looking only at a distribution of demand functions, indexed by type. Consider again the case of vertical heterogeneity, and denote $p = D(q,\theta)$ as a type-θ consumer's demand curve for quality. By definition, $D(q,\theta) \equiv u_q(q,\theta)$. The relevant condition for profit maximization is now

$$D\big(q(\theta),\theta\big) - C_q\big(q(\theta)\big) = \frac{1 - F(\theta)}{f(\theta)} D_\theta\big(q(\theta),\theta\big).$$

Rearranging, this can be written in the more familiar form

$$\frac{P'(q(\theta)) - C_q(q(\theta))}{P'(q(\theta))} = \frac{1}{\eta(q(\theta),\theta)},$$

where $\eta = \frac{1-F}{f}\frac{D_\theta}{D}$ is the relevant elasticity of marginal demand for the $q(\theta)$ marginal unit. In the elasticity form, the intuitive connection between non-linear pricing and classic monopoly pricing is clear. In a large variety of competitive non-linear pricing models, the effect of competition is to increase this elasticity and hence reduce marginal distortions. To understand how this elasticity formula changes under competition, we separately examine the settings in which a consumer makes all purchases from a single firm, or commonly purchases from multiple firms.

6.2. Non-linear pricing with one-stop shopping

Suppose that in equilibrium, consumers purchase from at most one firm. For example, each consumer may desire at most one automobile, but may desire a variety of quality-improving extras (air conditioning, high performance stereo, luxury trim, etc.) which must be supplied by the same seller. In this setting of one-shop shopping, firms compete for each consumer's patronage. One can think of the consumer's decision in two stages: first, the consumer assigns an indirect utility of purchasing from each firm's product's line and associated price schedule, and second, the consumer visits the firm with the highest indirect utility (providing it is nonnegative) and makes his purchase accordingly.

6.2.1. One-dimensional models of heterogeneity

Assume for the present that all uncertainty in the above setting is contained in a one-dimensional parameter, θ, and that preferences for each firm j's products are given by $u^j(q_j, \theta) - P_j(q_j)$, $j = 1, \dots, n$. Given the offered schedules, the indirect utility of purchasing from each firm j is

$$v_j(\theta) = \max_{q_j} u^j(q_j, \theta) - P_j(q_j).$$

We let $v_0(\theta) = 0$ represent utility associated with not purchasing from any firm. Calculating the indirect utilities, firm j can derive the best alternative for each consumer of type θ, relative to the firm's offer:

$$\underline{v}_j(\theta) \equiv \max_{k \neq j} v_k(\theta),$$

where the utility from no purchase is included in the maximand on the right. The competitive environment, from firm j's point of view, is entirely contained in the description of $\underline{v}_j(\theta)$. The best response of firm j is the same as a monopolist which faces a consumer with utility $u(q, \theta) - P(q)$ and an outside option of $\underline{v}_j(\theta)$.

This monopoly restatement of firm i's problem makes clear a new difficulty: the outside option depends on θ. Economically, the presence of θ in the outside option means that it is no longer clear which consumer types will be marginally attracted to a firm's rival.[58] Fortunately, some guidance is provided as there exists a connection between

[58] A number of theoretical contributions in the incentives literature have developed the methodology of type-dependent participation constraints; see, for example, Lewis and Sappington (1989), Maggi and Rodriguez-Clare (1995) and Jullien (2000).

the nature of the participation constraint and the form of preference heterogeneity – horizontal or vertical.[59]

• *Horizontal heterogeneity* Consider a setting in which consumers are located between two firms such that closer consumers have not only lower transportation costs, but also a higher marginal utility of quality. For example, consumers without strong preferences between an Apple- or Windows-based desktop computer are also not willing to pay as much for faster processors or extra software packages in their preferred product line; the reverse is true for someone with strong brand preferences. This is a setting of horizontal heterogeneity. Formally, let θ represent a consumer's distance to firm 1 (and her "closeness" to firm 2); we assume that $u^1_\theta(q,\theta) < 0 < u^2_\theta(q,\theta)$. Because greater distance lowers the marginal utility of quality, we also have $u^1_{q\theta}(q,\theta) < 0 < u^2_{q\theta}(q,\theta)$. Holding q fixed, a consumer that is close to firm 1 and far from firm 2 obtains higher utility from firm 1 than firm 2, and has a higher marginal valuation of firm 1's quality than firm 2's. It follows that a low-θ (respectively, high-θ) consumer has a higher demand for firm 1's (respectively, firm 2's) product line.

An early and simple model of non-linear pricing by oligopolists in a setting of horizontal heterogeneity is developed in Spulber (1989), which we follow here.[60] Firms are evenly spaced on a circular market of unit size, and consumers' types are simply their locations on the market. Consider a consumer located between two firms, with the left firm located at 0 and the right one located at $\frac{1}{n}$. The consumer's utility from the left firm at price p is taken to be $u^1 = (z-\theta)q - P_1(q)$ and the utility derived from the right firm is $u^2 = (z - (\frac{1}{n} - \theta))q - P_2(q)$. Here, the base value of consumption, z, is known, but the consumer's location in "brand" space is private information. There is a single-crossing property in (q,θ) for each firm: nearer consumers enjoy a higher margin from consuming q.

Consider firm 2's problem. Taking $P_1(q)$ as fixed, we have $\underline{v}_2(\theta) = \max\{0, v_1(\theta)\}$, where $v_1(\theta) = \max_q (z-\theta)q - P_1(q)$. Using the envelope theorem, we know that $v_1'(\theta) = -q_1(\theta) \leqslant 0$, so $\underline{v}_2(\theta)$ is decreasing. As a result, if the marginal type, $\tilde{\theta}$, is indifferent between the two firms, then firm 1 obtains market share $[0, \tilde{\theta})$ and firm 2 obtains the share $(\tilde{\theta}, \frac{1}{n}]$. This partition implies that the determination of market share and the allocation of quality are separable problems. Price competition between the local duopolists is *entirely* focused on the marginal consumer. Here, each firm will trade off the gain derived from the additional market share captured by raising this marginal consumer's utility against the cost of lowering prices to all inframarginal consumers.

[59] Several papers have drawn upon this distinction in one form or another; see, for example, Borenstein (1985), Katz (1985), and Stole (1995).

[60] Spulber (1984) also considers spatial non-linear pricing with imperfect competition, but models imperfect competition by assuming firms are local monopolists within a given market radius and that the market radius is determined by a zero-profit condition. Unlike Spulber (1989), this approach to spatial competition ignores the interesting price effects of competition on the boundaries. Norman (1981) considers third-degree price discrimination with competition under a similar model of spatial competition.

This classic tradeoff determines the value of $\underline{v} = v_1(\tilde{\theta}) = v_2(\tilde{\theta})$. Given the equilibrium partition and utility of the marginal consumer, $\underline{v}$, each firm will allocate $q(\theta)$ as if they were a second-degree price-discriminating monopolist constrained to offer $v(\theta) \geqslant \underline{v}$. As Spulber (1989) emphasizes, the resulting quality allocations are equivalent to those of a monopolist operating over the given market shares. Given the quality allocation is unchanged between competition and monopoly, the marginal price schedules are the same whether the market structure is an n-firm oligopoly or an n-plant monopolist. Only the *level* of prices will be lower under competition, leaving positive surplus to the marginal "worst-type" consumer.

A few remarks are in order. First, a multi-product monopolist may choose not to cover the market, while every consumer would otherwise be served under oligopoly, so we must be careful to consider market coverage in making welfare conclusions. Second, fixing the number of distinct product lines, n, and assuming that the market is covered under monopoly and oligopoly, social welfare is unaffected by the market structure. Under competition, consumer surplus is higher and profits are lower, but the aggregate surplus is unchanged from a multi-product monopoly selling the same n product lines. Third, as the number of product lines, n, increases and more brands become available, the distance between brands decreases. The marginal customer then moves closer to her nearest brand, leading to a reduction in quality distortions. Of course, more product lines typically come at a social cost, which raises a final point: In a free-entry model with fixed per-plant costs of production. Social welfare may decrease from excessive entry.

• *Vertical heterogeneity* Suppose instead that unobservable heterogeneity is vertical rather than horizontal; i.e., every firm ranks the consumer types identically. Formally, $u^j_{q\theta}(q_j, \theta) > 0$ and $u^j_\theta(q_j, \theta) > 0$ for $j = 1, \ldots, n$. Given that all firms rank the consumer types equivalently and θ does not represent differentiated tastes for brands, the source of product differentiation is not immediate. Two approaches to modeling imperfect competition emerge in such a setting.[61] The first assumes firms have different comparative advantages for serving customer segments; e.g., Stole (1995). The second assumes that the firms are ex ante symmetric in their productive capabilities, but in an initial stage the firms commit to a range of qualities before the choosing prices, generating endogenous comparative advantages that soften price competition; e.g., Champsaur and Rochet (1989). We consider each approach in turn.

Consider a duopoly where firm 1 has a commonly known comparative advantage over firm 2 for an identifiable consumer segment. As a simple example, suppose that a consumer obtains $u^1(q_1, \theta) = \theta q_1 + z - P_1(q_1)$ from firm 1 and $u^2(q_2, \theta) = \theta q_2 - P_2(q_2)$

[61] Locay and Rodriguez (1992) take a third approach. They assume that buyers must consume goods in groups (e.g., a family or club), and that the group chooses a firm (one-stop shopping) based on some group-welfare norm. Competition occurs between firms for groups and drives profits to zero. With zero profits there remains intra-group price discrimination to allocate costs.

from firm 2, although the cost of production is $C(q) = \frac{1}{2}q^2$ for both firms. In equilibrium, firm 2 offers $P_2(q) = C(q)$ and the consumer's associated indirect utility becomes $\underline{v}_1(\theta) = \frac{1}{2}\theta^2$. Firm 1, in order to make any sales, must offer at least $\frac{1}{2}\theta^2$ to any type it wishes to serve. Straightforward techniques of optimization with type-dependent participation constraints verify that in this equilibrium, $P_1(q) = C(q) + z$, providing that the consumer who is indifferent between the two firms chooses to purchase from firm 1. In contrast to the setting of horizontal heterogeneity, the participation constraint binds for *every* type of consumer. One may also note that the equilibrium allocation is efficient; it is known with certainty that firm 1 extracts all the consumer's residual surplus, z. Consumers nonetheless obtain considerable information rents given the strong competitive pressures from firm 2.

This model of vertical heterogeneity is perhaps too simple, because neither firm has a comparative advantage on the margin of quality, and thus the firms are perfectly competitive. Firm 1 only extracts rents on its comparative advantage, the additive component of z, which can be extracted without distortion given full information about z. A more general model would allow variations in the marginal comparative advantages of the firms. Along these lines of inquiry, Stole (1995) assumes that consumers are located on a unit circle with n evenly-spaced oligopolists *but* each consumer's location is observable so that firms can offer delivered, non-linear prices conditioned on location. For a consumer segment located at $x \in [0, \frac{1}{n}]$, suppose that the utility of consuming from the first firm is $u^1 = (\theta - x)q - P_1(q)$, while the utility of consuming from the second firm is $u^2 = (\theta - (\frac{1}{n} - x))q - P_2(q)$. Firms furthermore have symmetric costs of production, say $C(q) = \frac{1}{2}q^2$. A reasonable conjecture would have the consumer purchasing from the nearest firm (say, firm 1), while the more distant firm offers its product line at cost and makes no sales, $P_2(q) = C(q)$. Now it is less clear for which types the participation constraint will bind. The closer firm now faces a competitive pressure which guarantees consumer surplus of at least $\underline{v}_1(\theta) = \frac{1}{2}(\theta - (\frac{1}{n} - x))^2$, which is increasing in θ.

For the moment, suppose the nearer firm offers the monopoly quality schedule, assuming that the outside option only matters for the lowest type, θ_0, and that θ is distributed uniformly on $[\theta_0, \theta_1]$. Straightforward calculations reveal that $q_1(\theta) = 2\theta - \theta_1 - x$. The envelope theorem implies that the slope of the consumer's indirect utility function from firm 1 is $v_1'(\theta) = q_1(\theta)$; consequently, there must be parameter values (e.g., $\frac{1}{n} > 2x + \theta_1 - \theta_0$) such that the participation constraint binds for only the lowest type. More generally, an interior value of $\hat{\theta}$ exists such that the participation constraint binds for all $\theta < \hat{\theta}$, and is slack otherwise. When this happens, it must be the case that $q_1(\theta) = \underline{v}_1'(\theta)$ over the determined interval, which in turn requires that q_1 is less distorted than it would be without the binding constraint. While the calculation of this interval relies upon control-theoretic techniques, it helps us understand how competition affects distortions. Here, the rival firm's offer has an additional competitive effect, actually increasing quality for the lower end of consumer types. When the number of firms increases, the firms become closer and the rival offer becomes more attractive, binding over a larger interval as the differentiation between firms decreases.

While these two simple examples of vertical heterogeneity may be of applied interest, they fail to adequately portray the richness of results that can arise in a setting of vertical heterogeneity when firms have different comparative advantages on the margin. For example, a comparative advantage such as different marginal costs of supplying quality leads to a reasonable conjecture that the firms would split the consumer market. However, the effects of competition are more subtle than in the simpler, horizontal-heterogeneity setting with symmetric firms.

Turning to the case of endogenous comparative advantage, we follow Champsaur and Rochet (1989) and consider a two-stage-game duopoly in which firms commit to quality ranges $Q^j = [\underline{q}_j, \bar{q}_j]$, $j = 1, 2$ in the first stage, and then compete using price schedules properly restricted to these intervals in the second stage. Let $\pi^j(Q^1, Q^2)$ be the equilibrium profits in the second stage given the intervals chosen in the first. Champsaur and Rochet (1989) demonstrate that for any given first-stage quality intervals, there is an equilibrium to the second-stage price game with well-defined payoff function $\pi^j(Q^1, Q^2)$, and that in the equilibrium, firms typically find it optimal to leave quality gaps: e.g., $\underline{q}_1 \leqslant \bar{q}_1 < \underline{q}_2 \leqslant \bar{q}_2$. In the presence of a gap, firm 1 sells to the lower interval of consumer types with a lower quality product line while firm 2 serves the higher end with higher qualities. More remarkably, they show under a few additional conditions that when a gap in qualities exist, the profits of the firms can be decomposed into two terms:

$$\pi^1(Q^1, Q^2) = \pi^1(\{\bar{q}_1\}, \{\underline{q}_2\}) + \pi^1(Q^1, [\bar{q}_1, \infty)),$$
$$\pi^2(Q^1, Q^2) = \pi^2(\{\bar{q}_1\}, \{\underline{q}_2\}) + \pi^2((-\infty, \underline{q}_2], Q^2).$$

The first term corresponds to the payoffs in a traditional single-quality product-differentiation game. If this was the only component to payoffs, firms would choose their qualities to differentiate themselves on the margin and soften second-stage price competition; this is pure differentiation profit. The second term is independent of the other firm's strategy and represents the surplus extracted from consumers situated entirely in the area of local monopoly; this is pure segmentation profit along the lines of Mussa and Rosen. In many settings, the Chamberlinian incentive to differentiate products in the first term dominates the incentive to segment consumers within the served interval. For example, when preferences are as in Mussa and Rosen (1978), with $u^j(q, \theta) = \theta q$, $C(q) = \frac{1}{2}q^2$ and θ uniformly distributed, Champsaur and Rochet (1989) show that in equilibrium each firm makes a positive profit but offers a unique quality. Although non-linear pricing is an available strategy, both firms optimally discard this option in the first stage to increase profits in the second. Competition acts to reduce choice.

6.2.2. *Multidimensional models of heterogeneity*

A shortcoming of one-dimensional models is that they are inadequate to capture both privately-known brand preferences and privately-known marginal values of consumption. Furthermore, the lack of compelling conclusions from the one-dimensional modeling approach (particularly the vertical setting) is partly due to the ad hoc manner of modeling product differentiation across firms. Ideally, we would derive economic implications from a model which contains both horizontal and vertical unobservables with a more general allowance for product differentiation.

Two approaches have been taken by the literature. The first relies upon simulations to uncover the basic tendencies of price discrimination.[62] Borenstein (1985), for example, considers a closely related model with heterogeneity over transportation costs (or "choosiness") as well as value.[63] Using simulations in both second- and third-degree frameworks, he concludes that sorting over brand preferences rather than vertical preferences leads to a greater price differential when markets are very competitive. Borenstein and Rose (1994) develop a similar model to study the impact of competition on price dispersion and conclude from numerical results that dispersion increases for reasonable parameter values.

A second modeling approach to product differentiation uses the well-known discrete-choice approach and incorporates vertical heterogeneity along the lines of Mussa and Rosen (1978). By assuming brand preferences enter utility additively (as in the discrete-choice literature), enough additional structure on preferences arises to provide tractable solutions. In this spirit, Rochet and Stole (2002) develop a methodology for calculating non-linear price schedules when preferences take the discrete-choice form of $u(q_j,\theta) - P_j(q_j) - \xi_j$, and ξ_j represents a brand-specific shock to the consumer when purchasing from firm j.

Each consumer has a multidimensional type given by $(\theta, \xi_1, \dots, \xi_n)$. As before, let $v_j(\theta) \equiv \max_q u(q_j,\theta) - P_j(q)$ represent a type-θ consumer's indirect utility of purchasing from firm j, excluding brand-specific shocks. When considering a purchase from firm j, the consumer's outside option is given by

$$\underline{v}_j(\theta,\xi) \equiv \max_{k\neq j}\bigl\{0, v_1(\theta) - \xi_1, \dots, v_n(\theta) - \xi_n\bigr\} + \xi_j.$$

The competitive environment, from firm j's point of view, is entirely contained in the description of $\underline{v}_i(\theta,\xi)$.

First, consider the monopoly case of $n = 1$ and suppose that ξ_1 is independently distributed from θ according to the distribution function $G(\xi)$ on $[0,\infty)$. A monopolist facing a class of consumers with these preferences has a two-dimensional screening problem. The program itself, however, is very easy to conceive. For any non-linear pricing schedule, $P_1(q)$, there is an associated indirect utility, $v_1(\theta) = \max_q u(q,\theta) - P_1(q)$. Because a consumer will purchase if and only if $v_1(\theta) \geqslant \xi_1$, the monopolist's market share conditional on θ is $G(v_1(\theta))$. The monopolist's objective in terms of $q(\theta)$ and $v_1(\theta)$ becomes

$$\max_{\{q,v_1\}} \mathrm{E}_\theta\bigl[G\bigl(v_1(\theta)\bigr)\bigl(u\bigl(q(\theta),\theta\bigr) - C\bigl(q(\theta)\bigr) - v_1(\theta)\bigr)\bigr],$$

62 E.g., Borenstein (1985), Wilson (1993), among others.

63 Armstrong (2006) provides further analysis in this spirit.

subject to incentive compatibility conditions that $v_1'(\theta) = u_\theta(q(\theta), \theta)$ and $q(\theta)$ is non-decreasing. There is no participation constraint because participation is endogenous. Now $v_1(\theta_0)$ is no longer chosen to equal the outside option of zero (a corner condition in a standard monopoly program), but is instead chosen to satisfy a first-order condition. In a classic tradeoff, a higher utility level (equivalent to shifting $P_1(q)$ downward) reduces the profitability of all inframarginal consumers, but increases market share by raising indirect utilities.

To determine the appropriate first-order conditions of this problem, one needs to appeal to control-theoretic techniques. The resulting Euler equation is a second-order non-linear differential equation with boundary conditions, and generally does not yield a closed-form solution. Nonetheless, Rochet and Stole (2002) demonstrate that in the Mussa and Rosen (1978) model, in the presence of additive utility shocks, the equilibrium quality allocation lies between the first-best solution and Mussa–Rosen solution without additive uncertainty ($\xi_1 \equiv 0$). In this sense, the addition of random effects reduces the monopolist's distortions. While it is true that leaving consumers with more surplus reduces profits for any given rate of participation, raising consumer surplus on the margin has a first-order beneficial effect of increasing the rate of participation. The endogenous participation rate implies it is less profitable to extract surplus from consumers and, therefore, it is no longer as valuable to distort quality in order to extract surplus.[64]

Returning to the setting of competition, we can now analyze models incorporating product differentiation, heterogeneity over brand preferences and heterogeneity over preferences for quality. Several papers have taken this approach in one form or another, including Schmidt-Mohr and Villas-Boas (1999), Verboven (1999), Armstrong and Vickers (2001), and Rochet and Stole (2002). For example, consider a duopoly with two firms on the endpoints of a Hotelling market of unit length, populated with consumers, each with unit transportation costs equal to τ. Let the consumer's location, x, in this interval take on the role of the additive shock. Specifically, $\xi_1 = \tau x$ and $\xi_2 = \tau(1 - x)$, where x is distributed according to some distribution $G(x)$ on $[0, 1]$. As before, firm j makes profit of $u(q(\theta), \theta) - C(q(\theta)) - v_j(\theta)$ for each consumer of type θ who purchases. A consumer will purchase from firm 1, only if $v_1(\theta) - \tau x \geqslant \max\{0, v_2(\theta) - \tau(1 - x)\}$. Hence, the probability that a consumer of type θ visits the firm $j \neq k$ is given by the participation function:

$$G_j(v_1, v_2) = \begin{cases} G\bigl(\min\{\frac{v_1}{\tau}, \frac{1}{2} + \frac{v_1 - v_2}{2\tau}\}\bigr), & \text{for } j = 1, \\ 1 - G\bigl(\min\{\frac{v_2}{\tau}, \frac{1}{2} + \frac{v_2 - v_1}{2\tau}\}\bigr), & \text{for } j = 2. \end{cases}$$

The two arguments in each of the minimands represent the cases of local monopoly and local competition, respectively.

[64] Interestingly, these problems may generate a lower interval of pooling, even with the standard restrictions of quadratic preferences and uniformly distributed θ in Mussa and Rosen (1978).

The participation function gives rise to a competitive non-linear pricing game with a well-defined normal form in quality and utility allocations. Each duopolist j chooses the functions (q_j, v_j) to maximize

$$\mathrm{E}_\theta\big[G_j\big(v_1(\theta), v_2(\theta)\big)\big(u\big(q_j(\theta), \theta\big) - C\big(q_j(\theta)\big) - v_j(\theta)\big)\big],$$

subject to the requirement that $v_j'(\theta) = u_\theta(q_j(\theta), \theta)$ and $q_j(\theta)$ is non-decreasing. The monopoly methodology of Rochet and Stole (2002) can be directly applied to solve for each firm's best-response function, which in turn can be used to determine the equilibrium price schedules. Generally, closed-form equilibrium solutions are not available, and we must resort to numerical routines to determine solutions. The form of the solution is similar to those of monopoly when the market is not fully covered: the duopoly allocations of quality lie between the case of monopoly and the first-best, with lower marginal prices for quality than the monopolist in Mussa and Rosen (1978). As firms become less differentiated (τ decreases), the duopoly solution converges to the full-information, first-best allocation. Hence, duopoly lies between the monopoly and socially-efficient allocations.

Two final remarks are in order. First, this discrete-choice approach to competition with a single dimension of vertical uncertainty is quite flexible. It can easily be extended to oligopolies with general distributions of ξ. In such an n-firm oligopoly, firm i's market share is represented by $G_j(v_1, \ldots, v_n) \equiv \mathrm{Prob}[u_j - \xi_j \geqslant \max_{k \neq j} u_k - \xi_k]$, and the analysis proceeds as before. It can also easily be adapted to explore questions about price–cost margins and add-on pricing, as discussed in Section 6.3 below.

Second, and more fundamental, a precise solution for these games can be determined in one instance, as independently noted by Armstrong and Vickers (2001) and Rochet and Stole (2002).[65] Suppose that the firms are symmetric and that the market is entirely covered in equilibrium. Define the following inverse hazard rate which captures firm j's ability to profit from its random brand effect as

$$H_j(u_1, \ldots, u_n) \equiv \frac{G_j(v_1, \ldots, v_n)}{\frac{\partial}{\partial v_j} G_j(u_1, \ldots, u_n)}.$$

If this function is homogeneous of degree zero in indirect utilities for each firm (i.e., $\frac{\mathrm{d}}{\mathrm{d}v} H_j(v, \ldots, v) = 0$ for each j), then non-linear, cost-plus-fixed-fee prices, $P_j(q) = C(q) + F_j$, form a Nash equilibrium. Such homogeneity naturally arises when the fixed-effects distributions are symmetric. For example, in our Hotelling duopoly above, $H_j(v, v) = \tau$ and the equilibrium prices are $P(q) = C(q) + \tau$. The similarity with the uniform-pricing, single-product Hotelling game is remarkable. Duopolists earn profits over their locational advantage, but because they have no competitive advantage in supplying quality, they do not gain from distortions on this margin. This result of cost-plus-fixed-fee pricing, however, depends critically upon firm symmetries and upon market coverage. Changes in either of these assumptions will open up the possibility that firms distort qualities in their battle for market share.

65 Verboven (1999) finds a related pricing result: given exogenous quality levels and cost symmetries between duopolists, price is equal to cost plus a uniform markup.

6.3. Applications: add-on pricing and the nature of price–cost margins

Several papers use multidimensional discrete-choice frameworks to explore specific price discrimination questions. We consider here the contributions in Verboven (1999) and Ellison (2005).

Verboven (1999) uses this framework to make predictions about absolute and relative price–cost margins, and how these margins move with respect to quality. According to the received theory of monopoly non-linear pricing, the monopolist's absolute price–cost margins, $P(q) - C(q)$, increase with quality, *but* the percentage price–cost margins, $(P(q) - C(q))/P(q)$, typically *fall* with q. This finding is certainly true for the Mussa–Rosen (1978) setting in Section 6.1, and it is also true for a monopolist choosing two qualities and selling to two types of consumers, $\theta \in \{\underline{\theta}, \bar{\theta}\}$.[66] However, this theoretical prediction seems at odds with reality. For example, Verboven (1999) presents evidence from the European automobiles that the margins on quality add-ons are higher than the margins on base products. This leads one to reject the simple monopolistic model of second-degree price discrimination and conclude that the percentage price–cost margins rise with quality for this market.

In response, Verboven (1999) makes two changes to the basic monopoly model to create an alternative theory that better fits the data and provides a remarkably simple model of competition with non-linear pricing. First, assume that consumers have both a vertical heterogeneity component, θ, and a horizontal fixed effect for each product line. Second, assume that high-quality prices are unobservable by consumers. For example, it may be that prices for quality add-ons are not advertised and would be costly to learn before arriving at the point of sale. Ellison (2005) refers to a setting with this second assumption as an "add-on pricing" game.

The first modification requires distributional assumptions. Rather than following Verboven (1999), we use a simpler set of distributional assumptions to the same effect. We assume that θ takes on only two equally likely types, $\theta \in \{\underline{\theta}, \bar{\theta}\}$ with $\bar{\theta} > \underline{\theta}$, and that brand preferences derive from a Hotelling model of differentiation; i.e., the firms are positioned on the endpoints of a Hotelling market of length 1, consumers are uniformly distributed and must expend transportation costs of τ per unit-distance traveled.[67] The firms can sell only two exogenously given qualities, q_1 and q_2 with $\Delta q = (q_2 - q_1) > 0$, at costs of $c_2 \geqslant c_1$, respectively. For the high type of consumer, we also suppose the efficiency of a quality add-on: $\bar{\theta}\Delta q > c_2 - c_1$. Applying the results of Armstrong and Vickers (2001) and Rochet and Stole (2002), if the market is covered

[66] Note that this result for the two-type case relies upon the monopolist optimally choosing qualities with smooth, convex cost function. For arbitrary qualities, it is no longer necessarily true. In Verboven (1999), the underlying type distribution for θ is continuous and only two exogenous qualities are offered. Here, the result of decreasing relative price–cost margins again emerges.

[67] These different assumptions do not change Verboven's main theoretical conclusions and allow us to more closely compare Verboven (1999) to recent work by Ellison (2005).

and consumers observe the full price schedules, then equilibrium prices are cost-plus-fixed-fee. It follows that equilibrium prices under duopoly with fully advertised price schedules are $p_2 = c_2 + \tau$ and $p_1 = c_1 + \tau$, and incentive compatibility constraints are non-binding. Absolute price–cost margins are constant but, as in monopoly, percentage price–cost margins fall with quality.

To this duopoly model, Verboven (1999) adds a second modification, similar to that in Lal and Matutes (1994): while consumers costlessly observe the base-quality price, they cannot observe the high-quality price without expending an additional search cost. Consumers correctly anticipate the high-quality product prices and in equilibrium have no incentive to search, regardless of the insignificance of the search cost. As a result, the individual firms behave as monopolists on the high-quality item. Under some reasonable conditions for types and costs, the firms will set a price that makes the high-type consumer indifferent between consuming the high- and low-quality products: $p_2 = p_1 + \bar{\theta}\Delta q$. The low-quality price now serves a new role: it provides a credible signal about the unobserved high-quality price. Each firm, taking the equilibrium prices of its rival as given, $\{p_1^*, p_2^*\}$, chooses its low-quality price to maximize the following expression (after substitution of $p_2 = p_1 + \bar{\theta}\Delta q$ and $p_2^* = p_1^* + \bar{\theta}\Delta q$):

$$(p_1 - c_1)\left(\frac{1}{2} + \frac{p_1^* - p_1}{2\tau}\right) + (p_1 + \bar{\theta}\Delta q - c_2)\left(\frac{1}{2} + \frac{p_1^* - p_1}{2\tau}\right).$$

Solving for the optimal price (and imposing symmetry), we have $p_1^* = \bar{c} + \tau - \frac{\bar{\theta}}{2}\Delta q$ and $p_2^* = \bar{c} + \tau + \frac{\bar{\theta}}{2}\Delta q$, where $\bar{c} \equiv (c_1 + c_2)/2$.

Two interesting results follow when there is incomplete information about add-on prices. First, relative price–cost margins increase with quality if and only if competition is sufficiently strong, $\tau < (\bar{\theta}\Delta q - \Delta c)\bar{c}/\Delta c$. This result is in sharp contrast to the monopoly and fully-advertised duopoly pricing games. Second, although Verboven (1999) does not stress this result, the presence of incomplete information about add-on prices does not raise industry profits; instead, average prices are unchanged. Indeed, for any fixed price differential, $p_2 - p_1$, the first-order condition for profit maximization entirely pins down the average price; the average price equals the average cost plus τ. The ability to act as a monopolist on the high-quality item gets competed away on the low-type consumers; the result is similar to Lal and Matutes' (1994) for loss-leader pricing.

It is perhaps surprising that the presence of incomplete information about high-quality prices does not increase profits, especially given that the reasoning in Diamond (1971) suggests unobservable pricing generates monopoly power in other contexts.

In order to study the strategic effects of unobservable add-on pricing further, Ellison (2005) uses a similar model to the one presented above but with the key difference of heterogeneity, γ, over the marginal utility of income: $u = q - \gamma p - \tau x$, where x is the distance traveled to the firm. Defining $\theta = 1/\gamma$, these preferences can be normalized to $u(q, \theta) = \theta q - p - \theta\tau x$. While this formulation has the same marginal rate of substitution between money and quality as Verboven's (1999) setting, a consumer with higher marginal utility of income (and therefore a lower marginal willingness to pay for quality) now *also* is less sensitive to distance. This vertical heterogeneity parameter captures price sensitivities with respect to a competitor's price and to a firm's own price. This reasonable modification of preferences also eliminates Verboven's (1999) profit neutrality result.

To see why this matters, we can introduce two distinct terms, τ_1 and τ_2, to capture the sensitivities of each market.[68] The first-order condition requires

$$\left(\frac{1}{2} - \frac{1}{2\tau_1}(p_1 - c_1)\right) + \left(\frac{1}{2} - \frac{1}{2\tau_2}(p_2 - c_2)\right) = 0.$$

Given the unobservability of add-on prices, profit maximization and incentive compatibility require a positive price differential, $p_2 - p_1 = \bar{\theta}\Delta q > 0$, and the marginal effect of a price change will be positive in market 1 and negative in market 2. In Verboven's (1999) setting, $\tau_1 = \tau_2 = \tau$, because there is no heterogeneity over brand sensitivities. The effect on profits from a marginal reduction in p_1 is equal to the effect of a marginal increase of p_2. It is optimal that the average price is unchanged and that the individual prices are equally distorted from $\bar{c} + \tau$. In contrast, after normalizing utility, Ellison's (2005) setting has $\tau_1 = \underline{\theta}\tau$ and $\tau_2 = \bar{\theta}\tau > \tau_1$. Now, a small reduction in p_1 has a greater effect on profit than an equal increase in p_2 does. Hence, the base price is less downward distorted than the high-quality price is upward distorted. The price dispersion is not centered around $\bar{c} + \tau$, and the net result is an increase in the average price (and profit) from unobservable add-on prices [Ellison (2005)]. While the profit neutrality result in Verboven (1999) is quite interesting, it should be applied cautiously given the plausibility of the preferences in Ellison (2005).

6.4. *Non-linear pricing with consumers in common*

In the previous section, the models were cast with the discrete-choice, one-stop-shopping assumption that assigns each consumer to at most one firm in equilibrium. The only conduit for competitive effects was through the outside option; once a consumer chose to purchase from a firm, the offers of other firms became irrelevant. This assumption generated a natural separability in the equilibrium analysis. In some settings, however, one-stop-shopping is an inappropriate assumption. As an extreme example, one could imagine two firms selling complementary goods such as a monopoly vendor of software and a monopoly vendor of computer hardware. In a less extreme example, two firms may sell differentiated products that are substitutes, but it is efficient for the customer to consume some output from each seller. In both cases, the consumer is likely to purchase from both firms in equilibrium, and the non-linear price schedule offered by one firm will typically introduce a competitive externality on its rival's sales *at every margin*.

[68] We assume the sensitivities are not too different from one another.

6.4.1. One-dimensional models

Most common agency models consider competition between two principals (e.g., price-discriminating duopolists) for a common agent's activities (e.g., consumer's purchases) when there is one dimension of uncertainty over the agent's preferences.[69] In equilibrium, the consumer purchases goods from *both* firms, which introduces a new difficulty: one firm's contract can negatively impact the screening effectiveness of the other's.[70]

The most interesting and tractable setting for such one-dimensional models are when (i) both firms care about the same dimension of preference uncertainty, and (ii) consumption of one firm's good affects the marginal utility of consuming the other firm's good. An example of the first condition arises when the consumer's marginal utility of income (e.g., high marginal utilities of income may imply high price elasticities of demand for all goods) is relevant. An example of the second condition arises when the goods are either substitutes (i.e., $u_{q_1 q_2}(q_1, q_2, \theta) < 0$) or complements (i.e., $u_{q_1 q_2}(q_1, q_2, \theta) > 0$). If there is no interaction in the consumer's utility function, then the firms are effectively monopolists over their products and competition is not economically meaningful.

In the common-agency game, each firm j simultaneously offers the consumer a nonlinear price schedule, $P_j(q_j)$, for the purchase of good q_j. The consumer decides how much (if any) he wishes to buy of the two goods, and then makes his purchases simultaneously. Importantly, firms cannot condition their price schedule on the consumer's choices from the rival.

Suppose that the consumer's utility is quasi-linear and characterized by

$$u(q_1, q_2, \theta) - P_1(q_1) - P_2(q_2),$$

[69] Stole (1991), Martimort (1992), and Martimort and Stole (2005) present the basic analysis. Other related papers, covering a variety of applications, include Gal-Or (1991), Laffont and Tirole (1991), Biglaiser and Mezzetti (1993), Bond and Gresik (1996), Martimort (1996), Mezzetti (1997), Calzolari (2004), and Martimort and Stole (2003). An early paper by Calem and Spulber (1984) considers a common agency setting in which firms are restricted to offering two-part tariffs.

[70] For completeness, one needs to distinguish between *intrinsic* and *delegated* common agency games. This distinction was first noted by Bernheim and Whinston (1986) in the context of common agency and moral hazard. When the common agency game is intrinsic, the agent is assumed to be unable to accept only one of the two principals' offers. This is an appropriate assumption, for example, in regulatory settings where the regulated firm can either submit to all governmental regulatory bodies or exit the industry. When common agency is delegated, the agent has the additional options of contracting with just one or the other principal. When firms cannot monitor a consumer's purchases with a rival, the delegated common agency game is more appropriate. As noted by Martimort and Stole (2005), however, the distinction has no impact on the equilibrium allocations of $q_j(\theta)$ chosen by participating consumers at each firm. The distinction does matter if one is interested in consumer surplus (which is higher under delegated agency) or market participation when coverage is incomplete (delegated agency games may generate more market coverage than intrinsic agency games). Of course, when the goods are perfect complements on the extensive margin, such as arguably in the example of monopoly computer software and hardware firms, the games are strategically equivalent since a consumer would never choose to purchase from only one firm.

which satisfies a one-dimensional single-crossing property in each (q_j, θ) pair and is increasing in θ. Appealing to previous arguments, if q_2 was fixed, firm 1 would construct a non-linear pricing schedule to induce consumers of type θ to select $q_1(\theta)$, satisfying the relationship

$$u_{q_1}\big(q_1(\theta), q_2, \theta\big) - C'\big(q_1(\theta)\big) = \frac{1-F(\theta)}{f(\theta)} u_{q_1\theta}\big(q_1(\theta), q_2, \theta\big).$$

Generally, however, when $u_{q_1 q_2} \neq 0$, the choice of q_2 will depend upon the offer of $P_1(q)$.

We proceed, as before, by converting the competitive problem into the more familiar and tractable monopoly program. To this end, take firm 2's pricing schedule as fixed and define the consumer's best-response function and indirect utility, given (q_1, θ):

$$\hat{q}_2(q_1, \theta) = \arg\max_{q_2} u(q_1, q_2, \theta) - P_2(q_2).$$
$$v_1(q_1, \theta) = \max_{q_2} u(q_1, q_2, \theta) - P_2(q_2).$$

The indirect utility function, $v_1(q, \theta)$, is continuous and increasing in both arguments. It is straightforward to check that if the goods are complements, then $v_1(q, \theta)$ satisfies the single-crossing property.[71] If the goods are substitutes, then whether single-crossing is satisfied must be checked in equilibrium. For a wide variety of preferences, this concern is not a problem so we cautiously proceed by setting it aside. The end result is that firm 1's optimization problem is identical to that of a monopolist facing a consumer with preferences $v_1(q, \theta)$.[72] Competitive effects are embedded in this indirect utility function, much as they are embedded in the outside option $\underline{v}_j(\theta)$ when there is one-stop shopping.

Suppose for the sake of argument that $\hat{q}_2$ is continuous and differentiable and $v_1(q, \theta)$ satisfies the single-crossing property. Then, using the monopoly methodology, firm 1's optimal price-discriminating solution is to choose $q_1(\theta)$ to satisfy

$$\frac{\partial v_1(q_1(\theta), \theta)}{\partial q_1} - C_q\big(q_1(\theta)\big) = \frac{1-F(\theta)}{f(\theta)} \frac{\partial^2 v_1}{\partial q_1 \partial \theta}\big(q_1(\theta), \theta\big).$$

Using the equilibrium condition that $q_2(\theta) = \hat{q}_2(q_1(\theta), \theta)$ and applying the envelope theorem to replace the derivatives of v_1 with derivatives of $\hat{q}_2$, we obtain pointwise in θ:

$$\begin{aligned} &u_{q_1}(q_1, q_2, \theta) - C_q(q_1) \\ &\quad = \frac{1-F(\theta)}{f(\theta)} \left(u_{q_1\theta}(q_1, q_2, \theta) + u_{q_1 q_2}(q_1, q_2, \theta) \frac{\partial \hat{q}_2(q_1, \theta)}{\partial \theta} \right). \end{aligned} \tag{2}$$

[71] Formally, complementarity and single-crossing implies that $u(q_1, q_2, \theta) - P_1(q_1) - P_2(q_2)$ is supermodular in (q_1, q_2, θ). Hence, the maximized function is also supermodular.

[72] A few technical issues regarding the associated virtual surplus function – namely strict quasi-concavity and supermodularity – must also be addressed; see Martimort and Stole (2005), for details.

Comparing this result to the analogous monopoly equation, (1), we see that the presence of a duopolist introduces a second information-rent effect: $u_{q_1 q_2} \frac{\partial \hat{q}_2}{\partial \theta}$.

Suppose for the moment that the duopolists' goods are substitutes: $u_{q_1 q_2} < 0$. Because $\hat{q}_2$ is increasing in θ, the second term is negative and reduces the standard distortion. Hence, when the products are substitutes in the consumer's preferences, distortions are reduced by competition. Alternatively, if the goods were complements, the distortions would be amplified. Intuitively, selling an extra margin of output to a lower type requires that the firm reduce the marginal price of output for all consumers (including higher types), and in so doing, reduce inframarginal profit. The reduction in inframarginal profit, however, is offset by the fact that a marginal increase in q_1 causes the consumer to lower q_2 marginally, which consequently lowers the information-rent term u_θ.

In a broader sense, the result shares the same spirit as Bertrand equilibria in pricing games with differentiated, single-product duopolists. If the goods are imperfect substitutes, we know the presence of competition reduces purchasing distortions, while if the goods are complements, distortions increase. This intuition goes back at least as far as Cournot (1838). The present argument suggests that this single-price intuition is robust to the introduction of more complicated non-linear pricing and multi-product firms.

6.4.2. *Multidimensional models*

One can easily think of examples in which the two-dimensional preference uncertainty is more appropriate because each firm wants to segment on a different dimension of consumer tastes. In these settings, the interaction of marginal utilities of consumption may introduce a common agency setting worthy of study. Unfortunately, this approach shares many of the same technical difficulties with multidimensional screening models and so has received little attention. A notable exception is the paper by Ivaldi and Martimort (1994).[73] The authors construct a model which avoids many of these technical difficulties by employing a clever change of variables to allow aggregation of consumer heterogeneity into a one-dimensional statistic.[74]

A simple version of Ivaldi and Martimort's (1994) model makes this technique clear. Suppose that there are two competing firms, $i = 1, 2$, each producing one good and offering non-linear pricing schedules $P_i(q_i)$ to the population of consumers. A consumer has two-dimensional private information, (θ_1, θ_2), and preferences for consumption of the two goods given by

$$u = \theta_1 q_1 + \theta_2 q_2 - \frac{1}{2} q_1^2 - \frac{1}{2} q_2^2 + \lambda q_1 q_2 - P_1 - P_2,$$

[73] Miravete and Röller (2003) successfully apply a similar methodology to their study of the U.S. cellular telephone industry. A related competitive setting in which aggregation usefully converts a multidimensional problem into a single dimension can be found in Biais, Martimort and Rochet (2000).

[74] Ivaldi and Martimort (1994) empirically fit this model to data from the French energy market.

with $|\lambda| < 1$. For the moment, suppose firms are restricted to offering quadratic price schedules. Taking the price schedule of firm 2 as given, $P_2(q_2) = \alpha_2 + \beta_2 q_2 + \frac{\gamma_2}{2} q_2^2$, it follows that the type (θ_1, θ_2) consumer's first-order condition for choice of q_2 is given by

$$\theta_2 - q_2 + \lambda q_1 = \beta_2 + \gamma_2 q_2.$$

Solving for q_2 and substituting in the first-order condition for the choice of q_1, yields

$$\theta_1 - q_1 + \frac{\lambda}{1 + \gamma_2}(\theta_2 - \beta_2 + \lambda q_1) = P_1'(q_1).$$

We can define a new measure of heterogeneity as $z_1 \equiv \theta_1 + \frac{\lambda\theta_2}{1+\gamma_2}$, and use it as a one-dimensional sufficient statistic for firm 1's consumer preferences. The two-dimensional problem has thus been simplified and standard methods can be employed. Furthermore, providing that z_1 follows a Beta distribution with parameter λ, Ivaldi and Martimort (1994) show that firm 1's optimal contract is indeed quadratic.[75] The conclusions of the model are quite simple: an increase in λ (tantamount to making the goods closer substitutes) causes the duopolists to reduce price margins, further suggesting that our intuition from the differentiated Bertrand model is robust to multidimensional types and to larger strategy spaces which include non-linear price schedules.

7. Bundling

It is well known that a multiproduct monopolist can increase its profit by engaging in some form of bundling, even when demands for the component products are independently distributed.[76] The intuition of monopoly bundling is well known. Take a monopolist selling two distinct goods, for example, who can offer them for sale individually or as a bundle, with the bundle price being less than the individual prices. Such pricing effectively segments the market into three groups: those with moderately high valuations for both goods who buy the bundle, those with high valuations for one good and low valuations for the other who buy at the individual prices, and those who do not purchase. One can think of this pricing strategy as a form of non-linear pricing with quantity discounts: the first unit is for sale at the individual price, and the second unit is for sale at a reduced price equal to the difference between the bundle price and the sum

[75] While this condition places rather strong restrictions on the equilibrium distribution of (θ_1, θ_2), one could utilize the simple aggregation approach for more general distributions, providing one was content to restrict strategy spaces to quadratic price schedules.

[76] McAfee, McMillan and Whinston (1989) provide a general set of results in this context. See also Stigler (1963), Adams and Yellen (1976), Schmalensee (1984), Armstrong (1999), Armstrong and Rochet (1999) and Bakos and Brynjolfsson (1999) for more on monopoly bundling strategies. For a discussion of the same effect in the context of regulation, see Section 4.5 of Armstrong and Sappington (2007) in this volume.

of the individual prices.[77] Moreover, if consumer reservation values are independently distributed across goods, as the number of goods increases, the law of large numbers implies a homogenizing effect as it reduces consumer heterogeneity. Mixed bundling with a large number of goods allows the monopolist to extract almost all of the consumer surplus, as shown by Armstrong (1999).[78]

When bundling is introduced in markets with imperfect competition, additional effects arise. In what follows, there are three pricing strategies to evaluate. A firm can offer "components pricing" in which each product is sold for a separate price and there is no discount for multiple purchases from a single firm; a firm can practice "pure bundling" (or "tying") by offering only a package of goods for a bundled price; and a firm can practice "mixed bundling" by offering both component prices and bundle discounts. It is also helpful to proceed by separately examining these strategies in the context of multiproduct duopoly and in the context of multiproduct monopoly with the threat of entry by single-product firms.

7.1. Multiproduct duopoly with complementary components

Suppose that there are two firms in an industry, a and b, each producing in two distinct markets, 1 and 2. We assume, however, that the two component goods are perfect complements. For example, market 1 consists of two brands of stereo receiver and market 2 consists of two brands of speakers. Assuming that the goods are compatible, consumers have preferences over the four possible combinations of goods that make up a system.[79]

Consider our three marketing strategies: components pricing, pure bundling, and mixed bundling. In the first strategy, firm a offers the pair of component prices $\{p_{1a}, p_{2a}\}$; under pure bundling, firm a offers a single price, p_{12a}; and under mixed bundling, firm a offers three prices, $\{p_{1a}, p_{2a}, p_{12a}\}$. Absent the ability to publicly commit to an overall marketing strategy before prices are chosen, each firm individually prefers to choose mixed bundling for reasons familiar to a monopolist. Such a choice, however, may lead to lower industry profits than had the firms chosen component pricing. Matutes and Regibeau (1992) make this point as do Anderson and Leruth (1993) for different demand structures.[80] That industry profits may be lower is reminiscent of

[77] Formally, optimal pricing in these environments quickly becomes intractable because sorting occurs over a multidimensional space. See Armstrong and Rochet (1999) and Rochet and Stole (2003) for a survey of the multidimensional screening literature and the results on bundling by a monopolist.

[78] When marginal costs are zero, there is no social loss from selling consumers only pure bundles, as valuations will exceed marginal costs on every component. Hence, for information goods which typically have very low marginal costs, the homogenizing effect of pure bundling is especially attractive. Bakos and Brynjolfsson (1999, 2000) emphasize this point.

[79] The issue of the choice of compatibility is addressed in Matutes and Regibeau (1988, 1992) and Economides (1989).

[80] Matutes and Regibeau (1992), in a model of Hotelling product differentiation, show that when the components are compatible, mixed bundling by both duopolists generates lower industry profits than pure component

Thisse and Vives (1988) and other asymmetric best-response models in which price discrimination causes intense competition. In mixed-bundling case, however, there is no clear notion of weak and strong market asymmetries, so the intuition for why mixed bundling lowers profits relative to the other strategies is not immediate. To understand, suppose that a firm switches from pure components pricing to mixed-bundling. Such a firm will increase its profits (holding the prices of the rival fixed) by choosing its bundle price to be than lower the total of its pure component prices and its new component prices to be higher than before. The result is that the rival's residual demand for mixed-systems will fall. If the rival anticipates the other firm's mixed bundling strategy, it will lower its component prices. In the end, mixed bundling reduces industry profits on net. Of course, if the market is covered, mixed bundling also reduces social welfare relative to pure component pricing.

The previous analysis suggests that firms may have an incentive to commit to either pure bundling or pure components pricing in order to avoid the intense competition of mixed bundling. Matutes and Regibeau (1988) and Economides (1989) take up this issue in a dynamic game which allows firms to commit to either pure bundling or pure components pricing prior to choosing prices. They find that pure components pricing raises industry profits relative to pure bundling, and that it is a dominant strategy equilibrium for each firm to choose component pricing.

The economic intuition for their result is simple. Suppose under components pricing that a firm a reduces its price for product 1 by Δp. The result is that the demand for firm a's market-1 good increases without any effect in market 2. Under pure bundling, if firm a reduces its system price by Δp, the demands for its goods in both markets increase. In short, demand is more elastic when firms practice pure bundling. Profits are lower as a result.

Matutes and Regibeau (1992) and Anderson and Leruth (1993) generalize the game to allow for a commitment to mixed-bundling, in addition to allowing pure-components and pure-bundling strategic commitments. A similar economic intuition is present in both papers; mixed bundling is unprofitable from an industry perspective, and a commitment to pure component pricing may arise in equilibrium. Matutes and Regibeau (1992) find that depending upon costs, it is an equilibrium for firms to commit to either pure component or mixed bundling strategies in the initial stage.[81] In a different model of demand, Anderson and Leruth (1993) find that a commitment to pure-component pricing always arises in equilibrium, and industry profits are higher than if commitment does not exist and mixed-bundling occurs.

pricing. Anderson and Leruth (1993), find a similar relationship when preferences for differentiation are drawn from Logit distributions.

[81] When costs are low, a "prisoner's dilemma" exists between the strategies of mixed bundling and components pricing, resulting in firms committing to mixed bundling. For intermediate costs, one firm chooses mixed bundling, the other chooses component pricing, and for high costs both firms choose component pricing.

7.2. Multiproduct monopoly facing single-product entry

Consider the setting of an incumbent monopolist facing the threat of entry in one of its two markets. What are the incumbent's incentives to offer bundled prices? Does the answer depend upon the incumbent firm's ability to commit?

One of the first in-depth studies of the value of a commitment to pure bundling ("tying") is found in Whinston (1990).[82] Whinston addresses the question of whether tying its market-1 good with a product sold in a second (potentially duopoly) market is a profitable strategy to maintain monopoly in both markets. The classical response to this question has been that if the second market exhibits perfect competition and marginal cost pricing, such bundling cannot be valuable to the monopolist. Moreover, profits are reduced if there are some bundle-purchasing consumers whose value of good 2 is lower than the marginal cost of production.

Whinston's model departs from the classical argument by assuming that competition in market 2 is imperfect. In the first model of Whinston (1990, Section I), the monopolist's commitment to bundle its products in two markets lowers the profits of any duopolist who may enter market 2. Because the consumer's valuation of the monopolist's market-1 good is assumed to be independent of his market-2 valuation, and because the monopolist's market-2 good is an imperfect substitute for the entrant's good, tying causes the monopolist to price aggressively following entry. A commitment to sell only a pure bundle makes the monopolist more aggressive in market 2. Under bundling, each additional market share has an added value equal to the profit margin created in market 1. Since the value of a marginal market-2 sale is higher when products are tied, the incumbent prices more aggressively and lowers the profits of firm b. For a range of entry costs, the potential entrant will remain out of the market if and only if the monopolist in market 1 makes such a commitment. Of course, such a commitment carries a corresponding cost to the incumbent. Having succeeded in foreclosing entry, the monopolist is now left to maximize profits over the two markets using only a pure bundle price.

A similar entry-deterring effect of tying is explored in Choi and Stefanadis (2001). Suppose that the goods in the two markets are perfect complements, and that a potential entrant exists for each market. An entrant competes in a market only if it has an innovation that makes its component cheaper to produce than the monopolist's. If both entrants succeed in innovating, the monopolist is displaced and earns zero profits. If only one succeeds, however, the monopolist is able to practice a prize squeeze and extract some of the entrant's social contribution, providing its products are not tied. Suppose that the monopolist can make a commitment to tie its products before entry is decided, and that the probability of an innovation depends upon the investment by the potential entrant. Then the monopolist will tie its goods if its ability to extract rents in a price squeeze is

[82] Carlton and Waldman (2002) develop and extend the ideas in Whinston (1990) to understand how bundling complementary products can be used to preserve and create monopoly positions in a dynamic setting.

sufficiently poor. The tradeoff is a simple one: tying reduces the incentives to invest in innovation and entry, but a if a single firm enters, tying prevents the monopolist from squeezing the entrant.

The above examples illustrate how a commitment to pure bundling may deter entry. If entry occurs, of course, the incumbent would like to abandon its tying strategy so credible commitment is critical. As the papers on multiproduct duopoly and mixed bundling suggest, however, an incumbent firm without commitment ability would choose mixed bundling as a statically optimal strategy, and this choice may reduce duopoly profits sufficiently to deter entry. Whinston (1990, Section II(B)) considers a variant of his earlier model with a heterogeneous captive market, showing the possibility that bundling will be ex post profitable with entry, so commitment is unnecessary. In this setting, bundling may sufficiently reduce the profitability of market 2 for the potential duopolist and deter entry. A similar idea of entry deterrence also appears in the discussion of Matutes and Regibeau (1992) in the context of mixed bundling. Because mixed bundling lowers industry profits relative to pure components pricing, a prohibition against price discounts for bundles would raise the likelihood of entry.[83]

Bundling impacts not only the entry decision, but it may also affect the post-entry profitability of an incumbent. Consider the issue of entry accommodation. Whinston (1990, Section II(A)) makes the point that the strategy of pure bundling will be useful in softening competition following entry. As a simple example, one can imagine intense competition on market 2 without bundling (because the firms' market-2 goods are homogeneous). Now bundling may generate a form of vertical differentiation with the bundled product representing a higher "quality" product with additional features. With such vertical differentiation, pricing in market 2 may be less intense. In this way, a commitment to pure bundling may be an ideal accommodation strategy.

Other authors have found similar accommodating effects from commitments to sell a pure bundle. Carbajo, de Meza and Seidmann (1990) construct a model in which goods are homogeneous in market 2, but values for the goods in market 1 and 2 are perfectly correlated. Pure bundling segments the market into high-valuation consumers purchasing the bundle and low valuation consumers purchasing the single product from firm b. If the cost of production in market 2 is not too much greater than in market 1 and demand is linear, then firm a will commit to bundling, prices will rise in market 2 and consumer surplus will decrease. Chen (1997a) presents a similar model in which duopolists who can produce in both markets play a first-stage game over whether to sell good 1 or a pure bundle of goods 1 and 2; as before, market 2 is a perfectly competitive market. The pure-strategy equilibrium exhibits differentiation with one firm choosing good 1 and the other offering the pure bundle. Again, bundling serves to soften competition by introducing product differentiation. Importantly, the product differentiation

[83] The papers of Nalebuff (2004) and Bakos and Brynjolfsson (2000) demonstrate that pure bundling may be more profitable than component pricing for a multiproduct incumbent, but pure bundling reduces a single-market entrant's profitability. Mixed bundling is not considered.

role of bundling in these models arises because firms commit to sell only the pure bundle; mixed bundling would undermine product differentiation.[84]

8. Demand uncertainty and price rigidities

The pricing strategies studied in the preceding sections are well-known forms of price discrimination. In the present section, we consider a setting which on the surface is less related to price discrimination – specifically, aggregate demand uncertainty with non-contingent (or rigid) pricing.

Imagine that a firm is facing a continuum of heterogeneous consumers, each with unit demands, and that these demands have a common component of uncertainty. For any given realization of the aggregate uncertainty, the market demand curve is downward sloping. We will use $D_s(q)$ to indicate the market demand curve in state s, where $s = 1, \dots, S$ and the probability of a state occurring is given by f_s, $\sum_s f_s = 1$. The firm cannot discriminate over the interconsumer heterogeneity because of the unit demand assumption. The firm may, however, be able to set its uniform price conditional on the realized demand state. With such contingent pricing, the firm would be acting like a third-degree price discriminator where each market is associated with a different demand state. The analysis would mirror that in Section 3.

Suppose instead that firms cannot practice contingent pricing and must fix their prices prior to the realization of aggregate demand. Although firms cannot directly price discriminate by state, they can accomplish some discrimination indirectly by offering buckets of output at various prices. For example, in a low demand state, only the low priced output is purchased. In a high demand state, high-priced output is purchased after the low-priced output is sold out. A higher average price results in the higher demand states. In a sense, firms are indirectly price discriminating across states of aggregate demand by offering fixed amounts of output at a variety of prices.

To focus our discussion, consider our non-contingent pricing assumption applied to a market of homogeneous goods in which aggregate demand uncertainty exists. Following the approach taken by Prescott (1975), Eden (1990) and Dana (1998, 1999a, 1999b), we assume that each firm $i = 1, \dots, n$ offers a distribution of prices and quantities, $q_i(p)$, where $q_i(p)$ gives the number of units available from firm i at price p. We denote the cumulative supply function (i.e., the total amount of output supplied at a price equal to or less than p) as $Q_i(p)$. Let $q(p) = \sum_{i=1}^n q_i(p)$ and $Q(p) = \sum_{i=1}^n Q_i(p)$.

Note that the output-distribution strategy $q_i(p)$ is *not* a non-linear price schedule in the sense of Section 6. In fact, $Q_i(p)$ represents something closer to a supply function as it gives the total number of units supplied by firm i at prices no greater than p. Even so, $Q_i(p)$ is *not* a supply function in the neoclassical sense either, because each firm

[84] Reisinger (2003) presents a demand model that allows general correlations of brand preferences across products to determine when bundling will soften or intensify competition.

sells its output at a variety of prices along the curve $Q_i(p)$, and typically some rationing occurs as too many customers line up to purchase the lowest priced items.

The firms anticipate the effects of demand uncertainty and offer a distribution of output at different prices. If demand is unusually low, a small measure of consumers shows up and purchases the cheapest priced units; if demand is unusually large, many consumers show up (first buying up the cheap items, then the ones more dear) eventually driving the price of each firm's goods upward.[85] The greater the positive demand shock, the larger the average selling price will be.

The market for airline tickets is a good example of this phenomenon. In their revenue management programs, airlines try to accomplish several objectives – properly price the shadow costs of seats and planes, effectively segment the market using a host of price discrimination devices (e.g., Saturday night stay-over restrictions, etc.), and quickly respond to changes in aggregate demand. This latter objective is accomplished by offering buckets of seats at different prices. Thus, if a convention in Chicago increases demand for airline tickets on a given weekend from New York to Chicago, the low-priced, restricted-fare economy buckets quickly run dry, forcing consumers to purchase otherwise identical seats at higher prices.[86]

In the demand uncertainty setting with ex post price rigidities, multiple prices are offered in any given aggregate demand state. Therefore, we need a rationing rule for allocating goods to consumers before proceeding. Three different assumptions of rationing have been considered in this literature: proportional, efficient and inefficient. Proportional rationing requires that all consumers willing to buy at a given price are equally likely to obtain the limited quantities of the good. Because we have assumed

[85] Alternatively, one could model demand uncertainty in a setting in which each customer selects a firm knowing that stock-outs occur with some probability and the customer has no recourse to visit another firm. In these settings, firms can compete on availability through their reputation and pricing strategies. See, for example, the papers by Carlton (1978), Deneckere and Peck (1995) and Dana (2001b), in which firms compete in both price and availability. Because these settings are further removed from the methodology of price discrimination, we do not discuss them here.

[86] Two related sets of work should also be mentioned and distinguished before proceeding. The first concerns the optimal flexible price mechanism for responding to demand uncertainty. For example, an electrical utility may be capacity constrained in periods of high demand, but it can sell priority contracts to end users to allocate efficiently the scarce output in such periods. Wilson (1993, chs. 10–11) provides a detailed survey of this literature. To my knowledge, no work has been done which examines the effect of competition on such priority mechanisms, although some of the results from the literature on competitive non-linear pricing would be relevant. The second related set of models analyzes supply-function games and equilibria. In these games, firms submit neoclassical supply functions and a single price clears the market in each demand state. The most influential paper on such supply-function equilibria is by Klemperer and Meyer (1989) [see also their earlier paper, Klemperer and Meyer (1986)]. The fundamental difference between supply-function games and the output-distribution games which are the focus of the present section is that, in the former, a Walrasian auctioneer determines the unique market clearing price, while in the latter, a set of prices is available and rationing exists at all but the highest chosen price. Although in both settings average price increases with demand, in a supply-function equilibrium there is no price variation within any aggregate demand state. To preserve focus, we leave this interesting literature aside.

that our consumers have unit demands, this is equivalent to assuming that consumers arrive in random order and purchase at the lowest available price. Efficient rationing assumes that the highest value customers show up first.[87] Finally, inefficient rationing assumes that those with the lowest valuation for consumption arrive first (perhaps because they have lower valuations of time relative to money, and so can afford to stand in line). We focus on proportional and efficient rationing.

We begin with the monopoly setting to illustrate how a distribution of outputs at various prices can improve upon uniform pricing and mimic second-degree price discrimination. We then explore the perfectly competitive setting to understand the effect of competition and the zero-profit condition on equilibrium pricing, as in Prescott (1975). Following Dana (1999b), we encapsulate these models into one general model of oligopoly, with monopoly and perfect competition as extremes.

8.1. Monopoly pricing with demand uncertainty and price rigidities

Consider a monopoly setting in which there are two states of aggregate demand: $D_s(q)$, $s = 1, 2$, where $D_2(q) \geqslant D_1(q)$. Within each demand state, consumers have unit demands but possibly different reservation prices. There is a constant marginal cost of production, c, and a cost of capacity, $k \geqslant 0$. The marginal cost, c, is only expended if production takes place and capacity exists; k must be spent for each unit of capacity, regardless of production. We assume that $D_1(0) > c+k$, so that the highest demanding customers value the object above the marginal production and capacity costs in the lowest demand state.

Note that in a standard non-linear pricing problem, a monopolist facing two consumer types with demands $D_1(q)$ and $D_2(q)$ would typically offer a menu of two price–quantity pairs to screen the buyers and extract more information rents on the margin. Similarly, in our aggregate demand uncertainty setting with non-contingent pricing, a monopolist would want to implement the same allocation when the consumers are replaced with mathematically equivalent markets. This is not possible, however, because of consumer heterogeneity within each demand state.[88] The monopolist, however, can still achieve a similar albeit less profitable result offering distributions of output and prices.

For simplicity, first suppose that rationing is efficient. In our two-state example, the monopolist chooses buckets of output and corresponding prices to solve

$$\max_{\{q_1,q_2\}} f_1\big(D_1(q_1)-c\big)q_1 + f_2\big(D_2(q_1+q_2)-c\big)q_2 - k(q_1+q_2),$$

[87] "Efficient" rationing is so named because it guarantees that there is never an ex post misallocation of goods among consumers. The term is a slight misnomer, as we will see, in that the efficient rationing rule does not guarantee that the allocation is ex post efficient between consumers and firms; that is, in most demand states some capacity will be unsold, although the marginal consumer values the output above marginal cost.

[88] The fact that the firm cannot discriminate over consumer heterogeneity is related to the discussion in Section 5.

subject to $p_1 = D_1(q_1) \leqslant p_2 = D_2(q_1 + q_2)$ (i.e., prices are increasing with demand). The first-order conditions (ignoring the monotonicity constraint) are

$$D_1(q_1)\left(1 - \frac{1}{\varepsilon_1(q_1)}\right) = c + k - f_2 D_2'(q_1 + q_2)q_2,$$

$$D_2(q_1 + q_2)\left(1 - \frac{1}{\varepsilon_2(q_2)}\right) = c + \frac{k}{f_2}.$$

Note that in the high-demand state, $s = 2$, the marginal cost of capacity is $\frac{k}{f_2}$; i.e., the marginal cost of capital in the high-demand state multiplied by the probability of the high-demand state must equal the cost of producing the capacity. Interestingly, the marginal price in the high-demand state is set at the state-contingent optimal monopoly price, while the price in the low-demand state is biased upward from the optimal price (and hence output is distorted downward, relative to a state-contingent monopolist). Hence, the outcome is reminiscent of second-degree price discrimination, where the monopolist distorts quality downward for the low-type consumer. Also note that if k is sufficiently large, the requirement that $p_2 \geqslant p_1$ is satisfied in the relaxed program; otherwise, no price dispersion arises.

Consider the case of multiplicative demand uncertainty explored in Dana (1999b) in which demand is characterized by $q = X_s(p) = sX(p)$. Holding price fixed, the elasticity of demand is not affected by demand shocks. To take a numerical example, suppose that $X(p) = 4 - p$, $s_1 = 1$, $s_2 = 2$, $c = 1$, $k = 1$; if both states are equally likely, then the profit-maximizing state-contingent prices are $p_1 = 3$ and $p_2 = \frac{7}{2}$. However, when prices cannot directly depend upon the demand state and rationing is efficient, then optimal monopoly prices are $p_1 = \frac{46}{15}$ and $p_2 = \frac{56}{15}$.[89]

Now consider proportional rationing under monopoly, as in Dana (2001a). Because all consumers have an equal chance of purchasing at the low price of p_1 in the high demand state, the residual demand at p_2 is $X(p_2)(1 - \frac{q_1}{X_2(p_1)})$ at p_2. An additional economic effect arises. It is now possible that the low-demand customers obtain some of the low-priced goods, thereby increasing the residual demand in the high-demand state. As a result, the monopolist can do better with proportional rationing than with efficient rationing.[90] The monopolist's program is to maximize

$$\max_{\{p_1, p_2\}} (p_1 - c - k)X_1(p_1) + f_2\left(p_2 - c - \frac{k}{f_2}\right)X_2(p_2)\left(1 - \frac{X_1(p_1)}{X_2(p_1)}\right),$$

[89] Note that care must be taken in comparing these prices. With contingent pricing, all output sold in state 2 transacts at p_2. With non-contingent pricing, the highest price of output sold in state 2 is p_2, but some output is sold at p_1 as well.

[90] Better still, the monopolist extracts even more of the intrastate rents in the case of inefficient rationing. With one state, for example, the monopolist will extract all consumer surplus with inefficient rationing by posting one unit for each price on the demand curve.

subject to $p_2 \geqslant p_1$. Here, we switch to maximizing prices in order to rotate the high-state demand curve inward under proportional rationing; the switch is notationally less cumbersome. Quantities at each resulting price are determined recursively: $q_1 = X_1(p_1)$ and $q_2 = X_2(p_2)(1 - \frac{q_1}{X_2(p_1)})$.

The result that monopoly profits are higher under proportional rationing compared to efficient rationing is general. With proportional rationing, some low-demand consumers purchase the low-priced items in the high-demand state, raising the average price to high-demand customers. Returning to our previous example, the optimal monopoly prices under proportional rationing are $p_1 = 3$ and $p_2 = \frac{7}{2}$.[91]

8.2. *Competition with demand uncertainty and price rigidities*

Now consider the polar extreme of no market power – perfect competition. Assume there are S demand states, $s = 1, \ldots, S$, ordered by increasing demand, with probability f_s and cumulative distribution $F(s)$. In a free-entry, perfectly competitive equilibrium, no firm can make positive expected profit for any output sold with positive probability. As Prescott (1975), Eden (1990), and Dana (1998, 1999b) have shown, this no-profit condition completely determines equilibrium prices.[92]

Given an equilibrium distribution of output, suppose that the units offered at the price p sell in states s' and higher; it follows that the probability these units sell equals $1 - F(s' - 1)$. The zero-profit condition in this case is that $(p - c)[1 - F(s' - 1)] = k$. Hence, we can index the price by state and obtain

$$p(s) = c + \frac{k}{1 - F(s - 1)},$$

where $p(1) = c + k$. Competitive prices equal the marginal cost of production plus the marginal expected cost of capacity.

Two remarks on the perfectly competitive case are significant. First, consider the dispersion of the competitive prices. In our two-state, multiplicative-uncertainty numerical example, the competitive prices are $p_1 = c + k = 2$ and $p_2 = c + \frac{k}{1-F(s_1)} = c + \frac{k}{f_2} = 3$. These prices are more dispersed than the monopoly prices under proportional rationing (recall, $p_1 = 3$ and $p_2 = \frac{7}{2}$). Dana (1999b) shows this result is general: competition generates more price dispersion than monopoly pricing when aggregate demand uncertainty is coupled with non-contingent pricing.

Second, except in the lowest demand state, price exceeds marginal cost, c. Because prices are inflexible ex post, this means that some firms will have unsold capacity priced above marginal cost, and consumption will be inefficiently low. Hence, regardless of

[91] Again care must be taken in comparing these prices to the state-contingent prices (which are identical), as the former represent the highest purchase price in each state while the latter represent the price of all output sold in that state.

[92] This analysis displays striking similarities to the Butters model of advertising discussed in the chapter by Bagwell (2007) in this volume.

the rationing rule, price inflexibility implies that consumption will be inefficiently low relative to the flexible-price benchmark in almost all states.

So far, we have said nothing about the rationing rule under perfect competition; the zero-profit condition is enough to determine the spot prices across states: $\{p(1), \ldots, p(S)\}$.[93] Regardless of rationing rule, prices in a perfectly competitive market with demand uncertainty and ex post price rigidities vary by the state of aggregate demand and firms make zero profits. Prices are at *effective marginal cost*, where effective marginal cost includes the expected cost of adding capacity for a given state in addition to the familiar marginal cost of production. Of course, while capacity is priced efficiently, the market allocation is not Pareto efficient because ex post rationing may generate misallocations across consumers.

Finally, we turn to oligopoly. Dana (1999b) constructs an oligopoly model with symmetric firms in environments of multiplicative demand uncertainty and proportional rationing, which includes perfect competition and monopoly as special cases. When uncertainty is multiplicative and rationing is proportional, the residual demand function for a given firm i can be calculated given the output distributions offered by the remaining firms, $q_{-i}(p)$. Using this residual demand function, Dana (1999b) calculates the symmetric equilibrium and shows that it ranges from the monopoly setting ($n = 1$) to the perfectly competitive setting as $n \to \infty$. Remarkably, Dana (1999b) also shows that the support of prices increases as n increases, as suggested in our two-state example with perfect competition. The resulting relationship between price dispersion and competition generalizes to models of oligopoly.

The result is consistent with Borenstein and Rose's (1994) finding in the airline industry of increased price dispersion as the number of competing firms on a given route rises. Hence, the price dispersion in airline pricing may not be attributable to standard second- or third-degree price discrimination arguments, but instead represents an optimal response to aggregate demand uncertainty with price rigidities.

[93] A competitive equilibrium also requires that the output supplied at each price level is such that the residual demand is zero across all states. With efficient rationing, the residual demand at a price $p(s)$, given cumulative output purchased at lower prices, $Q(p(s-1))$, is $X_s(p(s)) - Q(p(s-1))$. Hence, equilibrium requires that

$$q\big(p(s)\big) = \max\big\{X_s\big(p(s)\big) - Q\big(p(s-1)\big), 0\big\},$$

with $q(p(1)) = X_1(c+k)$. Alternatively, in a world of proportional rationing, residual demand at $p(s)$ is

$$RD_s\big(p(s)\big) = X_s\big(p(s)\big)\left(1 - \sum_{j=1}^{s-1} \frac{q(j)}{X_j(p(j))}\right).$$

Equilibrium requires this to be zero in each state, which provides a recursive relationship to determine the quantities offered at each spot price.

9. Summary

While the extremes of perfect competition and monopoly are invaluable tools for understanding the economic world around us, most economic activity takes place in the realm in between these poles. One need not search very far within this sphere of imperfect competition to find numerous examples of the price discrimination strategies described in this chapter. Given the significance of these practices, an understanding of the interaction of price discrimination and competition – and how this interaction affects profits, consumer surplus, market structure and welfare – is an integral topic in industrial organization. This chapter documents many theories where (under imperfect competition) price discrimination increases welfare, providing that markets are not foreclosed. That said, even this finding is not without exceptions and counterexamples. At times, it may be frustrating that truly robust theoretical predictions are a rarity due to the additional effects of imperfect competition on our classic price-discrimination theories. In many circumstances the theories cannot provide definitive answers without additional empirical evidence. Conclusions regarding profit and welfare typically depend upon the form of consumer heterogeneity, the goods for sale, and the available instruments of price discrimination. Nonetheless, in the end the theories inform by making these dependencies clear.

The theoretical research to date also makes clear that we should not expect that the predictions of monopoly price discrimination theory will survive empirical tests using data from imperfectly competitive markets. The most interesting empirical question is that which comes after data rejects the monopoly discrimination theory: "What is the best alternative theory of price discrimination under imperfect competition?" Here, provocative combinations of theoretical and empirical work lie before us.

Acknowledgements

I am grateful to Jim Dana, Wouter Dessein, J-P. Dube, Glenn Ellison, David Genesove, Joyce Van Grondelle, David Martimort, Canice Prendergast, Markus Reisinger, Jean-Charles Rochet, Klaus Schmidt, Dan Spulber, Achim Wambach, Michael Whinston, and seminar participants at the Center for Economic Studies, Ludwig-Maximilians-Universität, Munich, Germany for helpful comments. I am especially indebted to Mark Armstrong and Audris Wong for their many helpful comments and insights. Financial support received from the National Science Foundation, the University of Chicago, GSB, and from the CES.

References

Acquisti, A., Varian, H. (2005). "Conditioning prices on purchase history". Marketing Science 24, 367–381.
Adams, W.J., Yellen, J.L. (1976). "Commodity bundling and the burden of monopoly". Quarterly Journal of Economics 90, 475–498.

Aghion, P., Bolton, P. (1987). "Contracts as a barrier to entry". American Economic Review 77, 388–401.
Aguirre, I., Espinosa, M., Macho-Stadler, I. (1998). "Strategic entry deterrence through spatial price discrimination". Regional Science and Urban Economics 28, 297–314.
Anderson, S., de Palma, A., Thisse, J.-F. (1992). Discrete Choice Theory of Product Differentiation. MIT Press, Cambridge, MA.
Anderson, S., Leruth, L. (1993). "Why firms may prefer not to price discriminate via mixed bundling". International Journal of Industrial Organization 11, 49–61.
Armstrong, M. (1999). "Price discrimination by a many-product firm". Review of Economic Studies 66, 151–168.
Armstrong, M. (2006). "Recent developments in the economics of price discrimination". In: Blundell, R., Newey, W., Persson, T. (Eds.), Advances in Economics and Econometrics: Theory and Applications, Ninth World Congress, vol. 2.
Armstrong, M., Rochet, J.-C. (1999). "Multi-dimensional screening: A user's guide". European Economic Review 43, 959–979.
Armstrong, M., Sappington, D.E.M. (2007). "Recent developments in the theory of regulation". In: Armstrong, M., Porter, R. (Eds.), Handbook of Industrial Organization, vol. 3. North-Holland, Amsterdam (this volume).
Armstrong, M., Vickers, J. (1993). "Price discrimination, competition and regulation". Journal of Industrial Economics 41, 335–359.
Armstrong, M., Vickers, J. (2001). "Competitive price discrimination". RAND Journal of Economics 32, 579–605.
Bagwell, K. (2007). "The economic analysis of advertising". In: Armstrong, M., Porter, R. (Eds.), Handbook of Industrial Organization, vol. 3. North-Holland, Amsterdam (this volume).
Baker, J. (2003). "Competitive price discrimination: The exercise of market power without anticompetitive effects (comment on Klein and Wiley)". Antitrust Law Journal 70, 643–654.
Bakos, Y., Brynjolfsson, E. (1999). "Bundling information goods: Pricing, profits and efficiency". Management Science 45, 1613–1630.
Bakos, Y., Brynjolfsson, E. (2000). "Bundling and competition on the Internet: Aggregation strategies for information goods". Marketing Science 19, 63–82.
Banerjee, A., Summers, L. (1987). "On frequent flyer programs and other loyalty-inducing arrangements". Working Paper, No. 1337. Harvard Institute for Economic Research (HIER).
Baumol, W., Swanson, D. (2003). "The New Economy and ubiquitous competitive price discrimination: Identifying defensible criteria of market power". Antitrust Law Journal 70, 661–686.
Bernheim, D., Whinston, M. (1986). "Common agency". Econometrica 54, 923–943.
Besanko, D., Dube, J.-P., Gupta, S. (2003). "Competitive price discrimination strategies in a vertical channel using aggregate retail data". Management Science 49, 1121–1138.
Bester, H., Petrakis, E. (1996). "Coupons and oligopolistic price discrimination". International Journal of Industrial Organization 14, 227–242.
Bhaskar, V., To, T. (2004). "Is perfect price discrimination really efficient? An analysis of free entry". RAND Journal of Economics 35, 762–776.
Biais, B., Martimort, D., Rochet, J.-C. (2000). "Competing mechanisms in a common value environment". Econometrica 68, 799–838.
Biglaiser, G., Mezzetti, C. (1993). "Principals competing for an agent in the presence of adverse selection and moral hazard". Journal of Economic Theory 61, 302–330.
Bliss, C. (1988). "A theory of retail pricing". Journal of Industrial Economics 36, 375–391.
Bond, E., Gresik, T. (1996). "Regulation of multinational firms with two active governments: A common agency approach". Journal of Public Economics 59, 33–53.
Borenstein, S. (1985). "Price discrimination in free-entry markets". RAND Journal of Economics 16, 380–397.
Borenstein, S., Rose, N. (1994). "Competition and price dispersion in the U.S. airline industry". Journal of Political Economy 102, 653–683.

Brander, J., Eaton, J. (1984). "Product-line rivalry". American Economic Review 74, 323–334.
Busse, M., Rysman, M. (2005). "Competition and price discrimination in Yellow Pages advertising". RAND Journal of Economics 36, 378–390.
Cabolis, C., Clerides, S., Ioannou, I., Senft, D. (2005). "A textbook example of international price discrimination". Working Paper, July 2005. Department of Economics, University of Cyprus.
Calem, P., Spulber, D. (1984). "Multiproduct two-part tariffs". International Journal of Industrial Organization 2, 105–115.
Calzolari, G. (2004). "Incentive regulation of multinational enterprises". International Economic Review 45, 257–282.
Caminal, R., Matutes, C. (1990). "Endogenous switching costs in a duopoly model". International Journal of Industrial Organization 8, 353–373.
Carbajo, J., de Meza, D., Seidmann, D. (1990). "A strategic motivation for commodity bundling". Journal of Industrial Economics 38, 283–298.
Carlton, D. (1978). "Market behavior with demand uncertainty and price inflexibility". American Economic Review 68, 571–588.
Carlton, D., Waldman, M. (2002). "The strategic use of tying to preserve and create market power in evolving industries". RAND Journal of Economics 33, 194–220.
Champsaur, P., Rochet, J.-C. (1989). "Multiproduct duopolists". Econometrica 57, 533–557.
Chen, Y. (1997a). "Equilibrium product bundling". Journal of Business 70, 85–103.
Chen, Y. (1997b). "Paying customers to switch". Journal of Economics and Management Strategy 6, 877–897.
Chen, Y. (1999). "Oligopoly price discrimination and resale price maintenance". RAND Journal of Economics 30, 441–455.
Cheung, F., Wang, X. (1999). "A note on the effect of price discrimination on entry". Journal of Economics and Business 51, 67–72.
Choi, J.P., Stefanadis, C. (2001). "Tying, investment, and the dynamic leverage theory". RAND Journal of Economics 32, 52–71.
Clerides, S. (2002). "Price discrimination with differentiated products: Definition and identification". International Journal of Industrial Organization 20, 1385–1408.
Clerides, S. (2004). "Book value: Inter-temporal pricing and quality discrimination in the U.S. markets for books". Economic Inquiry 42, 402–412.
Cohen, A. (2001). "Package size and price discrimination: Evidence from paper towels". Working Paper. University of Virginia.
Cooper, J., Froeb, L., O'Brien, D., Tschantz, S. (2005). "Does price discrimination intensify competition? Implications for antitrust". Antitrust Law Journal 72, 327–373.
Corts, K. (1998). "Third-degree price discrimination in oligopoly: All-out competition and strategic commitment". RAND Journal of Economics 29, 306–323.
Cournot, A. (1838). Recherches sur les principes mathématiques de la théorie des richesses. English ed. Bacon, N. (Ed.), Researches into the Mathematical Principles of the Theory of Wealth, MacMillan, New York, 1897.
Courty, P., Li, H. (2000). "Sequential screening". Review of Economics Studies 67, 697–717.
Crawford, G., Shum, M. (2001). "Empirical modeling of endogenous quality choice: The case of cable television". Working Paper.
Dana Jr., J.D. (1998). "Advance-purchase discounts and price discrimination in competitive markets". Journal of Political Economy 106, 395–422.
Dana Jr., J.D. (1999a). "Using yield management to shift demand when the peak time is unknown". RAND Journal of Economics 30, 456–474.
Dana Jr., J.D. (1999b). "Equilibrium price dispersion under demand uncertainty: The roles of costly capacity and market structure". RAND Journal of Economics 30, 632–660.
Dana Jr., J.D. (2001a). "Monopoly price dispersion under demand uncertainty". International Economic Review 42, 649–670.
Dana Jr., J.D. (2001b). "Competition in price and availability when availability is unobservable". RAND Journal of Economics 32, 497–513.

De Fraja, G. (1996). "Product-line competition in vertically differentiated markets". International Journal of Industrial Organization 14, 389–414.
DeGraba, P. (1990). "Input market price discrimination and the choice of technology". American Economic Review 80, 1246–1253.
Deneckere, R., Peck, J. (1995). "Competition over price and service rate when demand is stochastic: A strategic analysis". RAND Journal of Economics 26, 148–162.
Dessein, W. (2003). "Network competition in nonlinear pricing". RAND Journal of Economics 34, 593–611.
Diamond, P. (1971). "A model of price adjustment". Journal of Economic Theory 3, 156–168.
Diamond, P., Maskin, E. (1979). "An equilibrium analysis of search and breach of contract. I. Steady states". Bell Journal of Economics 10, 282–316.
Dupuit, J., (1849). Annales des ponts et chaussées, 17. Translated in: "On Tolls and Transport Charges". International Economic Papers, Macmillan, London, 1952.
Economides, N. (1989). "Desirability of compatibility in the absence of network externalities". American Economic Review 79, 1165–1181.
Eden, B. (1990). "Marginal cost pricing when spot markets are complete". Journal of Political Economy 98, 1293–1306.
Ellison, G. (2005). "A model of add-on pricing". Quarterly Journal of Economics 120, 585–637.
Farrell, J., Klemperer, P. (2007). "Coordination and lock-in: Competition with switching costs and network effects". In: Armstrong, M., Porter, R. (Eds.), Handbook of Industrial Organization, vol. 3. North-Holland, Amsterdam (this volume).
Fudenberg, D., Tirole, J. (1991). Game Theory. MIT Press, Cambridge, MA.
Fudenberg, D., Tirole, J. (2000). "Customer poaching and brand switching". RAND Journal of Economics 31, 634–657.
Fudenberg, D., Villas-Boas, M. (2005). "Behavior-based price discrimination and customer recognition". In: Handbook of Economics and Information Systems. North-Holland, Amsterdam. In press.
Gabszewicz, J., Thisse, J.-F. (1979). "Price competition, quality and income disparities". Journal of Economic Theory 20, 340–359.
Gabszewicz, J., Thisse, J.-F. (1980). "Entry, (and exit) in a differentiated industry". Journal of Economic Theory 22, 327–338.
Gal-Or, E. (1983). "Quality and quantity competition". The Bell Journal of Economics 14 (2), 590–600.
Gal-Or, E. (1991). "A common agency with incomplete information". RAND Journal of Economics 22, 274–286.
Gale, I., Holmes, T. (1992). "The efficiency of advance-purchase discounts in the presence of aggregate demand uncertainty". International Journal of Industrial Organization 10, 413–437.
Gale, I., Holmes, T. (1993). "Advance-purchase discounts and monopoly allocation of capacity". American Economic Review 83, 135–146.
Galera, F. (2003). "Welfare and output in third-degree price discrimination: A note". Working Paper.
Gilbert, R., Matutes, C. (1993). "Product-line rivalry with brand differentiation". Journal of Industrial Economics 41, 223–240.
Goldberg, P. (1995). "Product differentiation and oligopoly in international markets: The case of the U.S. automobile industry". Econometrica 63, 891–951.
Goldberg, P., Verboven, F. (2005). "Market integration and convergence to the law of one price: Evidence from the European car market". Journal of International Economics 65, 49–73.
Graddy, K. (1995). "Testing for imperfect competition at the Fulton fish market". RAND Journal of Economics 26, 75–92.
Gul, F. (1987). "Noncooperative collusion in durable goods oligopoly". RAND Journal of Economics 18, 248–254.
Holmes, T. (1989). "The effects of third-degree price discrimination in oligopoly". American Economic Review 79, 244–250.
Holton, R. (1957). "Price discrimination at retail: The supermarket case". Journal of Industrial Economics 6, 13–31.

Hotelling, H. (1929). "Stability in competition". Economic Journal 39, 41–57.
Hurdle, G., McFarland, H. (2003). "Criteria for identifying market power: A comment on Baumol and Swanson". Antitrust Law Journal 70, 687–696.
Ivaldi, M., Martimort, D. (1994). "Competition under nonlinear pricing". Annales d'Economie et de Statistique 34, 71–114.
Johnson, J.P., Myatt, D.P. (2003). "Multiproduct quality competition: Fighting brands and product-line pruning". American Economic Review 93, 748–774.
Jullien, B. (2000). "Participation constraints in adverse selection models". Journal of Economic Theory 93, 1–47.
Katz, M. (1984). "Price discrimination and monopolistic competition". Econometrica 52, 1453–1471.
Katz, M. (1985). "Firm-specific differentiation and competition among multiproduct firms". Journal of Business 57, S149–S166.
Katz, M. (1987). "The welfare effects of third-degree price discrimination in intermediate good markets". American Economic Review 77, 154–167.
Klein, B., Wiley, J. (2003a). "Competitive price discrimination as an antitrust justification for intellectual property refusals to deal". Antitrust Law Journal 70, 599–642.
Klein, B., Wiley, J. (2003b). "Market power in economics and in antitrust: Reply to Baker". Antitrust Law Journal 70, 655–660.
Klemperer, P. (1992). "Equilibrium product lines: Competing head-to-head may be less competitive". American Economic Review 82, 740–755.
Klemperer, P., Meyer, M. (1986). "Price competition vs. quantity competition: The role of uncertainty". RAND Journal of Economics 17, 618–638.
Klemperer, P., Meyer, M. (1989). "Supply-function equilibria in oligopoly under uncertainty". Econometrica 57, 1243–1278.
Kotler, P. (1994). Marketing Management, eighth ed. Prentice-Hall, New York.
Laffont, J.-J., Tirole, J. (1991). "Privatization and incentives". Journal of Law, Economics, and Organization (Special Issue) 7, 84–105.
Laffont, J.-J., Rey, P., Tirole, J. (1998). "Network competition: Price discrimination". RAND Journal of Economics 29, 38–56.
Lal, R., Matutes, C. (1994). "Retail pricing and advertising strategies". Journal of Business 67, 345–370.
Lederer, P., Hurter, A. (1986). "Competition of firms: Discriminatory pricing and location". Econometrica 54, 623–640.
Leontief, W. (1940). "The theory of limited and unlimited discrimination". Quarterly Journal of Economics 54, 490–501.
Leslie, P. (2004). "Price discrimination in Broadway Theatre". RAND Journal of Economics 35, 520–541.
Lewis, T., Sappington, D. (1989). "Countervailing incentives in agency problems". Journal of Economic Theory 49, 294–313.
Liu, Q., Serfes, K. (2004). "Quality of information and oligopolistic price discrimination". Journal of Economics and Management Strategy 13, 671–702.
Locay, L., Rodriguez, A. (1992). "Price discrimination in competitive markets". Journal of Political Economy 100, 954–965.
Lott, J., Roberts, R. (1991). "A guide to the pitfalls of identifying price discrimination". Economic Inquiry 29, 14–23.
MacLeod, B., Norman, G., Thisse, J.-F. (1988). "Price discrimination and equilibrium in monopolistic competition". Intenational Journal of Industrial Organization 6, 429–446.
Maggi, G., Rodriguez-Clare, A. (1995). "On countervailing incentives". Journal of Economic Theory 66, 238–263.
Mankiw, N.G., Whinston, M. (1986). "Free entry and social inefficiency". RAND Journal of Economics 17, 48–58.
Martimort, D. (1992). "Multi-principaux avec anti-selection". Annales d'Economie et de Statistique 28, 1–38.
Martimort, D. (1996). "Exclusive dealing, common agency, and multi-principals incentive theory". RAND Journal of Economics 27, 1–31.

Martimort, D., Stole, L. (2003). "Contractual externalities and common-agency equilibria". In: Advances in Theoretical Economics, vol. 3. Berkeley Electronic Press. http://www.bepress.com. Article 4.
Martimort, D., Stole, L. (2005). "Market participation under delegated and intrinsic common agency games". Working Paper.
Maskin, E., Riley, J. (1984). "Monopoly with incomplete information". RAND Journal of Economics 15, 171–196.
Matutes, C., Regibeau, P. (1988). "Mix and match: Product compatibility without network externalities". RAND Journal of Economics 19, 221–234.
Matutes, C., Regibeau, P. (1992). "Compatibility and bundling of complementary goods in a duopoly". Journal of Industrial Economics 40, 37–54.
McAfee, P., McMillan, J., Whinston, M. (1989). "Multiproduct monopoly, commodity bundling, and correlation of values". Quarterly Journal of Economics 104, 371–383.
McManus, B. (2004). "Nonlinear pricing in an oligopoly market: The case of specialty coffee". Working Paper. Olin School of Business, Washington University.
Mezzetti, C. (1997). "Common agency with horizontally differentiated principals". RAND Journal of Economics 28, 323–345.
Miravete, E. (1996). "Screening consumers through alternative pricing mechanisms". Journal of Regulatory Economics 9, 111–132.
Miravete, E., Röller, L.-H. (2003). "Competitive nonlinear pricing in duopoly equilibrium: The early U.S. cellular telephone industry". Working Paper.
Mussa, M., Rosen, S. (1978). "Monopoly and product quality". Journal of Economic Theory 18, 301–317.
Nahata, B., Ostaszewski, K., Sahoo, P. (1990). "Direction of price changes in third-degree price discrimination". American Economic Review 80, 1254–1258.
Nalebuff, B. (2004). "Bundling as an entry barrier". Quarterly Journal of Economics 119, 159–187.
Nevo, A., Wolfram, C. (2002). "Why do manufacturers issue coupons?: An empirical analysis of breakfast cereals". RAND Journal of Economics 33, 319–339.
Nilssen, T. (1992). "Two kinds of consumer switching costs". RAND Journal of Economics 23, 579–589.
Norman, G. (1981). "Spatial competition and spatial price discrimination". Review of Economic Studies 48, 97–111.
Oren, S., Smith, S., Wilson, R. (1983). "Competitive nonlinear tariffs". Journal of Economic Theory 29, 49–71.
Phlips, L. (1983). The Economics of Price Discrimination. Cambridge Univ. Press, Cambridge, UK.
Pigou, A.C. (1920). The Economics of Welfare. Macmillan, London.
Prescott, E. (1975). "Efficiency of the natural rate". Journal of Political Economy 83, 1229–1236.
Reisinger, M. (2003). "The effects of product bundling in duopoly". Working Paper.
Rey, P., Tirole, J. (2007). "A primer on foreclosure". In: Armstrong, M., Porter, R. (Eds.), Handbook of Industrial Organization, vol. 3. North-Holland, Amsterdam (this volume).
Robinson, J. (1933). "The Economics of Imperfect Competition". Macmillan, London.
Rochet, J.-C., Stole, L. (2002). "Nonlinear pricing with random participation". Review of Economic Studies 69, 277–311.
Rochet, J.-C., Stole, L. (2003). "The economics of multidimensional screening". In: Dewatripont, M., Hansen, L. (Eds.), Advances in Economics and Econometrics: Theory and Applications, Eighth World Congress, vol. 1. Cambridge Univ. Press.
Rosenthal, R. (1980). "A model in which an increase in the number of sellers leads to a higher price". Econometrica 48, 1575–1580.
Rossi, P., Allenby, G. (1993). "A Bayesian approach to estimating household parameters". Journal of Marketing Research 30, 171–182.
Rossi, P., McCulloch, R., Allenby, G. (1996). "The value of purchase history data in target marketing". Marketing Science 15, 321–340.
Salop, S. (1977). "The noisy monopolist: Imperfect information, price dispersion and price discrimination". Review of Economic Studies 44, 393–406.

Salop, S. (1979). "Monopolistic competition with outside goods". Bell Journal of Economics 10, 141–156.

Salop, S., Stiglitz, J. (1977). "Bargains and ripoffs: A model of monopolistically competitive price dispersion". Review of Economic Studies 44, 493–510.

Salop, S., Stiglitz, J. (1982). "A theory of sales: A simple model of equilibrium price dispersion with identical agents". American Economic Review 72 (5), 1121–1130.

Schmalensee, R. (1981). "Output and welfare effects of monopolistic third-degree price discrimination". American Economic Review 71, 242–247.

Schmalensee, R. (1984). "Gaussian demand and commodity bundling". Journal of Business 57, S211–S230.

Schmidt-Mohr, U., Villas-Boas, M. (1999). "Oligopoly with asymmetric information: Differentiation in credit markets". RAND Journal of Economics 30, 375–396.

Schwartz, M. (1990). "Third-degree price discrimination and output: Generalizing a welfare result". American Economic Review 80, 1259–1262.

Shaffer, G., Zhang, Z.J. (1995). "Competitive coupon targeting". Marketing Science 14, 395–416.

Shaffer, G., Zhang, Z.J. (2000). "Pay to switch or pay to stay: Preference-based price discrimination in markets with switching costs". Journal of Economics & Management Strategy 9, 397–424.

Shaked, A., Sutton, J. (1982). "Relaxing price competition through product differentiation". Review of Economic Studies 49 (1), 3–13.

Shaked, A., Sutton, J. (1983). "Natural oligopolies". Econometrica 51 (5), 1469–1484.

Shepard, A. (1991). "Price discrimination and retail configuration". Journal of Political Economy 99, 30–53.

Spence, M. (1976a). "Product differentiation and welfare". Papers and Proceedings of the American Economic Review 66, 407–414.

Spence, M. (1976b). "Product selection, fixed costs, and monopolistic competition". Review of Economic Studies 43, 217–235.

Spulber, D. (1979). "Noncooperative equilibrium with price discriminating firms". Economic Letters 4, 221–227.

Spulber, D. (1984). "Competition and multiplant monopoly with spatial nonlinear pricing". International Economic Review 25, 425–439.

Spulber, D. (1989). "Product variety and competitive discounts". Journal of Economic Theory 48, 510–525.

Stahl, D. (1989). "Oligopolistic pricing with sequential consumer search". American Economic Review 79, 700–712.

Stigler, G. (1963). "United States v. Loew's Inc.: A note on block-booking". The Supreme Court Review 1, 152–157.

Stigler, G. (1987). A Theory of Price. Macmillan, New York.

Stiglitz, J. (1989). "Imperfect information in the product market". In: Schmalensee, R., Willig, R.D. (Eds.), Handbook of Industrial Organization, vol. 1. North-Holland, Amsterdam, pp. 769–847. Distributed in the U.S. and Canada by Elsevier Science, New York.

Stole, L. (1991). "Mechanism design and common agency". Working Paper.

Stole, L. (1995). "Nonlinear pricing and oligopoly". Journal of Economics & Management Strategy 4, 529–562.

Taylor, C. (2003). "Supplier surfing: Competition and consumer behavior in subscription markets". RAND Journal of Economics 34, 223–246.

Thisse, J.-F., Vives, X. (1988). "On the strategic choice of spatial price policy". American Economic Review 78, 122–137.

Tirole, J. (1988). The Theory of Industrial Organization. MIT Press, Cambridge, MA.

Varian, H. (1980). "A model of sales". American Economic Review 70, 651–659.

Varian, H. (1985). "Price discrimination and social welfare". American Economic Review 75, 870–875.

Varian, H. (1989). "Price discrimination". In: Schmalensee, R., Willig, R.D. (Eds.), Handbook of Industrial Organization, vol. 1. North-Holland, Amsterdam, pp. 597–654. Distributed in the U.S. and Canada by Elsevier Science, New York.

Verboven, F. (1996). "International price discrimination in the European car market". RAND Journal of Economics 27, 240–268.

Verboven, F. (1999). "Product-line rivalry and market segmentation – With an application to automobile optional engine pricing". Journal of Industrial Economics 47, 399–426.
Villas-Boas, M. (1999). "Dynamic competition with customer recognition". RAND Journal of Economics 30, 604–631.
Ward, M. (2003). "Symposium: Competitive price discrimination (Editor's note)". Antitrust Law Journal 70, 593–598.
Whinston, M. (1990). "Tying, foreclosure, and exclusion". American Economic Review 80, 837–859.
Wilson, R. (1993). Nonlinear Pricing. Oxford Univ. Press, Oxford, UK.
Winter, R. (1997). "Colluding on relative prices". RAND Journal of Economics 28, 359–371.
Yoshida, Y. (2000). "Third-degree price discrimination in input markets: Output and welfare". American Economic Review 90, 240–246.

Chapter 35

MARKET STRUCTURE: THEORY AND EVIDENCE

JOHN SUTTON

London School of Economics

Contents

Handbook of Industrial Organization, Volume 3
Edited by M. Armstrong and R. Porter

DOI: 10.1016/S1573-448X(06)03035-4

Abstract

This chapter reviews the literature which has developed around the 'bounds approach' to market structure over the past fifteen years. The focus of this literature lies in explaining cross-industry differences in concentration, and in the size distribution of firms. One of the main ideas involved is that a study of these cross-industry differences offers a powerful way of uncovering the operation of some key competitive mechanisms.

Keywords

Oligopoly, Industrial structure, Manufacturing, Advertising, R&D, Size distribution, Endogenous sunk costs, Bounds approach

JEL classification: L13, L16, L60, M37

1. Introduction

Why are some industries dominated worldwide by a handful of firms? Why is the size distribution of firms within most industries highly skewed? Questions of this kind have attracted continued interest among economists for over half a century. One reason for this continuing interest in 'market structure' is that this is one of the few areas in economics where we encounter strong and sharp empirical regularities arising over a wide cross-section of industries. That such regularities appear in spite of the fact that every industry has many idiosyncratic features suggests that they are molded by some highly robust competitive mechanisms – and if this is so, then these would seem to be mechanisms that merit careful study. If ideas from the IO field are to have relevance in other areas of economics, such as International Trade or Growth Theory, that relevance is likely to derive from mechanisms of this robust kind. Once we ask, "what effect will this or that policy have on the economy as a whole?", the only kind of mechanisms that are of interest are those that operate with some regularity across the general run of markets.

The recent literature identifies two mechanisms of this 'robust' kind. The first of these links the nature of price competition in an industry to the level of market concentration. It tells us, for example, how a change in the rules of competition policy will affect concentration: if we make anti-cartel rules tougher, for example, concentration will tend to be higher. (A rather paradoxical result from a traditional perspective, but one that is quite central to the class of 'free entry' models that form the basis of the modern literature.)

The second mechanism relates most obviously to those industries in which R&D or Advertising play a significant role, though its range of application extends to any industry in which it is possible for a firm, by incurring additional fixed and sunk costs (as opposed to variable costs), to raise consumers' willingness-to-pay for its products, or to cut its unit variable cost of production. This mechanism places a limit on the degree to which a fragmented (i.e. low concentration) structure can be maintained in the industry: if all firms are small, relative to the size of the market, then it will be profitable for one (or more) firm(s) to deviate by raising their fixed (and sunk) outlays, thus breaking the original 'fragmented' configuration.

In what sense can these mechanisms be said to be 'robust'? Why should we give them pride of place over the many mechanisms that have been explored in this area? These questions bring us to a central controversy.

1.1. The bounds approach

The first volumes of the *Handbook of Industrial Organization*, which appeared in 1989, summed up the research of the preceding decade in game-theoretic IO. In doing so, they provided the raw materials for a fundamental and far-reaching critique of this research program. In his review of those volumes in the *Journal of Political Economy*, Sam Peltzman pointed to what had already been noted as the fundamental weakness of the project [Shaked and Sutton (1987), Fisher (1989), Pelzman (1991)]: the large majority of the results reported in the game-theoretic literature were highly sensitive to certain more or less arbitrary features of the models chosen by researchers.

Some researchers have chosen to interpret this problem as a shortcoming of game-theoretic methods per se, but this is to miss the point. What has been exposed here is a deeper difficulty: many outcomes that we see in economic data are driven by a number of factors, some of which are inherently difficult to measure, proxy or control for in empirical work. This is the real problem, and it arises whether we choose to model the markets in question using game-theoretic models or otherwise [Sutton (2001c)]. Some economic models hide this problem by ignoring the troublesome 'unobservables'; it is a feature of the current generation of game-theoretic models that they highlight rather than obscure this difficulty. They do this simply because they offer researchers an unusually rich menu of alternative model specifications within a simple common framework. If, for example, we aim to model entry processes, we are free to adopt a 'simultaneous entry' or 'sequential entry' representation; if we want to examine post-entry competition, we can represent it using a Bertrand (Nash equilibrium in prices) model, or a Cournot (Nash equilibrium in quantities) model, and so on. But when carrying out empirical work, and particularly when using data drawn from a cross-section of different industries, we have no way of measuring, proxying, or controlling for distinctions of this kind. When we push matters a little further, the difficulties multiply: were we to try to defend any particular specification in modeling the entry process, we would, in writing down the corresponding game-theoretic model, be forced to take a view (explicitly or implicitly) as to the way in which each firm's decision was or was not conditioned on the decisions of each rival firm. While we might occasionally have enough information about some particular industry to allow us to develop a convincing case for some model specification, it would be a hopeless task to try to carry this through for a dataset which encompassed a broad run of industries. What, then, can we hope to achieve in terms of finding theories that have empirical content? Is it the case that this class of models is empirically empty, in the sense that any pattern that we see in the data can be rationalized by appealing to some particular 'model specification'?

Two responses to this issue have emerged during the past decade. The first, which began to attract attention with the publication of the *Journal of Industrial Economics* Symposium of 1987, was initially labeled 'single industry studies', though the alternative term 'structural estimation' is currently more popular. Here, the idea is to focus on the modeling of a single market, about which a high degree of information is available, and to 'customize' the form of the model in order to get it to represent as closely as possible the market under investigation. A second line of attack, *which is complementary to* (rather than an alternative to) the 'single industry approach',[2] is offered by the bounds approach developed in Sutton (1991, 1998), following an idea introduced in Shaked and Sutton (1987). Here, the aim is to build the theory in such a way as to focus attention

[2] On the complementarity between these two approaches, see Sutton (1997a).

on those predictions which are robust across a range of model specifications which are deemed 'reasonable', in the sense that we cannot discriminate a priori in favor of one rather than another on empirical grounds (Sutton, 2000).

A radical feature of this approach is that it involves a departure from the standard notion of a 'fully specified model', which pins down a (unique) equilibrium outcome. Different members of the set of admissible models will generate different equilibrium outcomes, and the aim in this approach is to specify *bounds* on the set of observable outcomes: in the space of outcomes, the theory specifies a *region*, rather than a point. The question of interest here, is whether the specification of such bounds will suffice to generate informative and substantial restrictions that can be tested empirically; in what follows, it is shown that these results: (i) replicate certain empirically known relations that were familiar to authors in the pre-game theory literature; (ii) sharpen and re-specify such relations; and (iii) lead to new, more detailed empirical predictions on relationships that were not anticipated in the earlier literature.

1.2. Scope and content

The literature on market structure is extensive, and the present chapter does not offer a comprehensive overview. Rather, it focuses heavily on two leading strands in the literature, in which it has proved possible to bring together a robust theoretical analysis with sharp empirical tests. The first of these relates to the cross-industry studies pioneered by Bain (1956) which lie at the heart of the structure–conduct–performance tradition (Section 2). The second relates to the size distribution of firms, first studied by Gibrat (1931) (Section 3). In Section 4, we look at the area of market dynamics, where it has proved much more difficult to arrive at theoretical predictions of a robust kind, but where a substantial number of interesting empirical regularities pose a continuing challenge for researchers.

Two notable literatures that lie beyond the scope of this review are the Schumpeterian literature, and the organizational ecology literature. On the (close) relations between the bounds approach and the Schumpeterian literature, see Sutton (1998, pp. 29–31) and Marsili (2001). A good overview of current work in the organizational ecology literature will be found in Carroll and Hannan (2000). Critiques of the bounds approach will be found in Bresnahan (1992), Schmalensee (1992) and Scherer (2000).

2. The cross-industry literature

2.1. Background: the Bain tradition

The structure–conduct–performance paradigm, which began with Bain (1956), rested on two ideas. The first idea involved a one-way chain of causation that ran from structure (concentration) to conduct (the pricing behavior of firms) to performance (profitability).

High concentration, it was argued, facilitated collusion and led to high profits. To explain why these high profits were not eroded by entry, the second idea came into play: it was argued that high levels of concentration could be traced to the presence of certain 'barriers to entry'.

In Bain's 1956 book, these barriers were associated with the presence of scale economies in production, a factor that can be taken as an exogenous property of the available technology. Attempts to account for observed levels of concentration by reference to this factor alone, however, were clearly inadequate: many industries, such as the soft drinks industry, have low levels of scale economies in production, but have high levels of concentration. This prompted a widening of the list of candidate 'barriers' to include inter alia levels of advertising and R&D spending. The problem that arises here, is that these levels of spending are not exogenous to the firms, but are the outcomes of the firms' choices. It is appropriate, therefore, to model these levels as being determined jointly with the level of concentration as part of an equilibrium outcome; this is a central feature of the modern game-theoretic literature. To appeal to observed levels of advertising or R&D as an 'explanation' for high concentration levels is a mistake.

The central thrust of the structure–conduct–performance literature lay in relating the level of concentration to the level of profitability (profits/fixed assets, say) across different industries. Here, it is necessary to distinguish two claims.

The first relates to the way in which a fall in concentration, due for example to the entry of additional firms to the market, affects the level of prices and so of price–cost margins. Here, matters are uncontroversial; that a fall in concentration will lead to a fall in prices and price–cost margins is well supported both theoretically and empirically. [While theoretical counter-examples can be constructed, they are of a rather contrived kind; see Rosenthal (1980).] To test this idea it is appropriate to look at a number of markets for the same product, which differ in size (the number of consumers), so that larger markets support more sellers. It can then be checked whether prices and so price–cost margins are lower in those larger markets which support more sellers. The key body of evidence is that presented in the collection of papers edited by Weiss (1989). For a comprehensive list of relevant studies, see Schmalensee (1989, p. 987).

A second, quite different (and highly controversial) claim relates to the net profit of firms (gross profit minus the investment costs incurred in earlier stages), or their rates of return on fixed assets. In the 'free entry' models used in modern game-theoretic literature, entry will occur up to the point where the gross profits of the marginal entrant are just exhausted by its investment outlay. In the special setting where all firms are identical in their cost structure and in their product specifications, the net profit of each firm will be (approximately)[3] zero, whatever the level of concentration. This symmetric setup provides a useful point of reference, while suggesting a number of channels through which some relationship might appear between concentration and profitability. [For a discussion on this issue see Sutton (2001c); on the current dubious status of this

[3] I.e. up to an integer effect, which may in practice be substantial [Edwards and Starr (1987)].

concentration/profitability relationship, see Schmalensee's contribution to volume II of this Handbook Schmalensee (1989).]

A separate strand of this early literature focused in explaining concentration by reference to the 'barriers' just mentioned. Notwithstanding the objections noted above, it is of interest that regressions of this kind generated one rather robust statistical regularity, and one long-standing puzzle.

The statistical regularity is one that appears in cross-industry regressions between concentration, and a series of explanatory variables that include: (i) some measure of scale economies relative to market size (usually the cost of a single plant of 'minimum efficient scale' – the 'set-up cost' – divided by total industry sales revenue), and (ii) a measure of advertising intensity (usually the ratio of total industry advertising to industry sales revenue). Regressions of this kind suggest a clear positive relation in respect of setup costs/market size, and a rather weak positive relation in respect of the advertising–sales ratio [Sutton (1991, p. 124)]. One of the implications of the models considered below is that these relations should indeed be observed in such a (misspecified) regression [Sutton (1991, pp. 127–128)]. The puzzle that appears in regard to such regressions relates to the results obtained when the industry-wide R&D/sales ratio is included as an additional explanatory variable; typically, it turns out to be uncorrelated with concentration. A large literature developed during the 1970s and '80s in which concentration was regressed on the R&D/sales ratio (without including such additional factors as the ratio of setup costs to market size, or the advertising/sales ratio). This literature generated no generally agreed conclusions; in volume II of this Handbook, Cohen and Levin (1989, p. 1075) note that most papers on the question report a positive relation, though some find a negative relation, and others argue for a non-monotonic relation.[4] Results change substantially when industry-specific effects are controlled for, but there is no general agreement on what kind of control variables are appropriate though many authors favor including some index of "technological opportunity". Most tellingly, once such control variables are included, the partial correlation between R&D intensity and concentration is extremely weak. The authors cite the example of Scott's (1984) study, which found that "line of business concentration and its square explained only 1.5 percent of the variance in R&D intensity across 3388 business units, whereas two-digit industry effects explained 32 percent of this variance". This suggests that the cloud of observations on which such regressions are being run is so diffuse as to cast doubt on the usefulness of the exercise.

One of the central themes in what follows relates to a simple resolution of this issue, following Sutton (1998). It is argued that there are two problems with the idea of examining simple correlations between R&D and concentration: (a) it is vital to control for the fact that some markets, as conventionally defined in this literature, are single well-defined markets in the economic sense, while others are more complex, incorporating

[4] This claim should be distinguished from the claim for a U-shaped relation (across firms rather than industries) between R&D intensity and an index of the intensity of competition based on price–cost margins, posited by Aghion et al. (2005), as shown in their Figure 1.

various clusters of substitute goods ['competing groups' in Caves's (1986) terminology], and this must be controlled for, and (b) there are many further factors that impinge on the relationship between R&D and concentration, some of which are difficult to control for, so that the appropriate specification is a 'bounds' relationship rather than a conventional regression relationship. Once these two issues are addressed, a clear and straightforward picture emerges (Section 2.6).[5]

2.2. Some preliminary examples

The analysis developed below is based on multi-stage game models of a standard kind; before turning to formalities, we begin with a few elementary examples. The simplest setup involves a two-stage game of the following form. There are N_0 ($\geqslant 2$) firms. At stage 1, each firm chooses an action 'enter' or 'don't enter'. A firm choosing not to enter receives a payoff (profit) of zero. At stage 2, all those firms who have entered compete for consumers.[6] The firms offer a homogeneous product, which is produced by all firms at the same constant level of marginal cost $c \geqslant 0$. The payoff of a firm is given by the profit earned in stage 2, minus a sunk cost $\varepsilon > 0$ associated with the firm's entry at stage 1.

To complete the specification of the model, we model demand for the product by assuming that all consumers have a utility function of the (Cobb–Douglas) form,

$$U = x^{\delta} z^{1-\delta}$$

defined over two goods, the good x that is the focus of our analysis, and some outside good z. It follows from the form of the utility function that consumers spend a constant fraction δ of their incomes on good x, independently of the price of x. To avoid technical problems in the case where only one firm enters, assume that some 'imported' good is available at some (high) price p_0 that is a perfect substitute for x, so that consumers make no purchases of x if $p > p_0$. The price p_0 now serves as a monopoly price in the model.

Now denote total consumer expenditure on x as S, where S serves as a measure of the size of the market. We can now write the market demand schedule as

$$X = S/p,$$

where p denotes market price and $X \equiv \sum x_j$ is the total quantity sold by all firms.

We characterize equilibrium as a perfect Nash equilibrium of the two-stage game. Taking as given the number N of firms who have entered at stage 1, we solve for a (symmetric) Nash equilibrium in quantities at stage 2 (Cournot equilibrium). A routine

[5] For an alternative view that proposes the degree of appropriability of R&D returns as the relevant 'missing variable'; see Lee (2005).

[6] Thus a strategy takes two forms: either 'don't enter', or 'enter; and choose an action in the second stage as a function of the decisions taken by firms at the first stage (in effect, as a function of the number of entrants)'.

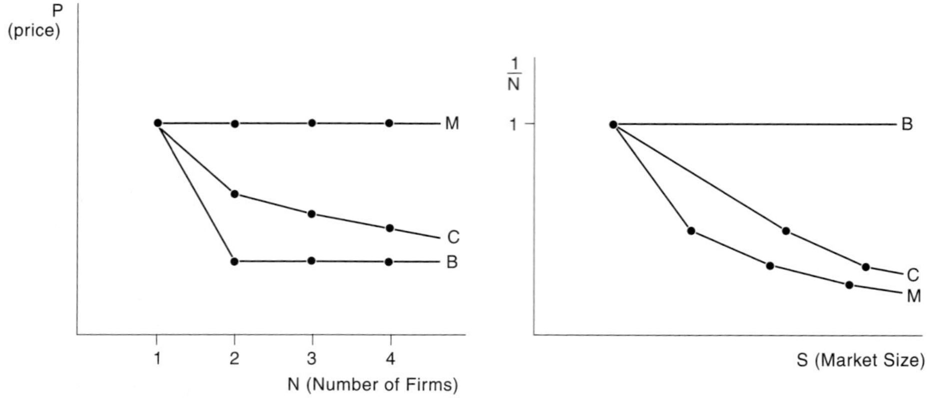

Figure 35.1. Equilibrium price as a function of the number of entrants, N, and equilibrium concentration ($1/N$) as a function of market size, for three simple examples (B = Bertrand, C = Cournot, M = joint profit maximization).

calculation leads to the familiar result that, at equilibrium, price falls to marginal cost as N rises. (Figure 35.1, left panel, schedule C; the calculation is set out in Appendix A.) The equilibrium profit of firm i in the second stage subgame is given by S/N^2. Equating this to the entry fee $\varepsilon > 0$ incurred at stage 1, we obtain the equilibrium number of entrants as the largest integer satisfying the condition $S/N^2 \geqslant \varepsilon$. As S increases, the equilibrium number of firms rises, while the 1-firm concentration ratio $C_1 = 1/N$ falls monotonically to zero (Figure 35.1). It is also worth noting that output per firm rises with S, and that the number of firms rises less than proportionally with S; these observations are central to the literature on 'market size and firm numbers' (see below, footnote 17).

Now consider an alternative version of this model, in which we replace the 'Cournot' game by a Bertrand (Nash equilibrium in prices) model at stage 2. Here, once two or more firms are present, equilibrium involves at least two firms setting $p = c$, and all firms earn zero profit at equilibrium. Here, for any size of market S that suffices to support at least one entrant, the only (pure strategy) equilibrium for the game as a whole involves exactly one firm entering, and setting the monopoly price (Figure 35.1, schedule B).[7]

Finally consider a third variant of the model, in which we replace our representation of the second stage subgame by one in which all firms set the monopoly price.[8] Now, for any number N of firms entering at stage 1, we have that price equals p_0, and each firm receives a fraction $1/N$ of monopoly profit; the number of entrants N is the number which equates this to ε, as before (Figure 35.1, schedule M).

[7] Mixed strategy equilibria are discussed in Section 3.

[8] This can be formalized by replacing stage 2 by an infinite horizon stage game, and invoking the basic 'Folk theorem' result [see, for example, Tirole (1990)].

Figure 35.2. Alternative equilibria in a Hotelling-type model of horizontal production differentiation.

The results illustrated in Figure 35.1 serve to introduce an important result. We can interpret a move from the monopoly model to the Cournot model, and then to the Bertrand model, as an increase in the 'toughness of price competition', where this phrase refers to the functional relationship between market structure, here represented by the 1-firm concentration ratio $C_1 = 1/N$, and equilibrium price.[9] An increase in the toughness of price competition (represented by a downward shift in the function $p(N)$ in the first panel of Figure 35.2), implies that for any given level of market size, the equilibrium level of concentration $C_1 = 1/N$ is now higher (Figure 35.2, second panel). This result turns out to be quite robust, and it will emerge as one of the empirically testable predictions of the theory in what follows (Section 2.4).

All the cases considered so far have involved firms that produce a homogeneous product. We may extend the analysis by considering products that are ('horizontally') differentiated, either by geographic location, or by way of product characteristics that cause some consumers to prefer one variety, while others prefer a different variety, their prices being equal. When we do this, a new feature appears, since models of this kind tend to exhibit multiple equilibria. For any given market size, we will in general have a set of equilibrium outcomes; the case in which N firms each offer a single variety arises as one possible outcome, but there will usually be additional equilibria in which a smaller number of firms each offers some set of products.

The simplest way to see this point is by thinking in terms of the classic Hotelling model, in which products are differentiated by their locations along a line [Figure 35.2; see Sutton (1991, pp. 38–39)]. Imagine a 'single product firm' equilibrium in which firms occupy a set of discrete locations A, B, C, D, E, etc. We can construct, for example, a new equilibrium in which every second location is occupied by a single ('multiproduct') firm. There will now be an equilibrium in which prices are the same as before. This firm's profit function is additively separable, into functions which represent the separate contributions from each of its products, and the first-order condition for profit maximization coincides with the set of first-order conditions for the firms owning products A, C, E, etc. in the original setup. If the original 'single-product firm' configuration constituted an equilibrium of the two-stage game, so too will this 'high concentration' configuration in which our multi-product firm owns every second product.

[9] This phrase refers, therefore, to the 'form of price competition' which is taken as an exogenously given characteristic of the market. It will depend on such background features of the market as the cost of transport of goods, and on such institutional features as the presence or absence of anti-trust laws. [On the determinants of the 'toughness of price competition' see Sutton (1991, ch. 6).] In particular, it does not refer to the equilibrium level of prices, or margins, which, within the two-stage game, is an endogenous outcome. For a novel application of this concept, see Raith (2003).

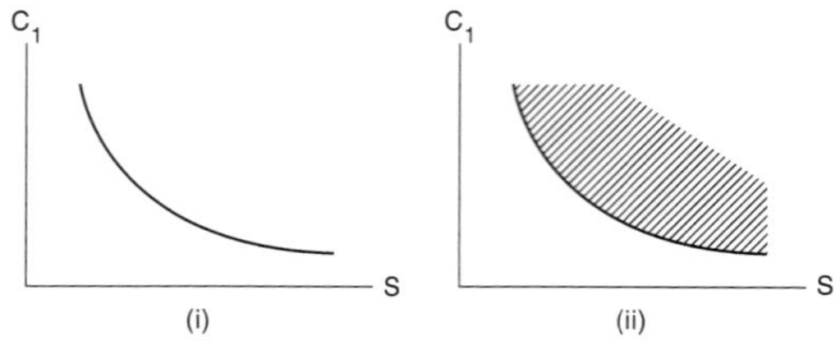

Figure 35.3. The relation between market size S and concentration C_1, in (i) a homogeneous goods model, and (ii) a model of horizontal product differentiation. In the latter case, the only restriction that we can place on the concentration–size relationship is a 'bounds' relationship.

Now in this setting, the functional relationship between concentration and market size, illustrated in Figure 35.1, must be replaced by a lower bound relationship. The lower bound is traced out by a sequence of 'single product firm' equilibria; but there are additional equilibria lying above the bound (Figure 35.3).[10]

This Hotelling example illustrates a general problem in relation to modeling the final-stage subgame. Here we face two questions: (a) what is the best way to represent price competition (à la Cournot, à la Bertrand, or otherwise)? (b) if products are differentiated, are they best modeled by means of a Hotelling model, or a non-locational model that treats all varieties in a symmetric fashion,[11] or otherwise? This is the first problem that motivates the introduction of a Bounds approach.

A second problem that strengthens the case for such an approach relates to the form of the entry process. In the above examples, we have confined attention to the case of 'simultaneous entry'. If we replace this by a 'sequential entry' model, the (set of) equilibrium outcomes will in general be different. For example, in the setting of (horizontal) product differentiation, there may (or may not) be a tendency in favor of 'more concentrated' equilibria, in which the first mover 'pre-empts' rivals by introducing several varieties [Schmalensee (1978); for an extended example, see Sutton (1998, ch. 2 and Appendix 2.1.2)].

The main burden of the analysis developed in the next section is concerned with framing a theory that gets around these two sources of difficulty. Before proceeding to a general treatment, however, there is one final example that is worth introducing.

[10] One comment sometimes made about this setup is that we might hope, by introducing a 'richer' model specification, or by appealing to characteristics of individual firms, to arrive at a model that led to some particular (i.e. unique) equilibrium. However, to justify any specific model of this kind – since many such models might be devised – we would need to appeal to information about the market and the firms that we would be unlikely to have access to, at least in a cross-industry study. Thus we are led back once again to the problem of 'unobservables'.

[11] Examples of such 'symmetric' models include the models of Dixit and Stiglitz (1977), and the 'linear demand model' discussed in Shubik and Levitan (1980), Deneckere and Davidson (1985), Shaked and Sutton (1987) and, in a Cournot version, in Sutton (1998).

2.2.1. A quality choice model

A key feature that has not arisen in the examples considered so far relates to the possibility that firms might choose to incur (additional) fixed and sunk costs at stage 1 with a view to improving their competitive positions in the final-stage subgame. This kind of expenditure would include, for example, outlays on R&D designed to enhance the quality, or technical characteristics, of firms' products; it would include advertising outlays that improve the 'brand-image' of the product; and it would include cost-reducing 'product innovation' in which R&D efforts are directed towards the discovery of improved production methods.

We can illustrate this kind of situation by extending the simple Cournot model introduced above, as follows. Suppose all consumers have the same utility function of the form

$$U = (ux)^{\delta} z^{1-\delta}$$

defined over two goods, where u represents an index of perceived quality for good x. Increases in u enhance the marginal utility derived from this good. We will refer to this first good x as the "quality" good, in order to distinguish it from the "outside" good, z.

Rival firms are assumed to offer single goods of various qualities. Let u_i and p_i denote the quality and price respectively of firm i's offering. Then, the consumer's decision problem can be represented as follows: given the set of qualities and prices offered, it is easy to show that the consumer chooses a product that maximizes the quality–price ratio u_i/p_i; and the consumer spends fraction δ of his or her income on this chosen quality good, and fraction $(1-\delta)$ on the outside good. Total expenditure on the quality goods is therefore independent of their levels of prices and perceived qualities and equals a fraction δ of total consumer income. Denote this level of total expenditure on quality goods by S.

The first step in the analysis involves looking at the final stage of the game. Here, the qualities are taken as given (having been chosen by firms at the preceding stage). Equilibrium in the final stage of the game is characterized as a Nash equilibrium in quantities (Cournot equilibrium). A feature of this equilibrium is that, since each consumer chooses the good that maximizes u_i/p_i, the prices of all those products enjoying positive sales at equilibrium must be proportional to their perceived qualities, that is, $u_i/p_i = u_j/p_j$ for all i, j.

The calculations are set out in Appendix B; here, we summarize the relevant properties of the solution. In the final stage subgame, some number of products survive with positive sales revenue; it may be the case that products with qualities below a certain level have an output level of zero, and so profits of zero, at equilibrium. Denoting by N the number of firms that enjoy positive sales ('survive') at equilibrium, the final stage profit of firm i is given by

$$\left\{1 - \frac{N-1}{u_i} \frac{1}{\sum(1/u_j)}\right\}^2 \cdot S. \tag{2.1}$$

Associated with this equilibrium is a threshold level of quality $\underline{u}$; all 'surviving' products have $u_i > \underline{u}$ and all products with $u_j \leqslant \underline{u}$ have an output of zero at equilibrium. The sum in the above expression is taken over all 'surviving' products, and N represents the number of such products. The threshold $\underline{u}$ is defined by adding a hypothetical $(N+1)$th product to the N surviving products, and equating the profit of good $N+1$ to zero, viz. $\underline{u} = u_{N+1}$ is implicitly defined by[12]

$$\frac{1}{\underline{u}} = \frac{1}{u_{N+1}} = \frac{1}{N}\sum_{1}^{N+1}\frac{1}{u_j} \quad \text{or equivalently} \quad \frac{1}{\underline{u}} = \frac{1}{N-1}\sum_{1}^{N}\frac{1}{u_j}.$$

Now consider a 3-stage game in which each of the N_0 potential entrants decides, at stage 1, to enter or not enter, at cost $F_0 > 0$. At stage 2, the N firms that have entered choose a quality level, and in so doing incur additional fixed and sunk costs. Denote by $F(u)$ the total fixed and sunk cost incurred by an entrant that offers quality u, where u lies in the range $[1, \infty)$ and

$$F(u) = F_0 u^\beta, \quad u \geqslant 1.$$

Thus the minimum outlay incurred by an entrant equals F_0 (>0).

Given the qualities chosen at stage 2, all firms now compete à la Cournot in stage 3, their gross profit being defined as above. A firm's payoff equals its net profit (gross profit minus the fixed and sunk outlays incurred).

A full analysis of this model will be found in Sutton (1991, ch. 3). Here, we remark on the key feature of the relationship between market size and concentration. At equilibrium, N firms enter and produce a common quality level u. For small S, the level chosen is the minimum level $u = 1$, and the size–structure relation mimics that of the basic Cournot model. But once a certain critical value of S is reached, the returns to incurring fixed outlays on quality improvement rise, and the level of u rises thereafter with S. The number of firms N, on the other hand, remains constant: the 'convergence' effect, whereby the (lower bound to the level of) concentration falls to zero as $S \to \infty$, breaks down. Increases in market size are no longer associated with a rise in the number of firms; rather, the expenditures incurred by each firm rise, while the number of firms remains unchanged (Figure 35.4).[13] It is this breakdown of the convergence property that will form the central theme of Section 3.

[12] The number of products that survive can be computed recursively by labeling the products in descending order of quality, so that $u_1 \geqslant u_2 \geqslant u_3 \geqslant \cdots$ and considering successive candidate sets of surviving products of the form $(u_1, u_2, \ldots, u_k)$. For each such set there is a corresponding value of $\underline{u}$; the set of surviving products is the smallest set such that the first excluded product has a quality level $u_{k+1} < \underline{u}$.

[13] Chapter 3 of Sutton (1991) analyses a wider range of cost functions of the form $a + bu^\beta$, which illustrate a number of different forms that the concentration–size relationship can take. Here, I have confined attention to the simplest case, in order to provide a preliminary illustration of the 'non-convergence' result. The only new feature arising when we move to this wider set of cost functions is that the right-hand segment of the lower bound need not be flat; it may rise or fall towards its asymptotic level (which depends on β alone and not on F_0).

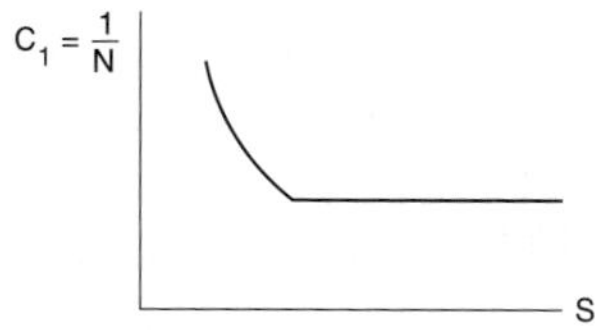

Figure 35.4. Market size and the (one-firm) concentration ratio in the 'quality competition' example.

2.2.2. *A limiting case*

An interesting 'limiting case' of this example is obtained by letting $\beta \to \infty$. Here, the effectiveness of fixed outlays in raising product quality is arbitrarily low. In the limit, such spending has no effect, and the optimal choice for all firms is to set $u = 1$, its threshold value. Here, the equilibrium collapses to that of the simple Cournot example considered earlier, in which firms paid an exogenously given entry fee, here equal to F_0, to enter. It is natural from the point of view of the theory to interpret the 'exogenous sunk cost' model considered above as a limiting case arising within the general ('endogenous sunk cost') model.

2.2.3. *Extensions*

The idea embodied in the 'quality competition' example is more general than might appear to be the case at first sight. The key idea lies in the notion that a firm can increase its gross (i.e. final stage) profit by incurring additional fixed and sunk costs at stage 1. This idea carries over immediately to a setting in which firms offer a homogeneous product, and where each firm can reduce its unit cost of production at stage 2 by incurring additional fixed outlays at stage 1 ['process innovation'; see Dasgupta and Stiglitz (1980), and Sutton (1998, ch. 14)].

More generally, we may combine both these channels in a single model, by characterizing each firm by a pair of numbers (c_i, u_i) denoting its unit cost of production, and its 'perceived quality', which we can label as the firm's 'capability' in some particular market. We can then model firms as 'competing in capabilities' [Sutton (2001b)].

Finally, these ideas can be extended in a straightforward way to the analysis of 'learning by doing' and 'network externalities', as discussed in Section 4 below.

2.3. *A theoretical framework*

In this section, we move to a general treatment. We specify a suitable class of multistage games, and consider a setting in which the fixed and sunk investments that firms make are associated with their entering of products into some abstract 'space of products'. This setup is general enough to encompass many models used in the literature. For example, in a Hotelling model of product differentiation, the (set of) action(s) taken by a firm would be described by a set of points in the interval [0, 1], describing the location of its products in (geographic) space. In the 'quality choice' model considered above, the action of firm i would be to choose a quality level $u_i \geqslant 1$. In the model of 'competing in capabilities', the firm's action would be to choose a pair of numbers (u_i, c_i) and so on (Sutton, 2001a).

2.3.1. A class of stage-games

We are concerned with a class of games that share the following structure: There are N_0 players (firms). Firms take actions at certain specified stages. An action involves occupying some subset, possibly empty, of "locations" in some abstract "space of locations", which we label A. At the end of the game, each firm will occupy some set of locations.

The notation is as follows: a location is an element of the set of locations A. The set of locations occupied by firm i at the end of the game is denoted $\mathbf{a}_i$, where $\mathbf{a}_i$ is a subset of A viz. $\mathbf{a}_i \subset A$. If firm i has not entered at any location then $\mathbf{a}_i$ is the empty set, i.e. $\mathbf{a}_i = \emptyset$. Associated with any set of locations is a fixed and sunk cost incurred in entering at these locations. This cost is strictly positive and bounded away from zero, namely, for any $\mathbf{a}_i \neq \emptyset$, $F(\mathbf{a}_i) \geqslant F_0 > 0$. The outcome of the game is described by an N_0-tuple of all locations occupied by all firms at the end of the game. Some of the entries in this N_0-tuple may be null, corresponding to firms who have not entered the market. In what follows, we are concerned with those outcomes in which at least one firm has entered the market and are interested in looking at the locations occupied by the firms who have entered (the "active" firms). With that in mind, we label the number of active firms as N ($\geqslant$1), and we construct an N-tuple by deleting all the null entries, and re-labeling the remaining firms from 1 to N. The N-tuple constructed in this way is written as $(\mathbf{a}_i) = (\mathbf{a}_1, \mathbf{a}_2, \ldots, \mathbf{a}_n)$ and is referred to as a "configuration".

The payoff (profit) of firm i, if it occupies locations $\mathbf{a}_i$, is written

$$\Pi\big(\mathbf{a}_i \mid (\mathbf{a}_{-i})\big) - \mathbf{F}(\mathbf{a}_i),$$

where $(\mathbf{a}_{-i})$ denotes $(\mathbf{a}_1, \ldots, \mathbf{a}_{i-1}, \mathbf{a}_{i+1}, \ldots, \mathbf{a}_N)$. The function, $\Pi(\mathbf{a}_i \mid (\mathbf{a}_{-i}))$ which is non-negative everywhere, is obtained by calculating firms' equilibrium profits in some final stage subgame (which we refer to as the "price competition subgame"), in which the $\mathbf{a}_i$ enter as parameters in the firms' payoff functions. It is defined over the set of all configurations. The second argument of the profit function is an $(N-1)$-tuple $(\mathbf{a}_{-i})$, which specifies the sets of locations occupied by each of the firm's rivals. Thus, for example, if we want to specify the profit that would be earned by a new entrant occupying a set of locations $\mathbf{a}_{N+1}$, given some configuration $\mathbf{a}$ that describes the locations of firms already active in the market, we will write this as $\Pi(\mathbf{a}_{N+1} \mid \mathbf{a})$. If, for example, only one firm has entered, then $(\mathbf{a}_{-i})$ is empty, and the profit of the sole entrant is written as $\Pi(\mathbf{a}_1 \mid \emptyset)$, where $\mathbf{a}_1$ is the set of locations that it occupies. A firm taking no action at any stage incurs zero cost and receives payoff zero. In writing the profit function $\Pi(\cdot)$ and the fixed cost function $F(\cdot)$ without subscripts, we have assumed that all firms face the same profit and cost conditions, i.e. a firm's payoff depends only on its actions, and those of its rivals; there are no 'firm-specific' effects. (Since our focus is on looking at a lower bound to concentration, it is natural to treat firms as symmetric; asymmetries between firms (i.e. firm-specific effects) will tend to lead to levels of concentration that are above the bound we specify here.)

We are interested in examining the set of configurations that satisfy certain conditions. These conditions will be defined in a way that does not depend upon the order of the entries in **a**. Two configurations that differ only in the order of their elements are equivalent, in the sense that each one satisfies the conditions if and only if the other does.

2.3.2. Assumptions

We introduce two assumptions on the games to be considered. The first assumption relates to the payoff function Π of the final-stage subgame, on which it imposes two restrictions. Restriction (i) excludes 'non-viable' markets in which no product can cover its entry cost. Restriction (ii) ensures that the number of potential entrants N_0 is large. (The role of this assumption is to ensure that, at equilibrium, we will have at least one inactive player, so that $N < N_0$.) Denote the configuration in which no firm enters as $\emptyset$.

ASSUMPTION 1. (i) There is some set of locations $\mathbf{a}_0$ such that

$$\Pi(\mathbf{a}_0 \mid \emptyset) > F(\mathbf{a}_0).$$

(ii) The sum of final stage payoffs received by all agents is bounded above by $(N_0 - 1)F_0$, where N_0 denotes the number of players and F_0 is the minimum setup cost (entry fee).

The second assumption relates to the rules specifying the stages at which firms may enter and/or make investments:

ASSUMPTION 2 (extensive form). We associate with each firm i an integer t_i (its date of 'arrival'). Firm i is free to enter any subset of the set of products A at any stage t, such that $t_i \leqslant t \leqslant T$.

This assumption excludes a rather paradoxical feature that may arise in some basic 'sequential entry' models, where a firm would prefer, if allowed, to switch its place in the entry sequence for a later position [Eaton and Ware (1987)]. In practice, firms are always free to delay their entry; this assumption avoids this anomalous case by requiring that a firm arriving in the market at stage t is free to make investments at stage t and/or at any subsequent stage, up to some final stage T (we exclude infinite horizon games).[14,15]

2.3.3. Equilibrium configurations

The aim of the present exercise is to generate results that do not depend on (a) the details of the way we design the final-stage subgame, or (b) the form of the entry process. To handle (a), we work directly in terms of the 'solved-out profit function' of the final-stage subgame, introduced as our profit function $\Pi(\cdot)$ above. To deal with (b), the entry process, we introduce an equilibrium concept that is defined, not in the space of strategies (which can only be specified in the context of some particular entry process), but in the space of outcomes, or – more precisely – configurations. The key idea here is this: the set of 'equilibrium configurations' defined below includes all outcomes that can be supported as a (pure strategy, perfect) Nash equilibrium in any game of the class defined by Assumptions 1 and 2 above. In what follows, we develop results which show that certain ('fragmented') market structures cannot be supported as equilibrium configurations – and so they cannot be supported as (pure strategy, perfect) Nash equilibria, irrespective of the details of the entry process.

Now there are two obvious properties that must be satisfied by any pure strategy, perfect Nash equilibrium within this class of models. In what follows, we define the set of all outcomes satisfying these two properties, as follows:

DEFINITION. The N-tuple $\mathbf{a}$ is an *equilibrium configuration* if:

(i) Viability[16]: For all firms i,

$$\Pi\big(\mathbf{a}_i \mid (\mathbf{a}_{-i})\big) - F(\mathbf{a}_i) \geqslant 0;$$

(ii) Stability: There is no set of actions $\mathbf{a}_{N+1}$ such that entry is profitable, viz. for all sets of actions $\mathbf{a}_{N+1}$,

$$\Pi(\mathbf{a}_{\mathrm{N}+1} \mid \mathbf{a}) - F(\mathbf{a}_{N+1}) \leqslant 0.$$

[14] The intuition underlying this assumption is worth noting: it says that *any* firm can enter any set of products at stage T of the game, taking as given all products entered by itself and its rivals at earlier stages. It is important to note that the actions involved here are ones that involve firms' incurring sunk costs (irreversible investments). This should be distinguished from the notion used in the 'contestability' literature, where an entrant is allowed to take incumbents' current *prices* as given [Baumol, Panzar and Willig (1982)]. This is not assumed here; price competition is modeled by reference to some weak restrictions on the solved-out profit function for the final stage subgame.

[15] The question of whether the results obtained in this multistage game setting will hold good in a dynamic game setting, in which there is no 'final' stage after which no further investments occur, is considered is Section 6.

[16] It is worth noting that the viability condition has been stated in a form appropriate to the 'complete information' context in which we are working here, where exit is not considered. In models where exit is an available strategy, condition (i) must be re-stated as a requirement that profit net of the *avoidable* cost which can be saved by exiting should be non-negative.

PROPOSITION 1 (inclusion). *Any outcome that can be supported as a (perfect) Nash equilibrium in pure strategies is an equilibrium configuration.*

To see why Proposition 1 holds, notice that 'viability' is ensured since all firms have available the action 'do not enter'. Assumption 1(ii) ensures that there is at least one firm that chooses this action at equilibrium; while if the stability condition does not hold, then a profitable deviation is available to that firm: given the actions prescribed for its rivals by their equilibrium strategies, it can profitably deviate by taking action $\mathbf{a}_{N+1}$ at stage T.

2.4. *The price competition mechanism*

We can now formalize the discussion of the 'price competition' mechanism introduced in the examples of Section 2.2 above, following Selten (1983) and Sutton (1991, ch. 2).[17] We confine attention, for ease of exposition, to the class of 'symmetric' produce differentiation models.[18] In these models, each firm chooses some number n of distinct product varieties to offer, and incurs a setup cost $\varepsilon > 0$ for each one. The profit of firm i in an equilibrium of the final stage subgame can be written as

$$S\pi\big(n_i \mid (n_{-i})\big).$$

Now consider a family of such models, across which the form of price competition in the final stage subgame differs. We consider a one-parameter family of models that can be ranked in the following sense: we define a family of profit functions parameterized by θ, denoted by

$$\pi\big(n_i \mid (n_{-i}); \theta\big).$$

An increase in θ shifts the profit function downwards, in the sense that, for any given configuration we have that if $\theta_1 > \theta_2$, then

$$\pi\big(n_i \mid (n_{-i}); \theta_1\big) < \pi\big(n_i \mid (n_{-i}); \theta_2\big).$$

[17] These ideas are also developed in the literature on 'market size and firm numbers' pioneered by Bresnahan and Reiss (1990a, 1990b) and Berry (1992), which is very closely related to the bounds approach; for a discussion see Sutton (1997a) and the contribution of Berry and Reiss to this volume. Specifically, this literature holds constant the nature of the price competition regime, and focuses on how an increase in market size affects outcomes. It is a generic property of single-product firm models with exogenous sunk costs, that an increase in market size leads to a fall in price–cost margins, and so, in a symmetric equilibrium, to a rise in the output of each firm, as the product of output and the price–cost margin must suffice to allow recovery of the sunk cost (as in the Cournot example of Section 2.1). A recent paper by Campbell and Hopenhayn (2005) examines this effect empirically. When we turn to a multi-product firm setting, the issues of interest relate to the range of market sizes over which alternative configurations can be supported as equilibria [for example, Shaked and Sutton (1990)]. Recent empirical studies by Mazzeo (2002) on motels and Manuszak (2002) on the evolution of the U.S. brewing industry explore these issues.

[18] Such models include for example the linear demand model [for a Bertrand version see Shubik and Levitan (1980), Shaked and Sutton (1982); for a Cournot version see Sutton (1998)], and the model of Dixit and Stiglitz (1977).

The parameter θ denotes the 'toughness of price competition' in the sense that an increase in θ reduces the level of final stage profit earned by each firm, for any given form of market structure (i.e. configuration).

We now proceed as follows: for each value of S, we define the set of configurations satisfying the viability condition, viz.

$$S\pi\left(n_i \mid (n_{-i}); \theta\right) \geqslant \varepsilon \quad \text{for all } i. \tag{2.2}$$

For each configuration, we define an index of concentration. For concreteness, we choose the 1-firm sales concentration ratio C_1, defined as the share of industry sales revenue accounted for by the industry's largest firm. We now select, from the set of configurations satisfying (2.2), the configuration with the lowest (or equal lowest) value of C_1, and we define this level of concentration as $\underline{C}_1(S; \theta)$. This construction defines the schedule $\underline{C}_1(S; \theta)$, which forms a lower bound to concentration as a function of market size. Assuming that π is increasing in C_1, then it follows immediately from Equation (2.2) that an increase in θ shifts this schedule upwards.

Say we begin, then, with an equilibrium configuration in some market. Holding the size of the market constant, we introduce a change in the external circumstances of the market which implies a rise in θ; for example, this might be a change in the rules of competition policy (a law banning cartels, say), or it might be an improvement in the transport system that causes firms in hitherto separated local markets to come into direct competition with each other (as with the building of national railway systems in the nineteenth century, for example).

If the associated shift in θ is large enough, then the current configuration will no longer be an equilibrium, and some shift in structure must occur in the long run.

At this point, a caveat is in order: the theory is static, and we cannot specify the dynamic adjustment path that will be followed once equilibrium is disturbed.

All that can be said is that restoration of the stability and viability conditions requires a rise in concentration.[19] We may distinguish two candidate mechanisms that may bring this about: the exit of some firm(s), and/or the consolidation of others via mergers and acquisitions. This argument relies upon the link between concentration and price (and so gross profit per firm), whose theoretical and empirical status was noted in Section 2.1 above.

2.4.1. *Empirical evidence*

The most systematic test of this prediction is that of Symeonidis (2000, 2001), who takes advantage of an unusual 'natural experiment' involving a change in competition

[19] The speed of adjustment by firms will be affected inter alia by the extent to which the setup cost ε is sunk, as opposed to fixed. If ε is a sunk cost, then a violation of the viability constraint will not require any adjustment in the short run; it is only in the long run, as the capital equipment needs to be replaced, that (some) firms will, in the absence of any other structural changes, no longer find it profitable to maintain their position, and will exit. If ε is partly fixed, rather than sunk, then exit is likely to occur sooner.

law in the UK in the 1960s. As laws against the operation of cartels were strengthened, a rise in concentration occurred across the general run of manufacturing industries. Symeonidis traces the operation of these changes in detail, and finds a process at work that is consistent with the operation of the response mechanisms postulated above.

Sutton (1991) reports some 'natural experiments' affecting particular industries in the wake of the spread of the railways in the late nineteenth century. The salt industry, both in the U.S. and Europe, went through a process of consolidation in the wake of these changes. First prices fell, rendering many concerns unviable. Attempts to restore profitability via price coordination failed, due to 'free riding' by some firms. Finally, a process of exit, accompanied by mergers and acquisitions, led to the emergence of a concentrated industry [Sutton (1991, ch. 6)].

The history of the sugar industry offers some interesting illustrations of the way in which differences in the competition policy regime affected outcomes. In the U.S., it follows a similar pattern to that of the salt industry over the same period. In Continental European countries, on the other hand, a permissive competition policy regime allowed firms to coordinate their prices, thus permitting the continuance of a relatively fragmented industry into the twentieth century. The Japanese market provides an unusually informative natural experiment, in that it went through three successive regimes in respect of competition policy. A tight cartel operated in the period prior to the First World War, and concentration was low. In the inter-war years, the cartel broke down and concentration rose. In the years following the Second World War, however, the authorities permitted the industry to operate under a permissive 'quota' regime; and this relaxation in the toughness of price competition encouraged new entry, and a decline in concentration [Sutton (1991, ch. 6)].

2.5. *The escalation mechanism*

We now turn to a general statement of the 'non-convergence' result introduced in the 'quality choice' example of Section 2.1. The analysis is developed in two steps. In this section, we consider a 'classical' setting in which each firm offers a (single) product within the same market, and all these products are substitutes. In Section 2.6 we will turn to a more complex setting in which the market comprises several distinct product groups, or 'submarkets'. Here, then, each firm's action takes one of two forms, 'do not enter' or 'enter with quality u_i', where u_i is chosen from the interval $[1, \infty)$.

The outcome of firms' actions is described by a configuration

$$\mathbf{u} = (u_1, \dots, u_i, \dots, u_N).$$

We associate with every configuration $\mathbf{u}$ a number representing the highest level of quality attained by any firm, viz.

$$\hat{u}(\mathbf{u}) = \max_i u_i.$$

We summarize the properties of the final-stage subgame in a pair of functions that describe the profit of each firm and the sales revenue of the industry as a whole. Firm i's final stage profit is written as

$$\Pi(u_i \mid (\mathbf{u}_{-i})) \equiv S\pi(u_i \mid (\mathbf{u}_{-i})) \geqslant 0,$$

where $\mathbf{u}_{-i}$ denotes the $N-1$ tuple of rivals' qualities, and S denotes the number of consumers in the market.[20] Total industry sales revenue is denoted by

$$Y(\mathbf{u}) \equiv Sy(\mathbf{u}).$$

It is assumed that any firm entering the market incurs a minimum setup cost of F_0 and that increases in the quality index above unity involve additional spending on fixed outlays such as R&D and advertising. We choose to label this index so that the fixed outlay of firm i is related to the quality level u_i according to

$$F(u_i) = F_0 u_i^{\beta}, \quad \text{on } u_i \in [1, \infty), \text{ for some } \beta \geqslant 1.$$

We identify the level of spending on R&D and advertising as

$$R(u_i) = F(u_i) - F_0.$$

The economics of the model depends only on the composite mapping from firms' fixed outlays to firms' profits, rather than on the separate mappings of fixed outlays to qualities and from qualities to profits. At this point, the labeling of u is arbitrary up to an increasing transformation. There is no loss of generality, therefore, in choosing this functional form for $R(u_i)$.[21] (The form used here has been chosen for ease of interpretation, in that we can think of β as the elasticity of quality with respect to fixed outlays.[22])

To avoid trivial cases, we assume throughout that the market is always large enough to ensure that the level of sales exceeds some minimal level for any configuration, and that the market can support at least one entrant. With this in mind, we restrict S to the domain $[1, \infty)$, and we assume, following Assumption 1 above.

ASSUMPTION 3. The level of industry sales associated with any non-empty configuration is bounded away from zero; that is, there is some $\eta > 0$ such that for every configuration $\mathbf{u} \neq \emptyset$, we have $y(\mathbf{u}) \geqslant \eta > 0$ for all $\mathbf{u} \neq \emptyset$.

[20] The motivation for writing the profit function (and the industry sales revenue function) in this form (i.e. multiplicative in S), derives from an idea which is standard throughout the market structure literature: firms have flat marginal cost schedules, and increases in the size of the market involve an increase in the population of consumers, the distribution of consumer tastes being unaltered. Under these assumptions, a rise in the size of the population of consumers S shifts the demand schedule outwards multiplicatively and equilibrium prices are independent of S.

[21] There is, however, a (mild) restriction in writing $F(u_i)$ as $F_0 u_i^{\beta}$ rather than $F_0 + b u_i^{\beta}$, as noted in footnote 14 above. See Sutton (1991, ch. 3) for details.

[22] Rather than represent F as a single function, it is convenient to use a family of functions parameterized by β, since we can then hold the profit function fixed while varying β to capture changes in the effectiveness of R&D and advertising in raising final stage profits.

This assumption, together with Assumption 1(i), implies that the level of industry sales revenue $Sy(\mathbf{u}) \geqslant S\eta$ in any equilibrium configuration increases to infinity as $S \to \infty$.

2.5.1. A non-convergence theorem

In what follows, we are concerned with examining whether some kinds of configuration $\mathbf{u}$ are unstable against entry by a 'high-spending' entrant. With this in mind, we investigate the profit of a new firm that enters with a quality level k times greater than the maximum value $\hat{u}$ offered by any existing firm. More specifically, we ask: What is the minimum ratio of this high-spending entrant's profit to current industry sales that will be attained *independently* of the current configuration $\mathbf{u}$ and the size of the market?

For each k, we define an associated number $a(k)$ as follows.

DEFINITION. $a(k) = \inf_{\mathbf{u}} (\pi(k\hat{u} \mid \mathbf{u}))/(y(\mathbf{u}))$.

It follows from this definition that, given any configuration $\mathbf{u}$ with maximal quality $\hat{u}$, the final-stage profit of an entrant with capability $k\hat{u}$, denoted $S\pi(k\hat{u} \mid \mathbf{u})$, is at least equal to $a(k)Sy(\mathbf{u}) = a(k)Y(\mathbf{u})$, where $a(k)$ is independent of $\mathbf{u}$ and S.[23]

The intuition is as follows: k measures the size of the quality jump introduced by the new 'high spending' entrant. We aim to examine whether such an entrant will earn enough profit to cover its fixed outlays, and so we want to know what price it will set, and what market share it will earn. This information is summarized by the number $a(k)$, which relates the gross (final-stage) profit of the entrant, $S\pi(k\hat{u} \mid \mathbf{u})$, to pre-entry industry sales revenue, $Sy(\mathbf{u}) = Y(\mathbf{u})$. Since we wish to develop results that are independent of the existing configuration, we define $a(k)$ as an infimum over $\mathbf{u}$.

We are now in a position to state:

THEOREM 1 (non-convergence). *Given any pair $(k, a(k))$, a necessary condition for any configuration to be an equilibrium configuration is that a firm offering the highest level of quality has a share of industry sales revenue exceeding $a(k)/k^{\beta}$.*

PROOF. Consider any equilibrium configuration $\mathbf{u}$ in which the highest quality offered is $\hat{u}$. Choose any firm offering quality $\hat{u}$ and denote the sales revenue earned by that firm by $S\hat{y}$, whence its share of industry sales revenue is $S\hat{y}/SY(\mathbf{u}) = \hat{y}/Y(\mathbf{u})$.

Consider the net profit of a new entrant who offers quality $k\hat{u}$. The definition of $a(k)$ implies that the entrant's net profit is at least

$$aSy(\mathbf{u}) - F(k\hat{u}) = aSy(\mathbf{u}) - k^{\beta} F(\hat{u}),$$

where we have written $a(k)$ as a, in order to ease notation.

[23] It is worth noting that the above definition implies that $a(1) = 0$. To see this, notice that we can choose a configuration in which all n firms, and our new entrant, offer quality 1, so that all have the same profit. The ratio between the profit of any firm, and total industry sales revenue, can now be made arbitrarily small by letting $n \to \infty$. Since $a(k) \geqslant 0$ is defined as the infimum over all configurations u, it follows that $a(1) = 0$.

The stability condition implies that this entrants' net profit is non-positive, whence

$$F(\hat{u}) \geqslant \frac{a}{k^{\beta}} Sy(\mathbf{u}).$$

But the viability condition requires that each firm's final-stage profit must cover its fixed outlays. Hence the sales revenue of the firm that offers quality $\hat{u}$ in the proposed equilibrium configuration cannot be less than its fixed outlays:

$$S\hat{y} \geqslant F(\hat{u}) \geqslant \frac{a}{k^{\beta}} Sy(\mathbf{u})$$

whence its market share

$$\frac{S\hat{y}}{Sy(\mathbf{u})} \geqslant \frac{a}{k^{\beta}}.$$

This completes the proof. □

The intuition underlying this result is as follows: if the industry consists of a large number of small firms, then the viability condition implies that each firm's spending on R&D is small, relative to the industry's sales revenue. In this setting, the returns to a high-spending entrant may be large, so that the stability condition is violated. Hence a configuration in which concentration is "too low" cannot be an equilibrium configuration. This result motivates the introduction of a parameter, which we call alpha, as the highest value of the ratio a/k^{β} that can be attained by choosing any value $k \geqslant 1$, as follows.[24,25]

DEFINITION. $\alpha = \sup_k (a(k))/k^{\beta}$.

We can now reformulate the preceding theorem as follows: since the one-firm sales concentration ratio C_1 is not less than the share of industry sales revenue enjoyed by the firm offering quality $\hat{u}$, it follows from the preceding theorem that, in any equilibrium configuration, C_1 is bounded below by α, independently of the size of the market, viz.

$$C_1 \geqslant \alpha. \tag{2.3}$$

[24] The reason for introducing the supremum over k is as follows: some 'sizes of jump', measured by k, may be profitable for the deviant, while other are not. In seeking to characterize a lower bound to concentration, we seek to eliminate configurations that can be broken by a high-spending entrant using *any* value of k.

[25] In defining alpha, we have for convenience taken the limits in a particular order: we first seek a pair k, $a(k)$ which hold for *all* configurations; alpha is then defined by taking the supremum over k. This begs the question: what if, as the quality level(s) of firms rise(s), we could always find a suitable pair k, $a(k)$, but only by choosing a different (larger) value of k, as quality levels increase? It is possible to construct an example of the kind, in which there is a lower bound to concentration which is strictly positive – even though there is no single pair k, a (k) with $a(k) > 0$ as defined above. This indicates that there is a (slight) restriction introduced in defining alpha in the present manner. (In other words, the restriction stated in (2.3) below always holds, but in some (rather special) circumstances a tighter version of the restriction is valid.)

INTERPRETING ALPHA

In an industry where alpha is strictly positive, a high-spending entrant can achieve a profit exceeding some fixed proportion of current industry sales *independently of the number of low-spending rivals.* If the industry consists of a large number of firms, all with a small market share, then this arrangement can be disrupted by the arrival of a single 'high spender'; the profits of such a high spender cannot be eroded to zero by the presence of low spenders, however many are present. Even if the prices of the low quality products fall to the unit (variable) cost of production, at least some fraction of consumers will be willing to pay a price premium for the high-quality product.[26]

The interpretation of alpha hinges on the question: can the profit of a high-spending firm be diluted indefinitely by the presence of a sufficiently large number of low-spending rivals?

A loose but useful analogy is provided by thinking of a lottery in which N players buy tickets costing \$1, and one winner draws a prize of predetermined value Y. The expected payoff to a high-spending individual who buys k tickets while the remaining $(N - 1)$ players buy one ticket each is equal to $kY/[k + (N - 1)]$. For any k, this can be made arbitrarily close to zero by choosing N sufficiently high. This captures the nature of an industry where alpha equals zero: the returns to a high-spending firm can be diluted indefinitely by the presence of many

Equation (2.3) constitutes a restatement of the basic non-convergence result developed in the preceding theorem. In the light of this result, we see that alpha serves as a measure of the extent to which a fragmented industry can be destabilized by the actions of a firm who outspends its many small rivals in R&D or advertising. The value of alpha depends directly on the profit function of the final stage subgame, and on the elasticity of the fixed cost schedule. Hence it reflects both the pattern of technology and tastes and the nature of price competition in the market. We noted earlier that the results do not depend on the way we label u, but only on the composite mapping from F to π. To underline this point, we can re-express the present result as follows: increasing quality by a factor k requires that fixed outlays rise by a factor k^β. For any given value of β, write k^β as K. We can now write any pair $(k, a(k))$ as an equivalent $(K, a(K))$ pair. Alpha can then be described as the highest ratio $a(K)/K$ that can be attained by any choice of $K \geqslant 1$.

[26] It is worth emphasizing that our assumption on the cost structure states that a higher value of u involves an increase in fixed (and sunk) outlays; it does not involve a rise in the unit variable cost of production. It is natural in the present context to ask: what if a rise in quality involves both a rise in fixed outlays, and a rise in unit variable cost. The answer is: if the latter effect is small, there will still be an $a(k)$, k pair as defined above, and the 'non-convergence' result still holds. But if the rate at which unit variable cost rises with u is sufficiently steep, then $a(k)$ will fall to zero for all k. This idea lies at the heart of the literature on vertical product differentiation [Shaked and Sutton (1982)]. [For an overview of the main ideas, see Sutton (1991, pp. 70–71) and the references cited therein.]

low-spending rivals. It is possible, to in this setting, to have an equilibrium configuration in which a large number of firms each purchase a single ticket – so that if we measure concentration in terms of the number of tickets purchased, we have a fragmented industry.

In contrast to this, consider the Cournot model with quality described in Section 2.2 above. Here, if we begin from a configuration in which N firms have qualities not exceeding $\hat{u}$, and introduce an $(N+1)$th firm with quality $k\hat{u}$, then the profit of this entrant can be computed from Equation (2.1) of the text as

$$\pi(k\hat{u} \mid u) = \left\{1 - \frac{N}{k\hat{u}} \frac{1}{\sum_1^N \frac{1}{u_j} + \frac{1}{k\hat{u}}}\right\}^2 \cdot S.$$

Now for any N and any set of qualities $u_1, \ldots, u_N$ none of which exceed $\hat{u}$, the expression on the r.h.s. cannot be less than

$$\left\{1 - \frac{1}{k}\right\}^2 \cdot S$$

whence, noting that industry sales revenue equals S, we have

$$a(k) = (1 - 1/k)^2 > 0 \quad \text{for } k > 1.$$

2.5.2. *An ancillary theorem*

Within our present context of a classical market in which all goods are substitutes, the interpretation of alpha is straightforward. The parameter $a(k)$ measures the degree to which an increase in the (perceived) quality of one product allows it to capture sales from rivals. Thus the statement, within this context, that there exists some pair of numbers k and $a(k) > 0$ satisfying the above conditions requires only very weak restrictions on consumer preferences [for a detailed justification of this remark, by reference to a specific representation of consumer preferences, see Sutton (1991, pp. 74–76)].[27] The question of interest is: how costly is it, in terms of fixed outlays, to achieve this k-fold increase in u? This is measured by the parameter β. With this in mind, we proceed to define a family of models, parameterized by β, as follows: we take the form of the profit function, and so the function $a(k)$, as fixed, while allowing the parameter β to vary. We assume, moreover, that for some value of k, $a(k) > 0$. The value of $\alpha = \sup_k a(k)/k^\beta$

[27] What is required is that at least some fraction of consumers will be willing to pay some price in excess of unit variable cost c for the good of quality $k\hat{u} > \hat{u}$, whatever the prices ($\geqslant c$) of all rival goods. It is intuitively clear that this will be the case once some fraction of consumers are willing to switch from rival substitute goods, in response to a quality increase. In a simple 'vertical product differentiation' model such as the Cournot model with quality, this result is immediate (see Box). A formal statement of the (weak) restrictions on consumer preferences required to ensure this result in the more complex setting that combines vertical and horizontal product attributes is set out in Sutton (1991, p. 75).

varies with β. (The case $\alpha = 0$ can be treated as a limiting case as $a(k) \to 0$ or $\beta \to \infty$.)

We are now in a position to develop an ancillary theorem whose role is to allow us to use the observed value of the R&D and/or advertising to sales ratio to proxy for the value of β. The intuition behind the ancillary theorem is this: if the value of β is high, this implies that the responsiveness of profit to the fixed outlays of the deviant firm is low, and under these circumstances we might expect that the level of fixed outlays undertaken by all firms at equilibrium would be small; this is what the theorem asserts.

We establish this by showing that certain configurations must be unstable, in that they will be vulnerable to entry by a low-spending entrant. The idea is that, if spending on R&D and advertising is ineffective, then a low spending entrant may incur much lower fixed outlays than (at least some) incumbent firm(s), while offering a product that is only slightly inferior to that of the incumbent(s). The ancillary theorem allows us to fix some threshold level for the ratio of R&D plus advertising to sales, and consider the set of industries for which the ratio exceeds this threshold level: we may characterize this group as being 'low β' and so 'high alpha' industries, as against a control group of industries in which R&D and advertising levels are (very close to) zero. It is this result which leads to the empirical test of the non-convergence theorem.

Before stating the theorem however, some preliminary development is necessary, since the proof of the ancillary theorem rests on an appeal to the entry of a low-spending firm. This raises a technical issue: suppose, for the sake of illustration, that the underlying model of the final stage subgame, whose properties are summarized in the profit function $\pi(\cdot)$, takes the form of the elementary 'Bertrand model'. In this setting, if all firms offer the same quality level, once one firm is present in the market, no further entry can occur; for any entry leads to an immediate collapse of prices to marginal cost, and so the entrant can never earn positive margins, and so cover the sunk cost incurred in entering. In what follows, we will exclude this limiting case. (To exclude it is harmless, relative to the theory, since the theory aims to place a lower bound on the 1-firm concentration ratio; and if we are working in this 'Bertrand limit', then the 1-firm concentration ratio is necessarily unity, as we saw in Section 2.2.)

To define and exclude this limiting case, we need to specify the relationship between the profit earned by an entrant, and the pre-entry profit of some active firm (the 'reference firm').

Consider an equilibrium configuration in which the industry-wide R&D (or advertising) to sales ratio is x (>0). Within this industry, we select some reference firm whose R&D and advertising outlays constitute a fraction x (or greater) of its sales revenue. There must be at least one such firm in the industry, and since this firm must satisfy the viability condition, it must earn a gross profit of at least fraction x of its sales revenues in order to sustain its level of R&D and advertising.

Now consider an entrant that offers the same quality level as the reference firm. Insofar as entry reduces prices, this entrant will enjoy a lower price–cost margin than that earned by the reference firm in the pre-entry situation. But, for a sufficiently high value of x, we assume that the entrant will enjoy some strictly positive price–cost mar-

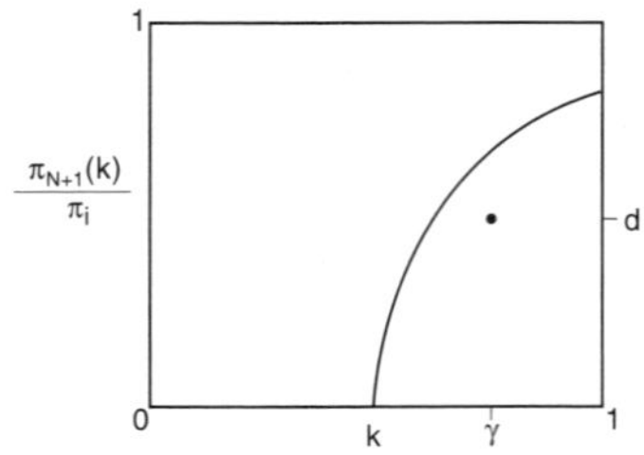

Figure 35.5. The relative profit of a low-quality entrant. The incumbent firm, labeled i, offers quality u_i and earns (pre-entry) profit π_i. The entrant, labeled firm $N+1$, offers quality ku_i and earns profit $\pi_{N+1}(k)$.

gin, so that its final stage profit is strictly positive (this is what fails in the 'Bertrand limit').

This is illustrated in Figure 35.5. The horizontal axis shows the ratio between the quality of the entrant's product, and that of the reference firm; k varies from 0 to 1, with a value of 1 corresponding to the entrant of equal quality. Our assumption states that for $k = 1$, the entrant's post-entry profit is strictly positive. On the vertical axis, we show the ratio of the entrant's profit to the pre-entry profit of the reference firm.[28] Our exclusion of the Bertrand limit states that, for $k = 1$, this ratio is strictly positive. We further assume that the entrant's profit varies monotonically with its quality, and so with k. It then follows that we can depict the entrant's profit as a function of k as a curve; the assumption states that this curve does not collapse inwards to the bottom right-hand corner of the diagram (the 'Bertrand limit'). Specifically, it says that there is some value of x, such that if the pre-entry price–cost margin exceeds x, then there is some point in the interior of the square such that the curve we have just described lies above this point.

We state this formally as follows.

ASSUMPTION 4. There is some triple (x, γ, d) with $0 < x, \gamma < 1$, and $0 < d < 1$, with the following property: suppose any firm i attains quality level u_i and earns final-stage profit π_i that exceeds a fraction x of its sales revenue. Then an entrant attaining a quality level equal to $\max(1, \gamma u_i)$ attains a final-stage profit of at least $d\pi_i$.

The ancillary theorem linking the R&D (or advertising)/sales ratio to the parameter β now follows.

THEOREM 2. *For any threshold value of the R&D (or advertising)/sales ratio exceeding* $\max(x, 1-d)$, *where x and d are defined as in Assumption* 4, *there is an associated*

[28] It is convenient to work in terms of this ratio, so as to state the assumption in a way that does not involve the size of the market S.

value of β^* such that for any $\beta > \beta^*$, no firm can have an R&D/sales ratio exceeding this threshold in any equilibrium configuration.[29]

A proof of this theorem is given in Sutton (1998, ch. 4). An implication of Theorem 2 is that an industry with a high R&D (or advertising)/sales ratio must necessarily be a high-alpha industry. With this result in place, we are now in a position to formulate an empirical test of the theory: Choose some ('sufficiently high') threshold level for the R&D (or advertising)/sales ratio (written as R/Y in what follows), and split the sample of industries by reference to this threshold. All industries in which alpha is close to zero will fall in the low R/Y group, and so for this group the lower bound to the cloud of points in (C, S) space should extend to zero as $S \to \infty$. For all industries in the group with high R/Y, on the other hand, the value of β will lie below β^*, and so the lower bound to concentration will be bounded away from zero by $C_1 \geqslant a(k)/k^{\beta}$.

In pooling data across different industries, it is necessary to 'standardize' the measure of market size by reference to some notion of the minimum level of setup cost F_0, which we write as ε. A practical procedure to represent this as the cost of a single plant of minimum efficient scale, and to write the ratio of annual industry sales revenue to minimum setup cost as S/ε. This leads to the prediction illustrated in Figure 35.6; tests of this prediction are reported in the next section.[30,31]

It is interesting to consider the relationship between this prediction and the traditional practice of regressing concentration on a measure of scale economies to market size (essentially S/ε), together with a measure of advertising intensity and R&D intensity. Such regressions indicated that concentration fell with S/ε, and rose (weakly) with the advertising–sales ratio [Sutton (1991, p. 124)]. It can be shown that, under the present theory, these results are predicted to emerge from the (misspecified) regression relationship. [For a full discussion, see Sutton (1991, Annex to ch. 5).]

[29] It may be helpful to illustrate the ideas of Assumption 4 and Theorem 2 by reference to a numerical example: suppose $x = 0.04$ and $d = 0.95$ (intuitively: entry reduces prices only slightly). Say we select all those industries with R&D sales ratios exceeding $\max(x, 1 - d) = 0.05$, whence we can find at least one incumbent firm i, that spends at least 5% of its sales revenue Sy_i on R&D or advertising. Now suppose we let $\beta \to \infty$, so that these fixed outlays become completely ineffective. Then an entrant to this industry can, by spending nothing on such fixed outlays, enjoy a positive net profit. Its final-stage profit falls short of the pre-entry final-stage profit of the incumbent by at most $0.05S\pi_i$, but its saving on fixed outlays relative to the incumbent is at least $0.05Sy_i > 0.05S\pi_i$, whence its net profit exceeds the pre-entry net profit of the incumbent, which is non-negative. It follows that, once β is 'sufficiently large', the pre-entry configuration is not an equilibrium configuration.

[30] For a discussion of alternative measures of setup cost, see Sutton (1991, pp. 93–99).

[31] A further practical issue arises in relation to the use of the (theoretically appropriate) 1-firm concentration ratio C_1. Since official statistics never report this, for reasons of confidentiality, it has long been customary in IO to use a readily available measure such as C_4. The prediction shown in Figure 35.7 still applies, here, of course.

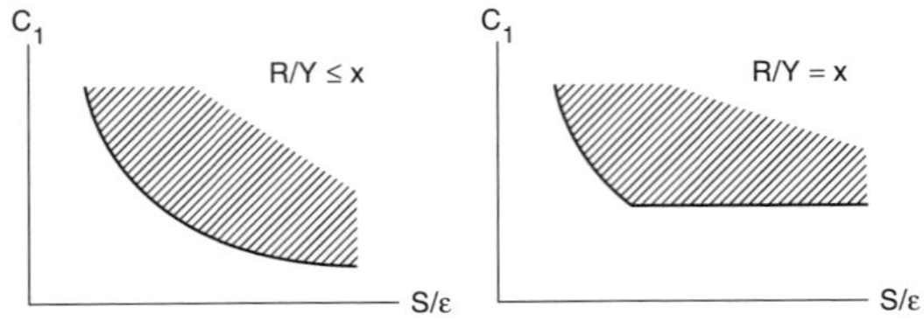

Figure 35.6. The 'bounds' prediction on the concentration–market size relationship.

2.5.3. Empirical evidence

We have developed this first version of the non-convergence theorem in a context in which the classical market definition applies, i.e. the market comprises a single set of substitute goods, so that an increase in fixed and sunk outlays enhances consumers' willingness-to-pay for all its products in this market. Now this condition will apply strictly only in rather special circumstances. One setting in which it applies to a good approximation is that of certain groups of advertising-intensive industries. Here, even though the market may comprise a number of distinct product categories, the firm's advertising may support a brand image that benefits all its products in the market. (A similar argument applies in R&D intensive industries when scope economies in R&D operate across different groups of products in the market; see below, Section 2.6.)

The first test of the non-convergence theorem [Sutton (1991, ch. 5)] was carried out on a dataset for 20 industries drawn from the food and drink sector, across the six largest Western economies. The industries were chosen from a single sector so as to keep constant as many extraneous factors as possible. The food and drink sector was chosen because, alone among the basic 2-digit SIC industry groups, it is the only one in which there is a nice split between industries that have little or no advertising (sugar, flour, etc.) and industries that are advertising-intensive (breakfast cereals, petfood, etc.).

Data was compiled from market research reports, combined with company interviews. The industry definitions used are those which are standard in the market research literature, and these correspond roughly to 4-digit SIC definitions. All industries for which suitable data could be assembled were included. The size of each market was defined as the number of 'minimum efficient scale' plants it would support, where the size of a m.e.s. plant was measured as the median plant size in the U.S. industry.

The sample was split on the basis of measured advertising sales ratios into a control group ($A/S < 1\%$) and an experimental group ($A/S \geqslant 1\%$); though the large majority of industries in the latter group had advertising–sales ratios that were very much higher than 1%.

The data from the study is illustrated in Figure 35.7, which shows the scatter of observations for the control group (upper panel) and the experimental group (lower

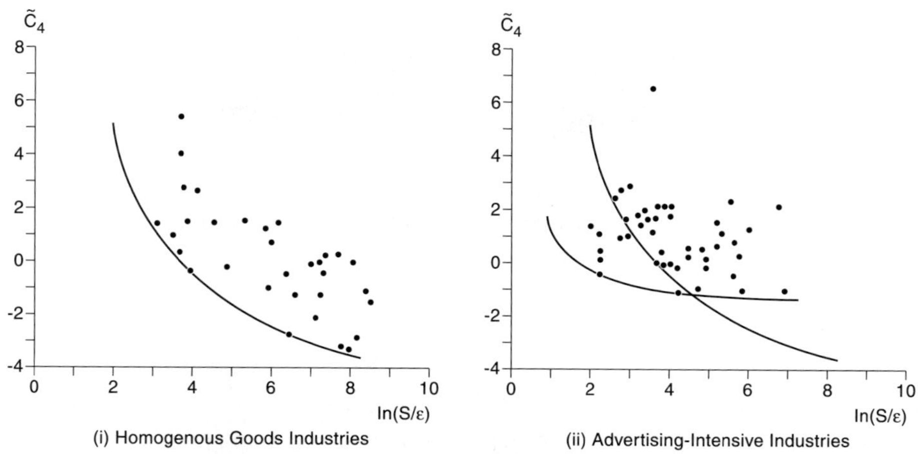

Figure 35.7. A plot of $\tilde{C}_4$ versus S/ε for advertising-intensive industries (ii) and a control group (i). The fitted bound for the control group is reproduced in panel (ii) for comparison purposes.

panel) on plots of (a logit transformation[32] of) the 4-firm concentration ratio. A fitted lower bound[33] for the control group indicates an asymptotic value for $\underline{C}_4(S)$ in the limit $S \to \infty$ which is 0.06%; the corresponding lower bound for the experimental group is 19%, which is significantly different from zero at the 5% level.[34]

The non-convergence property has also been investigated by Robinson and Chiang (1996), using the PIMS data set, a dataset gathered by the Strategic Planning Institute

[32] The logit transformed value $\tilde{C}_4 = \ln(C_4/(1 - C_4))$ is defined on $(-\infty, +\infty)$ rather than $[0, 1]$ and this may be preferred on econometric grounds.

[33] Following Smiths' (1985, 1988, 1994) maximum likelihood method. Techniques for bounds estimation are discussed in Sutton (1991, ch. 5), and Sutton (1998, ch. 4). An alternative method which has some attractive features from a theoretical viewpoint, but which has less power than that of the maximum likelihood methods described by Smith, is that of Mann, Scheuer and Fertig (1973); see Sutton (1998) for details. Both these approaches are sensitive to the presence of outliers, and for this reason some authors, including Lyons, Matraves and Moffat (2001), favor alternative methods that have proved useful in the estimation of frontier production functions. A very simple method of attack is provided by quantile regression methods, which Giorgetti (2003) has recently applied, in combination with maximum likelihood methods, to examine the lower bound to concentration for a sample of manufacturing industries.

[34] These findings have been questioned for the case of the U.S. food and drink sector by Rogers (2001). Rogers reports a regression of concentration against market size/setup costs, for 40 4-digit SIC industries in this sector, over five census years and finds that advertising raises the level, but not the slope of this relationship. He interprets this result as reflecting claims by Rogers and Ma (1994) and Rogers and Tockle (1999) that food and drink advertising in the U.S. has been losing its effectiveness over time and/or that merger activity in non-advertising intensive food and drink industries has led to a narrowing of the difference in concentration between these two groups of industries. Rogers also notes that a possible reason for the difference in findings relative to Sutton (1991) lies in problems of market definition for some of the 4-digit SIC industries in the sector. [Such problems arise when SIC industries comprise both advertising intensive and non-advertising intensive submarkets; see, for example, Giorgetti (2003).]

representing a wide range of firms drawn mostly from the Fortune 1000 list. Firms report data for each of their constituent businesses (their operations within each industry, the industry being defined somewhat more narrowly than a 4-digit SIC industry); for a discussion of the PIMS dataset, see, for example, Scherer (1980).

The unit of observation here is the individual business, and the sample comprises 1740 observations. The sample is split into a control group (802 observations) in which both the advertising–sales ratio and the R&D–sales ratio for the business lie below 1%. The remaining ('experimental') groups comprise markets where one or both ratios exceed 1%.

Within the control group, the authors set out to test whether an increase in the 'toughness of price competition' raises the lower bound $\underline{C}_k(S)$. They do this by using three proxies for the 'toughness of price competition': price competition is tougher if (1) the product is standardized rather than customized, (2) the product is a raw or semi-finished material, or (3) buyer orders are infrequent. The findings of the study are:

(i) the 'non-convergence' property is confirmed for all 'experimental' groups,
(ii) the asymptotic lower bound for the control group converges to zero, but
(iii) when the control group is split into the 'tough' and 'non-tough' price competition sub-groups, it is found that tougher price competition shifts the bounds upwards (as predicted by the theory), but the asymptotic lower bound to concentration for the 'tough price competition' group is now strictly positive, i.e. it does not converge to zero asymptotically, contrary to the predictions of the theory. Instead, the (3-firm) concentration ratio converges to an asymptotic value of 10%, intermediate between that for the 'weak price competition' control group, and the values found for the 'experimental groups' (15.8%–19.6%). (The authors add a caveat to this conclusion, noting that this finding may reflect data limitations in their sample.)

An investigation of the non-convergence property by Lyons and Matraves (1996) and Lyons, Matraves and Moffat (2001) uses a data set covering 96 NACE 3-digit manufacturing industries for the four largest economies in the European Union, and a comparison group for the U.S. Splitting the sample by reference to observed levels of the advertising–sales ratio and R&D–sales ratio as in Robinson and Chiang, the authors estimate a lower bound to concentration for each group.

A key novelty of this study is that it attacks the question of whether it is more appropriate to model the concentration–size relationship at the E.U. level, or at the level of national economies (Germany, UK, France, Italy). The authors construct, for each industry, a measure (labeled 't') of intra-EU trade intensity. They hypothesize that, for high (respectively low) values of t, the appropriate model is one that links concentration in the industry to the size of the European (respectively national) market. They proceed to employ a maximum likelihood estimation procedure to identify a critical threshold t^* for each country, so that according as t lies above or below t^*, the concentration of an industry is linked to the size of the European market, and conversely. Within this setting, the authors proceed to re-examine the 'non-convergence' prediction. They find that 'a very clear pattern emerges, with ... the theoretical predictions ... receiving clear support' [Lyons, Matraves and Moffat (2001)].

The key comparison is between the asymptotic lower bound to concentration for the control group versus that for the experimental groups. Over the eight cases (4 countries, E.U. versus National Markets) the point estimate of the asymptotic lower bound for the control group lies below all reported[35] estimates for the three experimental groups, except in two instances (advertising-intensive industries in Italy, advertising and R&D intensive industries in France); in both these cases the reported standard errors are very high, and the difference in the estimated asymptotic value is insignificant.

2.6. Markets and submarkets: the R&D vs concentration relation

The theory set out above rests on the classical definition of a market as comprising a set of goods, all of which are substitutes. We may reasonably apply this model to, for example, a narrowly defined market in which firms' advertising outlays create a 'brand image' that benefits all the firms' offerings in the market. But once we turn to the case of R&D intensive industries, the formulation of the theory developed above becomes inadequate. For in this setting, once we define the market broadly enough to incorporate all substitute goods, we may, for example, be left with various sets of products, each of which requires some distinct technical know-how. Here, each firm must choose not only its level of R&D spending, but the way in which its R&D efforts should be divided among the various product groups ('submarkets'). These different R&D programs may, or may not, contain common elements, leading to 'economies of scope' in R&D across different submarkets. On the demand side, too, there may be linkages across submarkets: it may, for example, be the case that products within each sub-group are close substitutes, but some products from different subgroups are weak substitutes. It is tempting to dismiss all such problems as a 'question of aggregation' by suggesting that we should analyze competition and market structure at the level of the submarket. However, the logic of partial equilibrium analysis lies in defining a market broadly enough to justify taking as given what is going on in other markets; this was the idea behind Joan Robinson's classic definition of a market by reference to a 'break in the chain of substitutes'. Here, however, firms' actions in one submarket will have an effect on the profits of firms in other submarkets, and so on their strategic choices.

The idea of responding to these problems by working at a lower level of aggregation becomes increasingly unattractive as we move to the context of markets where the pattern of linkages across submarkets is relatively complex; for a discussion of these difficulties, see Sutton (1998, pp. 14–16, 165). The only satisfactory way forward in this setting lies in building these features into the theory. In what follows, we extend the model of the preceding section by introducing the notion of a set of 'technological trajectories', and their associated 'submarkets' as follows.

[35] Some cases are unreported due to lack of a sufficient sample size.

The capability of firm i is now represented by a set of quality indexes, its quality index on trajectory m (equivalently, in submarket m), being denoted by $u_{i,m}$, where m runs from 1 to M. A firm's capability is represented by the vector

$$\mathbf{u}_i = (u_{i,1}, \ldots, u_{i,m}, \ldots, u_{i,M})$$

and a configuration is written as $\mathbf{u} = (\mathbf{u}_1, \ldots, \mathbf{u}_i, \ldots, \mathbf{u}_N)$.

The firm's fixed cost can now be written as the sum of the costs incurred on each trajectory,[36] viz.

$$\sum_m F_0 u_{i,m}^{\beta}.$$

A full discussion of the theory, within this more complex setting lies outside the scope of this chapter; for details, the reader is referred to Sutton (1998, ch. 3). Here, attention is confined to an informal account of the key idea, which concerns the way in which we represent the idea of 'linkages' across submarkets.

To motivate ideas, we begin by raising some questions. We begin with linkages on the demand side. Suppose, firstly, that the products in the different submarkets are relatively close substitutes. We might expect intuitively, in this setting, that as firms advanced along one trajectory, they might 'steal' market share from firms operating along other trajectories. Can a process of this kind lead to the emergence of a single 'dominant trajectory', and so to high concentration at the level of the market as a whole?

At the other extreme, suppose the products in the different submarkets are poor substitutes. Here, an obvious limiting case arises, in which the market becomes separable into a number of independent submarkets – and we might expect that, even if each of these constituent submarkets is concentrated, the fact that different firms may be present in different submarkets makes possible an outcome in which the market as a whole is highly fragmented.

Similar questions arise in respect of linkages on the supply side, i.e. when there are economies of scope in R&D across the different submarkets. A simple way of introducing such scope economies into the analysis is to replace the above additive cost function by a sub-additive function. For example, we may suppose that a firm's quality index on trajectory m is a function of its spending both on trajectory m, and – to some degree – on its spending on other trajectories. As with linkages on the demand side, the presence of such scope economies can influence the degree to which a concentrated outcome emerges in the market as a whole.

It will be clear at this point that a general depiction of the nature of the linkages that may be present between submarkets would be rather complicated. It turns out, however, that for our present purposes a very simple representation proves to be adequate. This

[36] For simplicity, I will confine attention to a setting in which all the submarkets are treated symmetrically. The additive form of the cost function implies that there are no economies of scope in R&D; the introduction of such scope economies is considered below.

involves introducing a new parameter σ, defined on the interval [0, 1], which represents the strength of linkages between submarkets. Our 'class of models', which was parameterized by β above, will now be parameterized by the pair (β, σ). The focus of analysis will lie in distinguishing between two cases: where σ is 'large', and where σ becomes close to zero, the latter case being identified with the limiting case where the market consists of a set of 'independent submarkets'.

Before introducing this new parameter, we first pause to define precisely what is meant by a 'submarket' and its associated 'technological trajectory', in the context of the present theory. We do this by asserting the existence of some pair of numbers k_0 and $a(k_0)$ which play the role of the k and $a(k)$ pair in our preceding discussion – but which relate, not to the market as a whole, but to any specific submarket. In other words, we assume that a firm that raises its capability along some technical trajectory, i.e. raises the quality u of its product(s) in some associated submarket, will thereby steal sales from other products *in the same submarket*; but we leave open the question of what happens in respect of products in other submarkets. This captures the idea that products within the same submarket are close substitutes, and incorporate the same technology.

ASSUMPTION 5. There is a pair (a_0, k_0) with $a_0 > 0$, $k_0 > 1$ such that in any configuration $\mathbf{u}$ with maximum quality $\hat{u}$ attained along trajectory m, an entrant offering quality $k_0\hat{u}$ along trajectory m will achieve a final-stage profit of at least $a_0 S y_m(\mathbf{u})$, where $S y_m(\mathbf{u})$ denotes the (pre-entry) total sales revenue in submarket m.

We augment the set of assumptions introduced in the preceding section by two additional assumptions, whose role is to introduce the parameter σ, and to pin down the distinction between the two cases just described.

Assumption 6 introduces the substitution parameter. For each configuration $\mathbf{u}$ define the configuration $\mathbf{u}^{(m)}$, in which firms' capabilities on trajectory m are as in $\mathbf{u}$, but all other trajectories are unoccupied (so that goods in category m face no competition from goods in other categories). The following intuition motivates Assumption 6: removing substitute products does not decrease the demand for products of any category[37]; and in the special case where goods in different groups are poor substitutes, the demand for products in any particular group is unaffected by the prices and qualities of goods in other groups.

ASSUMPTION 6. (i) For any $\sigma \geqslant 0$

$$y_m\left(\mathbf{u}^{(m)}\right) \geqslant y_m(\mathbf{u}),$$

whereas for $\sigma = 0$, this relation holds as an equality.

(ii) As $\sigma \to 0$, the ratio

$$\frac{y_m(\mathbf{u})}{y_m(\mathbf{u}^{(m)})}$$

converges to 1, uniformly in $\mathbf{u}$.

[37] We ignore any demand complementaries throughout.

Part (i) of the assumption says that removing products in other submarkets does not diminish the sales of products in submarket m. Part (ii) of the assumption says that when σ is close to zero, the removal of products in other submarkets has a negligible effect on the sales of products in submarket m.

The next assumption constitutes the key step. What it does is to pin down the concept of σ as a measure of the strength of linkages between trajectories, and in particular to identify the limiting case where $\sigma \to 0$ as that of independent submarkets (or trajectories). We introduce this idea by re-examining the case of a low-quality entrant. We now ask: how low can the quality ratio fall before this entrant's final-stage profit becomes zero? Here it is appropriate to consider the cases of entry both along trajectory m, and along a different trajectory. In the case of entry along the same trajectory, we might expect that there is some quality ratio $\gamma_0 > 0$ sufficiently low that a product of quality less than $\gamma_0\tilde{u}$ could not earn positive profit in competition with a product of quality $\tilde{u}$. In the case of entry along a different trajectory, this should still be true if the products associated with different trajectories are substitutes. However, if $\sigma = 0$, so that demand for each product category is independent of the prices and qualities of products in other categories, then this would no longer be so. This motivates:

ASSUMPTION 7. For any $\sigma > 0$, there exists a quality ratio $\gamma_0 \in (0, 1]$ such that a product of quality $\gamma\tilde{u}$, where $\gamma \leqslant \gamma_0$, cannot command positive sales revenue if a rival firm offers a product of quality $\tilde{u}$ on any trajectory.

REMARK. Assumption 7 is the only assumption that restricts the way in which the profit function $\pi(\cdot)$ varies with the parameter σ. The restriction is very weak; in particular, it imposes no monotonic relationship between σ and $\pi(\cdot)$. Rather, it simply imposes a certain restriction for any strictly positive value of σ, thereby leaving open the possibility that this restriction breaks down in the limit $\sigma \to 0$.

The intuition behind this assumption may be made clearer by noting what would follow if γ_0 were equal to zero (i.e. if Assumption 7 could not be satisfied for any strictly positive γ_0). This would imply that we could find some pair of products whose qualities were arbitrarily far apart, both of which could command positive sales at equilibrium. Assumption 7 states that this can happen only if σ is close to zero.[38]

The intuition behind the assumption is clear, in regard to the case where the linkages are on the demand side, i.e. where the products are substitutes. The formulation of the assumption is designed, however, to capture both these demand–side linkages, and supply–side linkages operating via scope economics in R&D. To see the intuition regarding these latter linkages, consider a high-spending firm operating in another submarket, whose R&D spending in that submarket enhances its product quality in submarket m. Once again, the low-quality firm in submarket m may be unable to achieve

[38] This assumption can be illustrated using Figure 35.6 above, as follows: it states that for $\sigma > 0$, the curve showing the relative profit earned by a new (low quality) entrant will meet the horizontal axis at some strictly positive value of γ. For $\sigma = 0$, it may meet at the origin.

positive profit if this rival's relative spending, and so its quality level, in its primary submarket is sufficiently high. If the strength of these (scope economy) linkages is vanishingly small however, this is no longer the case; an arbitrarily wide gap between a low-quality product in submarket m, and a high-quality product in some other submarket is consistent with the former product's viability.

Within this framework, we can now develop a version of the non-convergence theorem appropriate to the setting of markets that contain many submarkets. To do this, we need to extend the set of 'observables' R/Y and C_1 used in the preceding section, to incorporate a third parameter, labeled h, which measures the degree to which the equilibrium outcome is seen to involve a breaking up of the market into a greater or lesser number of submarkets.

We define a 'homogeneity index', labeled

$$h = \max_m \frac{y_m(\mathbf{u})}{y(\mathbf{u})}.$$

Here, h represents the share of industry sales revenue accounted for by the largest product category. If all products are associated with the same trajectory, then $h = 1$. If there are many different trajectories, each associated with a small product group, then h is close to zero. We now state the reformulated version of the non-convergence theorem.

THEOREM 3. *In any equilibrium configuration, the one-firm sales concentration ratio satisfies*

$$C_1 \geqslant \frac{a_0}{k_0^\beta} h.$$

The proof of this theorem mimics that of Theorem 1 above, and is omitted here.

It is worth noting that, while β and σ are exogenous parameters that describe the underlying pattern of technology and tastes in the market, h is an endogenous outcome. The intuition is as follows: if σ is very high, so that submarkets are very closely linked, the process of competition among firms on different trajectories will lead to the emergence of a single dominant trajectory, so h will be high, and C_1 will be high also. But if σ is close to zero, firms in one submarket have little or no influence on those in another. One possible form of equilibrium is that in which a different group of firms operate in each submarket, so that h is low, and C_1 is low also. This is not the only possible outcome: another equilibrium involves having the same group of firms in each submarket, so that h is low but C_1 is high.

2.6.1. Some illustrations

The new idea that arises when we move beyond the classical market to this more complex setting is that two polar patterns may emerge in high-technology industries. The first is the pattern of 'R&D escalation' along a single technical trajectory, leading to a high level of concentration – this was the pattern explored in the preceding section.

The second is a pattern of 'proliferation' of technical trajectories and their associated submarkets. The key point to note is that the structure of submarkets emerges endogenously: specific illustrations may be helpful here.

The history of the aircraft industry from the 1920s to the end of the pre-jet era in the late 1950s illustrates the first pattern. The industry of the 1920s and early 1930s featured a wide variety of plane types: monoplanes, biplanes and triplanes; wooden planes and metal planes; seaplanes and so on. Yet buyers were primarily concerned with one key attribute: the "cost per passenger per mile". So once one design emerged which offered the best prospects for minimizing this target (the DC3), the industry quickly converged on a single technical trajectory [the details of this case are set out in Sutton (1998, ch. 16)].

The other polar pattern is illustrated by the Flowmeter industry, an industry characterized by a high level of R&D intensity, which supports a large number of firms, many of whom specialize in one, or a few, of the many product types (submarkets) that co-exist in the market. Different types of flowmeter are appropriate for different applications, and the pattern of 'substitution' relationships among them is complex and subtle [see Sutton (1998, ch. 6)]. The focus of R&D spending in the industry is associated with the introduction of new basic types of flowmeter, which offer advantages to particular groups of buyers. Thus the pattern here is one of 'proliferation' rather than escalation; the underlying pattern of technology and tastes is such that the industry features a large number of submarkets.

2.6.2. Empirical evidence II

Theorem 3, together with Theorem 2 above, implies an empirical prediction regarding the joint distribution of concentration, R&D intensity, and market segmentation (Figure 35.8). Suppose we take a group of industries within some large economy for which the R&D/sales ratio lies above some (high, though unspecified) cutoff value. Theorem 2 implies that associated with the cutoff level of R&D intensity, there is some associated value of β^* such that for all industries in this group, $\beta \leqslant \beta^*$. Theorem 3 then implies that for all industries in this group

$$C_1 \geqslant \frac{a_0}{k_0^{\beta}} \cdot h.$$

If we define a control group of industries for which R&D intensity is low, this group should contain some industries for which the value of β is high. Here, according to the theory, the lower bound to concentration converges to zero as the size of the economy becomes large,[39] independently of the degree of market segmentation, as measured by h. Hence if we examine such a group, for a large economy, we expect to find that concentration can be close to zero independently of h (Figure 35.8).

[39] Recall that $k_0 > 1$ and $a(k_0) > 0$; the fact that $a(1) = 0$ was noted in footnote 23 above.

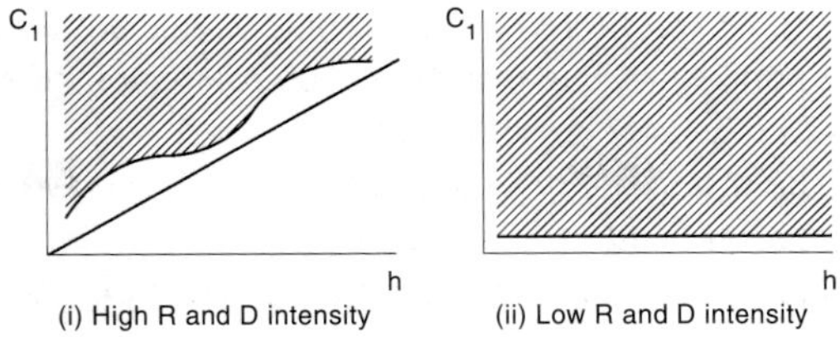

Figure 35.8. The empirical prediction.

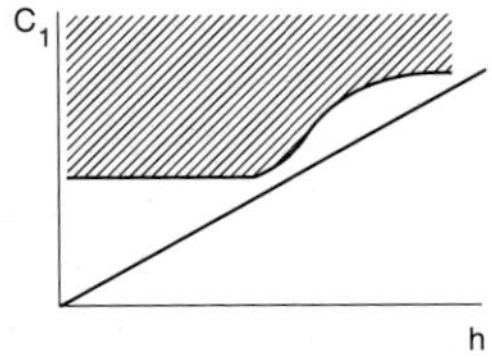

Figure 35.9. The effect of scope economies in R&D.

There is one important caveat, however. Linkages between submarkets are of two kinds: those on the demand side (substitution) and those on the supply side (scope economies in R&D). Our empirical measure of the parameter h relates only to demand side effects; the identification and measurement of scope economies in R&D across submarkets would not be feasible in practice, and so the above test has been formulated in a way which neglects these supply-side linkages. But if such linkages are present, how is the prediction illustrated in Figure 35.8 affected? It is easy to show that the presence of such linkages will lead to an upward shift in the lower bound in the region of the origin, as illustrated in Figure 35.9, so that we will no longer find points in the bottom left-hand corner of the diagram [for details, see Sutton (1998, ch. 3)].

Sutton (1998) reports empirical evidence on the C_4, h relationship for U.S. 5-digit manufacturing industries in 1977.[40] The control group consists of the 100 5-digit industries for which the combined advertising and R&D to sales ratio was least ($\ll 1\%$). The experimental group consists of all industries with an R&D/sales ratio exceeding 4% (46 industries). The value of h is computed as the ratio of the sales of the largest 7-digit product group to the sales of the industry.[41] The results are illustrated in Figure 35.10,

[40] This is the only census year that coincides with the short period for which the Federal Trade Commission's Line-of-Business program was in operation, so that figures for R&D intensity computed at the level of the business, rather than the firm, are available, albeit only at the 4-digit level. It is also, fortunately, the case that for that year, sales by product group at the 7-digit level were reported in the Census of Manufactures, thus allowing h to be computed for each 5-digit industry.

[41] The level of aggregation at which submarkets should be defined in estimating h should be low enough to ensure that the firms in that submarket offer competing (groups of) products. Working at the lowest available (7-digit) level seems appropriate, on this criterion. In defining the market, it is appropriate to work at a level of aggregation corresponding to a 'break in the chain of substitutes', and here it is probably best to use the 4-digit or 5-digit SIC level as the best available approximation in official statistics.

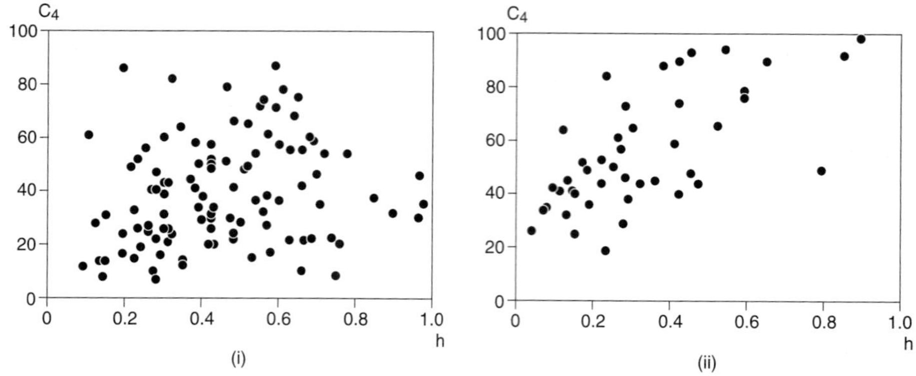

Figure 35.10. The (C_4, h) relationship for R&D-intensive industries (ii) and for a control group (i).

and they show a clear pattern of the form predicted.[42] A test of the same form as that reported above, following Smith's (1985, 1988) maximum likelihood method, indicates that the slope of the ray bounding the observations from below is significantly different from zero at the 5% level; the same results holds for the logit-transformed measure $\tilde{C}_4 = \ln(1/(1 - C_4))$.

A recent study investigating this relationship is that of Marin and Siotis (2001), who use the Chemintell data base to build up a dataset covering 102 markets in the chemicals sector in Europe (Germany, UK, Italy, France and Spain). Taking the European market as the relevant market, and splitting the sample into a 'low R&D' control group[43] of 42 industries and a 'high R&D' group of 60 industries, the authors examine the (C_1, h) relationship by carrying out a 'frontier analysis' exercise, within which they examine whether h affects the lower bound to concentration differently as between the control group and experimental group. They show that the lower bound rises with h in the experimental group, but is independent of h in the control group, consistently with the prediction illustrated in Figures 35.8 and 35.10[44].

As in the scatter diagrams from Sutton (1998) shown in Figure 35.10, the scatters shown by Marin and Siotis show an absence of points in the region of the origin for

[42] The outlier to the center right in the lower panel of Figure 35.10 is SIC 35731 (Electronic Computers). The recorded h index for this industry may be anomalous. The reported four-firm concentration ratio for SIC 35731 (Electronic Computers) fell from 75 percent in 1972 to 49 percent in 1977. The U.S. Department of Commerce's *Industrial Outlook* for 1977 noted that this industry's product lines had already fragmented into mainframes, minicomputers, etc. This was not reflected in the seven-digit product listings until the classification was revised in 1987. From that date, the measured h-index is much lower.

[43] The cutoff level chosen for the R&D/Sales ratio is 1.8%; the authors choose this level on the basis of a detailed examination of R&D spending figures, together with patent data.

[44] They also replicate the form of test used in Sutton (1998) by examining whether the ratio C_1/h is bounded away from zero for the experimental group; here, they report that the lower bound to the ratio is significantly different to zero at the 1% level.

the R&D intensive group. As noted above, this is consistent with the presence of scope economies across (at least some) submarkets in low-h industries; and in the presence of such scope economies, the asymptotic lower bound to $C_1(S)$ will lie above zero, in datasets collected at the level of the 'market'; nonetheless, as Marin and Siotis show, there is an important loss of information involved in applying the $C_1(S)$ relation at this level (i.e. without controlling for h).

2.6.3. Some natural experiments

It is of interest, as before, to look to some case histories of industries in which an exogenous shock led to a rise in the lower bound to concentration. As emphasized already, the theory does not specify any dynamic adjustment path to a new equilibrium. It does, however, specify the form of the 'profitable deviation' that becomes available to firms once the exogenous shock arises. Here, we expect to see a process of escalating R&D outlays among the firms. Checking that the exogenous shock sparks off such a process provides us with an ancillary test of the theory; if such a process is not in evidence, then the explanation offered by the theory for any subsequent rise in concentration is implausible.

The theory indicates that the (asymptotic) lower bound to concentration depends on two parameters, β, measuring the effectiveness of R&D (or advertising) in raising technical performance (or perceived quality), and σ, which measures the strength of linkages between submarkets. It is of interest, therefore, to investigate natural experiments which are driven by each of these parameters.

The photographic film industry affords a nice example of a shift in β, associated with the advent of color film in the 1960s. Up to the early 1960s, black and white film was dominant, and the technology of production was well established. There was little incentive to spend on R&D, as the quality of existing film was high, and few consumers were willing to pay a premium for higher quality film. Color film, on the other hand, was in its infancy, and quality was poor. As quality began to rise, its share of the market increased, and it became clear that it would in due course come to dominate the market. As this became apparent to firms, their R&D efforts escalated, and following a process of exit, and consolidation by merger and acquisition, the global industry came to be dominated by two firms (Kodak and Fuji).

A natural experiment involving a shift in σ is provided by the telecommunications sector. Up to the end of the 1970s, it had been standard practice for each major producer of switching systems to operate domestic procurement policies that strongly favored local firms. A shift in the U.S. policy marked by the breakup of AT&T in 1982, however, was seen – both within the U.S. and elsewhere – as signaling a likely move towards more deregulated markets, in which domestic procurement would no longer be the rule. In terms of the theory, this is equivalent to the joining-up of hitherto separated submarkets (and so to a rise in σ). The aftermath of these events saw an escalation of R&D efforts in the next generation of switching devices, and a rise in global concentration levels, to the point where the world market came to be dominated by five firms by the early 1990s. [The details of both these cases will be found in Sutton (1998, ch. 5).]

2.6.4. Case histories

A series of recent studies have examined the evolution of structure in particular industries by reference to the 'endogenous sunk costs' framework. Bresnahan and Greenstein (1999) apply the model to the computer industry, Motta and Polo (1997) to the broadcasting (television) industry, while Matraves (1999) explores the pharmaceutical industry as an example of a 'low-alpha' industry [see also Sutton (1998, chs. 8 and 15) for the pharmaceuticals and computer industries, respectively]. Bakker (2005) explores the early history of the European film ('movie') industry, and explains the decline of the industry at the advent of the 'talkies' era by reference to an 'escalation effect' in which the U.S. film makers took the lead. The early history of the aircraft industry, explored in Sutton (1998, ch. 16), offers a nice example of 'escalation and shakeout', which was first documented systematically in the classic analysis of Almarin Phillips (1971).

3. The size distribution

A curious feature of all the models considered so far lies in the role played by outcomes in which all firms are of the same size. The bounds defined in Section 2 were generated by outcomes of this type, yet it is rare to encounter such an outcome in practice. Most industries are characterized by a fairly skew distribution, with a small number of relatively large firms. It is this observation that motivates the traditional growth-of-firms literature that began with the seminar contribution of Gibrat (1931).

In contrast to the game-theoretic models considered so far, which place strategic interactions at the heart of the analysis, the growth-of-firms tradition begins by abstracting from all such effects. Implicitly or explicitly, it works in a framework in which the market consists of a number of independent 'island' submarkets, each large enough to support a single production plant. It models the evolution of market structure by looking at a population of firms, each of which grows over time by taking up a succession of these discrete 'investment opportunities'. At the heart of the analysis lies a simple point: if firms enter a market over time, the recent arrivals will have had fewer of these opportunities, and will on average be smaller. In other words, the mere disparity in firms' ages is a source of size inequality. It will turn out in what follows that the size inequality deriving from this point alone will place sharply defined limits on the size distribution. The degree to which this mechanism induces inequality in firms' sizes turns on the question: how will the current size of an already active firm (as measured by the number of investment opportunities it has already take up on different islands) affect the likelihood that it will be the one to take up the next 'investment opportunity'?

3.1. Background: stochastic models of firm growth

The 'growth-of-firms' tradition generated a major literature during the 1950s and '60s which crystallized in the work of Simon and his several co-authors [see Ijiri and Simon (1964, 1977), Sutton (1997b)]. The Simon model provides a useful point of departure in assessing the later literature. It assumes a framework in which the market consists of a sequence of independent opportunities, each of size unity, which arise over time. As each opportunity arises, there is some probability p that it will be taken up by a new entrant. With probability $(1 - p)$ it will be taken up by one of those firms already in the market ('active firms'). The size of any (active) firm is measured by the number of opportunities it has already taken up. There are two assumptions:

(i) Gibrat's Law: the probability that the next opportunity is taken up by any particular active firm is proportional to the current size of the firm.

(ii) Entry: the probability that the next opportunity is taken up by a new entrant is constant over time.

Assumption (ii) is rather arbitrary, though it may be a reasonable approximation. Simon regarded it merely as providing a useful benchmark, and presented various robustness tests showing that 'reasonable' departures from the assumed constancy of p would have only a modest effect on the predictions of the model. The predictions are driven crucially by assumption (i) (Gibrat's Law). What this leads to is a skew distribution of the Yule type, and Simon presented various empirical studies for the U.S. which suggested that it provided a good approximation to the size distribution of large manufacturing firms.

The goodness of fit of the size distribution provides only indirect evidence for Gibrat's Law. A second strand of the literature of the 1950s and '60s focused on the direct investigation of Gibrat's Law, by looking at the relation between firm size and growth over successive years in a panel of firms. While various studies of this kind cast doubt on the idea that proportional growth rates were independent of firm size, no clear alternative characterization emerged.

These questions were re-explored during the 1980s, when researchers obtained access to U.S. census data which allowed them to examine the growth of manufacturing establishments (plants) as a function of both size and age.[45] These new studies suggested a more subtle characterization, which involves two statistical regularities. The first regularity relates to survival rates: it was found that the probability of survival increases with firm (or plant) size, while the proportional rate of growth of a firm (or plant) conditional on survival is decreasing in size. The second regularity relates to age and size: for any given size of firm (or plant), the proportional rate of growth is smaller according as the firm (or plant) is older, but its probability of survival is greater.

These new findings prompted new interest in theoretical models of firm growth. An obvious candidate model was the recently published 'learning' model of Jovanovic

[45] Evans (1987a, 1987b), Hall (1987), Dunne, Roberts and Samuelson (1988).

(1982). In the Jovanovic model, a sequence of firms enters the market. Each firm has some level of 'efficiency' (its unit cost of production), but it does not know what its relative efficiency is prior to entering. Over time, the profits it achieves provide information on its relative efficiency. More efficient firms grow and survive. Less efficient firms 'learn' of their relative inefficiency, and (some) choose to exit.

This model provides a qualitative description of a process of excess entry followed by some exit, and this was the aspect of the model which made it attractive as a vehicle for discussing the new empirical results. As to the size distribution of firms, the model said little: it would depend on inter alia on unobservables, such as the initial distribution of 'efficiency levels'.

Other attempts to model from growth and the size distribution using strategic models led to a similar conclusion: results depended delicately on industry-specific features that would be difficult to control for in cross-industry studies [Hjalmarsson (1974), Selten (1983)].

In parallel with these theoretical developments, new appraisals on the empirical evidence on the size distribution led to a complementary conclusion. In the second volume of this Handbook, Schmalensee (1989) concluded that attempts to fit the data on size distributions for different industries led to the conclusion that 'no one form of distribution fits all industries well'.

It is these findings which motivate the search for a weaker, bounds type, characterization in what follows.

3.2. *A bounds approach to the size distribution*

The approach introduced in Sutton (1998) proceeds in two steps. The first step, set out in this section, remains within the traditional growth-of-firms framework, and explores the consequences of replacing Gibrat's Law with a weak inequality restriction on the size–growth relationship (labeled the 'provisional hypothesis'). In the second step, set out in the next section, we return to a game-theoretic setting, and show how this restriction arises naturally from a more fundamental 'symmetry principle' within the special context of a market that comprises many (approximately) independent submarkets.

The traditional literature began with the question: how does the size of a firm affect the likelihood that it will be the one to enter the next 'island' market? Rather than offer a direct answer, we take a different approach. Since we aim to find a bound in the space of outcomes, corresponding to the least unequal distribution of firm size, it is natural to ask what would happen if we treated all firms symmetrically, i.e. if we supposed, in particular, that a firm's past history on other islands had no effect on its future prospects. Now this is clearly not a good description of what will happen *on average*, since in many if not most markets the firm that is already operating on other islands will have an advantage, via economies of scale or learning effects, say, over its smaller rivals. To allow for this, however, we introduce our replacement for Gibrat's Law in the form of an inequality constraint.

Gibrat's Law states that if there are two incumbent firms, A and B, whose sizes (as measured by the number of opportunities they have taken up so far) are denoted n_A and n_B, then the probability that firm A (respectively B) takes up the opportunity is proportional to the current size of firm A (respectively B). In what follows, this assumption is replaced by the restriction:

(i)a The provisional hypothesis: the probability that the next market opportunity is filled by any currently active firm is non-decreasing in the size of that firm.

Stated in terms of growth rates, Gibrat's Law assumes that a firm's *proportional* growth rate is independent of its size; the present 'provisional hypothesis' states that a firm's *absolute* growth rate is non-decreasing in firm size.

It is shown in Sutton (1998, ch. 10) that this modified Simon model leads, in the limit where the number of opportunities becomes large, to a size distribution which features a certain minimum degree of inequality in the size distribution of firms. Specifically, it leads to the prediction that the Lorenz curve must lie farther from the diagonal than a limiting 'reference curve', which is defined by the relationship

$$C_k \geqslant \frac{k}{N}\left(1 - \ln \frac{k}{N}\right), \tag{3.1}$$

where C_k is the k-firm concentration ratio (which here represents the fraction of all opportunities taken up by the k largest firms in the industry), and N is the number of firms. (The case of equal sizes would correspond to $C_k = k/N$, and here the Lorenz curve lies on the diagonal.)

This result has two interesting features:

1. The lower bound to concentration is *independent* of Simon's entry parameter p which represents the probability that any opportunity will be taken up by a new entrant. Here, this parameter affects average firm size but not the shape of the size distribution or the associated concentration measures. This contrasts sharply with the traditional literature on the size distribution of firms, which led to a family of size distributions of varying skewness, parameterized by p. Simon's work linked this parameter to empirical estimates of the entry rate of new firms. Other early models also led to a *family* of size distributions; in Hart and Prais (1956), for example, the lognormal distribution's variance could be linked to the variance of the distribution of shocks to firm size between successive periods. The present setup contains no free parameters whose measurement might be subject to error; it leads to a quantitative prediction regarding the lower bound to concentration, conditional only on the assumed constancy of the entry rate (condition (ii)).
2. Various countries publish data on k-firm concentration ratios for several different values of k. The present result implies that the various k-firm ratios are all bounded below by a curve which approximates the above reference curve. In what follows, we take advantage of this in pooling data for various reported k-firm concentration ratios.

One final comment is in order. So far, we have confined attention to a setting in which all opportunities are identical, so that a firm's size can be measured by the number of opportunities that it captures. What if opportunities differ in size?

Suppose that the size of each opportunity is given by an independent random draw from some distribution, and consider two distributions in which the size of a firm is measured (a) by a count of the number of opportunities that it has taken up (i.e. the distribution considered in the preceding discussion), and (b) by the sum of the sizes of the opportunities it has taken up.[46]

It can be shown [Sutton (1998, Appendix 10.4)] that the Lorenz curve associated with distribution (b) lies further from the diagonal than that of distribution (a). In other words, the heterogeneity of opportunities simply adds an additional component to the inequality in the size distribution. This will cause a greater degree of inequality in firm sizes; it will not lead to a violation of the bounds specified by the above formula.

The results described in this section emerge from a re-working of the traditional growth-of-firms literature, in which Gibrat's Law is replaced by a weak inequality constraint on the size-growth relationship (condition (i)a). How does this relate to a game-theoretic analysis? This is the subject of the next section.

3.3. The size distribution: a game-theoretic approach

The bridge from the 'stochastic process' model just explored, to a game-theoretic analysis, rests on the idea of 'markets and submarkets', developed in Section 2.6 above. Here, we focus on the limiting case of a market that contains many independent submarkets, between which there are no linkages, either on the demand side or the supply side. In this setting, all strategic interactions occur *within* submarkets, rather than across submarkets.

The simplest context of this kind is the one used in the growth-of-firms approach, where each submarket consists of a single island market supporting one plant. The results for this case generalize immediately to the setting in which each submarket supports several plants. We begin, then, with the single plant case, and suppose that the island submarkets open up in succession over time. We distinguish between firms that already operate one or more plants ('active firms') and those who do not. The size of an 'active' firm is measured by the number of plants it already operates.

The key idea relates to the analysis of entry to a single island market, where our pool of potential entrants consists of all the currently active firms. Loosely, what we want to explore is the idea that each of these active firms has the same probability of occupying

[46] For the sake of concreteness, we might consider each opportunity to involve an investment of one unit, and to generate a level of sales revenue that was described by a independent random draw from some distribution. We can then interpret distribution (i) as the 'size distribution by assets', and distribution (ii) as the 'size distribution by sales'.

the next island submarket, independently of their histories in other submarkets, and so independently of their sizes.[47]

This idea mirrors the 'provisional hypothesis' of the preceding section, where the minimal degree of size inequality occurred when the probability of taking up the next opportunity was independent of firm size.

In a game-theoretic setting, we can generate the appropriate entry probabilities directly by focusing on symmetric equilibria; here the probabilities emerge naturally as part of the symmetric (mixed strategy) equilibrium. To see how this works, recall the (static) game-theoretic analysis of a single island market large enough to support exactly one firm: if we confine attention to pure strategy equilibria, there are several asymmetric equilibria, in which firm 1 (or 2, or 3) enters while all other firms do not enter. There is also one symmetric equilibrium, in which each firm uses the same mixed strategy (of the form 'enter with probability p, do not enter with probability $(1 - p)$'). Building on this idea, it is straightforward to generate mixed strategy equilibria, in a suitably constructed dynamic entry game, which has the feature that exactly one firm enters, and where the probability of being the entrant is the same for all firms [Sutton (1998, ch. 11)].

The key novelty of the game-theoretic approach is that it allows us to examine situations in which each island submarket can support several firms between which there may be various kinds of strategic interactions. For example, along the equilibrium path of the game, it may be that the first firm to enter 'pre-empts' further entry (either permanently or temporarily). It may be that a sequence of firms enter, each with a different number of products, these products being entered at a series of discrete times [see Sutton (1998, ch. 11) for examples of this kind]. Once a firm has entered its first product, then, it is no longer symmetric with firms that have not yet entered on this island, and it may (and in general will) play a pure strategy in the subgame that follows its entry. But there is one generic feature that must always hold, which relates to the set of firms that have not yet entered. It must be the case, at any decision point at which entry occurs, along the equilibrium path of the game, that each of these firms has the same probability of being selected as the entrant.

This suggests a simple nomenclature: we can think of the potential entrants as taking up 'roles' in the game, and we can name these roles as 'first entrant', 'second entrant' and so on. Along the equilibrium path of the game, the firm filling a particular role ('first entrant' say) may for example enter a higher number of plants than a firm playing a different ('second entrant') role, so that roles differ in size. The key assumption, labeled the 'symmetry' principle, relates to the allocation of roles to new entrants: all potential entrants are treated equally in role assignment.[48]

[47] Since we are looking at a lower bound to concentration we are, as before, abstracting from all other forms of asymmetry between the firms; as noted earlier, any such 'firm specific-effects' tend to lead to a higher level of concentration, and so on in characterizing a lower bound, it is natural to abstract from such effects.

[48] Formally this requirement is expressed in a manner analogous to the Selten–Harsanyi restriction for games with affine subgames: we require that the strategy used by each firm induces the same strategy for each submarket (independently of the history of actions in other submarkets) [Harsanyi and Selten (1988)].

In Sutton (1998, ch. 13), a formal model is presented in which firms enter a series of submarkets, subject to the above principle. It is shown that, irrespective of the nature of (the game played in) each submarket, the limiting form of the size distribution, where a firm's size is measured on the number of roles it occupies, converges to a geometric distribution. Where all the roles are identical, as in the 'single plant per island' setting, then the limiting Lorenz curve satisfies (3.1) above as an equality. Once roles differ in size, however, the Lorenz curve moves further from the diagonal, and (3.1) is satisfied as an inequality.

We have, therefore, two ways of arriving at this limiting Lorenz curve, which derive respectively from (i) the 'provisional hypothesis' of the preceding section, and from (ii) the 'symmetry' principle for markets with independent submarkets. The two lines of attack are complementary, and it is useful in empirical investigations to bear in mind the intuitions underlying each approach. The game-theoretic model pertains only to the context of markets with many (approximately) independent submarkets, and in this context it provides a vehicle for investigating the size distribution both *within* submarkets (where the bounding Lorenz curve does not apply) and for the market as a whole (where it does). This leads to some sharp tests of the theory, as we note below.

One advantage of combining the first ('growth of firms') treatment of this issue with the game-theoretic model, is that it focuses attention on an alternative interpretation of what drives the result on the limiting Lorenz curve. In order to violate the 'inequality' relationship that replaces Gibrat's Law, and so this limiting Lorenz curve, we need to have a setting in which large firms suffer a systematic disadvantage relative to smaller rivals, in respect of their absolute growth rates. Even in markets that do *not* contain 'many independent submarkets', we would not *normally* expect to see a violation of this kind; such violations might be expected only in rather special circumstances (see below).

One final technical remark is in order, regarding the role of 'independence effects' in the above analysis. We have worked here in terms of a setup containing many independent submarkets. Yet it is rare in economics to encounter a market in which the submarkets are strictly independent. Nonetheless, across the general run of 4- or 5-digit SIC industries in the U.S., it is in most cases easy to identify various submarkets (in product space, or in geographic space) which are approximately independent [for a definition of the concept of 'approximate independence', see Sutton (1998), Barbour, Holst and Janson (1992)].[49] It is of considerable relevance in the present context to note that the results developed above do *not* require that the submarkets be independent, but only that they be approximately independent.

[49] A simple illustration may be helpful: let $\ldots, x_{-1}, x_0, x_1, x_2, \ldots$ be independent random variables. Define the set of random variables θ_i as follows: for a fixed $\tau > 1$, let θ_i be a linear combination of $x_{i-\tau}, x_{i-\tau+1}, \ldots, x_{i+\tau}$. Now the θ_i are approximately independent. (Note that θ_1 is not independent of θ_2 as both depend on x_1; but θ_i is independent of all θ_j, where $j \leqslant i - 2\tau$ or $j \geqslant i + 2\tau$.) This example is of particular economic interest in the context of geographically separated submarkets.

3.4. The size distribution: empirical evidence

The empirical predictions may be summarized as follows:

1. A reference curve exists which bounds the Lorenz curve away from the diagonal ((3.1) above). There are two alternative sufficient conditions[50] for this curve to apply:
   (a) The *absolute* growth rate is non-decreasing in firm size;
   (b) The market comprises many (approximately) independent submarkets.
2. The Lorenz curve will lie strictly further from the diagonal than the reference curve, if either of two conditions hold:
   (a) If the *absolute* growth rate is strictly increasing in firm size. (The presence of economies of scale or scope will lead to an effect of this kind.)

   The second condition relates to the 'independent submarkets' model:
   (b) If different roles within submarkets (i.e. 'first mover', 'second mover', etc.) are associated with different sizes of businesses *within* each submarket, then again the Lorenz curve for the market as a whole will lie strictly beyond the reference curve.

In the context of markets containing many submarkets, an additional and more powerful test of the theory can be formulated. This depends on identifying conditions under which a game-theoretic model would predict that, within each individual submarket, the bound defined by the reference curve would be violated (in the sense that the Lorenz curve should lie on, or close to, the diagonal). In Sutton (1998, ch. 2), a sufficient set of conditions for this to hold is developed.[51] In this context we have the twin prediction that:

3. (a) The Lorenz curves for individual submarkets lie close to the diagonal;
   (b) The Lorenz curve for the market as a whole lies at or beyond the reference curve.

The above 'bounds' prediction has been tested using data for manufacturing industries in the U.S. and Germany [Sutton (1998, ch. 13)]. A comparison of the U.S. and German cases is of particular interest in testing a 'bounds' prediction, since it is well known that, among those countries that produce high quality census of manufactures data, the average level of industrial concentration is relatively high in the U.S., and relatively low in Germany. Hence if we pool all observations for (C_k, N), where N denotes

[50] Assuming, following Simon's 'benchmark case' assumption, that the fraction of opportunities filled by new entrants is constant over time; if this fraction is decreasing over time, the bound may be violated (Section 3.1).

[51] Specifically, the results are developed for the class of 'symmetric' product differentiation models (Dixit–Stiglitz model, Linear demand model, etc.). These models can be interpreted as pertaining to markets where the submarkets are small in the sense that all firms' market areas are overlapping. Within this class of models, it is shown that if (a) the products are close substitutes, and (b) the toughness of price competition is low, then irrespective of the form of the entry process, the only form of equilibrium is one where each entrant offers a single product.

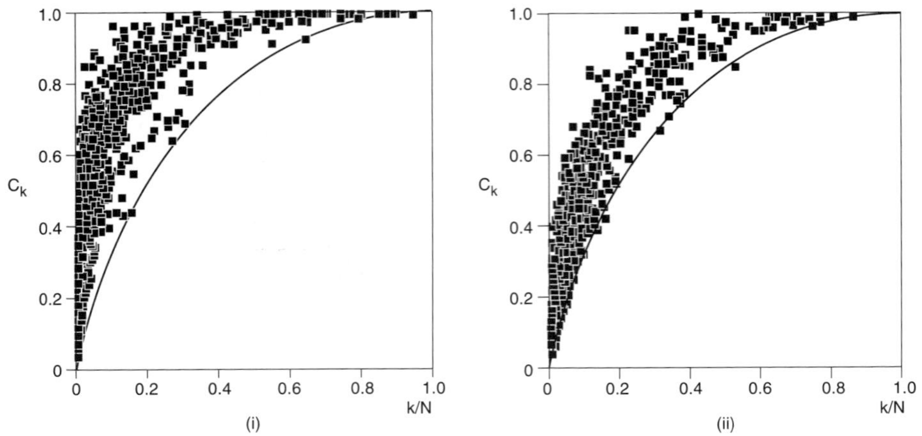

Figure 35.11. Panel (i) shows the scatter diagram of C_k against k/N for pooled data ($k = 4$, 8 and 20) for the United States 1987, at the four-digit level. The Lorenz curve shown on these figures is the reference curve (3.1). Panel (ii) shows data for Germany, 1990 ($k = 3, 6, 10$ and 25).

the number of firms, and C_k is a k-firm concentration ratio, then the resulting 'cloud' of points in (C_k, N) space for the U.S. will lie much farther above the diagonal than will the cloud for German data. Yet if a 'bounds' approach is appropriate, then we should find that the edge of the two clouds should lie on the predicted reference curve above. From Figure 35.11, which shows the data for the U.S. and Germany, it is clear that this is the case.

A second way of testing the prediction is by examining the induced relationship between C_k and C_m, where $m > k$, as described in Sutton (1998, ch. 10, Proposition 10.3). This test has the advantage of relying only on the (relatively easy to measure) concentration ratios, and not on the (much more problematic) count of firm numbers. The test procedure involves substituting m and C_m into the reference curve (3.1) to infer a corresponding value of N; then inserting this value of N, and k, in (3.1) we obtain a lower bound to C_k conditional on C_m, which we label $\underline{C}_k(C_m)$.

Results for this conditional prediction are shown in Figure 35.12. An interesting feature of these results appears when the residuals, $C_4 - \underline{C}_4(C_{50})$, are plotted as a histogram (Figure 35.13). It is clear that the histogram is strong asymmetrical, with a sharp fall at zero, where the bound is reached. Such a pattern of residuals can be seen, from a purely statistical viewpoint, as a 'fingerprint' of the bounds representation, suggesting that on statistical grounds alone, this data would be poorly represented by a conventional 'central tendency' model which predicted the 'center' of the cloud of points, rather than its lower bound.

These predictions on the 'reference curve' bound can be derived from a modified model of the traditional kind, without reference to game-theory, or to the 'independent submarkets' model as we saw above. A more searching test of the 'independent submarkets' model developed above is provided by focusing on a market that comprises

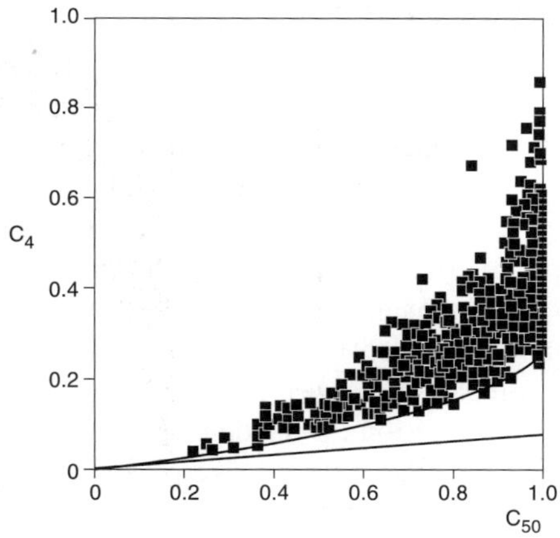

Figure 35.12. An alternative test of the bounds prediction, using data for U.S. manufacturing at the five-digit level, 1977 by reference to a scatter diagram of C_4 versus C_{50}. The solid curve shows the lower bound $C_4(C_{50})$ predicted by the theory. The ray shown below this curve corresponds to the symmetric equilibrium in which all firms are of equal size.

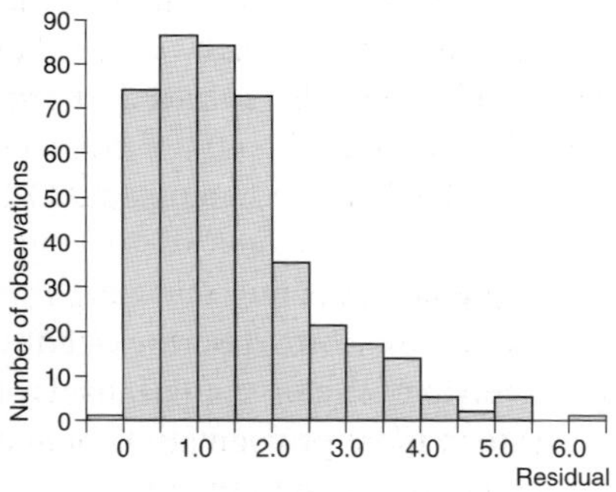

Figure 35.13. A histogram of differences between the actual concentration ratio C_k and the predicted lower bound $C_k(C_{50})$ for the data in Figure 35.12.

many submarkets, and which also satisfies a set of 'special conditions' under which a game-theoretic analysis predicts that the Lorenz curves for individual submarkets must lie close to the diagonal.[52] The U.S. cement market, which satisfies these conditions well, is examined for 1986 in Sutton (1998, ch. 13). It is found that, of 29 states[53] having more than one plant, all but one have Lorenz curves lying closer to the diagonal than the reference curve; yet at the aggregate level, the Lorenz curve for the U.S. as a

[52] See above, footnote 51.

[53] In Sutton (1998), data at state level for the U.S. was chosen as the size of the typical state is of the same order as the typical 'shipping radius' for cement plants.

whole lies almost exactly on the reference curve. These results are consistent with the predictions of the 'independent submarkets' model.

A number of recent studies have re-examined these predicted relations on the size distribution. De Juan (2002, 2003) examines the retail banking industry in Spain, at the level of local (urban area) submarkets (4977 towns), and at the regional level. As in the case of the cement market, described above, conditions in the retail banking industry appear to satisfy the special conditions under which individual submarkets will have Lorenz curves close to the diagonal. A question that arises here is, how large a town can be considered as an (independent) submarket in the sense of the theory? A large city will presumably encompass a number of local submarkets. Rather than decide a priori on an appropriate size criterion for the definition of a submarket, the author sets out to 'let the data decide' on the threshold size of a submarket. With this in mind, she carries out a regression analysis across all towns with population sizes in the range 1000–5000 inhabitants, distinguishing between two sets of explanatory variables: decomposing the number of branches per town into the product of the number of branches per submarket, and the number of submarkets per town, she postulates that the number of branches per submarket depends on population density and the level of per-capita income, while the number of submarkets per town depends (non-linearly) on the population of the town. The results of this regression analysis are used to fix a threshold that determines a sub-set of 'single submarket towns'. For this sub-set of towns, she finds that 96% are 'maximally fragmented' (i.e. the Lorenz curve lies on the diagonal).

The analysis is then extended to larger towns; using a map of branch locations, cluster analysis methods are used to identify alternative 'reasonable' partitionings of the area of the town into 'local submarkets'. Examining one typical medium-size town in this way, she finds that 71% of those local submarkets are maximally fragmented. Finally, the analysis is extended to the level of major regions, each of which comprises many towns; here, the Lorenz curves for each region are found to lie farther from the diagonal than the reference curve.

Buzzacchi and Valletti (2006) examine the motor vehicle insurance industry in Italy. Here, the institutional framework of the industry is such as to produce an administratively determined set of submarkets: each vehicle is registered within one of 103 provinces, and owners are required to buy insurance within their own province; moreover, over nine-tenths of premia are collected through local agents within the province. The authors develop a model of strategic interaction to model competition within submarkets. At the submarket level they find, consistently with their model, that Lorenz curves for the 103 provinces lie almost wholly between the reference curve and the diagonal. At the national level, however, the Lorenz curve lies farther from the diagonal than the reference curve defined by Equation (3.1), as predicted.

In an interesting extension of the analysis, the authors examine, for a set of 13 European countries, the conditional prediction for the lower bound to C_5 as a function of C_{15}; the results show that the cloud of observations lies within, but close to the predicted (conditional) lower bound (as in Figure 35.12).

While all the empirical tests considered so far deal with geographic submarkets, Walsh and Whelan (2001) deal with submarkets in product space: specifically, they look at retail market shares in carbonated soft drinks in Ireland. Within this market, they identify 20 submarkets; and they justify this level of definition of submarkets by reference to an estimation of cross–price elasticities, by reference to an estimated model of demand.[54]

In this market, the special conditions set out above do not apply; and so the expectation under the theory is that the Lorenz curves for submarkets should not stand in any special relationship to the reference curve; in fact, these submarket level Lorenz curves lie in a widely dispersed cloud that extends from the diagonal to well beyond the reference curve. Here, the authors make a important distinction, relative to the theory, in distinguishing between the Lorenz curve based on a count of roles, versus the curve based on sales data. The latter incorporates, as noted earlier, an additional variance component associated with the dispersion in role size, and is expected to lie farther from the diagonal than the reference curve. One unusual feature of this study is that the authors can follow year-to-year fluctuations in role size. It is shown that

(i) the Lorenz curve based on role size is stable from year to year and is very close to the reference curve defined by (3.1);
(ii) the Lorenz curve based on sales data lies farther from the diagonal, and is relatively volatile over time. This finding is consistent with prediction 2(b) above.

In two recent papers, Ellickson (2006, 2007) presents a wide-ranging analysis of the U.S. supermarket industry. The point of departure of the analysis lies in his finding that supermarket concentration in local markets (defined by reference to their range of distribution to stores) exhibits the 'non-convergence' property. The author considers several alternative models to explain observed structure (horizontal product differentiation, capacity competition, product proliferation models, etc.), and rejects each of these in favor on an 'endogenous sunk cost' model. He conjectures that the important element in these costs relates to the development of more efficient (chain-level distribution systems based in part of information technology).

Ellickson then goes on to distinguish two groups of firms in the industry: those (large firms) which compete in such investments at the chain-level, and the 'fringe' of (smaller) firms that do not. He argues that the latter group of firms should be well represented by the 'independent submarkets' model, but the former group should not (as their firm-level investments create economies of scope across local submarkets). He then examines the Lorenz curves for each group, while using the characteristics of the empirical Lorenz curves to determine the dividing line between the two groups. It is found that the dividing line corresponds well to the distinction between firms that operate distribution networks organized at the national chain level, and those which do not.

[54] One caveat is in order here, insofar as many of the firms involved here are foreign firms, and so it is less easy to imagine the entry process in terms of the model set out above.

4. Dynamics of market structure

The two literatures considered up to this point have been concerned with explaining cross-sectional regularities of two different kinds. Each one leads to a constraint on the pattern of outcomes seen in cross-industry data sets. These constraints can be meshed together in a straightforward way, to provide a unified analysis of cross-industry patterns [Sutton (1998, ch. 14)].

In this section, we turn to questions of dynamics. Here, the link between theory and evidence is much less tight. This reflects the fact that the problems posed by unobservables (such as the beliefs of firms and the way this impinges on entry decisions, etc.) pose much more serious problems, and it is notoriously difficult to arrive at robust theoretical results that place testable restrictions on the data.

4.1. Dynamic games

To what extent can the results of the multi-stage game models developed in Section 2 above be carried over to a 'dynamic games' framework, in which firms spend on fixed outlays in each successive period, while enjoying a flow of returns in each period that reflects the current quality and cost levels of the firm and its rivals? This is a difficult question, which has been explored from two angles. In Sutton (1998, ch. 13), a dynamic game is set out in which an exogenously fixed 'imitation lag' T is imposed, in the sense that if a firm raises its R&D spending at time t, then the resulting quality jump occurs only at time $t + T$; rivals do not observe the expenditure at time t, but do observe the quality jump at time $t + T$. The point of this model is to expose the nature of the implicit assumption that is made in choosing a multi-stage framework: the results of such a framework can be mimicked in the dynamic game set up by letting the lag T become large. In other words, the multi-stage game framework implicitly excludes certain kinds of equilibria that may arise in dynamic games. It is therefore of particular interest to ask: to what extent might ('new') forms of equilibria appear in an unrestricted dynamic game, that could undermine the non-convergence results developed above? The issue of interest turns on the appearance of 'underinvestment equilibria', as described in Sutton (1998). Here the idea is that firms 'underspend' on R&D, because rivals strategies prescribe that any rise in R&D spending by firm 1 at time t will result in a rise by its rivals at period $t + 1$. It is shown in Nocke (2006) that this kind of equilibrium can indeed appear in a suitably specified dynamic game in which firms can react arbitrarily quickly to rivals' actions. This leads to a reduction in the lower bound to concentration relative to the equivalent multi-stage game model; but the 'non-convergence theorem' developed above in the multi-stage game setting continues to hold good in the dynamic game.

A different approach to modeling industry equilibrium as a dynamic game has been introduced by Ariel Pakes and his several coauthors [see in particular Ericson and Pakes (1995)], which provides inter alia an alternative vehicle within which to explore the evolution of structure in a dynamic setting. The examples based on this approach which have appeared in the published literature to date employ profit functions that, in the language of the present review, have a value of alpha equal to zero. In some recent work, however, Hole (1997) has introduced the simple 'Cournot model with quality' example of Section 2.2 above into the Pakes–Ericson framework. The results show, in the context of a 3-firm example, as the parameter β falls (so that alpha rises), the outcomes cluster in a region in which two firms account for an arbitrarily high fraction of sales. These results provide an analog of the 'non-convergence theorem' in a stochastic, dynamic setting. (For a discussion of the approach, see the contribution by Ariel Pakes and Uli Doraszelski to this volume.)

4.2. Learning-by-doing models and network effects

Two special mechanisms often cited in the literature as leading to a concentrated market structure are the learning-by-doing mechanism, and the network effects mechanism. [See, for example, Spence (1981), Fudenberg and Tirole (1983, 1985), Cabral and Riordan (1994), Gruber (1992, 1994).] It is shown in Sutton (1998, chs. 14 and 15) that these two mechanisms can be represented in simple 2-stage game models that are identical in structure ('isomorphic'). The idea is that the firms plays the same 'Cournot' game in each period, but each firm's second period cost function (in the learning-by-doing model) or the perceived quality of its product (in the network effects model) is affected by its level of output (sales) in the first period. This induces a linkage between the profit earned in the first period, and in the second. This effect is precisely analogous to the 'escalation mechanism' described above; we can think of the profit foregone in period 1 (as the firm raises its output beyond the level that maximizes first period profit) as an 'opportunity cost' analogous to the fixed cost $F(u)$ in the 'quality competition' model of Section 2.2 above. [This analogy is spelt out precisely in Sutton (1998, ch. 14, footnote 1, p. 351).] Beyond this simple 2-stage game characterization, however, the analysis of these games becomes more complex. The contribution of Cabral and Riordan (1994) is noteworthy, in that it gives a full characterization of the dynamics of the process in a learning-by-doing context.[55]

A central theme in the associated literature relates to the idea that small changes in initial conditions may have large effects on outcomes. ('History dependence.') This theme has been extensively explored by David (1975), David and Bunn (1990) and Arthur (1989). From an analytical viewpoint, this phenomenon can be seen as pertaining to a wide rate of games featuring an 'escalation' mechanism of the kind explored in Section 2.[56] A crisp theoretical characterization of this idea comes from the dynamics of patent–race games, of the form developed by Harris and Vickers (1985, 1987).

[55] Albeit at the cost of working in a setting in which a single indivisible unit is sold in each period, and attention is confined to symmetric equilibria.

[56] For some cases of 'history dependence' in this setting, see Sutton (1991, ch. 9).

4.3. Shakeouts

One of the most striking features of industry dynamics is the occurrence of 'shakeouts', a phenomenon documented and characterized in considerable depth by Klepper and his several co-authors [Klepper and Graddy (1990), Klepper and Simons (2005)]; as a new industry develops, the number of producers tends first to rise to a peak and later falls to some lower level. The extent and timing of this 'shakeout' varies widely across product markets. In some cases, it comes early in the life of the product, and is very sharp. In others, it is relatively muted, or does not occur at all. For example, the market for lasers, which is characterized by a large number of submarkets corresponding to lasers designed for different applications, shows no 'shakeout'; rather, the number of firms rises steadily over time. In the terminology of Section 2 above, this is a low-alpha industry. By contrast, the early history of the 'high-alpha' aircraft industry was marked by a very sharp shakeout [Sutton (1998, ch. 15)]. It seems the 'shakeout' process can plausibly be seen as part of a dynamic adjustment process associated with the evolution of concentration, and models of 'shakeout effects' can by seen as dynamic counterpoints of the static models of the 'escalation effect' of Section 2 above.

Two types of models have been postulated for shakeouts. The first is due to Jovanovic and MacDonald (1994) who begin by stating that Klepper's data on shakeout cannot be accounted for by appealing to the 'learning' model of Jovanovic (1982). Instead, the authors postulate a model in which early entrants employ a common technology which after some time is superseded by a new technology. The new technology offers low unit costs, but at a higher level of output per firm (scale economies). The transition to the new technology involves a shakeout of first generation firms, and the survival of a smaller number of firms who now employ the new large-scale technology. By calibrating the model against the data for the U.S. tire industry, the authors can simulate successfully the number of firms, and the movement of stock prices over time.[57]

The model of Klepper (1996) combines a stochastic growth process for firms, who enter by developing some new variant ('product innovation'), with the idea that each firm may spend some fixed costs to lower its unit cost of production ('process innovation'). Assuming some inertia in sales, and some imperfection in capital markets, those firms whose current sales are larger find it profitable to devote more fixed costs to process innovation (because the fixed costs incurred are spread over a larger volume of sales). As the larger firms cut their unit production costs, some smaller firms are no longer viable, and these exit, generating the 'shakeout'.

4.4. Turbulence

A striking feature of industry dynamics is that, across different industries, there is a positive correlation between gross entry rates, and gross exit rates, i.e. the 'churning' of

[57] A recent model which focuses on explaining the temporal pattern of hazard rates for exit in this industry is that of Tong (2000).

the population of firms is greater in some industries than others. However, most of this entry and exit has little effect on the largest firms in the industry.[58]

Within any one country, quite a strong correlation usually exists between entry and exit rates by industry. Geroski (1991), for example, reports a correlation coefficient of 0.796 for a sample of 95 industries in the UK in 1987. The most comprehensive data on this issue comes from a compilation of country studies edited by Geroski and Schwalbach (1991). The cross-country comparisons afforded by this study indicate that there is at least a weak correspondence between the ranking of industries by turbulence in different countries. This is important in that it suggests that there may be some systematic, industry-specific, determinants of turbulence levels.

These results have prompted interest in the determinants of turbulence (defined conventionally in this literature as the sum of gross entry and gross exit rates) across different industries. At least four types of influence are likely to be involved:

(a) Underlying fluctuations in the pattern of demand across product varieties or plant locations.
(b) The displacement of existing technologies (modes of production) by alternatives.
(c) The displacement of existing products by new and superior substitutes.
(d) Fluctuations in relative efficiency (productivity) levels across firms.

Of these, the first factor may be of primary importance, but while it is easy to model, it is very difficult to measure or control for empirically. The second and third factors pose some interesting questions in terms of modeling. Some new models have been developed recently, but these have not yet led to empirically tested claims regarding the influence of industry characteristics on the degree of turbulence. The effect of a displacement of production technologies has been modeled by Lambson (1992), who considers an industry facing exogenous shocks to relative factor prices, which occur at infrequent intervals. Firms incur sunk costs in building a plant using a given technology, and when factor prices change, an entrant – knowing that factor prices shift rarely – may find it profitable to enter the industry and displace incumbents. In this kind of model, the level of sunk costs incurred by firms will influence entry and exit rates, conditional on the volatility of industry demand.

The third factor listed above relates to the idea that (some) exit may be induced by entry, as new and superior product varieties displace existing products. This is a basic idea discussed in the vertical product differentiation literature. The key theoretical question is why the old varieties cannot continue to retain a positive market share at some price, given that their costs of product development are sunk. Such varieties would indeed continue to survive in a 'horizontal' product differentiation model, but this is not generally true in a 'vertical' product differentiation model [Gabszewicz and Thisse (1980), Shaked and Sutton (1982)].

58 The volatility of market shares among large firms has been less widely studies. An important early study was that for Caves and Porter (1978), which used the PIMS data-set. See also the studies by Steven Davies (1991) and David and Haltiwanger (1992).

The mechanism that has been explored most fully in the literature is that involving shocks to the relative efficiency (productivity) levels across firms. This is a central feature of the "passive learning" version of the Ericson–Pakes model discussed above. It is also the mechanism underlying the model of Hopenhayn (1992); a recent extension of the Hopenhayn model has been used by Asplund and Nocke (2006) to examine, both theoretically and empirically, the way in which changes in market size affects the rate of firm turnover.

5. Caveats and controversies

5.1. *Endogenous sunk costs: a caveat*

One procedure that has become common in the literature, following Sutton (1991), is to treat industries as falling into two discrete groups, those in which advertising and R&D are unimportant, and those in which they play a substantial role. Schmalensee (1992), in reviewing Sutton (1991), referred to these as type I and II industries, respectively.

In tandem with this nomenclature, it has become common to identify these two groups of industries as being represented by the 'exogenous sunk cost' model and the 'endogenous sunk cost model,' respectively. This leads to some confusion, since it begs the question: are not all sunk costs endogenous? (A firm can decide, for example, on its level of plant capacity, or its number of manufacturing plants.) While it is helpful in empirical testing to split the sample into two groups, it is worth noting that the underlying theoretical model is one of 'endogenous sunk costs'; and that the 'exogenous sunk cost model' is just a simplified representation of a special limiting case of the endogenous sunk cost model, corresponding to the limit $\beta \to \infty$ as noted in the text [Shaked and Sutton (1987)]. What matters to the level of concentration is not the 'endogeneity of sunk costs', but the value of α, which may be zero *either* because β is high, *or* because σ is low.

5.2. *Can 'increasing returns' explain concentration?*

The appeal of 'increasing returns' as a 'general' explanation for observed levels of market concentration is highly problematic, since different authors use this term in different ways. At one extreme, the term is used in its classic sense, to refer to the idea that the average cost curve is downward sloping. This feature holds good in all the models described above, including those cases where the lower bound to concentration falls to zero in large markets. It follows that an appeal to 'increasing returns' in this sense does not provide an explanation for high levels of concentration in large markets.

Another sense in which the term is used arises in empirical work, where it is said to be important to discover whether there are increasing returns to R&D. The implication behind this concern seems to be that the presence or absence of increasing returns could carry implications for market structure, with increasing returns being linked to high concentration.

What does "increasing returns" mean in this context? This is rarely spelled out, but what is often measured is a technical relation between R&D spending and some output measure, such as a count of patents. In terms of the present theory, diminishing returns in this sense are consistent with any value of alpha – and indeed, in the examples used above, we used a diminishing returns form for the function linking R&D spending to product quality.

Another sense in which we might interpret "increasing returns to R&D" would be to look, in the spirit of the present theory, at the relation between a firm's R&D spending and the gross profit it earns as a result of that spending. Within the theory, this relation can take either a diminishing returns form, or an S-shaped form (first increasing, then diminishing). Either shape is consistent with both low and high values of alpha. It would seem, then, that looking to increasing returns as an explanation for high concentration levels is not a helpful way forward.

5.3. Fixed costs versus sunk costs

It has been suggested that many of the features of the models described above should carry over to a setting in which costs are fixed but not sunk [Schmalensee (1992), Davies and Lyons (1996)]. It is not clear that any *general* claim of this kind can be supported by reference to a formal analysis, so long as we identify the '2-stage' (or multistage) game framework with the 'sunk cost' interpretation. [For a discussion of this point see Sutton (1991), and for a response, see Schmalensee (1992).] If costs are fixed but not sunk, it seems appropriate to model firms' actions by reference to a 1-shot game in which firms take simultaneous decisions on entry and prices. This captures the notion introduced in the Contestability literature by Baumol, Panzar and Willig (1982). It is crucial to results of this literature that sunk costs be *exactly* zero. The Bertrand example of Section 2 illustrates how an arbitrarily small departure from this assumption can change the qualitative features of equilibrium outcomes.[59] In practice, it seems to be extremely difficult to find any industry in which sunk costs are zero; for a recent attempt to quantify the extent to which fixed outlays are sunk, see Asplund (2000).

6. Unanswered questions and current research

In the light of the preceding discussion, there are four areas that are worth noting as being potentially fruitful areas for future research:

[59] If the sunk cost of entry is exactly zero in the Bertrand example, then any number $n \geqslant 2$ of firms will enter, and price will coincide with marginal cost.

Bounds and 'single industry studies' It was noted above that there is a deep complementarity between the bounds approach, and the single industry studies (or 'structural estimation') approach. The first aims at a low level characterization of some mechanisms that operate in a more or less uniform way across a wide range of industries. The latter approach focuses on 'model selection', its aim being to arrive at a richly specified model that captures various industry-specific factors. Building a bridge between the two levels offers some interesting challenges. This can in principle be worked upon from either end: by adding structure to a 'bounds model' or by uncovering, through the accumulation of evidence from different industries, some new candidate generalizations. One strand of current research in this area involves the study of 'limits to monopolization'. This line of inquiry is motivated by the empirical observation that we rarely see industries in which a single firm has a market share close to unity in large markets; the gradual 'fade-out' of the scatter diagrams in Figure 35.7 above as we move to the top right of the diagram illustrates this point. Research to date has been limited, but suggests that the mechanisms involved here are of a relatively delicate (industry-specific) kind [Nocke (2000), Vasconcelos (2002)].

The variance of growth rates While the growth-of-firms literature has focused considerable attention to the relation between the size of a firm and its *expected* growth rate, it was not until quite recently that attention was directed to the dispersion (variance) of firms' growth rates, and the way this varied across different size classes. A seminal paper appeared in *Nature* in 1996 which drew attention to a striking empirical regularity, in the form of a simple 'power law' relationship [Stanley et al. (1996)]. The interpretation of these results remains controversial, and deserves further scrutiny [for one candidate explanation, see Sutton (2001c), and for a dissenting view, Wyart and Bouchard (2002)]. A second empirical regularity reported in Stanley et al. (1996) relates to the shape of the distribution of proportional growth rates. The authors reported, for the Compustat data-set on U.S. corporations, a distribution of the double-exponential type. A recent contribution by Fu et al. (2005) combines the notion of 'independent submarkets' with Gibrat's Law to develop a candidate explanation for the distribution of firm growth rates.[60] It is perhaps because virtually all papers on these topics have appeared in physics, rather than economics journals, that this important strand in the recent literature has received less attention in the IO literature than it merits.[61]

60 Firms are represented as a collection of business units operating in different sub-markets; and Gibrat's Law is applied both to the sales of each individual business, and to the firm's introduction of new businesses. The pharmaceutical industry offers a unique context for testing such a model, since (approximately) independent business units can be identified with different 'therapeutic groups' within the industry [Sutton (1998)]. The authors show that the model leads to a form of distribution of firm growth rates that is double-exponential close to the origin, but has power-law ('fat') tails; and this predicted form fits the data very closely.

61 Another, less justifiable, reason for this lack of impact may be that the best candidate models are 'statistical', rather than ones based on (profit maximizing) firm behavior. But there is no reason why some economically interesting relationships should not derive from primitive and robust features of markets, in-

The size distribution revisited Notwithstanding the fact that the size distribution of firms varies widely across industries, there is continuing interest in characterizing the shape of the aggregate distribution of firm size for the economy as a whole. Axtell (2001) uses comprehensive data from the U.S. Census to show that the aggregate distribution conforms well over its entire range to a Pareto (i.e. power law or scaling) distribution with an exponent slightly above unity. While, as Axtell notes, there are various stochastic growth processes based on Gibrat's Law that converge to a distribution of this form, a deeper challenge lies in reconciling the apparent uniformity of the aggregate distribution with the fact that quite different patterns are observed within different industries.[62]

Market dynamics I: turbulence In this area, our knowledge remains quite limited. The key empirical finding is that the ranking of industries by the degree of (entry–exit) turbulence is broadly similar across countries. This strongly suggests that there are industry-specific factors at work in molding this pattern; the elucidation of the factors driving this pattern is one of the most intriguing challenges for future research.

Market dynamics II: market shares and market leadership A second aspect of market dynamics relates to fluctuations over time in the pattern of market shares within an industry. While a considerable literature has been devoted to developing stochastic models of market share dynamics, the main challenge lies in uncovering statistical regularities that can provide a focus for the interplay of theory and evidence in this area. One unresolved debate of long standing relates to the 'persistence of leadership' question: to what extent should we expect a market share leader to retain the leadership position over time? To what degree does leadership persist in practice? On what factors does the persistence of leadership depend? For a review of these issues in the context of an empirical investigation, see Sutton (2007).

Mergers One topic that has not been covered explicitly in this chapter is 'mergers and concentration'.[63] The reason for this is that robust results of the kind emphasized here remain elusive in regard to the motives and mechanisms underlying merger activity. This longstanding area of investigation continues to pose challenges in respect of the

dependently of whether or not firms are profit maximizers. Nonetheless, it is all the more interesting, against this background, to probe the status of Gibrat's Law, and alternative postulates of this kind, relative to models of profit maximizing firms (see footnote 64 below).

[62] Against this background, a recent contribution by Cabral and Mata (2003) is of particular interest. Using data for the Portuguese manufacturing sector, they explore the way in which the size distribution evolves over time within various industries. A further strand in the recent literature relates to the use of new data sources to examine the size distribution of firms in developing countries; see, for example, Van Biesenbroeck (2005).

[63] Mergers enter the picture developed above in two ways: (a) as one of adjustment mechanisms driving a rise in concentration when exogenous influences shift the lower bounds upwards, and (b) as a factor leading to outcomes 'inside the bound' (see the discussion relating to Figures 35.2 and 35.3 above).

characterization of mechanisms that operate in a systematic way both over time and across the general run of industries.

Capabilities A new strand in the literature seeks to relate the market structure literature to the notion of firms' 'capabilities' [Nelson and Winter (1982)]. It was noted in Section 2.2 that we can think of a firm's capability as being represented, in one sense, by its levels of productivity and product quality in each market in which it operates. More fundamentally, the term 'capability' relates to the set of 'shared know-how' embodied in a set of individuals within the firm, from which these levels of productivity and quality derive. In the language of the present chapter, this raises the challenge of opening the 'black box' represented by the fixed cost schedule $F(\cdot)$ that maps a firm's quality and productivity levels into its fixed (R&D) outlays. One payoff from moving to this deeper level of analysis is that we might arrive at a better understanding of the problems of 'markets dynamics' discussed above.[64] A firm's growth and survival, in a world in which demand and supply conditions fluctuate across the several markets in which it may operate, will depend not only on its observed levels of productivity and quality in the sub-markets or product groups in which it currently operates, but on the underlying know-how that will determine its levels of productivity and quality in other (new) product groups to which it may move. Developing a satisfactory theoretical and empirical analysis of these issues would seem a natural next step relative to the current literature.

Acknowledgements

I would like to thank Volker Nocke, Rob Porter, Michael Raith, and Tomasso Valletti for their extremely helpful comments on a preliminary draft.

Appendix A: The Cournot example

The profit of firm i in the second stage subgame is

$$(p-c)x_i = \left(S \Big/ \sum x_j - c\right)x_i. \tag{A.1}$$

Differentiating this expression w.r.t. x_i we obtain the first-order condition,

$$-\frac{S}{(\sum x_j)^2} \cdot x_i + \frac{S}{\sum x_j} - c = 0. \tag{A.2}$$

64 An interesting implication of a 'capabilities' view is that it suggests a robust and natural naturalization of (a weak form of) Gibrat's Law as an outcome of profit maximization: for if the firm's depth and breadth of know-how is both a driver of its current range of activities, and of its comparative advantage across the range of new market opportunities that arise over time, then the expansion of activities taken in equilibrium by profit maximizing firms may show the rough proportionality to their current sizes that is observed in practice.

Summing Equation (A.2) over i, and writing $\sum x_j$ as X, we obtain

$$\sum x_j \equiv X = \frac{S}{c}\frac{N-1}{N}. \tag{A.3}$$

It follows from (A.2), (A.3) that all the x_i are equal, whence $x_i = X/N$, whence

$$x_i = \frac{S}{c}\frac{N-1}{N^2} \quad \text{and} \quad p = c\left\{1 + \frac{1}{N-1}\right\} \quad \text{for } N \geqslant 2. \tag{A.4}$$

Substituting (A.4) into (A.1) and rearranging, it follows that the profit of firm at equilibrium equals S/N^2.

Appendix B: The Cournot model with quality

The profit function may be derived as follows. The profit of firm i is

$$S\pi_i = p_i x_i - cx_i = \lambda u_i x_i - cx_i, \tag{B.1}$$

where

$$\lambda = S\Big/\left(\sum_j u_j x_j\right). \tag{B.2}$$

To ease notation it is useful to express the first-order condition in terms of λ. With this in mind, note that

$$\frac{\mathrm{d}\lambda}{\mathrm{d}x_i} = -\frac{S}{(\sum_j u_j x_j)^2}\frac{\mathrm{d}}{\mathrm{d}x_i}\left(\sum_j u_j x_j\right) = -\frac{Su_i}{(\sum_j u_j x_j)^2} = -\frac{u_i}{S}\lambda^2. \tag{B.3}$$

Now the first-order condition is obtained by differentiating (B.1), viz.

$$\frac{\mathrm{d}\pi_i}{\mathrm{d}x_i} = \lambda u_i + u_i x_i \frac{\mathrm{d}\lambda}{\mathrm{d}x_i} - c = 0.$$

On substituting for $\frac{\mathrm{d}\lambda}{\mathrm{d}x_i}$, from (B.2) and (B.3), and rearranging, this becomes

$$u_i x_i = \frac{S}{\lambda} - \frac{cS}{\lambda^2}\frac{1}{u_i}. \tag{B.4}$$

Summing over all products, we have,

$$\sum_j u_j x_j = \frac{NS}{\lambda} - \frac{cS}{\lambda^2}\sum_j (1/u_j).$$

But from (B.2) we have $\lambda = S/(\sum_j u_j x_j)$ whence $\sum_j u_j x_j = S/\lambda$ so that

$$\frac{S}{\lambda} = \frac{NS}{\lambda} - \frac{cS}{\lambda^2}\sum_j (1/u_j)$$

whence

$$\lambda = \frac{c}{N-1} \sum_j (1/u_j). \tag{B.5}$$

Substituting this expression for λ into (B.4) we have on rearranging that

$$x_i = \frac{S}{c} \cdot \frac{N-1}{u_i \sum_j (1/u_j)} \left\{ 1 - \frac{N-1}{u_i \sum_j (1/u_j)} \right\}. \tag{B.6}$$

Setting the expression in brackets equal to zero leads to a necessary and sufficient condition for good i to have positive sales at equilibrium, as described in the text. By ranking firms in decreasing order of quality, and considering successive subsets of the top $1, 2, 3, \ldots,$ firms, we can apply this criterion to identify the set of products that command positive sales at equilibrium. Denoting this number by N henceforward, we can now solve for prices, using $p_i = \lambda u_i$, whence from (B.5) we have

$$p_i - c = \left\{ \frac{u_i}{N-1} \sum_j (1/u_j) - 1 \right\} c. \tag{B.7}$$

Inserting (B.6) and (B.7) into the profit function

$$\pi_i = (p_i - c) x_i$$

and simplifying, we obtain

$$\pi_i = \left\{ 1 - \frac{N-1}{u_i} \frac{1}{\sum_j (1/u_j)} \right\}^2 S. \tag{B.8}$$

References

Aghion, P., Bloom, N., Blundell, R., Griffith, R., Howitt, P. (2005). "Competition and innovation: An inverted-U relationship". Quarterly Journal of Economics 120, 701–728.

Arthur, W.B. (1989). "Competing technologies, increasing returns, and lock-in by historical events". Economic Journal 99, 116–131.

Asplund, M. (2000). "What fraction of a capital investment is sunk costs?". Journal of Industrial Economics 48, 287–304.

Asplund, M., Nocke, V. (2006). "Firm turnover in imperfectly competitive markets". Review of Economic Studies 73, 295–327.

Axtell, R. (2001). "Zipf distribution of U.S. firm sizes". Science 293, 1818–1820.

Bain, J.S. (1956). Barriers to New Competition. Harvard Univ. Press, Cambridge, MA.

Bakker, G. (2005). "The decline and fall of the European film industry: Sunk costs, market size and market structure, 1890–1927". Economic History Review 58, 310–351.

Barbour, A.D., Holst, L., Janson, S. (1992). Poisson Approximation. Clarendon Press, Oxford.

Baumol, W.J., Panzar, J.C., Willig, R.D. (1982). Contestable Markets and the Theory of Industry Structure. Harcourt Brace Jovanovich, San Diego.

Berry, S. (1992). "Estimation of a model of entry in the airline industry". Econometrica 60, 889–917.

Bresnahan, T.F. (1992). "Sutton's sunk costs and market structure: Price competition, advertising and the evolution of concentration". RAND Journal of Economics 23, 137–152.
Bresnahan, T.F., Greenstein, S. (1999). "Technological competition and the structure of the computer industry". Journal of Industrial Economics 47, 1–40.
Bresnahan, T.F., Reiss, P.C. (1990a). "Entry in monopoly markets". Review of Economics Studies 57, 531–553.
Bresnahan, T.F., Reiss, P.C. (1990b). "Do entry conditions vary across markets?". Brookings Paper on Economic Activity 3, 833–881.
Buzzacchi, L., Valletti, T. (2006). "Firm size distribution: Testing the 'independent submarkets model' in the Italian motor insurance industry". International Journal of Industrial Organization 24, 809–834.
Cabral, L., Riordan, M. (1994). "The learning curve, market dominance and predatory pricing". Econometrica 62, 1115–1140.
Cabral, L.M.B., Mata, J. (2003). "On the evolution of firm size distribution: Facts and theory". American Economic Review 93, 1075–1089.
Campbell, J.R., Hopenhayn, H.A. (2005). "Market size matters". Journal of Industrial Economics 53, 101–122.
Carroll, R., Hannan, M.T. (2000). The Demography of Corporations and Industries. Princeton Univ. Press, Princeton.
Caves, R.E. (1986). "Information structures of product markets". Economic Inquiry 24, 195–212.
Caves, R.E., Porter, M.E. (1978). "Market structure, oligopoly and the stability of market shares". Journal of Industrial Economics 26, 289–313.
Cohen, W.M., Levin, R.C. (1989). "Innovation and market structure". In: Schmalensee, R., Willig, R. (Eds.), Handbook of Industrial Organization, vol. 2. North-Holland, Amsterdam, pp. 1059–1107.
Dasgupta, P., Stiglitz, J. (1980). "Industrial structure and the nature of innovative activity". Economic Journal 90, 266–293.
David, P. (1975). "Clio and the economics of QWERTY". American Economic Review Proceedings 75, 332–337.
David, P.A., Bunn, J.A. (1990). "Gateway technologies and the evolutionary dynamics of network industries: Lessons from electricity supply history". In: Heertje, A., Perlman, M. (Eds.), Evolutionary Technology and Market Structure: Studies in Schumpeterian Economics. University of Michigan Press, Ann Arbor, pp. 121–156.
Davies, S.W. (1991). "The dynamics of market leadership in UK manufacturing industry, 1976–86". Report Series. London Business School, Centre for Business Strategy.
Davies, S.W., Lyons, B.R. (1996). "Industrial Organization in the European Union: Structure, Strategy and the Competitive Mechanism". Oxford Univ. Press, Oxford.
Davis, S.J., Haltiwanger, J. (1992). "Gross job creation, gross job destruction and employment reallocation". Quarterly Journal of Economics 57, 819–863.
De Juan, R. (2002). "Entry in independent submarkets: An application to the Spanish retail banking market". Economic and Social Review 33, 109–118.
De Juan, R. (2003). "The independent submarkets model: An application to the Spanish retail banking market". International Journal of Industrial Organization 21, 1461–1487.
Deneckere, R., Davidson, C. (1985). "Incentives to form coalitions with Bertrand competition". RAND Journal of Economics 16, 473–486.
Dixit, A.K., Stiglitz, J.E. (1977). "Monopolistic competition and optimum product diversity". American Economic Review 67, 297–308.
Dunne, T., Roberts, M.J., Samuelson, L. (1988). "Patterns of firm entry and exit in U.S. manufacturing industries". RAND Journal of Economics 19 (4), 495–515.
Eaton, B.C., Ware, R. (1987). "A theory of market structure". RAND Journal of Economics 18, 1–16.
Edwards, B.K., Starr, R.M. (1987). "A note on indivisibilities, specialization and economies of scale". American Economic Review 93, 1425–1436.
Ellickson, P. (2006). "Quality competition in retailing: A structural analysis". International Journal of Industrial Organization 24, 521–540.

Ellickson, P. (2007). "Does Sutton apply to supermarkets?". RAND Journal of Economics. In press.
Ericson, R., Pakes, A. (1995). "Markov-perfect industry dynamics: A framework for industry dynamics". Review of Economic Studies 62, 53–82.
Evans, D.S. (1987a). "The relationship between firm growth, size and age: Estimates for 100 manufacturing industries". Journal of Industrial Economics 35 (4), 567–581.
Evans, D.S. (1987b). "Tests of alternative theories of firm growth". Journal of Political Economy 95 (4), 657–674.
Fisher, F.M. (1989). "Games economists play: A noncooperative view". RAND Journal of Economics 20, 113–124.
Fu, D., Pammolli, F., Buldyrev, S.V., Riccaboni, M., Matia, K., Yamasaki, K., Stanley, H.E. (2005). "The growth of business firms: Theoretical framework and empirical evidence". Proceedings of the National Academy of Sciences of the United States of America 102, 18801–18806.
Fudenberg, D., Tirole, J. (1983). "Learning-by-doing and market performance". Bell Journal of Economics 14, 522–530.
Fudenberg, D., Tirole, J. (1985). "Preemption and rent equalization in the adoption of new technology". Review of Economic Studies 52, 383–402.
Gabszewicz, J.J., Thisse, J.F. (1980). "Entry (and exit) in a differentiated industry". Journal of Economic Theory 22, 327–338.
Geroski, P. (1991). Market Dynamics and Entry. Basil Blackwell, Oxford.
Geroski, P., Schwalbach, J. (1991). Entry and Market Contestability. Basil Blackwell, Oxford.
Gibrat, R. (1931). "Les inégalités économiques ; applications : aux inégalités des richesses, à la concentration des enterprises, aux populations, des villes, aux statistiques des familles, etc., d' une loi nouvelle, la loi de l' effet proportionnel". Librairie du Recueil Sirey, Paris.
Giorgetti, M.L. (2003). "Quantile regression in lower bound estimation". Journal of Industrial Economics 51, 113–120.
Gruber, H. (1992). "Persistence of leadership in product innovation". Journal of Industrial Economics 40, 359–375.
Gruber, H. (1994). Learning and Strategic Product Innovation: Theory and Evidence from the Semiconductor Industry. North-Holland, London.
Hall, B. (1987). "The relationship between firm size and firm growth in the U.S. manufacturing sector". Journal of Industrial Economics 35 (4), 583–606.
Harris, C., Vickers, J. (1985). "Perfect equilibrium in a model of a race". Review of Economic Studies 52, 193–209.
Harris, C., Vickers, J. (1987). "Racing with uncertainty". Review of Economic Studies 54, 1–21.
Harsanyi, J.C., Selten, R. (1988). A General Theory of Equilibrium Selection in Games. MIT Press, Cambridge, MA.
Hart, P.E., Prais, S.J. (1956). "The analysis of business concentration: A statistical approach". Journal of the Royal Statistical Society (Series A) 119, 150–181.
Hjalmarsson, L. (1974). "The size distribution of establishments and firms derived from an optimal process of capacity expansion". European Economic Review 5 (2), 123–140.
Hole, A. (1997). "Dynamic non-price strategy and competition: Models of R&D, advertising and location". Unpublished Ph.D. Thesis. University of London.
Hopenhayn, H.A. (1992). "Entry, exit and firm dynamics in long run equilibrium". Econometrica 60, 1127–1150.
Ijiri, Y., Simon, H. (1964). "Business firm growth and size". American Economic Review 54, 77–89.
Ijiri, Y., Simon, H. (1977). Skew Distributions and the Sizes of Business Firms. North-Holland, Amsterdam.
Jovanovic, B. (1982). "Selection and the evolution of industry". Econometrica 50 (3), 649–670.
Jovanovic, B., MacDonald, G.M. (1994). "The life cycle of competitive industry". Journal of Political Economy 102 (2), 322–347.
Klepper, S. (1996). "Entry, exit, growth and innovation over the product life cycle". American Economic Review 86 (3), 562–583.

Klepper, S., Graddy, E. (1990). "The evolution of new industries and the determinants of market structure". RAND Journal of Economics 21 (1), 27–44.

Klepper, S., Simons, K. (2005). "Industry shakeouts and technological change". International Journal of Industrial Organization 23, 23–43.

Lambson, V. (1992). "Competitive profits in the long run". Review of Economics Studies 59, 125–142.

Lee, C.-Y. (2005). "A new perspective in industry R&D and market structure". Journal of Industrial Economics 53, 1–25.

Lyons, B.R., Matraves, C. (1996). "Industrial concentration". In: Davies, S.W., Lyons, B.R. (Eds.), Industrial Organization in the European Union: Structure, Strategy and the Competitive Mechanism. Oxford Univ. Press, Oxford.

Lyons, B.R., Matraves, C., Moffat, P. (2001). "Industrial concentration and market integration in the European Union". Economica 68 (269), 1–26.

Mann, N., Scheuer, E., Fertig, K. (1973). "A new goodness-of-fit test for the two-parameter Weibull or extreme-value distribution with unknown parameters". Communications in Statistics 2 (5), 383–400.

Manuszak, M.D. (2002). "Endogenous market structure and competition in the 19th century American brewing industry". International Journal of Industrial Organization 20, 673–692.

Marin, P., Siotis, G. (2001). "Innovation and market structure: An empirical evaluation of the 'Bounds approach' in the chemical industry". Working Paper. Universidad Carlos III de Madrid and CEPR.

Marsili, O. (2001). The Anatomy and Evolution of Industries. Edward Elgar, Cheltenham.

Matraves, C. (1999). "Market structure, R&D and advertising in the pharmaceutical industry". Journal of Industrial Economics 47, 169–194.

Mazzeo, M.J. (2002). "Product choice and oligopoly market structure". RAND Journal of Economics 33, 221–242.

Motta, M., Polo, M. (1997). "Concentration and public policies in the broadcasting industry: The future of television". Economic Policy 25, 295–334.

Nelson, S., Winter, D. (1982). "An Evolutionary Theory of Economic Change". Harvard Univ. Press, Cambridge, MA.

Nocke, V. (2000). "Monopolization and industry structure". Working Paper. Nuffield College, Oxford.

Nocke, V. (2006). "Collusion and dynamic (under)investment in quality". RAND Journal of Economics. In press.

Pelzman, S. (1991). "The Handbook of Industrial Organization: A review article". Journal of Political Economy 99, 201–217.

Phillips, A. (1971). Technology and Market Structure: A Study of the Aircraft Industry. D.C. Heath, Lexington, MA.

Raith, M. (2003). "Competition, risk and managerial incentives". American Economic Review 93, 1425–1436.

Robinson, W., Chiang, J. (1996). "Are Sutton's predictions robust?: Empirical insights into advertising, R&D and concentration". Journal of Industrial Economics 44 (4), 389–408.

Rogers, R. (2001). "Structural change in U.S. food manufacturing, 1958–1977". Agribusiness 17, 3–32.

Rogers, R.T., Ma, Y.R. (1994). "Concentration change in an area of lax antitrust enforcement: A comparison of two decades: 1967 to 1977 and 1977 to 1987, evidence from the food processing industries". Paper presented at the Northeast Regional Research Project NE-165 Research Conference, Montreal, Quebec.

Rogers, R.T., Tockle, R.J. (1999). "The effects of television advertising on concentration: An update". New York Economic Review 30, 25–31.

Rosenthal, R. (1980). "A model in which an increase in the number of sellers leads to a higher price". Econometrica 48, 1575–1579.

Scherer, F.M. (1980). Industrial Market Structure and Economic Performance, second ed. Rand McNally, Chicago.

Scherer, F.M. (2000). "Professor Sutton's technology and market structure". Journal of Industrial Economics 48, 215–223.

Schmalensee, R. (1978). "Entry deterrence in the ready-to-eat breakfast cereal industry". Bell Journal of Economics 9, 305–327.

Schmalensee, R. (1989). "Inter-industry differences of structure and performance". In: Schmalensee, R., Willig, R. (Eds.), Handbook of Industrial Organization, vol. 2. North-Holland, Amsterdam, pp. 951–1009.

Schmalensee, R. (1992). "Sunk costs and market structure: A review article". Journal of Industrial Economics 40, 125–133.

Scott, J.T. (1984). "Firm versus industry variability in R&D intensity". In: Zvi, G. (Ed.), R&D Patents and Productivity Change. University of Chicago Press for the National Bureau of Economic Research, Chicago.

Selten, R. (1983). "A model of oligopolistic size structure and profitability". European Economic Review 22 (1), 33–57.

Shaked, A., Sutton, J. (1982). "Natural oligopolies". Econometrica 51, 1469–1484.

Shaked, A., Sutton, J. (1987). "Product differentiation and industrial structure". Journal of Industrial Economics 36, 131–146.

Shaked, A., Sutton, J. (1990). "Multiproduct firms and market structure". RAND Journal of Economics 21, 45–62.

Shubik, M., Levitan, R. (1980). Market Structure and Behavior. Harvard University Press, Cambridge, MA.

Smith, R.L. (1994). "Nonregular regression". Biometrika 81, 173–183.

Smith, R.L. (1985). "Maximum likelihood estimation in a class of non-regular cases". Biometrika 72, 67–90.

Smith, R.L. (1988). "Extreme value theory for dependent sequences via the Stein–Chen method of Poisson approximations". Stochastic Processes and Their Applications 30, 317–327.

Spence, A.M. (1981). "The learning curve and competition". Bell Journal of Economics 12, 49–70.

Stanley, M.R., Nunes Amaral, L.A., Buldyrev, S.V., Harlin, S., Leschorn, H., Maass, P., Salinger, M.A., Stanley, H.E. (1996). "Scaling behaviour in the growth of companies". Nature 319 (29), 804–806.

Sutton, J. (1991). Sunk Costs and Market Structure. MIT Press, Cambridge, MA.

Sutton, J. (1997a). "Game theoretic models of market structure". In: Kreps, D., Wallis, K. (Eds.), Advances in Economics and Econometrics, Proceedings of the World Congress of the Econometric Society. Tokyo, 1995. Cambridge Univ. Press, Cambridge, pp. 66–86.

Sutton, J. (1997b). "Gibrat's legacy". Journal of Economics Literature 35, 40–59.

Sutton, J. (1998). Technology and Market Structure. MIT Press, Cambridge, MA.

Sutton, J. (2000). Marshall's Tendencies: What can Economists Know?. MIT Press, Cambridge, MA.

Sutton, J. (2001a). "Rich trades, scarce capabilities: Industrial development revisited" (Keynes Lecture, 2000). In: Proceedings of the British Academy, vol. III (2000 Lectures and Memoirs), pp. 245–273. Reprinted in: Economic and Social Review 33 (1) (2002) 1–22.

Sutton, J. (2001b). "The variance of firm growth rates: The scaling puzzle". Physica A 312, 577–590.

Sutton, J. (2001c). "Market Structure and Performance". In: International Encyclopaedia of the Social and Behavioral Sciences. Elsevier, Amsterdam.

Sutton, J. (2007). "Market share dynamics and the "persistence of leadership" debate". American Economic Review 97, 222–241.

Symeonidis, G. (2000). "Price competition and market structure: The impact of restrictive practices legislation on concentration in the U.K.". Journal of Industrial Economics 48, 1–26.

Symeonidis, G. (2001). The Effects of Competition: Cartel Policy and the Evolution of Strategy and Structure in British Industry. MIT Press, Cambridge, MA.

Tirole, J. (1990). Theory of Industrial Organization. MIT Press, Cambridge, MA.

Tong, J. (2000). "Submarkets, shakeouts and industry life cycle". Sticerd Discussion Paper EI/26. London School of Economics.

Van Biesenbroeck, J. (2005). "Firm size matters: Growth and productivity growth in African manufacturing". Economic Development and Cultural Change 53, 545–583.

Vasconcelos, H. (2002). "Three essays on collusion and mergers". Unpublished Ph.D. Thesis. European University Institute, Florence.

Walsh, P.P., Whelan, C. (2001). "Portfolio effects and firm size distribution: Carbonated soft drinks". Economic and Social Review 33, 43–54.

Weiss, L. (Ed.) (1989). Concentration and Price. MIT Press, Cambridge, MA.

Wyart, M., Bouchard, J.P. (2002). "Statistical models for company growth". Available at SSRN: http://ssrn.com/abstract=391860 or doi:10.2139/ssrn.391860.

Chapter 36

ANTITRUST POLICY TOWARD HORIZONTAL MERGERS[1]

MICHAEL D. WHINSTON

Northwestern University and NBER
e-mail: mwhinston@northwestern.edu

Contents

[1] This chapter draws on material in Chapter 3 of Whinston (2006).

Handbook of Industrial Organization, Volume 3
Edited by M. Armstrong and R. Porter

DOI: 10.1016/S1573-448X(06)03036-6

Abstract

Recently there has been a notable increase in interest in antitrust law in much of the world. This chapter discusses antitrust policy toward horizontal mergers, the area of antitrust that has seen some of the most dramatic improvements in both economic tools and the application of economics in enforcement practice. The chapter discusses theoretical considerations, merger laws and enforcement practices, econometric methods for analyzing prospective horizontal mergers, and evidence concerning the ex post effects of actual horizontal mergers.

Keywords

Horizontal mergers, Mergers, Market power, Price effects, Unilateral effects, Coordinated effects, Efficiencies, Merger guidelines, Antitrust, Merger simulation

JEL classification: L10, L13, L40, L41

1. Introduction

The last thirty years have witnessed a dramatic movement in much of the world toward unregulated markets, and away from both state ownership (in the former Eastern Block, in South and Central America, and elsewhere) and state regulation (in North America and many European countries). Not coincidentally, they have also witnessed, especially recently, a notable increase of interest in antitrust law.

Antitrust laws (known as "competition" laws outside the United States) regulate economic activity. These laws' operation, however, differs in important ways from what is traditionally referred to as "regulation". Regulation tends to be industry-specific and to involve the direct setting of prices, product characteristics, or entry, usually after regular and elaborate hearings. By contrast, antitrust law tends to apply broadly, and focuses on maintaining basic rules of competition that enable the competitive interaction among firms to produce desirable outcomes. Investigations and intervention are exceptional events, that arise when those basic rules may have been violated.

Antitrust laws can roughly be divided into two types: those concerned with "collusion" (broadly defined) and those concerned with "exclusion". The former category focuses on ways in which competitors may be able to reduce the level of competition among themselves. Its main concerns are price fixing (cartels) and horizontal mergers. The latter category focuses on ways in which a dominant firm may reduce competition by excluding its rivals from the marketplace, either fully, or by more partially reducing their competitiveness. It focuses on practices such as predatory pricing, exclusive dealing, and tying.

In this chapter, I discuss antitrust policy toward horizontal mergers. Of all the areas of antitrust, this is the one that has seen the most dramatic improvement in recent years in both economic tools and the application of economics in enforcement practice.

I begin in Section 2 by discussing the key theoretical issues that arise in evaluating proposed horizontal mergers. Central to those considerations is the fact that while horizontal mergers may reduce firms' incentives for competitive pricing, they can also create important efficiencies. In Section 3, I provide an overview of merger laws and enforcement practices, with a particular focus on antitrust agency enforcement guidelines. The development of those guidelines in many countries has led to a substantial improvement in the application of economic principles to merger enforcement practices. In Section 4, I discuss ways in which econometric evidence can be used to answer some of the key questions that arise in these guidelines. In Section 5, I instead look at empirical techniques that seek to move beyond the guidelines' frameworks for evaluating prospective mergers. One of those methods, merger simulation, represents a particularly promising direction for enforcement practice. In Section 6, I discuss what we know about the effects of actual mergers. While enforcement focuses on analyzing prospective mergers, surprisingly little work has examined the impact of consummated mergers ex post, a critical step for improving enforcement practice. Here I discuss what is known about both price effects and efficiencies. Finally, I end the chapter in Section 7 with some concluding remarks on future directions in the analysis of horizontal mergers.

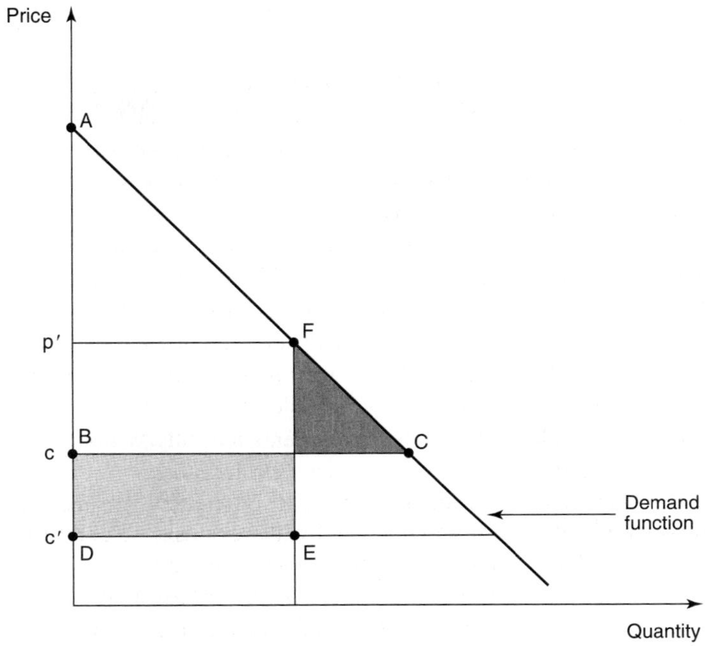

Figure 36.1. The Williamson tradeoff.

2. Theoretical considerations

2.1. *The Williamson trade-off*

The central issue in the evaluation of horizontal mergers lies in the need to balance any reductions in competition against the possibility of productivity improvements arising from a merger. This trade-off was first articulated in the economics literature by Williamson (1968), in a paper aimed at getting efficiencies to be taken seriously.[2] This "Williamson trade-off" is illustrated in Figure 36.1.

Suppose that the industry is initially competitive, with a price equal to c. Suppose also that after the merger, the marginal cost of production falls to c' and the price rises to p'.[3] Aggregate social surplus before the merger is given by area ABC, while aggregate surplus after the merger is given by area ADEF. Which is larger involves a comparison

[2] At that time, concern over the fate of small (and often inefficient) businesses frequently led the courts to use merger-related efficiencies as evidence *against* a proposed merger.

[3] We assume here that these costs represent true social costs. Reductions in the marginal cost of production due, say, to increased monopsony power resulting from the merger would not count as a social gain. Likewise, if input markets are not perfectly competitive, then reductions in cost attributable to the merger must be calculated at the true social marginal cost of the inputs rather than at their distorted market prices.

between the area of the shaded triangle, which is equal to the deadweight loss from the post-merger supracompetitive pricing, and the area of the shaded rectangle, which is equal to the merger-induced cost savings. If there is no improvement in costs, then the area of the rectangle will be zero and the merger reduces aggregate surplus; if there is no increase in price, then the area of the triangle will be zero, and the merger increases aggregate surplus. Williamson's main point was that it does not take a large decrease in cost for the area of the rectangle to exceed that of the triangle: put crudely, one might say that "rectangles tend to be larger than triangles". Indeed, in the limiting case of small changes in price and cost, differential calculus tells us that this will always be true; formally, the welfare reduction from an infinitesimal increase in price starting from the competitive price is of second-order (i.e., has a zero derivative), while the welfare increase from an infinitesimal decrease in cost is of first-order (i.e., has a strictly positive derivative).

Four important points should be noted, however, about this Williamson trade-off argument. First, a critical part of the argument involves the assumption that the pre-merger price is competitive; i.e., equal to marginal cost. If, instead, the pre-merger price p exceeds the pre-merger marginal cost c then we would no longer be comparing a triangle to a rectangle, but rather a trapezoid to a rectangle (see Figure 36.2) and "rectangles are not bigger than trapezoids"; that is, even for small changes, both effects are of first-order.[4] Put simply, when a market starts off at a distorted supra-competitive price, even small increases in price can cause significant reductions in welfare.

Second, the Williamson argument glosses over the issue of differences across firms by supposing that there is a single level of marginal cost in the market, both before and after the merger. However, since any cost improvements are likely to be limited to the merging firms, it *cannot* be the case that this assumption is correct both before and after the merger, except in the case of an industry-wide merger. More importantly, at an empirical level, oligopolistic industries (i.e., those in which mergers are likely to be scrutinized) often exhibit substantial variation in marginal cost across firms. The import of this point is that a potentially significant source of welfare variation arising from a horizontal merger is entirely absent from the Williamson analysis, namely the welfare changes arising from shifts of production across firms that have differing marginal costs; so-called, "production reshuffling". We will explore this point in some detail shortly.

Third, the Williamson analysis takes the appropriate welfare standard to be maximization of aggregate surplus. But, as we will discuss in more detail in Section 3, a question about distribution arises with the application of antitrust policy. Although many analyses of mergers in the economics literature focus on an aggregate surplus standard, enforcement practice in most countries (including the U.S. and the E.U.) is closest to a consumer surplus standard.[5] If so, then no trade-off needs to be considered: the merger should be allowed if and only if the efficiencies are enough to ensure that price does not increase.

[4] Specifically, the welfare loss caused by a small reduction in output is equal to the price–cost margin.

[5] On this point, see also the discussion in Baker (1999a).

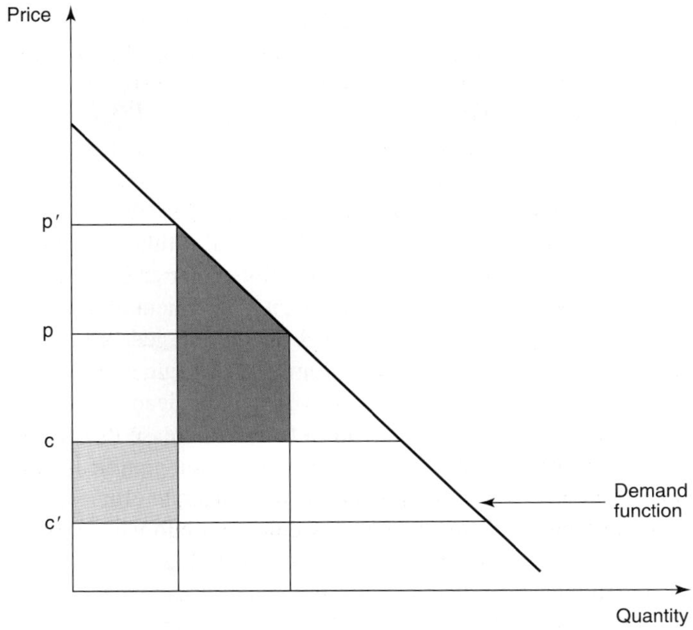

Figure 36.2. The Williamson tradeoff when the pre-merger price exceeds marginal cost.

Finally, the Williamson argument focuses on price as the sole locus of competitive interaction among the firms. In practice, however, firms make many other competitive decisions, including their choices of capacity investment, R&D, product quality, and new product introductions. Each of those choices may be affected by the change in market structure brought about by a merger. We will return to this point later in this section.

2.2. Static ("unilateral") effects of mergers

Careful consideration of these issues requires a more complete model of market competition. The simplest class of models in which we can formally analyze the effects of horizontal mergers are static oligopoly models. The general presumption in such models is that, absent efficiencies, prices will rise following a merger. The reason for this presumption is that, holding rival prices or outputs fixed, a merger between sellers of substitute goods will lead them to internalize the negative externality that more aggressive pricing or output choices has on the merger partner.[6]

[6] Throughout I focus on mergers of sellers. The same principles apply to mergers of buyers, who have an incentive to reduce demand to lower prices. In some cases, firms that are vertically integrated participate in the market as both buyers and sellers. For a discussion of that case, see Hendricks and McAfee (2000).

Translating this price-increasing effect into an increase in equilibrium prices requires some further "regularity" assumptions. For example, we will see shortly that, absent efficiency improvements, a merger raises price under fairly weak regularity conditions in the Cournot model of simultaneous quantity choices among producers of a homogeneous good. In differentiated price competition models, matters are a little more complicated. The internalization caused by the merger (the fact that some of the sales lost due to a product's price increase are captured by other products now owned by the merged firm) implies that the merged firm will have an incentive to raise the price of any one of its products holding fixed the prices of all of its other products and the prices of rivals.[7] To insure that all prices in the market rise it is sufficient to know that – holding rival prices fixed at any levels – the merger causes the merged firm to raise all of its prices, and that best responses are "upward sloping" (strategic complements). The latter condition implies that the merged firm's price increases lead rivals to increase their prices, which in turn causes the merged firm to further increase its own prices, and so on. These two conditions will hold, for example, if the pricing game is supermodular.[8]

What are the welfare effects of a merger that does generate efficiencies? Farrell and Shapiro (1990) provide such an analysis for the special case in which competition takes a Cournot form. [For related analyses, see Levin (1990) and McAfee and Williams (1992).] They investigate two principal questions: First, under what conditions are cost improvements sufficiently great for a merger to reduce price? As noted earlier, this is the key question when one adopts a consumer surplus standard. Second, can the fact that proposed mergers are profitable for the merging parties be used to help identify mergers that increase aggregate surplus? In particular, one difficult aspect of evaluating the aggregate welfare impact of a merger involves assessing the size of any cost efficiencies. The merging parties always have an incentive to overstate these efficiencies to help gain regulatory approval (or placate shareholders), and these prospective claims are hard for an antitrust authority to verify. But since only the merging parties realize these efficiency gains, it might be possible to develop a *sufficient* condition for a merger to enhance aggregate surplus that does not require investigation of claimed efficiencies by asking when the merger has a positive net effect on parties other than the merging firms.

[7] The share of the lost sales of product A that are captured by product B when A's price increases is known as the *diversion ratio* from product A to product B.

[8] With constant unit costs, a *sufficient* condition for supermodularity with multiproduct firms is that the demand function for each product j satisfies $\partial D_j(p_1, \dots, p_N)/\partial p_k \partial p_r \geqslant 0$ for all product prices p_k and p_r. This sufficient condition is satisfied in the case of linear demands, but in few other standard models. For example, it is not satisfied in the Logit model. With single product firms, one can sometimes establish instead supermodularity of the log-transformed game [see, for example, Vives (1999) and Milgrom and Roberts (1990)]. That is the case, for example, for the single-product Logit model. Unfortunately, this method does not extend to the case of multiproduct firms. Deneckere and Davidson (1985) provide conditions that imply that a merger increases all prices with symmetrically differentiated products. As a general matter, it appears relatively easy to get non-increasing best responses in the type of random coefficient models that are often used in merger simulations (see Section 5.1). For example, if a rival's price increase causes relatively poor consumers to shift to a firm's product, the firm's optimal price may well fall.

Consider the first question: When does price decrease as a result of a merger in a Cournot industry? To be specific, suppose that firms 1 and 2 contemplate a merger in an N-firm industry and, without loss of generality, suppose that their pre-merger outputs satisfy $\hat{x}_1 \geqslant \hat{x}_2 > 0$. Following Farrell and Shapiro, we assume that the equilibrium aggregate output increases if and only if, given the pre-merger aggregate output of non-merging firms $\hat{X}_{-12}$, the merger causes the merging firms to want to increase their joint output. The following two assumptions are sufficient (although not necessary) for this property to hold[9]:

(A1) The industry inverse demand function $P(\cdot)$ satisfies $P'(X) + P''(X)X < 0$ for all aggregate output levels X.

(A2) $c_i''(x_i) > P'(X)$ for all output levels x_i and X having $x_i \leqslant X$, and for all i.

Letting $\hat{X}$ be the aggregate pre-merger output in the market, the pre-merger Cournot first-order conditions for these two firms are

$$P'(\hat{X})\hat{x}_1 + P(\hat{X}) - c_1'(\hat{x}_1) = 0, \tag{1}$$

$$P'(\hat{X})\hat{x}_2 + P(\hat{X}) - c_2'(\hat{x}_2) = 0. \tag{2}$$

[9] Formally, (A1) and (A2) have the following implications:

(i) Each firm i's profit maximization problem, given the joint output of its rivals X_{-i}, is strictly concave and therefore has a unique solution. Moreover, letting $b_i(X_{-i})$ denote firm i's best-response function, $b_i(\cdot)$ is non-increasing and $b_i'(X_{-i}) \in (-1, 0)$ at all X_{-i} such that $b_i(X_{-i}) > 0$.

(ii) The equilibrium aggregate output is unique. To see this, define each firm i's *aggregate output best-response function* as $\lambda_i(X) = \{x_i\colon x_i = b_i(X - x_i)\}$. For a given level of aggregate output X, this function gives the output level for firm i that is consistent with X if firm i is playing a best response to its rivals' joint output. By observation (i), this output level is unique, is non-increasing in X, and is strictly decreasing in X wherever $\lambda_i(X) > 0$. The equilibrium aggregate output is then the unique solution to $\sum_i \lambda_i(X) = X$.

(iii) For any set of firms I, define its *equilibrium best-response function*

$$b_I^e(X_{-I}) \equiv \left\{ \sum_{i\in I} x_i\colon x_i = b_i(X_{I/\{i\}} + X_{-I}) \text{ for all } i \in I \right\}.$$

This gives, conditional on X_{-I}, the (unique) aggregate output for firms in set I that results if all of the firms in set I are playing best responses. It is the solution to $\sum_{i\in I} \lambda_i(X_I + X_{-I}) = X_I$. From this, one can see that $b_I^e(\cdot)$ is non-increasing and $b_I^{e\prime}(X_{-I}) \in (-1, 0)$ whenever $b_I^e(X_{-I}) > 0$, just like the individual best-response functions.

(iv) The pre-merger equilibrium joint outputs of the merging and non-merging firms $(\hat{X}_{12}, \hat{X}_{-12})$ are the unique solution to

$$b_{12}^e(\hat{X}_{-12}) = \hat{X}_{12}, \qquad b_{-12}^e(\hat{X}_{12}) = \hat{X}_{-12}.$$

The post-merger equilibrium joint outputs $(\overline{X}_{12}, \overline{X}_{-12})$ are the unique solution to

$$b_M(\overline{X}_{-12}) = \overline{X}_{12}, \qquad b_{-12}^e(\overline{X}_{12}) = \overline{X}_{-12},$$

where $b_M(\cdot)$ is the best-response function of the merged firm. Given the properties of these best-response functions noted in observation (iii), aggregate output increases after the merger if and only if $b_M(\hat{X}_{-12}) > b_{12}^e(\hat{X}_{-12})$.

Adding these two conditions together, we have

$$P'(\hat{X})(\hat{x}_1 + \hat{x}_2) + 2P(\hat{X}) - c_1'(\hat{x}_1) - c_2'(\hat{x}_2) = 0. \tag{3}$$

Now suppose that the merged firm's cost function will be $c_M(\cdot)$. Assuming that the merged firm's profit function is concave in its output [which is also implied by (A1) and (A2)], its best response to $\hat{X}_{-12}$ is greater than the sum of the two firms' pre-merger outputs $\hat{x}_1 + \hat{x}_2$ if and only if

$$P'(\hat{X})(\hat{x}_1 + \hat{x}_2) + P(\hat{X}) - c_M'(\hat{x}_1 + \hat{x}_2) > 0, \tag{4}$$

or, equivalently [using (3)], if

$$c_2'(\hat{x}_2) - c_M'(\hat{x}_1 + \hat{x}_2) > P(\hat{X}) - c_1'(\hat{x}_1). \tag{5}$$

Since $c_1'(\hat{x}_1) \leqslant c_2'(\hat{x}_2) < P(\hat{X})$ [this follows from the pre-merger first-order conditions (1) and (2) and the fact that $\hat{x}_1 \geqslant \hat{x}_2 > 0$], this can happen only if

$$c_M'(\hat{x}_1 + \hat{x}_2) < c_1'(\hat{x}_1). \tag{6}$$

Condition (6) is a stringent requirement. It says that for price to fall the merged firm's marginal cost at the pre-merger joint output of the merging firms must be below the marginal cost of the more efficient merger partner. To better understand this condition, suppose that the merged firm has the *same* marginal cost as the more efficient merger partner (at the pre-merger output levels) and think about each of their incentives to increase output marginally. A marginal increase in output has the same incremental cost and is also sold at the same price for the two firms. However, the accompanying reduction in the market price is more costly for the merged firm than it would be for the more efficient merger partner because the merged firm sells more. Since the more efficient merger partner did not find it worthwhile to further increase its output before the merger, neither will the merged firm. Hence, for the merged firm to increase its output above the pre-merger level, it must have a lower marginal cost than the more efficient merger partner.

From condition (6), we can see that some kinds of mergers can *never* reduce price. First, as is no surprise, a merger that reduces fixed, but not marginal, costs cannot lower price. For example, imagine that before the merger each of the merging firms has cost function $c(x) = F + cx$, while the cost function of the merged firm is $c_M(x) = F_M + cx$, where $F_M < 2F$. By (6), this merger cannot reduce price.

More interesting, however, a merger that involves "no synergies" – that is, whose only efficiencies involve a reallocation of output across the firms so that

$$c_M(x) = \min_{x_1', x_2'} \left[c_1(x_1') + c_2(x_2')\right] \quad \text{s.t.} \quad x_1' + x_2' = x, \tag{7}$$

also will not result in a lower price. To see why, consider the simple case where the merging firms have increasing marginal costs. If, after the merger, both merger partners' plants remain in operation, efficient production involves equating the marginal costs of the two firms. This must result in the merged firm's marginal cost lying between the marginal costs of the two merger partners. Hence, condition (6) cannot be satisfied in this case. If, on the other hand, one of the merger partner's plants is shut down after the merger to save on fixed costs, then the other plant will be producing more than its pre-merger level. Since marginal costs are increasing, (6) once again cannot hold. More generally, Farrell and Shapiro show that a merger that involves no synergies must raise price whenever (A1) and (A2) hold.[10]

Let us now turn to the second question by supposing that the merger does increase price. Under what circumstances does it nevertheless increase aggregate surplus? To see this, suppose that firms in set I contemplate merging. Let x_i denote firm i's output and let $X_I = \sum_{i \in I} x_i$. Now consider the effect of a small reduction in the output X_I of the merging firms, say $dX_I < 0$ (by our previous assumptions, if price is to increase – and hence aggregate output is to decrease – it must be that the output of the merging firms falls), and the accompanying reduction in aggregate output $\mathrm{d}X < 0$. Let $\mathrm{d}x_i$ and $\mathrm{d}p$ be the corresponding changes in firm i's output (for $i \notin I$) and the price.

The key step in Farrell and Shapiro's analysis is their use of the presumption that proposed mergers are profitable for the merging firms.[11] If this is so, then we can derive a *sufficient condition* for the merger to increase aggregate surplus based on the *external effect* of the merger on non-participants; that is, on consumers and the non-merging firms. Specifically, the welfare of non-participants is given by

$$E = \int_{P(X)}^{\infty} x(s)\,\mathrm{d}s + \sum_{i \notin I} \bigl[P(X)x_i - c_i(x_i)\bigr]. \tag{8}$$

If a privately profitable merger increases E, then it increases aggregate surplus.

[10] A proof of this result goes as follows: Given the pre-merger aggregate output of firm 1 and firm 2's rivals, $\hat{X}_{-12}$, let $(\bar{x}_1, \bar{x}_2)$ denote the merged firm's best response. Also, let $b_i(\cdot)$ be the pre-merger best-response function of firm i for $i = 1, 2$. Observe, first, that after the merger we must have $\bar{x}_1 \leqslant b_1(\bar{x}_2 + \hat{X}_{-12})$ and $\bar{x}_2 \leqslant b_2(\bar{x}_1 + \hat{X}_{-12})$. (Formally, this can be established using a simple revealed preference argument; intuitively, the merged firm reduces both of its plants' outputs below their unmerged best responses since it internalizes the externality that each plant's output has on its other plant.) Now suppose, contrary to our hypothesis, that $\bar{x}_1 + \bar{x}_2 > \hat{x}_1 + \hat{x}_2$. Clearly $\bar{x}_i > \hat{x}_i$ for either $i = 1$ or $i = 2$; without loss of generality, suppose that $\bar{x}_2 > \hat{x}_2$. Then

$$\bar{x}_1 \leqslant b_1(\bar{x}_2 + \hat{X}_{-12}) < b_1(\hat{x}_2 + \hat{X}_{-12}) = \hat{x}_1.$$

But, $\bar{x}_1 < \hat{x}_1$ implies that

$$\bar{x}_1 + \bar{x}_2 \leqslant \bar{x}_1 + b_2(\bar{x}_1 + \hat{X}_{-12}) < \hat{x}_1 + b_2(\hat{x}_1 + \hat{X}_{-12}) = \hat{x}_1 + \hat{x}_2,$$

a contradiction.

Spector (2003) shows that if one adds the assumption that the merger is profitable (as we do below when considering effects on aggregate surplus), then price cannot fall after a merger that involves no synergies even if entry occurs after the merger.

[11] Note that in the Cournot model a merger need not increase the profits of the merging firms because of rivals' resulting output expansion [Salant, Switzer and Reynolds (1983); see also Perry and Porter (1985)].

To examine the effect of the merger on E, Farrell and Shapiro study the external effect of a "differential" price-increasing merger. That is, they examine the effect on E of a small reduction in output by the merging parties, $\mathrm{d}X_I < 0$, along with the accompanying differential changes in the outputs of rivals, $\mathrm{d}x_i$ for $i \notin I$. These changes $\mathrm{d}x_i$ arise as the non-merging firms adjust their optimal outputs given the reduction in the merged firms' output $\mathrm{d}X_I < 0$. Under Farrell and Shapiro's assumptions, these changes reduce the overall output in the market: $\mathrm{d}X = \mathrm{d}X_I + \sum_{i \notin I} \mathrm{d}x_i < 0$. Totally differentiating (8) we see that their effect on E is

$$\mathrm{d}E = -\hat{X} P'(\hat{X})\,\mathrm{d}X + \sum_{i \notin I} \hat{x}_i P'(\hat{X})\,\mathrm{d}X + \sum_{i \notin I} \big[P(\hat{X}) - c_i'(\hat{x}_i)\big]\,\mathrm{d}x_i. \tag{9}$$

The first two terms in (9) are, respectively, the welfare loss of consumers and welfare gain of the non-merging firms due to the price increase. The former is proportional to consumers' total purchases $\hat{X}$, while the latter is proportional to the non-merging firms' total sales $\sum_{i \notin I} \hat{x}_i$. The third term in (9) is the change in the non-merging firms' profits due to production reshuffling. Combining the first two terms and replacing the price–cost margin in the third term using the first-order condition for the non-merging firms we can write

$$\begin{aligned}
\mathrm{d}E &= -\hat{X}_I P'(\hat{X})\,\mathrm{d}X + \sum_{i \notin I} \big[-P'(\hat{X})\hat{x}_i\big]\,\mathrm{d}x_i \\
&= -P'(\hat{X})\,\mathrm{d}X \left[\hat{X}_I + \sum_{i \notin I} \hat{x}_i \left(\frac{\mathrm{d}x_i}{\mathrm{d}X}\right)\right] \\
&= -P'(\hat{X})\hat{X}\,\mathrm{d}X \left[s_I + \sum_{i \notin I} s_i \left(\frac{\mathrm{d}x_i}{\mathrm{d}X}\right)\right],
\end{aligned} \tag{10}$$

where s_i is firm i's pre-merger market share (s_I is the collective market share of the firms in set I), and $\frac{\mathrm{d}x_i}{\mathrm{d}X}$ is the (differential) change in non-merging firm i's output when industry output changes marginally.[12] Thus, $\mathrm{d}E \geqslant 0$ if and only if

$$s_I \leqslant -\sum_{i \notin I} s_i \left(\frac{\mathrm{d}x_i}{\mathrm{d}X}\right). \tag{11}$$

Farrell and Shapiro establish (sufficient) conditions under which signing this differential effect at the pre-merger point is sufficient for signing the global effect.[13] Note one very important aspect of condition (11): it establishes that a merger is welfare-enhancing

[12] $\frac{\mathrm{d}x_i}{\mathrm{d}X}$ is equal to $\lambda_i'(\hat{X})$, the derivative of firm i's aggregate output best-response function (see footnote 9). We get $\frac{\mathrm{d}x_i}{\mathrm{d}X}$ from implicitly differentiating the expression $P'(X)x_i + P(X) - c_i'(x_i) = 0$. Note that $\frac{\mathrm{d}x_i}{\mathrm{d}X} = (\frac{\mathrm{d}x_i}{\mathrm{d}X_{-i}})/(1 + \frac{\mathrm{d}x_i}{\mathrm{d}X_{-i}})$, where $\mathrm{d}X_{-i} \equiv \sum_{j \neq i} \mathrm{d}x_j$ and $\frac{\mathrm{d}x_i}{\mathrm{d}X_{-i}}$ is the slope of firm i's best-response function $b_i'(X_{-i})$.

[13] In particular, this is so if $[P''(\cdot), P'''(\cdot), c_i''(\cdot), -c_i'''(\cdot)] \geqslant 0$.

without the need to quantify the efficiencies created by the merger since the sign of the external effect is purely a function of pre-merger market shares and the non-merging firms' reactions to the merging firms' output reduction.

As one example, consider a situation with a (weakly) concave inverse demand function $[P''(\cdot) \leqslant 0]$ and constant returns to scale for the non-merging firms. We then have $\frac{\mathrm{d}x_i}{\mathrm{d}X} = -[1 + P''(X)x_i/P'(X)] \leqslant -1$ for all i, and so the external effect $\mathrm{d}E$ is non-negative when

$$s_I \leqslant \sum_{i \notin I} s_i \left(1 + \frac{P''(X)x_i}{P'(X)}\right) = (1 - s_I) + \frac{P''(X)X}{P'(X)} \sum_{i \notin I} (s_i)^2$$

or

$$s_I \leqslant \frac{1}{2}\left\{1 + \frac{P''(X)X}{P'(X)} \sum_{i \notin I} (s_i)^2\right\}. \tag{12}$$

Since, $P''(\cdot) \leqslant 0$, this condition holds whenever the merging firms have a share below $\frac{1}{2}$.[14]

As another example consider a situation with the linear inverse demand function $P(X) = a - X$ in which the cost function for a firm with k units of capital is $c(x, k) = \frac{1}{2}(x^2/k)$. (A merger of two firms with k_1 and k_2 units of capital results in a merged firm with $k_1 + k_2$ units of capital.) Farrell and Shapiro show that in this case the external effect is non-negative if

$$s_I \leqslant \left(\frac{1}{\varepsilon}\right) \sum_{i \notin I} (s_i)^2; \tag{13}$$

that is, if the share of the merging firms is less than an elasticity-adjusted Herfindahl–Hirschman index of the non-merging firms.

Observe that in these two examples the external effect is more likely to be positive when the merging firms are small and the non-merging firms are large. This is so because of two effects. First, there is less of a welfare reduction for consumers and the non-merging firms in aggregate resulting from a given price increase when the output of the merging firms is low (to first-order, this welfare reduction for consumers and non-participating firms is proportional to the output of the merging firms, X_I). Second, after the merger, the output of the non-merging firms increases. Since in the Cournot model larger firms have lower marginal costs in equilibrium [this follows from (1) and (2)], the effect of this reshuffling of production on non-merging firms' profits is more positive when the non-merging firms are large. It is also noteworthy that the external effect is more likely to be positive when the shares of the non-merging firms are more concentrated.[15]

[14] If the inverse demand function is linear, then $\mathrm{d}E$ is also negative whenever $s_I > 1/2$.

[15] Note that when a merger will instead *lower* price, $\mathrm{d}E$ is positive when the reverse of condition (11) holds. In that case, a merger is more likely to have a positive external effect when the merging firms are large

Conditions (12) and (13) are simple conditions that require only readily available data on pre-merger outputs and information on the market demand function. Indeed, when demand is linear, checking condition (12) requires information only on market shares [and condition (12) necessarily holds whenever $s_I \leqslant 1/2$].[16] However, the precise forms of these tests are very special and depend on having a great deal of a priori information about the underlying demand and cost functions. For more general demand and cost specifications, condition (11) requires that we also know the slopes of the non-merging firms' best-response functions [in order to know $(\frac{\mathrm{d}x_i}{\mathrm{d}X})$]. These slopes are significantly more difficult to discern than are pre-merger outputs and the elasticity of market demand.

Several further remarks on the Farrell and Shapiro method are in order. First, using the external effect to derive a sufficient condition for a merger to be welfare enhancing depends critically on the assumption that proposed mergers are privately profitable. To the extent that agency problems may lead managers to "empire build" to the detriment of firm value, this assumption may be inappropriate.[17]

Second, this approach relies as well on the assumption that all of the private gains for the merging parties represent social gains. If, for example, some of these gains arise from tax savings [see Werden (1990)] or represent transfers from other stakeholders in the firm [Shleifer and Summers (1988)], this assumption would be inappropriate.

Third, Farrell and Shapiro use the assumption that the merger is profitable in only a limited way. By asking when the external effect is positive, they provide a sufficient condition for a merger to increase aggregate surplus that requires no consideration at all of efficiencies. More generally, an antitrust authority that cannot verify claimed efficiencies directly might use the fact that a merger is profitable to update its beliefs about the extent of likely efficiencies. It could then ask whether the merger results in an increase in expected aggregate surplus given this updated belief.

Fourth, the Farrell and Shapiro analysis is based on the strong assumption that market competition takes a form that is described well by the Cournot model, both before and after the merger. Many other forms of price/output competition are possible, and – as mentioned when discussing the Williamson trade-off – important elements of competition may occur along dimensions other than price/quantity. There has been no work that I am aware of extending the Farrell and Shapiro approach to other forms of market

and the non-merging firms are small (and hence, not very efficient). In fact, Levin (1990) shows that (in an environment with constant returns to scale) if the most efficient non-merged firm is less efficient than the merged firm and price falls following the merger, then the merger necessarily increases aggregate surplus.

[16] Although they bear some superficial resemblance to the concentration tests that appear in the DOJ/FTC Merger Guidelines (see Section 3), conditions (12) and (13) differ from the Guidelines' tests in some significant ways, such as the fact that increases in the concentration of non-merging firms can make the merger more desirable socially.

[17] In this regard, it appears from event study evidence that, on average, mergers increase the joint value of the merging firms, although there is a large variance in outcomes across mergers [Andrade, Mitchell and Stafford (2001), Jensen and Ruback (1983)]. One might take the view, in any case, that antitrust policy should not concern itself with stopping mergers based on unresolved agency problems within the merging firms.

interaction. The papers that formally study the effect of horizontal mergers on price and welfare in other competitive settings [e.g., Deneckere and Davidson (1985) and some of the papers discussed in Section 2.3] all assume that there are no efficiencies generated by the merger.[18]

Finally, there is some evidence that the efficiency consequences of production reshuffling that Farrell and Shapiro's analysis focuses on may well be important in practice. Olley and Pakes (1996), for example, study the productivity of the telecommunications equipment industry following a regulatory decision in 1978 and the breakup of AT&T in 1984, both of which facilitated new entry into a market that essentially had been a (Western Electric) monopoly. They document that productivity varied greatly across plants in the industry. More significantly from the perspective of the Farrell and Shapiro model, Olley and Pakes show that there was a significant amount of inefficiency in the allocation of output across plants in the industry once market structure moved away from monopoly.[19]

2.3. Mergers in a dynamic world

One of the notable aspects of the Farrell and Shapiro model is its static nature. A number of interesting and important issues arise when one thinks of mergers in a more dynamic context. Many of these issues have received only limited attention.

2.3.1. Repeated interaction ("coordinated effects")

In Farrell and Shapiro's Cournot model, mergers necessarily raise price [under regularity conditions (A1) and (A2)] in the absence of any merger-induced efficiencies. This need not be true when firms interact repeatedly and tacit (or even explicit) collusion is a possibility. (In antitrust lingo, a merger's effects on tacit collusion are referred to as "coordinated effects", in contrast to the "unilateral effects" the merger has on static pricing incentives.) In such cases, as Davidson and Deneckere (1984) note, mergers can be a double-edged sword: they reduce the merging firms' direct incentives for cheating on tacit agreements, but they may also raise firms' profits when collusion breaks down, and thus indirectly increase the temptation to cheat, especially for non-merging firms. Because of these effects, a merger that generates no efficiencies can potentially lead all prices in a market to fall.

Analyzing the effects of a merger on firms' abilities to sustain collusion typically requires a model in which firms can be asymmetric.[20] Several recent papers have stud-

[18] One exception is Gowrisankaran (1999) who allows for a merger-specific "synergy" (effectively, a reduction in fixed costs) in his computational model of endogenous mergers.

[19] In particular, efficiency in this sense *decreased* as the industry went from monopoly to a more competitive market structure. However, overall industry productivity increased over time as capital was reallocated toward more efficient firms.

[20] An exception is when a merger combines firms with the same constant returns to scale technology as in Salant, Switzer and Reynolds (1983).

ied such models. Compte, Jenny and Rey (2002), for example, consider the effects of horizontal mergers in a repeated Bertrand model with firms having differing capacity constraints; Vasconcelos (2005) examines a repeated Cournot game in which firms' cost functions $c(x, k)$ depend both on their output x and capital k (a merger of firms i and j leads to a merged firm with capital $k_i + k_j$); Kuhn (2004) explores a model of repeated price setting with symmetrically differentiated products in which a merger joins the product lines of the merging firms. These papers focus on classes of equilibria in which each firm's profit along any equilibrium path (either collusive or punishment) is a constant share of aggregate profit. This simplifies the analysis of equilibria since the set of subgame perfect equilibrium values for the firms is one-dimensional. (Moreover, all firms agree on what is the "best" equilibrium within this class.)

For example, in the Compte, Jenny and Rey paper, market demand is $Q(p) = 1$ if $p \leqslant 1$ and 0 if $p > 1$. Each firm i has capacity k_i and can produce output at zero cost up to capacity. There are N firms, with $k_1 \leqslant \cdots \leqslant k_N$ and $K \equiv \sum_j k_j \geqslant 1$. The firms play a repeated simultaneous price choice game. In such a game, if any collusion is possible, it is possible to sustain perfect collusion in every period (a price of 1). Compte, Jenny and Rey therefore focus on characterizing the lowest discount factor δ at which collusion is feasible.

There are two cases to consider in their model. First, if $K_{-N} \equiv \sum_{j \neq N} k_j \geqslant 1$, then any set of $N - 1$ firms has enough capacity to supply all of demand. In that case, the static Nash equilibrium yields profits of zero to all firms, and represents the worst possible punishment for a deviation. Collusion is then feasible if and only if

$$\hat{\pi}_i(1) \leqslant \frac{\alpha_i \pi(1)}{1 - \delta} \quad \text{for all } i,$$

where $\hat{\pi}_i(1) = \min\{k_i, 1\} \equiv \hat{k}_i$ is firm i's profit from an optimal deviation when all other firms charge a price of 1 ($\hat{k}_i$ is firm i's "effective" capacity), α_i is firm i's market share, and $\pi(1) = 1$ is the aggregate profit in each period when all firms charge a price of 1. Substituting these values and dividing by α_i, collusion is feasible if and only if

$$\max_i \frac{\hat{k}_i}{\alpha_i} \leqslant \frac{1}{1 - \delta}.$$

Thus, the firm that constrains collusion is the firm with the largest ratio of effective capacity to market share. Collusion is easiest to sustain when this ratio is the same for all firms, that is, when each firm i's market share is equal to its share of effective capacity: $\alpha_i = \hat{k}_i / \hat{K}$, where $\hat{K} = \sum_i \hat{k}_i$. Hence, the lowest discount factor at which collusion is feasible is

$$\underline{\delta} = \frac{\hat{K} - 1}{\hat{K}}. \tag{14}$$

Condition (14) tells us that when $K_{-N} \geqslant 1$, so that punishments for deviation always lead to a payoff of zero, mergers can never harm the prospects for collusion (note that a merger can never increase $\hat{K}$). Moreover, a merger of firms i and j who both have strictly positive capacities will make collusion easier whenever they can supply the entire market after the merger ($k_i + k_j > 1$).

In the second case, $K_{-N} < 1$, so there is no longer a zero-profit static Nash equilibrium. Determining when collusion is feasible then requires that we also determine the worst possible punishment. Following techniques in Abreu (1986), these worst punishments involve a "stick-and-carrot" structure. Specifically, the best and worst equilibria, which involve per period discounted aggregate profits of $\bar{v}$ and $\underline{v}$, have the following structures: If any collusion is possible, the best equilibrium involves the firms all charging price $\bar{p} = 1$ in every period if no deviation has occurred in the previous period (so $\bar{v} = 1$), and reverting to the worst equilibrium if a deviation has occurred. The worst equilibrium involves all firms charging some price $\underline{p} < 1$ for one period. If no firm deviates, they then revert to the best equilibrium; if, instead, some firm deviates, the worst punishment is restarted.[21] In this case, collusion is sustainable if and only if there is a punishment value $\underline{v}$ such that for all i,

$$(\hat{k}_i - \alpha_i) \leqslant \left(\frac{\delta}{1-\delta}\right)\alpha_i(1-\underline{v}), \tag{15}$$

$$\max\{1 - K_{-i}, 0\} \leqslant \alpha_i \underline{v}. \tag{16}$$

Condition (15) is the condition needed for firm i not to deviate from the collusive price $\bar{p} = 1$ (the best deviation involves selling $\hat{k}_i$ units at a price slightly below 1). It says that the gain from a one-period deviation $(\hat{k}_i - \alpha_i)$ is less than the present discounted value of the loss from reverting to the worst equilibrium in the next period. Condition (16) is the condition needed for firm i not to deviate from the punishment price $\underline{p}$ (the best deviation involves charging a price $p = 1$ and selling $\max\{1-K_{-i}, 0\}$ units). It says that the payoff in the first period of deviating must be less than the firm's per period payoff in the worst equilibrium. Since deviation leads to a restarting of the worst equilibrium, this insures that a deviation is not profitable. Dividing by α_i and looking for the firms for which these constraints are tightest, we see that collusion is possible if and only if

$$\max_i\left(\frac{\hat{k}_i}{\alpha_i}\right) - 1 \leqslant \left(\frac{\delta}{1-\delta}\right)(1-\underline{v}), \tag{17}$$

$$\max_i\left(\frac{\max\{1 - K_{-i}, 0\}}{\alpha_i}\right) \leqslant \underline{v}. \tag{18}$$

Note that the firm that imposes a constraint on collusion at the collusive price $\bar{p} = 1$ may be different than the firm that imposes the constraint at the punishment price $\underline{p}$. Putting conditions (17) and (18) together tells us that collusion is feasible if and only if

$$\left(\frac{\delta}{1-\delta}\right) \geqslant \frac{\max_i(\frac{\hat{k}_i}{\alpha_i}) - 1}{1 - \max_i(\frac{\max\{1-K_{-i},0\}}{\alpha_i})}. \tag{19}$$

[21] If there is a lower bound on prices (such as $\underline{p} \geqslant 0$), then the punishment period may need to last more than one period.

Collusion is easiest at the market shares $(\alpha_1, \ldots, \alpha_N)$ that minimize the right-hand side of (19). The numerator, reflecting incentives to deviate from the collusive price, is minimized when shares are proportional to effective capacities, as before. The denominator, reflecting incentives to deviate from the punishment price, is minimized when shares are proportional to each firm's minimax payoff, $\max\{1 - K_{-i}, 0\}$. Compte, Jenny and Rey show that the collusive incentives dominate, so that collusion is easiest when shares are again proportional to effective capacities. This makes the numerator on the right-hand side of (19) equal $(\hat{K} - 1)$. The denominator, on the other hand, equals $[1 - (1 - K_{-N})\hat{K}/\hat{k}_N]$, which reflects the fact that with shares proportional to effective capacities, it is the largest firm that has the highest incentive to deviate from the punishment.[22] This implies (using the fact that $K_{-N} + \hat{k}_N = \hat{K}$ when $K_{-N} < 1$) that the lowest discount factor at which collusion is feasible is

$$\underline{\delta} = \frac{\hat{k}_N}{\hat{K}}. \tag{20}$$

Condition (20) has a striking implication: when $K_{-N} < 1$, only mergers that involve the largest firm matter for the ease of sustaining collusion (since no other mergers change $\hat{K}$ when $K_{-N} < 1$) and any merger that causes the largest firm to grow larger starting from an initial size at which it is unable to serve the entire market makes collusion *harder* (by raising $\hat{k}_N$ and possibly lowering $\hat{K}$). The reason is that it is the largest firm that constrains the ability to punish when shares are proportional to effective capacities. Indeed, the value of the worst punishment is $\underline{v} = \hat{K}(1 - K_{-N})/\hat{k}_N$. For example, when the largest firm approaches having nearly all of the industry capacity, so that $\hat{k}_N \to \hat{K}$ and $(1 - K_{-N}) \to 1$, it becomes impossible to punish deviations from collusion ($\underline{v} \to 1$).

The fact that asymmetry, and thus mergers involving the largest firm, can harm collusion arises as well in the papers by Vasconcelos (2005) and Kuhn (2004). As in Compte, Jenny and Rey, the reason is the punishment effect: the largest firm often has the greatest incentive to deviate in a punishment phase. Intuitively, it bears the largest cost from the punishment.

While these papers have significantly increased our understanding of the factors affecting collusion with asymmetric firms, the restricted classes of equilibria they analyze could give misleading results. For example, an optimal collusive scheme might involve different shares for a firm in collusive and punishment phases, or even different prices for different firms within a given period. In general, one must also confront the issue of how firms select which equilibrium to play among the various feasible collusive equilibria. The last section of Kuhn (2004) uses computational techniques to look at the

[22] To see this formally, substitute $\alpha_i = \hat{k}_i/\hat{K}$ into the denominator of (19) and observe that for any $i \neq N$, $\max\{1 - K_{-N}, 0\}/\hat{k}_N \geqslant \max\{1 - K_{-i}, 0\}/\hat{k}_i$ if $K_{-i} \geqslant 1$, while if $K_{-i} < 1$ then

$$\frac{\max\{1 - K_{-N}, 0\}}{\hat{k}_N} = \frac{1 - K_{-N}}{\hat{k}_N} \geqslant \frac{1 - K_{-N}}{k_N} \geqslant \frac{1 - K_{-i}}{k_i} = \frac{\max\{1 - K_{-i}, 0\}}{\hat{k}_i}$$

(the second weak inequality follows because $K > 1$).

effect of mergers when firms use Nash bargaining to select from among the full set of collusive equilibria in a linear version of his model. More work in this direction, both analytical and computational, would be useful.

2.3.2. Durable goods

The Farrell and Shapiro analysis focuses on non-durable goods. Many mergers, however, occur in durable goods industries. Two issues arise when merging firms operate in a durable goods market. First, consumers' abilities to delay their purchases in anticipation of future price reductions affect the ability to exercise market power. As emphasized by Coase (1972), this may mitigate – sometimes completely – the ability of a durable good monopolist to earn positive profits. On the other hand, consumers' abilities to delay their purchases may make tacit collusion among durable good oligopolists *easier* by reducing the sales enjoyed by a deviating seller. This occurs because consumers who anticipate that a price war is about to break out will delay their purchases. Indeed, Gul (1987) and Ausubel and Deneckere (1987) show that in some cases durable good oligopolists may be able to sustain a higher price than can a durable good monopolist.

The second issue concerns the welfare costs of horizontal mergers that do increase market power. Carlton and Gertner (1989) point out that used goods may constrain the pricing of even a monopolist whose market power is not otherwise constrained by the factors noted by Coase. Indeed, when new goods depreciate in quantity but not in quality (so that used goods may be combined to yield equivalent consumption value to new goods) and the market is initially at a competitive steady state, even a newly-formed monopolist will not be able to raise price above the competitive level until the current stock of used goods depreciates. If it depreciates slowly, or if entry is likely to occur before too long, then even a merger to monopoly will have small welfare effects. In contrast, Gerstle and Waldman (2004) show that when used goods are of lower quality than new ones and consumers differ in their willingness to pay for high quality, a newly-formed monopolist will be able to raise price right away, and that welfare losses are larger than in the setting studied by Carlton and Gertner.

2.3.3. Entry

In most market settings, merging firms need to worry about the possibility of new entry following their merger. This can affect both the set of proposed mergers and their welfare consequences.

The possibility of post-merger entry reduces the set of profitable mergers. It also affects the average characteristics of profitable mergers. Werden and Froeb (1998), for example, in an exploratory study of mergers and entry, observe that mergers that lead to entry are rarely profitable in the absence of efficiency improvements. Thus, the set of profitable mergers when entry is possible is likely to be more heavily weighted toward mergers that reduce costs.

Consider now how the possibility of entry affects the welfare evaluation of mergers. If we are interested in a consumer surplus standard, the possibility of new entry increases the likelihood that a given merger will lower price. If we are interested in an aggregate surplus standard, however, the possibility of entry need not make a given merger more attractive. To see why, consider the standard two-stage model of entry with sunk costs [as in Mankiw and Whinston (1986); see also, Mas-Colell, Whinston and Green (1995, ch. 12)], and for simplicity imagine that competition takes a Cournot form, that firms have identical constant returns to scale technologies, and that the merger creates no improvements in efficiency. In this setting, the short-run result of two firms merging is an elevation in price, while the long-run effect (once entry can occur) is the entry of exactly one additional firm and a return to the pre-merger price. However, in this setting, we know that entry incentives are generally excessive [see Mankiw and Whinston (1986)]: too many firms enter the industry in a free-entry equilibrium. This implies that the merger's effect on aggregate surplus is *worse* when entry is possible than when it is not.

We will see shortly (in Section 3.1.3) that easy entry conditions tend to make antitrust agencies more receptive to a merger. If the goal is to maximize aggregate surplus, would such a presumption make sense given the above observation? One reason it might is related to Farrell and Shapiro's idea of conditioning on a proposed merger being profitable. In particular, if easier entry causes profitable mergers to involve, on average, greater efficiencies, then mergers that are proposed in markets with easy entry may nonetheless be more likely to increase aggregate surplus (and consumer surplus too).

2.3.4. Endogenous mergers

There is a fairly large literature that tries to endogenize the set of mergers that will occur in a market in the absence of any antitrust constraint [see, for example, Mackay (1984), Kamien and Zang (1990), Bloch (1996), Yi (1997), Gowrisankaran and Holmes (2004)]. One key observation in this literature is that an unregulated merger process may stop far short of full monopolization. The reason is a "hold-out" problem: if potential acquirees anticipate that the acquirer will be purchasing other firms, thereby raising the market price, they may insist on such a high price for their own firm as to make their acquisition unprofitable. Indeed, in some cases, this may mean that no mergers occur at all.[23]

This literature has some potentially important implications for Farrell and Shapiro's analysis of the welfare effects of proposed horizontal mergers. For example, observe that when Farrell and Shapiro assume that a proposed merger is profitable for the merging parties they do this under the assumption that this merger is the only merger that can happen. In a dynamic context in which other mergers may follow the currently proposed merger (or, may occur if it is *not* consummated), what it means for a merger to be

[23] This point is also related to the literature on contracting with externalities [e.g., Segal (1999)].

"profitable" is that the merger must increase the sum of the two firms' values. This is not the same as saying that the merger is profitable in the absence of other mergers. Moreover, the external effect of the merger may differ markedly from Farrell and Shapiro's calculation of the change in E. For example, it may include changes in the amounts that non-merging firms are paid later when they themselves are acquired.

This literature also suggests that there may be some subtle effects from a change in an antitrust authority's rules for blocking mergers. Such a change may have not only a direct effect on the set of consummated mergers through a change in treatment when a given merger is proposed, but may also change the set of permissible mergers that are actually proposed.

2.3.5. Other competitive variables

Focusing on dynamics, one can begin to consider other, more long-run aspects of competition among firms, such as capacity investment, R&D, and new product development. In principle, a merger's effect on welfare may be as much or more through changes in these dimensions as through changes in prices/outputs. Some progress on these issues has been made through the use of computational techniques. Berry and Pakes (1993), for example, discuss simulations of a dynamic oligopoly model with capacity investment in which a merger's long-run effects on profitability and welfare through changes in investment indeed swamp its static price/output competition effects. Further work along these lines can be found in Gowrisankaran (1999), who also attempts to endogenize the merger process itself. Some consideration of non-price variables has recently been introduced into merger analyses through the concept of "innovation markets" [Gilbert and Sunshine (1995)].

2.3.6. Multimarket contact

Finally, in a dynamic world in which tacit collusion is possible, a merger may affect pricing in a market not only by changing within-market concentration, but also by changing the extent to which multiproduct firms compete against one another in multiple markets. Bernheim and Whinston (1990), for example, show theoretically that, in some cases, multimarket contact can improve firms' abilities to sustain high prices by pooling the incentive constraints that limit tacit collusion. Some evidence of multimarket contact effects is provided by Phillips and Mason (1992) and Evans and Kessides (1994). The latter study provides evidence that the price increases that arose from a series of horizontal mergers in the U.S. airline industry in the 1980s were to a significant degree due to multimarket contact effects.

3. Merger laws and enforcement

Merger laws and enforcement developed at very different times in different countries. Antitrust scrutiny of horizontal mergers started before 1900 in the U.S., but much later in most other countries. For instance, mergers were first subject to review in the United Kingdom in 1965, in Germany in 1973, in Australia in 1974, and in Israel in the late 1980s. The E.U. did not have a merger control law until 1990. Yet, despite this fact, in recent years there has been a striking convergence in merger laws and enforcement around the globe toward a model in which mergers are evaluated prospectively for their potential competitive harms according to fairly similar standards. In many – although not all – respects, this convergence has been toward the U.S. model of merger review. In this section, I begin by reviewing that approach. I next describe merger control in the E.U. I then discuss some of the main areas of differences in other countries, with a particular focus on one important area of difference, the choice of a welfare standard. Finally, I look briefly at enforcement experience in the U.S. and the E.U.

3.1. U.S. merger laws and the DOJ/FTC guidelines

Horizontal mergers were first regulated in the United States with passage of the Sherman Act in 1890. Section 1 of the Sherman Act states that "Every contract, combination in the form of trust or otherwise, or conspiracy, in restraint of trade or commerce among the several states, or with foreign nations, is hereby declared illegal...". This vague prohibition authorized the U.S. courts to develop a common law of antitrust to fulfill the statute's intent, and the courts soon used it to rule some horizontal mergers (particularly among railroads) illegal. (The U.S. courts also applied Section 1 of the Sherman Act to price fixing, exclusive contracts, and other anticompetitive "agreements".)

The vagueness of the Sherman Act's prohibitions, however, resulted in pressure for further legislation, leading in 1914 to passage of the Clayton and Federal Trade Commission Acts. The Clayton Act more specifically prohibits certain practices including, in its Section 7, mergers where "the effect of such acquisition may be substantially to lessen competition, or tend to create a monopoly" in any line of commerce. The Federal Trade Commission Act created the Federal Trade Commission (FTC) as a specialist agency to enforce the antitrust laws. The central substantive provision guiding the FTC's enforcement actions is Section 5 of the Act which states that "Unfair methods of competition in or affecting commerce... are hereby declared illegal". The U.S. courts interpret Section 5 as applying to anything that is a Sherman Act or Clayton Act violation.[24]

Three types of sanctions can be imposed in U.S. antitrust cases: criminal penalties, equitable relief, and monetary damages. Sherman Act offenses are felonies, and the Department of Justice (DOJ), but not the FTC, can seek criminal penalties for them. (Violations of the Clayton Act and FTC Act are not crimes.) In practice, however, criminal penalties are sought only for overt price fixing and are not relevant for horizontal merger enforcement.

[24] The courts also interpret Section 5 of the FTC Act as applying as well to somewhat "lesser" acts that violate the "spirit" of the Sherman and Clayton Acts. That broader interpretation seems not to matter, however, in the area of merger enforcement. The FTC also applies Section 5 to consumer protection issues, such as misleading advertising and fraud.

Equitable relief entails undoing a wrong that has occurred, or preventing future harm, for example, by requiring divestiture of a merger that has already been consummated or by preventing firms from merging in the first place. In practice, nearly all antitrust remedies in horizontal merger cases involve equitable relief.

Both the DOJ and private parties can sue in the federal courts for equitable relief for violations of either the Sherman or Clayton Acts. The result of such a proceeding, should the plaintiff prevail, is a court issued *decree*. (Often, however, settlement negotiations result instead in a *consent decree* prior to a court decision in a case.[25])

The FTC can also seek equitable relief. Here the procedure is somewhat different and involves a quasi-judicial administrative proceeding within the agency in front of what is known as an "administrative law judge", in which the FTC staff and the accused firms present evidence. The administrative law judge then issues an opinion, which is then reviewed by the Commission, consisting of five commissioners appointed by the President for seven-year terms. The Commission can approve or change (in any way) the administrative law judge's decision, and is then empowered to issue a "cease and desist" order if it finds that violations have occurred. Like lower court rulings for DOJ or private party suits, these cease and desist orders can be appealed by the firms to the appellate courts. In practice, however, the FTC merger review process often involves a court hearing much earlier than that, since for mergers that it has concerns about which have not yet been consummated the FTC nearly always seeks a preliminary injunction in federal court to prevent the parties from merging until after its internal proceeding is completed.

Finally, private parties who prove in court that they were injured due to Sherman and Clayton Act offenses can recover treble damages. In addition to providing a means for compensating parties injured by antitrust violations, these penalties help to create an additional army of private enforcers of the antitrust laws (moreover, an army that is perhaps more aware of when violations are occurring than are the governmental enforcement agencies). Treble damages rarely arise from horizontal mergers, however, because merger notification requirements (discussed next) mean that most illegal mergers are now blocked before they are consummated.

Since the Hart–Scott–Rodino Act of 1976, parties to mergers that exceed certain size thresholds must notify the DOJ and FTC of their intention to merge. Currently, notification is required if the acquired company exceeds \$212.3 million in assets, or if the acquired company exceeds \$53.1 million in assets and the annual sales or assets of the larger of the acquirer and acquired firms exceeds \$106.2 million and of the smaller exceeds \$10.7 million. The parties must then wait 30 days before consummating their merger (15 days if it is a cash tender offer). Prior to that time limit, the agencies can

[25] One important issue that I do not discuss is the crafting of effective remedies. A report by the FTC [Federal Trade Commission (1999)] studies factors that have led divestitures to be more or less effective as a merger remedy. Recently, the European Commission has also completed such a study [European Commission (2005)].

issue a request for additional information. Once the parties have complied with this so-called "second request", an additional 30-day waiting period begins (15 days for a cash tender offer) to give the agencies time to object to the merger before it is consummated. In practice, there is a great deal of flexibility in the duration of the second request phase because it depends on when compliance is deemed to be complete. In fact, since at this point in the process the parties are usually eager to appear cooperative in the hope of persuading the agencies to their point of view, they will often agree to delay the date of official compliance, or agree to delay merging for more than 30 days after they have complied.

The agencies tend to divide their review of notified horizontal mergers by industry to take advantage of industry-specific expertise. One somewhat odd feature of this division of responsibility between the two agencies is that different procedures apply to the two agencies' reviews of mergers, with the DOJ's need to go to court contrasting with the FTC's ability to conduct its own quasi-judicial administrative proceeding within the agency. This difference is tempered in practice, though, by the fact that both agencies need to go to federal court to obtain a preliminary injunction.

In addition to these federal antitrust statutes, state attorney generals can also use their individual states' antitrust laws to attack a merger that affects commerce in their state. Indeed, nothing in principle prevents a state's attorney general from doing so even after the DOJ or FTC has approved a merger.

The DOJ and FTC have periodically issued guidelines outlining the method they would follow for evaluating horizontal mergers. The most recent *Horizontal Merger Guidelines* were issued jointly in 1992, with a revision to the section on efficiencies in 1997.[26] The *Guidelines* first took a form resembling their present one in the early 1980s. The changes to the *Guidelines* introduced at that time dramatically increased the level of economic sophistication in horizontal merger review. The *Guidelines* have also greatly influenced the approach toward merger review adopted by antitrust authorities in other countries.

In practice, the approach followed by the DOJ and FTC in their merger reviews has an enormous effect on the set of mergers that are actually consummated. Antitrust cases are extremely expensive and often long affairs. As a result, once the DOJ or FTC announce that they will seek to block a merger, few firms decide to incur the costs and time required to fight in court. (Nearly all of the remaining mergers are dropped or settled if the agencies win a preliminary injunction in court.)

The merger analysis described in the *Guidelines* consists of four basic steps:

1. Market definition.
2. Calculation of market concentration and concentration changes.
3. Evaluation of other market factors.
4. Pro-competitive justifications.

[26] A copy of the Guidelines can be found at: http://www.usdoj.gov/atr/public/guidelines/horiz_book/hmg1.html and http://www.ftc.gov/bc/docs/horizmer.htm.

3.1.1. Market definition

For simplicity suppose that the two merging firms produce widgets. The DOJ and FTC will first ask the following question:

> Would a hypothetical profit-maximizing monopolist of widgets impose at least a small but significant and non-transitory increase in the price of widgets given the pre-merger prices of other products?

In practice, a "small but significant and non-transitory increase in price" (the "SSNIP test") is usually taken to be 5% of the pre-merger price. If the answer to this question is yes, then widgets is the relevant market. If the answer is no, then the agencies add the next closest substitute product (the product that would gain the most sales as a result of a 5% increase in the price of widgets) and ask the question again for this new larger potential market. This process continues until the answer to the question is yes. The idea is to arrive at a "relevant market" of products in which a merger potentially could have an anticompetitive effect.[27]

In this example, the two firms were both producing the homogeneous product widgets. Sometimes they will be producing imperfect substitutes, say widgets and gidgets (or products sold in imperfectly overlapping geographic areas). The DOJ and FTC will start by asking the same question for each of these products separately. The merger is "horizontal" if this leads to a market definition in which the two products are both in the same market.

So far we have assumed that the merging firms each produce a single product. In many cases, however, they will be multi-product firms. The DOJ and FTC will follow the same procedure for each product they produce.

The market definition procedure described in the *Guidelines* makes a number of seemingly arbitrary choices to resolve potential ambiguities (and in some cases leaves these ambiguities unresolved). For example, consider the 5% price increase test. If an oil pipeline buys oil on one end, transports it, and sells it at the other, is the "price" the total price charged for the oil at the end, or is it the net price for the transportation provided? Note that if oil is supplied competitively, then the basic economic situation is not affected by whether the pipeline buys oil and sells it to consumers, or charges oil companies for transportation with the oil companies selling delivered oil to consumers. Yet, which price is chosen matters for the *Guidelines*' market definition procedure. The *Guidelines* explicitly discusses this example, and opts for the net price of transportation. In contrast, in discussing retail mergers, the *Guidelines* opt for looking at the increase

[27] One thorny issue is what to do if widget producers are successfully colluding (tacitly) before the merger. Applying the SSNIP test directly, one would conclude that widgets is not the relevant market. This might be appropriate if one expects collusion to continue forever, in which case a merger cannot make matters worse in widgets. But if that collusion might at some point break down, a merger would prevent those price decreases from happening. In response to this concern, the *Guidelines* state that if it appears that firms are currently colluding, then the relevant comparison price for the SSNIP test would be a "competitive" price.

in retail prices, rather than the (implicit) net price of retail services. As another example, should the test be that the hypothetical monopolist raises price on all products by at least 5%, or that it does so for at least one of them? Here the *Guidelines* require that at least one price including one of the products of the merging parties increase by at least this amount. It is in some sense difficult to know what is the "right" way to resolve these (and other) ambiguities, because the *Guidelines*' procedure – while intuitive – is not based directly on any explicit model of competition and welfare effects.

3.1.2. Calculating concentration and concentration changes

Once the DOJ or FTC has defined the relevant market, the next step is to calculate the pre- and post-merger concentration levels. To do so, the DOJ and FTC will include all firms that are producing currently as well as all likely "uncommitted entrants"; i.e., firms that could and would readily and without significant sunk costs supply the market in response to a 5% increase in price. Pre-merger shares are then calculated for each of these firms, usually on the basis of sales, although sometimes based on production, capacity (or, more generally, asset ownership), or (when uncommitted entrant responses are important) likely sales shares in response to a hypothetical 5% price increase. Using these pre-merger shares, say $(s_1, \dots, s_N)$, the DOJ and FTC then calculate the following concentration measures:

Pre-merger Herfindahl–Hirschman index: $\text{HHI}_{\text{pre}} = \sum_i (s_i)^2$.

Post-merger Herfindahl–Hirschman index: $\text{HHI}_{\text{post}} = \sum_i (s_i)^2 - (s_1)^2 - (s_2)^2 + (s_1 + s_2)^2 = \sum_i (s_i)^2 + 2s_1 s_2$.

The change in the Herfindahl–Hirschman index: $\Delta\text{HHI} = \text{HHI}_{\text{post}} - \text{HHI}_{\text{pre}} = 2s_1 s_2$.

The levels of these measures place the merger in one of the following categories:

$HHI_{post} < 1000$: These mergers are presumed to raise no competitive concerns except in exceptional circumstances.

$HHI_{post} > 1000$ *and* < 1800: These mergers are unlikely to be challenged if the change in the Herfindahl–Hirschman index is less than 100. If it exceeds 100, then the merger "potentially raises significant competitive concerns", depending on consideration of other market factors.

$HHI_{post} > 1800$: These mergers are unlikely to be challenged if the change in the Herfindahl–Hirschman index is less than 50. If it is between 50 and 100, then the merger "potentially raises significant competitive concerns", depending on consideration of other market factors. If the change exceeds 100, it is presumed that the merger is likely to be anti-competitive without evidence showing otherwise.

Recalling that in a symmetric oligopoly the Herfindahl–Hirschman index is equal to 10,000 divided by the number of firms in the market, an index of 1000 corresponds to 10 equal-sized firms; an index of 1800 corresponds to 5.6 equal-sized firms. A change of 100 in the Herfindahl–Hirschman index would be caused by the merger of two firms with roughly a 7% share; a change of 50 would be caused by the merger of two firms with a 5% share.

The Guidelines therefore establish "safe harbors" for merging firms (i.e., cases in which a challenge is declared to be "unlikely") as well as some initial presumptions of anticompetitive harm. Actual enforcement practice has been more lenient than these numbers may suggest. This is due, in part, to the DOJ and FTC's consideration of other market factors and pro-competitive justifications, to which we now turn.

3.1.3. Evaluation of other market factors

Calculation of pre-merger concentration and its change due to the merger is only the starting point of the DOJ and FTC's investigations. After calculating these concentration figures, the DOJ and FTC consider a number of other factors affecting the likely competitive impact of the merger. These include:

Structural factors affecting the ease of sustaining collusion (tacit or explicit). These include factors such as homogeneity of products, noisiness of the market, and others that influence the ease of sustaining collusion [see, for example, Hay and Kelley (1974) and Whinston (2006, ch. 2)]. Generally, the DOJ and FTC are more concerned about mergers in markets in which tacit or explicit collusion is easier to sustain. One might wonder, however, whether mergers in markets in which collusion is easier should necessarily be of greater concern. After all, relatively little competitive harm can come from a merger in a market in which it is already easily for the firms to sustain the joint monopoly outcome. Put differently, the relevant question is the extent to which the merger is likely to increase prices. Market conditions that make collusion easier in general need not make the price effect of a merger larger.

Evidence of market performance. Although not explicitly mentioned in the *Guidelines*, the DOJ and FTC often consider empirical evidence showing how the level of concentration in such a market affects competitive outcomes in assessing the likely competitive effects of a merger. We will discuss this type of evidence further in Section 4.2.

Substitution patterns in the market. The DOJ and FTC will ask whether the merging firms are closer substitutes to each other than to other firms in the market. This is a way to avoid discarding important information about substitution patterns, as might occur by simply calculating concentration figures. In markets with product differentiation (and unit demands), a merger changes pricing incentives when the products of the merging firms are the first and second choices, at prevailing prices, of a significant share of customers. The agencies will look to demand estimates, marketing studies, business documents, and other evidence to determine the extent to which this is true.[28]

[28] The *Guidelines* also state that the agencies "will presume that a significant share of sales in the market are accounted for by consumers who regard the products of the merging firms as their first and second choices" when the merger falls outside of the safe-harbor regions described above and the merging firms have a combined share of at least 35 percent.

Substitution patterns between products in and out of the market. The DOJ and FTC will ask whether there is a large degree of differentiation between the products just "in" and just "out" of the market. This is, in a sense, a way of softening the edges of the previous determination of the relevant market; that is, it is a way of making the "in-or-out" decision regarding certain products less of an all-or-nothing proposition. To the extent that there are not close substitutes outside the market, there is a greater potential for the exercise of market power.

Capacity limitations of some firms in the market. Here the aim is to avoid the loss of important information about the competitive constraint provided by the merging firms' rivals that might occur from a simple calculation of market concentration. If a rival is capacity constrained, one would expect it to be less of a force in constraining any post-merger price increase. Also, as discussed in Section 2.3.1, capacity constraints can affect the degree to which a merger facilitates tacit or explicit collusive pricing.

Ease of entry. Here the DOJ and FTC will consider the degree to which entry involving sunk costs might preclude anticompetitive effects arising from the merger. (Recall that "uncommitted" entrants, who have insignificant sunk costs, are included in calculating market shares.) The question they ask is whether, in response to a 5% price increase, entry would be likely to occur within 2 years that would drive price down to its pre-merger level. As discussed in Section 2.3.3, this makes sense with a consumer surplus welfare standard, but there is a question about how the ease of entry should affect merger analysis if the goal is to instead maximize aggregate surplus.

3.1.4. Pro-competitive justifications

The principal issue here is the consideration of efficiencies. The DOJ and FTC typically adopt a fairly high hurdle for claimed efficiencies because it is relatively easy for firms to claim that efficiencies will be generated by a merger, and relatively hard for antitrust enforcers to evaluate the likelihood that those efficiencies will be realized. How efficiencies should be factored into the analysis of a merger depends on the welfare standard adopted by the agencies. The 1997 revisions to the DOJ/FTC *Guidelines*, while somewhat ambiguous, suggest that the efficiencies need to be sufficient to keep consumer surplus from decreasing for a merger to be approved.[29] With such a consumer surplus

[29] The *Guidelines* state that "The Agency will not challenge a merger if cognizable efficiencies are of a character and magnitude such that the merger is not likely to be anticompetitive in any relevant market. To make the requisite determination, the Agency considers whether cognizable efficiencies likely would be sufficient to reverse the merger's potential to harm consumers in the relevant market, e.g., by preventing price increases in that market". Note, however, that this test is stated as a sufficient condition for approving a merger, not as a necessary one. This ambiguity may seem a bit odd, but is probably deliberate. The agencies have some prosecutorial discretion, and can approve mergers that the courts might block. While the courts' standard is not totally clear either, it surely leans more toward a consumer surplus standard than is the preference of the economists at the agencies. In addition, there may be some difference in the standards applied by the DOJ and the FTC, with the FTC more inclined toward a consumer surplus standard than the DOJ. (Since the

standard, for example, reductions in the merging firms' fixed costs do not help a merger gain approval; only reductions in marginal costs matter.

Regardless of whether a consumer or aggregate surplus standard is followed, the efficiencies that are counted must be efficiencies that could not be realized easily by less restrictive means, such as through individual investments of the firms, through joint production agreements, or through a merger that includes some limited divestitures.

One concern in mergers that claim significant operating efficiencies (say through reductions in manpower or capital) is whether these reductions alter the quality of the products produced by the firms. For example, in a recent merger of two Canadian propane companies having roughly a 70% share of the overall Canadian market, the merging companies proposed consolidating their local branches, reducing trucks, drivers, and service people. These would be valid efficiencies if the quality of their customer service did not suffer, but if these savings represent instead a move along an existing quality–cost frontier, they would not be valid efficiencies from an antitrust standpoint.

3.2. Merger control in the E.U.

While merger control began in the E.U. only in 1990, today the E.U. has a highly developed merger control policy that often represents a critical hurdle for large companies who wish to merge. Merger review in the E.U. is handled by the European Commission, and the investigative process by the Competition Directorate General ("DG Comp") within the Commission. In 2004, the E.U. adopted a new merger control regulation (the "ECMR"; Regulation 139/2004) that changed somewhat the substantive test applied to merger review, and also made some procedural and investigative reforms.[30] At the same time, the Commission published merger review guidelines and adopted some internal institutional changes designed to improve its decision-making.[31,32] The current E.U. policy resembles the U.S. approach in many respects, although with some significant differences.

E.U. merger policy applies to all mergers involving companies whose sales surpass certain size thresholds. Specifically, a merger between two firms has a "community dimension" if the combined entity has at least 5 billion Euros in worldwide sales and

agencies tend to specialize in reviewing mergers in different industries, this would have the effect of applying somewhat different standards in different industries.) On this issue, see also Werden (1997).

30 These reforms involved the referral process described below and also increased the Commission's powers to compel production of information.

31 The old and new merger regulations, the Commission's guidelines, and other related documents can be found at http://europa.eu.int/comm/competition/mergers/legislation/regulation/#regulation. For an introduction to E.U. merger review and the new ECMR, see Parisi (2005). For a discussion of E.U. merger policy prior to these changes, see Motta (2004).

32 The internal institutional reforms were designed to improve decision-making by, for example, creating a new chief economist position and forming an internal review panel, distinct from the investigating team, for each merger investigation.

if each firm has sales of at least 250 million Euros in the E.U., unless each merging firm has more than two-thirds of its E.U. sales in the same Member State.[33] If these thresholds are not met, the merger still has a community dimension if (i) the combined entity has sales of more than 2.5 billion Euros worldwide and more than 100 million Euros in sales in at least three Member States, and if (ii) each of the merging parties has at least 100 million Euros in sales in the E.U. and at least 25 million Euros in sales in each of at least three of the member states considered under (i), unless each merging party has more than two-thirds of its sales in the E.U. in the same Member State. When these thresholds are met, the parties must notify the European Commission of their merger and await approval before consummating their merger. The Commission then has exclusive jurisdiction over the case. These notification and jurisdiction rules contrast with the U.S. process in two respects. First, notification and jurisdiction coincide in the E.U. (every merger to which E.U. law applies must be notified). In contrast, in the U.S., the FTC and DOJ need not be notified of mergers that are smaller than the Hart–Scott–Rodino thresholds, even though these mergers are still subject to the U.S. antitrust laws (there are no size thresholds that limit application of the U.S. laws). Second, in the U.S., individual states' Attorney Generals may attempt to block a merger under their state's laws at the same time that the DOJ or FTC is reviewing the merger under the U.S. antitrust laws.

When these size criteria are not met, the merger is handled by the individual national competition authorities. However, the regulation also includes a "referral" process, whereby Member States may request that the European Commission handle review of a notified merger. In addition, in advance of notification, the merging firms may request referral to the Commission if they would otherwise have to notify the competition authorities in at least three individual Member States. In this case, if none of the Member States objects, the merger is deemed to have a community dimension and the Commission has exclusive jurisdiction over its review. There are also provisions for partial or complete referrals of merger reviews from the Commission to individual Member States who may have either a particular interest or particular expertise in the review of a merger.

The basic review procedure resembles in broad outline that at the FTC, in that the Commission investigates a proposed merger, holds an internal hearing, and reaches a decision. There are a few important differences though. First, the review procedure in the E.U. is subject to much stricter time deadlines than is review in the U.S. The procedure involves two phases. The Commission has 25 working days to either approve a notified merger or, if it has serious doubts, open a "Phase II" investigation.[34] If it does open such an investigation, it has 90 more working days to reach a decision. This deadline can be extended by up to 20 days with the parties' consent, but – unlike in the U.S. – not by more than this.[35] If the Commission fails to reach a decision by this deadline,

[33] These size thresholds, and those in the next sentence, exclude value-added taxes.

[34] This deadline is extended to 35 working days if the parties submit proposed conditions for their merger (such as limited divestitures) or if there was a referral request.

[35] The total period can be extended to 105 working days if conditions are offered.

the merger is deemed to have been approved. Second, unlike in the U.S., the parties have the right to access the Commission's investigative file during the Phase II review process. In the U.S., any such access comes only as part of the usual discovery process should the merger end up in court. Third, the E.U. has the power to block a merger on its own. Courts become involved only if someone appeals the Commission's decision.[36] This contrasts with the U.S. situation in which even the FTC must go to court to get a preliminary injunction. As a result, the U.S. courts play a decisive role in merger review with greater frequency than in the E.U. Historically, the appeals process in Europe has been very slow, often taking a number of years, so that few merging parties have appealed Commission decisions in the hopes of still merging.[37] Starting in 2000, however, a new expedited appeals process was instituted which may end up altering the extent of court review in the E.U.[38]

Until recently, the substantive test for reviewing mergers in the E.U. was focused on the notion of "dominance". In the E.U.'s original merger regulation, mergers were "incompatible with the common market", and hence could be prohibited, when the merger would "create or strengthen a dominant position as a result of which effective competition would be significantly impeded in all or a substantial part of the European Union". Dominance is

> ... a situation where one or more undertakings wield economic power which would enable them to prevent effective competition from being maintained in the relevant market by giving them the opportunity to act to a considerable extent independently of their competitors, their customers, and, ultimately, of consumers.

For a single firm, a market share of over 50% is presumptively "dominant", while a share between 40–50% will often be. (In a few cases, a share below 40% has been held to be dominant.) Under the original merger regulation, the concept of dominance was used to get at both unilateral and coordinated effects. First, a merger creating a single dominant firm could be illegal because of its creation of market power leading to unilateral effects. In addition, through the concept of "collective dominance", the regulation could be used to block mergers that were likely to lead to significant coordinated effects. However, it was unclear whether the original regulation could be used to attack mergers that were likely to give rise to unilateral effects without creating a dominant firm. (For example, a merger of the second and third largest firms in an industry in which the three largest firms have shares of 40, 15, and 15 percent.)

The substantive test in the new ECMR makes clear that the regulation applies to such situations. The new test prohibits mergers that would

[36] These appeals go first to the Court of First Instance, and then to the European Court of Justice. Unlike in the U.S., where only the merging parties can appeal a decision blocking a merger, third parties have standing to appeal Commission decisions in the E.U. (both those blocking and allowing the merger).

[37] In some cases, parties have instead appealed just to reverse the Commission's finding that they are dominant, so as not to be subject to heightened antitrust scrutiny in the future (an example is the appeal of the Commission's ruling in the 2001 GE-Honeywell case).

[38] In the other direction, as noted earlier, in Europe third parties have standing to appeal Commission decisions. In the U.S., only the merging parties have this right.

significantly impede effective competition, in particular as a result of the creation or strengthening of a dominant position, in the common market or a substantial part of it.

The new language makes illegal all mergers that "significantly impede effective competition", paralleling the U.S. "substantial lessening of competition" test, while still retaining the existing jurisprudence of "dominance" based rulings.[39]

The Commission's new merger guidelines (combined with its 1997 market definition notice) describe its approach to implementing this test.[40] They parallel the U.S. *Guidelines* closely, including in their approach toward efficiencies. Nonetheless, there are some differences. Reflecting the dominance-based aspects of the ECMR, the Commission's guidelines contain a greater emphasis on the merged firm's market share than do the U.S. *Guidelines*. A combined share above 40% is likely to meet the criteria for being dominant. In the other direction, a combined share below 25% is presumed not to significantly impede effective competition, except in cases of collective dominance. The Commission guidelines also state HHI criteria that set initial presumptions about a merger (although there is language stating that these are not "presumptions"). The Commission is unlikely to have concerns with mergers in which the post-merger HHI is below 1000. It is also unlikely to have concerns with mergers in which the post-merger HHI is between 1000 and 2000 and the change in the HHI is below 250, or in which the post-merger HHI is above 2000 and the change in the HHI is below 150, except in exceptional cases where other factors mitigate these presumptions. These cutoffs are more lenient than those in the U.S. *Guidelines*, although perhaps not more lenient than the actual practice of the U.S. agencies. Also, while stated only as safe-harbor regions, when viewed as also delineating the set of mergers over which the Commission *may* have concerns, these thresholds are clearly stricter than the old dominance test of 40%. (The post-merger HHI in a market in which there is a firm with a 45 percent share, for example, cannot be lower than 2000.[41])

Three other differences from the U.S. *Guidelines* are that (i) supply substitution is formally included in the market definition step, while in the U.S. it is considered only later in the calculation of shares and concentration, (ii) the presence of buyer power is stated explicitly as a factor that may mitigate any increase in market power among sellers in a market due to a merger, and (iii) the possibility of foreclosure is explicitly considered in the E.U. guidelines, while it is not mentioned in the U.S. *Guidelines*.[42]

[39] As the preamble to the new ECMR puts it, the notion of a significant impediment to competition extends "beyond the concept of dominance, only to the anti-competitive effects of a concentration resulting from non-coordinated behavior of undertakings which would not have a dominant position on the market concerned".

[40] The market definition notice is at http://europa.eu.int/comm/competition/antitrust/relevma_en.html.

[41] Kuhn (2002) argues that this tightening of the standard for legality motivated many of those who favored the change in the substantive test.

[42] For a discussion of the issue of foreclosure, see the chapter by Rey and Tirole in this volume. The U.S. also has vertical guidelines that can apply to a merger that involves vertical issues. In practice, though, the European Commission has been more open to considering foreclosure issues in merger cases than have the U.S. agencies.

Despite these differences, the test for legality of a merger under the new ECMR and the Commission's merger guidelines is now close to that in the U.S.

3.3. *Differences across other countries*

The pattern in other countries as well has been toward a substantial convergence in antitrust law and enforcement towards the U.S. focus on whether a merger causes a "substantial lessening of competition" and the framework of the U.S. *Horizontal Merger Guidelines*. Nonetheless, as in the case of the E.U., there are still some significant areas of difference across countries. These include notification requirements, methods of adjudication, and the formal legal test in the laws themselves, as well as elements of different countries' antitrust authorities' procedures for evaluating mergers such as market definition tests, thresholds of presumption (e.g., safe harbors), and the consideration given to the "other factors" listed (and other factors not listed) in the U.S. *Guidelines*.

One of the most significant ways in which most countries differ from the U.S. model is in the formal process of adjudication. Few countries have anything resembling the odd mix of procedures in the U.S. In some cases, such as the E.U. procedure discussed above, the procedure resembles the FTC proceedings, in which a specialist agency analyzes the facts and renders a decision, which can then be appealed to a court. In other countries, such as Canada, the specialist agency must bring a case to a separate tribunal. Nearly always, however, this tribunal specializes in antitrust matters, unlike the U.S. situation in which the DOJ and the FTC (for preliminary injunctions) bring merger cases in federal courts that hear many types of cases.

A second important difference concerns the formal welfare standards embodied in different countries' laws. The differences in standards show up most clearly in how they consider efficiencies (although, as I noted above, they should probably also affect the consideration of entry). As we have seen, the U.S. is closest to applying a consumer welfare criterion to mergers, so that efficiencies are a defense only to the extent that they are likely to prevent price increases (or, more generally, prevent any reduction in consumer surplus). The E.U. adopts this same criterion. Australia, however, considers the change in aggregate surplus as part of a "public benefits" test for determining whether to allow mergers that are expected to raise price (it also considers other factors, such as effects on exports). New Zealand also considers a merger's effects on aggregate surplus. Until the recent *Superior Propane* case, Canada had a very explicit aggregate surplus standard. Now, however, Canada applies a "balancing weights" approach, in which the Competition Tribunal is supposed to apply weights to consumer and producer surplus that reflect the "social" weight to be accorded to transfers between consumers and shareholders. These weights may differ from one merger to another, reflecting, for example, the relative wealth of consumers and shareholders in a particular merger.

3.3.1. *Theoretical perspectives on the welfare standard for merger review*

It is striking that while most economists would regard maximization of aggregate surplus as the natural standard for merger review, most merger reviews around the world actually apply something close to a consumer surplus standard. Distributional concerns could, of course, lead to something close to a consumer surplus standard. The economics literature also contains some analyses that suggest economic reasons why even a society interested in aggregate surplus might prefer to commit its antitrust authority to a consumer surplus standard.

Besanko and Spulber (1993) provided the first such argument. They study a setting in which the merging parties know more about the efficiency improvement generated by their merger than does the antitrust authority. Specifically, suppose that the merging firms observe the merger's "type" θ, where θ is drawn from set $[\underline{\theta}, \bar{\theta}] \subset \mathbb{R}$ according to distribution $F(\cdot)$, but the antitrust authority does not.[43] A merger of type θ results in a change in the joint profit of the merging firms equal to $\Delta\pi(\theta)$, a change in consumer surplus equal to $\Delta CS(\theta)$, and a change in aggregate surplus equal to $\Delta S(\theta) = \Delta\pi(\theta) + \Delta CS(\theta)$. Higher θ mergers are more efficient, so that these functions are all increasing in θ. The cost of proposing a merger is $k > 0$. [This cost is not included in $\Delta S(\theta)$ and $\Delta\pi(\theta)$.] Since only profitable mergers will ever be proprosed, we can restrict attention to mergers with $\Delta\pi(\theta) \geqslant k$.

The merger review game proceeds as follows: First, after observing θ, the merging firms decide whether to propose their merger. Then, the antitrust authority chooses a probability α that the merger is approved.

As a starting point, suppose that the antitrust authority uses an aggregate surplus standard in making its decision. To focus on the interesting case, suppose that there is some uncertainty at the time of the antitrust authority's decision about whether the merger increases aggregate surplus. Specifically, suppose that $E[S(\theta)] < 0$ so that on average the merger lowers aggregate surplus, while $S(\bar{\theta}) > 0$ so that the most efficient merger would raise aggregate surplus. Consider equilibria in which the approval probability is positive: $\alpha^* > 0$.[44] Any such equilibrium has a cut-off structure: if the probability of approval is α, the proposed mergers are those with types $\theta \geqslant \hat{\theta}(\alpha)$, where $\alpha \cdot \Delta\pi(\hat{\theta}(\alpha)) = k$. It also must have a probability of approval below 1 ($\alpha^* < 1$) since if approval was certain all merger types would be proposed, which would instead lead the agency to reject all mergers (recall that $E[\Delta S(\theta)] < 0$). Since $\alpha^* \in (0, 1)$, the antitrust authority must be *indifferent* about approving the merger given the set of merger types that are actually proposed in the equilibrium. That is, if α^S is the approval probability and θ^S is the cut-off type we must have

$$E\big[\Delta S(\theta) \mid \theta \geqslant \theta^S\big] = 0 \tag{21}$$

and

$$\theta^S = \hat{\theta}\big(\alpha^S\big). \tag{22}$$

[43] One can think of the type θ as representing the informational asymmetry that persists after the agency conducts its merger review.

[44] There is always also an equilibrium in which the agency approves no mergers ($\alpha^* = 0$) and no mergers are ever proposed. I ignore this equilibrium in what follows.

Condition (21) has a startling implication: merger activity in this situation *must reduce* aggregate surplus since proposed mergers on net generate no improvement in aggregate surplus, but incur proposal costs. Even banning all merger activity would be better.

In contrast, consider what happens if the agency commits to evaluating mergers based on a consumer surplus standard. In that case, an approval probability α^{CS} and cut-off type θ^{CS} is an equilibrium if

$$E\big[\Delta CS(\theta) \mid \theta \geqslant \theta^{CS}\big] = 0$$

and

$$\theta^{CS} = \hat{\theta}\big(\alpha^{CS}\big). \tag{23}$$

In any such equilibrium, merger activity must increase aggregate surplus since that change equals

$$\begin{aligned}
&\big[1 - F\big(\theta^{CS}\big)\big]\big\{\alpha^{CS} E\big[\Delta S(\theta) \mid \theta \geqslant \theta^{CS}\big] - k\big\} \\
&\quad = \big[1 - F\big(\theta^{CS}\big)\big]\big\{\alpha^{CS} E\big[\Delta CS(\theta) \mid \theta \geqslant \theta^{CS}\big] + \alpha^{CS} E\big[\Delta\pi(\theta) \mid \theta \geqslant \theta^{CS}\big] - k\big\} \\
&\quad > \big[1 - F\big(\theta^{CS}\big)\big]\big[\alpha^{CS} \Delta\pi\big(\theta^{CS}\big) - k\big] \\
&\quad = 0.
\end{aligned}$$

Thus, here, a commitment to a consumer surplus standard actually increases aggregate surplus.

A few caveats are in order, however. First, a consumer surplus standard does not always improve things. In particular, for mergers whose effect on aggregate surplus is necessarily positive [because $S(\underline{\theta}) > k$], the equilibrium of the merger game when the agency uses a aggregate surplus standard maximizes aggregate surplus by approving all mergers, while the equilibrium when the agency uses instead a consumer surplus standard will reject some mergers whenever $E[\Delta CS(\theta)] < 0$. Second, when there is uncertainty about the effect of a merger on aggregate surplus, a better outcome than that generated by a consumer surplus standard can be achieved using merger filing fees. These can implement the same set of proposed mergers as the consumer surplus standard, but without the cost of rejecting good (high θ) mergers with positive probability.

Two more recent papers of this type are Neven and Roller (2002) and Lyons (2002). Neven and Roller (2002) study a model of lobbying [along the lines of Grossman and Helpman (1994) and Bernheim and Whinston (1986)] in which firms (both the merging firms and competitors) can attempt to influence the antitrust authority but consumers are unable to do so. The antitrust authority cares both about its mandated goal and the firms' "influence" payments (these may be thought of as the implicit promises of future employment, etc.). Intuitively, if lobbying is efficient (so that a dollar payment is worth a dollar to the authority), an authority with a consumer surplus mandate will end up maximizing aggregate surplus because it will maximize the sum of consumer surplus and influence payments, and those influence payments will reflect firms' profitabilities

Table 36.1
Recent merger enforcement experience in the U.S. and E.U.

	U.S.			E.U.		
Year	Transactions	Blocked	Modified	Transactions	Blocked	Modified
1997	3702	19	39	172	1	9
1998	4728	25	57	235	2	16
1999	4642	22	54	292	1	27
2000	4926	26	53	345	2	40
2001	2376	8	46	335	5	23
2002	1187	12	21	279	0	15
2003	1014	18	17	212	0	17
Total	22,575	130	287	1870	11	147

Sources: U.S. data are from the FTC/DOJ annual reports to Congress ("Merger Enforcement" section), available at http://www.ftc.gov/bc/hsr/hsrinfopub.html. E.U. data are from http://europa.eu.int/comm/competition/mergers/cases/stats.html.

from merger approval.[45] Lyons (2002), on the other hand, notes that firms can choose which mergers to propose and can be expected to propose the most profitable merger among those that will be allowed. Restricting the set of allowed mergers through a consumer surplus standard can in some cases lead firms to propose mergers that increase aggregate surplus by more than the mergers they would choose under an aggregate surplus standard.

3.4. *Enforcement experience*

Table 36.1 summarizes enforcement experience in the U.S. and E.U. from 1997 through 2003.

The U.S. agencies handled more than ten times as many cases as did the E.U. during this period. This is no doubt due in large part to the substantially lower notification thresholds in U.S. law than in the E.U. merger regulations. The number of notified transactions reached its high in both the U.S. and E.U. in the year 2000, with the drop after that much more precipitous in the U.S. than in the E.U. Over the 1997–2003 period 0.6% of notified transactions (130 out of 22,575) were blocked by the U.S. agencies, and another 1.3% (287 out of 22,575) were approved subject to conditions that modified the original proposed merger (e.g., through partial divestitures). In the E.U., notified transactions were about as likely as in the U.S. to be blocked (0.6%), but much more

[45] Neven and Roller actually focus on cases in which both lobbying and the ability to monitor the antitrust authority's adherence to its mandated goal are imperfect.

likely to be modified (7.9%).[46] This could reflect a difference between the merger review approaches of the U.S. agencies and the European Commission, but is also likely to reflect the fact that the mergers handled by the European Commission are, on average, much larger than those handled by the U.S. agencies because of the different notification thresholds.

In the U.S., the number of blocked or modified mergers as a percentage of notified mergers rose slightly in 2001–2003 relative to 1997–2000, going from 1.6% to 2.0%. Whether this was because of a change in the type of mergers being pursued, the change from the Clinton to the Bush administration (not likely), or the fact that the agencies' personnel were handling fewer cases is not clear. In contrast, this percentage fell from 9.4% in 1997–2000 to 7.3% in 2001–2003 in the E.U.[47]

4. Econometric approaches to answering the *Guidelines*' questions

There are two principal areas in which econometric analysis has been employed in applying the DOJ/FTC *Guidelines* and similar guidelines in other countries. These are in defining the relevant market and in providing evidence about the effects of increased concentration on prices. In this section, I discuss these methods.

4.1. Defining the relevant market

Suppose that we have a collection of substitute products (goods $1, \ldots, N$) that include the products of the merging firms. To answer the *Guidelines*' market definition question we want to study whether a hypothetical profit-maximizing monopolist of some subset of these products would raise price by at least 5%, taking the prices of other firms as fixed (at their pre-merger levels). We can do this if we know the demand and cost functions for these products, and the pre-merger prices of all N products.

To answer the *Guidelines*' question, we must first estimate the demand functions for these products. The simplest case to consider arises when we are considering a hypothetical monopolist of a single homogeneous product, say widgets, which is differentiated from the products of all other firms. In this case, we only need to estimate the demand function for widgets, which is given by some function $x(p, q, y, \varepsilon)$, where p is the price of widgets, q is a vector of prices of substitute products, y is a vector of exogenous demand shifters (e.g., income, weather, etc.), and ε represents (random) factors not observable by the econometrician. For example, a constant elasticity demand function (with

46 The "transactions" columns in Table 36.1 report the number of notified transactions in each year, not the number of decisions reached in each year. The number of decisions in each of these years in the E.U. were: 142 in 1997, 238 in 1998, 270 in 1999, 345 in 2000, 340 in 2001, 273 in 2002, 231 in 2003. Thus, 0.6% of E.U. decisions blocked and 8.0% of E.U decisions modified proposed mergers over this period. The U.S. does not report the total number of decisions in each year (as our earlier discussion indicated, a decision is a less well-defined event in the U.S.).

47 The number of blocked or modified mergers as a percentage of total decisions in the E.U. fell from 9.8% in 1997–2000 to 7.1% in 2001–2003.

one substitute product and one demand shifter) would yield the estimating equation

$$\ln(x_i) = \beta_0 + \beta_1 \ln(p_i) + \beta_2 \ln(q_i) + \beta_3 \ln(y_i) + \varepsilon_i, \tag{24}$$

where i may indicate observations on different markets in a cross-section of markets or on different time periods in a series of observations on the same market.[48]

Several standard issues arise in the estimation of Equation (24). First, as always in econometric work, careful testing for an appropriate specification is critical. Second, it is important to appropriately control for the endogeneity of prices: the price of widgets p is almost certain to be correlated with ε because factors that shift the demand for widgets but are unobserved to the econometrician will, under all but a limited set of circumstances, affect the equilibrium price of widgets.[49] The most common direction for the bias induced by a failure to properly instrument in estimating Equation (24) would be toward an underestimation of the elasticity of demand because positive shocks to demand are likely to be positively correlated with p.[50] Observe, however, that if we were to estimate instead the inverse demand function

$$\ln(p_i) = \bar{\beta}_0 + \bar{\beta}_1 \ln(x_i) + \bar{\beta}_2 \ln(q_i) + \bar{\beta}_3 \ln(y_i) + \varepsilon_i, \tag{25}$$

then since the equilibrium quantity x is also likely to be positively correlated with ε, we would expect to underestimate the *inverse* demand elasticity – that is, *over-estimate* the demand elasticity. (Indeed, the difference between these two estimates of the demand elasticity is one specification test for endogeneity.) This observation leads to what might, in a tongue-in-cheek manner, be called the *Iron Law of Consulting*: "Estimate inverse demand functions if you work for the defendants and ordinary demand functions if you work for the plaintiffs". What is needed to properly estimate either form are good cost-side instruments for the endogenous price/quantity variables; that is, variables that can be expected to be correlated with price/quantity but not with demand shocks.

Matters can become considerably more complicated when the product set being considered includes differentiated products. If the number of products in the set is small, then we can simply expand the estimation procedure just outlined by estimating a system of demand functions together. For example, suppose that we are considering a hypothetical monopolist of widgets and gidgets, and that there is a single substitute product. Then, in the constant elasticity case, we could estimate the system

$$\ln(x_{wi}) = \beta_{10} + \beta_{11} \ln(p_{wi}) + \beta_{12} \ln(p_{gi}) + \beta_{13} \ln(q_i) + \beta_{14} \ln(y_i) + \varepsilon_{1i}, \tag{26}$$

$$\ln(x_{gi}) = \beta_{20} + \beta_{21} \ln(p_{gi}) + \beta_{22} \ln(p_{wi}) + \beta_{23} \ln(q_i) + \beta_{24} \ln(y_i) + \varepsilon_{2i}. \tag{27}$$

48 More generally, such an equation could be estimated on a panel data set of many markets observed over time.

49 This correlation will not be present, for example, if the firms have constant marginal costs and engage in Bertrand pricing prior to the merger.

50 The discussion in the text takes the price of the substitute q as exogenous. However, this price may also be correlated with ε and may need to be instrumented.

The main difficulty involved is finding enough good instruments to identify the effects of the prices p_w and p_g separately. Usually one will need some variables that affect the production cost of one product and not the other (or at least that differ significantly in their effects on the costs of the two products).

As the number of products being considered expands, however, estimation of such a demand system will become infeasible because the data will not be rich enough to permit separate estimation of all of the relevant own and cross-price demand elasticities among the products (which increase in the square of the number of products). In the past, this was dealt with by aggregating the products into subgroups (e.g., premium tuna, middle-line tuna, and private label tuna in a merger of tuna producers) and limiting the estimation to the study of the demand for these groups (the prices used would be some sort of price indices for the groups). Recently, however, there has been a great deal of progress in the econometric estimation of demand systems for differentiated products. The key to these methods is to impose some restrictions that limit the number of parameters that need to be estimated, while not doing violence to the data.

Two primary methods have been advanced in the literature to date. One, developed by Berry, Levinsohn and Pakes (1995) [see also Berry (1994)], models the demand for the various products as a function of some underlying characteristics.[51] For example, in the automobile industry that is the focus of their study, cars' attributes include length, weight, horsepower, and various other amenities. Letting the vector of attributes for car j be a_j, the net surplus for consumer i of buying car j when its price is p_j is taken to be the function

$$u_{ij} = a_j \cdot \beta_i - \alpha_i p_j + \xi_j + \varepsilon_{ij}, \tag{28}$$

where β_i is a parameter vector representing consumer i's weights on the various attributes, α_i is consumer i's marginal utility of income, ξ_j is a random quality component for car j (common across consumers) that is unobserved by the econometrician, and ε_{ij} is a random consumer/car-specific shock that is unobserved by the econometrician and is independent across consumers and cars. The parameters β_i and α_i may be common across consumers, may be modeled as having a common mean and a consumer-specific random element, or (if the data are available) may be modeled as a function of demographic characteristics of the consumer.[52] The consumer is then assumed to make a choice among discrete consumption alternatives, whose number is equal to the number of products in the market.

[51] Berry, Levinsohn and Pakes build on previous work by Bresnahan (1987), as well as a large literature on discrete choice and product characteristics [see, e.g., McFadden (1981) and the references therein]. For further reading on these methods, see Ackerberg et al. (in press).

[52] If individual-level demographic and purchase data are available, then the parameters in (28) can be estimated at an individual level; otherwise, the population distribution of demographic variables can be used with aggregate data, as in Nevo (2001).

Berry, Levinsohn and Pakes (1995), Berry (1994), and Nevo (2000a, 2000b, 2001) discuss in detail the estimation of this demand model including issues of instrumentation and computation. The key benefit of this approach arises in its limitation of the number of parameters to be estimated by tying the value of each product to a limited number of characteristics. The potential danger, of course, is that this restriction will not match the data well. For example, one model that is nested within Equation (28) is the traditional logit model (take β_i and α_i to be common across consumers, assume that $\xi_j \equiv 0$, and take ε_{ij} to have an extreme value distribution). This model has the well-known independence of irrelevant alternatives (IIA) property, which implies that if the price of a good increases, all consumers who switch to other goods do so in proportion to these goods' market shares.[53] This assumption is usually at odds with actual substitution patterns. For example, it is common for two products with similar market shares to have distinct sets of close substitutes. Berry, Levinsohn and Pakes discuss the example of a Yugo and a Mercedes (two cars) having similar market shares, but quite different cross-elasticities of demand with a BMW. If the price of a BMW were to increase, it is likely that the Mercedes's share would be affected much more than the share of the Yugo.[54] A good deal of work in this literature has focused (successfully) on how to estimate versions of this model that have richer substitution patterns than the logit model. For example, by allowing consumers to differ in their β_i coefficients, the model generates more reasonable substitution patterns, since the second choice of a consumer who chooses a BMW (and, hence, is likely to value highly horsepower and luxury) is much more likely to be a Mercedes than a Yugo because the Mercedes's characteristics are more similar to the characteristics of the BMW.

The second method is the multi-stage budgeting procedure introduced by Hausman, Leonard and Zona (1994) [see also Hausman (1996)]. In this method, the products in a market are grouped on a priori grounds into subgroups. For example, in the beer market that these authors study, beers are grouped into the categories of premium beers, popular-price beers, and light beers. They then estimate demand at three levels. First, they estimate the demand within each of these three categories as a function of the prices of the within-category beers and the total expenditure on the category, much as in Equations (26) and (27). Next, they estimate the expenditure allocation among the three categories as a function of total expenditure on beer and price indices for the

[53] To see this, recall that in the logit model, the demand of good k given price vector p and M consumers is

$$x_i(p) = M\frac{e^{a_k\cdot\beta-\alpha p_k}}{\sum_j e^{a_j\cdot\beta-\alpha p_j}},$$

so the ratio of the demands for any two goods j and k is independent of the prices of all other goods.

[54] The fact that two products with the same market shares have the same cross-elasticity of demand with any third product in fact follows from the additive i.i.d. error structure of the Logit model [which implies that they must have the same value of $(a_j\cdot\beta-\alpha p_j)$], not the extreme value assumption. The extreme value assumption implies, however, the stronger IIA property mentioned in the text.

three categories. Finally, they estimate a demand function for expenditure on beer as a function of an overall beer price index.

In this method, the grouping of products into categories (and the separability and other assumptions on the structure of demand that make the multi-stage budgeting approach valid) restricts the number of parameters that need to be estimated. This allows for a flexible estimation of the substitution parameters within groups and in the higher level estimations. On the other hand, the method does impose some strong restrictions on substitution patterns between products in the different (a priori specified) groups. For example, the substitution toward products in one group (say, premium beers) is independent of which product in another group (say, popular price beers) has experienced a price increase.

To date there has been very little work evaluating the relative merits of these two approaches. One such study is Nevo (1997), who compares the two methods in a study of the ready-to-eat cereal industry. In that particular case, he finds that the Berry, Levinsohn and Pakes characteristics approach works best (the multi-stage budgeting approach produces negative cross-price elasticities for products like Post's and Kellogg's Raisin Bran cereals that are almost surely substitutes), but it is hard to know at this point how the two methods compare more generally.

The second step in answering the *Guidelines*' market definition question is estimation of firms' cost functions. This can, in principle, be accomplished directly by estimating cost functions, or indirectly by estimating either production functions or factor demand equations. Like estimation of demand, these methods all must confront endogeneity issues; selection issues can also arise.[55] One additional problem with the cost side, however, is often a lack of necessary data. The output and price data needed for demand estimation tend to be more readily available than the cost or input information needed to determine a firm's cost function.

Without the ability to directly estimate firms' cost functions, we can still estimate marginal costs if we are willing to assume something about firms' behavior. For example, suppose we assume that firms are playing a static Nash (differentiated product) pricing equilibrium before the merger and that each firm i produces a single product before the merger.[56] Then we can use the fact that the firms' prices satisfy the first-order conditions

$$\big(p_i - c_i'\big(x_i(p)\big)\big)\frac{\partial x_i(p_i, p_{-i})}{\partial p_i} + x_i(p) = 0 \quad \text{for } i = 1, \dots, N \tag{29}$$

to derive that

$$c_i'\big(x_i(p)\big) = p_i + \left[\frac{\partial x_i(p_i, p_{-i})}{\partial p_i}\right]^{-1} x_i(p) \quad \text{for } i = 1, \dots, N. \tag{30}$$

[55] See Olley and Pakes (1996) and Griliches and Mairesse (1995) for discussions of these issues.

[56] The same type of inference can be made with multi-product firms using a somewhat more complicated equation. See Nevo (2001).

This gives us an estimate of firms' marginal costs if we are willing to assume that marginal costs are approximately constant in the relevant range.[57]

Given estimated demand and cost functions for the products controlled by the hypothetical monopolist, and the pre-merger prices of other products, one can compute the hypothetical monopolist's profit-maximizing prices and compare these to the pre-merger prices of these products to answer the *Guidelines*' 5% price increase market definition question.

The econometric tools to estimate demands and costs, particularly in an industry with extensive product differentiation, are fairly recent. Moreover, time is often short in these investigations. As a result, a number of simpler techniques often have been applied to try to answer the *Guidelines*' market definition question. The simplest of these involve a review of company documents and industry marketing studies, and informally asking customers about their likelihood of switching products in response to price changes. These methods, of course, are likely to produce at best a rough sense of the degree of substitution between products.[58,59]

Two other methods include examining price correlations among a set of products and, for cases in which the issue is geographic market definition, looking at patterns of trans-shipment. Both of these have serious potential flaws, however.

To consider the use of price correlations, imagine that we have two cities, A and B, that are located 100 miles apart. City B has a competitive widget industry that produces widgets at a cost per unit of c_B. There is a single widget producer in city A who has a cost per unit of c_A. These costs are random. The demand at each location i is $x_i(p) = \alpha_i - p$ and there is a cost t of transporting a widget between the cities.

Imagine, first, that the transport cost is infinite, so that the markets are in fact completely distinct. Then the price in market A will be $p_A^m = (\alpha_A + c_A)/2$ and the correlation between the prices in market A and market B will be

$$\frac{\operatorname{cov}(p_A, c_B)}{\sqrt{\operatorname{var}(p_A)\operatorname{var}(c_B)}} = \frac{\frac{1}{2}\operatorname{cov}(\alpha_A, c_B) + \frac{1}{2}\operatorname{cov}(c_A, c_B)}{\sqrt{\operatorname{var}(p_A)\operatorname{var}(c_B)}}. \tag{31}$$

If, for example, α_A is fixed and $c_A = c_B \equiv c$, then the correlation will equal 1 (perfect correlation) even though the markets are completely distinct. (This is just the case of a common causal factor, in this case the level of marginal cost.)

Suppose instead that t is random, that $\alpha_A = 1$ and $c_A = c_B \equiv c$, and that for all realizations of t we have $(c + t) < \frac{1}{2}$. In this case, the price in market B fully constrains

[57] Alternatively, given a behavioral assumption, one can try to econometrically infer costs by jointly estimating demand and the firms' supply relations as discussed in Bresnahan (1989).

[58] More formal consumer survey methods can also be used; see, for example, the discussion in Baker and Rubinfeld (1999).

[59] Rough estimates of the degree to which customers would switch in response to a given price increase and of the firms' price–cost margins can be used to ask whether the price increase would be profitable for the hypothetical monopolist. This is the essence of "critical loss analysis" [Harris and Simons (1989)]. For a critique of common uses of critical loss analysis, focusing on the importance of checking if those rough estimates of customer switching and margins are consistent with the firms' pre-merger behavior, see Katz and Shapiro (2003) and O'Brien and Wickelgren (2003).

the price in market A so that $p_A = c + t$. If t and c are independently distributed, then the correlation between the prices in the two markets is

$$\frac{\mathrm{cov}(c+t, c)}{\sqrt{\mathrm{var}(c) + \mathrm{var}(t)}\sqrt{\mathrm{var}(c)}} = \frac{\mathrm{var}(c)}{\sqrt{\mathrm{var}(c) + \mathrm{var}(t)}\sqrt{\mathrm{var}(c)}}. \tag{32}$$

Hence, if var(c) is small, the correlation between the prices will be nearly zero, despite the fact that market A is fully constrained by the competitive industry in market B. On the other hand, if the variance of t is instead small, then the correlation will be close to 1. Yet – and this illustrates the problem – whether it is var(c) or var(t) that is small has no bearing on the underlying competitive situation.

A problem with looking at trans-shipments is also illustrated by this last case since no trans-shipments take place in equilibrium despite the fact that market A is fully constrained by market B.

4.2. *Evidence on the effects of increasing concentration on prices*

To help determine the likely effects of a proposed merger, the DOJ and FTC (and the merging parties) often examine evidence on the effects of concentration in similar markets. These studies typically follow the "structure–conduct–performance" paradigm of regressing a measure of performance – in this case price – on one or more measures of concentration and other control variables.[60] A typical regression seeking to explain the price in a cross-section of markets $i = 1, \ldots, I$ might look like

$$p_i = \beta_0 + w_i \cdot \beta_1 + y_i \cdot \beta_2 + CR_i \cdot \beta_3 + \varepsilon_i, \tag{33}$$

where w_i are variables affecting costs, y_i are variables affecting demand, and CR_i are measures of the level of concentration (the variables might be in logs, and both linear and non-linear terms might be included). In the most standard treatment, these variables all are treated as exogenous causal determinants of prices in a market. As such, and given the mix of demand and cost variables included in the regression, it has become common to refer to the regression results as "reduced form" estimates, with the intention of distinguishing them from "structural" estimates of demand and supply relationships [see, for example, Baker and Rubinfeld (1999)]. Given the results of regression (33), the impact of the merger on price is typically predicted from (33) using pre and post-merger measures of concentration, where post-merger concentration is calculated by assuming that the merged firms' post-merger share is equal to the sum of their pre-merger shares (e.g., that the HHI changes from $\mathrm{HHI}_{\mathrm{pre}}$ to $\mathrm{HHI}_{\mathrm{post}}$).

Regressions such as these have seen wide application in horizontal merger cases. In the FTC's challenge of the Staples/Office Depot merger, for example, this type of regression was used by both the FTC and the defendants.[61] In that merger the focus was on whether these office "superstores" should be considered as a distinct market (or

[60] The use of price in structure–conduct–performance studies was most forcefully advocated by Weiss (1990).
[61] For an interesting discussion of the use of econometric evidence in the case, see Baker (1999b).

"submarket") or whether these stores should be viewed as a small part of a much larger office supply market. The parties used this type of regression to examine the determinants of Staples' prices in a city.[62] In that case, an observation of the dependent variable was the price of a particular Staples store in a particular month; the concentration measures included both a measure of general concentration in the office supply market and measures of whether there were office supply superstores within the same Metropolitan Statistical Areas and within given radiuses of the particular Staples store.

As another example, when the Union Pacific railroad (UP) sought to acquire the Southern Pacific railroad (SP) in 1996 shortly after the merger of the Burlington Northern Railroad (BN) and the Sante Fe Railroad (SF), many railroad routes west of the Mississippi River would go from being served by three firms to being served by two firms in the event of the merger, and some would go from being served by two firms to one firm. The merging parties claimed that SP was a "weak" railroad, and that it did not have a significant competitive effect on UP in any market in which BN/SF was already present. To bolster this claim, the merging parties conducted this type of study of UP's prices, where the concentration variables included separate dummy variables indicating exactly which competitors UP faced in a particular market.[63]

Although this method has provided useful evidence in a wide range of cases, it can suffer from some serious problems. A first problem has to do with the endogeneity of concentration. In fact, (33) is *not* a true reduced form. A true reduced form would include only the underlying exogenous factors influencing market outcomes and not concentration, which is an outcome of the competitive process.[64] Indeed, in many ways Equation (33) is closer to estimation of a supply relation, in the sense discussed in Bresnahan (1989). To see this, consider the case in which demand takes the constant elasticity form $X(p) = Ap^{-\eta}$, all firms are identical with constant unit costs of c, and firms play a static Cournot equilibrium. Then we can write an active firm's first-order condition as

$$p = c - P'(X)x_i = c + \frac{s_i}{\eta} p = c + \frac{H}{\eta} p, \tag{34}$$

where $P(\cdot)$ is the inverse demand function and s_i is firm i's market share which, given symmetry, equals the Herfindahl–Hirschman index, which I denote here by H. As in Bresnahan (1989), we can nest this model and perfect competition by introducing a conduct parameter θ and rewriting (34) as

$$p = c + \theta \frac{H}{\eta} p.$$

[62] The data were actually a panel of stores over time, rather than just a single cross-section or time series as in Equation (33).

[63] The case was presented before the Surface Transportation Board, which has jurisdiction over railroad mergers.

[64] Often some of the other right-hand side variables are endogenous as well. For example, in studies of airline pricing, it is common to include the load factor on a route – the share of available seats that are sold – as a right-hand side variable affecting costs.

Thus,

$$p = \left(\frac{\eta}{\eta - \theta H}\right)c, \tag{35}$$

where the term in parentheses represents the proportional mark-up of price over marginal cost. Taking logarithms, we can write (35) as

$$\ln(p) = \ln(c) + \ln(\eta) - \ln(\eta - \theta H). \tag{36}$$

Suppose that marginal cost takes the form $c = \bar{c}e^{\varepsilon}$, where ε is an unobservable cost component and $\bar{c}$ is either observable or a parameter to be estimated.[65] Then (36) becomes

$$\ln(p) = \ln(\bar{c}) + \ln(\eta) - \ln(\eta - \theta H) + \varepsilon, \tag{37}$$

which has a form very close to (33), the main difference being the interaction between the concentration variable H and the demand coefficient η. Estimating Equation (33) might then be considered a linear approximation to this supply relation.

The problem in estimating (37) is that, because of its endogeneity, H is likely to be correlated with the cost shock ε, causing least-squares estimation to produce inconsistent (i.e., biased) parameter estimates. Specifically, since the number of firms in a market is determined by the profitability of entry, H will be related to the level of costs in the market. To derive consistent parameter estimates in this case we need to find instrumental variables that are correlated with H but not with the unobserved costs ε. Possibilities include the "market size" variable A, and measures of the cost of entry.

Even if we can find such instruments, however, the model we used to derive Equation (37) assumed that firms are symmetric. This is problematic, since (aside from a Cournot industry with identical constant returns to scale firms) either the pre-merger or the post-merger situation is likely to be asymmetric. When we allow for asymmetries, however, a firm's supply relation is unlikely even to take a form like (33), in which rivals' prices or quantities affect the firm's pricing only through a concentration measure like H. If so, (33) will be misspecified.

Another potential problem with using estimates of (33) to predict merger-induced price changes arises because of unobservable strategic choices by firms. For example, firms often will make strategic decisions that affect costs, such as conducting R&D or investing in capacity. These decisions, say k, typically will depend on the degree of competition in a market; that is, in a sample of markets they may be described by some function $k^*(H, \cdot)$. Looking back at Equation (37), if k is unobserved by the econometrician, it will end up in the unobserved term ε. Since $k^*(\cdot)$ depends on H, this induces a correlation between ε and H that cannot readily be instrumented for, because variables that are correlated with H almost always will be correlated with k and hence with ε.

65 More generally, we could model the cost term $\bar{c}$ as a function of observed variables and parameters.

Thus, even if firms are symmetric and H really is exogenous in our sample of markets, our parameter estimates will be inconsistent.

Is this a problem? One might argue that the answer is no. After all, if H is really exogenous, then the least-squares estimates still tell us the expectation of price conditional on H (and observable demand and cost factors). Since this is what we really want to know – the total effect of a change in H on price, including any effects due to induced changes in k – perhaps we are fine? The problem is that this is true only if the merger will change the strategic choices k in accord with the function $k^*(H, \cdot)$ that holds in the data. This may or may not be the case. For example, $k^*(H, \cdot)$ may reflect the long-run equilibrium choice of k given H, but k may be very different from this in the short and medium run after the merger.

For instance, consider the UP/SP example. One important factor for the determination of prices on a route is the level of aggregate capacity available on that route (such as tracks, sidings, and yards); higher capacity is likely to lead to lower prices, all else equal. In the pre-merger data, this aggregate capacity level is likely to be correlated with the number and identity of competitors on a route. For example, aggregate capacity probably is larger when more firms are present. Hence, in a regression that includes the number of firms on a route, but not capacity, some of the effect that is attributed to an increase in concentration likely results from the fact that, across the sample of markets, higher concentration is correlated with lower capacity levels. But in a merger, while the number of firms will decrease on many routes, the level of capacity on these routes may well remain unchanged (at least in the short-run). If so, the regression would predict too large an elevation in price following the merger.

Finally, there is also a problem when we turn to using the estimates for predicting the price change due to a merger. The actual post-merger equilibrium level of H is unlikely to equal HHI_{post}, the level calculated by simply assuming that the post-merger share of the merged firms is equal to the sum of their pre-merger shares. Indeed, in the Cournot model we know that (without synergies) H will *not* be equal to HHI_{post}, since the merged firms' combined share will fall. As one simple example, in the case of an N-firm symmetric Cournot industry with constant returns to scale, the post-merger Herfindahl–Hirschman index will be $1/(N-1)$, while $\text{HHI}_{\text{post}} = 2/N$. We can deduce the true merger-induced change in concentration if we have structural estimates of demand and supply relations. But, as we will see in the next section, if we have estimates of these relations we also can use them to directly predict post-merger prices, and so there would not be much point to using (33).

Given the relative ease and widespread use of this method, one might hope that it gives at least approximately correct answers despite these problems. It would be good to know more than we now do about whether this is right.[66]

[66] See Peters (2003) for one look at this question.

5. Breaking the market definition mold

When they were introduced, the *Guidelines* greatly improved the U.S. agencies' analysis of proposed horizontal mergers. At the same time, we have seen that their market definition-based process, while intuitive, is not based on any explicit model of competition and welfare effects. Given this fact, it is natural to ask whether there are other techniques that do not require this type of market definition exercise and examination of concentration changes. In this section, we examine three alternative techniques that economists have proposed for evaluating the likely effects of a merger. These are merger simulation, residual demand estimation, and the event study approach. Of these three, merger simulation seems particularly promising.

5.1. Merger simulation

If we are really going the route of estimating demand and cost functions to answer the *Guidelines*' market definition question (as in Section 4.1), why not just examine the price effects of the merger directly using these estimated structural parameters? That is, once we estimate a structural model of the industry using pre-merger data, we can *simulate* the effects of the merger. Doing so, we also can avoid a costly debate over what should be "in" and "out" of the market.

Conceptually, simulating the price effects of a merger is simple: given demand and cost functions for the various products in the market and an assumption about the behavior of the firms (existing studies typically examine a static simultaneous-move price choice game), one can solve numerically for the equilibrium prices that will emerge from the post-merger market structure. For example, if firms 1 and 2 in a three-firm industry merge, the equilibrium prices (p_1^*, p_2^*, p_3^*) in a static simultaneous price choice game will satisfy (the notation follows that in the discussion of differentiated product demand systems in Section 4.1)

$$(p_1^*, p_2^*) \quad \text{solves} \quad \max_{p_1, p_2} \sum_{i=1,2} \left[p_i x_i\left(p_1, p_2, p_3^*, q, y\right) - c_i\left(x_i\left(p_1, p_2, p_3^*, q, y\right)\right)\right],$$

and

$$p_3^* \quad \text{solves} \quad \max_{p_3} \ p_3 x_3\left(p_1^*, p_2^*, p_3, q, y\right) - c_3\left(x_2\left(p_1^*, p_2^*, p_3, q, y\right)\right).$$

Given explicit functional forms for the demand and cost functions, fixed-point algorithms (or, in some cases, explicit solutions using linear algebra), can be used to find post-merger equilibrium prices. [More detailed discussions of the method can be found in Hausman, Leonard and Zona (1994), Nevo (2000b), and Werden and Froeb (1994).] Going one step further, one also can ask how large a marginal cost reduction must arise from the merger to prevent consumer surplus from falling (or, with an aggregate surplus standard, what combinations of fixed and marginal cost reductions are necessary to prevent aggregate surplus from falling). With the recent advances in estimating structural models, this approach is gaining increasing attention.

There are, however, three important caveats regarding this method. First, correct estimation of demand is essential for the quality of any predictions through simulation. Demand estimates will be more reliable when the simulation does not have to rely on out-of-sample extrapolation; that is, when the merger does not cause prices to move outside the range of prior experience.

Second, a critical part of the simulation exercise involves the choice of the post-merger behavioral model of the industry. One can base this behavioral assumption on estimates of behavior using pre-merger data, a technique that has a long history in the empirical industrial organization literature [see, for example, Bresnahan (1987, 1989) and Porter (1983)].[67] A serious concern, however, is that the firms' behavior may *change* as a result of the merger. For example, the reduction in the number of firms could cause an industry to go from a static equilibrium outcome (say, Bertrand or Cournot) to a more cooperative tacitly collusive regime. In principal, this too may be something that we can estimate if we have a sample of markets with varying structural characteristics. But, to date, those attempting to conduct merger simulations have not done so.

Third, as previously discussed, pricing is likely to be only one of several important variables that may be affected by a merger. Entry, long-run investments in capacity, and R&D may all be altered significantly by a merger. The empirical industrial organization literature is just beginning to get a handle on these dynamic issues. To date, no actual merger simulation has included them. Nonetheless, dynamics is a very active area of research, and it may not be long before this begins to happen. [For a discussion of a simulation of merger effects in a dynamic model with capacity investments using assumed parameter values see Berry and Pakes (1993).]

In recent work, Peters (2003) evaluates the performance of these simulation methods by examining how well they would have predicted the actual price changes that followed six airline mergers in the 1980s. The standard merger simulation technique, in which price changes arise from changes in ownership structure (given an estimated demand structure and inferred marginal costs) produces the price changes shown in Table 36.2 in the column labeled "Ownership Change".[68] The actual changes, in contrast, are in the last column of the table, labeled "actual $\%\Delta p$". While the merger simulation captures an important element of the price change, it is clear that it predicts the price changes resulting from the various mergers only imperfectly. For example, the U.S. Air–Piedmont merger (US–PI) is predicted to lead to a smaller price increase than either the Northwest–Republic (NW–RC) or TWA–Ozak (TW–OZ) mergers, but the reverse actually happened.

Peters next asks how much of this discrepancy can be accounted for by other observed changes that occurred following the merger, such as changes in flight frequency

[67] Alternatively, one could simply compare the actual pre-merger prices with those predicted under various behavioral assumptions, as in Nevo (2000b).

[68] See Peters (2003) for a discussion of how different assumptions about the demand structure affect these conclusions.

Table 36.2
Simulated and actual price changes from airline mergers

	Component effects of average percent relative price change in overlap markets					
Merger	# of markets	Ownership change	Observed changes	Change in μ	Change in c	Actual $\%\Delta p$
NW–RC	78	19.8	−1.4	0.9	−10.1	7.2
TW–OZ	50	20.8	−2.2	−0.8	−1.0	16.0
CO–PE	67	6.4	0.7	0.2	20.5	29.4
DL–WA	11	7.6	−1.5	−0.5	6.0	11.8
AA–OC	2	4.7	−3.6	−1.8	7.6	6.5
US–PI	60	12.7	2.0	−1.9	6.7	20.3

Source: Peters (2003).

or entry, by including these observed changes in the post-merger simulation. The column labeled "observed changes" in Table 36.2 reports the answer. As can be seen there, these observed changes account for little of the difference.[69]

Given this negative answer, Peters then looks to see whether changes in unobserved product attributes (such as firm reputation or quality, denoted by μ in the table) or in marginal costs (denoted by c in the table) can explain the difference. The changes in unobserved product attributes can be inferred, using the pre-merger estimated demand coefficients, by solving for the levels of these unobserved attributes that reconcile the post-merger quantities purchased with the post-merger prices. Given the inferred post-merger unobserved product attributes, Peters can solve for the Nash equilibrium prices that would obtain were product attributes to have changed in this way, assuming that marginal costs remained unchanged. (Observe that since the post-merger unobserved product attributes are obtained entirely from the demand side, these computed equilibrium prices need not equal the actual post-merger prices.) As can be seen in the column labeled "change in μ", this accounts for little of the difference between predicted and actual prices.

Finally, Peters can infer a change in marginal cost by calculating the levels of marginal costs that would make the computed Nash equilibrium prices equal to the actual post-merger prices. (This is done by including all of the previous changes, including the inferred changes in unobserved product attributes μ, and solving for marginal costs using the Nash equilibrium pricing first-order conditions, as in the discussion of econometric approaches to market definition in Section 4.1.) The price change in the column labeled "change in c" reports the size of the change if these marginal cost changes are included in the simulation, omitting the product attribute changes. As can be seen in

[69] It should be noted, however, that Peters looks only at the year following consummation of the merger. These changes may be more significant over a longer period.

the table, the changes due to changes in c represent a large portion of the discrepancy between the initial simulation and the actual price changes.

It should be noted, however (as Peters does), that an alternative interpretation of these results is that it was firm conduct rather than marginal costs that changed post-merger. For example, this seems most clear in the case of the CO–PE merger, where the acquired airline was suffering serious financial difficulty prior to the merger. In that case, prices undoubtedly increased not because of a true marginal cost change, but rather because of a change in the previously distressed firm's behavior. Changes in behavior may have occurred in the other mergers as well. At the very least, however, Peters's study suggests directions that are likely to be fruitful in improving prospective analyses of mergers.

It seems clear that as techniques for estimating structural models get better, merger simulation will become an increasingly important tool in the analysis of horizontal mergers. How quickly this happens, however, and the degree to which it supplants other techniques, remains to be seen. My sense is that it is likely that before too long these techniques, and their further refinements, will constitute the core of merger analysis, at least for cases in which data and time limitations are not too severe.

5.2. *Residual demand estimation*

Another technique that does not follow the *Guidelines*' path, but that also avoids a full-blown structural estimation, is the residual demand function approach developed by Baker and Bresnahan (1985). Specifically, Baker and Bresnahan propose a way to determine the increase in market power from a merger that involves separately estimating neither the cross-price elasticities of demand between the merging firms' and rivals' products nor cost function parameters. As Baker and Bresnahan (1985, 59) put it:

> Evaluating the effect of a merger between two firms with $n-2$ other competitors would seem to require the estimation of at least n^2 parameters (all of the price elasticities of demand), a formidable task.... That extremely difficult task is unnecessary, however. The necessary information is contained in the slopes of the two single-firm (residual) demand curves before the merger, and the extent to which the merged firm will face a steeper demand curve.... The key to the procedures is that the effects of all other firms in the industry are summed together. ... This reduces the dimensionality of the problem to manageable size; rather than an n-firm demand system, we estimate a two-firm residual demand system.

To understand the Baker and Bresnahan idea, it helps to start by thinking about the residual demand function faced by a single firm (i.e., its demand function taking into account rivals' reactions), as in Baker and Bresnahan (1988). Specifically, consider an industry with N single-product firms and suppose that the inverse demand function for firm 1 is given by

$$p_1 = P_1(x_1, x_{-1}, z), \tag{38}$$

where x_1 is firm 1's output level, x_{-1} is an $(N-1)$-vector of output levels for firm 1's rivals, and z are demand shifters. To derive the residual inverse demand function facing firm 1, Baker and Bresnahan posit that the equilibrium relation between the vector x_{-1} and x_1 given the demand variables z and the cost variables w_{-1} affecting firms $2, \ldots, N$ can be denoted by

$$x_{-1} = B_{-1}(x_1, z, w_{-1}). \tag{39}$$

For example, imagine for simplicity that there are two firms in the industry ($N = 2$). If equilibrium output levels are determined by either a static simultaneous-choice quantity game or by a Stackleberg game in which firm 1 is the leader, then (39) is simply firm 2's best-response function. Substituting for x_{-1} in (38) we can then write firm 1's residual inverse demand function as

$$p_1 = P_1\big(x_1, B_{-1}(x_1, z, w_{-1}), z\big) \equiv R_1(x_1, z, w_{-1}). \tag{40}$$

For example, in the simple case in which z and w_{-1} are both scalar variables, we might estimate this in the simple constant elasticity form:

$$\ln(p_{1i}) = \gamma_0 + \gamma_1 \ln(x_{1i}) + \gamma_2 \ln(z_i) + \gamma_3 \ln(w_{-1,i}) + \varepsilon_i. \tag{41}$$

Baker and Bresnahan would then look to the estimate of γ_1, the quantity elasticity of the residual inverse demand function, as a measure of the firm's market power.[70]

Note that since x_1 typically will be correlated with ε, we will require an instrument for x_1. Moreover, since the rivals' cost variables w_{-1} are already in the estimating Equation (41), this will need to be a cost variable that affects *only* firm 1, say w_1. Unfortunately, such an instrument is often hard to find.

Figure 36.3 depicts the idea of what identifies the residual demand function $R_1(\cdot)$. Imagine that firms other than firm 1 produce a homogeneous product, that firm 1's product may be differentiated, and that the N firms compete by simultaneously choosing quantities. By holding fixed the demand variable z and the cost variables w_{-1} for firm 1's rivals, the estimating Equation (41) effectively holds fixed the rivals' aggregate best-response function, which is labeled as $\bar{B}_{-1}(\cdot)$ in Figure 36.3.[71] A shift in the cost variable for firm 1 from w_1' to $w_1'' < w_1'$ shifts firm 1's best-response function outward as depicted in Figure 36.3. This increases x_1 from x_1' to x_1'' and reduces the sum of the rivals' joint output X_{-1}. The slope of the residual demand function is then equal to the ratio of the resulting change in firm 1's price to the change in its quantity. For example, if rivals have constant returns to scale and act competitively, and if firm 1's product is not differentiated from its rivals' products, then $\bar{B}_{-1}(\cdot)$ will be a line with slope -1, and the coefficient γ_1 estimated in Equation (41) will be zero since any decrease in firm 1's output will be met by a unit-for-unit increase in its rivals' output.

[70] A similar derivation to that above can be done to derive instead a residual ordinary (rather than inverse) demand function.

[71] That is, the function $\bar{B}_{-1}(\cdot)$ is the sum of the quantities in the vector function $B_{-1}(\cdot)$.

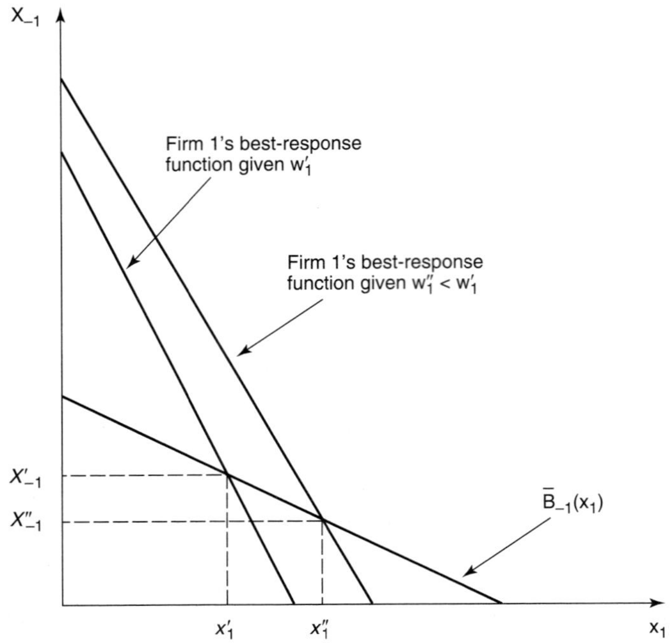

Figure 36.3. The idea behind the Baker–Bresnahan residual demand function estimation.

While clever, there are at least two serious potential problems with this approach in addition to the difficulty of finding suitable instruments. First, the "equilibrium relation" between firm 1's output x_1 and its rivals' outputs x_{-1} may not take the form in (39). For example, if there are two firms ($N = 2$) and outputs are determined via a Stackleberg game with *firm* 2 as the leader, then firm 2's output will depend on all of the variables that affect firm 1's best-response function (i.e., including w_1), not just on (x_1, z, w_2).

Second, unless firm 1 is *actually* a Stackleberg leader, the output chosen by firm 1 in equilibrium will *not* be the solution to $\max_{x_1}[R_1(x_1, z, w_{-1}) - c_1]x_1$. For example, if outputs actually are determined in a simultaneous (Cournot) quantity choice game, the residual demand function derived from this procedure will not have any direct correspondence to the actual price–cost margins in the market.

Baker and Bresnahan's procedure for evaluating a merger expands on this idea. Imagine, for simplicity, an industry in which initially there are three firms, and suppose that firms 1 and 2 will merge and that firm 3 will remain independent (the idea again extends to any number of independent firms). Now suppose that the inverse demand functions for firms 1 and 2 are

$$p_1 = P_1(x_1, x_2, x_3, z) \tag{42}$$

and

$$p_2 = P_2(x_1, x_2, x_3, z). \tag{43}$$

As before, suppose that firm 3's best-response function is

$$x_3 = B_3(x_1, x_2, z, w_3). \tag{44}$$

Substituting as before we can write

$$p_1 = R_1(x_1, x_2, z, w_3), \tag{45}$$

$$p_2 = R_2(x_1, x_2, z, w_3). \tag{46}$$

Equations (45) and (46) give the residual inverse demands faced by merged firms 1 and 2, taking into account firm 3's reactions to their price choices. Given estimates of these equations, Baker and Bresnahan propose evaluating the merger by computing the percentage price increase for each of the merging firms caused by a 1% reduction in *both* of their outputs, and comparing this to the two merging firms' single-firm residual inverse demand elasticities (as derived above); if these elasticities are much greater in the former case, they conclude that the merger increases market power.

Unfortunately, this method for evaluating post-merger market power suffers from the same problems as in the single-firm case. Moreover, an additional problem emerges with the method Baker and Bresnahan use to compare pre- and post-merger market power: since both of the merging firms could not have been Stackleberg leaders prior to the merger, the single firm residual inverse demand elasticities clearly are not directly related to pre-merger mark-ups.[72]

Taken together, these various problems make the residual demand approach less useful than merger simulation.

5.3. The event study approach

A third empirical technique that does not follow the *Guidelines*' method, examines the effect of a merger without *any* kind of structural estimation. The simple idea, originating in Eckbo (1983) and Stillman (1983), is as follows: A merger that will raise the prices charged by the merging firms is good for rivals, while one that will lower these prices is bad for them. Hence, we should be able to distinguish these two cases by looking at rivals' stock price reactions to the merger announcement and any subsequent enforcement actions. (Eckbo and Stillman looked at these reactions for a number of mergers and found no positive effects on rivals, and therefore concluded that most mergers are not anticompetitive.)

[72] In the special case in which the merged firm will act as a Stackleberg leader, we can however use the estimates of (45) and (46) to derive the post-merger prices by solving $\max_{x_1,x_2} \sum_{i=1,2}[R_i(x_1, x_2, z, w_3) - c_i]x_i$ for the merged firm's optimal quantities (x_1^*, x_2^*) and then computing $p_1^* = R_1(x_1^*, x_2^*, z, w_3)$ and $p_2^* = R_2(x_1^*, x_2^*, z, w_3)$.

Although a simple technique (it uses the standard event-study method), it has a number of potential pitfalls. The first has to do with the power of the test. McAfee and Williams (1988), for example, examine what they argue was an "obviously anticompetitive merger" and find no evidence of statistically significant positive stock price reactions by rivals. They argue that the problem is that the rivals may be large firms with highly variable stock returns so that the power of the test may be low; i.e., we should not take the lack of statistically significant reactions in rivals' stock prices to mean that the merger will not raise prices.[73]

Another issue has to do with what the literature calls "precedent effects". If a merger is announced, this may convey information about market (or regulatory) conditions more generally. For example, consider the announcement of an efficiency-enhancing merger. This announcement may indicate not only that the merged firms' costs will fall, but also that the other firms in the industry are likely to follow their example by merging themselves. Typically, the resulting reduction in all firms' costs will lead to both lower prices and higher profits. Thus, the informational content of this announcement – what it says about likely future mergers and their effects – will lead rivals' stock prices to *increase* upon announcement of this price-reducing merger.[74]

In the other direction, there is a possibility that a merger that increases the size of a firm could also increase the likelihood of anticompetitive exclusionary behavior. For example, in a "deep pocket" model of predation in which the size of a firm's asset holdings affects its ability to predate on rivals [e.g., Benoit (1984), Bolton and Scharfstein (1990)], a merger might increase the likelihood that rivals are preyed upon. This could lead to negative returns for rival stock values from announcement of a merger that would increase price in the long run.

These interpretational difficulties can be substantially avoided by looking instead at *customer* stock prices as done by Mullin, Mullin and Mullin (1995). Doing so allows one to look directly at the stock market's expectation of the changes in price (as well as any non-price dimensions of buyer surplus such as quality) arising from the merger. Mullin, Mullin and Mullin study the United States Steel (USS) dissolution suit that was filed in 1911. They begin by identifying thirteen potentially significant events in the history of the case, and then narrow their focus to five events by restricting attention to those events that caused a statistically significant movement in USS's stock price. The five events are described in Table 36.3, which also indicates with a (+) or a (−) whether the event is associated with an increase or a decrease in the probability of dissolution.

[73] Another reason for finding no effects on rivals is that the merger announcement might be anticipated. This can be checked by looking to see if the announcement had any effect on the stock prices of the merging firms.

[74] In principal, we can try to distinguish between anticompetitive and precedent effects by looking for differential stock–price responses among rivals: competitive effects should be felt more strongly by rivals that compete more closely with the merging firms. In this way, Prager (1992) finds evidence of precedent effects in her study of the 1901 merger between Great Northern Railway and the Northern Pacific Railway. One caveat, however, is that in some cases the precedent effect also may be more relevant for these same firms.

Table 36.3
Event descriptions

Variable		Description
USSRUMOR	(+)	Wall Street reacts to rumors that U.S. Steel will voluntarily dissolve and the following day the *New York Times* reports that U.S. Steel and the Department of Justice (DOJ) are negotiating the voluntary dissolution. Neither the DOJ nor U.S. Steel comments on these reports initially. September 20–21, 1911
USSDEN	(−)	U.S. Steel announces that it is not contemplating dissolution and believes that it is not guilty of antitrust violations. September 26, 1911
DISSUIT	(+)	The DOJ files the dissolution suit against U.S. Steel. On the same day, U.S. Steel officially announces that it will cancel the Great Northern lease and lower the freight rates on iron ore as had been previously reported. October 26, 1911
SCTREARG	(−)	The Supreme Court orders reargument in several large antitrust cases before it, including the U.S. Steel case. May 21, 1917
SCTDEC	(−)	The Supreme Court affirms the district court decision in U.S. Steel's favor. March 1, 1920

Source: Mullin, Mullin and Mullin (1995).

They then examine the effects of these events on the stock market values of four sets of firms: steel industry rivals, railroads, the Great Northern Railway, and street railway companies. Examining steel industry rivals follows the Eckbo–Stillman method.[75] Railroads and street rail companies, in contrast, were both customers of USS, in that they bought significant quantities of steel.[76] The event responses of these groups to the five events are shown in Table 36.4, which also shows the response of USS to each event.[77] As can be seen in the table, the responses of steel industry rivals are generally insignificant. The railroad stocks, however, respond to these events in a statistically and economically significant way, and in a direction that suggests that dissolution of USS would lower steel prices.

Two further points are also worth noting. First, while Mullin, Mullin and Mullin found significant effects on customers, it should be noted that finding no statistically significant customer stock–price response to a merger's announcement may not indicate the absence of a price effect: if customers are themselves producers, any price increases

[75] The set of steel rivals excludes the Great Northern Railway which had a complicated relationship with USS due to USS's lease of the Great Northern Railway's iron ore holdings. Mullin, Mullin and Mullin examine the effects of the events on the Great Northern Railway separately, which are not reported here.

[76] The railroads were both customers and suppliers to USS since a great deal of steel was shipped by rail. Mullin, Mullin and Mullin argue that the effects on both suppliers and customers should be in the same direction because they would both depend only on the change in the output of steel.

[77] Street rail stock prices were available only toward the end of the sample period. Note also that Table 5 in their paper, from which the results in Table 36.4 are drawn, also reports the effect of these events on the Great Northern Railway.

Table 36.4
Average estimated event responses

Event	Steel rivals	Railroads	Street rails
USSRUMOR	0.00374	0.02033	
	(0.1782)	(3.0246)	
USSDEN	0.00903	−0.01320	
	(0.4316)	(−1.9742)	
DISSUIT	−0.03532	0.01260	
	(−1.6874)	(1.8828)	
SCTREARG	0.06233	−0.01860	
	(1.7707)	(−0.7394)	
SCTDEC	0.04260	−0.02858	−0.02551
	(1.3366)	(−1.7453)	(−0.3533)

Source: Mullin, Mullin and Mullin (1995).
Note: t-statistics are in parentheses.

may be fully passed on to final consumers. In addition, as noted in the McAfee–Williams critique, the power of such a test may be low. Second, similar kinds of tests could also be run, looking instead at effects on firms that produce complements to the products of the merging firms.

Any suggestion that an antitrust authority should primarily rely on event–study analyses presumes that stock market participants are able to forecast the competitive effects of mergers more accurately (and faster) than is the agency, perhaps a questionable assumption.[78] Less extreme is the idea that an antitrust authority might use event–study evidence as just one source of information, perhaps as a check on its own internal analysis and any opinions obtained directly from industry and stock market participants.

6. Examining the results of actual mergers

All of the foregoing discussion has focused on a *prospective* analysis of horizontal mergers. It is natural to ask, however, what we know, looking *retrospectively*, about their *actual* effects. Such analyses can be useful for at least two reasons. First, they can guide our priors about the likelihood of mergers being anticompetitive or efficiency-enhancing (ideally, as a function of their characteristics). Second, we can use this information to assess how well various methods of prospective merger analysis perform, as the Peters (2003) paper discussed in Section 5.1 does for merger simulation.

Unfortunately, the economics literature contains remarkably little of this kind of analysis. In the remainder of the chapter, I discuss some studies that have looked at

[78] The studies in Kaplan (2000), for example, illustrate how the stock market's initial reaction to a merger is often a poor forecast of the merger's ultimate profitability.

either price or efficiency effects in actual mergers (none look at both). This is clearly an area that could use more research.[79,80]

6.1. Price effects

A small number of studies have analyzed the effects of actual mergers on prices. Many of these have focused on the airline industry, where a number of high-profile mergers occurred in the mid-1980s and price data are publicly available because of data reporting regulations. Borenstein (1990) studies the effects of the mergers of Northwest Airlines (NW) with Republic Airlines (RC) and Trans World Airlines (TW) with Ozark Airlines (OZ) in 1985 and 1986. In both cases, the merging airlines had their major hub at the same airport: Minneapolis served as the hub for both NW and RC; St. Louis was the hub for TW and OZ.[81] Both mergers began in 1985 with final agreements reached in the first quarter of 1986, and received regulatory approval (from the Department of Transportation) in the third quarter of 1986. Table 36.5 shows the average "relative prices" before and after the mergers for four categories of markets, defined by whether both merging firms were active competitors in the market before the merger (defined as each firm having at least a 10% market share on the route prior to the merger and shown in the first column of the table) and by whether they faced any competition before the merger (whether there were "other firms" in the market is shown in the second column of the table). The "relative prices" columns record for the third quarters of 1985, 1986, and 1987 the average over markets in the respective category of the percentage difference between the average price for the merging firms in that market and the average price for a set of markets of a similar distance (throughout the table, standard errors are in parentheses). The "av. change" over 1985–1987 is the average over markets in the respective category of the percentage difference between the 1987 "relative price" in the market and the 1985 "relative price".[82]

The results in Table 36.5 reveal very different experiences following the two mergers. Prices increased following the NW–RC merger, but not following the TW–OZ merger. Looking at the different categories in the NW–RC merger, (relative) prices increased by 22.5% on average in markets which were NW and RC duopolies prior to the merger.[83]

[79] Pautler (2003) surveys some articles that I do not discuss here, including studies looking at profitability, stock price reactions, and other effects.

[80] To the extent that the limited amount of work is due to a lack of data, one way to enhance our knowledge (or at least that of the enforcement agencies) may be for the enforcement agencies to require parties to approved (or partially approved) mergers to provide the agencies with information for some period of time after their merger.

[81] NW and RC accounted for 42% and 37% respectively of enplanements at Minneapolis; TW and OZ accounted for 57% and 25% of enplanements at St Louis.

[82] Note that this average price change is therefore not equal to the change in the average relative prices reported in the relative price columns.

[83] Werden, Joskow and Johnson (1991) also look at these two mergers. Using somewhat different techniques from Borenstein, they also find that the NW–RC merger increased prices substantially, while the TW–OZ

Table 36.5
Merging airlines' price changes at their primary hubs

	Other firms	Mkts	Relative prices[a] 1985	1986	1987	Av. change[a] 1985–1987
NW&RC	Yes	16	3.1 (2.8)	0.2 (4.5)	10.1[d] (5.9)	6.7 (4.3)
NW or RC	Yes	41	14.3[b] (2.6)	21.2[b] (3.5)	19.9[b] (2.8)	6.0[c] (2.6)
NW&RC	No	11	15.2[d] (8.2)	32.1[b] (10.3)	37.8[b] (7.5)	22.5[b] (5.2)
NW or RC	No	16	27.0[b] (6.7)	36.6[b] (9.5)	39.4[b] (7.1)	12.0[c] (5.5)
Total		84	14.7[b] (2.3)	21.5[b] (3.3)	24.1[b] (2.7)	9.5[b] (2.1)
TWA&OZ	Yes	19	−1.3 (6.1)	−2.7 (4.0)	3.2 (4.6)	4.6 (7.5)
TWA or OZ	Yes	29	10.5[c] (4.0)	4.7 (4.2)	5.7 (4.4)	−3.0 (3.1)
TWA&OZ	No	9	39.6[b] (7.5)	55.5[b] (13.2)	27.4[b] (2.4)	−5.8 (6.4)
TWA or OZ	No	10	56.0[b] (12.0)	61.4[b] (11.8)	33.5[b] (8.1)	−12.3[c] (4.0)
Total		67	17.8[b] (4.0)	17.9[b] (4.6)	12.1[b] (3.0)	−0.0 (3.5)

Source: Borenstein (1990).
[a]Shown in percent.
[b]Significant at 1-percent level (two-tailed test).
[c]Significant at 5-percent level (two-tailed test).
[d]Significant at 10-percent level (two-tailed test).

It is also noteworthy that prices also increased on routes in which NW and RC did not compete prior to the merger. This could reflect a price-constraining effect of potential entry prior to the merger, increased market power arising from domination of the hub airport after the merger, or in the case of markets in which they faced competitors, the effects of increased levels of multimarket contact with competitor airlines. Borenstein

merger had smaller (but, in their case, still positive) price effects on routes on which the merging firms were active competitors. Peters (2003) also reports price changes for these same mergers in his study of six mergers during this period. His data show instead that prices increased 7.2% and 16% in the NW–RC and TW–OZ mergers, respectively, in markets that were initially served by both merging firms. Peters reports that they increased 11% and 19.5%, respectively, in markets where these firms faced no pre-merger competition.

also notes that the prices of other airlines on these routes displayed a pattern very similar to the pattern seen for the merging firms in Table 36.5.

Kim and Singal (1993) expand on Borenstein's analysis by examining the price changes resulting from fourteen airline mergers that occurred from 1985 to 1988. Table 36.6 depicts the average of the changes in the relative prices for routes served by the merging firms compared to all other routes of similar distance. The table is divided horizontally into three sections: The first "full period" section looks at the change in (relative) prices from one quarter before the first bid of the acquirer to one quarter after consummation of the merger; the second "announcement period" section looks at changes from one quarter before the first bid of the acquirer to one quarter after this bid; the third "completion period" section looks at changes from one quarter before consummation to one quarter after. The table is also vertically divided into two sections. The left section looks at the merging firms' (relative) price changes, while the right section looks at rivals' (relative) price changes on the routes served by the merging firms. Within each of these sections, (relative) price changes are computed separately, depending on whether one of the merging firms was financially distressed prior to the merger. Descriptions of the variables in Table 36.6 are in the notes to the table.

Looking at price changes for the merging firms, we see that relative prices rose by an average of 3.25% over the full sample period in mergers involving firms that were not financially distressed. They rose substantially more (26.25%) in mergers involving a financially distressed firm. The announcement period and completion period changes are interesting as well. One might expect market power effects to be felt prior to the actual merger (as the management teams spend time together), while merger-related efficiencies would occur only after completion. For mergers involving "normal firms" we indeed see that prices rise in the announcement period and fall – although not as much – in the completion period.[84] (The patterns for mergers involving a failing firm are more puzzling.) Price changes for rival firms again follow similar patterns. Kim and Singal also examine through regression analysis the relationship between the change in relative fares and the change in the Herfindahl–Hirschman index. Consistent with the efficiency interpretation just given, they find that for mergers involving "normal firms", the size of the price elevation during the announcement period is highly correlated with the change in concentration induced by the merger, while the fall in prices during the completion period is unrelated to this change.

Finally, Kim and Singal break the merging firms' routes into four categories depending on whether the route involves a common hub airport for the merging firms (if so, it is a "hub" route) and whether the merging firms both served the route prior to the merger (if so, it is an "overlap" market). Table 36.7 depicts their results on (relative) price changes (in percentages) for the full period. Notably for mergers involving

[84] It is perhaps a little surprising, however, that substantial efficiencies would be realized so soon after completion. Moreover, there is some evidence [Kole and Lehn (2000)] that these mergers may have led to increases rather than decreases in marginal costs.

Table 36.6
Changes in relative fares of merging and rival firms

Variable	Merging firms: All mergers	Merging firms: Mergers between normal firms	Merging firms: Mergers with a failing firm	Rival firms: All mergers	Rival firms: Mergers between normal firms	Rival firms: Mergers with a failing firm
Full period:						
Sample size	11,629	8511	3118	8109	5578	2531
Relative fares, beginning	0.9602* (0.8238*)	1.0325* (0.8982*)	0.7626* (0.6883*)	0.9140* (0.8645*)	0.9745* (0.9218*)	0.7807* (0.7588*)
Relative fares, ending	1.0159* (0.8850*)	1.0529* (0.9309*)	0.9148* (0.8015*)	0.9831* (0.9287*)	1.0085 (0.9472*)	0.9272* (0.8944*)
Relative fare changes Lfarchg (percentage)	9.44* (9.75*)	3.25* (3.76*)	26.35* (20.66*)	12.17* (11.20*)	5.94* (4.42*)	25.90* (23.71*)
Announcement period:						
Sample size	7214	5832	1382	4891	3730	1161
Relative fares, beginning	0.9792* (0.8575*)	0.9855* (0.8636*)	0.9530* (0.8376*)	0.9444* (0.8945*)	0.9499* (0.9093*)	0.9268* (0.8487*)
Relative fares, ending	1.0270* (0.8947*)	1.0754* (0.9440*)	0.8228* (0.7337*)	0.9807* (0.9208*)	1.0345* (0.9634*)	0.8079* (0.7882*)
Relative fare changes Lfarchg (percentage)	5.54* (3.81*)	11.32* (10.38*)	−18.85* (−17.66*)	5.06* (3.77*)	12.64* (9.73*)	−19.28* (−14.80*)
Completion period:						
Sample size	7557	6140	1417	5304	4105	1199
Relative fares, beginning	0.9874* (0.8657*)	1.048* (0.9273*)	0.7247* (0.6528*)	0.9496* (0.8938*)	1.0201* (0.9507*)	0.7081* (0.7046*)
Relative fares, ending	0.9640* (0.8683*)	0.9652* (0.8724*)	0.9590* (0.8541*)	0.9764* (0.9296*)	0.9776* (0.9286*)	0.9725* (0.9332*)
Relative fare changes Lfarchg (percentage)	0.21 (3.31*)	−9.00* (−6.82*)	40.11* (38.36*)	6.10* (7.13*)	−5.36* (−3.72*)	45.34* (43.24*)

Source: Kim and Singal (1993).
Notes: Relative fare is the ratio of the fare on the sample route to the weighted average fare in the control group. The relative fares are measured at the start and end of each observation period. Lfarchg is the mean of the differences between the sample and control routes in the natural logs of the ratio of fares at the end to the beginning of each period. All numbers not in parentheses represent unweighted means of the variable. All numbers in parentheses are means weighted by the number of passengers on each route. For relative fares, statistical significance is tested using the t statistic with reference to a mean of 1.00, and for Lfarchg the significance is with reference to a mean of zero.
*Statistically significant at the 1-percent level (two-tailed test).

Table 36.7
Relative fare changes for four categories of routes

Period and subsample	Mean Lfarchg, percentage [sample size]: Merger between normal firms	Merger with a failing firm	Mean Lhhichg, percentage [sample size]: Merger between normal firms	Merger with a failing firm	Regression coefficient (t statistic)**: Constant	Normal × Lhhichg	Fail × Lhhichg	R^2_{adj}
Merging firms: full period								
Hub/overlap	−0.33 [193]	48.91* [180]	36.35* [193]	20.13* [180]	0.3174 (9.00)	−0.4891 (−6.69)	0.0920 (1.00)	0.101
Hub only	−11.01* [291]	40.23* [331]	1.89 [291]	5.81* [331]	0.1604 (6.99)	−0.0461 (−0.45)	0.0837 (0.72)	−0.002
Overlap only	3.92* [1205]	40.12* [566]	22.49* [1205]	19.92* [566]	0.1535 (11.89)	−0.1370 (−4.56)	0.3512 (5.28)	0.044
Neither	3.84* [6822]	18.28* [2041]	0.84* [6822]	4.02* [2041]	0.0690 (16.59)	0.1945 (12.12)	0.1548 (3.38)	0.016

Source: Kim and Singal (1993).
Notes: Lfarchg is deserbed in Table 36.6. Lhhichg is the difference between the sample and control routes in the natural logs of the ratio of the Herfindahl–Hirschman index at the end to the beginning of each period.
*Statistically significant at the 1-percent level (two-tailed test).
**$\text{Lfarchg}_i = \alpha + \beta_1 \text{Normal}_i \times \text{Lhhichg}_i + \beta_2 \text{Fail}_i \times \text{Lhhichg}_i + \varepsilon_i$.

normal firms, prices fall on "hub only" routes (i.e., non-overlap routes involving a common hub) and they have no change on hub/overlap routes. (Moreover, Kim and Singal show that these price reductions come entirely during the completion period.) These changes strongly suggest the presence of merger-related efficiency benefits. "Overlap only" markets show a price change like that seen in Table 36.6 for the full sample. Finally, note that routes that are neither a hub route nor an overlap route also experience price increases of this magnitude. These may reveal the effect of increased multimarket contact.[85]

Peters (2003), which was largely focused on evaluating merger simulation techniques (see Section 5.1), also documents the service changes and entry events that followed six of these mergers. Peters shows that flight frequency tended to decrease in markets that initially were served by both merging firms, and increase in markets that initially were served by only one of the merging firms.[86] The mergers also led to entry, although

[85] Evans and Kessides (1994) perform a structure–conduct–performance-style study of the relationship between airline prices and both concentration and multimarket contact during this period and find positive and economically significant price effects from both factors. Their findings also provide indirect evidence on the effects of the airline mergers during this period because most of the changes in concentration and multimarket contact in their sample were attributable to mergers.

[86] Borenstein (1990) and Werden, Joskow and Johnson (1991) report similar changes in service following the NW–RC and TW–OZ mergers.

changes in the number of rivals were only statistically significant for three of the mergers.

Banking is another industry in which firms are required to provide the government with data on their operations. Prager and Hannan (1998) study the price effects of mergers in the U.S. banking industry from January 1992 through June 1994. They examine the change in deposit rates for three types of deposits, NOW accounts (interest-bearing checking accounts), MMDA accounts (personal money market deposit accounts), and 3MOCD accounts (three-month certificates of deposit).[87] Hannan and Prager separately examine the effects of "substantial horizontal mergers" in which the Herfindahl–Hirschman index in the affected market increases by at least 200 points to a post-merger value of at least 1800, and "less substantial mergers", in which the Herfindahl–Hirschman index increases by at least 100 points to a post merger value of at least 1400 and which were not "substantial mergers". Their price data are monthly observations on deposit interest rates from October 1991 through August 1994. Their estimating equation takes the form

$$\text{ratchg}_{it} = \alpha + \sum_{t=2}^{T} \delta_t I_t + \sum_{n=-12}^{+12} \beta_n SM_{\text{int}} + \sum_{n=-12}^{+12} \gamma_n LSM_{\text{int}} + \varepsilon_{it},$$

where $\text{ratchg}_{it} = \ln(\text{rate}_{it}/\text{rate}_{i,t-1})$ and rate_{it} is bank i's deposit rate in period t, I_t is a dummy variable taking value 1 in period t and 0 otherwise, SM_{int} is a dummy variable taking value 1 if bank i was exposed to a substantial horizontal merger in month $t+n$, and LSM_{int} is a dummy variable taking value 1 if bank i was exposed to a less substantial horizontal merger in month $t+n$.[88] The results from this estimation can be seen in Table 36.8, where the merger exposure effects are presented in three aggregates: the pre-merger period ($n=-12$ to $n=0$), the post merger period ($n=1$ to $n=+12$), and the total period.

The results indicate that substantial mergers reduce the rates that banks in a market offer. This effect is largest for NOW accounts (approximately a 17% reduction in rates), for which customers arguably have the strongest attachment to local banks, and least for three-month CD's (less than 2% reduction in rates, and not statistically significant). Notably, however, Prager and Hannan find that less substantial mergers increase rates paid in the market. One possible interpretation of this difference is that these mergers involve efficiencies (which allow banks, in the absence of other effects, to increase their rates), but the effects of these efficiencies on prices are more than offset by an increase in market power for substantial mergers. Unlike in Kim and Singal (1993), the direction of these effects is the same in the pre and post-merger period. Finally, although the results in Table 36.8 do not distinguish between the price changes for merging firms

[87] MMDA accounts have restricted check-writing privileges.

[88] In fact, matters are somewhat more complicated than this, because the pricing data are at the bank level, not the market (SMSA) level. Hence, the merger exposure variables are actually weighted averages (by deposits) of the exposures that a given bank i has in the various markets in which it operates.

Table 36.8
Price effects of "substantial" and "less than substantial" bank mergers

	NOW			MMDA			3MOCD		
	Coefficient	t-statistics	Probability > $\|t\|$	Coefficient	t-statistics	Probability > $\|t\|$	Coefficient	t-statistics	Probability > $\|t\|$
Pre-merger effect									
Substantial mergers	−0.0865	−1.431	0.159	−0.0139	−0.429	0.670	0.0023	0.129	0.898
Lesser mergers	0.0585	2.050	0.046	−0.0081	−0.459	0.648	0.0148	0.877	0.385
Post merger effect									
Substantial mergers	−0.0882	−2.348	0.023	−0.0765	−4.349	0.000	−0.0178	−0.687	0.495
Lesser mergers	0.0368	1.326	0.191	0.0042	0.135	0.893	0.0443	1.689	0.098
Total effect									
Substantial mergers	−0.1747	−2.413	0.020	−0.0905	−2.317	0.025	−0.0155	−0.450	0.655
Lesser mergers	0.0953	2.422	0.019	−0.0038	−0.109	0.913	0.0590	1.728	0.091
Number of observations		13,313			13,498			12,972	
Number of banks		435			443			433	
Average observations per bank		30.60			30.47			29.96	
Regression R^2		0.0896			0.1409			0.3586	

Source: Prager and Hannan (1998).

Notes: OLS with robust standard errors[1]; dependent variable: ratchg_{it}. Each regression includes 33 month indicators and 25 weighted merger indicators ($I[t = m]$ for $m = 2$ to 34 and I [bank i "exposed" to merger in month $t - n$], $n = -12, \ldots, 0, \ldots, 12$). Coefficients for these variables are not reported in order to conserve space.

[1]The estimation technique employed here allows for the possibility of error correlation across observations within the same state.

and their rivals, Prager and Hannan find that these two groups had similar price effects, paralleling the Borenstein (1990) and Kim and Singal (1993) findings on this point.

In a recent paper, Focarelli and Panetta (2003) study bank mergers in Italy during the years 1990–1998 and their effects on deposit rates. Like Kim and Singal (1993) and Prager and Hannan (1998), they separately look at announcement (which they call "transition") and completion periods. However, they look at a much longer time period after the merger when examining the completion period (for each merger, they consider the effects until the end of their sample), arguing that a long time period may be required to realize efficiencies from merger. Like Kim and Singal they find evidence of market power effects during the announcement/transition period as deposit rates fall during this period. However, they find that in the long run these mergers increased deposit rates. Thus, in this case, the price-reducing effects of merger-related efficiencies seem to have dominated the price-increasing effects of increased market power.

Some recent studies have been done as well in other industries in which price data are available. Hosken and Taylor (2004) study the effects of a 1997 joint venture that combined the refining and retail gas station operations of the Marathon and Ashland oil companies. Specifically, they examine retail and wholesale price changes in Louisville, Kentucky, a city where this merger raised concentration significantly (the wholesale Herfindahl–Hirschman index increased from 1477 to 2263; the retail index increased by over 250, ending up in the 1500–1600 range). They conclude that there is no evidence that the merger caused either wholesale or retail prices to increase.[89] In contrast, Hastings (2004) finds that rivals' prices increased following ARCO's 1997 acquisition (through long-term lease) of 260 stations from Thrifty, an unbranded retailer. Vita and Sacher (2001) document large price increases arising from a 1990 merger between the only two hospitals in the city of Santa Cruz, California. The acquirer in this case was a non-profit hospital. Hospital markets, which also have data publicly available because of regulatory requirements, have also been the subject of some other work evaluating price and service effects of mergers; see Pautler (2003).[90]

There is one important caveat to the interpretations we have been giving to observed price changes in these studies: throughout, we have been assuming that the product remains unchanged. An alternative explanation for price increases or decreases instead may be that the merger led to changes in the quality of the merged firms' products. Thus, rather than market power, price increases may reflect quality improvements; and rather than cost reductions, price decreases may reflect quality degradation. That said, many of the papers we have discussed document patterns that tend to rule out such interpretations of their findings. For example, the price increases during the Kim and

[89] Wholesale prices did increase significantly 15 months after the merger, but the authors argue that this was due to an unrelated supply shock.

[90] In an older study, Barton and Sherman (1984) document the price changes that occurred following the 1976 and 1979 acquisitions of two competitors by a manufacturer of two types of duplicating microfilm. They provide evidence consistent with price increases following the merger. The data they use comes as a result of a 1981 FTC antitrust suit seeking to reverse the acquisitions.

Singal (1993) announcement period are unlikely to come from quality improvements. Likewise, Focarelli and Panetta (2003) explicitly examine and reject the hypothesis that the long-run increases in merging banks' interest rates that they document are due to quality degradation.

In summary, the literature documenting price effects of mergers has shown that mergers can lead to either price increases or decreases, in keeping with the central market power versus efficiency trade-off that we have discussed. There is also some evidence that more substantial mergers are more likely to raise prices. The use of post-merger evidence to evaluate techniques for prospective merger analysis, as in Peters (2003), is unfortunately much more limited.

6.2. Efficiencies

Just as with price effects, remarkably little has been done examining the effects of horizontal mergers on productive efficiency. Indeed, here the evidence is even thinner. Most of the work examining the efficiency effects of mergers has examined mergers in general, rather than focusing on horizontal mergers. The effects need not be the same. On the one hand, there may be greater potential for synergies when the merging firms are in the same industry.[91] On the other hand, since horizontal mergers may increase market power, even efficiency decreasing horizontal mergers may be profitable for merging firms.

Work examining mergers in general has typically found that there is a great deal of heterogeneity in merger outcomes. Some mergers turn out well, others very badly.[92] As well, the average effects are sensitive to both the time period examined and the particular sample of mergers studied. Perhaps the best-known study of post-merger performance is Ravenscraft and Scherer (1987), who document using the FTC's Line of Business data (collected for just three years, from 1974–1976) a dramatic decline in post-merger profitability of acquired lines of business, which generally were highly successful prior to acquisition. Ravenscraft and Scherer's sample, however, largely consisted of acquisitions from the conglomerate merger wave of the 1960s. Two different studies have examined data from the years following this conglomerate merger wave, Lichtenberg and Siegel (1987) and McGuckin and Nguyen (1995). Lichtenberg and Siegel examine the effect of ownership changes on statistically estimated total factor productivity at the plant-level using the Census Bureau's Longitudinal Establishment Data (LED) for the years 1972–1981. (Total factor productivity is determined in much of their work as the residual from estimation of a Cobb–Douglas production function.) As can be seen in Table 36.9 (where "year t" is the year of the merger), in contrast to the Ravenscraft and

[91] One reason for greater synergies simply may be that the managers of the acquiring firm are more likely to understand the business of the acquired firm; see, for example, Kaplan, Mitchell and Wruck (2000).

[92] This is also consistent with the event–study analysis of stock price returns, which finds wide variation in how the market evaluates announced mergers. At the same time, as the case studies in Kaplan (2000) document, a merger's performance may end up very different from the stock market's initial forecast.

Table 36.9
Differences in mean levels of productivity between plants changing ownership in year t and plants not changing ownership

Year	Level of productivity (residual)[a]	Year	Level of productivity (residual)[a]
$t-7$	−2.6 (4.00)	$t+1$	−2.9 (6.06)
$t-6$	−3.0 (5.06)	$t+2$	−2.7 (6.00)
$t-5$	−3.4 (6.50)	$t+3$	−2.5 (4.97)
$t-4$	−3.3 (6.77)	$t+4$	−1.9 (3.52)
$t-3$	−3.3 (7.40)	$t+5$	−1.9 (3.23)
$t-2$	−3.6 (8.71)	$t+6$	−1.8 (2.57)
$t-1$	−3.7 (9.59)	$t+7$	−1.2 (1.16)
t	−3.9 (9.10)		

Source: Lichtenberg and Siegel (1987).
[a] t-statistics to test H_0: difference equals 0 (in parentheses).

Scherer findings, they find that acquired plants were less productive than industry averages prior to acquisition, but had productivity increases that brought them almost up to the industry average after the acquisition. This may reflect the undoing of Ravenscraft and Scherer's inefficient conglomerate mergers.

The LED database, however, contains primarily large plants. McGuckin and Nguyen (1995) study the same question using instead the Census Bureau's Longitudinal Research Database (LRD) for the years 1977–1987. They restrict attention to mergers occurring between 1977 and 1982 and focus on the food manufacturing industry (SIC 20). This sample includes many more small plants than in Lichtenberg and Siegel's analysis. It also includes plants that only operated during part of the sample period (an "unbalanced panel"), while Lichtenberg and Siegel used a balanced panel (a balanced panel may worsen selection biases). However, instead of a measure of total factor productivity most of their analysis uses labor productivity (the average product of labor relative to the industry average product), which can be affected by shifts in the mix of inputs. In contrast to Lichtenberg and Siegel, McGuckin and Nguyen find that acquired plants have above-average productivity prior to acquisition, although they find that this is not true when they restrict attention to large plants like those studied by Lichtenberg and Siegel. Like Lichtenberg and Siegel, they find post-merger productivity improvements.

Unfortunately, neither of these studies deals with endogeneity or selection issues when estimating productivity, which can seriously bias productivity estimates [see Olley and Pakes (1996)]. In addition, neither of these studies considers separately the effects of horizontal mergers. In fact, ideally we would like to know how horizontal mergers affect productivity *conditional* on their structural attributes (e.g., potential for increasing market power).

There have been a few studies looking at efficiency effects of horizontal mergers. Most of these have focused on the banking industry. In general, these studies have found little evidence that, on average, mergers of banks that operate within the same local markets increase those banks' efficiencies. [See, for example, Berger and Humphrey (1992) and Peristiani (1997), as well as the discussion in Pautler (2003).]

A recent study that also examines horizontal mergers explicitly is Pesendorfer (2003), which studies a horizontal merger wave in the paper industry during the mid 1980s. Rather than estimating productivity directly, Pesendorfer tries to infer pre- and post-merger productivity using the firms' capacity choices. (Much as we discussed in Sections 4.1 and 5.1, he infers marginal costs from the Cournot-like first-order conditions for capacity choice.) This is an interesting idea, but it is unfortunately not entirely convincing in his application. This is true for several reasons. First, the investment first-order conditions he uses are entirely static, while investment choices are likely to be affected by dynamic considerations. Second, his procedure relies on an assumed investment cost function (this might not be necessary if one instead has panel data). Finally, one cannot distinguish whether the changes in marginal cost he derives reflect shifts of the plant's marginal cost function or movements along an unchanging function.

In summary, the evidence on the efficiency effects of horizontal mergers provides little guidance at this point. There is reason, however, to be hopeful that we will learn more soon. Recent work, most notably Olley and Pakes (1996), has greatly improved our ability to estimate productivity [see also Levinsohn and Petrin (2003)]. The examination of the productivity effects of horizontal mergers seems a natural (and highly valuable) direction for this work to go.

7. Conclusion

A great deal of progress has been made in recent years in our ability to analyze prospective mergers. A better theoretical understanding of the trade-off between market power and efficiencies, the development of merger simulation techniques, some initial steps towards understanding a range of dynamic issues, and a few investigations of the effects of actual mergers have all been significant steps forward. At the same time, as the discussion has made clear, there are a number of important and interesting areas that clearly need further research. Continued theoretical work on mergers in dynamic settings, incorporation of non-price variables and changing firm behavior into merger simulation techniques, further evidence on the price and efficiency effects of mergers (particularly conditional on a merger's attributes), and additional work using ex post merger experiences to evaluate methods for prospective merger analysis are all high priorities.

Acknowledgements

I thank Mark Armstrong, Jonathan Baker, Michael Black, Patrick Bolton, Dennis Carlton, Richard Caves, Luke Froeb, Neil Gandal, Ken Heyer, Kai-Uwe Kuhn, Aviv Nevo, Volker Nocke, Ariel Pakes, John Parisi, Paul Pautler, Craig Peters, Robert Porter, Simon Priddis, Patrick Rey, Tom Ross, Spencer Waller, Greg Werden, and Abe Wickelgren for their comments, help, and suggestions. Fan Zhang provided excellent research assistance. I also thank the NSF, the Searle Foundation, and the Toulouse Network for Information Technology for their financial support.

References

Abreu, D. (1986). "Extremal equilibria of oligopolistic supergames". Journal of Economic Theory 39, 191–223.

Ackerberg, D., Benkard, L., Berry, S., Pakes, A. (forthcoming). "Econometric tools for analyzing market outcomes". In: Heckman, J.J. (Ed.), Handbook of Econometrics, Elsevier, Amsterdam. In press.

Andrade, G., Mitchell, M., Stafford, E. (2001). "New evidence and perspectives on mergers". Journal of Economic Perspectives 15, 103–120.

Ausubel, L.M., Deneckere, R.J. (1987). "One is almost enough for monopoly". RAND Journal of Economics 18, 255–274.

Baker, J.B. (1999a). "Developments in antitrust economics". Journal of Economic Perspectives 13, 181–194.

Baker, J.B. (1999b). "Econometric analysis in FTC v. staples". Journal of Public Policy and Marketing 18, 11–21.

Baker, J.B., Bresnahan, T.F. (1985). "The gains to merger or collusion in product-differentiated industries". Journal of Industrial Economics 33, 427–444.

Baker, J.B., Bresnahan, T.F. (1988). "Estimating the residual demand curve facing a single firm". International Journal of Industrial Organization 6, 283–300.

Baker, J.B., Rubinfeld, D.L. (1999). "Empirical methods used in antitrust litigation: Review and critique". American Law and Economics Review 1, 386–435.

Barton, D.M., Sherman, R. (1984). "The price and profit effects of horizontal merger: A case study". Journal of Industrial Economics 33, 165–177.

Benoit, J.-P. (1984). "Financially constrained entry in a game with incomplete information". RAND Journal of Economics 4, 490–499.

Berger, A.N., Humphrey, D.B. (1992). "Megamergers in banking and the use of cost efficiency as an antitrust defense". Antitrust Bulletin 37, 541–600.

Bernheim, B.D., Whinston, M.D. (1990). "Multimarket contact and collusive behavior". RAND Journal of Economics 21, 1–26.

Bernheim, B.D., Whinston, M.D. (1986). "Menu auctions, resource allocation, and economic influence". Quarterly Journal of Economics 101, 1–31.

Berry, S.T. (1994). "Estimating discrete choice models of product differentiation". RAND Journal of Economics 25, 242–262.

Berry, S., Pakes, A. (1993). "Some applications and limitations of recent advances in empirical industrial organization: Merger analysis". American Economic Review Papers and Proceedings 83, 247–252.

Berry, S., Levinsohn, J., Pakes, A. (1995). "Automobile prices in market equilibrium". Econometrica 63, 841–890.

Besanko, D., Spulber, D. (1993). "Contested mergers and equilibrium antitrust policy". Journal of Law, Economics, and Organization 9, 1–29.

Bloch, F. (1996). "Sequential formation of coalitions in games with externalities and fixed payoff division". Games and Economic Behavior 14, 90–123.

Bolton, P., Scharfstein, D. (1990). "A theory of predation based on agency problems in financial contracting". American Economic Review 80, 93–106.

Borenstein, S. (1990). "Airline mergers, airport dominance, and market power". American Economic Review 80, 400–404.

Bresnahan, T.F. (1987). "Competition and collusion in the American automobile industry: The 1955 price war". Journal of Industrial Economics 35, 457–482.

Bresnahan, T.F. (1989). "Empirical methods in industries with market power". In: Schmalensee, R., Willig, R. (Eds.), In: Handbook of Industrial Organization, vol. II. Elsevier, Amsterdam.

Carlton, D., Gertner, R. (1989). "Market power and mergers in durable goods industries". Journal of Law and Economics 32, S203–S226.

Coase, R.H. (1972). "Durability and monopoly". Journal of Law and Economics 15, 143–149.

Compte, O., Jenny, F., Rey, P. (2002). "Capacity constraints, mergers, and collusion". European Economic Review 46, 1–29.

Davidson, C., Deneckere, R. (1984). "Horizontal mergers and collusive behavior". International Journal of Industrial Organization 2, 117–132.

Deneckere, R., Davidson, C. (1985). "Incentives to form coalitions with Bertrand competition". RAND Journal of Economics 16, 473–486.

Eckbo, B.E. (1983). "Horizontal mergers, collusion, and Stockholder wealth". Journal of Financial Economics 11, 241–273.

European Commission (2005). "Merger remedies study". Available at: http://europa.eu.int/comm/competition/mergers/legislation/remedies.htm.

Evans, W.N., Kessides, I.N. (1994). "Living by the 'golden rule': Multimarket contact in the U.S. airline industry". Quarterly Journal of Economics 109, 341–366.

Farrell, J., Shapiro, C. (1990). "Horizontal mergers: An equilibrium analysis". American Economic Review 80, 107–126.

Federal Trade Commission (1999). "A study of the commission's divestiture process". Available at: http://www.ftc.gov/os/1999/08/divestiture.pdf.

Focarelli, D., Panetta, F. (2003). "Are mergers beneficial to consumers? Evidence from the market for bank deposits". American Economic Review 93, 1152–1172.

Gerstle, A.D., Waldman, M. (2004). "Mergers in durable-goods industries: A re-examination of market power and welfare effects". Mimeo.

Gilbert, R.J., Sunshine, S.C. (1995). "Incorporating dynamic efficiency concerns in merger analysis: The use of innovation markets". Antitrust Law Journal 63, 569–602.

Gowrisankaran, G. (1999). "A dynamic model of endogenous horizontal mergers". RAND Journal of Economics 30, 56–83.

Gowrisankaran, G., Holmes, T.J. (2004). "Mergers and the evolution of industry concentration: Results from the dominant-firm model". RAND Journal of Economics 35, 561–582.

Griliches, Z., Mairesse, J. (1995). "Production functions: The search for identification". NBER Working Paper No. 5067.

Grossman, G., Helpman, E. (1994). "Protection for sale". American Economic Review 84, 833–850.

Gul, F. (1987). "Noncooperative collusion in durable goods oligopoly". RAND Journal of Economics 18, 248–254.

Harris, B.C., Simons, J.J. (1989). "Focusing market definition: How much substitution is necessary?". Research in Law and Economics 12, 207–226.

Hastings, J. (2004). "Vertical relationships and competition in retail gasoline markets: Empirical evidence from contract changes in Southern California". American Economic Review 94, 317–328.

Hausman, J.A. (1996). "Valuation of new goods under perfect and imperfect competition". In: Bresnahan, T., Gordon, R. (Eds.), The Economics of New Goods. In: Studies in Income and Wealth, vol. 58. National Bureau of Economic Research, Chicago.

Hausman, J., Leonard, G., Zona, J.D. (1994). "Competitive analysis with differentiated products". Annales D'Economie et de Statistique 34, 159–180.

Hay, G., Kelley, D. (1974). "An empirical survey of price-fixing conspiracies". Journal of Law and Economics 17, 13–38.

Hendricks, K., McAfee, R.P. (2000). "A theory of bilateral oligopoly, with applications to vertical mergers". Mimeo.

Jensen, M.C., Ruback, R.S. (1983). "The market for corporate control: The scientific evidence". Journal of Financial Economics 11, 5–50.

Kamien, M.I., Zang, I. (1990). "The limits of monopolization through acquisition". Quarterly Journal of Economics 105, 465–500.

Kaplan, S.N. (Ed.) (2000). Mergers and Productivity. University of Chicago Press, Chicago.

Kaplan, S.N., Mitchell, M.L., Wruck, K.H. (2000). "A clinical exploration of value creation and destruction in acquisitions: Organizational design, incentives, and internal capital markets". In: Kaplan, S.N. (Ed.), Mergers and Productivity. University of Chicago Press, Chicago.

Katz, M.L., Shapiro, C. (2003). "Critical loss: Let's tell the whole story". Antitrust 17, 49–56.

Kole, S., Lehn, K. (2000). "Workforce integration and the dissipation of value in mergers: The case of USAir's acquisition of piedmont aviation". In: Kaplan, S.N. (Ed.), Mergers and Productivity. University of Chicago Press, Chicago.

Kim, E.H., Singal, V. (1993). "Mergers and market power: Evidence from the airline industry". American Economic Review 83, 549–569.

Kuhn, K.-U. (2002). "Reforming European merger review: Targeting problem areas in policy outcomes". Journal of Industry, Competition, and Trade 4, 311–364.

Kuhn, K.-U. (2004). "The coordinated effects of mergers in differentiated products markets". Working Paper #34. John M. Olin Center for Law and Economics, University of Michigan Law School.

Levin, D. (1990). "Horizontal mergers: The 50-percent benchmark". American Economic Review 80, 1238–1245.

Levinsohn, J., Petrin, A. (2003). "Estimating production functions using intermediate inputs to control for unobservables". Review of Economic Studies 70, 317–341.

Lichtenberg, F.R., Siegel, D. (1987). "Productivity and changes in ownership of manufacturing plants". In: Brooking Papers on Economic Activity: Special Issue on Microeconomics. The Brookings Institution, Washington, DC.

Lyons, B.R. (2002). "Could politicians be more right than economists?: A theory of merger standards". Working Paper CCR 02-1. Revised Centre for Competition and Regulation.

Mackay, R.J. (1984). "Mergers for monopoly: Problems of expectations and commitment". Mimeo.

Mankiw, N.G., Whinston, M.D. (1986). "Free entry and social inefficiency". RAND Journal of Economics 17, 48–58.

Mas-Colell, A., Whinston, M.D., Green, J.R. (1995). Microeconomic Theory. Oxford Univ. Press, New York.

McAfee, R.P., Williams, M.A. (1988). "Can event studies detect anticompetitive mergers?". Economics Letters 28, 199–203.

McAfee, R.P., Williams, M.A. (1992). "Horizontal mergers and antitrust policy". Journal of Industrial Economics 40, 181–186.

McFadden, D. (1981). "Econometric models of probabilistic choice". In: Manski, C., McFadden, D. (Eds.), Structural Analysis of Discrete Data. MIT Press, Cambridge, MA, pp. 198–272.

McGuckin, R.H., Nguyen, S.V. (1995). "On productivity and plant ownership change: New evidence from the longitudinal research database". RAND Journal of Economics 26, 257–276.

Milgrom, P., Roberts, J. (1990). "Rationalizability, learning, and equilibrium in games with strategic complementarities". Econometrica 58, 1255–1278.

Motta, M. (2004). Competition Policy: Theory and Practice. Cambridge Univ. Press, Cambridge.

Mullin, G.L., Mullin, J.C., Mullin, W.P. (1995). "The competitive effects of mergers: Stock market evidence from the U.S. steel dissolution suit". RAND Journal of Economics 26, 314–330.
Neven, D.J., Roller, L.-H. (2002). "Consumer surplus vs. welfare standard in a political economy model of merger control". Mimeo.
Nevo, A. (1997). "Demand for ready-to-eat cereal and its implications for price competition, merger analysis, and valuation of new goods". Ph.D. Dissertation. Harvard University.
Nevo, A. (2000a). "A practitioner's guide to estimation of random coefficients logit models of demand". Journal of Economics and Management Strategy 9, 513–548.
Nevo, A. (2000b). "Mergers with differentiated products: The case of the ready-to-eat cereal industry". RAND Journal of Economics 31, 395–421.
Nevo, A. (2001). "Measuring market power in the ready-to-eat cereal industry". Econometrica 69, 307–342.
O'Brien, D.P., Wickelgren, A.L. (2003). "A critical analysis of critical loss analysis". Antitrust Law Journal 71, 161–184.
Olley, G.S., Pakes, A. (1996). "The dynamics of productivity in the telecommunications equipment industry". Econometrica 64, 1263–1298.
Parisi, J.J. (2005). "A simple guide to the EC merger regulation of 2004". Antitrust Source, available at: http://www.abanet.org/antitrust/source/01-05/jan05_full_source.pdf.
Pautler, P.A. (2003). "Evidence on mergers and acquisitions". Antitrust Bulletin 48, 119–221.
Peristiani, S. (1997). "Do mergers improve the X-efficiency and scale efficiency of U.S. banks? Evidence from the 1980s". Journal of Money, Credit, and Banking 29, 326–337.
Perry, M.K., Porter, R. (1985). "Oligopoly and the incentive for horizontal merger". American Economic Review 75, 219–227.
Pesendorfer, M. (2003). "Horizontal mergers in the paper industry". RAND Journal of Economics 34, 495–515.
Peters, C. (2003). "Evaluating the performance of merger simulation: Evidence from the U.S. airline industry". Working Paper #32. Northwestern University, Center for the Study of Industrial Organization.
Phillips, O., Mason, C. (1992). "Mutual forbearance in experimental conglomerate markets". RAND Journal of Economics 23, 395–414.
Porter, R.H. (1983). "A study of cartel stability: The joint executive committee, 1880–1886". Bell Journal of Economics 14, 301–314.
Prager, R.A. (1992). "The effects of horizontal mergers on competition: The case of the Northern Securities company". RAND Journal of Economics 23, 123–133.
Prager, R.A., Hannan, T.H. (1998). "Do substantial horizontal mergers generate significant price effects? Evidence from the banking industry". Journal of Industrial Economics 46, 433–452.
Ravenscraft, D.J., Scherer, F.M. (1987). Mergers, Sell-offs, and Economic Efficiency. Brookings Institution, Washington, DC.
Salant, S., Switzer, S., Reynolds, R. (1983). "Losses from horizontal mergers: The effect of an exogenous change in industry structure on Cournot-equilibrium". Quarterly Journal of Economics 98, 185–199.
Segal, I. (1999). "Contracting with externalities". Quarterly Journal of Economics 114, 337–388.
Shleifer, A., Summers, L.H. (1988). "Breach of trust in hostile takeovers". In: Auerbach, A. (Ed.), Corporate Takeovers: Causes and Consequences. University of Chicago Press, Chicago, pp. 33–56.
Spector, D. (2003). "Horizontal mergers, entry, and efficiency defenses". International Journal of Industrial Organization 21, 1591–1600.
Stillman, R. (1983). "Examining antitrust policy towards horizontal mergers". Journal of Financial Economics 11, 225–240.
Taylor, C.T., Hosken, D.S. (2004). "The economic effects of the Marathon–Ashland joint venture". Mimeo.
Vasconcelos, H. (2005). "Tacit collusion, cost asymmetries, and mergers". RAND Journal of Economics 36, 39–62.
Vita, M.G., Sacher, S. (2001). "The competitive effects of not-for-profit hospital mergers: A case study". Journal of Industrial Economics 49, 63–84.
Vives, X. (1999). Oligopoly Pricing: Old Ideas and New Tools. MIT Press, Cambridge, MA.

Weiss, L.W. (Ed.) (1990). Concentration and Price. MIT Press, Cambridge, MA.

Werden, G. (1990). "Antitrust policy toward horizontal mergers: A comment on Farrell and Shapiro". Paper No. 90-4. Department of Justice Economic Analysis Group Discussion.

Werden, G. (1997). "An economic perspective on the analysis of merger efficiencies". Antitrust 11, 12–16.

Werden, G., Froeb, L. (1994). "The effects of mergers in differentiated products industries: Logit demand and merger policy". Journal of Law, Economics, and Organization 10, 407–426.

Werden, G., Froeb, L. (1998). "The entry-inducing effects of horizontal mergers: An exploratory analysis". Journal of Industrial Economics 46, 525–543.

Werden, G.J., Joskow, A.S., Johnson, R.L. (1991). "The effects of mergers on prices and output: Two cases from the airline industry". Managerial and Decision Economics 12, 341–352.

Whinston, M.D. (2006). Lectures on Antitrust Economics. MIT Press, Cambridge, MA.

Williamson, O.E. (1968). "Economies as an antitrust defense: The welfare tradeoffs". American Economic Review 58, 407–426.

Yi, S.-S. (1997). "Stable coalition structures with externalities". Games and Economic Behavior 20, 201–237.

AUTHOR INDEX

n indicates citation in a footnote.

SUBJECT INDEX